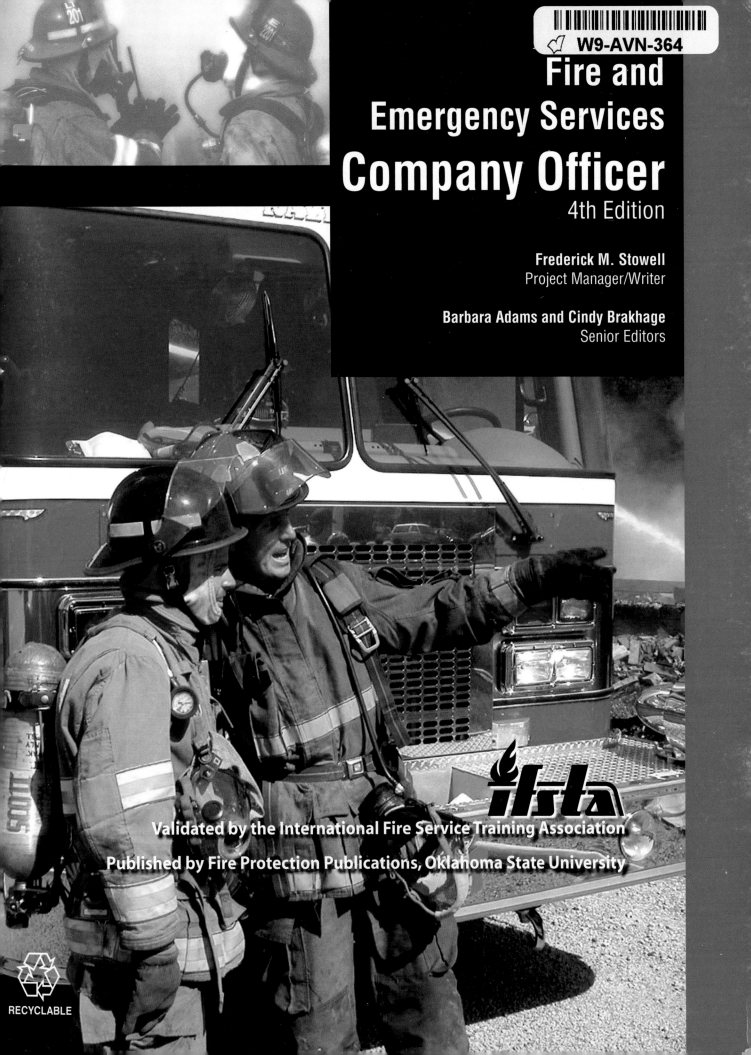

W9-AVN-364

Fire and Emergency Services
Company Officer
4th Edition

Frederick M. Stowell
Project Manager/Writer

Barbara Adams and Cindy Brakhage
Senior Editors

Validated by the International Fire Service Training Association

Published by Fire Protection Publications, Oklahoma State University

RECYCLABLE

The International Fire Service Training Association

The International Fire Service Training Association (IFSTA) was established in 1934 as a *nonprofit educational association of fire fighting personnel who are dedicated to upgrading fire fighting techniques and safety through training.* To carry out the mission of IFSTA, Fire Protection Publications was established as an entity of Oklahoma State University. Fire Protection Publications' primary function is to publish and disseminate training texts as proposed and validated by IFSTA. As a secondary function, Fire Protection Publications researches, acquires, produces, and markets high-quality learning and teaching aids as consistent with IFSTA's mission.

The IFSTA Validation Conference is held the second full week in July. Committees of technical experts meet and work at the conference addressing the current standards of the National Fire Protection Association and other standard-making groups as applicable. The Validation Conference brings together individuals from several related and allied fields, such as:
- Key fire department executives and training officers
- Educators from colleges and universities
- Representatives from governmental agencies
- Delegates of firefighter associations and industrial organizations

Committee members are not paid nor are they reimbursed for their expenses by IFSTA or Fire Protection Publications. They participate because of commitment to the fire service and its future through training. Being on a committee is prestigious in the fire service community, and committee members are acknowledged leaders in their fields. This unique feature provides a close relationship between the International Fire Service Training Association and fire protection agencies, which helps to correlate the efforts of all concerned.

IFSTA manuals are now the official teaching texts of most of the states and provinces of North America. Additionally, numerous U.S. and Canadian government agencies as well as other English-speaking countries have officially accepted the IFSTA manuals.

ISBN 0-87939-281-9   Library of Congress Control Number: 0879392819

Fourth Edition, First Printing, April 2007   *Printed in the United States of America*

10   9   8   7   6   5   4   3   2   1

If you need additional information concerning the International Fire Service Training Association (IFSTA) or Fire Protection Publications (FPP), contact:

Customer Service, Fire Protection Publications, Oklahoma State University
930 North Willis, Stillwater, OK 74078-8045
800-654-4055   Fax: 405-744-8204

For assistance with training materials, to recommend material for inclusion in an IFSTA manual, or to ask questions or comment on manual content, contact:

Editorial Department, Fire Protection Publications, Oklahoma State University
930 North Willis, Stillwater, OK 74078-8045
405-744-4111   Fax: 405-744-4112   E-mail: editors@osufpp.org

Chapter Summary

Part A Fire Officer Level I

Part B Fire Officer Level II

Appendices

Table of Contents

Preface

The fourth edition of the IFSTA **Fire and Emergency Services Company Officer** manual is written to assist fire and emergency services personnel in meeting the job performance requirements of the standard National Fire Protection Association (NFPA) 1021, *Standard for Fire Officer Professional Qualifications* (2003). It provides the basic level of knowledge that is required for Level I and Level II fire officers and officer candidates.

It should be understood that this manual serves as an educational foundation for certification at each level and as professional development for personnel currently in those positions. Additional reading and course work are highly recommended for all fire officers regardless of their assigned functions or positions within the fire and emergency services organization.

Acknowledgement and special thanks are extended to the members of the IFSTA validation committee. The following members contributed their time, wisdom, and knowledge to the development of this manual:

IFSTA Fire and Emergency Services Company Officer Fourth Edition
IFSTA Validation Committee

Chair

Gary Wilson
Fire Rescue Training Institute
University of Missouri
Columbia, Missouri

Vice Chair

Mike Brackin
Personnel Standard Commission
Alabama Fire College
Tuscaloosa, Alabama

Secretary

Ed Kirtley
Oklahoma State University/Fire Service
Training
Stillwater, Oklahoma

Committee Members

Wil Dane
Denham Springs Fire Department
Denham Springs, Louisiana

Stan Fernandez
City of San Rafael Fire Department
San Rafael, California

Christopher A. Garrett
Richmond Fire and Rescue Services
Richmond, Virginia

Todd Iremonger
Clark County Fire District No. 6
Vancouver, Washington

Bob Madden
Bend Fire and Rescue
Bend, Oregon

Manick Noormahamud
Toronto Fire Services
Toronto, Ontario, Canada,

Darren Olquin
San Ramon Valley Fire Protection District
San Ramon, California

Mark S. Pare
Providence Fire Department
Cranston, Rhode Island

Lawrence L. Preston
Maryland Fire and Rescue Institute
University of Maryland
College Park, Maryland

Willie (Billy) G. Shelton, Jr.
Virginia Department of Fire Programs
Glen Allen, Virginia

Steve Sloan
North Carolina Office of State Fire Marshal
Raleigh, North Carolina

The following individuals contributed their assistance and comments as reviewers for this manual:

David Covington, San Antonio (TX) Fire Department

Rick Dunn, South Carolina Fire Academy

Craig Hall, United States Air Force, Scott Air Force Base (IL)

Nancy Trench, Fire Protection Publications (FPP)

The following individuals and organizations contributed information, photographs, and other assistance that made completion of this manual possible:

Andrews Air Force Base (MD) Fire Department

Danny Atchley, Oklahoma City (OK) Fire Department

Steve Baker

Benny Deal, Midwest City (OK) Fire Department

Bob Esposito

Manuel Fonseca, Nashville Fire Department

Dennis Foth, Sverdrup Technologies

Dr. Richard Gist, Kansas City (MO) Fire Department

Bonnie Hudlet

Jeff Kilfoyle

Bill Lellis

Chad Love

Mike Mallory, Tulsa (OK) Fire Department

Chris E. Mickal, New Orleans (LA) Fire Department

Rick Montemorra, Mesa (AZ) Fire Department

Paul Ramirez, Phoenix (AZ) Fire Department

Dave Rohr

Dr. Jessica A. Stowell, University of Oklahoma (Tulsa)

Greg Terrill

William Zieres, Missouri Division of Fire Safety

Williams Fire and Hazard Control, Inc

Federal Emergency Management Agency (photographers):

Robert J. Alvey	Marvin Nauman
George Armstrong	Jason Pack
Jocelyn Augustino	Michael Rieger
Roman Bas	Bri Rodriguez
Andrea Booher	Liz Roll
Win Henderson	Asron Skolnik
Robert Kaufman	Anjanette Stayten
Bill Koplitz	Mark Wolfe
Bob McMillan	

Central Florida Fire Academy

Conoco, Inc.

Fire Service Training, Oklahoma State University

Florida Department of Agriculture and Consumer Services

Fort Belvoir (VA) Fire Department

Fuquay-Varina (NC) Fire Department

International Association of Fire Fighters

International Association of Fire Chiefs

Iowa Fire Service Training Bureau

Lab Safety Supply, Inc.

National Aeronautics and Space Administration

Naval Fire District, Washington, D.C.

PowerTrain, Inc.

    Dan Kennedy

    Juli Tompkins

San Ramon Valley (CA) Fire Protection District

Tyndall Air Force Base (FL) Fire Department

United States Air Force

    Kamaile Chan

    Lou Czarnecki

    David Clifford

    Stacey Harter

    Michele Lacerda

    Chris Mills

    Jim Podolske

Volunteer Fireman's Insurance Services

Additionally, gratitude is extended to the following members of the FPP project team whose contributions made the final publication of this manual possible:

Fire and Emergency Services Company Officer Project Team

Project Manager/Staff Liaison/Writer
Fred Stowell, Senior Technical Editor

Editors
Barbara Adams, Senior Editor
Cindy Brakhage, Senior Editor

Technical Reviewer
Jeff Fortney, Senior Technical Editor

Proofreaders
Cindy Brakhage, Senior Editor
Michelle Skidgel, Instructional Developer

Curriculum Development
Bill Robinson, Curriculum Coordinator
Melissa Noakes, Curriculum Developer
Beth Ann Fulgenzi, Curriculum Developer

FPP Photographers
Jeff Fortney, Senior Technical Editor
Tom Ruane, Senior Technical Editor
Fred Stowell, Senior Technical Editor

Production Manager
Don Davis

Illustrators and Layout Designers
Ann Moffat, Production Coordinator
Ben Brock, Senior Graphic Designer
Clint Parker, Senior Graphic Designer
Lee Shortridge, Senior Graphic Designer

IFSTA Projects Coordinators
Craig Hannan and Ed Kirtley

Library Researchers
Susan F. Walker, Librarian
Jenny Brock, Senior Data Control Technician
Caleb Bates, Student Technician

Editorial Assistant
Tara Gladden

Introduction

The fire and emergency services professions have a long and established heritage in culture and society. Traditions that are deeply rooted in that heritage continue to influence the organization, structure, operations, and titles used in the services. For instance, the fire and emergency services organization is based on a scalar structure that assigns rank in a hierarchy of authority that is similar to a pyramid (**Figure I.1**).

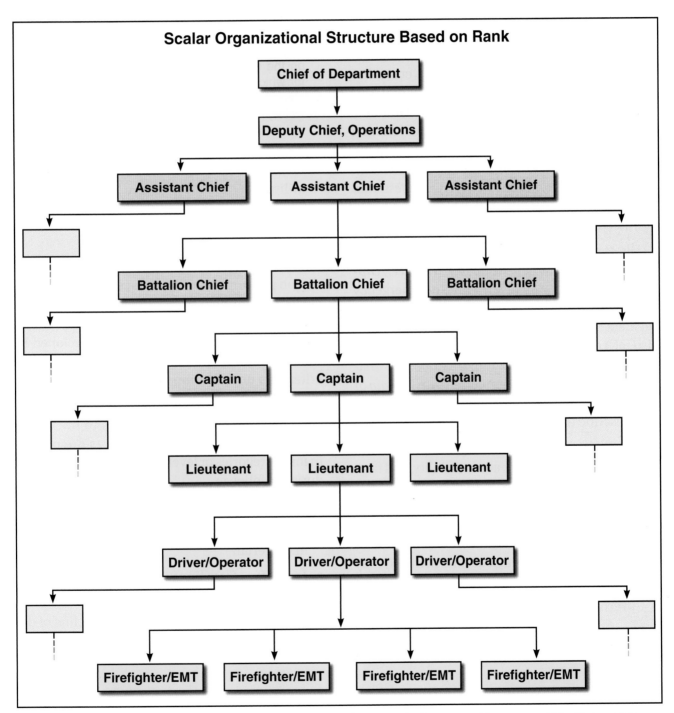

Figure I.1 The typical hierarchy of most fire and emergency services organizations resembles a pyramid that is based on rank as well as function.

The base of the pyramid rests on the firefighter or emergency medical technician (EMT) while at the top or peak of the pyramid is the fire chief, fire commissioner, or director of public safety. Between these extremes are the specialists such as fire apparatus driver/operators, supervisors, and midlevel managers.

Rank Designations

The first-level supervisor in this hierarchy is the company officer who is responsible for the operation of a single unit and the personnel assigned. This unit may be an apparatus and a crew that perform rescue, fire suppression, ventilation, salvage and overhaul, or medical services. Or it may be a small workgroup that performs a staff function (duties that primarily provide support within the organization) such as training or administration. NFPA 1021, *Standard for Fire Officer Professional Qualifications* (2003), uses the designation *Fire Officer I* to describe the first-level supervisor.

The terms used to designate the rank of this individual are generally *lieutenant, engineer, captain*, or a similar term. In large fire and emergency services organizations, a second-level or mid-management supervisor may also exist. This person is also referred to as a company officer and will have greater responsibility and authority than the first-level supervisor and will be referred to as *captain* or *senior captain*. NFPA 1021 uses the term *Fire Officer II* to describe this supervisor/manager.

The determination and assignment of duties, responsibilities, authority, accountability, and rank designations for all fire and emergency services personnel belong to the authority having jurisdiction (AHJ). In some instances, the employer and the labor/employee representative discuss and/or negotiate job duties for various ranks. An AHJ may be one of the following:

- Governing board
- Municipal, state/provincial, or federal political authority

International Fire Service Ranks

Within the fire and emergency services worldwide, designations of rank vary widely. In some organizations, the rank titles are similar to those used in the United States and are based on military rank structures. This situation is particularly true in nations that place the fire and emergency services under the jurisdiction of the military.

Other organizations may use terms that are more closely aligned with the function or duty of the position. For instance, the London (England) Fire Brigade uses the titles *station manager, watch manager A*, and *watch manager B*, depending on the number of personnel, units, or facilities for which the officer is responsible. In short, an officer's title may vary depending on the local history and culture and the organization's position within the jurisdiction.

- Military command structure
- Private for-profit company
- Private nonprofit governing board

The AHJ creates the organization, establishes the job performance criteria for each position, develops promotional systems, and hires and trains personnel to staff the organization. Many jurisdictions use standards that have been developed by the National Fire Protection Association (NFPA) as criteria for organizational responsibilities and job performance requirements (JPRs).

The NFPA standard that applies to fire officer qualifications is NFPA 1021. It places fire officers in four categories or levels based on their assigned duties as follows:

- *Level I* — First-line supervisor (supervisor)
- *Level II* — Midlevel supervisor (supervisory/ managerial)
- *Level III* — First-line manager (managerial/administrative)
- *Level IV* — Department manager or chief of department (administrative)

While Level I and Level II, the topics of this manual, are considered company officers, Level III qualifications are generally considered battalion/district chiefs, assistant chiefs, or deputy chiefs. Level III chief officers may be in charge of geographic areas within a response area, a specific number of companies or stations, or administrative functions such as training, public fire and life-safety education, or administration within the organization.

The Level IV designation is reserved for the officer who is in charge of the organization or chief of the department. Fire Officer Level III and IV requirements are addressed in the IFSTA **Chief Officer**, 2nd edition, manual.

The largest single officer group within the fire and emergency services is that of company officer. Level I and Level II officers provide the first level of supervision for line functions including the following:

- Fire suppression
- Search and rescue
- Emergency medical services (EMS)
- Fire prevention
- Public fire and life-safety education
- Fire cause determination and arson investigation

These officers also supervise and manage staff functions such as operations, planning, training, logistics, administration, and finance. They have direct contact with the majority of the organization's members and represent the administration to the membership. They are also in contact with external customers, citizens that the organization was created to protect and assist. Therefore, in addition to fire and emergency skills, they must also have the following knowledge and skills:

- Interpersonal communication skills
- Knowledge of basic administrative functions
- Supervisory and leadership skills
- Ability to plan and organize

A further distinction that may exist between supervisory and managerial company officers is based on whether the position provides services to external or internal (employees) customers. The terms *line* and *staff* have been adopted to describe the relationship created by this distinction:

- *Line functions* — Provide services directly to external customers based on the organization's mission statement and goals.
- *Staff/support functions* — Provide services to the line units (internal customers) based on the objectives established to attain the organization's goals.

In some fire and emergency services organizations, the duties and responsibilities assigned to company officers may blur and overlap. The result may be an organization that has only one level of company officer who must perform the activities NFPA has assigned to both levels. In other organizations, the Level I officer may be assigned to a line function and be in charge of a fire-suppression company, while a Level II officer is assigned additional administrative duties.

Regardless of the arrangement, all company officers should have the same knowledge and skills that will permit them to safely and effectively provide the services that the authority and citizens expect. Professional development that provides the ability to progress through the ranks should also be available to all personnel. Company officers should remember the old adage that they are *students of the position they aspire to, stewards of the position they hold, and teachers of those who are subordinate to them.*

Knowledge, Skills, and Abilities

The company officer must possess certain knowledge, skills, and abilities and have the ability to apply them to their assigned tasks. Specifically, a company officer must have the following knowledge, skills, and abilities:

- Understand the structure, policies, and procedures of the fire and emergency services organization and the larger governmental entity of which it is a part.

- Know how to communicate effectively orally and in writing in both routine and emergency situations.

- Know the fundamentals of human resources management.

- Know how to protect the safety and health of company personnel.

- Know basic building construction and building systems such as heating, ventilating, and air-conditioning (HVAC) as well as fire-protection systems.

- Have an understanding of the planning process, inspection procedures, investigation techniques, and public fire and life-safety education.

- Know how to deliver company-level emergency services to the public.

- Know how to deliver company-level training in order to maintain a high degree of company proficiency.

While knowledge and skills can be learned from manuals and courses, *abilities* are the outcomes of the applications of knowledge and skills. Abilities are based on experience and work ethic and develop over time. As an example, an officer must experience a variety of situations before becoming comfortable and confident with the application of the decision-making process.

This manual provides the information necessary to attain and perfect these skills. It provides the knowledge that is required to meet NFPA JPRs that will lead to Fire Officer Level I and Level II certifi-

cations. The numbers of the JPRs are listed at the beginning of chapters where they are referenced. Learning objectives, located at the beginning of each chapter will assist the reader in focusing on the appropriate topic and knowledge. **Appendix A** contains a guide that coordinates the learning objectives and JPRs to the specific page of the chapter that relates to the requirements.

The reader should also be aware of the difference between *training* and *education*. Both are essential for safe, effective, and efficient delivery of emergency services. Both are also essential for career advancement within the emergency services. And both are interrelated although different in scope and purpose. However, both are different in definition and application. Besides training and education, the officer must also realize the importance of *certification*.

Training

Fire and emergency services personnel are most familiar with the concept of *training*, which is instruction that emphasizes job-specific learning objectives and traditional skills-based teaching. Some knowledge-based learning occurs in the form of learning about topics such as fire behavior, symptoms of illnesses, causes of accidents, and so on.

The knowledge is then applied to the learning of skills such as fire suppression, patient care, and safe behavior in hazardous environments. Firefighters, driver/operators, and paramedics can be trained to perform their assigned duties and responsibilities. Training and practice helps to ensure that they become effective, efficient, and confident in the performance of their duties.

Education

Education, on the other hand, involves instruction that emphasizes knowledge-based learning objectives that are *not* tied to a specific job. Education is related to concepts such as management styles, budget process, governmental theories, or history.

Education is received initially in primary and secondary schools (K–12), colleges, and universities. Because of the shift in responsibilities, new company officers may be required to attend and complete various college-level courses. Continuing education is essential to advancement within the fire and emergency services officer levels.

Fire and Emergency Services Higher Education (FESHE) Model Curriculum

The U.S. Fire Administration/National Fire Academy (USFA/NFA), working in conjunction with universities, created the FESHE model curriculum. Degree-granting institutions are encouraged to use this model curriculum to develop college-level programs for the fire and emergency services. Currently, model curriculums have been developed for Associate and Bachelor Degrees. The model curriculum is a portion of a professional development program that provides a consistent career path for members of the fire and emergency services nationally.

Certification

Certification is the result of tests or assessments that are given to personnel to determine their abilities to apply knowledge and skills in various situations. Career advancement or mobility within the profession depends on certification.

All officers should attempt to acquire and maintain the appropriate levels of certification required by their organizations. They should also perform the following actions:

• Support professional development for the personnel assigned to them.

• Motivate personnel to attain the required certification, training, and education.

• Continue their own professional development to improve their skills.

• Set the best possible example for subordinates.

Manual Organization

The organization of the manual assists in the creation and use of a curriculum or curriculums for Fire Officer Level I and Level II courses. The manual is divided into two parts: Part A contains information that is specific to Level I certification. Part B contains information that is specific only to Level

II certification. Students who are using this text to certify for Level II Fire Officer are encouraged to review the sections in Part A that relate to the Level II requisite knowledge such as the chapters on communications, ethics, and leadership.

Each chapter is preceded by a page containing the lesson objectives and a chapter table of contents. These are provided to assist the reader in navigating the chapter and focusing on the material that is considered essential for the company officer to master. The following is a list of the chapter topics addressed in the manual.

Part A   Fire Officer Level I

Chapter 1: Transition to the Role of Company Officer

Chapter 2: Leadership

Chapter 3: Supervision

Chapter 4: Logic, Ethics, and Decision-Making

Chapter 5: Legal Responsibilities and Liabilities

Chapter 6: Interpersonal Communications

Chapter 7: Oral Communications

Chapter 8: Written Communications

Chapter 9: Administrative Functions

Chapter 10: Safety and Health Issues

Chapter 11: Organizational Structure

Chapter 12: Company-Level Training

Chapter 13: Human Resources Management

Chapter 14: Labor/Management Relations

Chapter 15: Community Relations and Public Fire and Life-Safety Education

Chapter 16: Records Management

Chapter 17: Preincident Planning

Chapter 18: Incident Scene Communications

Chapter 19: Incident Scene Management

Chapter 20: Incident Scene Operations

Chapter 21: Postincident Activities

Part B   Fire Officer Level II

Chapter 22: Management Activities

Chapter 23: Types and Forms of Government

Chapter 24: Interagency and Intergovernmental Cooperation

Some of the information provided in this manual exceeds the minimum requirements set in the NFPA JPRs for Level I and Level II Fire Officers. The information is considered to be educationally sound and intended to *raise the bar*. For example, the term *ethics* is used infrequently in the standard. The IFSTA validation committee believed that the topic was critical for all fire officers and, therefore, included it as a complete chapter with logic and decision-making. Additional material is provided in the appendices, suggested reading list, and glossary at the end of the manual.

Resources

Additional educational resources to supplement this manual are available from the International Fire Service Training Association (IFSTA) and Fire Protection Publications (FPP). These resources include a study guide that is available in both hardcopy and electronic formats, which will assist readers in mastering the contents of this manual.

A full curriculum is available for instructors and training agencies to facilitate the teaching of the concepts and techniques described in this manual. Clip art, photos, and illustrations that are found in the manual are available on a Compact Disc–Read-Only Memory (CD-ROM) for use by instructors as well as an instructor's guide for teaching Level I and Level II Fire Officer topics.

Terminology

IFSTA has traditionally provided training materials that are used throughout the U.S. and Canada. In recent years, the sales of IFSTA materials have expanded into a truly international market and resulted in the translation of materials into German, French, Spanish, Japanese, Hebrew, Turkish, and Italian. Writing the manuals, therefore, requires the use of *Global English* that consists of words and terms that can be easily translated into multiple languages and cultures.

This manual is written with the global market as well as the North American market in mind. Traditional fire service terminology, referred to as *jargon*, must give way to more precise descriptions and definitions. Where jargon is appropriate, it will be used along with its definition. The glossary at the end of the manual will also assist the reader in understanding words that may not have their roots in the fire and emergency services. The sources for the definitions of fire-and-emergency-services-related terms will be the *NFPA Dictionary of Terms* and the IFSTA **Fire Service Orientation and Terminology** manual.

Due to the many job titles and ranks that are used to describe a company officer, the IFSTA validation committee decided to use specific terms rather than titles to describe Level I and Level II officers. The Level I officer will be referred to by the term *supervisor* and the Level II officer will be referred to as *manager*. The difference in the meaning of the terms is presented in Chapter 3, Supervision, and Chapter 22, Management Activities.

Purpose and Scope

The *purpose* of **Fire and Emergency Services Company Officer,** 4th Edition, is to provide emergency services personnel with basic information necessary to meet the JPRs of NFPA 1021 for Level I and Level II Fire Officers. The chapters contain information that is specific to the duties generally assigned to first-line supervisors and midlevel managers and includes material that is not directly addressed in the JPRs.

The *scope* of the manual is to provide Level I and Level II Fire Officer candidates and current fire and emergency services company officers with basic supervisory and managerial knowledge. This knowledge is necessary to develop skills for ensuring safe, efficient, and effective leadership during emergency operations and nonemergency activities as well as the daily administration within the organization.

The knowledge of fire behavior, essential fire-fighting skills, and basic emergency medical skills is assumed to have been acquired before moving to the fire officer level. Company officers must be knowledgeable in the following areas:

- Concepts of management, leadership, ethics, and human relations
- Basic administrative duties
- Community risk, awareness, and demographics
- Emergency response duties
- Teaching of skills and knowledge to company personnel

Key Information

Various types of information in this manual are given in shaded boxes marked by symbols or icons. See the following definitions:

Company Officer Sidebar

Sidebars give additional relevant information that is more detailed, descriptive, or explanatory than that given in the text.

Company Officer Information

Information boxes give facts that are complete in themselves but belong with the text discussion. It is information that may need more emphasis or separation. They can be summaries of points, examples, calculations, scenarios, or lists of advantages/disadvantages.

Company Officer Case History

A case history analyzes an event. It can describe its development, action taken, investigation results, and lessons learned. Illustrations can be included.

Company Officer Key Information

Key information is a short piece of advice that accents the information in the accompanying text.

Three key signal words are found in the text: **WARNING, CAUTION,** and **NOTE.** Definitions and examples of each are as follows:

- **WARNING** indicates information that could result in death or serious injury to fire and emergency services personnel. See the following example:

WARNING
Live-fire training must adhere to the requirements set forth in NFPA 1403, *Standard on Live Fire Training Evolutions* (Current edition).

- **CAUTION** indicates important information or data that fire and emergency service responders need to be aware of in order to perform their duties safely. See the following example:

CAUTION
Fire and emergency responders must be familiar with the physiological, emotional, and technological limitations caused by the use of respiratory protection equipment to prevent injury or death.

- **NOTE** indicates important operational information that helps explain why a particular recommendation is given or describes optional methods for certain procedures. See the following example:

NOTE: This information is based on research performed by the International City/County Managers Association, Inc.

Referenced NFPA Standards and Codes

One of the basic purposes of IFSTA manuals is to allow fire and emergency services personnel and their departments to meet the requirements set forth by NFPA codes and standards. These NFPA documents are referred to throughout this manual. References to information from NFPA codes are used with permission from National Fire Protection Association, Quincy, MA 02169. This referenced material is not the complete and official position of the National Fire Protection Association on the referenced subject, which is represented only by the standard in its entirety.

It's All About You

Anyone who is familiar with the IFSTA manuals will realize the text infrequently uses pronouns like *she*, *he*, *him*, *her*, or *you*. This edition of Fire and Emergency Services Company Officer is no different.

However, the reader must realize that this manual is all about YOU. You must make yourself part of the manual. You must learn the information, make it your own, and apply it to your job. As a company officer, regardless of level, function, or assignment, you must be able to perform in a professional and competent manner.

To be professional, you must do the following things:

• Be a leader.

• Have a personal set of values that can be expressed as an ethical code.

• Have the ability to make decisions quickly.

• Balance the safety of your subordinates against the welfare of the community you serve.

• Stay abreast of the technological and operational changes that are taking place in your profession.

• Be able to take responsibility.

• Be able to admit when you are wrong.

• Be able to forgive others when they are wrong.

• Know your job.

• Be prepared for any situation or contingency that may arise.

• Understand the concepts of duty, honor, ethics, and integrity.

• Be accepting of others.

• Be able to delegate responsibility.

As a fire and emergency services company officer, you are the bridge between the administration of the organization and the people who provide the essential services of the organization. You are a supervisor and a subordinate — someone who assigns tasks and then helps to physically perform them.

Your community, your organization, and your subordinates depend on you. You must not let them down. And you must not let yourself down. At the end of each shift, you should be able to answer affirmatively the question *Have I been the best that I can be?*

Transition to the Role of Company Officer

Chapter Contents

Learning Objectives

1. Recall the importance of the company officer.

2. Select facts about the challenges a new company officer will encounter.

3. Indicate the types of expectations facing a new company officer.

4. Identify solutions that may need to be attained by a new company officer.

5. Recall the individuals or groups to which a company officer may be responsible.

6. Compare the Fire Officer Level I and Level II human resources management duties.

7. Compare the Fire Officer Level I and Level II community and government relations duties.

8. Compare the Fire Officer Level I and Level II administration duties.

9. Compare the Fire Officer Level I and Level II inspection and investigation duties.

10. Compare the Fire Officer Level I and Level II emergency service delivery duties.

11. Compare the Fire Officer Level I and Level II health and safety duties.

Chapter 1
Transition to the Role of Company Officer

When a firefighter, driver/operator, or emergency medical technician (EMT)-paramedic assumes the role of company officer, a transition occurs that is one of the most challenging within the fire and emergency services. Although the promotion from one position to the next may be immediate, the transition is not. The transition from follower to supervisor occurs over time and requires many personal changes and adjustments. Making the transition requires that a new officer know the following elements:

- Understand the importance of the position of company officer.

- Recognize the challenges, expectations, and solutions created by the transition.

- Know the responsibilities of a company officer.

- Know the duties of a company officer.

This chapter discusses each of these elements of the *slide across the seat* transition. See the key information box for one person's experience.

Transition: Slide Across the Seat

For some people the *slide across the seat* transition may be faster than for others. When I was promoted to fire-equipment operator in my career department, I left one station as a firefighter and arrived at a new station for the next shift as an acting company officer. Fortunately, the majority of the crew had more years of experience than me, and the company responded to very few emergency calls. Those facts offset the lack of knowledge, skills, and abilities that I would have needed as a company officer. As an acting company officer, the first shift was very unnerving for me.

Importance of the Company Officer

Company officers perform critically important roles in the fire and emergency services. These roles are important to the personnel they supervise, the administration they support, and the public they serve. The company officer is often the first and, in some cases, only contact with the fire department that external customers may have in their lifetimes. Therefore, a first impression made by a company officer may make or break the organization's reputation (**Figure 1.1**).

Figure 1.1 Company officers sometimes provide the public with the first and often strongest impression of the fire and emergency services organization. Therefore, it is important for the officer to be courteous and professional when interacting with the public.

Recognizing the importance of the position and its responsibilities is critical to performing the duties of a company officer. Filling the position requires leadership talents, ethical qualities, and supervisory skills that many new officers will have to develop.

At the same time, a new officer must be careful not to develop an attitude of superiority. This attitude can be the result of an internal self-perception of importance. If a superior attitude develops, an officer will find that the transition may be much longer and more difficult than expected.

As a Supervisor

Fire and emergency response units are generally close-knit, held tightly together by the bonds of friendship, experience, tradition, professionalism, and a mutual mission. Much like a family, the members of the unit feel a mutual respect and desire to protect each other from harm. They also look to the company officer to make decisions that will protect and provide them with a safe, happy, and comfortable work environment.

As a supervisor, the company officer is much like a parent figure to the members of the unit. The company officer performs the following functions:

- Provides leadership
- Acts as a role model
- Gives advice
- Provides representation for members to the administration
- Negotiates conflicts
- Applies counseling or coaching when necessary

All of these functions take place continuously, with some conflicting with others. However, one of the most important tasks of a company officer is to ensure the safety of the unit's members at all times, especially during emergency operations (**Figure 1.2**). The company officer must be able to balance the acceptable level of risk to the unit with fulfilling the objectives assigned. Completing assignments and bringing the unit's members home safely require skills that must be developed quickly during the transition period.

Figure 1.2 The company officer must make decisions that are based on the safety of all emergency responders at the emergency incident scene. The results of the unit's actions must be balanced against the level of risk to which the unit is exposed.

As a Subordinate

A new company officer will have had experience as a subordinate. Following orders, completing tasks, and using initiative wisely should have been mastered and will have influenced the promotion to company officer. At the same time, a new company officer is not only a *supervisor* but also a *subordinate*. A company officer is responsible for the members of the unit and their actions and activities. That responsibility cannot be delegated to another member of the organization or unit.

The organization's administration expects the company officer to apply supervisory skills to control the unit and effectively deploy it to complete assigned objectives. These objectives may mean performing training drills, conducting fire and life-safety inspections, or providing emergency care through medical, rescue, or fire-suppression activities.

The company officer is also expected to administer policies, rules, and regulations and enforce them when necessary. The new role of supervisor, representing the administration to the unit, requires the ability to lead in a way that provides sound results.

As a subordinate, a company officer is expected to execute the orders of superior officers (**Figure 1.3**). This fact may place a company officer in the

Figure 1.3 Implementing the policies and orders of the organization requires the company officer to communicate the organization's expectations and reasons for the policy or order.

position of having to enforce what others perceive as unpopular or unfair policies or orders. An officer must remember that being a supervisor is not a popularity contest. Nor should officers question or publicly criticize policies or orders that they believe to be unfair; this action can provide a negative example for both subordinates and peers.

As a Public Servant

Research indicates that the public has greater contact with members of local government than with any other government level. The company officer and members of a unit are the first direct contacts the public will have with the fire and emergency services of a local government. Many times, that contact occurs when members of the public are experiencing their worst day.

The company officer may interact with the public by providing services such as the following:

- Issuing burning permits
- Inspecting facilities
- Providing public fire and life-safety education
- Investigating suspicious fires
- Providing emergency care to victims of hazardous incidents

In the company officer, the public sees and judges the entire organization. How that initial contact develops and the results of it are crucial to the impressions that the public will have of the organization.

As a public servant, a new company officer must have an understanding of the role of public servant and also ensure that the unit's members understand this role. They must apply the concepts of customer service that are so important in private industry for keeping customers happy and staying in business.

The company officer should consider the fire and emergency services organization a service-oriented corporation. Members of the public (external customers) expect an efficient delivery of those services for the money they have invested in property taxes, fees, or donations. The company officer and members of a unit must always remember who their customer is and that the customer provides them with the resources to perform their jobs **(Figure 1.4)**.

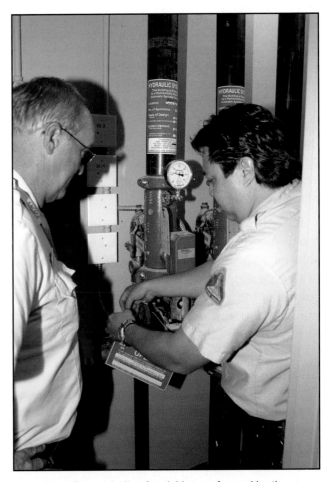

Figure 1.4 The majority of activities performed by the fire and emergency services organization will bring the company officer into direct contact with the public. The inspection of fire-suppression systems in commercial buildings is just one of the services the company officer may perform.

This concept of customer service applies to volunteer as well as career organizations. Members of the fire service are held accountable to deliver a service that meets the needs of the organization's external customers.

Challenges, Expectations, and Solutions

The transition to company officer includes challenges, expectations, and potentially the search for successful solutions. Making a successful transition is important to the organization because the company officer is the vital connecting link between the unit and the administration of the organization. It is also important to the new officer because it represents future promotional opportunities that may lead to greater managerial responsibility. Finally, success is important to the members of the unit because it represents a change in cultures of the unit and the type of leadership to which its members may be accustomed.

The move from the backseat or driver's seat to the officer's seat brings with it not only challenges but expectations. The personal challenges and expectations may be external (held by subordinates and superiors) or internal (within the personality of the new officer).

Both the challenges and expectations can make the transition difficult for all concerned. In seeking solutions, the new company officer must be aware of the challenges and how to meet them. Finding solutions for external and internal expectations may be more difficult to identify but are equally as important.

Challenges

Challenges that a new officer will encounter consist of learning and applying concepts such as the following:

- *Leadership* — As a firefighter or EMT-paramedic, personal leadership may have been part of an informal association with other members of a unit working as a team. As an officer, leadership is a tool that is used to ensure that the unit operates safely, effectively, and efficiently.

- *Ethics* — As an officer, ethical conduct takes on great importance because the officer is a role model for subordinate members of the unit, peers, and even the public.

- *Supervision* — Supervision at the company officer level may be the most difficult type of supervision one can encounter. The move from being supervised to supervising while still under the supervision of higher officers can seem overwhelming.

- *Responsibility* — Taking responsibility for personal actions changes because the new officer now must take responsibility for the actions of subordinates.

- *Authority* — A new officer must learn what authority is legitimately assigned to the position and how to apply it in a fair and equitable manner.

Of course, some of these concepts apply to all members of the emergency services organization and society in general. Ethical conduct should definitely apply to everyone in society. Each of the preceding topics is addressed in detail in the appropriate chapters throughout the remainder of this manual. A suggested reading list is provided at the end of the manual.

Most of the challenges facing the new company officer will be interpersonal in nature. They will be the result of changes in relationships between members, perceptions, and group expectations on the part of those involved in the change and evolution of a new unit based on the changes. The transition also presents personal challenges for the new company officer.

Relationship Changes

For the officer who is promoted or selected from within the organization, the challenge will be to make the change from unit member to unit leader. The relationship between peers and friends will shift to a relationship between supervisor and subordinate.

The change may be strained due to jealousies that occur because other members believe they deserved the position or because the new officer uses a style of leadership that is perceived to be inadequate and may not fit with the new unit. Or the leadership style may be one that conflicts with certain subordinates. To meet this challenge, the company officer must both learn correct interpersonal skills to communicate with members of the unit and practice a form of leadership that is appropriate to the situation **(Figure 1.5)**.

Another shift in relationships that can create a challenge occurs when the unit must respond to an emergency. During the majority of the work shift, members of the unit are training or performing routine duties involving station or apparatus maintenance. The type of leadership and supervision is more situational in nature. When the unit responds to an emergency, however, the dynamics of the relationship change; directions must be given and responded to quickly with appropriate action. It is not a time for questioning or objecting to an assignment.

When the emergency is over, the relationship returns to the form it had during routine station life. The difference between the two forms of supervision is that station life is relationship-oriented while the emergency is task-oriented and based on knowledge, skills, and abilities of members of the unit.

Challenges may also occur when there is a change in work schedules. Some organizations on the U.S. West Coast are moving from a 24-hour-on/24-hour-off work schedule to one based on 48 hours on duty with 96 hours off work. Working together for an extended period may have benefits such as being able to complete a project. At the same time, friction between members may occur that will consume the energy and attention of the officer for the entire work shift. The officer must be flexible enough to work within formal changes to the work schedule or within artificially created situations caused by extended emergency operations such as those experienced during the World Trade Center or Hurricane Katrina incidents.

What is Expected and What is Right

One challenge to a new officer is ensuring that the members of the company do what is expected and what is right. The challenge, in other words, is how do you deal with the fact that the booster tank was not *topped off* by the previous shift?

In volunteer, combination, or industrial organizations, the relationships that exist at an emergency scene will be drastically different from the relationships that exist on a daily basis. Spouses, siblings, parents/children, and close friends must be able to adjust from a friendly relationship to one of authority **(Figures 1.6 a and b, p. 18)**.

The relationship may even require the exchange of supervisory roles as the employer and employee leave a place of work and respond to an emergency. The employee may become the company officer, and the employer becomes the firefighter. Mutual respect and the ability to take and give orders are essential for the success of this type of relationship change. It will be necessary for both parties to recognize the change and to react accordingly.

Figure 1.5 New company officers are usually faced with the challenge of determining the appropriate interpersonal style to use when interacting with unit members. One style will not be effective in all types of situations.

Figures 1.6 a and b The relationship between company officers and their subordinates is vastly different in emergency and nonemergency situations. (a) At an emergency, the company officer must give direct commands, and subordinates must react accordingly. (b) Assigning station duties or determining when to make an appointment for an inspection can occur in a more relaxed atmosphere. *Photo a courtesy of District Chief Chris Mickal.*

Incident Command System Implementation

When the Incident Command System (ICS) is implemented, it is possible that a chief officer may be under the operational authority of a company officer, or a captain may be responsible to a lieutenant when the individual has a specialty that is required by the situation. These relationships are based on the concept that qualifications, experience, specialized knowledge, and training are more important than rank during emergency incidents. Company officers should consult their standard operating procedure/standard operating guideline (SOP/SOG) for clarification of their organization's policy.

Perceptions

Perceptions can create another challenge for a new officer. Members of a unit will have perceptions of the ability of the new officer based on personal opinions, experiences, or even rumors. Perceptions are subjective, often based on emotions and not on facts, and can be difficult to overcome. Members may also have a perception of the relationship between them and the new officer as a result of the previous relationship as friends and peers. They may expect that their friendship will allow them access to privileges or a freedom from strict policies enforced by the organization.

Unless the officer establishes an understanding regarding the relationship and the enforcement of policy, the unit will suffer. True friendship, however, should never result in a situation that places either the officer or subordinates in such a negative situation.

An officer, too, may have perceptions that can cause relationship problems with personnel. An officer may believe that the appropriate leadership model is based on authority and that *rank has its privileges*. There may also be the belief that rank immediately requires respect and that subordinates and former peers must acknowledge the new status.

An authoritarian approach in any type of organization can be disastrous to the officer, the unit, and the organization. This is another example of how an officer must use skill and observation regarding the most appropriate method of leading each member of the unit.

Group Dynamics

Finally, the dynamics of the unit will present challenges to the new officer and its members. The group dynamics may change as the new officer attempts to replace a long-time company officer who may have been highly respected and revered by members of the unit. Attempting to duplicate the actions of the previous officer can create resentment and loss of respect for the new officer.

Making sweeping changes in order to create a *new* unit can also be unsuccessful and cause the unit to suffer. The new officer should use the opportunity to verbalize personal expectations, establish priorities, and listen to crew member expectations. The officer must understand the experience-level and educational and generational differences within the crew.

Traditions

A new company officer may be faced with the challenge that is best expressed in the words *we never did it that way before*. At the same time, the officer may be tempted to use this same phrase as a response to orders or policies issued by the organization. Simply stated, this challenge is a barrier to change. To overcome the barrier, the officer must be able to explain why it is important to make the change, how the change will benefit the crew, and how the change will benefit the community.

Personal Factors

Making the transition to company officer creates a variety of personal challenges for the new fire officer. If this transition is not managed properly, it can result in antagonism, jealousy, and the loss of friendships. To overcome these personal challenges, the new officer must perform the following actions:

- ***Commit to the responsibilities, duties, and requirements of the supervisory position*** — Learn about, be interested in, and be dedicated to the position.

- ***Show loyalty to the organization*** — Support the leadership team and political authority. Do *not* openly criticize the organization, management, or decisions that are made by it. *Examples:*
  - Show respect and loyalty to subordinates by listening to their concerns, ideas, opinions, or complaints.
  - Validate subordinates' concerns by helping them come to a conclusion regarding their issues. When the concerns are valid, share them with the management team.
  - Show loyalty towards company personnel by giving them a voice to share their concerns, ideas, opinions or complaints. As a supervisor, the company officer is now part of the management structure in the organization, acting as the ears of the organization.

- ***Support all types of education and training*** — Seek opportunities to learn and also provide them to other members of the organization. All supervisors, regardless of their level, perform the following three functions simultaneously:
  - Stewards of the position that they hold
  - Teachers of those they supervise
  - Students of the positions to which they aspire

- ***Guard conversations*** — *Never* say anything, both on and off the job, that would bring dishonor onto a person, a position, or the organization. Do *not* disclose information that is confidential, in particular information concerning subordinates. Consider information confidential unless told otherwise.

- *Accept criticism graciously and accept praise, honors, and advancement modestly* — Admit mistakes and errors and take responsibility for them. Do *not* take credit for the accomplishments of others.

- *Lead by example* — Realize that setting a positive example is the key to successful leadership of any organization. This concept cannot be stressed strongly enough. That positive example must be founded on a consistent adherence to a set of moral, ethical, and social values. See Chapter 4, Logic, Ethics, and Decision-Making, for a discussion of ethics.

- *Praise in public; discipline in private* — *Never* discredit subordinates in front of their peers. Causing anyone personal embarrassment or humiliation in public can destroy any type of relationship.

Acting Company Officer

It is important to remember that the position of acting company officer or acting officer-in-charge is different from that of company officer. The acting officer may not have the level of authority of a company officer while still having the same responsibility. Experience gained as an acting officer can help prepare for the higher position, but it will not provide all of the necessary knowledge.

Expectations

Like the challenges, expectations take many forms. There are the external expectations of subordinates, peers, family, superiors, and the public at large. Some of the expectations are very unreasonable and may result in conflicts. For instance, former close firefighter peers may expect a new officer to overlook policy infractions because of friendship **(Figure 1.7)**.

Family members may not realize the added responsibility that results in more time at work or the increased stress generated by the new role. Their expectations of time and attention from the new company officer may prove to be unrealistic and unattainable. This situation may be the case when an officer changes from a 24/48 (or similar) work

Figure 1.7 Former peers may expect the new company officer to make decisions that are based on personal relationships rather than organizational policies or good management practice. This expectation can result in added stress for the new officer and requires the application of good interpersonal skills when a unit member wants to act like a friend or an equal.

shift to an 8-hour work day. The family, and even the officer, may not be prepared for the change.

Administrators may expect a new officer to automatically know how to lead, supervise, and perform the duties of a company officer without any additional training. The public will expect the new officer, like the former officer, to have answers to all questions and provide the same level of service without any time for transition. A company officer should be prepared to seek assistance from more experienced personnel or from the administration or training divisions when necessary.

Internal expectations, however, may be the most difficult to overcome. Assuming the position of company officer may cause an individual to improperly use the authority of the position, resulting in an abuse of power. Rank may also be confused with respect, something that must be earned and returned. Finally, a new officer may expect to be treated as invaluable to the operation of the organization.

New company officers may expect that they can *change the world*, setting their expectations beyond reach or reason. Realistic company officers know that the only person they can truly change is themselves, and in doing so create the opportunity for greater change. Bringing expectations into line with reality requires the realization that some expectations are unattainable or unreasonable.

At the same time, real expectations can be met through education, training, and effort. This manual will assist a new officer in meeting realistic personal internal expectations and external ones that are within reason. At the same time, a new officer will learn how to manage the unreasonable expectations and reach a compromise with the people who hold them.

Solutions

Every new company officer will be faced with some or perhaps all of these challenges and expectations. It will take time to develop new relationships and establish new unit spirit. To overcome these challenges and expectations, a new company officer will have to consider the following solutions:

- Communicate effectively.
- Apply appropriate supervisory techniques.
- Manage effectively.
- Project a command presence (**Figure 1.8**).
- Develop an appropriate leadership style.
- Show respect for others.
- Be loyal to the company, organization, and community.
- Be a positive and ethical role model at all times.
- Live by a personal and professional code of ethics.
- Set high yet attainable standards.
- Value diversity in people and situations.
- Praise accomplishments.
- Listen to others.
- Commit to education and training.
- Remain humble.

Figure 1.8 During emergency incidents, the company officer must project a command presence that gives subordinates confidence that the officer has made the correct decision.

Some of these solutions will be easy to attain, while others may require a fundamental change in the officer. By applying and practicing the skills in this list, an officer will provide the type of role model that the company, organization, and profession will recognize and try to emulate. Attaining these skills will require the officer to recognize what is lacking and work to develop it.

A new officer should rarely resort to using rank as a reason for compliance. Instead, the officer should establish relationships based on mutual respect for the abilities of members of the unit and the officer. An officer may have already established a reputation for good leadership, strong interpersonal skills, and fair supervision as an acting company officer. This previous relationship can provide a bridge for the new officer, even though there is a long distance between acting company officer and actual company officer.

A new officer should always remember that respect must be earned. However, it is also possible that members of the unit may decide to respect the position and not the person filling it. Then the new officer will have to work to gain the personal respect of the members.

Responsibilities

Regardless of the fire officer level or the type of fire and emergency services organization, all company officers have certain responsibilities. They have responsibilities to the following people or groups:

- **Subordinates** — Provide primarily a safe work environment by adhering to and enforcing safety regulations; also represent the needs of their subordinates to the organization and provide the following elements so that subordinates are effective as individuals and as a team:

  — Ethical leadership

  — Fair and just supervision

  — Educational and training opportunities

- **Organization** — Administer properly all policies and procedures of the organization; represent the organization to members of the unit and the public.

- **Public** — Provide effective and efficient professional service to the public; be conscious of the fact that the public provides the resources to the organization and that officers are stewards of those resources.

- **Profession** — Serve as visible representatives and role models, like all members of the fire and emergency services. The public and the organization's members judge the profession by the actions of its officers.

- **Family** — Listen to expectations and needs when relying on families for support and understanding; communicate the responsibility, authority, and requirements of the new position.

- **Themselves** — Live by a set of ethical standards and values that are based on the accepted moral values of the community if they expect their subordinates to live by them; respect themselves and abide by their convictions if they expect the same from others.

By understanding their responsibilities and the people they are responsible to, company officers will be able to perform the duties that are assigned to them. Those duties are generally outlined in the section that follows.

Duties

According to NFPA 1021, *Standard for Fire Officer Professional Qualifications* (2003), the duties of a company officer may be divided into general categories that apply to all fire officer levels (I through IV). The IFSTA **Chief Officer**, 2nd edition, manual contains information on these categories as they apply to the Level III and Level IV Fire Officers, while this manual addresses Level I and Level II. The categories are as follows:

- Human resources management
- Community and government relations
- Administration
- Inspection and investigation
- Emergency service delivery
- Health and safety

Each category is further divided into job performance requirements (JPRs) that guide the officer in the performance of the duties. Within each JPR are requisite knowledge and skills used to create officer training programs, establish evaluation and promotional criteria, and create learning objectives like those found at the beginning of each chapter in this manual.

Besides the duties delineated in NFPA 1021, additional duties may be assigned to the company officer. Examples of these are included in the Miscellaneous section later in this chapter.

Human Resources Management

As first-level supervisors for a group of employees, Level I Fire Officers must be able to perform the following duties involving human resources management:

- Provide effective supervision for both emergency and nonemergency activities.
- Assign tasks.
- Evaluate personnel performance.
- Provide company-level training activities.
- Administer policies and procedures efficiently and equitably.
- Recommend actions when situations exceed their authority or ability.
- Act as a project manager in certain situations.
- Provide professional development opportunities for members.
- Initiate or assist with personnel transfers, personal benefits (such as annual, sick, injury, and family leaves), changes in those benefits, awards and commendations, disciplinary actions, and labor/management issues (including grievances).

In addition to the Level I duties, the Level II Fire Officer must also perform the following human resources management duties:

- Evaluate personnel performance and ensure that employees perform to the best of their abilities **(Figure 1.9)**.
- Prepare projects and divisional budgets.

Community and Government Relations

As a visible representative of the governmental authority and the department, a Level I Fire Officer must be able to respond to citizen inquiries and complaints in an efficient and courteous manner. The officer must also be able to present public fire and life-safety educational programs for the benefit of members of the community **(Figure 1.10)**. The officer must realize that the success of any fire and emergency services organization is directly proportional to its community involvement.

Although NFPA 1021 does not assign the Level II Fire Officer any additional duties in this category, it is very likely that this officer will perform the same functions as the Level I Fire Officer. Knowledge of community demographics and cultural diversity, the services provided by the local authority, and the means of processing public requests is essential to all fire officers. In addition, fire officers in small

Figure 1.9 Performance evaluations provide feedback to employees and improve personal performance. Company officers are responsible for evaluating personnel under their command.

Figure 1.10 Nonemergency activities such as the presentation of fire and life-safety education programs are essential parts of a company officer's duties.

departments may be responsible for reporting to members of the local authority or interacting with managers in other departments within the jurisdiction such as Public Works, Human Resources, or Finance and Revenue.

Administration

A Level I Fire Officer must administer the administration's policies, procedures, and orders at the unit level. The officer observes the application of these administrative documents and recommends changes to them as necessary. A company officer maintains records of unit activities and prepares reports based on these records. Another administrative function is assisting with the preparation of the organization's budget by monitoring the unit's resources and documenting the consumption and cost of providing those resources.

Administrative duties generally assigned to a Level II Fire Officer may include the following:

- Develop budgets (based on the information provided by Level I Fire Officers).

- Evaluate the resource needs of assigned units.

- Purchase materials and equipment that will meet the needs of the unit.

- Maintain records on purchases.

The Level II Fire Officer may also be responsible for the development of policies and procedures that result in the efficient and effective use of resources and provide the public with the required services. Finally, the officer may be required to provide the media with information regarding emergency incidents or department activities based on organizational policies, standard operating procedures, and media guidelines. The ability to apply planning concepts and project the needs and resources into the future will be necessary in performing all of these functions.

Inspection and Investigation

When Level I Fire Officers are assigned to a fire-suppression incident, they are also responsible for the initial fire cause determination or investigation process **(Figure 1.11)**. That duty requires that the following actions be performed:

- Secure incident scene.

- Preserve evidence.

- Interview witnesses and emergency personnel.

- Notify a fire investigator when the situation warrants it.

Figure 1.11 Incident scene security is important to ensure the safety of the public and protect evidence that may be required for legal actions.

A Level I Fire Officer may also have to control the salvage and overhaul activities of emergency responders to prevent the destruction of evidence. Incidents that involve criminal activity such as acts of terrorism or the operation of illegal drug laboratories require that the following actions be taken:

- Notify the appropriate law enforcement agency.

- Designate the scene as a *crime scene.*

- Maintain security of the scene until fire investigation personnel arrive.

A Level II Fire Officer may be required to perform the following duties:

- Conduct a preliminary investigation of a fire scene.

- Analyze all available information.

- Determine the point of origin and cause of the fire.

Each state may have different requirements for fire marshals, which determine how much of an investigation may be done. Company officers must be familiar with the local rules, regulations, and restrictions.

This Level II Fire Officer may also be assigned fire and life-safety inspections, which requires performing the following duties:

- Understand building construction.

- Understand and apply the jurisdiction's building and fire codes **(Figure 1.12)**.

- Identify types of hazards and fire-protection systems.
- Apply fire and life-safety regulations to all types of occupancies.

Emergency Service Delivery

The duty most often associated with the company officer is that of responding to and managing emergency incidents of all types. The Level I Fire Officer is generally in charge of the first unit arriving at an incident and must perform the initial size-up of the situation, establish the Incident Command System (ICS), and allocate resources to control the incident. To help a Level I Fire Officer evaluate the situation, it is important that preincident planning has taken place.

The Level I Fire Officer is also responsible for the inspection of all potential hazardous sites within the unit's response area and the creation of a preincident plan for each. This plan is shared with other units and command officers (Level II and Level III) who may respond to the same incident.

Upon arrival, the fire officer must develop and initiate an incident action plan (IAP) and incident safety plan (ISP) and establish the ICS in accordance with local policy (**Figure 1.13**). Following the incident, the fire officer conducts a postincident analysis for incidents involving a single unit or participates in an analysis under the leadership of a command officer when the situation involved additional resources.

Figure 1.12 Company officers may be assigned the task of inspecting new construction and renovations to commercial and multifamily properties. They must have a thorough knowledge of the local building and fire codes as well as knowledge of building construction.

Figure 1.13 The first-arriving company officer at any emergency incident scene is responsible for establishing the Incident Command System used by the organization.

Working with Level I Fire Officers, the Level II Fire Officer performs the following duties:

- Develop preincident plans for multiunit operations.

- Assign resources to effectively control incidents.

- Conduct postincident analyses using information gathered from all responding units.

This officer may also be responsible for interagency coordination at incidents that involve units or resources from other levels of government, other departments within the authority having jurisdiction (AHJ), or emergency responders from other jurisdictions. This duty requires knowledge of the available resources, knowledge of protocols for acquiring those resources, and existing mutual aid agreements.

Health and Safety

Ensuring the health and safety of all personnel is an essential responsibility and duty for all fire officers. For Level I Fire Officers, this duty requires performing the following actions:

- Apply health and safety standards daily.

- Implement safety-related policies and procedures.

- Monitor personnel to ensure that safety guidelines are followed.

- Report all situations that involve job-related injuries or fatalities.

- Act as a role model by personally adhering to accepted health and safety practices.

Safety must become second nature for all personnel in all types of emergency and nonemergency situations. Safety policies are nonnegotiable, and the importance of safety cannot be overemphasized.

In response to an alarming increase in line-of-duty deaths (LODD), the International Association of Fire Chiefs (IAFC) and 13 affiliated organizations called for the first national *safety stand down* on June 21, 2005. The purposes of the stand down were as follows:

- Focus attention on firefighter line-of-duty deaths.

- Promote programs that address wellness and safety, proper apparatus and equipment maintenance, and safe operations.

- Promote safe behaviors in both emergency and nonemergency activities.

This safety stand down continues to be a part of many fire and emergency service organizations on a regular basis. See Chapter 10, Safety and Health Issues, for further information on safety in the fire and emergency services.

The Level II Fire Officer must know and understand the jurisdiction's health and safety policies, potential risks and hazards that result from unsafe practices, and methods for mitigating such risks and hazards. The primary health and safety duties for this officer are analyzing unit accident and injury reports and recommending steps to prevent their reoccurrence.

Miscellaneous

Depending on the size of the organization, company officers may be assigned other duties that are not specifically mentioned in NFPA 1021. Company officers may be assigned to training divisions, medical response units, or specialized rescue or hazardous materials units or to administrative duties such as the following:

- Performing preconstruction plan reviews (**Figure 1.14**)

- Issuing permits or licenses

- Acting as liaison to other agencies or organizations

Figure 1.14 In some jurisdictions, fire and emergency services company officers review and approve preconstruction plans or the private fire protection systems portions of those plans.

They may be responsible for reporting to the local governing body to provide information and advice. In any case, the ability to project a professional image to the public, to stakeholders, and to peers is essential for the organization and the officer.

Summary

The company officer holds a position that is unique in the fire and emergency services and supervisory positions in general. As a member of a unit, the officer must perform the same tasks that other members perform such as donning personal protective equipment (PPE), advancing hoselines, searching for victims, or administering medical care.

At the same time, the officer is a member of management performing the functions of a first-level supervisor, evaluating personnel, providing training, and developing budget requests to name just a few duties. The company officer is also a representative of the unit to the administration, the administration to the unit, and the organization to the public.

In each of these roles, an officer must make decisions, act ethically, and apply supervisory and management skills to provide a professional service to the public and members of the unit. Finally, the company officer must understand and adhere to acknowledged standards of leadership. Leader, supervisor, manager, and unit member are all roles that a company officer must learn to play effectively and simultaneously.

Leadership

Chapter Contents

Learning Objectives

1. Match leadership terms to their definitions.

2. Recall information about the leadership trait theory.

3. Select facts about the behavior theory of leadership.

4. Identify characteristics of various situational leadership theories.

5. Choose correct responses about the principle-centered leadership theory.

6. Match levels of leadership to their definitions.

7. Identify characteristics of the basic leadership, situational leadership, social-change, and alpha leadership models.

8. Select facts about developing leadership skills.

9. Select facts about developing leadership concepts.

10. Identify various types of power.

11. Identify personality attributes needed and steps to be taken to achieve command presence.

Job Performance Requirements

This chapter provides information that addresses the following job performance requirements of NFPA 1021, *Standard for Fire Officer Professional Qualifications* (2003):

Chapter 5 Fire Officer II

5.2.1 (A)

Chapter 2
Leadership

People ask the difference between a leader and a boss. The leader leads, and the boss drives.

–Theodore Roosevelt

Leadership has been called *a trait, a behavior, a skill, a talent, a characteristic,* and *an art.* The names of people who are considered leaders fill volumes of books on history, management, politics, and psychology. While definitions and examples of leadership abound, one thing is certain: In the fire and emergency services, leadership is essential.

The company officer must be able to recognize what effective leadership is and how to apply it during emergency and nonemergency functions. Leadership is critical in emergency situations where personal risks are high and hazardous conditions can change rapidly. Control of personnel is essential to ensure that injuries are kept to a minimum, accountability is assured throughout the operation, and operational goals are attained **(Figure 2.1)**. In nonemergency operations and during daily work activities, leadership is essential for using resources efficiently, ensuring a safe and healthy environment, and preventing interpersonal disputes that can weaken a unit's effectiveness.

Company officers must understand various leadership theories and models, types of power, supervisory methods, and management skills and apply them daily. This chapter provides an overview of leadership and its application by company officers. Chapter 3, Supervision, discusses supervision techniques as they apply to both Fire Officers I and II. Chapter 22, Management Activi-

ties, discusses management functions and skills and their applications. Appendix O, Management Theories, provides an overview of management theory development.

The terms *leading, supervising,* and *managing* are used to describe various approaches to the duties assigned to company officers. While both supervising and managing are similar in their

Figure 2.1 Effective control of emergency incident scenes depends on leadership, the application of the Incident Command System, and incident action plans (either written or not) that the incident commander (IC) uses to manage the incident.

definitions and are sometimes used interchangeably, this manual will limit the use of each. See the information box for definitions.

Supervising is most closely related to the act of directing, overseeing, or controlling the activities of other individuals, a basic function of the Level I Fire Officer as a first-line supervisor. Managing, on the other hand, will be applied to the control of a project, program, situation, or organization, a function often associated with the Level II Fire Officer.

Techniques for supervising personnel and managing projects, programs, situations, and organizations abound and are taught in university courses and business seminars. Leading, on the other hand, is not easily taught or learned. It is based on personality traits or characteristics that must be developed by the individual.

Leadership Definitions

- **Supervising** — Act of directing, overseeing, or controlling the activities and behavior of employees who are assigned to a particular supervisor

- **Managing** — Act of controlling, monitoring, or directing a project, program, situation, or organization through the use of authority, discipline, or persuasion

- **Leading** — Act of controlling, directing, conducting, guiding, and administering through the use of personal behavioral traits or personality characteristics that motivate employees to the successful completion of an organization's goals

Some organizational theorists, psychologists, and behavioral scientists believe that leaders can effectively supervise and manage but that managers and supervisors cannot always lead. The sections that follow provide the company officer with a basic understanding of the history of the development of leadership theory, leadership models that are appropriate to the emergency services, and an explanation of power and how it is applied through leadership. Also included is a presentation of leadership concepts and skills development for the company officer.

The application of leadership will be illustrated in the appropriate context in the rest of this manual through the use of examples. To be successful, however, the company officer must go beyond this manual with self-directed reading and study in the concepts of leadership.

Theories

The nineteenth and twentieth centuries saw the rise of the industrial age and the development of the behavioral sciences. Part of this development included studies into organizational management and leadership. Theories were developed that attempted to define leadership and apply it to the operation of business, industry, government, and the military.

Successive theories replaced earlier ones as more studies and improved research methodology produced more information on the concept of leadership. Some of the resulting theories have been based on traits, behavior, quality management, situations, principles, and levels. The sections that follow provide a brief historical perspective of the development of leadership theory.

Leadership Traits

Throughout the 1900s, sociologists, psychologists, and organizational theorists attempted to determine the specific character traits that make a person an effective leader. During a period of 70 years, more than 300 studies were done to pinpoint traits that were consistently found in all leaders.

The disadvantage of the trait approach is that no single trait was found to be consistently present in all examples. At the same time, no direct connection could be established between a particular trait and effective leadership. The advantage to this approach is that the traits, when emphasized in an example, provide multiple role models for the student of leadership to study.

Leadership skills can be developed through modeling by consciously observing role models and then applying the observed leadership traits through practice. Successful leaders in private industry, political leaders, military leaders, athletic team leaders, social activists, and religious leaders all provide examples of some if not all of the traits listed in the information box.

Examples of Leadership Traits

- **Supervisory ability** — Applying the four functions (planning, organizing, directing, and controlling) of management to accomplish the objectives through the efforts of others

- **Decisiveness** — Solving problems and making informed decisions

- **Intelligence** — Using common sense, logic, and reason in making decisions

- **Self-assurance** — Demonstrating self-confidence and self-esteem when making decisions

- **Initiative** — Accomplishing goals and objectives with a minimum of supervision

- **Desire for professional success** — Gaining additional responsibility within the organization through hard work

- **Integrity** — Applying consistently a set of morals or values to the decision-making process and doing the right thing

- **Personal security** — Knowing that the leader is secure in the position and does not feel threatened by subordinates, peers, or the political environment

- **Sense of priority** — Determining what must be accomplished first and maintaining focus on the outcome

- **Vision** — Having a dream or concept of the way things can or should be

- **Industriousness** — Accomplishing seemingly insurmountable tasks

- **Interpersonal skills** — Communicating ideas and getting along with others

- **Empowerment** — Sharing authority and responsibility with other members of the organization

- **Innovation and creativity** — Seeking continuously new and imaginative methods for accomplishing the mission of the organization

- **Consistency** — Applying procedures, policies, rewards, and discipline evenly and fairly over time

- **Preparedness** — Always being prepared for any potential situation and having contingency plans in place to resolve it

- **Living in the future** — Anticipating change and meeting it in a proactive manner (concerned with *what will be* more than *what has been*)

Historical examples abound in the pages of biographies as well as the stylized characters of folk stories. Because of the importance of leadership in management, many volumes are available that focus on individuals who have demonstrated leadership traits, how they used those traits, and the effect they had on organizations or situations.

Behavioral Leadership

The behavioral theory of leadership was developed in the 1940s and includes several styles and theories, including, among others, the following:

- *Basic leadership style* — Includes autocratic, democratic, and laissez-faire categories

- *Two-dimensional leadership styles* — Includes job-centered and employee-centered models

- *Contingency leadership theory* — Believes that no single best style exists

- *Contemporary leadership styles* — Includes charismatic, transformational, transactional, and symbolic theories

- *Theory X* — Bases theory on the average worker disliking work

- *Theory Y* — Bases theory on the average worker believing work is natural

- *Theory Z* — Bases theory on involved workers performing without supervision

Each of these styles may be the result of the presence of (or lack of) some of the leadership traits listed. Company officers should know the strengths and weaknesses of each theory and style and be capable of applying the principles that are most appropriate in any given situation.

The key to successfully applying the different theories to real situations is to remember that each theory or style is valid in the right situation within the variables of the situation. The seven behavioral leadership styles and theories listed are described in the sections that follow.

Basic Leadership Style

This style is one of the most familiar and groups leaders into three categories that are recognizable to most members of the fire and emergency services. The following basic leadership style categories can be effectively used based on the situation to which they are applied:

- *Autocratic* — The leader tells subordinates what to do and how to do it with little or no input from them. If this is the dominant leadership style used, it may result in significant challenges from subordinates. This style is appropriate for emergency operations but lacks effectiveness in daily operations. *Example:* Giving emergency scene orders and commands

- *Democratic* — The leader includes employees in the decision-making process and allows them to work with the least amount of supervision necessary. This style is appropriate for both day-to-day and special emergency operations such as hazardous materials or technical rescue incidents where knowledge and skills are more important than rank.

- *Laissez-faire* — In French, it literally means *to allow to do*. The leader leaves employees to make all the decisions and does *not* supervise them at all. This style is appropriate for routine station or community tasks. However, if it is the dominant leadership style, it can result in a loss of respect from followers and has the potential for a challenge from a strong informal leader. It should never be used at emergency incidents.

When the basic leadership theory is applied, the three leadership styles can be placed on a continuum or line/scale. The continuum is shown in the Basic Leadership Model section, p. 41.

Two-Dimensional Leadership Style

This style is a theory based on independent studies done at Ohio State University and the University of Michigan in the late 1940s. It is represented by a four-quadrant chart that compares the degree of job structure to the degree of employee consideration (also referred to as *job-centered* and *employee-centered*).

Depending on the amount of emphasis placed on getting the job done through an autocratic approach or allowing employees full authority (as in the laissez-faire approach), this type of leadership style can be plotted on a graph. This model was used as the basis for a number of the situational-leadership models that were developed beginning in the 1950s and continuing into the 1970s (**Figure 2.2**). See Situational Leadership and Situational Leadership Model sections.

Contingency Leadership Theory

This theory was developed in the 1950s and is based on the belief that there is no single best leadership style. Application of this theory requires that the situation be matched to the leadership style. Factors that affect the success or failure of a particular leadership style include answers to the following questions:

- How good is the relationship between the leader and subordinates?

- Is the task structured or unstructured?

- Is the leader working from a position of strong or weak power?

Contemporary Leadership Styles

This category consists of theories that are currently popular in the field of management studies. Although the following theories may not be readily applied in the fire and emergency services, the company officer should be able to recognize them when dealing with leaders in the political and business communities:

- *Charismatic* — Inspires follower loyalty and creates an enthusiastic vision that others work to attain. Leaders have strong personalities, and it is sometimes difficult to separate the personality of the leader from that of the organization. When the leader dies or leaves the organization, it is difficult to find a replacement that can live up to the image of the charismatic leader.

- *Transformational* — Depends on continuous learning, innovation, and change within the organization. This leader works to involve followers in the change process, challenge them to attain their full potential, and create follower satisfaction and growth while still meeting

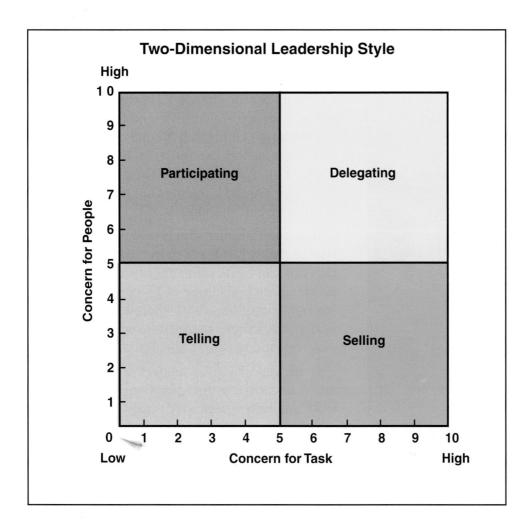

Two-Dimensional Leadership Style

Figure 2.2 Two-Dimensional Leadership Style Model.

organizational goals. True transformational leadership is a rare quality, yet it can be found at different organizational levels. Like charismatic leaders, these leaders are often identifiable by their dedicated followers. See Alpha Leadership Model section.

- *Transactional* — Involves an exchange between a leader and followers in which followers perform tasks effectively in exchange for rewards provided by the leader. It is a style that can be used by first-line supervisors and middle-level managers who have the authority or ability to provide rewards (**Figure 2.3, p. 36**).

- *Symbolic* — Bases theory on a strong organizational culture that holds common values and beliefs. Leadership starts at the top of the organization and extends downward to the first-line supervisor. Employees and subordinates have full faith and trust in the leadership of the organization. Leaders are viewed as infallible. The

difficulty associated with this type of leadership is that employees fail to question leadership decisions or to speak openly when management makes apparent errors.

Theory X and Theory Y

In his book *The Human Side of Enterprise*, Dr. Douglas McGregor contrasted two attitudes about leadership: Theory X and Theory Y. Each theory describes the beliefs that some leaders have about their subordinates, their needs, and their motivations. McGregor said that leaders develop leadership styles based on one of two views.

The Theory X leader basically believes as follows:

- The average worker is inherently lazy, dislikes work, and will avoid it whenever possible.

- Because of their inherent dislike of work, most workers must be coerced into performing adequately by threats of punishment.

Figure 2.3 Company officers can use the transactional leadership style to motivate subordinates to perform to their personal best. *Courtesy of District Chief Chris Mickal.*

- Only a small part of the worker's intelligence, ingenuity, and imagination is ever harnessed, but with proper leadership, workers will excel.

Theory X and Theory Y represent both ends of the leadership spectrum, and few if any leaders subscribe completely to one or the other. In fact, most leaders exhibit styles that reflect both theories. Both theories have their disadvantages. McGregor's X and Y theories fail except when applied to specific individuals.

In reality, a leader who is said to be a *Theory X type* probably just leans more toward that direction but still holds some Theory Y views as well. The opposite is also true of *Theory Y types.* Under the right conditions, both theories have application in the fire and emergency services as well as in private industry.

Generally, Theory X leaders are theoretically more concerned with production or the results of labor and believe that they must constantly push their workers to perform because workers are not self-motivated. Theory Y leaders are also theoretically more concerned with people and believe that workers will be motivated to produce because it is human nature, unless they are stifled by management.

- The average worker prefers to be closely supervised and shuns responsibility because of a general lack of ambition.

In contrast, the Theory Y leaders believe as follows:

- The average worker does *not* inherently dislike work — in fact, workers feel work can be as natural as play or rest.

- Workers will perform adequately with self-direction and self-control without coercion.

- Workers will support organizational objectives if they associate those objectives with their personal goals.

- The average worker learns not only to accept responsibility but, in fact, also learns to seek responsibility.

Theory Z

In the 1980s, in response to Theories X and Y, William Ouchi coined the term *Theory Z leadership.* He spent years researching Japanese companies and American companies that used Japanese leadership styles. Japanese firms have enjoyed a high level of commitment and production from their workforce using the Theory Z philosophy.

The basic principle behind Theory Z leadership is that involved workers are the key to increased productivity and that each worker can perform autonomously (without supervision) because all workers are trustworthy. The basic concepts of Theory Z include the following:

- Leadership style that focuses on the people

- Employees remaining with the company for life

- Close relationship between work and social life

- Workers' goal to produce economic success nurtures togetherness

- Participative approach to decision-making

Theory Z principles certainly have a place in the fire and emergency services because operations involve personal commitment, strategic planning, and tactical teamwork with personnel working toward a common goal. Emergency responders rely on each other to resolve emergency incidents safely, efficiently, and effectively.

They also spend a great deal of time together, which results in the formation of a family-type relationship. This inevitable bonding reinforces their mutual interdependence and promotes a commitment to work for the common good.

One problem that has been associated with Theory Z leadership is a resistance to change. Once a pattern or method has been established, it is difficult to introduce any deviation from the established pattern. Similarly, it is difficult to incorporate new innovations or equipment into the system. However, these dilemmas can be overcome through training.

A weakness in the Theory Z concept is that the leader is expected to alter the situation to meet the style rather than altering the style to meet the situation. Theory Z fails if workers do not exhibit the total unity and commitment to the organization and each other that is required to be continuously successful. This theory was a predecessor of the situational leadership theory and model (see Situational Leadership and Situational Leadership Model sections).

Total Quality Management and Leadership

The development of management theories in the post-World-War-II era paralleled the development of leadership theories. One of the leaders in both areas was Dr. W. Edwards Deming who is credited with helping Japan rebuild its economy after the war.

Although his theory, known as *total quality management (TQM)*, is primarily a management theory and model, it depends on the application of strong leadership that is employee-focused. He connected organizational results to the happiness of workers, which is now a cornerstone of successful businesses. See Chapter 22, Management Activities, for further information on TQM.

Situational Leadership

Situational leadership theories were developed to overcome the shortcomings found in the previous theories. Leadership theorists attempted to determine the appropriate style of leadership based on the type of situation. Theories within this category include leadership-continuum, path-goal, and results-based leadership.

Leadership-Continuum Theory

This theory was developed in 1973 by R. Tannebaum and W. H. Schmidt and is used to determine which leadership style (ranging from autocratic to democratic leadership) a leader should apply to a situation. As a model, this theory can be applied to the fire and emergency services if each style is appropriately applied to the correct situation.

Traditional leaders historically tend to be autocratic at all times. Leaders that embrace empowerment understand that it is possible to move along a continuum from one extreme to another, using the most effective and efficient leadership style based on the specific situation. Unlike the basic leadership style mentioned earlier, the leadership-continuum theory does not utilize the laissez-faire style.

Traditionally, weaknesses of this leadership theory have included the following:

- Requires the leader to be a good judge of situations and people in order to select the appropriate style of leadership

- Assumes that the leader has all the information necessary to make a decision or to act

- Assumes that there are no other external political or social forces that can effect the situation

- Oversimplifies a complex situation by making it into a two-dimensional situation

When this theory is applied, it can become two-thirds of the balanced leadership continuum found in the Basic Leadership Model section. The list of leader actions begins from the autocratic end of the continuum and continues as follows:

- *Makes the decision and announces it without discussion or employee involvement (Tell)* — Applies to an emergency-scene situation that requires immediate action

- *Makes the decision and then sells it to employees based on why it is in the organization's best interest (Sell)* — Works when the leader is supporting a decision made by a higher authority such as the implementation of a new departmental policy

- *Presents ideas to members and invites their questions (Consult)* — Clarifies a decision the leader has made to subordinates

- *Presents a tentative decision to members that is subject to change (Consult)* — Desires some member participation such as duty assignments

- *Presents the problem to members, asks for suggestions, and then makes the decision based on the best recommendation (Consult)* — Allows members to provide alternative ideas while allowing the leader to make the final selection (**Figure 2.4**)

- *Defines limits on a decision and asks members to make the decision (Share)* — Uses the consensus process to develop facility specifications

- *Sets limitations and allows members to make all decisions without interference (Share)* — Requires the leader and members to agree upon the limitations and the leader to feel comfortable empowering subordinates with the decision-making process

Figure 2.4 Company officers can take advantage of the experience and knowledge of their subordinates by consulting with them to determine the best solution for a problem.

Path-Goal Theory

This theory was developed in 1971 by Robert House and is based on employees' perceptions of the unit's goals and objectives. These perceptions are composed of situational factors. The leader then determines the best of four styles to use in influencing members in the accomplishment of those goals.

The following situational factors determine the leadership style that results in the achievement of goals and objectives:

- *Subordinate* — Consists of answers to the following questions:
  — How much authority does the member desire in deciding what tasks to perform and how to perform them?
  — How much influence do members believe they have in achieving goals?
  — How much necessary ability (skills) do members have to achieve goals?

- *Environmental* — Consists of the actual authority the leader has in relationship to the subordinate, the type of task (one-time or repetitive), and how much other members of the group are involved in the completion of the task.

This theory has the same disadvantage as the leadership-continuum theory: Both require that the leader must be extremely accurate in using good judgment to determine the appropriate leadership style. The leader determines which of the following four leadership styles best applies to the situation (**Figure 2.5**):

- *Directive* — Leader gives specific guidance to subordinates.

- *Supportive* — Leader shows concern for subordinates.

- *Participative* — Leader asks for suggestions from subordinates.

- *Achievement-oriented* — Leader establishes high goals and expects high performance from subordinates.

Results-Based Leadership Theory

This theory was developed by Dave Ulrich, Jack Zenger, and Norm Smallwood and explains that leadership ability should not be judged by personal

Leadership Styles Chart

Directive	Supportive	Participative	Achievement-Oriented
An autocratic approach that is required when • Members want and expect strong authority. • The task is complex. • Members have low-skill abilities. **Examples:** • May be applied to a hazardous materials incident where complete control of all personnel is required. • May be applied for new recruits just entering the fire and emergency services.	Useful when members • Do not want or perceive the need for strong authority. • Have high-skill abilities. • The task is fairly simple. • May be appropriate when personnel know the daily routine and are allowed to complete their tasks without supervision. **Examples:** • When a senior officer arrives at a minor incident where the incident commander has been established and has full knowledge necessary to handle the situation, the senior officer does not assume command from the subordinate. • Also useful in mentoring newly promoted company officers who may be highly competent in the technical aspects of fire fighting, but need guidance in their newfound role as a leader/supervisor.	Used with highly skilled members who want to be involved in the decision-making process. **Examples:** Works with a committee that is given the responsibility to draft a policy or procedure.	Leader sets difficult but achievable goals. **Examples:** Is valuable when members • Are accepting of strong authority. • Are rewarded for their achievements. • Have high-skill levels.

Figure 2.5 Descriptions and examples of four leadership styles.

traits alone but by the results those traits have on the success of the organization. According to the authors, effective leadership is the result of personal attributes multiplied by the results. The criteria used for judging a leader's success is based on the following:

• How well the leader balances the demands of employees, the organization, customers, and investors (in a public nonprofit situation, it would be internal customers, external customers, stakeholders, and the organization)

• How well the leader connects the results to the strategy of the organization

- How well the results conform to long- and short-term goals
- How well the results support the organization instead of the leader's personal gain

Principle-Centered Leadership

This theory of leadership developed during the past two decades is based on the writings of Stephen Covey. Referred to as either *principled* or *principle-centered leadership,* it focuses on the use of basic values or principles to lead an organization. It suggests that there are certain core ethical values on which individuals base decisions and live their lives.

Principal-centered leadership focuses on value-driven leadership and proactively living one's own life versus enduring a reactive life, always feeling controlled by another's actions. These values may be the foundation for the organization's mission statement or code of ethics (see Chapter 4, Logic, Ethics, and Decision-Making). In any case, they must be held by other members of the organization for principled-centered leadership to be effective.

The theory states that the leader uses these values to guide internal and external personal relations, make decisions, create policy, and determine success. Examples of these values include the following:

- Integrity
- Excellence
- Respect for the individual
- Harmony
- Loyalty
- Faith
- Honesty
- Courage

Covey applied this leadership theory to management as well in his book *Seven Habits of Highly Effective People.* See Chapter 22, Management Activities, for more on this application.

Leadership Levels

During the late 1990s, Jim Collins researched leadership in successful companies. The results of this research, published in his book *Good to Great,* prompted him to create a hierarchy of leadership based on the traits of various leaders and the successes of their organization. The levels of that hierarchy from bottom to top are as follows:

- *Level 1 leader — Highly capable individual:* Person who makes productive contributions through talent, knowledge, skills, and good work habits
- *Level 2 leader — Contributing team member:* Person who contributes individual capabilities to the achievement of group objectives and works effectively with others in a group setting
- *Level 3 leader — Competent manager:* Person who organizes people and resources toward the effective and efficient pursuit of predetermined objectives
- *Level 4 leader — Effective leader:* Person who catalyzes commitment to and vigorous pursuit of a clear and compelling vision, stimulating higher performance standards
- *Level 5 leader — Executive:* Person who builds enduring greatness through a paradoxical blend of personal humility and professional willpower

While all levels of leaders are distinguished by characteristics mentioned in this chapter, Collins notes that the Level 5 leader has characteristics that the others do not. Those characteristics include the following:

- Ambition for the organization rather than personal ambition
- Development of subordinates who will become successful successors
- Personal modesty and humility
- Driven to make the company succeed
- Diligence to ensure organizational success regardless of the amount of effort required
- Success attributed to factors other than themselves but takes full responsibility for failures

It should be apparent that the characteristics that Collins attributes to a Level 5 leader are value-driven and can be compared to Stephen Covey's principled-centered leadership theory. The Level 5 leader has strong personal character and humility and is focused on a vision of a goal.

The apparent advantages of this theory are that it achieves long-term, lasting, and superb results. The disadvantages are that it requires a great deal of time and personal investment on the part of the leader who, in the end, does not get any personal credit.

Although not all fire officers will become a Level 5 leader as defined by Collins, it does provide an example to strive for. It is essential that a company officer continually focus on the leadership style, model, and characteristics that will result in an efficient and effective operational unit and ensure that the organization meets the expectations of customers and goals of the organization.

Models

Many theories exist on what leadership is as well as how to apply any one theory to an organization. Many of these theories appear similar to each other due to the cumulative effect of their development over time. Some theories have developed into models for effective leadership.

What distinguishes a model from a theory is that a model has been proven through application, while theories contain only hypotheses that still need to be proven or disproved. With the knowledge of leadership theories, a company officer can select the model that can best be applied to a specific situation, type of decision-making process, or group of subordinates.

Basic Leadership Model

The basic leadership model is based on the theory that divides leaders into three categories: autocratic, democratic, and laissez-faire (see Basic Leadership Style section). This model can be effectively used in the fire and emergency services based on the situation to which it is applied.

Like any part of life, leadership can be placed on a continuum or line/scale from one extreme to another. The extremes of the leadership/management line are autocratic on one end and laissez-faire on the other. Company officers will find themselves at various points along this line throughout their careers and even on any given workday in their lives.

For a company officer to be a *balanced leader*, it is necessary to approach leadership from a moderate or centered point on the line **(Figures 2.6 a–c, p. 42)**. The balanced leader is concerned with getting work accomplished while considering the welfare and happiness of members of the unit. Therefore, the leader involves subordinates in the decision-making process and allows them to work with a minimum amount of supervision.

The key information box shows the characteristics of each leadership category that composes the leadership continuum. The company officer may recognize these characteristics from past experience with other supervisors or superiors.

Balanced Leader Continuum		
Autocratic	**Democratic**	**Laissez-Faire**
Controlling	Minimal control	No control
Makes all decisions	Involves employees	Makes no decisions
Work-oriented	Balanced concerns	People-oriented

Balanced leadership fosters respect and trust within a unit. A *unit* may be a *company, section, workgroup,* or other organizational component. Democratic leadership also implies that the situational leadership model discussed in the next section is a valuable tool that permits a company officer to vary the amount of leadership required based on the situation and ability of members of the unit.

The balanced leader leads by example. Company officers will never ask subordinates to do anything that they themselves have not done or would not do. This example also means that the company officer follows the rules, regulations, policies, and procedures of the department/organization and applies them fairly and evenly to all members of the unit. Decisions must be based on accurate information and withstand the application and scrutiny of logic.

Finally, the examples set by the company officer, and all fire officers, must be ethical and based on the values, beliefs, and morals of the organization and society. Officers who strive to balance their leadership principles will follow the continuum and use the three basic leadership theory categories at the appropriate time.

Figures 2.6 a–c A balanced leader uses the most appropriate leadership style for the situation. At an emergency incident, the company officer (a) uses an autocratic style by issuing orders that will result in immediate action, (b) employs a democratic style by consulting with personnel who have specialized knowledge or training, or (c) takes a hands-off approach and allows personnel to do the tasks they are trained for and capable of doing. *Photos a and b courtesy of San Ramon Valley Fire District.*

Situational Leadership Model

Based on the two-dimensional and situational leadership theories, this model, developed in the 1970s, depends on matching the leader's style to the maturity of the members of the unit or subordinates **(Figure 2.7)**. This approach was developed by Paul Hersey and Ken Blanchard as an extension of the Ohio State University study mentioned earlier.

The term *maturity* used in this context does not refer to age or emotional stability but rather to the competence, commitment, technical ability, and willingness of subordinates to do the task. The maturity of the employee (also referred to by Hersey and Blanchard as *follower readiness*) is based on the following two elements:

- First is the *ability* (determined by knowledge, skills, and experience) of the employee to perform the task.

- Second is the *willingness* of the employee to perform the task. Commitment and motivation determine the willingness level.

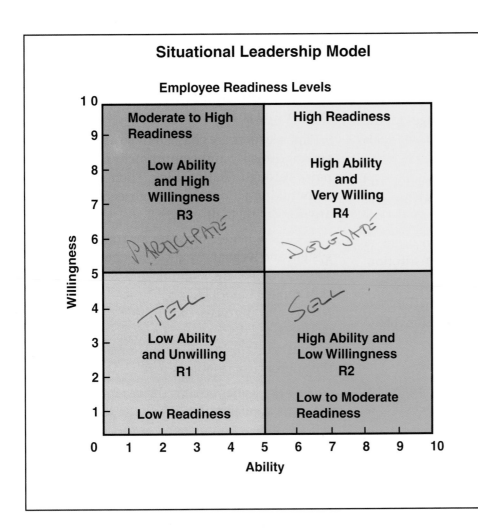

Figure 2.7 Situational Leadership Model.

The authors established four readiness levels based on these two elements. Based on the four levels of readiness, the leader may decide to use one of the following four leadership styles:

- *Telling* — Uses autocratic approach

- *Selling* — Uses refined autocratic approach that involves convincing members that the task is appropriate and justified

- *Participating* — Relies on input from members in determining how the task should be accomplished

- *Delegating* — Uses limits set by leader and allows members to determine how the task will be accomplished

Situational leadership allows a company officer to be flexible in selecting a style that best suits the situation and the employees who are involved. The leader is expected to examine each situation and choose the appropriate action to accomplish the task.

The ability and willingness of members to comply are also factors that influence the choice of styles. Not all employees are skilled or knowledgeable enough to be involved in every participatory management situation. Each member will have a different commitment level based upon the readiness level for which they have been trained.

Also, some employees resent the totally autocratic approach and rebel through various means. The company officer must have a sound understanding of the members of the unit and their abilities and be knowledgeable enough to use the style best suited to the situation.

Social-Change Model

Developed by members of the higher education community in the 1990s and based on theories like principle-centered leadership, the social-change model is regarded by some as the leadership model for the future. It is a value-based model of leadership that places service at the core for social change. This model has been used in university student affairs organizations and nonprofit organizations that focus on social problems and the need for change.

The model's purpose is to make changes for the betterment of others through leadership. The goals of the social-change model are as follows:

- Promote in the individual self-knowledge and an understanding of one's interests, talents, and values.

- Increase leadership competence in order to cause positive cultural change in an institution, community, or society.

Corresponding to and interacting with the goals are seven critical values that are subdivisions of the model's three areas:

- *Individual* — Critical values:

  — *Consciousness of self and others:* Awareness of values, emotions, attitudes, and beliefs that motivate people to action

  — *Congruence:* Consistency of thoughts, feelings, and actions toward others

  — *Commitment:* Personal investment of time and energy for the duration of the project

- *Group* — Critical values:

  — *Common purpose:* Shared goals and values defined by the active participation of members of the group

  — *Collaboration:* Application of mutual trust as a means of empowering others and oneself

  — *Controversy with civility:* Acknowledgment that group members will inevitably hold different views and that differences must be addressed in a civil values-based, respectful manner

- *Community/society* — Critical value: *Citizenship:* Acknowledgment that the members of the group have both individual rights and responsibilities to the community

Alpha Leadership Model

The alpha leadership model is a continuation of the transformational theory mentioned previously (see Contemporary Leadership Styles section). The model was developed in 2002 by Robert Deering and is based on the concept that the leader involves followers in the process of accomplishing a goal within the limits of the system. Thus, it is a relationship between four elements: leader, followers, system, and goal.

Alpha leaders are characterized as persons who generate loyalty and commitment from subordinates through relationships. Their subordinates enjoy taking action even though leaders never ask anything of them directly.

An alpha leader must be aware of the larger system and its goals by applying one of three core skills: anticipating, aligning, and acting. The first skill applied is *anticipating*. The leader anticipates trends and patterns that indicate problems or challenges in the system. The leader must have the mental agility to recognize the problem and assign the appropriate resources to it.

Next the leader applies the second skill: *aligning*. This application requires the leader to have self-awareness and recognizes the leader's affect on others. Aligning requires the leader to establish strong relationships with other members of the group and create conditions that permit each person to succeed.

Finally, the leader applies the third core skill: *acting*. The leader begins by applying the 80/20 Rule (also known as *Pareto's Principle*) by committing 80 percent of the effort on 20 percent of the tasks that are important. The leader is also proactive, rather than reactive, and listens to feedback from subordinates and customers. The leader remains focused on the goal at all times.

Alpha leaders understand the organization's goal and they align people and resources to achieve it. They are always open to suggestions and new ideas that allow them to be proactive towards all types of situations.

Skills Development

The first step in developing leadership skills is to create a list of accepted leadership traits like those mentioned previously (see Leadership Traits section). This list becomes the criteria or benchmark standard that is compared to the individual. The company officer also uses the standard as a checklist of personal leadership traits. Of course, this method is very subjective and can be influenced by individual differences, perceptions, and personal bias.

Another method would involve an anonymous survey of the company officer's subordinates, peers, and superiors in a 360-degree feedback evaluation that includes objective responses to questions about the officer's leadership traits (see information box). This method, too, can be very subjective.

A final method involves the use of professionally developed and administered personality profiles such as the Myers-Briggs Profile or the Acumen Survey. Personality profiles should never be self-administered or analyzed. They must be used under the direction of trained human resources personnel.

It is common to use a combination of these methods. The results should be compiled by a disinterested third party such as the organization's human resources department.

Once a company officer has determined the characteristics that are present and those that are lacking, it is time to develop a strategy for improving on the weaker skills. The fact that not all leaders are outstanding in all situations should also be remembered. For example, while some military

leaders have been exceptional field commanders, they have been less than adequate administratively or politically.

Depending on the area that appears to need attention, an officer may choose to follow any number of paths to improvement such as the following:

- *Courses* — One approach may involve taking a course in a specific subject such as interpersonal or intercultural communication or organizational theory. Courses on these topics focus on improving skills that are basic to the leadership function. These courses are usually

360-Degree Feedback Evaluation

The purpose of a 360-degree feedback evaluation is to provide a performance evaluation based on the observations of people who are associated with the person who is being evaluated. The information is gathered from people who have direct professional contact with the person, which may include peers, subordinates, employees, members of other agencies, and members of the public who are in reasonably constant contact with the individual.

The information that is gathered is based on the performance they observe. Written survey forms or oral interviews can be used to gather the information. Interview and survey questions should be open-ended so that they do not limit the response to a *yes* or *no* answer.

Responses must remain confidential to protect the people who are providing the information. It also ensures that they will speak freely and not hesitate to provide constructive criticism.

Feedback evaluations and interpretation of results need to be administered and performed by a professional trained in this technique. The organization's human resources department can usually provide this service.

Before considering or attempting this type of evaluation, a leader should possess a high degree of self-confidence. Furthermore, respondents to the evaluations must have confidence in the leader before an honest assessment will be performed. If respondents are concerned about retaliation, an honest evaluation will not occur.

offered though local colleges, universities, the National Fire Academy (NFA), or state/provincial or regional training associations.

- **Seminars/workshops** — Another approach is to attend seminars or workshops on leadership, diversity, and decision-making.

- **Literature readings** — A third method involves reading available literature on leadership and leaders to determine how to implement personal change.

- **Counselors/mentors** — Finally, it may be advantageous to work on personal traits with a counselor to help change or reinforce values and beliefs. A mentor, particularly one who exemplifies positive leadership capabilities, can also be helpful in providing guidance and feedback on leadership traits **(Figure 2.8)**.

Concepts

While the traits of a leader (see Leadership Traits section) may not exist in every individual, they can be developed and gathered into concepts that are fundamental to a good leader. The most basic of leadership traits can be summarized in five concepts: The good leader (1) sees opportunities that others do not, (2) identifies challenges early, (3) communicates effectively, (4) plans for success, and (5) builds trust with others. A fire officer who has these traits will be able to lead a workgroup, company, or unit successfully. Descriptions of these concepts are as follows:

- **Sees opportunities** — Involves having a vision that views situations from all angles while still understanding that tradition can provide direction.

- **Identifies challenges** — Involves recognizing potential problematic situations ranging from personality conflicts to political intrigue that may confront the workgroup, company, or unit. Recognition requires monitoring not only the internal but also the external climate of the organization much as a meteorologist tracks potential storms on a radar screen.

- **Communicates** — Involves not only being able to express ideas clearly but also being able to listen to and interpret feedback from others who are either internal or external to the organization.

Figure 2.8 The company officer can be a strong influence in the lives of subordinates by providing counseling and mentoring, which involves the ability to listen to people and hear their concerns.

Effective communication is the basis for all successful supervisors, managers, and leaders. Without good communication skills, a company officer will miss opportunities and challenges and, therefore, serve only as an autocratic leader.

- **Plans for success** — Involves generating plans, implementing them, and evaluating their effectiveness. Effective planning saves energy, time, resources, lives, and frustration. Planning is the sign of an organized and confident leader.

- **Builds trust** — Creates an environment of mutual trust not only within the organization but also within the community, service area, and profession. A company officer can create this environment in the following ways:

  — Lead by example and with integrity.

  — Place trust in the people who have earned it.

  — Respect others.

— Value fairness.

— Emphasize personal leadership.

— Support the political and administrative leadership.

— Grasp the importance of the overall situation by visualizing the big picture.

A company officer must also be able to recognize the difference between a *leader* and *manager*. Sara White has articulated one version of the difference in an article in a professional pharmacist's journal.* She stated differences as follows:

- Managers administer; leaders innovate.

- Managers ask how and when; leaders ask what and why.

- Managers focus on systems; leaders focus on people.

- Managers ensure that things are done right; leaders ensure that the right things are done.

- Managers maintain; leaders develop.

- Managers rely on control; leaders inspire trust.

- Managers have a short-term perspective; leaders have a long-term perspective.

- Managers accept the status quo; leaders challenge the status quo.

- Managers have an eye on the bottom line; leaders have an eye on the horizon.

- Managers are the classic good soldiers; leaders are their own people.

- Managers are copies; leaders are originals.

Because the company officer is a supervisor, manager, and leader, it is important to remember the differences of each role and act appropriately. This knowledge will put the officer on the road to great leadership that is common to successful leaders and includes the following actions:

- *Challenge the system* — Determine first that the system, or part of it, needs to be improved.

- *Inspire a shared vision* — Share next the vision for change in words that can be understood by subordinates.

---

* Courtesy of Sara J. White, M.S., FASHP (Master of Science, Fellow of the American Society of Health-System Pharmacists).

- *Enable others to act* — Give subordinates the tools and methods to solve the problem or make the change.

- *Model the way* — Show how to do it through personal example when the work becomes hard.

- *Encourage the heart* — Share the glory with the subordinates' hearts, while keeping the pains within the leader's heart.

- *Establish priorities* — *Examples:*

— The top priority is the emergency response.

— The second priority is preemergency readiness, including training, planning, and maintenance.

— The third priority is administration, including facility maintenance, documentation, etc.

Power Types

According to Webster's Dictionary, *power* is the *possession of control, authority, or influence over others.* Those with power can give advice, offer rewards, or threaten subordinates with a variety of sanctions. However, leaders often do not have to actually exercise their power. Instead, the subordinate's perception of the leader's power is sufficient to produce the desired effect.

Power itself is not inherently bad. The reasons for which power is exercised may be judged to be *good* or *bad*, and the use of power can be *effective* or *ineffective*. When people perceive power as something *bad*, they may be thinking either that the use of power is ineffective or that the motives of those exercising the power are questionable. According to psychologists John French and Bertram Raven, there are five types of power: reward, coercive, identification, expert, and legitimate.

Effective and successful leaders recognize the types of power and how they can be used to motivate subordinates. The company officer who adheres to the situational or basic leadership models will find that some types of power are rarely required.

Reward

Power is based on one person's perception of another's ability to grant rewards. Perceived power increases in direct relation to the amount of rewards an employee sees a leader or supervisor controlling. Leaders who have or are perceived to have this power can use it to motivate their subordinates to be more productive.

Results depend on the strength of subordinates' desires for these rewards and their perceptions of the leader's ability to provide them. Examples of organizational rewards that employees may seek include the following:

- Getting a raise or bonus
- Being promoted to a more responsible job (**Figure 2.9**)
- Getting an expanded operating budget
- Gaining trust or respect
- Gaining additional authority

Coercive

Power is based on subordinates' perceptions of the leader's authority to punish. The strength of coercive power is not necessarily proportional to the authority to punish but rather to subordinates' perceptions of the leader's authority to punish. Coercive power will not be required if the officer is respected and trusted to make the right decisions and is supportive of subordinates. Examples of coercive power are as follows:

- Verbal or written reprimand for substandard work performance
- Suspension without pay
- Withholding a promised or expected reward such as a raise or promotion
- Termination

Identification

Power is derived from someone's desire to identify with and emulate another. Celebrities are used to sell merchandise or deliver public service messages because of their identification power. They can influence members of the public because people want to identify with and be like famous spokespersons. In the same way, fire and emergency service leaders who are respected and well-liked can strongly influence others; therefore, these leaders have an obligation to give sound advice and set a good example for subordinates to follow.

Another form of identification power is *referent* or *personal power,* which is one's perception that they have power because of a relationship with someone who does have power. For example, a company officer may be a neighbor of the mayor. The fire chief and others may perceive the company officer has power in the form of influence because of this relationship.

Expert

Power is based on one person's perception that another's knowledge and expertise can help in the first person's endeavors. Knowledge is power, and those who have knowledge also have power. In any given situation, the one with the most knowledge often has the most power, even if that person does not have the most authority.

Fire and emergency services officers should know what special knowledge, skills, and abilities that their subordinates have. They should be willing to act as a facilitator to help these subject-matter experts when the need for their expertise arises. For example, a hazardous materials expert may be placed in a position of authority over others of superior rank during a hazardous materials incident (**Figure 2.10**).

Figure 2.9 Promotions, awards, and recognition can be strong motivators for all employees regardless of rank.

The same may be true of any function requiring highly specialized knowledge or expertise. In certain situations, a formal leader will accede to a subordinate who has greater knowledge about a subject, process, or situation.

Another form of knowledge power is *information power*. This power is based on the perception that a person or group controls information that is needed to perform a duty or activity.

Legitimate

Power is derived because of the organizational structure of the department/organization (also called *organizational authority* or *position power*). The legitimizing agency (department/organization) vests legitimate power in company officers in order to conduct the functions assigned to their units.

Company officers may derive power from a variety of sources, depending upon their individual leadership strengths and weaknesses. Those who rely on their legitimate or position power alone are not likely to be successful. They should strive to develop the ability to exercise all forms of power as each situation demands.

Subordinates will accept the legitimate power based on the perception that the officer has been deemed worthy of the position. Legitimate power is derived from one of the following three sources:

- Shared values
- Acceptance of a social structure
- Sanction of a legitimizing agent

Command Presence

Command presence is the complex ability to identify the components of a situation, assess the need for action, determine the nature of the necessary intervention, and initiate the action — and also to be perceived as having the ability necessary to take this action. The term is generally associated with the military or law enforcement personnel.

Effective fire and emergency services leaders can have command presence in all of their assigned emergency and nonemergency duties **(Figure 2.11)**. They are able to instill in others the valid belief that everything will be okay simply by their presence at the emergency. To achieve command presence, it is necessary to have the following six personality attributes:

Figure 2.11 Displaying a command presence helps to build confidence in the listener and establishes credibility in the speaker and the topic. Both are essential when it is important to convey a message such as fire safety to children or adults.

Figure 2.10 The company officer should rely on personnel who have specialized training and knowledge. In situations such as hazardous materials incidents, rank is less important than knowledge.

- **Self-confidence** — Leaders' self-images contribute to the images others have of them. Self-confidence is developed by thorough self-examination and having a clear appraisal of oneself.

- **Trustworthiness** — Subordinates must be able to trust the decisions made by the leader. This trust is based on the leader's experience and the experience subordinates have had with the leader.

- **Consistency** — Leaders must be consistent in decisions, actions, and relationships.

- **Responsibility** — Leaders must accept responsibility for the outcome of decisions and actions. Ultimate responsibility cannot be delegated.

- **Acceptance** — Leaders must accept limitations (personal, situational, and political) that cannot be overcome. Accepting that a solution may not be available and then working with the next best alternative requires flexibility on a leader's part.

- **Expertise** — Skills and abilities that are based on knowledge and experience are essential to command presence. Attempting to bluff through a situation can result in unacceptable losses.

Along with these personality characteristics, leaders can take the following eight steps to create command presence:

Step 1: Know what the situation is.

Step 2: Know what resources are available to apply to the situation.

Step 3: Know the strategy and tactics required to resolve the situation.

Step 4: Listen to all points of view.

Step 5: Make the decision.

Step 6: Take responsibility for the decision.

Step 7: Implement the decision.

Step 8: Evaluate the decision.

This eight-step approach can be applied to all types of situations from emergency responses to the development of a budget. Command presence will ensure confidence from subordinates, the administration, and the public.

Summary

When a member of the fire and emergency services is selected, elected, or promoted to the rank of company officer, that person's worldview changes. Both responsibility and authority increase with the new position. To make this transition, a company officer must have a strong foundation based on self-awareness, which will then provide the emotional stability required to be an effective leader.

A company officer must be able to recognize the various leadership models and the theories they are based on and determine which model is best by considering the situation, personnel, the organization, and personal leadership abilities. A company officer must be able to put all the theories and concepts into action and lead by example. Leading by example, based on accepted values, morals, and ethical standards, while focusing on and communicating an attainable vision, ensures that the officer will create a work environment that will foster mutual trust and respect.

The recognition of leadership skills development, leadership concepts, and the types of power and their use are also important knowledge areas for company officers. Finally, recognizing, understanding, and adopting command presence will apply leadership concepts to everyday situations.

Robert F. Hamm on Leadership

Beginning in 1967, IFSTA published *Leadership in the Fire Service*. This manual was edited by Everett Hudiburg and based on lectures presented by Robert F. Hamm. Mr. Hamm was a journalist, minister, and instructor in fire service training in Indiana. Although the terminology used in the manual may be outdated by today's standards, the concepts are not. The following is based on part of his lecture titled "The Successful Leader Today."

Mr. Hamm believed that a leader could be recognized by his or her actions and attitudes. Some of those actions and attitudes include the following:

- *Speech* — Speech in this instance refers to how the leader speaks to others. A leader's manner of speech is intended to help, inspire, and challenge subordinates to perform at their best. A leader is never condescending when addressing others.

- *Courtesy* — A leader is courteous and polite when dealing with other people. Phrases like *Please, Thank you*, and *You are welcome* are used at all times when appropriate.

- *Friendliness* — Mr. Hamm believed that nothing was more contagious than friendliness. If a person is friendly, it will then be easy to make friends.

- *Loyalty* — A true leader is loyal to subordinates, the organization, and the community. Loyalty is based more on actions than on words. However, loyalty also means being aware of imperfections and problems that must be corrected rather than blindly accepting them. Blind loyalty, as stated in the chapter, can take a person or group on the *Road to Abilene*.

- *Dependability* — A leader is dependable in all aspects of life. Promises are kept, assignments are completed, confidences are maintained, and words match actions.

- *Tactfulness* — A leader exhibits tact by being considerate of the feelings of others and in the handling of delicate situations. Tact requires the use of sound judgment, common sense, and kindness rather than direct force of authority.

- *Enthusiasm* — Like friendliness, enthusiasm is contagious. A leader approaches life, duty, and the task at hand with intense interest, determination, zeal, and fervor. Mr. Hamm quoted Ralph Waldo Emerson in saying *Nothing great was ever achieved without enthusiasm*.

- *Understanding* — Finally, a leader understands other people and accepts them for who they are and where they are in life. A leader understands that perfection is often sought but sometimes not achieved. Understanding is walking a mile in someone else's shoes.

Supervision

Chapter Contents

Learning Objectives

1. Distinguish between *supervision* and *management*.

2. Recall the basic challenges common to most supervisory positions.

3. Identify responsibilities required of a company officer to ensure an efficient and stable unit.

Job Performance Requirements

This chapter provides information that addresses the following job performance requirements of NFPA 1021, *Standard for Fire Officer Professional Qualifications* (2003):

<u>Chapter 4 Fire Officer I</u>

4.1.1

4.2.6(A)

Chapter 3
Supervision

In the previous chapter, leadership theories and models that apply to the fire and emergency services were introduced. Along with leadership, supervision and management are the other two important skills for fire officers in fire and emergency service organizations to have. These skills are different, but use of each affects the success of the others, making them interconnected. All three skills benefit from the application of the functions of management created by Henri Fayol, which include planning, organizing, controlling, researching, analyzing, directing, and evaluating.

This chapter describes supervision and the skills required to execute it effectively. It is important to remember that the type of organization (volunteer, combination, career, military, or industrial) creates a need for a flexible supervisory approach. Management theory and application will be discussed in Chapter 22, Management Activities.

A *supervisor* is anyone who is responsible for the activities of one or more subordinate employees. In the fire and emergency services, NFPA 1021, *Standard for Fire Officer Professional Qualifications* (2003), specifies that Fire Officers I, II, III, and IV are all considered supervisory personnel.

The definitions of the terms *supervision* and *management* are similar and often used interchangeably. However, this manual uses the terms to describe two distinctly different fire officer responsibilities as follows:

- *Supervision* — Includes the processes of directing, overseeing, and controlling the activities of other individuals and is basic to the successful completion of the duties assigned to a Level I Fire Officer.

- *Management* — Refers to the administration and control of projects, programs, situations, or organizations. Level II Fire Officers are often assigned management duties of administering a function such as public fire and life-safety education or logistics in a small department or managing an incident scene involving multiple units or agencies.

It should be noted, however, that a Level I Fire Officer may be required to manage a single-company incident or project and should be familiar with basic management principles. Training in supervision and management techniques is readily available at university and business seminars. Both techniques require the application of leadership theories and models as discussed in Chapter 2, Leadership.

Supervision Definitions

- *Supervising* — Act of directing, overseeing, or controlling the activities and behavior of employees who are assigned to a particular supervisor

- *Managing* — Act of controlling, monitoring, or directing a project, program, situation, or organization through the use of authority, discipline, or persuasion

- *Leading* — Act of controlling, directing, conducting, guiding, and administering through the use of personal behavioral traits or personality characteristics that motivate employees to the successful completion of an organization's goals

- *Following* — Act of being a team player while working toward a common goal

At the same time, a company officer is also a *follower*, that is, a subordinate to others **(Figure 3.1)**. Understanding that an officer has multiple responsibilities and some are the same as those performed by company members will help the officer develop the leadership skills mentioned previously. The definition of each term is repeated in the information box, p. 55.

Challenges

Most Level I Fire Officers have the responsibility for supervising fire-company-level personnel or small groups of around four people. The experience gained at this level creates the foundation for supervising larger and more complex groups as the officer advances to Level II and above.

The number of personnel who are directly supervised varies according to position and function, abilities of the employees, and complexity of the specific environment or situation. The efficient assignment of subordinates to a supervisor is referred to as *span of control*. Generally, the best span of control consists of three to seven subordinates with five being the preferred number. See the Span of Control section in Chapter 11, Organizational Structure, and Manageable Span of Control section in Chapter 19, Incident Scene Management, for more information.

As a first-level supervisor, a company officer has the following basic challenges that are common to most supervisory positions:

- Establishing priorities
- Anticipating problems
- Establishing and communicating goals and objectives
- Involving employees in the process of establishing goals and objectives
- Creating an effective team from the unit by fostering a positive environment through the use of sound leadership, team development, and management techniques **(Figure 3.2)**
- Creating job interest within a unit by motivating group members through dedication, positive attitude, commitment, and perseverance; accomplished through empowering, rewarding, coaching, mentoring, and celebrating accomplishments

In addition, the company officer provides an example to the group by demonstrating sound leadership characteristics. The sections that follow discuss each of the basic supervisory challenges and the responsibilities and tasks that are necessary to meet them.

Establishing Priorities

Essential to meeting all challenges is the establishment of priorities. A company officer's priorities are based primarily on the mission statement of the organization. Having priorities helps the company officer maintain focus on the important activities. Time can be managed more effectively, and energy can be directed toward the goals and objectives that will provide the greatest good for the unit and community.

Priorities also help an officer maintain a positive mental attitude. Stress and frustration can be reduced because the officer does not have to deal with competing issues that are not high on the priority list. Having priorities will also assist the

Figure 3.1 Company officers are both leaders and followers. As such, they represent the link between members of the unit and the organization's administration, which may be the battalion/district chief.

Figure 3.2 It is essential that the company officer and members of the unit develop into a team. In many emergency incidents, the unit will be operating alone and will have to depend on its teamwork to be successful. *Courtesy of San Ramon Valley Fire District.*

personal protective equipment (PPE) and tools with which to respond, and developing preincident plans for occupancies and hazards within the response area **(Figure 3.3)**.

- *Application of efficient organizational skills* — Included in this category are the completion of reports and records, station maintenance, and other administrative duties assigned to the officer.

By establishing and relating these priorities to personnel, newly appointed, promoted, or assigned company officers can frame their expectations in a manner that make exceptions unlikely. Company officers who adhere to these activities are setting strong examples for members of their units and will be leading by example.

Figure 3.3 Training is key to being prepared for emergency responses. The ability to use equipment (such as personal protective equipment) properly, follow established procedures, and respond quickly to commands depends on good training.

Anticipating Problems

One challenging aspect of supervision is anticipating, mitigating, and solving problems. The problems may involve resolving personnel disputes, scheduling resources, meeting deadlines, or dealing with the public to mention a few. A

officer in anticipating problems and establishing the unit's goals and objectives.

In the fire and emergency services, the company officer should recognize that activities can be categorized into three levels of priority: emergency response, preparation for emergency response, and organizational duties. To meet these priorities, the company officer considers the following preparation activities:

- *Mental preparation for emergency response* — To meet this first priority, the company officer and members of the unit must be mentally and emotionally prepared to respond to any type of emergency situation at any time during their work shift.

- *Direct preparation for emergency response* — These activities include training and drilling as a team, preparing the apparatus, obtaining supervisor must be able to recognize the potential for a problem, determine a fair and equitable solution, and then apply appropriate principles to remedy the problem.

When a problem arises suddenly, it is necessary to react to the situation and attempt to resolve it quickly. Such actions taken by supervisors need to be corrective, progressive, and lawful.

To anticipate a personnel problem means that company officers must listen emphatically, which means they must monitor the unit closely, know individual members, and be aware of symptoms of stress, jealousy, harassment, dissatisfaction, anger, and disrespect for others. When the first sign of a problem arises (such as excessive griping, abuse of sick leave, or loss of enthusiasm), a supervisor must be able to respond in a proactive manner. Failure to recognize and take appropriate action allows a problem to grow.

This proactive approach may consist of counseling with employees, listening to grievances, and suggesting solutions **(Figure 3.4)**. Obviously, the first step is to be a good listener. If the problem is very complex or outside the skills of the supervisor (such as financial, marital, or substance-abuse-related situations), the supervisor needs to follow the organization's policy by referring the employee to the organization's employee assistance program (EAP) or human resources department.

When a situation occurs quickly and requires immediate action, a supervisor should attempt to defuse the situation and exhibit good command presence. Individuals who are angry or emotional will not hear rational solutions to problems. Once the individual or involved parties are calm, counseling can begin to determine the root cause of the incident and find a solution. In all cases, a complete record of the incident and counseling session should be kept to protect all parties involved and the supervisor from unsubstantiated accusations at a later date.

Establishing and Communicating Goals and Objectives

A company officer must be able to establish certain short-range objectives, based on the established priorities listed earlier, to meet the goals assigned to the unit. The company officer applies the steps of the planning process to develop the unit's short-range objectives, which are based on the overall long-range goals of the organization.

Objectives should be attainable, clearly stated, measurable, and within the capability of the unit. Realistic time frames for completion of the objectives must be established and adhered to. These objectives, along with the goals of the organization, must be communicated to members of the unit.

Communicating the goals and objectives for nonemergency projects and then tracking the progress toward meeting those objectives can be accomplished in a number of the following ways:

- Communication can take place through group meetings where the information is passed on verbally **(Figure 3.5)**.

- Written task sheets can be provided to each member of the unit. Individual assignments and deadlines are included on the sheets.

- Objectives can be incorporated into graphs or timelines that are posted on a bulletin board in the work area and updated as deadlines are met. When members of a unit are located at remote work sites, objectives can be distributed electronically and the graphs displayed for all members to access.

Company officers who communicate goals and objectives clearly and provide periodic progress reports (feedback) to members of the unit will find that the group works more efficiently and effectively toward a common goal. In addition,

Figure 3.4 Counseling personnel should always be done in private. Depending on the complexity of the individual's problem, the company officer may attempt to resolve it or refer the individual to the employee assistance program.

supervisors who involve employees in the process of establishing objectives will find that employees have more incentives to fulfill the objectives.

At emergency incidents, a company officer must communicate instructions clearly and concisely. Subordinates must be able to understand the goals and objectives of the operation based on the directions that are given. There is usually no time for subordinates to ask questions in emergency situations. Therefore, the instructions should be as complete and easily understood as possible **(Figure 3.6)**.

Figure 3.5 The company officer should communicate project goals and objectives through meetings with unit members. This approach allows members to ask questions, clarify misunderstandings, and become part of the solution.

Figures 3.6 Commands given at emergency incidents should be clear and concise. The company officer must ensure that the person receiving the order fully understands what is expected and what must be done.

Involving Employees in the Process

Supervisors can involve employees in the process of establishing goals and objectives in one of the following three methods:

- *Simply require the employee to accomplish a specific task* — Relies on the concept that the supervisor knows the best practice to perform the task and has all the information necessary to make the decision and that the employee is thoroughly trained in performing the task as required. This method has been the traditional method in the military, fire service, and business field during much of the past century. *Factors:*

  — In an emergency situation where time is critical and reaction must be immediate, this autocratic leadership method may still be an option.

  — However, regular use of this method for non-emergency tasks can serve as a disincentive and lead to employee resentment.

- *Delegate tasks* — Allows the employee to select the specific method for accomplishing the task. Similar to the first method, but involves giving the employee the authority to accomplish the task and accepting the fact that the employee is capable of deciding how to do it. *Considerations:*

  — Delegation of authority helps to promote an atmosphere of team spirit within the unit.

  — It also gives the employee a sense of value and self-respect, while allowing the supervisor more time and energy to deal with more urgent problems.

  — Delegation works very well in emergency situations when subordinates are experienced and the company officer has confidence in their abilities.

- *Use democratic leadership principles* — Gives members of the unit an opportunity to establish goals and objectives during the planning stage. Initially, the chief of the department and senior management team establish the organizational goals and determine the major objectives for each division of the organization for a specific time period. *Process:*

— Each division chief meets with officers in charge of the units within the division and communicates the objectives that apply to them. In some cases, objectives that are assigned to one division affect the operation of another division.

— Ultimately, it may become the responsibility of the company officer and members of the unit to develop the objectives that directly affect them.

— Recommended objectives are then transmitted back through the chain of command and, if adopted, added to the rest of the organization's objectives.

In the democratic leadership approach, for example, a company officer may be involved in the decision-making process for purchasing a new fire apparatus. The company officer must gather information from members of the unit, coordinate efforts with all work shifts, and provide an objective set of requirements from the standpoint of the people who will use the apparatus. The company officer involves each member of the company on each work shift through a brainstorming process that uses the knowledge, skills, and experience of each member.

In this method, the company officer is a member of the unit and also facilitator and coach by guiding the unit toward the objective of developing the apparatus specifications. From the standpoint of daily operations, members of the unit can also assist in the development of operational policies and procedures, including use, care, and maintenance of the apparatus and logistical support (**Figure 3.7**).

Creating an Effective Team from the Unit

Each supervisor is responsible for a unit based on the organizational function of the various divisions of the organization. Although a unit may vary in size from as few as four people to as many as an entire division, a company officer will usually supervise the smallest of these groups. These units are the basis for the organization's table of organization (see a sample in **Appendix B**).

Fire and emergency services personnel generally think in terms of *companies* when they think of the basic unit of the organization. Companies

Figure 3.7 The democratic approach to leadership provides everyone in the unit with the opportunity to contribute to the decision-making process. The company officer acts as a facilitator during group sessions such as apparatus or facility-design discussions.

are usually composed of three or more people and assigned to a vehicle or apparatus. They are also assigned specific tasks based on the unit's functions. The term *unit* is used in this manual to include all types of assignments, including fire suppression, search and rescue, or emergency medical services (EMS).

Companies or units may also be thought of in terms such as *workgroups* or *teams*. These terms may be applied to both line and staff units such as emergency response and administration. The personnel in these groups compose a team. The company officer must work to create an atmosphere that is conducive to team building. Descriptions are as follows:

- *Workgroups* — Groupings of people with the common purpose of completing specific objectives within the organization. Workgroups are provided with the necessary facilities, equipment, and other resources needed to accomplish their assigned tasks. It is the responsibility of the individual company officer to build a team from the workgroup.

- *Team building* — Process of overcoming inherent individual differences (such as age, experience, rank, job classification, education, gender, ethnicity, religion, politics, and personal interests) within the unit and empowering members to make decisions for the benefit of the

- If difficulties in the private lives of employees start to have negative effects on the workgroup, intervene with care.

- If there are problems of a personal nature, refer employees to the appropriate employee assistance program, human resources department, or other behavioral counseling services for assistance.

Creating Job Interest Within a Unit

The company officer can create job interest within a unit in a number of ways. Some effective methods include empowering employees, providing rewards and incentives, coaching, counseling and mentoring members of the unit, and celebrating accomplishments.

Creating Job Interest: Definitions

- *Coaching* — Informal process of giving motivational direction, positive reinforcement, and constructive feedback to employees in order to maintain and improve their performances and ensure successful performances

- *Counseling* — Formal process that involves activities that assist participants in identifying and resolving personal, behavioral, or career problems that are adversely affecting performance

- *Mentoring* — Process used to prepare capable individuals for advancement within the organization through the direction of a positive role model

Empowering Employees

Empowering employees is a form of delegation that allows subordinates to take responsibility for their actions and decisions. It helps to build self-esteem and motivation within the employee. It is based on the concept of giving decision-making power to employees instead of having the supervisor retain it.

Empowering employees requires the supervisor to relinquish some authority and have confidence in employees' skills, judgment, and abilities. By empowering employees, the supervisor is helping to increase their self-image and productivity.

If members of a unit have not experienced the empowerment process, it is important for the company officer to begin with small attainable projects. The following steps can be used:

Step 1: Identify the problem or decision that must be made. The solution must be attainable and one that will benefit the majority of members.

Step 2: State that all solutions will be considered but the best one will be adopted. Tell the unit that they must prioritize the suggested solutions and include a contingency in the event the best choice cannot be used.

Step 3: Explain the reality that outside forces may prevent the adoption of some results. Lack of personnel, funds, or time as well as political considerations are among the barriers to implementation.

Utilizing an employee's special talents can both empower and involve the employee in a project more deeply. For instance, personal skills such as photography, calligraphy, computer skills, or other hobbies may be a means for allowing employees to add more to the project.

Empowerment gives an employee a vested interest in the project and organization. As an internal customer, the employee's success is directly linked to the success of the organization.

Rewarding Employees

Generally, supervising fire officers do not have authority to grant raises, give time off, or provide any type of monetary rewards for employees, but that fact does not mean that they cannot provide rewards and incentives for good work within the unit. *Incentives* are those things earned through effort or participation.

Rewards are critical as motivational techniques in volunteer and combination or career departments/organizations **(Figure 3.10, p. 64)**. Some reward and incentive examples are as follows:

- Make public acknowledgements of accomplishments.

- Hold group gatherings or parties to create cohesiveness and spirit.

- Make positive statements on the skills and abilities of members of the unit to improve self-esteem. Recognition by a supervisor is a good motivator.

- Make appropriate comments on an employee's job performance evaluation, which can result in future monetary rewards.

- Acknowledge a unit's or an individual's accomplishments to the organization's administration.

The size or value of the incentive is not the critical part of providing incentives for accomplishments; it is the mere fact that the company officer made an effort to acknowledge an individual's contribution to a group or project. Reward and award programs are critical to the volunteer staffing component and improve morale in combination and career departments/organizations.

The organization should have a series of reward and award programs. The company officer should be aware of the programs that are available and use them. However, rewards and awards must be earned in order to validate the incentive. When a person is presented with a reward or award that is not truly earned, disrespect is shown to that individual as well as other individuals who deserved the recognition.

It is important to give rewards as soon as possible following the accomplishment. Delaying the award or reward lessens the value of the recognition. The company officer must be consistent in the types of rewards given, situations that result in the presentation of them, and justifications for giving them.

Coaching Employees

Coaching is an informal process of giving motivational direction, positive reinforcement, and constructive feedback to employees in order to maintain and improve their performances and ensure successful performances. To be effective, the feedback needs to be positive, immediate, direct, and frequent. As a coach, the company officer teaches and directs the subordinate through encouragement and advice **(Figure 3.11)**.

An effective coach helps a subordinate establish a goal and determine how to reach the goal and provides suggestions when they are requested.

Figure 3.11 Coaching is an easy method for motivating employees and ensuring their continued commitment to the organization through their personal success.

Figure 3.10 People are motivated by rewards. Those rewards can be as simple as a public acknowledgement of an accomplishment or as formal as a promotion and pay increase.

Telling the subordinate what to do and how to do it is not as effective because the subordinate will not feel like taking responsibility for the process. The situational leadership model can be applied to coaching as the leader allows the subordinate to make decisions under the leader's guidance. See Chapter 2, Leadership.

Counseling Employees

Counseling is a formal process that involves activities that assist participants in identifying and resolving personal, behavioral, or career problems that are adversely affecting performance. Sessions may be scheduled on a periodic basis such as annually, before a promotional examination, or when the subordinate exhibits unacceptable behavior.

Counseling should occur in private, and a record should be kept of the session. The company officer must adhere to the policies, procedures, and rules for counseling that have been established by the jurisdiction. The company officer must also be familiar with the labor/management agreement regarding the right to union representation during counseling sessions as well as the grievance procedures established by the agreement.

The following four-step method of counseling can be used in the fire and emergency services:

Step 1: ***Describe the current performance*** — Describe levels in a positive manner. Specifically state the required behavior and expectations. Explain how and why current behavior is not acceptable. Specify how behaviors can be improved by using specific examples.

Step 2: ***Describe the desired performance*** — State in detail exactly what action is expected or required in order to provide clear direction for the employee.

Step 3: ***Gain a commitment for change*** — Ask the employee to agree to the new level of performance. In some cases, this commitment could be considered a contract and become part of the employee's formal personnel record.

Step 4: ***Follow up the commitment*** — Observe the employee following the counseling session to determine whether performance improves or schedule a follow-up meeting to discuss progress. If change does not occur, subsequent counseling sessions may be required. If unacceptable behavior continues after subsequent counseling, refer the situation to the next level of administration, based on the organization's counseling policy and the labor/management agreement.

Mentoring Employees

The primary purpose of mentoring is to prepare capable individuals for advancement within the organization through the direction of a positive role model. Mentoring programs enhance management skills, improve productivity, and encourage diversity **(Figure 3.12)**.

Experienced supervisors can mentor in the following ways:

- Provide role models for future leaders.
- Provide guidance in career choices.
- Assist in gaining specialized training.
- Provide outside resources.
- Make challenging work assignments.
- Monitor the achievements of subordinates.

Both mentors and subordinates should participate voluntarily and be enthusiastic and supportive of the program. If mentoring is approached as a

Figure 3.12 Company officers act as mentors by providing a positive role model for their subordinates.

mandatory activity, the individuals involved may be resentful or participate only partially. Mandatory participation may cause a mentor to be a negative role model.

In some business texts, it is suggested that a mentor should not be a direct supervisor to the subordinate. However, in the military, the concept of mentoring begins with the immediate supervisor. According to the *U.S. Air Force Promotion Fitness Examination Guide,* a mentor is *a trusted counselor or guide.*

In the Air Force mentoring model, the immediate supervisor is designated as the primary mentor for each subordinate in a unit. This designation in no way restricts the subordinate's desire to seek additional counseling and professional development advice from other sources or mentors.

Supervisors must make themselves available to subordinates who seek career guidance and counsel. The accomplishments of both the mentor and subordinate should be acknowledged throughout the process.

Celebrating Accomplishments

When objectives are met, celebrate their accomplishment as soon as possible. This celebration signals the completion of a project and shows members of the unit that their contributions are important. Announce the completion of the project to the rest of the organization and congratulate participants on the results. Do not overuse celebrations because they will lose their value.

Responsibilities

All supervisors have specific major responsibilities to an organization regardless of its type. No activity, project, or incident is finished until all assigned tasks have been completed. By accomplishing each of these responsibilities, the company officer can ensure an efficient and stable unit. Several of these responsibilities are listed as follows:

- *Set a clear and positive example for subordinates* — Become the primary role model for members of the unit. Actions must be ethical and value-driven.

- *Define expectations* — Tell subordinates the level of actions that are expected. Stated

expectations are the criteria that all unit and individual activities are judged against.

- *Receive assignments and complete a task or objective efficiently and effectively* — Accept the responsibility for assignments and ensure that assignments are completed. See task completion outline following this list.

- *Promote and maintain health and safety policies within the workplace* — Ensure the safety and well-being of all unit personnel. Determine the appropriate action to alter the situation when a member of the unit is physically unfit to perform assigned duties (based on job-related standards and hiring criteria) or exhibits unsafe behavior. *Methods:*

  — Provide an example of safe and healthy conduct for subordinates by personally adhering to safety policies.

  — Make safety and health issues part of the planning for task and assignment completion.

  — Ensure that the organization's safety and health regulations are enforced consistently and employees are held accountable for safety violations and/or failing to maintain a safe working environment.

- *Develop an environment of cooperation and teamwork* — Maintain a cooperative team environment, which is essential to fulfilling the unit's assignments effectively and efficiently. Exert positive leadership to ensure that the unit works together.

- *Develop and maintain the company as an integral part of the organization* — Form the unit into a team, and fit the team into the rest of the organization. Understand how the unit depends on and supports other units within the division and organization. This understanding helps to create a cohesive organization with common shared objectives and goals.

- *Promote skills development, skills maintenance, and skills improvement in employees* — Provide psychomotor training on a constant basis to ensure individual and unit proficiency **(Figure 3.13)**.

- *Maintain discipline and ensure that policies and procedures are adhered to at all times* — Ensure that personnel adhere to rules, regulations, policies, and procedures that are essential to the orderly operation of any organization. Ensure that subordinates conform to requirements. At the same time, provide a positive example by conforming to them also.

- *Establish the perimeters of behavior* — Establish the limits of behavior. Ensure that subordinates know what activities are permitted and which ones are forbidden.

- *Ensure that activities are directed toward organizational goals* — Monitor activities assigned to the unit to ensure that they ultimately contribute to the organization's mission statement and goals. The achievement of emergency, nonemergency, and organizational goals depends on individual companies or units.

- *Promote the pursuit of educational and professional opportunities* — Encourage, support, and provide opportunities for career advancement and professional development. The future of any organization depends on the training of new personnel.

- *Promote credentialing and certification as opportunities to enhance an individual's professionalism* — Encourage subordinates to obtain certification in areas that are essential to fulfilling the mission of the company and the organization.

- *Maintain files and records and prepare reports* — Ensure that the unit's activity reports are properly prepared and records are retained at the unit level. Government regulations mandate the retention of certain types of records and the submittal of reports to various agencies. These records must be accurate, complete, timely, and confidential (where necessary) **(Figure 3.14)**. All records have the potential of becoming legal documents and most, with the exception of medical records, may become public.

The company officer is responsible for completing the tasks or ensuring that delegated tasks have been completed. Completing a task requires the application of the planning, organizing, controlling, and evaluating skills that are outlined as follows:

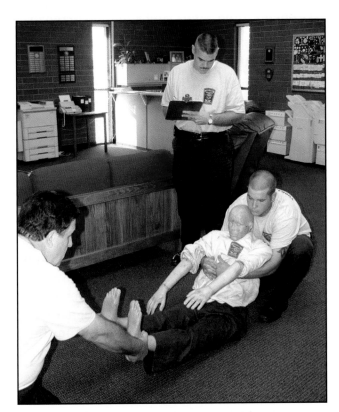

Figure 3.13 The company officer ensures that members of the unit have the skills required to perform their duties. Training and skills evaluations should be part of the daily routine.

Figure 3.14 A very important part of a company officer's duties is maintaining records. To be useful, records must be accurate, complete, timely, and, when required, confidential.

- Establish and communicate the plan for task completion to employees. The plan contains the sequence of steps, the time schedule for step completion, and the assignment of duties, responsibility, and authority.

- Ensure that the schedule is realistic with attainable objectives. Base attainable objectives on the application of available resources, including personnel, funding, time, and materials.

- Organize employees to work as a team with an objective or a goal in focus. Leadership and the creation of team spirit are essential to the success of the unit.

- Delegate the appropriate amount of responsibility and authority to employees, which gives a sense of ownership in the project. However, final responsibility and authority always remains with the company officer.

- Evaluate the quality and completion of the task. Monitor progress to determine whether the plan is being followed or a change must be made to resolve unforeseen difficulties. Use tools such as flow charts or program evaluation and review technique (PERT) charts to track the completion of each step of the project.

Elements

Company officers must exhibit strong, positive leadership qualities at all times. A company officer leads by example and must adhere to a standard of ethical, moral, and legal behavior that motivates subordinates to do the same. In addition, some key elements must be part of the company officer's supervisory style such as the following:

- Encourage employee participation in the decision-making process.

- Delegate or involve members of the unit in planning.

- Respect the judgment of employees.

- Teach, enforce, and follow health and safety rules.

- Be a coach and mentor to employees.

- Show consideration for diversity within the unit.

- Acknowledge accomplishments.

- Treat each member of the unit fairly and equitably.

- Intervene in the private lives of the members of the group *only* when problems are affecting the workplace. Referral to the organization's EAP is usually the most effective method for assisting employees on how to resolve personal problems.

- Keep accurate records.

- Keep lines of communication open at all times.

- Do not contribute to or allow situations that make other people feel uncomfortable or impose upon their personal dignity.

- Provide positive motivation for subordinates.

Above all, a supervisor must be consistent in the application of these elements. A lack of consistency will ultimately undermine a company officer's authority and ability to lead. Inconsistency can create relationships within the unit that distract attention from the primary goals of the organization and take energy, time, effort, and attention to repair.

Summary

Company officers must understand the principles of supervision of individuals. This chapter applied best business practices to the concept of supervision to provide a fundamental understanding. The company officer or officer candidate can use this material as a springboard to further studies through college-level classes, workshops, seminars, and literature readings on the various subjects addressed.

Company officers must know and be able to apply supervisory skills to gain the greatest advantage from subordinates and the unit. The development of a team atmosphere and the application of leadership skills will result in the creation of an effective, efficient, and cohesive emergency response or administrative unit.

Robert F. Hamm on Delegation

In the IFSTA *Leadership in the Fire Service* manual, Robert F. Hamm presented a lecture titled "The Job of Delegating." In the lecture, Mr. Hamm correctly states that delegating is one of the most difficult tasks for many people and requires hard work to do it right. To be successful, supervisors must be able to delegate tasks along with the authority to perform them.

Mr. Hamm suggests that there are some accepted rules for delegating tasks. These rules are paraphrased as follows:

- *Handing out assignments* — Assignments must be clearly and concisely stated and include what is to be done, when it is to be completed, and what the expected results are. A leader must be careful, however, not to tell the subordinate exactly how to perform the task, which is considered *micromanaging* and does not permit the subordinate to exercise any creativity or initiative in performing the task.

- *Handing out credit* — A leader is generous with praise and credit that is deserved. Even if a task is not completed to the level of expectations of the leader, a sincere word of praise about what was accomplished should be given. Constructive feedback is much easier to accept when it is accompanied by praise.

- *Allowing for mistakes* — Delegating tasks should be based on the ability of the subordinate to accomplish it. This fact is especially important if the task is critical to the mission or specialized in nature. A task should never be assigned to a person who is not trained, qualified, or certified to perform it. However, a leader must accept the fact that errors can occur. In order for personnel to develop and improve their skills, they must be able to learn from their mistakes; and a leader must provide constructive feedback to them.

- *Putting oneself into the hands of others* — A supervisor must trust the abilities and judgment of subordinates and demonstrate confidence in them. Subordinates must also realize that the supervisor has trust in them, and they must make the best effort possible to perform the task properly.

- *Never stressing failure* — Stressing the negative, the potential for failure, or the potential result of failure creates a self-fulfilling prophecy; that is, the person who is given a task sees no other option but to fail. When a task is delegated, a supervisor should stress the positive results, the abilities of the subordinate to complete the task, and the challenge the task provides to the subordinate.

- *Remaining relaxed* — A supervisor should always remain relaxed when delegating a task. This attitude demonstrates that the officer is confident and comfortable with the ability of the person who is assigned the task.

- *Being a teacher* — In order to delegate tasks, a supervisor must ensure that subordinates have the knowledge, skills, and abilities necessary to perform them. Therefore, the officer must be able to instruct subordinates or mentor them properly. Teaching in this respect is passing on knowledge and skills gained from experience.

Logic, Ethics, and Decision-Making

Chapter Contents

Learning Objectives

1. Match to their definitions terms associated with logic

2. Identify the four types of reasoning.

3. Identify types of fallacies.

4. Identify facts about ethical conduct.

5. Select facts about an ethics program.

6. Place in correct order the steps for dealing with ethical issues.

7. Recall the elements of making a decision.

8. Select correct responses about the steps of the decision-making process.

9. Identify barriers to decision-making.

10. Identify the questions of the four-way test for ethical decision-making.

Job Performance Requirements

This chapter provides information that addresses the following job performance requirements of NFPA 1021, *Standard for Fire Officer Professional Qualifications* (2003):

Chapter 4 Fire Officer I

4.1.1

Chapter 4
Logic, Ethics, and Decision-Making

By the beginning of the twenty-first century, the terms *logic* and *ethics* had become widely used by electronic and print media in North America. News articles and electronic media programs discussed the use of logic in decision-making by corporate leaders. Ethics (or the lack of them) were applied not only to the business community but also to the political leaders of the nation and world. The continuing reference of these two terms indicates the importance of the topics in a modern society. But the roots of logic and ethics are far older than a person may suspect.

Logic and *ethics* are terms that find their origin in the Ancient Greek civilization of the sixth century B.C.E. They were considered by the philosophers of the time to be essential to a strong human character. Definitions were as follows:

- *Logic* (or *logos*) — Ability to reason and present a strong argument in favor of or against a position. It was also the ability to recognize fallacies in the arguments of others and thereby be able to refute or correct the opposing position.

- *Ethics* (or *ethos*) — Analysis of the principles of human conduct in order to be able to determine between *right* and *wrong*.

A third part of this philosophy of the human character is *pathos*, the ability to have empathy or sympathy for another person and make arguments based on emotional appeals. While all three are important, only logic and ethics as they apply to company officers in the fire and emergency services are discussed in this chapter.

Decision-making is a constant part of everyday life. Whether decisions are mundane (like deciding what to have for a meal) or critical (like those made at an emergency incident), company officers are constantly deciding between various choices to arrive at a desired outcome. Because the decision-making process depends heavily on the use of logic and ethical choices, a discussion of the process is also included in this chapter.

Logic

As mentioned, *logic* is the ability to use rational thinking and reasoning to determine the correct answer to a problem. It is also the ability to develop an argument in favor of a position while at the same time being able to see the fallacies or falsehoods surrounding an opposing view.

Both equally important elements of logic are discussed in this section. First, the steps necessary to reason through a situation are applied to the decision-making process. Second, the various theories of fallacies are discussed and various examples provided.

Reasoning

When a person is faced with making a decision or persuading others to support a particular decision, it is essential to apply logic in the form of reasoning to arrive at a decision. There are four general types of reasoning: inductive, deductive, causal, and analogical (**Figure 4.1, p. 74**). Recognizing and learning to use each type will help the company officer in making sound and defensible decisions.

Inductive

Inductive reasoning is a process that arrives at a general conclusion based on a foundation of specific examples or data. This approach depends on supporting evidence that consists of statistics,

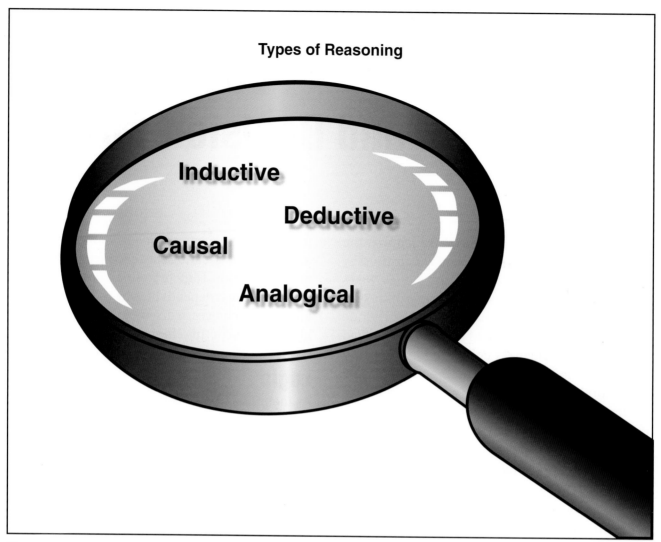

Types of Reasoning

Inductive

Deductive

Causal

Analogical

Figure 4.1 The four types of reasoning that are used to reach a logical conclusion or make a decision are shown.

facts, and examples to arrive at the conclusion. Documentation is essential to the inductive reasoning approach to decision-making. For example, if a fire officer wants to convince a governing body that the fire department should purchase a new 100-foot (30 m) aerial device, a case has to be built on basic facts such as the following:

• Types and heights of structures to be protected

• Age of the current aerial device/lack of an aerial device

• Cost of maintenance for the current aerial device

• Cost of maintenance for the proposed unit

• Operating cost comparison between the existing and proposed units

• Number of incidents where the current unit was used

• Training costs

• Safety concerns

• Current design criteria and NFPA standard requirements

• Warranty coverage of the new unit

With these specific facts, an officer can create a structural foundation for the request that will be difficult to undermine or refute. Because facts and statistics are so important to the case, they must be recent, typical, appropriate, accurate, and specific. *Statistics* are the numbers that are gathered as raw data to support the argument. See Chapter 25, Analyses, Evaluations, and Statistics, for more information.

In developing an argument, the use of statistics, however, can be misused and manipulated to support an argument and bias a decision. To prevent the misuse of statistics, the fire officer must ensure that the following elements are considered:

- *Reliable sources* — Use documented, unbiased sources from organizations/departments such as NFPA, U.S. Fire Administration (USFA), U.S. National Institute for Occupational Safety and Health (NIOSH), U.S. Census Bureau, U.S. Department of Labor, International Association of Fire Fighters (IAFF), and International Association of Fire Chiefs (IAFC).

- *Valid data* — Use data that are validated to support decisions and use commonly accepted methods to perform the analysis.

- *Accurately interpreted statistics* — Explain and present statistics clearly so that they are understandable and not misleading. Clearly explain what the statistics represent. *Example:*

  — When the U.S. government states that the unemployment rate is only 4 percent, it can sound very impressive, given the total population of the nation.

  — However, that 4 percent does not take into account the people who are not in the labor force (referred to as *hardcore unemployed*), that is, the number of people who are not actively looking for work. The actual number of people who are not employed will be much higher.

- *Legible statistics* — Make statistics easy for the audience or reader to see, read, visualize, and comprehend. Use graphs, charts, and tables for clarification (**Figure 4.2**).

Deductive

Deductive reasoning is the process of reaching a specific conclusion based on a general statement or principle. It is usually developed in the form of a *syllogism* (a three-part statement that consists of a *major premise, minor premise,* and *conclusion*). This type of reasoning depends on the acceptance that the major and minor premises are true. If they are true, then the conclusion must be true.

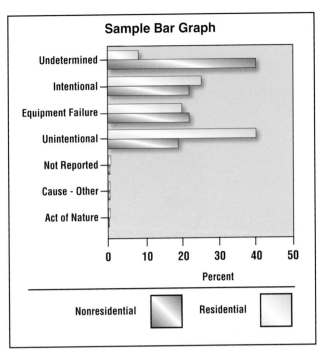

Figure 4.2 Graphs are an effective way of presenting statistics to an audience.

The following is an example of deductive reasoning:

Major Premise: *All buildings taller than seven stories are considered to be high-rise buildings.*

Minor Premise: *The building code requires that all high-rise buildings have sprinklers.*

Conclusion: *Therefore, all new buildings over seven stories tall must have sprinklers.*

If the first sentence (major premise) is considered to be true and the second sentence (minor premise) is considered to be true, then the third sentence (conclusion) must also be true. Because deductive reasoning requires that people agree on the truth of the two premise statements (and truth is subjective), it is more difficult to make decisions or arguments based on deductive reasoning.

Causal

Causal (or *cause-and-effect*) reasoning is a process that is based on the relationship between two or more events in such a way that it is obvious one caused the other to occur (**Figure 4.3, p. 76**). Decisions or arguments based on causal reasoning may be structured in one of two ways: Either from a known cause to a predicted result or from a known result backward to a suspected cause.

Causal Reasoning

CAUSE

EFFECT

Figure 4.3 Causal reasoning can be used to determine the root cause of an incident.

The key to effective causal arguments is in establishing a factual, direct link between the cause and effect. Without that link, the argument is subject to criticism and debate and will fail. Because causal reasoning looks at specific occurrences and draws general conclusions from them, it is considered a form of inductive reasoning.

It is sometimes easier to reason from the cause to a predicted effect, especially if there is sufficient supporting documentation. For instance, it can be argued that closing fire stations will create longer response times, which in turn will result in increased fire loss and casualties. This reasoning is based on nationally collected data on the relationship between response times and severity of fire losses.

When working from the known result backwards, it is necessary to find the link to the cause, which may be harder than it appears. In many cases, the link is created solely to prove that a presumed cause is true. For instance, a department head may want to *prove* that the increase in dollar loss due to fire during the past year is the result of the closing of fire stations when, in fact, the increase may be due to the value of the properties involved.

Extreme care must be taken in working from effect back to cause because bias created by a presumption may influence the process. The company officer responsible for the initial cause determination of a fire must be very careful in the use of this type of logic. Fire investigators are particularly experienced at this type of process because they must use the evidence of an actual fire and work back to determine its cause.

Analogical

Analogical reasoning is based on a comparison between two similar cases. It infers that what is true in the first case will also be true in the second case. This type of reasoning is usually found in the persuasive type of argument or speech (See Chapter 7, Oral Communications). When using analogical reasoning, it is important to ensure that the example being cited has sufficient similarities to the proposed solution to assure its validity.

For instance, the following argument is valid if the first statement is true and all other comparisons are equal:

First Case: *Elmira has a building code that requires residential sprinkler systems in all new construction of residential structures.*

Second Case: *Since it was enacted, the number of fires in residential structures has decreased by 20 percent.*

Conclusion: *Therefore, enacting a sprinkler requirement in our community would result in a similar decrease in fires.*

Fallacies

Whether a company officer is making a decision, developing an argument in favor of a decision, or listening to an opposing argument or position, recognizing fallacies is an important skill. A *fallacy* is false or fallacious reasoning that occurs when someone attempts to persuade others without sufficient supporting evidence or by using irrelevant or inappropriate arguments.

So pervasive is the use of fallacies that speech communication professionals have documented over 50 types of fallacies. The following fallacies are only a few of those frequently used:

- **Causal** — Makes a faulty connection between the cause and effect; also referred to in Latin as *post hoc, ergo propter hoc* (which means *after this, therefore,* or *because of this*). Just because one event follows another chronologically does not mean that the first caused the second to occur. *Example:*

  — *The Soviet Union collapsed after instituting state atheism. Therefore, we must avoid atheism for the same reasons.*

  — Atheism was not considered one of the causes for the collapse of the Communist political structure.

- **Bandwagon** — Tries to make the statement that *everyone* is doing something or believes something so that makes it the correct point of view or activity. *Example:*

  — *Everyone is going to the party, so you should let me go too.* This argument is a favorite of teenagers.

  — *If everyone jumped off a cliff, would you want to jump off too?* This typical response is what many parents say to the first argument.

- **Straw man** — Makes a weak, easily refuted statement to take attention away from the main point, thus creating a distraction from the main point. *Example:*

  — A proponent of a new library uses the statement: *There are those who don't care if children read.*

  — The person is creating a straw man that everyone can attack without having to develop a strong factual case for the library itself.

- **Hasty generalization** — Makes an argument or conclusion that is based on insufficient or non-existent evidence; can also result in stereotyping. *Example:*

  — *My Uncle Fred is lazy; therefore, all men named Fred are lazy.*

  — Because one person is lazy does not mean that all persons of the same nationality, race, gender, or ethnic background have the same trait.

- **Red herring** — Occurs when someone uses irrelevant facts to distract the listener from the main issue; is the staple of many politicians who are asked a specific question and then avoid answering it by raising other issues. *Example:*

  — *You may claim that the death penalty is an ineffective deterrent against crime — but what about the victims of crime?*

  — *How do you think surviving family members feel when they see the man who murdered their son kept in prison at their expense? Is it right that they should pay for their son's murderer to be fed and housed?*

- **Non sequitur** — Concludes something that simply does not follow the main premise of the argument; Latin for *it does not follow. Example: The city council should not build a new fire station because the city cannot afford to keep the swimming pools open during the summer.*

- **Slippery slope** — Consists of a series of worsening consequences that are assumed will result from the initial decision or action. *Example: You can never give anyone a break. If you do, they will continuously take advantage of you and finally they will walk all over you.*

Fallacies like those listed appear in media reports, analyses, advertising pieces, political speeches, and even in formal organizational reports. The company officer should take time to carefully listen to or read arguments that are presented for consideration.

Arguments that contain fallacies lack credibility and factual support and should be suspected of containing fallacious reasoning. When developing a report or oral argument, a company officer must ensure that the facts support the argument and that fallacies are not present.

As supervisors, company officers will also find that their subordinates use fallacies to gain approval or influence officers in making decisions relative to their proposals or requests.

The perceptive company officer can use this opportunity to develop subordinates by correcting their approaches and identifying the weaknesses of their arguments. If in fact the request is within reason, a company officer can guide the subordinate in the proper method to argue the point or concern.

Ethics

As mentioned earlier, *ethics* (sometimes called *moral philosophy*) is the philosophical principle that is used to determine correct and proper behavior by the members of a society. From the viewpoint of the ancient Greek philosophers, ethics is the glue that holds a civilization together. Without ethics, there would be chaos, and civilization (or society) would dissolve **(Figure 4.4)**.

Ethics played a large role in early Greek society and, therefore, the civilization of North America, which is based strongly on the writings of the Greek philosophers. Unfortunately, the examples that tend to appear in the news media are predominately examples of the *lack* of ethical conduct more than anything else. The lack of ethical conduct may be the cause of some or all of the following incidents that occur in many societies:

- Insider stock trading
- Pork-barrel political programs
- Sexual harassment
- Racial/ethnic/gender discrimination

Figure 4.4 Ethics is the foundation of most modern societies.

Because the fire and emergency services are not immune to these same types of situations, it is essential that all fire officers understand the importance of ethical conduct and how to adhere to it. This section deals with individual and organizational ethical conduct and issues in the fire and emergency services, discusses the ethics program, discusses how to write a code of ethics for an organization, and provides examples of codes of ethics.

Ethical Conduct

The basis for ethics is the socially accepted beliefs, morals, and values of a community or society. Ethical standards express the level of conduct all members of society are expected to follow. In brief, they are statements of what is right and proper conduct for the individual in all relationships and activities. This conduct may involve relationships with others, the decision-making process, or simply choosing between *right* and *wrong*. Few decisions are as clear, and most involve many choices that fall into the *gray* range between the two extremes.

Classic examples abound of situations that challenge basic ethical standards. Picking up coins that are found on the street is an activity that most people have experienced. But do they have a right to keep the found change? What if the denomination is more than a dollar or $5? At what point of value should the found money be reported and to whom should it be reported? In another example, is it appropriate for a fire inspector to accept gifts from the owners or occupants of structures in appreciation for their services? If so, what is the maximum value of these gifts?

The fire and emergency services are not immune to the need for ethical standards of conduct. Because of the position of respect and honor that the services and their members have in North America and other regions of the world, it is important that all members attempt to live up to an ethical code of conduct.

The company officer must remember that society tends to expect a higher level of ethical conduct from members of the fire and emergency services. Even the media tends to identify individuals as *firefighters* or *emergency medical technicians (EMTs)* while other professionals are rarely identified by their professions. In most cases, the emphasis has been on the heroism of the firefighter or EMT. However, instances involving unethical conduct on the part of the emergency responder have also been prevalent.

Before a company officer can implement an organization's ethical code of conduct, it is necessary to understand three basic components of ethics: origins of personal ethics of individuals, causes of unethical conduct, and how people justify unethical conduct in themselves and an organization. These components are important not only in recognizing unethical conduct in others but also internally within the company officer.

Personal Ethics Origins

Ethics and ethical behavior are learned traits. They are transmitted to an individual from many sources. The primary source is the family, which instills personal values and morals. Other sources are organized religions, educational institutions, society, and peers (**Figure 4.5**).

The values that are instilled by these sources remain with the individual for life unless the person consciously alters them. Examples of ethical values include the following:

- Honesty
- Integrity
- Impartiality
- Fairness
- Loyalty
- Dedication
- Responsibility

- Accountability
- Perseverance
- Frugality
- Faithfulness
- Heroism
- Patriotism
- Morality

Some of these values are the same as those listed in Chapter 2, Leadership, in the Leadership Traits and Behavioral Leadership sections. These values are generally accepted by most cultures and societies of the world to be important to the existence of a civilized society. As the ancient Greek philosophers asserted: Without ethics, society would dissolve into chaos. The same is true of organizations that lack values or a commitment to ethics.

Figure 4.5 Individuals learn ethical behavior from many sources. Primary to these sources is the family.

Ethics: Three-Step Check

Step 1: *Is it legal?* — Will I be violating civil law, professional standards, or departmental policy?

Step 2: *Is it fair to all concerned?* — Is it balanced? Is it fair in the long term as well as the short term? Does it promote win-win relationships?

Step 3: *How will it make me feel about myself?* — Will it make me proud? Would I feel good if my decision was published in the newspaper? Would I feel good if my family know about it?

Unethical Conduct Causes

In order to create a culture based on ethical behavior, a company officer must understand what contributes to unethical behavior. The potential for unethical conduct on the part of individuals and organizations, including the fire and emergency services, is limitless and too often realized, especially in profit-driven private enterprise.

Researchers in private industry have documented the causes of unethical behavior in organizations. Some of these causes are summarized as follows:

- **Behaviors that violate ethical standards** — The use of bribery or payoffs to ensure that an organization is awarded a lucrative contract is rewarded in the form of promotions or bonuses. The unethical conduct is not only on the part of the business representative who makes the bribe or payoff but also on the part of the organization's employee who accepts it. Bribes and payoffs are not always used to purchase this type of influence. Gifts, trips, and promises of future employment are also forms of bribery.

- **Bottom-line mentality** — For some organizations, financial success in the form of profits may be all that matters, and any action (ethical or otherwise) is justified if a profit is made for the organization. Thus, ethical standards simply become obstacles that must be overcome in the name of profits. Although making a profit does not motivate the fire and emergency services, staying within the constraints of budgets does. *Examples:*

  — Making the organization *look good on paper* to the political authority can create situations where unethical conduct may occur.

  — In the political public arena, the *political bottom line* is a similar cause where decisions are intended to influence the electorate in favor of a politician at the eventual expense of the same voters.

  — *Pork-barrel projects* are government expenditures that may appear to have little or no real value other than to enhance the image of a politician and gain more votes. In the end, citizens may have to pay higher taxes or lose other benefits to support the project.

- **Exploitive mentality** — An attitude in some private and public organizations encourages people to use others in order to succeed. It tends to promote negative stereotyping, undermine compassion, and create a selfish attitude. This attitude may take the form of telling lies about people, starting and spreading rumors, or taking credit for the work of another person.

Quality Service: The Bottom Line

Company officers should remember that *providing quality service* is the *bottom line* in the fire and emergency services. Quality service adds value to the company, organization, and authority having jurisdiction (AHJ).

There are as many reasons for unethical conduct in individuals as there are examples of unethical actions. Research in the speech communication discipline indicates that there are four main reasons for lying. The same following reasons can describe most forms of unethical conduct on the part of individuals in general:

- **Basic needs** — Gain objects that fulfill an individual's basic needs such as food, money, clothing, or other items.

- **Affiliation** — Create, prolong, or avoid social relationships. For example, the hazing that young college students may have to go through to join a fraternity or sorority may result in the unethical treatment of those students.

- **Self-esteem** — Increase the perceived competence of an individual in the eyes of others such as falsifying records, cheating to make a higher score on a test, or spreading gossip that belittles another person.

- **Self-gratification** — Increase an individual's personal enjoyment. *Examples:* illegal gambling, substance abuse, and theft.

Personal Justifications

When the culture of an organization or society rewards unethical conduct, it is easy to understand how individuals can engage in these types of activities. The individual accepts the benefits of such actions and then justifies them internally.

Justification also occurs when a person is trying to make a decision (whether ethical or unethical). Common justifications for unethical conduct include the following:

- Pretending that the action is legal or ethical

- Believing that the action is really in the best interest of the organization or individual

- Believing that the action is okay because no one will ever find out about it

- Expecting that the organization will support the action if it is ever discovered
- Believing that the action is acceptable because everyone else is doing it
- Believing that the end (result) justifies the means (method) even if the means are unethical

When the individual has justified the unethical action internally, it then becomes easier to commit the action and any similar subsequent actions. To overcome these attitudes, the organization must create a culture that encourages and rewards ethical conduct and disciplines unethical conduct.

Promotional Systems

At the former University of Michigan Fire School (the state training authority before the current Fire Fighters Training Council), a student in a fire officer class discussed his personal experience with promotional systems. The student was preparing to take a competitive promotional examination that consisted of a written test, interview, and skills test. He contrasted the current process to that of his former fire department that promoted strictly by seniority.

He said that in his former department, information, training, and ideas were shared openly because there was no reason not to do so. However, in his current department, there was no sharing of information. To do so could cause someone else to have a higher score on the promotional examination and keep the candidate from getting a promotion.

Ethics Program

Creating an ethical culture requires the creation of an ethics program that includes an organizational and individual code of ethics. Surveys of the business community have determined that organizations that have a formal ethics program have a strong ethical culture. Employees of these organizations have a positive opinion of the ethical performance of the organization and its senior managers.

An ethics program is essential to any fire and emergency services organization and justifies any reasonable expense in resources. Company officers are responsible for adhering to the elements of the ethics program and for communicating the program to their subordinates.

Elements

An ethics program contains certain elements that make it effective. To ensure that the organization maintains an ethical culture, the ethics program needs to include a written code of ethics or ethics policy. This code is a brief, one- or two-page statement of the values that govern the organization and the expectations desired in the actions of management and the membership.

The various program elements are summarized as follows:

- *Distinguish between what is ethical and legal* — Laws are usually written to enforce ethical conduct. However, creating laws tends to occur after the conduct has become a threat to the organization or society. The laws are a reaction to the situations that develop over time.

- *Enforce program provisions* — The ethics program must come from as well as have the full support of both the chief of the organization and senior management personnel. They must follow the same standards that they require of members and recognize and reward ethical behavior. They must also discipline anyone who does not follow them.

- *Conduct formal training* — This element communicates the ethical behavior through mandatory participation in the training and the program. Thus, employee participation from the beginning is a requirement of the program.

- *Involve employees* — Employees of the organization need to be involved in the development and implementation of the program.

- *Evaluate and revise* — The program must be continuous with reevaluations, revisions, and alterations as required.

Code of Ethics

An essential part of the ethics program is the written code of ethics. Codes of ethical conduct have been established by the International Association of Fire Chiefs (IAFC), the American Society for Public Administration (ASPA), and the U.S. House of Representatives to name a very few. Expressing the organization's code of ethics in written form provides the administration, employees, and the public with a visible standard to abide by. A code of ethics is specific to the organization that creates it. Sample codes of ethics are included in **Appendix C**.

The brief list that follows provides company officers with an idea of what is expected of them, their subordinates, and their organizations. Generally, topics that may be addressed in fire and emergency services codes of ethics include the following:

- Relationships between members
- Relationships with the public
- Use of governmental property
- Acceptance of gifts and favors
- Conflict of interest
- Financial disclosures
- Information management
- Discrimination in hiring, promoting, discipline, or relations
- Upholding public trust
- Upholding national, state/provincial, or local laws, statutes, or ordinances
- Upholding and supporting bylaws, rules, regulations, policies, and procedures of the department/organization
- Loyalty to the government, department/organization, fellow firefighters/emergency responders, and community
- Professionalism
- Integrity
- Truthfulness
- Obedience at the station and emergency
- Criminal activity

Ethical Issues

The existence of a code of ethics strengthens the ethical culture of the organization but does not guarantee that ethical questions will not continue to challenge the organization or its employees as generations change. Training employees in the importance of making ethical decisions, how to make those decisions, and how to recognize and respond to unethical actions on the part of others provide valuable tools for dealing with such issues (**Figure 4.6**).

However, company officers must be able to manage issues when they arise. The use of logic and reasoning must be supplemented by the use of ethical decision-making. Use the following steps when dealing with an ethical dilemma:

Step 1: *Recognize and define the situation* — Determine the answers to the following questions: What is it? What has caused it? Who is involved? What are the potential results?

Step 2: *Obtain all the facts surrounding the situation* — Conduct an objective investigation to gather the details of the event.

Step 3: *List all possible options necessary to respond to the situation* — Develop this list by brainstorming with other members of the department if time allows. In emergency situations, the officer may have to rely on personal experience to develop such a list.

Step 4: *Compare each option to established criteria* — Use benchmarks such as legality, morality, benefit, and justification as criteria.

Step 5: *Select the best option that meets the criteria* — Make the decision.

Figures 4.6 Many organizations now require that employees attend ethics classes. The company officer may be required to teach an ethics class or explain ethics policies to subordinates.

Step 6: *Double check the decision* — Ask more subjective questions such as *How would I feel if my family/spouse/friends found out about this?* and *How would I feel if this decision was reported in the local/national media?*

Step 7: *Take action and implement the decision* — Ensure that the factual foundation is firm, criteria are met, and potential for exposure is minimized so that the best decision, based on the information gathered, is made.

Fire officers lead primarily by example and the most important example they can provide to their organization and community is ethical decision-making and action. An organization's culture is only as sound as the example set by the officers who are in positions of leadership and authority. This example means that fire officers must establish and adhere to goals that are ethical.

Those goals must be based on sound factual evidence and reasoning. Officers must be honest in their presentation of their decisions, both in communicating the decision and results of the decision. Honesty generates acceptance for the decision and builds trust in the officer who made that decision.

It is important for all individuals to be guided by a strong set of beliefs, values, and morals. They must be able to recognize and use ethical behavior in relationships, in decision-making, and as leaders.

Of all the axioms for guiding people ethically, the most applicable is the one spoken by Confucius (K'ung Ch'iu) in the sixth century B.C.E. (**Figure 4.7**). When asked by a student, *Is there one expression that can be acted upon until the end of one's days?* Confucius answered: *There is* shu: *do not impose on others what you yourself do not want.*

In Western civilization that same ethical axiom is known as the Golden Rule: *Do unto others, as you want them to do unto you.* In any civilization, culture, or society, this axiom is a valid ethical strategy to follow.

The responsibility for the development of an ethical culture within the organization belongs to everyone in the organization. The administration must support, communicate, and personally adhere to the adopted code of ethics. Formal training for all personnel must be provided beginning with entry-level employee training and extending to fire officer training courses.

Annual refresher classes that focus on various ethical questions should be part of the organization's training schedule. At the company level, the fire officer should work to create an ethical culture in the relationship between crew members. Discussions of ethical questions can be used to promote the permanent existence of an ethical culture.

Thought to Consider

If you would be ashamed for your parents, spouse, or friends to read about an unethical activity that you were involved in, then you should not take part in the activity.

Figure 4.7 Confucius is responsible for the basic ethical premise: *Do not impose on others what you yourself do not want.*

Decision-Making

Decision-making is a daily activity for company officers and other members of the fire and emergency services **(Figure 4.8)**. An individual makes some of those decisions for personal reasons such as career advancement, while other decisions are made for the good of the organization such as prioritizing a budget. Other decisions are group decisions made by members of the management staff or a project team. An individual or a group, depending on the situation, may be responsible for making a decision.

How a decision is made, however, will contain the same elements and follow the same process steps. Those elements and steps are similar to those mentioned in the Logic and Ethics sections of this chapter. Some barriers to decision-making also exist, and they are discussed along with the phenomenon known as the *Abilene Paradox.* The four-way test is also described as a means of testing the ethical value of a decision.

Figure 4.8 Company officers must make immediate and accurate decisions during emergency incidents.

Elements

Effective leaders must understand the decision-making process and apply it to a variety of situations. To understand and apply the process, the company officer must be able to answer four basic questions about a situation (the basic assessment), understand the unit or organization that the situation involves, and understand decision-making models.

Basic Assessment

A situation or problem that requires a decision has the following four basic elements that the company officer must consider in assessing a situation:

- ***Is the decision within the authority of the company officer?*** — Some decisions that effect the organization or community are the responsibility of superior officers rather than supervisors and managers. The company officer should not attempt to make decisions that are the responsibility of others. Likewise, the company officer should not pass decisions up the chain of command that are within that officer's level of responsibility and authority.

- ***Is there sufficient information available about the situation or problem to make an informed decision?*** — The lack of information can lead to a hasty and potentially disastrous decision. An effective leader should take the time to collect as much information as possible from any sources available before making a decision. For example, this action is called *size-up* in an emergency situation.

- ***How will the decision affect the unit or organization?*** — This question involves knowing the potential outcome of the decision before it is made. To answer this question, the company officer must have satisfactorily answered the previous question and applied logic to determine the variety of outcomes that are possible.

- ***Is the problem worth the effort?*** — The situation needs to be worth the time, resources, risk, and commitment to even address. *Examples:*

  — At an emergency incident, the answer to this question is the difference between committing to an offensive or a defensive strategy.

  — In the administrative function, the answer to this question may involve implementing an inexpensive fitness or wellness plan in the hopes of offsetting the high costs of on-the-job injuries.

Members of the Unit

The company officer must understand the morale, mood, and capabilities of the members of the unit. This understanding comes from the following actions:

- Monitoring members

- Listening to concerns

- Watching for symptoms of stress, fatigue, loss of interest, resistance to change, and other signs that a problem may exist

By gauging the morale of the unit, the company officer will be able to determine how to correct any potential problem, motivate members of the unit, and introduce a change model. It also means that some decisions may have to be postponed if the group is not able to perform the necessary function demanded by the decision. For example, the implementation of a hazardous materials first responder program will have to wait until the organization is trained and equipped to meet the requirements of such a function.

Decision-Making Models

Generally, problems are based on the following three considerations:

- Whether decisions are generic (programmed) or exceptional (nonprogrammed):
  — *Generic:* Decisions that are routine or recurring are usually made based on existing standards, rules, regulations, procedures, or policies of the organization. *Example:* Implementing the Incident Command System (ICS) at all emergency incidents
  — *Exceptional:* Decisions that involve a nonrecurring, nonroutine, unique, and significant situation. *Example:* Involving the emergency expenditure of funds to purchase a replacement apparatus when an existing unit is destroyed

- Conditions to which decisions are subject

- Choice of decision-making models used to solve the problem

The conditions that affect decisions are classified as follows:

- *Certainty* — Decisions have known results and require specific resources. Generic decisions usually involve certainty.

- *Risk* — Decisions will have probable consequences, although there is the possibility of unknown outcomes. Exceptional decisions will have risk.

- *Uncertainty* — Decisions have completely unknown consequences, usually because of a lack of information. Exceptional decisions will have both risk and uncertainty.

Two generally accepted decision-making models are taught in business management courses: rational model and bounded rationality model. In the *rational* or *classical model,* the leader gathers information and makes the decision based on the best possible alternative to the situation. This type of decision model is usually applied to the exceptional (nonprogrammed) decisions that have the potential for high risk or uncertain outcomes **(Figure 4.9)**.

The *bounded rationality model* allows the leader to select the decision that will satisfy the minimal requirements of the situation. This type of decision model is usually applied to generic (programmed) decisions that have certain outcomes **(Figure 4.10, p. 86)**.

Figure 4.9 Nonprogrammed decisions are regularly made at emergency incidents where the outcome is uncertain.

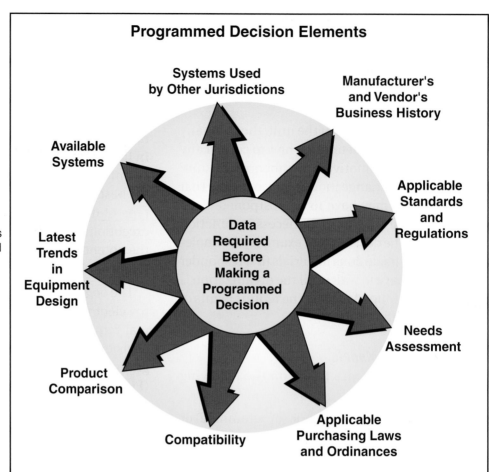

Programmed Decision Elements

Systems Used
by Other Jurisdictions

Manufacturer's
and Vendor's
Business History

Available
Systems

Applicable
Standards
and
Regulations

Latest
Trends
in
Equipment
Design

Data
Required
Before
Making a
Programmed
Decision

Needs
Assessment

Product
Comparison

Compatibility

Applicable
Purchasing Laws
and Ordinances

Figure 4.10 A programmed decision is based upon various types of data that are gathered through thorough research of the available information.

Both models can be applied when making an individual or group decision. The use of a group in the decision-making process is basic to the *participatory management* style that is part of democratic management. As the name implies, members of the unit are involved or participate in the process.

This form of empowerment has the added benefit of increasing personal commitment to the process and provides members with a feeling of self-worth. Empowerment can occur when generic decisions such as purchasing equipment are made by a committee or when nonemergency duty assignments are made within a group. Group decisions have both advantages and disadvantages to the organization that a fire officer needs to understand (see information box).

Group Decision-Making

Advantages	Disadvantages
Better decisions	Slower process
Improved information	Time may be wasted
Improved alternatives	Decision may only meet the minimum requirements
Improved understanding of the decision	
Increased commitment to the decision	Domination by a group member
Improved morale within the group	Potential for conformity
	Perceived stigma of not being part of a team
Increased motivation	Disenchantment with the group process
Trains members in the process	
	Potential barricade created if a member does not agree with the final decision

The company officer must remember that the use of the group decision-making method does not mean that the officer has given up any authority or responsibility for the final decision. Leadership means accepting full responsibility for all decisions made by the leader, unit, or organization.

Process Steps

The steps of the decision-making process should lead to an action rather than a decision; that is, making a decision that is not implemented is simply having a good intention. The action step fulfills that good intention. The steps of the process are described in the sections that follow.

Classify the Problem

Just like decisions, problems may be either generic (programmed) or exceptional (nonprogrammed). In either case, sufficient information must be gathered to classify the problem as generic or exceptional. Descriptions are as follows:

- *Generic problem classification* — One that is recurring and may even be the symptom of a larger problem. It can usually be solved through the application of a rule, policy, or principle. *Example:* Increase in job-related back injuries

- *Exceptional problem classification* — One that may only occur once. But it must be dealt with by a response that is peculiar to or customized for that problem. *Example:* Chemical spill caused by a transport vehicle accident

Define the Problem

In this step, the problem is given a name or definition. In order to ensure that the definition is accurate, compare it to all observable facts. All of the facts must be gathered and analyzed. Definitions are as follows:

- *Generic problem definition* — Requires more data to determine the specific problem, which may have an underlying major problem, and note a trend such as injuries that have occurred when individuals attempt to lift heavy items without assistance.

- *Exceptional problem definition* — Requires that information related to the specific event be gathered quickly. In the example of a chemical spill, information such as the type of material involved, quantity, flammability, and environmental data (among others) helps to define the specific problem and contributes to the decision-making process. Trends will not usually play a part in defining this type of problem.

List Alternative Options

When the problem has been classified and defined, various responses must be determined. In some instances, alternative options are limited by the nature of the situation or availability of resources. The leader may have to establish limits based on knowledge of the internal or external political climate, available resources, or time available to implement the solution. However, in most instances (such as with the generic type of problem), alternatives may be limitless.

If time is available, then all potential solutions should be listed. Ranking the solutions by assigning values to each based on a predetermined set of criteria helps in making the selection of the best response. It is important for company officers to realize that spending too much time developing a long list of alternative options is unproductive time management.

Determine the Best Response

The *best response* is the one that will fully and completely correct the problem. This response is the one that is technically, morally, ethically, legally, politically, and financially correct. The company officer should also understand that some situations require a multidimensional solution.

For example, in a case of lifting-related back injuries, the best response (and also a multidimensional solution) may be to purchase back-support belts for all members of the organization and provide training on proper lifting techniques or when it is proper to use two employees to lift an object. The best response to a chemical spill might be the direct application of a foam chemical agent to blanket the spill.

However, the best response may not be possible and a compromise or concession must be made to correct the problem. For example, the organization may not be able to purchase the necessary quantity of back-support belts in the current budget;

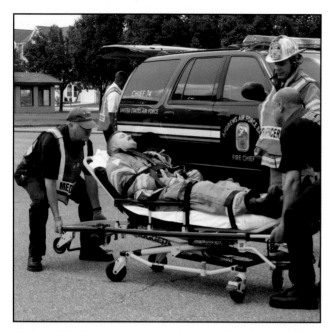

Figure 4.11 Most organizations have policies that require a minimum number of responders to lift a victim, the use of mechanical aids such as collapsible gurneys, or the wearing of back-support braces.

therefore, it may be necessary to provide a policy that mandates that all lifting over a certain weight be performed by teams of two or more individuals (**Figure 4.11**). Training in this type of lifting would then have to be provided.

The first choice should always be the right response. For example, a lack of foam concentrate may prevent the immediate blanketing of the chemical spill, in which case, evacuation of the area by all personnel may be the first decision until sufficient concentrate arrives. The second choice will be a compromise or concession.

Because the response seldom fully and completely corrects the problem, the company officer needs to balance the effort or cost in resources against the result. In those cases, the officer selects the response that has the most significant advantages and the least number of significant disadvantages.

Convert the Decision Into an Action
This step is the key element that changes an intention into an active decision. It requires that a commitment be made to assign responsibility for the implementation of the decision, allot the necessary resources to the decision, establish measurements for success, and hold people responsible for the implementation.

In the example involving back injuries, implementation may be assigned to the health and safety officer or the training division. The measurements would be the number of lifting-related back injuries during the subsequent time period.

Responsibility for the action in the chemical spill example would be assigned to the operational chief officers commanding the various components of the incident. The measurements would be the successful containment, blanketing, and removal of the chemical hazard.

Test the Action Against the Desired Outcome
Through feedback from participants and personal observation, the officer determines whether the decision has effectively solved the original problem. This test may be immediate in the exceptional situation such as the application of a sufficient blanket of foam over a chemical spill. It may also take time as in the case of reducing lifting-related back injuries through policy, training, additional equipment, or additional personnel.

Feedback and observation would also inform the company officer whether other problems have been created by the initial decision. In the situation involving the chemical spill, those problems may involve environmental pollution, evacuation and relocation costs, or safety-related situations.

Generic problems may have side effects that involve finances, morale, or perception problems. Because the use of back-support belts in the first example may represent a change in operating conditions, members of the organization who view their use as an invasion of their rights to choose how to perform certain tasks may resist the change. When resistance or other problems become apparent, the decision-making process may need to be reevaluated.

Barriers
Making decisions can be difficult because of the personal barriers that exist within the individual. Some of these barriers are *psychological (internal)* while others are generated by the *organizational culture (external)*. An understanding of the vari-

ous types of barriers helps the company officer to recognize them and overcome them before they derail the process.

It is possible, though, that some barriers cannot be overcome, causing the company officer to be willing to accept that fact and work within the constraints they pose. The sections that follow describe the barrier types and a paradox.

Psychological (Internal) Barriers

Internal barriers are the result of psychological conflicts within the individual; these barriers are described as follows:

- *Fear* — Becomes one of the main personal barriers to making a decision. It may be the fear of failure, fear of embarrassment or personal ridicule, fear of physical harm, fear of public exposure, or any number of other consequences that may result from making what is perceived to be a bad decision. Most of these fears are unfounded and exist only in the mind of the individual. *Overcoming fear:*
  — Ask the question, *What is the worst thing that can happen?*
  — Answering this question can place the situation in the context of real consequences, minimize the stress caused by irrational fears, and make the decision easier.

- *Ego or self-esteem* — Prevents effective decision-making. Too much ego can lead to overconfidence that causes the individual to ignore the advice of others. For example, dictators usually succumb to bad decision-making because of an inflated ego. Considering others' opinions or perspectives is not a sign of weakness or indecisiveness but shows an officer's ability and desire to gather as much information as possible before making a decision and taking action. On the other hand, a lack of self-esteem leads to indecisiveness. In this case, the individual does not have the self-confidence necessary to make a decision and is afraid of being criticized for the final decision, regardless of whether it is right or wrong. *Controlling ego and building self-esteem:*
  — Employee assistance program counseling
  — Outside professional counselor
  — Strong personal commitment

- *Indecisiveness* — Means that events will overtake the need for the decision. When indecisiveness occurs, the problem may overwhelm the available resources. Making a best-judgment decision and taking action, even if the decision and action later prove to be wrong, is better than allowing inaction to take control of the situation. *Examples:*
  — A less-than-perfect decision can be more effective than no decision at all.
  — A less-than-perfect decision can be improved upon and might prevent missing an important window of opportunity for the organization, unit, or leader.

- *Distrust* — Causes lack of trust in one's own ability to make a correct decision and in others to provide accurate information to implement a decision. Distrust is a result of low self-esteem and can cause paralysis and keep any decision from being made. Good decisions require that full trust be placed in the abilities of everyone involved in the process.

- *Antagonism* — Means that active opposition to a decision by others causes the decision-maker to compromise even though the compromise might not be the best solution to the problem. Antagonism may be the result of ego, personality differences, or jealousy. *Overcoming antagonism:*
  — Provide clear, concise communications with those involved.
  — Listen to the concerns and ideas of others and accept them as valid, which reduces the potential threat of an antagonistic response to the decision.

- *Jealousy* — Causes an individual to act irrationally and block the suggestions of others. The decision-making ability of a committee can be crippled if one or more of the members are jealous or resentful. *Overcoming jealousy:*
  — Display good communication skills.
  — Treat others with respect.

- *Unethical motives* — Involves personal gain, enhanced self-image, and personal protection at the expense of others. Bad decisions can be generated when the reason for making them is unethical. This barrier requires an insistence that decisions be motivated by and based on an ethical foundation. Personal agendas need to be subordinated to the good of the organization and solution of the problem.

Decisions Not Allowed

When I was a Battalion Chief in a small Texas community, I was told by the chief, *If it is not covered in the standard operating procedure (SOP), you can't do it!* When I asked if he meant that I was to discount 30 years of training, education, and experience and only do what was written, he said *Yes!*

This example illustrates the fact that some organizations and managers will not allow decisions to be made. This type of culture will cause young officers to be afraid to make a decision.

Organizational (External) Barriers

External barriers that exist outside the individual may be created by how a situation is organized. These barriers are described as follows:

- *Lack of data* — Includes the lack of accurate, sufficient, or timely information. The lack of data can result in making no decision, making the wrong decision, or accepting a compromise that is not adequate to completely resolve the problem. Overcome this barrier by gathering the most accurate, reliable, recent, and unbiased information.

- *Lack of accurate analysis* — Leads to an unacceptable decision even if data is accurate, recent, or sufficient. Every effort must be made to look at the total picture of the incident or problem based on all available information to determine the correct relationship of the various parts.

- *Lack of resources* — Delays decisions if necessary resources are not available. The lack of finances, personnel, time, and equipment or the inability to enforce the decision can keep the most effective decision from being made and permit the implementation of an unacceptable compromise. A lack of resources may require that the decision be implemented in phases or postponed until the required resources are available **(Figure 4.12)**.

- *Lack of management/membership support* — Dooms decisions to failure from the start. Lack of support (such as in the area of allocation of resources) will simply result in a good intention that does not become an action. Support from upper management or the membership is built through the use of team building, open communication, and the empowerment of the membership. Depending on the issue or initiative, building support can start from the bottom up or the top down.

Figure 4.12 Flammable liquids fires are extremely difficult to control under any circumstances. A lack of resources such as an insufficient quantity of foam concentrate can result in a fire that can spread to exposures and destroy more product before it is extinguished or burns all available fuel. *Courtesy of Williams Fire and Hazard Control, Inc.*

- **Lack of commitment**—Leads to ineffective decisions. The personal commitment of the decision-maker and those affected by the decision are required in order to have effective decisions. The use of oral and written communication skills and public statements of commitment create the image of commitment necessary to ensure acceptance of the decision.

- **Lack of capacity**—Lacks the authority or ability to make a decision in some cases. *Examples:*

  — The ability to provide raises may rest with the human resources or finance departments of the governing authority and the administration of the organization instead of the company officer.

  — The ability to enforce local building and fire codes on federal government property that is located within the local jurisdiction may rest with other officials. Overcoming this barrier may require the building of political alliances inside and outside the organization.

Compromise

There are some instances when compromise is unacceptable. Examples might include situations involving questions of ethics and safety. In these cases, the company officer may be forced to make what others perceive to be unpopular decisions.

Abilene Paradox

The *Abilene Paradox* (a popular theory developed by Jerry B. Harvey from personal experience) explains why members of a group may go along with a decision even when they believe it to be a bad one rather than dissent against the group. Because the individual members of the group do not want to appear out of step or are afraid that their opinion is flawed, they will not voice their concern or opposition to the group's decision **(Figure 4.13)**.

The prime historical example of this occurred in the U.S. with the administration of President Richard M. Nixon when the president's advisors approved the Watergate break-in. In later interviews, the participants all admitted that it was a bad idea

Figure 4.13 The *Abilene Paradox* is an analogy for the inability of groups to question a decision that many of the group members believe is wrong.

that they personally opposed but did not want to object to in the meeting. Symptoms of the Abilene Paradox (also known as the *inability to manage agreement*) are as follows:

- Group members agree individually in private about the problem facing the organization.

- They also agree individually in private about the actions that are required to solve the problem.

- However, they fail to accurately communicate their private desires and beliefs to one another.

- Because members have failed to communicate their private desires, the group makes decisions that are counterproductive and may be unethical.

- The process then frustrates the members of the group.

- The cycle continues to repeat itself unless it is corrected through accurate communication.

The use of empowerment and openness of communication during the committee decision-making process helps to reduce the chance that poor decisions will be made. The company officer must work to overcome these barriers to ensure that the correct decisions are made and implemented. The implementation of the right response can be ensured in the following ways:

- Open, honest, direct, and appropriate communication
- Membership involvement
- Appropriation of resources
- Ethical foundation
- Accurate, well-analyzed data

Four-Way Test

To test the ethical foundation of a decision (either personal or professional), it may be beneficial for the individual to follow a simple four-step process. In 1943, Rotary International adopted as part of their by-laws (deleted in a 1980 revision) a four-way test for ethical decision-making. To determine if a decision is ethical, answer the following four questions:

- Is it the truth?
- Is it fair to all concerned?
- Will it build goodwill and better relationships?
- Will it be beneficial to all concerned?

By answering *yes* to these questions, the potential that the decision is the correct one is greatly increased. This test, however, is not a code of ethics according to Rotary International but only a guideline for a high standard of human relations.

It may be more appropriate to create a four-way test for the fire and emergency services fire officer that is slightly different. Mentally testing all decisions against this or any accepted standard helps to ensure that a decision is at least ethically sound and justifiable. The questions to ask are as follows:

- Is the decision based on well-analyzed facts?
- Is the decision based on ethical values held by the organization and the community?
- Will the decision build strong internal and external relationships and generate the appropriate image of the organization?
- Will the decision benefit everyone affected by it?

Summary

Company officers must have the respect and support of the members of the organization, the senior management staff, the community, and their peers. Through the application of logic and ethics, company officers can gain this level of respect and support.

Logical, well-reasoned decision-making will provide the company officer with the ability to generate public, political, and internal support for the needs of the unit, organization, membership, and community. It will also provide the company officer with the ability to recognize and refute illogical comments about the organization.

Further, a strong and valid ethical and moral personal belief system is the *bottom line* for all relationships. The relationships that a company officer has are no exception. To maintain the public's trust and a positive public image of the fire and emergency services, every fire officer must adhere to a personal and professional code of ethics. Finally, applying both logic and ethics to the decision-making process will increase the likelihood that a decision is the best one and that it will be accepted and implemented.

Values

Values can be defined as *learned, relatively enduring, and emotionally charged moral concepts that help people in making decisions and planning actions.* The priorities people set and the choices they make are based on their personal and community values. Because codes of ethics and the decision-making process are based on values, it is important to remember the following key points about them:

1. *All values are learned* — The primary source of values is the family, followed by friends, formal education, work, and religious activities. Beyond these sources are the written and oral histories of the society or community to which the person belongs, including myths, folk tales, and factual historical events.

2. *Values are enduring* — While values may be forgotten and altered as people mature and have additional life experiences, they are difficult to ignore or change. The values acquired as a child continue to be present throughout a person's life.

3. *Values may not be consciously known by the individual or society* — Values may be established and adhered to but not stated openly; that is, a person may not be able to state the value and yet may act upon it consistently.

4. *Values tend to be consistent* — Therefore, society and individuals maintain values that are compatible. Values that are not compatible or consistent are generally ignored or excluded by society or the individual.

5. *Values establish what is morally desirable in society* — That is, they create a set of criteria that define what is considered good or bad, right or wrong, or moral or immoral. This set of criteria guides human conduct. However, such criteria can also be the cause of conflict because individuals and societies may define the criteria differently.

6. *Values are emotionally charged* — Emotions that are generated by personal values are subjective and sometimes viewed by others as irrational. Emotions express how people view a value. Something that is loved is loved with passion, while something that is hated is avoided and despised. Emotionally charged values can also prevent an appreciation and acceptance of values or cultures that are different from one's own.

7. *Values are great motivators within the individual and society as a whole* — Value-based motivation can result in acts of extreme heroism and bravery or acts that may be against the commonly held values of the community or society.

8. *Values influence personal behaviors, actions, or responses* — Although there may be other influences on personal behavior, such as self-esteem, role definitions, laws, and peer influence, values form the basis for the choice in behaviors.

Legal Responsibilities and Liabilities

Chapter Contents

Learning Objectives

1. Select facts about the major sources of law.

2. Identify the seven classifications of laws.

3. Match to their definitions legal terms.

4. Recall various forms of liability

5. Select facts about federal and statutory laws of importance to a company officer's duties.

6. Identify national consensus standards that relate to emergency services.

Chapter 5
Legal Responsibilities and Liabilities

As supervisors and public employees, a great many company officers' day-to-day activities are governed by a variety of laws, ordinances, and regulations. Company officers and their subordinates are subject to federal, state/provincial, and local laws/ordinances (Canadian municipal bylaws) as well as their organization's policies, rules, and regulations. To make matters even more difficult, these laws, ordinances, and regulations are not interpreted or applied uniformly in all jurisdictions. Also, the court interpretations of many of these laws change over time.

It is essential for company officers to understand the basic concepts of law, including the sources and classifications of laws in the U.S. and Canada and the difference between criminal and civil law. They should also be aware of the various types of liability, the so-called *Fireman's Rule,* and the application of governmental immunity.

Also important to company officers are the U.S. and Canadian federal laws and national consensus standards that apply to how company officers and emergency responders conduct themselves while on duty. Consensus standards and model building and fire codes are also of importance to company officers who write equipment specifications or inspect occupancies in their jurisdictions. Company officers in other countries must research and follow the laws, standards, and regulations that apply in their particular jurisdictions.

The Law

All organized societies depend on some mechanism to ensure that members of the group live in harmony and peace. The legal system is composed of courts, judges, attorneys, and laws and is the primary mechanism for ensuring harmony and peace in the majority of the world's societies in the 21st century. The purpose of the legal system and laws is to create a structure for the resolution of conflict and ensure the safety of the members of society.

Laws exist at all levels of society. International laws regulate the relationship between national governments, national laws regulate the relationship between states/provinces to ensure fair and equitable treatment of all citizens, state/provincial laws regulate the activities of citizens within their borders, and local laws and ordinances establish the legal framework for life within the community **(Figure 5.1)**.

Figure 5.1 Laws exist throughout society. Some are represented by common symbols such as traffic control signs that have a direct affect on the safety of citizens.

Generally, laws come from a number of sources, including written constitutions, legislative actions, court decisions, and governmental agencies. The laws are divided into categories depending on the type of conflict or situation (criminal or civil) the law is intended to govern or control. Laws also establish liability, requiring citizens to take responsibility for their own actions.

While some people may argue that society has too many laws, restricting the freedom of its members, it can also be argued that the members of society are too erratic and independent to live in communities without restrictions imposed by legal frameworks. In either case, the company officer is an active participant in society and must be familiar with the types of laws that govern the community, the fire and emergency services organization, and ultimately the officer.

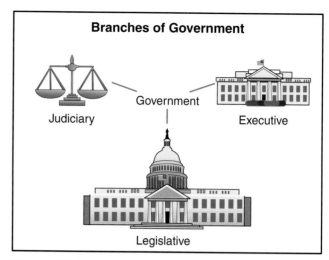

Figure 5.2 The three branches of government.

Legal Definitions

- *Law* — Rule of conduct or procedure established by custom, agreement, or authority.
- *Legal system* — Body of rules and principles governing the affairs of a community and enforced by a political/judicial authority. *Example*: International law.

Sources of Law

In general, the major sources of laws in North America and much of Europe are federal and state/provincial constitutions (which provide judicial decisions and legislative actions) and government agencies. In North America, the federal governments of Canada and the U.S. as well as all the provinces, states, and territories base their laws on these sources.

Federal and State/Provincial Constitutions

The federal constitutions in both the U.S. and Canada are the basic *laws of the land*. The constitution describes the organization of the federal government, the powers assigned to each branch of the government, and the powers ascribed to the states or provinces. The U.S. Constitution contains a Bill of Rights that defines individual rights and freedoms of citizens in broad and general terms. All laws enacted by Congress/Parliament, state/provincial legislatures, or local entities must be consistent with the respective federal constitution.

The federal court system and, ultimately, the U.S. Supreme Court is the arbiter in matters of constitutional law in the U.S. The constitutions of the U.S. and Canada each create a federal governmental structure consisting of three branches — legislative, executive, and judicial (**Figure 5.2**). State/provincial governments mirror this structure and have similar constitutions to the federal constitution. In general terms, the *legislative branch* creates laws and the *executive branch* implements, administers, and enforces them. The *judicial branch* interprets the laws.

Legislative Actions

Statutory laws are the result of legislative actions such as those laws passed by the U.S. Congress, Canadian Parliament, state or provincial legislatures, or local entities (counties, municipalities, towns, etc.). The authority to create these laws stems from the federal constitutions of both countries. These laws, referred to as *statutes* or *ordinances*, may be revised or repealed by the body that enacted them. They are also subject to interpretation by the state/provincial or federal judiciary.

For instance, a local municipality has the right (as a subagency of the state) to enact and enforce laws regarding open burning, fireworks (sale, possession, and use), or occupancy limitations. However, a local ordinance may not be in conflict with a federal or state law.

Judicial Decisions

By definition, *common law* (also known as *case law*) is that body of law that is based on tradition, custom, usage, and decisions of the judicial courts within a particular country, society, or culture. Therefore, common law consists of laws that were developed by judicial decisions rather than legislative action (statutory law). Judicial decisions are subject to the changes in society and views of individual members of the judiciary.

When a judge is asked to rule on a question before the court, the judge reviews prior decisions on similar questions. In essence, the prior decisions form a precedence upon which future decisions are based.

Government Agencies

Within the limits of the statutory laws that created them, federal, state/provincial, and local government agencies such as U.S. Occupational Safety and Health Administration (OSHA), U.S. Environmental Protection Agency (EPA), state fire marshal's offices, and local code enforcement departments are empowered to create and enforce rules and regulations to implement the legislation for which they are responsible.

These rules and regulations, known as *administrative laws*, have the force of law. For instance, the local fire marshal's office can create and enforce, with the authority of the municipality, the regulations regarding the storage of flammable and combustible liquids **(Figure 5.3)**.

Classifications of Laws

Laws are further divided into seven classifications **(Figure 5.4)**. The decisions and actions of all fire and emergency services personnel are controlled by and subject to each of these classifications. Therefore, it is essential that personnel be familiar with the following classifications of laws and how they affect their work:

- *Substantive* — Deals with actual issues by establishing principles, defining duties and obligations, and creating and defining the limitations of rights within a society. These laws are established by legislative and government agencies and constitutions. *Examples:*

Figure 5.3 Administrative laws regulate such activities as the storage and transportation of flammable and combustible liquids.

Figure 5.4 Seven classifications of laws commonly found in North America.

— *Tort:* Duty of care provided to another party

— *Contract:* Offers and the acceptance of offers

- **Procedural** — Defines the judiciary rules or mechanisms used to enforce substantive laws. They are established by legislative actions and constitutions. In the U.S., the federal courts follow the procedures set forth in the *Federal Rules of Civil Procedures,* while the states codify their rules in similar documents. The laws include the following information, among other things:

— Where to file a case

— What may be filed

— When filings may be made

— How the case will be handled

- **Common** — Bases laws in the U.S., Canada, and many other former British colonies (including federal, state, provincial, and local law) on English Common Law, which was spread throughout the world by British colonizers. Although common law was traditional or customary, much of it has become statutory law through adoption and codification by various legislatures. *Examples:*

— Common law exists in all Canadian provinces except Quebec and in all U.S. states except Louisiana (both of which were influenced by the early French settlers and base their laws on the Napoleonic Code).

— Common law marriage was once widespread in the American colonies and the U.S. but currently only exists in 10 states and the District of Columbia. It has been outlawed in the remaining states and territories.

- **Statutory** — Pertains to laws enacted by legislative bodies of government. *Examples:*

— *U.S. federal level:* Created the U.S. Fire Administration (USFA), OSHA, EPA, Equal Employment Opportunity Commission (EEOC), and the Internal Revenue Service (IRS)

— *Canada federal level:* Created federal agencies similar (but not identical) to those in the U.S., including Occupational Health and Safety (OH&S), Natural Resources, Atomic Energy Commission, Canadian Transportation Commission, National Energy Board, and Revenue Canada.

— *State/provincial level:* Created tax codes, marriage laws, voting laws, motor vehicle laws, gaming laws, hunting regulations, health and safety laws, and laws governing the formation of special districts for fire protection, sanitation, recreation, education, etc.

— *Local level:* Created ordinances that adopt a particular edition of a building or fire code, establish speed limits on local streets and roads, require business licenses, and adopt the fire and emergency services organization's annual budget.

- **Administrative** — Pertains to laws created by government agencies and used to enforce and implement statutory law. They define the extent of the powers and responsibilities held by administrative agencies in performing their assigned responsibilities. Obviously, as exemplified by the IRS and OSHA, the power that these enforcement agencies wield can be significant. Career and volunteer company officers and their subordinates are fully accountable under these laws. *Examples:*

— OSHA regulations in the *Code of Federal Regulations (CFR),* such as Title 29 (Labor) Part 1910.120 (hazardous waste operations), contain the administrative laws that protect workers — including firefighters — in high-hazard industries **(Figure 5.5)**.

— Agencies such as EPA, EEOC, and others are empowered to create and enforce administrative laws to fulfill their missions.

- **Criminal** — Protects society as a whole from wrongful actions (also known as *penal law*). These laws are established by legislative action at all levels of government and are in the tradition of common and civil laws. Substantive criminal law defines the act and punishment for various crimes. Criminal laws extend from those that define petty theft to the degrees of murder as well as the following:

— Hate crimes

— Smuggling

— Embezzlement

— Acts of terrorism

Figure 5.5 The health and safety of fire and emergency services personnel are just two of the topics covered by Occupational Safety and Health Administration (OSHA) regulations. The proper use of respiratory protection such as self-contained breathing apparatus (SCBA) is part of those regulations.

- *Civil* — Defines relationships between individuals or groups and helps to resolve disputes between parties (also known as *noncriminal laws*). They are established by legislative action rather than judicial decisions. Relationships regulated by civil law include the following:

— Property rights

— Contracts

— Taxation

— Privacy

While it is possible for the same act to be a violation of both criminal and civil laws, most actionable behavior is either one or the other. The difference between criminal and civil law is rela-

tively simple. Criminal law deals with the rights and responsibilities of individuals toward society, and civil law deals primarily with private rights and responsibilities. More detailed differences are as follows:

- *Criminal law* — Means by which society protects itself; its penalties are sometimes monetary (fines), loss of freedom (jail), or both. Criminal actions (*prosecutions*) are brought by the government (representing the people) against an individual or group. The defendant's guilt must be proven *beyond a reasonable doubt.*

- *Civil law* — Means by which individuals seek redress, usually in the form of monetary damages, from other individuals, corporations, or the government. Civil actions (*suits*) are usually brought by an individual against another individual or group, although there are *class action* suits on behalf of many individuals with a common complaint. The standard of proof is *a balance of probabilities* or *a preponderance of evidence.*

Liability

The thought of being held liable can be very frightening for a person or an organization. The term *liability* is usually associated with being sued or taken to court by another person or group. However, all persons live with some type of liability constantly. A liability is a legal obligation or responsibility.

For instance, parents are obligated to ensure that their children are educated, fed, clothed, and housed. Company officers are responsible for performing their duties in a professional manner. Subordinates are responsible for executing orders and performing the tasks assigned to them. All of these examples imply liability.

There are numerous forms of liability from the legal standpoint. They include criminal, civil, tort, negligence, and personal. The company officer should be familiar with each of these and with the application of the so-called *Fireman's Rule* and governmental immunity. Each of these topics is covered in the sections that follow.

Legal Terminology

- **Plaintiff** — Party (also known as *claimant* or *complainant*) who initiates a lawsuit (also known as *action*) before a court

- **Defendant** — Any person or institution against whom an action is brought in a criminal or civil court of law; person being sued or accused

- **Liability** — State of being legally obliged and responsible

- **Tort** — Civil wrong or breach of duty to another person as defined by law

- **Proximate cause** — Effective or primary cause of loss or damage or an unbroken chain of events between the occurrence and resulting damage

- **Negligence** — Failure to exercise the same care that a reasonable, prudent, and careful person would under the same or similar circumstances

- **Malfeasance** — Commission of an unlawful act; *committed* by a public official

- **Misfeasance** — Improper performance of a legal or lawful act

- **Nonfeasance** — Failure to act when under an obligation to do so; refusal (without sufficient cause) to do that which is a legal duty

- **Standard of care** — Level of care a *reasonable person* would use under similar circumstances; standard of behavior upon which the theory of negligence is based

- **Sovereign immunity** — Doctrine that the federal, state/provincial, or local government is immune to lawsuit unless it gives its consent

- **Vicarious liability** — Situation that occurs when one person is held responsible for the actions or inactions of another individual; also applies to the liability incurred by an organization for the actions or inactions of an employee

Criminal Liability

Criminal laws are codified in a criminal or penal code and everyone within the jurisdiction is subject to these laws. Typical criminal laws are those against arson, murder, rape, robbery, theft, embezzlement, fraud, kidnapping, extortion, drunk driving, and many other antisocial acts. These laws are intended to protect members of society from acts that would place their lives and/or property in serious jeopardy.

While there are numerous federal criminal laws such as those against tax violations, civil rights violations, racketeering, drug trafficking, mail fraud, and a number of other offenses that may involve the crossing of state/provincial boundaries, most criminal laws are administered by individual states/provinces. Acts that are defined as criminal vary from state to state and province to province; therefore, it is imperative that company officers know the laws of their state or province and how those laws have been interpreted.

When a criminal act applies to public servants, it is called *malfeasance*. It is generally used in connection with public officials who embezzle public funds, accept bribes, or break laws in connection with their duties.

Regardless of whether a law is state, provincial, or federal or how it is interpreted in a given state or province, one principle applies in all criminal cases — *an employee cannot be required by his or her employer to commit a crime*. Therefore, if an employee commits a crime while on duty, the employee and not the employer is responsible.

In some cases, employers may defend employees in a civil action, but they cannot and will not defend an employee in a criminal action. On the other hand, supervisors are not responsible for the criminal acts of their subordinates unless the supervisor was aware of the act and failed to stop the criminal conduct or participated in it. Regardless of the circumstances, company officers and their subordinates, career or volunteer, are never justified in breaking the law or committing a crime.

Civil Liability

The basis for all civil law is the fact that anyone, including individuals, corporations, associations, government agencies, and even convicts in prison, has the right to sue anyone else. There need only be an unresolved issue and someone to be held accountable.

Civil actions can involve any claim of loss (usually financial) and may be based on failure to perform a service or failure to exercise due caution. If a carpenter fails to perform work after having been paid for the work, the person who hired the carpenter can sue to recover the money paid and, perhaps, punitive damages as well.

Figures 5.6 Punitive damages are intended to hold a person responsible for actions that have harmed another person in some way. If the person whose actions have resulted in harm is found guilty, that person will be responsible for paying for all damages and expenses incurred by the victim.

Punitive damages are intended to *punish* the offender. If someone's car is damaged by someone else's recklessness or carelessness, the person suffering the damage can sue the other party for the cost of repairs, medical expenses if an injury resulted, rental car expenses, etc. **(Figure 5.6)**. Employees who feel that they have been sexually harassed can sue the offender for damages even if the plaintiff suffered no monetary loss.

Tort Liability

Most civil actions against fire and emergency services organizations are related to tort liability. A *tort* is a civil wrong or injury. The main purpose of a tort action is to seek payment for property damaged or destroyed, personal injuries, or lost income. The following elements must exist for a valid tort action:

- The defendant must owe a legal duty to the plaintiff.

- There must be a breach of duty; that is, the defendant must have failed to perform or properly perform that duty.

- The breach of duty must be a proximate cause (one that in a naturally continuous sequence produces the injury or damage and without which the injury or damage would not have occurred) of the accident or injury that resulted.

- The plaintiff must have suffered damages as a result.

When a citizen files a tort against a government agency such as the fire and emergency services organization, each of these elements must be proven. The first element (duty) is relatively easy to establish in an emergency-incident-related tort because the organization has jurisdiction over the fire-suppression, rescue, and related activities at the incident.

Duty is also relatively clear regarding the delivery of medical aid and in the area of emergency response to hazardous materials incidents. Public emergency services have a responsibility and duty to provide for the safety of the citizens in the jurisdiction.

Proving that the plaintiff has suffered damages (fourth element) may also be easy to prove, although determining the amount of damages may be difficult. Direct loss such as medical expenses or the value of property can easily be shown. It may be more difficult to place a monetary value on long-term care, rehabilitation, or psychological or stress-related suffering. Juries can be very liberal in awarding money based on projected difficulties for the plaintiff.

The question of causation may be more difficult to establish. Breach of duty does not have to be the only cause. In fact, most accidents are the result of multiple factors. However, juries have been known to view the issue of proximate cause very liberally when the injuries are substantial or emotionally charged such as when a child is badly injured. If a jury is emotionally sympathetic to the plaintiff, it may be satisfied with a weak connection between cause and effect, which will strain the criteria for proximate cause.

Negligence Liability

Negligence — breach of a legal duty — is the major issue in most tort liability cases. When a person possesses a greater amount of expertise than others, that person's legal duty is then proportionately greater. Therefore, the *standard of care* for which an emergency medical technician (EMT) would be responsible is the standard that a reasonable, prudent, and careful EMT would be expected to meet and not that of a paramedic or doctor **(Figure 5.7)**.

One of the key questions in negligence is the adequacy of performance. There are two ways in which one can be judged negligent: wrongful performance (*misfeasance*) or the omission of performance when some act should have been performed and was not (*nonfeasance*). Examples are as follows:

- Misfeasance occurs when an individual has the knowledge, ability, and legal authority to act but performs the act incorrectly. For instance, an EMT who is trained to use an automatic external defibrillator (AED) but uses it improperly resulting in further injury to a patient may be subject to negligent liability based on misfeasance.

- Nonfeasance would occur if a company officer failed to order the overhaul of a structure even though all indicators suggested that a reignition was possible. That officer could be held liable for property damage resulting from the reignition of the fire because proper overhaul techniques were not used.

A critical issue in negligence liability is the care with which a company officer's responsibilities are discharged. If conduct or performance falls below a reasonable standard of care, the responsible persons and/or organizations may then be held liable for injuries and damages that resulted from such conduct. While there are factors that may limit company officers' abilities to act, they have a responsibility to act in a manner that is reasonable, based on the information at hand and the resources available.

When a potentially hazardous condition exists, the reasonableness of action must take into account the following factors, particularly when resources are not available to correct all such conditions:

- Gravity of harm posed by the condition
- Likelihood of harm
- Availability of a method and/or equipment to correct the situation
- Usefulness of the condition for other purposes
- Burden of removing the condition

Many items of information may be brought into court to aid in establishing the prevailing standard of care. Some of the strongest types of evidence are national consensus standards (such as those from National Fire Protection Association [NFPA], American National Standards Institute [ANSI], etc.) and the organization's own guidelines and policies. A reasonable and prudent person would be expected to follow these guidelines. See National Consensus Standards section.

Sources of information that may help to establish the standard of care include the following:

- Agency directives and policies
- Directives of a superior agency (legal mandates)
- Guidelines and policies of other agencies (locally accepted practices)
- Guidelines and standards developed by professional organizations (such as NFPA)
- Professional texts and manuals (such as IFSTA manuals)
- Professional journals
- Research publications
- Opinions of expert witnesses

It is the responsibility of the fire and emergency services organization to train its members to an accepted standard of care. It is the responsibility of the company officer and members of the organization to maintain their levels of knowledge and skills to continually meet this standard.

Figure 5.7 Emergency responders are responsible for providing the level of care to which they are trained. They can be held legally liable for not providing that care if they fail or refuse to do so.

Personal Liability

The duty owed to the public for a reasonable standard of care extends to all parties that are responsible for abating hazardous situations and delivering emergency care. Parties include individual employees of public agencies and private contractors.

Basically, everyone has an obligation to conduct themselves in a manner that does not cause harm or further injury to any other person. Anyone who violates this general duty of care may be liable for damages.

If a court or jury decides that an individual is liable, a judgment of damages can then be returned against the individual. Recovery of punitive or exemplary (serving as a warning) damages is one reason for suing an individual employee, especially when the public agency is prohibited from paying such damages.

However, as a practical matter, government employees are not often held responsible for payment of awards. Because an individual's assets are small compared to those of the government, the organization is more likely to be targeted for recovery of damages. However, it is quite possible for the municipal government to successfully apply the rule of *governmental immunity*, leaving the employee(s) involved open to personal liability. See Governmental Immunity section. Nevertheless, being named as a defendant in a lawsuit is a serious matter.

Fireman's Rule

At the opposite end of the liability spectrum is the question of whether a property owner is liable for a firefighter's injuries suffered while fighting a fire or controlling an emergency caused by the property owner's negligence. In most jurisdictions, the courts have held property owners immune from liability because of the so-called *Fireman's Rule.*

This doctrine holds that firefighters, rescuers, and other emergency responders know the risks involved and are trained to deal with those risks; therefore, they are not entitled to redress (compensation for injuries) from the property owner for injury suffered as a result of performing their duty. The exception to this doctrine is if the injury was the result of a crime such as arson or the property owner's gross negligence or willful and wanton disregard for the firefighter's safety.

For example, if the property owner knew that the burning building contained explosives but failed to inform firefighters of them, the owner would probably be held liable for any damages if firefighters were injured by a subsequent explosion **(Figure 5.8)**. Some courts and jurisdictions have expanded the Fireman's Rule to include emergency medical services (EMS) providers and law enforcement personnel.

At the same time, several states have overturned the Fireman's Rule or severely limited its application. Company officers should contact

Figure 5.8 Property owners may be held liable for injuries to emergency responders if negligence can be proven. For example, improper storage or marking of hazardous materials could be considered a liable condition. *Courtesy of District Chief Chris Mickal.*

their local and state/provincial legal departments to determine the current use of this rule in their response area.

Governmental Immunity

As mentioned earlier, much of U.S. and Canadian law evolved from English Common Law. One of the most relevant doctrines that made the transition was that of *sovereign immunity*. Originally conceived to protect British royalty, this doctrine holds that *a sovereign is exempt from suit, not because of any formal conception or obsolete theory, but on the logical and practical ground that there can be no legal right against the authority that makes the law on which the right depends.* In other words, the sovereign (monarch) can do no wrong. For centuries, this doctrine has been extended to protect any legally constituted government from liability.

In the U.S. and Canada, the doctrine of sovereign immunity had the effect of holding any federal, state, provincial, or local government immune from liability in tort (noncriminal) cases. The practical effect was that any government entity or agency (or agent thereof) was immune from liability for any action taken in an official capacity even if the action was negligent.

For example, under sovereign immunity, a fire and emergency services organization and its members would be immune from liability if a fire engine ran a red light during an emergency response and collided with a vehicle that had the legal right-of-way. Even though such an act would normally be considered negligence under statutory law, the sovereign immunity doctrine would protect the organization and its members from liability.

However, in 1946, the U.S. government waived its immunity from liability in tort cases and allowed the litigation of such claims in federal courts. Even after the federal government's decision, most states maintained their immunity from suits for tortious injury to persons or property.

In the ensuing decades, however, the doctrine of sovereign immunity has been eroded through legislative modification and (in some cases) outright abolition by judicial decisions. In some states, the concept of sovereign immunity has been declared unconstitutional.

Whether and how immunity applies to local jurisdictions such as counties, cities, and towns varies because of differences in state law. In some instances, immunity is afforded to local jurisdictions on the basis that their immunity derives directly from the state. However, when a state loses its immunity, its local jurisdictions lose theirs as well. As a result, some incorporated municipalities have been held to be fully responsible for the tortious acts of their agents, just like any other corporation.

The concept of governmental immunity from tort claims continues to change. Several mechanisms have been established that reflect the prevailing opinion that government entities should assume some responsibility for the negligence of their agents and employees. The current status of governmental immunity laws in various states is one of the following:

- Doctrine of immunity still in force
- Limited liability by means of a tort claims act:
  — Suits instituted as prescribed by statute
  — Suits brought before a special tribunal
  — Suits authorized only within prescribed limits
- Legislative claims boards — Approves valid claims made by citizens against the state
- Abandonment of immunity — Remedy left to the courts as if the state were a private citizen

It is important for company officers and their subordinates (including volunteers) to realize that they — as individual employees — may also be held liable. Although firefighters and other emergency responders are usually immune from liability as long as they act *within the scope of their authority,* they may be held liable if they commit an act on the job that is so much at variance with their training and organizational policy as to constitute gross negligence. For example, if a fire engine arrives at a fire unprepared such as without water in its tank, the organization and engine crew might *not* be immune from liability.

In such cases, plaintiffs must show that the firefighters acted with complete disregard for their training and the organization's standard operating procedures (SOPs). In more than one case, individual firefighters have been found liable under a punitive damages award that actually punishes the firefighter for such improper behavior.

In these actions, the government agency is precluded from paying the fine for the individual. Today, the continuing trend away from sovereign immunity continues, and tort and/or negligence liability applies to governmental functions in all but a few jurisdictions.

To protect themselves and their subordinates from possible liability, company officers must learn what laws and regulations apply to their official activities and how the courts in their area have interpreted these laws. Because new laws and regulations are enacted each year, existing ones are revised or repealed, and the courts clarify the applicability and limitations of these laws through their interpretations and rulings, staying current is an ongoing responsibility of all company officers.

It is an important responsibility for company officers because they and their subordinates will be held accountable for complying with existing laws, especially in the areas of environmental protection and civil rights. In all situations, ignorance of the law is no excuse and does not afford protection.

Federal Laws

Company officers at all levels of government have particular interests in a number of federal administrative and statutory laws. Because these laws are of such importance to the discharge of a company officer's duties, it is assumed that they know these laws or that they should know them, and they may be held personally liable for failing to follow any of them. The federal laws that are of significance to most company officers are those that relate to protecting health and safety, the environment, and their subordinates' employment rights.

There may be state laws that also deal with the same or similar areas, but it is beyond the scope of this manual to discuss the specific variations in state laws. Because state laws may be more or less restrictive than federal laws in a given area, company officers should learn what laws are applicable in their jurisdictions, how those laws are interpreted locally, and what those laws require of them.

U.S. federal administrative laws are contained in the *Code of Federal Regulations (CFR)*. It is the codification of the general and permanent rules established by the executive departments and agencies of the federal government. It is divided into 50 titles that represent broad areas subject to federal regulation. Each volume of the *CFR* is updated once each calendar year and is issued on a quarterly basis.

The major health and safety laws in the U.S. are administrative laws created by OSHA. The major environmental laws are those of EPA. The major laws involving employment rights are those in Title VII of the Civil Rights Act of 1964, the EEOC, the Americans with Disabilities Act (ADA), and the Fair Labor Standards Act (FLSA). EMS providers are regulated by the U.S. Department of Transportation (DOT) that has developed certification requirements. Similar laws exist in Canada and its provinces.

Occupational Safety and Health Administration

As mentioned earlier, OSHA regulations for which company officers are responsible are contained in Title 29 (Labor) of the *CFR*. Title 29 contains regulations that are designed to protect the safety and health of all workers including firefighters and emergency responders. Part 1910.120 of Title 29 addresses training requirements and emergency response requirements for hazardous materials incidents. Company officers are responsible for knowing and following all of these regulations.

Part 1910.134 addresses operations that require the use of respiratory protection when working in situations that are confirmed or suspected of being immediately dangerous to life or health (IDLH). Along with NFPA 1500, *Standard on Fire Department Occupational Safety and Health Program*, this part is the basis for the *two-in/two-out rule* for interior fire attack and has wide application to many fire department activities.

Part 1910.146 addresses operations in confined spaces, including incidents involving tanks, bins, grain elevators, trenches, elevator shafts, or collapsed structures. Obviously, this part addresses many of the emergency activities in which fire and emergency responders become involved. Therefore, it is extremely important that company officers be familiar with its requirements (**Figure 5.9, p. 108**).

Figure 5.9 Confined-space search and rescue operations are subject to Occupational Safety and Health Administration (OSHA) safety regulations. *Courtesy of U.S. Federal Emergency Management Agency, FEMA News Photo Roman Bas, photographer.*

Environmental Protection Agency

The EPA regulations protecting the environment are contained in Title 40 (Protection of Environment) *CFR*. These laws and regulations deal with how hazardous substances are stored and shipped. They also contain regulations designed to protect the environment by governing how contaminants are contained, cleaned up, and disposed of.

Company officers come under these regulations whenever they must deal with releases of contaminants into the environment. Company officers and their subordinates can be held personally liable if they fail to follow these regulations during an incident **(Figure 5.10)**.

Figure 5.10 Federal or state/provincial environmental protection regulations influence how responders control and clean up hazardous materials spills.

For example, if company members fail to contain a spilled contaminant and allow it to run into and contaminate a waterway, they can be held liable. Likewise, if they simply flush a contaminant down a sewer or storm drain instead of containing it and disposing of it as required, they may be held liable.

Civil Rights Act

The Civil Rights Act of 1964 was the most comprehensive legislation of its type in U.S. history. From a public employment perspective, one of the most important parts of the Act is Title VII, which eliminated discrimination on the basis of race, color, national origin, religion, and sex (gender). In 1967, the category of age (40–70) was added to this list, and in 1978, pregnancy was added. To enforce these and other antidiscrimination laws, the Act created the EEOC.

Title VII, Presidential Executive Orders, and court decisions based on the Act, combined to place the following two obligations on employers:

- ***Do not discriminate in employment*** — Ensure that everyone has an equal chance to be hired based on qualifications.

- ***Eliminate the present effects of past discrimination*** — Take positive steps to seek, recruit, select, develop, reward, and retain individuals who were formerly denied employment opportunities because of their race, color, national origin, religion, gender, or age.

Equal Employment Opportunity Commission

The EEOC was charged with protecting the rights of all workers — especially those in what are called *protected classes* (see information box) such as the following:

- Women

- Minorities

- Workers over age 40 and under age 70

- Those with disabilities

It is illegal to discriminate in the recruitment, selection, promotion, or termination of anyone in one of these classes. One of the EEOC's first actions was to draft the administrative laws necessary to create and implement *affirmative action,* actions to increase the number of women and minorities (considered underutilized portions of the workforce) hired into jobs that were formerly occupied by white males exclusively.

Definition: Protected Class

Protected class is a class or group characteristic that may not be used as the sole reason for an employment decision unless it constitutes a bona-fide occupational qualification. State and federal antidiscrimination laws currently identify the following protected groups: race, color, creed, religion, ancestry, national origin, sex, marital status, age, disability, and veteran status. Some states and organizations prohibit discrimination on the basis of sexual orientation.

Affirmative Action

Affirmative action does *not* mean that employment standards have to be lowered. It only requires that the standards for recruitment, selection, and promotion be *essential* for the work and based on work-related criteria (**Figure 5.11**). Volunteer fire and emergency services organizations, like their career counterparts, are prohibited from discriminating against or excluding anyone from membership who can pass the job-related criteria. Historically, there have been four primary areas of employment discrimination: disparate treatment, adverse impact, sexual harassment, and reasonable accommodation.

Disparate Treatment

Disparate treatment (also called *differential treatment*) simply means treating an applicant or employee differently than those of another race, gender, religion, etc. Some examples of disparate treatment might be the following:

- Asking a female applicant different questions than male applicants are asked

- Denying employment to an older applicant because the applicant *might* have a greater tendency of being ill and can use large amounts of sick leave or require more health benefits

Figure 5.11 Federal law requires that all preemployment physical ability testing be based on job-related activities. A valid test could be performing a stair climb while wearing weight equivalent to the weight of protective equipment that increases the applicant's heart rate. *Courtesy of Rick Montemorra.*

- Denying employment to a single parent because that person *might* need time off to care for a sick child

- Denying employment to a woman because she is pregnant

- Requiring more or less work from an employee than is required of those of a different race

Adverse Impact

This type of discrimination occurs when an employer uses a test or other screening device that initially is not intended to discriminate but adversely affects members of one of the protected classes more than other applicants or employees. Some examples of adverse impact might be the following:

- Requiring a high school diploma may affect members of some minority groups because fewer of them may have finished high school.

- Requiring EMT, Firefighter I, or other professional certifications may affect single parents who cannot attend these classes because of child-rearing demands.

- Using tests written in English may affect Hispanics, Asians, and other minorities who speak or read English as a second language.

- Using minimum height and weight requirements may affect more women than men and more Hispanic and Asian men than Caucasian men.

- Using performance tests that involve lifting, jumping, and climbing (in excess of the actual job requirements) may affect protected class applicants.

Employers are required by EEOC regulations to use employment standards and screening devices that are directly related to performing the job successfully. Any standard or device that adversely affects a greater percentage of those in a protected class than it does other applicants or employees must be *proven* by the employer to be job-related.

Sexual Harassment

One of the obvious differences between the composition of fire and emergency services organizations today and those of a generation ago is *gender*. Females comprise an ever-increasing proportion of career and volunteer emergency services organizations **(Figure 5.12)**. This shift in the composition of the workforce has also resulted in the application of federal Civil Rights Act Title VII laws regarding discrimination.

Title VII specifically prohibits gender-based discrimination, and the courts have ruled that on-the-job harassment is a form of discrimination. According to the law, there are two forms of sexual harassment that result in discrimination. The company officer has several supervisory roles and responsibilities regarding this type of discrimination.

Quid pro quo. This form consists of any overt, unwanted, or unwelcome sexual behavior or advances toward a worker by someone who has the power to reward or punish the worker. A stated or implied promise of a reward (promotion, salary increase, etc.) for sexual favors or a penalty (demotion, termination, etc.) for a refusal is clearly sexual harassment and is illegal under Title VII. The fact that sex between a worker and a supervisor or employer was *consensual* does not mean that it was necessarily *welcome*. Some examples are as follows:

- If a worker consented to sex because of an implied threat of punishment for not cooperating, it is still sexual harassment under the law.

- Harassment does not have to involve sexual intercourse; it can be any of a number of unwanted and unwelcome acts — touching, fondling, or rubbing one's body against a subordinate's.

- Harassment can even be sexually explicit language, images, or gestures. On-the-job behavior does not have to be sexual in nature to be considered harassment.

Hostile work environment. This form occurs when speech or conduct is *severe* (considered objectionable by a reasonable person) or *pervasive* (widespread, common, or repeated) enough to create a hostile or abusive work environment. The courts define a hostile work environment by whether a reasonable person, in the same or similar circumstances, would be offended by the conduct. In addition, any supervisors, regardless of gender,

Figure 5.12 The number of females in the fire and emergency services has been increasing over the past decades. Similarly, they are represented in all ranks from firefighter to chief of the department.

who refer to their subordinates of the opposite sex in derogatory, vulgar, and/or sexual terms are engaging in sexual harassment. Essentially, any overt or covert gender-related behavior that creates a hostile work environment is considered to be sexual harassment under Title VII and is against the law. Not all sexual harassment involves supervisors and their subordinates — a hostile work environment can be created by anyone. Some examples are as follows:

- Male supervisors frequently referring to female subordinates as *bimbos* or *chicks*

- Female supervisors rolling their eyes, throwing up their hands in mock frustration, and shouting *men!* when a male subordinate makes a mistake

- Inappropriate conduct of a sexual nature, including sexually oriented jokes and sexually explicit e-mail, screen savers, posters, cartoons, and graffiti; any unwanted verbal and physical contact

- *Retaliation* by a supervisor or other member of the organization resulting from a sexual harassment or hostile workplace report

- Employees are engaging in sexual harassment if they do any of the following actions:
  - Displays sexually explicit or suggestive photographs or images in the workplace
  - Frequently makes remarks about another coworker's anatomy
  - Frequently uses profane language or tells *dirty* jokes
  - Frequently berates female firefighters' abilities or plays practical jokes on them
  - Continues sexual harassment even when told that the behavior is offensive
  - Allows sexual harassment to continue after it has been reported
  - Allows any type of discrimination that creates a hostile work environment

Although there are no federal laws prohibiting discrimination based on sexual orientation, a Presidential Executive Order specifically outlaws this type of discrimination within the U.S. federal government. At the state and local levels, 15 states and more than 124 municipalities prohibit discrimination based on sexual orientation. Company officers should be aware of the local discrimination laws and work to protect the privacy and personal rights of all employees regardless of sexual orientation.

Supervisory roles and responsibilities. Company officers are responsible for creating and maintaining a work environment that is free of inappropriate and unlawful behavior. When any firefighter reports hostile work behaviors, company officers must act upon the report. Company officers must ensure the physical, mental, and emotional safety of all members of the unit. As supervisors, they have the following roles and responsibilities that they must perform to ensure that retaliation, harassment, or hostility does not exist in the workplace:

- Communicate openly and honestly appropriate behavior expectations in the workplace.

- Treat all employees with dignity and respect.

- Create, maintain, and accept nothing less than a positive and supportive work environment.

- Promote participation by all employees in work activities that benefit the individual, the unit, and the organization.

- Assign work equitably and provide opportunities for professional growth.

- Assign work so that diverse views are represented in decision-making when possible.

- Communicate promotional and developmental opportunities to subordinates.

- Identify and eliminate conditions that might contribute to a hostile work environment.

- Identify, eliminate, and prevent discrimination of all types.

- Act immediately upon all reports of sexual harassment or inappropriate behavior.

- Serve as a role model for behavior that promotes appropriate behavior that leads to a productive and hospitable work environment (**Figure 5.13, p. 112**).

Figure 5.13 The company officer must act as a role model for subordinates. Creating a positive and hospitable work environment is essential to a strong team.

Reasonable Accommodation

Under EEOC regulations, employers are required to do what is *reasonable* to accommodate their employees' differences. Among the differences that must be accommodated, if reasonably possible, are the following:

• Religious differences

• Gender-based differences

• Differences based on permanent physical or mental impairment

The point of the Title VII legislation is that employers should make every reasonable effort to accommodate differences among their employees. Court decisions continue to define and clarify exactly what constitutes *reasonable accommodation* in any given situation.

Years after the Civil Rights Act was passed, the reasonable accommodation requirements relating to workers with physical or mental disabilities were incorporated into a separate body of legislation: ADA. See Americans with Disabilities Act section.

North America is a diverse society composed of men and women of various races, religions, nationalities, and ethnicity. Some religions require their adherents to keep the Sabbath — that is, they cannot work from sunset on Friday until after sunset on Saturday. If it is reasonable, these individuals should be allowed to adjust their hours of work to accommodate their religious obligations.

Both male and female personnel now occupy many fire stations that were originally designed and constructed to house only men. Many of these stations do not have separate toilet and shower rooms or separate dormitories, so these facilities must be shared.

Some reasonable means of accommodating men and women sharing fire station facilities, such as reversible signs for lavatory doors saying, *Occupied/Unoccupied,* must be provided. Portable walls may be used to partition common dormitories into sleeping cubicles that afford a greater degree of privacy. When new stations are built or existing ones are significantly remodeled, separate facilities should be included.

Under the Pregnancy Discrimination Act of 1978 and the Family Medical Leave Act (FMLA) of 1993, female firefighters must be given the same pregnancy leave and maternity leave benefits as female workers in other professions. In addition, the FMLA provides a similar leave benefit for males under certain circumstances.

The issue of mothers breast-feeding infants while on duty is a state/provincial issue rather than a national issue. Because some states and provinces have laws permitting breast-feeding in public, company officers should become aware of the state/provincial laws, local ordinances, and organization's policies regarding this activity.

Americans with Disabilities Act

The ADA of 1990, along with the Canadian Charter of Rights and Freedoms, are intended to reduce or eliminate discrimination based on physical or mental disabilities. As discussed in the Reasonable Accommodation section, these laws require reasonable accommodation for persons with permanent disabilities **(Figure 5.14)**. A temporary disability such as drug or alcohol abuse or even a broken limb does not qualify.

In those businesses and government buildings in the U.S. and Canada where the laws apply, reasonable accommodation means the following:

• Existing barriers to access must be removed.

• Barriers may not be included in new construction.

Figure 5.14 As public buildings, fire and emergency services facilities must be accessible to citizens with physical limitations. Designated parking spaces and automatic door actuators (shown) are just two of the accommodations required by law.

- Auxiliary aids must be provided for people with vision, speech, or hearing impairments or with any other physical or mental impairment that limits activity.

However, the ADA does not apply to all businesses and groups. The federal government, Native American tribes, and private clubs are exempt. In general, the Act's requirements include two major categories: public accommodation and employment.

Public Accommodation

Most retail and service businesses are considered to be public accommodations according to the Act. Typical public accommodations are as follows:

- Hotels and motels
- Restaurants
- Grocery stores
- Retail shops
- Offices
- Fire stations

To comply with ADA regulations, these establishments may have to provide entry/egress ramps, doorways and corridors that are wider than standard ones, lever-operated door hardware, grab rails in bathrooms, and telephones accessible to those in wheelchairs, to name a few. Any business, regardless of size, that is considered to be a public accommodation must comply with the regulations — provided that compliance is not *too expensive, disruptive, or difficult and reasonable efforts have been made to comply.*

Company officers may become involved in the public accommodations category of ADA regulations if they are involved in the plan review or inspection of new construction projects. They may be required to specify the exit requirements for a public building that must meet both ADA and building/fire code regulations.

Company officers may also be involved in the design of a new fire station or remodeling of an existing one. While ADA requirements will be mandatory for the new facility, requirements may be waived or altered for the remodel project, depending on the cost and feasibility of meeting the requirements.

Employment

Company officers may also be directly involved in the application of ADA regulations if they are part of the process of hiring new employees. The organization is bound by ADA employment regulations and may be held liable for failure to comply with them.

The essence of the employment category of ADA is that employers cannot discriminate against qualified applicants because of their disabilities; however, the employment regulations only apply to organizations with 15 or more *full-time* employees. The disabled must have equal access to employment opportunities, promotions, and fringe benefits. This access may mean that a hearing-impaired applicant may have to be provided with an interpreter (signer) for the employment interview.

However, ADA *does not* require that unqualified or under-qualified applicants be hired. ADA regulations require that the most qualified applicant be hired based on education, experience, and ability.

Fair Labor Standards Act

While not part of the Civil Rights Act (or Title VII), FLSA regulations are very important for all company officers in career and combination organizations with five or more employees. The FLSA of 1938 guaranteed that workers in the private sector would be paid overtime at a time and one-half salary rate if they worked more than 40 hours in 1 week. However, FLSA did not apply to state and local public employees until a decision by the U.S. Supreme Court in 1985.

Because of the atypical work schedules of police and firefighters, Congress passed an exemption to the 40-hour rule for local public safety agencies. The FLSA workweek was set at 43 hours for police and 53 hours for firefighters. EMS personnel are also covered by FLSA if they are an integral part of a public fire protection or police agency, but volunteer firefighters, rescue, and some EMS personnel and employees of private corporations contracted to provide protective services are not.

Some training activities outside of the normal work schedule are covered by FLSA, but others are not. A fire and emergency services organization's executive and administrative personnel (management) are not covered by FLSA because they are usually not entitled to overtime pay.

While company officers are rarely involved in the administration of FLSA regulations, it is critical that they have some understanding of what the regulations require. It is also important that company officers keep accurate records of who is on duty at any given time and what their work assignments are. These records may be used in court proceedings involving overtime pay disputes.

National Consensus Standards

A number of fire and emergency service industry associations and organizations develop and publish consensus standards and information that directly relate to many emergency activities. While these standards and other publications do not have the force of law unless adopted by the jurisdiction's governing body, they are recognized as authoritative documents and industry standards.

In tort liability cases, these publications may be used to establish the standard of care required. This means that fire and emergency services organizations and their personnel may be found to be liable if they failed to follow these standards — even if the documents were not adopted locally. Most of the national consensus standards that relate to fire and emergency service activities are developed by the following organizations:

- National Fire Protection Association (NFPA)
- ASTM International (orginally known as the American Society for Testing and Materials [ASTM])
- Underwriters Laboratories Inc (UL)
- Underwriters' Laboratories of Canada (ULC)
- International Code Council (ICC)
- Canadian Commission on Building and Fire Codes (CCBFC)
- U.S. Department of Defense (DoD)

In Canada, approvals are given by the Standards Council of Canada (SCC) and American National Standards Institute (ANSI), which facilitate standards development through the consensus process. Each Canadian province adopts approved standards independently from the Canadian federal government.

Model building and fire codes address the design, construction, and use of buildings and their service systems such as heating, ventilating, and air-conditioning (HVAC), fire protection, plumbing, and electrical. The codes provide local, state, and federal officials with consensus codes that establish nationally accepted standards that may be modified locally as needed.

Definition: Industry Standard

Industry standard — Procedures and criteria recognized as acceptable practices by peer professional, credentialing, or accrediting organizations.

National Fire Protection Association

The majority of the national consensus standards that fire and emergency services organizations in the U.S. and Canada use are developed and published by NFPA. When the need for a standard is recognized, the association invites a number of volunteers with expertise in that field to form a committee to develop a draft. The completed draft is then made available to the public for review and comment. The public comments are reviewed by the committee, and they may or may not be incorporated into the finished document.

The final version of the standard is then submitted to the NFPA general membership for adoption. Although there are hundreds of NFPA standards, some of the ones used most often by fire and emergency services organizations are the following:

- NFPA 1, *Uniform Fire Code*™
- NFPA 70, *National Electrical Code*®
- NFPA 101, *Life Safety Code*®
- NFPA 704, *Standard System for the Identification of the Hazards of Materials for Emergency Response*
- NFPA 901, *Standard Classifications for Incident Reporting and Fire Protection Data*
- NFPA 921, *Guide for Fire and Explosion Investigations*
- NFPA 1001, *Standard for Fire Fighter Professional Qualifications*
- NFPA 1002, *Standard for Fire Apparatus Driver/ Operator Professional Qualifications*
- NFPA 1003, *Standard for Airport Fire Fighter Professional Qualifications*
- NFPA 1021, *Standard for Fire Officer Professional Qualifications*
- NFPA 1031, *Standard for Professional Qualifications for Fire Inspector and Plan Examiner*
- NFPA 1033, *Standard for Professional Qualifications for Fire Investigator*
- NFPA 1035, *Standard for Professional Qualifications for Public Fire and Life Safety Educator*
- NFPA 1041, *Standard for Fire Service Instructor Professional Qualifications*

- NFPA 1051, *Standard for Wildland Fire Fighter Professional Qualifications*
- NFPA 1061, *Standard for Professional Qualifications for Public Safety Telecommunicator*
- NFPA 1403, *Standard on Live Fire Training Evolutions*
- NFPA 1404, *Standard for Fire Service Respiratory Protection Training*
- NFPA 1410, *Standard on Training for Initial Emergency Scene Operations*
- NFPA 1500, *Standard on Fire Department Occupational Safety and Health Program*
- NFPA 1521, *Standard for Fire Department Safety Officer*
- NFPA 1561, *Standard on Emergency Services Incident Management System*
- NFPA 1581, *Standard on Fire Department Infection Control Program*
- NFPA 1582, *Standard on Comprehensive Occupational Medical Program for Fire Departments*
- NFPA 1600, *Standard on Emergency Management and Business Continuity Programs*
- NFPA 1710, *Standard for the Organization and Deployment of Fire Suppression Operations, Emergency Medical Operations, and Special Operations to the Public by Career Fire Departments*
- NFPA 1720, *Standard for the Organization and Deployment of Fire Suppression Operations, Emergency Medical Operations, and Special Operations to the Public by Volunteer Fire Departments*
- NFPA 1901, *Standard for Automotive Fire Apparatus*
- NFPA 1906, *Standard for Wildland Fire Apparatus*
- NFPA 5000, *Building Construction and Safety Code*®

There are many other NFPA standards that relate to specific areas within the fields of fire and emergency services. Each one is important in its own way. Company officers should familiarize themselves with the complete list of NFPA standards and study in detail those that specifically apply to their responsibilities. Most U.S. fire and emergency services organizations maintain a complete set of current NFPA standards.

In addition to standards, NFPA publishes handbooks that provide examples and illustrations that help people interpret the standards. These handbooks may also be introduced in legal proceedings to demonstrate accepted industry practices. Some of the handbooks that may be used by company officers include the following:

- *Uniform Fire Code™ Handbook* (NFPA 1, 2006)
- *Life Safety Code® Handbook* (NFPA 101, 2006)
- *National Fire Alarm Code® Handbook* (NFPA 72, 2002)
- *National Electric Code® Handbook* (NFPA 70, 2005)
- *Automatic Sprinkler Systems Handbook* (NFPA 13, *Installation of Sprinkler Systems*, 2002)
- *Fire Protection Handbook™*, 2003

American National Standards Institute

ANSI is a private, nonprofit organization that administers and coordinates the voluntary standardization and conformity assessment system. While ANSI does not develop consensus standards, it does accredit member organizations that do. The consensus process is guided by ANSI's principles of consensus, due process, and openness and includes an appeals process for manufacturers who wish to contest test results of their products or materials.

Some of the ANSI standards that are most relevant to the fire and emergency services are as follows:

- Z87.1-2003, *Practice for Occupational and Educational Personal Eye and Face Protection Devices*
- Z88.2-1992, *Practices for Respiratory Protection*
- Z88.10-2001, *Respirator Fit Test Methods*
- Z88.8-1995, *Performance Criteria and Test Methodologies for Air Purifying Respirators* or Z88.8-200X, *Test Methodologies for Air Purifying Respirators*
- Z89.1-2003, *Industrial Head Protection*

Many ANSI standards are cross-referenced between NFPA and OSHA documents. For instance Z88.2-1992, *Practices for Respiratory Protection*, is referenced in the following documents:

- NFPA 1404, *Standard for Fire Service Respiratory Protection Training*
- NFPA 1981, *Standard on Open-Circuit Self-Contained Breathing Apparatus for Fire and Emergency Services*
- OSHA 29 *CFR* 1910.134, Respiratory Protection

ASTM International

ASTM International is a consensus-based standards writing and testing organization. ASTM International develops testing processes that are used by other testing organizations in the development of safety products. Some of the fire and emergency services publications that ASTM International offers include the following:

- ASTM F2412-05, *Standard Test Methods for Foot Protection*
- WK4867, *Guide to Relating Protection Levels A, B, C, and D to National Fire Protection Association Protection Levels*
- WK517, *New Specification for Protective Clothing for Incidents Involving Bio-Terrorism Agents*

A Work Item (WK) may be a new standard or revision to an existing standard that is under development by a committee. ASTM publishes WK descriptions in the interest of openness as well as to solicit input from interested stakeholders who may not be members of the committee.

Underwriters Laboratories Inc.

Founded in 1894, UL is an independent, not-for-profit product-safety testing and certification organization. Products that bear the UL label have been tested for their intended use and are certified as safe. UL also provides third-party testing and certification for in-service equipment, such as annual testing of ground ladders, apparatus fire pumps, and aerial devices on a five-year cycle **(Figure 5.15)**.

UL has developed more than 800 standards for safety. Some of its standards that directly relate to the fire and emergency services are as follows:

Figure 5.15 Third-party organizations can provide annual ground ladder testing to meet NFPA requirements.

- UL 92 (1993) *Standard for Safety Fire Extinguisher and Booster Hose*

- UL 260 (2004) *Standard for Safety Dry Pipe and Deluge Valves for Fire-Protection Service*

- UL 262 (2004) *Standard for Safety Gate Valves for Fire-Protection Service*

- UL 268 (1996) *Standard for Safety Smoke Detectors for Fire Alarm Signaling Systems*

- UL 299 (2002) *Standard for Safety Dry Chemical Fire Extinguishers*

- UL 1626 (2001) *Standard for Safety Residential Sprinklers for Fire-Protection Service*

- UL 2244 (1999) *Standard for Safety Aboveground Flammable Liquid Tank Systems*

International Code Council

The ICC was formed in 1994 by the merger of three building and fire-code organizations. The intention was to provide greater consistency of code content and greater acceptance of model codes

Figure 5.16 Company officers may be assigned the duty of reviewing and approving new construction and building renovation plans. The company officer must have a working knowledge of the building, fire, and life-safety codes that have been adopted by the local jurisdiction.

by governmental officials. Company officers who work in areas that have adopted the ICC codes or any other building and fire code should become familiar with code requirements (**Figure 5.16**). Fire and life safety inspections are based on the contents of the following codes:

- *International Building Code®*

- *ICC Electrical Code®*

- *International Existing Building Code®*

- *International Fire Code®*

- *International Mechanical Code®*

- *International Property Maintenance Code®*

- *International Residential Code®*

- *International Urban-Wildland Interface Code™*

- *International Zoning Code®*

U.S. Department of Defense

Company officers who work for or respond to military bases located in the U.S. should be familiar with requirements generated by the DoD, including the following:

- Unified Facilities Criteria (UFC) 3-600-01, *Design: Fire Protection Engineering for Facilities*

- UFC 1-200-01, *Design: General Building Requirements*

The UFC manuals are similar to the model building codes and the NFPA building and fire codes. They provide planning, design, construction, operations, and maintenance criteria for structures built on federal military bases and reservations. The manuals apply to all service commands having military construction responsibilities **(Figure 5.17)**.

Standards Council of Canada

While many Canadian fire and emergency service agencies use the NFPA professional qualifications standards for training and certification — either as written or as reference material for locally written standards — none are *law* in Canada. ANSI standards are recognized in Canada but are normally used as references in Canadian codes. Transport Canada (TC) is responsible for a number of key acts and regulations that govern Canada's transportation system.

The SCC is a federal Crown corporation with the mandate to promote efficient and effective standardization, which is the development and application of standards — publications that establish accepted practices, technical requirements, and terminologies for products, services, and systems. Standards help to ensure better, safer, and more efficient methods and products and are essential elements of technology, innovation, and trade. The SCC also represents Canada's interests in standards-related matters in foreign and international forums.

For automotive fire apparatus, for example, NFPA standards may be used, but those of ULC are used more often because ULC does testing and certification while NFPA does not. In general, standards approved by SCC are the basis for regulations that influence fire and emergency services organizations and operations. These standards may be developed by the following organizations:

- Canadian Standards Association (CSA)
- Underwriters Laboratories of Canada (ULC)
- Canadian General Standards Board (CGSB)
- Bureau de Normalisation du Quebec (BNQ)

Figure 5.17 Facilities on military bases and reservations are subject to the requirements of the Unified Facilities Criteria (UFC).

Underwriters' Laboratories of Canada

ULC is an independent, not-for-profit third-party product safety testing and certification organization. ULC is accredited by the SCC under the National Standards System. ULC provides various types of testing including aerial, fire pump, and ground ladder testing. All ULC standards are developed by committees composed of a balance of manufacturers, users, inspection authorities, and the general public, representing major interests across Canada.

Canadian Commission on Building and Fire Codes

The Canadian Commission on Building and Fire Codes (CCBFC) develops and maintains six of Canada's model construction and fire codes. The CCBFC is similar to the ICC in the U.S. and oversees the work of several standing committees, special purpose committees, and task groups. As a consensus standards organization, CCBFC members are volunteers and selected from across Canada and appointed by the National Research Council (NRC).

Summary

As public servants and employees, company officers must be aware of and able to reference the laws that apply to them and their profession. They must know where to find federal, state/provincial, and local laws governing emergency operations, environmental protection, and civil rights and become familiar with them. Company officers must be very familiar with laws pertaining to sexual harassment, disparate treatment, and related personnel laws specific to their organization, jurisdiction, and state/province.

Company officers must also be able to find, reference, apply, and interpret the intent of laws at any given time while performing their job functions. This responsibility includes decisions made during emergency operations. Limited immunity from tort liability may or may not exist for company officers performing their official duties, but they should not depend on its existence.

While company officers are generally not liable for the illegal actions of their subordinates, if a company officer knew or should have known about such activity — and permitted it to continue — the company officer is also liable. Company officers should not fear doing their jobs, but they should be aware that they are accountable for any actions that they perform or fail to perform.

Interpersonal Communications

Chapter Contents

Learning Objectives

1. Identify the six basic elements of all forms of communication.

2. Select facts about the five purposes for interpersonal communication.

3. Identify correct responses about words as symbols.

4. Recall information about the cultural concept of words.

5. Select facts about the actions that a company officer can take to improve verbal communication skills.

6. Select correct responses about the nonverbal component.

7. Select facts about the actions that a company officer can take to improve nonverbal communication skills.

8. Recall information about the listening process and improving listening skills.

9. Apply the interpersonal communication model to an emergency situation scenario.

10. Apply the interpersonal communication model to a nonemergency situation.

Job Performance Requirements

This chapter provides information that addresses the following job performance requirements of NFPA 1021, *Standard for Fire Officer Professional Qualifications* (2003):

<u>Chapter 4 Fire Officer I</u>

4.2.1

4.2.1(A)

4.2.2

4.2.2(A)

Chapter 6
Interpersonal Communications

To be an effective leader, a fire officer must be able to communicate with others. The three most common forms of communication are informal interpersonal, formal oral, and written. Communication skills rank directly below leadership ability in the skills most employers desire of new employees.

Most of the daily tasks company officers perform involve some form of continual communication such as the following:

- *Communicating at an emergency scene* — Has a direct effect on the safety and efficiency of their crews

- *Writing reports and keeping records* — Affects how company officers are perceived by their supervisors and the rest of the organization

- *Dealing with citizen inquiries or complaints (especially under stressful circumstances)* — Affects whether a citizen complaint is handled successfully or the citizen files a complaint against the officer for an inappropriate comment

- *Making public fire and life-safety education presentations* — Provides critical life-safety information to external customers and enhances the public image of the fire and emergency services organization

- *Receiving orders from superiors and communicating them to subordinates* — Ensures the effective and efficient administration of the organization

The effectiveness with which company officers communicate affects their relations with their supervisors, subordinates, and the public. In short, for company officers to be effective, they must understand and apply the principles and techniques of effective communication.

Each of these communication categories (interpersonal, oral, and written) are the subject of hundreds of books, thousands of articles, and numerous college-level degree programs. This chapter provides a brief overview of interpersonal communication through communicating effectively and listening skills.

The topics of formal oral communication will be addressed in Chapter 7, Oral Communications, while written communication is addressed in Chapter 8, Written Communications. While reading and studying material on communications is helpful, practicing the skills through application also helps to integrate them into the officer's personal abilities.

Communicating Effectively

Interpersonal communication is the communication that takes place between two people who have established a relationship, and it occurs on a daily basis in the lives of all people who live in groups. A relationship may be between parent/child, employer/employee, husband/wife, friends, or even two people over the telephone (**Figure 6.1, p. 124**).

Interpersonal communication consists of casual language, casual nonverbal clues, spontaneity, and frequent changes of the roles of speaker and listener. The tone of the conversation can change based on the perceptions of the two parties, moving from congenial to angry.

Therefore, it is important that all individuals understand and master the skills involved in interpersonal communication. So important are these skills that NFPA 1021, *Standard for Fire*

Figure 6.1 Telephone conversations are only one of the ways that company officers interact with people on a daily basis.

Officer Professional Qualifications, has added them to the Fire Officer Level I and Level II job performance requirements for the position of company officer.

To understand the dynamics of interpersonal communication, it is best to participate in a college-level course on the subject. Such a course involves not only reading and learning the concepts but also practicing them through role-play situations. The sections that follow explain the basic concepts and principles of interpersonal communication in a brief overview, give interpersonal communication purposes, and discuss both verbal and nonverbal components.

Communication Basics

Interpersonal communication consists of the following six basic elements:

- Sender
- Message
- Medium or channel
- Receiver
- Interference
- Feedback to the sender

Five of the elements of the process are essential to effective interpersonal communication to occur. Understanding the remaining element, interference, allows the participant to recognize and overcome this potential barrier to effective communication. The sections that follow discuss the elements as they apply to interpersonal communication **(Figure 6.2)**.

Sender

The *sender* (referred to in some speech communication texts as the *speaker*) originates a *message* by encoding or turning thoughts and mental images into words. The words are selected based on the perceived ability of the *receiver* (also known as the *listener*) to understand the message. See Message and Receiver sections.

For example, a parent speaking to a child will use words that are simple and easy to understand. On the other hand, an incident commander on the fireground will use brief, specific commands in jargon to which firefighters can quickly react **(Figures 6.3 a and b)**.

Message

The *message* is the meaning, idea, or concept that a speaker is attempting to communicate to the listener (receiver). While most people think of a message as the spoken word, it actually consists of nonverbal factors or clues as well.

The message may be transmitted by auditory (spoken or heard), visual (sight), tactile (touch), olfactory (smell), gustatory (taste), gestural (a motion), or any combination of these means. An effective message includes a combination of these elements that conveys the same idea to the listener or receiver. See Receiver section.

Medium or Channel

The *medium* or *channel* is the path that a message takes between the sender and the receiver. In most interpersonal communication situations, the channel is usually face to face. Both the sender and the receiver can take advantage of the various means by which the message is conveyed, leading to better understanding.

In the fire service, messages are often conveyed by other means such as telephone or radio. When radio communication was first introduced into the fire service, simplified *10-codes* were used to ensure that orders were fully understood. The 10-codes were locally developed and agreed upon.

Communication Model

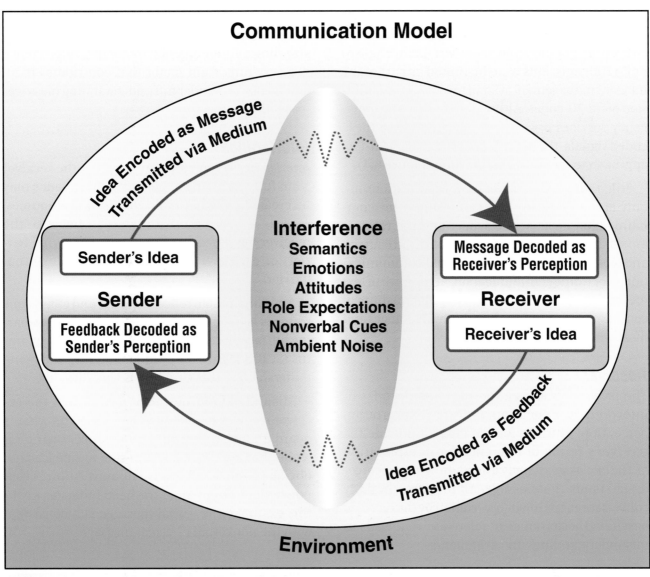

Idea Encoded as Message Transmitted via Medium

Interference
Semantics
Emotions
Attitudes
Role Expectations
Nonverbal Cues
Ambient Noise

Sender's Idea

Sender

Feedback Decoded as Sender's Perception

Message Decoded as Receiver's Perception

Receiver

Receiver's Idea

Idea Encoded as Feedback Transmitted via Medium

Environment

Figure 6.2 The components of the Communication Model can be represented by an oval which depicts the relationship between six basic elements.

Figures 6.3 a and b How a person communicates depends largely on who the listener is and the situation. (a) A parent will choose simple language when talking with a child. (b) A company officer will use specific, direct commands that may contain jargon when giving orders at an emergency incident.

As departments started to respond with neighboring organizations, it became apparent that the codes were not the same. *Clear-text* (plain English) radio transmissions were instituted as part of the incident management system to replace the confusion of the 10-codes. Although some fire and emergency services organizations may still use these coded signals, the preferred choice is the clear-text approach to radio communication **(Figure 6.4)**.

Still, radio and telephone communications are only auditory means and can result in miscommunication because the sender and the receiver are separated by distance, are out of visual contact, and lack the advantage of nonverbal communication. Electronic communication, in the form of text messaging, is also becoming a popular medium of communication and can have both advantages and disadvantages as well.

Receiver

The *receiver* receives a message and decodes or interprets it. Education, cultural background, perception, attitude, and context all provide the receiver's frame of reference for interpretation of the message, which affects how the receiver understands the message. All too often in daily conversation, it is misinterpretation by the receiver, based on these frames of reference, that leads to misunderstandings and arguments.

Good listening skills (discussed later in the chapter) are essential for overcoming misunderstandings. At emergency incidents, interference is a very important factor that contributes to an emergency responder misunderstanding messages (see following section).

Interference

Interference is a factor that prevents the receiver from fully receiving a message. Interference may be created by either *internal* or *external* sources. Messages may be misunderstood because the receiver has a hearing impairment (internal barrier) or excessive noise is in the area (external barrier).

A common occurrence in the fire and emergency services is the use of handheld radios while wearing full facepiece self-contained breathing apparatus (SCBA) **Figure 6.5)**. Understanding and being understood in this situation is very difficult.

Misunderstandings also occur when the receiver receives mixed messages based on what is heard and what is seen. For instance, saying *yes* while shaking the head from side to side leads to obvious confusion because in most cultures that nonverbal movement of the head indicates *no*. In this example, the verbal message is inconsistent with the nonverbal or visual message.

Figure 6.4 The use of radio communications to personnel and units who may be out of sight of the incident commander (IC) requires the use of clear-text messages that must be repeated by the listener to ensure that the message was properly understood.

Figure 6.5 Communicating either directly or by radio can be difficult when wearing respiratory protection. The speaker must speak clearly and with increased volume to be understood.

Overcoming internal or external interference is challenging for the receiver. To overcome an internal barrier, the receiver must focus on what the sender is saying, listen carefully, provide feedback immediately, and use nonverbal factors or clues to emphasize and acknowledge understanding of the message. In the case of hearing disability, as mentioned earlier, a person should use hearing aids or increase the volume on radio or telephone equipment.

Controlling external interference in a nonemergency situation may include turning off an air conditioner, closing a window or door, or moving the conversation to a quieter location. At an emergency incident, it may be very difficult, if not impossible, to control external interference. Some alternatives include the following:

- Turning off audible warning devices at the incident

- Using communication headsets or earpieces

- Relying on agreed-upon hand signals

- Increasing the volume of communication equipment

However, some situations may involve so much interference that face-to-face communication is the only solution (**Figure 6.6**). In these cases, messengers can be used to communicate with units that are located remotely from the command post. Each situation has to be approached as a special situation requiring special solutions.

Figures 6.6 The most effective method for issuing orders at an incident is in person.

Feedback to the Sender

The response (called *feedback)* is important to the continuation of the conversation. Feedback completes the communication process, resulting in an ongoing cycle that can be illustrated with a loop. The message's effect will be obvious to the sender by the auditory, visual, gestural, or tactile response of the receiver.

If feedback is positive, the desired result will then be achieved. If it is negative, then confrontation or misinterpretation may result. The sender will have to regroup and alter the wording of the message to ensure that it is properly understood.

Interpersonal Communication Purposes

There are five general purposes for interpersonal communication: learn, relate, influence, play, and help. Brief descriptions are as follows:

- *Learning*— Acquire knowledge or skills. When a member of a fire and emergency services organization needs to know how to complete a purchase order, for instance, asking a member of the purchasing department or branch will result in the transfer of knowledge.

- *Relating* — Establish a new relationship or maintain an existing one. When new personnel are hired, they must be welcomed into the organization. Establishing a personal relationship, whether in a career, combination, or volunteer organization, is important to giving a new employee a feeling of belonging, which increases loyalty to the group.

- *Influencing* — Control, direct, or manipulate behavior. Company officers influence others in situations that involve the following actions (to mention a few):
  — Giving commands at the incident scene
  — Counseling a subordinate
  — Instructing citizens in the use and importance of smoke detectors
  — Conducting annual fitness reviews

- *Playing*— Create a diversion and gain pleasure or gratification. In the context of using verbal humor to reduce stress, most fire and emergency responders are accustomed to using interpersonal communications in a playful manner during their daily work schedules.

- *Helping* — Minister to the needs of another person or console someone in the time of tragedy or loss. Consoling victims, relatives, or other emergency workers in situations that involve injuries, deaths, or losses is part of the duties of fire and emergency services responders **(Figure 6.7)**.

For a conversation to work properly, both the sender and the receiver must agree on its purpose. Agreement is usually implied by the situation such as the classroom situation in which the teacher and student agree that the purpose of the relationship is for the student to learn.

In some cases, the purpose must be stated to ensure that both parties understand it fully. A situation that involves influencing the actions of a subordinate would require that the subordinate understand that the purpose of the conversation involves a change of attitude, activity, or behavior.

Figure 6.7 The ability to listen and provide consolation to victims in times of crisis are important traits for all emergency responders.

Verbal Component

The verbal message depends on the symbols that are used to convey it; those symbols are words. *Words* create a mental image of something, someone, some activity, or some concept. Words also depend on the contexts in which they are spoken.

Other words influence the meaning of the word, as does the situation in which the word is spoken. For instance, the word *duck,* when spoken while pointing at a group of birds flying overhead is used to symbolize the visual image. However, when it is spoken as a command in a hazardous situation, it means *look out* or *get down.*

An understanding of the use of words, though, is only the beginning step when an officer wants to improve verbal communication skills. The most effective improvements involve the following elements:

- Understanding the other person's view
- Taking responsibility for personal thoughts and feelings
- Respecting the thoughts and feelings of others
- Being accurate and clear when speaking
- Focusing on the other person
- Controlling emotions when interacting with others

To accomplish these changes, the company officer has to acknowledge both personal strengths and weaknesses and practice making the necessary changes. It is important to understand words as symbols, cultural concepts of words, and how to improve verbal skills.

Words as Symbols

Many people think of communication as consisting of only the words they speak. Research by communication professionals, however, indicates that words (the verbal component of the communication process) only provide the receiver with 7 percent of the message. Nonverbal actions provide the remaining 93 percent (see Nonverbal Component section). This fact does not mean that words are not important because they are.

Without words, it would be impossible to accurately and effectively convey the total message. Therefore, company officers must understand both the power and the weakness of words as part of a message. Words as symbols have the following characteristics:

- *Arbitrary* — A word may not mean the same to all people; meaning may even change over time from generation to generation and region to region. Male generic language such as *fireman* has evolved into *firefighter* or *policeman* has evolved into *police* or *law enforcement officer* as professions have grown to include women.

- *Ambiguous* — Word meanings are not specific or do not have agreed-upon definitions. The term *Yankee* means one thing to a baseball fan, another to someone living in Asia, and a far different meaning to someone from the state of Georgia. Translations of books into English and even British books sold on the American market are sources of examples of ambiguity in words. *Examples:*

  — The British use the term *boot* to refer to what Americans call the *trunk* of a vehicle.

  — The word *love* is simple in other languages where there are specific words for the various types of love. In North America, the word *love* must have other words added to make it specific as in *brotherly love* or *romantic love*.

- *Abstract* — Meanings are generalizations rather than concrete or tangible meanings. *Example:*

  — Consider the tool used by firefighters to pry open doors or windows. Moving from the abstract to the more specific, they are *tools*, *forcible entry tools*, *door openers*, *crowbars*, or *pry bars*.

  — Depending on the number and variety of tool types carried on an apparatus, the number and type of tool that the listener may respond with can vary if the request is too general.

  — Thus the use of the abstract word *tool* would be avoided and a more specific term such as *pry bar* would be substituted (**Figure 6.8**).

To be effective communicators, company officers must select and use words that accurately symbolize the image that they are trying to convey. This word selection is particularly important when speaking to people who do not have a shared experience with the speaker. Explaining how a smoke detector works to someone who does not have a background in fire science requires less technical terms than explaining the concept to another emergency responder.

Company officers should always be aware of their audience or listener. The terms that are common to the fire and emergency service may have another meaning or no meaning at all to the general public. Avoid technical language and fire service jargon when speaking with the public, elected officials, the news media, and others from outside the profession.

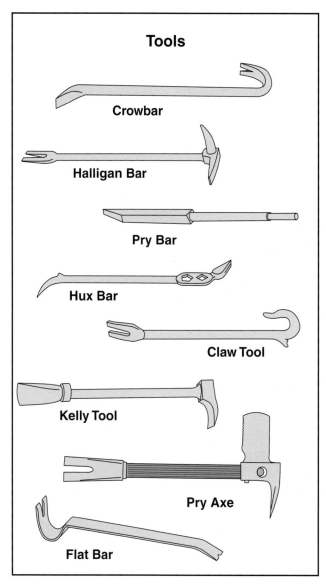

Figure 6.8 To communicate effectively, company officers must be able to use specific terms that the listener can interpret correctly the first time. *Hand me that tool* is less effective than *Hand me the Halligan.*

Obsolete Terms and Their Replacements

Fireman	Firefighter
Manpower	Personnel
To Man	To Staff
Nozzleman	Nozzle Operator
Ladderman	Firefighter
Manhole	Maintenance Hole

Cultural Concepts of Words

The meaning or symbolism that people place on words depends on their cultural backgrounds. Generally, the meanings of words used in North American English are based on a Eurocentric culture (European-based worldview). Therefore, words have been used to compare other people with this traditionally dominant group. The result has been the common use of terms that place these *others* at subordinate positions in society by stereotyping or generalizing certain characteristics or traits of a group of people.

Gender, ethnicity, age, religion, political association, education, and regional background are several ways that people are stereotyped by language. Avoid words that draw attention to these classifications in a negative context in all types of communication. To demean, put down, or degrade people based on the words they use will only build barriers to real communication. It is more productive to attempt to understand other persons and show respect for their cultural backgrounds.

It is vitally important for the company officer to understand the symbolism of language and the effect that it can have when speaking to and about members of specific groups. As a leader who provides an example for members of the organization, the company officer must not use language that stereotypes people or groups.

At the same time, company officers must not tolerate the use of this type of language by subordinates or other members of the organization. The use of stereotypes creates the perception of a hostile work environment that is a major impediment to successful leadership. Slurs, innuendos, name calling, and inappropriate jokes and comments are no longer accepted or tolerated in the workplace. It is unprofessional, unacceptable, and illegal.

As mentioned in the previous chapter, laws exist at all levels of government that prohibit statements that can be construed as being discriminatory, salacious, or hostile or create a hostile environment. As a leader and role model, company officers must avoid making such statements or allowing them from others.

Verbal Skills Improvement

To ensure strong interpersonal relationships at work, at home, and in the community, the company officer must develop verbal skills that build understanding. Learning to communicate based on a few guidelines helps everyone develop relationships and increase organizational effectiveness and efficiency. To improve verbal skills, it is necessary to practice the following guidelines:

- *Engage in dual perspective* — Be aware of the receiver's frame of reference. Recognize the listener as having a different culture and attempt to relate to it rather than diminish it or make fun of it.

- *Take responsibility for personal feelings and thoughts* — Do not blame someone else for personal feelings and thoughts. Use language that is *I*-based such as *I believe . . . .* or *I think . . . .* Avoid phrases such as *You hurt me* or *You disappoint me* and focus instead on ownership of the feelings and the cause of those feelings such as *I am disappointed by your actions.*

- *Show respect for the feelings and thoughts of the other person* — Avoid trying to apply personal feelings to another person such as saying, *I know how you feel.* Because people have feelings based on their personal life experiences, it is almost impossible for anyone to know how a person feels. Being empathetic is a more appropriate approach and acknowledges feelings or emotional states. Understand and respect their positions and build upon those concepts to create strong relationships. A better way of responding in this type of situation is to say, *I'm sorry you have to go through this.*

- *Try to gain accuracy and clarity in speaking* —Avoid abstract vernacular language or phrases that can cause misunderstandings. Avoid generalizations that result in stereotypes such as *All lawyers are crooks.* Generalizations are in themselves false. Be clear and accurate in all types of communication.

- *Be aware of any special needs of the receiver* — Speak slowly and clearly while facing a person if the person is deaf or hard of hearing for example. This procedure makes it easier for the person to read lips. Do *not* exaggerate lip or mouth movements because this action is *not* helpful and may even make the words more difficult to understand.

- *Avoid speaking or addressing a problem while angry or emotional* — Pause and place the conversation on hold until emotions are under control. Emotions can cause a speaker to say things that are untrue or hurtful, using words as weapons. This *timeout* allows both parties to get a better perspective of the situation.

Nonverbal Component

Speech communication research indicates that nonverbal communication transmits from 55 to 93 percent of the message. The nonverbal elements are 55 percent of the message, while the vocal tones and inflections are 38 percent (**Figure 6.9**). This research would suggest that nonverbal clues are more important than the verbal message, which is only 7 percent of the total message. The nonverbal message may even overpower the verbal message. Nonverbal clues consist of the following elements:

- *Kinesics* — Body motion and position

- *Paralanguage or vocalics* — Vowel sounds or tones used to create the verbal message

- *Self-presentation* — Clothing, touch, use of time, and control of the speaker's environment

An understanding of the importance of each of the elements of nonverbal communication assists the company officer in recognizing and interpreting those signals, therefore, improving nonverbal communication. While it is important for the company officer to understand each of the elements of nonverbal communication, paralan-

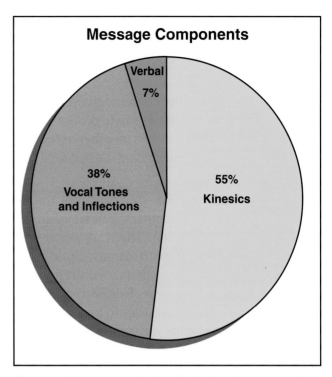

Figure 6.9 As indicated in this illustration, the nonverbal component of most messages provides the listener with the greatest percentage of the message.

guage and self-presentation are beyond the scope of this manual. Information on these topics may be found in speech communication textbooks or on the Internet.

Kinesics

The main elements of kinesics include eye contact, facial expression, gestures, posture, and poise. Kinesics can project a person's self-perception, emotional state, approachability, or cultural background. Descriptions are as follows:

- *Eye contact* — The eyes are said to be the *windows of the soul*, giving others access to the most personal emotions of the person to whom they are talking. In Eurocentric cultures, good eye contact can convey self-confidence, honesty, trust, and credibility. Averting one's gaze can indicate deceit, lying, insecurity, or anxiety. However, eye contact is also a function of cultural background. Therefore, the use of eye contact must be appropriate to the situation, the relationship, and the culture. *Examples:*

— The term *shifty eyed* has been coined to describe someone who *cannot* be trusted because of a lack of eye contact.

— Many Native American or Asian societies believe that it is disrespectful to make direct eye contact with a person who is *not* of the same status.

— In the wrong context, too much eye contact can be as damaging as too little. Staring or leering into the eyes of a member of the opposite sex can be considered too personal and intimidating.

- **Facial expression** — The face can show the six basic emotions: happiness, sadness, surprise, fear, anger, and disgust. The term *poker face* indicates a person who can disguise those emotions so effectively that others misinterpret the person's words or actions. To effectively communicate the correct message in a relationship, the facial expressions must match the verbal message. Because people learn to manipulate their words but not their nonverbal clues, the listener will often believe these clues over the words.

- **Gestures** — Many people *talk with their hands*. It is even considered a cultural stereotype in some cultures. In situations where noise prevents verbal communication, gestures are effectively used to send messages such as *come here* and *stop*. When personnel are establishing a helicopter landing zone, for example, directions for the helicopter pilot are often given with hand signals. Understanding the types of gestures and the critical role they play in communication allows the listener to understand the speaker more clearly **(Figure 6.10)**. Gestures used in North America play the following five different roles in communication:

— *Emblems:* Gestures that take the place of verbal communication. The thumbs-up gesture is accepted as meaning *okay* while a shrug of the shoulders means *I don't know* or *I don't care*. Some gestures that are acceptable in the U.S. have different meanings, both positive and negative, in other cultures.

— *Illustrators:* Gestures that are used to emphasize or assist in the understanding of the verbal message. An example is when an angler says, *That bass was at least 18 inches long!* and spreads his hands the same distance apart.

— *Affect displays:* Gestures that go with a verbal expression of feeling. These displays are generally unconscious such as a facial grimace of pain when a person pinches a finger.

— *Regulators:* Gestures that are used to control the flow of the verbal conversation. In this case, it is part of the feedback the listener or audience provides that tells the speaker to continue, expand on the information, or finish. Gestures consist of shifts in posture, shifting of eye contact, head movement, nodding, or raising the eyebrows.

— *Adaptors:* Gestures (usually unconscious) that are used to relieve stress in a speaker such as wringing the hands, tapping the foot, scratching the head, or stroking the face.

- **Posture** — Persons sitting or standing erect can create the impression of having a great deal of self-confidence and authority. Slouching or standing with stooped shoulders makes a person appear insecure, disinterested, or intimidated **(Figure 6.11)**.

- **Poise** — Poise is the accumulation of all the other nonverbal elements into one image of self-confidence and authority. Poise is gained by mastering the skills of interpersonal and speech communications. Mastery of these skills helps to overcome the nervousness that some people experience when they are put into situations that involve speaking in public or meeting strangers.

Nonverbal Communication Improvement

Improving personal nonverbal communication skills begins with self-reflection and observation. Company officers should apply the following general concepts:

- **Eye contact** — Learn to maintain eye contact while speaking to people. Also recognize that some cultures find direct eye contact to be disrespectful. Learn to modify the use of eye contact when it is appropriate.

- **Body language** — Convey an image of self-confidence by standing tall and erect. Slouching or keeping hands in trousers pockets can be interpreted as being tired, depressed, or uninterested.

Figure 6.10 When the company officer is attempting to emphasize a relationship or an item, gesturing can help the listener visualize it better. In this photo, the speaker may be describing the width of a ladder rung or the length of a piece of rope.

Figure 6.11 Confidence and authority are communicated when the speaker stands erect while speaking. Slouching or leaning on the podium can give the impression of insecurity or a lack of caring.

- *Facial expression* — Learn to match facial expressions to the message.

- *Gestures* — Identify and control gestures that are annoying or distracting to others. Learn to use gestures to emphasize and illustrate the message.

- *Poise* — Create poise by building self-confidence and overcoming any fear associated with public speaking or dealing with strangers. Poise is accomplished through practice and a command of the information or topic in the message.

- *Personal appearance* — Maintain a professional appearance at all times, set an example for subordinates, and require the same level of professionalism from subordinates.

- *Touch* — Become conscious of the effect that touch can have on others, both positive and negative.

- *Proximity* — Be aware of the cultural differences that determine the use of space and apply it appropriately.

- *Use of time* — Adjust the application of time based on the individuals or groups that are being dealt with. If it is necessary to maintain strict control over time, explain the requirements to all who are concerned.

Determine which areas need improvement and then make appropriate changes. By improving personal skills, the company officer can then project an effective image that invites and enhances interpersonal relationships. At the same time, understand that the nonverbal communication that other people portray may not fit these concepts exactly.

People are the products of their home environments and do not fit neatly into stereotypes that are associated with some of these generalities. This concept also applies to cultural values, morals, ethics, and work habits as well as nonverbal clues. For instance, not all people living in the South speak with a drawl and not all people from the West like rodeos or barbeque.

Cultural Views of Time

Traditionally, cultural views of the use of time can be divided into the following two categories:

- **Monochronic** — Eurocentric cultures view time *monochronically;* that is, time is compartmentalized with events scheduled in succession (linear) and allotted specific amounts of time. This concept explains why meetings must begin on time and why it is not acceptable to be late for an appointment.

- **Polychronic** — Cultures that are *polychronic* (such as some Middle Eastern, Latin American, and Native American societies) do not place these same restrictions on time. Time is viewed as cyclical. They believe that punctuality is not important, schedules do not have to be adhered to strictly, and interruptions are acceptable.

Listening Skills

Of all the communication skills discussed in this manual, listening is probably the most important. Research indicates that most people remember only 50 percent of a message 24 hours after they hear it and only 25 percent after 48 hours. Because listening constitutes approximately 42 percent of a person's average day, improving listening skills is essential to effective communication (**Figure 6.12**). To maximize success as leaders, company officers must master good listening skills.

Many people confuse hearing and listening. Although both activities involve the use of the auditory senses through the use of the ears, they are *not* the same. Definitions are as follows:

- *Hearing* — Physiological process that involves sound waves striking the eardrums. The majority of the sound waves that enter the ear consist of noise. People hear all sounds around them such as music playing in an elevator, air passing through an air-conditioning system, or traffic on the street. Most are ignored, creating only a dull background noise to the sounds the listener is actually focusing on.

- *Listening* — Active part of the communication process that includes attending, understanding, remembering, evaluating, and responding to a speaker. Once a company officer has learned

the various parts of the listening process, it will be possible to apply them to improve existing listening skills.

Attending

Attending is basically paying attention to the message. It means focusing on the speaker and ignoring other distractions. In a controlled environment such as a counseling session in an office setting, focus may be easy to accomplish.

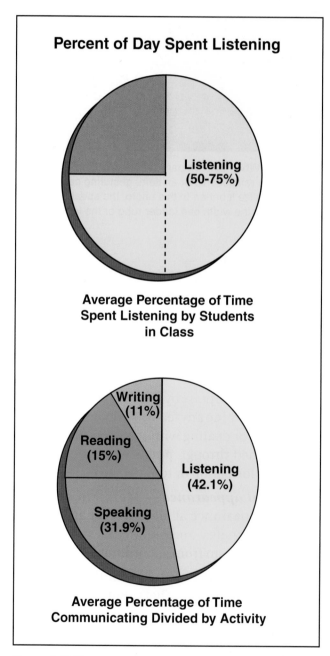

Figure 6.12 The average person spends approximately 42 percent of the day listening. The figures in this illustration vary depending on the methodology used to gather the data.

For example, closing a window or door can shut out traffic noise or turning off a radio and lowering the volume of dispatch speakers during the session can eliminate distractions. Visual distractions such as clutter on the desk or memorabilia in the office can be removed before the session begins.

Controlling the environment of an emergency scene is much more difficult, which means that the listener must concentrate much harder on the speaker. This concentration is particularly important when the communication is occurring over the radio.

Some suggestions for improving the attending step are as follows:

- ***Be ready to listen*** — Look at the speaker if possible. Think about the speaker and what is being said. Visualize the situation or event that the speaker is talking about.

- ***Listen to the complete message*** — Wait until the speaker has finished delivering the message before responding.

- ***Maintain eye contact*** — Listen to both the verbal and nonverbal messages.

- ***Remove physical barriers*** — Sit in chairs that are at right angles to one another. Sitting behind a desk can place a physical and psychological barrier between the listener and the speaker (**Figure 6.13**).

- ***Listen to one speaker at a time*** — Try to listen to only one person at a time. Dividing attention between multiple speakers will guarantee that parts of the messages will be lost.

Figure 6.13 To improve interpersonal communications, the company officer should attempt to remove any physical barriers. Sitting at right angles is one approach to removing barriers.

Understanding

Understanding consists of decoding the message and assigning meaning to it. It involves the following actions:

- Organizing the message into a logical pattern

- Observing the nonverbal clues to help with the meaning of the message

- Asking questions to clarify the meaning of the message

When a message is important or the receiver is unsure of the importance of the message, the receiver can respond by repeating the message word for word or paraphrasing it. *Paraphrasing* is restating the message in different words but keeping the same meaning.

Paraphrase the message back to the speaker to ensure that understanding is clear. This action is both polite and articulate; it means you both listened *and* understand what was said.

Remembering

Remembering what has been said is critical for the message to have the correct effect. To assist in remembering, repeat the information. When possible, take notes, which is an effective and important way to help with retention of messages.

Note-taking is particularly important in interviews or performance evaluations. Always keep a small notepad available for writing information, whether in the office or at emergency incidents (**Figure 6.14, p. 136**).

Another method for remembering specific information is the use of *mnemonics*, a system or technique to improve memory. One useful mnemonic device consists of reducing a phrase to the first letters of each word of the phrase. An example that is familiar to most fire officers is *RECEO*, the basic steps of fire scene operations: Rescue, Exposure, Confinement, Extinguishment, and Overhaul.

Evaluating

Evaluating the message involves critically analyzing the message to determine how factual it really is. To evaluate a message, the listener must be able to separate facts from opinions; use the following definitions:

Responding

Responding to the speaker completes the communication process and means an exchange of roles (the listener becomes the speaker and vice versa). Without any response, the speaker does not know if the message was received, understood, or will be acted upon.

The response needs to be both verbal and nonverbal to indicate that the message was understood. A response may also occur during the understanding step of the process when a question is asked or the message is paraphrased. A response can also occur in the remembering step to help retain the message.

Improving Listening Skills

Practicing good listening skills is the best way to improve them. Listen to speeches or stories on audiotape and try to repeat the key elements. Practice taking notes at meetings or speeches to improve note-taking skills. These actions help to overcome the barrier created by information overload by pinpointing the essential elements of the message.

When listening to a speaker, try to focus on the speaker and the message. The greatest distraction is the listener's internal *voice*. This voice may be responding to something that was said earlier or something the listener would like to say. It could just be daydreaming. While this internal monologue is underway, the words of the speaker are being ignored.

To overcome this barrier, first identify it. Try responding to the speaker by asking questions or paraphrasing what has been said. When responding is inappropriate such as it would be with a formal speech, take notes of the key points.

Before small group meetings or individual counseling sessions, the company officer should remove barriers to listening in the room where the meeting will take place. This is especially true when conducting training sessions. These barriers may include the following (**Figure 6.15**):

- Noise-producing equipment
- Visual distractions such as posters on the walls
- Uncovered or open windows with exterior views
- Cell phones, pagers, and radios

Figure 6.14 An effective way to keep track of critical information is to write it down. When conducting interviews or listening to instructions, the company officer can use a notepad to write important points such as names, times, locations, and observations.

- *Facts* — Verifiable data that can support the decision-making process. A radio report that an engine company has reached the seat of the fire and is applying water to it can be verified by the observation that the smoke has changed from black to gray.
- *Opinion* — Generalization that may not be verifiable without additional data. The report from a witness that everyone is out of a structure cannot be verified without a thorough search of the building.

Analysis of the message depends on the following factors:

- Personal experience of the listener
- Other available information
- Interpretation of the nonverbal clues from the speaker
- Credibility of the speaker

During company-level training exercises, try to identify barriers to communication, both over the radio and at the command post. Training exercises that re-create fireground conditions help to identify potential barriers and provide an opportunity to identify solutions.

As part of a postincident evaluation, determine ways to improve listening skills for those involved in an incident (**Figure 6.16**). The incident safety officer and/or critique officer is responsible for identifying communication problems, reporting them, and suggesting ways to overcome them during postincident analyses.

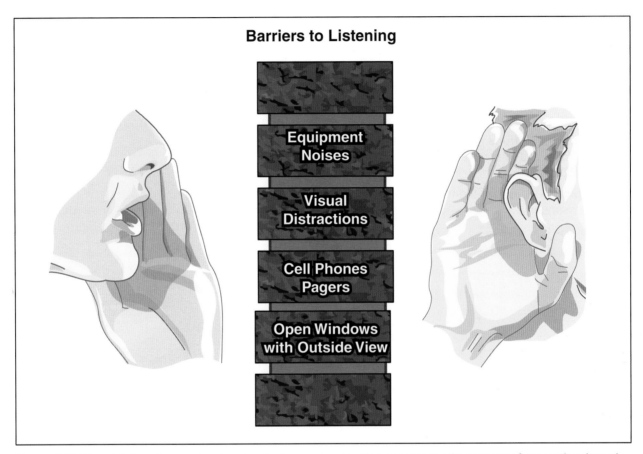

Figure 6.15 Like a brick wall, some barriers to effective communication can prevent the message from getting through.

Figure 6.16 During a postincident critique, communication problems discovered during the analysis of an incident should be discussed. Solutions to improving incident communications should be recommended.

The company officer should work to overcome psychological barriers such as prejudice by accepting others as they are and not as people think they should be. Prejudice based on preconceived concepts of dress, voice, or attitude can be major barriers to hearing what a speaker has to say.

Barriers to Listening

- *Information overload* — Identify the essential elements of the message.

- *Personal Concerns* — Focus on the speaker and the message rather than personal concerns or thoughts.

- *Outside distractions* — Take control of the environment and remove as many distractions as possible.

- *Prejudice* — Focus on the message and not the messenger.

Summary

As a foundation to other types of communication, an understanding of effective interpersonal communication is important to all fire officers. The concepts can be applied to emergency and nonemergency situations, counseling and mentoring subordinates, professional development, and improving relations with external customers of the organization.

All company officers must master the basic interpersonal communication skills in order to be effective leaders. In addition, officers will find these skills appropriate in all areas of their lives and gain the benefits that good communication skills bring to all relationships.

Guidelines for Listening

Numerous articles and books have been written about the art of listening, its importance, and how to improve the ability to listen. The following are just a few of the suggested guidelines for being an active listener:

- **Be attentive to the speaker** — Nonverbal behavior, including eye contact, relaxed posture, and a friendly facial expression, creates a positive atmosphere. An attentive attitude causes the speaker to feel relaxed, important, self-confident, and secure.

- **Be interested in the speaker's needs, ideas, and concerns** — Listen with understanding and mutual respect. Do not let personal bias or opinions become a barrier to listening.

- **Pay close attention to individual inferences, facts, and judgments made by the speaker** — These factors can provide an insight into what the speaker considers important.

- **Provide clear verbal evidence that listening is taking place** — Such evidence includes the following actions:
  - Giving constructive feedback
  - Being able to paraphrase what the speaker has said
  - Being able to ask questions for clarification
  - Asking probing or challenging questions about statements made by the speaker

- **Show respect for the speaker** — When providing feedback, use an inclusive, friendly, and sharing tone.

- **Do not exaggerate, distort, or state out of context what the speaker said when repeating statements.**

- **Be prepared to detect fallacies in logic and reasoning on the part of the speaker** — If necessary, ask for sources or citations for facts or conclusions that may appear to be inaccurate or improperly used.

- **Acknowledge what has been said in an honest, clear, timely, respectful, and relevant manner when the speaker is finished** — Feedback of this type is important in the communication process and assures the speaker of the importance of what has been said.

- **Listen from a caring attitude** — An active listener allows the speaker to express ideas and feelings while assuming a nonjudgmental, noncritical attitude. Ask questions for clarity but do not cross-examine the speaker.

- **Act like a mirror** — A good listener summarizes what the speaker has said to ensure a complete understanding of what was said.

- **Do not become personally involved in the speaker's problem** — Becoming personally involved may cause the listener to jump to conclusions and become judgmental, resulting in anger and hurt feelings on the part of both speaker and listener.

- **Use verbal cues** — Verbal cues include such feedback as *I see*, *right*, or *that's interesting*. It is also helpful to encourage the speaker to elaborate on the topic by saying *Tell me more about it*, *I'd like to hear what you're thinking*, or *I'd be interested in your opinion*.

Oral Communications

Chapter Contents

Learning Objectives

1. Identify elements of the speech communication process.

2. Distinguish between interpersonal communication and speech communication.

3. Identify characteristics of effective speakers.

4. Match to their definitions the three types of formal speeches.

5. Select facts about the persuasive speech.

6. Recall the principles used in the informative speech.

7. Identify facts about various speaking opportunities available to the company officer.

8. Recall information about public relations speeches.

9. Place in order the steps of the speech preparation process.

10. Choose correct responses about the steps of the speech preparation process.

Job Performance Requirements

This chapter provides information that addresses the following job performance requirements of NFPA 1021, *Standard for Fire Officer Professional Qualifications* (2003):

Chapter 4 Fire Officer I

4.2.5(B)

4.3.3(A)

4.4.1(A)

4.4.2(B)

4.6.1(B)

4.6.2(B)

4.6.3(B)

4.6.4(B)

4.7.1(B)

4.7.2(B)

Chapter 5 Fire Officer II

5.4.4(A)

5.4.4(B)

Chapter 7
Oral Communications

While interpersonal communication deals with the everyday interaction between individuals, *oral communication* is the process of presenting formal oral presentations or speeches to groups. Company officers may be required to make oral presentations to administrative bodies (such as the city council or county board of commissioners), management groups, work teams, or citizens' organizations. The purpose of the presentation may be to improve community relations or provide training for unit personnel. The size of the group may vary from small (less than 12) to large (several hundred).

Some of the theories of interpersonal communication also apply to oral communication such as the basic communication model and the concepts of listening and feedback. To be effective when making oral presentations, company officers should learn and practice the concepts presented in this chapter. The quality of the presentation can mean acceptance or rejection of a proposed budget, policy, or program: The more effective the presentation, the greater the possibility that a proposal will be accepted.

Making an oral presentation is simply making a speech in public. In fact, the two terms, *oral communication* and *speech communication* can be used interchangeably. Because public speaking is the number one fear of many people, it will be necessary to overcome that fear through an important part of oral communication: practice **(Figure 7.1)**. By taking every advantage to speak in public, to small groups, or to the news media, company officers will gain more confidence and improve delivery skills.

In addition to an understanding of the speech communication process, company officers need to be familiar with the characteristics of an effective speaker. Research has shown that these characteristics are present in most good speakers. Company officers need to recognize the types of speeches they may be called upon to make (including informative and persuasive speeches).

They must also be aware of the potential opportunities that will be available to them (and sometimes required of them) to make speeches. Finally, it is important for the officer to learn and practice the speech preparation process. This process takes an idea and develops it into an effective speech by following specific steps.

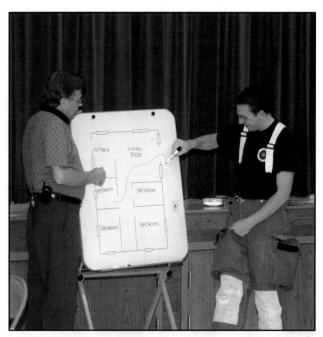

Figure 7.1 Company officers have many opportunities to speak in public. Fire and life-safety presentations provide a chance to practice and improve public speaking skills.

Speech Communication Process

To begin with, the speech communication process, which is similar to the interpersonal communication process discussed in the previous chapter, is composed of seven basic elements. By keeping these basic elements in mind, the company officer can become more effective in presenting ideas and information by controlling the elements of the communication process. The basic elements are as follows:

- **Sender** — Person who originates the process (also referred to as the *speaker* or *source*) by translating ideas and images into words that an audience can understand.

- **Receiver** — Individuals or group of individuals who compose an audience (also referred to as the *listener* or *audience*) **(Figure 7.2)**. It is their responsibility to be effective listeners and translate the words into mental images that they can relate to.

- **Message** — Content of the speech, idea, or information that the sender wants the audience to hear. It consists of both the verbal and nonverbal symbols used by the sender.

- **Medium** or **channel** — Path the message takes between the sender and receiver. It is both visual and auditory and may be face to face, over a videoconferencing link, or by way of a speakerphone. *Examples:*

— *Visual channel:* Includes graphs, slides, transparencies, PowerPoint® presentations, and any other visual aid employed by the sender. It also includes the posture, facial expressions, gestures, and clothing worn by the sender.

— *Auditory channel:* Consists of the message chosen by the sender and the vocal inflections, rate, and quality used by the sender.

- **Feedback** — Response by the audience to the message presented by the sender. It may consist of laughter, applause, facial expressions, head nodding, or questions. Feedback provides the sender with the knowledge that the message has been received and whether it has been understood. Feedback completes or perpetuates the communication process.

- **Context** — Communication environment that includes the physical location, time, and attitude of both the sender and receiver. *Examples:*

— *Physical location:* May consist of a well-lit, comfortable auditorium with soft seats or an informal meeting area in a station apparatus room with metal folding chairs **(Figure 7.3)**

— *Time of day:* Has an affect on the mental awareness of the audience or its attentiveness; an audience is less attentive immediately following a meal than at other times of the day

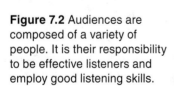

Figure 7.2 Audiences are composed of a variety of people. It is their responsibility to be effective listeners and employ good listening skills.

Figure 7.3 Not all presentations are made in an auditorium or classroom. The company officer may find that an apparatus room is more appropriate to the topic being presented.

Comparisons Between Interpersonal Communication and Speech Communication

Interpersonal Communication	Speech Communication
Casual language	Formal language
Casual nonverbal clues	Formal nonverbal clues
Spontaneous	Intentional
Roles between sender and receiver can change frequently	Roles of sender and receiver are consistent and may not change

— *Attitude of the sender:* Can be affected by illness, apprehension, or enthusiasm

— *Attitude of the receiver:* Can be the same as that of the sender, who may have heard rumors of impending layoffs or reassignments

- *Interference (or noise)* — Anything that interferes with the accurate transmission of the message. *Examples:*

— External environmental noise such as air-handling units, intercom paging systems, phones, traffic, or machinery or talking, laughing, or coughing from the audience

— Internal noises, including the listeners' hunger, drowsiness, or personal concerns that cause their minds to focus on other issues instead of the message

Characteristics of Effective Speakers

Analyses of effective speakers throughout history have shown that they all tend to have similar speaking traits or characteristics. This section assists in the development of these characteristics as they relate to oral communication. Characteristics include the following:

- *Audience-centered* — The speaker knows the audience and adapts the topic, speech organization, presentation style, and personal appearance to this audience. This characteristic

requires that the speaker learn as much as possible about the audience, determine what the audience needs to know about the subject, and determine the purpose of the presentation before the development of the speech.

- *Good development of ideas* — Effective speakers are also effective thinkers; they use their thinking skills to create interesting, appealing, and memorable ways of presenting their information. *Examples:*

— Use relevant examples.

— Use appropriate humor.

— Tell stories to which the audience can relate.

— Use effective metaphors.

- *Good organization of ideas* — The structure of the speech varies depending on the purpose of the speech. See Types of Speeches and Organize the Speech sections. *Examples:*

— A well-organized persuasive speech gains the audience's attention, provides the necessary background information, illustrates the situation, and offers a solution to the situation.

— An informative speech may be organized topically or according to the complexity of the subject.

- *Best choice of words* — Words (as much as any other part of the communication process) convey the message. The choice of the right words ensures that the message stands a good chance of being understood. *Examples:*

- It is important to not speak above the intellectual level of the audience by using words they might not understand.

- It is just as important that the speaker not talk below the level of the audience, insulting their intelligence by being too basic.

- **Good delivery skills** — An effective speaker uses more than words to convey the message. Enthusiasm for the subject is essential to communicating the message. It makes the audience want to listen and ensures that audience members do not let their minds drift and ignore the speaker. Enthusiasm is conveyed by the following:

  - Eye contact

  - Facial expressions

  - Voice inflections (changes in tonal quality to emphasize ideas and thoughts)

- **Good research skills** — An effective presentation must be based on reliable data and analysis. The use of reliable data builds credibility for the speaker and the topic and can help to ensure compliance with the speaker's proposal. Research skills include the following:

  - Locating the appropriate data **(Figure 7.4)**

  - Analyzing the data

  - Applying the data to the topic

  - Including the data into the body of the speech or into visual aids that support the speech

- **Appropriate use of humor** — Effective speakers use appropriate humor to create a relaxed atmosphere and get the attention of the audience. However, avoid inappropriate humor that offends members of the audience. Humor that is appropriate in one setting may not be acceptable in another. The sensitivity of comments and actions must always be a consideration in any communication setting. Inappropriate humor that may have been considered acceptable in the past is no longer tolerated in fire and emergency services organizations.

- **Critical thinking skills** — These skills are necessary to convert the data that has been gathered into an effective argument or concept. The basic concepts of critical thinking can be taught, but to become a personal skill, it must be practiced

Figure 7.4 Effective presentations are based on reliable information. Research and analysis must be thorough and accurate to ensure that information is reliable.

through the analysis of speeches, presentations, and even advertising, looking for flaws in logic such as incorrect conclusions based on the data provided. Critical thinking skills are necessary for the following concepts:

- Evaluating ideas

- Recognizing fallacies

- Developing theories

- Recognizing relationships between various data

- Prioritizing options

- Understanding causes and effects

Types of Speeches

In some instances, elements of one speech type may be introduced into another type to increase interest, provide variety, or emphasize a point. The following speeches are three accepted types of formal speeches:

- **Persuasive** — Use a strong argument based on reliable data in order to create a change in belief, behavior, or attitude).

- **Informative** — Give the audience definitions, descriptions, explanations, or information that teach a topic.

- **Entertainment** — Use humorous stories or anecdotes.

The types may be remembered by the acronym *PIE*. Although there are a number of other types of speeches that are based on these three types, the company officer will generally only need to know the persuasive and informative types of speeches to accomplish the assigned functions of a Level I or Level II Fire Officer.

Persuasive

The persuasive speech may be the most difficult to develop and at the same time the most important type of speech an officer can give. It is intended to cause change by describing a problem and supplying a solution (**Figure 7.5**).

The persuasive speech is based on the theory called *Monroe's Motivated Sequence Pattern* developed by Alan Monroe in the 1930s. Developed properly, Monroe's sequence can be the basic outline for persuading a group to follow a desired course of action.

The sequence is not an absolute formula and may require modification based on an audience analysis (see Analyze the Audience section under Speech Preparation Process section). Briefly, the sequence is as follows:

I. *Attention*— Gain the attention of the audience in the introduction, which is usually a memorable statement, analogy, statistic, or story.

II. *Need* — Describe the problem (how it developed and who is affected by it) and demonstrate a need for a change in the current situation. This need is the main idea of the speech.

III. *Satisfaction*— Present the best solution, providing sufficient information and evidence to allow the audience to understand how it accomplishes the goal. Satisfaction is the second main idea of the speech. Evidence may consist of the following:
 — Examples
 — Statistics
 — Testimonies by experts

IV. *Visualization*— Describe the best solution for the problem and where it has been successfully used previously. Provide a vivid example of the results and how it will affect members of

Figure 7.5 One important use of the persuasive speech is convincing the public to change a behavior that will result in a safer community. When making a public presentation, the company officer should decide on the appropriate clothing for the occasion and audience; a uniform may not always be the best choice.

the audience. This step may also visualize the results that would occur if the required action were not taken. Visualization is the third main idea.

V. *Action* — Make an appeal for change by providing the audience with the basic steps needed to accomplish the change, which is the basis of the conclusion of the speech. The action steps must be easy and manageable for the audience to attain.

Informative

These speeches are the easiest to develop when the process listed in the Speech Preparation Process section is followed and supporting data is accurately compiled and analyzed. The informative speech is the type used most often by company officers to perform the following duties:

● Provide status reports.

● Describe events.

● Give project updates.

● Provide unit-level training (**Figure 7.6, p. 148**).

● Educate the public and media.

Informative speeches are classified by the topics they cover. Typically, informative speeches are about the following topics:

- **Ideas**—Speeches about ideas tend to be abstract and attempt to explain principles, theories, and concepts. A typical topic might be *Fuels Management* or *Explanation of the Emergency Medical Services (EMS) System*. The organization of the speech is accomplished by using either one of the following ways:

  — *Topical:* Using logical subdivisions

  — *Complex:* Moving from simple to more complex

- **Objects** — An objects-type speech is used to explain a tangible object such as a nozzle or apparatus-mounted fire pump. The organization may be topical or spatial (moving from one part to another) **(Figure 7.7)**.

- **Procedures** — A procedures-type speech describes how something works or outlines a process. This speech is usually organized chronologically. *Topic examples:*

  — How to develop a budget

  — How to operate an elevating platform

- **People**—A speech about a person may be a general overview of that person's life or may focus on one specific event intended to illustrate a value or skill. The organization may be chronological or topical.

- **Events** — An events-type speech is used to describe an actual event such as the Chicago fire of 1871, Hurricane Katrina in 2005, or a specific hazardous materials incident. The organization is generally chronological, but it may also be divided into logical subsections. For instance, in the case of an incident, an explanation of the activities of the various units assigned to it may be used to describe the overall operation.

A speaker effectively conveys the informative message to an audience by using certain principles. Mastering these principles improves the delivery of any informative speech, but the topic must be well supported with evidence (facts and data on which the topic is based). The evidence must be accurate, current, and appropriate to the subject matter. See Gather Supporting Evidence section.

The informative speech principles are outlined as follows:

- **Adapt the topic to the audience** — Know the audience and purpose of the speech. Adaptation is the basis for all audience-centered speeches.

- **Motivate the audience to listen to the speech** — Provide motivation in the introduction to the speech by asking a question such as *What if you had a fire and nobody came to help?*

- **Use redundancy**—Use a concept generally used in teaching, which is to tell the audience what the message is (introduction), deliver the message (speech body), and tell the audience what the message was (conclusion).

- **Use simple-is-better concept** — Deliver ideas in simple phrases rather than complex ones to allow the audience to grasp and retain them longer.

Figures 7.6 Unit-level training is an effective way of maintaining skills and providing information about new policies, procedures, or equipment.

Figure 7.7 An informative presentation on a topic such as the operation of a thermal imaging camera provides the basic information that personnel can then practice during training evolutions.

- ***Organize the topic in a logical manner*** — Organize complex ideas and concepts logically, that is, organize by divisions, in a chronological order, spatially, or from general to specific. Main ideas should be balanced evenly within the speech. See Organize the Speech section.

- ***Use clear transitions to move the listener through the topic*** — Link one division with the next and make the flow of ideas smooth. For instance, a transition for a talk on foam operations might be *Now that we know how foam acts to impede combustion, let's see how it can be effectively applied to the fire.* These types of transitions are sometimes called *backward and forward* transitions.

- ***Use both verbal and nonverbal reinforcement of ideas*** — Emphasize the importance of specific ideas by stating, *This is the most important point I will make* or *Remember this point.* At the same time, changes in vocal inflection, volume, or rate or the use of a pause or gesture can help to emphasize the point.

- ***Use an even flow to deliver the information*** — Organize the speech to present information evenly rather than in clusters of facts or details.

The audience must have time to interpret and process the information before receiving additional concepts. This principle is particularly important when the information is new or unfamiliar to the audience. Presenting too much information initially causes the following reactions:

— Overwhelms members of the audience

— Distracts them

— Causes them to lose attention

- ***Build on the familiar*** — Relate new information to knowledge that the audience already has because familiarity with common knowledge makes the new information more understandable and relatable.

- ***Use visual aids*** — Use a variety of visual aids, charts, presentation software visuals (such as PowerPoint®), slides, or illustrations to emphasize the topic (**Figure 7.8, p. 150**). The majority of people are visual learners and retain what they see more than what they hear. *Considerations:*

— Make visual aids simple, direct, informative, and appealing. The general rule (6 by 6) for

Guidelines: Develop Effective Visual Aids

- Use typefaces or fonts that are readable, consistent, and large enough to read at a distance. Font size depends on the size of the presentation room and projection screen. Avoid the use of all uppercase letters.

- Follow the *6 by 6 Rule*: Use a maximum of six lines down and six words across the viewing area.

- Limit the text to phrases and not complete sentences. The text helps the audience focus on the key points of the presentation. The oral presentation expands on these phrases.

- Create one heading for each slide or image. Expand with subheadings or illustrations such as graphs, charts, photographs, or clipart.

- Keep the backgrounds simple so they do not conflict with the text or graphics.

- Keep the color compatible with the text and graphics. Do not select colors that clash or distract the attention of the audience. The choice of color also

helps to convey a message: Red indicates danger, yellow indicates caution, blue indicates serenity, etc.

- Use transitions and animations sparingly because they can overpower the message that a slide is attempting to convey.

- Use variety in the composition of the various elements on the slides by interspersing graphs, charts, photographs, and clipart to create interest.

- Use parallel structure on each slide: Start phrases with nouns and start bullets with verbs, which make the points easier to link together.

- Use handouts of the slides as necessary. Handouts can be particularly helpful when presenting complex or detailed concepts. The audience can make appropriate notes using handouts based on the slides; however, handouts can also become distractions by giving the audience something to look at other than the presentation. An option is to distribute them at the conclusion of the presentation.

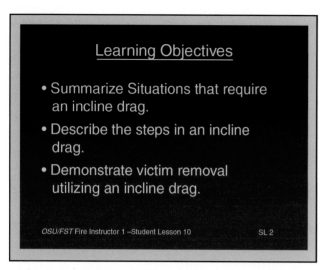

Figure 7.8 Presentation software provides the company officer with an easy and effective way to add interest to speeches and can be used for most topics. *Courtesy of Fire Service Training, Oklahoma State University.*

Figure 7.9 Some reports to governing bodies are intended to provide information about the status of projects such as the construction of new facilities or the implementation of a fire and life-safety program. *Courtesy of Benny Deal.*

the quantity of text on a slide or PowerPoint® visual is six lines of not more than six words each.

— Limit PowerPoint® visual transitions, animations, and sound effects, which are very interesting visually, but can become distracting if overused.

Speech Opportunities

Company officers may have the opportunity to present public speeches on many occasions. Opportunities may include presentations of reports to governing boards, public relations talks to community groups, and providing public information to the news media. Each of these occasions requires a different approach, although the basic public-speaking skills remain the same.

Report Presentations

The general purpose of presenting a report is to provide information. For instance, it may be the presentation of a status report on a project or proposed changes to a policy or procedure (**Figure 7.9**). The presentation might also require the use of the skills used in the persuasive speech, which may involve presenting a budget request to the governing board and persuading them to adopt it.

Reports may also be presented internally when the status of a project or program must be reported to the administration or to various committees or management teams. Generally, steps that result in successful reports are as follows:

Step 1: *Make an immediate statement of purpose* — The audience is there to hear a report on a specific situation so state the situation clearly and concisely at the beginning of the speech.

Step 2: *Explain how the information that the report is based upon was gathered* — This step establishes credibility and allows the audience to focus on the report itself.

Step 3: *Present possible solutions to the situation* — The most important part of this type of presentation may be outlining a new course of action or recommending changes in procedures or policies. If one solution is preferable, use persuasive techniques to then guide the audience to the same conclusion.

Step 4: *Tell the specific benefits for and effects on the audience* — Explain what the benefits are to increase the likelihood that the audience will listen and pay attention.

Step 5: *Anticipate any objections or questions that might arise* — Have an understanding of the members of the audience and their individual concerns and agendas. It is also important to have the necessary information to answer questions. However, if information is not available, do not attempt to answer immediately. Simply state that the information will be available at a later date.

Step 6: ***Provide a written copy of the report to the audience*** — Include an executive summary at the beginning, which allows members of the audience to follow the key points in the report.

Public Relations Speeches

Company officers must keep in mind that the image of the organization depends not only on the quality of service provided but also on a positive image and relationship with the community. Public relations speeches help to maintain this relationship by keeping the public informed and addressing community concerns when they arise.

This speech may be informative or persuasive in nature. It is similar to the presentation of a report discussed previously. The only difference is the audience. While a report is normally given to an authority or group of coworkers, the audience for a public relations speech is the general public.

Members of this audience will not have copies of the presentation but will certainly have questions and sometimes criticisms for the speaker. It is essential that the speaker is prepared and keeps a positive and noncombative attitude during the presentation.

Public Information Speeches

Another public speaking opportunity with which company officers sometimes have to cope is speaking with the media. The occasion may be a planned and prearranged press conference or it may be a spur-of-the-moment interview at the scene of an incident. In any case, the company officer must be prepared for this possibility and represent the department well as a spokesperson **(Figure 7.10)**.

To create a positive working relationship between the organization and the local media, it is advantageous to provide opportunities to learn each other's profession. Members of the media and the organization will gain a better understanding of the responsibilities and challenges the other party faces. These opportunities can be provided through the following methods:

- Conducting monthly cross-training meetings

- Inviting members of the press to address organizational meetings

- Conducting *ride-along* programs that permit reporters to observe day-to-day operations

Speaking with or being interviewed by the media can be a challenge. The media can be either a friend or an enemy. Company officers should work with the media, be honest and forthright, and follow organizational policies and procedures that outline media relations.

Some organizations have a designated public information officer (PIO) assigned to answer media questions on large incidents **(Figure 7.11, p. 152)**. If the organization has a PIO on scene, company officers should politely direct questions and interview requests to that person.

Figure 7.10 Interviews that are given during emergency incidents are generally unrehearsed and may require the company officer to answer questions about the cause of an incident.

Figure 7.11 Most fire and emergency services organizations have fire officers who are assigned as public information officers (PIOs). However, there are occasions when the PIO is not available and the company officer who is on scene may be required to speak to the news media.

If there is no PIO assigned or available, company officers should follow organizational policies and procedures when being interviewed. The following guidelines will be helpful to company officers who are assigned to give interviews:

- Remember that there is no such thing as *off the record*. Anything said to a reporter can be quoted. Do not be misled by the friendly reporter who says *Just between us . . . .*

- Beware when asked leading questions. Sometimes reporters will use this tactic to get the answer they want. Listen to the questions carefully and thoughtfully and answer *yes* or *that's correct* only if the facts in the questions are 100 percent accurate and no inaccurate conclusions have been drawn.

- Avoid getting into disagreements or becoming defensive with reporters. Defensiveness may suggest that information is being withheld even when it is not.

- Do *not* be led into answering questions beyond the officer's area of knowledge or expertise. Refer such questions to those who have the necessary information or offer to find the answer — and always follow through.

- Avoid using esoteric fire service terminology (jargon). When a technical term must be used, explain its meaning at the time it is used.

- Be as frank and open as possible without divulging confidential information about victims' identities, possible fire cause, etc. Honesty is the best policy.

- Do *not* answer *What if* questions. Do *not* answer hypothetical questions by explaining that you are not prepared to speculate.

- Listen for false or misleading information in reporters' questions. If a question contains false information, politely discount the misinformation and provide accurate information.

- Beware of the forced-choice question. If either way of answering a question would be inaccurate, then answer with a separate, factual response. Be tactful, but refute false information.

- Do *not* volunteer information, especially if it is speculative. For example, prematurely suggesting to the media that a fire is possibly of electrical origin could have an adverse affect if an arson case is later developed from that fire.

- Be prepared. Rehearse your interview technique, and try to improve delivery.

- Remove sunglasses when being interviewed on camera or off. When communicating with anyone, it is important for individuals to be able to see the speaker's eyes.

- Make sure to provide a good background of an apparatus or incident scene when being interviewed on camera.

- Be familiar with the organization's policy on any type of information that must be kept confidential such as patient information that is regulated by the Health Insurance Portability and Accountability Act (HIPPA).

- Seek additional training on the specific duties of a PIO.

NOTE: For more information on this topic see the IFSTA **Public Information Officer** manual and the Incident Command System (ICS) 220-2, *Information Officer Checklist* (**Appendix D**).

Speech Preparation Process

Just as there is a formal speech communication process and specific characteristics for effective speakers, there is also a process for preparing a speech. The key to this process is the audience. During each step of the process, the speaker must remain focused on the intended audience.

Canned speeches (those prepared for all occasions and audiences) will not be effective because each audience and each occasion is different. Never fall into the habit of using the same speech over and over again. However, previously given speeches can be retained, modified for similar occasions, and reused.

This practice is used by many nationally known speakers when presenting similar presentations. Analyze the audience and create a new speech for them. Once the speaker knows the audience, then a speech can be developed.

Following a logical sequence in the preparation of an oral presentation helps to ensure the success of the speech. The steps of the speech preparation process are as follows:

Step 1: Select the topic.

Step 2: Determine the purpose.

Step 3: Generate the main ideas.

Step 4: Develop the central idea.

Step 5: Gather supporting evidence.

Step 6: Organize the speech.

Step 7: Rehearse the speech.

Step 8: Deliver the speech.

Step 9: Evaluate the speech.

Analyze the Audience

As mentioned previously, the key to a successful oral presentation is thorough audience analysis. In a society as diverse as the one established in North America (which is based on many cultures), it is very unlikely that an audience will be homogeneous (all alike). Age, gender, ethnic background, socioeconomic status, educational level, political affiliation, and religious beliefs (among others) set people apart.

Even within the fire and emergency services, various cultural differences exist. In addition to the differences listed previously, the fire and emergency services are composed of volunteers, career personnel, firefighters, emergency medical responders, specialists, rookies, operational unit members, labor organization members, and administrators. Job titles, functions, and affiliations create artificial differences that can have an effect on the operation of an organization.

Knowing the various cultures and subcultures that compose an audience goes a long way toward acceptance of the ideas that are presented. Elements of an audience analysis are described in the sections that follow and include the following:

- Demographics
- Attitudes, beliefs, and values
- Physical settings
- Audience adaptations

Demographics

Demographics include age, gender, religion, education, and cultural/ethnic/racial backgrounds. Knowing the demographics of a group is one way of analyzing the audience (**Figure 7.12, p. 154**).

For instance, if the majority of a group was born before 1950, references to events of the 1960s may help form a bond of understanding between the speaker and the audience. When the audience is composed primarily of women, positive comments concerning issues specific to women as they relate to the topic would then be appropriate. In each case, relating the topic or issue to the needs, concerns, and background of the audience helps to generate acceptance of the topic.

Sources for demographic information include the following:

- Federal, state, and local governments
- Libraries
- Colleges and universities
- Internet

Attitudes, Beliefs, and Values

Audience analysis also includes an understanding of the attitudes, beliefs, and values of a group's members. What are their likes and dislikes? How do they perceive what is true and false? What are their core values on good, bad, right, and wrong?

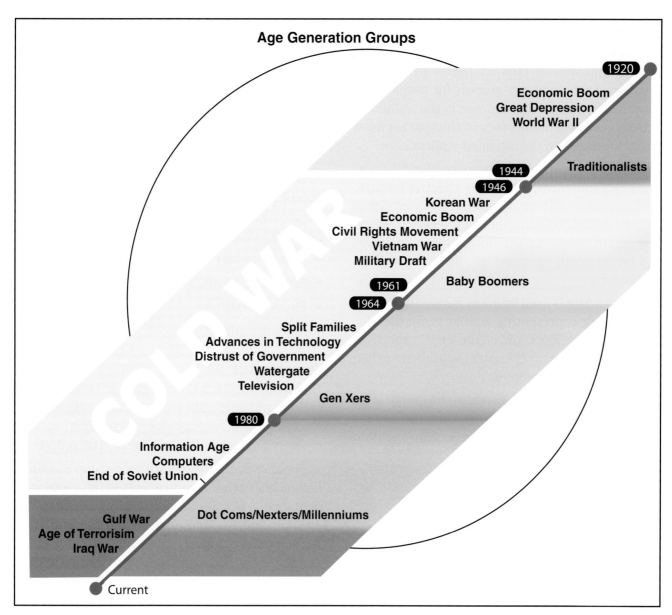

Age Generation Groups

1920

Economic Boom
Great Depression
World War II

Traditionalists

1944
1946

Korean War
Economic Boom
Civil Rights Movement
Vietnam War
Military Draft

Baby Boomers

COLD WAR

1961
1964

Split Families
Advances in Technology
Distrust of Government
Watergate
Television

Gen Xers

1980

Information Age
Computers
End of Soviet Union

Gulf War
Age of Terrorisim
Iraq War

Dot Coms/Nexters/Millenniums

Current

Figure 7.12 Each of the four generations depicted have been defined or affected by specific events that occurred during their lifetimes. At the same time, the events of the previous generation may also have a direct affect on their values and beliefs.

When members of the group are familiar to the speaker (other company officers for instance), it may be fairly easy to determine these attitudes, beliefs, and values. Chances are they are shared with the speaker because of similar backgrounds, age, or gender. It is also easy to discuss these issues with members of the audience before developing the presentation.

When the audience is composed of members of the community unknown to the speaker (such as the board of county commissioners or a neighborhood association), consider a more formal analysis.

If members of the group are public figures (politicians for instance), review the comments that they made during political campaigns and public statements they made on fire-related issues.

Analyze audiences that are not composed of public figures by looking at the reason the group exists such as its mission statement (if it has one), bylaws, or publicity that it has generated. Generally, the members of such a group hold similar attitudes, beliefs, and values.

Physical Settings

Knowing the audience also includes knowing the environment in which the presentation is given. This knowledge provides the speaker with some control over how the audience hears the topic.

Make a preliminary trip to the site and discuss the physical arrangement with the people in charge of the facility. Make certain that audio/visual equipment is provided and in working order. Determine whether technical assistance is available or someone who knows how to operate the equipment will be available during the presentation **(Figure 7.13)**.

Ensure that the climate is comfortable and lighting is appropriate to the presentation. Determine whether there will be any environmental noise that could prevent the speaker from being heard and understood. Ensure that seating is adequate and comfortable.

Audience Adaptations

Knowing the audience extends to the actual presentation of a speech. The feedback portion mentioned earlier lets the speaker know whether the message is being heard and understood as intended.

Knowing the audience and developing (or adjusting) the speech to fit them is important in all types of presentations. Some of the indicators of audience involvement with the speaker include the following:

- *Eye contact* — Helps the listeners engage in the topic. Loss of eye contact by audience members is an indication that they have lost interest or don't understand the topic.
- *Facial expressions* — Indicate agreement or disagreement and are involuntary for the most part, which makes them good indicators.
- *Restlessness* — Results from loss of interest in the topic or excessive length of the speech. Short presentations that are to the point are preferred over long, rambling speeches.
- *Nonverbal responses* — Include applause, head nodding, and gesturing.
- *Verbal responses* — Can be loud or subdued, depending on the group and situation. Responses may take the form of heckling comments or questions.

Select the Topic

Selecting the topic of an oral presentation by a company officer is generally an easy step. The topic is usually a function of the officer's position or duties. Therefore, the topic will take the form of something the officer is required to talk about. In any case, the topic must be clearly defined before the speech is developed. Examples include the following:

- A company officer in an administrative position may be required to make budget presentations and project status reports to the jurisdiction's administrative body.

Figure 7.13 Before giving any speech or presentation, the company officer should tour the room or area. The location of light controls, sound systems, and the need for technical assistance should be noted during the tour.

- An assistant fire marshal may make presentations on changes in the fire prevention code or new open-burning laws to the fire chief, fire marshal, or administrative body.

- A company officer assigned to a line unit may be required to speak to a neighborhood association within the response area on the need to support a sales tax to provide a new truck or an additional station.

Determine the Purpose

The general purpose of a speech is similar to the informative and persuasive types of speeches mentioned earlier. Like the selection of the topic, the purpose is likely to be a function of job responsibilities and predetermined (in some cases) by someone else. For instance, the specific purpose of the speech may be to inform the audience about the topic.

Understanding the purpose assists in creating the final speech. If the topic is an upcoming sales-tax election, the general purpose would then be to generate support of the issue. The specific purpose would be to inform members of the audience about the importance of the election, benefits, and effects on each person. This purpose statement needs to be clear and concise and included in the introduction of the speech.

Generate the Main Ideas

To begin organizing the speech, look at the specific purpose of the speech and determine whether it has logical divisions; that is, how many ideas are required to support the purpose. By listing them, the structure of the speech will begin to take shape.

For example, when considering the purpose given in the previous section (sales-tax election information), main ideas might include answers to the following questions:

- What will be the effect of a sales-tax increase?

- How much will it cost each year?

- What does it apply to?

- How long will it last?

- How will it be used?

- What will it buy?

- How soon will results be visible?

Next, look at the specific purpose and develop the reasons for supporting it. In this example, supporting reasons are likely to be as follows:

- Reduced response times

- Lower vehicle maintenance costs

- Increased personnel safety

- Additional services

Finally, establish the steps necessary to accomplish the specific purpose. This sequence may result in a chronological arrangement of the material or an actual step-by-step progression similar to the steps used for donning respiratory protection for example (**Figure 7.14**).

Once these three criteria have been applied, determine which ideas best support the purpose and develop the organization of the speech around them. See Organize the Speech section.

Figure 7.14 A presentation on how to use a new piece of equipment such as a power saw will usually follow a sequence based on each step of the operation.

Develop the Central Idea

The central idea is the reason for the speech. The central idea is similar to the thesis statement used in writing, which is discussed later in Chapter 8, Written Communications. It tells the audience what the speech is about and develops from the main ideas that were generated previously. To be effective, the central idea must be a statement (and not a question) presented in one complete sentence. Use specific language rather than vague generalities, and state the two or three main points of the speech.

Finally, relate the central idea to the audience. For instance, the central idea of the sales-tax example given earlier might be *Supporting the halfpenny sales tax will provide the community with increased fire protection.*

Gather Supporting Evidence

Just telling the audience to support a sales-tax increase is not enough to convince them to vote for it. The central idea must be supported by facts and data that are easily understood by the audience. Facts and data need to support the assumption that an action must be taken or the information provided is accurate. Once gathered, the supporting evidence must be incorporated into the speech in a logical manner.

Gathering data is the research phase of speech preparation. It involves locating, reading, analyzing, and recording the data that supports the central idea. Sources for the information may be the following **(Figure 7.15)**:

- Departmental/organizational or jurisdictional annual reports
- Budget documents
- Response-time reports

- National or regional fire databases
- Community demographics
- Federal/state/provincial/local legal mandates

In all cases, the sources of the information must be recorded in the speech preparation documents. In addition, the accuracy of information must be ensured. Citing an inaccurate source can be destructive to the speech and reputation of the speaker.

Insert the appropriate supporting data (with citations) into the appropriate section of the speech outline. Although citations may not be used during the speech, it is important to have them available if a question concerning the information is raised.

When quoting statistics and testimony, citations must be given in the speech. The supporting data can be incorporated into the body of the speech in a number of ways such as the following:

- *Brief example* — Short statement (perhaps a sentence or two) that illustrates the central idea or one of the main ideas.

- *Hypothetical situation* — Fictitious situation that illustrates a general idea or the results of an action or inaction. Use it very carefully because

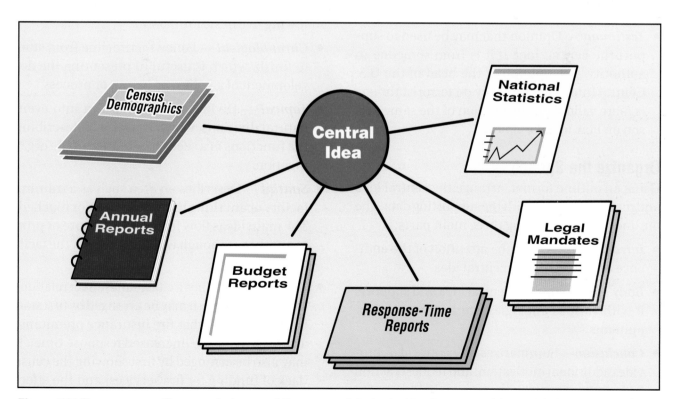

Figure 7.15 The company officer may find some of the sources listed valuable when researching a topic for a presentation.

it is difficult to prove based on data. Indicate that the situation is hypothetical by introducing it with *for instance* or *let us suppose.*

- *Analogy* — Story that compares one situation with another. Use carefully, especially when comparing one group with another, to support an intended outcome. Ensure that the two situations that are being compared are truly alike. The analogy may have been based on only one factor when many others have a greater affect on the outcome.

- *Statistics* — Numbers that summarize data and are used to show trends. Statistics probably provide the bulk of the data that company officers rely on in their oral presentations. Statistics shown with visual aids carry greater importance and are more memorable than those included in the body of the speech (see information box). However, statistics can be used to the benefit of an argument while not accurately illustrating the situation. Consider the example given earlier:

  — If 75 percent of those interviewed supported the sales-tax increase, it sounds very favorable.

  — If only four people were interviewed from a city of 7,500, how valid is the statistic?

- *Testimony* — Opinion that may be used to support the central idea if it is from someone in authority. The opinion of the head of the U.S. Central Intelligence Agency on terrorist threats is more valid than the opinion of the same person on how to bake a pie.

Organize the Speech

Using an outline format, arrange the central idea and main ideas along with the supporting data. The outline has the following three main parts:

- *Introduction* — Gets the attention of the audience and presents the central idea

- *Body* — Develops the central idea and supports it with various analogies, stories, statistics, or opinions

- *Conclusion* — Summarizes the central idea, provides additional motivation, and requests action from the audience (in the case of the persuasive speech)

Statistics Factors

It is possible that no matter how accurate the statistics or how detailed the information, it may be impossible to overcome a preconceived, inaccurate idea held by an audience. Factors to consider when using statistics in oral presentations include the following:

- Keep statistics to a minimum because too many numbers will distract or confuse the audience.

- Use round numbers to make statistics easier to understand, and always preface the number with the words *approximately* or *just over/under.*

- Use graphs and charts to show trends in the statistics **(Figure 7.16)**.

- Present statistics through visual aids such as PowerPoint® presentations, slides, transparencies, or easel pad charts of graphs, tables, or raw numbers.

- Show numbers in relation to other information such as the per capita income of the community or increases in cost per square foot (square meter) when sprinkler systems are required in homes.

The speech can be organized into one of the following five basic formats:

- *Chronological* — Follows a timeline from start to finish, which is useful in presenting the development of a policy, program, or process.

- *Topical* — Divides the central idea into even, natural divisions, which is useful in describing the functions of a section or branch of the organization.

- *Spatial* — Describes an area such as a training facility or anything that can be seen or touched. The main ideas flow from one structure or prop to another as though walking through the facility.

- *Causal* — Describes a cause-and-effect relationship. For example, it may be arranged by first stating the effect (higher fire insurance premiums) and then the cause (increased response time). It may also be arranged by first showing the cause (lack of funding for fire services) and the effect (increased fire loss in the community).

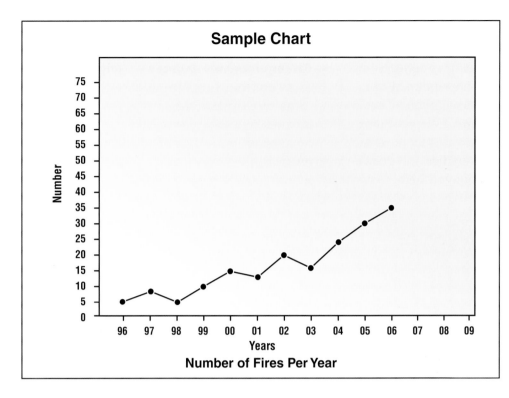

Sample Chart

Number

Years

Number of Fires Per Year

Figure 7.16 Charts can be an effective means for depicting trends based on statistics.

- *Problem/solution* — States a problem followed by the solution (which is used in the persuasive speech). The order may be reversed to emphasize the problem.

Once a format is selected, the material in the speech may be further organized by using one of the following strategies:

- *Primacy* — Place the most important information at the beginning of the body of text, which psychologically tells the listener that this information carries the greatest weight.

- *Recency* — Place the most important information at the end of the body of text. By placing the information at the end, it is the last thing absorbed by members of the audience and remains fresh in their minds.

- *Complexity* — Move from the simple ideas or concepts to the more complex, which is useful when describing a process that requires a basic understanding of theories.

- *Specificity* — Move from general to specific or specific to general, which may be used to relate statistics to individual members of the audience, such as first stating the national debt in dollars and relating it then to the amount that each member of the audience is responsible for.

- *Soft-to-hard evidence* — Move from opinions or inferences to facts and statistics; may take the form of a hypothetical situation that is supported then by specific figures.

Once a strategy has been determined, develop the outline into a form that can be followed in a presentation. Write the specific ideas, facts, and figures that need to be conveyed to the audience. Include transitions from one main idea to the next. Backward and forward transition statements help the flow of the speech by signaling the listener that a new idea is about to be presented.

Do *not* attempt to write the speech in manuscript form unless it is given by reading directly from the page (see Deliver the Speech section). The use of note cards or an outline can help to make the presentation appear more spontaneous and interesting. The use of a PowerPoint® slide show can be advantageous because it allows the speaker to view the outline plus additional notes that the audience cannot see. Remember, though, it is a tool and not a crutch.

Once the speech is completely organized, have someone else in the organization listen to it or read the outline to ensure that it is accurate, logical, and understandable. Make any corrections at this point.

Rehearse the Speech

Just as an athlete practices a specific play before a game, the company officer needs to rehearse a speech before presenting it. The rehearsal may include an audience (such as other staff members) or it can be recorded on videotape. Either of these methods helps the speaker develop better presentation skills by illustrating nonverbal and vocal problems that can easily be changed before the final presentation.

A simple approach is to practice in front of a mirror where the speaker can observe and correct any nonverbal habits that may be distracting for the audience. Practicing the speech will also help to determine the length of the presentation and adjust it according to the allotted time.

As mentioned earlier, public speaking causes the greatest fear in people. Referred to as *speech anxiety*, it manifests itself with an increased breathing rate, a rapid heartbeat, excess perspiration, an upset stomach, and a quivering voice. Rehearsing a speech helps to overcome this anxiety. Other ways of overcoming anxiety include the following:

- Knowing the audience
- Being prepared
- Being organized
- Visualizing success
- Focusing on the message and not the fear
- Acting calm and confident

Deep breathing exercises before presenting the speech can also help relax a nervous speaker. Another reassuring thought is that the company officer (when properly prepared) most likely knows more about the topic than the audience does. In any case, giving a speech is less hazardous than fighting a fire.

Deliver the Speech

Company officers who are not accustomed to speaking before groups may find that membership in organizations like Toastmasters International will provide the opportunity to improve their abilities. Besides the actual delivery of a speech, other delivery issues include nonverbal aspects of the delivery, vocal delivery, and physical appearance of the speaker.

The actual delivery of a speech can take the following four forms:

- *Extemporaneous delivery* — Relying on notes or an outline allows the speaker to speak conversationally. It is the preferred delivery style that works best in the majority of situations. The notes or outline are based on the process that has been outlined previously. This method is taught in most public speaking courses.

- *Memorizing the text* — Unfortunately, this approach takes a great deal of effort and results in a stiff and stilted speech. It is also very easy to lose one's place or omit an important fact or statistic. Memorization may be useful for short presentations like presenting an award, but it should not be used for longer, more important speeches.

- *Impromptu delivery* — When a speaker is unprepared or caught off guard (such as at a press conference), this approach can be used. It requires a great deal of knowledge and the ability to mentally access that knowledge quickly and accurately. A speaker does not need to use this method when there is sufficient time to prepare a speech.

- *Reading the text* — Although used in certain situations, this form is rarely used by company officers in dealing with the public or other fire service personnel. *Disadvantages:*

  — Reading causes the speaker to concentrate on the manuscript and lose eye contact with the audience, placing a barrier between the speaker and the audience.

  — Words lack inflection and become monotonous.

  Exceptions:

  — It may be necessary to read a prepared statement to ensure that the audience gets the exact message and nothing is left to chance.

  — Speeches written for political figures are usually read using a teleprompter to allow the speaker to look at the audience while reading the text. However, this tool is rarely available for company officers.

Nonverbal Delivery

Because the nonverbal message is as important as the verbal message, speakers must be aware of their eye contact, facial expressions, gestures, posture, and poise. Eye contact is the most important of these five elements of nonverbal communication and is essential for all forms of interpersonal and public oral communication. It conveys concern and sincerity and adds to the speaker's credibility.

Descriptions of nonverbal messages are as follows:

- *Eye contact* — Maintaining eye contact with members of the audience communicates sincerity, trust, and credibility and shows that the speaker is concerned about the listeners. When speaking to a large group, consider the following actions:

  — Scan the audience while speaking.

  — Stop and speak directly to various individuals.

  — Look directly at the person who asks a question when answering specific questions.

  — Do *not* look over the audience or stare into space (an action that indicates that the speaker does not need or want contact with the audience).

- *Facial expressions* — Research indicates that facial expressions are culturally universal. They can express each of the six basic emotions (happiness, anger, fear, disgust, surprise, and sadness) in generally the same way. Therefore, facial expressions need to mirror the content of the verbal message that is being delivered, which will then emphasize the message. *Inappropriate facial expressions:*

  — When an opposite verbal message is spoken, it leads to confusion on the part of the audience or (worse) loss of trust in the speaker.

  — For instance, smiling broadly while announcing layoffs or station closings would be extremely inappropriate.

- *Gestures* — Many people *talk* with their hands as they speak with their mouths. However, most people, regardless of ethnic background, emphasize their words with gestures. In public speaking, gestures can be useful and appropriate when not overdone. Practice gestures during the rehearsal of a presentation (**Figure 7.17**). Again, video taping the rehearsal helps a speaker establish the appropriate gestures. *Guidelines:*

- *Appropriate:* Use large broad gestures for a large group, especially if the room is large. Casual, less dramatic movements would be appropriate for a small group.

- *Variety:* Use gestures to enumerate, describe, symbolize, and point. Use both hands, not just one.

- *Consistent:* Make the gestures exciting when the words and vocal tone are exciting. When the tone is subdued, match it with the appropriate gesture.

- *Definite:* Make a gesture look like it was intentional, matching the message. Tentative gestures convey a lack of confidence on the part of the speaker.

- *Natural:* Make gestures flow with the message and make them relaxed rather than rigid. Avoid pounding the fist or slashing the air with the hand.

- *Not too many:* Overusing gestures looks forced and detracts from the intended message.

Figure 7.17 Because gestures can be overused and therefore distracting to the audience, the company officer should practice using them for the greatest effect. *Courtesy of U.S. Federal Emergency Management Agency, Jocelyn Augustino, photographer.*

- **Posture**—Communication studies indicate that a speaker's posture communicates significant information to the audience. One study has indicated that the stance a speaker takes reflects on that person's credibility. Standing erect with the head up helps project the voice, making the speaker easier to understand. The speaker's stance needs to be natural and relaxed based on the circumstances of the speech, environment, and formality or informality of the occasion. *Actions to avoid:*

  — Slouching

  — Shifting from foot to foot

  — Drooping the head

- **Poise**—Poise is the accumulation of all the other nonverbal elements into one image of self-confidence and authority. A discussion of poise is in the Kinesics section of Chapter 6, Interpersonal Communications.

Vocal Delivery

If a message is important enough to warrant a formal speech, then it needs to be interesting, heard, and understood. The voice is the medium for accomplishing these tasks through *vocal delivery:* a matter of timing, variety, and practice.

Listening to famous speeches, watching comedians deliver monologues, and listening to politicians can provide examples of how to use vocal delivery to convey the message to the audience. In some cases, it may be necessary to modify vocal delivery in order to meet the needs and size of an audience.

For example, when speaking through an interpreter, provide periodic breaks in the delivery to allow the interpreter time to insert a translation of what was just said. When speaking to an audience of deaf or hearing-impaired persons with the assistance of a sign-language interpreter, it is not necessary to provide the breaks; however, it is helpful to avoid speaking too rapidly. In both cases, it may be helpful to meet with the interpreters ahead of time to discuss or provide the content of the speech as well as determine what can be done to make their work more effective.

Descriptions of vocal delivery elements are as follows:

- **Hearing** — Speak loud enough to overcome the barriers of external noise and room size. If a sound system is used, test it before the presentation to ensure that the speaker can talk at a normal volume and still be heard. If a sound system is not available, then the speaker must project the voice (directing the words at an intended point in the audience) and speak to the last row in the audience. Projecting is not the same as yelling.

- **Understanding** — Articulate and use accepted pronunciation as follows:

  — *Articulation:* Make the sounds of words clear and distinct. A lack of articulation can result in the audience not understanding some words and misinterpreting the message.

  — *Pronunciation:* Use proper sounds that form specific words. Mispronouncing words may be the result of a regional influence (such as an accent), an ethnic influence, or simply bad habits that have developed over time. Just as people are judged by their appearance, they are also judged and classified by their speech patterns.

- **Interesting** — Use *pitch* (how high or low the voice is) and *inflection* (applying pitch to various words) to maintain the listener's attention by keeping the speech from being monotone and monotonous. The rate or speed at which the speaker talks also adds variety. *Considerations:*

  — Speaking too slowly can make a speech drag and seem boring.

  — Speaking too fast may frustrate listeners who miss vital words or cannot follow words quickly.

  — Using the speed of phrases within the context of the speech adds interest and contrast between the phrases.

  — Using silence, in the form of pauses between phrases, can add suspense and emphasize the previous statement, allowing the listener time to reflect on it.

  — Repeating an important statement can provide the needed emphasis to help listeners remember certain information.

Physical Appearance

It is an accepted belief that people are judged by their appearance. Because most fire and emergency services personnel wear uniforms, the public expectation is that the uniform symbolizes the knowledge and experience of the fire and emergency services. In essence, the uniform adds credibility to the speaker and topic. When a company officer makes a presentation to an audience composed of nondepartmental people, a well-maintained, clean, and pressed dress uniform is an important asset (**Figure 7.18**).

In certain circumstances when a uniform might intimidate the audience or when the topic is not related directly to the department/organization, a dress suit would be more appropriate. In any case, the speaker never dresses more casually than members of the audience.

Evaluate the Speech

Effective speakers usually evaluate their speeches to determine whether the following three essential goals have been met:

- *Speech must be understood by the audience* — It must be clear, concise, logical, and memorable. This goal requires good development and presentation skills.

- *Speech must achieve its intended purpose* — It must inform or motivate the audience to an intended action. Presentation of critical information in a logical sequence will ensure that the purpose is achieved.

- *Speaker's efforts must be ethical* — A speaker must use accurate and appropriate supporting facts and not rely on fallacies. Ethical speakers will state the purpose of the speech in order to not confuse the audience and provide alternative solutions to a problem if more than one is possible.

If one of these goals was not achieved, then the speaker must determine why and correct the problem before giving the speech again. A simple approach to determining the effectiveness of a presentation is the use of audience surveys.

Although not always possible or appropriate, surveys can be used when public education presentations are made or training classes are

Figure 7.18 There will be occasions when presentations must be made while wearing full dress uniforms. Solemn occasions such as funerals or annual fallen firefighter ceremonies as well as retirements and graduations are just some of those events.

presented. Otherwise, the speaker can rely on the comments of members of the audience who can provide an informal view of the effectiveness of the presentation.

Summary

At some point in their careers, company officers will be responsible for making an oral presentation. Formal presentations may take the form of project progress reports to an administrative body, public relations media presentations, training sessions for unit personnel, or public information presentations to members of the public.

To be effective, the company officer must be able to deliver the information so that the audience understands and acts upon the presentation. The success of the presentation depends on the officer's understanding of the types of speeches, the speech presentation process, and the characteristics of an effective speaker. Finally, the company officer must take the time to practice giving speeches through a variety of speaking opportunities.

Written Communications

Chapter Contents

Learning Objectives

1. Match to their definitions terms associated with written communication.

2. Identify parts of an outline.

3. Identify common paragraph transitions.

4. Identify generally accepted writing guidelines.

5. Select facts about writing memos and e-mail messages.

6. Select correct responses about writing letters.

7. Given scenarios, write a letter, memo, and e-mail relating to the fire service.

8. Identify guidelines to follow when writing a press release.

9. Given a scenario, write a news release about a fire and emergency services event.

10. Select facts about various types of reports.

11. Write a report on a specific fire department topic.

12. Select facts about executive summaries, agendas, and minutes.

13. Identify basic information to be included in a policy or procedure.

14. Recall information about requests for proposals (RFPs) and bid specifications.

Job Performance Requirements

This chapter provides information that addresses the following job performance requirements of NFPA 1021, *Standard for Fire Officer Professional Qualifications* (2003):

Chapter 8
Written Communications

As part of their assigned duties, company officers must prepare written communications including reports (status, postincident, etc.), requests for proposals (RFPs), bid specifications, executive summaries, and press releases as well as letters, memorandums (memos), electronic mail (e-mail) messages, meeting agendas, minutes, policies, and procedures. Written communications must be accurate, concise, and professional in appearance.

Based on the appearance and quality of the document, a reader will gain an impression of the ability and credibility of the company officer and the organization. While some officers may be fortunate enough to have clerical staff to assist with the development and writing of a final document, most company officers have to research, draft, finalize, and edit each document that carries their signature.

Company officers should consider enrolling in technical or business writing courses at their local college or vocational school to assist in mastering the skills necessary to be an effective writer. The information provided in this chapter can form a foundation for those courses of study and give an officer a set of basic tools to use in the interim.

Documents are written for specific purposes: to educate, persuade, inform, or enlighten. The ability to write effectively helps to ensure that the intended purpose is attained. Effective writing is a skill that is learned and maintained through continual practice.

This chapter describes the writing process, which includes organizing the document and writing it by applying accepted guidelines to make it interesting and understandable. The types of documents discussed include memos and e-mail messages, letters, press releases, reports, executive summaries, agendas, minutes, policies and procedures, and RFPs and bid specifications.

Document Organization

The first step in writing any document is to determine the audience, scope, and purpose. Most company officers are familiar with the terms *scope* and *purpose* because they are found in NFPA standards and IFSTA manuals; they are the foundations for those documents. Using scope and purpose statements and an audience definition, the basic organization of the document is then outlined.

Audience, Scope, and Purpose

The *audience* may be an individual (such as a supervisor or subordinate), internal group (such as staff members or labor representatives), or external audience (such as the municipal governing body or the readership of a national trade journal). Knowing the audience helps to keep the writer (and the document) audience-focused. An audience-focused document is written to the needs, concerns, and levels of understanding of the readers (**Figure 8.1, p. 168**).

The *scope* of the document is the subject or topic and how broad or narrow the coverage of it is. The topic may be an upcoming meeting or an article on a recent emergency incident. The scope is stated in the thesis statement of the document. As mentioned earlier, the thesis statement is similar to the central idea of a speech.

Figure 8.1 When writing any document, the company officer should focus on the audience or recipient of the document (in this case a chief officer). Knowing the audience will influence the tone, detail, and style used in the document.

The *purpose* is why the document is being written. It establishes what the writer wants to accomplish such as informing the audience of an event or describing a new method or procedure.

Outline

Once the audience, scope, and purpose have been determined, the writer then creates the basic organization of the document. The briefest of outlines includes the following parts (**Figure 8.2**):

- *Introduction* — Tells the reader what the topic of the document is through the thesis statement. The main points that support the topic may also be included. The introduction gets the reader's attention, provides motivation, and focuses the reader on the topic, which can be accomplished by doing the following:

  — State a fact or cite an example.

  — Raise a question.

  — Note a common misconception.

  — Make a bold assertion or statement of opinion.

- *Body* — Includes the information, data, and supporting material for the topic. The body is divided into subtopics or main points that support the topic. Each subtopic is supported by facts, data, or examples.

- *Conclusion* — Summarizes the main points of the document and may include a call to action to motivate the reader. The conclusion brings the document to finality and closure. Do *not* introduce new material in the conclusion of the document because it would leave questions unanswered.

The application of this format is similar to the standard training model used by the fire and emergency services, the military, and most educational organizations. This model is referred to as *this is what I am going to tell you* (introduction), *this is what I am telling you* (body), and *this is what I just told you* (conclusion). It allows the reader to fully understand the subject of the document.

This basic outline can be expanded then to include additional main points that support the topic sentence in the introduction. Smooth transitions should be used to tie the three parts of the document together, leading the reader from the introduction into the body and then to the conclusion. See Paragraph Transitions section.

Outlining the document helps the writer establish the logical flow of the material, placing the strongest points at the beginning and then supporting each point with additional data. Outlines must be balanced with a minimum of two points under each heading. If there is only one point, it becomes part of the heading and is not included as a separate entry. Balance also applies to the use of bullets, numbers, or letters (if there is no *2*, then there is no *1*).

Whenever possible, headings need to be expressed in parallel form; that is, nouns need to be made parallel with nouns, verb forms with verb forms, adjectives with adjectives, and so on. Although parallel structure is desired, logical and clear writing should not be sacrificed simply to maintain parallelism. Reasonableness and flexibility of form is preferred to rigidity.

Document Writing Guidelines

Once the outline is developed, the text is created within the framework of the outline. The text is divided into paragraphs that are composed of sentences. *Paragraphs* are visual reference points that indicate a subdivision of the topic for the reader. Just as the introduction contains the thesis

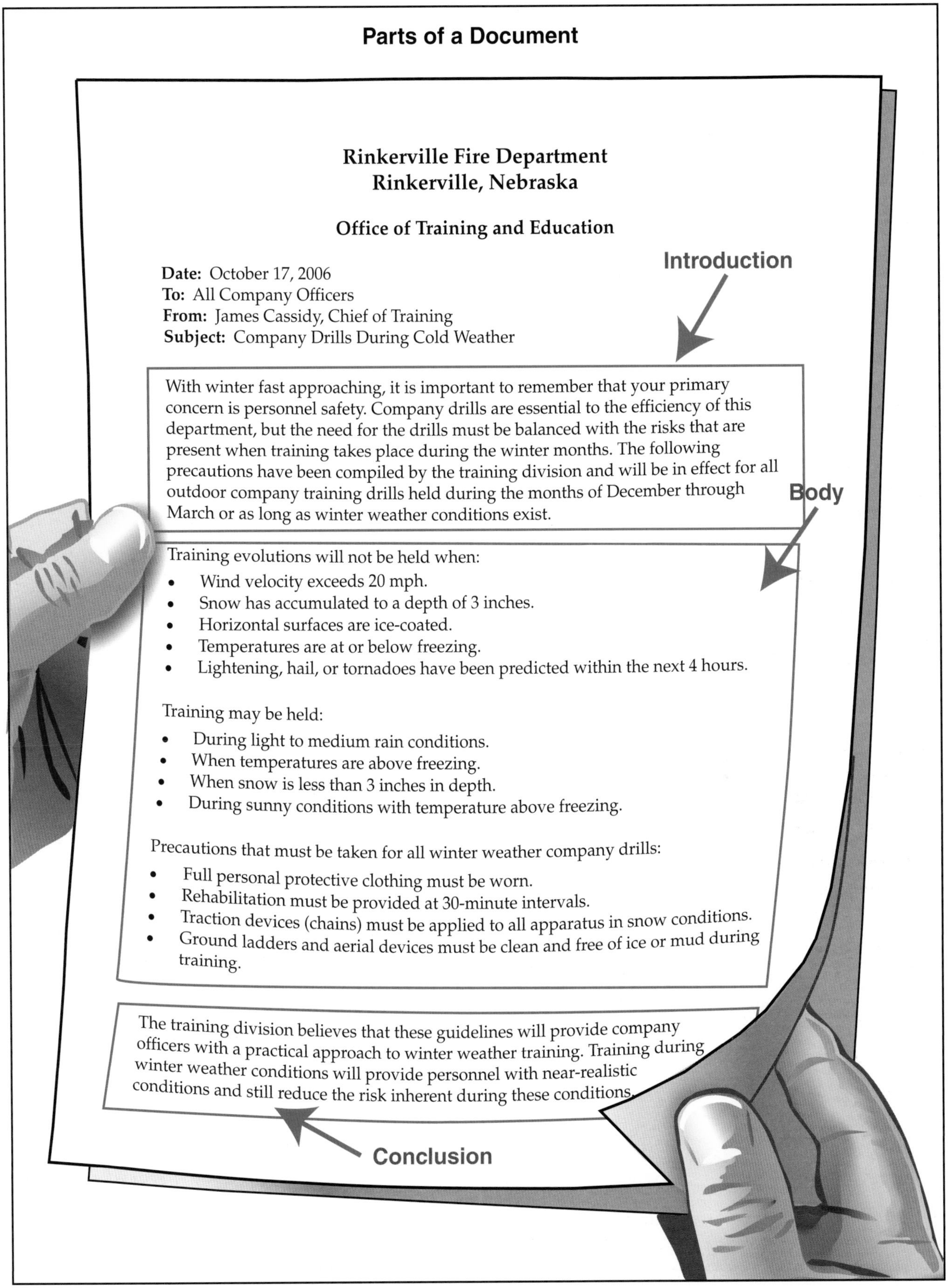

Parts of a Document

Rinkerville Fire Department
Rinkerville, Nebraska

Office of Training and Education

Introduction

Date: October 17, 2006
To: All Company Officers
From: James Cassidy, Chief of Training
Subject: Company Drills During Cold Weather

With winter fast approaching, it is important to remember that your primary concern is personnel safety. Company drills are essential to the efficiency of this department, but the need for the drills must be balanced with the risks that are present when training takes place during the winter months. The following precautions have been compiled by the training division and will be in effect for all outdoor company training drills held during the months of December through March or as long as winter weather conditions exist.

Body

Training evolutions will not be held when:
- Wind velocity exceeds 20 mph.
- Snow has accumulated to a depth of 3 inches.
- Horizontal surfaces are ice-coated.
- Temperatures are at or below freezing.
- Lightening, hail, or tornadoes have been predicted within the next 4 hours.

Training may be held:
- During light to medium rain conditions.
- When temperatures are above freezing.
- When snow is less than 3 inches in depth.
- During sunny conditions with temperature above freezing.

Precautions that must be taken for all winter weather company drills:
- Full personal protective clothing must be worn.
- Rehabilitation must be provided at 30-minute intervals.
- Traction devices (chains) must be applied to all apparatus in snow conditions.
- Ground ladders and aerial devices must be clean and free of ice or mud during training.

The training division believes that these guidelines will provide company officers with a practical approach to winter weather training. Training during winter weather conditions will provide personnel with near-realistic conditions and still reduce the risk inherent during these conditions.

Conclusion

Figure 8.2 The basic outline for most documents contains three parts: Introduction, Body, and Conclusion.

statement, each paragraph needs to contain a topic sentence that announces and controls the content of the paragraph. For variety, the topic sentence may occur at the beginning, in the middle, or at the end of a paragraph.

The number of paragraphs depends on the number of subdivisions in the outline. There is no rule for the number or length of paragraphs in a document. However, paragraphs that are too long tend to slow the reader, while those that are too short create an impression of a choppy and disjointed document. The average paragraph is 75 to 125 words long, which is long enough for a topic sentence and four or five supporting sentences.

Tying paragraphs together with transitional ideas helps to maintain the flow and rhythm of a document. In addition to transitions, the writer needs to consider general text development guidelines that are used by most good writers.

Paragraph Transitions

Transitional words usually come at the end of one paragraph and then at the beginning of the next paragraph **(Figure 8.3)**. Some common transitions used at the end of a paragraph to indicate summation include the following (grouped by similarity):

Figure 8.3 Transitions are words that provide a bridge or connection between each paragraph in a document.

- *After all*, *all in all*, and *all things considered*
- *Briefly* and *by and large*
- *Finally*
- *In any case*, *in any event*, *in brief*, *in conclusion*, *in short*, *in summary*, *in the final analysis*, and *in the long run*
- *On balance* and *on the whole*
- *To sum up* and *to summarize*

Transitions that may be used at the start of a paragraph can be categorized by the comparison or relationship that they are intended to indicate. Some of them include the following:

- ***Show contrast or qualification*** — Examples: *on the contrary, however, in contrast, still, yet, contrarily, notwithstanding, but, nevertheless, in spite of, on one hand, on the other hand, rather, or, nor, conversely, at the same time,* and *while this may be true*

- ***Indicate continuity*** — Examples: *besides, furthermore, in other words, next, similarly, at first, first of all, to begin with, in the first place, at the same time, for now, for the time being, the next step, in time, in turn, later on, meanwhile, then, soon, in the meantime, later, while, earlier, simultaneously,* and *afterward*

- ***Show cause and effect*** — Examples: *thus, consequently, as a result, for this reason, so that, with the result that, hence, accordingly, therefore, so, because, since, due to, in other words,* and *then*

- ***Indicate exemplification*** — Examples: *for example, for instance, in fact, to illustrate, namely, in other words, in particular, specifically,* and *such as*

Text Development

Some generally accepted writing guidelines that assist in the development of the text are as follows:

- ***Be clear*** — Write what is meant and mean what is written. Clarity is essential in all forms of communication. Do not use *doublespeak* — a form of camouflage — to hide the real message.

- ***Get to the point*** — State the topic of the document quickly. Most readers do not want to wade through a great deal of information before they know why they are reading the document.

- **Use a minimum of words to convey the message** — Eliminate superfluous details or wordiness. A concise document that uses the least number of words gets more attention than one that is filled with unnecessary words.

- **Write in a conversational tone** — Use words, terms, and phrases that the audience is familiar with and understands. Do not use slang or colloquial expressions.

- **Use a friendly and positive tone** — Gain support for the topic of the message.

- **Avoid archaic language** — Use words, terms, and phrases that are current to the message and audience.

- **Avoid jargon** — Tailor the words to the audience, which is especially important when writing to an audience that is unfamiliar with departmental or organizational terminology.

- **Avoid long sentences and the use of numerous commas within sentences** — Divide long sentences into shorter ones. Average sentences are usually 17 words in length.

- **Write in an active voice** — Make the document come *alive*. A phrase such as *It has been decided to* leaves the reader wondering who made the decision. It also hides the responsibility for the decision, which is the same as removing the actors from a play. *Better choice:*
  - Have the subject of the sentence perform the action.
  - For example, the sentence could read as follows: *The ladder captain and I plan to . . . .*

- **Use parallel structure** — Use the same pattern of words to show that two or more ideas have the same level of importance, which can occur at the word, phrase, or clause level. Be consistent in the wording of documents. The use of ideas of equal weight or value creates balance and rhythm that aid in delivering the meaning of the message. The usual way to join parallel structures is with the use of coordinating conjunctions such as *and* or *or.*

- **Always proofread a document before finalizing it** — Never send a letter, memo, or report immediately after writing it. Have someone else proofread it if possible. It is even advisable

Figure 8.4 Letters, memos, e-mails, and reports reflect on the credibility of the writer and the organization. The company officer should always take time to proofread and correct all documents before they are published.

to set the document aside and read it the next day. Use of the spell-check and grammar-correction tools in word-processing programs is highly recommended; however, they do not take the place of proofreading (**Figure 8.4**). *Methods:*
- Print the document and read it.
- Read the document backwards, although this method can be difficult for someone who is not experienced with it.

- **Use bullets, numbers, or other indicators for key points** — Call attention to key points and enable the reader to focus on them. These indicators are accepted methods for emphasizing key points or lists within a document. The information that is emphasized needs to be parallel such as each point starting with an active verb like *develop, demonstrate, evaluate,* etc.

- **Use appendices for additional information** — Place documentation, tables, graphs, forms, examples, and methodology in appendices. This placement helps to reduce clutter that may occur in technical reports.

- **Retain a copy of the written document** — Keep a copy of the memo, letter, report, or other document in electronic form or hard copy in a filing cabinet (or both). In either case, organize files to permit quick retrieval of the document.

Specific Document Types

Generally, the document organization and writing guidelines mentioned earlier can be applied to all memos and e-mail messages, letters, press releases, reports, and executive summaries. Agendas and minutes of meetings take a slightly different form because they use a chronological format to either schedule or report the results of a meeting.

Procedures, policies, and RFPs or bid specifications require a more formal style usually dictated by the authority having jurisdiction. If the jurisdiction does not have a formal style for these documents, model forms may be found in technical writing manuals, found on the Internet, or acquired from other organizations. Manufacturers usually supply model bid specifications formats upon request.

Memos and E-mail Messages

In private industry, a memo is a quick and relatively simple way of transmitting a message within an organization. It has the benefit of being brief and providing a written document that describes *what, where, when, who, why,* and sometimes *how.*

Memos are valuable because they cause the writer to commit to a certain course of action. They also provide a chain of communication and evidence of action on a specific topic.

Before all levels of supervisors and managers began using computers, memos were handwritten notes created by the manager or typed documents created by the secretarial staff at the direction of the manager. Today, memos are generally written by the manager, which saves time and creates direct communication between the writer and audience.

It is an odd phenomenon, but newly appointed or promoted managers tend to write more memos and e-mail messages (commonly referred to as *e-mails*) than necessary. Perhaps it is to acknowledge their added authority and responsibility or just establish the presence of new managers in the structure. Whatever the case, newly promoted company officers need to take a course in business communication or attend a workshop on memo or e-mail writing to assist in the transition from receiver of memos to creator of memos.

Memos are generally sent by electronic means rather than hard-copy documents in interoffice mail, which speeds the communication process still further. Therefore, the methods for writing memos and e-mails are generally the same (**Figure 8.5**). However, it is important for an organization to have an e-mail policy that includes information on proper e-mail etiquette.

It is easy to circumvent the chain of command using the e-mail system. Company officers must remember to stay within the organization's chain of command when sending electronic communications.

The e-mail policy needs to become part of the organization's policy and procedures manual and include enforcement, training, and monitoring elements. Company officers must be familiar with the policy and adhere to it. An e-mail policy is important for an organization for the following three reasons:

- *Professionalism* — Proper creation and use of e-mails help to convey professional images of departments or organizations.

- *Efficiency* — E-mails (like memos that get to the point) provide the necessary information and do not require further explanation, thus adding to the efficiency of the organization.

- *Liability protection* — An e-mail policy that explains content, use, and distribution guidelines can prevent legal actions based on the perceptions of a hostile workplace or libelous or slanderous statements.

Figure 8.5 Electronic correspondence or e-mails have become the primary means of written communication in many organizations.

A memo or an e-mail has one purpose: to accomplish a task. Therefore, it needs to be short and to the point. If an e-mail is too lengthy or wordy, the message may be ignored, particularly if a person receives a lot of e-mails. Memos and e-mails can follow standard formats, but it is important to remember their value and be aware of several cautions about their contents. The majority of memos or e-mails can be written to give the following six pieces of information:

- *Who* — Assign responsibility for the task or action. This item is sometimes implied in the address line that states *To.*

- *What* — Tell the task or action that is expected or has been accomplished.

- *When* — Tell the date and time the action is expected to take place. It may also name a deadline for the action.

- *Where* — Tell the location of the task or action. This item may not always be necessary.

- *Why* — Explain the reason for the action.

- *How* — Detail the steps to be followed in implementing the task or action. This item may or may not be necessary, depending on the topic of the memo.

Parts of a Memo or E-mail: Example

A meeting *(what)* of the Apparatus Committee *(who)* will be held in the conference room at the Fire Department Headquarters *(where)*. The meeting will begin promptly at 9 a.m. and last 3 hours *(when)*. The purpose of the meeting is to review specifications for the new ladder apparatus included in this year's capital budget *(why)*. The proposed specifications will be compared to the appropriate NFPA standards, department needs analysis, and operational procedures *(how)*.

General Formats

Because of the importance of memos in the world of business, preprinted forms have been created that permit the writer to simply fill in the blanks. These forms have evolved into computer-generated templates. The writer simply inserts the correct information into the form, saves the finished product under the appropriate name, and mails it electronically to a person or an audience or prints it for distribution.

Templates include the company, organization, or section name at the top, space for the date the memo is created, space for the name(s) of the recipient(s), space for the name of the writer, and space for the subject of the memo. Two of these spaces fulfill the part of the memo referred to earlier as *who;* that is, the person(s) to whom the memo is intended and the writer of the memo **(Figure 8.6, p. 174)**.

Value

The value of the memo or e-mail exceeds the actual message because it also tells about the ability of the writer. Therefore, it is important to ensure that the memo or e-mail carry a strong and professional image of the writer. The writer needs to proofread the memo or e-mail before issuing it. When proofreading, look for the following items:

- *Correct spelling* — The spell-check function of most word-processing programs can be very valuable, but it can also miss errors that involve the use of words like *to, two,* and *too* or *do, dew,* and *due.*

- *Correct punctuation* — Missing commas and the misuse of semicolons, colons, or other punctuation marks may not be obvious to the writer but may appear as glaring errors to the receiver.

- *Correct grammar* — Grammar may be the most difficult item to correct due to education, background, or regional usage. Most modern word-processing programs have a grammar function as part of the spell-check function. If the writer has access to a grammar text or a reference handbook, it is advisable to check any phrases that appear to be questionable.

- *Neatness* — The appearance of the finished printed document is similar to the physical appearance of a speaker: It projects self-respect, professionalism, and personal image (or the lack thereof).

- *Consistent format* — A consistent and attractive format reflects well on the writer and the organization.

Rinkerville Fire Department

311 South High Street
Rinkerville, Ohio
73313-9909

Phone: 555-555-3000
Fax: 555-555-3001
E-mail: ChiefFD@rinkerville.oh.us

Memorandum

Date:

To:

From:

Subject:

Rinkerville Fire
Department
Established 1935

Figures 8.6 A simple template or format can be used for both memos and e-mails. The template should provide a space for the name of the recipient, writer, topic, date, names of other interested parties, and the text of the message.

- *Concise/accurate content* — The body of the memo or e-mail (the reason it was written) needs to be clear, concise, logically arranged, and to the point. Information included must be accurate and worth putting into written form.

Cautions About Contents

While memos and e-mails are important to internal communication, they can also be a source of embarrassment and legal difficulties. Consider the following cautions about their contents:

- *Never put into writing anything that cannot be made public* — Open meeting laws and public records laws make all documents available to the media, government agencies, and the public. Some specific exceptions to this rule include certain communications with legal counsels, certain personnel documents, and personal medical records.

- *Do not use memos or e-mails for criticisms, reprimands, or personal communications that are best communicated in person* — *Never* hide behind memos or e-mails to deliver bad news. Memos or e-mails may be appropriate methods for warnings regarding inappropriate behaviors because they provide written documented proof that a supervisor warned an employee.

- *Never use sexist, racist, or inappropriate language in memos or e-mails* — This language represents unprofessional conduct and can result in legal action and embarrassment for the department or organization and the individual.

- *Delegate memo or e-mail writing to a member of the organization who can effectively write them if the company officer cannot* — Writing correct memos or e-mails may be a personal weakness. Continue the practice of delegating

E-mail Tips

- Be concise and to the point.
- Answer a question fully when responding.
- Always use proper spelling, grammar, and punctuation.
- Make the message personal.
- Use templates for frequently used responses to save time.
- Answer all e-mails (like phone calls) quickly.
- Do *not* attach unnecessary files.
- Always use proper structure and format.
- Avoid the use of all capital letters, which indicates the writer is angry (all capitals symbolize yelling).
- Read the message before it is sent to ensure that it is complete and correct.
- Do *not* use the *reply-to-all* function if only one person is the intended recipient.
- Avoid abbreviations and emoticons (symbolic pictures made from keyboard characters) because they are not professional.
- Be careful to format the message so that it is easily readable.

- Avoid the use of colors or fonts that make the message difficult to read.
- Do *not* create or forward chain letters.
- Do *not* request delivery and read receipts unless it is absolutely necessary.
- Do *not* ask to recall a message.
- Do *not* copy and send a message or attachment without permission.
- Do *not* discuss confidential information.
- Write in the active voice rather than the passive.
- Use a meaningful subject line to indicate the contents to the reader.
- Stay with one general subject per message.
- Use short sentences.
- *Never* send or forward messages containing libelous, slanderous, defamatory, offensive, racist, sexist, or obscene comments or statements.
- *Never* reply to or forward spam (unsolicited e-mail).
- Do *not* use a signatory line at the end of a memo; it is not necessary.
- Keep records of communications by saving e-mails in both electronic (compact disc–read-only memory [CD-ROM] or diskette) and hardcopy forms.

someone else until further training for the company officer on writing memos and e-mails is completed.

- **Have memos and e-mails proofread** — This practice ensures greater accuracy of the material.

- **Remember that e-mails cannot be withdrawn once they are sent and will exist forever** — Technology exists that can recover material from physically destroyed computer hard drives and reformatted disks. Therefore, nothing should be put into e-mails that the writer does not want made public at some time in the future. In legal cases, subpoenaed e-mail has been a source of embarrassment and even dismissal.

Letters

While memos and e-mails are for internal use, letters are generally used with persons, groups, and agencies outside the organization. Letters are longer, more formal, and tend to represent the entire organization rather than a specific branch or section. The contents of letters may be similar to memos and e-mails or include information that is normally found in a report.

Because the letter is representative of the entire organization, it is essential that it be professional and flawless. Letters are official documents and require the attention that a report or executive summary gets. Recommended methods for ensuring that the letter properly reflects the image of the organization are as follows:

- Proofreading the letter

- Reviewing the letter for accuracy in the content

- Having the letter approved by a superior when necessary

When writing any document, even those with sensitive information intended for only a limited audience, always assume that the letter will become public at some point. Therefore, never write anything that will be embarrassing to the organization. Letters, although written by individuals, reflect the image of the organization.

Most organizations (private or public) provide some form of official stationery for the purpose of writing letters. Use computer word-processing programs to customize letter templates to fit the letterhead or official stationery. Letters may then be printed directly onto the stationery or onto a separate page that is then copied onto the letterhead.

Various types of letters may be required by the organization, and most have an accepted format. A number of general considerations apply to letters to ensure that they reflect the proper image.

Comparing the Memo or E-mail and Letter

Memo or E-mail	Letter
Brief	Long
Internal Audience	External Audience
Informal	Formal
Represents Subunits	Represents the Total Organization

Accepted Format

The physical arrangement of the elements of a letter depends on the organization's letterhead stationery and the policy or procedure to which the organization adheres. The accepted format for most business letters consists of the following parts (**Figure 8.7**):

- **Heading** — Consists of the company letterhead or return address, and may include the filing or reference number of the document.

- **Opening** — Includes the date, address block of the recipient, attention line, and salutation.

- **Body** — Contains the message; it is further divided into the following parts that may be contained in one or more paragraphs:

  — *Introduction*: Tell the reader the purpose of the letter; be clear, direct, and specific in stating it. Use the document writing guidelines mentioned earlier.

  — *Body*: Give the supporting documentation for the subject, including such information as what is expected of the reader, what the expected outcome will be, how the outcome will affect the reader, why the subject is important, and basic facts that support the

Parts of a Letter

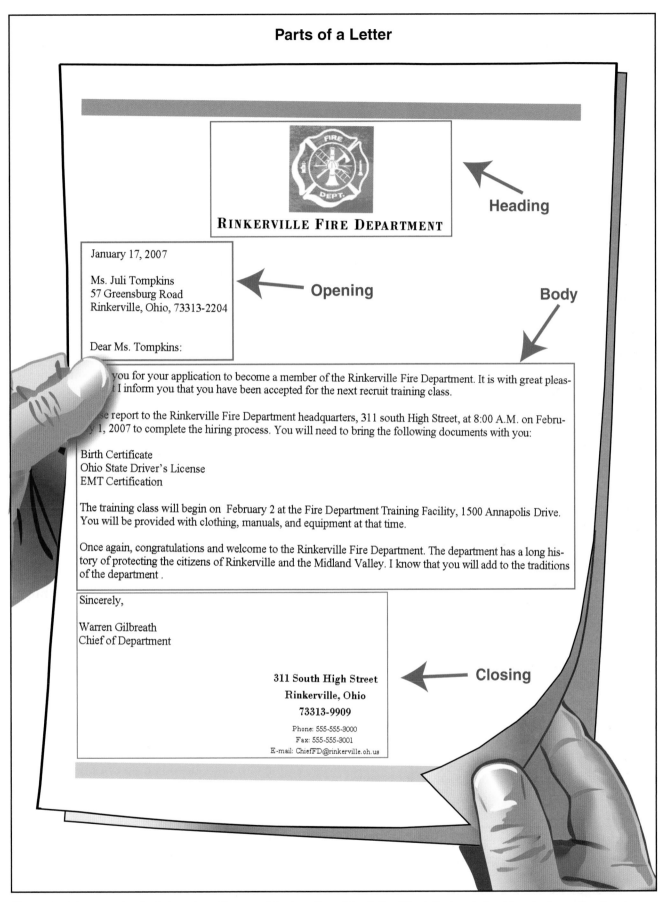

Figure 8.7 The organization's letterhead is part of the heading of the letter. The letterhead should project a professional image of the organization.

subject. This information varies depending on the letter's purpose. Attachments may also be included with the letter and referred to in the body of the letter. Attachments usually include:

○ Brochures

○ Tables, graphs, or photographs

○ Maps or diagrams

○ Detailed technical information that is too extensive for the letter itself

— *Conclusion:* Summarize the letter simply; it may call for a specific action on the part of the reader. The conclusion needs to be brief and to the point like the introduction.

- *Closing* — Contains the complimentary closing and the writer's signature, name, and title (if appropriate, include contact information: phone numbers, fax number, pager number, etc.); may include the filing or reference information if it is not contained in the heading. Postscripts, usually afterthoughts or personal notes, may also be included in the closing.

Types

A company officer will be required to write a variety of letter types as part of the position or function. A few that may be required are listed as follows:

- *Problem* — States either a problem and requests a solution or solves a problem from the reader by suggesting a solution.

- *Denial* — Gives basically a rejection notice; may be sent to individuals who have applied for a job or vendors who have not received a contract or bid award.

- *Customers* — Gives written information for individuals or organizations to which the department or organization provides a service such as plans reviews, permits, or inspections.

- *Promotion* — Promotes the organization; generally, a sales letter that states the positive features of the organization.

- *Praise and evaluation* — Congratulates the reader or provides an evaluation of the reader's work or proposal.

- *Persuasion* — Convinces the reader to follow some desired course of action.

- *Thank you* — Acknowledges the gratitude that the individual or organization has for assistance or courtesy on the part of another person or organization.

- *Form* — Fulfills a specific function based on a standardized format and is created in advance. The subject may be any of the topics mentioned in this list; however, form letters must be personalized to have impact and retain a positive image of the organization in the mind of the reader.

General Considerations

Regardless of the type of letter, the following general considerations should be taken into account:

- *Consider the tone of the letter* — Convey emotion to the reader in keeping with the message. However, *never* write an angry or critical letter because anger causes the reader to become defensive, block out the message, and respond in kind.

- *Be sincere in the message* — Establish and support the credibility of the writer and the organization. Do *not* make claims that cannot or will not be accomplished.

- *Make the letter reader-centered (audience-focused)* — Make it clear and easy to read. Get to the point quickly and do *not* waste the reader's time.

- *Express praise easily and always say "please" and "thank you"* — Strengthen relationships between the writer, organization, and the reader (common courtesy).

- *Admit mistakes and take responsibility* — Admit that an error has been made and then explain how the mistake will be corrected to the reader's satisfaction. Taking responsibility is the most ethical approach that an individual or organization can take; however, do not be overly self-deprecating (that is, do not make comments that create an image of consistent and continuing mistakes).

- *Make the letter personal when possible* — Use personal pronouns like *I, you,* and *us* rather than impersonal words like *the writer* or *the company.*

Press Releases

Fire and emergency services organizations that do not have a full-time public information officer (PIO) may assign company officers the task of preparing press or news releases **(Figure 8.8)**. However, the media usually will not print a prepared statement verbatim (word for word). They may use a few direct quotes, but they will edit the release and make it fit their particular editorial style. In this editorial process, the information in the original release may be distorted.

In most cases, reporters prefer to gather facts relating to the incident and write the story themselves. When supplying the facts relating to an incident, company officers are in fact being interviewed, and they should use the guidelines provided in the Public Information Speeches section of Chapter 7, Oral Communications.

If a reporter asks for a prepared press release on a particular event or topic, it can be submitted in outline form — leaving it to the reporter to fill in details — or it can be submitted in narrative form as though it were a script. Regardless of which form is used, the content should be limited to the facts of the event or topic and should be as simple and straightforward as possible.

In preparing a press release, use the following guidelines:

- Summarize the information in the first sentence by answering the questions *who, what, when, where,* and *why*. Information does not necessarily have to be in that order.

- Use the inverted pyramid style of organization by putting the most important facts first and the least important ones last.

- Limit sentence length to no more than 20 words.

- Write no more than four or five lines per paragraph; one-sentence paragraphs are acceptable.

- Use active voice (*Fire Chief Jones announced . . . .* instead of *It was announced by Fire Chief Jones . . . .*).

- Write clearly and concisely; avoid flowery language and technical terms or jargon (use *hazardous materials* instead of *haz mat* and *National Fire Protection Association* instead of *NFPA*).

- Be sure that all direct quotes and paraphrased statements are properly attributed.

Credibility of a press release or any other document can be lessened by errors such as poor grammar, incorrect spelling, and wandering or random

Figure 8.8 A press release is used to provide the news media with an accurate and timely notice of upcoming events of interest to the public.

thoughts. To prevent these errors, a company officer can perform the following actions:

- Proofread the document and then proofread it a second time.
- Have someone else proofread the document if there is time.
- Include any photo opportunities there might be and when they will occur.
- Include a telephone number where a reporter can call and ask additional questions.
- Keep press releases short, concise (no more than two pages in length), and easy to read.
- Provide information to the organization's PIO to write press releases when the company officer is not responsible for writing them.
- Check the organization's standard operating procedure/standard operating guideline (SOP/SOG) for press release format and release criteria.

For more information on the preparation of press and news releases, see the IFSTA **Fire and Life Safety Educator** and the **Public Information Officer** manuals. Besides these valuable resources, the company officer should also review Chapter 7, Oral Communications, and textbooks on speech communication.

Reports

Besides memos and e-mails, reports constitute the bulk of the writing produced by most company officers. Some reports are simply forms that are completed with specific information concerning an incident or event. Other reports are more like essays, written in narrative, paragraph form and requiring greater thought and organization than form reports.

Form-Based

Most company officers are responsible for the completion of form-based reports on a daily basis **(Figure 8.9)**. The reports may consist of incident reports, injury reports, fire investigation reports, training reports, internal or external inspection reports, or attendance reports. Recorded on computers or hard-copy forms, the officer is required to place specific information into spaces or fields.

Form reports require certain writing skills that may be taken for granted. Some of these skills are as follows:

- *Legibility*— Text must be printed or typed rather than in script.
- *Accuracy* — Times, addresses, names, quantities, and events must be correct.
- *Completeness*— All available information must be included.
- *Objectivity* — Text must express facts and not opinions; it cannot be subjective.

All form reports must be considered legal documents that may be needed in a court of law. Therefore, the writer needs to retain a copy of the report and any other notes made at the time of the incident. Personal notes may prove beneficial if the writer is called to testify. Remember that personal notes can be subpoenaed if used in court.

Narrative

A narrative report may be the result of a form report or it may be generated as part of a project or analysis. Topics may include staff reports, technical reports, detailed incident reports, resource allocation analyses, or business, master, strategic, or work plans. Narrative reports are written in essay form and are similar to the oral presentations described in Chapter 7, Oral Communications.

The first step in preparing a narrative report is to determine the purpose of the report, which is usually the result of a request from a superior officer, the local authority, or a state/provincial or national authority. Therefore, the purpose may be to supply information that is required by a specific time.

In some cases, the report is required on a set time schedule such as annually or semiannually. In other cases, the company officer may decide to provide a report that informs the audience of progress on a project or proposed project.

In any event, the writer must decide who the intended audience will be. Knowing the audience determines the amount of detail used, format, and tone of the report. An annual report to the local authority will be formal with details of costs, services, and needs. A brief project update to the administrative staff will be short and informal

A | FDID ☆ | State ☆ | MM DD YYYY Incident Date ☆ | Station | Incident Number ☆ | Exposure ☆ | ☐ Delete ☐ Change ☐ No Activity | **NFIRS–1 Basic**

B Location Type ☆

☐ Check this box to indicate that the address for this incident is provided on the Wildland Fire Module in Section B, "Alternative Location Specification." Use only for wildland fires.

Census Tract ⌷⌷⌷⌷-⌷⌷

☐ Street address
☐ Intersection
☐ In front of
☐ Rear of
☐ Adjacent to
☐ Directions
☐ US National Grid

Number/Milepost | Prefix | Street or Highway | Street Type | Suffix

Apt./Suite/Room | City | State | ZIP Code

Cross Street, Directions or National Grid, as applicable

C Incident Type ☆
Incident Type

D Aid Given or Received ☆ ☐ None

1 ☐ Mutual aid received
2 ☐ Auto. aid received
3 ☐ Mutual aid given
4 ☐ Auto. aid given
5 ☐ Other aid given

Their FDID | Their State
Their Incident Number

E₁ Dates and Times   Midnight is 0000

Check boxes if dates are the same as Alarm Date.

	Month	Day	Year	Hour	Min
Alarm ☆					

ALARM always required

☐ Arrival ☆

ARRIVAL required, unless canceled or did not arrive

☐ Controlled

CONTROLLED optional, except for wildland fires

☐ Last Unit Cleared

LAST UNIT CLEARED, required except for wildland fires

E₂ Shifts and Alarms
Local Option

Shift or Platoon | Alarms | District

E₃ Special Studies
Local Option

Special Study ID# | Special Study Value

F Actions Taken ☆

Primary Action Taken (1)

Additional Action Taken (2)

Additional Action Taken (3)

G₁ Resources ☆

☐ Check this box and skip this block if an Apparatus or Personnel Module is used.

	Apparatus	Personnel
Suppression		
EMS		
Other		

☐ Check box if resource counts include aid received resources.

G₂ Estimated Dollar Losses and Values

LOSSES: Required for all fires if known. Optional for non-fires.   None

Property $ ⌷⌷⌷,⌷⌷⌷,⌷⌷⌷ ☐
Contents $ ⌷⌷⌷,⌷⌷⌷,⌷⌷⌷ ☐

PRE-INCIDENT VALUE: Optional

Property $ ⌷⌷⌷,⌷⌷⌷,⌷⌷⌷ ☐
Contents $ ⌷⌷⌷,⌷⌷⌷,⌷⌷⌷ ☐

Completed Modules
☐ Fire–2
☐ Structure Fire–3
☐ Civilian Fire Cas.–4
☐ Fire Service Cas.–5
☐ EMS–6
☐ HazMat–7
☐ Wildland Fire–8
☐ Apparatus–9
☐ Personnel–10
☐ Arson–11

H₁ ☆ Casualties ☐ None

	Deaths	Injuries
Fire Service		
Civilian		

H₂ Detector
Required for confined fires.

1 ☐ Detector alerted occupants
2 ☐ Detector did not alert them
U ☐ Unknown

H₃ Hazardous Materials Release ☐ None

1 ☐ **Natural gas:** slow leak, no evacuation or HazMat actions
2 ☐ **Propane gas:** <21-lb tank (as in home BBQ grill)
3 ☐ **Gasoline:** vehicle fuel tank or portable container
4 ☐ **Kerosene:** fuel burning equipment or portable storage
5 ☐ **Diesel fuel/fuel oil:** vehicle fuel tank or portable storage
6 ☐ **Household solvents:** home/office spill, cleanup only
7 ☐ **Motor oil:** from engine or portable container
8 ☐ **Paint:** from paint cans totaling <55 gallons
0 ☐ **Other:** special HazMat actions required or spill > 55 gal (Please complete the HazMat form.)

I Mixed Use Property ☐ Not mixed

10 ☐ Assembly use
20 ☐ Education use
33 ☐ Medical use
40 ☐ Residential use
51 ☐ Row of stores
53 ☐ Enclosed mall
58 ☐ Business & residential
59 ☐ Office use
60 ☐ Industrial use
63 ☐ Military use
65 ☐ Farm use
00 ☐ Other mixed use

J Property Use ☆ ☐ None

Structures
131 ☐ Church, place of worship
161 ☐ Restaurant or cafeteria
162 ☐ Bar/tavern or nightclub
213 ☐ Elementary school, kindergarten
215 ☐ High school, junior high
241 ☐ College, adult education
311 ☐ Nursing home
331 ☐ Hospital

341 ☐ Clinic, clinic-type infirmary
342 ☐ Doctor/dentist office
361 ☐ Prison or jail, not juvenile
419 ☐ 1- or 2-family dwelling
429 ☐ Multifamily dwelling
439 ☐ Rooming/boarding house
449 ☐ Commercial hotel or motel
459 ☐ Residential, board and care
464 ☐ Dormitory/barracks
519 ☐ Food and beverage sales

539 ☐ Household goods, sales, repairs
571 ☐ Gas or service station
579 ☐ Motor vehicle/boat sales/repairs
599 ☐ Business office
615 ☐ Electric-generating plant
629 ☐ Laboratory/science laboratory
700 ☐ Manufacturing plant
819 ☐ Livestock/poultry storage (barn)
882 ☐ Non-residential parking garage
891 ☐ Warehouse

Outside
124 ☐ Playground or park
655 ☐ Crops or orchard
669 ☐ Forest (timberland)
807 ☐ Outdoor storage area
919 ☐ Dump or sanitary landfill
931 ☐ Open land or field

936 ☐ Vacant lot
938 ☐ Graded/cared for plot of land
946 ☐ Lake, river, stream
951 ☐ Railroad right-of-way
960 ☐ Other street
961 ☐ Highway/divided highway
962 ☐ Residential street/driveway

981 ☐ Construction site
984 ☐ Industrial plant yard

Look up and enter a Property Use code and description only if you have NOT checked a Property Use box.

Property Use ⌷⌷⌷ Code

Property Use Description

NFIRS–1 Revision 01/01/05

Figure 8.9 First page of a two-page sample form used by the National Fire Incident Reporting System (NFIRS). (Continued on p. 182)

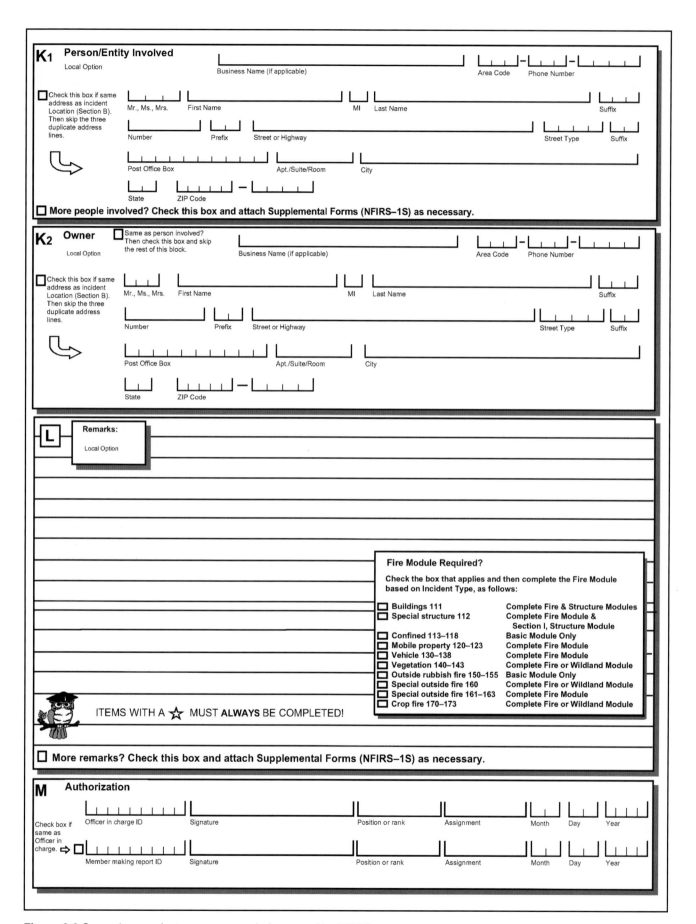

Figure 8.9 Second page of a two-page sample form used by NFIRS.

and include only information that has developed since the last report. Jargon (profession-specific words and terms) needs to be limited to internal audiences and not used at all for readers outside the organization.

The next step is to determine the format for the report. Types of narrative reports include the following:

- **Justification** — Focuses on why a certain course of action was taken or should be taken. The report begins with the situation or problem and then provides the solution to the problem and steps taken (or that should be taken) to gain the solution. *Examples:*
  — Budget request
  — Purchase recommendation
  — After-action report

- **Recommendation** — States the problem, provides a variety of solutions, and then recommends the best solution based on the available criteria. *Example:* station-location report.

- **Progress** — Provides an overview of the current status of a project. It is chronological in nature, beginning with a description of the project and proceeding through the individual steps to the current point or actual completion. The audience should be able to visualize the development of the project. *Example:* Progress reports required on long-term projects such as the development of a health and fitness program.

- **Progress and justification** — Combines the two forms into one by providing justification for the project, describing the steps to complete the project, and including justification for any changes in the project development (**Figure 8.10**).

- **Description** — Describes a process, project, or item that gives the audience a detailed image of the subject. *Examples:*
  — Describe a new apparatus design.
  — Describe each of the steps necessary to implement a rapid intervention team policy.

With the purpose and format determined, the topic is then thoroughly researched. Background data is assembled from previous reports, personal experience, interviews, analysis, and other

Figure 8.10 A narrative report may contain information on the progress of a project such as the construction of a new fire station or a request for additional funding to complete the project. *Courtesy of Rick Montemorra.*

documents. Include source citations in the form of footnotes and endnotes to provide credibility and direct the audience to the original material.

Footnotes have the advantage of keeping the information on the same page and making it easier for the reader to find. Endnotes have the advantage of keeping all the notes and citations together in one list at the end of the paper. Endnotes can also contain a larger amount of information, including graphs or tables that cannot be contained in a footnote.

Once the subject has been researched, an outline is developed based on the format. As mentioned earlier, an outline is a balanced framework around which the body of the subject is constructed. Each main topic in the outline is supported by at least two subtopics.

Regardless of the type of report, it follows the basic format: introduction, body, and conclusion. The narrative report, when complete, also includes a brief review or executive summary.

Executive Summaries

An *executive summary* is a brief review of the key points in a report, a technical paper, bid specifications, or an analysis that provides an audience such as senior managers an opportunity to understand the main points of the document without having to read the entire document. Executive summaries are usually provided to supervisors or administrative bodies by the authors of the original reports and attached to the fronts of reports or papers.

An executive summary ensures that the essential information contained in the report is read. It acts as an attention-getter that may spur the audience to read the full report and provides senior management with the main points necessary when justifying the report to the media, public, or legislative body.

The executive summary is basically the main topic statement of the report followed by bullets denoting the main points **(Figure 8.11)**. If it were compared to an outline, the main points would be the capital letters of the outline.

It needs to be brief (no longer than two pages), easy to read, and focused on the facts rather than the opinions expressed in the paper. The conclusion of the summary is the recommendation or suggested action found in the paper or report.

An executive summary may also be an analysis of a technical report by a reviewer other than the original author. In this case, the writer may be asked to provide an interpretation of the key points to assist in the decision-making process. The reviewer would follow the executive summary format but include analytical comments in the summary's conclusion.

Agendas

An *agenda* outlines activities proposed for a meeting or event. Agendas should be specific, be sequential, and include the main points that are to be addressed during the meeting. State/provincial or local open-meeting laws may require that agendas contain very specific information and be publicly posted a set period of time before the meeting. The agenda can also serve as the basic framework for the minutes of the meeting.

Minutes

Minutes are the accurate records of the topics covered, decisions made, and assignments given during meetings. Minutes establish the *who, what, when, where, how,* and *why* of the meeting. They

provide paper trails in the event of legal actions and form the basis for the program development process.

The meeting may be a performance review between two individuals or a committee meeting composed of any number of people. In all cases, minutes are important records of the events.

When required, meetings could be tape-recorded. This audio (or sometimes video) record is then transcribed into written minutes. At the same time that recordings are being made, a written set of minutes is also made. This redundancy ensures that the important points are written in case the recording is not understandable or the transcribing secretary misses a point.

Written minutes begin with the formal agenda of the meeting. Some people like to use this agenda on which to make notes for the minutes. This method is very efficient because it allows the agenda to become the outline for the minutes when they are transferred into a computer or word processor. Minutes include the following items:

- Date and time
- Committee name or title
- Names of attendees
- Names of excused members
- Names of absentees
- Guest speakers
- Location
- Purpose (if no agenda is provided)
- Old business (listed by topic)
- Action items and individual assignments
- New business
- Date, time, and location for next meeting

Minutes, like an executive summary, focus on the key points of meetings. They do not include everything that was said by every member during discussions of the key points **(Figure 8.12, p. 186)**. Everything said is contained in the audio/visual recording of the meeting. Each agenda item includes the topic, any important information to support the topic, and the decision of the committee on the topic.

Yosemite National Park
Environmental Impact Statement
Executive Summary

Introduction

This Environmental Impact Statement (EIS) presents several alternatives to implement National Park Service (NPS) fire policies in Yosemite National Park and in the El Portal Administrative Site, hereafter referred to as the Project Area. The EIS supports the implementation document for the fire program: the fire management plan. The fire management plan would be prepared and approved subsequent to the issuance of a Record of Decision for the EIS.

Most of Yosemite National Park is designated Wilderness, but it also includes and is adjacent to road and trail corridors, historical sites, residential communities and businesses, and administrative and recreational areas of several jurisdictions. Fire management reflects this diversity of land use. This document proposes alternatives for management of wildland and prescribed fire, protection of human life and property, restoration and maintenance of fire-dependent ecosystems, and reduction of hazardous fuels. It also examines the environmental impacts of each alternative.

Purpose of the Fire Management Plan

The purpose and goals of the Yosemite fire management program include the following:

- To develop a plan that is consistent with NPS wildland fire management policy and adheres to guiding principles from the Federal Fire Policy. These principles include the following:

  — Firefighter and public safety is the first priority in every fire management activity.

  — Wildland fire is an essential ecological process and natural change agent.

  — Fire management plans, programs, and activities support land and resource management plans and their implementation.

  — Sound risk management is a foundation for all fire management activities.

  — Fire management programs and activities are economically viable, based on values to be protected, costs, and land and resource management objectives.

  — Fire-related plans and activities should be based upon the best available science.

  — Fire management plans and activities incorporate public health and environmental quality considerations.

  — Federal, state, tribal, local, and interagency coordination and cooperation are essential.

In accordance with the Federal Fire Policies, the Yosemite fire management program would specifically:

- Execute a fire management program that provides for the safety of firefighters and the public, including safe operations and safe fire-management-related facilities (e.g., helibases, fire camps, fire stations).

- Use wildland and prescribed fires to restore and maintain park ecosystems to target conditions.

- Reduce the risk of fire to cultural resources (e.g., historic buildings and pictographs) through fuel reduction, prescribed burning, or fire suppression to prevent fires from damaging cultural resources. Fire would also be used as a tool to manage cultural landscapes.

- Reduce the risk of catastrophic fire to wildland/urban interface (WUI) communities by the use of prescribed fire and mechanical fuel reduction techniques.

- Ensure that fire management planning and operations support the goals and objectives of resource and wilderness management programs.

Source: http://www.nps.gov/archive/yose/planning/fire/noframes/executivesummary.htm

Figure 8.11 Example of an executive summary.

Figure 8.12 Minutes for meetings may be typed directly into a computer, written by hand, or recorded on audio or video media.

Minutes need to be accurate, brief, and easy to read. If action items are assigned to individuals, details such as the specific assignment, resources needed, and completion dates are then included.

Meetings that involve a small group of people (such as a performance review or a project assignment meeting) may not require a written agenda. But the meeting should result in minutes that capture the decisions and assignments that are agreed upon, which is essential when either the subordinate or supervisor is expected to complete a specific task within a specified timeframe. In essence, the minutes may constitute a contract between the two parties.

Policies and Procedures

The majority of fire and emergency services organizations have policies and procedures in written form within the organization. Depending on the definition adopted by the authority having jurisdiction, the document may be called *standard operating procedures (SOPs), standard operating guidelines (SOGs), policies and procedures manual (PPM),* or *general orders (GOs).* These documents contain the mission statement, responsibilities, and authority of the organization and each of its branches and functional positions.

Policies may include everything from sick leave to the smoking policy of the organization. Procedures manuals are used to describe specific pro-

cesses step by step. They exist in training manuals, operational manuals, and maintenance manuals (to mention a few).

Basic Format

All policy and procedures documents have some basic similarities. Generally, the policies and procedures manual contains the following:

- Statement of purpose
- Statement of scope
- Contents page
- Procedures or policies organized by specific topic or function
- Appendices that contain copies of forms that are referred to in the body of the text

Structurally, each page contains basic information at the top that assists the reader in navigating the document (see sample format). This basic information includes the following:

- *Subject* — What the policy or procedure is about
- *Procedure number* — Number assigned to the specific procedure for tracking purposes
- *Dates* — Original date of implementation plus any revision dates
- *Supersedes* — Procedure number that is replaced by the current page
- *Approvals* — Initials of the authority approving the policy or procedure
- *Distribution* — List of persons or groups to whom the policy or procedure is issued
- *Applicability* — Persons or groups to whom the policy or procedure applies
- *Pages* — Number indicating the position within the document, usually indicated as *1 of 12* and so on
- *Revision* — Indication of whether the current page is original or a revision
- *Forms used* — Indication of the appropriate form used to fulfill the policy or procedure

Sample Policy/Procedures Format			
Class A Foam Usage			**#2002-5**
Date: 12/05/2002	**Revised:** 03/03/2003	**Supersedes:** #1999 -12	**Approval**: fms
Page: 1 of 5	**Distribution:** All Branches		**Forms:** none
Revision: yes	**Applicability:** Operations Branch		

   A. Class A foam will be used on all structural fires.

   B. Application rates will be based on the type of nozzle used.

   C. Replacement foam will be requested from Supply at the termination of the incident.

Revisions

Because the policy and procedures manuals must be revised periodically, the number and location of each copy must be available to the administration. The responsible manager creates and maintains a master list of the manuals containing the individual tracking numbers and locations.

When new pages are distributed, they are signed for to verify receipt, and all personnel are notified that changes have been made **(Figure 8.13)**. If the changes or additions are major, then training accompanies the new policy or procedure. Organizations that distribute revisions by e-mail need to establish a tracking method to ensure that all personnel and sites have received, read, and understand the material.

A preferred method for maintaining and updating the policy and procedures manual is to save it to a network server to which all personnel have access. With this system, personnel are assured of having the current version of each policy or procedure.

A notice is sent to all work units every time a policy or procedure is added or updated in order that all personnel will be aware of the change. Of course, this system is an option only if the department has the necessary equipment.

Requests for Proposals and Bid Specifications

A *request for proposal (RFP)* defines the needs of the department or organization and allows manufacturers or their authorized distributors to decide if they can meet bid specifications. *Bid specifications* include the specific equipment requirements of the department or organization plus the legal requirements of the finance or purchasing officer of the jurisdiction.

Writing RFPs and bid specifications is a very technical skill **(Figure 8.14, p. 188)**. Errors in writing bid specifications can result in the purchase of equipment that does not meet the needs of the fire or emergency services organization. It is highly recommended that the person or group that is

Figure 8.13 Company officers are responsible for maintaining the policy and procedures manual assigned to their station or unit. When new policies are enacted, the company officer compares any new policy statements with existing ones and informs all members of the unit about the changes.

- Cannot meet delivery deadlines
- Cannot provide the required performance bonds
- Lack the established financial support to complete the contract
- Have a documented history of contract violations

The RFP process reduces the number of bidders to those companies that are capable of meeting the bid specifications. Before writing an RFP, the responsible officer or committee needs to consult both legal counsel and the authority's purchasing laws to determine what kinds of controls can legally be placed on bids or bidders. The selection of bidders may not be subjective or arbitrary. A sample RFP is found in **Appendix E**, Sample Request for Proposal.

Bid Specifications

Legal requirements (sometimes referred to as *boilerplate*) define the legal obligations and requirements that are necessary to meet specifications. They are required in all bid specifications. Personnel of fire and emergency services organizations do not develop these particular sections of the specifications but need to be aware of them and their affect on potential bidders. Requirements for bidders may include the following:

- Attendance at prebid meetings
- Warranties
- Liability or performance bonds
- Specified delivery times
- Payment schedules
- Financial statements

The development of the bid specifications for required equipment is the responsibility of the fire and emergency services department/organization. The language must be clear and concise. Each detail of the design requirement must be included, and nothing can be assumed (**Figure 8.15**).

Specifications that are vague or too general can create problems for the organization. Bidders could propose products or services that do not meet the organization's needs. This situation could lead to formal protests of the selection process by unsuccessful bidders and include legal action.

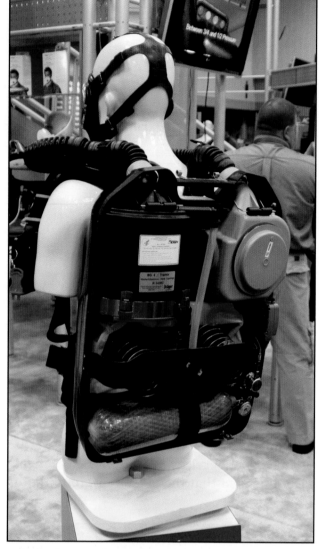

Figure 8.14 A request for proposal (RFP) provides potential bidders with enough information to decide whether they can provide the equipment (such as respiratory protection equipment) or service requested by the fire and emergency services organization.

assigned the task of writing RFPs or developing bid specifications be thoroughly trained in the process.

Proposals

An RFP must have a specific schedule outline, including bid dates, delivery dates, provisions for supplying units for scheduled evaluations, and training dates for technicians and training officers. An RFP also allows the jurisdiction to have control over the companies that can bid based on the responses to the RFP and participation in prebid meetings. Companies are eliminated from consideration in the following situations:

Figure 8.15 Bid specifications for capital purchases such as apparatus must be complete, detailed, and specific while still providing all eligible vendors the opportunity to bid on the item.

Some of the topics included in bid specifications are as follows:

- NFPA standard, National Institute for Occupational Safety and Health/Mine Safety and Health Administration (NIOSH/MSHA) standard, or American National Standards Institute (ANSI) certification for the intended use

- Number of units to be purchased

- Design requirements

- Delivery date

- Warranty

- Accessories

- Training for maintenance technicians

- Training for operational personnel

- Startup parts inventory

- Acceptance testing

- Technical support

- Nonperformance clause

If a specific feature that meets valid operational requirements is only available from a single manufacturer, an option for bidding an equal alternative or a method to take exception to the specifications must be included. At the same time, if no exceptions are allowed, it should be stated and justified in the specifications.

Including too many specifications that only one manufacturer can meet results in a restrictive bid that may be prohibited by the purchasing ordinances or laws of the jurisdiction. If a specific brand of equipment is the only type that meets the needs of the department or organization, then the finance or purchasing officer of the jurisdiction may be able to grant an exemption for a sole- or single-source bid and declare that specific brand as the jurisdiction's standard.

Most fire equipment manufacturers provide sample bid specifications forms as a guide. The company officer or bid specifications committee needs to be aware that these samples may be written in such a way that only that manufacturer can meet them.

Bid specifications usually have to be approved by the jurisdiction's finance or purchasing officer. Once approved, the purchasing department issues bid requests to qualified bidders and sets a date for the opening of the bids. The bids may only be returned to and handled by the purchasing department. Once received, the qualified bids are given to the purchasing officer or committee for evaluation.

Some other purchasing methods may be available to the department or organization. They include purchasing through state/provincial government agencies that buy in bulk or have a generic design specification.

Another approach is to work with neighboring departments or organizations to develop a mutually acceptable specification that all departments or organizations can use. This form of cooperative purchasing can reduce the cost of development and price of the product.

Summary

Written communications, regardless of the form they take, are basic to the daily operation of a modern fire and emergency services organization. The company officer will be expected to provide written reports, official letters, policy recommendations, RFPs, bid specifications, and other documents that can become the basis for decision-making on the part of superiors.

Accuracy and professional appearance are critical elements of all written communications. In the end, they provide a record of the activities of the officer and the organization.

Administrative Functions

Chapter Contents

Learning Objectives

1. Select facts about the main objectives of the customer service concept.

2. Identify various information-gathering methods.

3. Identify steps to be taken in interpreting information.

4. Apply the customer service concept to a citizen inquiry.

5. Select facts about written policies and procedures.

6. Recall information about the policy and procedures revision and monitoring process.

7. Given a scenario, recommend changes to an existing policy or implement a new departmental policy.

8. Identify various budget systems and types.

9. Identify revenue sources.

10. Select facts about the steps of budget development.

11. Prepare a budget request for a specific fire service need.

Job Performance Requirements

This chapter provides information that addresses the following job performance requirements of NFPA 1021, *Standard for Fire Officer Professional Qualifications* (2003):

Chapter 4 Fire Officer I

4.1.1

4.3.3

4.3.3(B)

4.4.1

4.4.3(A)

Chapter 9
Administrative Functions

Company officers who are assigned to either staff or line functions are required to perform similar administrative functions. Those functions include providing customer service, preparing and administering policies and procedures, and preparing or assisting in the preparation of the organization's budget. Each of these functions is essential to the operation of the organization and is described in this chapter.

Customer Service Concept

In the business community, customer service is based on providing a product or service that meets the needs of a group of people called *customers:* people who use and consume a product or service. These customers then provide feedback to the business on the quality and value of the product or service and their satisfaction with it. For fire and emergency services organizations, customers include internal employees, external beneficiaries, and stakeholders **(Figure 9.1, p. 194)**. Customer service includes the following objectives:

- Identify and target the customer base (see Customer Base section), generate productive professional relationships with those customers, and develop and implement strategic plans with clear, attainable goals and objectives.

- Form individualized relationships with stakeholders (governing body members; see Customer Base section) and partnerships with other concerned agencies and provide the highest level of customer service to the greatest number of customers.

- Provide employees with the information they need to know about customers' needs, wants,

and desires (see Customer Needs, Wants, and Desires section) and build relationships between employees and customers.

The concept of customer service is valuable to any organization and basic to business management theory taught in colleges and universities. In the private sector (nongovernment entity), good customer service is essential for a business to remain competitive and profitable. In the business world, shareholders (people who own stock in the business) place value on the *bottom line* or the profit or loss of the business. The bottom line is also the basis for good business profits and investments for the future. The bottom line in the public sector (government entity) is the level of customer service and the resulting satisfaction.

Surveys have shown that businesses that place a high value on customer service have a higher return on sales and greater control of the marketplace than those that place a lower emphasis on it. Knowing who the customers are and understanding what they need and want determine how well businesses compete with each other for sales and profits. In the public sector, knowing the customer's needs and wants determines the types of services that must be provided and the quality of those services.

The public must believe that they are getting quality service for the money they pay in the form of taxes and fees. Competition exists in the form of changes that the public can demand when services do not meet their expectations. Examples could include changes in the organization's leadership and organizational structure or privatization of the fire and emergency services organization.

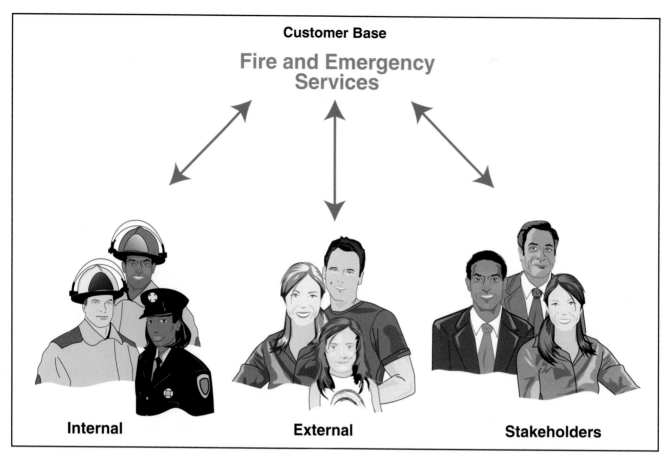

Customer Base

Fire and Emergency Services

Internal   **External**   **Stakeholders**

Figure 9.1 In the fire and emergency services, customers are not limited to members of the community. Customers may be internal, external, or members of special interest groups known as *stakeholders*.

All fire officers must understand the basic concept of customer service. They must be able to perform the following actions:

- Define the customer base.

- Identify what all customers need, want, and desire.

- Monitor the delivery of the organization's services as it relates to these needs, wants, and desires.

Information-gathering methods and information interpretation are additional elements of the customer service concept. Additional information on customer service is included in Chapter 15, Community Relations and Public Fire and Life-Safety Education.

Customer Base

It is important to define who the customers are and monitor their changing attitudes (see Customer Needs, Wants, and Desires and Service-Delivery

Monitoring sections). All fire and emergency services organizations have the following three types of customers:

- ***Internal customers*** — Employees and members of the organization. These customers may include emergency personnel, administrative staff, officers, or members of the bargaining unit **(Figure 9.2)**. Each group will have its own wants and needs. For instance, as members of the bargaining unit, emergency responders will want a contract that contains wages and benefits that they believe to be fair and equitable. Members of the administrative staff may need communication devices such as cellular phones and pagers. *Determine composition:*

  — Create a demographic database from general information on employees.

  — Use an internal survey or compile general information provided at the time of hiring. The questions used to gain this information must fall within federal hiring guidelines.

— Collaborate and work together to meet the goals of the organization when it is a combination volunteer/paid department. Use polls, informal conversation, questionnaire data, training data, etc. to determine the variables to make this collaboration successful.

- *External customers* — Members of the general population within the service area who are beneficiaries of the services provided as well as people responsible for providing the majority of the funds needed to operate the organization. They are not, however, a homogeneous group of people who have the same needs, wants, and desires. They are composed of a wide variety of smaller groups based on a number of characteristics. Determine service area demographics by gathering information on the demographics from numerous governmental sources including the most recent national census. *Examples:*

  — These customers may be residents of the service area or nonresidents who commute into the service area to work, shop, or visit.

  — They may also be part of stakeholder groups such as an active voting block, a specific age group such as senior citizens, or an organization like the Parent Teacher Association (PTA).

- *Stakeholders* — Members of the political body who govern the organization or influence it through legislation, nongovernmental agencies, community groups, standards-making organizations, and businesses that provide services to the organization (**Figure 9.3**). Political bodies include national, state/provincial, regional, and local governments.

Customer Needs, Wants, and Desires

The needs, wants, and desires of people are not a constant or static laundry list — they vary with the individual customer from day to day and even moment to moment. This variability is a reason why it is important to define who the customers are and monitor their changing attitudes.

Monitoring these attitudes requires the leadership of the organization to understand the way the population views the need for services and whether they have the means to pay for them (see Service-Delivery Monitoring section). Several methods are available for gathering information on customer needs/wants/desires (see Information-Gathering Methods section).

Many states/provinces have suffered revenue shortfalls because citizens voted to change the tax structure and limit the amount and method for raising funds while still expecting the previous levels of service. See the information box, p. 196, for a comparison of needs/wants/desires.

Figure 9.3 Stakeholders are not only members of the local government or the insurance industry but also members of groups that can be directly influenced by the fire and emergency services organization. For instance, members of the construction industry are affected by building and fire codes enacted by the local government on behalf of the fire service.

Figure 9.2 Internal customers are the members of the organization. They can be further divided by their job title, rank, or membership in the labor organization.

Needs/Wants/Desires

Humans have basic needs, some of which are outlined by Maslow in his *Hierarchy of Needs* diagram. At the same time, humans also possess general wants and very specific desires. These three terms are often confused with one another, especially in the minds of individuals. A comparison of needs, wants, and desires is as follows **(Figure 9.4)**:

- I need transportation.
- I want a car.
- I desire a luxury sport utility vehicle (SUV).

It is necessary for fire officers to recognize the real *needs* of the customers (which must be provided) and separate them from *wants* (which are nice but not necessary) and *desires* (which are usually unnecessary and unrealistic). All three must be recognized and respected, but only the needs must be met.

Internal Customers

Internal customers want both tangible and intangible benefits: fair compensation, reasonable benefits, and position security as well as a challenging professional career or volunteer experience. Additionally, they want a safe work environment, ethical leadership, the dignity that comes from respectful management, and the feeling of being an integral part of an organization.

In career and combination organizations, the labor/management agreement and/or civil service process where one exists satisfies most of the tangible needs. Chief officers, company officers, and members who compose the workgroup supply the intangible needs.

External Customers

While the specific needs of external customers vary, the basic needs are generally protection of their lives and property from the effects of fires and other hazards and access to competent emergency medical care. As the demographics of the service area change, services will have to keep pace with them. Meeting these needs determines the following elements:

- Services an organization provides
- Level of staffing required to provide those services
- Location of facilities
- Types of equipment and apparatus needed
- Total costs to provide the services

Stakeholders

Stakeholders' needs include retaining political power within the jurisdiction by representing the interests of their constituents, justifying the collection of revenues based on the level of service

Figure 9.4 Needs, wants, and desires may state basic criteria in different ways.

provided, and responding to the complaints and requests of constituents. If the fire and emergency services organization fails to provide or keep pace with the service needs of the public, it is perceived that elected officials are unable to manage the organization.

This perception can create a political crisis and loss of confidence that could result in a new group of politicians being voted into office at the next election. If political officials cannot justify the services provided with the current tax base, the public may vote to alter the taxation rate, possibly causing further cutbacks in services. Finally, if the public perceives that services are inadequate, they will complain directly to their elected officials.

In all of these situations, stakeholders could attempt to control or change the fire and emergency services organization to the detriment of the fire officers and members. Civil service laws or labor/management agreements can reduce the potential for some of these changes. Forced changes could include the following:

- Firing administrative officers
- Reducing personnel staffing
- Altering work schedules
- Changing the organization's responsibilities

Other stakeholders such as nonprofit or nongovernmental agencies look to the fire and emergency services organization for assistance and support for various types of projects for which they cannot succeed alone. For instance, the Project Safe Place™ program depends on fire stations in some communities to provide a refuge for youths in crisis. The Muscular Dystrophy Association works with members of the fire service to raise funds for muscular dystrophy research **(Figure 9.5)**.

Other agencies have partnerships that benefit the organization and the agency as well as the public. The insurance industry benefits from its support of the fire and emergency services organization by the reduction in dollars due to fire, which translates into lower insurance claims.

Stakeholders may also be groups of people who are directly or indirectly affected by decisions made by the jurisdiction on behalf of the fire and emergency services organization. For instance,

Figure 9.5 The Muscular Dystrophy Association (MDA) Fill-the-Boot Campaign is symbolic of the relationship between the fire service and a nonprofit organization. *Courtesy of Bonnie Hudlet.*

members of the construction trades are affected by changes in building and fire codes that relate to building construction or fire-safe work activities. The construction industry is directly affected by the changes in building codes that require fire detection or suppression systems in all new construction or renovations of old buildings.

Information-Gathering Methods

Information on the needs/wants/desires of customers can be gathered through a passive method where the organization simply waits for a customer to express a specific need, want, or desire. This approach takes very little effort in terms of time or money.

The problem with this approach is that it is reactive, is crisis-oriented, and can be biased. By the time a customer has expressed an opinion, the problem may already exist and will require an immediate change, in some cases a knee-jerk reaction.

At the same time, if the organization bases needs/wants/desires on individual requests, they may not form a consensus of the needs/wants/desires/expectations of the majority of the community. Therefore, funds, time, and effort may be inappropriately expended on a need/want/desire that does not benefit the greatest number of people.

A second approach is more active by taking the initiative and seeking information on a regular basis from internal and external customers and stakeholders. This approach may be accomplished in numerous ways including periodic meetings, surveys, and informal interviews.

Each of these ways is based on the concept of feedback mentioned earlier in this manual. Listening to feedback is a primary method for determining the needs/wants/desires of any of the three groups of customers. The company officer is usually involved in the collection of information using the feedback approach.

Meetings

Periodic meetings benefit the organization by allowing customers to be involved in the decision-making process. Internal customers view this as empowerment that can improve their morale and productivity. Examples include meetings such as the following:

- Supervisor and an employee
- Division manager and subordinates **(Figure 9.6)**
- Administration and labor organization representatives

External customers can be involved in the decisions that determine desired service levels, staffing and station-location requirements, and

policy changes that affect code enforcement. Stakeholders can view the meetings as a continuing commitment by the fire and emergency services organization to the needs of other groups and agencies. The meeting format can be an open-forum, permitting comments from all those attending or a small-group decision-making process that involves brainstorming activities.

Surveys

Conducting surveys is another source of information on the needs/wants/desires of customers. The customer survey determines the services that external customers believe that the organization should provide. In order for a survey to have meaning, the surveyed population must be representative of the jurisdiction. Additionally, an expert should develop the survey and provide analysis of survey responses.

The survey can be distributed by mail (commonly with utility bills), by hand at shopping centers or county fairs, or directly to customers by on-duty personnel. Many organizations use postincident service evaluation cards as another form of survey. Another approach for gaining customer input is electronic feedback. Customers can complete survey forms online and automatically submit them to the organization **(Figure 9.7)**.

Figure 9.7 Surveys may be completed and returned online, by mail, or in person.

Figures 9.6 Internal customers need to believe that they are a part of the decision-making process. Frequent meetings between chief officers and subordinates help to improve communications, feedback, and morale.

Benefits of customer surveys include the following:

- Provides a written response to the specific questions surrounding customer needs/wants/desires

- Is relatively inexpensive to develop

- Is useful in describing the needs/wants/desires of a large population or service area

- Can be administered from remote locations using mail, e-mail, or telephone

- Demonstrates that results may be statistically significant even when analyzing multiple variables because the survey involves a large customer base

- Asks a variety of questions about a given topic, giving considerable flexibility to the analysis

- Obtains more precise measurements when using standardized questions (enforces uniform definitions or descriptions upon customers); ensures that similar data can be collected from groups and then interpreted comparatively (between group study)

- Eliminates customer subjectivity greatly because standardized questions provide all customers with the same stimulus or focus

The survey is an excellent tool when limitations are recognized and it is used in conjunction with other methods of determining customer needs/wants/desires. Some limitations include the following:

- Surveys usually result in a less than 70 percent return rate. Generally those who are very satisfied or very dissatisfied (more likely) with the service provided return most surveys.

- An active and coordinated response by a small and vocal minority can result in a skewed image of the needs of the majority.

- Surveys usually limit the response to the questions listed on them, therefore making them inflexible.

- In order for any survey to have validity, a professional who knows how to develop unbiased questions must develop it.

Informal Interviews

Informal interviews are opportunities for supervisors to learn from employees if changes are needed in the work environment, policies, or other work-related issues. The results of these interviews are usually the first indications of what may become trends if they affect others in the workgroup.

Trends may also become apparent when gathering information from members of the community, other agencies, other departments/organizations, or vendors. For instance, informal interviews with other fire officers in neighboring communities may provide an overview of fire-related incidents that appear to be intentionally set.

Information Interpretation

Gathering information on customers and their needs/wants/desires is only the beginning of the customer service process. Those needs/wants/desires must then be channeled through a series of steps that include the following:

- Analyze information and separate realistic needs from wants and desires.

- Compare needs to the current operating procedures and the organization's mission statement to determine whether they are within the responsibility and authority of the organization.

- Prioritize needs based on importance.

- Develop programs or plans that will satisfy individual needs.

- Allocate funds necessary to establish programs or implement plans.

- Merge similar needs and combine with the appropriate element of the organization's operating procedures.

A list of valid customer needs can be included as input in the systems-process model, which is based on the change model discussed in Chapter 22, Management Activities. However, it is essential that needs be accurate and adequately separated from the less realistic wants, and desires. Like the *desirable SUV* mentioned in the earlier information box example, fulfilling a desire may cost more than its benefit.

Service-Delivery Monitoring

To determine the success or failure of any change in service made as the result of customers recognizing a need and separating it from their wants and desires, the organization monitors the outcome of the change. Monitoring a change occurs over the life of the change, usually on a specified time period such as monthly, semiannually, or annually.

The methods for monitoring the change are similar to those used to gather the information on customer needs/wants/desires — meetings, interviews, and surveys, etc. When feedback indicates that needs are being adequately and efficiently met, monitoring will then be used to determine whether they change over time, requiring an alteration in the service level in the future.

The customer-satisfaction survey differs from the survey used to determine the needs/wants/desires of the community. The satisfaction survey includes questions that focus on quality of the service that the customer has received from the organization. A sample customer-satisfaction survey form is found in **Appendix F.**

Policies and Procedures

For the effective and efficient operation of any fire and emergency services organization and use of resources through standardized systems, written policies and procedures are essential. They place into writing the expectations of the organization based on its organizational model and strategic and operational plans. The following methods can be used to ensure that policies and procedures are fully understood and complied with:

- Distribute in written or electronic format.

- Communicate to all members.

- Post in a conspicuous place in all facilities.

As mentioned in Chapter 8, Written Communications, policies and procedures are known by a variety of names including *standard operating procedure (SOP), standard operating guideline (SOG), administrative policies and procedures,* or simply *policies and procedures.* Regardless of the title, they must contain information that is current and appropriate.

Therefore, the organization should have a process to evaluate the need for creating new policies and procedures and revising existing ones. Policies and procedures are continually monitored for effectiveness. Organization members should also be familiar with the difference between policies, procedures, orders, and directives.

Company officers must explain organizational policies and procedures to subordinates and new employees as part of their indoctrination (**Figure 9.8**). In addition, whenever company officers learn of a new law or regulation from any level of government, they have an obligation to inform their superiors about it. This action allows the organization's administration to determine whether new organizational policies and procedures are needed in order to comply with the new legislation.

In some jurisdictions, accepted practices that deviate from written policies or procedures may legally become a policy or procedure. This devia-

Figure 9.8 The company officer should inform subordinates of any changes in policies and procedures when they occur. It is also good practice to review existing policies and procedures periodically.

tion is an application of the common law tradition described in Chapter 5, Legal Responsibilities and Liabilities.

Policies

A *policy* is a guide to decision-making within an organization. Policies originate with top management in the organization and are disseminated to lower levels for implementation. These policies not only aid in decision-making, but they also define the boundaries and standards that the administration expects company officers and members to use **(Figure 9.9)**.

Policies are created when formal written guidelines or criteria are needed for the operation of the organization. Periodically, changes in the operation of the organization may require changes in policies.

Policies may be traditional or unwritten in some situations. Some policies are the result of government regulations. A policy analysis is performed when changes in operations require changes in policies. Policies are placed in manuals or databases.

Some policies result from an appeal to management for guidance in making decisions about exceptional situations. For instance, a company officer who does not know how a certain situation should be handled might refer the matter to a superior. Appeal is made upward until someone in the hierarchy is reached who has the authority to make the decision.

The decision-maker may write a policy for handling similar cases in the future. A company officer may make a decision in order to resolve a problem, and this decision serves as a precedent that evolves into organizational policy, which is often the case.

The company officer's duty regarding policies is to understand and apply them fairly, consistently, and with discretion. Correct interpretation and application of organizational policies may require consultation (through the chain of command) with the administration. Formal instruction in organizational policies and their interpretations is necessary for all members of the organization.

Figure 9.9 Policies set the boundaries and standards to which personnel adhere. Examples of policies are mandatory use of respiratory protection, nontobacco use while on duty, and participation in a physical fitness program.

Policy Analysis

A *policy analysis* determines whether current policies are effective and enforceable. It also determines whether resulting problems are caused by the lack of policies. This analysis usually takes place when an organization is experiencing some type of internal difficulty.

This analysis process takes time and effort and may even require the use of an outside agency such as the authority's legal department or human resources department. Generally, though, if the problems are not severe, the fire or emergency services organization can form an internal committee or task force to provide the analysis.

Unwritten Policies

Unwritten policies, sometimes called *organizational norms* or *past practices*, are a result of tradition within the organization. Such policies are implied in the routine activities of the organization. Implied policies develop where no clear policy exists. This situation is especially true in organizations where policies are not written or when written policies are out of date.

A past practice can result from a single incident, decision or action. An officer should consult with superiors, association/labor representatives, or a human resources specialist before making a decision that may affect the entire organization.

Unwritten policies can come to have as much force as though they were written. Employee organizations may also desire to use an unwritten past practice as a tool to mold written standards or establish a precedent for settling grievances. It becomes apparent how deeply rooted tradition is when an organization tries to change from traditional implied policies to newer written ones.

Government Laws or Ordinances

Policies are sometimes imposed upon fire and emergency services organizations by federal mandates, state/provincial regulations, or local government laws or ordinances. For example, equal employment opportunity practices have been imposed by the federal government through the Fair Labor Standards Act (FLSA) and the Americans with Disabilities Act (ADA).

Many state governments are now adopting federal standards for the control of hazardous materials. Local codes and ordinances also affect operations of fire and emergency services organizations.

Policy Manual

Policies must be communicated to make the administration's intent clear. Policies that are drafted and placed in a manual or database give members of the organization a reference point for decision-making.

Collectively, these policies form the organization's policy manual. Organized, well-drafted policies promote consistent uniform practices throughout the organization and more predictable outcomes in the field.

Procedures

While a policy is a guide for decision-making, a *procedure* is a detailed plan of action — a written communication that is similar and closely related to a policy. A procedure details in writing the steps to follow in conducting organizational policy for some specific, recurring problem or situation. Procedures are better developed at the company level because these individuals will be responsible for following and implementing procedures to meet certain policies.

For instance, most organizations with personnel departments require those seeking employment to first apply at the personnel office. This procedure for processing new applicants then directs the personnel department (and it, in turn, directs the applicant) through the successive steps that must be followed in the application process.

Most fire and emergency services organizations provide personnel with specific, detailed information about how specific situations should be handled. Development and use of SOPs allow an organization to make the best use of its human resources. Having a consistent point of reference helps all members of the organization perform to a measurable standard.

Misunderstandings about techniques, responsibilities, and procedures are reduced by referencing a specific SOP. Emergency response and operations at incidents require clear, decisive action on the part of incident commanders, company officers, and firefighters.

SOPs provide the direction on which specific actions are based. They are the basis for much of the company-level skills training such as initial fire attack, use of the Incident Command System (ICS), rapid intervention crew (RIC) procedures, fireground search and rescue, and others (**Figure 9.10**).

Revision Process

To ensure that policies and procedures are flexible enough to adapt to changes in the operating environment and organizational requirements, a process for revising them should be established. The revision process is included in the policy or procedures manual or database and is based on answers to the following questions:

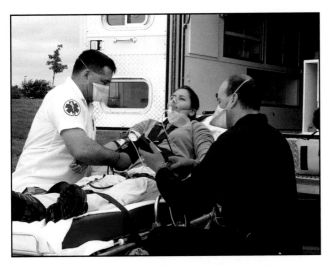

Figure 9.10 Written procedures include the activities personnel must perform to meet established policies. A policy that requires emergency medical services (EMS) personnel to wear personal protective equipment (PPE) can be supported by a procedure that defines the specific type of PPE such as medical masks and gloves when transporting a patient.

- When does the policy or procedure need to be revised? Is there a specific timetable?

- What conditions or circumstances would cause a policy or procedure to need revision?

- How should the policy or procedure be revised: completely, partially, or not at all?

Indications that a policy or procedure needs to be revised may include the following:

- Internal/external customer complaints

- Increase in policy or procedure infractions

- Injuries or property loss due to a failure of the policy or procedure

- Change in the resources used to accomplish the task

- Change in the problem that the policy or procedure was intended to solve

- New technology

- Legal mandates

When it becomes apparent that a policy or procedure must be revised, replaced, or abandoned, the actual process steps can be based on the steps used in the decision-making process (see Chapter 4, Logic, Ethics, and Decision-Making). The National Fire Academy (NFA) suggests using the following simplified model:

- *Define the problem* — Determine the weakness or deficiency of the current policy or procedure.

- *Collect information* — Gather data on various methods to address the problem. Sources may include NFA, other departments or agencies with similar policies or procedures, or the business community.

- *Generate alternative options* — Develop at least two alternative solutions that are intended to resolve the problem based on the collection of information.

- *Evaluate alternative options* — Compare the alternative solutions to the desired result.

- *Select one option* — Choose the option that best corrects the problem. Also select a second best option as a contingency or alternate solution.

Monitor Process

The policies and procedures of the organization (like most elements of the administrative function) must be continually monitored for effectiveness. Policies and procedures are most effective if they are dynamic documents, that is, documents that are subject to constant scrutiny, review, and revision.

Responsibility for the monitoring of all policies and procedures rests with the chief officers of the organization. They should be familiar with the content, application, and effects of the policies they use to manage the organization. They should also be aware of the proper procedures for performing tasks assigned to them and members of their command. However, company officers must communicate any concerns or problems with the policies and procedures to their supervisors.

As stated earlier, company officers are the first level of supervision within the organization. It is their responsibility to administer policies and procedures and report any problems that occur when using or enforcing them. Infractions and unauthorized alterations of policies and procedures should be noted and reported by company officers for the purpose of reinforcing existing policies and procedures or revising them to meet changing conditions.

Orders and Directives

In both nonemergency and emergency situations, company officers may issue many orders and directives (either written or verbal). However, on the fireground or at other emergency incidents, they are both considered mandatory because of the seriousness of the situation. Both orders and directives are needed to conduct organizational functions.

Orders are based upon the authority delegated to the fire officer to implement organizational policies and procedures **(Figure 9.11)**. Compliance is mandatory because an order is based upon a policy or procedure. A *directive* is not based on a policy or procedure; it is more in the nature of a request. Directives are not mandatory except during emergency situations.

Issuing orders at an emergency incident is an important supervisory duty for company officers. When an order is understood and executed, tactical objectives and strategic goals are accomplished. Besides accomplishing goals and objectives, orders aid in training and developing cooperation. Properly given orders result in the need for less supervision in the future as members learn what is expected of them.

It is important that company officers control their emotions when issuing orders at emergencies. Detection of any anxiety, uneasiness, or extreme

Figure 9.11 During emergency operations, fire officers give orders that direct the activities of personnel. Violating an order is not only unlawful, it can also be unsafe and result in unforeseen consequences for other members of the unit.

excitement in company officers can affect the emotional stability and performance of firefighters in their companies.

Emergency incident orders must be issued calmly and be clear, concise, and complete. This duty requires strong leadership abilities and a command presence on the part of the fire officer. See Chapter 2, Leadership, for a detailed discussion of command presence.

Another important supervisory duty of company officers involves issuing and enforcing unpopular orders. The administration sometimes establishes policies and procedures that may adversely affect firefighters. It usually falls to company officers to issue and enforce these orders. As mentioned in Chapter 1, Transition to the Role of Company Officer, if company officers are to do their jobs well, they must be willing to put aside their personal feelings and support the administration's position.

This support by company officers must not be halfhearted or obviously forced. Officers must give genuine support or remain neutral to the decision. One of the best ways that company officers can develop this kind of support for an unpopular order is to find out why the order was issued. Chief officers do not issue orders frivolously, so they must have good reasons for issuing a controversial one.

Company officers should make every effort to find out what those reasons are. With that information, they can explain the necessity for the order and answer any questions that their subordinates might have about the new order.

Budget Process

Every fire and emergency services organization, from the smallest volunteer company to the largest fire department, must have a budget with which to operate. The term *budget* can be defined as a planned quantitative allocation of resources for specific activities. Therefore, in the broadest of definitions, it is the allocation of all resources (time, space, equipment, facilities, apparatus, personnel, funding, and research) to the completion of a task.

In this manual, budgets refer to the narrow financial budget that lists both proposed expenditures (personnel pay, benefits, facilities, apparatus, materials, utilities, and insurance) and expected revenue sources. Budgets are formal statements of the costs of operating and the expected revenues needed to meet those costs.

The revenues that fund the organization's budget may come from a variety of sources. In the case of a volunteer company, the revenues may come from fundraising events such as bake sales, pancake breakfasts, and benefit dances or golf tournaments and/or private and corporate donations **(Figure 9.12)**. In most combination and career fire and emergency services organizations, funding comes from tax revenues, fees for services, government subsidies and grants, and similar sources.

According to the job performance requirements of NFPA 1021, *Standard for Fire Officer Professional Qualifications,* company officers must be able to prepare a budget request to obtain the items needed to operate their particular companies. To accomplish this task, the company officer must understand the types of budgets normally used in public administration, types of revenue sources available, and the steps of the budget process itself. Local laws and ordinances vary, but the basic budgetary theory remains the same among jurisdictions.

Figure 9.12 Volunteer fire and emergency services organizations depend on a variety of revenue sources including pancake breakfasts and bake sales. In addition to raising operating funds, these events raise community awareness of the organization and provide opportunities for recruiting and public fire and life-safety education. *Courtesy of Iowa Fire Service Training Bureau.*

Historically, the company officer has not had direct control over the funds allotted at the company level by the budget. In recent years, however, an increasing number of jurisdictions have assigned budget responsibilities to the company officer.

The benefits to the organization include the reduction of delays in performing general maintenance and obtaining disposable items. It also provides some experience for company officers to work with a budget and make decisions accordingly.

Company officers must monitor the use of materials, ensure that adequate stocks are available, and purchase replacement supplies in a timely manner. They must always conform to the purchasing and inventory laws and ordinances of the authority having jurisdiction (AHJ).

The budgets of government jurisdictions are more than lists of proposed expenditures and expected revenue. They perform three vital functions for government by (1) describing and identifying the relationship between different tasks, (2) providing assistance in the decision-making process, and (3) clarifying political power. Most budgets perform the following functions:

- Anticipate future expenditures based on the goals and objectives of the jurisdiction or organization.

- Review the effectiveness of past budget performance.

- Establish and reinforce governmental policy.

- Assign responsibility for the accomplishment of goals and objectives.

Systems and Types

In both the government and business sectors in North America, many terms are used to describe budgets. The terms vary depending on the source or the organization using them. In general the following two phrases describe budgets:

- *Budget system* — Model or format to which a budget process conforms

- *Budget type* — Description of how costs or revenues are divided between capital and operational purchases

Budget Systems

Budget systems are the general formats to which a jurisdiction's budget process conforms. Each system provides the same result through a variety of approaches. Some may contain elements of other systems. Typically, those systems are known by the following names:

- *Line-item budgeting* — Consists of lists of revenue sources and proposed expenditures for the budget cycle **(Figure 9.13)**

- *Zero-based budgeting (ZBB)* — Requires all expenditures to be justified at the beginning of each budget cycle

- *Matrix budgeting* — Involves a variety of independent units assigned to a limited duration project.

- *Program budgeting* — Uses separate categories of programs or activities

- *Performance budgeting* — Uses categories of function or activity based on projected performance

- *Planning programming budgeting system (PPBS)* — Links planning and budgeting through program development

Budget Types

In general, two types of budgets are used by public organizations: capital budgets (projected major purchases) and operating budgets (recurring expenses of day-to-day operation). Company officers may be responsible for preparing budget requests to obtain the items needed to operate their particular unit or station.

Typical items that might be included would be operating materials, utilities, fuel, or replacement tools. Personnel costs (wages and benefits) would not be included in these requests since they are calculated by the administrative division of the organization.

This preparation usually involves the relatively simple process of updating the requests from the previous year's budget to reflect current needs.

Training Budget

Organization: _____   Year: _____

Department: _____   Submitted by: _____

Annual training allotment: _____

| 1Q Budget: | $0 | 3Q Budget: | $0 | Total Budget: | $0 |
| 2Q Budget: | $0 | 4Q Budget: | $0 | | |

1st Quarter Training Budget

Line	Item	Description/Justification	Qty.	Unit Cost/Rate	Total
1	Courseware development				$0
2	Courseware purchase				0
3	Certification				0
4	Train-the-trainer				0
5	Hardware purchase				0
6	Facility rental				0
7	Instructional materials				0
8	Technical equipment				0
9	Consulting fees				0
10	Instructor fees				0
11	Content acquisition				0
12	Travel				0
13	Per diem				0
14					0
15					0
				Grand Total	$0

Figure 9.13 Sample line-item budget. These budgets may simply be a listing of items and projected costs or include a narrative about each item. Both approaches may be required during the budget-development phase.

Requests developed by various company officers are collected by chief officers at the next level of the organization and submitted to the administration. Requests from the various divisions of the organization are combined to form a single budget request. A percentage that represents the rate of inflation based on the federal government's cost-of-living estimate is usually added to the request as a means of covering any increase in the cost of products and materials.

It is important that all company officers participate in this process. Company officers can share the workload with other fire officers and reduce the chances that something is omitted. Once a budget is approved, it is difficult to purchase anything that was not requested.

Capital. A *capital budget* includes projected major purchases — items that cost more than a certain specified amount of money and are expected to last more than 1 year (usually 3 or more years). Fire apparatus and vehicles, equipment, and facilities are typical capital items for fire and emergency services organizations **(Figure 9.14)**. Many jurisdictions have multiyear capital improvement plans or projects (CIPs) for these and other major investments. The final decision on what is purchased is made by the governing body based on the justification provided by the administration of the fire and emergency services organization. Revenues for capital purchases may come from a variety of sources such as the following:

- Set percentage of the annual revenues (shared between the various departments within the jurisdiction such as street, public works, or fire) used to operate the jurisdiction

- Special tax dedicated to capital purchases such as a multiyear CIP or a dedicated sales tax

- Special grants, assessments, or bond issues

Operating. An organization's *operating budget* is used to pay for the recurring expenses of day-to-day operations **(Figure 9.15)**. The largest

Figure 9.15 Operating budgets allocate funds for the purchase of supplies, tools, and equipment that are valued at less than an established price. Janitorial supplies, EMS supplies, hand tools, and personal protective equipment (PPE) are among the items purchased with operating funds.

Figure 9.14 Capital items include apparatus, facilities, and equipment that exceed an established value per unit. Many organizations permit apparatus to be specified that are fully equipped with tools, fire hose, and radio equipment. Others only allow the vehicle to be purchased with capital funds while the equipment is purchased with operating funds.

single item in the operating budget of most career organizations is personnel costs — salaries and benefits. In many organizations, personnel costs (sometimes called *personnel services*) represent as much as 90 percent of the operating budget. Considering that noncash (fringe) benefits cost some jurisdictions an amount equal to 50 percent of a person's base salary, it is easy to understand why the personnel-services category represents such a high percentage of the budget. Operating budgets also pay for the following:

- Utilities
- Office supplies
- Apparatus and vehicle fuel
- Janitorial supplies
- Contract services for the maintenance of apparatus and facilities
- Other items needed to function on a daily basis

Revenue Sources

All government jurisdictions depend on some type of revenue to provide the services that citizens require. The majority of jurisdictions depends on property, sales, or income taxes (or a combination of these) as the primary source of revenue. Trust funds, enterprise funds, restricted funds, sinking funds, bond sales, grants/gifts, foundations, or fundraisers may supplement or replace this revenue.

Tax Revenues

Traditional sources of revenue that government organizations depend on include property taxes, use fees, sales taxes, and income taxes. These taxes tend to provide a rather stable and predictable source of revenue that is available to all levels of government. They are not, however, completely immune to changes in the economy or taxpayer revolts.

Company officers must be aware of the trends in revenue collection in order to develop realistic budget projections and program goals. It may be necessary to actively support an increase in taxation by justifying it based on the required level of services. Gaining support for tax increases requires accurate data collection and public presentations that are objective and factual.

Descriptions of the various tax revenue sources are as follows:

- **Property taxes** — Ad valorem (Latin for *according to the value*) tax levied against the owner of real or personal property; major source of revenues for state and municipal governments. *Historical factors:*

  — They have been very dependable, increasing with the value of property as determined by the most recent sales price or periodic evaluations by tax assessors.

  — Because of voter disapproval, the past 25 years have seen changes that have resulted in stagnation or regression in property-tax revenues.

- **Sales taxes** — Tax levied by a state or city on the retail price of an item, collected by the retailer; generally levied at municipal and state levels of government and may be the primary revenue source for operating budgets. They are also a target for citizen groups who demand tax reform.

- **Personal income taxes** — Taxes on personal income collected by the federal government, most state/provincial governments, and some municipal governments; have been the subject of some voter concern and are directly affected by the economy and political trends. *Decreased revenue causes:*

  — Job layoffs

  — Reductions in work hours

  — Loss of overtime benefits

  — Tax cuts resulting from legislative action or a vote of the people

- **Special purpose tax levy** — Levy based on the assessed value of property specified as *millage* ($1/$1,000 property valuation) and collected by the local government for a specified government purpose such as the operation of the fire department or ambulance service; applies for a specified time period and is submitted to voters for approval. A special taxing authority can be used to support rural fire-protection districts.

- **Fees** — Money collected to support services; includes building permits, plans reviews, reports, vehicle registrations, building inspections/reinspections, hazardous materials responses,

Figure 9.16 Containing and controlling spilled hazardous materials can be extremely expensive due to state/provincial and federal environmental and safety regulations. The cost of containment can usually be collected from insurance carriers or owners of transport or manufacturing companies. *Courtesy of Steve Baker.*

emergency medical services (EMS) responses, and even fire protection services (subscription services for emergency response) **(Figure 9.16)**. Fees may be collected by the individual organization or the finance and revenue department and then credited to the appropriate organization.

Trust Funds

A *trust fund* is an account whose assets are managed by a trustee or a board of trustees for the benefit of another party or parties. Funds are governed by applicable federal and state/provincial laws and the legal document that established the trust.

Funds that are derived from donations and gifts are placed into the account. They may be further divided into categories such as undesignated gifts, broadly designated gifts, and specifically designated gifts, depending on the wishes of the donor. Thus a donation may be designated for the purchase of a new piece of equipment, construction of a new facility, or simply for the operation of a one-time program such as cardiopulmonary resuscitation (CPR) classes for the community.

Trust funds are usually intended for one-time purchases and not for recurring operating expenses. Trust funds are either *general* for perpetual and long-term trust funds or *specific* for short-term trust funds.

Perpetual trusts are funds from which only income (interest) from capital may be expended. *Long-term* trusts are funds from which both income and capital may be expended. Any capital spent from long-term trusts must be defined as expendable. *Short-term* trusts are funds that are spent in the current year for some expressed purpose.

Another form of trust fund is the *employee pension* fund that provides retirees with an income based on years of service, age, and contributions. Both the jurisdiction and the employee usually make contributions to the fund over the length of the employee's service.

Enterprise Funds

An *enterprise fund* is established to finance and account for the acquisition, operation, and maintenance of government facilities and services that are entirely or predominantly self-supporting by user fees such as water and sewer service fees. Enterprise funds may also be established when a jurisdiction has decided that periodic determinations of revenues earned, expenses incurred, and/or net income are appropriate.

Government-owned utilities and hospitals are ordinarily accounted for by enterprise funds. The ambulance transportation component of EMS is often sustained or supplemented by an enterprise fund when the service is provided by a government agency **(Figure 9.17, p. 210)**.

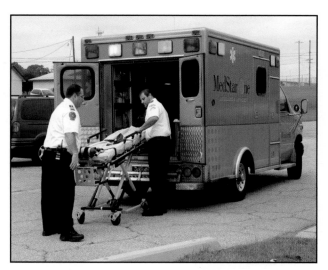
Figure 9.17 Enterprise funds can be used to provide ambulance services to a community.

An *auxiliary enterprise* is an entity that exists to furnish services to the population of a service area and charges a fee related to the cost of the service. Auxiliary enterprise accounts are operated on an annual budget based on the estimate of operating income and expense, including bond-interest expense and provisions for bond retirement if applicable. Fire-protection subscriptions (annual dues or fees paid by residents for fire protection similar to home-owner's insurance) may be used to create auxiliary enterprise funds.

Restricted Funds

Restricted funds are deposited into accounts that are created to receive money from a single source such as building or smoke-detector inspections. The money is collected by the fire and emergency services organization and deposited into a restricted account. Only the organization can withdraw funds from that account, and it can only be used for very specific expenses such as fire and life-safety program costs.

Sinking Funds

A *sinking fund* is an account that receives a specified amount of revenue that will be used in the future to pay off a jurisdiction's indebtedness. For example, when a municipality sells bonds to build a new fire station, funds must be accumulated from sales or property tax to buy the bonds back with interest at a specific date in the future (see Bond Sales section). Although not sources of revenue

for local governments, sinking funds are part of the budget of most state/provincial and municipal governments and provide funds for the operation of fire and emergency services organizations.

Bond Sales

A *bond* is a promise to repay the principal along with interest on a specified date, that is, when the bond reaches *maturity*. Some bonds do not pay interest, but all bonds require a repayment of principal. When an investor buys a bond, that person becomes a creditor of the jurisdiction that sold the bond. The federal government, states/provinces, counties/parishes, municipalities, public corporations, and many other types of institutions sell bonds to fund programs and projects.

Bonds are divided into different categories based on tax status, credit quality, issuer type, maturity, and whether they are secured/unsecured as well as other classification methods. U.S. government treasury bonds (T-Bonds) are generally considered the safest unsecured bonds because the possibility of the U.S. Treasury defaulting on payments is almost zero.

Some bonds are tax-exempt such as those typically issued by municipal, county, or state/provincial governments. These interest payments are not subject to federal income tax and sometimes are not subject to state or local income tax.

In some jurisdictions, members of the electorate must approve the sale of bonds. Bond sales are linked to specific purchases such as apparatus or land. This type of single-use funding may be an alternative to tax revenues when there is strong voter sentiment against property, sales, or income tax increases.

Grants/Gifts

Many fire and emergency services organizations supplement their general budgets with *grants* that are either private or corporate donations or subventions (subsidies) from national or state/provincial governments to these organizations to meet specific needs. For example, in some states a portion of all fire-insurance premiums paid to the insurance industry is returned to local fire and emergency services organizations to pay for training and training-related materials.

In many jurisdictions, service clubs and other civic organizations donate funds to purchase specialized equipment such as hydraulic rescue tools or semiautomatic defibrillators. It is important that funds donated for capital purchases are used for that purpose only — and not for operating expenses.

Grants are available from both government and nongovernment organizations (NGO) for specific purposes. Examples are as follows:

- Government grants such as those provided by the U.S. Fire Administration (USFA), the U.S. Department of Homeland Security (DHS), or U.S. Department of Transportation (DOT) provide local emergency responders with training and equipment necessary to deal with a variety of incidents.

- Nongovernment organizations or nonprofit organizations provide grant money to fund programs such as civilian CPR training through fire and emergency services organizations **(Figure 9.18)**.

The application process for obtaining grants can be challenging, especially for small organizations. Grant writing is very specialized and success requires a skilled professional grant writer.

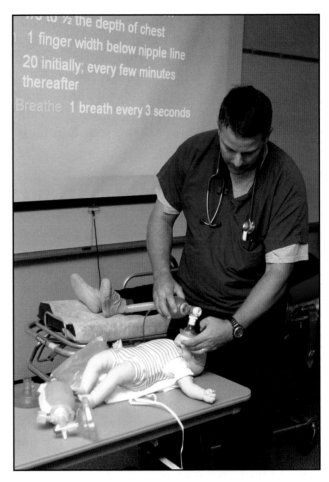

Figure 9.18 Fire and emergency services organizations provide training to external customers through nongovernmental grants. One of the better known training activities funded in this manner is CPR training.

Fire Grants

Currently, the U.S. Fire Administration (USFA), through the U.S. Department of Homeland Security (DHS), offers the following three types of grants to fire and emergency services organizations:

- ***Assistance to Firefighters Grant (AFG)*** — Grant to assist fire departments in protecting the health and safety of the public and fire-fighting personnel from fire and fire-related hazards. Grants are awarded directly to fire departments of a state. They are awarded on a competitive basis to applicants qualifying in the following ways:

  — Addressing AFG program priorities

  — Demonstrating financial need

  — Demonstrating benefits derived from their projects

- ***Staffing for Adequate Fire and Emergency Response (SAFER) Grant*** — Grant to hire additional firefighters and emergency responders. Grants are awarded directly to volunteer, combination, and career fire departments to enhance their ability to attain 24-hour staffing and thus assure their communities have adequate protection from fire and fire-related hazards. The grants help grantees attain this goal in the following ways:

  — Hiring of firefighters

  — Recruiting and retaining volunteer firefighters

- ***Fire Prevention and Safety (FP&S) Grants*** — Grants to enhance the safety of the public and firefighters with respect to fire and fire-related hazards. These grants are part of the AFG program. The primary goal is to reach high-risk target groups in order to mitigate the high incidences of fire death and injuries.

While many grants are based on specific needs, such as hazardous materials response training, other federally and state/provincial supported programs operate largely through consolidated funding streams, normally referred to as *block grants.* Under this methodology, funding is made available for defined purposes but with minimum conditions.

The use and support for block grants have increased in recent years. They meet the need for flexibility at the program level. Block-grant funding minimizes the bureaucratic aspects of the budgeting process because those outside the performance chain are presumed accountable for fund expenditures. Block grants recognize that those who do the work and spend the funds are accountable, responsible, and best qualified to make such decisions.

At the same time, block grants ensure community involvement in the application process. An example of a program funded by a block grant is a senior-citizen safety awareness program that provides education as well as smoke detectors or fire extinguishers to participants.

Foundations

The fire and emergency services are not as familiar with foundations as a source of revenue as other sources. However, in certain situations they can provide considerable funding. When researching available foundations, company officers should realize that foundations want to make a difference. As such, a foundation's scope is limited and application requirements are quite extensive.

Foundations usually focus on specific projects or innovative ideas. They usually have a specific target area of interest and geographic area in which to support projects. It is a waste time to solicit funds from a foundation if the organization is not within its scope or geographic area.

There are several different types of foundations. In general, foundations are organized as private, corporate, community, or operating. They usually have boards of directors and will give potential recipients information on their scopes and geographic distribution areas.

Many state governments publish an annual listing of foundations operating within their jurisdictions. These reports contain valuable information including the scope of the grants, target area and audience, value of the grants, application deadlines, and contact information.

Fundraisers

Fundraising is most often an activity used by volunteer or combination organizations to supplement or provide operating revenues. Fundraisers usually take the form of local events such as social events, bingo, raffles, and requests for donations. Some organizations have annual bean or pancake suppers that serve as public-relations events as well as fundraisers.

In some areas, fire and emergency services organizations sponsor circuses and other events and share the proceeds with organizers of the events. The greatest danger in these cosponsored events is that the telephone solicitations required to sell tickets may result in negative responses from the public that will focus on the organization and not the telephone marketers.

Process Steps

Budget development is an involved and ongoing process. Company officers work together along with chief officers, other staff members, and citizen representatives to create annual budgets. The process is generally divided into understandable steps. The six steps involved in the budget process are planning, preparing, implementing, monitoring, evaluating, and revising.

Plans

Throughout the year, administrative personnel who are responsible for budget preparation maintain records and make notes on the implementation of the current budget. Depending on local conditions or legal requirements, the budget process begins in earnest 3 to 5 months before the end of the current *fiscal year:* The established period of time when an organization's annual financial records begin and end such as July 1 to June 30 or October 1 to September 30.

At the beginning of the planning process, the jurisdiction should have a fairly clear idea of estimated revenues, based upon the following factors:

- Tax projections
- Expected grants and subsidies from the state/provincial or federal government
- Expected fees for services
- Bond sales
- Funds from other sources

Preparation

Estimated revenues from all sources are translated into preliminary budget priorities by the jurisdiction's finance and revenue department. The chief/manager of the fire and emergency services organization may be informed of general fiscal conditions and what parameters to work within during department budget planning and preparation sessions.

As part of the preparation process, company officers will be required to submit estimates of the funds they will need to operate their units, stations, or programs and their request justifications. The officers should keep in mind the following two types of spending that exist in any organization:

- *Fixed-cost spending* — Mandated purchases or costs such as assessments to the sinking fund, personnel wages, and personnel benefits
- *Discretionary spending* — Spending that occurs after fixed costs are paid; may include the purchase of new equipment or the upgrade and/or implementation of a new program

An important point relating to preparing budget requests is that requests should *not* be inflated or overestimated. To help taxpayers and their elected representatives make informed decisions about how tax revenues are spent, fire and emergency services organization officers have a responsibility to make every budget request as accurate and realistic as possible and present that request in the format expected by administrators and elected officials.

All requests should be kept as simple as possible. The simplest, most direct language should be used. In the narrative description of the services and their funding requirements, the language should be written so that anyone can understand it — no use of acronyms or fire and emergency services jargon.

Those who ultimately decide to approve or disapprove these requests may have little or no knowledge of fire and emergency services terms. If a request is not approved or is reduced, it should be done on the merits of the program — not because the request could not be understood.

In most jurisdictions, funding requests for capital items are separated from operating expenses as mentioned earlier. Even though these two categories must be separated, they are submitted as part of the same organizational budget request. Once all data are compiled and translated into specific requests for specific programs and activities, the first draft of the budget request is finished.

Because this request will be thoroughly scrutinized, along with the requests from every other department/organization in the jurisdiction, its chances for approval are increased when the document is as complete and correct as possible. Therefore, before the budget request is submitted for external review by the jurisdiction, prudent administrators insist that each organizational budget request first go through a diligent internal review.

Justification. Justifying a budget request requires documentation and supporting evidence that proves to even the most casual listener that the request is valid. Thorough research is the basis for this documentation (**Figure 9.19, p. 214**). This information is not only used to justify the budget request, it is also the information that was used to prepare the budget in the first place. Accurate research and internal records maintenance provide strong bases for both activities.

Internal review. In this context, *internal* refers to the fire and emergency services organization as well as the parent organization to which it may be assigned such as the department of public safety. The fire and emergency services organization's budget request is thoroughly reviewed by the parent organization's administrator, the chief/manager of the department/organization, or staffs of both organizations. After the internal review, the

Figure 9.19 Replacing a piece of apparatus that has been damaged or destroyed in an accident may seem simple. However, the organization still has to justify the replacement cost and show that other alternatives, such as replacing it with an older reserve unit, are not cost-effective. *Courtesy of Mike Mallory.*

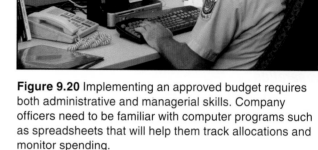

Figure 9.20 Implementing an approved budget requires both administrative and managerial skills. Company officers need to be familiar with computer programs such as spreadsheets that will help them track allocations and monitor spending.

budget is incorporated into the combined budget request for the entire parent organization and submitted to the jurisdiction's governing body for an external review. *Review elements:*

- Determine whether the data available justify the request.
- Consider alternative approaches to providing the same services or alternative sources of revenue.
- Consider potential questions that may be asked by the governing body and develop answers based on sound arguments.

External review. The *external* review is the final review that the budget-request document receives. The governing body of the jurisdiction schedules one or more public hearings so that citizens of the jurisdiction can have input into the decisions on the budget. The budget may be sent back to the administrator to be revised in light of citizen concerns. The governing body then considers both revenues and expenditures and may adjust either or both to balance the budget and meet the needs of citizens. When citizen concerns have been addressed and the budget is balanced, the governing body approves the budget and it becomes law.

Implementation

Once the budget has been approved and adopted, the administrator, department heads, managers, and supervisors (company officers) will have the

funds with which to turn the vision reflected in the budget into reality. They must use their administrative and managerial skills to implement the budget (**Figure 9.20**).

In addition to important fiscal details, the approved and adopted budget represents a plan for the organization's operation for the fiscal year. Many chief officers take this opportunity to meet with personnel to review the budget and explain what it means to the organization's operation. In organizations that are too large to make a mass meeting practical, a written or videotaped budget message from the chief/manager may serve the same purpose.

Regardless of how it is accomplished, the importance of communicating this message cannot be overemphasized. Company officers participate in the communication process by explaining the adopted budget to subordinates and clarifying any misconceptions that may exist.

The budget tells those who must function within its limitations whether new personnel can be hired, staff cuts will be necessary, vacant positions can be filled, and new equipment can be purchased. In addition, the budget requests that were approved or disapproved may provide an indication about how the jurisdiction perceives the services provided by the organization — or they may simply reflect fiscal reality.

The budget message should include any specific praise or criticism by the organization's jurisdiction. While the praise may be gratifying, the criticism may be more valuable. If criticism is viewed objectively, it can serve as a way to focus future priorities and performance within the fire and emergency services organization.

Monitor Process

The budget process does not end with the implementation of the budget. The budget must be monitored to determine its effectiveness and prevent a budgetary crisis in the event of a change in the economic environment.

Typically, individual departments/organizations within the jurisdiction are informed only of the expenditures of their allotted budgets. Most jurisdictions print and distribute monthly account statements that indicate the account balances in each program, line item, or category of the budget. This accounting allows the fire officer responsible for budget administration to track purchasing trends and ensure that accounts are not overspent.

With the addition of computer-based accounting programs, this monitoring control can become a more frequent check performed on a weekly or daily basis with feedback provided to budget managers. In addition, many organizations now keep such budget-accounting information in electronic form on computer servers accessible to department managers. This electronic version provides more current information and eliminates the need for much of the printing and distribution that was done in the past.

Evaluation

Evaluating the effectiveness of a budget is actually part of the monitor process. When applied to the purchase of materials, an evaluation can be as simple as determining that the proper amount and quality of materials are available in a reasonable amount of time. When it is applied to programs and performance, it requires a cost/benefit analysis that compares the total effort necessary to produce desired results.

The individual project manager, chief/manager of the department/organization, or an auditor assigned by the jurisdiction may perform evaluations. The results of the evaluation can be used to justify program changes, additional funding for programs, or elimination of programs that are deemed cost-prohibitive.

Revision

There is always the possibility that a budget will have to be revised during the budget cycle. Causes may include the following:

- Decrease in revenue
- Increase in operating costs
- Underestimation of actual costs
- Increase in service requirements
- Change in labor/management agreement
- Unforeseen or catastrophic occurrence

Because budget expenditures must be in line with actual revenue, the most likely result of a change will be to revise the costs of operations or capital purchases. The process for revising the budget is defined by local ordinance or policy. However, the options and actions listed in the Monitor Process section can be applied to each of these reasons for revisions.

Records should be maintained on all changes and revisions in the budget during the cycle. These records are necessary for improving the accuracy of future budget preparations and provide a history of the current budget.

Summary

Company officers are responsible for numerous administrative functions in fire and emergency services organizations of all sizes. To effectively execute these functions, company officers must be familiar with the customer service concept, the creation and implementation of policies and procedures, and the budget development process in effect in their jurisdictions.

These administrative functions may not be as exhilarating as fire suppression or search and rescue, but they are critical to the operation of the organization. All three functions are influenced by or affect the three groups of customers: internal, external, and stakeholder. It is essential for the company officer, as the first level of supervision and a representative of the organization to the public, to understand the needs of these groups and be able to win and maintain their goodwill and support.

Safety and Health Issues

Chapter Contents

Learning Objectives

1. Identify facts about emergency scene casualties and nonemergency workplace casualties.

2. Identify facts about safety initiatives and resources that focus on ensuring a safe work environment.

3. Recall various safety policies and procedures.

4. Distinguish among activities to ensure a safe work environment at the emergency scene, en route to and from the emergency scene, and at facilities.

5. Select facts about information included in a safety and health program.

6. Select facts about maintaining an effective infectious disease control program.

7. Recall information about conducting accident investigations.

8. Identify facts about collecting data and completing accident report forms.

9. Select facts about investigating injuries, illnesses, and exposures.

Job Performance Requirements

This chapter provides information that addresses the following job performance requirements of NFPA 1021, *Standard for Fire Officer Professional Qualifications* (2003):

<u>Chapter 4 Fire Officer I</u>

4.7.1

4.7.1(A)

4.7.2

4.7.2(A)

Chapter 10
Safety and Health Issues

In order to fulfill their basic mission of protecting the lives of the population they serve, fire and emergency responders must first protect themselves. An injured or incapacitated responder cannot assist a victim and, at the same time, requires aid and resources that would otherwise be dedicated to that victim.

Because of their position in the organizational structure, company officers are responsible for their own safety and health and that of each person in their companies. They must be familiar with the accident investigation policies and procedures of their organizations. Company officers must also know the following information:

- Common causes of personal injuries and accidents that affect members
- Local safety policies and procedures
- Basic workplace safety
- Components of an infectious disease control program

While emergency scene safety receives a great deal of attention, nonemergency safety is equally important. Injuries and fatalities can, and do, occur at the fire station, training facility, and other facilities while personnel are performing daily nonemergency activities. Creating and maintaining a safe work environment in the daily nonemergency activities result from identifying personal risks in the facilities, activities, and behaviors and controlling or eliminating them through policies and procedures.

Cardiac arrest is the leading cause of firefighter fatalities, while overexertion or stress that results in heart attacks and strokes is the leading cause of firefighter injury. Reducing these injury and fatality causes is the responsibility of the organization and each individual. An effective method is the implementation of a health and wellness program by the organization. The program includes education in and the application of proper nutrition, exercise, and the cessation of the use of tobacco products of all types.

As members of an *all-risk profession*, company officers are responsible for fostering a positive safety and health environment. Company officers must be able to influence their subordinates' perceptions regarding compliance with the organization's safety and health policies and procedures. Therefore, company officers *must* set a good example by seriously complying with the safety and health issues of the department.

This chapter begins by discussing the casualties that result from unsafe acts followed by a review of the most commonly applied fire service safety standards. Typical safety policies and procedures, workplace safety, and initial accident investigations are addressed. The infectious disease control program is also discussed. Finally, the process for investigating accidents and injuries is provided.

Emergency Services Casualties

Casualties occur at emergency incidents, in transit to and from incidents, during training, and during work shifts at the station and other facilities **(Figure 10.1, p. 220)**. Company officers must be aware of statistics that support the claim that fire fighting is a dangerous profession. Knowing these figures and the causes of casualties help fire officers provide company-level safety training and instruction that will reduce and perhaps eliminate these consequences.

Figure 10.1 Casualties include both fatalities and injuries. Injuries received at emergency incidents account for approximately half of the total injuries reported by emergency responders each year.

The company officer can also use programs and resources such as the Everyone Goes Home initiative, the FirefighterCloseCalls.Com and EMSCloseCalls.Com web sites, and the concept of the Firefighter Safety Stand Down to generate an interest in safe work behaviors. The result can be the application of safety policies and procedures that ensures a safe work environment.

Emergency Scene Casualties

A report published in March 2004 by RAND Worldwide (a professional provider of services designed to improve productivity and increase safety through review and consultation) stated that fire and emergency responder injuries during emergency operations in the U.S. amounted to approximately 88,000 incidents, half of the total fire and emergency responder injuries reported per year. Of these, 2,000 injuries were potentially life-threatening.

The types of injuries included trauma, cuts and bruises, burns, asphyxiation, and thermal stress. The majority of injuries occurred during fire attack and search and rescue activities. Incident reports indicated that personnel involved in emergency medical services (EMS) activities were most likely to suffer sprains, strains, back injuries, and exposures to infectious or communicable diseases.

According to information provided by the U.S. Fire Administration (USFA) in January 2006, 106 firefighters died during 2005 while on duty compared to 117 firefighters who died in 2004. Since 1977, the trend indicates a fluctuation from a high in 1978 (171) to a low in 1992 (77). Between 2000 and 2006 the average has been 107 lives lost per year (this average does *not* include the 344 firefighters killed in the September 11, 2001, terrorist attack). Regardless of the highs, lows, and averages, authorities agree that these numbers are too high and thus unacceptable (**Figure 10.2**).

The two leading causes of fatalities to firefighters are the result of motor vehicle accidents and heart attacks resulting from physical stress. In 2005,

Figure 10.2 Each year over 100 funerals are held for emergency responders who die in the line of duty.

stress-related fatalities were at the highest level in over 10 years, accounting for 40 percent of all line-of-duty deaths (LODD). Emergency incident fatalities accounted for 20 percent of the fatalities since 1977.

In many fire and emergency services organizations, EMS responses account for between 50 and 80 percent of emergency-response volume. These incidents result in only 3 percent of firefighter fatalities. Trauma accounts for the deaths of 50 percent of firefighters who were involved in EMS operations at the time of their fatal injuries; another 38 percent involved in EMS operations died from heart attacks.

Nonemergency Workplace Casualties

Nonemergency casualties include any fatalities or injuries that occurred while performing administrative duties, training, code enforcement and inspections, maintenance, or other nonincident-related situations. In 2004, 37 firefighters were killed in these types of accidents. Tragically, many of these occurred during training evolutions.

Between 1987 and 2003, training-related injuries increased by nearly 21 percent. Approximately 7,000 injuries occurred in 2001 during training exercises. The leading type of injury was strain/sprain (51 percent) followed by wound/cut/bleeding/bruise (20 percent). Heart attacks and strokes only constituted 1 percent of the training-related injuries reported in May 2003 by USFA **(Figure 10.3)**.

Training-related fatalities, which are about 10 percent of all annual firefighter LODD, have risen in recent years. The leading cause of training-related fatalities has been heart attacks followed by traumatic injuries.

Terminology

Accident is a term that is frequently used to describe an unplanned, uncontrolled event resulting from unsafe acts and/or unsafe occupational conditions, either of which may result in injury, death, or property damage. Accidents may be the result of adverse conditions in the environment (weather, terrain, or situation), equipment/material malfunction, or the result of human error (ignorance, carelessness, or mental/emotional/physical difficulties).

Some safety professionals prefer to use the term *incident* to refer to such events and contend that all incidents are preventable and controllable. With proper training, skills development, care and maintenance of equipment, adhering to safety regulations, and a proactive attitude toward safety, accidents or incidents can be controlled, reduced, or even eliminated.

Therefore, another definition of *accident* could be occurrences and their causes that may lead to property damage or personal injuries that may be divided into two categories: injury and noninjury. Company officers are responsible for protecting themselves and their personnel from accidents by emphasizing safe actions and activities and enforcing safety regulations.

Figure 10.3 Injuries that occur during training exercises can be prevented. The use of full protective clothing and equipment and safe behaviors can reduce or eliminate most types of physical injuries. Heart attacks and strokes can be reduced by changes in personal behaviors and lifestyles.

Safety Initiative

In response to the increasing numbers of fire and emergency services casualties, the National Fallen Firefighters Foundation, in cooperation with USFA, hosted a summit in March 2004 involving approximately 200 leaders from throughout the nation's fire service. The summit resulted in the development of strategic initiatives that will be undertaken in an effort to meet the following goals:

- Reduce firefighter fatalities by 25 percent over the next 5 years.

- Reduce firefighter fatalities by 50 percent over the next 10 years.

The resulting initiative can be condensed into 16 objectives that have been titled *Everyone Goes Home*. Company officers are essential to the achievement of these objectives and they must be familiar with and support them. The objectives are paraphrased as follows:

1. Define and advocate the need for cultural change within the fire service relating to safety, incorporating leadership, management, supervision, accountability, and personal responsibility.

2. Enhance the personal and organizational accountability for safety and health throughout the fire service.

3. Focus greater attention on the integration of risk management with incident management at all levels, including strategic, tactical, and planning responsibilities.

4. Empower all firefighters to stop unsafe practices.

5. Develop and implement national standards for training, qualifications, and certification (including regular recertification) that are equally applicable to all firefighters based on the duties they are expected to perform.

6. Develop and implement national medical and physical fitness standards that are equally applicable to all firefighters based on the duties they are expected to perform.

7. Create a national research agenda and data-collection system that relate to the initiatives.

8. Utilize available technology wherever it can produce higher levels of safety and health.

9. Thoroughly investigate all firefighter fatalities, injuries, and near misses.

10. Ensure that grant programs support the implementation of safe practices and/or mandate safe practices as an eligibility requirement.

11. Develop and champion national standards for emergency response policies and procedures.

12. Develop and champion national protocols for response to violent incidents.

13. Ensure that firefighters and their families have access to counseling and psychological support.

14. Ensure that public education receives more resources and is championed as a critical fire and life-safety program.

15. Strengthen advocacy for the enforcement of codes and the installation of home fire sprinklers.

16. Ensure that safety is a primary consideration in the design of apparatus and equipment.

Firefighter Close Calls

One of the statistics that has *not* been tracked regarding firefighter injuries is the number of close calls that could have easily resulted in injury or fatalities. A *close call* is any event that came close to resulting in an injury or fatality. To address this issue several individuals formed web sites called FirefighterCloseCalls.Com and EMSCloseCalls.Com. At these sites, firefighters and EMS personnel can log close calls they had and review close calls of other responders in an attempt to prevent similar types of injuries and fatalities in the future **(Figure 10.4)**.

Firefighter Safety Stand Down

As a result of an alarming increase in firefighter fatalities during the first 5 months of 2005, the International Association of Fire Chiefs (IAFC) sponsored a Firefighter Safety Stand Down on June 21, 2005. When significant safety issues needed to be addressed, the Stand Down (an idea taken from the military) was to have departments eliminate

Figure 10.4 Firefighter close calls are rarely reported. However, the data collected on close calls can help to determine trends in improper behavior or procedures. *Courtesy of San Ramon Valley Fire Protection District.*

- NFPA 1500, *Standard on Fire Department Occupational Safety and Health Program*
- NFPA 1561, *Standard on Emergency Services Incident Management System*
- NFPA 1581, *Standard on Fire Department Infection Control Program*
- NFPA 1983, *Standard on Fire Service Life Safety Rope and Equipment for Emergency Services*
- NFPA 1852, *Standard on Selection, Care, and Maintenance of Open-Circuit Self-Contained Breathing Apparatus (SCBA)*

The company officer should be familiar with the local safety policies and procedures and their applications. Training sessions should be held periodically to ensure that unit members are familiar with the policies and procedures. Practical training evolutions and company-level training should include the use of all appropriate safety policies.

Basic to all safety policies and procedures is the establishment of a safety and health program. The safety and health program is comprised of smaller programs or components that focus on specific areas of safety and health. The first is the accident, injury, and illness prevention program that provides hazard information and training for responders. Of growing importance to fire and emergency responders is the medical or infection exposure control program that protects responders from disease. Finally, the safety and health program includes a comprehensive physical fitness and wellness program to improve the health of employees and alter behavior patterns that may increase the likelihood of injury or illness.

The task of managing the safety and health program is usually assigned to the health and safety officer (HSO). The task of reporting the effectiveness of the program to the HSO belongs to the company officer.

Basic Workplace Safety

Workplace safety consists of activities that ensure a safe work environment and protect employees from job-related injuries, illnesses, and exposures to infectious diseases and hazardous materials. It is the ultimate responsibility of the organization's management to provide a safe workplace. This goal

nonemergency functions for the day and focus this time on the safety issues in their department. See **Appendix G** for an example of the Richmond Fire and Emergency Services 2005 Safety Stand Down.

As a result of the first Firefighter Safety Stand Down, many fire and emergency services organizations have instituted regular, company-level safety training. Some organizations require a set period of time dedicated to a single safety topic per work shift. Others use an entire work shift per month for the same purpose. In both cases, the company officer is responsible for providing safety instruction and training.

Due to the success of the 2005 Stand Down, a second Stand Down was scheduled on June 21, 2006. Its purpose was to increase awareness of the need for safety and call attention to the unacceptably high number of LODD that occurred the previous year.

Safety Policies and Procedures

The organization's safety policies and procedures should be based on NFPA safety standards, including but not limited to the following:

is attained through training, policies, procedures, and maintenance of facilities and equipment. However, it is the responsibility of the company officer to implement training requirements, policies, and procedures and report the need for any maintenance or the replacement of unsafe equipment.

For fire and emergency responders, the workplace is *not* a single location — it is rather multiple locations connected by routes of transportation. The organization and company officer have no control over the majority of these locations. Only the organization's facilities, stations, and apparatus can be directly controlled and made as safe as possible. Therefore, the workplace can be generally divided into emergency scene, en route to and from emergency scene, and facilities.

The company officer must be familiar with the organization's safety and health program. This program applies to all areas of the workplace and provides information and methods for ensuring that a safe work culture is developed.

Figure 10.5 A strict and properly administered physical fitness program combined with good nutrition can reduce the likelihood of strokes and heart attacks.

Emergency Scene

The statistics for fire and emergency responder casualties provided at the beginning of this chapter indicate that the majority of fatalities occur at emergency scene incidents and are the result of cardiac arrest due to overexertion. To reduce emergency scene casualties, the company officer must approach safety from the following two directions:

- First, the primary cause of fatalities must be addressed through education, fitness, and wellness. The company officer must ensure that members of the unit are aware of the risks posed by the following conditions:

  — Improper nutrition

  — Lack of weight control

  — Lack of physical fitness **(Figure 10.5)**

  — Use of tobacco, which contributes to heart disease

- Second, during the emergency incident, the company officer must monitor subordinates to ensure that they do not become physically stressed. When symptoms of overexertion occur, personnel must be removed from the operation

and placed in a rehabilitation area. If symptoms are acute, the individual may require transportation and hospitalization.

Other emergency scene injuries can be prevented or reduced through the application of policies and procedures that regulate emergency scene activities. Personnel must be provided with the correct level of personal protective equipment (PPE), respiratory protection, and tools to safely and properly perform their duties. The company officer is responsible for ensuring that all personnel use the equipment that has been provided **(Figure 10.6)**.

Operational procedures must also be implemented to ensure as safe a work environment as possible. Some of these include the following:

- Lockout/tagout procedures to prevent unexpected energization, start-up, or release of stored energy

- Two unit members or mechanical devices to lift objects or victims who are over a predetermined weight

- Appropriate protective clothing when performing certain tasks; may include eye protection, hand protection, or ice cleats worn on boots or shoes

Figures 10.6 The company officer is responsible for ensuring that all members of the unit have proper personal protective equipment (PPE) and that it is in good condition and worn for the correct hazards.

- Heavy items mounted in lower compartments on apparatus
- Respiratory protection program
- Two in/two out program
- Establishment of an initial rapid intervention crew or team (IRIC/IRIT) at the incident
- Activation of personal alert safety system (PASS) devices
- Breathing air conservation procedures
- Establishment of a personnel accountability system (tags, Personal Accountability Report [PAR] count)

En Route to and from Scene

Apparatus and vehicle accidents are also responsible for many fatalities and injuries while personnel are en route to the incident. The emergency services

Figure 10.7 Driver/operator training and proper maintenance of apparatus are necessary elements if the number of accidents involving apparatus is to be reduced. *Courtesy of Mike Mallory.*

organization can control some of these accidents through apparatus design and maintenance and driver/operator training and certification.

Accidents involving privately owned vehicles (POVs) are more difficult to control. Volunteer and combination organizations can provide emergency lighting and audible warning devices as well as defensive driving training for responders. Policies regarding the use of warning devices and maximum response speeds can also help prevent accidents. The most effective means, though, is to change the culture that creates an extreme sense of urgency in responders, which could cause them to drive unsafely **(Figure 10.7)**.

Company officers must work to change this culture. In both career and volunteer organizations, units have been involved in accidents when driver/operators attempted to exceed the speed limit or not stop at controlled intersections. The company officer must always remember that both the officer and the driver/operator are responsible for the operation of the apparatus, and the officer has ultimate authority over the company and its safety.

Facilities

The one workplace where the organization has the greatest influence is in the organization's facilities. Fire stations, training centers, administrative offices, and maintenance buildings all have inherent features or activities that may contribute to an accident, injury, illness, or fatality. Proper maintenance is one of the best methods for providing a safe workplace. The company officer or building manager is responsible for reporting the need for repairs and ensuring that they are completed. Annual facility inspections are generally the responsibility of the HSO (**Figure 10.8**).

Training in safe methods for cleaning the facility, performing external lawn care, and storing materials and equipment are duties of the company officer. Safe procedures must be established for the following actions:

- Using warning signs for wet surfaces
- Using power and hand tools
- Using sharp instruments in the kitchen
- Climbing stairs or using slides or slide poles
- Cleaning upper story windows
- Replacing filters in heating, ventilating, and air-conditioning (HVAC) units
- Cleaning apparatus
- Parking apparatus in the facility
- Lifting heavy objects
- Repairing tools

Figure 10.8 Annual inspections of the organization's facilities, including shop areas, mechanical spaces, and storage areas, are usually the responsibility of the health and safety officer (HSO). The company officer is responsible for ensuring that the facility is clean and that repairs are reported and completed when they are needed.

Safety and Health Program

The company officer is also responsible for providing subordinates with information on the organization's safety and health program. Among the information that should be given to employees is the following:

- How and when to report injuries, including instruction on the location of first-aid facilities
- How to report unsafe conditions and practices
- Proper care, use, selection, and maintenance of personal protective equipment (PPE) along with its limitations
- Proper actions to take in the event of emergencies, including the routes of exiting areas during emergencies
- Identification of hazardous gases, chemicals, or materials along with instructions on their safe use and emergency action following accidental exposure
- Description of the organization's entire safety and health program (including its various components)
- On-the-job review of the practices necessary to perform initial job assignments in a *safe manner*
- Procedures to follow when exposed to blood-borne pathogens
- Proper procedures for lifting and back care
- Proper handling and use of power tools
- Rules and regulations regarding the use of vehicles in both emergency and nonemergency situations
- Approved safety procedures for incidents involving trenching/shoring and confined-space rescues
- Safety procedures designed to provide fall protection (**Figure 10.9**)
- Descriptions of the types of respiratory equipment and their use

Infectious Disease Control Program

Some occupational illnesses can be the result of exposures to individuals who or situations that are capable of transmitting an infectious disease. To control and manage this potential threat to the

Figure 10.9 The use of caution signs can reduce the potential for falls in the organization's facilities. All personnel should be made aware of the importance of safe procedures when cleaning or performing maintenance work.

safety and health of the organization's members, it is essential that an infectious disease control program be established. This program may also be called a medical exposure program and is regulated by NFPA 1581, *Standard on Fire Department Infection Control Program*.

A designated infection control officer is responsible for developing and managing this program. The infection control officer ensures that an adequate infection control plan is developed and all members are trained and supervised in the plan. The HSO or other fire officer who has the knowledge, training, and skills to fulfill the required duties may fill this position.

The program begins with a written infection (exposure) control plan that clearly explains its intent, benefits, and purposes. The plan must cover the standards of exposure control such as the following:

- Education and training requirements
- Vaccination requirements for potential threats such as anthrax or hepatitis B virus, annual flu vaccinations and tuberculosis (TB) inoculations

- Documentation and record-keeping requirements
- Cleaning, decontamination, and disinfection of personnel and equipment
- Exposure control and reporting protocols

Exposure reports must be maintained in a record-keeping system. Due to the fact that some symptoms may not become apparent for many years following exposure, these records must be maintained for 30 years following termination or retirement of an employee. These records are confidential and may only be released to the member or a designated representative.

Records are also maintained for training that involves the proper use of PPE, exposure protection, postexposure protocols, and disease modes of transmission as they relate to infectious diseases. The HSO and safety and health committee are required to annually review the infectious disease plan, updates, protocols, and equipment.

Investigation Policies

As defined previously, accidents are unplanned, uncontrolled events resulting from unsafe acts and/or unsafe occupational conditions, either of which may result in injury, death, or property damage. To reduce the potential for accidents to occur or to reduce the severity of accidents, the organization must develop and implement an accident investigation policy and procedure.

Too often, investigators only seek to identify who, if anyone, is responsible for the incident. This approach does nothing to prevent a reoccurrence or to address the *root cause* (basic reason) for the incident.

The policy should define accidents, establish the authority for investigating each type of accident, and establish a procedure for accident investigation. A managing company officer (Level II Fire Officer), the HSO, and the safety and health committee will have the ultimate authority for accident analysis. The supervising company officer (Fire Officer I), however, will have the responsibility for performing the initial accident investigation based on the procedure.

Accident investigations are not limited to accidents according to NFPA 1500. The company officer is also responsible for investigating job-related injuries and illnesses, fatalities, and exposures to infectious diseases and hazardous materials or atmospheres.

Accidents

When an accident occurs, an investigation is conducted to determine the root cause or the most basic reason for the accident and its source or origin. Accident investigations should be objective, impartial, and directed toward fact-finding, not fault-finding **(Figure 10.10)**. Several reasons to investigate workplace accidents are to identify and document the following conditions:

- Behavior or condition that caused an accident (root cause)
- Previously unrecognized hazards
- Apparatus/equipment defects or design flaws
- Additional training needs
- Improvements needed in safety policies and procedures
- Facts that could have a legal impact on an accident case
- Historical trends

When a workplace accident investigation is conducted, all participants and witnesses should be interviewed and all relevant factors documented.

Prominent among these is the human factor (personal characteristics). To conduct a thorough and comprehensive investigation, the investigators must have some knowledge of human behavior.

Human Factors

Safety research in private industry has shown that accidents happen frequently to some people and infrequently to others. This research indicates that accidents are *not* uniformly distributed throughout the workforce. Workers who fail to control the factors leading to an accident because of mental, psychological, or physical reasons will be involved in accidents more often than other workers. These workers are described as *accident prone*.

The accident-prone phenomenon can be explained by the term *human factors*, which are an individual's attributes or personal characteristics that cause the individual to be involved in more or fewer accidents than other individuals. In most cases, an organization can mitigate negative human factors through motivation, training, or technical revision. Human factors that often contribute to accidents have been classified into the following three broad categories:

- *Improper attitude* — Includes willful disregard, recklessness, irresponsibility, laziness, disloyalty, uncooperativeness, fearfulness, oversensitivity, egotism, jealousy, impatience, obsession, phobia, absentmindedness, excitability, incon-

Figure 10.10 The company officer should gather information regarding all accidents and injuries as soon as possible following an incident. Observations of the physical area of the incident, interviews with those involved, and inspections of any tools or equipment involved form the basis of the incident report.

sideration, intolerance, or mental unsuitability in general. Readjusting any of these attitudes or personality traits through counseling, training, or discipline can lead to accident reduction.

- *Lack of knowledge or skill* — Includes insufficient knowledge, misunderstandings, indecision, inexperience, poor training, or failure to recognize potential hazards. These problems can be reduced or eliminated through training.

- *Physically unsuited* — Includes problems of hearing, sight, weight, height, illness, allergies, slow reactions, disabilities, intoxication, or physical limitations in general. Correcting these physical limitations can often reduce accident rates. If they cannot be corrected, personnel should not be assigned to tasks where their limitations might create a hazard or be potentially dangerous to themselves or others.

An organization's effectiveness in mitigating the human factors that lead to accidents often depends upon a number of other factors. Some of these factors include time and resources committed to developing and implementing safety policies and procedures, safety training, and certification on the safe use of equipment. Safety training must be documented and the policies and procedures enforced.

Company officers should also be aware that the National Institute for Occupational Safety and Health (NIOSH) requires that an investigation be made of all incidents involving firefighter LODD. In addition, NIOSH may require that additional training be provided within the organization to change any contributing behavioral characteristics that may have caused a fatality.

Accident Scene Control

When the incident involves serious personal injuries, the victim must first be stabilized and transported to a health care facility for medical treatment **(Figure 10.11)**. Minor injuries may be treated at the scene. The company officer next ensures that the accident scene is secured and all equipment, clothing, or vehicles are left in place.

If conditions require that vehicles be moved, an attempt to photograph or at least sketch the location of each vehicle should be made. The company officer must remember that anything that

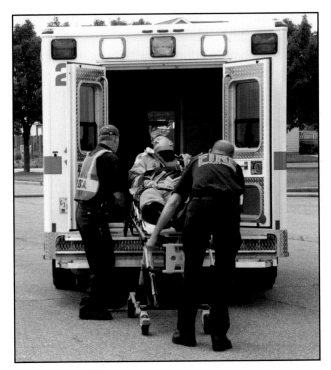

Figure 10.11 When a member of the unit is injured, the first duty of the company officer is to provide proper medical treatment. This treatment may require that the injured responder be transported immediately to a medical care facility.

was involved in the incident is evidence first for reconstructing the accident and preventing future accidents and second for supporting potential legal cases that may result.

Accurate Data Collection

The accident, injury, illness, and fatality statistics that are used to analyze accidents and determine trends are only as accurate as the original information that is gathered by investigating company officers. Company officers must follow the prescribed procedures and properly complete accident investigation forms provided by the jurisdiction.

The form may be a simplified version that permits the officer to enter words into blanks and complete a narrative account of the incident. Forms may also be designed so that they are similar to the National Fire Incident Reporting System (NFIRS) forms that require the use of predesignated codes to describe an incident. In either case, the form should be designed to record the essential information for accidents, injuries, illnesses, or fatalities.

In conducting an investigation, company officers collect basic information about the participants, event, or incident. The investigation should provide the following information:

- **General information** — Items:
  - Date and time of incident
  - Type of incident, illness, injury, or fatality
  - Location and emergency response type
  - Names of witnesses and their accounts of the situation
- **Employee characteristics (participant)** — Items:
  - Name and unit assignment (company/shift)
  - Age and gender
  - Rank/function
  - Personal protective clothing or equipment in use
- **Environmental information** — Items:
  - Weather and temperature
  - Day or night conditions
  - Noise and visibility
  - Terrain
- **Apparatus/equipment information** — Items:
  - Type of equipment involved
  - Age and condition
  - Location
  - Maintenance history
  - Distinguishing characteristics

A narrative description of the incident is the final portion of the investigation report. This narrative includes observations on the part of the officer, eye-witness reports, participant interviews, and information from other sources such as law-enforcement reports and dispatch information **(Figure 10.12)**.

Data gathered by the company officer is transmitted through the system to the HSO or Fire Officer II who uses the information to analyze the accident, job-related injuries and illnesses, fatalities, and exposures. Documentation must be retained and signed by the investigating officer.

Figure 10.12 Accident forms are generally available in hardcopy and electronic formats. The company officer should transcribe notes from the investigation onto the proper form and then check the results for accuracy.

Injuries, Illnesses, and Exposures

When a member of the unit experiences a job-related injury, illness, or exposure, the first duty of a company officer is to ensure prompt medical treatment for the individual. When the injury, illness, or exposure is serious, the individual must be transported to the closest available medical facility. Once the company officer has provided for the treatment of the member, an investigation can commence.

Investigations of job-related injuries, illnesses, or exposures generally include gathering the same information in the same way as accident investigations. Some differences may exist depending on the nature of the incident. For instance, an investigation into a claim that involves an illness that is perceived to be job-related may require more time and the services of a specialty organization such as one that samples air or water. These types of investigations may occur at some time after the event. The company officer must focus on the idea that information gained from the investigation may lead to the discovery of an environmental cause for the illness.

An exposure investigation may occur immediately following the incident or at some point in the future when symptoms of exposure appear in the individual. Accurate and thorough documentation of all incidents and exposures is basic to any current or future investigation.

An example of a long-range investigation involves the occurrence of cancer in a predominately high number of personnel who worked at a single station in one city. The symptoms did not appear until many years after some had retired. Attempts to determine the cause of the trend included water and air sampling, testing for asbestos, and a review of all emergency responses the members had been on. Tragically, no evidence of a single cause was ever determined.

Summary

An efficient and effective fire and emergency services organization depends on a safe, healthy, physically fit, and emotionally stable membership. It is the responsibility of the company officer to ensure a safe working environment though training, education, equipment, policies, procedures, leadership, and supervision. This safe environment is accomplished through the development and implementation of a comprehensive safety and health program that contains individual components to address both the obvious and obscure hazards to the health and well being of the members.

The organization must also make physical fitness a reality through the implementation of a holistic employee physical fitness and wellness program. The wellness component includes proper nutrition, back care, heart and lung disease awareness, and stress-reduction counseling. The organization should work to address all areas of health and wellness both through prevention and education. Through these efforts, the organization can reduce injuries, reduce fatalities, reduce health and lost-time costs, and improve the morale of the membership.

Company officers must make safety and health their primary concerns for their subordinates. To do so, they must set the example for others to follow and ensure that all operations are performed in a way that is consistent with standard operating procedures/standard operating guidelines (SOPs/SOGs) and safe practices.

Organizational Structure

Chapter Contents

Learning Objectives

1. Match to their definitions the organizational principles used by most fire and emergency services organizations.

2. Choose correct responses about organizational structure within the fire and emergency services.

3. Identify purposes of fire protection organizations.

4. Identify public fire and emergency services organizations.

5. Identify private fire and emergency services organizations.

6. Match to their definitions various types of staffing.

7. Select facts about the three types of resource allocation.

Job Performance Requirements

This chapter provides information that addresses the following job performance requirements of NFPA 1021, *Standard for Fire Officer Professional Qualifications* (2003):

Chapter 4 Fire Officer I

4.1.1

Chapter 11
Organizational Structure

Fire and emergency services organizations are composed of diverse and sometimes complex groups of people. These people are organized in a manner intended to provide the highest level of service to their customers at the lowest possible cost. The smallest unit of the organization is generally called a *company*. Company officers are responsible for directing the members of their companies or units in ways that achieve this high level of service. In order to accomplish this task, company officers must understand the structure of their organizations, where their units are located in them, and how their units relate to other organizational parts.

The discussion of a fire and emergency services organization's structure may be divided into two views: How it is funded and how it is staffed. Funding determines whether the organization is classified as public or private, while staffing indicates whether personnel are considered career (paid for their services) or volunteers.

Regardless of whether a fire and emergency services organization is public or private or is staffed by career or volunteer personnel (see Staffing section), it must have some type of formal structure. The structure provides a management framework for the organization and defines how it will plan and operate to meet its mission. This structure also determines how the organization will interact with other organizations or government agencies, both internal and external to the jurisdiction (that is, agencies within the local government of which the fire and emergency services organization is a part and agencies that are a part of another governmental authority).

This chapter discusses the basic principles of organizational structure, purposes and classifications of fire and emergency services organizations, and how organizations are staffed. Resource allocation issues are also discussed.

Basic Principles

In any society, people deal with organizational structures in one form or another. From participating in recreational sports programs to living within family groups, everyone participates in structured activities daily. Organizational structure is important to the fire and emergency services because it permits the effective, organized, and efficient use of resources. Teamwork and esprit de corps, quality leadership, effective discipline, and efficient operations are all important to emergency response personnel, and the organizational structure must accommodate these traits.

Knowledge of the basic principles of organizational structure can help the company officer or officer candidate understand how fire and emergency services organizations are structured. The principles are based on organizational theory, research, and practice in both public and private organizations. Principles discussed include the following:

- *Scalar structure* — Chain of authority
- *Line and staff personnel* — Two distinct groups
- *Decision-making authority* — Legal ability to make and implement decisions
- *Unity of command* — Each subordinate must have only one supervisor

- ***Span of control*** — Limits the number of subordinates that one individual can effectively supervise
- ***Division of labor*** — Large jobs divided into smaller tasks for individual assignment

In most public fire and emergency services organizations in North America, the top official carries the title of *chief* or, in some cases, *commissioner,* or *chief executive officer (CEO)*. Whatever title given, the CEO must ensure that the organization has an adequate structure and management system, including required policies and procedures, to govern the operation of the organization in support of its mission.

All fire chiefs or CEOs strive for unity within the organization. To ensure that personnel work together effectively, written standard operating procedures/standard operating guidelines (SOPs/SOGs) are required. These procedures/guidelines are used to define organizational policy and describe behavioral and performance expectations of employees. However, cooperation among company members is based not only upon following organizational guidelines but also on the trust that results from the consistent application of sound organizational principles.

Scalar Structure

The term used to describe the common organizational structure in the fire and emergency services is *scalar,* which is defined as *having an uninterrupted series of steps* or a *chain of authority.* The scalar organization is a paramilitary, pyramid-type of organization with authority centralized at the top. Decisions are directed down from the top of the organizational structure through intermediate levels to the base of the structure. Information, in turn, is transmitted up from the bottom through the structure to the positions at the top.

Typically, emergency services are scalar organizations (**Figure 11.1**). Companies are organized in the scalar manner: They are located with other

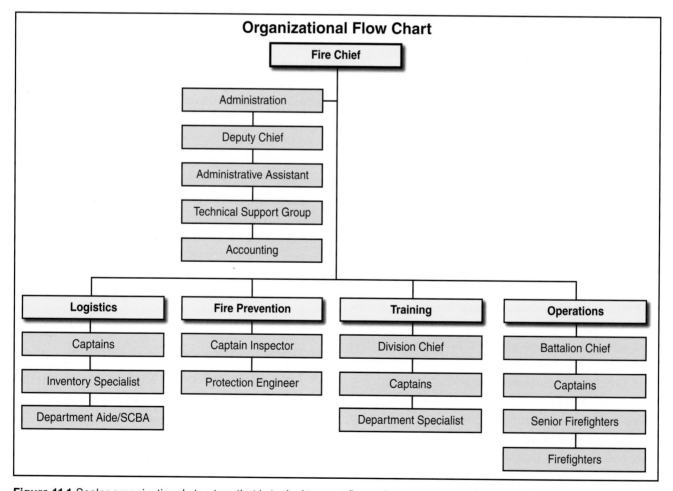

Figure 11.1 Scalar organizational structure that is typical to most fire and emergency services organizations.

companies in a scalar battalion/district, each battalion/district is combined with others to form a work shift, and each shift is organized to provide services to the response area. However, operations do not always follow the rigid scalar form. In the pure form of the scalar principle of management, there is an unbroken chain — or scale — of supervisors from the top of the organization to the bottom. This chain models the flow of authority, and any action or communication taking place in the group should follow these well-defined lines of authority.

In many cases, direct communication at lower organizational levels allows for quicker actions and reactions. So, within this scalar structure, certain decision-making authority is delegated to lower levels, and communication is enhanced. The true scalar structure is well-suited for dealing with emergency situations for the following reasons:

- Span of control is maintained (see Span of Control section).

- Information is centralized for decision-making (see Decision-Making Authority section).

- Functional chain of command is maintained (see Unity of Command section).

Line and Staff Personnel

Line and *staff* are terms that refer to the traditional organizational concept that separates fire and emergency services personnel into the following two distinct groups:

- *Line personnel* — Those who deliver services to the public or external customers (see Chapter 9, Administrative Functions); typical functions include fire suppression, emergency medical services (EMS), inspections, education, and investigations **(Figure 11.2a)**

- *Staff personnel* — Those who provide support to the line personnel or internal customers (see Chapter 9, Administrative Functions); typical functions are training, logistics, and personnel administration **(Figure 11.2b)**

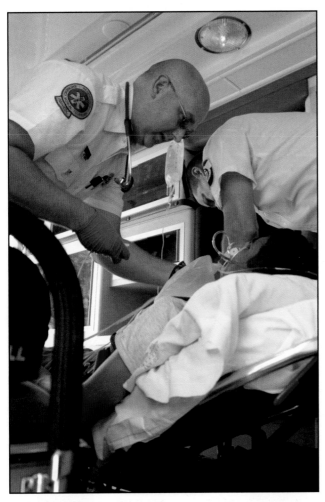

Figure 11.2a The activities of line and staff personnel are generally determined by the customers they serve. Line personnel such as EMS responders serve external customers of the organization.

Figure 11.2b Staff personnel such as training officers provide support for internal customers or members of the organization. Staff officers may also fulfill line functions such as providing training to external customers in the form of fire and life-safety or CPR training. *Courtesy of Benny Deal.*

With the addition of new roles and responsibilities, the distinction between line and staff functions becomes less distinct. Company officers have traditionally reported to a battalion chief or other line supervisor during all their emergency activities and routine nonemergency activities. However, it is not uncommon for company officers to also report to a staff officer when the company is engaged in some specialized activity (such as code enforcement, public education, hydrant inspection programs, etc.) that is under the authority of that particular staff officer. This reporting practice is sometimes called *functional supervision*.

In small organizations, and especially in combination (both career and volunteer personnel) departments and volunteer (all volunteer personnel) organizations, staff duties may also be assigned to line personnel. This assignment of duties may also result in functional supervision.

Decision-Making Authority

Authority refers to the legal ability of an individual to make and implement decisions for which the individual is held accountable; there are two types: centralized and decentralized (**Figure 11.3**). The

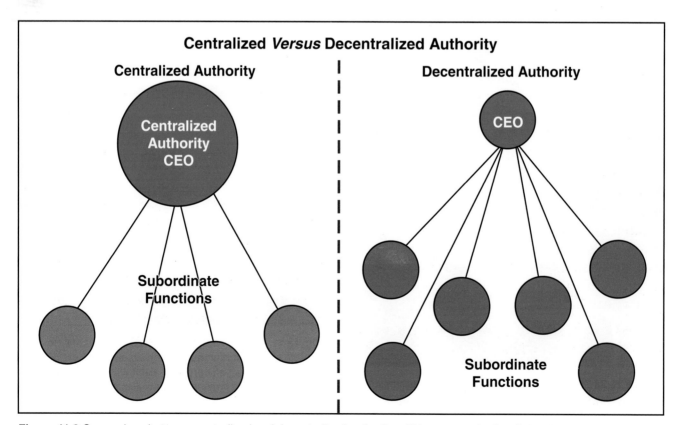

Figure 11.3 Comparison between centralized and decentralized authority within an organizational structure.

difference between the two types is the level at which decisions are made. Descriptions are as follows:

- **Centralized authority** — Decisions are made by one person at the top of the structure. Centralized authority works well in very small organizations such as an individual fire company, but in large organizations the leader's span of control may be exceeded unless decision-making authority is delegated.

- **Decentralized authority** — Decisions are allowed to be made at a lower level (basically delegation of authority), with the effects of the decisions reported through the structure. For decentralized authority to work effectively, the fire chief or CEO must ensure that all members understand the direction, values, and goals of the organization.

Centralized

Regardless of the level where decision-making authority is located, accountability for decisions is almost always centralized. The fire chief or CEO of the organization delegates to officers the authority to make decisions and implement plans, but the fire chief or CEO is still accountable for any decisions made.

As a general rule, no one in a fire and emergency services organization has absolute authority to avoid accounting to a higher authority. Even the fire chief or CEO is accountable to the local governing body and ultimately to the public.

Decentralized

Even though authority is granted at different levels *to accomplish specific tasks*, decentralized authority has limits. The fire chief or CEO might give the authority to make policy changes to a deputy, assistant, or battalion/district chief while granting authority to service equipment to the company level.

The chief or CEO may also decentralize the authority to make certain decisions only in specific areas. For example, a fire chief may dictate what tasks are to be performed but delegate to the company officer the authority to decide when and in what order the tasks are performed.

Decentralization of authority allows for the expeditious handling of most matters. When decisions are made at lower levels in an organization, upper management personnel are freed to concentrate on more important matters. The details resulting from a decision do not have to be reported, but the effects of the decision do.

For example, depending upon the size and organizational structure of the fire and emergency services organization, a fire chief usually *does not* need to know that the maintenance department is going to replace two pistons and six valves on Engine 7185. However, the fire chief *may* need to know that an engine will be out of service for an extended period for maintenance.

Ideally, decision-making authority should be delegated to the lowest organizational level possible. However, with decentralization of authority, the possibility of a duplication of effort exists. To avoid this duplication, policies must define what decisions can be made and under what conditions. A review system must also be established to ensure accountability and study the effects of decentralized decisions.

Delegation of Authority

Because the company officer may feel an obligation or commitment to guarantee that every task is completed, the decision to delegate authority to finish a task is often difficult. There may be doubt in the officer's mind that the delegated task will be completed in a manner that meets the standards of the organization. Feelings like these are natural and show that the officer is genuinely interested in doing a good job. Challenges such as delegating tasks can be alleviated through a good training program that not only builds knowledge, skills, and abilities but also trust.

When delegating a task, an officer must exercise some discretion to ensure that the assigned employee is *capable of doing the job*. The officer should attempt to pick the right person for the right job. However, officers should look for opportunities to delegate tasks that challenge subordinates to build their knowledge and skill set as well as their confidence.

Delegation of an assignment must be accompanied with appropriate authority and trust that the individual will achieve the desired results using proper methods. It is difficult for anyone to accomplish a task without being given the necessary authority to complete the assignment.

Another important consideration in the delegation of authority is to make the objective clear to the individual being given the assignment. The company officer should describe the task and its relationship to the overall goal or objective. In addition, the officer must make clear what resources are available and what time and safety constraints apply to the assignment.

Unity of Command

Unity of command is a management principle that states that each subordinate must have only one supervisor (**Figure 11.4**). If an employee is required to report to more than one supervisor, the employee and the supervisors may face a number of difficult situations. The most common of these difficult situations created by the lack of unity of command are the following:

- The employee follows the last order received, even though the previous order has not been performed. Thus, the first assignment is incomplete but the supervisor who ordered it thinks that it has been done.

- The employee executes the task poorly while trying to do two (perhaps conflicting) tasks at once.

- The employee plays the supervisors against each other so that neither supervisor knows exactly what the employee is doing, and the employee may do little or no work.

- The employee becomes frustrated while attempting to follow the conflicting orders of different supervisors and gives up both tasks.

As each of these scenarios illustrates, violation of the *unity of command* principle leads to confusion and frustration by both subordinates and supervisors. Conversely, organizations structured so that each worker reports to only one supervisor provides adequate direction and accountability, which then allows all workers to be more productive and efficient. Unity of command depends on the use of two other concepts: chain of command and functional supervision.

Figure 11.4 The basic principle of unity of command is that a subordinate must have only one supervisor.

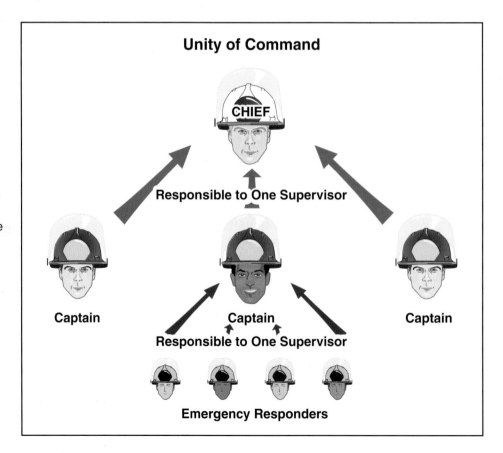

Chain of Command

The *chain of command* is the pathway of responsibility from the top of the organization to the bottom and vice versa. Although each member reports to one supervisor directly, every member is still responsible to the fire chief or CEO indirectly through the chain of command.

With unity of command, supervisors can divide the work into specific job assignments without losing control. The fire chief or CEO can issue general orders that filter through the chain of command and translate into specific work assignments for the various ranks down through the organizational structure.

A type of breach of the unity of command principle, commonly known as an *end run*, occurs when a subordinate sidesteps the immediate supervisor and takes a problem directly to an officer higher in the chain of command. While there may be circumstances that make it necessary for a subordinate to take this action, it is generally an attempt to circumvent the chain of command, which is usually destructive to organizational unity and cohesiveness.

In most cases, the superior officer should instruct the subordinate to follow the chain of command and take the problem to the immediate supervisor. However, if the immediate supervisor is part of the problem with which the subordinate is seeking help, the subordinate *may* be justified in going over the supervisor's head. Usually, however, sidestepping actually excludes the person who is best able to solve the problem — the immediate supervisor.

For these reasons, it is important for all officers to make their subordinates aware of the proper method of handling problems through the chain of command. In turn, they must be willing and able to handle their subordinates' problems. To reduce the likelihood of being sidestepped in the chain of command, officers should do the following:

- Be available to listen to their subordinates' problems.
- Listen to problems sincerely, and give them full consideration.
- Take action and let employees know that something is being done.

- Take a problem to the next level in the chain of command when it cannot be solved at the officer's level of authority.

Functional Supervision

One deviation from the unity of command principle is *functional supervision*: When personnel are assigned by their supervisor to perform duties that fall under the authority of another supervisor, the subordinates are allowed to report to the second supervisor on matters relating to that function. For example, if company personnel are assigned to perform code enforcement inspections, it is more efficient for them to direct their questions to and coordinate their activities with the fire prevention supervisor *while they are performing those duties.*

At all other times and for all other activities, they still report to their regular supervisor. Obviously, for this arrangement to work, both supervisors must communicate with each other and closely coordinate their activities.

Span of Control

Span of control is the number of subordinates that one individual can effectively supervise. This principle applies equally to supervising the crew of a single company or the officers of several companies under the direction of an incident commander (IC). There is no absolute rule for determining how many subordinates that one person effectively can supervise. The number varies with the situation but is usually considered to be somewhere between three and seven.

While a wider span of control can have advantages in nonemergency operations, it is not recommended for the majority of emergency operations. The National Incident Management System-Incident Command System (NIMS-ICS) model is based on a span-of-control ratio of one supervisor to three to seven subordinates or functions with an optimum of five (**Figure 11.5, p. 242**). The variables that affect span of control in any given situation are as follows:

- *Ability and experience of the supervisor*
- *Ability and experience of subordinates*

Figure 11.5 During emergency operations, the optimum span of control is five positions per supervisor. When this number is exceeded, authority should be delegated and reporting responsibilities reassigned to maintain the optimum span of control.

- *Nature of the task* — Characteristics:
  — Urgency
  — Conditions under which it must be performed, including the geographical area that subordinates may be working within
  — Complexity
  — Rate at which it must be performed
  — Similarity/dissimilarity to tasks being performed by others

- *Proximity of subordinates to the supervisor and each other*

- *Consequences of a mistake*

When the tasks being performed are relatively simple and repetitive, all workers are well-trained, and workers are performing the same or similar tasks, then effective supervision is easier. Further, when subordinates are working close enough to the supervisor or other coworkers that they can ask questions or get help easily, little supervision may be required. When mistakes by workers are of little consequence, one person can probably supervise the maximum number of subordinates effectively.

Effective supervision is extremely difficult in the following circumstances:

- Tasks being performed are very complex.

- Workers' level of training is minimal.

- Workers are performing dissimilar tasks.

- Workers are widely separated from the supervisor and each other.

These variables may be manageable in some cases. However, when the consequences of a worker's mistake could result in fatalities or injuries, the level of supervision required limits the number of subordinates that one person can effectively supervise to the absolute minimum.

Examples of the span-of-control principle can be seen at emergency incidents: Proper span of control is evident when a company officer supervises the members of one engine company (between three and six subordinates, depending on local policy), a strike team leader supervises the five company officers in charge of the engines in a strike team, a division supervisor commands five strike teams and/or task forces, etc.

However, the emergency incident can also show the effects of allowing span of control to be exceeded: At a major incident, the IC fails to organize the incident scene resources in a way that allows authority to be delegated appropriately. The IC attempts to directly control all on-scene units, makes every decision at all levels, and is soon overwhelmed by the myriad details of the operation. This situation can cause the following conditions:

- Chaos at the incident scene

- Breakdowns in communication and coordination

- Duplication of effort by units *freelancing* (operating on their own without consulting command officers) at will

- Confused, inefficient operation at best and perhaps losses of life and property

Most administrators recognize that the span of control has limits and expect authority to be delegated. It is also realized that those accepting delegated authority will make mistakes. As a general rule, when authority is delegated and accepted earnestly, mistakes made by the subordinates should be considered as subjects for training rather than discipline.

Division of Labor

The *division-of-labor* principle consists of dividing large jobs into smaller tasks that are then assigned to specific individuals. In the fire and emergency services, division of labor is important for the following reasons:

- Assigns responsibility
- Prevents duplication of effort
- Makes specific, clear-cut assignments

To accomplish the work assignments within a fire and emergency services organization, the assignments are divided into groups that may be based on the following elements:

- *Type of task* — Organizations commonly place emergency work tasks into similar groups such as engine, truck, and rescue/EMS companies and assign personnel and equipment to handle these tasks. Several types of companies are used for specific purposes. An example is the arrangement of engine and truck (ladder) companies in the emergency response division **(Figure 11.6)**. Each company is responsible for performing certain tasks that help meet the general objectives of the organization.

- *Geographical area* — Assignments exist in the arrangement of districts or battalions within the organization's response area. Each district contains the number of engines, trucks/ladders, ambulances, and specialty units required to protect the occupancies within it.

- *Time of year or season* — Assignments might include a public education program that focuses on the use of heating appliances in winter. During the period when temperatures drop and people start to light or use furnaces, operate space heaters, and use other heating appliances, public fire and life-safety educators would focus their attention on safety topics involving this equipment.

- *Available resources* — Another consideration is the number of people needed to accomplish the assigned tasks. Emergency services organizations typically assign teams of responders to each company. Each team is responsible for performing the duties assigned to that company.

Figures 11.6 Truck or ladder companies perform specialized tasks such as vertical ventilation, search and rescue, salvage, and elevated fire streams. *Courtesy of District Chief Chris Mickal.*

- *Skills specialization* — Tasks cannot simply be assigned at random because few people are capable of doing all things well. Consideration must be given to using the best person available for the job. An effective way of handling anticipated work assignments is to train individuals to perform particular jobs. Special training and specific jobs are used extensively in the fire and emergency services. *Examples:*

  — Personnel within a particular company may be trained for specific specialties such as emergency medical technician (EMT).

  — Hazardous materials teams are now common in many fire and emergency services organizations.

Common divisions in an emergency service organization include emergency response services, community services, and internal services.

Within each work assignment group, subgroups are assigned to meet the requirements of the more specific tasks assigned to the particular work assignment group.

For the division-of-labor principle to be effective, all positions within the organization must be clearly defined. Analyzing each position is the key to identifying all the skills and knowledge necessary for that job. Job analyses and job descriptions are critical to assist personnel in performing their many tasks. All personnel must know what their specific responsibilities are and understand what is expected of them.

It is important to provide adequate cross-training so that the various company members are able to perform other tasks with proficiency. One of the advantages of cross-training is that it enables different companies to work together well because each company officer understands the capabilities, requirements, and needs of the other.

Fire and Emergency Services Organizations: Purposes

All fire and emergency services organizations share several common purposes. How the authority having jurisdiction (AHJ) attempts to accomplish those purposes determines the type of emergency services organization it establishes and how it staffs that organization. The AHJ may decide to establish a single organization that provides all types of emergency services or a number of smaller organizations that specialize in specific types of services.

Some functions may even be assigned to other departments or agencies within the jurisdiction. For example, all new construction plan reviews may be the responsibility of the building inspections department, or the fire investigation function may be vested with the police department.

Some of the more common purposes include the following:

- Providing adequately equipped and trained fire-suppression capabilities appropriate to customer requirements, local hazards and conditions, and reasonable budgetary allocations

- Providing non-fire-suppression-type emergency services such as emergency medical care, technical rescue, and hazardous materials response **(Figure 11.7)**

- Conducting fire and life-safety education programs to improve customer awareness

- Conducting fire and life-safety inspections of various types of occupancies to ensure building and fire code compliance

- Investigating fires to determine origin and cause and detect possible maliciously intentional situations that indicate criminal intent

- Coordinating customers' total fire protection systems, including review of new construction and development to ensure that materials and designs provide adequate fire-suppression systems, hydrants, apparatus access, separations between structures, and means of egress

- Advising local government in matters of fire protection and public life safety, including the need for additional resources, laws, and ordinances to support fire protection and life safety

- Establishing and maintaining agreements with public and private entities for coordinated responses and mutual aid (see Resource Allocation section)

- Preparing the organization and the community to react or respond to natural and human-caused disasters or emergencies

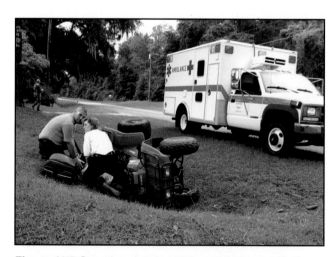

Figure 11.7 Over the past decade, emergency medical responses have increased to the point that many fire departments are assuming the functions originally performed by public and private ambulance services.

Fire and Emergency Services Organizations: Classifications

At the broadest level, fire and emergency services organizations can be classified as either *public* or *private*. As mentioned previously, this classification is determined by how the organization is funded. The sections that follow describe some of the more common forms of public and private organizations.

Public fire and emergency services organizations provide services to the public and are funded by the public through the collection of taxes and fees. The public fire and emergency services organization is the most common class in North America.

Private fire and emergency services organizations are not funded through public taxes but instead receive funds raised through the sale of services, contracts, and revenue provided by the parent organization. The services are provided to a single firm or facility and not to the general public.

The private fire and emergency services organization may, however, provide services to the general public through a mutual aid agreement with the local municipal or county fire and emergency services organization. A *mutual aid agreement* is a written agreement that obligates participants to provide personnel, equipment, and apparatus when requested by any of the participants (see Resource Allocation section).

There are three major categories of private fire and emergency services organizations. First, some industrial complexes and military installations may choose to maintain fire and emergency response resources to protect their properties rather than relying solely or partially on local public fire and emergency services organizations for such protection.

The second type is a for-profit business that owns emergency response equipment and hires firefighters or emergency responders to provide fire protection for the public under contract with government agencies. Generally, for-profit organizations provide EMS and medical transport services to municipalities and counties.

The third type of organization is the smallest category of all types of fire protection and emergency services — the private, nonprofit fire and emergency services organization. These organizations meet the U.S. government requirements for nonprofit 501(c)(3) Public Benefit Corporations and are staffed by career and volunteer members.

Public

About nine out of ten firefighters are employed by municipal or county fire and emergency services organizations according to the U.S. Department of Labor. The fire and emergency services organization may actually be an organizational unit within a larger jurisdiction or it may be a self-contained entity.

The primary means of categorizing public fire and emergency services organizations is by the jurisdiction the organization serves. In the context of this manual, the term *jurisdiction* has two distinct connotations. First, it refers to the area served by a fire and emergency services organization; that is, its response area. Second, it refers to the authority that gives the organization the legal right to exist, provide emergency services, and take the actions necessary to ensure adequate protection.

In the first sense, the jurisdiction of a fire and emergency services organization may be clearly tied to a level of government such as a municipal fire and emergency services organization operating within the physical boundaries of a city and with the authorization of its municipal government. However, because fires and other emergencies do not recognize territorial and legal boundaries, fire and emergency services organizations are often organized across jurisdictional boundaries.

Some areas have shared jurisdictional responsibilities such as state/provincial-protected forest land within the boundaries of a city or fire district. Some of the more common public jurisdictions that provide fire and emergency service protection include the following:

- *Municipal (city)* — Functional division of the lowest level of local government
  - Traditional fire department
  - Public safety department
  - Fire protection district

- **County** — Political subdivision of a state/province that operates under its jurisdiction
- **Fire district** — Special government body authorized by a state/province to exist and operate in order to provide fire and life-safety protection to a geographic area or region within the state/province
- **State/provincial** — Territory occupied by one of the constituent administrative districts of a nation whose rights are defined by a constitution
- **Federal** — National governments of the U.S. and Canada; each provides services to its citizens
- **Tribal** — Term that describes the governmental structure of Native American and Aboriginal Peoples of North America

Municipal (City)

Municipalities are protected by a variety of types of fire and emergency services organizations. Staffing for any of these organizations or departments may be career, combination, or volunteer (See Staffing Section). Varieties include the following:

- **Traditional departments** — The term *municipal fire department* (sometimes known as *bureau of fire* or *fire bureau*) refers to a functional division of the lowest level of local government such as a city, town, township, village, or incorporated or unincorporated community that is authorized at the state/provincial level to form a fire and emergency services organization. This level is the most common jurisdiction for fire and emergency services organizations. *Funding and staffing:*
  — The municipal department or organization operates as part of the local government and receives funding, authority, and oversight from that body.
  — Typically, the personnel who staff career or combination fire departments are municipal employees.
- **Public safety departments** — These departments are typically under the direction of a single department head who is responsible for both law enforcement and fire and emergency services within the jurisdiction. These departments resemble combination fire and emergency

services organizations in that some personnel are full-time, career firefighters whose numbers are supplemented by full-time, career law enforcement officers when there is a fire or other emergency. *Details:*
  — Public safety departments usually train and equip their law enforcement officers to function as firefighters under the supervision of fire and emergency services organization company officers and command officers who have no law enforcement duties or training.
  — The *fire bureau* designation, while sometimes used in the same context as *fire department* (as noted earlier), is technically a subdivision of the public safety department. The public official who manages the public safety department will be in charge of the law enforcement bureau, medical bureau, fire bureau, or emergency management bureau. This type of organizational structure is less common than the structure of municipal fire departments.
- **Fire protection districts** — These districts include the municipality within the response area and may be countywide or regional. See Fire District section.

As a departmental agency within municipal government, most public fire and emergency services organizations exhibit an organizational structure that reflects the local governmental structure. The department head generally oversees the operation of the organization and serves as the principal interface between it and the rest of the municipal government.

The size of the public fire and emergency services organization depends primarily on the size of the population and geographic area served, factors such as special fire protection requirements (heavy industry, use and transportation of hazardous materials, etc.), and the number of services to be provided as determined by the local governing body. All fire and emergency services organizations maintain one or more *fire stations* — sometimes called *houses* or *halls* — from which personnel and equipment respond.

Large organizations may operate several stations throughout their service area as well as have separate facilities for administration, training, and other functions **(Figure 11.8)**. Large organizations may have personnel who specialize in such areas as hazardous materials response, technical rescue, emergency medical care, arson investigation, and fire safety/code enforcement inspections. Combination departments may have career response personnel who are certified as driver/operators of the apparatus they drive, while other responders are volunteers who respond to the incident or station when called.

To provide a wide variety of services, large organizations may have administrative and functional subdivisions such as districts, divisions, battalions, companies, and special squads or teams. These subdivisions may be under the supervision of fire officers with a variety of titles or ranks such as *chief officers, majors, captains,* or *lieutenants.*

In small organizations, personnel may be called upon to serve in multiple roles to provide a full range of services. For example, in these organizations an officer who is in charge of emergency response units may also be the fire marshal in charge of fire and life-safety code enforcement.

Funding to support the operation of a full-time, career or combination fire department is part of the municipal budget and is usually obtained through the collection of taxes. However, some communities also charge subscription fees for fire and emergency services or bill users for at least part of the cost of providing an emergency response — particularly for emergency medical responses and nonemergency (ambulance) transfers. The department's budget generally is set on an annual basis and must address all department expenses, including apparatus and equipment purchases and maintenance, operating expenses, and funding for personnel wages and benefits.

County

The second level in local government is normally the county. Fire and emergency services organizations at this level are becoming more common **(Figure 11.9)**. County fire and emergency services organizations generally protect large areas of unincorporated land that contain large populations such as Los Angeles (CA) County or Anne Arundle (MD) County. Small municipalities within the county may also contract with the county for fire and life-safety services.

The county fire and emergency services organization may exist to augment small town and rural fire departments, or it may consolidate them into a single response organization. With the creation

Figure 11.8 In large communities, fire stations built in the 1920s and 1930s are still in use. Those old facilities may be used to house administrative offices when the need for emergency response in the neighboring community decreases due to shifts in population.

Figure 11.9 County fire and emergency services organizations provide protection to both rural and small municipal communities within their jurisdictions. *Courtesy of the U.S. Federal Emergency Management Agency, Jocelyn Augustino, photographer.*

of local offices of emergency preparedness to meet the challenges of homeland security and disaster preparedness, consolidation of emergency services is becoming more common. In particular, the office of emergency preparedness can provide a cost-efficient approach to purchasing specialized response apparatus and equipment funded by federal grant money.

Fire District

In the fire service, terms used to describe fire and emergency services organizations that are *not* under the jurisdiction of a municipal, county, state/provincial, or federal government vary throughout North America. Three of the common types are described as follows:

- *Fire district* — Serves the same purpose as the county fire and emergency services organization in some states/provinces but is *not* directly related to a single county government. Fire districts may be formed as a portion of a county or may overlap county boundary lines to serve a special shared need such as a large manufacturing plant on the border between two counties. In effect, the district is a special government body authorized by the state/province to exist and operate in order to provide fire and life-safety protection to a geographic area.

- *Fire protection district* — Describes a political subdivision monitored by a board of directors and authorized by state statute. The residents in the district elect directors and tax is paid annually just like residents who live in a municipality pay school or library taxes. Unlike the fire district mentioned earlier, funding is dedicated to the fire protection district and not shared with other agencies or departments.

- *Voluntary fire association* — Responds to emergencies that occur on the property of subscription holders and depends on a subscription or membership fee for its funding base. This approach is very similar to the fire departments of the 1800s that were operated by insurance companies.

For the purpose of this manual, the term *fire district* will be used to describe all three of these organizations. Generally, these three types of fire districts operate under a board of trustees or commissioners who represent the residents of the district. The board oversees the organization, administers funding, sets policy, and otherwise determines its operation.

Funding may come from a district tax or subscription fee or may be taken from city, county, or state/provincial taxes. In most cases, the district is established through a vote of the people living in the district, frequently with board members being elected and taxes approved at the same time.

Staffing for the fire district organization may be provided by full-time career, volunteer, or combination personnel. Some stations may function in one way while others function differently, especially when the district absorbs existing municipal or county fire and emergency services organizations during its creation. Unlike municipal and county fire and emergency services organizations, fire districts do not have the support services provided by a municipal services center for apparatus maintenance, station maintenance, etc. Fire districts must provide these services themselves or contract with private providers.

Some fire districts may contract for fire protection services with other municipal, county, or state agencies. They serve as a taxing authority and transfer revenue to the contracted agency. Funding from general revenues is shared with other agencies within the fire district.

State/Provincial

Fire and emergency services organizations authorized and operated at the state/provincial level may provide either emergency or nonemergency response services. Generally, state/provincial emergency fire-suppression companies are organized for forest, wildland, and urban-interface fires. They may include permanently staffed engine and water tender apparatus or on-call aircraft and helicopters that are used for aerial support of land-based fire-suppression companies.

Nonemergency services include a state/provincial fire marshal's office that provides inspection and investigation services in areas that do not have municipal- or county-level services. State/provincial training academies provide fire and emergency services training to all departments within the jurisdiction. Training at this level may include certification to a number of NFPA professional qualification levels and/or specialty training and certification in areas such as hazardous materials responder, fire department safety officer, or technical rescue technician.

Federal

Federal fire and emergency services exist to protect federal lands and property. They include forestry units and organizations stationed on military facilities. Nationally organized urban search and rescue teams that are prepositioned to respond within 24 hours of any event are maintained by the U.S. government. In addition, the U.S. Fire Administration (USFA) provides training courses for all career, volunteer, and combination organizations through the National Fire Academy (NFA) as well as the Emergency Management Institute (EMI).

The U.S. Department of Defense (DoD) operates more than 200 fire and emergency services organizations on military installations in the continental U.S. **(Figure 11.10)**. These organizations provide structural fire protection on military installations, airport crash/rescue services, or port facilities and ships. In addition, these military fire and emergency services organizations may also provide fire protection off base under mutual aid agreements with local civilian fire and emergency services organizations (see Resource Allocation section).

With the continuing reshaping of the U.S. military establishment in the early 21st century, military fire and emergency services organizations have also changed. Fire and emergency services protection is increasingly supplied by civil service (nonmilitary) personnel, civilian contractors, or local municipal organizations. On facilities in foreign countries, local citizens are hired and trained to meet DoD certification **(Figure 11.11)**. Upper-level positions are filled by military personnel.

In the U.S., some DoD fire and emergency services organizations are being used during large-scale emergencies for fire protection and emergency recovery duties, which includes not only the DoD fire departments but also uniformed military personnel working along with local fire and emergency services organizations. These assignments are the results of a presidential order that made DoD serve as mutual aid providers to their neighboring jurisdictions.

The Canadian Defense Department oversees military and civilian fire and emergency services organizations operating in 35 installations in and around North America. These organizations provide structural protection, airfield rescue and fire fighting, vehicle extrication, and hazardous materials response for land-based installations. They also provide fire-fighting teams for maritime vessels that carry aircraft. These organizations operate with neighboring communities through mutual aid agreements (see Resource Allocation section).

Figure 11.10 The U.S. Department of Defense (DoD) maintains fire and emergency services training facilities to support the fire protection efforts of all branches of the military. One of those training facilities is located at Goodfellow Air Force Base in Texas. *Courtesy of Louis F. Garland Fire Training Academy, Goodfellow Air Force Base, Texas.*

Figure 11.11 Fire and emergency services organizations operated by DoD provide the same types of services that nonmilitary fire and emergency services organizations do.

Tribal

Tribal governments have sovereignty over their designated lands in accordance with agreements with the U.S. and Canadian federal governments. They also have agreements with the state/provincial governments within whose boundaries they exist.

According to the Bureau of Indian Affairs (BIA), U.S. Department of the Interior, there are 562 federally recognized Native American tribal governments within the U.S. Many reside on the 55.7 million acres of land that is held in trust by the U.S. government. On these reservation lands, the BIA trains, equips, and funds fire and emergency services organizations that are staffed by members of the tribe living on that reservation. These organizations provide the same types of services that are provided by municipal, county, and state fire and emergency services organizations (**Figure 11.12**).

In Canada, the Department of Indian and Northern Affairs provides similar support to the 633 officially recognized bands of Aboriginal Peoples of Canada (also known as *First People*). Tribal land and government reserves exist in all provinces and territories of Canada.

Private

While there are fewer private emergency services organizations than there are public ones, they still provide the same types of services and must meet similar NFPA standards for training and operations. Private emergency services organizations generally fall into one of the following three categories:

- *Fire and emergency services organization* — Serves a very limited area such as a single business or industrial facility (fire brigade) and is staffed and funded by the parent business or agency (**Figure 11.13**).

- *For-profit fire and emergency services organization* — Contracts with other entities to provide fire protection services to businesses owned by a third party (either commercial or government) such as a municipality, refinery, chemical plant, or airport.

- *Private, nonprofit fire and emergency services organization* — Provides protection to municipalities, counties, and regions throughout North America; receives funds through donations, grants, or contracts with municipalities, businesses, or individuals within the service area.

Industrial Fire Brigades

Many commercial facilities such as oil refineries, chemical processing plants, research facilities, marine port facilities, and airports (both public and private) maintain industrial fire brigades or other emergency response teams. These teams or

Figure 11.12 Native American tribal governments provide fire protection for residents of tribal land under the authority of the U.S. Bureau of Indian Affairs.

Figure 11.13 Industrial fire brigades are trained, equipped, and maintained by a parent business or agency for the facility being protected. Chemical and petroleum processing and storage facilities are examples of industrial sites that may have their own fire-fighting resources.

brigades may be established in accordance with NFPA 600, *Standard on Industrial Fire Brigades*, 2005 edition, and NFPA 1081, *Standard for Industrial Fire Brigade Member Professional Qualifications*, 2001/2006 edition.

Reasons for establishment include the following:

- Inability or unwillingness of the local community to provide the needed resources

- Need to have a more immediate response than the local public fire and emergency services organization can or will provide

- Need to protect special hazards that require knowledge and capabilities beyond those of the local public fire and emergency services organization

- Remoteness from any public fire and emergency services organization

- Reduced insurance rates

- Reduction of potential liabilities

- Compliance with Federal Aviation Administration (FAA) regulations at airports

Consequently, these businesses maintain their own facilities, personnel, apparatus, and equipment to respond to fires and other emergency incidents. Often, such firms are willing to enter into mutual aid agreements and collaborate with public fire officials to develop fire and hazardous materials protection plans involving their facilities (see Resource Allocation section).

Because of these agreements, company officers may respond with private industrial fire brigades in order to provide fire protection for these facilities and the surrounding area. Company officers should become acquainted with the mutual aid agreement, facility personnel, equipment, and operating procedures that might be involved in such a response (see Resource Allocation section). It is also important that they ensure that equipment and communications are compatible between public and private organizations.

For-Profit Fire and Emergency Services Organizations

The private sector is delivering more and more services that were once considered government functions, including delivering mail, collecting refuse, and operating correctional facilities. An increasing number of government entities are finding it less expensive or more convenient to contract with private industry to provide these services, which also include fire and emergency services **(Figure 11.14)**. Some of the organizations include the following:

- Wackenhut Services, Inc.
- ProTech Fire Services
- Rural/Metro

Figure 11.14 Companies that are trained and equipped for controlling specialized types of hazards, such as petroleum fires, contract to provide fire protection to industrial facilities that do not have internal fire brigades.

While still not the norm, it is not uncommon for cities to contract with private for-profit organizations to provide some services such as fire suppression, rescue, and EMS that are traditionally provided by public fire and emergency services organizations. This trend is likely to continue, and public fire and emergency services organizations must realize that their very survival as entities may depend on their ability to deliver services to their customers more efficiently. State and federal forestry and parks departments are increasingly using contracted fire resources for support at large fires.

Nonprofit Fire and Emergency Services Organizations

Nonprofit fire and emergency services organizations consist of both career and volunteer personnel and serve various areas or regions. Some of the organizations include the following:

- Tidewater (VA) Emergency Medical Services Council

- Spring Valley (CA) Volunteer Fire Department

- Bay Leaf (NC) Fire Department

- CE-Bar (TX) Volunteer Fire Department

- Alburtis (PA) Fire Company

- Hillsdale (MI) Rural Fire Association, Inc.

- Granville (OH) Volunteer Fire Department

Funding for nonprofit fire and emergency services organizations must meet the requirements of the U.S. tax code for 501(c)(3) organizations. Funding may come from donations, fundraisers, subscriptions, contracts, or grants. Current U.S. Department of Homeland Security rules permit these organizations to request and receive Fire Act Grant funds and assistance.

Staffing

Regardless of whether the fire and emergency services organization is public or private, the organization must be staffed in order to function. Some emergency responders receive pay and benefits for their work and are commonly called *career* firefighters while others serve on a strictly voluntary basis. In this context, the term *professional* refers to a level of competence or expertise, behavior, and appearance and may apply equally to career and volunteer personnel. An organization may be fully staffed with career personnel, volunteer personnel, or a combination of both career and volunteer personnel.

Career (Full-Time) Organizations

Most large cities and some counties and private industries operate full-time, career fire and emergency services organizations (**Figure 11.15**). The municipality, county, or industry maintains facilities and equipment to support fire protection and emergency services and employs firefighters and other personnel to provide those services. Personnel are fully paid by the jurisdiction.

In addition to salary, personnel in career organizations are likely to receive benefits that may include life and medical insurance, retirement plans, paid vacation and sick leave, and other entitlements. Some or all of the staff may work for the city, county, or industry under a periodically renewed contract, which is often negotiated on behalf of the workers by a labor union.

Another characteristic of full-time, career fire and emergency services organizations is that their fire stations are staffed continuously. Emergency response personnel live in the fire stations while

Figure 11.15 Career fire and emergency services organizations are composed of personnel that work full time for the organization. *Courtesy of the U.S. Federal Emergency Management Agency, Anjanette Stayten, photographer/FEMA News Photo.*

United States Fire and Emergency Services Organizations, 2003

Type of Staffing	Number of Organizations	Number of Personnel
Career (100% career firefighters)	2,016	296,850
Mostly Career (51–99% career firefighters)	1,588	Unknown
Mostly Volunteer (1–50% career firefighters)	5,283	Unknown
Volunteer (0% career firefighters)	21,651	800,050
Total	**30,542**	**1,096,900**

Note: It is estimated that 12 percent of all fire departments are career or mostly career and protect 61 percent of the population. At the same time, 88 percent of fire departments are volunteer or mostly volunteer and protect 39 percent of the population.

Source: For personnel numbers: NFPA's *Survey of Fire Departments for U.S. Fire Experience, 2003*. For organization numbers: U.S. Fire Administration National Fire Department Census, 2003. Figures released in 2006 indicate that the number of registered fire departments is 24,296 or 81 percent of the estimated total of departments in the U.S.

Canadian Fire and Emergency Services Organizations, 2005

Type of Staffing	Number of Organizations	Number of Personnel
Career	95	23,694
Combination	213	Unknown
Volunteer	3,184	84,314
Total	**3,492**	**108,008**

Source: Canadian Association of Fire Chiefs

hourly wage or a set fee per response. This approach to compensation may also be used to pay part-time personnel in full-time, career organizations

A variation of career organization staffing is the use of public safety officers. In this variation, the fire command/management officers, company officers, and apparatus driver/operators are full-time, career fire personnel, while the firefighters are law enforcement officers who are trained and equipped to function as firefighters. In a sense, public safety officers are similar to volunteer firefighters in combination departments.

Public safety officers perform their normal law enforcement patrol duties until a fire is reported. When they carry their fire-fighting personal

they are on duty. The organization may also maintain administrative offices with personnel that work more conventional business hours.

Some career organizations employ personnel on a part-time basis to supplement the response force during peak emergency periods based on the time of day, day of the week, or season. Some organizations use short-term, full-time (seasonal) employees to provide service during wildland fire seasons. These terms of employment are usually 3 to 6 months in duration **(Figure 11.16)**.

Some fire and emergency responders work on an *on-call* basis. Under this method, a responder does *not* reside at the fire station but is summoned to the fire station or emergency scene by means of a telephone call, pager, or community signal. Personnel are paid for responding, usually with an

Figure 11.16 Wildland fire-fighting operations may be conducted by career, full-time, part-time, or seasonal personnel. Some organizations such as the state/provincial forestry department hire trained wildland firefighters under contract for the duration of the wildland fire season. *Courtesy of the U.S. Federal Emergency Management Agency, Andrea Booher, photographer.*

protective equipment (PPE) in their patrol cars, they can then respond directly to the fire scene and work under the supervision of a company officer.

Volunteer Organizations

Volunteer organizations operate with volunteers who perform all the required functions without pay (**Figure 11.17**). A volunteer organization may operate as a department of the local government, but most are totally independent from government agencies within the areas they serve.

According to the U.S. Fire Administration, 70 percent of fire and emergency services organizations are staffed by volunteer firefighters. The organization may be a municipal, county, or nonprofit organization and serve a wide range of geographic areas.

In some cases, a town may provide a facility to be used as a fire station and may even buy and maintain fire-suppression equipment. In other cases,

Figure 11.17 Volunteer fire and emergency services organizations generally meet weekly to train and practice skills such as apparatus driving and placement.

the volunteer organization meets its expenses without support from municipal funds. Money may come from donations, subscription fees paid by people in the community, billing for all or part of response costs, and fundraising events such as bake sales, pancake breakfasts, dinners, dances, or fairs.

Oversight of the volunteer organization comes from the local entity that supports the organization or from an independent association or governing board. However, some volunteer organizations are nonprofit corporations governed by boards of directors.

In most cases, volunteer organizations do not maintain fire stations that are continuously staffed. Personnel respond from home or workplace to emergencies when summoned by pagers, telephone calls, or community signals. Designated personnel go to the fire station and drive the apparatus to the emergency scene, while others may report to the fire station or directly to the scene. The majority of communities in the U.S. and Canada provide fire protection through volunteer fire organizations.

Combination Departments

By definition, a *combination department* is one in which some of the firefighters and emergency responders receive pay while other personnel serve on a voluntary basis. These organizations, whether public or private, function with a combination of both paid personnel and volunteers.

For example, a mostly volunteer organization may pay driver/operators or part of the salary of a dispatcher/telecommunicator who is shared with the law enforcement organization. A full-time career department may also maintain a cadre of volunteers trained in fire suppression, rescue, emergency medical care, scene control, or other areas.

In some combination departments, there may be more paid firefighters than unpaid firefighters. In some, the highest ranking officer is a volunteer who exerts primary control over the organization; in others, control is exercised by a full-time paid chief. The distribution of responsibilities and relative percentages of paid and unpaid personnel can vary greatly from one combination department to another.

Combination organizations provide staffing and receive funding in accordance with the dominant aspect of their organization. Thus, combination departments that are operated primarily as full-time, career organizations tend to staff their stations continuously and use budgeted tax dollars to fund their operations. Those organizations that primarily use volunteers tend to have no one or only limited numbers of responders residing in their fire stations.

In some cases, departments are actually operated on a *paid-on-call* basis. Functionally, the paid-on-call organization resembles a volunteer organization in that the fire stations are minimally staffed and emergency personnel are normally summoned to the emergency scene or fire station by pagers, telephones, or community signals. Fiscally, it resembles a full-time, career organization because most or all paid-on-call organizational funding comes from a local government agency or association.

Resource Allocation

Many factors affect the degree to which a fire and emergency services organization is able to provide all of the services required by a jurisdiction. A primary consideration for most organizations is fiscal limitations. Many jurisdictions face financial constraints that make it necessary for government leaders to evaluate the extent to which fire and emergency services protection can be provided to the public. Additional factors concern the methods by which these services are provided.

Because fire and life-safety protection is just one of the many services that a local government's budget must support, government leaders have to determine the distribution of funds to satisfy these different requirements. This requirement frequently results in compromises in the individual services in order to provide a reasonable overall balance in meeting the jurisdiction's various needs.

Therefore, one of the roles of the company officer and other fire officers is to make the best possible use of available resources, which involves the following elements:

- Protecting personnel and equipment
- Conserving materials and supplies
- Planning for the most cost-effective and efficient use of resources

The result of this approach will be the fulfillment of the organization's mission at the minimum level of funding. One of the most common techniques for extending the organization's budget has the following two parts:

1. Fund only the minimum number and types of resources needed to deal with those emergencies that are most likely to occur within the jurisdiction.

2. Rely on agreements with other jurisdictions and agencies to supplement the organization's resources for unusually large or exceptional incidents.

Agreements with other jurisdictions or agencies are normally formal, written plans that define the roles of the participants. Agreements can be categorized as mutual aid, automatic aid, or outside aid.

Mutual Aid

Mutual aid is the result of a reciprocal agreement between two or more fire and emergency services organizations. The agreements may be local, regional, state/province wide, or interstate/interprovince, and the organizations may or may not have contiguous boundaries. The mutual aid *agreement* defines how the organizations will provide resources in various situations and how the actions of the shared resources will be monitored and controlled.

Responses under a mutual aid agreement are usually on an *on-request* basis (**Figure 11.18, p. 256**). As the term implies, on-request assistance is provided only when an organization asks for assistance such as when its resources are depleted by an unusually large incident or a number of simultaneous small incidents. Under these agreements, the requested agency may, at its option, dispatch the requested aid. When the organization receiving the request has or is likely to have to commit its resources within its own boundaries, the request for mutual aid may be denied.

Figure 11.18 Requests for mutual aid are usually made by the incident commander at the scene and requested through the organization's telecommunications center. The center maintains a list of agencies and the types of resources that they can provide under mutual aid agreements. *Courtesy of Paul Ramirez.*

The most common reasons why fire and emergency services organizations enter into mutual aid agreements besides to receive federal or state funding are as follows:

- *Allows sharing of limited or specialized resources between neighboring jurisdictions* — For example, adjoining fire and emergency services organizations sometimes work together to acquire selected apparatus, equipment, or personnel resources that are required to support their overall missions but whose utilization is limited to the point that none of the individual cooperating organizations could justify the expenditure.

- *Addresses the need for neighboring jurisdictions to assist each other when a response requirement exceeds the primary jurisdiction's capabilities* — For example, an organization may also require assistance from another because of the size or nature of an emergency. Some fires may involve such a large area or structure that they exceed the response capabilities of the responsible jurisdiction or an emergency may result in more casualties than the primary jurisdiction can evacuate and treat.

- *Addresses occupancies within a jurisdiction that may be considered target hazards or high-risk facilities* — For example, a facility may store and use substances that could pose a serious health risk to the public. If the facility is located near the boundary of another jurisdiction or prevailing winds or waterways are likely to transport contaminants into an adjoining jurisdiction, the affected organizations may choose to establish mutual aid agreements.

- *Addresses the situation where an organization may require assistance when its resources are deployed at an incident and a second, simultaneous emergency occurs* — In effect, a second organization may provide backup response for subsequent emergencies in the event that the primary jurisdiction's resources are already committed.

- *Allows organizations to meet NFPA, Insurance Services Office (ISO), and other requirements for staffing, apparatus availability, response times, etc. through shared resources* — For example, an agreement between a municipality protected by a volunteer organization and an adjacent career-protected municipality could provide greater constant protection for the first community and supplemental protection for the second one.

- *Provides a quicker response when other fire and emergency services organizations are closer to the emergency site than are the primary jurisdiction's resources* — For example, the agreement between two bordering municipalities could establish response areas that overlap the actual city limits of each. This agreement would establish responses based on travel time rather than jurisdiction.

- *Defines responses for areas on the boundaries between adjacent jurisdictions* — For example, a mutual aid agreement between two neighboring municipalities can establish which jurisdiction will respond to certain types of emergencies that occur in the unincorporated areas between them.

- *Defines response methods for fire and emergency services organizations within a jurisdiction such as a military base or corporate fire protection agency (fire brigade) within a city's limits* — For instance, the agreement between a municipality and a large refinery within its boundaries could establish the municipal response in support of a fire at the refinery. At the same time, it could establish the response of specialized foam fire-fighting units from the refinery to a hazardous materials incident within the municipality.

Company officers may be asked to assist in the development and maintenance of mutual aid plans. At a minimum, these plans should specify the following actions:

- Define roles of each organization, including incident management and chains of command.

- Establish operating guidelines.

- Define lines and methods of communications.

- Include common terminology, references, specifications, equipment compatibility, and other factors that may directly affect the effectiveness of the different organizations in working with each other.

- Provide maps, evacuation routes, hydrant locations and data, details of potentially affected systems (sewers, railroads, waterways, etc.), and similar information useful in a response outside of one's jurisdiction.

- Address insurance and legal considerations that may affect the agreement.

- Establish additional nonemergency agreements such as training and routine communications as required.

Additionally, mutual aid plans should be reviewed periodically to ensure that they remain current and up to date. Both the creation and maintenance of mutual aid agreements require personnel to work with other organizations and agencies, including their own and other governmental jurisdictions. Because all mutual aid agreements are contracts, they must be reviewed and approved by the legal departments of both organizations.

In some cases, implementation of new policies or ordinances may be necessary to support the mutual aid agreements. To be most effective, all fire and emergency services organizations participating in these agreements should conduct joint training exercises so that differences in equipment and procedures may be identified and rectified before a major incident occurs.

Emergency Management Assistance Compact (EMAC) and Mutual Aid Box Alarm System (MABAS)

Two forms of mutual aid agreements that have been created in the past 50 years in the U.S. are the EMAC and MABAS. Each is designed to provide a framework for responding to major disasters. EMAC was successfully employed during the U.S. hurricane emergencies in 2005.

EMAC was created in 1996 by an act of Congress as the first national disaster-relief compact since the Civil Defense and Disaster Compact of 1950. EMAC is a national agreement that links the resources of each individual state together. When the governor of one state declares a disaster, relief and response aid is made available from other partner states. The compact is designed to provide rapid and flexible deployment of aid to the stricken area.

MABAS is a much older mutual aid compact, dating from the 1960s. It is an agreement between the fire and emergency response agencies of Northern Illinois and Southern Wisconsin. The participating communities, counties, and agencies agree to perform the following procedures:

- Maintain a predetermined level of staffing.
- Use the Incident Command System (ICS).
- Use common terminology and operating procedures.
- Operate on a common radio frequency during mutual aid incidents.

Responding agencies work under the command and dispatch control of the stricken community. MABAS is under the direction of an executive board composed of members of the various partners.

Automatic Aid

Automatic aid results from a formal, written agreement between fire and emergency services organizations that share a common boundary. *Automatic aid* occurs whenever certain predetermined conditions occur. For example, automatic aid may be initiated whenever an emergency is reported along a mutual jurisdictional boundary, especially in areas where the actual boundary line is unclear. An agreement may provide for automatic aid in the event of any fire involving a given number of alarms.

Automatic aid agreements may also be required at specific facilities such as airports, oil refineries, or chemical manufacturing plants. A major incident at one of these facilities may virtually ensure that the resources of the primary jurisdiction will be exceeded so that any incident involving that facility will lead to an automatic response by other agencies.

Outside Aid

Outside aid is similar to mutual aid except that payment rather than reciprocal aid is made by one jurisdiction to the other. Outside aid is normally addressed through a signed contract under which one jurisdiction agrees to provide aid to another in return for an established payment that is normally an annual fee but may be on a per-response basis. Otherwise, the outside agreement differs little from the mutual aid agreement.

The agreement should define the following elements:

- Conditions under which support will be provided: automatic or on request
- Terms for conducting the response: command and communication, standard operating procedures/standard operating guidelines (SOPs/SOGs), legal considerations, etc.

Summary

Fire and emergency services organizations will not be able to fulfill their missions and achieve their goals effectively and efficiently without a valid organizational base. There are several ways in which emergency services organizations may be organized to achieve their assigned goals: public, private, career, volunteer, and combination.

Regardless of how they are organized, they all function with the same organizational principles: unity of command, span of control, and division of labor. Other principles involve scalar structure, line and staff personnel, and decision-making authority. These principles are important not only at emergency incidents but also in the daily nonemergency routines. For company officers to be effective leaders, they must know and use these principles in both emergency and nonemergency situations.

Company officers can also help reinforce the culture of the organization by building a strong work ethic within the unit. Officers can delegate projects to subordinates that help teach planning, organizing, directing, and coordinating projects.

Division of Labor in the Fire and Emergency Services

Division of labor provides the organization with a means of efficiently assigning resources to the completion of nonemergency programs and projects and emergency incidents. The application of the division of labor in nonemergency programs and projects is identical to the use of the concept in business and industry. Individuals or units are provided the materials, funds, and authority to complete certain specific tasks. The people assigned to complete the tasks have specific knowledge and skills required to perform the tasks. Examples of this type of division of labor in the fire and emergency services include plans review, code enforcement, training, finance, and public information.

The division of labor at emergency incidents may become blurred, however, due to the urgency of the situation and the fact that fire and emergency services personnel are cross-trained to perform multiple tasks. Division of labor at emergency incidents is based on the unit more than the individual; that is, truck or ladder companies are trained and equipped to perform ventilation, search and rescue, salvage, and other nonsuppression tasks. Engine company personnel are trained and equipped to locate and extinguish fires or mitigate the emergency. However, they may also be assigned the task of opening windows for limited ventilation or performing search and rescue.

At the company or unit level, division of labor may be less obvious. While the driver/operator is responsible for the placement of the apparatus and operating the pump or aerial device, it is also possible that the driver/operator may be assigned search or command duties if the apparatus is not placed in operation. Company officers responsible for command at an incident may find themselves operating the nozzle, performing forcible entry, or setting a ladder. These situations occur when units have limited staffing or crew members have already been assigned other tasks. In these cases, division of labor becomes less important than accomplishing the immediate task.

Company officers must realize that the concept of division of labor is necessary for the efficient use of resources. At the same time, they must realize that it is necessary to be flexible and personnel may need to be assigned to tasks they do not normally perform. Such assignments must also be based on the knowledge, skills, and abilities of personnel as well as their technical qualifications and certification. Under no circumstances should anyone be assigned or attempt to perform a task for which they are not trained, qualified, or certified.

Company-Level Training

Chapter Contents

Learning Objectives

1. Distinguish between the two levels of fire and emergency services training.

2. Recall information about the four-step method of instruction.

3. Select facts about lesson plans.

4. Identify various methods of training.

5. Direct employees during a training evolution.

Job Performance Requirements

This chapter provides information that addresses the following job performance requirements of NFPA 1021, *Standard for Fire Officer Professional Qualifications* (2003):

Chapter 4 Fire Officer I

4.2.3

Chapter 12
Company-Level Training

Training is a key to safe, efficient, and effective fire and emergency services operations. The role of the company officer in providing training is so important that NFPA 1021, *Standard for Fire Officer Professional Qualifications*, requires that all Fire Officer I candidates complete Instructor I training as defined in NFPA 1041, *Standard for Fire Service Instructor Professional Qualifications*.

Fire officers and officer candidates can refer to the IFSTA **Fire and Emergency Services Instructor** manual, 7th edition, for a detailed presentation of formal instructor training. This chapter provides an overview of the topic as it applies to Fire Officer I and is based on information that is contained in that manual.

Fire and emergency services training consists of two levels or types of training: formal courses and continuing education. First and primary to the success of the organization are the formal training courses that are usually presented by the organization's training staff or training officer. Organizations that do *not* have internal training personnel should have state or regional training agencies available that can provide formal training for them.

Formal training consists of entry-level, emergency medical technician (EMT), driver/operator, officer, instructor, and specialized training. Certified fire and emergency services instructors present the formal training courses. The courses may be presented at the organization's training facility, at a regional or state/provincial training agency, at the National Fire Academy (NFA), on site at the fire station, or through distance learning via television or computer-accessed Internet connections.

Specialty training topics such as hazardous materials or aircraft rescue may be presented at facilities that are equipped with training props to simulate the specific type of emergency or hazard **(Figure 12.1)**. Vocational schools, colleges, and universities may also be used to provide courses that they are equipped to teach.

Continuing education is the second level or type of training and consists of the continuous refresher training that is the responsibility of the company officer. The information that is presented may consist of presentations of new policies or procedures, reviews of safety procedures, company drills, or practical skills evolutions.

The goal of company- or unit-level training is to maintain the high level of knowledge, skills, and ability that each member of the unit had upon completion of the formal entry-level training.

Figure 12.1 State/provincial, regional, and large metropolitan training facilities usually have the props that are required for specialized training such as the application of foam at vehicle fires.

Company-level training should also provide the opportunity to develop mastery of those skills **(Figure 12.2)**. At the same time, company-level training may be used to integrate new company members into the unit and improve the teamwork of the unit.

Many times, the training that is accomplished at the company level is substandard, and the only opportunity firefighters and emergency responders have to maintain or perfect their skills is through actual emergency responses, which is a double-edge sword. First, if the emergency responder is at a station with very few calls, the skills will not be retained. Second and perhaps most important is that many skills learned at the company level may have led to bad habits that contradict what was taught at recruit school. While the old adage of *this is how we do it in the real world* is used by many company officers, the truth is that this type of attitude contributes to firefighter injuries and fatalities.

Figure 12.2 Company-level training is intended to maintain the mastery of skills that were acquired during formal entry-level training. Skills such as proper lifting techniques should be practiced regularly during work shifts.

Company officers MUST ensure that the company-level training conducted meets the standards of the organization and matches what is taught during recruit training. According to NFPA 1201, *Standard for Providing Emergency Services to the Public*, 2004, the organization must evaluate the effectiveness of its training programs. Part of this evaluation includes the teaching skills of the company officer. The company officer must possess good leadership skills, teaching skills, and enthusiasm to create a team from the individuals that compose the company. By combining the knowledge that the fire officer has already learned from this manual about leadership, supervision, and safety with the information contained in this chapter on training, the officer will have a strong foundation for developing an effective company.

This chapter includes an overview of how the company officer determines the type of training needed by the company, the elements of the four-step method of instruction, lesson plans and how to modify them, and various training methods. Training methods include presentations, discussions, demonstrations, and practical training evolutions in the context of company-level drills.

During company-level training, the company officer and members of the unit assume new roles. Although they still have a supervisor/subordinate relationship, the company officer is now in the role of instructor or teacher and company members are now students. In the remainder of this chapter, unit members may be referred to as *students* to emphasize this role in the relationship.

Training Needs Determination

Most company-level training needs will be established by the organization. This determination is based on a number of considerations including the following:

- Legally mandated training
- Performance during emergency operations
- Annual refresher or recertification requirements
- Postincident analysis reports
- Personnel evaluation reports
- Changes in operational procedures

- Implementation of new policies, procedures, or equipment

- Changes in the types of services delivered by the organization

- Job task analyses

- Preparation for the next level of authority or advancement

- New personnel assignments based on transfers, promotions, or newly hired personnel

Occasionally, the company officer may have the responsibility for determining the training needs for the unit. This determination will be based either on the same criteria used by the training division or personal observation by the company officer of the unit's need for remedial training based on a previous emergency response. The company officer will have to follow a process that includes the following steps:

Step 1: Determine the type of service, skill, or task that must be performed.

Step 2: Compare that new level of performance to the current level.

Step 3: Design the type of training that will raise the knowledge, skills, and abilities of company personnel to a new level.

The training division or the state/provincial training agency may be able to provide the training materials once the need is determined. For example, the company may have been assigned a new automatic transmission pumping apparatus to replace an older model with standard transmission. The operation of the new apparatus would be different in both the driving and pumping modes. On each work shift, the company officer would have to determine the driver/operator's familiarity with the operation of the new apparatus. The training might include the following actions:

- Reading the vehicle's operations manual

- Learning the operation of the vehicle from a manufacturer's representative

- Practicing driving the vehicle

Additional training in the operation of the pump would have to be provided until the driver/operator was proficient **(Figure 12.3)**. The company officer, with the help of the manufacturer's representative

Figure 12.3 When a new apparatus is placed into service or existing vehicles are reassigned, company personnel are trained in the proper use of the apparatus. Training officers generally provide this type of training such as explaining the operation of the pump.

or a member of the training or apparatus maintenance staff, would write learning objectives that the driver/operator would have to meet to show proficiency in the operation of the vehicle.

Four-Step Method of Instruction

Although there are numerous teaching models used for instructional delivery, one of the most effective and the one provided in the IFSTA **Fire and Emergency Services Instructor** manual is the four-step method of instruction. Instructors use this model to develop lesson plans and as a process for teaching lessons and courses. Company officers can use the process for effective company-level training. The model consists of the following four steps:

Step 1: *Preparation*— Establish lesson relevancy to the job by introducing the topic, gaining the students' attention, and stating the learning objectives. How the students will be evaluated should also be mentioned. This step also includes the self-preparation that the instructor or company officer takes before beginning the lesson or class. *Instructor preparation* includes the following activities:

— Reading the lesson plan

— Gathering any additional information that may be required

— Assembling the audiovisual training aids and props

— Practicing the skills that will be taught

Step 2: *Presentation* — Present the information to be taught using an orderly, sequential outline. Select the teaching method that is appropriate to the learning styles of the students and the topic being taught. Presentation can be combined with the next and most important step, application. Generally, the presentation choices available are as follows:

— Lecture

— Illustrated lecture

— Discussion

— Demonstration

— Learning activities such as role-playing when the topic benefits from these approaches

Step 3: *Application* — Provide opportunities for learning through activities, exercises, discussions, work groups, skill practices, practical training evolutions, and similar learning activities. The purpose is to reinforce the student's learning. Most learning takes place during the application step, making this step critically important.

Step 4: *Evaluation* — Have students demonstrate how much they have learned through a written, oral, or practical examination or test. The purpose is to determine whether students achieved the lesson objectives or course outcomes. Instructors or company officers can base most evaluations on observation of individual skills and practical training evolutions unless they administer an examination that has been provided by the training division. Determine how well students have performed skills or evolutions and provide them with feedback to assist them in improving those skills.

Generally, the company officer will be provided with a lesson plan that contains the basic elements, including the learning objectives. The format of most lesson plans will follow the four-step method

of instruction. Company officers should be prepared to alter the lesson plan to meet the existing conditions. However, they should *never* alter the four-step method of instruction.

Lesson Plans

The lesson plan is basic to all teaching. It is essentially a road map that guides the instructor, teacher, or company officer through the topic. The lesson plan is the vehicle that the company officer will use to deliver the required training regardless of whether it is simply a lecture presentation on a new policy, a demonstration of a piece of equipment, or a practical training evolution intended to improve company teamwork.

Lesson plans are generally developed by the training division or purchased as part of an existing curriculum. However, all company officers must be familiar with the basic components of a lesson plan in order to use and modify it when necessary. Company officers should review the lesson plan and clarify any points that they do not understand with the training division (**Figure 12.4**).

Planning what topic and how much to teach is a prelude to instruction. Planning a lesson helps company officers carefully think about what to teach and strategies for teaching. Most company officers cannot just walk into a classroom and begin teaching without some plan as to what they will do, where they will go with the information, and how they will get there.

Teaching without a plan gives no guarantee that course objectives will be met or students will actually learn what is required by the course outcomes or job performance requirements (JPRs). JPRs describe the level of performance that is required to perform a specific *job* and are grouped into *duties* as established by the NFPA professional qualifications for a position in the fire and emergency services.

For instance, NFPA 1021 organizes a group of similar jobs into a category or duty called *Human Resources Management*. One of the JPRs under this duty (4.2.3) requires that the Fire Officer I be able to direct personnel in a training evolution. To accomplish this duty, an officer must be able to communicate effectively to pass along requisite

Firefighter I   Student Lesson 9

1. Preparation

Topic:	Ground Ladders
Time:	1 hour
Level of Instruction:	Application
Learning Objective:	Inspect a ladder as part of a maintenance schedule.
Resources Needed:	Ladder to be inspected — ladder should be old enough to show some wear and tear
	Stick of chalk for marking defects
	Two sawhorses
	Important: Set up ladder on sawhorses in demonstration area before class begins.
Prerequisites:	Completion of ladder lifts and carries, as tested in Skill Sheets 9-2 through 9-8
References:	NFPA 1001, Fireground Operations 5.3.6
	Essentials of Fire Fighting, Chapter 9
Summary:	Regular and proper cleaning of ladders is more than a matter of appearance: Dirt or debris from a fire may collect and harden, making the ladder sections inoperable. Ladders should be cleaned and inspected after each use. They should also be inspected on a regular monthly basis.
Assignment:	Additional practice, if needed
Comments:	If time permits, consider showing the video *Ground Ladders*.

2. Lesson Outline

A. Maintenance

    1. Keep ground ladders free of moisture.

    2. Do not store or rest ladders in a position where they are subjected to exhaust or engine heat.

    3. Do not store ladders in any area where they are exposed to the elements.

    4. Do not paint ladders except for the top and bottom 12 inches (300 mm) of the beams for purposes of identification or visibility.

B. Cleaning ladders

    1. Clean ladders after every use and before inspecting.

    2. Use a soft-bristle brush and running water for cleaning.

    3. Wipe the ladder dry, checking for defects.

C. General maintenance, inspection, and repair

    1. Maintenance means keeping ladders in a state of usefulness or readiness

    2. Repair means either restoring or replacing that which has become inoperable.

    3. Ladders meeting NFPA 1931 are marked by the manufacturer with a certification label on the ladder beam.

    4. All firefighters should be capable of performing routine ladder maintenance.

Page 1 of 2

Figure 12.4 Sample lesson plan, p. 1. (Continued on p. 268)

5. Only trained ladder repair technicians should perform ladder repairs.
6. Firefighters should clean ladders after each use; dirty ladders cannot be properly inspected.
7. Firefighters should inspect ladders after each use and monthly.
8. There are two methods of determining whether metal ladders have been exposed to high temperatures.
    a. Water boils when sprayed on the ladder
    b. Heat indicator label has changed color
9. Only trained fire service personnel or an approved testing organization should service test fire service ground ladders.

  D. Inspecting specific ladder types
1. Ground ladders
    a. Check heat sensor labels on metal and fiberglass ladders for a color change indicating heat exposure.
    b. Check rungs for snugness and tightness.
    c. Check bolts and rivets for tightness.
    d. Check welds for any cracks or apparent defects.
    e. Check beams and rungs for cracks, splintering, breaks, gouges, checks, wavy conditions, or deformation.
2. Wood ladders/ladders with wood components
    a. Look for areas where the varnish finish has been chafed or scraped.
    b. Check for darkening of the varnish (indicating exposure to heat).
    c. Check for dark streaks in the wood (indicating deterioration of the wood).
3. Roof ladders
    a. Make sure that the roof hook assemblies operate with relative ease.
    b. Check for signs of rust, deformities, and looseness of parts.
4. Extension ladders
    a. Make sure the pawl assemblies work properly.
    b. Look for fraying or kinking of the halyard.
    c. Check the snugness of the halyard cable when the ladder is in the bedded position.
    d. Make sure the pulleys turn freely.
    e. Check the condition of the ladder guides and for free movement of the fly sections.
    f. Check for free operation of the pole ladder staypole toggles and check their condition.

  E. Summary

    Summarize lesson by reviewing:
    • Names of ladder parts
    • Maintenance and inspection guidelines

Part 3. Evaluation

Distribute and administer Chapter 9 Written Test to evaluate candidate mastery of the cognitive content of the lesson.

Administer Chapter 9 Performance Test at scheduled time. Record competency ratings on competency profile.

Figure 12.4 Sample Lesson plan, p. 2.

knowledge and give directions or orders to subordinates during the company drill to impart requisite skills.

Generally, the company officer will be provided with a training schedule and lesson plans for a specific topic to be taught at the company level **(Figure 12.5)** (see Training Schedules section). Many times, the officer may not receive a lesson plan but simply be told to make a presentation on a new policy or another topic. In this instance, the officer should rely on a model lesson plan, experience, and the assistance of the training division to create the presentation.

Using a lesson plan does *not* ensure fulfillment of objectives either, but it increases the odds of success. Without planning the lesson ahead of time, company officers may find that they are lacking important support equipment or supplemental materials, which means that they cannot properly teach or demonstrate a skill. The result

Sample Company-Level Training Schedule

Tompkins Valley Fire Department
Company Training Schedule

April

Sunday	Monday	Tuesday	Wednesday	Thursday	Friday	Saturday
1A	2B Ground ladder raises	3C Ground ladder raises	4A Ground ladder raises	5B SCBA care and maintenance	6C SCBA care and maintenance	7A SCBA care and maintenance
8B	9C Attack line deployment	10A Attack line deployment	11B Attack line deployment	12C Forcible entry	13A Forcible entry	14B Forcible entry
15C	16A Highway safety	17B Highway safety	18C Highway safety	19A PPV concepts and use	20B PPV concepts and use	21C PPV concepts and use
22A	23B Fire cause determination	24C Fire cause determination	25A Fire cause determination	26B Training Center Multicompany training evolutions	27C Training Center Multicompany training evolutions	28A Training Center Multicompany training evolutions
29B	30C Physical fitness evaluations, company training cancelled					

Each lesson plan is designed to provide 4 hours of training utilizing presentation, discussion, and demonstration techniques. Company officers should schedule daily training for the most effective results. Training may take place between 0800 and 2000 hours.

Figure 12.5 Sample company-level training schedule of required or suggested training topics. An appropriate lesson plan is included with the schedule.

for both the company officer and students is that time is wasted because appropriate teaching and learning could *not* take place.

It may become necessary for the company officer to modify or alter a lesson plan. Modification may be necessary for the following reasons:

- Time is not available to present the lesson completely. Modification may include dividing the topic into smaller components and creating a brief review for each of the topics.

- Audiovisual aids that are required in the lesson plan may not be available. An alternate teaching method or approach may need to be created to replace the missing training aid.

- A lesson plan may be outdated and not accurately represent the current process or policy. The company officer may need to rewrite the lesson plan, with administrative approval, to meet the current situation.

- Members of the audience may not respond to the teaching methods listed in the lesson plan. The company officer may need to substitute a different teaching method that will provide a better learning experience for students (see Methods of Training section).

- Environmental conditions may prevent the presentation of the lesson plan as originally intended. Inclement weather may force the company officer to modify the practical training evolutions for use in an apparatus room or other enclosed space.

The company officer should document the reason for modifications, type of modifications, and result of the modifications. This information should be forwarded to the training division or agency. When the lesson plan is part of a certification program or course, the company officer should consult with the training division before making any modifications that could jeopardize certification.

Methods of Training

Among other methods, company-level training may consist of presentations, discussions, demonstrations, or practical training evolutions. The sections that follow provide a description of the key elements of each of these methods. The company officer should review all of the training material that has been provided for the topic, practice the required method, and request any assistance necessary before starting the lesson.

Although the presentation method is the most familiar to instructors and students, not all lessons will follow that format. Some lessons may benefit from the discussion or demonstration methods. In some cases, several methods will be used together to present a topic in a variety of ways, which is one approach that can be used when the student group is large and possesses a variety of learning styles. Company officers must be aware of how their company members learn and how to best teach them.

Presentations

Some presentations will take the form of a lecture that may be illustrated with audiovisual training aids such as electronic slide shows or videos. Pads and easels can be used to list important items. Company officers must be aware of their own presentation skills and use their strengths to maximize the student learning experience. Before beginning a presentation, the company officer should ensure that the space is appropriate to the presentation in the following ways:

- Ensure that the seating arrangement is comfortable and that all participants can see the officer and any visual aids (**Figure 12.6**).

- Ensure that all distractions (both audible and visual) are removed, which includes turning off televisions, lowering the volume of station radios and intercoms, and closing windows that might allow outside noises into the room.

- Reduce glare that might obstruct the view of videos, and ensure that lighting can be modified to improve viewing of any visual aids.

- Have all training aids and props readily accessible and in working condition.

- Ensure that room temperature is in a comfortable range.

During the presentation, the company officer should use accepted instructional delivery methods such as those presented in the IFSTA **Fire and Emergency Services Instructor** manual. Some delivery method considerations include the following:

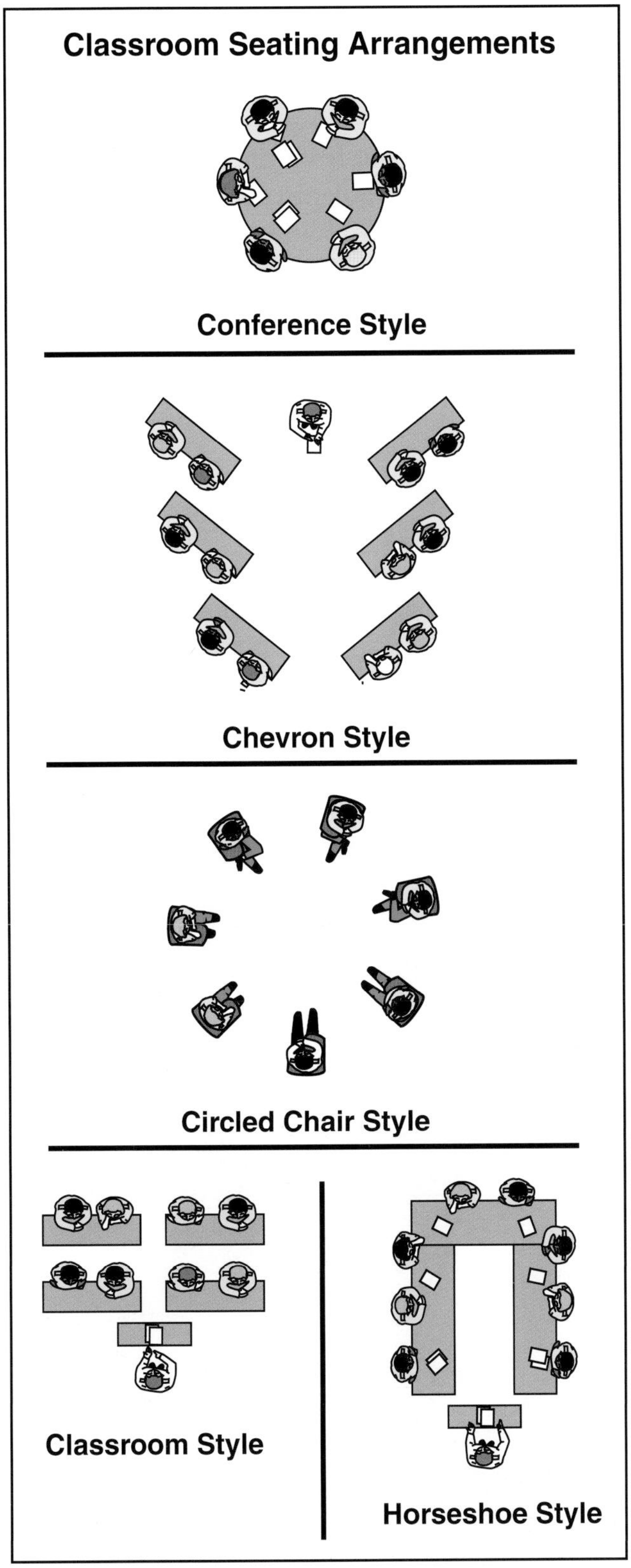

Classroom Seating Arrangements

Conference Style

Chevron Style

Circled Chair Style

Classroom Style

Horseshoe Style

Figures 12.6 The company officer should select the seating plan that is most appropriate for the topic, class size, and available space.

- Use the lesson plan as a basis for the presentation.
- Speak to the students; make eye contact with them.
- Do not speak to easels or dry-marker boards when writing on them; face the audience while speaking (**Figure 12.7**).
- Use vocal variation to emphasize key points.
- Summarize key points and concepts.
- Ask questions and solicit questions from students to keep them actively involved.
- Focus on the audience, notice body language and facial expressions, and listen to students' questions.
- Use examples that relate the topic to students and their jobs.
- Motivate students to learn the material by showing them how it will benefit them both personally and professionally.

Figure 12.7 It is very difficult for students to hear or understand what is being said when an instructor talks while writing on a dry-marker board and faces away from the audience.

Discussions

The *discussion* format allows interaction between the teacher and students and among students. A discussion is a less formal approach to teaching; however, it is not less structured. Learning objectives must still be attained and a lesson plan followed.

The company officer must plan the discussion based on the topic and time allowed for it. Because discussions can be time-consuming, the company officer must ensure that time is used efficiently and the topic is specific enough to provide students with the necessary information to conduct a discussion.

The discussion format that company officers will most likely use is the *guided discussion* where the company officer acts as the facilitator and presents a topic to the students **(Figure 12.8)**. The members of the group discuss ideas in an orderly exchange controlled or guided by the company officer. The intent of this type of discussion is to gain knowledge from other group members, modify their own ideas, or develop new ones.

As facilitator, the company officer's role is to guide the discussion and meet the lesson objectives in the following ways:

- Keep the discussion on the topic.
- Add pertinent details.

- Ask thought-provoking questions.
- Analyze conversations to ensure understanding.

Topics that benefit from the discussion format might include the implementation of a new policy or procedure, a postincident critique, an event within the jurisdiction that may have an effect on the unit, or trying to develop solutions to a problem that is affecting the company or organization. Discussions are an excellent way to involve company personnel in the decision-making process.

Demonstrations

A *demonstration* is the act of showing how to do something or how something operates or acts. It is a basic means for teaching manipulative (psychomotor) skills, physical principles, and mechanical functions **(Figure 12.9)**. It can be used effectively to show the operation of tools, equipment, apparatus, or materials and show the results of their use.

Figure 12.8 The company officer acts as facilitator during discussions by calling on students, keeping the discussion focused on the topic, making notes, and providing illustrations that help to clarify the topic.

Figure 12.9 Demonstrations can show how an item works or is used. Students participate by repeating the steps demonstrated by the instructor.

To use the demonstration method effectively, company officers should follow a few guidelines. **Table 12.1** shows the guidelines for the two critical areas: preparing and demonstrating.

Company officers may also elect to have members of their company who are trained in specialized skills give demonstrations. Following the prescribed lesson plan, a certified EMT could give refresher training in cardiopulmonary resuscitation (CPR). A member of the hazardous materials team could provide Awareness-Level hazardous materials training for fire company personnel. With this approach, the company officer can involve subordinates in the teaching process, providing them with additional teaching skills and experience.

Table 12.1
Demonstration Method

Prepare	Demonstrate Skill
1. Know clearly what is to be demonstrated and its learning objective. 2. Be proficient in every step of the demonstration by practicing in advance with other company officers or personnel who will be involved in the teaching. 3. Acquire all equipment and accessories, ensure that they work, and arrange them for use. 4. Arrange the room or demonstration area so that all participants can see and hear the demonstration.	1. Begin the demonstration by linking new information with the students' current knowledge. 2. Explain what the demonstration will show the group how to do. 3. Explain why the skill is important. 4. Demonstrate the skill once at normal speed. 5. Repeat the demonstration step by step while explaining each step slowly. 6. Repeat the demonstration again while a class member or the group explains each step. 7. Consider using a video camera and large-screen monitor when the group is large in order to allow students to see the process up close or observe small details. 8. Allow students the opportunity to ask questions and clarify any misunderstandings. 9. Ask for a student volunteer to demonstrate the skill while explaining the steps. Give reassurance by coaching and guiding the student through the process. Offer suggestions or corrections during the demonstration. 10. Provide the opportunity for students to practice, and allow them to supervise and correct each other as they become skilled. Again, closely monitor student activities when students practice potentially dangerous skills for the first time. 11. Reassemble the group and demonstrate the skill one more time at normal speed and/or one more time slowly as the group explains the steps as a summary. Relate the skill to the learning objective and performance on the job.

Practical Training Evolutions

Practical training evolutions (sometimes called *company drills*) are essential for providing safe and efficient fire and emergency services to the public. Therefore, they are key elements in any fire and emergency services organization's training program. Practical training evolutions may be simple (involving one company or a single type of evolution) or complex (involving multiple units or a series of evolutions). Practical training evolutions fulfill the following two primary requirements for the emergency services organization:

- *Hands-on* training required in applicable NFPA standards and Occupational Safety and Health Administration (OSHA) regulations and mandated by professional associations and local jurisdictions that have authority over the training function

- Practical training evolutions that allow students to apply the knowledge and practice the skills they have learned in the classroom.

Generally, company-level practical training evolutions reinforce the skills that were learned during formal training sessions and help company members learn to work together (**Figure 12.10**). In addition, realistic practical training evolutions promote enthusiasm, morale, confidence, and team spirit among fire and emergency service responders.

Practical training evolutions are also opportunities for personnel and units from various agencies, organizations, and jurisdictions to train together for potential joint operations. Multicompany evolutions should include all units within the assigned response area and be monitored by instructors, safety officers, and chief officers. Company officers can, and should, develop multicompany evolutions that involve small numbers of units such as a simulated fire requiring two fire engines pumping water in tandem to a scene (**Figure 12.11**).

Figure 12.10 Company-level drills can be held at a variety of locations, including unused parking lots. Hose lays, pumper hookups, and apparatus positioning are just some of the drills that the unit can practice.

Figure 12.11 Multicompany training exercises help to improve the coordination of units that normally respond together. Company officers can gain experience in commanding multiple units and applying the Incident Command System.

The company officer should select training locations that enhance the student's learning experience and reflect actual locations and emergency conditions in which the unit may operate. To ensure the proper level of realism while maintaining personnel safety, the company officer must plan the training evolutions based on established criteria. At the same time, the officer must maintain control of the training evolution at all times. Finally, the company officer must be creative in selecting the resources needed to develop a realistic learning experience.

Simple Evolutions

Simple training evolutions involve small numbers of students performing a single task that requires only a few skills (**Figure 12.12**). Examples include the following:

- Lifting and setting ground ladders
- Using portable fire extinguishers
- Lifting and moving patients
- Forcing entry through doors
- Taking and recording patients' vital signs
- Deploying and advancing attack hoselines
- Driving and parking fire apparatus

Figure 12.12 A ladder raise, whether performed by one-person or multiple people, is an example of a simple training evolution. Proper safety precautions should always be applied to every training evolution.

These types of training evolutions may involve from one to five active participants. The evolution is repeated until the participant(s) are able to perform it without error. When more than one participant is involved, students rotate positions so that each has the opportunity to experience and practice each part of the skill.

The company officer begins the evolution by explaining the learning objectives, demonstrating the evolution, relating the evolution to the classroom presentation, and emphasizing the safety requirements for the evolution. If the evolution involves more than one participant, the demonstration may require the use of an experienced group of responders to perform the evolution for students to observe.

While monitoring the actual evolution, the company officer should immediately stop and correct any performance weaknesses or errors. The sooner corrections are made, the more likely students are to recognize problems and adjust their behaviors. Safety infractions are always acknowledged and corrected immediately.

Simple training evolutions should be performed as though participants were involved in a real emergency incident, which means that the appropriate personal protective equipment (PPE) is worn during the evolution. All policies and procedures that would affect personnel are applied during the training evolution, including the National Incident Management System-Incident Command System (NIMS-ICS) (see information box, p. 276). Practical training evolutions should also be practiced with both the minimum and maximum levels of staffing that the organization requires.

For instance, if an engine company is staffed by one person who may arrive at the incident ahead of the rest of the crew, that scenario should be part of the training. If a company is normally staffed by four people but has a minimum level of three, both scenarios should be practiced. By following these suggestions, students will practice and learn the skills they are required to use when they are on duty.

Complex Evolutions

Complex training evolutions may involve multiple units, agencies, or jurisdictions in scenarios that require high levels of cooperation and coordination. Company officers may be involved in planning and participating in these types of evolutions. Some examples of complex scenarios are as follows:

- Automatic or mutual aid responses
- Large area structure fires
- Structural collapses
- Natural disasters such as floods, tornados, or earthquakes
- Hazardous materials incidents
- Human-caused disasters, including terrorist attacks
- Large area forest, wildland, or urban interface fires
- Transportation incidents such as aircraft crashes, bus or truck accidents, or shipboard fires **(Figure 12.13)**

Any practical evolution that involves multiple teams of fire or emergency services responders automatically demands the use of the NIMS-ICS. With this system, all participants and observers are accounted for and kept under control. Evolutions that are complex, involve large numbers of participants or units, or may involve dangers inherent in the exercise itself demand incident management.

The use of NIMS-ICS during practical training evolutions has two benefits: First, it helps ensure the safety and accountability of participants. Second, it acquaints participants with the operation of the system. Participants can take this training experience and apply what they have learned at the scene of an actual emergency.

The company officer should adapt NIMS-ICS to fit the requirements of the particular type of evolution. In the case of any evolution that holds the potential for injuries, the use of NIMS-ICS is an absolute necessity.

Locations

Company officers may use a wide variety of sites for practical training evolutions. The most obvious place to perform evolutions is at the station in the apparatus room, in a large indoor classroom (dormitory or living room), or on the parking lot/driveway. Each of these spaces is ideal for training with fire hose, portable fire extinguishers, ground ladders, or other equipment.

Interior rooms can be arranged for search and rescue training by covering participants' self-contained breathing apparatus (SCBA) facepieces with facepiece covers or black tape and turning off lights in the room. Most stations will have a fire

Figure 12.13 Complex training evolutions involving aircraft incidents require coordination and planning as well as space to create a truly realistic training experience.

hydrant on the property for pumping evolutions and deploying and charging hoselines.

Other remote training sites may include a wide variety of locations and types that may meet the organization's needs. The company officer or the training division may have a list of available remote sites that include the following information:

- Location
- Name of owner/representative
- Availability (access and time)
- Water supply source
- Possible types of training evolutions that the site could support

In any of these examples, the company officer must coordinate the training with the administration, training division, and property owner. Examples of potential remote training sites and possible training uses include the following:

- *Parking lots* — Driver/operator training, supply and attack hose deployment, and vehicle extrication operations **(Figure 12.14)**
- *Subdivisions under construction* — Driver/operator and building construction training
- *Abandoned/condemned structures* — Ventilation and forcible-entry training
- *Military or government-owned reservations* — Wildland fire suppression, off-road driver/operator training, and joint military and fire department training

- *Airports* — Aircraft crash/fire/rescue, driver/operator, and foam fire-suppression training
- *Grain elevators/silos* — Technical and rope-rescue and grain bin/elevator rescue training
- *Industrial sites* — Confined-space rescue, technical and rope rescue, hazardous materials, and fire-suppression training as well as joint-training evolutions with the local industrial fire brigade
- *Wildlands* — Wildland fire-suppression and off-road driver/operator training (may involve joint activity with controlled burns)
- *Structures under demolition* — Building collapse, ventilation or forcible entry, and rapid intervention team training
- *Vehicle salvage yards* — Vehicle extrication operations **(Figure 12.15)**
- *Parking garages* — Standpipe operations and high-angle rescue training
- *Commercial buildings in the service area that are for sale and unoccupied* — Search and rescue, hoseline deployment, and tactical simulation operations
- *Warehouses and aircraft hangars* — Large area search, rapid intervention, hoseline deployment, and tactical simulation operations

Figure 12.14 Unused parking lots can be used for driver/operator training and hose deployments.

Figure 12.15 Vehicle salvage companies can provide wrecked vehicles for extrication training. If it is not possible to move a vehicle to a training facility, training can take place on the salvage company's property.

Some of these remote sites will be available for repeated use while others will provide only a onetime training opportunity. In all cases, the appropriate permission to gain access and train on any remote site must be obtained in advance from the property owners or their agents.

Remote-site training locations must meet the requirements for environmental protection regarding water runoff, soil contamination, and air pollution. Company officers must consult the agencies responsible for these environmental regulations and determine the required precautions and permits. They must also monitor weather conditions to ensure that adverse weather, limited visibility, icing, and temperature extremes do not increase risks to participants, citizens, or exposures.

Company officers must not attempt a live-burn training exercise without approval from the administration and the training division. They must adhere to the requirements of NFPA 1500, *Standard on Fire Department Occupational Safety and Health Program*, and NFPA 1403, *Standard on Live Fire Training Evolutions*, regarding safety during live-burn training exercises. Safety is the primary concern during any and all practical training evolutions.

Planning Factors

When planning practical training evolutions, company officers must take many factors that contribute to a safe and effective learning experience into consideration. These factors include the following:

- *Safety* — Level of realism in the training evolution must balance with the level of risk to the safety and health of students. In all cases, safety must take precedence over realism. Safety means not only the use of proper PPE but planning the evolution with safety as a key component of the evolution. The safety factor cannot be overemphasized in planning training.

- *Learning objectives* — Practical training evolutions must result in students meeting the learning objectives of the lesson. If the evolution does not meet these criteria, time and effort are wasted. A lesson plan must be created to help define the learning objectives.

- *Justifications*—Meeting the learning objectives is just one justification for the evolution. The training must meet other criteria too, including cost/benefit, legal requirements, positive community perception, and allotment of resources.

- *Supervision*—Every training evolution must be supervised and monitored by company officers. The larger the evolution, the more supervisors are required for supervision. A guideline based on NFPA 1403 requirements that can help in planning for the evolution is an instructor-to-student ratio of one to five.

- *Resources/logistics*—The plan must provide for all the resources necessary to perform the tasks and complete the evolution, which is especially critical for evolutions that occur at remote sites. *Requirements:*
  — Water supply quantities must be calculated based on the requirements of NFPA 1142, *Standard on Water Supplies for Suburban and Rural Fire Fighting*.
  — Apparatus, tools, extinguishing agents, and personnel must be available at the site.
  — Rest and rehabilitation resources for all participants as well as emergency medical resources must be planned for and brought to the site.
  — Sufficient time must be provided to complete the evolution.

- *Weather* — Company officers must plan to hold evolutions when the weather will not be a distraction or create a safety hazard and be prepared to alter their plans when the weather becomes inclement.

- *Legal requirements* — Considerations include those laws, regulations, or standards that cause the training to occur and those that limit, constrain, or prohibit training evolutions. Legal requirements that place limitations on training evolutions include environmental laws, zoning, building and fire codes, and ownership. The legal requirements that cause the training to occur define the following:

— Type of training that must take place

— Minimum amount of time that must be used for training

— Evaluation criteria used to determine if training was successful

- **National Incident Management System-Incident Command System (NIMS-ICS)** — In order for a training evolution to mirror the actual events that take place at an emergency incident, an evolution must adhere to an accepted command structure. Whether the evolution is intended to involve a single company, multiple companies, or multiple agencies and jurisdictions, NIMS-ICS must be established and followed.

- **Exposures** — Remote training locations will have exposures that must be considered when planning a practical training evolution that involves the release of smoke, embers, water, or other residue. Exposure protection must be provided during all live-fire evolutions. *Other considerations:*

  — The movements of smoke and fire embers on wind currents may affect residents living in the area.

  — Water runoff could contaminate drinking water supplies or create a slipping or skidding hazard.

- **Evaluations/critiques** — Lesson plans should include an opportunity for company officers and participants to evaluate evolutions and their performances in the following ways:

  — Assist students to attain proficiency and address weaknesses.

  — Assist the training division in determining the effectiveness of the particular evolution.

  — Assist company officers in determining their own effectiveness in teaching and supervising a practical training evolution.

  — Provide models of the critique process for all participants to become familiar with when they are involved in emergency incident critiques **(Figure 12.16)**.

Experienced fire and emergency service responders are generally task-oriented and cooperative students. They enjoy working as a team

Figure 12.16 Training evolutions should end with an evaluation and critique of the evolution. The critique is an opportunity for participants to comment on the effectiveness of the operation and learn from any errors that were made.

or group and accomplishing an assigned task with others. These personal traits have important implications for planning practical evolutions. The company officer should apply the following guidelines when planning a practical evolution and establishing the desired learning objectives for experienced personnel during company drills:

- Give each participant the opportunity to have input and influence the final learning outcome based on the established learning objectives. Participants must know their roles and the desired learning objectives of the training evolution.

- Do *not* assign too many participants to specific tasks. Keep all participants busy, and eliminate or greatly reduce *stand-around time*.

- Provide a safe staging area for students and an observation area for nonparticipants.

- Maintain a suitable instructor-to-participant ratio. The exact ratio varies with the type of evolution, although the ratio (one to five) given earlier may be used as a gauge.

- Assign a safety officer to monitor all training activities. Having a safety officer is a requirement of NFPA 1500 and good fire and emergency services practice. The company officer will assume this role even if the training only involves one company (a single resource) under the requirements of NIMS-ICS.

- Ensure that training participants have the necessary skill levels and knowledge needed for a particular training evolution. *Examples:*
  - Participants who are *not* familiar with the specialized knots needed for high-angle rescue require additional training before participating in such a course or training evolution.
  - Prerequisites may have to be satisfied before students are allowed to participate in an evolution. A complete review of each individual's training record will reveal those who are qualified to participate in advanced exercises. This review encompasses JPRs and prerequisite skills and knowledge.
  - The company officer may want to request that the training division provide prerequisite training for any personnel who do *not* meet the required knowledge level.

- Design the practical evolution so that a positive outcome is possible. Assigning a task that is very difficult or impossible to accomplish provides a limited learning experience.

- Provide a summary of what has been learned and what can be carried into the operational environment and actual emergency setting. This summary may be an opportunity for a discussion of the training scenario and its results.

- Videotape the training evolution if possible to assist with the critique and for future use as a visual training aid.

- Document all company-level training accurately, including times, topics, participants, and results. See Chapter 16, Records Management, for a detailed discussion of this topic.

Evolution Control

Both simple and complex practical training evolutions must be controlled. Controlling an evolution involves the following elements:

- *Supervising* — Provide direct supervision over participants to ensure that the correct skills are used safely during the evolution.

- *Monitoring* — Observe the progress of the evolution to ensure that all lesson objectives are performed and accomplished.

- *Teaching* — Use the evolution to teach by including related or new information for students when appropriate.

- *Managing* — Apply the elements of NIMS-ICS to control the evolution as though it was an actual emergency situation.

Resources

Ideas for practical training evolutions should be available from the training division or from the state/provincial training agency. NFA may also be a source for evolutions as well as the NFPA standards. Fire Protection Publications (FPP) also publishes a very good manual called *The Sourcebook for Fire Company Training Evolutions*. This manual contains predesigned training sessions that can be completed within 2 to 3 hours.

Training Schedules

The company officer should also consider how and when to schedule the training. In some fire and emergency services organizations, the company-level training schedule may be established by tradition. A specific time during each shift may be dedicated to training. In the case of volunteer or combination organizations, that time may be a weekday evening or a weekend morning or afternoon.

Other organizations may delegate the selection of the training time to the company officer or district/battalion chief. If the company officer has this type of flexibility, the following considerations should be taken into account when scheduling the training:

- Allow enough time for the topic to be taught, practiced, and learned.

- Ensure that the time allowed for the lesson matches the time mandated by the training division/agency for the specific topic.

- Select a time that should be relatively free from distractions.

- Select a time when personnel can focus on the topic and practice skills. Research indicates that students are at their peaks between 10 a.m. and noon. Most company officers recognize that personnel are less likely to learn and respond in the time immediately after a meal and later in the evening.

- Schedule training when the majority of participants are available.

- Schedule joint training with other units in the same station or district. This approach results in the best use of time and talent since two or more company officers can *team teach* the topic (officers instruct the portions of the topic with which they are most familiar).

- Include enough time for rest breaks and rehabilitation (**Figure 12.17**).

Figure 12.17 Training evolutions can be very exhausting, especially during the summer. Schedule rest and rehabilitation breaks at regular intervals. Provide liquids and monitor participants' physical conditions.

- Notify the district/battalion chief, operations chief, and dispatch/telecommunications center if it will be necessary to take the unit out of service during the training or leave the response area. Ensure that units are available to respond in place of out-of-service units. Another approach is to have a reserve unit available to respond while a primary unit is out of service.

- Schedule training at a location with limited distractions

Summary

Most fire and emergency services instructors recognize the fact that the amount of training that is mandated and required can exceed the amount of time available to provide it. Therefore, the organization's company officers are essential in the training process if training goals are to be attained. At the same time, company-level training is one of the best methods available for building teamwork and ensuring that the company will operate safely and effectively during emergency situations. The company officer must work to provide the mandatory level of training while building teamwork within the company.

Training drills are also a good way for an officer to evaluate the skills of unit personnel. By observing the crew, the officer can spot trends, strengths, weaknesses, and habits that can be altered, reinforced, or supported to benefit the unit. It is the responsibility of the company officer to instill teamwork, leadership, resourcefulness, and pride so that the unit can operate safely and efficiently, whether performing a simple drill or participating in a complex drill with other units, divisions, or organizations.

Human Resources Management

Chapter Contents

Learning Objectives

1. Match to their definitions types of plans.

2. Recall information about company-level planning.

3. Select facts about issues involving personnel assignments.

4. Select facts about promotion and retention.

5. Select correct responses about performance evaluations.

6. Select correct responses about specific human resources issues a company officer may face.

7. Respond to scenarios about human resources policies and procedures.

8. Select facts about conflict management.

9. Recall information about discipline as it applies to the company officer.

Job Performance Requirements

This chapter provides information that addresses the following job performance requirements of NFPA 1021, *Standard for Fire Officer Professional Qualifications* (2003):

<u>Chapter 4 Fire Officer I</u>

4.2

4.2.4(B)

4.2.5

4.2.5(A)

4.2.5(B)

4.2.6

4.2.6(A)

4.2.6(B)

Chapter 13
Human Resources Management

Human resources are the most important resources available to the fire and emergency services organization. *Human resources* are the personnel that compose the organization. They perform the duties and tasks assigned to the organization and provide the services to the organization's customers. They may be volunteers or career personnel who perform either emergency or nonemergency duties. Company officers are part of those resources. At the same time, they have those same resources available to them to perform the duties assigned to their companies or units.

As a manager of human resources, the company officer must be able to communicate with, supervise, train, evaluate, discipline, and ensure retention of personnel assigned to the company. These skills are applied to all of the activities that the unit performs. The company officer plans and prioritizes the activities needed to meet the mission of the organization. At the same time, personnel safety must always be a consideration for the company officer. Interpersonal communication is one of the most important of these skills and was discussed in depth in Chapter 6, Interpersonal Communications.

An overview of the planning function, elements of human resources policy management, and behavior management are given in this chapter. Elements addressed include new employee duty assignments, conflict management, specific human resources policies, discipline, promotions, retention, and performance evaluations. This chapter provides both career and volunteer company officers with the knowledge necessary to effectively and efficiently use their personnel to accomplish the unit's assigned tasks.

Laws that affect personnel issues were presented in Chapter 5, Legal Responsibilities and Liabilities. The theories and applications of supervision were presented in Chapter 3, Supervision, while company-level training was described in Chapter 12, Company-Level Training. Finally, Chapter 10, Safety and Health Issues, included information on safety and health issues such as stress and other problems that can affect personnel.

Career and volunteer fire officers are faced with very similar challenges when dealing with the personnel under their command. However, in two instances, the challenges for each are different: First, career fire officers must be familiar with labor/management policies and agreements (See Chapter 14, Labor/Management Relations) as well as state/provincial and federal human resources laws. Second, volunteer fire officers must be aware of the means for attracting and retaining volunteers. Fire officers who work for a combination organization will benefit from the information presented for both instances.

Planning Function

Planning is a managerial function that determines in advance what an organization, a group, or an individual should do and how it will get done. It is the foundation of the management process, which includes planning, organizing, leading, and controlling. Planning must be completed before the rest of the process is undertaken. To be effective, plans must be implemented. While it is the responsibility of chief officers and the administrative staff to develop formal organizational plans, it is the responsibility of company officers to implement them.

Company officers must know the types of plans used by the organization, how the planning process works, how to apply it at the company or unit level, and the process for altering existing plans. The planning process provided in this chapter may be applied to both emergency and nonemergency activities.

Plan Types

The generally accepted basic classification of plans is based on the frequency with which they are used. Therefore, two broad categories can be established: standing plans and single-use plans. Plans may also be categorized as strategic, operational/administrative, and contingency. Plan descriptions are as follows:

- *Standing* — Develop policies, procedures, and rules that are used frequently. The creation of policies, procedures, and rules helps to ensure the consistent and equal application of authority while defining responsibility within the organization. The company officer relies on the results of standing plans to manage the day-to-day emergency and nonemergency activities of the unit.

- *Single-Use* — Accomplish a specific objective such as the development of a program, project, or budget (**Figure 13.1**). These plans are usually intended to reach an objective within a short period of time. Company officers may be assigned the implementation of various single-use plans such as a voluntary home fire and life-safety program.

- *Strategic* — Chart the course of the organization over an indefinite future that is divided into definite time components. The plan attempts to take into account the external factors that will affect the organization such as changes in the economy, demographics, service requirements, hazards, and technology. *Characteristics:*

  — Strategic plans are based on trends and expectations of the future environment, but external factors are somewhat unpredictable and some unforeseen events will occur.

  — Strategic planning, while relying on the best judgment of the planning committee based

on analysis of the available information, must be designed to be flexible and responsive to change.

  — Strategic plans must be communicated to members of all units, and those portions of the plans that are assigned to a particular unit must be implemented through the use of operational and administrative plans (see following bullet).

- *Operational/administrative* — Focus on *how* objectives will be accomplished as opposed to strategic plans that focus on *what* the organization will do. Operational/administrative plans are concerned with those factors that are within the control of the organization, objective, and fact-based while strategic plans are subjective.

Figure 13.1 A budget is an example of a single-use plan that the company officer may develop. Budgets are created for specific time periods, usually one year, although multiyear budgets may be developed for special projects such as the construction of new facilities or replacement of apparatus.

- **Contingency**—Create alternative plans that can be implemented in the event of uncontrollable circumstances. These plans attempt to prepare for the worst possible situations. Company officers should be aware of contingency plans for the most likely emergency situations that could occur. For instance, in case a natural disaster interrupts the organization's communications system, company officers must be aware of alternative methods for communicating with other units or the dispatch/telecommunications center.

The Planning Process

There are many planning models available to the company officer. One common model includes five steps that guide the company officer through the planning process. This type of model is usually presented graphically to illustrate the relationships of the component parts. The purpose of this five-step model (or any other similar program-planning model) is to provide planners with a systematic approach to decision-making. The model can be applied to either emergency or nonemergency situations. The five-step planning model includes the following steps:

Step 1: *Identify*— Select a problem that requires a response. The problem may be an emergency situation such as a victim trapped in a motor vehicle accident or a nonemergency incident such as an interpersonal conflict between crew members. These examples will be referenced in the following steps.

Step 2: *Select*— Choose the appropriate response to the problem, which requires choosing the goals, outcomes, and objectives required to meet them.

— *Emergency example:* Successfully extricating the trapped victim

— *Nonemergency example:* Resolving the interpersonal conflict

Step 3: *Design*— Determine the steps required to meet the goals, outcomes, and objectives previously selected.

— *Emergency example:* Stabilizing the vehicle, protecting the victim, determining the proper extrication methods, and positioning the tools for use

— *Nonemergency example:* Determining the appropriate location for counseling, collecting information about the conflict from other crew members, and requesting participants to attend the counseling session at a designated time

Step 4: *Implement* — Perform the selected activity or supervise crew members in the activity that will mitigate the problem.

— *Emergency example:* Supervising or participating in the activities that will stabilize, protect, and ultimately extricate the victim

— *Nonemergency example:* Participating in the counseling session by mediating the conflict resolution between crew members

Step 5: *Evaluate*— Determine the effectiveness of the activities in meeting the goals or outcomes. Effectiveness may be immediate such as the successful extrication of the victim or prolonged such as the improved relationship of crew members.

The five-step planning model can be represented as a circular path or as a flowchart (**Figure 13.2** and **Figure 13.3, p. 288**). The results of the evaluation may indicate the need for some changes in the activities. When changes are identified, a new analysis is used to begin the cycle again. See Chapter 15, Community Relations and Public Fire and Life-Safety Education, for more information on the five-step planning process.

Using the previous emergency-situation example, if the victim is still trapped after the roof and door of the vehicle have been cut away, it may be necessary to use a hydraulic ram to spread the dashboard and firewall away from the seat. In the nonemergency-situation example, the counseling session may *not* have the desired results and participants may need professional counseling by a human resources specialist.

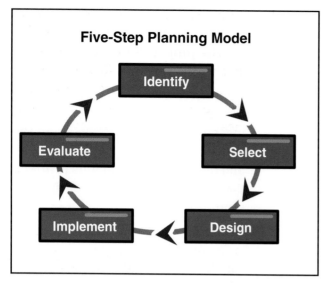

Figure 13.2 The five-step planning model may be represented as a circular path creating a never-ending process.

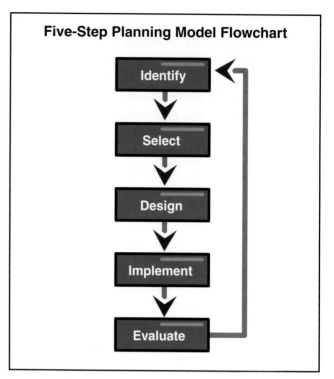

Figure 13.3 A flowchart may also be used to represent the five-step planning model.

Company-Level Planning

The company officer can apply the planning process to both emergency and nonemergency situations with different approaches. While nonemergency planning can take time and involve the input of all company members and may result in a consensus opinion, emergency incident action planning must be immediate with limited input and result in a command decision.

All planning should be documented by the company officer. Documentation provides evidence of the decisions that were made and serves as a guide for future planning. Should the results of the planning fail to meet the required goal, the documentation will assist in determining why the plan needs to be altered and how to do it.

Emergency Incident

Emergency incident planning involves two distinct activities that occur at two different times: preincident and at the incident scene. First, the company officer and crew members participate in preincident planning. Preincident planning is similar to nonemergency planning because it is *not* immediate and can have input from multiple sources, including members of the company and external sources. The results of preincident planning provide the background information for emergency incident action planning.

For example, the company inspects target hazards within the response area, prepares attack plans based on potential types of hazards, and prepares surveys that increase the unit's knowledge of hazards present in the various sites or facilities. The first three steps of the planning process can be applied during the inspection: Site hazards are *identified*, appropriate actions are *selected*, and the best actions are *designed* into an overall action plan with equal input by crew members **(Figure 13.4)**. The company officer can then assign tasks to crew members based on information gathered in the inspections and the knowledge, skills, and abilities of each person.

These task assignments must be flexible to meet changes in staffing that occur due to vacations and sick leaves. At the same time, the location or type of incident, such as chemical spills, fires, collapses, etc., will require a specific action by the unit. For instance, a fire may occur in any part of a structure. Some potential locations of a fire may be close to the main entrance while others may be close to a service entrance, or a fire can be located where there is no entrance such as an attic space. A fire may also block a means of egress for employees, requiring an immediate rescue response.

Second, once an incident occurs and the company is on scene, the company officer puts the preincident plan for this type of incident into effect and mentally applies the planning process steps to create an incident action plan: The problem is identified, a goal is selected, objectives are designed, activities are implemented, and the results are evaluated for effectiveness. Input is continuously requested from personnel at the scene to help determine that objectives are being met **(Figure 13.5)**. However, the company officer is making all decisions in an autocratic manner. Decisions are based on the internal application of the planning process steps.

Nonemergency Activities

Like the preincident planning mentioned previously, activities for nonemergency situations can be determined through the steps of the planning process, using input from members of the crew. For instance, the company may have been assigned the duty of inspecting all commercial establishments

within their response area by the end of the month **(Figure 13.6)**. The company officer can apply the planning process to the goal of making the inspections in the specified time while still meeting other requirements such as company-level training. The members of the company can provide their ideas on the best means to meet all obligations.

Figure 13.5 At an emergency incident, the company officer assigns tasks based on the incident action plan (IAP). This plan defines the strategic goals and tactical objectives and ensures that they are met by appropriate activities.

Figure 13.4 Part of the planning process can also be applied to the development of preincident plans. Three steps that can aid in preincident planning are identify, select, and design.

Figures 13.6 The planning process can also be applied to nonemergency activities such as the inspection of a commercial facility.

Plan Alterations

Because company officers implement the plans, they are most aware of the need for changes or alterations. Plans may be altered for the following reasons:

- *Existing conditions may warrant the immediate alteration of an operation* — The company officer uses personal experience and knowledge to recommend making a change. The recommendation is documented by including a description of the situation, justification for the alteration, and a description of the outcome based on the proposed alteration.

- *Original requirements are not being effectively met* — The company officer can recommend to a superior or to the administrative staff that the plan be reassessed and altered. The recommendation is documented with a detailed description of the requirements, justification for the alteration, and a description of the outcome based on the proposed alteration.

Human Resources Policy Management

Company officers are involved with human resources management or relations in one form or another during their service careers. This situation exists in volunteer, combination, and career organizations regardless of whether they are public or private organizations. As supervisors, company officers have to deal directly with the administration of human resources management policies involving new employee duty assignments, promotions, retention, and performance evaluations.

Other human resources policy issues include duty exchange, vacation leave, sick leave, and wellness leave. The company officer must also be familiar with the symptoms of substance abuse, indications of a hostile work environment, and excessive absenteeism. Grievance issues, which are human resources topics and considered part of the labor/management topic, are discussed in Chapter 14, Labor/Management Relations.

New Employee Duty Assignments

The company officer must be familiar with the policies that regulate new employee duty assignments within the organization. As a first-line supervisor, the officer will be responsible for a number of duty assignments for new personnel. Most fire and emergency services organizations require a probationary training period for new personnel. The company officer will be responsible for ensuring that personnel on probation receive the required training and supervision. The officer must also help new personnel adjust to the work environment, learn new duties and responsibilities, and become part of the company or unit.

First Duty Assignments

Following the entry-level training period, new fire-fighting and emergency-response personnel are assigned to operational units. The first duty assignment is usually with an emergency-response fire-fighting company, usually an engine or ladder/truck company. Some organizations have a policy to place new personnel on very active units to provide first-hand experience quickly. Other organizations believe that it is better to place new personnel in less active areas to allow them time to get accustomed to station life and duties.

Whichever duty-assignment policy is followed, it is important to make the new employee's initial introduction as smooth as possible. Initial impressions and experiences affect a firefighter/emergency responder's development, motivation, and retention.

Probationary Periods

The majority of fire and emergency services organizations have probationary periods for entry-level fire-fighting and emergency-response personnel. Long used in career organizations, many progressive volunteer and combination organizations now use probationary periods for new volunteer and on-call personnel. These periods are usually 6 to as much as 18 months in length and allow the organization to evaluate the ability of the probationary employee to fulfill job requirements.

The probationary period begins at the end of entry-level fire-fighting and emergency-response training. The probationary period is an opportunity for first-line supervisors to provide guidance while at the same time observe and evaluate the work habits of new employees **(Figure 13.7)**. The probationary period is also an opportunity for the company officer to provide training and information that may not have been addressed in the formal entry-level training.

Company officers are responsible for establishing work assignments for new personnel assigned to their units. Because emergency response is the primary mission of the unit, it is important that new firefighters/emergency responders are told the tasks they must perform at emergency incidents. Specific emergency-incident tasks are assigned to new employees and practiced with other members of the crew.

New personnel must also be familiar with the location of equipment stored on the apparatus and how it is used. This type of fundamental company-level training is the responsibility of the company officer and should take precedence over all other task-related training.

The new company member must also learn the many duties and tasks required in nonemergency activities. Apparatus and equipment care and cleaning, facility cleaning, and duties such as standing radio watch and interacting with external customers are included in these activities. Initially, explaining these duties may be the direct responsibility of the company officer.

Some training instruction may be delegated to an appropriate member of the company. For instance, apparatus care and cleaning can be taught and supervised by the driver/operator. Emergency medical services (EMS) responsibilities such as inventory control, material request procedures, and equipment decontamination can be taught by the senior emergency medical technician (EMT) assigned to the apparatus or station **(Figure 13.8)**.

Duties that are infrequent and nonemergency in nature such as developing preincident surveys or public education activities can be taught after the emergency-response activities are taught. The company officer can instruct new members before the nonemergency events occur.

Assigning a mentor to new employees is an excellent method of ensuring that knowledge is passed on. A *mentor* is an experienced member of the unit who can provide personal instruction and encouragement to a new employee.

In addition, the activities of new employees should be documented. An organization may have a *sign off* or *task book* that helps the organization monitor training and accountability. The sign off book may have items as simple as emptying a dishwasher to subjects as diverse as explaining the organization's uniform and grooming standards or specific tasks related to deploying a rescue line.

Figure 13.7 In career and volunteer organizations, the company officer must work closely with new personnel to ensure that they fully understand their duties and follow established policies and procedures.

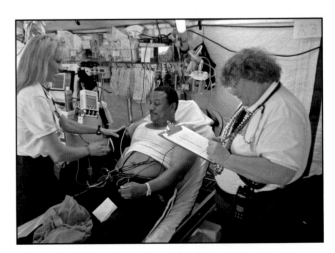

Figure 13.8 Experienced personnel can be assigned the task of supervising and observing the activities of new personnel. *Courtesy of U.S. Federal Emergency Management Agency, Marvin Nauman, photographer.*

The probationary period usually ends with a formal written test and performance evaluation administered by the training division. The company officer may also be required to provide a performance evaluation of the new employee based on observations made during the probationary period. In the event that the probationary employee cannot successfully complete the training or is unable to meet minimum job requirements, termination can occur at that time in career organizations, contingent on labor/management agreements.

Work Environments

The employee work environment is also important because a hostile environment can cause resentment and conflict. New employees must be given the opportunity to *fit in* and become contributing members of the unit. This situation is especially true when the organization is in the process of diversifying its membership. Because a diverse workforce may be different for some current members, change management is an important part of diversification. The company officer must ensure that the change process occurs smoothly, and new employees are properly assimilated into the unit.

Expectations

While the organization is responsible for creating a positive work environment, it is also responsible for providing the proper training for new personnel in the basics of station life. They should be made aware of the expectations that the company officer, other employees, and the organization have of them such as the following:

- Reporting to work on time
- Performing assigned station duties
- Working as part of a team
- Paying attention to details and following through with assignments
- Respecting authority
- Taking personal responsibility
- Maintaining a positive attitude
- Respecting confidentiality
- Treating others like they themselves want to be treated

The company officer must communicate these expectations to the new employee in clear, concise, and understandable terms. These expectations should also be provided in written form. To ensure that expectations are understood, an officer must seek feedback from the employee. At the same time, the company officer must provide the support and leadership that the probationary firefighter/emergency responder needs. Supporting those needs means becoming familiar with the employee's background and values.

Promotions

The company officer should take an interest in the career choices of personnel in the unit. With the aid of the training division or state/provincial training agency, the company officer can provide promotional information on the types of courses subordinates should attend and certifications that would be most helpful. A timeline should be developed so that subordinates have the following information:

- Eligibility requirements
- Approximate schedules of promotional examinations
- Required length of service at the current rank before a higher rank can be attained
- Other career paths that are available

Depending on personal abilities and interests, subordinates may be more successful and advance faster in nonemergency response positions within the organization. It is a responsibility of company officers to help subordinates investigate all possibilities. Both counseling and mentoring are effective approaches to career path development. Information on both of these techniques is included in Chapter 26, Human Resources Management II.

Retention

All types of fire and emergency services organizations are faced with the challenge of retaining members. The investment in the training and equipping of new members must be realized in the form of continuous and long-term service. In addition, the premature loss of experienced personnel affects the organization due to the loss of knowledge, skills, and leadership ability.

Keys to Success

The following chart is a brief summary of expectations that are considered keys to success for an organization. It is divided into general, company officer, and emergency response categories. The chart was adapted from a memo to all company officers of the Clark County (WA) Fire District No. 6.

Expectations

General	Company Officers	Emergency Response
• If it doesn't feel right, it probably isn't. • Make expectations known, and ensure that they are clear and reasonable. • Stop problems before they get out of hand. • Set goals and reach them. • Be honest. • Be the best you can be. • Lead by example! • Give crews what they need to succeed (resources, training, advice, etc.). • Seek answers before passing judgment on another's actions or decisions. • Do the right thing. • Discipline when necessary ... praise when appropriate. • Don't make excuses ... learn from your mistakes and move on. • Manage time effectively (and share the plan with the crew). • Communicate! • Develop an effective team. • Participate in mandatory physical fitness workouts. • TRAIN! TRAIN! TRAIN! • Wear proper uniforms. • Utilize the chain of command. • Participate in all chores. • Keep apparatus and stations orderly and clean. • Complete incident reports as soon as possible after returning from an incident. • Understand that the job is more than just showing up.	• Maintain proper management of emergency scenes. • Manage training events effectively. • Be available by cell phone when away from the station. • Ensure timeliness and accuracy of all documentation. • Attend officer meetings. • Complete performance evaluations. • Be a leader as well as a supervisor.	• Respond promptly 24 hours a day. • Know your response area (streets, businesses, and target hazards). • Use proper radio procedures. • Perform size-ups when needed — provide an update when appropriate. • Remember priorities: Size-up, resources, water supply, and command (apparatus placement). • Look for that little extra customer service opportunity on every response. • Adjust the response code or level as appropriate (Code 1, Recall, or Add Apparatus). • Maintain crew integrity — no freelancing or independent operations! • Understand and use the passport accountability system. • Wear full protective clothing (hoods, self-contained breathing apparatus [SCBA], personal alert safety system [PASS] devices, and universal precautions). • Be aggressive ... but BE SAFE! • Return the company to service as soon as possible when released from the emergency scene. • Self-dispatch when aware of any emergency situation and if it is the correct thing to do. • Correct emergency dispatches when necessary by providing additional information. • Keep the battalion chief informed of any changes to response capability. • Announce water supply location only if needed. • Perform primary and secondary searches by different crews. • Use proper terminology to describe crews or locations • Repeat face-to-face orders on the tactical radio channel for crew location and accountability. • Notify the Incident Commander (IC) when entering a building or using self-contained breathing apparatus (SCBA). A Rapid Intervention Team (RIT) will monitor air times. • Split crews by engine name and engine name B (Example: *E61* and *E61-B*). • Send companies without an assignment to Level 1 staging. • Ensure that pump operators wear proper personal protective equipment (PPE). • Know the incident location (check map if necessary). • Ensure that all apparatus are on the correct operations radio channel. • Never go to the scene empty-handed.

Retention is particularly important to organizations that depend on volunteers because of the ever-shrinking pool of new applicants. At the same time, career organizations may lose personnel to higher paying nonemergency jobs or to other fire and emergency organizations that have better benefits or wages. While chief officers must make retention part of their planning process and part of the organization's culture, the company officer must work to ensure that company personnel are satisfied with their accomplishments and feel needed.

Planning for retention involves determining the needs of members and then providing for those needs. When needs are social (as is the case with many volunteers), fire officers must create events that satisfy that need. When needs involve secure jobs with advancement potentials (as is the case with many career personnel), educational opportunities and a variety of advancement paths are necessary. Company officers can use counseling sessions to assist career personnel in selecting the appropriate educational and promotional opportunities to reach their career goals.

To create a culture of retention, it is important to first know why people want to become firefighters/emergency responders. Knowing people's motivations helps to identify factors that can satisfy those personal needs. Creating a positive, inclusive, and participatory atmosphere also helps. People need to want to come to work at the start of the shift **(Figure 13.9)**. Among other things, they want to be challenged by daily tasks, find variety in their work assignments, and enjoy the people they work with. Company officers are responsible for creating this atmosphere.

There are many reasons why people join the fire and emergency services. Some of these reasons are as follows:

- Desire for achievement
- Need for a sense of belonging
- Personal recognition
- Financial reward
- Security
- Guaranteed retirement benefit

Figure 13.9 The company officer is responsible for creating and maintaining a positive and cooperative work environment. This environment can be accomplished through open communication and permitting subordinates to take part in the decision-making process.

- Personal challenge
- Advancement
- Responsibility
- Community service
- Family tradition
- Increased sense of self-worth
- Fun
- Excitement
- Organizational membership benefits

Not all of these reasons or motivations are present in all applicants, and some motivations may not be a guarantee for a successful fire-fighting or emergency-response career. For instance, the fact that other members of the family have been in the organization does *not* mean that the applicant will make a good firefighter/emergency responder. Because an applicant is or has been a member of another organization also does *not* guarantee the person will be *a fit* within another one.

Performance Evaluations

Performance evaluations are important parts of human resources management. Evaluations may be informally impromptu or formally scheduled. A Fire Officer I will have the opportunity to provide impromptu informal evaluations through the observation of a subordinate's daily activities. When behaviors warrant, coaching or counseling can be employed to reinforce proper habits or correct improper habits.

Formal performance evaluations are held on a specific schedule, usually annually. Other opportunities for formal evaluations could occur before a promotional examination or when improper behavior that has not improved through informal evaluations needs to be corrected.

According to NFPA 1021, *Standard for Fire Officer Professional Qualifications,* the responsibility for formal performance evaluations rests with the Level II Fire Officer. However, in some organizations the Level I officer also has this responsibility. Company officers should consult their organization's policies governing performance evaluations. Information on formal procedures is included in Chapter 26, Human Resources Management II.

Specific Human Resources Policies

Human resources policy issues that a company officer may face are the same as those faced by any supervisor. Some, such as duty exchange, vacation leave, sick leave, and wellness, involve the interpretation and application of organizational policies. Others, such as hostile work environments, substance abuse, and absenteeism, are the result of improper behaviors. Each type of issue must be addressed immediately to prevent the recurrence of infractions or development of a potentially destructive situation within the unit.

Duty Exchange

Many career and combination organizations permit employees of similar rank and training to exchange duty shifts or portions of shifts. If a labor/management agreement exists, the specific requirements for the duty exchange may be included. One of the main reasons for including duty exchange in the agreement is the requirement by

Figure 13.10 Due to federal laws and labor/management agreements, the company officer must maintain an accurate record of personnel duty exchanges.

the federal Fair Labor Standards Act (FLSA) for employers to maintain accurate records of hours worked **(Figure 13.10)**. See Chapter 14, Labor/Management Relations for more information.

Company officers should instruct subordinates on the proper duty-exchange procedures based on the labor/management agreement or organizational policy. The policy or agreement may include requesting permission from the company officer, providing the name and qualifications of the person who will be substituting, indicating the date and length of exchange, and stating the date and time the obligation will be repaid.

The company officer must document and monitor duty exchanges to ensure that they are conducted properly. Documentation is very important when the organization has a limit to the number of exchanges an employee can have during a specified length of time such as a single pay period.

Vacation Leave

Vacation leave (annual leave) is accrued by an employee based on the length of service and/or the labor/management agreement. Vacation leave requests are usually made by all employees near the beginning of the calendar year and granted according to seniority and rank. Requests are usually made in writing. Requests may be denied for valid reasons such as insufficient staffing or mandated training during the period of the request. Company officers must adhere to the organization's policy for granting vacation leave and the labor/management agreement requirements if one is in effect.

Requests for unscheduled vacation leave may occur at any time. Granting vacation leave in these circumstances may be at the discretion of the company officer or may require permission from a higher ranking officer. Requests may be denied based on staffing levels or training requirements of the unit, division, or organization.

Sick Leave

Employees may request sick leave in advance, immediately before a work shift, or during a work shift. The company officer must follow local policy for granting sick leave to employees. In some cases, dependent sick leave (when a member of the employee's immediate family is ill or requires assistance) may also be considered as part of the sick-leave benefit **(Figure 13.11)**.

Requests in advance of a work shift can occur when an employee has a planned medical procedure such as elective surgery or a medical evaluation or examination. Depending on the organization's policy, these requests may have to be in writing and provided to the company officer a specified period of time in advance.

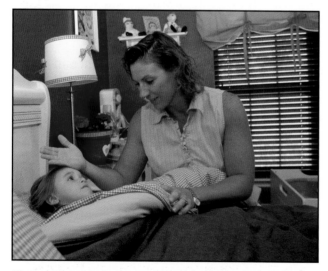

Figure 13.11 Most career fire and emergency services personnel have sick-leave benefits. Dependent sick leave may also be part of the employee benefits.

Sick leave that is requested immediately before a work shift can have the greatest affect on staffing. The company officer should *not* request that any employee report for duty when they have requested sick leave; however, if a pattern of sick-leave requests develops, the company officer may request that the employee provide evidence of the nature of the illness in the form of a medical release. This requirement may be found in the organization's sick-leave policies or labor/management agreement.

Employees that become ill during a work shift also pose problems. Depending on the nature of an illness and how incapacitated an employee is, the company officer may have to make a difficult decision. Options may be limited by the local sick-leave policy or labor/management agreement. The employee may be requested to remain on duty if the illness is minor or go to a physician or minor emergency medical center for evaluation. When staffing levels permit or the illness is more serious, an employee may be released from duty and either sent home or to an emergency room for treatment.

Depending on organizational policy or labor/management agreement requirements, employees may be required to provide a physician's approval before returning to work. This requirement may be based on the nature of the illness or length of time an employee has been on sick leave. Company officers must adhere to the policy or agreement when allowing an employee to return to work. Documentation should also be kept on sick-leave requests, sick-leave use, and return-to-duty requirements. Evidence of proper dependent sick-leave use may also be required.

Wellness Leave

Some organizations may separate sick leave from wellness leave depending on their definition or the labor/management agreement. Wellness leave may apply to doctor's appointments, examinations/evaluations, elective surgery, physical fitness evaluations, physical rehabilitation, or psychological counseling such as that provided by the employee assistance program (EAP). Requests for wellness leave will probably be made in writing in advance.

The company officer must follow local policy in granting this type of leave. While each employee may be allowed a prescribed amount of annual wellness leave, maintaining mandated unit staffing levels is also a major consideration.

Hostile Work Environment

One of the greatest challenges to supervisors and managers in the past half century has been dealing with situations involving hostile work environments that exist when employees in the workplace are subject to a pattern of exposure to offensive conduct or behavior by any member of the workforce. This condition is an outgrowth of the sexual-harassment situations that began to appear as women entered male-dominated work environments. Policies have been expanded to protect all employees from hostile or abusive actions.

The condition is further aggravated if supervisors or managers take no steps to discourage or discontinue such behavior. Federal and state/provincial mandates have reinforced the need for change throughout North America.

Sexual harassment, as mentioned in Chapter 5, Legal Responsibilities and Liabilities, involves both hostile work environments and attempts by supervisors to use their powers to gain sexual favors from employees. Failure to follow proper procedures can have legal repercussions on both officers and organizations. Company officers must know and understand the following elements:

- Laws that govern workplace behavior
- Behaviors that constitute sexual harassment and create a hostile environment
- Local reporting process for sexual harassment charges
- Employee rights in such cases

Eliminating a hostile environment and preventing sexual harassment are responsibilities of all members of the organization. Company officers must monitor their own activities as well as those of unit members (**Figure 13.12**). Actions that they can take as supervisors were listed in Chapter 5, Legal Responsibilities and Liabilities. Additional actions include the following:

- Ensure that the organization's sexual-harassment policy is clearly stated to all employees and posted in a highly visible location in the station or facility.
- Be aware of warning signs that sexual harassment is occurring. These signs include the following:
  — Display of sexually-oriented pictures, objects, or written materials
  — Frequent jokes of a sexual nature
  — Open use of sexual innuendos or pressure for dates
  — Routine occurrences of sexually-oriented profanity
- Take corrective action immediately and decisively.

Figure 13.12 A hostile work environment can be caused by many situations. The company officer must be aware of warning signs and take immediate action before the situation becomes worse.

- Inform employees who are engaging in inappropriate behavior that it is an infraction of the organization's policies and will not be tolerated.

- Inform superiors and document all information regarding incidents and attempts to resolve them if behaviors continue.

- Request additional or remedial training in the organization's policy regarding sexual harassment or hostile environments.

Company officers can make a major error when they ignore any behavior that may contribute to a hostile work environment. Situations that are ignored rarely go away and actually become worse.

Substance Abuse

Substance abuse includes the improper use of alcohol and drugs. Because alcohol and drugs impair judgment and slow reaction times, their effects are not only on the individual but also on those who work and live with the individual as well as the public.

The U.S. Fire Administration (USFA) estimates that as many as 10 percent of the 1.1 million firefighters in the U.S. may be abusing drugs. The International Association of Fire Fighters (IAFF) estimates that 75 percent of the total firefighter population in the U.S. has used either drugs or alcohol. Similar figures are available for the rest of the emergency response services.

Company officers must be aware of the symptoms of drug and alcohol use and recognize them when they occur among subordinates. They must also be aware of the root causes for substance abuse and attempt to address these problems before abuse occurs. However, company officers must remember that they are not psychologists or professional counselors. When a problem becomes apparent, they must refer subordinates to the organization's EAP.

The cause of substance abuse can be any number of problems. The symptoms that indicate an employee is involved with substance abuse of any kind will vary depending on the type of substance (**Figure 13.13**). Different drugs produce different effects resulting in slight variations in outward indications.

Any one symptom may not be enough to indicate substance abuse but should be enough to suggest that there may be a problem. Some signs and symptoms are specific to opiates and narcotics and are distinct from those experienced with central nervous system stimulants like cocaine or depressants like alcohol.

To offset the potential danger of substance abuse, the fire and emergency services organization should establish a written policy as part of the EAP in the employee physical fitness and wellness program. The policy must include control mechanisms that provide rehabilitation procedures for employees as well as reporting and privacy procedures (**Figure 13.14**).

Some organizations have established periodic, random drug testing for all employees. The medical department of the jurisdiction usually has this testing done by contracted healthcare facilities. It is essential that the results of this testing (like all medical records of members) are kept confidential. The company officer may be aware of when unit members are required to take these tests and must keep this knowledge in strictest confidence. A process should be established within the program whereby members who refuse to participate or who become repeat offenders following rehabilitation may have their employment terminated.

Absenteeism

Absenteeism may be an indication of a serious problem that an employee is having trouble coping with or it may be the result of circumstances beyond the employee's control. The first step is for the company officer to gather all the information concerning a particular incident.

If an employee was absent for a reason that was beyond the employee's control such as severe weather, severe illness or injury, or a missed airline flight, then the company officer should counsel with the employee, stressing the importance of contacting the supervisor or other officer in these circumstances. The company officer should let the employee know that the organization will, within its policies and procedures, work to assist the employee.

If the cause of an absence was a personal problem, then the company officer should refer the employee to the EAP for counseling. If the situa-

Substance Abuse	
Symptoms	**Causes**
General Substance Abuse: • Change in circle of friends • Reclusive behavior — long periods spent in self-imposed isolation • Long, unexplained absences • Lying and stealing • Involvement on the wrong side of the law • Deteriorating family relationships • Obvious intoxication, delirium, incoherence, or unconsciousness • Changes in behavior and attitude • Decrease in job or school performance **Specific to Opiate and Narcotic Abusers:** • Accelerated heart rate • Constricted pinpoint pupils • Relaxed or euphoric state that may lead to a dangerous level of respiratory depression resulting in coma or death **Others:** • Dilated pupils • Restlessness • Hyperactivity • Euphoria • Slurred speech • Disabled coordination • Decreased attention span • Impaired judgment	• Low self-esteem • Financial difficulties • Domestic problems • Physical or emotional addiction • Peer pressure • Perception that substance use is acceptable • Stress • Self-doubt

Source: Government information from the U.S. National Library of Medicine in the Public Domain.

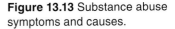

Figure 13.13 Substance abuse symptoms and causes.

Figure 13.14 When substance abuse is suspected, the company officer should counsel with the subordinate privately. Depending on local policy, the subordinate should be referred to the organization's employee assistance program (EAP) for professional help when necessary.

tion cannot be resolved or the employee is absent repeatedly, then the company officer should recommend that some form of discipline be enacted. In all cases, records of the incident and subsequent interviews should be maintained.

Behavior Management

Very few people have identical personalities, values, and behaviors. The differences between people can result in many types of conflict that must be resolved if people are going to live and work together. The company officer is responsible for ensuring that unit members can overcome differences and learn to resolve conflicts.

Behavior management involves both conflict management and discipline activities on the part of the company officer. Both activities require the company officer to be familiar with the organization's human resources policies and procedures and any labor/management agreement that may be in affect as well as have strong leadership skills.

Conflict Management

One of the responsibilities of all company officers is managing conflict. Conflict occurs when people are in opposition or disagreement. To be able to control or resolve these situations, supervising company officers must understand conflict management styles, steps to resolving conflict, and methods of negotiating internal conflict resolution. Conflict management skills are essential to resolving situations that involve personnel conflict regardless of the cause.

Management Styles

Each generally accepted conflict management style used in the business community is based on the concern for the other party and oneself. These concerns result in three types of behavior that are defined as follows **(Figure 13.15)**:

- *Passive (nonaggressive) behavior* — Occurs when people hide their own emotions so that others do not know how they feel. The goal of passive behavior is to appease others and avoid conflict at any cost. *Examples:*

— Failing to defend their rights

— Failing to express honest feelings, thoughts, and beliefs and, consequently, permitting others to violate their rights

— Expressing one's thoughts and feelings in such an apologetic, diffident, self-effacing manner that it devalues them

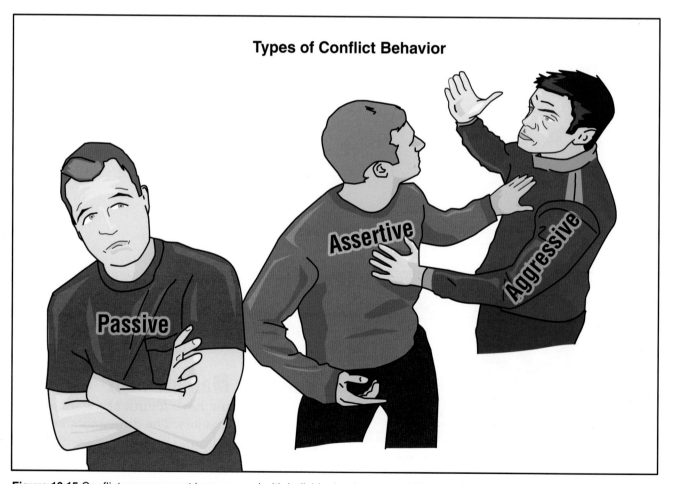

Figure 13.15 Conflict management is concerned with individuals who may exhibit one of three types of behavior: passive, aggressive, or assertive.

- *Aggressive behavior* — Occurs when people express their emotions openly by using threatening behaviors toward people or objects, which results in the violation of others' rights. The goal is to dominate the situation or other person and win, which forces the other person to lose (*win-lose* situation). *Examples:*
  - Exhibiting behavior that is often dishonest and inappropriate such as shaking a fist in another person's face or shouting at, striking, or physically intimidating another person
  - Humiliating, degrading, or belittling persons in a conflict to ensure winning
  - Overpowering persons so they become weaker or less able to express thoughts and beliefs and defend their needs and rights

- *Assertive behavior* — Occurs when people express their emotions honestly and defend their rights without hurting others. The goals of assertion are communication and mutual respect, fair play, and compromise between the rights and needs of the two parties involved in the conflict. The personal rights of other people are not violated, while the thoughts, feelings, and beliefs of the individual are expressed in an honest and appropriate manner.

Conflict management styles may include any one or more of five types. **Table 13.1, p. 302,** lists descriptions and example situations. Definitions are as follows:

1. *Avoiding conflict* — Taking a nonassertive or passive approach; people may deny that a problem exists, refuse to take a stand on a situation, or mentally or physically withdraw from a situation. The result is a *lose-lose* situation because the conflict is never resolved.

2. *Accommodating conflict* — Appeasing other persons by passively giving in to their positions. The result is a *lose-win* situation because the second person's needs are met at the expense of the first person.

3. *Forcing conflict* — Relying on an aggressive and uncooperative approach to conflict management, resulting in a *win-lose* situation. The forcing style can damage relationships, create animosity, and result in a single-solution response to problems.

4. *Negotiating conflict* — Reaching a compromise solution that all parties can agree upon. The supervisor is moderately assertive and cooperative. The result is a decision that causes everyone to compromise on some things while benefiting on others. The conflict is resolved relatively quickly and relationships are maintained.

5. *Collaborating conflict* — Sharing of information openly and honestly, which usually results in the best solution to the conflict (also referred to as the *problem-solving* style). While the previous styles involve the personal interests of the parties involved, this style is focused on the best interests of the organization, community, or service area.

Conflict Resolution Steps

When conflict occurs, it is best to resolve it as soon as possible. The longer the company officer waits to confront a problem, the greater the effort that will be required to find a solution. The decision-making process discussed in Chapter 4, Logic, Ethics, and Decision-Making, can be very helpful as the basis for managing conflict. Using that process, the six steps of conflict resolution are as follows:

Step 1: *Classify/identify the problem* — Determine what type of conflict is involved, and identify participants.

Step 2: *Define/diagnose the problem* — Determine the amount of time, skills, effort, and resources required to resolve an issue. Determine whether a conflict is a symptom of a deeper and more involved problem.

Step 3: *List alternative options* — Determine whether an issue should be resolved through collaboration, negotiation, force, accommodation, or avoidance. Determine which conflict management style is most appropriate to the problem. In the event the selected style is not effective, determine which style is the next best choice.

Step 4: *Determine the right response/appropriate conflict management style* — Select the appropriate style. Knowing the advantages and disadvantages of each style

Table 13.1
Conflict Management Styles

Number	Style	Description	Example Situations
1	***Avoiding Conflict*** (taking a nonassertive or passive approach)	• Although it may appear that the benefit of avoiding conflict is to maintain relationships, the relationships will suffer in the long term. • The longer the conflict goes unresolved, the greater the strain on the relationship and the lower the work efficiency of those involved. • All conflict should be resolved as soon as possible	Some situations in which avoidance may be necessary and acceptable are as follows: • The conflict is trivial and does not affect the tasks being done. • The company officer or supervisor does not have a high stake in the issue that is causing the conflict. • There is no time to attempt to resolve the conflict due to other priorities. • The conflict may damage or compromise an important relationship. When the relationship is important, avoidance provides the time necessary to balance the importance of the conflict with the importance of the relationship and determine a logical resolution to the conflict. • The emotions involving the conflict are very high. The avoidance approach will permit both parties to gain control of their emotions before attempting to resolve the conflict.
2	***Accommodating Conflict*** (appeasing others by passively giving in to their positions)	• While the initial benefit may be maintaining relationships, the result may be counterproductive. • It is possible that the person who is giving in had the better solution for the situation. • Continuing to accommodate others also results in the loss of leadership and influence in the group. • Too much accommodation on the part of anyone involved in a conflict might result in a compromised solution and the potential for animosity or resentment.	Situations that may be appropriate to the accommodating style of conflict management are as follows: • The person employing it prefers to be a follower and not a leader in this situation. • The company officer or supervisor does not have a high stake in the issue that is causing the conflict. • There is limited time to resolve the conflict. • The conflict may damage or compromise an important relationship. It may be appropriate to balance the importance of the relationship with the importance of the situation that is causing the conflict. • The senior person involved in the conflict is an autocratic manager who uses the forcing style of conflict management.

Continued

Table 13.1 (continued)

Number	Style	Description	Example Situations
3	***Forcing Conflict*** (relying on an aggressive and uncooperative approach)	• If the person using this style is correct, the solution may be the best possible one. • However, if the opposite is true, the solution may be disastrous. • In any event, the potential for damaged personal relationships is very high for the person using this style.	Some situations that may require the forced style of conflict management are as follows: • The issue is extremely important, and the final decision will be an unpopular one. • The support of others is not important to the outcome of the decision. • Maintaining relationships is not important. • Conflict resolution is urgent, and there is no time for debate or discussion.
4	***Negotiating Conflict*** (reaching a compromise solution that all parties can agree upon)	• The disadvantage is that the solution may not be the best one for the organization or unit. • Also, if this style is used too often, it causes the people or groups involved to ask for more than they need, knowing they will not get it. • This approach has become symbolic in some labor-management negotiations.	The appropriate uses of the negotiating style are as follows: • The issues are complex and critical. • There are no clear or simple solutions to the situation. • All parties to the conflict are interested in different solutions. • All parties have similar power within the organization. • The resulting solution will be temporary. • The time to resolve the conflict is short.
5	***Collaborating Conflict*** (also called the *problem-solving* style) (sharing of information openly and honestly)	• The advantage of this style is that it usually results in the best possible solution. • The disadvantage is that it takes mutual trust, time, skills, and effort to use it. • It is the most difficult of the styles to implement, yet it is also the most rewarding. • Collaboration requires that all parties are willing to work for the goals of the organization or unit and provide all the information that is necessary to make the final decision. • In most organizations, this style requires a change in culture, which has to originate at the highest level.	Situations that can be addressed with the collaborative style are as follows: • The situation demands the best possible solution without a compromise. • The parties involved are committed to cooperation for the good of the organization. • The maintenance of relationships is very important. • There is sufficient time to implement the collaborative process. • The conflict is a peer-based conflict.

and the situations that are appropriate to each will help in making this decision. If possible, base the decision on common ground such as overlying goals of the organization.

Step 5: ***Convert the decision to an action*** — Implement the chosen conflict management style. If a situation requires an immediate and forceful response, give direction to those involved and expect them to follow it. If there is time, gather information and pursue a negotiated or collaborative agreement. The result of the process must be a decision that all parties will adhere to either through force, when necessary, or through agreement.

Step 6: ***Test the action against the desired outcome*** — Implement the decision and test the results against the agreed-upon outcome.

Internal Conflict/Dispute Resolution

The company officer may not always be able to resolve a conflict or may even be a participant in the conflict. In these instances another approach will be required. Traditionally, conflict resolution has followed a formal process that may be part of the organization's policy and procedures manual or the labor/management agreement. Unfortunately, if the conflict is not resolved internally, the situation may result in a costly and time-consuming legal confrontation.

The alternative to this situation is an internal conflict or dispute resolution process. Although there are a number of variations, one of the most effective has been the *peer-mediation process*. The parties in the conflict voluntarily appear before a team composed of other organizational employees who are specially trained in the mediation process **(Figure 13.16)**.

This proactive approach helps to create an organizational culture of peace and concern for the rights and needs of the membership. This approach is also progressive and in keeping with the participatory management style that is becoming prevalent in the fire and emergency services of the twenty-first century. Some benefits of this process can be as follows:

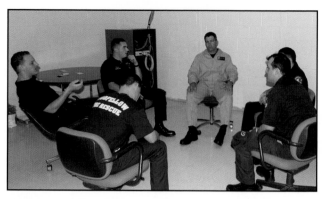

Figure 13.16 One form of conflict resolution is peer mediation. It is a voluntary process that requires the parties in conflict to discuss the problem in the presence of other members of the unit and permit the group to resolve the problem.

- ***Relationships are maintained*** — Results are consensus based and tend to be long lasting.
- ***External publicity is avoided*** — Conflict remains within the organization. Participants are spared from unflattering publicity.
- ***Costly litigation is avoided*** — Process occurs outside the judicial system and depends on mutual agreement for enactment of the resolution.
- ***Organization and participants control the process*** — Participants and the organization control the selection of the type of mediation, topic of the mediation, and resolution of the mediation.
- ***Participants control the resolution*** — Outcome of the conflict is determined by the membership and not by an external group.

Discipline

Discipline is often thought of as punishment; however, the vast majority of the discipline imposed is done to correct inappropriate behavior, not to punish persons. The word *discipline* comes from the root word *disciple* — a *learner*. One dictionary definition of discipline is *training that corrects;* therefore, the main purpose of discipline is to educate. Discipline in the fire and emergency services is designed to fulfill the following purposes:

- Educate and train.
- Correct inappropriate behavior.

- Provide positive motivation.

- Ensure compliance with established rules, regulations, standards, and procedures.

- Provide direction.

Corrective disciplinary actions should be taken in a manner that is progressive and lawful. Corrective action is required when an employee disobeys established rules or performance requirements. All discipline should start with an investigative interview to gather information regarding the situation or behavior that appears to require a change.

There are many possible reasons why personnel may break the rules or not comply with procedures. Some (but not all) of these reasons include the following:

- *Resentment* — Created when wages and working conditions are (or are perceived to be) substandard, bitter labor/management disputes have occurred, difficult contract negotiations have occurred, or rules are being unfairly or inconsistently applied

- *Boredom* — Caused when there is too little work or too little interest in the work

- *Ignorance* — Created when there is a lack of knowledge of the job requirements and/or the rules of conduct

- *Stress* — Caused by personal problems (on or off the job) that affect job performance

Investigatory Interview

An *investigatory interview* is one in which a supervisor questions an employee to obtain information that could be used as a basis for discipline. Employee rights during an investigatory interview may be established by the organization's human resources policies, the labor/management agreement, or state/provincial laws. The Weingarten Rights apply in all cases in the U.S. (see information box).

Investigatory Interview: Weingarten Rights

When disciplinary counseling or an investigatory interview is necessary, the company officer should be aware that the Weingarten Rights apply. The Weingarten Rights are the result of a U.S. Supreme Court ruling in the 1975 case of the *National Labor Relations Board (NLRB) v J. Weingarten,* which guarantees the employee the right to union representation during an investigatory interview or counseling session. However, the supervisor is *not* obligated to inform the employee of this right. It is the responsibility of the employee to request the presence of a union representative.

If an employee has a reasonable belief that discipline may result from answers that are given in the investigatory interview, the employee has the right to request union representation before the interview continues. When an investigatory interview occurs, the following rules apply:

Rule 1: The employee must make a clear request for union representation before or during the interview. The employee cannot be punished for making this request.

Rule 2: After the employee makes the request, the supervisor has the following three options:

— Grant the request and delay the interview until the union representative arrives and has a chance to consult privately with the employee.

— Deny the request and end the interview immediately.

— Give the employee a choice of having the interview without representation or ending the interview.

Rule 3: If the supervisor denies the request and continues with the interview, this action may constitute an unfair labor practice and the employee has a right to refuse to answer questions. An employee cannot be disciplined for such a refusal but is required to sit through the interview until the supervisor terminates the interview. Leaving before this time may constitute an act of punishable insubordination.

Progressive

Most public entities have laws requiring some form of progressive discipline, although it may not be called by that name. In general, *progressive discipline* starts with training/education to correct the first instance an employee fails to meet performance standards or violates the rules of conduct. Discipline then progresses to punitive (formal sanction) measures if there are additional offenses.

However, even in organizations using progressive discipline, a sufficiently serious first offense (theft, assault, gross negligence, etc.) may result in termination. The action should always fit the offense, so the initial response may be corrective (written notice) or punitive. Progressive leadership and participatory management can help to ensure that punitive discipline is seldom used within the organization.

Progressive discipline usually involves the following three levels:

- *Preventive action* — Hold an individual counseling interview to correct the inappropriate behavior as soon as it is discovered and prevent it from becoming a pattern or progressing to a more serious offense **(Figure 13.17)**. *Process:*

  — Ensure that the employee understands both the rule that was violated and the organizational necessity for the rule during the interview.

  — Explain exactly what is expected of the employee in the future and what may happen if the rule is violated again.

  — Document the interview in a written record.

- *Corrective action* — Use corrective action when an employee repeats a violation for which preventive action was taken or commits a different violation. It may also be used if an employee commits a serious violation as a first offense. Corrective action differs from preventive action primarily in that it is always done in writing. Give the employee a letter in person or send one by certified mail with a return receipt requested to guarantee that it is received. The letter includes the following information:

  — Description of what transpired in the preventive interview if one was held

  — Description of what the employee is or is not doing that violates organizational rules

  — Review of organizational policy regarding the possible consequences if the behavior continues or a change in behavior fails to meet organizational standards

  — Statement informing the employee that a copy of the letter will be placed in the employee's personnel file

Figure 13.17 Progressive discipline begins with the company officer counseling with the subordinate. The purpose of the counseling session, held in private, is to inform the subordinate of the inappropriate behavior, explain the expectations for improved behavior, and gain assurance that the subordinate fully understands the situation.

- *Punitive action* — Give the employee notice of possible sanctions. Use this action when an employee either continues to exhibit inappropriate behavior, despite earlier corrective efforts, or commits a very serious violation of organizational rules as a first offense. Put the employee on notice that this behavior cannot and will not be tolerated. After meeting all mandated procedural rules and employee protection requirements, consider the range of possible sanctions as follows:
  — Formal written reprimand (similar to corrective letter except it is considered severe and formal discipline)
  — Fine (specific monetary payment)
  — Suspension (time off without pay)
  — Demotion (loss of rank)
  — Termination (dismissal from organization)
  — Prosecution (legal action that may result in a large fine or jail time)

Of the three levels of progressive disciplinary action, the company officer is most likely to use preventive action. It is less likely that the company officer will have the authority to apply either corrective or punitive action. However, the officer will have to recommend to higher authorities the appropriate action based on documented evidence of misbehavior by the employee.

Legal

All discipline must meet legal requirements; discipline may only be administered for violations of written policies, procedures, rules, regulations, standard operating procedures/standard operating guidelines (SOPs/SOGs), and verbal orders. If there is no valid requirement, there is no basis to discipline an employee. Discipline that is administered for any other reason may result in the action being overturned by a superior officer or a court of law.

The company officer should also be aware that not every possible violation by an employee must be covered by a specific written policy or regulation. Most SOPs/SOGs include a general duty clause that simply prohibits actions or behaviors that are considered unprofessional or

Formal Discipline

In many organizations when violations are serious such as safety violations that cause injuries or property losses, the company officer may be required to either administer immediate formal discipline or notify the next level supervisor. Formal discipline may include a written reprimand or suspension of the employee with pay, pending the outcome of investigations. However, state/provincial and federal laws are designed to protect employees from arbitrary and capricious disciplinary actions. All fire officers must recognize that employees are entitled to the following information and considerations:

- Written *notice of proposed action*
- *Reasons therefore*
- Copy of the charges and materials upon which the action is based
- *Right to respond* (either orally or in writing) to the authority initially imposing discipline

Once these requirements have been met, discipline may be imposed without a hearing unless the employee requests one. A hearing is where evidence is provided or given; it is not intended to be an adversarial proceeding. Instead, it is meant to be informational — to minimize the risk of error in a supervisor's initial decision because of a lack of information. The employee, or designated legal or union representative, may provide additional information and respond to the specific charges before discipline is imposed.

inappropriate. For example, there are generally no rules against dumping garbage on a supervisor's desk. But such action by an employee could result in disciplinary action even without a written policy against it because the action is considered inappropriate and unacceptable to the average person.

In career organizations that are bound by labor/management agreements, procedures for disciplinary actions may be a part of the agreement. If the company officer does not follow the agreement procedures when administering a disciplinary action (even a minor one), a grievance may be lodged by the subordinate or the labor representative, which may prevent any future action against the employee on that issue.

Summary

Supervising a fire and emergency services company or unit demands strong leadership and interpersonal skills from the company officer. The officer must be able to apply these skills to the human resources management process. The process includes developing plans for the most effective use of personnel in both emergency and nonemergency operations, supervising new employees during their probationary periods, administering human resources policies, and applying behavior management techniques for conflict management and discipline. Because human resources issues involve the organization's members, it is essential that the company officer know both the human resources policies and procedures and the labor/management agreement that is in effect.

Robert F. Hamm on Evaluating Subordinates

In his lecture titled "Evaluation — Duty of Fire Service Officers," Robert F. Hamm provided a list of characteristics or things to consider when evaluating a subordinate for promotion. Mr. Hamm also believed that individuals can use this same list as a self-evaluation either in preparation for promotion or simply to determine whether they are performing to the best of their abilities. When evaluating the subordinate, can the company officer answer the following questions positively?

- Performs well in the current position? Accepts the duties and responsibilities that are part of the present job?
- Has the ability to solve problems and adapts to new situations and conditions?
- Gets along with others?
- Seeks greater responsibility and takes on tasks that are beyond the current level of responsibility?
- Has administrative abilities and organizes tasks efficiently?
- Uses time properly and completes projects and tasks within the time allotted?
- Responds positively to change, both personal and organizational?
- Has the ability to make friends?
- Has an enthusiastic attitude about work?
- Exhibits loyalty to the unit, peers, and the organization?
- Exhibits self-control and self-restraint?
- Has an open-mind; accepts the views and opinions of others?
- Exhibits impartial and fair judgment?
- Exhibits a dependable nature; keeps promises, schedules, and rules?
- Has the ability to solve problems?

While this is not an exhaustive list of characteristics, it does provide a company officer with a framework for thinking about the ability of subordinates to assume higher levels of responsibility. The characteristics that a company officer looks for in others should mirror those that the company officer exhibits.

Labor/Management Relations

Chapter Contents

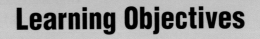
Learning Objectives

1. Identify components of the history of the labor movement in North America.

2. Recall information about the negotiating process.

3. Select facts about grievance procedures.

Job Performance Requirements

This chapter provides information that addresses the following job performance requirements of NFPA 1021, *Standard for Fire Officer Professional Qualifications* (2003):

Chapter 4   Fire Officer I

4.1.1

Chapter 14
Labor/Management Relations

The development of labor-related organizations dates to the Middle Ages in Europe, around 1100 CE. Guilds and craft unions were formed for the benefit of their members and provided training as new members joined. The traditions of guilds and craft unions spread to North America as immigrants arrived from Europe in the 1600s.

Organized labor unions have been part of the North American employment culture for over 100 years. They developed during the Industrial Revolution as a response to the working conditions in heavy industry that seemed to take advantage of the worker without providing the benefits that are today considered fundamental to employment in any occupation. Today, those benefits include fair wages, employee safety, job security, and noncash (tangible) benefits.

In the early 20th century, public-sector workers began to organize into labor unions in order to gain better salary levels and some of the same benefits that private-sector workers enjoyed. Today, many fire and emergency services personnel in career, industrial, and combination organizations are represented by labor unions that handle collective bargaining or contract negotiations for the membership **(Figure 14.1)**.

The current relationship between most labor unions and organizational management or authority is very different from that in the early years. In many situations, the leadership of both the fire and emergency services organization and labor union work very closely together to provide members with a safe work environment. Budgets are prepared with the cooperation of labor unions, creating an atmosphere of open communications.

Grievances (complaints) are dealt with through an established process, resulting in fair and equitable resolutions.

Chief officers in career organizations are sometimes in the position of representing the management perspective while still being members of the *bargaining unit* (term used in labor/management agreements to indicate the union). Some labor/management agreements exclude only the fire chief and one designated assistant from the bargaining unit.

In other fire and emergency services organizations, all chief officers are either excluded from the bargaining unit or included in their own fire officers' unions. Company officers are generally members of the bargaining unit, although some may belong to a fire officer's union along with the chief officers.

Figure 14.1 Many career fire and emergency services personnel are represented by labor unions that represent their members in contract negotiations.

Figure 14.2 Company officers may be involved in contract negotiations as members of the labor union or they may simply be represented by the union. Knowledge of the negotiations process and what the contract contains are important as both an employee and a supervisor.

Company officers must be knowledgeable in the history of the labor movement, labor/management process, laws governing it, and principles of negotiations **(Figure 14.2)**. They must also know the differences between private and public labor unions and grievance procedures as defined by the labor/management agreement or the organization's human resources policies. This chapter discusses these issues.

History of the Labor Movement

The company officer may find the history of the labor movement in North America extremely interesting. In both the U.S. and Canada, workers organized as a result of the harsh treatment given them by industrialists. At the same time, the owners of major businesses resisted the creation of unions and enlisted the aid of federal and state/provincial governments in an attempt to stop unionization. Some of the confrontations between workers and management turned violent **(Figure 14.3)**. Victories and defeats on both sides stiffened the resolve of both union and management to continue the struggle.

In the early years of the twentieth century, workers who joined a union in the U.S. took significant risks. At that time, employers had the legal right to fire any worker whom they believed might be engaging in union activities — and they did not hesitate to do so. In fact, many employers required job applicants to sign a pledge that they would *not*

THE HOMESTEAD RIOT.—Drawn by W. P. Snyder after a Photograph by Dabbs, Pittsburg.—[See Page 678.]
THE PINKERTON MEN LEAVING THE BARGES AFTER THE SURRENDER.

Figure 14.3 In the beginning of the labor movement, conflict between workers and management sometimes resulted in violence. The Homestead Riot of 1892 is an example of one such confrontation. *Courtesy of the U.S. Library of Congress Prints and Photographs Division, Washington, D.C.*

join a union. If they broke the pledge, they were fired. Before 1932, these *yellow-dog contracts*, as these pledges were called by the unions, were upheld and enforced by the courts.

The New Deal, created during the first term (1932–1936) of President Franklin D. Roosevelt, introduced a period of significant change in national labor relations that would last well beyond the New Deal era itself. Over the following three decades, several key pieces of legislation were enacted that greatly expanded the rights of workers and curtailed the power of employers. The most prominent of these laws were the following:

- Norris-La Guardia Act of 1932
- National Industrial Recovery Act (NIRA) of 1933
- Wagner-Connery Act of 1935 (commonly referred to as the *Wagner Act*)
- Fair Labor Standards Act (FLSA) of 1938
- Taft-Hartley Act of 1947
- Landrum-Griffin Act of 1959

Together with some antitrust legislation, these laws formed the basis for labor relations as we know them today. Similar laws were enacted in Canada as a result of the Great Depression and resulting economic uncertainty.

Norris-La Guardia Act

The Norris-La Guardia Act made yellow-dog contracts unenforceable by any U.S. court. In doing so, the Act established the legal principle that an employee cannot be forced into a contract by the employer in order to either obtain or keep a job. In addition to making yellow-dog contracts unenforceable, the Act made it almost impossible for an employer to obtain a court injunction to prevent a work stoppage (strike). Before the Act, employers could get an injunction not only against strikes but also against protest demonstrations (picketing) as well.

Even with the passage of the Norris-La Guardia Act, employers could still threaten and fire workers for engaging in union activities. But with the Act in force, unions had the right to strike, picket, and boycott employers without interference from the courts.

National Industrial Recovery Act

The Great Depression was at its peak in 1933 with an unemployment rate of over 25 percent of the population. In an attempt to revitalize the U.S. economy, President Roosevelt persuaded Congress to pass the National Industrial Recovery Act (NIRA). NIRA guaranteed unions the right to conduct collective bargaining. Roosevelt wanted this legislation in order to increase wages and thus maintain workers' purchasing power.

The Act was also a windfall for organized labor, and workers joined unions affiliated with the American Federation of Labor (AFL) and the new Congress of Industrial Organizations (CIO) in large numbers. However, in 1935, the Supreme Court ruled that the NIRA was unconstitutional and voided it.

Wagner-Connery Act

Following the Supreme Court's decision on NIRA, Senator Robert Wagner (NY) immediately introduced the Wagner-Connery Act, which was quickly passed by Congress. The Wagner Act included the following provisions:

- Allowed workers to decide, by a majority vote, who would represent them in the bargaining process
- Established the National Labor Relations Board (NLRB)
- Defined unfair labor practices and gave the NLRB the power to hold hearings, investigate such practices, and issue decisions and orders concerning them
- Prohibited management from interfering with or coercing employees who tried to organize
- Required management to bargain with a recognized union, although management was not obligated to agree to any of the union's demands
- Outlawed yellow-dog contracts entirely (the Norris-La Guardia Act had only made them unenforceable)

The Wagner Act was an attempt to restrain management and equalize the power of both management and labor. However, the Act did *not* impose penalties for any violations, nor did it provide the NLRB with any real power to enforce its decisions or orders. The Act did *not* become effective until it went before the courts.

For example, the NLRB decided that a group of employees had been fired in violation of the Wagner Act—but it was not until the courts agreed with the NLRB that the employees were reinstated with back pay. In 1937, a Supreme Court decision in the case of *Steelworkers v. Jones & Laughlin Steel* found that the Wagner Act was constitutional).

During the late 1930s and early 1940s, union membership grew under the protection of the Wagner Act and favorable court decisions. However, shortly after World War II, a series of major strikes threatened the transition of the economy from war production back to a peacetime orientation. These strikes made it apparent that with government protection and favorable court decisions, unions had grown substantially stronger than their management counterparts. In an attempt to restore some balance, the U.S. Congress passed the Taft-Hartley Act of 1947 over President Harry S. Truman's veto. The new Act amended the Wagner Act and imposed violation penalties on unions (see Taft-Hartley Act section).

Fair Labor Standards Act

The Fair Labor Standards Act (FLSA) was passed in 1938 to guarantee that workers in the private sector would receive overtime pay at one and one-half times their normal rate of pay for work beyond 40 hours in 1 week. However, the Act did not apply to state and local public employees until a U.S. Supreme Court decision in 1985. The effect of the Act is primarily related to how firefighters and other emergency services workers are classified and compensated.

The FLSA defines employees as either *exempt* or *nonexempt* based on certain criteria. Nonexempt employees are entitled to overtime pay, while exempt employees are not. Most employees included by the FLSA are nonexempt, while some are not. Some jobs are classified as exempt by definition such as executives, administrative personnel, highly skilled computer-related employees, and licensed professionals (doctors, lawyers, architects, engineers, and certified public accountants among others).

In addition, managers who hire and fire employees and who spend less than half their work time performing the same duties as their employees are typically also exempt employees. In general, the more responsibility and independence or discretion an employee has, the more likely the employee is to be considered exempt.

For most employees, however, whether they are exempt or nonexempt depends on the following factors:

- How much they are paid
- How they are paid
- What kind of work they do

Taft-Hartley Act

The Taft-Hartley Act provided specific penalties for NLRB violations, including fines and imprisonment. In addition, Taft-Hartley modified the Wagner Act in the following areas:

- *Union representation* — Gives workers the right to choose *not* to join a union, thus outlawing the closed shop (union membership required for employment). It limits representation elections (which are held to determine whether a union should — and which union would — represent employees) to one per year. The Act also gives employers the right to express their *views, arguments, or opinions* about union membership as long as such *expression contains no threat of reprisal or force or promise of benefit.*

- *Unfair labor practices* — Protects employees from being pressured by unions to join. Employees are also protected from having to pay exorbitant union dues or initiation fees. Employees who refuse to join a union are protected against possible union reprisals. The Act requires unions to *bargain in good faith* as the Wagner Act had previously required employers to do.

- *Bargaining procedures* — Provides for a 60-day cooling-off period in which the existing contract remains in effect when initial negotiations for the renewal of a labor contract fail to produce a new agreement. Negotiations for contract renewal normally start 60 days before a contract expires. If an impasse is reached after 30 days of negotiating, the Federal Mediation and Conciliation Service must be notified of the dispute. See Negotiation Process section for more information.

- *Regulation of unions' internal affairs* — Makes information on rules regarding union membership requirements, dues, initiation fees, elections, etc. available to the federal government as well as to the membership.

- *Strikes during a national emergency* — Keeps workers on the job while they are trying to settle a dispute when a strike would affect a key industry or put the health and safety of the nation in jeopardy. The president can invoke the Act in these situations.

Definitions

- **Union** — Organization of employees authorized to bargain with an employer for working conditions; usually formed based on the type of profession or job

- **Open shop** — Business or industrial establishment for which employment is *not* restricted to a particular trade union membership; also an agreement under which union membership is *not* required

- **Closed shop** — Business or industrial establishment whose employees are required to be union members or agree to join the union within a specified time after being hired; technically an agreement that requires membership before employment (closed shop is now illegal everywhere in North America)

- **Union shop** — Agreement that requires an employee to join the union at some point after the employment relationship begins; legality depends on the state and existence of a *right-to-work law*

- **Right-to-work law** — Prohibits employers or unions from requiring workers to belong to a union in order to have a job (currently 21 states have right-to-work laws permitted by Section 14(b) of the Taft-Hartley Act)

- **Bargaining unit** — Group of employees who are represented by a union or labor organization

- **Collective bargaining** — Negotiation between organized employees and their employer to determine wages, hours, benefits, and working conditions

- **Strike** — Work stoppage that results from a coordinated refusal on the part of employees to perform assigned work

- **Lockout (shutout)** — Withholding of work from employees and the closing of a workplace by an employer during a labor dispute; an employer's counterpart to a union's strike

Landrum-Griffin Act

Following the merger of the AFL and CIO in 1955, widespread corruption was found in older union locals. As a reaction to these revelations, Congress passed the Landrum-Griffin Act of 1959 (officially known as the *Labor-Management Reporting and Disclosure Act*). The Act included the following requirements:

- Union members' *bill of rights* to ensure that unions are run in a democratic manner

- Disclosure report listing union assets and names and personal assets of every union officer and employee that is annually sent to the federal government; in addition, employers report any financial relationship they have with a union or union representative

- Guidelines establishing minimum requirements for elections and responsibilities and duties of all union officers and officials

- Taft-Hartley Act Amendments: Severely restricts secondary boycotts, union security (contract clauses that ensure the union's continued survival, that is, mandatory membership), and recognition picketing (picketing of companies where a rival union is already recognized)

NOTE: The Taft-Hartley Act outlawed closed shops, although it permitted *union shops* that require employees to join the union within 30 days of being hired. State right-to-work laws prohibit unions and employers from requiring employees to belong to a union in order to obtain and retain a job.

Private and Public Labor Unions

The rapid and sustained growth of private-sector labor unions (as described earlier) and the continued opposition to the recognition of public-employee labor unions continued in the post-World War II era. By the mid-1950s, however, public-sector labor unions began to be established due to changes in federal and state/provincial laws. Although public-sector labor unions are similar to, and sometimes affiliated with, private-sector labor unions, differences between the two categories exist.

Public-Sector Labor Unions

Despite the fact that private-sector labor unions had prospered in the years immediately before, during, and immediately after World War II, membership in public-employee labor unions lagged far behind. In the mid-1950s, fewer than 1 million government employees were members of labor unions.

In January 1962, President John F. Kennedy issued an executive order that gave federal employees the right to bargain collectively for the first time. Then in 1969, President Richard M. Nixon further expanded the rights of federal public-employee unions by establishing a Federal Labor Relations Council (similar to the NLRB for unions in the private sector).

A number of states enacted public-sector collective bargaining laws during the same period — mostly from 1959 through the mid-1970s. The result of these executive orders, along with a changing social climate, was that public-employee unions grew to more than 4 million members by 1970.

Even though public-employee strikes were illegal in most states, several major cities experienced strikes by public employees, including sanitation workers, teachers, police, and firefighters, in the late 1960s. In 1968, the International Association of Fire Fighters (IAFF) union rescinded its 50-year-old rule prohibiting strikes by its affiliated locals.

NOTE: The position of the IAFF concerning impasse situations and subsequent job actions by its local affiliates is very clear as a result of convention action taken by delegates at previous conventions. These delegates represent the supreme authority of the IAFF. The delegates have mandated that the IAFF has no authority either to sanction or disapprove strikes or other types of job actions. The authority for such decisions, as well as the responsibility, rests entirely in the hands of the local affiliates.

In 1970, employees of the U.S. Postal Service went on strike. Even though the strike was illegal and the postmaster general was forbidden by law to negotiate with the strikers, he did so anyway. The final result was that strikers were reinstated without penalty and even received raises. In addition, Congress recognized the American Postal Workers Union (APWU) as the bargaining agent for postal employees. This action proved that even the federal government was no longer immune from strikes.

In 1981, members of the Professional Air Traffic Controllers Organization (PATCO) went on strike over a variety of issues. This action severely hampered commercial flight operations at U.S. airports.

When members failed to return to work as ordered, President Ronald Reagan fired all striking members and decertified the union. This action clarified the Reagan Administration's view of labor relations.

In response, employers stiffened their resolve against what they perceived as the growing militancy of public-employee unions, and they increased their efforts to pass right-to-work laws. In 1997 President Clinton mandated the establishment of labor-management relations councils with all federal employees including firefighters.

Differences Between Public and Private Labor Unions

Although labor unions exist in both public and private sectors and are responsible for negotiating member benefits with management, there are differences between the two categories **(Figure 14.4)**. First, in the public sector, the fire and emergency services organization usually has a monopoly on fire protection in the community or response area. This monopoly means it is often the only source of fire or rescue services available to the public.

Second, these fire and emergency services are extremely vital to the public. This vital service is one of the reasons why governments initially hesitated in giving public-sector employees the right to organize and bargain collectively. It is also why public-safety employees have seldom been given the right to strike, a tool that most private-sector labor organizations still have.

A third difference is that public-sector collective bargaining is more likely to involve the courts, depending on the structure of the state collective bargaining law. In recent years, there has been an increase in court involvement in public-sector collective bargaining.

Finally, the law governing collective bargaining in the public sector is *not* as uniform as laws governing the private sector. State/provincial laws now address most collective bargaining in the public sector.

In the collective-bargaining process, teams from management and the labor union attempt to negotiate an agreement that the membership then votes upon to approve or reject. In the public sector, the process does not end there. The agreement

Differences in Collective Bargaining	
Public Sector	**Private Sector**
• Lack of competition — service provider has a monopoly	• Competitive market — services are designed to meet the competition
• Service is extremely vital — the community depends on the service for their personal life safety	• Services may be important but are not vital — the community may elect to do without the service or find an alternative service to meet their needs
• Disputes are usually resolved in the court system — labor/management laws sometimes require that disagreements must be presented in courts of law	• Disputes are sometimes resolved in the court system — due to the cost of litigation, both labor and management may prefer to resolve the dispute without the assistance of the legal system
• Collective bargaining laws are not uniform — the laws may exist at the national or state/provincial levels but will vary from state/province to state/province	• Collective bargaining laws are generally uniform — the laws, primarily at the national level, are equally applied across the nation.

Figure 14.4 Public- and private-sector labor unions vary in a number of ways.

must also be ratified by the local governing body, the state/provincial legislature, or whatever body holds ultimate responsibility to the public.

The IAFF has also pointed out that there is a difference in the strategy used by the labor union during negotiations. In the private sector, labor union representatives often argue that there is too much of a gap between the organization's profits and workers' wages, salaries, and benefits. Since there is no profit motive in the public sector, that argument is not effective for labor negotiators. Instead, they often argue that the public-sector employees are worth more than they are paid. This argument is usually based on a market survey of similar delivery areas with similar types of fire and emergency services organizations.

Nevertheless, the public labor union's negotiations goal is still the same: improvement in employees' working conditions **(Figure 14.5)**. This goal, in turn, affects personnel recruiting, morale, retention, and discipline as well.

Figure 14.5 Improving working conditions is a major concern of the labor unions that represent fire and emergency services personnel. The issues involving safety and health are particular concerns. One such issue is the use of hearing protection when operating apparatus pumps.

Firefighter Unions

The history of labor relations in North America has been anything but stable. Sometimes relations are amicable; sometimes they are bitterly hostile. Labor and management have continued to coexist because each one needs the other. The major firefighter unions are no exception.

Some full-time career firefighters are represented by the International Brotherhood of Teamsters and others by the American Federation of State, County, and Municipal Employees (AFSCME). However, most career firefighters belong to locals affiliated with the International Association of Fire Fighters (IAFF), which is affiliated with the AFL-CIO and the Canadian Labor Council.

The IAFF differs from most private-sector unions in the relationship of its national and international levels to the individual locals. In private-sector unions, the parent organization exercises considerable control over the operation of each local. In the IAFF, its international officers help organize locals and when invited to do so, help resolve local labor disputes. It also strives to improve pay, pensions, working conditions, and firefighter health and safety, while allowing the locals considerable autonomy.

Unlike most private-sector unions, the IAFF also allows supervisors (company officers) to be members of the union, and they are included in the bargaining unit. IAFF locals are organized democratically, permitting members to vote to select their officers, decide initial positions to be taken in collective bargaining, and ratify contracts.

Contract Negotiations

Labor unions and the fire and emergency services organization regularly enter into negotiations to establish contracts between the two. The negotiating process (also known as the *collective bargaining process*) determines the working conditions, wages, and benefits for the duration of the contract, usually 1 year or more. The contract also establishes the rights of both management and the union.

The company officer should be familiar with the negotiating process, the importance of open communication, and employee involvement in the process. Not only will the company officer, who is a member of the labor union, benefit from the process but the company officer may also be an active participant.

Negotiation Process

The purpose of labor/management negotiations is to create a contract between the management of the organization and the employees who are represented by the labor union. That contract defines the responsibilities and obligations of both parties to the agreement and specifically defines employee wages, salaries, benefits, and working conditions. The elements of the negotiation process include the following:

- ***Bargaining session schedule*** — Sessions are scheduled after the labor union issues a formal call for proposals, typically about 60 days before the bargaining sessions are expected to begin. These dates are arbitrary and should provide sufficient time before the end of the existing contract to complete negotiations. Some negotiations begin as early as 9 months before the end of the contract. *Extensions:*

  — Current contracts are normally extended without a formal call for negotiations.

  — Extensions are based on the duration language contained in the contract such as *Agreement shall, upon ratification by the appropriate authorities of each party, remain in full force and effect until such time as the parties enter into, and have ratified or arbitrated, a successor agreement.*

- ***Contract content*** — Labor/management agreements usually have sections that address the following five areas:

  — *Routine clauses:* Constitutional items such as the preamble and purpose of the agreement, terms covered by the agreement, reopening conditions, and amendments

  — *Clauses affecting labor union security:* Items that describe the bargaining unit that the agreement covers; list the steps by which a labor union is recognized as an employee representative

  — *Clauses describing the rights and prerogatives of management:* Items that recognize that management has the right to decide matters that the agreement does *not* address

  — *Sections that describe how the department/organization will handle employee grievances (complaints):* Items regarding discipline, termination, and the process for filing a grievance

— *Sections that list the conditions of employment:* Areas such as wages, salaries, and fringe benefits; hours, holidays, vacations, and sick leaves; apprenticeships and training practices; hiring and firing policies; safety issues; and strikes and lockouts

- *Representation* — Bargaining teams usually represent labor and management. *Team composition:*

  — *Management team:* IAFF suggests that this team be composed of a high-ranking personnel officer, financial expert or budget analyst, and lawyer. The chief of the organization or another upper-level official should also be on the management team to be available for consultation.

  — *Labor union team:* A team that is selected or elected by the union membership may include the president of the union, members with experience in bargaining, and the union's legal counsel.

- *Preparation* — Both labor and management gather information that will support their positions. Data is collected throughout the year. Preparation is key to success in the process. Information is gathered on the following elements:

  — Wages paid in similar organizations in similar sized markets

  — Cost of current wages and benefits

  — Provisions of the current contract

  — Employee grievances

  — Past bargaining sessions

  — Representatives of the opposite side

- *Proposal presentation* — Some experts suggest that each side enter the bargaining session with proposals to present to the opposite negotiators as well as a list of new and continuing demands that they want to discuss. Presenting such lists allows each team to be proactive and take the initiative rather than reacting to the proposals of the other side.

- *Scope of bargaining* — Three categories of topics are included in contract negotiations as follows:

  — *Mandatory:* Items that *must be* bargained for. Either side can force the other to bargain over mandatory subjects; includes wages, hours, and other terms and conditions of employment.

  — *Permissive:* Items that *may be* bargained for. Either side can refuse to bargain over these items, and the other side cannot force them to discuss them. However, if both sides can agree, they are free to bargain and reach an agreement. When the item is signed, it becomes binding. For example, the right of employees to wash their personal cars while on duty may be considered a permissive item.

  — *Illegal:* Items that *cannot be* bargained for. Even if both sides agree, the item cannot be enforced.

- *Handling an impasse* — Despite good-faith negotiations by management and labor, bargaining can hit an *impasse* (sticking point over which neither side is willing to compromise). Mediation and fact-finding are the most common means of resolving impasses in the public-safety sector. Arbitration and strikes may also be used to resolve an impasse, although strikes by public employees are generally prohibited by state/provincial and federal laws (see information box, p. 322).

Open Communications

The negotiating process is basically one of communication. Both sides have to make certain the messages they transmit are the ones received; if they are not, misunderstanding occurs. The process can fail because people are individuals with internal barriers of communication based on different attitudes, experiences, values, beliefs, biases, and assumptions. Those same barriers can prevent a message from being received as intended.

Other barriers such as being defensive or preoccupied may affect receivers. People may also have emotional blocks or hold stereotyped views that get in the way of understanding **(Figure 14.6, p.**

Impasse Resolution

Descriptions of methods for overcoming an impasse are as follows:

- **Mediation** — A third, neutral party (mediator) talks with each side and discovers the real issues and concerns that are stalling negotiations. Mediators are usually provided by the U.S. and Canadian Federal Mediation and Conciliation Services or a state/provincial agency that has the same function. The results of mediation, however, are not binding on either party. *Mediator duties:*

  — Clarifies misconceptions that one side holds about the positions of the other and gets both sides talking again in hopes of leading them to reconciliation and a contract

  — Uses information from other labor disputes around the country to move one or both sides away from unrealistic and untenable positions

  — Provides both sides access to high-ranking officials and improves the chances for a contract settlement

- **Fact-finding** — Arbitrators (authoritative persons) look at facts and then develop suggested solutions (similar to arbitration). However, these suggestions are not binding. The procedure identifies facts that can convince government officials and other policy-making bodies to make concessions in return for a settlement. Neither management nor labor is forced to make a serious effort to come up with its strongest offers; therefore, the procedure may not resolve a dispute, and suggestions might not satisfy either party.

- **Arbitration** — Arbitrators hear evidence from both sides in the dispute and determine a binding solution. Neither management nor labor particularly likes the procedure because it takes the final decision out of their control, but state/provincial laws or municipal charters or ordinances sometimes require arbitration. *Elements:*

  — *Final offer arbitration:* Involves each side offering what is supposed to be its most generous offer on each issue to be resolved. The arbitrator must choose one of the offers on each issue without compromise. The procedure theoretically forces each side to make realistic proposals while coming close to what its final offer on each issue would be.

  — *Single arbitrator or panel:* Both sides usually choose names from a list supplied by a professional organization such as the American Arbitration Association, Canadian International Institute of Applied Negotiations, or similar state/provincial organizations.

  — *Strike-off procedure:* Each side alternately strikes a name from a list of professional arbitrators until the required number is left.

- **Strike** — The labor union can use a work stoppage as the last resort when it sees no other way around an impasse or wants to pressure management to grant concessions. Strikes by public employees are against the law in most states and provinces. Bans against strikes have helped to prevent them, and their numbers have decreased significantly in recent years. In the past, a central issue was usually the primary cause of a strike, and management leaders would attempt to stall the strike by reacting to the first indications of employee discontent by identifying that issue. Historically, strikes by fire and emergency services personnel have lasted an average of 3 to 7 days. Strikes were generally caused by the following issues:

  — Problems with wages and hours

  — Disputes over job benefits

  — Unhappiness about pay parity with other internal departments such as law enforcement

  — Unhappiness about the way management handles labor issues such as recognizing a labor union or defining the bargaining unit

323). Their expectations could prevent them from receiving the message accurately.

IAFF has suggestions for solving communications problems that are valid for both sides of the negotiation process, and they parallel those communication techniques discussed in Chapter 6, Interpersonal Communications. Three ways suggested by IAFF are as follows:

- ***Ensure quality communications*** — Think before speaking and select the right word and phrases, accompanied by the right voice inflections and facial expressions, to ensure a message is delivered as intended.

- ***Understand the audience*** — Know to whom the message is intended so it can be tailored to match the receivers and ensure that it is received and understood correctly.

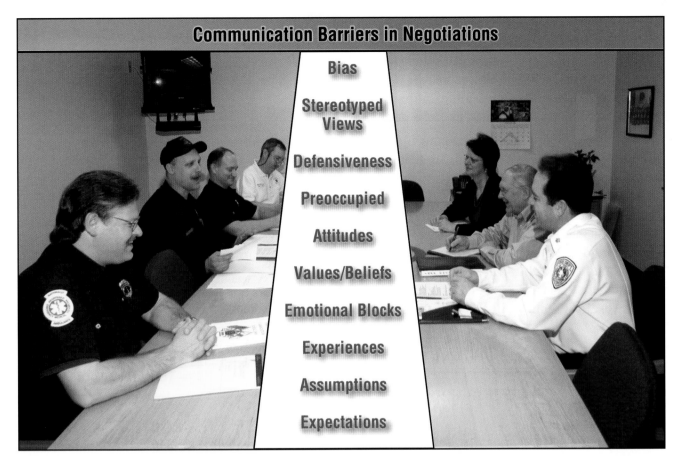

Communication Barriers in Negotiations

Bias

Stereotyped Views

Defensiveness

Preoccupied

Attitudes

Values/Beliefs

Emotional Blocks

Experiences

Assumptions

Expectations

Figure 14.6 Barriers can prevent open communications in labor/management negotiations.

- *Hold two-way dialogues* — Relay the message and then use questions to ensure that the other side understands. Listen for feedback, watch for nonverbal signals, and focus on the context as well as the content of the message.

Employee Involvement and Participation

Collective bargaining can result in a compromise in which one side or the other believes that it has lost in the process. This perception of a *win-lose* type of confrontation can generate resentment within the organization with both membership and management viewing each other on a *them-us* basis. This perception is detrimental to the working efficiency of the organization.

To avoid the potential loss of organizational cohesion, leaderships of both labor and management should consider an alternative approach that will result in what is termed *mutual gains bargaining*. This type of bargaining requires both parties to continually focus on the welfare of the public.

The Phoenix (AZ) Fire Department in the mid-1980s developed a model for labor/management relations that included this approach. Developed jointly by the department and the leadership of Phoenix Firefighters Union Local No. 493, the process is called *Relations by Objectives (RBO)*. The main goal is to foster an open, respectful, and trusting relationship between members of the bargaining unit and department management. Together they can create plans that will meet the needs of the public, the organization, and the union and its members.

Although RBO does not involve contract negotiations, it is the cornerstone of a progressive labor/management environment. About the same time, a program developed in the Mesa (AZ) Fire Department created a labor-management partnership based on RBO and other private-sector business models. The partnership created teams that researched issues and made decisions on the delivery of service to both internal and external customers.

By involving the membership of the organization in the decision-making process, both labor and management can create an atmosphere of mutual trust and respect. This atmosphere improves contract negotiations because it forces both sides to work in partnership for the benefit of the public.

A model example of this is the continued cooperation between the IAFF and International Association of Fire Chiefs (IAFC). They have established joint-development teams that created the Candidate Physical Ability Test (CPAT) and the Peer Fitness Training (PFT) Certification Program, which provide standards that are consistent with the unique health, and fitness needs of the fire and emergency services. The PFT program is part of the IAFF/IAFC Joint Wellness/Fitness Initiative **(Figure 14.7)**.

Joint IAFF/IAFC Initiatives

The following are some of the notable projects initiated jointly by the IAFF and the IAFC:

- IAFF/IAFC Fire Service Joint Labor Management Wellness-Fitness Initiative

- National Fire Fighter Near-Miss Reporting System

- International Fire Fighter Safety Stand-Down (2005-Present)

- Emergency Vehicle Safety Initiative — driving safety

- Project FIRES (Firefighter Integrated Response Equipment Systems) Personal Protective Equipment (1976-1980's)

- Project HEROES (Homeland Emergency Response Operational and Equipment Systems) Personal Protective Equipment (2002-Present)

- Multiphase Study on Firefighter Safety and the Deployment of Resources: Multiyear research project to study the link between firefighter safety and resource deployment including community risk assessment and planning

Figure 14.7 The IAFF and the IAFC have jointly sponsored a number of programs that are intended to improve fire and emergency responder health and welfare.

Proactive Labor/Management Relations

Some fire and emergency services organizations participate in a monthly labor and management meeting. The meetings were born from the idea that problems could be discussed openly in an informal forum where decision-makers gather. Benefits include the following:

- Personnel can hear first-hand information from the fire chief and union representatives.

- Major problems are discussed and resolutions are explored.

- Minor problems are identified and solved early.

- Rumors are dispelled quickly before they gain momentum.

- Interested parties can take advantage of this environment to bring forth new ideas and find resources for projects.

Grievance Procedures

Grievance procedures are usually included in the labor/management agreement or they are part of the organization's policy and procedures manual. As supervisors, company officers are part of the grievance process. A *grievance* is a complaint by an employee on one or more of the following issues:

- Demotion

- Suspension without pay

- Termination with cause

- Work assignments that violate the labor/management agreement, law, or departmental/organizational policy

- Conditions of work or employment that violate the labor/management agreement, law, or departmental/organizational policy

Grievances may be filed when employees believe that they have been unjustly disciplined. It is important for both the company officer and an employee to follow the discipline and grievance procedures that have been adopted by the organization and/or are part of the labor management agreement. These procedures include the application of the Weingarten Rights. See Chapter 13, Human Resources Management, for additional information on this requirement.

Because state labor laws or labor/management agreements define grievance procedures, examples may vary widely. However, all model procedures contain the same general elements such as filing period, testimony, witnesses, representation, and review steps.

The grievance procedure needs to be effective, consistent, and provide an equitable resolution. Company officers must be aware of the grievance procedures in effect in their organization and be prepared to follow them in the event they are needed. Organizations with strong labor/management relationships tend to resolve issues before they get to the grievance level.

Filing Period

The grievance procedure must specify the time period for filing a grievance following a serious incident or after an individual becomes aware that an incident may fit the list of issues listed earlier or is in the labor/management agreement. As an example, the following wording could be used in a policy and procedures manual:

A grievance must be initiated within fifteen (15) workdays after the employee receives notice or becomes aware of the action that is the basis for the grievance. If the employee is not satisfied with the decision at any step, the employee must carry the grievance forward to the next step within fifteen (15) workdays after receiving the written decision. If the employee does not carry the grievance forward within fifteen (15) workdays, the grievance procedure shall be terminated and the grievance disposed of in accordance with the last written decision. For purposes of this procedure, the term workdays refers to Monday through Friday.

Testimony, Witnesses, and Representation

A provision for the employee to provide information, request witness testimony, or have a member organization or legal representative present needs to be included in the procedure. As an example, the following wording could be used in a policy and procedures manual:

At every step, the employee may testify and present witnesses and materials in support of his/her position. The testimony of an employee, given either on his/her own behalf or as a witness for another employee, will not subject an employee to retaliatory action. At every step, the employee may be accompanied by an employee representative.

Review Steps

Although the time frames given might differ in various types of fire and emergency services organizations, the specific review steps that an employee follows should be part of the grievance procedure and may include the following:

Step 1: **Request review by immediate supervisor.**

a. Within fifteen (15) workdays after an employee receives notice or becomes aware of the action that is the basis for a grievance, the employee initiates a grievance, typically by completing a Grievance Form (which may be obtained from the human resources department), submits it to the human resources department, and provides a copy to his/her immediate supervisor. In some jurisdictions, grievances are initiated simply by verbally notifying the supervisor that an employee is *filing a grievance.*

b. Within fifteen (15) workdays after receipt of the Grievance Form, the immediate supervisor and the employee meet and discuss the grievance in a face-to-face meeting. A nonrepresented management member may become involved if there are contractual issues.

c. The supervisor completes a written decision within fifteen (15) workdays after the face-to-face meeting. If the supervisor fails to respond or if the decision is not satisfactory to the employee, the employee may carry the grievance process forward to Step 2.

Step 2: Request review by next higher level of management.

    a. If the employee is not satisfied with the result of Step 1, the employee must notify the human resources department that he/she wants further review within fifteen (15) workdays after receiving the written decision at Step 1. Within fifteen (15) workdays after receiving notice that the employee wants further review, the human resources department schedules a face-to-face meeting for the division head/vice president and the employee to discuss the grievance.

    b. Within fifteen (15) workdays after the face-to-face meeting, the division head/vice president issues a written decision that includes specific reasons for the decision.

Step 3: Request grievance hearing.

    a. If the decision is not satisfactory, the employee may elect to have a grievance hearing either before a panel of departmental/organizational members or an administrative judge under the conditions of the local jurisdiction's policies within fifteen (15) workdays after receiving the written decision at Step 2. The employee must notify the human resources department in writing whether he/she wants a hearing before an employee panel or an administrative judge. An arbitrator or fact finder, rather than a grievance panel, might review grievances filed within the context of a labor/management agreement. For an employee panel, the human resources department selects the panel members, convenes the hearing and arranges for the grievance to be heard.

    b. The director of the human resources department or his/her designee chairs the employee panel. The employee panel may include staff nonexempt employees, staff exempt employees, or a combination of both exempt and nonexempt employees. Members representing the unit where the grievance originates may not serve on the employee panel.

    c. The employee panel, judge, or arbitrator shall hear the grievance within fifteen (15) workdays after the date on which the employee submits his/her written request to the human resources department. The decision of the institutional panel or commission is subject to review by the chief of the organization.

Step 4: Receive review of decision by the chief of the organization — The recommendation of the employee panel, judge, or arbitrator is forwarded to the chief of the organization. The chief notifies the grievant of the final decision within fifteen (15) workdays.

Both the employee and management must adhere to each step of the grievance procedure. It is also important that accurate records be maintained on the grievance process and the event that caused it. Company officers must be fully aware of the rights of the employee under the grievance process, which is provided for the protection of employees. Failure to follow grievance procedures will almost always have a negative consequence on the company officer or employee who fails to follow procedures.

Summary

Company officers are in a unique situation compared to supervisors in most private-sector labor unions that exclude supervisors from membership in the union. Because company officers represent management as supervisors but are also eligible for union membership, they must often walk a very fine line. This position makes it imperative that they know what contracts and agreements are in effect between the fire and emergency services organization and the labor union and what each side's rights and responsibilities are under those agreements.

Company officers should also have some knowledge of labor relations in general and about firefighter unions in particular. They should have knowledge of typical contract issues and the various means available for resolving those issues. Company officers should also be prepared to be active participants in any initiative directed toward building a cooperative relationship between labor and management in their organization. Finally, company officers must be aware of the grievance process in effect in their organization, whether it is based on policy or a labor/management agreement.

Community Relations and Public Fire and Life-Safety Education

Chapter Contents

Learning Objectives

1. Recall information about community demographics and the diversity of a community.

2. Respond to scenarios about community needs.

3. Select facts about the purpose and scope of a public fire and life-safety education program.

4. Identify different types of public education programs.

5. Select correct responses regarding the five-step process in creating a public education program.

6. Give a fire and life-safety presentation.

7. Select facts about dealing with customer concerns, complaints, and inquiries.

8. Respond to scenarios about concerns of citizens.

9. Select facts about the public information officer (PIO) and media relations.

Job Performance Requirements

This chapter provides information that addresses the following job performance requirements of NFPA 1021, *Standard for Fire Officer Professional Qualifications* (2003):

Chapter 4 Fire Officer I

4.3

4.3.1

4.3.1(A)

4.3.1(B)

4.3.2

4.3.2 (B)

4.3.3

4.3.3(B)

4.3.4

4.3.4(A)

Chapter 15
Community Relations and Public Fire and Life-Safety Education

As part of the many duties of company officers, community relations and public fire and life-safety education are important aspects that help build relationships with the community served. The concepts of customer service are applied to these topics with the intent of strengthening the bonds between the emergency services organization and the external customer, usually citizens. Company officers and crew members are the first, and sometimes only, contacts that citizens have with the fire and emergency services organization.

To establish this relationship, the company officer must first know who the external customers are as well as the environment where they live and work. The company officer must recognize and understand the demographics of the service area.

Next, the officer must be able to use the appropriate method for dealing with customer concerns and complaints. The goodwill of the organization and the credibility of the officer depend on the resolution of citizen concerns, both large and small. In some cases, complex citizen complaints or concerns may need to be handled by a designated member of the administration such as the public information officer (PIO) or civil affairs officer.

Finally, the officer must be able to provide fire and life-safety information and advice to citizens. This assistance may be in the form of formal public education programs for specific groups or single responses to citizens in need of information. This chapter provides the company officer with the basic general concepts and ideas that can then be applied to specific situations involving both community relations and public fire and life-safety education.

Community Demographics

Understanding the composition of the community requires a basic knowledge of *demographics*: results of a statistically-based study of a population. The population is categorized into groups based on physical, social, or economic characteristics such as the following:

- Age
- Sex
- Marital status
- Family size
- Education
- Geographic location
- Occupation

Demographics are used in marketing and business to define a target audience for a product or service. In public service, they are used to determine the specific groups within the service area in order to properly serve their needs. Often, generic public safety education programs are ineffective because diversity and cultural beliefs are not considered when public fire and life-safety education programs are modified to meet the needs of each population group.

Sources for demographic data on the national, state, and local levels in the U.S. are as follows:

- U.S. Census Bureau
- U.S. Department of Labor
- U.S. Department of Health and Human Services
- State, regional, and local government agencies

In Canada, sources include the Canadian Census Bureau and provincial, regional, and local government agencies. The most recent data were compiled following the 2000 U.S. census and the 2001 Canadian census. Information is also available in almanacs that are privately published and accessible through public library systems, on the Internet, or at retail outlets.

Appropriate Terminology

The meaning of the terms *sex* and *gender* are sometimes confused. Sex is a biological fact and, in the case of humans, is defined as *male* and *female.* Gender refers to the culturally and socially defined roles and responsibilities of males and females based on characteristics that are attributed to each group. These roles and responsibilities may be self-perceptions that the individual holds or society enforces.

U.S. Population

The 2000 census indicates that the U.S. population has rapidly diversified **(Figure 15.1)**. Women comprise over 53 percent of the population and slightly less than 47 percent of the workforce. Foreign-born population in the U.S. has increased by 28.3 million in the decade prior to 2000 with most originating in Asia and Latin America. The

percentage of immigrants living in the U.S. in 2000 was 10.4 percent.

Recent data indicate that 70 percent of the Asian-American population is first- or second-generation immigrants. While the current non-Hispanic white population comprises 69 percent of the total population, it will comprise less than 50 percent by the year 2030, according to estimates.

In addition, the population is aging as members of the Baby-Boom Generation (those born between 1946 and 1964) get older **(Figure 15.2)**. In many cases, members of this group are not retiring at the traditional retirement age and are continuing to work or changing professions. Households headed by single women increased by 25 percent in the 1990s, while the traditional family (father, mother, and 2.5 children) decreased by 24 percent. As all of this information indicates, the composition of our society is dynamic and continues to change.

Because demographics vary regionally and between urban, suburban, and rural areas, it is necessary to research the community that the emergency response organization serves to determine the exact composition of its population. For instance, in California and some major U.S. cities, Caucasians are already less than 50 percent of the population. The largest numbers of Asians and Hispanics live in California, while Oklahoma has the largest population of Native Americans.

U.S. census data is readily available and can be used to develop a demographic profile of the local community or service area. Census data can be assessed through the federal government's web site and the specific postal zip code for the area in question. Data within each region can be divided by language, literacy levels, and disabilities or other topics.

Canadian Population

The Canadian population is also diversifying rapidly and becoming a multiethnic, multicultural society **(Figure 15.3)**. According to the 2001 Canadian census, Canada has 5.4 million foreign-born residents living there. This percentage (18.4 percent) is the highest in 70 years.

Canadians consist of 200 distinct groups that are referred to as minorities in addition to those of English and French ancestry. The primary source

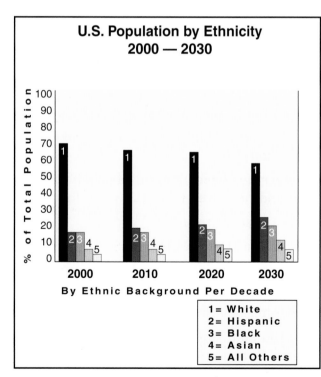

Figure 15.1 Graph showing U.S. population by ethnicity projections from 2000 to 2030. Percentages of Hispanic, Black, and Asian background populations are increasing.

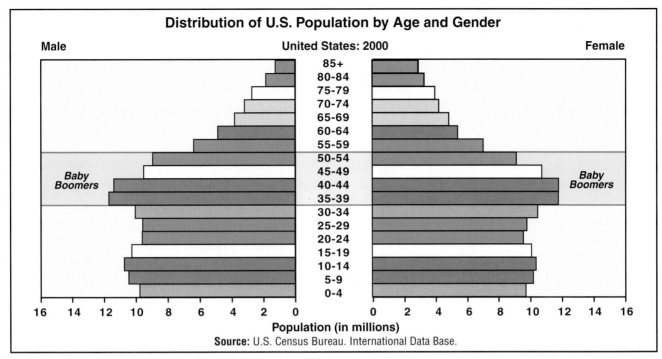

Distribution of U.S. Population by Age and Gender

Male | United States: 2000 | Female

85+
80-84
75-79
70-74
65-69
60-64
55-59
50-54
45-49
40-44
35-39
30-34
25-29
20-24
15-19
10-14
5-9
0-4

Baby Boomers (left and right)

16 14 12 10 8 6 4 2 0   0 2 4 6 8 10 12 14 16

Population (in millions)

Source: U.S. Census Bureau. International Data Base.

Figure 15.2 As the population of the U.S. ages, the so-called Baby Boom Generation now nears the traditional retirement age. Since the 2000 census, many members of this generation are continuing to work.

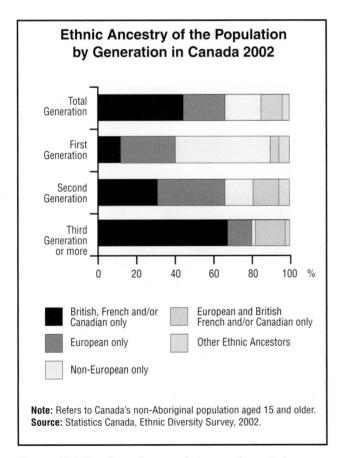

Ethnic Ancestry of the Population by Generation in Canada 2002

Total Generation
First Generation
Second Generation
Third Generation or more

0   20   40   60   80   100   %

■ British, French and/or Canadian only
◱ European and British French and/or Canadian only
▨ European only
▢ Other Ethnic Ancestors
□ Non-European only

Note: Refers to Canada's non-Aboriginal population aged 15 and older.
Source: Statistics Canada, Ethnic Diversity Survey, 2002.

Figure 15.3 The Canadian population continues to become increasingly diverse. The ethnic ancestry of the Canadian population by generation in 2002 is shown.

for immigrants in the past 50 years has been Asia, which contributed 58 percent of all immigrants. The three largest immigrant groups are Chinese, South Asian, and Black. The majority of all immigrants are of working age or between 25 and 64 years of age.

Community Diversity

Customers who comprise the community or service area that the fire and emergency services organization protects may be as diverse as the total population of the world. Cultural classifications that are used to define diversity include the following:

- Age
- Gender
- Sexual orientation
- Ethnicity
- Race
- Religion
- Politics
- Socioeconomic level
- Education

Company officers and members of the fire and emergency services organization must be aware of the various groups that comprise their *community*. For company officers, the community is not just the area encompassed by their immediate response area. The community includes the composition of the organization's area of responsibility. With a mobile and shifting population, the area of responsibility includes individuals who commute into the area, live in the area and work elsewhere, or are only in the response area temporarily such as university students, tourists, or migrant workers.

Diversity can be either a benefit or barrier within a community. As a benefit, it provides multiple viewpoints upon which to expand society. The diversity of language, cultural customs, and cultural values should be viewed as assets rather than as a series of barriers. Listening to others, constantly being open to new ideas, and respecting differences strengthen an organization and its members and increase the bonds with the various elements of the community.

Diversity can also create barriers between service providers and customers. A lack of understanding creates a *them-us* mentality that separates people. Many times, people are classified by the language they use or their attitude and perceived priorities of what is important to them. The inability to speak or understand the language of a population makes it extremely difficult to resolve issues or provide services. People who speak the dominant language can be classified by their accents and stereotyped by generic perceptions.

Cultural Classifications

As listed earlier, classifications are used to define diversity within the community. Because people tend to congregate with others who have similar interests, neighborhoods in urban areas can be classified by some of these same terms. Even in rural areas, the residents will have some of the same interests and needs. As a community ages, so does the neighborhood, eventually transitioning to a younger one with different needs.

Fire and emergency services tend to change in response to the changing face of the community. For instance, a neighborhood comprised of elderly residents will have more need for medical services while a neighborhood comprised of young families will need fire and life-safety programs directed toward children.

Company officers must be familiar with their response areas, know the demographic composition of the community, and be flexible enough to provide the services that all members of the community need and deserve **(Figure 15.4)**. As the organization's representatives in the neighborhood, company officers and their crew members should recommend public relations and fire and life-safety education programs to the administration when the need becomes apparent. An

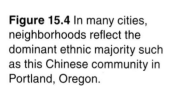
Figure 15.4 In many cities, neighborhoods reflect the dominant ethnic majority such as this Chinese community in Portland, Oregon.

example of a model neighborhood program is the Village Fire Company Concept developed by the Richmond (VA) Fire and Emergency Services (see information box).

Richmond (VA) Fire and Emergency Services: Village Fire Company Concept

The *Village Fire Company Concept* is an organizational management model that uses a decentralized approach to service delivery. The concept was taken from historical practices when small towns and villages were protected by firefighters and fire apparatus were housed in a single fire station somewhere near the center of town. Many times, these fire stations served the communities as gathering spots for citizens to conduct village business or bond together during social events. Members of the village fire company knew all aspects of the village — its people, places, and things — and took personal responsibility for protecting the village from fires and other disasters.

It doesn't matter if a fire department has one fire station or forty-fire stations, the model remains the same. Because most fire departments have a primary response district (or first-due area), the model focuses on having officers and firefighters of each individual fire company accept that same level of responsibility and ownership of their *village* as their predecessors did so many years ago.

This model provides company officers and firefighters with the ability to build relationships within the community and gain that intimate knowledge of the village they protect. While the overall direction of the organization remains the responsibility of the fire chief, company officers are responsible for much of the decision-making and planning for fire protection in their village.

Many of the supporting operations, such as fire code enforcement and fire and life-safety education program delivery (which are traditionally provided by other divisions within a department), become the responsibility of members of the individual *village fire companies*. All company members are expected to aggressively seek opportunities to interact with the community and make their respective fire stations an integral part of their village.

Languages

Although English is the most common language in North America and a very common second language in other parts of the world, there are still groups of people who are not proficient in the use of English. In both urban and rural areas of North America, workers cluster together in communities and neighborhoods speaking the native tongue in which they are most accustomed. The most common non-English language in the U.S. is Spanish, while in Canada it is French. Various other languages spoken in North America include Chinese, Russian, Vietnamese, Korean, Italian, German, and Laotian.

The advantage to having a multilingual community is the availability of resources for translators. These individuals can be volunteers or paid translators on call to assist at emergencies. They may also be used to translate written educational materials, assist in interviews, or train personnel in the culture of the various language groups.

Company officers should be aware of the process for contacting translators for assistance at emergency incidents or when needed to resolve a customer concern, complaint, or inquiry. Lists of translator services may be maintained at the stations, on the apparatus, or with the telecommunications center. Simultaneous translation may also be available via telephone service through the telecommunications center.

In order to communicate with individuals who have hearing impairments, company officers may need to have knowledge of American or international sign languages **(Figure 15.5, p. 336)**. American Sign Language (ASL) is used in the U.S. and English-speaking areas of Canada. There is no one true international sign language, although there is a growing trend in Europe to develop one that can be used throughout the European continent. Training in ASL is available and should be provided for personnel.

Text telephones (TTYs) and telecommunications devices for the deaf (TDDs) as well as amplified phone sets are also available to allow hearing-impaired individuals to place emergency phone calls. Company officers and crew members must have a working knowledge of this type of equipment if

Figure 15.5 Company officers will often come in contact with citizens who have speech or hearing disabilities. Sign-language interpreters are essential for communicating with the hearing impaired. *Courtesy of Rick Montemorra.*

TTY Versus TDD

The proper notation for *TTY* is *TeleTYpewriter,* which refers to both the old model teletypewriter and the new model *TDD (Telecommunication Device for the Deaf).* TTY is the culturally preferred term used by most deaf and hard-of-hearing users. The term *TDD* implies that only deaf people use the device when in fact there are also users who are hard of hearing.

The traditional TTY will only work on analog mobile phone networks and not on digital networks. A special digital TTY mode must be used with digital mobile phones.

Jeryl Lynn Brown, a North Carolina Justice Academy Instructor/Coordinator, suggests the following procedures for receiving TTY calls:

- Ask clarifying questions, one at a time.
- Use vocabulary that is easy to understand.
- Keep sentence structure simple. For many TTY/TDD users, English may be a second language.
- Avoid using English idioms. For instance, rather than saying *stand by,* type *PLS HD* or *PLS HLD* (please hold).
- Process the call just like calls are processed for hearing callers. Use phrases like *stay calm* and inform the caller that *help is on the way* as soon as possible. Continue to periodically reassure the caller.

Figure 15.6 Text telephones and telecommunications devices (TTYs) may be located in fire stations or the organization's telecommunications center.

it is installed in their station. They should also be aware of people living within their response area who have TTY and TDD equipment in their homes. This information should be provided by the telecommunications center, administration, public phone company, or a social services organization that provides the equipment **(Figure 15.6)**.

The diversity of language means that fire and emergency services personnel must communicate in a variety of languages. Telecommunications centers must provide personnel who are multilingual to take accurate information over the telephone.

Emergency responders should also have the ability to communicate with customers in the language in which the customer is most proficient. This type of communication is accomplished either by having bilingual or multilingual members trained on each unit or providing them with a contact person who can respond as a translator via the telecommunications center.

NOTE: The company officer should always try to communicate with a citizen before requesting a translator. However, the company officer and crew members must know who to contact and how to make contact with a translator if needed.

Cultural Customs

All cultures have customs that make them unique in the world. Some of those cultural customs include the use of time, space, and nonverbal communications. It is important for fire and emergency services personnel to recognize and understand the culture of the groups in their areas and how they use these characteristics.

While the dominant culture of North America values time as a precious commodity and places importance on being *on time,* some cultures do not. Therefore, within certain cultures, meetings do not always begin at the specified hour and minute. This time consideration has to be taken into account when meetings with specific groups are planned.

Some ethnic groups view personal space considerations differently than many North Americans. While the European American (generally descended from the English, French, and Northern Europeans) considers personal space (within 18 inches [457 mm]) to be reserved for family members, many other cultures do not **(Figure 15.7)**. Some are quite comfortable carrying on a conversation with a stranger within that distance.

On the other hand, access to sleeping quarters for women may be restricted by gender in the home of a Muslim family. Company officers must consider this restriction especially when responding to medical emergencies. Company officers must balance the need for immediate action to save a life with the potential for violating a cultural custom.

The various interpretations of nonverbal signals or communications by ethnic groups have been a topic of discussion for many years. Crossing one's legs and exposing the sole of the foot or shoe is considered rude in many societies. Hand gestures such as the *okay* sign made with the thumb and forefinger of the hand have an offensive meaning to some groups.

While it is impossible to record and memorize all of the differences that various cultures have, it is important to recognize that there are differences. Involving members of the various cultural groups in cultural sensitivity training for fire and emergency personnel is one way of connecting groups with the organization and providing training at the same time. It may also be beneficial to create

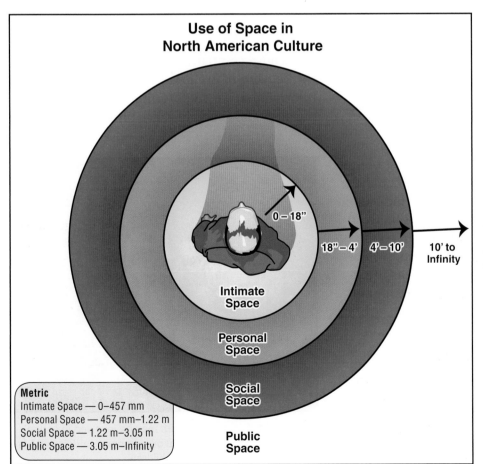

Figure 15.7 Company officers should understand the concept of personal space as it applies to various cultural groups within their response areas.

small workgroups representing the organization and different cultural groups to discuss cultural traits, values, and characteristics.

Many communities sponsor cultural events that showcase the various foods, music, dances, and customs of various cultures. German Oktoberfests, Mexican fiestas, Chinese new years, and international food fairs are just a few examples of celebrations that increase awareness of a particular culture while providing an entertaining atmosphere.

Cultural Values

Cultural groups have unique ethical and moral values based on their own traditions. Some of those traditions are founded on religious tenets, while others are based on relationships. An understanding of cultural values and traditions is important when an organization interacts with a particular ethnic group.

Cultural values can be defined as learned, long-lasting, and emotionally charged moral concepts that assist people in making decisions, forming judgments, and preparing to act. They provide people with the foundation on which to live their lives. Values are primarily passed through the family from one generation to the next. They may be based on religious beliefs, common sense, traditions, or even folklore. Some values are gained through formal education while others are acquired from peers.

Company officers should realize that values are as much a product of the individual's background as they are of the cultural group with which they associate themselves. For instance, some individuals place a great deal of value on acquiring material possessions even though that value is in conflict with their ethnic heritage. At the same time, values that were important to ancestors, such as bringing honor to the parents, may transcend time and location.

Public Fire and Life-Safety Education

While there are many ways to enhance an organization's public image, the means most often used by fire and emergency service organizations is *public fire and life-safety education:* one of the most cost-effective safety activities of any fire and emergency services organization. In terms of public relations, it is an ideal way for the organization to enhance its public image while providing a valuable public service. Actively seeking opportunities to interact with the community in this way can generate a tremendous amount of goodwill for the organization.

Three of the most effective means of providing fire and life-safety information and enhancing the organization's image through public education are group presentations, media programs, and direct assistance. Company personnel, sometimes in cooperation with the fire and life-safety educators of the organization, can make presentations within their response area **(Figure 15.8)**. At the same time, they can provide individual assistance to people who have questions or concerns about safety.

NOTE: Funding for fire and life-safety programs is currently available from the U.S. Department of Homeland Security, Preparedness Directorate's Office of Grants and Training. The primary goal of the Assistance to Firefighters Grant (AFG) Program's Fire Prevention and Safety Grant (FP&S) is to reach high-risk target groups in order to mitigate the high incidences of death and injuries.

Because company officers may be involved in the delivery of fire and life-safety programs and information, it is important for them to know the purpose and scope of these programs, the three

Figure 15.8 Company officers may be involved in school visits, assisting public education personnel in delivering fire and life-safety messages to children.

types of public education, company-level education activities, and the application of the planning process in public education. Each of these topics is discussed in the following sections.

Purpose and Scope

The *purpose* of a fire and life-safety education program is to inform members of the community or service area about the fire and life-safety hazards they face and what they can do to mitigate those hazards — that is, help them change their behaviors in a way that results in fewer fires, injuries, and property losses within the community. Messages can be easily divided into the following three general categories that can be applied to all types of hazards:

- *What to do in the event a fire or other emergency occurs* — Example: Take shelter in the center of a house when a tornado is approaching or dial 9-1-1 in the event of a fire.

- *How to prevent a fire or emergency from occurring* — Example: Store oily rags in a closed metal container or keep cleaning materials and medicines out of the reach of children.

- *How to persuade others to use fire or life-safety behaviors* — Example: Help children understand the importance of using a home escape plan or help an elderly family member understand how to extinguish a grease fire.

Instead of attempting to educate the entire community as a whole, it is more practical and effective to divide the community into smaller, more manageable target groups. These groups may include the following people:

- Preschoolers
- School children
- Young adults
- Adults
- Older adults (age 65 or older)
- Homeowners
- Apartment tenants
- People with disabilities
- Public- and private-sector employees
- Medical and nursing facility personnel

- Members of religious organizations
- Members of service clubs
- Members of civic organizations

The *scope* of the programs should reflect the needs of the community or service area that they are designed to serve. For example, if the community is adjacent to wildland areas or incorporates developments in the wildland/urban interface, the programs should include information about fire-safe roofing, defensible space, and similar topics. If there are ethnic neighborhoods in the community, fire and life-safety materials may need to be printed in the groups' native languages. Programs used to educate the various groups listed may focus on the following topics:

- Home fire-escape planning **(Figure 15.9, p. 340)**
- Babysitting safety
- Cooking hazards
- Clothing fires
- Elder care
- Juvenile firesetting
- Scald prevention
- First aid for burns
- Cardiopulmonary resuscitation (CPR) training
- Home fire-safety inspections
- Smoke alarm and carbon monoxide detectors
- Fire extinguisher use
- Home fire sprinkler systems
- Community Emergency Response Teams (CERTs)
- Water and ice safety
- Infant/child car-seat safety and installation
- Bicycle safety
- Fall prevention

The fire and life-safety education program must be well planned and conscientiously delivered if it is to accomplish its purpose. Such programs must be based on specific, measurable goals and objectives and focused on specifically identifiable groups. The goals and objectives are established by the organization with input from target audiences.

Figure 15.9 Information on developing home fire-escape plans are available for all types of residences including houses, apartments, and manufactured housing units. *Courtesy of Florida Department of Agriculture and Consumer Services.*

For example, a goal of a 50-percent reduction in fires and burn injuries to residents of boarding homes for the aged might develop into two programs — one intended to educate the residents of these facilities and another for their staffs. Another goal could be that everyone who attends the local Kiwanis meeting would test their home smoke alarms on the same day as the meeting.

Fire and emergency services organizations can significantly reduce the number of fires and medical emergencies and the resulting deaths, injuries, and property losses through the delivery of carefully designed public fire and life-safety education programs. At the same time, the organization can benefit from a positive, high-profile, and proactive image in the eyes of the public.

Group Presentations

Every opportunity to deliver a fire and life-safety message to a community group is also a good way to learn about the people in that group and develop a positive relationship with them. This opportunity creates a situation where the efforts of understanding the community and public relations merge to generate a *win/win* situation. Civic groups, service clubs, neighborhood associations, and other organizations are often looking for speakers to address their meetings, and these engagements can provide the company officer with numerous opportunities to make fire and life-safety presentations (**Figure 15.10**).

From the community-awareness standpoint, it is important that the fire and emergency services responders who serve the local area or neighborhood make these presentations. These presentations provide emergency-response personnel with an opportunity to interact directly with people from local neighborhoods.

From a public-relations standpoint, it may be more important that these presentations be made by public-education specialists within the organizations in order to maintain consistency in the message and its delivery to all neighborhoods throughout the community. If company officers are trained to deliver effective fire and

Figure 15.10 Sparky the Fire Dog® is a familiar concept that is used to instruct children in fire and life-safety information.

life-safety messages in this way, the number of available speakers within the organization is greatly increased.

Joint presentations by emergency-response personnel and public-education specialists will also provide benefits to those involved. Regardless of how and by whom these presentations are made, it is most important that every opportunity be used to make them.

News Media Programs

Live and/or prerecorded fire and life-safety messages delivered by fire and emergency services personnel through the various news media should be used frequently to increase public awareness while enhancing an organization's public image. As a condition of their operating licenses, electronic broadcast media (radio, television, and cable) in the U.S. are required to set aside a certain amount of their broadcast time for public service announcements (PSAs) or messages.

Many fire and emergency services organizations across North America have taken advantage of these opportunities. Company officers may be given the opportunity to research, develop, and deliver these messages.

In communities across the nation, fire and emergency services personnel host weekly or monthly fire and life-safety programs on the local public-service cable television channel. One example is the monthly *Greeley Code 4* program presented on the government-access channel in Greeley, Colorado. The show is a joint venture between the Union Colony Fire Rescue Authority, the Greeley Police Department, and the public information department of the City of Greeley.

The Virginia Beach (VA) Fire Department produces *Safety Connection*, a television program that appears several times a week locally and has been provided to other outlets worldwide. These shows and many others help fire and emergency services organizations provide fire and life-safety information directly to the public and increase the image of the organizations and the fire and emergency services profession.

Other means of distributing fire and life-safety messages include safety newsletters, inserts in utility bills, and ads on buses, in subway trains and stations, and on billboards. Public relations firms can generally provide information on the effectiveness of each method for reaching the greatest number of citizens or target groups. Some messages may be most effective in English while others may need to be translated into one of the 16 first (primary) languages that are spoken in the U.S. according to the 2000 census. *Primary* or *first language* is a person's native language or mother tongue that was first learned by the person as a child and then passed from one generation to the next.

Direct Assistance

Members of volunteer, combination, career, and other types of emergency services organizations are viewed by the public as experts in fire and life safety. Because of this image, the public relies on them for information, assistance, and advice when confronted with safety issues. Company officers should be prepared to provide this assistance whether on or off duty **(Figure 15.11, p. 342)**.

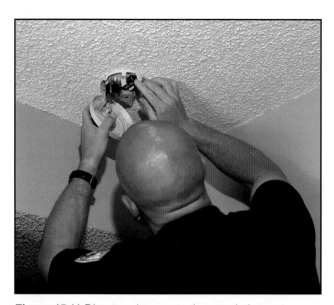

Figure 15.11 Direct assistance to the population may include the installation and periodic testing of battery-operated smoke alarms.

Assistance may involve replacing a battery in a smoke detector, recommending the size and type of fire extinguisher for an occupancy, or referring a citizen to the appropriate agency for aid. Direct assistance can go a long way in creating and maintaining goodwill with the community.

Company officers and crew members must remember that providing accurate information is extremely important. If the officer does not know the correct response to a question, it is acceptable to say *Let me find out and get back to you. I want to make certain that you get the right answer.*

Company-Level Participation

When properly trained in the concepts of fire and life-safety education, company officers can be valuable assets to the organization as well as the community they serve. Company officers play important roles in the development and delivery of fire and life-safety education. In fire and emergency services organizations that are *not* large enough to have a full-time fire and life-safety educator on staff, company officers and their subordinates can use on-duty time to develop and deliver these programs.

Because of their close contact with the community, company-level personnel can provide input that is very useful in developing program goals and objectives that target the most press-ing needs within their community and focusing program delivery on the most appropriate group or groups. When company-level personnel are assigned to deliver a program, they should be allowed to participate in its development. Company-level activities include the following:

- Hosting fire station tours
- Making school classroom visits
- Installing smoke alarms in residences
- Participating in activities during Fire Prevention Week in October

Five-Step Planning Process

Fire and life-safety program developers follow a structured and organized plan when creating programs. Such a plan is outlined in IFSTA's **Fire and Life Safety Educator** and **Fire and Emergency Services Instructor** manuals. Called the *five-step planning process,* it is the same process that the company officer uses for planning the use of human resources and making decisions (see Chapter 13, Human Resources Management).

The planning process provides for systematic planning and action. A common model is composed of the following five steps:

Step 1: **Identify** major fire and life-safety problems.

Step 2: **Select** the most cost-effective objectives for the education program.

Step 3: **Design** the program.

Step 4: **Implement** the program plan.

Step 5: **Evaluate** the program to determine impact.

These steps are not limited to public fire and life-safety education planning; they are also used in developing other types of plans and programs. In Chapter 13, Human Resources Management, the process was used to provide planners with a systematic approach to decision-making in both emergency and nonemergency situations.

In the five-step planning process, each step consists of several fact-finding activities and a decision. The fact-finding activities for public education involve answering a series of questions about the local jurisdiction and response area. A suggested *to do* list is included for each activity.

Company officers must be prepared to be flexible in the use of the five-step method. The suggested list identifies the sorts of tasks that will have to be done, but it is not a hard-and-fast checklist. Even though the five-step method can be used for planning any type of fire and life-safety education program, for the purposes of this discussion, the examples focus on fire- and burn-prevention themes.

Identification

In very active and/or high population areas, the use of graphing or mapping analytical software programs can help identify and visualize problem areas **(Figure 15.12)**. The identification step accomplishes two objectives: First, it helps to identify the most significant local fire and life-safety problems and concerns. Second, it helps to identify emerging issues such as the misuse of candles.

The following are some of the questions asked during the identification process with suggested action items:

- **What are the major fire and burn hazards?**
  - Research records on the causes of fires and burn injuries. For example, hospitals and emergency rooms in some states are required to report burn injuries to state agencies.
  - Identify the most frequent causes of fires and burn injuries.
  - Identify any patterns of local fires and burn injuries.

- **Where are the high-risk locations?**
  - Identify neighborhoods or building occupancy types with high fire and burn-injury risks. For example, the Oklahoma Smoke Alarm Study identified two postal zip code areas as targets for free smoke alarm installations.
  - Identify why the risks are above average.
  - Plan to concentrate resources in these high-risk locations.

- **When are the high-risk times?**
  - Identify certain times of day, week, or year with the highest incidences of fire loss or burn injuries. For example, one study focused on fires in large trash receptacles. The

Figure 15.12 Computer-based mapping programs can be useful in determining the types, locations, and frequency of hazards in the community or response area. *Courtesy of U.S. Federal Emergency Management Agency, George Armstrong, photographer.*

results indicated that fires were occurring immediately after the close of school on weekdays.
  - Identify types of fires occurring at these times.
  - Plan to concentrate fire-safety messages at these times.

- **Who are the high-risk audiences?**
  - Identify groups with higher fire death and injury rates than other groups.
  - Identify why certain victims have an above-average fire and injury rate.
  - Involve these groups in the fire education planning effort.

- **What is the high-risk behavior?**
  - Identify which behaviors — acts or omissions — cause fires and burn injuries.
  - Identify how behaviors can be changed.
  - Teach people exactly what to do and what *not* to do.

Education programs cannot change hazards that are substances or devices. For example, education simply cannot change the temperature of a cigarette lighter flame or the flammability of gasoline. However, *technology* may be used to change substances or devices. Education can influence some people to change some conditions or behaviors such as smoking in bed.

Hazards vs. Risks

In everyday conversation, the terms *hazard* and *risk* are often used interchangeably. Technically, however, hazards and risks describe two different things. The term *hazard* usually refers to the source of a risk. Examples of fire-related hazards include ignition sources (such as smoking materials or faulty electrical wiring) or behaviors (such as children playing with matches or persons overloading electrical outlets).

A *risk*, on the other hand, is the likelihood of suffering harm from a hazard. Risk can also be thought of as the potential for failure or loss. Fire-related risk is often expressed as the number of incidents, injuries, or deaths *per capita* (for each unit of the population). Depending upon the source of information, the per capita unit may be one person, a thousand people, or a million. To avoid comparing apples to oranges, public education planners must be clear as to what per capita means in each statistical table or report.

In other words, *risk* is the exposure to a hazard, and a *hazard* is a condition, substance, or device that can directly cause an injury or loss. For example, improperly stored caustic chemicals pose a hazard, whereas the person handling the chemicals is at risk of sustaining a chemical burn from them.

Other conditions such as age or disability are unchangeable. In those cases, a public educator develops programs to reduce the risk posed by exposure to the hazard. For example, a program to teach nursing home caregivers to supervise residents' smoking helps reduce the risk even though the hazards remain unchanged.

During the identification step, a picture of a community's biggest fire and life-safety problems will gradually begin to emerge. In some cases, answers to two or three of the earlier questions may combine to form a scenario (such as *inoperable smoke detectors in single-family homes* or *burn injuries from scalds to residents of the Pine Meadow Retirement Apartments*). In other cases, a single issue (such as *juvenile firesetting*) will emerge as the most severe problem.

Identifying which fire and life-safety problems to address is the critical first step in developing a targeted public education program. The answers lead to a decision: *What is the major fire or life-safety problem to be reduced through public education?*

Selection

The objective of the selection step is to choose the most cost-effective or achievable objectives for the public fire and life-safety education program. Being aware of the scope and limitations of available resources is important if planners are to be realistic about what an education program can accomplish.

As a result, the questions in the selection step focus on resources. In many ways, the selection step comes close to a primer on finding new resources, including funding, materials, and people, for public fire and life-safety education. Following are some of the questions and sample tasks considered in the selection step of planning:

- *Who are the potential audiences?*
  - Refer to high-risk audiences listed in the identification step.
  - Identify those who influence these high-risk victims.
  - Select the audience on which the public educator will have the greatest potential effect.

- *What are the potential costs and benefits of various training options?*
  - List alternative program objectives.
  - Identify what will be needed to achieve program objectives.
  - Review existing programs, and determine the advantages of purchasing educational materials versus creating them within the organization.
  - Determine cost of the needed fire-education materials.
  - Estimate loss-reduction effect of each program objective. Determine how much loss reduction can realistically be expected.

- *What resources are available within the community?*
  - Identify influential people in the community.
  - Identify those who speak the native language of the target group.
  - Identify signers for the hearing impaired.
  - List all local news media, service clubs, faith-based groups, and civic organizations.

— Make personal contact with key people and groups.

— Ask local businesses and organizations what materials, equipment, or personnel they could contribute to the program.

— Choose the most effective approach within limits of local resources.

By the end of the selection step, program planners will be able to reach a crucial decision: *the specific objectives of the education program.* The objectives should be clear, measurable, and attainable. In addition, answers to the questions in the selection step will be used to complete the design, implementation, and evaluation steps.

For example, information about major fire hazards and high-risk locations, times, victims, and behaviors will be very helpful when it is time to answer design step questions such as *What is the primary message?* In much the same way, insight about high-risk victims and potential audiences is critically important in deciding on the best formats, times, and places for education messages **(Figure 15.13)**.

Figure 15.13 Children (individually and in groups) are potential audiences for fire and life-safety messages. The primary message can be conveyed through formal presentations or one on one during station tours.

The selection and design steps are so closely related that it is sometimes difficult to distinguish one from the other. That relationship is normal. The important thing is to make sure that the program design is based on specific objectives selected to address a specific local problem.

Design

The design step is the bridge between planning a fire and life-safety education program and actually implementing it in the field. The objective of the design step is to develop the most effective means of communicating the program's message to the identified audience. In other words, this step is the time when the public educator decides what to say and how to say it, based on the message, audience, and available resources.

While it is possible that the company officer may be involved in designing an education program as part of an internal committee, it is more likely that the company officer will simply receive materials to present in a public forum or to visiting groups.

Implementation

The implementation step is where the day-to-day job of public fire and life-safety education happens. Most company officers will spend more of their time implementing and delivering these programs than in developing them. Planning the implementation step includes answering the following questions and identifying the associated tasks:

● *How will the target audience participate and cooperate in implementing the program?*

— Involve target groups in implementing programs.

— Tell target audiences what to expect.

— Reinforce messages through endorsement by local opinion leaders.

● *How will public educators be trained and scheduled?*

— Organize fire service personnel and volunteers from outside the fire service.

— Match community contacts with target audiences.

— Train people for their public education job.

- ***How will materials be produced and distributed?***

    — Assign production responsibilities.

    — Produce or purchase materials.

    — Distribute materials to public educators.

The actual teaching of a class is what the implementation step is all about. The presentation is the actual transfer of facts and ideas — making the subject come alive. The presentation should apply the lesson plan in the following ways:

- Explaining information
- Using supplemental training aids
- Demonstrating methods and technique

Company officers should use the most effective teaching methods and materials for each specific audience. They should apply the information found in Chapter 7, Oral Communications, and Chapter 12, Company-Level Training, to create interesting and informative presentations.

Evaluation

Evaluation is the *bottom line* of public fire and life-safety education. It is the point for measuring the effect of education programs and modifying them as needed. The techniques used to measure results may vary from obtaining immediate feedback from program attendees to monitoring long-term statistical trends. The former is valuable for its freshness and immediacy, but it lacks the objective validity of the latter.

To ensure that the education program actually works, a public educator will need to observe day-to-day program implementation. In this way, the company officer will be guided to the ultimate implementation decision: *monitoring and making ongoing adjustments and refinements to the program as needed during its implementation.*

Most company officers are more likely to be involved in obtaining immediate feedback from their audiences than in the collection and analysis of statistical data. Regardless of how feedback is obtained, it must be heeded.

While positive feedback may be very gratifying, negative feedback is far more valuable. With positive feedback, there is the possibility that those

responding are simply being polite and condescending. On the other hand, negative feedback indicates that something is wrong with the program message, its delivery, or both! Conscientious fire and life-safety educators must be willing to accept this sort of criticism constructively and review and adjust the program as needed.

Community Relations

Community relations involve another form of direct contact beyond public fire and life-safety education. As visible representatives of the jurisdiction, company officers and crew members will be the recipient of citizen concerns, complaints, and inquiries. How company personnel resolve these issues determines the image the public has of the organization. When dealing with the public, the company officer must always keep the importance of good customer service in mind **(Figure 15.14)**.

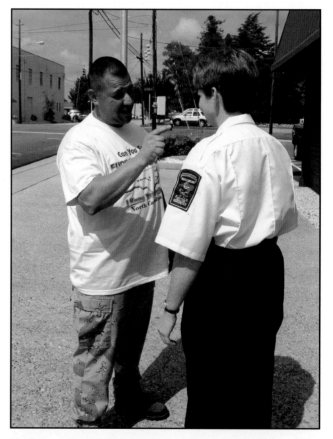

Figure 15.14 In some instances, the company officer may be faced with an angry or confrontational citizen. The company officer will have to use good interpersonal skills to defuse the situation, determine the real problem, and help the citizen to resolve the problem.

Customer Service Element

Resolving citizen concerns or complaints is an important element of customer service in the public sector. How these concerns or complaints are resolved determines to a great extent how the public views its fire and emergency services organization. Because fire and emergency organizations are committed to providing the highest level of service and the relationship between customer service and the organization's public image is valuable, it is critically important that all such issues be resolved as reasonably and as quickly as possible.

Customer Service Model

The Phoenix (AZ) Fire Department has developed a customer service philosophy that might serve well as a model for other fire and emergency services organizations. It has employed the customer service concept for many years and gained well-deserved credit for it. It provides an example for other fire officers and emergency services organizations. The following text is excerpted and adapted (with permission) from the *Essentials of Fire Department Customer Service* by Alan Brunacini:

1. Our essential mission and No. 1 priority is to deliver the best possible service to our customers.

2. Always be nice — treat everyone with respect, kindness, patience, and consideration.

3. Always attempt to execute a standard problem-solving outcome: quick/effective/skillful/safe/caring/managed.

4. Regard everyone as a customer.

5. Consider how you and what you are doing looks to others.

6. Don't disqualify the customer with your qualifications.

7. Basic organizational behavior must become customer-centered.

8. We must continually improve our customer service performance.

Concerns/Complaints/Inquiries

The term *citizen concerns* often translates into citizen *complaints;* that is, a citizen has a concern/complaint based on a perception of something the organization, service-area provider, or municipal-

ity has done — or *not* done. Issues may involve something directly under the control of the fire and emergency services organization such as burning regulations, inspections, or weed abatement. Questions on these issues are appropriate for the company officer to answer.

But the issue may also involve something over which the fire and emergency services organization has no jurisdiction — parking regulations for example. These concerns may be brought to the fire and emergency services organization simply because these personnel wear uniforms and badges that are similar to those worn by law-enforcement personnel and are perceived to be representatives of the jurisdiction as a whole. It may also be that the nearest fire station is the closest government facility to the citizen's residence (**Figure 15.15**).

Regardless of how or why a citizen complains to the fire and emergency services organization, company officers must be prepared to deal with the concern in a friendly, courteous, and profes-

Figure 15.15 The company officer must be prepared to answer questions or direct a citizen to the appropriate department or agency.

sional manner. Even if citizens are angry or upset, officers must remain calm and in control — allowing citizens to voice concerns or complaints in their own ways. However, if citizens become verbally abusive or threaten to resort to physical violence, officers should call for law-enforcement assistance.

One of the first skills required of company officers when dealing with irate citizens is effective listening. Company officers must develop the ability to hear or interpret what citizens mean, even when they are unable to articulate the concern clearly. This ability may require an extraordinary degree of familiarity with the different idioms used by people, which can be developed through community awareness or ability to read nonverbal language — or both.

Very often, just allowing a citizen to voice a complaint causes the person to become calm and able to look at an issue more rationally. The essential point is that company officers must try to understand the true nature of complaints in order to address them.

Once the real issue has been identified, the company officer can either resolve it or refer the citizen to the appropriate person or office. The proper resolution of all concerns, complaints, and inquiries, including those involving personnel acts or omissions, is a duty of all members of the organization. It is a responsibility of company officers to set an example of quality customer service for the members of their company to follow. Customer service is ethics in action with the public.

Resolutions

Concerns, complaints, and inquiries come in different forms. They may involve an employee's act or an omission. Concerns and complaints often stem from inquiries. If it is within a company officer's means and authority to satisfy a citizen's concern, complaint, or inquiry, then it needs to be done as soon as possible. Even if the issue must be referred to a higher authority or another department or agency, the company officer should take a personal interest in seeing that the concern, complaint, or inquiry is resolved as soon as possible to the citizen's satisfaction.

Resolution may require that the company officer speak on behalf of the citizen with whoever is empowered to deal with the citizen's issue. The citizen's concern becomes one of the company officer's most important responsibilities at that moment and must remain a focus until it is resolved.

If a concern or complaint is voiced during an emergency operation, it should *not* be allowed to interfere with the demands of the emergency. This situation requires tact because the company officer must explain without insulting the citizen that the emergency is more important at the moment than the complaint. Resolution of the concern or complaint should wait until the emergency incident is terminated.

It may be more likely that the organization may assign a company officer to investigate a concern regarding the organization's operations instead of citizens coming directly to a company officer. In this case, the company officer would have all of the resources of the organization to address the concern.

In order to refer a citizen to the appropriate authority, a company officer must be thoroughly familiar with the organizational and jurisdictional rules and regulations that apply. The company officer must also be knowledgeable of the full range of services that are available to citizens from the fire and emergency services organization and other governmental agencies (**Figure 15.16**). It is important to be aware of what is possible under existing regulations and what avenues are open to a citizen who has a problem.

The company officer's duty is to use every legal and ethical means within that officer's authority to satisfy a citizen's concern. To the extent required by organizational policy, the company officer must also document the complaint and its disposition. Such documentation may prove to be invaluable should the issue progress to litigation.

Employee Acts or Omissions

One class of citizen complaints is different from most (if not all) of the others — those that involve an act or omission by a member of the organization. Because of the sensitivity of these issues in terms of

Figure 15.16 Company officers and crew members should project a professional image at all times when dealing with the public. Personnel should remember that citizens are seeking assistance or information that is important to them.

The company officer who received the original complaint may or may not be involved in the incident's investigation. In either case, the officer should make it a personal responsibility to see that the complainant is informed (by the appropriate member of the organization) of the results when the investigation has been completed.

If the company officer receiving the original complaint is assigned the task of contacting the complainant, care must be taken to not divulge any information that may be considered privileged or confidential. Before contacting the complainant, the company officer needs to consult with the next level supervisor and/or the personnel department to clarify what information can and cannot be made public. The jurisdiction's legal department may also be able to provide guidance.

Public Inquiries

While sometimes similar to handling citizen concerns, resolving public inquiries is usually less challenging and confrontational. However, citizen concerns or complaints often begin with a seemingly straightforward inquiry. It is only when a citizen gets the anticipated response that the true nature of the inquiry is revealed. But, in most cases, citizen inquiries are just genuine requests for information or clarification.

Just like resolving concerns and complaints, company officers must develop the ability to hear what citizens mean as well as what they ask. Citizens are often *not* familiar with legal or regulatory language, and they simply may need to know how some particular regulation applies to them.

Once again, this process requires that a company officer be able to understand the true nature of the question and know what remedies are available under the circumstances. A company officer must know what forms may be required and be willing and able to assist a citizen in completing them if necessary.

Public Relations

In a very real sense, a public relations program markets the organization to the community **(Figure 15.17, p. 350)**. Its purpose is to acquaint the community with the organization's mission and show the organization, officers, members,

the organization's image, the concern for the rights of all involved, and possible litigation, these cases must be handled with extreme care.

The company officer receiving the complaint must know and follow the organization's policy to the letter. In most cases, policy requires that the process of formalizing a complaint begins by documenting the incident. The officer needs to elicit as much pertinent information as possible from the concerned customer regarding the alleged incident. Some organizations use a standardized form for this purpose.

When this form has been completed, the officer reassures the citizen that the complaint will be fully investigated and the citizen will be informed of the results. The officer then forwards the complaint form through channels to the appropriate individual or office.

Figure 15.17 The public receives most of its news and information through the broadcast news media, which can be an effective format for presenting the fire and emergency services organization, its activities, its services, and its programs to the public.

facilities, equipment, and operations in the best possible light. A positive public image can be the best possible tool during periods of budget cuts and layoffs.

Creating and maintaining a positive public image is accomplished through the use of a PIO and strong policy on news media relations. Whether the organization has a PIO or not, company officers should be familiar with the process and able to assume the duties and act in the position if required.

Marketing the fire and emergency services organization is also the responsibility of any labor union organization whether it's a formal labor union or a fraternal organization such as an auxiliary group. The organization should work closely with these groups to present the most professional and positive image of the fire and emergency services in the community.

Public Information Officer

While large career organizations may have the benefit of a full-time public relations specialist on staff, most organizations depend on the chief of the organization or senior staff member to fulfill the duties of PIO. A PIO has the responsibility of providing the public, via the news media, with information about the organization and its operations. To accomplish this duty successfully, the PIO must know the following information:

- Mission statement of the organization
- Generally accepted terminology used to describe all types of operations
- Names of television/radio/newspaper reporters, news media contacts, editors, and newsroom staff
- Deadlines for print publications and broadcast news programs
- Contact person for the various ethnic communities in the service area
- Basic marketing theory and image management
- Community calendar of events and opportunities for presentations

The company officer who functions as PIO or simply represents the organization at speaking engagements or presentations must have good communication skills **(Figure 15.18)**. Additional information on public information and education can be found in the IFSTA **Fire and Life Safety Educator, Public Information Officer,** and **Fire and Emergency Services Instructor** manuals.

Although the PIO is most visible to the news media and public in times of crisis when providing status reports during emergency incidents, this duty is actually only a small part of the responsibilities of the position. An ongoing duty involves

Figure 15.18 The public information officer (PIO) is often the symbol of the fire and emergency services organization. The community recognizes and associates that officer with stories about the organization.

ensuring that the community is continually aware of the organization and its nonemergency activities. Some potential opportunities to promote the organization publicly include the following:

- Opening a new fire station or training center
- Speaking at recruit academy graduation ceremonies
- Announcing personnel promotions
- Displaying new apparatus or equipment
- Recognizing personal achievements by members of the organization
- Recognizing the completion of specialized training
- Attending charitable activities
- Giving special recognition to those who retire
- Announcing changes in operational techniques
- Explaining expansion of services
- Forming joint partnerships with other public agencies or private organizations
- Demonstrating seasonal safety issues to the public such as holiday safety, candle safety, etc.
- Attending neighbor meetings and events such as opening day at a little league baseball season

An old axiom states that people remember and judge a person or organization by the last achievement of that person or organization. Therefore, it is essential that the last thing that the public hears about an organization is positive. Because this type of information is not delivered instantly, time to develop it is usually available so that it can be presented in the most professional manner possible. Every effort should be made to celebrate achievements in order to gain the best image for the organization.

All statements made to the public must be factual and truthful, which is the ethical approach and the one that wins the greatest support from the customer base. Examples of fire officers and other public officials who have attempted to hide information or distort the facts are prevalent. The results have been disastrous for both the organizations and individuals.

News Media Relations

Open and trusting relations between the fire and emergency services organization and the representatives of the news media are vital to good public relations. Editors, reporters, journalists, and broadcast personalities can support the organization through stories that portray it in a positive light. To meet the needs of both the news media and the fire and emergency services organization, some organizations have developed guidelines to strengthen the relationship between the two. See **Appendix H** for sample news media guidelines.

Members of the news media represent the public and have a right and an obligation to access emergency incidents and other events that involve public safety officials. In order to reduce potential conflict between news media representatives and fire and emergency services organization personnel at emergency incidents, the two groups need to establish a media task group to establish protocols to follow at incidents.

This task group would develop protocols for fire and emergency services organization personnel when working with news media representatives and for news media representatives when working at emergency incidents. These protocols would then be printed and distributed to members of both groups. The result should be improved cooperation and communication between members of both groups during crisis situations.

Both public safety officials and members of the news media have an obligation to the public, and that obligation is different for each group. The obligation of the fire and emergency services organization is to protect the safety and well-being of the public. The obligation of news media representatives is to protect the public's right to know.

Members of both professions are guided by strict ethical standards. Because their obligations are different, they must be sensitive to the needs and duties of the other profession. To gain this sensitivity or understanding, the established protocols should be incorporated into the fire and emergency services organization's training schedule and policy and procedures manual. Likewise, the news media should include the protocols in its policies, and instruct employees on how to follow it. **Table 15.1** gives some news media protocol examples.

Company officers should use these emergency scene public relations protocols to develop a working relationship with the local news media. Under no circumstances, however, should a member of an organization attempt to censor or improperly influence the news media either during the gathering of information or before its publication. Nor should any member of the organization provide classified information to the media without the permission of the head of the organization. All members, regardless of rank, must follow the organizational policy for the release of information to the public.

Summary

Company officers are usually the first line of contact with citizens in their community or response area. To effectively deal with the wants and needs of their customers, company officers must be familiar with the diverse composition of their community based on demographic evidence. Knowledge of the cultural backgrounds of the people living in the unit's response area will assist the company officer in providing public fire and life-safety programs, providing public relations information and events, and focusing on the customer service process.

Besides public fire and life-safety education and public relations, the company officer will have to be responsive to citizen concerns, complaints, and inquiries. Resolving some of these will require sensitivity to the citizen and diplomacy on the part of the company officer. Especially challenging will be resolving issues related to employee acts or omissions that involve customers and personnel. The company officer will have to use interpersonal skills, tact, and ethics in order to balance the interests of the customer and organization.

Table 15.1
News Media Protocols at an Emergency Incident

Public Safety Officials	News Media Members

• **Access** — Authorized news media personnel are allowed necessary access to properly witness and document emergency scenes in a safe manner, even when the general public has been denied access.
 	
• **Public property** — News media personnel have the responsibility and right under normal circumstances to photograph and report events that transpire on public property; however, this right does not permit them to do so in an unsafe or potentially dangerous manner. Do *not* provide these personnel with personal protective equipment (PPE) until they have been properly trained in its use.
 	
• **Editorial content** — Public safety officials should *not* restrict news photographers from taking photographs solely because they may disagree with the nature of the photograph. *Factors:*
  — The jobs of the news photographer and reporter are to gather information and take photographs.
  — Editors determine which photograph, video or movie footage, or information is used in the final article or story.
  — These decisions are based on the professional code of ethics to which the news media generally adheres.
 	
• **Deadlines** — A news media representative has the responsibility to collect and document as much information about an incident as possible as quickly as possible, which requires meeting deadlines for distribution of the news. *Factors:*
  — Sometimes it requires the collection of information that may seem irrelevant, unimportant, or even improper to the chief officer, company officer, or emergency responder.
  — News deadlines should *never* deter public safety officials from the obligation of notifying proper persons first in sensitive situations.
 	
• **Patient privacy** — Emergency responders must be knowledgeable of the terms of privacy policies and laws, such as the Health Insurance Portability and Accountability Act (HIPAA), and ensure that no one releases private information regarding patients' medical conditions.
	• **Credentials** — Media representatives need to have proper credentials and identify themselves to the incident commander (IC) or public information officer (PIO) upon arrival at an incident.
	
	• **Obstruction** — Journalists may not restrict, obstruct, or oppose public safety officers in the lawful execution of their duties. The following duties of a journalist are allowed:
	  — Being present at an emergency incident
	  — Taking photographs and videos
	  — Gathering information relative to the incident
	
	• **Crime-scene protection** — Police and fire officials have duties to perform under the law, and denial of access to crime scenes is sometimes necessary to an investigation because of crime-scene processing or collection of evidence. *Factors:*
	  — The reasons for such a denial should be explained to the news media.
	  — Access should be granted as soon as practical under the conditions.
	
	• **Pool situations** — Public safety officials may deny access to emergency scenes for public safety reasons. When the dictates of public safety allow only a limited representation of the news media, representatives of the news media present may create a pool arrangement and police it themselves. They should *not* place public safety officials in the position of resolving a dispute among themselves.
	
	• **Private property** — Members of the news media can photograph and witness arrests and emergencies on private property when the owner of such property does not object to their presence. If the owner does object, then all parties should take appropriate, courteous action to resolve the situation.
	
	• **Violations** — News media representatives apprehended for violating the law will be dealt with in the same manner as any other violator.

Records Management

Chapter Contents

Learning Objectives

1. Select facts about types of records normally maintained by a fire and emergency services organization.

2. Recall information about the components of the electronic storage/retrieval system.

3. Identify the steps in the management information system (MIS) process.

4. Distinguish between private and public records.

Job Performance Requirements

This chapter provides information that addresses the following job performance requirements of NFPA 1021, *Standard for Fire Officer Professional Qualifications* (2003):

Chapter 4 Fire Officer I
4.4.2(A)

Chapter 16
Records Management

Records management is the systematic control of an organization's records that ensures quick access to information when it is needed for decision-making or to fulfill legal requirements. The records management system allows the organization to perform the following actions:

- Operate efficiently and effectively.
- Prepare short-, medium-, and long-range plans.
- Meet legal obligations and requirements.
- Meet the expectations of internal and external customers and stakeholders.
- Identify and safeguard historically important records.
- Destroy redundant (duplicates other than a backup copy) or outdated records.
- Assign tasks, identify responsible individuals, and hold them accountable for their actions.
- Trace the evolution of a policy or procedure.

Company officers must understand the records management system that is used in their organization, the types of records that they are required to maintain, and how to access records in order to make decisions or justify actions. They should also be familiar with electronic data storage and recovery as well as the computer system in use by their organization.

The collection and use of records has many benefits to the fire and emergency services organization. Systematic management of records allows the organization to perform the following actions:

- Know what records the organization has and how to locate them easily.
- Increase operational efficiency and effectiveness.
- Save administrative costs, both in staff time and storage capacity.
- Support decision-making processes.
- Be accountable.
- Achieve strategic goals and objectives.
- Provide administrative continuity in the event of a disaster.
- Meet legislative and regulatory requirements.
- Serve as a historical record of the department.
- Protect the interests of internal and external customers and stakeholders.

Company officers are an integral part of the records management system. They are responsible for generating raw data and creating reports that become part of the system. They may also be responsible for analyzing information in the records for the purpose of assisting in decision-making or establishing trends. It is essential that company officers follow their organization's record management system and strive for accuracy in the collection of data that is used in records and reports.

This chapter provides the company officer with basic information on the records management system generally used by most fire and emergency services organizations. The management information system (MIS) or information technology (IT) system process is presented, including each of the functions of acquiring, analyzing, organizing, distributing, and storing data. Information storage and types of records are also presented and discussed as well as the conflict between public access to information and privacy concerns (**Figures 16.1 a and b, p. 358**).

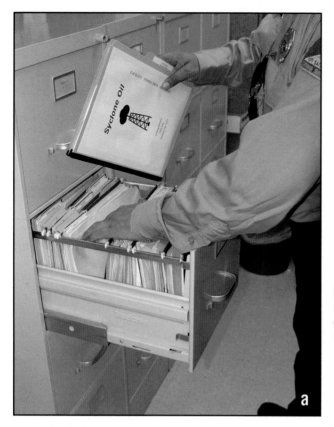

Figures 16.1 a and b Information management systems may include maintaining records (a) in hard-copy form in file cabinets, (b) in electronic format on computer systems, or by using a combination of both methods.

Management Information System Process

Data that are collected by company officers, chief officers, division and branch managers, and other members of the organizations are compiled in the MIS. This system was developed and maintained by professionals who specialize in information management. The MIS may exist as part of the administration of a municipality or governing body or it may be located within the fire and emergency services organization.

Company officers should have an understanding of the steps that the MIS process takes in acquiring, analyzing, organizing, distributing, and storing data and information. It is important to reemphasize the necessity of collecting accurate information. It is irresponsible to use inaccurate data to make critical decisions. The company officer should always remember the computer-age adage: *garbage in/garbage out!*

The record-keeping system requires training for all personnel involved in the collection of data. They need to know how to complete forms, what information to keep or discard, how to categorize the various documents, and how to cross-reference the information. Computer training is also necessary to ensure that records are entered into databases correctly.

Acquiring

Acquiring data is simply collecting it from the many sources available. A company officer is one of those many sources. Other sources inside the organization include the training, logistics, human resources, financial, dispatch, operations, inspection, investigation, and public information and education divisions.

Sources outside the organization include the jurisdiction's public works, streets/highways, law-enforcement, human resources, and finance and revenue departments and elected officials to name a few. Information may also be gathered from local newspapers, trade and professional journals, government agencies, and independent testing laboratories.

Most information is gathered on forms such as the NFIRS form, daily attendance forms, and inspection forms. Information may also be in other formats such as narrative reports. Videos, digital and film images, surveys, and site plans are collected to illustrate reports and forms.

Depending on the local jurisdiction's procedures, data may be collected by the district/battalion chief and submitted to the shift commander. At that point, the information is sorted and channeled to the appropriate officers within the administrative branch for analysis and action.

Acquiring Data Example

A hypothetical example can be used to illustrate the sources and means for acquiring data. This example is based on an actual emergency incident.

A nighttime fire has gutted the local BZ nightclub. Following the fire-suppression activities, it was determined by the company officer that the cause of the fire might be suspicious. The battalion/district chief agreed and authorized that fire investigators and law-enforcement officers be contacted. Both the fire investigators and law-enforcement personnel inspected the property and began the necessary background research. The information that needed to be gathered included the following:

- Time of the initial fire report, including an audiotape of the report
- Time of unit dispatch and arrival, also recorded on audiotape
- Incident report by first-arriving company officer
- Incident action plan
- Interviews with all emergency personnel responding to the scene
- Eyewitness interviews
- Company officer fire-cause determination report
- Fire-investigation report
- Law-enforcement investigation of property owner
- Property tax assessment (used to determine property value)
- Insurance company inspections and evaluations
- Last fire-prevention inspection report
- Videotapes from the club's security cameras
- Fire-detection and suppression-system information, including last inspection by the alarm and sprinkler companies

Analyzing

Depending on the type of information desired, the branch responsible for it will analyze the raw data that come from information collected on forms, in reports, on time sheets, etc. For instance, data contained in the average incident report include the time and type of incident and amount of loss.

The analysis, which can be performed by a computer program or manual calculations, looks at the relationship between key elements of the data and between similar information that is gathered from other incident reports. The final analysis may include a chart that relates the types of incidents to the time of day, loss based on the types of incidents, or loss based on the estimated response time. The resulting information can then show several justifications such as the following:

- Change in operational strategy
- Relocation of an existing station
- Change in the building code to require passive fire-suppression systems in existing structures similar to those identified in the raw data

If the analysis indicates that raw data are inaccurate or incomplete, a request for additional information may be sent back to the originating officer. If a trend of inaccurate or incomplete data

Data Analysis Example

In the BZ nightclub example, the various reports, interviews, audiotapes, and background research would be forwarded to the fire-investigations office. In some jurisdictions, this material may go to the law-enforcement authority. That office would then compile the data into a chronological form to create a picture of the situation that resulted in the fire. Examples are as follows:

- Information from the insurance provider might indicate that the owner had increased coverage on the property in the past 6 months.
- Information from the annual fire-prevention inspection might show that numerous code violations existed and had not been corrected by the time of the fire.
- The incident report completed by the first-arriving company officer might state that the fire was intense, and included the presence of the odor of gasoline once the fire was extinguished.

becomes apparent, it may be necessary to institute additional training in data collection.

Organizing

To ensure easy access to information, it must be organized or grouped into logical topics, which may result in cross-filing or cross-referencing information into various categories (**Figure 16.2**). If the information is maintained in hard-copy files, copies of the original forms and reports will be made and physically filed in the appropriate categories. A reference to the alternate locations can be made and attached to each file.

If the information is maintained in a computer system, links to the original information can be used to direct researchers to the location of the report. In both cases, backup files should be created and maintained to ensure business continuity in the event of a system failure or loss of the original reports.

When organizing the information, the officer(s) responsible for that task must keep in mind that some of the information in the files may be subject to privacy laws. For instance, personnel medical records that are linked to a hazardous materials or biological/medical exposure resulting from an incident will have restricted access. This access should be strictly controlled to prevent the accidental distribution of personal information.

Information Organization Example

In the BZ nightclub fire example, the information might be organized within the department or organization in the following two ways:

1. The individual reports might be organized by their primary topics; that is, the company officer's incident report would be filed with other incident reports in files based on date of incident, company responding, battalion/district response, or occupancy type.

2. Within the fire-investigations office, reports might be grouped by background information, incident reports, postincident reports, and other agency reports. A final file would contain all the information that would be required for any potential criminal court action. All reports would be cross-referenced between the various groups or categories.

Distributing

The information and reports that have been collected, analyzed, and organized are now distributed. Distribution can take the following two paths:

1. Take the reports to the branches of the organization that can benefit from the results of the analysis. For instance, training reports would be combined with attendance records and injury reports and distributed to the training division for action. That action might include the scheduling of training classes for members who had missed mandatory training or who reported an injury resulting from an incorrect activity that additional training can correct.

2. Take the reports to the archives for final storage.

Information Distribution Example

In the BZ nightclub fire example, information would first be sent to the legal branch of the jurisdiction for action. At the same time, information on the incident may be distributed within the organization to assist in future responses, inspections, and investigations.

For instance, the results of the investigation could be provided to the public information officer (PIO) for use with the news media. Results of the fire investigation could be used for training company personnel in recognizing intentionally set fires. The inspections branch might receive a report on the types of code violations that were present and with recommendations that other similar occupancies be inspected for the same types of violations.

Storing

Records are generally placed in storage and retained for a specific time period, depending on the type of record and legal requirements. Storage may be located in two places: active files and archives. *Active files* are those files that are required for day-to-day operations such as purchase requests and contracts. These files are usually maintained in the branch office for easy access. *Archives* are the repositories for records that may have historical value but are not required

MOUNT PROSPECT FIRE DEPARTMENT
FIRE PREVENTION BUREAU
112 E NORTHWEST HIGHWAY   MOUNT PROSPECT, IL 60056
847-818-5253   FAX: 847-818-5240

ADDRESS		SUITE #	INSPECTION DATE

NAME OF BUSINESS		INSPECTOR

BUSINESS LICENSE #	OCCUPANCY CLASSIFICATION	SHIFT/BADGE #

STRIP MALL/BUILDING COMPLEX NAME	BUSINESS HOURS

OWNER/MANAGER OF PROPERTY	OWNER/MANAGER ADDRESS	OWNER PHONE #

EMERGENCY CONTACT	EMERGENCY PHONE #1 (NO PAGERS)	EMERGENCY PHONE #2

	YES	NO	
FIRE ALARM SYSTEM?	☐	☐	FIRE ALARM/SUPPRESSION MONITORING COMPANY:_____
SPRINKLER SYSTEM?	☐	☐	PHONE #:_____ POSITION #:_____

			YES NO	APPROXIMATE
KNOX BOX?	☐	☐	HAZARD MATERIALS ON SITE? ☐ ☐	BLDG. SQ FOOTAGE:_____
FIRE PUMP?	☐	☐	TYPES:_____ QUANTITIES:_____	

	1.00			**3.00**			**5.00**
Fire Hydrant	**1.10**	**Exits**	**3.10**		Open Wiring	5.01
Obstructions/Condition	1.11	Improper Number	3.11		Cover off panel	5.02
Fire Lane	**1.20**	Blocked/Obstructed	3.12		Open junction boxes/outlets/ switches	5.03
Improper Markings	1.21	Locks	3.13		Extension cord use	5.04
Obstructed/Condition	1.22	Wrong door swing	3.14		Panel not accessible	5.05
Knox Box	**1.30**	Door needs repair	3.15		Broken conduit	5.06
Address	**1.40**	Arrangement	3.16		Panel not marked	5.07
		Exit Access	**3.20**		Ground fault	5.08
	2.00	Blocked/Obstructed	3.21		Explosion proof equipment	5.09
Sprinkler/Standpipe/Fire Pump	**2.10**	**Exit Enclosures (Stairs, etc.)**	**3.30**			**6.00**
Annual Test	2.11	Storage/Improper use	3.31		**Fire wall/Partitions**	**6.10**
Valves open/supervised	2.12	**Exit Signs**	**3.40**		Holes/cracks	6.11
Valves not labeled	2.13	Needs repair	3.41		Wrong rating	6.12
Valves not accessible	2.14	Improperly located	3.42		**Fire Doors/Frames**	**6.20**
No spare sprinkler/wrench	2.15	**Emergency Lights**	**3.50**		Annual test	6.21
Improper coverage	2.16	Needs repair	3.51		Need fire door	6.22
No inside bell	2.17	Inadequate Coverage	3.52		No fusible link	6.23
Fire Dept. Connection	**2.20**				Needs repair	6.24
Obstructed/Condition	2.21		**4.00**		**Ceiling**	**6.30**
Strobe/Condition	2.22	Improper Storage	4.01		Titles missing	6.31
Sign	2.23	Improper Dispensing	4.02		Holes/cracks	6.32
Not painted red	2.24	Ignition Sources	4.03			
Fire Alarm	**2.30**	Posting of "No Smoking" Signs	4.04			**7.00**
Annual Test	2.31	Fire Dept. Permit/Displayed	4.05		Housekeeping	7.01
Panel not accessible	2.32	**Spray Booths**	**4.10**		No posted occupancy limits	7.02
Panel not labeled/Zone map	2.33	Sprinklers/Residue	4.11		Compressed gas cylinders	7.03
Improper detector spacing	2.34	Ventilation/Booth	4.12		Kitchen filters	7.04
Other Fixed Suppression System	**2.40**	Filters/Residue	4.13		Improper storage	7.05
Semi/Annual Test	2.42				Gas meters	7.06
Not provided	2.43				Boiler certification	7.07
Portable Fire Extinguisher	**2.50**				Emergency fuel shutoff (gas station)	7.08
Annual Inspection	2.51					
Location	2.52					
Access/Obstruction	2.53					

Figure 16.2 Forms may be filed in multiple locations depending on the topic. The highlighted topics indicate the various files where this form could be located. *Courtesy of Mount Prospect (IL) Fire Department.*

for daily decision-making or report-writing. Old files placed in the archives should be organized by topic such as training, personnel, or incident **(Figure 16.3)**.

If a non-computer-based, manual system is developed, current records should be sorted by topic and filed accordingly. Copies should be made of all records and kept at remote sites in the event an incident destroys the original records. The jurisdiction may have a central file storage area that is available for the organization's use. Computer-based systems should have their data storage backed up (system file copies stored in other locations) on disk, tape, or alternate servers or printed for hard-copy files.

The organization should have a policy for the storage of records. The policy would state the length of time records remain in the active file and the point at which they are moved to the archives. The policy should also specify who has access to the various files and for what reason.

The company officer should always remember that sensitive files (information that is protected by law such as patient records) are always sensitive files, regardless of whether they are classified as active or archive. Archived files should have an established date for destroying them. Some files such as hazardous materials or biological/medical exposure reports have a legally mandated retention time.

Information Storage Example

Data collected on the BZ nightclub fire example would be stored initially in the fire-investigations branch in an active file. If the incident is one of many similar incidents, then access to the file is critical for establishing a trend.

Once the case is closed, either by legal action or determining that insufficient evidence is available to prosecute the responsible party, the file would be placed in the fire-investigations branch archive file. Similarly, the individual original reports would be stored in the appropriate files in the archives with cross-references to the master file.

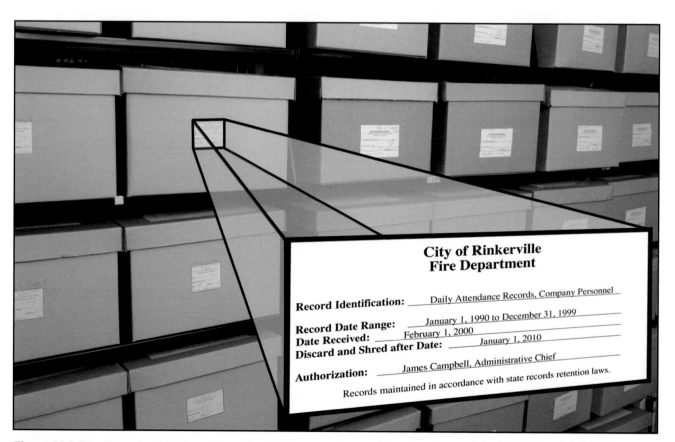

**City of Rinkerville
Fire Department**

Record Identification: _Daily Attendance Records, Company Personnel_

Record Date Range: _January 1, 1990 to December 31, 1999_
Date Received: _February 1, 2000_
Discard and Shred after Date: _January 1, 2010_

Authorization: _James Campbell, Administrative Chief_

Records maintained in accordance with state records retention laws.

Figure 16.3 Files that are stored in archives should have expiration-date labels on them. When the expiration date is reached, the files should be removed from storage and destroyed.

Information Storage

Records management or record keeping is just one element of the MIS that most organizations depend on today. The record-keeping function is the storing of information that is generated by the MIS. A wide variety of types of records are maintained by fire and emergency services organizations, addressing many topics such as those found in **Table 16.1, p. 364**. Company officers should be aware of the types of records that are maintained by their organizations and how they are organized. They must also be familiar with the tools used to create and access information when it is stored electronically.

Record Types

The main categories of records maintained by fire and emergency services organizations are budget, inventory, maintenance (preventive and corrective), activity, and personnel. Personnel records include categories such as training, performance, attendance, hazardous materials or biological/medical exposures, and medical.

Budget

Budget records include all information used to create them, budget status reports, past budgets, and budget requests that were not funded. Purchasing records, contracts, surplus sales, and other similar records should also be retained with this information.

Company officers should maintain the data they used to create their budget requests, justifications for requests, and processes used to generate requests. They should also maintain all records relating to purchases or purchase requests that they make. This information is necessary when federal grants are reviewed. A record of what is spent on each item must be maintained.

Inventory

Inventory and fixed-assets records are generally maintained by the administration or logistics branch of the organization. These records should be accurate and include information on all materials, equipment, facilities, land, and apparatus in the possession of the organization. However, each company officer should maintain a copy of all inventory records for the unit's apparatus, personnel, and facility.

Company officers may be responsible for performing periodic inventories of their areas of responsibility. Any changes in inventory must be noted and reported and, in some cases, justified.

In some organizations, a station or battalion may maintain an inventory of daily operating supplies. Depending on location, the facility may stock disaster preparedness supplies in the event of a natural disaster or other uncontrollable circumstances. The individual stations may have to operate for a number of hours without the ability to procure certain items **(Figure 16.4, p. 365)**. Therefore, the officer may need to establish and maintain an inventory of necessary supplies.

The officers in the station may also work with local vendors and companies in order to maintain the supplies' inventories in the station. The organization may already have certain vendors of choice that officers can contact to procure supplies.

Officers can often order supplies through an online program arranged through the organization and pay for them through a purchase order or with an organizational credit card. Some organizations (based on size) place the responsibility of operating a department purchasing program to company officers under the direction of a chief officer.

Maintenance

Fire and emergency services organizations keep maintenance records on stations and other facilities as well as on vehicles, tools, and equipment. Maintenance records are usually kept in two distinct but closely related categories: preventive and corrective.

Both sets of records hold significant legal value when a fire and emergency services organization has to go to court over an incident involving a piece of equipment owned by the organization. Records are usually maintained and analyzed by the logistics chief/manager.

Preventive maintenance is performed to prevent damage from occurring and extend the useful life of an item, vehicle, or facility by reducing wear. It is usually performed according to a predetermined

Table 16.1
Distribution of Topics in Various Record Types

Topic	Type of Record
Personnel	• Training (topic, date, location, participants, outcomes) • Performance (evaluations) • Attendance (daily personnel roster) • Hazardous materials or biological/medical exposure • Medical (examinations, injuries, illnesses)
Facilities	• Maintenance (preventive and corrective) • Budget (status, requests, purchasing contracts) • Inventory (fixed assets, equipment, supplies)
Vehicles	• Maintenance (preventive and corrective) • Budget (status, requests, purchasing contracts) • Inventory (fixed assets, equipment, supplies)
Equipment	• Maintenance (preventive and corrective) • Budget (status, requests, purchasing contracts) • Inventory (fixed assets, equipment, supplies)
Incidents	• Attendance (daily personnel roster) • Hazardous materials or biological/medical exposure • Medical (examinations, injuries, illnesses) • Incident reports • Emergency and nonemergency responses (historical record)
Functions	• Budget (status, requests, purchasing contracts) • Training (topic, date, location, participants, outcomes) • Attendance (daily personnel roster)
Activities	• Budget (status, requests, purchasing contracts) • Training (topic, date, location, participants, outcomes) • Attendance (daily personnel roster) • Inspections (historical record) • Investigations (historical record) • Emergency and nonemergency responses (historical record) • Communications
Administrative	• Budget (status, requests, purchasing contracts) • Inventory (fixed assets, equipment, supplies)

Figure 16.4 Company officers will be responsible for maintaining a record of the supplies on hand at their stations. They will also be responsible for either submitting a request for additional supplies or purchasing the replacement items when the supply level becomes low.

schedule. The need for preventive maintenance is obvious. Past experience, industry standards, and manufacturers' recommendations combine to form the basis for a schedule of periodic inspection and maintenance. Frequent inspection and cleaning often reveal incipient problems that are relatively easy and inexpensive to correct in their early stages.

The basis for preventive maintenance is record keeping. Records that are compiled during the preventive maintenance of apparatus, facilities, or pieces of equipment can provide the information necessary to predict a trend or justify a replacement **(Figure 16.5, p. 366)**.

Corrective maintenance (repairs) can be needed at any time. When an item is damaged or ceases to function, it must be repaired or replaced as soon as possible. Corrective maintenance is always possible due to an unforeseen event. Damage may occur because of an accident, overuse, operator error, or even abuse.

Deciding when or whether an item should be replaced or repaired is often based on its maintenance record and life expectancy. In either case, the corrective maintenance record is a critically important part of the decision-making process in the following ways:

- Showing that an item is relatively new would probably indicate that the item should be repaired

- Showing that an item is old and has a history of increasingly frequent failures or breakdowns may indicate the need to replace the item with something newer and more reliable

Preventive Maintenance Examples

A few of the countless examples of preventive maintenance that take place in an organization are as follows:

- Roofs of stations are inspected periodically, and any wear or damage is repaired in order to prevent costly water damage within the structure.

- Periodic inspection, cleaning, and maintenance of floor coverings, heating and air-conditioning systems, fire extinguishers, appliances, and septic systems will ensure that equipment and materials continue to function and operate efficiently until the end of their intended operational life cycles.

- The oil is changed in apparatus engines, and chassis are lubricated to reduce the likelihood of breakdowns that could be disastrous if they occurred during an emergency.

- Fire pumps are tested yearly, and this record shows the condition of the pump over time.

- To ensure accuracy, electronic meters (pump panel gauges, monitoring devices, and air-quality testing instruments) must be tested and calibrated on a manufacturer's recommended schedule.

- Preventive maintenance on gasoline-driven generators, power tools, ventilation fans, and other equipment can prevent breakdowns during an emergency incident.

- Fire hose is inspected and tested annually to prevent it from failing during an emergency incident.

- Wooden handles of tools are inspected and treated with linseed oil to keep them smooth and prevent dehydration that results in cracking and splintering.

- Ground ladders, respiratory breathing equipment, and personal protective equipment (PPE) are also inspected and tested on an annual basis and after each use to ensure their effectiveness during an emergency incident.

Figure 16.5 Preventive maintenance is based on accurate record keeping. Maintenance may be scheduled based on apparatus mileage, engine hours, calendar months, the manufacturer's recommendation, or an established industry standard. *Courtesy of Volunteer Fireman's Insurance Services.*

Motor Oil & Oil Filter Record

Date	Months Or Miles	Quarts Of Oil	Filter	Remarks

Lubrication Record

Date	Remarks	Date	Remarks

Printed in U.S.A.

C10:005

.. a subsidiary of the Glatfelter Insurance Group

VFIS

Emergency Vehicle
Maintenance Record Card

Vehicle Description _____ Manufacturer's Serial No. _____

Model Year _____ Plate No. _____

Tire Record

Make	Warranty (Life)	Date Installed	Odometer

Battery Record

Activity

Activity records are maintained at the company, district/battalion, and administrative levels of an organization. Each level supplies the next higher level with an accumulation of information until the records become part of the organization's information management section. Activity records are contained in the company/station logbook and on forms provided for each type of activity. Records include information about the following situations:

- Emergency and nonemergency responses
- Inspections
- Investigations
- Training
- Communications

This information provides the basis for planning and justifying budget requests. It is a historical record of all events, incidents, and projects that members of the organization participated in during a specific time period.

Personnel

Other than attendance records (daily personnel roster) and similar documents, personnel records are confidential. Company officers must be careful to protect that confidentiality by keeping all personnel records secure. Personnel records may be maintained at the company or district/battalion level, in the administrative office, in the medical or safety officer's office, or in the jurisdiction's human resources office.

The types of personnel records include training, performance, attendance, hazardous materials or biological/medical exposures, and medical. It is critical that personnel information be kept current. This information may be needed in the case of an emergency or a line-of-duty death (LODD).

Training. Training records are essential components of a successful training program. Not only do accurate records give an organization long-term inventories of its training activities, they may also be important and necessary in legal proceedings and management reviews such as those conducted by Insurance Services Office (ISO), International Fire Service Accreditation Congress (IFSAC), National Board on Fire Service Professional Qualifications (Pro Board), and International Association of Fire Chiefs/International City/County Management Association (IAFC/ICMA) accreditation program. Company-level training must be documented by the company officer and should include the following elements **(Figure 16.6)**:

- Topic of training session
- Time designated for training
- Date of training
- Location
- Participants
- Outcomes

Performance. Personal job-performance evaluations are part of an individual's personnel file maintained by the organization for each employee. The supervisor may also retain a copy for future job-performance evaluations. These records (like medical records) are confidential. Performance

Figure 16.6 Accurate training records, including attendance records, are the basis for personnel certification and organizational accreditation.

evaluations are an important part of an officer's ability to help steer a subordinate's career in a successful direction. Evaluations can help individuals in the following ways:

- Spot trends and habits in personal performance and behavior

- Help to reinforce good skills and discipline

- Correct unfavorable behaviors that could continue if individuals did not know they were deficient in their skills

- Help individuals improve their knowledge, skills, and abilities

Attendance. Daily attendance records for all personnel are maintained to provide data for the distribution of payrolls and benefits. Depending on the classification of an employee, a formal time card may be required as evidence of actual hours on duty. Other attendance records may be included in the company or unit logbook. Overtime, vacation leaves, compensatory (comp) time, duty exchanges (exchange of work shifts between members), and sick-leave benefits are based on the information that is included in daily attendance records.

Attendance records that support training requirements are also maintained. These records are evidence that an individual or unit has completed a specified number of hours of training in a specific topic such as respiratory protection or hazardous-materials response.

Volunteer and combination personnel should maintain accurate attendance records for both training and emergency operations. This practice ensures that participants receive credit for their participation in the activities. It can also establish a trend for nonparticipation that may result in changing training or activity schedules or termination from the department if applicable.

Hazardous materials or biological/medical exposure. Records that report significant individual exposures to hazardous materials such as smoke, chemicals, and biological, radiological, and nuclear materials are part of an individual's medical record. Exposure to patients with communicable diseases that may be transmitted through body fluids or airborne contact must also be reported. Because of the delayed effects of some of these hazards and the compounding effect of others,

these records must be accurate and retained by the organization for 30 years following the end of employment by individuals involved. Attendance records may also be used to support exposure records when a facility is determined to contain a toxic atmosphere such as a carbon monoxide leak from a gas-powered water heater.

Medical. Medical records are kept on all employees for the duration of their employment plus 30 years. The first information that is included in this record is the result of the preemployment medical examination. Periodic medical evaluations and examinations and post-medical-leave examinations are also included. The exposure reports mentioned earlier are also included in the medical file. The record is complete with the postemployment or termination medical examination. Company officers must record the following situations:

- All job-related injuries or illnesses that affect personnel assigned to them

- Illnesses that are not job-related when they result in the use of sick or injury leave

- Trends that might indicate the abuse of sick leave

Electronic Data Storage/Retrieval

Many fire and emergency services organizations are using some form of electronic data collection, analysis, organization, distribution, and storage/retrieval system to keep all types of records. They are also using computer-based word processors for writing reports and completing forms. Obviously, the company officers in these organizations must learn to use the computer-based system that their organizations use.

The variety of hardware and software available for electronic records management is almost overwhelming **(Figure 16.7)**. However, company officers are only responsible for learning to use the systems adopted by their organizations. Even though this task can still be daunting for some, it is one that company officers must undertake if they are to stay current and function at maximum efficiency.

In terms of hardware, company officers must learn to manipulate the components that are required to make any computer function. In terms

Figure 16.7 Advances in computer technology have resulted in the development of scores of types of data storage devices including external hard drives, miniature thumb drives, and rewritable compact discs (CDs) and digital video discs (DVDs).

of software, they must learn to use programs designed for the particular operating system adopted by their departments or organizations. Countless software programs are available for these systems, and many of them are *cross-platformed,* meaning they work on a variety of operating systems.

Most fire and emergency services organizations provide access to the Internet through their computer systems. Some organizations have internal networks called *intranets* that link all the organization's computers together to improve communication and share software and files. Company officers must understand the local as well as state/provincial and federal laws regarding the proper use of computer systems, access to the Internet, and various issues that are specific to the use of computers (see information box).

Hardware

Regardless of which type of computer an organization uses, the hardware that company officers must master is virtually the same. If the computers in the stations are stand-alone units — that is, they function independently and are not interconnected on a *local area network (LAN)* — each one has a *central processing unit (CPU).* Although it is easy to think of the monitor as the computer, it is the CPU that does the work.

Computer-Use Concerns

Company officers must be aware of certain situations that can result from using computers owned by the jurisdiction. They must also communicate these concerns to their subordinates to prevent any potential problems. The following list gives computer-specific concerns that company personnel must be aware of when using the organization's computer system:

- *Copyright* — Material found on the Internet may be copyright-protected. If a company officer wishes to use the material for training purposes or providing information in reports, it is important to gain permission from the original author or the agency that owns the web site (file or related group of files available on the World Wide Web).

- *Password Protection* — Each company officer may have an assigned password that provides access to either a computer or the Internet/intranet. Passwords are created to prevent the unauthorized use of a computer or access to records that are not public. Company officers must not provide their passwords to anyone else. If other unit members must have access to a computer, they should request their own personal passwords.

- *Viruses* — Computer systems, both public and private, are the target of viruses (infection/disruption programs) and spyware (private information access programs). Viruses and spyware disrupt computer systems or access information that is not normally available to the public. Company officers must ensure that the organization's computer security and protection programs (*firewalls* and *antivirus* and *antispyware programs*) are not compromised and must report any evidence that a virus or spyware is present on a computer.

- *Unauthorized use* — Company officers must adhere to all policies that define the appropriate use of an organization's computers and limit access to the Internet. Generally, only software that is licensed to an organization can be installed on its computers. Company officers should also track the use of computers by other personnel to ensure that they are not accessing unauthorized sites.

On networked systems, each station will have what is sometimes called a *dumb terminal* that is connected to a mainframe computer at some central data processing location — but the terminal or computer looks very similar to the stand-alone unit. In either case, in order to use the computer, a monitor is required. To issue commands to the CPU or mainframe, a keyboard and mouse are needed **(Figure 16.8)**.

To make the computer even more functional, one or more peripheral items are needed. *Peripherals* are ancillary devices connected to but not part of the computer. Typical peripherals are printers, modems, scanners, CD-ROMs (Compact Discs-Read-Only Memory) or zip drives (transfer and store large data files), and other similar devices. These devices allow the computer to print, transmit, reproduce, or store the data it processes. However, all of this hardware is of little value without the software to harness the computer's power.

Software

Software is the term used to describe coded programs that make computers perform various functions. Programs are available for storing, retrieving, and manipulating all sorts of data. Two common types of software programs that are very useful for company officers are spreadsheets and word processing.

Spreadsheet programs are well-suited for company-level record keeping, budgeting, scheduling, tracking, forecasting, and other numbers-related activities. Spreadsheets automatically perform certain mathematical functions whenever new data are entered. A new entry is automatically added to the previous total, and all other mathematical/statistical relationships are adjusted to reflect the new data. Spreadsheet programs are often bundled or sold all in one package. Programs are available for keeping the following records:

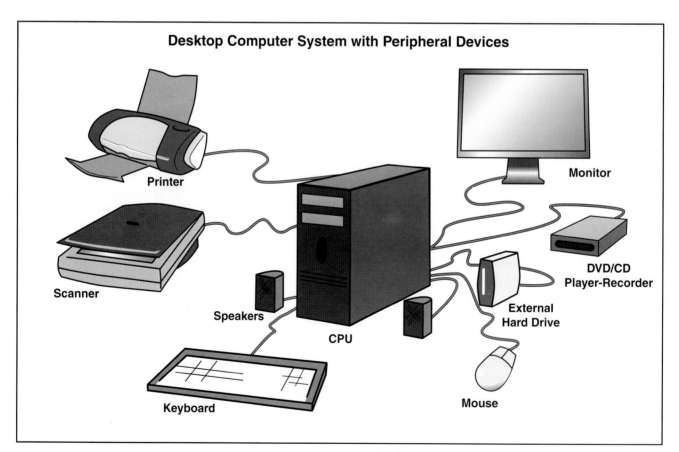

Desktop Computer System with Peripheral Devices

Printer

Scanner

Speakers

Keyboard

CPU

Monitor

DVD/CD Player-Recorder

External Hard Drive

Mouse

Figure 16.8 Computers are increasingly becoming parts of fire and emergency services facilities and operations. Company officers may have access to stand-alone computers or units that are interconnected with other computers within the organization.

- Training records
- Hose records
- Preventive maintenance records
- Inspection records
- Records of many other organizational functions

Word processing programs have allowed computers to replace typewriters as the means for writing reports and other documents. Word processors make composing, manipulating, and editing text so effortless that there is no longer any excuse for company officers turning in reports that are not well-organized, correctly punctuated, and free of spelling errors. Each department can design its own forms and keep this information on a computer.

The word processing and spreadsheet programs mentioned are commercial programs designed for all types of office and home use. Other commercially available types of programs include those that can create floor plans, illustrations, business cards, stationery, and publications such as newsletters and pamphlets. Many, if not all, of these programs have uses in the fire and emergency services profession.

While most organizations can make do with commercially produced programs, some software programs are specifically designed for fire and emergency services organizations, including the following:

- Database programs used for recording incidents in National Fire Incident Reporting System (NFIRS) format
- Inventory-control programs
- Records storage
- Inspections programs
- Training programs

More specialized and expensive than the commercial programs, these programs reduce the time and experience that it takes to create fire-service-specific templates. A longer learning curve may also be required for the average company officer to become proficient in using the specialized programs.

Internet and Intranet

The Internet is a worldwide network of computers that was established in 1969 to allow universities and other research institutions to quickly and easily share information with the U.S. military and defense contractors. Internet access is now available to the general public, and millions of computer users access it daily. The Internet is not a computer destination; it is a means by which individual computer users can communicate with others around the world. Users can perform the following functions:

- Send and receive electronic mail (e-mail) messages.
- Transfer data files.
- Access thousands of special-interest groups (including fire-service-related groups) and various *newsgroups* or *bulletin boards.*
- Download (transmit files from a central computer to a smaller computer) software programs.

There are countless groups, organizations, and individuals that can be accessed through the Internet **(Figure 16.9, p. 372)**. When company officers have questions relating to a particular topic, they can visit various web sites (files or related groups of files available on the World Wide Web) that can either provide the information needed or direct them to other sites on the Web (see information box, p. 372).

Individuals from groups of fire apparatus and equipment manufacturers or groups involved in emergency medical services (EMS), rescue, and other disciplines can ask questions of the entire group, and anyone in the group can respond to the question. The Internet provides an electronic open forum.

Many organizations now have internal computer networks called *intranets.* Like the Internet, the intranet permits the sharing of files, information, and programs between members of the organization. It may even be the basis upon which the MIS is built.

Figure 16.9 Professional organizations such as the IAFF maintain web sites that can provide company officers with information and links to other sites of interest. *Courtesy of International Association of Fire Fighters.*

ℹ️ **Internet-Specific Concerns**

Company officers must be aware of the following three areas where caution is advised when using the Internet:

1. The Internet contains sites that are inappropriate for access from work-related computers. In many jurisdictions such access is illegal and can result in an employee's termination.

2. The accuracy of some of the information found on the Internet is questionable. Always authenticate the information before using it to support or justify a recommendation.

3. Data and especially e-mail messages live forever on computers and in cyberspace. Even if a document has been erased, it can be recovered by trained computer personnel. Never put into writing anything that is inappropriate or illegal.

Privacy Versus Public Access

In this information age, people tend to think of all information as being public and accessible. Whether the information is in the form of tabloid articles on the private lives of celebrities or the internal decisions of giant corporations, the public

wants to know. At the same time, in general the public wants privacy. What people write in e-mails, what they say in private conversations, and what their opinions are on major issues are sometimes viewed as personal and private. It should be obvious that the desire for knowledge and privacy can come into conflict in today's society.

This conflict is apparent in government entities where the records that are generated by the organization, at taxpayer's expense, are generally considered public record and open to scrutiny. At the same time, some of the records deal with the private lives of the individuals who work for the organization. The company officer must be familiar with local, state/provincial, and federal laws that regulate both privacy and public access to data, reports, and records that they generate.

Privacy

Records that must be kept confidential include personnel files, individual training records, and medical files **(Figure 16.10)**. Access to these files must be limited. Training records may also be considered part of an individual's personal, private

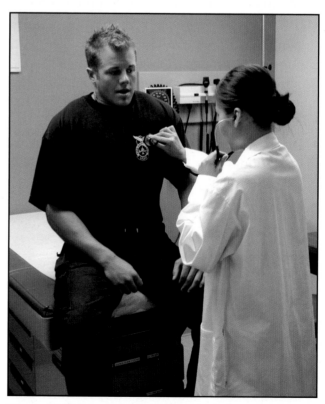

Figure 16.10 Personal medical files, including exposure reports, medical evaluations, and examination results, must be kept confidential.

employment file — a fact that requires an organization to limit access to training records. Even if local laws do *not* require this practice, organizations should develop and adopt policies that limit access to training records to only those personnel with a legal need to know.

Other personal information that is regulated to ensure privacy includes Social Security numbers and test scores. Many organizations no longer use an employee's Social Security number for records identification. The practice of using other identification methods reduces the opportunity for improper use or the potential for identity theft. Laws also protect the release of individuals' evaluation/testing scores.

In the U.S., the Family Education and Privacy Act prohibits the release of this type of personal information. Similarly, the Canadian province of Ontario has the Municipal Freedom of Information and Protection of Privacy Act (MFIPPA) that places the responsibility on instructors to know their duties and responsibilities under the applicable legislation within their jurisdictions. Scores and personal data are considered privileged information and are available only to management and a few other designated personnel with authorization and a specific need to know.

Public Access

While individual personnel records are confidential, other organizational records are not. Generally, open-meeting laws and open-records acts define the type of records that are available to the public and news media. The open-meeting law that is in effect in the jurisdiction will cause the official minutes and any other notes that were made as part of a meeting to be part of the public record. Care should always be taken in the recording of any information that might potentially become public.

Some records such as incident reports or fire investigations are available to individuals who own the involved properties or are involved in the incidents, unless specifically indicated to the contrary by statute. The exact definition and list of records that are available to the public are defined by the state/province. An example of the definition by one state is as follows:

Public record includes any writing containing information relating to the conduct of government or the performance of any governmental or proprietary function prepared, owned, used, or retained by any state or local agency regardless of physical form or characteristics: All budget and financial records; personnel leave, travel and payroll records; records of legislative sessions; reports submitted to the legislature; and any other record designated a public record by any official action by the Senate or the House of Representatives

Public records include virtually all records of agencies and jurisdictions within the state/province. Those records include documents, maps, photographs, videotapes, handwritten notes, letters, computer data (including e-mails), and all other records if they were created or held by a government organization **(Figure 16.11)**. Records of responses to emergency medical incidents present restricted-access issues because of the requirements for confidentiality.

Figure 16.11 Company officers often write notes during investigations regarding the location of evidence or personal observations. These notes, which may be used to write formal reports, are also subject to public access.

Exemptions to the open-records acts exist in many states, but they are limited and have been very narrowly interpreted by the courts. The laws presume that all records are open and place the burden on the jurisdiction to demonstrate that any requested materials are exempt. If a public record contains both exempt and nonexempt material, the exempt portion must be removed and the remaining nonexempt material disclosed.

All fire officers who are involved with the creation, storage, and distribution of records should be aware of the open-records laws enforced in their jurisdictions. Federal employees must be aware of the application of the Freedom of Information Act on U.S. government agencies. Examples of exemptions are as follows:

- Medical records and other materials involving matters of personal privacy
- Records relating to pending investigations
- Records required to be kept confidential by the federal government such as training, promotional, and educational records
- Trade secrets and certain information of a proprietary nature
- Research data, records, or information that has not been published, patented, or otherwise publicly disseminated

- Confidential evaluations submitted to a public agency in connection with the hiring of a public employee
- Investigative reports used by the organization as part of its quality-improvement effort

Company officers must be aware that any information that they collect regarding incidents, personnel evaluations or actions, or notes associated with citizen contacts may be subject to public access. It is critical that company officers be accurate and objective in the information they collect and observations they record. It is possible that the information may become part of a legal action and the officer might be required to testify on the validity of the information in a court of law.

Summary
Company officers are responsible for the collection of the raw data generated by their units' activities. Whether data are collected on forms or in narrative reports, it must be accurate, complete, and legible. Understanding the MIS process within their organizations helps ensure that they are collecting the correct data in the proper form. They must also be aware of privacy requirements and the public's right to know through public access.

Forms Development

Standardized forms ensure that information that is mandated by law and stored in the records management system is consistent and complete. Forms are based on the type of information that is outlined in the organization's policies or legal requirements of various governmental agencies. Forms may be purchased from office supply companies, provided by the authority having jurisdiction, or created by the company officer. In any case, the forms must be consistent with those used by the organization in both appearance and format.

Forms may be created for use in two formats: hard copy and computer-based. Both can be developed with a computer program that will create them in the desired format.

Hard-copy forms, such as course attendance forms or safety checklists, are completed by hand in pencil or ink. They are very simple to create and can be prepared in a word-processing program in a short time. Using the Table function, rows and columns are created, titled, and enlarged to accept the written entry or checkmark.

Computer-based forms are more difficult to create and may require a specialized computer program such as a database to generate the form. Computer-based forms are designed to not only collect but also sort information. Fields are assigned to specific questions in the form. Information placed into those fields, such as date, time, unit number, or type of training, must be consistent with the topic. Care must be taken in the creation of these types of forms so that the person completing the form provides accurate information in the proper category.

Forms should have fields that are consistent with other training forms used by the organization. For instance, Field 1 may always contain the date, Field 2 may always contain the instructor's name, Field 3 may always contain the student's name, and so on. The more consistent the assignment of data to specific fields, the easier the form will be to use and the easier the information will be to locate, analyze, and store.

A general set of guidelines for developing both hard-copy and computer-based forms includes the following:

1. Forms should have a meaningful title and have a form number that is consistent and registered with the organization. For example: *Course Evaluation Form, Form A-2004.03.revised*

2. In each cell or box, write the caption in the upper left corner of the cell. Provide an example as an illustration.

3. Define the information that is needed in each space or cell. For instance: *Course Date and Time*

4. Allow sufficient space for written responses in each cell. For vertical spacing allow 1 inch for three lines of handwriting. For horizontal spacing, allow 1 inch of space for every five characters with a maximum of ten characters per line.

5. Place checkboxes in front of each question.

6. Use adequate margins on each page, generally ⅜th of an inch on all sides.

7. Use screens or shaded areas to make the form visually appealing.

8. Include easy-to-understand instructions for the completion of the form.

9. Use 8-point fonts as a minimum size font.

10. Make the sequence and grouping of questions or cells logical and appropriate.

11. Keep the forms simple and uncluttered.

12. Use single words or brief phrases for the questions or captions.

13. Use familiar and understandable words, terms, and abbreviations.

14. Avoid ambiguities, idioms, compound questions, and technical terms.

15. Remember the audience who will use the form and keep it appropriate to them while still collecting the required information.

Preincident Planning

Chapter Contents

Learning Objectives

1. Select facts about preincident planning.

2. Match to their definitions the NFPA 220 types of building construction.

3. Match to their definitions the *International Building Code® (IBC®)* types of building construction.

4. Identify different types of roofs.

5. Choose correct responses about the preincident survey.

6. Select facts about conducting the preincident survey.

7. Select facts about fire loading.

8. Select facts about fire protection and structure ventilation systems.

9. Choose correct responses about water supply information that should be gathered during a preincident survey.

10. Select correct responses about developing preincident plans.

11. Apply the process of preincident planning to a facility.

Job Performance Requirements

This chapter provides information that addresses the following job performance requirements of NFPA 1021, *Standard for Fire Officer Professional Qualifications* (2003):

Chapter 4 Fire Officer I

4.6.1(A)

Chapter 17
Preincident Planning

The success or failure of emergency operations often depends upon the amount of knowledge that emergency personnel have about the environment in which they are operating, which is based on the amount of preincident planning that was done. Preincident planning allows emergency responders to anticipate the resources and procedures needed to meet specific demands within their jurisdictions.

Because every emergency incident is an uncontrolled situation, they are rarely identical. While similarities to other emergencies may exist, the exact circumstances surrounding an emergency may be different. To ensure that emergency personnel are able to recognize similarities and adapt to differences, it is important for them to know as much as possible about the potential incident scene before an incident occurs.

Although gathering information about a particular structure or occupancy during a preincident survey is often referred to as preincident planning, information gathering is only one part of the process. *Preincident planning* is the entire process of gathering and evaluating information, developing procedures based on that information, and ensuring that the information remains current. To obtain this information, company officers and unit personnel conduct preincident surveys of commercial, industrial, and institutional occupancies and high-risk (target) hazards within their response areas.

As mentioned, preincident planning involves more than just the preincident survey. Preincident planning actually consists of the following four separate functions:

1. Developing positive relationships with building owners/occupants

2. Conducting the preincident survey

3. Managing preincident data

4. Developing preincident plans

Basic to the preincident planning process, though, is an understanding of the difference between a preincident survey and a fire and life-safety code enforcement inspection. While some jurisdictions authorize company officers to perform both types of activities, most do not.

Company officers and unit personnel must also have an understanding of basic building construction and the building codes that regulate construction in the jurisdiction. Building codes define the type of construction that is used to build structures that will be used for specific purposes. These specific purposes determine the type of occupancy classification that will be assigned to the completed structure. Company officers will develop preincident plans based on the completed structure and its use.

Company officers should take advantage of the opportunity to survey buildings while they are under construction. These surveys provide opportunities to view and discuss various construction techniques and building components that will be hidden once those structures are complete.

The company officer should always obtain permission from the project manager or job superintendent before entering a construction site. Head, eye, and hearing protection may be required, and all safety regulations must be followed during the survey.

The company officer may find it helpful to refer to NFPA 1620, *Recommended Practice for Pre-Incident Planning* (2003). This recommended practice provides the information needed to conduct thorough preincident surveys and sample forms needed to develop comprehensive preincident plans from the information gathered during surveys.

This chapter discusses the preincident planning process, including the reasons for preincident surveys, how they differ from code enforcement inspections, how to prepare for preincident surveys, how to conduct them, and how to manage preincident data. Also discussed are basic building construction and building components that can contribute to fires and other emergencies and how these components can be used to control or limit the spread of fire.

Understanding Surveys and Inspections

Company officers and their department administrations need to understand the difference between preincident surveys and fire and life-safety code enforcement inspections. Preincident surveys are similar to fire and life-safety inspections, although surveys are not intended to locate code violations. If violations are discovered during a survey, the company officer may request that the owner/occupant correct the violation or simply report the problem to the authority's inspection division.

Preincident surveys and code enforcement inspections are sometimes conducted by the same personnel because some departments require their companies to perform both functions in one visit. However, preincident surveys and code enforcement inspections are conducted for entirely different purposes and should *not* be combined **(Figures 17.1 a and b)**.

Company-level personnel conduct preincident surveys for the following reasons:

• Become familiar with a structure or facility, its physical layout and design, any built-in fire protection systems, and any hazards that may exist.

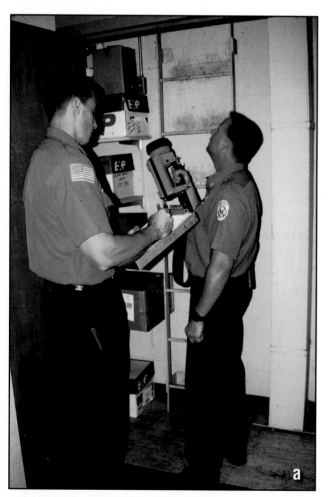

Figures 17.1 a and b Preincident surveys and code enforcement inspections accomplish two different goals: (a) Preincident surveys familiarize company personnel with the facilities in their response area and the potential hazards that they may contain. (b) Code enforcement inspections locate violations (either intentional or unintentional) of the local fire and life-safety code that could create hazards.

- Visualize and discuss how an emergency is likely to occur or a fire may behave in an occupancy and how existing strategies and tactics might apply to an incident at this occupancy.

- Identify the number and type of resources needed to handle an incident at a particular location.

- Identify critical conditions that were not noted during any previous facility surveys or have changed since the last survey.

When company-level personnel conduct a fire and life-safety code enforcement inspection, they become familiar with the occupancy simply by being there, but their attention is focused on code requirements for that occupancy. They are there to see that owners/occupants have done everything that the codes require to prevent fires from occurring and allow occupants to escape if an emergency does occur.

Understanding Basic Building Construction

Some of the most useful information that company officers should gather during a preincident survey is how the building is constructed. Because each type of building construction behaves differently under fire conditions, company officers must be able to identify the various types during the surveys. Knowing how stable or unstable different materials and assemblies are under fire conditions allows appropriate plans and procedures to be developed that will allow firefighters to do their jobs with the greatest possible level of safety.

Before a preincident survey, the company officer should review the applicable building code to determine the requirements that were applied to the structure when it was built. Old buildings may not meet current building codes although alterations must meet current requirements **(Figure 17.2)**.

The sections that follow provide a brief overview of the primary model building codes in use in the U.S. A discussion of structural building assemblies, lightweight construction, and other building components is included.

Figure 17.2 Over their life spans, old buildings may have been renovated or restored. Inspections of old buildings may require detailed research into the history of the structure and the application of building codes. In some instances, the fire and life-safety code currently in effect may take precedence over the original codes.

Building Construction Code Types

Model building codes provide municipalities and jurisdictions with the ability to control the construction and use of structures and ensure life safety for the occupants of these structures **(Figure 17.3, p. 382)**. Currently, model building codes, which include structural, electrical, plumbing, and safety requirements, are developed by two major organizations: National Fire Protection Association (NFPA) and International Code Council (ICC).

Local jurisdictions adopt the model codes, sometimes with alterations, and assign enforcement responsibilities to the building, electrical, plumbing, or fire inspections divisions or departments. The ICC publishes individual code books for building construction, electrical installation,

Figure 17.3 The design, construction, and use of all structures is regulated by the model building code adopted by the local jurisdiction. For instance, a parking garage may not be used as a place of residence without meeting current requirements for that type of occupancy.

plumbing installation, and many other building components. NFPA publishes similar code books as well as other standards.

Each model building code classifies building construction in different terms. In general, construction classifications are based upon materials used in construction and upon hourly fire-resistance ratings of structural components. Most building codes have the same five construction classifications described in this section, but some may use different terms to describe each classification.

NFPA 220, *Standard on Types of Building Construction* (2006), and the *International Building Code® (IBC®)* both use classifications that are consistent with those used in the National Fire Incident Reporting System (NFIRS). NFPA 220 uses

Roman numerals to designate the five major classifications (Types I through V). Each classification is further divided into subtypes using a three-digit Arabic number code or several letters. *IBC®* designates five construction types (Types I through V) with two subcategories (A and B) for each type with the exception of Type IV. In both classification systems, structures are composed of the following building elements:

- Structural frame
- Load-bearing walls, both interior and exterior
- Exterior nonbearing walls and partitions
- Interior nonbearing walls and partitions
- Floor assemblies
- Roof assemblies

NFPA 220 Classifications

NFPA 220 classifications designate five major building construction classifications that are then divided into subtypes that are based on the fire-resistance rating of the various structural components. The classifications begin with Type I, which is the most fire-resistive, and continue through Type V, which is the least fire-resistive. NFPA 220 construction classifications are described in the following list:

- *Type I construction* — Consists of structural members, including walls, columns, beams, floors, and roofs, that are made of noncombustible or limited combustible materials (also called *fire-resistive construction* in some codes) **(Figure 17.4)**. Buildings of this type were origi-

Figure 17.4 Type I building construction is the most fire-resistive of all types of construction. However, penetrations of fire assemblies (fire-rated walls, floors, and ceilings) can immediately compromise this high level of fire resistance.

nally designed to confine any fire and its resulting products of combustion to a given location. *Characteristics:*

— Because of the limited combustibility of the construction materials, the primary fuel load (total fuel available) is composed of the contents of the structure. See Fuel Loads section for more information.

— The ability of this construction to confine a fire to a certain area can be compromised by openings made in partitions and improperly designed heating, ventilating, and air-conditioning (HVAC) systems. See HVAC Systems section for more information.

• *Type II construction* — Consists of structural members similar to Type I except that the degree of fire resistance is lower (also called *noncombustible* or *noncombustible/limited combustible construction*). In some cases, materials with no fire-resistance rating (such as untreated wood) may be used. The heat buildup from a fire in the building can cause structural supports to fail. Another potential problem is the type of roof. *Characteristics:*

— Contents of the structure compose the primary fuel load.

— Roofs are often flat, built-up types that may contain combustible felt (tar paper) and roofing tar (**Figure 17.5**). Fire extension to the roof can eventually cause the entire roof to become involved and fail. See Roof Types section for more information.

• *Type III construction* — Consists of exterior walls and structural members that are portions of exterior walls that are made of noncombustible or limited combustible materials (commonly referred to as *ordinary construction*) (**Figure 17.6**). Interior structural members, including walls, columns, beams, floors, and roofs, may be completely or partially constructed of wood. The wood used in these members has smaller dimensions than that required for heavy timber construction (Type IV). Fire hazards can be reduced if fire-stops (solid materials) are placed inside concealed spaces to limit the spread of combustion byproducts. *Fire concerns:*

— Fire and smoke spreading through concealed spaces between walls, floors, and ceilings

— Heat conducting to concealed spaces through finish materials (drywall or plaster) or holes in finish materials, causing heat, smoke, and gases to spread to other parts of the structure

— Fire actually burning within concealed spaces and feeding on combustible construction materials in the space

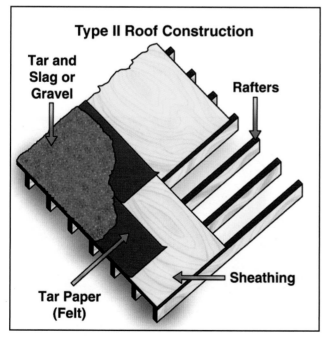

Figure 17.5 Materials that are commonly used in the roofs of Type II construction structures are generally combustible.

Figure 17.6 Type III construction consists of interior structural members that are constructed completely or partially of wood.

- **Type IV construction** — Consists of exterior and interior walls and their associated structural members that are of noncombustible or limited combustible materials (also called *heavy timber construction*) **(Figure 17.7)**. Other interior structural members, including beams, columns, arches, floors, and roofs, are made of solid or laminated wood with no concealed spaces. *Characteristics:*
  — Wooden members must have large enough dimensions to be considered heavy timber.
  — Dimensions that qualify as heavy timber vary (depending on the particular code being used) but are usually defined as being at least 8 inches (203 mm) in its smallest dimension.

- **Type V construction** — Consists of exterior walls, bearing walls, columns, beams, girders, trusses, arches, floors, and roofs made entirely or partially of wood or other approved combustible material **(Figure 17.8)**. Buildings are typically wood-frame structures used for various mercantile occupancies, most single-family and multifamily residences, and other free-standing structures up to about six stories in height. Just as in Type III construction, Type V construction differs from Type IV mainly in the smaller dimensions of the structural members.

International Building Code® Classifications

The *IBC*® designates five construction types with two subcategories for each type with the exception of Type IV. Each construction type is defined by the materials and fire performance of the building element of the structure. *IBC*® construction types are similar to the NFPA categories and range from Type I, which is most fire-resistive, to Type V, which is least fire-resistive. *IBC*® construction classifications are described in the following list:

- **Type I construction** — Consists of noncombustible materials characterized by the use of steel, iron, concrete, or masonry structural elements. *Subcategories:*
  — *Type IA:* Requires a 3-hour fire-resistance rating of the structural frame and load-bearing walls; floors must have a 2-hour fire-resistance rating; and roofs must have a 1½-hour fire-resistance rating (most stringent classification)
  — *Type IB:* Requires a 2-hour fire-resistance rating for the structural frame and load-bearing walls; floors must have a 2-hour fire-resistance rating; and roofs must have a 1-hour fire-resistance rating

- **Type II construction** — Consists of noncombustible materials but with a reduced fire-resistance rating when compared with Type I construction. Although the term is not completely accurate, this type is often referred to as a *1-hour building*, which means that bearing walls and floors have a 1-hour fire-resistance rating. *Subcategories:*
  — *Type IIA:* Requires noncombustible fire-resistive materials similar to Type I buildings insofar as the structural elements must be of steel, concrete, or masonry

Figure 17.7 Heavy timber or Type IV construction includes structural members that are made of solid or laminated wood members.

Figure 17.8 Single-family dwellings are examples of structures that use Type V construction.

— *Type IIB:* Requires approved noncombustible materials, but the materials used may have no assigned fire-resistance rating

• ***Type III construction*** — Consists of structural elements made of any materials permitted by the code. Exterior bearing walls must have a 2-hour fire-resistance rating. *Subcategories:*

— *Type IIIA:* Requires materials that will provide a 1-hour fire-resistance construction throughout the structure

— *Type IIIB:* Lacks the 1-hour fire-resistance construction requirement

• ***Type IV construction*** — Consists of structural elements of any type permitted by the code with exterior walls being constructed of noncombustible materials while interior building elements are constructed of solid or laminated wood having no concealed spaces (also known as *heavy timber* or *HT*). Buildings must have permanent partitions, and members of the structural frame must have a minimum fire-resistance rating of at least 1 hour. *Characteristics:*

— *Exterior walls:* May have fire-retardant-treated wood framing with a 2-hour fire-resistance rating or less

— *Wooden columns:* Requires a minimum 8-inch (203 mm) dimensioned lumber (not less than 6 inches [152 mm] nominal in width) when supporting a floor or not less than 8 inches (203 mm) nominal depth when supporting roof or ceiling loads only

— *Floor framing (including wood beams and girders):* Requires sawn or glued-laminated timber of at least 6 inches (152 mm) nominal depth and not less than 10 inches (254 mm) depth

— *Roof framing:* Requires wood-frame or glued-laminated arches for roof construction that rises from the floor with a minimum of 6 inches (152 mm) nominal width and 8 inches (203 mm) nominal depth for the first half of its length and then no less than 6 inches (152 mm) nominal dimension for the top half of its length

— *Roofs:* Must be constructed without concealed spaces

• ***Type V construction*** — Consists of structural elements and exterior and interior walls constructed of any materials permitted by the code (also known as *wood-frame construction*). *Subcategories:*

— *Type VA:* Requires a 1-hour fire-resistance rating for all structural elements except for nonbearing interior walls and partitions

— *Type VB:* May have non-fire-rated structural elements

Roof Types

The basic purpose of a roof is to protect the inside of a building from exposure to outside weather conditions. However, the roof also provides for a controllable interior environment, enhances the architectural style of a building, and contributes to the functional purpose of a building. An example of a roof designed around function is a domed roof over a sports arena.

The primary concern for firefighter safety is a roof's susceptibility to sudden and unexpected collapse because its supporting structure has been weakened by fire. Beyond that, the combustibility of the surface of a roof is a basic concern to the fire safety of an entire community. Roofs that can be easily ignited by flaming embers have been a frequent cause of major fires. Roof types include the following:

• Flat
• Pitched
• Arched
• Concrete
• Metal

Flat

Flat roofs may or may not have a slight slope to facilitate water drainage. They are most commonly found on commercial, industrial, and apartment buildings. Flat roofs are often penetrated by chimneys, vent pipes, shafts, scuttles, and skylights (**Figure 17.9, p. 386**). These roofs may be surrounded and/or divided by parapets. Roofs may also support water tanks, air-conditioning equipment, antennas, and other objects that add to a building's dead load (permanent building components).

The structural part of a flat roof (generally similar to the construction of a floor) consists of wooden, concrete, or metal joists (horizontal supporting members) covered with sheathing (layer of boards or other wood or fiber materials to strengthen the structure and serve as a base for an exterior weatherproof covering). The sheathing is often covered with a layer of insulating material that is always covered by a finish layer of some weather-resistant material.

In some installations, flat roofs do not employ joist and sheathing construction but are constructed of poured, reinforced or lightweight concrete, precast gypsum, or concrete slabs set within metal joists. Another form of flat roof, referred to as *lightweight construction* or *panelized roofing*, is discussed in the Lightweight Construction section.

Over time, flat roofs can deteriorate, resulting in water leaks and high maintenance costs. Some owners have resorted to constructing pitched roofs over existing flat roofs in order to provide better weather protection to the old roofs **(Figure 17.10)**. This type of construction results in a void where fires can spread rapidly and HVAC units could be hidden from view.

Figure 17.9 Commercial and industrial occupancies with flat roofs provide the company officer with an opportunity to inspect the roof for machinery items or any penetrations such as this vent.

Pitched

Pitched roofs have a peak along one edge or in the center, and a deck that slopes downward from the peak to one, two, or all edges. The slope of a pitched roof may vary from gradual to steep, but it is always more pronounced than those of flat roofs.

Pitched roofs consist of timber rafters or metal trusses (structural units made of several triangles) that run from the ridge to a wall plate on top of the outer wall at the eaves level. The rafters or trusses that carry the sloping roof can be made of various materials. Sheathing boards or panels are usually applied directly onto the rafters. Pitched roofs usually have a covering of roofing paper (felt) applied before shingles are laid. Shingle types may be wood, metal, composition, asbestos, slate, or tile **(Figure 17.11)**.

Figure 17.10 In recent years, it has become the practice to install metal pitched roofs over existing flat roofs. This practice conceals some of the machinery located on the roof and creates a hidden space where fires can spread undetected.

Figure 17.11 Residential roofs may consist of numerous types of coverings, including tile as shown here.

Pitched roofs on barns, churches, supermarkets, and industrial buildings are usually covered with shingles but may have rolled felt applied over the sheathing, which has been mopped with asphalt roofing tar. In other installations, instead of wood sheathing, gypsum slabs, approximately 2 inches (50 mm) thick, may be laid across metal trusses.

Arched

The arched type of roof is used on a wide variety of building types. One form of arched roof construction uses bow-string (bow-shaped) trusses as the main supporting members. The lower chord (bottom longitudinal member) of the truss may be covered with a ceiling to form an enclosed cockloft or roof space. Such concealed, unvented spaces may contribute to the spread of a fire and early failure of the roof (**Figures 17.12 a and b**).

Trussless arched roofs (sometimes called *lamella roofs*) are composed of relatively short timbers of uniform length. These timbers are beveled and bored at the ends where they are bolted together at an angle to form an interlocking network of structural timbers. This network forms an arch of mutually braced and stiffened timbers. Being an arch rather than a truss, the roof exerts a horizontal reaction in addition to the vertical reaction on supporting structural components.

In trussless arch construction, all parts of the underside of the roof are visible. A hole of considerable size may be cut or burned through the network sheathing and roofing without causing collapse of the roof structure. The loads are distributed to less damaged timbers around the opening.

Concrete

The use of precast concrete is very popular in certain types of construction. Precast roof slabs are available in many shapes, sizes, and designs. These slabs are hauled to the construction site and are ready for use. In other cases, the roof structure is formed and the concrete is poured on site.

Roofs of either precast or reinforced concrete are extremely difficult to breach, so another means of gaining access or ventilating the building should be used whenever possible. However, these roofs are virtually impervious to fire, so they are some of the most stable roof types.

A popular lightweight material made of gypsum plaster and portland cement mixed with fillers such as perlite, vermiculite, or sand provides a lightweight floor and roof assembly. This material is sometimes referred to as *lightweight concrete*. Lightweight precast planks are manufactured from this material, and the slabs are reinforced with steel mesh or rods. Lightweight concrete roofs are usually finished with roofing felt and a mopping of hot tar to make them weather-resistant.

Lightweight concrete roof decks may also be poured in place over permanent form boards, steel roof decking, paper-backed mesh, or metal rib lath. These lightweight concrete slabs are relatively easy to penetrate. Some types of lightweight concrete

Figures 17.12 a and b Arched roofs may conceal an attic space or be exposed from the interior. (a) From the exterior, there is no evidence of what the arched roof conceals. (b) An interior view shows the construction of the roof and the lack of protection if the roof is exposed to fire. *Photo b courtesy of Greg Terrill.*

can be penetrated with a hammer-head pick, power saw with concrete blade, jackhammer, or any other penetrating tool. These roofs are also very stable under fire conditions.

Metal

These roof coverings are made from several different kinds of metal and constructed in many styles. Light-gauge steel roof decks are most often supported on a framework of steel or wooden trusses **(Figure 17.13)**. Other types of corrugated roofing sheets are made from light-gauge cold-formed steel, galvanized sheet metal, or aluminum.

The light-gauge cold-formed steel sheets are used primarily for roofs of industrial buildings. Metal roofs on industrial buildings often have numerous roof openings such as skylights and hatches. Generally, metal roofs are lighter in weight per unit area than other types of roofs. Therefore, unless the supporting structure is weakened by fire, metal roofs may be less prone to collapse than other types of roofs. Metal roofs are a popular type when adding a pitched roof over an existing flat roof.

Lightweight Construction

Roof and floor construction in many commercial buildings no longer include conventional construction materials and designs. Conventional construction consisting of assemblies made of lumber has been replaced with what is called *lightweight construction*. In this type of construction, plywood panels (called *panelized roofing*) are supported by purlins (beams) between laminated wooden beams or gusseted wooden trusses that span from outside wall to outside wall **(Figure 17.14)**.

Figure 17.13 Lightweight steel roof decks are an economical solution when it is necessary to replace an existing composition shingle or flat roof. Metal roofs are found on both residential and commercial occupancies.

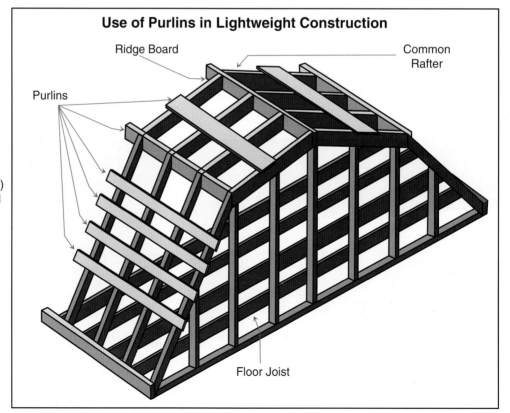

Use of Purlins in Lightweight Construction

Ridge Board

Common Rafter

Purlins

Floor Joist

Figure 17.14 Purlins (beams) are used in lightweight wood construction.

Conventional subfloor construction has been replaced by open web (diagonal member) trusses or wooden I beams. Compared to conventional construction, these systems are much lighter per unit area and are generally less prone to collapse. However, these lightweight components can fail rapidly when exposed to fire.

Roof or floor systems supported by open web trusses are prone to sudden and unexpected collapse if the unsupported bottom chord is subjected to downward force such as when firefighters inadvertently pull on them when pulling ceiling panels with pike poles.

According to the National Institute for Occupational Safety and Health (NIOSH), more than 60 percent of the roof systems in the U.S. are built using a truss system. By design, wooden truss systems contain a significant fuel load and are often hidden from sight. Fires in truss systems can burn for long periods before detection and can spread quickly across or through the trusses. Steel trusses are also prone to failure under fire conditions and may fail in less time than a wooden truss under the same conditions.

Building Components

Structures are not just composed of walls, floors, ceilings, and roofs. They also include electrical systems, plumbing systems, HVAC systems, and fire protection systems. While the company officer does not need to know the details of the electrical and plumbing systems, knowledge of HVAC and fire protection systems is essential. Because this knowledge is best obtained during preincident surveys, these systems are discussed in the Conducting Preincident Surveys section.

Preparing for Preincident Surveys

Good preparation for the preincident survey ensures that results will be valuable and the process will not inconvenience owners/occupants of the facility. The company officer should inform unit members in advance of the survey, discuss the survey process, list factors that should be considered during the survey, and assign duties if required.

Local policy may require, for instance, that one member of the unit remain with the apparatus during the survey. Communication between the company officer and the apparatus should be ensured in the event of an emergency dispatch.

The company officer should also prepare for the survey by gathering the tools and equipment that may be required for the inspection. If possible, the company officer should obtain a copy of the facility plot plan from the owners/occupants or the building code department.

Copies of the last code enforcement inspection and preincident survey should be consulted to provide a basis for identifying any changes or discrepancies during the survey. In addition, the company officer must contact the owners/occupants to explain the reason for the visit and establish a mutually acceptable time.

Consideration Factors

Preincident surveys are conducted to provide emergency response personnel with information about the occupancy that they will need should a fire or other emergency develop on the premises. During a survey, personnel should concentrate on the following factors:

- Where and how fires or other emergencies are most likely to occur
- How those emergencies are likely to develop
- What will likely happen as a result of a fire or emergency
- What will be needed in order to mitigate contingencies
- How building features such as fire walls and ventilation systems can be used to confine a fire to one section of the building
- What will be the best use of built-in fire protection systems such as automatic sprinklers
- What potential hazards to firefighter safety exist on the premises:
  — Hazardous materials or processes
  — High-voltage equipment
  — Unprotected openings
  — Metal-clad doors
  — Overhead power lines
  — Extreme elevation differences

- What firefighters will need to know about this occupancy in order to function safely if their vision is totally obscured by darkness and/or smoke

- Will the emergency services organization be adequately prepared to safely and successfully deal with the emergencies that are most likely to occur in this occupancy

- Will current strategic plans and tactical procedures be appropriate and adequate or will new ones need to be developed

- How a situation will change if the occupant load is significantly different from day to night

- Will an initial alarm assignment include sufficient resources

- Will specialized equipment or suppression agents be needed

- Will additional external resources or mutual aid be required

In some jurisdictions, the sheer number of commercial, multifamily residential, and industrial occupancies in each response area makes it virtually impossible for responsible companies to conduct preincident surveys in all of them. Therefore, companies must prioritize the occupancies to be surveyed.

The priorities are normally based on life-safety risk (including the risk to firefighters), property values at risk, and potential frequency and severity of fires or other emergencies occurring. Once these target hazards (occupancies with the highest priority) have been identified, the responsible companies can focus their efforts on those occupancies.

Facility Survey Equipment

Before a survey can be conducted, the company officer must be provided with the proper tools and equipment needed to gather and document the information necessary to develop a complete preincident plan. The equipment needed may vary depending upon what is specified in the organization's guidelines and the nature of the occupancy to be surveyed. However, most preincident survey kits (**Figures 17.15 a and b**) include the following supplies:

- *Writing equipment* — Tablet, pens, pencils, pencil sharpener, erasers, clipboard, and facility survey forms

- *Drawing equipment* — Engineering or graph paper, straightedge, and a copy of the NFPA standard symbols or those used by the organization

- *Other equipment* — Flashlight, water-pressure gauge, camera, and measuring tape or rangefinder

Figures 17.15 a and b Most preincident survey kits consist of (a) pencils, straightedges, erasers, a camera, tape measures, a flashlight, and (b) a water pressure gauge.

Members of the survey team will need at least one portable radio if they remain in service during the survey. They will also need appropriate personal protection such as helmets, eye protection, gloves, and hearing protection. Although some industrial facilities may provide safety glasses for visitors, company personnel should be properly equipped in the event the facility does not provide them.

Survey Schedules

In some fire and emergency services organizations, company officers are required to schedule their own preincident survey visits. In other organizations, scheduling is done by the battalion/district chief or a member of the administrative staff, and the company officer is merely informed of the arrangements. Either approach is acceptable. The former allows the company officer more control over the company's schedule, and the latter allows for an organization-wide coordination of effort. Regardless of who makes the arrangements, the visits should be scheduled at times that are convenient for the building owners/occupants **(Figure 17.16)**.

Figure 17.16 It is common courtesy to call the property owner/occupant and schedule the preincident survey at a time that is mutually acceptable to both parties.

For example, it would be counterproductive to schedule a preincident survey at a large retail store during the holiday shopping season. If owners/occupants are not unduly inconvenienced by the visit, they are more likely to cooperate with the survey team and be positively impressed with the effort. Even at the risk of inconveniencing the owners/occupants, however, visits should be scheduled at times that allow the survey team to obtain a realistic picture of activities that normally take place in the building and the normal number of occupants at various times of day and night.

Another consideration regarding the scheduling of preincident survey visits relates to the organization's fire and life-safety code enforcement activities. It would be unwise to schedule a preincident survey visit to any building that has had a recent code enforcement inspection — especially if the same personnel perform both functions. Owners/occupants may perceive the survey visit to be another inspection.

This misperception can make owners/occupants feel as though they are being harassed, so it is important to avoid this situation. For the same reason, it is also important that the company officer carefully explain to owners/occupants the reasons for the preincident survey, the planning process, and how owners/occupants will benefit.

To further increase community awareness, the organization should publicly announce that facility surveys will be conducted in specific areas. This announcement helps to promote the benefits of the program, prepare building owners/occupants for the surveys, and demonstrate that the organization is being proactive in attempting to improve fire safety and response capabilities.

Developing Positive Public Relations

Much of the success of the preincident planning program relies on establishing or fostering positive relationships from the time of arranging the preincident survey meeting to the time of contact with owners/occupants. Success also depends on the manner in which preincident survey team members conduct themselves and the image they project.

Survey teams must present a positive public image. Team members should stay together and conduct themselves in a professional and business-like manner throughout the survey. The company officer is responsible for ensuring that this process is performed.

Team members should be in a uniform appropriate to the situation. In mercantile and office buildings, clean and neat station uniforms are usually appropriate (**Figure 17.17**). In other occupancies, coveralls and safety equipment (helmets, safety glasses, etc.) may be needed. Generally, the mode of dress should be the uniform equivalent of what the owners/occupants wear.

The company officer must emphasize to the team that they are on the premises to do a job, not socialize among themselves or with owners/occupants of the facility. Team members should be friendly but not act as though the survey is a social visit. They should courteously answer any questions that are asked but avoid engaging in extended conversations that might keep owners/occupants from their work.

The survey may also be used as an opportunity to distribute fire and life-safety information. The information should be appropriate to the type of occupancy or a public education topic such as changing batteries in smoke detectors.

Fire and emergency services organizations that possess thermal imaging (infrared) cameras may want to consider using the devices as instructional aids during the survey. The device can be used to show owners/occupants potentially hazardous items such as electrical wiring that is overheated. It is also an opportunity for unit members to practice using the device (**Figure 17.18**).

Conducting Preincident Surveys

The company preincident survey process is usually based on an established procedure defined by the organization. The process varies between organizations and jurisdictions. Some organizations require that upon arrival at the survey location, company members remain at the apparatus while the company officer contacts the owners/occupants, confirms the appointment,

Figure 17.17 Because the company officer and unit members are representatives of the jurisdiction, it is important for them to dress and act in a professional way.

Figure 17.18 A thermal imaging (infrared) camera can be an effective tool for determining the existence and location of an electrical short or overloaded electrical circuit.

and reviews the survey procedure. The officer should inform the owners/occupants of how many company members will be involved in the facility survey and request any assistance the team may need **(Figure 17.19)**.

The company officer should also explain that (while the facility survey is not a code enforcement inspection) any serious fire or life-safety hazards found will have to be corrected. When serious hazards are found, the best approach is to attempt to obtain an on-the-spot correction and follow up with a memo to the fire prevention and inspection division. If compliance cannot be obtained, a fire inspector should be notified.

Preincident surveys should be made in a systematic and logical approach. Generally, the survey is divided between the exterior and interior of the structure. At a large facility such as a chemical plant, the survey may start with the exterior of the main plant building, proceed to the interior of the building, and then extend to other surrounding structures on the site.

During the survey, the company officer and crew members should note building components as they encounter them and remain focused on the consideration factors listed earlier. Specifically, they should look at ventilation systems, fire protection systems, and water supplies. While making the survey, firefighter safety hazards, structural conditions, fuel loading, and property conservation should also be considered.

Survey information may be gathered in a variety of methods, including checklists, written essay-style commentaries, sketches, photographs, or videos.

Survey Information Records

In order to collect and maintain the raw data during surveys, the company officer can rely on a variety of tools. First, information may be recorded on a form that collects specific information. This approach improves the chance that essential information is gathered. Second, field sketches should be made of the structure or facility showing its size, location, and components.

Finally, photographs or videos may be made of the structure or facility. The making of photographs and videos, however, must be with the express permission of the owners/occupants. Some processes and areas may be considered private by owners/occupants, and photographs may not be permitted in those locations.

Field Sketches

A *field sketch* is a rough drawing of a building that is prepared during the facility survey **(Figure 17.20, p. 394)**. This drawing should show general information about building dimensions and other related outside information such as the locations of fire hydrants, streets, water tanks, and distances to nearby exposures. All of the basic information for survey drawings that accompany the survey report should be shown on field sketches, but not all of the details need to be included.

Making field sketches on graph paper makes it easier to draw them to scale. Drawing to scale is not absolutely necessary but it helps to keep the drawing in proportion. This procedure will make it easier to transfer the information onto the survey drawings.

Photography

The organization should make the decisions on when and how to use photography in the preincident survey process. Some organizations choose to supplement their preincident survey sketches with

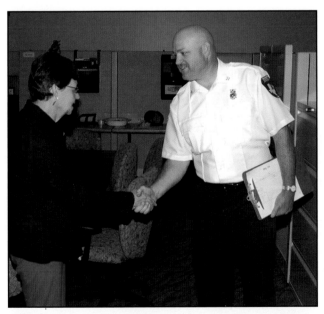

Figure 17.19 The first step in the preincident survey is to meet with the owner/occupant at the appointed time. No attempt to survey the facility should be made without the owner/occupant's knowledge.

photographs or videos. Using photography can provide some distinct advantages over sketches alone. Taking a photo or video is much faster than making a sketch, particularly when the subject is complicated. Also, a photograph will capture every visible detail. On the other hand, a photograph may capture too much detail and actually obscure the essential information in the picture.

Digital cameras can be used to create, edit, store, and reproduce photographs quickly and economically. Graphic symbols can be added to the photographs and images can be inserted into the preincident plan. Organizations that use apparatus-mounted computers can maintain all the necessary information for rapid retrieval during a response.

Videos can show relationships between buildings, manufacturing processes, and how the facility might appear as someone moves through it.

Videos and photographs can be used as training aids for other personnel who may respond to the facility in an emergency. Training scenarios can be based on the decisions that a responder would make while viewing a segment of a video.

Facility Exterior

After initial contact with the owners/occupants, company members can begin the exterior survey of the facility or building. Primarily, the exterior facility survey focuses on obtaining the necessary information to create a plot plan or compare observations to an existing plot plan. Buildings should be measured and their dimensions recorded, including distances from each building to exposures **(Figure 17.21)**. Note on the plot plan the locations of the following items:

- Fire hydrants and valves (see Fire Protection Systems and Water Supplies sections)
- Sprinkler and standpipe connections (see Fire Protection Systems and Water Supplies sections)
- Utility controls (shutoffs)
- Fences and landscaping
- Power lines
- Obstructions to property or structure access or egress
- Underground storage tanks
- Doors, windows, and fire escapes

Figure 17.20 Field sketches are created to show the relationship of structures on the site and means of access to them.

Figure 17.21 Tape measures or tape-measuring wheels can be used to obtain the exterior dimensions of the structure when developing a plot plan.

- Ornamental facings, awnings, or marquees
- Types of roof coverings that are visible from the exterior
- Heavy objects on roofs that are visible from the exterior
- Locations of gathering points for evacuating occupants

The exterior of a building is not a good vantage point for gathering building construction information. Many buildings are faced with brick or stone or covered with aluminum siding.

Site access is important and should be noted on the survey plot plan. Access information on items such as parking lots, driveways, bridges, and gates should be gathered along with information about any exposures. Private roadways and bridges do not always meet the weight requirements that are necessary on public thoroughfares for emergency apparatus.

Fire lanes may consist of solid-surface roads or marked lanes constructed with concrete egg-crate-shaped modules that are covered by grass and indistinguishable from regular turf. Alleyways may be narrow and have overhead obstructions, including exterior metal-frame fire escapes that can create barriers to emergency apparatus.

Fire protection systems in private structures must also be noted along with water supply sources and access capabilities to yard hydrants (privately owned) and valves located on private property. See Fire Protection Systems and Water Supplies sections for more information.

Building Interior

After the facility exterior has been surveyed, company personnel may move to either the building's top floor (or roof if it is accessible) or lowest floor (basement, subbasement, or ground floor) **(Figure 17.22)**. Unless dictated by organizational policy, the starting point for the interior survey is a matter of personal preference, but most people prefer to start on the top floor or roof.

Personnel then conduct the interior survey systematically working either upward or downward. They draw floor plans of each floor to show the locations of permanent walls, partitions,

fixtures, and machinery. Furniture should not be included on floor plans because their locations are not fixed.

The locations of any vertical shafts and horizontal openings should be noted. The locations of any fire protection equipment such as standpipe or sprinkler control valves should be included on the floor plan as should any occupant life-safety information (such as exit doors, fire control centers, fire extinguishers, or safe areas where occupants may be sheltered in place). See the Fire Protection Systems section for more information.

Life-safety information is collected in two basic topic areas: protection and evacuation of occupants and protection of firefighters (see the following section). Information about occupant protection that should be gathered and recorded during the interior survey includes the following:

- Locations and number of exits
- Locations of escalators and elevators

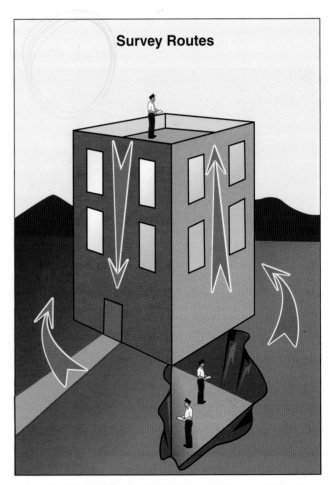

Figure 17.22 Structures may be surveyed internally from either top to bottom or bottom to top.

- Locations of windows and other openings suitable for rescue access

- Special evacuation considerations for disabled occupants, very old or very young occupants, and large numbers of occupants

- Locations of areas of safe refuge

- Flammable and toxic interior finishes or processes

Firefighter Safety Hazards

As survey personnel collect and record information about occupant life safety, they should also be gathering information about conditions in the building that may threaten their own safety **(Figures 17.23 a and b)**. Some of the potential life hazards to firefighters that should be noted are the following:

- Flammable and combustible liquids

- Toxic chemicals

- Biological hazards

Hazard Communications Symbols*	
Symbol	**Description**
	Biological Hazard
	Chemical Hazard
	Nuclear/Radiological Hazard
	Carcinogen/Cancer Hazard

* These symbols may be presented in a variety of colors and/or formats. For example, they will not always be seen in the center of a circle or rectangle.

b

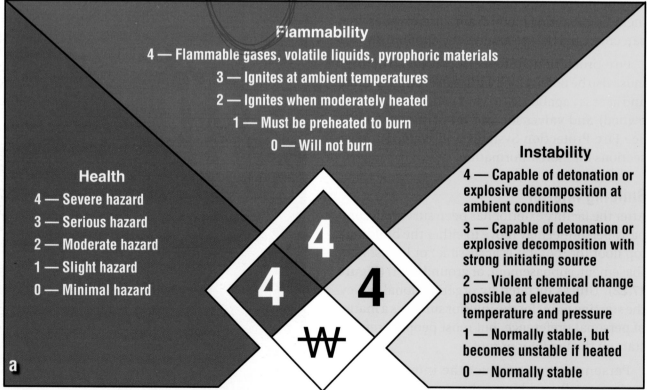

Figures 17.23 a and b Company officers should be familiar with the various types of hazard signage that may be present in the facilities they survey. Examples: (a) NFPA 704, *System for the Identification of the Hazards of Materials for Emergency Response,* numerical ratings and (b) hazard communications symbols.

- Explosives

- Reactive metals

- Radioactive materials

- Manufacturing processes that are inherently dangerous

Company personnel should also note building conditions that may present or contribute to hazardous situations. During the survey, the company officer should also record the materials and items that are not part of the structure but that contribute to the structure's fuel load.

Building Conditions

In addition to collecting and recording information about the contents of a building, the physical condition of the structure should also be noted. Conditions that may be hazardous to emergency responders during a fire include the following:

- Structural components that may fail during a fire or during high wind conditions

- Construction materials that might lose their strength when exposed to fire (unprotected steel, for example)

- Lightweight wood construction features

- Unsupported partitions or walls

- Roof construction that could fail quickly when exposed to fire or heavy loads such as a large snowfall

- Stacked or high-piled storage

- Heavy objects on roofs or suspended from interior roof structures that could cause roofs to collapse

- Heavy equipment that may fall through floors or cause floors to collapse

- Transformers and high-voltage electrical equipment vaults

- Large open areas (**Figure 17.24**)

- Building features that may confuse or trap firefighters during a fire such as the following:

  — Dead-end corridors or hallways

  — Open vats, pits, or shafts

  — Openings into underground utility shafts or tunnels

  — Multilevel floor arrangements

  — Mazelike room divisions or partitions

  — Alterations that disguise the original construction

Fuel Loads

The term *fuel load* represents the bulk of fuel available to burn and generally refers to the contents of a building. Because the materials used in the construction of most modern commercial and mercantile buildings contribute relatively little fuel to a fire, the major fuel sources are furnishings and other building contents.

When company officers observe and record the fuel load of buildings during preincident surveys (and subsequently devise plans for dealing with fires that may feed on this load), they are primarily

Figure 17.24 Open atriums may contribute to the spread of fire or toxic gases throughout a structure. New structures with this type of design will likely have fire-alarm, fire-detection, and automatic sprinkler systems in place to reduce the potential for fire spread.

addressing the fire-control considerations of preincident planning. See **Appendix I** for fire-flow calculation methods.

Because different materials behave differently during a fire, different fire-control procedures may have to be used depending upon what is burning. Therefore, knowing what combustibles a building contains can have a profound effect on firefighter safety and the tactics and strategies employed during a fire.

It may be impossible to identify a building's contents after a fire starts, so it is imperative that this information be gathered during preincident surveys. This practice is especially important in buildings where toxic, highly flammable, or explosive materials are stored or used. During preincident surveys, company officers should be sure to document the existence of large quantities of the following materials:

- Plastics
- Aerosols
- Compressed gases
- Explosives
- Flammable and combustible liquids
- Combustible dusts
- Corrosive/water-reactive materials

In today's society, most fuel loads are composed primarily of hydrocarbons, synthetics, and polyurethanes that contribute to a significant amount of heat release **(Figure 17.25)**. It is uncommon to find 100 percent of materials made from wood in structures. In these situations, the company officer must consider the following factors when conducting a preincident survey:

- Complexity of materials found in occupancies
- Possible need to conduct an aggressive initial fire attack
- Estimated burn time before arrival of first response units

The company officer should utilize the guidance of an owner/occupant (or representative) to assist in the determination of materials stored, their distribution within the structure, and any hazards they may cause. This person can also provide the necessary information on occupant policies regarding shutting down processes and production lines, fire-control procedures, and evacuation procedures and routes.

Ventilation Systems

Many types of structures, from single-family dwellings to large industrial buildings, have some form of climate control or HVAC system. These systems range from relatively small window-mounted units to huge commercial units that are as large as some small buildings. While the potential hazards to firefighters associated with large commercial units are widely recognized, even the small window-mounted units can be hazardous under certain conditions.

Figure 17.25 Products that are stored in warehouses may be tightly packed on high-stack storage racks or shelves, resulting in extreme concentrations of fuel loads. Some building codes require that high-stack products be protected by sprinkler systems within the shelving.

Therefore, firefighters must be familiar with the various types of HVAC systems in general and specific types of systems installed in buildings within their response areas **(Figure 17.26)**. Because HVAC systems can be used during emergency operations to remove contaminated atmospheres from a structure, company personnel should become familiar with the various types of HVAC systems and their operations.

The survey should also identify any built-in ventilation devices that can be used to control a fire or remove hazardous atmospheres from the structure. Finally, the company officer should be aware of any underflow air distribution systems that may be present.

HVAC Systems

While there are different types of systems used to control the climate within buildings, the ones of greatest interest to firefighters are the HVAC systems. The equipment in this category includes everything from small built-in fans and gas-fueled furnaces to heavy-duty combination units built into large residential, institutional, mercantile, and industrial structures. In general, the smaller the unit is, the smaller the potential risk is to firefighters.

For example, a window-mounted air conditioner may pose only two risks: electrical shock from a wiring short and physical injury if the unit falls from the window. Both risks may be easily controlled by turning off the electricity and removing the unit from the window when the surrounding structure has lost its ability to support it. For their own safety and that of others, firefighters need to be familiar with all of the various systems.

One reason that the acronym *HVAC* came into use was because the equipment needed to perform these three functions is often combined into a single system. This configuration produces significant savings because only one system of ducts is needed for all three functions. A common system of ductwork can have both positive and negative effects on structure fires.

On the positive side, HVAC ducts can be used to aid ventilating a burning building by expelling smoke from within the building — both during a fire and after it has been extinguished. On the

Figure 17.26 HVAC equipment may be located in mechanical rooms, in spaces within structures, on roofs of structures (as shown), or at ground level near structures.

negative side, if HVAC ducts are not controlled, smoke and fire can spread throughout a building through the ducts. Therefore controlling the HVAC ducts can be a critical element in successfully attacking and extinguishing a structure fire. Many HVAC ducts are equipped with fire/smoke detectors that automatically close dampers within the ducts during a fire.

Large built-in HVAC units can also be extremely hazardous to firefighters. Large commercial units increase the potential for structural collapse because some extremely heavy rooftop units were installed on old buildings that were not originally designed for the additional dead load.

Because of their sheer weight, HVAC units can crash down onto the floor below if the roof assembly supporting these massive units is weakened by fire. This collapse sometimes sets off a chain reaction in multistory buildings — each floor fails when the one above collapses onto it. Lacking the support of the floor assemblies between them, outer walls may then collapse inward onto the debris of the floors and roof. Outer walls can also suddenly collapse in an inward/outward pattern.

Correct and effective use of an HVAC system can limit the spread of smoke and fire gases, improve operating conditions for firefighters, and increase the likelihood of survival for building occupants. Although the actual manipulation of a building's HVAC system for smoke control should be left to the building engineer, firefighters should have an understanding of the HVAC system's capabilities and limitations. The building engineer should be consulted during preincident planning to help firefighters work more effectively with the engineer to use the system to best advantage during a fire. See Chapter 20, Incident Scene Operations, for more information on ventilation.

Built-In Ventilation Devices

Besides the HVAC system, some types of structures are equipped with built-in ventilation devices that are designed to limit the spread of fire, release heated fire gases, or control smoke and contaminated atmospheres. Roof and wall vents and curtain boards are most common in large buildings having wide, unbroken expanses of floor space. The standard that provides guidelines for the design and installation of smoke and heat venting equipment, NFPA 204, *Standard for Smoke and Heat Venting* (2002/2006), recommends using automatic heat-activated roof vents and curtain boards.

The existence of each of these devices should be noted in the preincident survey. Company officers need to become familiar with the specific types in use in their local areas. The various types of vents and curtain boards are described as follows:

- *Automatic roof and wall vents* — Release heat and smoke to the outside through vents that work automatically and are placed at the highest point of a roof or wall to limit the spread of fire within a building (**Figure 17.27**). Although some are now activated by smoke detectors, most still operate through the use of fusible links connected to spring-loaded or counterweighted cover assemblies. Operating sprinklers may slow

or prevent the activation of automatic roof vents. If they do not open automatically, firefighters will have to open them manually with manual-release mechanisms. *Characteristics:*

  - *Fusible links:* Separate when their designed fusing temperature is reached, allowing vent covers to open

  - *Automatic locking devices:* Ensure that vent covers remain open, even in gusty winds

- *Atrium vents* — Release heat and smoke from atriums (large, vertical openings in the center of structures such as high-rise hotels and office buildings) to the outside. Building codes in most areas require that atriums be equipped with automatic vents that are usually designed to be activated by either smoke or heat detectors.

- *Monitors* — Release heat and smoke to the outside from square or rectangular structures that usually penetrate the roofs of single-story buildings but may be found on high-rise buildings as well. They may have metal, glass, wired glass, or louvered sides. Monitors with solid walls should have at least two opposite sides hinged at the bottom and held closed at the top with a fusible link that allows them to fall open by gravity in case of fire. Those with glass sides rely upon the glass breaking to provide ventilation in case of a fire. If a fire does not generate enough heat to break the glass, it will have to be removed by firefighters.

- *Skylights* — Ventilate heat and smoke in the event of fire. Those equipped with thermoplastic panels or ordinary window glass can act as automatic vents because the temperature of a fire will melt the plastic or break the glass (**Figure 17.28**). Skylights without thermoplastic panels or automatic venting will have to be removed or glass panes will have to be broken. In skylights equipped with wired glass, panes may have to be removed from their frames.

- *Curtain boards* — Consist of fire-resistive half-walls (also known as *draft curtains*) that extend down from the underside of a roof to limit the horizontal spread of heat and smoke by confining them to a relatively small area directly over their sources (**Figure 17.29**). Curtain boards also concentrate heat and smoke directly under

Figure 17.27 Automatic vents may be located at the highest point of a roof or high on an exterior wall as shown here.

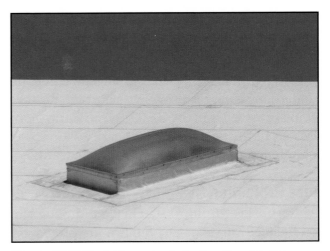

Figure 17.28 Skylights made of plastic will melt in fire or high-heat conditions, permitting the area to ventilate automatically.

Figure 17.29 Curtain boards or draft curtains are designed to prevent the spread of smoke and gases at the ceiling level. They work in conjunction with automatic roof vents.

automatic roof vents to accelerate the vents' activation and may also accelerate the activation of automatic sprinklers in the area. *Characteristics:*

— Extend generally a distance equal to at least 20 percent of the vertical distance from the floor to the roof but not lower than 10 feet (3 m) above the floor

— Areas encompassed will generally be those containing critical industrial processes and/or concentrations of flammable liquids or other hazardous materials with high fire potential

Underfloor Air Distribution Systems

Recent advances in HVAC system design have resulted in new ways of providing climate control in structures. The underfloor air distribution (UFAD)

system is one approach that is beginning to appear in newly constructed buildings and major structural renovations. The system introduces thermostatically controlled air into the space through openings in the floor. There are no overhead ducts or return air plenums, which allows an increase in ceiling heights. Return air passes through sidewall vents located adjacent to the HVAC system mechanical room.

Some architects and designers have raised a concern that UFADS pose a life-safety risk. If smoke is developing under a floor, it will be distributed into the space at floor level. As a deterrent, model building codes require smoke detectors in each space as well as in the mechanical rooms. Smoke detectors are not currently required in the UFAD distribution system.

Another concern is that water may enter the underfloor area, resulting in a short circuit that could cause a fire in the UFAD's electrical system. Design and installation must meet all existing code requirements to reduce this potential hazard.

Fire Protection Systems

An important item to be checked during the preincident survey is any built-in fire protection equipment or system. Because the survey is not a code-enforcement inspection, there is no need for the survey team to test this equipment, but rather merely note its presence and condition and evaluate its usefulness during a fire on the premises. Naturally, if the team observes some condition that would reduce the effectiveness of such equipment such as stock piled in a way that blocks one or more sprinklers, the situation should be reported to the owners/occupants. Suggestions for corrective actions should be included.

During the survey, personnel should remain focused on the primary mission of gathering information that will be needed by fire-suppression forces during a fire or other emergency on the premises. Some examples would be the need for specialized hose adapters or possible obstructions that may require greater lengths of fire hose.

For purposes of developing a preincident plan for the premises, the survey team should pay particular attention to the absence or locations and conditions of the following systems:

- *Fixed fire-extinguishing systems* — Include automatic sprinklers, carbon dioxide, dry chemical, halon-substitute flooding systems, etc., which may reduce the need for interior attack hoselines, but may increase the need for system support

- *Standpipe systems* — Include all classes of wet- and dry-pipe systems that permit the use of hoselines on upper floors and in remote areas of large-area structures; may allow firefighters to carry hose packs into a building rather than lay long attack hoselines from an engine outside

- *Fire detection and alarm systems* — Include all types of automatic detection systems for smoke, carbon monoxide, low oxygen content, and other situations that result in a toxic atmosphere and all types of systems used to alert occupants to the need to evacuate a structure or area. *Benefits:*

  — Fires can be detected and reported earlier

  — First-in units can arrive sooner

  — Firefighters could face smaller fires than might develop in the absence of such systems

The locations of specific items that should be included on the plot plan are as follows:

- Exterior fire department sprinkler and standpipe connections

- Pressure reducing valves

- Yard hydrants

- Sprinkler control and shutoff valves

- Types and quantity of spare sprinkler heads

- Fire pumps

- Fixed monitors and deluge devices

- Tanks containing extinguishing agents such as foam

- Interior standpipe connections and hose cabinets

- Types and sizes of standpipe hose connections

- Fire detection and alarm control panels or fire control centers (**Figure 17.30**)

- Self-closing fire doors

Water Supplies

Another critically important aspect of preincident planning relates to water supplies. Because water is still the cheapest, most widely available extinguishing agent, it will be the primary extinguishing agent used in most cases. If a facility is protected with sprinkler or standpipe systems, the required water supply should have been determined during the design and installation of the systems. However, changes in the demand for water, such as the construction of additional buildings using the same supply line, can reduce the actual water supply available to a facility.

Figure 17.30 The locations of fire alarm and detection panels or fire control rooms must be included on the plot plan.

Determining the availability and reliability of water supplies are key elements in the development of any preincident plan. The preincident survey of any given occupancy should gather the following water supply information:

• Locations of all water supplies

— Auxiliary water supplies

— Private water supply systems such as impounded bodies of water or wells

• Locations of water-system interconnections

— Hydrants, including hydrant main intake facing roadway **(Figure 17.31)**

— Fire protection system flow meters and alarms

— Other water-demand systems such as high-water demand processes that connect to the supply system

• Required fire flow based on construction type and fuel load information or on calculations done by owners/occupants

• Water supply system pressure (determined by reading the pressure at hydrants with a pitot gauge while flowing water from them)

• Available fire flow (determined by flowing a hydrant and determining water flow rates based on the pressure readings at the hydrant)

Figure 17.31 The company officer should also determine the locations and conditions of fire hydrants in the immediate area of the surveyed site. Obstructions should also be noted in the survey.

• Reliability of water supplies (determined by reading the water pressure at a variety of hydrants while simultaneously flowing water from them)

• Water supply utilization methods (how water is used and distributed within the facility)

The sizes and locations of water mains serving the occupancy should be determined. The public works department can provide this information based on the municipality's water atlas, a *map book* or online database of all waterlines in the jurisdiction.

Property Conservation

Another major consideration to be addressed during preincident surveys is property conservation. While conducting facility surveys, company officers and crew members should continuously ask themselves what can be done before a fire occurs and while it is being controlled in order to reduce property loss.

They should start by identifying the building's contents with the highest value. Depending upon the occupancy, these high-value items may include files and records, electronic equipment, machinery, merchandise, antiques, or any irreplaceable items. Such items may require that special salvage procedures be developed. For additional information on this topic, see the IFSTA **Fireground Support Operations** manual.

A major property conservation consideration that should be addressed during preincident surveys is the use of water as the primary extinguishing agent. Regardless of whether water is likely to be delivered by an automatic sprinkler system or fire department hoselines, its possible effects must be assessed.

In many cases, water used to extinguish a fire can do more damage than the fire itself. In addition to the damage that can be done to papers, books, and electronic equipment, a large quantity of water absorbed by materials in the building increases its weight and can threaten the building's structural integrity.

Dealing with this potentially significant safety consideration as well as the property conservation issue requires careful planning to avoid undesirable outcomes. A building may contain design features such as floor drains, scuppers, or other drains that can help prevent the accumulation of water. Stairways, halls, and other passages through which large volumes of water (including contaminated runoff) may be channeled to the outside should be noted during the surveys.

Managing Preincident Data

The three major tasks with any preincident plan involve gathering the data, entering the data into databases, and keeping the data current. Systems must be developed for managing the data that is gathered during site surveys and then used to produce preincident operational plans.

Some organizations use computer programs such as Computer-Aided Management of Emergency Operations (CAMEO®) to manage data regarding hazardous materials. Similar software is designed to assist in planning for other types of emergency responses, including Mapping

Applications for Response, Planning, and Local Operational Tasks (MARPLOT®). Programs such as FIREHOUSE Software® can be used to store and retrieve data relating to particular occupancies.

For organizations that have the necessary hardware, these computer programs can make the process of managing large quantities of preincident planning data much easier and make the information much more accessible when it is needed during an emergency. Essential data can be transmitted from the communications center to computer terminals mounted in apparatus responding to or on the scene. The following types of information can be transmitted:

- Directions to the scene
- Names of cross streets
- Locations of hydrants and other water supplies
- Water flow rates
- Unusual hazards on site
- Emergency phone numbers

However, even these sophisticated computer programs are only as good as the data they contain. When data are current, they can be extremely useful tools for incident commanders and company officers. But if the data is inaccurate or out of date, it may not only be useless, but it may even be dangerous.

Other organizations use hard-copy systems that usually consist of one or more binders filled with loose-leaf pages that contain essential information on the target hazards within the response area. They may be indexed by street address, business name, or some other method. These systems may be based on NFPA 1620 or a similar planning guide. These hard-copy systems, just like the computer-based programs, must also be kept current to be useful.

Businesses remodel or expand their facilities, add or eliminate equipment or processes, increase or reduce the amount of materials on the premises, or move to different locations. Any of these changes can invalidate existing preincident plans on these occupancies unless the plans are updated to reflect the changes.

In some areas, the business license and/or building permit processes help fire and emergency services organizations stay informed of business activity in their response areas. When people want to start businesses, they are required to apply for a business license. The application process is intended to identify the type of business to be conducted as well as provide information regarding materials and processes that will be part of the operation.

The licensing agency reviews business permit applications to ensure that the types of businesses are allowed in the proposed locations and all zoning, environmental, health, fire protection, and life-safety requirements have been met. The same requirements are true for individuals applying for building permits. Building permits are required for new construction and remodeling of existing structures.

The responsible agency reviews building plans to ensure that all code requirements are met. Both business license and building permit applications should be reviewed by the fire department so that information about new businesses and structures within the response area can be obtained.

One of the best ways of identifying changes in any business or building within the response area is by having the local fire company document and report any changes they observe in the course of their daily activities. These changes can then be reflected on any preincident plans that may have been developed for an affected occupancy. Building codes can provide guidance in determining a facility's primary occupancy use as opposed to the original intended use.

Developing Preincident Plans

Once the on-site visit is complete, the company officer is responsible for processing the information gathered by either using it to develop a preincident plan or forwarding it to those responsible for developing the plan. Preincident planning may involve a collective effort by all levels within the organization. The success of the entire preincident planning process depends upon the ability of the company to conduct adequate preincident surveys and the company officer's ability to process information and complete accurately written reports.

There are two general schools of thought about what should and should not be included in a preincident plan. Each of these approaches has certain advantages and disadvantages.

The first approach assumes that all interior structure fires behave in generally the same way and this behavior is predictable unless there is something in the fire environment to cause it to behave differently. Those who subscribe to this approach do not believe that a large volume of data about the building and its contents are necessary. Beyond certain essential information such as the basic floor plan and locations of utility controls, they only want to know what will make this fire behave differently than any other fire in a similar structure.

This approach has the advantage of being simple to develop, use, and maintain. Some incident commanders prefer this type of plan because they do not have to filter the essential information they need from many pages of extraneous data. The key to using this approach successfully is ensuring that the plan contains all essential data and enough additional information to make it complete. However, even with this *essentials-only* approach, the larger the structure and more complex the occupancy, the more data are needed to develop a complete plan (**Figure 17.32, p. 406**).

The other approach to preincident plan development is much more involved and structured (**Figure 17.33, p. 407**). It is more involved because the volume of information gathered on each structure and occupancy surveyed is extensive. It is more structured in that the same items of information are gathered on every structure and occupancy surveyed, regardless of how similar or different the structures are from each other.

The main advantage of this approach is that the likelihood of some critical item of information being omitted from the plan is extremely low. However, it may take the incident commander a considerable amount of time and effort during an emergency to find the critical information within a large mass of data.

Included in the preincident plan development process is the creation of illustrations of the floor and plot plans and elevations of the structure or facility, writing a survey report, and then con-

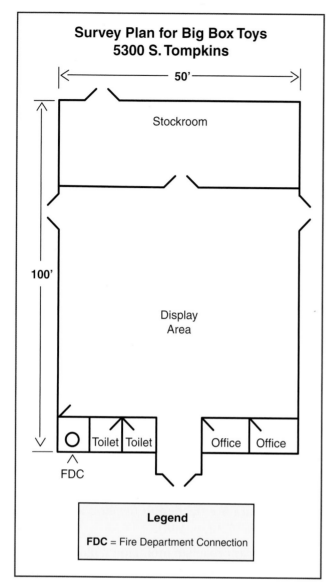

Figure 17.32 Survey plan showing only essential information.

verting the report into a preincident plan that can be easily used at an incident.

Facility Survey Drawings

While some of the information gathered during a preincident survey is compiled in the form of a written report, information about the building layout is more effectively described by a drawing or series of drawings that are included in the preincident plan. Three general types of drawings used to show building information are described as follows:

- *Plot plans* — Indicate how buildings are situated with respect to other buildings and streets in the area (**Figure 17.34a, p. 408**)

- *Floor plans* — Show the layout of individual floors, subfloors, and roofs (**Figure 17.34b, p. 409**)

- *Elevations* — Show side views of structures that depict the number of floors in buildings and grades of the surrounding ground (**Figure 17.34c, p. 409**)

Most building details can be shown on a floor plan drawing. When the survey is of a relatively small building, all the information can often be shown on one drawing. As the building size or complexity increases, the number of drawings needed to show the necessary detail clearly will also increase.

Every drawing or page of a set should be labeled with a title that clearly indicates the type of information that is included. The drawings should also include the date they were created. Producing the three types of drawings is a two-step process: making field sketches during the survey and then creating report drawings for the written report that is included in the preincident plan.

The drawings must be drawn to scale and show the essential details of the building and its surroundings. The details should be shown using the standard mapping symbols adopted by the organization. If a drawing is not labeled, a legend explaining the symbols must be included. If an item must be included for which there is no standard symbol, it should be indicated by a circled numeral. The numeral is then identified and explained in the legend.

The final drawing should be as visually simple as possible. Incident commanders must be able to determine the essential information quickly and do not have time to search through a multitude of details on the drawing.

Written Reports

After all drawings and any photographs have been compiled and labeled, a clear, concise written report must be prepared. In most cases, the cover of the report includes such basic information as the address of the building or occupancy, date of the facility survey, type of building, and name of the submitting officer. The form and content of the written report will be dictated by local policy.

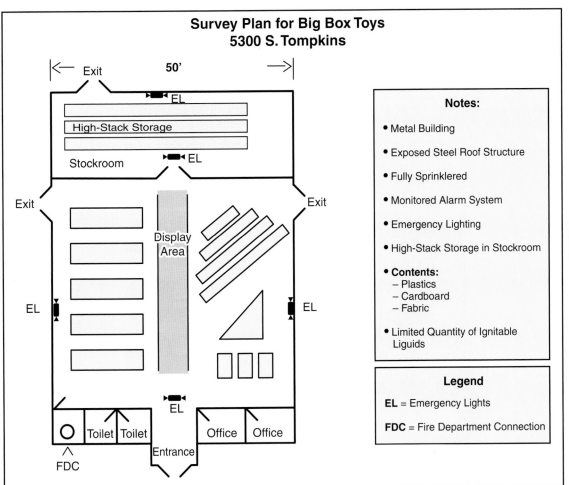

Survey Plan for Big Box Toys
5300 S. Tompkins

50'

Exit

EL

High-Stack Storage

Stockroom

EL

Exit

Exit

Display Area

EL

EL

Toilet | Toilet

Office | Office

EL

FDC

Entrance

Notes:

• Metal Building

• Exposed Steel Roof Structure

• Fully Sprinklered

• Monitored Alarm System

• Emergency Lighting

• High-Stack Storage in Stockroom

• **Contents:**
   – Plastics
   – Cardboard
   – Fabric

• Limited Quantity of Ignitable Liguids

Legend

EL = Emergency Lights

FDC = Fire Department Connection

Figure 17.33
Detailed survey plan.

As mentioned earlier, if organizational policy dictates that preincident plans contain only information that indicates how this occupancy is different from others, the written report should reflect that information. If policy dictates that the same type of information be included for each occupancy surveyed, the written report should give that information.

The detailed written report, containing all the information, sketches, photos, and videos, should be retained by the company officer and copies forwarded to the battalion/district chief, training division, inspections division, or other administrative office determined by local policy. The report then becomes the basis for the preincident plan.

Preincident Plans

The preincident plan should contain the essential information that will assist in the development of an incident action plan (IAP). The plan should be reproduced in a format that is easy to access and read. If the preincident plan is maintained in hardcopy format and kept in a Preplan Book in each of the apparatus, it may be one or two pages.

The address, cross streets, and business name or other identifying information should be at the top of the page. Occupancy type, construction type, hydrant locations, private fire protection systems, and special hazards can be listed in groups by topic for easy reference. The plot plan with access to the facility indicated on it should be on the main page or on a page of its own when it is very detailed.

When the preincident plan is maintained on a mobile data terminal (MDT) in the apparatus, the information should be organized in a similar fashion. The MDT can provide additional links to information specific to hazards that may be stored or used at each facility. The various electronic databases used to create these plans were provided in the Managing Preincident Data section.

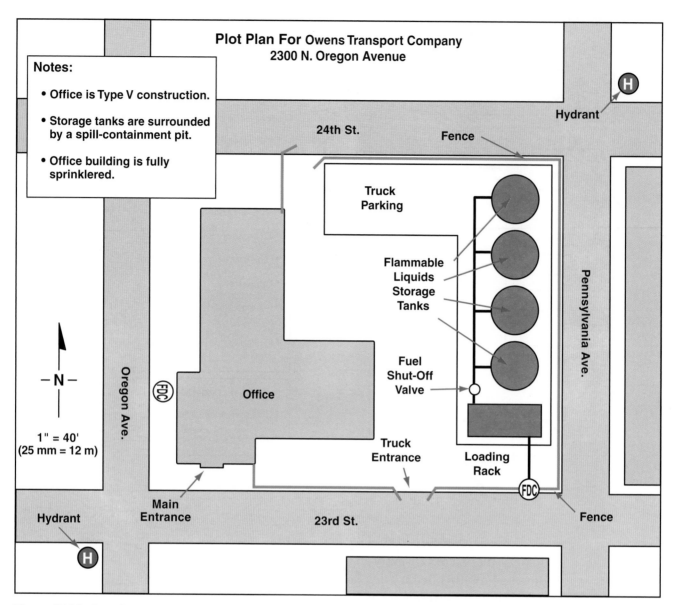

Figure 17.34a Sample plot plan depicting the structure and all adjacent streets, hydrants, structures, and access points.

Summary

The safety and effectiveness of emergency operations can be greatly enhanced when emergency responders have comprehensive and up-to-date information about the occupancies in which they may be required to operate. The more information they have, and the more reliable that information is, the better. The best way for this information to be gathered and transformed into a plan that will be useful during a fire or other emergency is through preincident surveys that involve company officers and members of their companies.

The preincident planning process provides reasonably accurate information and firsthand knowledge of structures or facilities for personnel who will be responding in the event of an emergency in the structure or facilities. At the same time, it trains personnel to recognize building construction types, fire protection system components, and building contents and manufacturing processes. A current and well-written preincident plan gives the company officer and members of the unit the information they need to devise and implement a successful IAP at the scene.

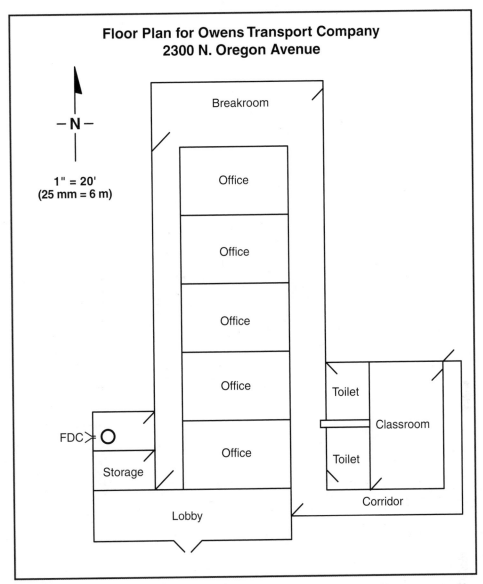

Figure 17.34b Sample floor plan indicating the access doors, interior wall arrangements, and other information.

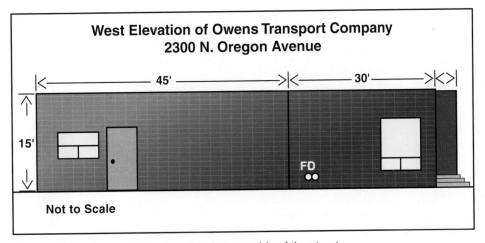

Figure 17.34c Sample elevation showing one side of the structure.

Incident Scene Communications

Chapter Contents

Learning Objectives

1. Recall information about interoperability.

2. Select facts about various types of communications equipment.

3. Identify correct radio communications procedures.

4. Select facts about the five *C*s of radio communication.

Job Performance Requirements

This chapter provides information that addresses the following job performance requirements of NFPA 1021, *Standard for Fire Officer Professional Qualifications* (2003):

Chapter 4 Fire Officer I

4.2.1(A)

Effective communication is critically important if emergency scene activities are to be conducted safely and efficiently. Company officers play a very important role in a fire and emergency services organization's incident scene communications because they transmit and receive the majority of incident scene messages.

Whenever the situation allows, the preferred method of communication is direct, face-to-face voice communication. However, the variety of environments in which firefighters and emergency responders must attempt to communicate usually makes it necessary for them to use some form of electronic communications.

Because each form of emergency scene communication has certain advantages and disadvantages, no one method or system is optimally effective in every situation. This situation means that emergency scene communications may involve everything from face-to-face oral communication to the use of very sophisticated satellite communication systems.

This chapter acquaints company officers with the issue of interoperability as well as the types of communications equipment they will be expected to use and proper procedures for using this equipment. This chapter discusses fire and emergency services radios, pagers, and alternative communications methods along with advanced technology communications systems.

Interoperability

Interoperability is the ability of a system to work with and use the parts or equipment of another system and is part of the requirements in the National Incident Management System (NIMS). When ap-

plied to communications at all fire and emergency services operations, interoperability means that radio equipment and frequencies must be compatible within the organization and between agencies. Coordinated responses to emergencies also require effective communication systems that have this ability. Strong partnerships and effective, interoperable communications enable all emergency response organizations and personnel to respond in a coordinated and disciplined manner.

Interoperability problems (mainly in the area of communications) were encountered during the Oklahoma City federal building bombing in 1995, the terrorist attack on the World Trade Center (WTC) in 2001, and Hurricane Katrina in New Orleans in 2005. During Hurricane Katrina, primary electrical power was lost initially, followed by the loss of auxiliary power generators that were disabled by floodwaters. Radio and cellular telephone towers were also damaged in the storm.

Local emergency response agencies in New Orleans were forced to share a small number of mutual aid radio channels that rapidly became overloaded with transmissions. Law enforcement and fire and emergency services were also plagued by the lack of compatibility with their surviving communications equipment **(Figure 18.1, p. 414)**.

Currently, radio frequencies that are assigned for public safety use are located in four areas of the radio spectrum that range from very low-band, very high frequency (VHF) in the 30–50 and 72–76 megahertz (MHz) ranges to 800 MHz (including frequencies from 806 to 869 MHz). No radios are available that can handle that wide range of frequencies, making it impossible for agencies using different frequencies to communicate with each other.

Figure 18.1 Incident command posts, such as this one established during Hurricane Katrina, may not have all the communications equipment and services normally associated with an emergency operations center (EOC). Controlling and communicating with units may require the incident commander to resort to less technical means such as keeping track of resources with note cards and using runners to convey messages. *Courtesy of District Chief Chris Mickal.*

To address some of these problems, the Federal Communications Commission (FCC) first ordered that all public safety (police, fire, and emergency medical services [EMS]) frequencies operating at 800 MHz be separated from commercial services operating within the same frequency range. The FCC next reallocated the 700 MHz (specifically 764 to 776 MHz and 794 to 806 MHz) bandwidth for public safety use.

By the end of 2007, television broadcasters currently operating at 700 MHz will transition to digital operations. The use of 700 MHz will provide operations free from interference (signal noise) for fire and emergency services organizations. These frequencies will permit radio reception within steel and concrete structures like the WTC.

Another challenge to communications interoperability is the migration from wideband to narrowband frequencies. This change is mandated by the FCC to allow more users to utilize the VHF spectrum by 2013. To meet this requirement, the Association of Public-Safety Communications Officials-International, Inc. (APCO International) developed the APCO Project 25, *Standards for Pub-*

lic Safety Digital Radio, which was adopted by the organization in 1995. The purpose of the standards is to improve interoperability between multiple agencies and increase the number of communication frequencies that are available during a major emergency.

Four key objectives in the development of the standards were as follows:

1. Provide enhanced functionality with equipment and capabilities focused on public safety needs.

2. Improve spectrum efficiency.

3. Ensure competition among multiple vendors through open systems architecture (layered hierarchical structure or model of a communications system that allows system design, development, installation, operation, improvement, and maintenance to be performed at a given layer or layers in the structure).

4. Allow effective, efficient, and reliable intra-agency and interagency communications.

In addition to the FCC requirements, the U.S. Department of Homeland Security (DHS) requires that any public safety communication equipment must meet APCO Project 25 criteria. One of those criteria is that radios must be digital and capable of operating at 12.5 kilohertz (kHz) (see information box for definitions).

From the standpoint of interagency operations, there are many mutual aid channels that have been allocated for regional or statewide use. At the same time, there are two nationwide channels currently available for major multiagency operations: the National Law Enforcement Emergency Channel at 155.475 MHz in high-band VHF and the Interagency Tactical Channel 13 at 866 to 868 MHz in the 800 MHz range. Company officers should ensure that their organizations have access to these channels and understand the communication protocols used on them.

Equipment

To be most effective at communicating on the emergency scene, company officers must be able to use the communications equipment they have at their disposal and know the standard communications procedures used by their jurisdiction. The sections that follow highlight some of the common types of communications equipment that company officers are expected to operate, including radios, pagers, alternative methods, and advanced technology systems.

Radios

Using some type of radio equipment is one of the most common forms of emergency scene communications. Radios provide instantaneous communication among emergency response companies, between those companies and the telecommunications center, and between companies and the rest of the emergency-scene organization through the chain of command. Instantaneous communication with portable radios (sometimes referred to as *walkie-talkies, handy-talkies,* or simply *portables*) enhances safety on the fireground or any other incident site. Properly operated and monitored radio communications provide the following advantages:

- Incidents can be quickly surveyed and evaluated.

- All parties involved in handling an incident can be informed or consulted.

- Orders, plans, and information can be quickly given or received to meet changing conditions.

- Personnel accountability can be maintained.

- Resources can be controlled and allotted efficiently.

The telecommunications center is the focal point for all emergency scene radio communications. Calls for assistance or to report an emergency are received at or channeled to the telecommunications center. The personnel, apparatus, and equipment needed to operate at emergency scenes are dispatched by the center's telecommunicator **(Figure 18.2)**. In general, the telecommunications center keeps track of all apparatus assigned to an incident and may be responsible for initiating a move-up or call-back system to provide coverage for response areas left unprotected. The center may also be responsible for activating a mutual aid agreement when additional resources are required.

In order for the system to function as designed, the telecommunications center must be aware of each unit's status at all times. There are a variety of means by which the telecommunicator may dispatch and keep track of the organization's resources. Most modern telecommunications centers

Figure 18.2 Telecommunications centers receive requests for service from the public, assign resources, provide information to responding units, and coordinate the use of transmission frequencies to emergency incidents. *Courtesy of U.S. Federal Emergency Management Agency, Jason Pack, photographer/FEMA News Photo.*

use some form of computerized system with an audiotape backup to manage their activities. These systems are commonly called computer-aided-dispatch (CAD) systems. The complexity of a CAD system in any jurisdiction is usually directly related to the size and activity level of that organization or jurisdiction.

The company officer should be aware of the changes that are occurring in the communications field to ensure greater compatibility between radio systems. APCO Project 25 standards regarding radio communications should be met. In addition, the officer must be familiar with radio frequencies and their use during emergencies. Finally, it is important to understand the types of radios (base, mobile, and portable) commonly used in the fire and emergency services, depending on the magnitude of the incident.

Radio Frequencies

While a relatively small-scale emergency operation can work effectively using a single radio frequency, this practice is *not* recommended. When the number of units from one organization assigned to a given incident increases or units from several different organizations are assigned to one incident, the use of additional frequencies is usually necessary.

Radio frequencies cannot be arbitrarily assigned and must not be unilaterally assumed by any operating unit during an incident. The assignment of frequencies reflects both preincident planning and the communications element of the incident action plan for that particular incident. Organizations that commonly respond together should have written working agreements for mutual frequency use and sharing.

The number of frequencies needed on any given incident depends on the number of resources involved and size of the incident command function needed for the incident. At large incidents, there may be as many as five major uses for radio communications. Each of the following areas may require one or more radio frequencies on large incidents:

- Command
- Tactical operations
- Support operations
- Air-to-ground communications (airport crash/rescue, wildland, or medical evacuation operations) **(Figure 18.3)**
- Air-to-air communications (wildland operations)
- Medical services

Figure 18.3 Effective communications between ground units, command posts, and aircraft involved in an emergency incident are essential. Air-to-ground coordination is not limited to wildland incidents as shown here. Aircraft may also be involved in evacuations, search missions, and structural fire suppression.

Fire and emergency services organizations may have anywhere from one to ten or more radio frequencies available for their use. Small, rural emergency response organizations that handle a low-call volume normally function on a single frequency. Larger organizations, or a group of smaller organizations that operate through the same telecommunications center, require a larger number of frequencies in order to operate efficiently.

In many cases, all emergency dispatch functions are on one frequency, routine operations are handled on a second frequency, and additional frequencies are available for large-scale incidents. At the incident commander's discretion, all communications at a large-scale incident may be switched to one of the extra frequencies to avoid interference from routine transmissions on the primary frequency.

Extremely large incidents may require multiple frequencies assigned to each incident. For example, all Command Section functions may be conducted on one channel, Operations Section communications carried on a second channel, and Logistics functions conducted on yet a third channel.

All organizations that routinely work together on emergency incidents must have the ability to communicate with each other by portable radio on common or mutual aid frequencies. In some cases, it may be necessary to provide mutual aid companies with portable radios once they are on the scene so that they may communicate with first-due companies.

Most urban emergency services organizations operate on the 800 MHz radio frequency, although some 400 MHz systems are still in operation around the country. As mentioned previously, 800 MHz radio systems have some disadvantages because of interference. At the same time, they have advantages in that frequencies can be *trunked* to provide a wider range of broadcast frequencies during an emergency (see sidebar for an explanation). Future use of the 700 MHz system will eliminate the disadvantages while retaining the advantages of the 800 MHz system.

Radio Trunking

In a *trunking system*, a set of channels shares the communications demands of the users. If no channel is free at the time a user makes a call, the call will be placed on hold for a few seconds until another channel becomes available. As a result, the user has less time to wait and enjoys better quality service. Trunking was developed because radio spectrum throughout the world was congested. Dynamic growth in mobile communications has made channel availability very difficult.

In trunking, each radio station transmits a control signal on a radio channel. Radio units have a number of traffic channels at their disposal for communication. When not in use, the radio unit is automatically tuned to the control signal. The unit's microprocessor can communicate with the system computer on this channel at any time.

If a user wishes to make a call, the unit transmits the request in the form of a data signal to the system computer. The computer finds the caller's desired correspondent and, by means of the control channel, checks for willingness to receive a call. When both parties are ready to communicate, the computer allocates the first available traffic channel.

When the call is terminated by either party, the radio unit sends a data signal releasing the channel. Radio stations may be interconnected to increase the service area to provide any size network up to a national or international level. Calls may also be made into other fixed-line networks such as telephone systems.

Base Radios

Base radios are normally operated from the jurisdiction's telecommunications center. However, at large-scale incidents that may have relatively long durations, a base radio may be assembled at a fixed location such as the incident command post (ICP) or incident base.

While these radios are typically scaled-down versions of the base radios found in a telecommunications center, they must be capable of monitoring and transmitting on all frequencies used on that particular incident. Depending on the area involved in the incident and the required range for radio communications, the base radio may need to be equipped with a sizable exterior antenna.

Base radios are also located in the various stations and facilities of the organization (**Figure 18.4**). These radios are used for nonemergency communications and as part of the dispatch system.

Mobile Radios

Mobile radios are mounted in vehicles, apparatus, and aircraft (both fixed and rotary wing) (**Figure 18.5**). Modern apparatus design usually includes the primary radio in the cab with remote stations at the pump panel, on the aerial device turntable, or in the basket of an elevating platform. Regardless of the position, the radio operator speaks through a handheld microphone or through a headset that is part of a vehicle intercom system. As with base stations, these radios should be capable of communicating on any frequency used on an incident.

At the very least, apparatus and personnel who are given specific functional or geographic assignments should be capable of communicating with each other and with their supervisors. Most modern mobile radios are capable of scanning, transmitting, and receiving on hundreds of frequencies. This capability is critical when working at large incidents with units from other jurisdictions that operate on frequencies that are different from local units.

Radios in aircraft may also be used on special incidents such as large-scale wildland fires, airport operations, or medical evacuations. However, because few if any company officers are expected to be able to operate aircraft radios (and those that are must be specifically trained), it is beyond the scope of this manual to address their use.

Portable Radios

Portable radios are handheld radios that allow personnel to remain in contact with each other, other units, the telecommunications center, and their supervisors when they are away from the mobile radio in the apparatus (**Figure 18.6**). As with mobile radios, portable radios may be operated on multiple channels. Current models of portable radios can scan, transmit, and receive on hundreds of channels.

Most portable radios have a very limited amount of transmitting and receiving power, usually only 1 to 5 watts (compared to the 100 to 150 watts of a typical mobile radio). Therefore, portable radios have a very limited range. When communicating from portable to portable, the range may be less than 1 mile (1.6 km). Communication distances between portable radios and mobile radios or base radios vary, depending on the capability of the mobile radio or base radio.

The range of portable radios may be extended using a repeater system. A repeater system receives a signal from a portable radio, boosts its power, and then transmits the signal to the receiver. The

Figure 18.5 Vehicle-mounted radios permit units to be in contact with the telecommunications center at all times. Radio speakers and sometimes microphones may be located at the pump panel or on the turntable and platform of aerial devices.

Figure 18.4 Base radio stations may be found in most fire and emergency services facilities.

Figure 18.6 Handheld or portable radios are essential to emergency scene operations. Portable radios permit the incident commander to control all units, gather information from remote locations at the incident, and improve the accountability of personnel.

following two primary types of repeater systems located in different locations are in common use:

1. *Apparatus* — Repeater system is part of the mobile radio in the apparatus assigned to the crew using portable radios. When a crew member transmits on a portable radio, the repeater system in the mobile radio boosts the radio's signal to its optimum power and rebroadcasts the signal.

2. *Geographical area* — Fixed or portable repeaters are located throughout a particular geographical jurisdiction. These repeaters receive signals from portable or mobile radios and boost their powers so that signals can be received by other portable, mobile, or base station radios.

Pagers

Pagers are most often used to notify volunteers, paid-on-call and off-duty career personnel, and staff officers to respond to the station or emergency incident scene. Pagers are available in a wide variety of types and sizes and are capable of making contact with an individual or a group of individuals selectively. Some pagers are activated by simply dialing a specific telephone number.

Most pagers used in the fire and emergency services are activated by a transmitter tone from the telecommunications center **(Figure 18.7)**. Pagers provide information to the user in one of two modes: voice message or text message.

Figure 18.7 Pagers have been a part of the fire and emergency services almost since they were introduced to the public. They are an inexpensive means of notifying personnel of an emergency or contacting someone.

Many volunteer fire and emergency services organizations use pagers that allow the user to monitor radio traffic on the dispatch frequency at all times. It is a good standard practice to broadcast emergency evacuation messages to all personnel over the dispatch frequency — in addition to the emergency scene frequency—because responders who do not have portable radios may be able to hear the message over their pagers.

Alternative Communications Methods

Because of the long duration of many large-scale emergency incidents, alternative communications systems may be used during these incidents. These alternative methods may also be necessary when the primary communication system is disrupted or must be abandoned, which might be the case after a hurricane or earthquake. The use of each of the following methods depends on the level of preparedness of the organization involved in the incident:

- Citizens band (CB) radios
- Amateur radio (ham) networks
- Land-based telephones
- Cellular telephones
- Satellite phones
- Fax machines
- Computer modems and wireless broadband connections

Citizens Band Radios

Some small, rural jurisdictions rely on CB radios as their primary mode of mobile communication. This practice is primarily because CB radios are relatively inexpensive and many small organizations do not have the financial resources to purchase standard mobile radios for their apparatus. In addition to their low cost, CB radios offer the following advantages to these organizations:

- CB radios are better than having no radios at all.
- Most modern CB radios have 40 channels, which allow different parts of the organization to operate on their own frequencies.
- Many personnel have CB radios in their personal vehicles, which can be a benefit when assembling a command structure.

Balanced against these advantages, CB radios have the following disadvantages:

- Members of the public may be operating on the same frequencies.
- Quality of the transmission may not be as clear as with standard fire and emergency services mobile radios.
- Range of effective communication is generally less than that of standard fire and emergency services mobile radios.
- CB radios are not intrinsically safe and may be a source of ignition in an explosive atmosphere.

Amateur Radio Networks

Ham operators are individuals who have access to extensive radio communications networks and equipment. They are licensed by the FCC to broadcast on specific frequencies and assigned

Communications After Hurricane Katrina

After Hurricane Katrina in 2005, many communications systems failed to operate due to the loss of infrastructure, the loss of power, and other circumstances such as the following:

- Communication towers were destroyed or damaged by flying debris and high winds.
- Auxiliary generators were damaged by floodwaters.
- Backup batteries became depleted of power.
- Amateur radio (ham) operators were evacuated or had no power or antennas.
- Portable radios, satellite phones, and cellular phones could not be recharged due to the lack of power.
- Systems that depended on land-based telephones and cable television systems such as telephones, fax machines, and computers were inoperable due to the loss of power and communication lines.

Under normal emergency conditions, some of these systems would be expected to continue to operate. However, a lesson learned as a result of Hurricane Katrina was that under catastrophic conditions, responders may have to improvise communications and resort to the use of runners to deliver messages.

call designations. Through their base stations and mobile and portable radios, ham operators can access repeaters, satellites, and telephone systems. These ham operators and their equipment are often available on a volunteer basis, but it may take several hours to mobilize them. Drills should be held with ham operators to practice notification and mobilization procedures.

In some areas, organized groups of ham operators are available and equipped to supplement or aid official emergency radio systems when the need arises. Fire and emergency services organizations that have access to a Radio Amateur Civil Emergency Service (RACES) chapter can usually mobilize an effective alternative radio system faster than those where individual ham operators must be notified one at a time.

RACES is administered by local, county, and state emergency management agencies and supported by DHS and the Federal Emergency Management Agency (FEMA). RACES, along with the Amateur Radio Emergency Service (ARES), provides radio communications for civil-preparedness purposes during periods of local, regional, or national civil emergencies.

Ham operators in a RACES chapter are also more likely to understand the needs of emergency providers and perform these functions more efficiently and effectively than non-RACES operators. RACES is an expansion of the Auxiliary Communications Service (ACS), which includes local government telecommunication services.

Land-Based Telephones

Public telephones or field telephones are sometimes used as a means of communicating at large-scale incidents, high-rise incidents, and shipboard and other confined-space incidents **(Figure 18.8)**. If radio communications break down, telephones may be an effective alternative. Even if radio communications are operational, it may be advantageous to communicate lengthy routine messages (ordering supplies, giving lengthy status reports, etc.) by telephone instead of obstructing emergency radio frequencies.

Land-based telephones are most commonly used when the incident base or ICP is located in a permanent structure that has telephone service.

Figure 18.8 Telephones that depend on wiring to transmit a signal are sometimes referred to as *land-based telephones*. They may be part of the local or regional telephone system or dedicated system within a structure or vessel such as the telephones found in elevators or fire control centers.

Temporary telephone service can also be established in an ICP or other location by telephone company personnel if it appears that an incident will be a lengthy operation.

Cellular Telephones

Advances in cellular telephone technology have made this type of telephone service affordable and commonplace in society. In some areas, cellular telephones are available where land-based phones are not. Cellular phones may be handheld or mounted in a vehicle. They allow people access to the world's telephone network without being hard-wired into a local telephone system.

Messages are transmitted as radio signals between the cellular phone and repeater/downlink equipment (*cell site*) that enters the call into the telephone system **(Figures 18.9 a and b, p. 422)**. Advanced technology now provides cellular telephones with the ability to capture and transmit photo and video images and access the Internet directly. These capabilities can provide company officers with rapid retrieval of information while not dominating a command radio frequency.

However, cellular telephones are *not* completely dependable. If the emergency scene is in an area that is not serviced by a cell site, no service is available. Even within a cell site area, there may be *dead spots* where reception is not

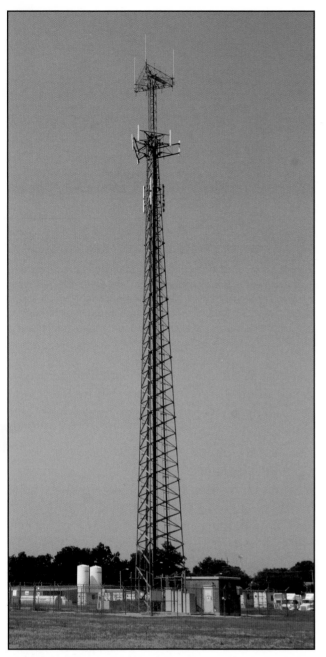

Figures 18.9 a and b Cellular telephone technology has made it possible for people to place phone calls from any location in the world that has access to the transmitted signal. However, when the signal is interrupted by the loss of (a) a permanent transmission tower, it will be necessary to acquire (b) a portable unit. *Photo b Courtesy of U.S. Federal Emergency Management Agency, Robert Kaufman, photographer.*

available. The loss of cell sites can also disrupt service, a situation that occurred in New York City on September 11, 2001.

Another major limitation is that incidents in densely populated areas tend to generate massive amounts of cellular telephone traffic from emergency providers and citizens alike. This situation occurred first in Oklahoma City in 1995 and again in New York City in 2001 when the number of

both emergency and nonemergency phone calls overloaded the system. This increase in traffic can quickly overwhelm existing cell-site equipment and block further calls from being made.

When an overload happens, cellular phone providers can provide equipment to temporarily boost the capacity of the systems. They can also provide special cellular telephones that have priority programming to ensure that every call made to or from these phones is completed. Fire and emergency services organizations should confirm the availability of these services during preincident planning.

As manufacturers of cellular phones continue to add more features to their units, other devices that offer combination features are being created and improved. In 1999, Research in Motion (RIM) developed the BlackBerry® personal digital assistant (PDA). This handheld unit offers wireless communication solutions and provides access to a wide range of applications including secure, wireless access to the following services:

- Electronic mail (e-mail)
- Data transfer
- Phone service
- Internet/intranet access
- Personal organizer

These units, and other similar devices, permit quick and efficient access to information that helps in decision-making. They also ensure that command personnel can transmit information over secure communications channels.

Satellite Telephones

On large-scale incidents, a satellite telephone system that is independent of land-based and cellular systems can be assembled. With the requisite equipment, this wireless telephone system can provide a reliable communications system that is free of the limitations and interference that characterize the other types of telephonic communications.

Some new generation telephones have the ability to operate as radios, communicating with other units within a limited area. A limitation to this type of system is that the user must know the specific phone numbers of each person on the network.

Fax Machines

Fax machines normally transmit signals over land-based telephone lines, but they may be operated through cellular telephone systems. Fax machines can be very useful for transmitting and receiving written documents such as situation status reports, building plans, hazardous chemical data,

and weather updates. At major emergency scenes, the incident base or ICP may have one or more fax machines.

Computer Modems and Wireless Broadband Connections

A *modem* (modulator/demodulator) converts the signal produced by one type of device (computer) to a form compatible with another device (telephone). This conversion allows a computer at the incident base, ICP, or other location to access databases and computer networks over a telephone line. Computer modems (like fax machines) may be attached to cellular or land-based telephone equipment.

Current technology also permits the use of computer modems for voice and image transfer, duplicating a cellular telephone link. Real-time photo and video images can also be transferred rapidly though this system.

Broadband is the name for any form of high-speed Internet access. Broadband connections are at least 10 times faster than modems. Increased speeds mean that images may be viewed on a computer screen in the full-screen size rather than a small, postage-stamp size. Preincident maps and photos can be transferred rapidly in a size that can be easily viewed. Web-based software programs and online file storage can be accessed from remote locations.

Broadband is available in the following four main types that all operate in different ways but provide very fast Internet access:

1. ***Asymmetric Digital Subscriber Line (ADSL)*** — Uses an existing phone line to provide high-speed Internet access

2. ***Cable modem*** — Uses fiber-optic cables that are shared with a television cable line; performs similarly to ADSL

3. ***Wireless*** — Connects a laptop computer equipped with an antenna and a wireless-fidelity (Wi-Fi) card to the Internet through a base station **(Figure 18.10, p. 424)**; provides the most effective way to access the Internet and data files that are maintained by the organization at an emergency incident scene

4. *Satellite* — Uses a satellite or dish-receiver to transmit information between a computer equipped with a modem and the source of the information (telecommunications center or Internet); provides transfer speeds that may be very fast but cost of the system may be prohibitive

Advanced Technology Communications Systems

In the past 20 years, communications technology has made significant advancements because of research and development efforts in private industry in general, the aerospace industry in particular, and the military. Although some of this technology may still be beyond the fiscal means of the majority of fire and emergency services organizations, much of it is affordable and available. Federal government grants have made new technology available to many organizations. Among the various types of new technology that benefit the fire and emergency services are the following:

- Mobile data terminal (MDT)
- Mobile data computer (MDC)
- Geographic information system (GIS)
- Global positioning system (GPS)

Mobile Data Terminal

An MDT is a radio-operated data terminal that allows a telecommunications center to transmit dispatch information, incident/patient status information, confidential messages that are not appropriate for verbal transmission over a radio, chemical information, and maps and charts to units at or en route to an incident scene. An MDT is the most common advanced communication technology used by the fire and emergency services **(Figure 18.11)**.

One style of MDT looks like a small personal computer mounted on a pedestal near a vehicle's dashboard. Another style resembles a laptop computer that can be pulled from the vehicle and used in a remote location if needed. Many MDTs are also equipped with status buttons that allow the telecommunications center to be aware of the unit's status (en route, on scene, available, etc.) without the need for verbal radio transmissions.

Mobile Data Computer

An MDC has all of the features of an MDT with the addition of a keyboard that allows two-way communication between the mobile units and the telecommunications center. Instead of the status buttons that an MDT uses to transmit its status, an MDC allows complete messages to be transmitted and received in the vehicle. This procedure facilitates two-way communications that are *not* appropriate for transmission over a radio.

Figure 18.10 Wireless technology connects computers to the Internet through a transmitter/receiver that is located on a base station. The effective distance between the remote computer and the base station will vary.

Figure 18.11 Mobile data terminals are finding increasing use in the fire and emergency services. Information regarding specific sites, hazards, and weather conditions are instantly available to the incident commander. *Courtesy of Rick Montemorra.*

Geographic Information System

A GIS is designed to provide a computer-readable description of geographic features in a particular area. A mobile computer can store data and on command display that data on specific segments of the area covered. In urban/suburban areas, addresses and occupancy information on individual structures may be stored in a GIS. This information may be useful to telecommunicators, responders, incident commanders, planning personnel, and technical specialists assigned to an incident.

Global Positioning System

A GPS receiver decodes satellite signals to establish a location. The location data is transmitted to an automatic vehicle locator (AVL) system at the telecommunications center. In a GPS, each vehicle is equipped with a GPS receiver and radio transmitter. The position of a vehicle is then shown on a map of the jurisdiction using the system.

These systems are generally capable of determining the location of a vehicle to within approximately 10 yards (9 m) of its actual position. Originally developed by the U.S. military as a means of tracking troops in combat, the GPS is now in use by civilian emergency services also.

GPS units are typically used in conjunction with computerized dispatch systems, MDTs, and GISs. There are several uses for a GPS. Two of the accepted uses are for tracking units at emergency scenes and dispatching the closest available units to an emergency. While the latter use is the most common, tracking units is being used more frequently than in the past. A GPS may also be used to track individual responders at incidents, making it easier to locate individuals who are lost or become unconscious.

Procedures

More important for company officers than a familiarity with communications equipment is a thorough knowledge of the procedures for using that equipment. Most fire and emergency services organizations have a communications management policy that defines the procedures and language to be used during both routine activities and emergency operations. By including communications in their standard operating procedures (SOPs), communication protocols are applied much more consistently. Communication procedures must accomplish the following two objectives:

1. Establish the use of specific common terms (clear text) that mean the same thing to all emergency response personnel.

2. Establish a system of transmitting periodic progress reports to keep all units current on the progress of an incident.

In clear text, specific terms are used to describe apparatus and standard operational modes and functions. For example, when a unit has been dispatched on an emergency call, the company officer transmits *Engine 7187 responding*. The term *responding* is only used for emergency response and *not* for routine, nonemergency movements. Nor should *en route* or any other term be used instead of *responding* when responding to an emergency call.

Many other terms have specific meanings and applications in clear text. Despite the fact that clear text has been in use for decades, some of the most common misuses of radio terminology occur in the area of resource identification. Some organizations refer to their *engines* as *trucks* even though the term *truck* is generally used to denote a *ladder company* (**Figure 18.12, p. 426**). Company officers have an obligation to learn and use correct radio terminology.

The adoption and use of clear text radio communication were made mandatory by the adoption of the NIMS-Incident Command System (ICS). This system is intended to increase the interoperability between all emergency services organizations at all levels of government. At major interagency incidents, all agencies must adhere to the NIMS-ICS communications procedures in states that have adopted NIMS. (See the National Incident Management System-Incident Command System section in Chapter 19, Incident Scene Management, for further information).

The company officer must be familiar with the radio communication protocols that have been adopted by the organization. Radio-use protocols are basic to effective emergency scene operations and also the basis for the ICS that is used by the

One Apparatus With Many Names

Ladder   Truck   Quint   Tower   Platform

Figure 18.12 Depending on local policy, the term used to designate an aerial device or the unit that staffs it may be one of a variety of terms.

organization. A discussion of general radio communication protocols and a set of five practices (the five *C*s) that ensure effective radio communications are included in the sections that follow.

Radio Communications

The purpose of emergency services radio communications is to allow units in the field to communicate with each other, with the telecommunications center, and with the incident chain of command during emergency operations. Being able to exchange critical or pertinent tactical information allows all elements of the organization to monitor the status of other units and overall operations.

The information exchanged can be task-related; for example, *Command, Engine 7; we need an additional supply line to support Truck 37's ladder pipe.* The information can also be a direct order based upon the decision of the incident commander; for example, *Communications, Penn Command; strike a third alarm. Have all companies report to Staging at 5th and Penn Streets.*

Individuals who operate radio equipment should realize that all radio transmissions can be monitored by the news media, the public, and the FCC. Radio operators should always be careful to *not* transmit any message that might reflect badly on the organization or provide patient information

that should remain confidential. Company officers are responsible for the radio discipline and conduct of their crews.

Examples exist of embarrassing and potentially damaging comments made in the presence of open microphones. Company officers and their subordinates must be careful in the presence of any radio and consider all microphones as open (activated) and transmitting.

Effective communications require a knowledge of basic radio communications, the ability to recognize and transmit essential information, and how to give direct orders over the radio. These topics are addressed in the sections that follow.

Basic Radio Communications

All emergency responders should be trained in the use of whatever radio equipment their organizations have. Regardless of whether they have been issued a portable radio or they normally do not operate department radios, emergency responders need to be able to use radios effectively if and when the need arises. Company officers are responsible for ensuring that every member of their crew is trained on the following topics:

- Basic radio operation and maintenance (changing batteries, replacing worn keypads, cleaning the unit, etc.)

- Radio frequency assignments and usage
- Organizational radio procedures
- Radio safety (ensuring that intrinsically safe radios are used in potentially explosive atmospheres and understanding that some radios may emit a low level of radiation during transmission that could pose a health hazard)

Obviously, it is important that all emergency responders be able to understand the operation of the various controls on the radio and quickly select different channels as the situation requires. They should also be capable of performing routine maintenance or care such as keeping radios clean and changing or recharging batteries (**Figure 18.13**).

Those who work in organizations that use multiple radio frequencies must know which frequencies are used for various functions. They must be

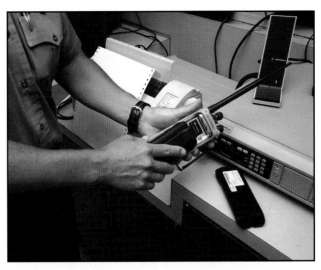

Figure 18.13 Most handheld radios are simple to operate. The company officer should be familiar with the use and maintenance of these radios, including how and when to change batteries and how to recharge them.

Single-Family Dwelling Fire Claims the Lives of Two Volunteer Firefighters (Ohio)

On February 5, 1998, two male volunteer firefighters (Victim No. 1 and Victim No. 2) died of smoke inhalation while trying to exit the basement of a single-family dwelling after a backdraft occurred. A volunteer engine company composed of four firefighters and one driver/operator were the first responders to a structure fire at a single-family dwelling located 3 miles from the fire department.

When the engine company arrived, one firefighter aboard reported that light smoke was showing from the roof. The four firefighters (including Victim No. 1) entered the dwelling through the kitchen door and proceeded down the basement stairs to determine the fire's origin. The four firefighters searched the basement, which was filled with light-to-moderate smoke.

A few minutes later, a fifth firefighter from Rescue 211 (Victim No. 2) joined the group. After extinguishing a small fire in the ceiling area, Victim No. 2 raised a ceiling panel, and a backdraft occurred in the concealed ceiling space. The pressure and fire from the backdraft knocked ceiling tiles onto the firefighters, who became disoriented and lost contact with each other and their hoseline.

Two firefighters located on the basement staircase exited the dwelling with assistance from two firefighters who were attempting a rescue. One firefighter was

rescued through an exterior basement door. The two victims' self-contained breathing apparatus (SCBA) ran out of air while they were trying to escape. Additional rescue attempts were made by other firefighters but failed due to excessive heat and smoke and lack of an established water supply. Both firefighters died of smoke inhalation and other injuries.

National Institute for Occupational Safety and Health (NIOSH) investigators concluded (see **Appendix J** for the complete NIOSH investigation report and recommendations) that in order to prevent similar incidents, fire departments should perform the following tasks:

- Utilize the first-arriving engine company as *the* command company and conduct an initial scene survey.
- Implement an incident command system with written standard operating procedures for all firefighters.
- Provide a backup hose crew.
- Provide adequate on-scene communications, including fireground tactical channels.
- Train firefighters in the various essentials of how to operate in smoke-filled environments, basement fire operations, dangers of ceiling collapse, ventilation practices, utilizing a second hoseline during fire attack, and identifying prebackdraft, prerollover, and preflashover conditions.
- Appoint an Incident Safety Officer.

able to differentiate among dispatch, tactical, and command frequencies and ensure that radios are always on the correct frequencies. This procedure is especially critical in situations where personnel may be in mortal danger from fires or other emergencies.

Figure 18.14 At all emergency incidents, radio communications should be short, concise, and easily understood. The larger the operation is, the greater the amount of radio transmissions and the possibility that transmissions and orders will be misunderstood or lost. *Courtesy of Paul Ramirez, Phoenix (AZ) Fire Department.*

Caution

Be sure that all personnel know the correct frequency to use for each function. Failure to use the correct frequency could result in no communication or a delay of assistance. Case histories (see example, p. 427) have shown that in some instances help for trapped firefighters was delayed because their calls for help were transmitted over the wrong radio frequency and not heard by units at the emergency scene.

Company officers must know and use their organization's radio procedures. These procedures should be used on a daily basis during both routine and emergency activities. If all members of the organization follow the established procedures on small, day-to-day incidents, using the procedures during major incidents will become routine.

It is also important for company officers to know the limitations of their radio equipment. Some types of transmissions require a *line-of-sight* between transmitter and receiver, while others may benefit from the use of a repeater system that strengthens the transmission. Some systems cannot penetrate structural members of some buildings, making transmissions impossible within the building and with radios outside the building. If the company officer determines that limitations exist, alternate communication methods should be located. Protocols should be established for working in areas that may obstruct transmissions.

Essential Information

One potential problem with the use of clear text is that some radio operators may become lax and begin to ramble when they are transmitting. Company officers should monitor their crews' radio

usage and see that personnel follow procedures and keep radio messages short and to the point **(Figure 18.14)**. Only essential information should be transmitted, and proper radio formats should be used.

For example, when an engine arrives at an emergency scene, the company officer should simply transmit, *Engine 3581 at scene.* When calling the telecommunications center or another unit, the company officer identifies the unit being called and then identifies the calling unit. For example, *Communications, Engine 7582.* After the other units acknowledges (*Go ahead 7582*), the company officer transmits the message. This method is sometimes referred to as *Hey you, it's me.* Many fire departments who have used this model for communications on the incident site contend that it eliminates units from pausing while waiting to hear to whom the next transmission is going.

Direct Orders

An example of a direct order: *Ladder 65, Operations — ventilate the roof.* A direct order can be made more explicit by adding extra information such as who is to carry out the task and why, how, when, and where it must be done. The officer issuing the order must decide how specific to make the order by considering the urgency of the task and capabilities of the individual or unit to whom the order is given.

The Five *C*s of Radio Communication

At an emergency incident scene, there is no time for company officers to stop and think about the correct method of communicating by radio. Therefore, they must follow effective and accepted communication protocols in day-to-day operations so that these skills will become second nature. The five *C*s of communication that every fire officer should practice when using radios are as follows:

- Conciseness
- Clarity
- Confidence
- Control
- Capability

Conciseness

Numerous functions must be performed at an emergency incident scene, and many will involve some form of communication. Therefore, communications must be kept as *concise* as possible or the assigned frequencies will become too congested with traffic to be of any use. To ensure conciseness, company officers must learn to plan their transmissions before keying the microphone (**Figure 18.15**). The following actions are recommended:

- Make messages task-oriented.
- Direct messages to companies — not individuals.
- Match messages to receivers.
- Keep messages specific.

Clarity

The *clarity* of a message adds to the overall effectiveness of all incident communications. Company officers should use standard terms and everyday language. When planning their transmissions, company officers should also strive to combine clarity with simplicity. For orders to be effective, they should describe only one task at a time before having the unit report back for additional tasks.

Orders issued to different units must be sufficiently spaced to avoid any question that separate orders are being transmitted. Emergency orders

Figure 18.15 To be concise, the incident commander should have in mind the message that needs to be conveyed. Writing the essential components of the message or referring to the incident action plan (IAP) can help keep the message on focus.

should be well-timed because many operations can be anticipated by an experienced company officer/incident commander, but the order that assigns units to those operations should not be issued until those operations are ready to be undertaken.

Confidence

Company officers must show confidence (also known as *command presence*) when using communication equipment, especially during emergency operations. When confidence is communicated, receiving units react with confidence. Company officers can communicate confidence by using a calm, natural tone and speaking at a controlled rate.

Control

Telecommunications can break down if it is not managed. The most important people responsible for controlling communications at the company level are the telecommunicator and incident commander. These key individuals should set a positive example for all units on the scene by following established radio protocols: At the beginning of a transmission, each unit must identify who they are calling and identify themselves; the receiver of the message should repeat or paraphrase the essence of the message back to the sender.

Requiring the receiver to acknowledge a message by repeating it reduces the chances of misunderstanding. This practice tells the sender that the message was understood as transmitted or alerts the sender that the message was not understood correctly and further clarification is necessary.

Capability

Effective communication depends on capable (well-trained) senders and receivers. But capability is *not* limited to technical proficiency; it also includes an ability to communicate, which means that company officers must be capable of listening effectively as well as initiating effective messages.

To perform these actions, company officers must be able to exercise the emotional control needed to remain calm under stress and emotional maturity to set a positive example by following established communication procedures.

Summary

Effective emergency incident scene communication is an essential part of operational effectiveness and safety. Company officers play a pivotal role in the communications process during these incidents. Not only do they transmit and receive most of the radio messages initiated during an incident, their crew members look to them for an example of how to use communications equipment properly and effectively. To fulfill this role, company officers must know what communications equipment is available to them, how to use it effectively, and how to be a positive role model for their crew members. They must practice the use of good communication techniques during nonemergency activities to ensure that they can communicate effectively during emergency operations.

Mobile Emergency Resource Support (MERS)

The U.S. Federal Emergency Management Agency (FEMA) provides communication equipment to local jurisdictions during large-scale emergencies such as hurricanes, tornadoes, or blizzards. One of the programs that FEMA offers is Mobile Emergency Response Support (MERS). The primary function of MERS is to provide mobile telecommunications, life-support, logistics, operational support, and power generation required for the on-site management of disaster response activities. In addition, MERS provides administrative support required by federal, state, and local responders in their efforts to save lives, protect property, and coordinate disaster operations.

Staged in six strategic locations, one with offshore capabilities, each of the MERS detachments can concurrently support a large Joint Field Office (JFO) and multiple field operating sites within a disaster area. MERS locations include Bothell, WA; Denver, CO; Maynard, MA; Denton, TX; and Thomasville, GA.

MERS assets include some 275 mobile units that provide emergency telecommunications, logistics, and operations support. Several truck-mounted generators, ranging from 20 to 400 kilowatts, provide enough power generation and distribution for several large facilities.

MERS detachments transport and distribute fuel via 1,200-, 2,200- and 3,500-gallon tankers. They can also transport water via 3,000-gallon tankers and, through a reverse osmosis purification unit, make brackish and saltwater safe and drinkable.

MERS also has Mobile Emergency Operation Vehicles (MEOVs) that are self-contained mobile communications vehicles. They contain power generation and satellite communications to provide mobile office support, including videoconferencing, at locations with no infrastructure. MEOVs are frequently matched with Mobile Disaster Recovery Center (MDRC) vehicles, providing power and communications so victims can register with FEMA.

FEMA Incident and Response Support Team (FIRST) vehicles are mobile communication vans used to provide command and control communication and real-time, rapid-needs assessment to FEMA leadership for quick-response support needs. This vehicle will be the first deployed along with the federal and state first responders on a Rapid-Needs Assessment (RNA) mission.

Company officers, along with the administration of the fire and emergency services organization, should be aware of these communication, administration, and logistics assets and the procedure for requesting them. Additional information is available from the FEMA web site. The information given in this sidebar was based on the FEMA Fact Sheet on MERS.

Incident Scene Management

Chapter Contents

Learning Objectives

1. Recall the common characteristics of the National Incident Management System-Incident Command System (NIMS-ICS).

2. Match to their definitions common terminology of the NIMS-ICS.

3. Select facts about the common characteristics of the NIMS-ICS.

4. Identify facts about incident priorities.

5. Select facts about incident size-up.

6. Identify the five steps in the size-up process as developed by Lloyd Layman.

7. Choose correct facts about the various scene-control methods.

8. Select from a list the variables that the officer may not be able to control when attempting to control traffic at an emergency scene.

9. Apply the NIMS-ICS model to an emergency incident plan.

10. Implement an incident action plan (IAP) at an emergency scene.

Job Performance Requirements

This chapter provides information that addresses the following job performance requirements of NFPA 1021, *Standard for Fire Officer Professional Qualifications* (2003):

Chapter 4 Fire Officer I

4.1.1

4.6.2

4.6.3(A)

4.6.3(B)

Chapter 19
Incident Scene Management

The safe and efficient management of any emergency incident requires that emergency responders gain control of the scene as quickly as possible and maintain that control throughout the incident. Successfully gaining and maintaining control of an incident scene is critically important to the successful outcome of any emergency. Unfortunately, emergency incidents are rarely the same, and a variety of problems may exist that will challenge the efficient management of them. The following problems may be difficult to overcome:

- Wide- and diverse-area emergency scene

- Multiple casualties

- Unstable structures or vehicles

- Leaking hazardous materials

- Debris strewn about

- Witnesses and curious bystanders (spectators) milling about

- Victims mixed with bystanders

- Treatment needs of victims

- Safety for those at the scene

Incident scene management applies to all types of emergency responses and all levels of resource commitment, ranging from single-resource situations to multijurisdictional and multiagency disasters that require many resources. By learning and applying incident scene management at single-resource situations, company officers will perfect the skills that can be applied to more complex situations.

The basis for safe and efficient incident scene management is the Incident Command System (ICS). Various forms of ICS (sometimes called the *Incident Management System [IMS]*) have been developed, adopted, taught, and implemented by fire and emergency services organizations for many years. Currently, the emphasis on the adoption and use of a standard ICS has been created by the adoption of the National Incident Management System (NIMS). Because the concept of incident management is so critical, the U.S. government mandated the use of ICS as a component of NIMS in 2004.

This chapter discusses the basic NIMS-ICS model, including the positions and functions that are needed at both small and large emergency incidents. Establishing priorities for incident scene management as well as initial incident size-up considerations and scene control are also addressed.

The actions of the first-arriving company officer are critical to the success of any emergency incident. That officer establishes the NIMS-ICS and makes decisions and takes actions that will influence the rest of the operation. Whether the company officer maintains command of the incident or transfers command to a senior or more experienced officer, the initial decisions must be reliable and based on the organization's incident scene management procedures.

National Incident Management System-Incident Command System

Essential to all emergency incident scene management is the management of emergency response resources: apparatus, personnel, equipment, and materials. NIMS-ICS establishes an organizational structure for all types of emergency incidents. Company officers must use

NIMS-ICS on all incidents no matter how small or large they are. Using the system on small, day-to-day incidents gives company officers opportunities to practice using it so that when large or complex incidents occur, the system will not seem foreign to emergency responders (**Figure 19.1**).

Every member of the organization, especially company officers, must be familiar with the system and trained in its application. In addition, all agencies with which mutual aid or automatic aid agreements are in force must know and use the same system. Achieving this familiarity may require extensive cross-training at all organizational levels among units of the participating agencies, especially at the company level.

The company officer must be familiar with the characteristics of the NIMS-ICS that have been adopted by the emergency services organization.

Figure 19.1 Effective resolution of large incidents, such as this wharf fire, requires the application of the NIMS-Incident Command System. *Courtesy of District Chief Chris Mickal.*

Common characteristics of the NIMS-ICS are as follows:

- Common terminology for functional structure
- Modular organization
- Common communications
- Unified command structure
- Incident action plan (IAP)
- Manageable span of control
- Predesignated incident facilities
- Comprehensive resource management
- Personnel accountability

Common Terminology for Functional Structure

Common terminology for organizational functional elements, position titles, facilities, and resources is essential for any command system, especially one that will be used by units from multiple agencies. The terms in the following lists describe organizational levels, resources, and leadership titles that need to be understood by all fire and emergency service responders

Organizational Levels

- *Command*—Act of directing, ordering, and/or controlling resources by virtue of explicit legal, agency, or delegated authority; also used to denote the organizational level that is in overall command (incident commander [IC]) of the incident. Lines of authority must be clear to all involved. Lawful commands by those in authority need to be followed immediately and without question.

- *Command Staff*— Incident management personnel who are in overall command of the incident; includes the public information officer, safety officer, and liaison officer who advise the IC.

- *General Staff*—Incident management personnel who represent the major functional Sections.

- *Section* — Organizational level having responsibility for a major functional area of incident management such as Operations, Planning, Logistics, Finance/Administration, and Information and Intelligence (this function may be designated as a section, a branch within Operations, or part of the Command Staff); organizationally located between *Command* and *Branch.* See the Information box, p. 438, for examples of the responsibilities and composition of the sections.

- *Branch* — Organizational level having functional/geographic responsibility for major segments of incident operations; organizationally located between *Section* and *Division* or *Group.* Branches are identified by Roman numeral or functional area (such as Command, Operations, etc.). *or sector*

- *Division* — Organizational level having responsibility for operations within a defined *geographic area;* organizationally between *Branch* and *single resources,* task force, or strike team. Resources assigned to a division report to that division supervisor. *Examples:*

  — Divisions are assigned clockwise around an outdoor incident with Division A at the front of the incident.

  — In multistory buildings, divisions are usually identified by the floor or area to which they are assigned: First floor is Division 1, second floor is Division 2, etc.

  — In a one-story building, the entire interior may be assigned as a division (Interior Division).

- *Group* — Organizational level, equal to division, having responsibility for a specified *functional* assignment at an incident (such as ventilation, salvage, water supply, etc.) without regard for a specific geographical area. When the assigned function has been completed, it is available for reassignment.

- *Unit* — Organizational level within the sections that fulfill specific support functions such as the resources, documentation, demobilization, and situation units within the Planning Section.

Resources

- *Resources* — All personnel and major items of equipment available (or potentially available) for assignment to incident tasks on which status is maintained; may be individual companies (single resources), task forces, strike teams, or other specialized units. *Factors:*

  — Resources are considered available when they have checked in at the incident and are not currently committed to an assignment.

  — It is imperative that the status of these resources is tracked so that they may be assigned when and where they are needed without delay.

- *Resource types* — Classification based on the capability of the resource. Resource types may refer to fire apparatus, crew transport (buses), hoseline crews, aircraft, hazardous materials units, fireboats, or ICS position assignments. Type I (1) resource is considered more capable than Type II (2), Type III (3), or Type IV (4). *Pumping apparatus examples:*

  — Type I engine is a structural fire-fighting apparatus with 1,000 gpm (3 785 l/min) pump capacity.

  — Type II engine may be an off-road grass-fire unit with 500 gpm (1 893 l/min) pump capacity.

  — Type III engine may be a 4-wheel drive vehicle with a 120 gpm (454 l/min) pump capacity **(Figure 19.2)**.

  — Type IV vehicle may be a commercial pickup with a skid-mounted 70 gpm (265 l/min) pump, tank, and hose reel.

- *Crew* — Specified number of personnel assembled for an assignment such as search, ventilation, or hoseline deployment and operations.

Figure 19.2 Type III off-road apparatus may be commercially produced or adapted by the local organization to meet local needs and financial resources.

The number of personnel assigned to a crew should be within span-of-control guidelines. A crew operates under the direct supervision of a crew leader.

- ***Single resources*** — Individual pieces of apparatus (engines, ladders/trucks, water tenders, bulldozers, air tankers, helicopters, etc.) and the personnel required to make them functional.

- ***Task force*** — Any combination of resources (engines, ladders/trucks, bulldozers, etc.) assembled for a specific mission or operational assignment **(Figure 19.3)**. All units in the force must have common communications capabilities and a designated leader. Once a task force's tactical objective has been met, the force is disbanded; individual resources are reassigned or released.

- ***Strike team*** — Set number of resources of the same kind and type (engines, ladders/trucks, bulldozers, etc.) that have an established minimum number of personnel. All units in the team must have common communications capabilities and a leader in a separate vehicle. Unlike task forces, strike teams remain together and function as a team throughout an incident.

Figure 19.3 Task forces are composed of a variety of resources; for example, a Type II pumping apparatus and a bulldozer operate in support of a hoseline crew at a wildland fire.

Leadership Titles

- ***Incident commander (IC)*** — Individual responsible for the management of all incident operations; primarily responsible for formulating the incident action plan (IAP) and coordinating and directing all incident resources to implement the plan and meet its goals and objectives

- ***Supervisor*** — Individuals responsible for command of a division or group within the Operations Section; may be assigned to an area initially to evaluate and report conditions and advise Command of the needed task and resources.

General Staff Composition and Duties

- ***Command*** — Incident commander (IC) and Command Staff positions, including public information officer, safety officer, liaison officer, and other positions as required.

- ***Planning Section*** — Responsible for the collection, evaluation, and dissemination of operational information and the preparation and documentation of the incident action plan (IAP); includes the resources, situation, demobilization, and documentation units as well as technical specialists

- ***Operations Section*** — Responsible for all tactical incident operations; includes branches, divisions or groups, and single resources

- ***Logistics Section*** — Responsible for providing facilities, services, and material support for the incident; includes the supply, food, ground support, communications, facilities, and medical units

- ***Finance/Administration Section*** — Responsible for financial, reimbursement, and administrative services to support incident management activities; includes the compensation/claims, procurement, cost, and time units

- ***Information and intelligence function*** — Responsible for managing internal information, intelligence, and operational security requirements supporting incident management activities; activated if necessary and may be the responsibility of a law enforcement official or unit; may be part of the Command Staff, part of the Planning Section, or assigned independently

Modular Organization

The NIMS-ICS is based on a *modular organization,* which means that the organization develops *from the top down* as additional functions are added based on the nature and scope of the incident. Developing from the top down means that the first officer on the scene may initially perform all of the NIMS-ICS functions required to control the incident.

If the incident increases in size or complexity, the IC then delegates functions to other officers as needed, building the structure based on the NIMS-ICS model. In most cases, the first-arriving company officer becomes the IC and directs both the strategic and tactical operations. The initial IC remains in charge of the incident until properly relieved or the incident is terminated.

The NIMS-ICS organization grows and expands as the incident grows. However, it should only grow as much as needed to maintain recommended span-of-control guidelines for any individual with supervisory responsibilities. Only those organizational positions that are required to manage the incident and bring it to a timely and successful conclusion need to be staffed.

Common Communications

A common means of communication is essential to maintaining control, coordination, and safety. NIMS requires that a common communications system include the ability to be understood and to contact all units or agencies that are assigned to the emergency incident. To ensure effective communications, all units must use clear text (specified phrases in plain English) rather than the 10-codes or any other agency-specific radio codes.

The NIMS-ICS also requires the establishment of a common incident communications plan that identifies different radio frequencies or channels to be used exclusively for specified organizational functions. To avoid the chaos that would result from all units attempting to receive and transmit on the same channel, the incident communications plan assigns specific channels to specific functions or units. Channels may be assigned for the following functions:

- Command
- Safety
- Tactical
- Support
- Ground-to-air
- Air-to-air

As part of the check-in procedure at an incident, all unit leaders should be given a copy of the communications plan for the incident. One of the most critical pieces of information to be distributed is the number of the safety channel. Someone in each unit must be designated to monitor this channel.

While most modern mobile and portable radios are capable of scanning, receiving, and transmitting over dozens of channels, not every organization is equipped with the latest communications equipment. If mutual aid units are not equipped with radios that can receive and transmit on the channels assigned to them in the plan, they must be issued portable radios that will function on those channels.

Unified Command Structure

A unified command structure is necessary when an incident involves or threatens to involve more than one jurisdiction or agency. For example, a fire that originates near the edge of a city may spread to an adjacent suburb or vice versa. However, these multijurisdictional incidents are not limited to fires.

A release of a hazardous vapor or gas may be carried by the wind into a neighboring jurisdiction. Likewise, if a flammable or toxic liquid enters a sewer or storm drain in one jurisdiction, it may flow into the next jurisdiction. Large-scale natural disasters such as Hurricane Katrina can easily affect multiple jurisdictions.

A unified command may also be appropriate within a single jurisdiction if multiple agencies are affected. For example, a hostage situation may be primarily a law enforcement incident, but if there is the possibility of a fire or explosion, the fire department may also have a legitimate interest in influencing the strategic and tactical decisions relating to the incident.

In a unified command structure, representatives of all affected agencies or jurisdictions share the Command responsibilities and decisions. They jointly establish the strategic goals for the incident and agree on the tactical objectives that must be achieved. In some agencies or jurisdictions, legal authority to act is vested in those occupying certain positions of responsibility. Unified command allows these individuals to interface with those who have the operational expertise required to resolve an incident.

As the fire and emergency services becomes more involved in all-hazard types of responses, it is essential that company officers become more aware of the unified command process. Even small incidents such as a fire in a residential structure that contains an illegal methamphetamine lab may result in a situation that requires the unified command approach. Cross-jurisdictional incidents will also place the company officer either in charge of or as part of a unified command.

Incident Action Plan

NFPA 1021, *Standard for Fire Officer Professional Qualifications,* requires the Fire Officer I to be able to develop an *initial action plan.* The NFPA term *initial action plan* means the same thing as the NIMS-ICS *incident action plan (IAP),* that is, a written or unwritten plan for the safe and efficient disposition of an emergency incident. Lloyd Layman and other authors have written extensively about the size-up process, and Layman uses the term *plan of operation* to describe the same concept (see Incident Size-up Considerations section). According to NFPA 1561, *Standard for Fire Department Incident Management System,* an IAP *establishes the overall strategic decisions and assigned tactical objectives for an incident.*

Even in a minor incident without a written IAP, the plan must be communicated to those who implement it. Company officers may be the very best persons to develop an IAP, but if they cannot communicate it to those who must implement it, the plan has no value.

An IAP is an integral part of NIMS-ICS, and implementing the plan affects how emergency resources are organized. All personnel assigned to an incident must function according to the IAP where strategic goals, tactical objectives, and support requirements for the incident are formulated. The first-arriving company officer takes the first steps in creating an IAP that can evolve as the incident expands to involve more resources.

Small incidents involving a few units and lasting short durations of time do not necessarily require *written* IAPs. However, components of the plan should be communicated to on-scene company officers to facilitate safe operations. Written IAPs are required in the following situations:

- Multiagency incidents
- Multijurisdictional incidents
- Resources are needed from multiple agencies or jurisdictions
- Incidents of long duration that require changes in shifts of personnel, units, or equipment

The IC determines the overall strategy for dealing with the incident and establishes the tactical objectives for meeting that strategy. The IAP contains all tactical and support activities required for the control of the incident (**Figure 19.4**). The plan is divided into operational periods consisting of specific time intervals. The duration of the operational periods may vary, depending on the complexity and type of incident, the estimated time to terminate the incident, the number of units and agencies involved, and environmental and safety considerations. Generally, operational periods may be as short as 2 hours or as long as 24 hours with the average being 12 hours.

IAPs usually contain the following elements that are documented in writing by completing the appropriate ICS forms:

- *Incident objectives (ICS 202)* — Lists clearly stated and measurable objectives to be achieved in the specific time interval
- *Organization assignment list (ICS 203)* — Lists descriptions of the ICS table of organization, including the units and agencies that are involved
- *Assignments list (ICS 204)* — Lists specific unit tactical assignments divided by branch, division, and group
- *Incident radio communications plan (ICS 205)* — Lists the basic radio channel assignments for use during the incident
- *Medical plan (ICS 206)* — Provides information on the location and staffing of the incident medical aid station, types of ambulance resources

INCIDENT OBJECTIVES	1. INCIDENT NAME *Billings Warehouse*	2. DATE PREPARED *1/25/2007*	3. TIME PREPARED *0925*

4. OPERATIONAL PERIOD (DATE/TIME)

1/25 0915 to Completion

5. GENERAL CONTROL OBJECTIVES FOR THE INCIDENT (INCLUDE ALTERNATIVES)

Contain fire to northwest corner of warehouse area

Use building fire suppression system to control and eliminate fire

Remove smoke and fire gases from structure to minimize damage to structure

Remove water from fire area

Conduct search of fire area when safe

6. WEATHER FORECAST FOR OPERATIONAL PERIOD

Clear, 35 F, Wind out of southwest at 5 mph, humidity 10%

7. GENERAL SAFETY MESSAGE

Be aware of potential roof collapse hazard

Respiratory protection & pass devices required in all operational areas.

ISO's assigned to all branches

Rehab located at corner of B-C

8. ATTACHMENTS (✓ IF ATTACHED)

☐ ORGANIZATION LIST (ICS 203)   ☐ ORGANIZATION LIST (ICS 203)   ☐ _____

☐ ASSIGNMENT LIST (ICS 204)   ☐ ASSIGNMENT LIST (ICS 204)   ☐ _____

☐ COMMUNICATIONS PLAN (ICS 205)   ☐ COMMUNICATIONS PLAN (ICS 205)   ☐ _____

202 ICS 3-80	9. PREPARED BY (PLANNING SECTION CHIEF) *J. E. FORTNEY*	10. APPROVED BY (INCIDENT COMMANDER) *E. C. KIRTLEY*

Figure 19.4 Sample incident action plan (IAP).

available, locations of on-site ambulances, and contact information for hospitals that are available

- **Operational planning worksheet (ICS 215)** — Lists resources available as well as tactical assignments and those resources that may be needed during the operational period

The IAP is maintained at the incident command post (ICP) and updated or revised as warranted or at the end of a specified time interval. At the end of the incident, the plan is used as part of the postincident analysis and critique. See **Appendix K** for copies of these ICS forms.

Manageable Span of Control

As mentioned in Chapter 11, Organizational Structure, *span of control* is the number of direct subordinates that one supervisor can effectively manage. Variables such as proximity, similarity of function, and subordinate capability affect that number. The number of subordinates can be higher in the following situations:

- Subordinates are within sight of the supervisor and are able to communicate effectively with each other

- Subordinates are performing the same or similar functions

- Subordinates are skilled in performing the assigned task

An effective span of control ranges from three to seven subordinates per supervisor, depending upon the variables just mentioned, with five considered to be the optimum number **(Figure 19.5)**. If an effective span of control is maintained, it is much easier for supervisors to keep track of their subordinates and monitor their safety.

Predesignated Incident Facilities

According to NIMS, several possible types of facilities can be established in and around an incident. The titles and functions of these facilities have been predesignated by the NIMS-ICS model. The types of facilities and their locations are determined by the requirements of the incident as outlined in the IAP. The most commonly used incident facilities are as follows:

- **Incident command post (ICP)** — Location from where all incident tactical operations are directed; located at or in the immediate vicinity of the incident site

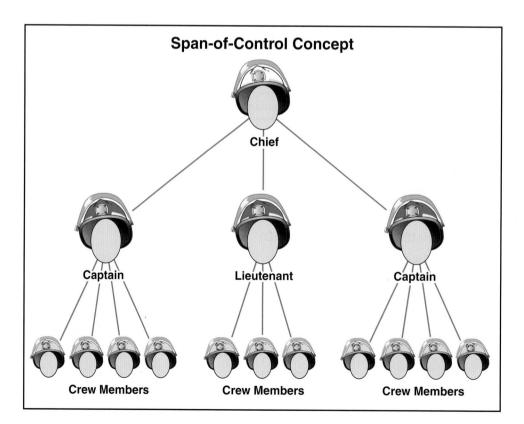

Figure 19.5 Example of the span-of-control concept.

Span-of-Control Concept

Chief

Captain Lieutenant Captain

Crew Members Crew Members Crew Members

- *Incident base* — Location (which remains fixed throughout the incident) to house equipment and personnel support functions; performs primary support activities; only one base is established per incident

- *Camps* — Locations (remote from the incident base) from which essential auxiliary support functions (such as providing food, sleeping areas, and sanitation) are performed at very large incidents; may relocate as needs of the incident dictate

- *Mobilization/staging areas* — Any location where resources (personnel, supplies, and equipment) are held in reserve while awaiting operational assignment. *Examples:*

  — *Wildland fires and other incidents:* Units in staging are on 3-minute availability **(Figure 19.6)**.

  — *High-rise fire:* Staging is located two floors below the fire floor.

- *Helibases* — Locations where helicopters are parked, serviced, maintained, and loaded; may be more than one on large incidents

- *Helispots* — Temporary locations where helicopters can land, refuel, and reload **(Figure 19.7)**

Comprehensive Resource Management

The purpose of comprehensive resource management is to provide the IC and General Staff with access to and control over all resources that are available to them. Resource management involves the ability to perform the following tasks:

- Establish systems for describing, inventorying, requesting, and tracking resources.

- Activate these systems before and during incidents.

- Dispatch resources before and during incidents.

- Deactivate or recall resources during or after incidents.

To make the best use of all incident resources, all company officers must keep incident command aware of the status of their units. The four following standard terms are used to report resource status:

Figure 19.6 Multiple staging areas were established during emergency operations in New Orleans following Hurricane Katrina. *Courtesy of District Chief Chris Mickal.*

Figure 19.7 Helispots are temporary helicopter landing sites. Supplies and personnel are loaded at these sites and refueling resources may be available as well.

1. ***In transit*** — Identifies resources that are en route to the incident but have not checked in at the incident command post (ICP) or staging area

2. ***Assigned*** — Performing an active assignment

3. ***Available*** — Ready for assignment (all resources in staging are available)

4. ***Out-of-service*** — Not ready for assignment (unable to respond)

The information that is transmitted by the units to the IC is recorded on the ICS assignment lists form (ICS 204) and the operational planning worksheet (ICS 215). When a plotting board depicting the incident site plan is used, magnetic markers representing the units are positioned on the plan to indicate location and status.

Personnel Accountability

An essential element of the NIMS-ICS is personnel accountability, which provides the efficient use of resources and the safety of all those involved in an incident. Company officers are responsible for knowing where their subordinates are at all times and what tasks they have been assigned. Therefore, the first-arriving company officer must establish the personnel accountability system for unit members and the expanding NIMS-ICS.

Several different types of accountability systems are in use. Emergency incident accountability systems are usually dictated by the organization's policies. Procedures for using an accountability system must be followed closely by all personnel. The IC is accountable for each company assigned to the incident **(Figure 19.8)**.

The NIMS-ICS provides a means of tracking the personnel resources assigned to a given incident. Personnel accountability includes all the following elements:

- ***Check-in*** — Requires all responders, regardless of affiliation, to check in to receive their assignments

- ***Incident action plan (IAP)*** — Identifies incident priorities and objectives, which dictate how tactical operations must be conducted

- ***Unity of command*** — Dictates that each responder has only one supervisor

- ***Span of control*** — Gives supervisors a manageable number of subordinates

- ***Division/group/crew assignment list*** — Identifies resources with active assignments in the Operations Section

- ***Resource status*** — Ensures that each company officer reports resource status changes as they occur

- ***Resource status unit*** — Maintains status of all incident resources

- ***Communications plan*** — Contains information on the assigned radio tactical channels; section, branch, and division designations; and communication protocols for the incident

When personnel at all levels in the emergency services organization operate according to these principles and procedures, personnel accountability and safety are maximized. As an incident grows from an initial alarm assignment to a major incident, these basic principles and procedures must continue to be applied.

Figure 19.8 The incident commander (IC) must know the location and status of all personnel at an emergency incident. An accountability system assists the IC in personnel management by visually depicting which personnel are at the incident and their assignments.

Incident Priorities

Incident scene management is an integral part of successfully resolving an emergency. Therefore, incident scene management should always reflect overall incident priorities (sometimes referred to as *incident objectives*). The priorities of incident scene management that are based on the mission statement of the organization are always conducted in the following order:

1. Life safety
2. Incident stabilization
3. Property conservation

Life Safety

Life safety is a multipart objective: It involves the safety of responders, victims, and bystanders. Life safety is the responsibility of everyone involved in an incident or at an incident scene. At an incident, life safety includes the following tasks:

- Protecting responders from the incident hazard or hazards while they are controlling it or them

- Removing victims from the incident hazard or hazards, providing appropriate medical care, and transporting them to a medical facility for additional treatment **(Figure 19.9)**

- Separating and protecting bystanders (witnesses, news media, family, and curiosity seekers) from the hazard or hazards

Incident Stabilization

Incident stabilization involves the decisions, resources, and activities that are required to control an incident. The first-arriving company officer begins the stabilization process by sizing up the incident based on information that is available (see Incident Size-up Considerations section). The company officer decides then on the tactical requirements of the incident and assigns resources to meet those requirements. In some cases, the stabilization activity may be implemented initially to ensure the life safety of victims who are trapped by the hazard.

Incident stabilization includes the following elements:

- Fire suppression
- Technical rescue or extrication

- Hazardous materials spill/leak control
- Vehicle or structural integrity
- Medical care for injured or ill victims
- Utility shutoff

Property Conservation

Property conservation is the result of incident stabilization activities. Property involved in an emergency incident will be exposed to less damage when the incident is controlled quickly. For instance, a structure fire that is confined to a single room and quickly extinguished with the minimum amount of water will result in a smaller amount of damage to the rest of the structure. Property conservation is accomplished through the following activities:

- Applying extinguishing agents properly and rapidly

- Using ventilation techniques properly

- Removing property from the hazardous area

- Protecting property in place by use of salvage covers

- Controlling and removing spilled hazardous materials with the least amount of contamination to the environment

Figure 19.9 The first consideration when setting incident priorities is life safety. Providing victims with medical aid and transport to a health-care facility when it is needed is part of the company officer's job.

Incident Size-up Considerations

To accomplish the incident priorities, the first-arriving company officer must know the type of emergency incident to which the unit has been assigned and then gather as much information as possible to make command decisions. *Size-up* is the ongoing process of evaluating an emergency situation to determine the following facts:

- What has happened
- What is happening
- What is likely to happen
- What resources will be needed to resolve the situation **(Figure 19.10)**.

Obviously, there are many different ways to fulfill these requirements. The process is continuous, beginning with the development of preincident plans for target hazards and continuing from the receipt of the alarm assignment until termination of the incident.

The company officer begins to actively size up the emergency when the alarm sounds and emergency notification is received. When a preincident plan for the emergency location exists, the company officer combines this information with information provided by the telecommunications center during unit dispatch. This information may include the description of the incident, weather conditions, and number of units assigned to the incident. At the same time, the company officer takes into account the unit's resources such as the number of personnel on duty and their knowledge, skills, and abilities plus the equipment and materials that may be needed to control the emergency.

An effective company officer is someone who not only can determine whether additional resources are needed but also determine the number of additional resources that will be needed by the time the current resources are operational at the scene. The lead/reflex time (amount of time to request and obtain additional resources) is a factor in this determination. Once on the scene, the company officer must also be proficient at determining how the hazard is developing, how rapidly it is expanding, and where it will be in both intensity and location when additional resources are operational at the scene if they are requested.

A company officer can use any number of size-up processes or models. Decades after Layman wrote his seminal work *Fire Fighting Tactics*, its principles are as valid as ever, and his traditional model is the one most commonly used today. In his book, Layman described the following considerations needed for analyzing any emergency situation:

- *Facts* — Things that are true
- *Probabilities* — Things that are likely to happen

Figure 19.10 In some instances, the facts of the incident situation may seem very obvious. The presence of heavy black smoke coming from a warehouse surrounded by personal vehicles indicates the need to account for occupants of the structure. *Courtesy of District Chief Chris Mickal.*

- *Own situation* — Officer's own knowledge about the situation

- *Decision* — Initial use of resources followed by supplemental resource needs

- *Plan of operation* — Information compiled into incident action plan (IAP)

Facts

The facts of the situation are things that are true. Facts are what the officer knows and is actually observing **(Figure 19.11)**. The majority of this information may be provided by the telecommunications center based on the report of the emergency. All of these items can and should be factored into the company officer's thought processes regarding the emergency. Some of these items include the following:

- Time (month, day, hour)

- Location (address, business name, landmarks)

- Nature of the emergency (fire, hazardous materials release, structural collapse, motor vehicle accident, medical emergency, etc.)

- Life hazard (occupants and responders)

- Exposures (adjacent uninvolved property)

- Weather (wind, temperature extremes, humidity, etc.)

- Number of potential trapped or injured victims

- Number of units being dispatched

The number of units being dispatched provides the company officer with an idea of the size or complexity of the incident. This information also gives the officer an idea of the number and type of resources that will be available to control the incident.

The company officer combines all of this information with any knowledge gained from building surveys, preincident plans, and training in fire or hazard behavior. If the company officer has any indication from the information available that additional or specialized resources are needed, a request should be made as soon as possible.

Based on facts, the company officer decides how closely to approach the source of the problem and how to make that approach **(Figure 19.12, p. 448)**. Consider the following examples:

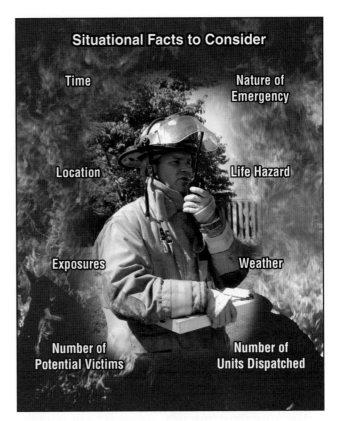

Figure 19.11 The company officer must consider multiple facts during the size-up process. These facts create the foundation for developing strategies and tactics to control an incident.

- *Wildland fire spreading rapidly* — Assessment may indicate that certain highway intersections need to be closed in order to keep nonemergency traffic away from the danger area and roads near the fire clear for emergency vehicles. Other considerations may include current and future weather conditions and the location of structures in the fire's path.

- *Hazardous materials release* — Assessment may indicate the need to approach upwind of the release, evacuate civilians from the immediate area, and request additional resources. Personnel who will be working closely to the release in order to control it must wear the proper level of personal protective clothing and have the correct level of training. First-arriving units may need to establish a control perimeter and remain outside the hazardous area.

- *Trench collapse* — Assessment may indicate the need to limit the approach of heavy fire apparatus in order to prevent further collapse.

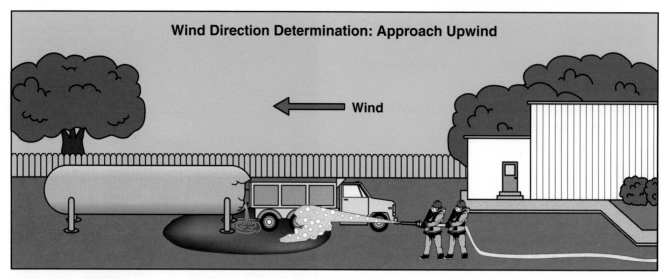

Figure 19.12 When possible, approach a hazardous materials spill from upwind.

- ***Motor vehicle accident*** — Assessment may indicate the need to deploy charged hoselines to control spilled fuel or protect against sparks emitted by power extrication tools.

- ***Working structure fire*** — Assessment may indicate the need to consider the possibility of structural weakness that could result in a roof or wall collapse. Other considerations are exposures that could be damaged by fire.

- ***Medical emergency*** — Assessment may indicate the need for responders to wear respiratory protection against airborne contaminates. In some situations, personal protection such as body armor may be required when there is a chance of civil unrest, criminal activities, or domestic violence directed at responders.

- ***Domestic dispute*** — Assessment may indicate the need for law enforcement protection or personal protective equipment (PPE).

Probabilities

Probabilities are things that are not known for certain, but based on the facts that are known, they are things that are *likely* to happen. Actual observation can transform a probability into a fact. To assist in making decisions, the following questions must be answered regarding the probabilities of a fire emergency situation:

- In which direction is the fire likely to spread, given fuel, weather, and topography?

- Are exposures likely to become involved?

- Are explosions likely and is a secondary explosion likely? Is a secondary collapse likely? Are aftershocks certain?

- Is an evacuation of people downwind likely to be needed?

- Are additional resources likely to be needed? If so, what types and how many?

Many of the decisions involved in the probabilities phase of a fire incident size-up can be made easier and the result more accurate when the officer making the decisions has some knowledge of the following factors:

- Fire behavior and smoke indicators (from past experience, training, and education)

- Building or topography involved (from preincident planning)

This knowledge is especially important if the building involved in fire has lightweight trusses and/or built-in fire protection. Many modern wood-frame buildings have lightweight truss components that have a tendency to fail early in a fire, creating a significant risk of early collapse for first-arriving crews. Also, knowledge of any built-in fire protection systems can suggest just how much first-arriving crews can rely on them. Unless these systems (automatic sprinklers, standpipes, fire hydrants, etc.) are regularly inspected and tested, they may not perform as designed.

Warning!

Firefighters may be injured or killed when fire-damaged roof and floor truss systems collapse, sometimes without warning. Firefighters should take the following steps to minimize the risk of injury or death during structural fire-fighting operations involving roof and floor truss systems:

- Know how to identify roof and floor truss construction.
- Report immediately the presence of truss construction and fire involvement to the incident commander (IC).
- Use a thermal imaging camera as part of the size-up process to help locate fires in concealed spaces.
- Use extreme caution and follow standard operating procedures (SOPs) when operating on or under truss systems.
- Open ceilings and other concealed spaces immediately whenever a fire is suspected of being in a truss system. Steps:
  - Use extreme caution because opening concealed spaces can result in backdraft conditions.
  - Always have a charged hoseline available.
  - Position between the nearest exit and the concealed space to be opened.
  - Be aware of the location of other firefighters in the area.
- Understand that fire ratings may not be truly representative of real-time fire conditions and the performance of truss systems may be affected by fire severity.
- Before emergency incidents, fire departments should take the following steps to protect firefighters:
  - Conduct preincident planning and inspections to identify structures that contain truss construction.
  - Ensure that firefighters are trained to identify roof and floor truss systems and use extreme caution when operating on or under truss systems.
  - Develop and implement SOPs to safely combat fires in buildings with truss construction.
- At the emergency incident, use the following procedures to protect firefighters:
  - Ensure that the IC conducts an initial size-up and risk assessment of the incident scene before beginning interior fire-fighting operations.
  - Evacuate firefighters performing operations under or above trusses as soon as it is determined that the trusses are exposed to fire, and move to a defensive mode.
  - Use defensive overhauling procedures after extinguishing a fire in a building containing truss construction.
  - Use outside master streams to soak smoldering trusses and prevent rekindles.

Source: National Institute for Occupational Safety and Health (NIOSH): "Preventing Injuries and Deaths of Fire Fighters Due to Truss System Failures," NIOSH Publication No. 2005-123.

Additional probabilities have developed in the past quarter century that must also be considered. While Layman was most concerned with structural fire incidents, today's emergency responders must consider many additional situations. Among them are the potentials for hazardous materials spills, fires, natural disasters, and chemical releases. Again, fuel, weather, and topography will influence the spread of these types of hazards (**Figure 19.13, p. 450**). Terrorist

Figure 19.13 Firefighters who are experienced in wildland fire fighting know that wind direction and velocity can change rapidly and unpredictably. *Courtesy of U.S. Emergency Management Agency, Andrea Booher, photographer/FEMA news photo.*

or illegal activities have also become a very real threat to responder safety and can determine courses of action.

Illegal Activities

The existence of illegal methamphetamine labs is now common across the U.S. They can be found in both urban and rural areas, operating in houses, apartments, sheds, and vehicles. The toxicity of the products, especially when involved in fire, creates hazardous atmospheres that demand the use of self-contained breathing apparatus (SCBA). Combined with this hazard is the likelihood that the operators of illegal drug labs may be armed, dangerous, and violent, which increases the risk faced by responders.

Terrorist Acts

Terrorist acts occurred in the U.S. before the September 11, 2001, attacks. They included the bombing of the federal building in Oklahoma City in 1995 and World Trade Center in New York City in 1993 and numerous attacks on abortion clinics, cosmetic testing laboratories, and construction sites **(Figure 19.14)**. The perpetrators of these attacks were both foreign and domestic and included animal-rights activists and ecoterrorists. These people represent the violent fringes of society.

The likelihood of more attacks increases the danger for emergency responders who may become targets of these attackers. The potential for secondary explosions that are intended to affect responders must be taken into consideration during the initial size-up. This terrorist tactic has been used frequently in the Middle East.

Company officers must be aware of the potential for these types of situations and use caution based on the real and potential dangers of the incident. When faced with a situation involving significant unknowns, the company officer must plan for possibilities rather than probabilities. This adjustment requires a more conservative approach for obvious safety reasons.

Figure 19.14 Acts of terrorism such as the bombing of the federal building in Oklahoma City have increased dramatically in the past decade.

Own Situation

The first-arriving officer's own situation is one set of facts that is known about the overall incident situation **(Figure 19.15)**. The following facts are among those to consider:

- Number and types of resources responding to or already at the scene

- Additional resources that are available immediately, with some delay, and with considerable delay

- Capabilities and limitations of resources (important factors in the development of an IAP)

- Assessment of the officer's own ability to deal with the situation based on training and experience

- Abilities of unit members

Figure 19.15 Some information available to the first-arriving company officer comes from a personal assessment of the officer's knowledge, skills, and abilities. Other information is based on the officer's knowledge of the abilities of unit members.

Decision

Even though Layman labeled this consideration in the singular, he went on to identify two or more separate decisions that must be made in the ongoing size-up process — an *initial decision* and one or more *supplemental decisions* based on the three incident priorities. Even the initial decision may be seen as having the following three segments:

1. Whether resources at the scene and those en route are adequate for the situation

2. How to deploy the resources already at the scene in the most effective manner

3. What to do with the resources that arrive (immediate deployment or staging)

As the incident progresses and the situation changes, supplemental decisions will have to be made. For instance, the IC needs to decide whether the initial deployment of resources is still producing the desired results or the deployments need to be changed. Also, on very large incidents (those lasting more than an operational period), consideration must be given to relief personnel, additional supplies, etc. More supplemental decisions will be required and more functional positions of NIMS-ICS may need to be activated when an incident continues for an extended period of time.

Plan of Operation

Information gathered in the size-up process serves no purpose unless it is used as a basis for making decisions about how to handle the incident. Depending upon the nature and scope of the incident, the plan of operation or IAP may be simple or complex. As mentioned earlier, the plan need not be in writing on relatively small, routine incidents (those involving only the initial assignment) — but there *must* be a plan. Large, complex incidents require a written IAP, often with numerous annexes. An IAP normally covers a single operational period, usually about 12 hours in duration.

Scene Control

Size-up of an incident determines the placement and positioning of apparatus (see Chapter 20, Incident Scene Operations), the assignment of resources (both initial and subsequent), and the methods that are required to control the incident scene. *Scene control* means controlling the environment in which responders must work and bystanders or victims may find themselves. Scene control is essential to ensuring the life safety of responders, victims, and bystanders.

Scene control begins with the establishment of the NIMS-ICS by the first-arriving company officer. The officer must establish and designate the perimeter of the hazard and divide it into control zones. Establishing control zones by setting boundaries and maintaining control over who enters and leaves these zones makes it easier to keep track of personnel in high-hazard areas.

Emergencies tend to also attract spectators, and maintaining control of a scene makes it easier to maintain their safety and provide important information to them in a safe area. Controlling the movements of nonemergency personnel near a high-hazard area contributes to life safety on the scene.

The methods used to establish and maintain scene control can vary almost as much as the incidents themselves. However, through experience, fire and emergency services personnel operating at countless emergency incidents have identified some scene-control methods that can be applied to most emergency incidents. These fundamental methods can be applied to several basic situations such as perimeter control, traffic control, crowd control, and on-scene occupant services.

An important decision that company officers must make when controlling any emergency scene is determining whether evacuating victims, bystanders, or nearby residents will be necessary. The various approaches to evacuation are addressed in Chapter 20, Incident Scene Operations.

Perimeter Control

There are numerous reasons to control the perimeter of an incident scene. Controlling the perimeter facilitates the use of a personnel accountability system. It also helps in accounting for victims and keeping the scene free of curious spectators.

Establishing three operating *control zones* (commonly labeled *hot*, *warm*, and *cold*) is the most common and effective way to control the perimeter

of an incident scene (**Figure 19.16**). The zones can be cordoned off with rope or fire line tape tied to signs, utility poles, parking meters, or any other objects readily available.

There is no specific distance or area that should be cordoned off for each zone or from the total incident scene. The zone boundaries should be established by taking into account the amount of area needed by emergency personnel to work, degree of hazard presented by elements involved in the incident, wind and weather conditions, and general topography of the area. The three zones can be described as follows:

- *Hot zone* — Area where resolving the problem takes place — fires are suppressed, hazardous materials releases are controlled and contained, vehicle extrication is performed, etc. Only personnel who are directly involved in disposing of the problem are allowed, which limits crowds and confusion at the most critical area of the scene. The size of the zone may vary greatly, depending upon the nature and extent of the problem. *Personnel requirements:*

  — Trained appropriately to manage the situation

  — Attired in complete personal protective equipment (PPE) designed for the specific hazard

  — Participated in a personnel accountability system implemented by the incident commander (IC) or incident safety officer (ISO)

- *Warm zone* — Area immediately outside the hot zone for personnel who are directly supporting the work being performed by those in the hot zone — limited to personnel who are operating hydraulic tool power plants, providing emergency lighting, and providing fire protection. These personnel are in full PPE and ready to enter the hot zone. In hazardous materials incidents, this zone is where a decontamination station is normally assembled.

- *Cold zone* — Area immediately surrounding the hot and warm zones — may include the incident command post (ICP) with a rapid intervention crew (RIC) nearby, public information officer's (PIO) location, rehabilitation area, and staging areas for personnel and portable equipment

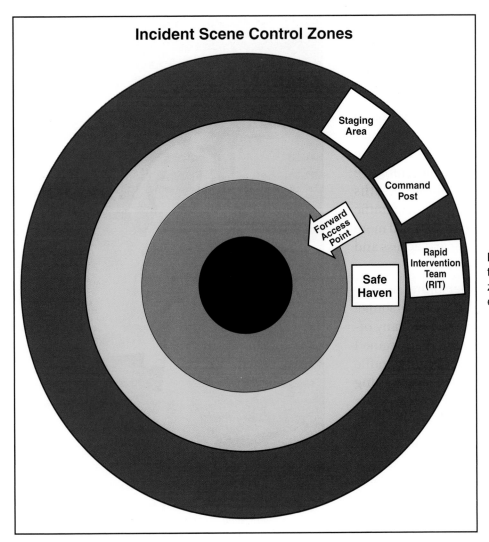

Incident Scene Control Zones

Staging Area

Command Post

Forward Access Point

Safe Haven

Rapid Intervention Team (RIT)

Figure 19.16 Illustration of the organization of control zones used for most types of emergency incidents.

(Figure 19.17). The outer boundary of this area would be the control line for the general public (crowd-control line). *Examples:*

— Backup personnel available to enter warm or hot zones

— Witnesses and family members of victims

— News media accompanied by the PIO or organization representative

NOTE: The term used to describe personnel or units that are given the task of locating and rescuing trapped emergency responders varies from agency to agency. *Rapid intervention crew (RIC), rapid intervention team (RIT),* and *initial rapid intervention crew (IRIC)* are among the terms that are presently in use. Because NFPA 1500, *Standard on Fire Department Occupational Safety and Health Program,* uses the term *RIC,* this manual will conform to that terminology. The

Figure 19.17 A rapid intervention crew (RIC) remains in the cold zone until needed.

term *IRIC* is also used to indicate the application of the requirement of such crews or teams to the first-arriving unit.

Traffic Control

A very important part of maintaining safety around an emergency scene is the control of vehicular traffic. Fire and emergency responders who have been struck by vehicles at incident scenes comprise a significant percentage of line-of-duty deaths (LODDs) and injuries. Controlling the flow of traffic makes operations at incident scenes proceed more smoothly and allows for more efficient access and departure of emergency vehicles.

Although law enforcement personnel usually control traffic, in some cases fire services personnel may have to perform this function. Company officers should ensure that unit members are trained in the basics of roadway safety and directing traffic around an incident (**Figure 19.18**). This training includes the proper placement of apparatus as barriers and use of traffic cones.

Personnel assigned to traffic control duties must also wear reflective safety vests. When engaged in vehicle extrication or other emergency operations, PPE with reflective stripes will provide the minimum visibility required by NFPA standards.

Figure 19.18 The correct use of traffic cones to redirect traffic, prevent access, and protect emergency responders is critical to incident scene safety.

///////////////////////

Caution

Company officers must ensure the safety of emergency responders and accident victims located on or near roadways, streets, or highways. Apparatus may be used to block traffic; traffic cones, signs, or flares may be used to divert traffic; *personnel must wear traffic vests when directing traffic;* **and law enforcement personnel** *should* **be asked to control traffic near the incident scene.**

Company officers must be aware that in some situations certain variables may need attention. The best approach to these situations is to make decisions based on the knowledge gained from preincident planning. Company officers also need to effectively communicate with law enforcement personnel about traffic safety needs at the incident scene.

The following variables may not be controllable, but both familiarization with the jurisdiction and training will improve the ability to manage them in a safe and effective manner:

● *Time of day* — Traffic congestion changes (in most areas) depend on the time of day. Darkness can affect the speed that traffic travels as well as visibility issues with apparatus. *Examples:*

— Traffic on arterial streets and highways leading into urban areas will be heaviest in the early morning when people are driving to work, while the lanes leading to the suburbs will be heaviest in the late afternoon when they return home (**Figure 19.19**).

— Streets near large plants or institutions that have three work shifts will be the most congested around shift-change times. This type of information should be on preincident plans for these facilities.

— School buses operate along predetermined routes before and after school hours. The locations of public or private schools where students are picked up or discharged by buses or private vehicles will be congested before and after school hours.

• *On-street parking* — Some cities control on-street parking by alternating the side of the street that can be used for parking. This information may be critical in old urban areas where streets are narrow and access is limited. Parking congestion may also vary by time of day. Residential areas may have more vehicles parked on the street at night, while office and commercial areas will be more congested during weekdays and retail shopping areas will be congested on weekends.

• *Weather conditions* — Extreme weather conditions such as heavy snowfalls, heavy rains that cause street flooding, or blowing dust near construction sites can affect traffic patterns and conditions. Conditions should be monitored during times of extreme weather. *Examples:*

— Become familiar with local snow-removal policies that designate which streets must be cleared first, parking restrictions, and other snow-removal rules.

— Mark roadways that can wash out or have low water fords over creeks on response maps **(Figure 19.20)**.

— Mark construction sites on maps to indicate potential street obstructions, limited access, dust, or heavy equipment on roadways.

• *Traffic flow patterns* — In some urban areas, the direction of traffic flow may be regulated, depending on the time of day or amount of traffic. Streets or lanes may become one-way during peak traffic times. These patterns have an affect on controlling traffic during an emergency and gaining access to an incident. Alternate access routes should be determined during preincident planning.

• *Roadway constrictions* — Many streets, roads, and highways have components that can slow, restrict, or block access to emergency apparatus. *Components:*

— *Bridges:* Weight restrictions can prevent the use of some bridges by vehicles and apparatus. Other restrictions can result from limited height access under bridge over-

Figure 19.19 Traffic congestion in most urban areas follows a pattern based on the time of day and day of the week. Company officers should be aware of the times and locations within their response area where traffic may slow or prevent timely responses.

Figure 19.20 Flood-prone roadways and areas where rainwater can collect can create barriers to emergency response vehicles and result in delayed responses. Local policy may prohibit driving apparatus into standing water that covers a street or road. *Courtesy of U.S. Federal Emergency Management Agency, Bob McMillan, photographer.*

passes. Privately owned bridges may not be designed to support the weight of emergency apparatus.

— *Low water dams:* Some roadways may have low water dams that permit water to flow across the road surface. During heavy rains, these roads may become completely impassible.

— *Railroad crossings:* Crossing grades may not be accessible to apparatus with low centers of clearance under the vehicle. Knowledge of train schedules, especially along sidings or spur lines that serve warehouses, may be sporadic. Some railroad spur lines have remotely controlled, unstaffed switch engines that may block crossings **(Figure 19.21)**.

— *Tunnels:* Consider tunnels from the view of access and as potential emergency scenes. A traffic accident, fire, or hazardous materials release from a transportation unit (either truck or train) in a tunnel can create a major incident that will require special equipment and training.

— *Parking lots and garages:* Parking lots and garages may not be designed to support the weight of emergency apparatus. Parking garages may have restricted minimum heights that prevent access of emergency apparatus, including ambulances.

Good coordination with the law enforcement agency will help alleviate problems with closing traffic lanes. In some areas, state and local road crews (departments of transportation or public works) provide incident response teams to manage traffic flow and safety.

Emergency incidents often do not involve vehicles nor are they always located on a street or roadway. They often occur inside buildings or in areas well off roadways. In these cases, it is important to park emergency vehicles in a way that does not interfere with the normal flow of traffic. See Chapter 20, Incident Scene Operations.

Each roadway variable requires effective and detailed preplanning to overcome potential barriers. Company officers must be familiar with all of these types of situations, record the locations and conditions on response maps, inform the tele-

Figure 19.21 Company officers must be aware of the location of railroad crossings and the general times that roadways may be blocked. Alternate routes should be noted on response maps.

communications center of changes resulting from construction or closures, and frequently check the locations for changes.

Crowd Control

In small incidents when evacuation is unnecessary, cordoning off the area as described previously will keep bystanders a safe distance from the scene and away from where emergency personnel are working. Once an area has been cordoned off, the boundary should be monitored to ensure that people do not cross it. Reasons for controlling individuals who were involved in an incident (and their family and friends) include the following:

• Keep individuals from wandering around the scene.

• Keep the uninjured from becoming injured.

- Provide a method of accounting for everyone involved in the incident.

- Obtain information from those involved in the incident.

- Separate witnesses from each other to prevent them from discussing what they saw and perhaps influencing each other to coordinate their stories.

When large-scale evacuations are not needed and there is no need for extensive traffic control, law enforcement personnel may be available to monitor the crowd-control line. It is preferable for law enforcement personnel to perform this function because they are trained to manage crowds and have the authority to make arrests if necessary.

Using emergency responders for crowd control may be necessary but should be avoided if possible. Emergency responders who are busy with crowd control are not available to help resolve the problem that brought them to the scene. Company officers should avoid placing emergency responders who have not yet been trained to manage crowds into these positions.

Incident Victims

People who are involved in an incident should be assessed by emergency medical personnel before being released from the scene **(Figure 19.22)**. This action is particularly important when an incident involves a release of hazardous or toxic materials.

Some symptoms may not become apparent for 24 or more hours. Without a local protocol to the contrary, anyone who refuses treatment or transportation to a medical facility should be asked to sign a release-of-liability form.

Spectators

Even in the most remote locations, spectators are often drawn to emergency scenes. Spectators are often quite curious and try to get as close to a scene as possible. All spectators should be restricted from getting too close to the incident for their own safety and that of victims and emergency personnel.

Friends/Relatives of Victims

Emergency scenes tend to be emotional situations that should be handled with care. This situation is particularly true when friends or relatives of victims are at the scene. These particular bystanders are often difficult to manage, but emergency responders should treat them with sensitivity and understanding. Relatives and friends of victims should be gently but firmly restrained from getting too close to the incident, and they should be kept some distance from the actual incident but still within the cold zone.

While friends or relatives may console each other, they should not be left entirely alone. A firefighter or other responsible individual should be assigned to stay with them until victims have been removed from the scene.

Figure 19.22 At incidents that involve a large number of victims, it is important to gather them into one location where their injuries can be prioritized and treated. Some victims may be transported to hospitals or released from the scene.

On-Scene Occupant Services

On-scene occupant services involve emergency responders seeing beyond the obvious physical affect of an incident on victims and witnesses and being aware of and sensitive to their mental and emotional conditions as well. Victims who are displaced from their homes should be medically evaluated and treated as needed and given shelter from the elements (perhaps in a department vehicle). The appropriate relief agencies should be called for further assistance (**Figure 19.23**).

In addition, emergency responders should help those directly involved to notify relatives perhaps by making a department cellular phone dedicated to this service available to them. Typically the cellular phone on scene is for incident management use only.

Emergency responders should also be aware of what those at the scene may have seen or experienced, including serious injuries or fatalities or major personal property losses (such as those during structure fires or collapses). Witnesses may also see responders performing tasks that they do not understand such as forcible entry, ventilation, the time involved in stabilizing victims before sending them to a medical facility, etc. It is an important part of occupant services to provide those at the scene with a reasonable explanation of *why* emergency responders are doing what they are doing.

In the case of structure fires, victims should also be given accurate and timely information about the progress of an incident and an estimate of when they might be able to reoccupy their property if it is possible. When it is safe to do so and personnel are available, property owners should be escorted through the damaged area so they can see for themselves. Some organizations have published *after-the-fire* brochures to help affected occupants understand what actions were taken and provide some recommendations for what to do when emergency responders leave the scene (**Figure 19.24**).

Emergency responders must be aware that their every action is being observed at an incident. Innocent jokes, laughter, horseplay, or even high-fives for a job well done can be misunderstood by those

Figure 19.23 Most communities have nonprofit organizations that provide assistance to victims of disasters or emergencies. *Courtesy of U.S. Federal Emergency Management Agency, George Armstrong, photographer.*

After the Fire!
Returning to Normal

FA-46

 FEMA

Figure 19.24 Brochures containing information that is helpful to victims of disasters are available from organizations like FEMA. Local fire and emergency services organizations may have material that is specific to local community services and agencies. *Courtesy of U.S. Federal Emergency Management Agency.*

at the scene. These seemingly innocuous gestures can make emergency responders appear uncaring and callous. Years of goodwill can be destroyed in a single moment.

Summary

Managing an emergency incident scene is one of the most important functions for the successful conclusion of an incident. Effective size-up based on sound decision-making and the implementation of the NIMS-ICS support the life-safety priority by protecting emergency responders from incident hazards, removing victims from hazards and providing medical care for them, preventing curious bystanders from wandering into hazardous areas, and evacuating people from potentially hazardous areas.

Incident scene management also supports other incident priorities by ensuring effective control and assignment of resources to stabilize the incident and conserve property. The implementation of the jurisdiction's NIMS-ICS also permits the effective and efficient use of available resources while providing for the expansion of the organization as other units, agencies, or jurisdictions become involved.

The company officer applies incident scene management during the initial size-up phase of the operation. Size-up begins when the alarm sounds and combines information from the preincident plan for specific hazards with information about the emergency provided by the telecommunicator. The incident size-up process considerations from Layman were described. The company officer uses scene control to ensure the efficient and safe resolution of the emergency incident, protect all persons on the scene, and provide access to occupant services.

Incident Scene Operations

Chapter Contents

Learning Objectives

1. Recall each of the elements of the Layman decision-making model.

2. Select facts about the application of size-up theory to three specific time periods.

3. Recognize condition indicators that may be present at a structure fire.

4. Identify facts about operational implementation.

5. Define various operational modes.

6. Select facts about various operational modes.

7. Recall facts about apparatus placement and positioning at structural fire scenes.

8. Select from a list guidelines for positioning apparatus at wildland fire scenes.

9. Identify considerations for positioning apparatus at hazardous materials incidents.

10. Recall facts about positioning apparatus at high-rise incidents.

11. Select from a list guidelines for the placement and positioning of apparatus at technical rescue incidents.

12. Identify considerations for positioning apparatus at aircraft incidents.

13. Choose correct facts about positioning apparatus at medical incidents.

14. Identify the incident termination activities of the company officer.

Job Performance Requirements

This chapter provides information that addresses the following job performance requirements of NFPA 1021, *Standard for Fire Officer Professional Qualifications* (2003):

Chapter 20
Incident Scene Operations

The company officer must be able to make decisions rapidly under extreme pressure. Even the smallest of emergency incidents can generate a great deal of stress within the officer who is attempting to establish the National Incident Management System-Incident Command System (NIMS-ICS), deploy resources, and determine the appropriate strategy and tactics to control the hazard. A company officer must employ proven leadership styles, proper resource management, supervisory skills, and knowledge of fire behavior and operational tactics in order to accomplish incident priorities efficiently, effectively, and safely.

One tool that will help the company officer make decisions is the Layman decision-making model. For over 50 years, this model has been successfully applied to all types of emergency situations. The company officer who can effectively apply this model to small incidents will be able to use the same process for large and complex incidents. The model (known by the acronym *RECEO-VS*) can be adapted for use in all types of hazardous situations. This chapter provides a detailed look at the model and how it is used.

The Layman decision-making model must be used with accurate information about the emergency incident. The company officer uses the size-up process introduced in Chapter 19, Incident Scene Management, to gather that information. The initial size-up includes gathering the following information:

- Preincident survey results about a particular structure, facility, or hazard

- Nature of the incident details provided in the alarm dispatch

- Visual indicators that the officer sees upon arrival **(Figure 20.1)**

Besides establishing the NIMS-ICS, performing size-up, and developing an IAP, the company officer implements the operational plan by determining the operational goals and objectives, selecting the form of command to assume and the operational mode to use. Correct placement and positioning of

Figure 20.1 Visual indicators may include the presence of smoke or evidence that the building is vacant such as the plywood coverings on the windows and doors of this house. *Courtesy of District Chief Chris Mickal.*

apparatus is necessary to the implementation of any operational mode. Improper placement may put apparatus and personnel in a hazardous location and can result in time lost if apparatus must be relocated.

Finally, this chapter provides information on the actions necessary to terminate an emergency incident. An incident is not terminated until the property has been returned to the possession of the owner and all emergency responders have been released from the site.

Layman Decision-Making Model

Fire and emergency services personnel respond to a wide variety of emergencies. In every emergency situation, whether it involves a fire, hazardous materials, rescue, vehicle extrication, or medical response, the priorities are basically the same: life safety, incident stabilization, and property conservation (as described in Chapter 19, Incident Scene Management).

To help in the decision-making process, the company officer applies Lloyd Layman's decision-making model: *RECEO-VS*. Layman recognized the need for identifying priorities in emergency situations. Even though his list of priorities is stated in fire-control terms, he also acknowledged that the same priorities could be applied to any type of emergency.

Life safety is always the first and highest priority, although rescue may not be the first *action* taken by the first-arriving unit. In some cases, it is necessary to control a fire, for example, before attempting a rescue. The second priority is to isolate and/or resolve the problem. If a fire can be controlled or hazardous materials release contained, then both the situation will be stabilized and the third priority — conserving property (which includes protecting the environment) — can be addressed. Once the incident is stabilized and contained, it is no longer a threat to exposures or adjacent properties.

Initially, Layman intended the term *RECEO* to be both a list of priorities *and* a sequence of operations, so he did not include *ventilation* and *salvage* in the list because they are *not* needed in every fire incident and are *not* always performed at the same point in the fire incidents when they are

used. Current application of the model includes ventilation and salvage as part of the process. The initials stand for the following priorities or operations:

- **Rescue** — Identifies the life-safety aspect of emergency incident priorities
- **Exposures** — Describes the need to limit an emergency incident to the property or area of origin
- **Confinement** — Describes the need to confine an emergency incident to the smallest possible area within the property of origin
- **Extinguishment** — Describes the activities needed to resolve an emergency incident
- **Overhaul** — Describes activities that restore an incident scene to a condition that is as nearly normal as possible
- **Ventilation** — Describes activities that control or modify the environment
- **Salvage** — Describes all actions taken to protect structures and contents from preventable damage

Emergency incidents that do not involve fire, such as an ignitable gas leak, only require the application of the appropriate operations. However, the sequence should be followed whenever possible.

Rescue

Rescue is the term that Layman used to identify the life-safety aspect of emergency incident priorities. In most fire and emergency service organizations, the term is taken to include humans, pets, and livestock. However, the term is not limited to occupants; it also includes emergency responders. The responder's life safety is the most important consideration because if a responder is disabled by an injury, that responder cannot rescue occupants or victims and consumes resources needed for victims.

Regardless of whether this position is valid or not, clearly the life safety of responders is *at least as* important as that of occupants. Therefore, company officers should neither expect nor allow their personnel to sacrifice themselves by taking unnecessary risks at an emergency incident scene. All personnel must conform to NFPA 1500, *Standard on Fire Department Occupational Safety and Health Program,* and Occupational Safety and Health Administration (OSHA) requirements for *two-in, two-out* (two responders must be available for rescue outside when two responders are inside a structure) and initial rapid intervention crew (IRIC) procedures.

Being the first and highest priority, life safety takes precedence over any and all other considerations, which means that, *if necessary,* a building may be allowed to burn for a period of time in order to facilitate a rescue. The same is true regarding firefighters — they should not be ordered into buildings that are already lost or any life-threatening situations to recover a body. No mere object is worth a human life.

Rescue focuses exclusively on the life-safety priority. One of the most important requirements of the rescue process is that the decision to attempt rescue must be declared over the radio in order to alert the telecommunications center and all other incoming units of the situation and the tactical decisions that were made. In fire incidents, search and rescue teams must take charged hoselines with them for their protection and that of those being rescued, not for fire attack purposes **(Figure 20.2)**.

The company officer must make some very difficult decisions when it is apparent that rescue operations may be required. First is to determine the

level of risk in which responders should be placed during the rescue (see Initial Risk Assessment section). Second is whether an evacuation should be required, either of a single structure or geographic part of the community. A decision may need to be made on whether survivors can be sheltered in place instead of evacuated. Some structures may have the necessary facilities to protect people such as pressurized stairwells.

Evacuation

Rescue may also require the evacuation of a building, neighborhood, or community during an emergency operation. Depending on the number of people involved and their conditions, evacuation can be relatively simple or very complex. After it has been determined that evacuation is necessary, the next determination is what area needs to be evacuated.

In the case of a structure fire, moving occupants either out of the involved building or to a safe haven within the building (shelter in place) may be all that is needed (see following section). However, in the case of a hazardous materials incident, a major wildland fire, or a natural disaster like Hurricane Katrina, a large number of people may have to be moved a considerable distance to ensure their safety **(Figure 20.3, p. 466)**.

Shelter in Place

The theory of *shelter in place* (also called *safe haven*) is that if there is too little time to conduct a full-scale evacuation, it may be just as effective to simply have occupants remain inside the protective cocoon of a building or in a protected portion of the building until the danger has passed. In case of a fire in a building, occupants who cannot exit the building can simply go to a predesignated safe area and await rescue by emergency responders. It is important that these areas be identified during preincident surveys and clearly indicated on preincident plans.

In response to the Americans with Disabilities Act (ADA), many new buildings and those that have undergone major renovation now include what are called *areas of rescue assistance.* These areas have certain minimum structural requirements (includ-

Figure 20.2 The first priority of any rescue is life safety, which means that emergency responders must wear the correct personal protective equipment and follow all policies and procedures regarding hazardous operations.

Figure 20.3 The extent of the damage caused to streets, roads, and transportation systems by Hurricane Katrina made evacuation by helicopter necessary. *Courtesy of U.S. Federal Emergency Management Agency, Michael Rieger, photographer.*

ing a means of communication) and fire protection features (fire-rated enclosures and doors) that effectively isolate them from the rest of the building. They provide a safe haven for occupants without having to leave the building.

A rather common application of shelter in place is in fires in the wildland/urban interface. Emergency responders and others who are in danger of being overrun by a fast-moving wildland fire can take refuge in a structure until the flame front passes. Even if the structure catches fire and eventually burns to the ground, it will protect occupants long enough for them to survive the flame front and escape the structure before it is completely consumed. Survivors will then be in a burned area that is relatively safe.

Another use of this concept is in the release of airborne contaminants in hazardous materials incidents. If a release has been stopped and all that remains is a windborne cloud of toxic vapor or gas, those inside buildings downwind of the release may be safer if they simply close all doors, windows, and vents, turn off heating, ventilating, and air-conditioning (HVAC) systems, and remain inside until the cloud passes. This type of shelter in place has limitations such as (1) vapors are flammable, (2) it will take a long time for gas to clear the area, and (3) buildings cannot be tightly closed. If these situations exist, occupants must then be evacuated from the site.

Exposures

Layman used the term *exposures* to describe the need to limit the fire or other emergency to the property or area of origin — that is, where the emergency began. Similar to the idea of sacrificing a building to facilitate a rescue, limiting the problem to the building or property of origin means taking, *if necessary,* defensive actions in order to save adjacent structures that are uninvolved or only slightly involved. If the first-arriving units have only enough resources to begin to resolve the incident or keep it from spreading — but not both — they should then focus their efforts on keeping the problem from spreading to uninvolved properties until additional resources arrive (**Figure 20.4**).

It may be that attacking the source of the problem is the best way to protect exposures, but if not, it is a lower priority than protecting the adjacent but uninvolved properties. Stopping oncoming traffic to protect the scene of a vehicle accident from being hit by other vehicles and thereby compounding the situation could be seen as addressing this priority.

Confinement

Confinement is the term that Layman used to describe the need to confine a fire or other problem to the smallest possible area within the property of origin. In the case of a structure fire, the priority is to confine the fire to the room of origin if possible.

When that option fails, confinement should be limited to the area or floor of origin with the building of origin being the last option. The principle can be applied to other types of emergencies as well — limiting a hazardous materials problem to the smallest area of the property in which it originated for example. The company officer must remember that it is necessary to confine the fire or hazard before it can be extinguished or eliminated.

Extinguishment

Even though Layman uses the fire-specific term *extinguishment,* the concept can be applied to any type of emergency. The concept is that of resolving the problem. It could mean extinguishing a fire, performing a rescue, stopping the flow of a hazardous material, or extricating the victims of a vehicle accident (**Figure 20.5**).

Overhaul

Layman carried his list of priorities beyond resolving the problem. He also included *overhaul:* restoring the scene to as nearly normal a condition as possible. In this phase of a fire-suppression operation, any and all hidden fire must be found and extinguished, smoldering contents or debris removed, and utilities (electricity and natural gas) turned off (**Figure 20.6**). Openings that were made to aid ventilation or force entry should be covered to protect the property from further damage by the elements and possible illegal entries.

The term *overhaul* can be applied to nonfire emergencies as well. After a hazardous materials release has been stopped, for instance, liquids must be cleaned up and packaged for proper disposal and any residues must be neutralized. In the case of a motor vehicle accident, the roadway must be cleared of debris and any spilled liquids must be picked up or neutralized so normal traffic flow can be restored. The overhaul phase of the operation can be made much easier when the proper resources are called to the scene based on an accurate initial or supplemental size-up.

Figure 20.5 Emergency personnel resolve emergencies by extinguishing a fire or extricating a victim trapped in a vehicle as shown in this photo. *Courtesy of Bob Esposito.*

Figure 20.4 Before extinguishing a hazardous materials fire, it may be necessary to cool and protect adjacent exposures. In this training photo, industrial fire brigade members apply hose streams to an exposure before attempting to turn off the flow of gas from a ruptured valve.

Figure 20.6 Overhaul includes removing any parts of a structure that may contribute to unsafe conditions. Even when a structure is totally destroyed, weakened structural members may need to be pulled down to prevent collapse.

Ventilation

Ventilation is a means of controlling or modifying the environment and spread of fire within a structure. Ventilation helps reduce the possibility of backdraft or flashover conditions, improves the chances of affecting a rescue by reducing hot gases and poisonous smoke, improves visibility for responders, and reduces property damage. Ventilation consists of those operations needed to replace a contaminated or heated atmosphere with normal air.

Ventilation can also be applied to releases of toxic or harmful gases within a structure. A structure's ventilation system can be used to expel the gases or positive-pressure ventilation fans may be used if the design of the structure permits it. Outside a structure, fans can be used to move and dissipate gases that have accumulated in low-lying areas.

The point to which a fire has progressed determines when ventilation is used; therefore, the ventilation process *floats*, meaning it can be used when needed during the implementation of the *RECEO* model. Ventilation must be coordinated with initial fire attack because ventilating a building too soon can cause rapid fire spread by introducing fresh air into the building before attack hoselines are in place. Yet, ventilation must not be started too late in a fire's progression or the positive effects of proper ventilation will be wasted.

Various types of ventilation involve opening doors or windows, cutting holes in roofs, and using mechanical ventilation fans or smoke ejectors to move fresh air into a building or pull contaminants out. In some instances, the building's HVAC system can be used to remove a contaminated or heated atmosphere.

Types

The option to ventilate a building must be made strategically, considering the personnel needed to perform the operation and type chosen: negative-pressure, positive-pressure, horizontal, or vertical.

- *Negative-pressure* — Technique using smoke ejectors to develop artificial circulation and pull smoke out of a structure; smoke ejectors are placed in windows, doors, or roof vent holes to pull the smoke, heat, and gases from inside the building and eject them to the exterior

- *Positive-pressure* — Method of ventilating a confined space by mechanically blowing fresh air into the space in sufficient volume to create a slight positive pressure within and thereby forcing the contaminated atmosphere out the exit opening (**Figure 20.7**)

- *Horizontal* — Any technique by which heat, smoke, and other products of combustion are channeled horizontally out of a structure by way of existing or created horizontal openings such as windows, doors, or other holes in walls

- *Vertical* (also called *top ventilation*) — Method of ventilating at the highest point of a building through existing or created openings and channeling the contaminated atmosphere vertically within the structure and out the top; uses holes cut in the roof and open building features such as skylights, roof vents, or roof doors

Figure 20.7 Positive-pressure ventilation replaces a contaminated atmosphere in a structure with fresh air. It can be used effectively during search and rescue operations to increase visibility and reduce high temperatures in a structure.

HVAC Systems Control

The HVAC systems of most buildings can both contribute to the hazardous situation or be used to minimize it. The company officer must recognize the type of hazard and how the HVAC system will affect it. It is important to consult the building engineer, if present, to determine how to control and use the system.

The heating system may consist of small gas-fired furnaces or large coal, coal oil, or gas-fired burners. Small gas-fired furnaces can usually be controlled by turning off the fuel at the gas meter. Electric heaters can usually be controlled by unplugging them or turning off the electrical service at the main panel. This procedure is also true for the large heating systems as well. Turing off the systems eliminates a source of fuel that can add to a fire or create a contaminated environment.

Air-conditioning systems are used to cool the interior environment. Electricity to these systems should be turned off to eliminate the fuel source.

The ventilation function of most HVAC systems is designed to move heated or cooled air throughout the structure and filter impurities out of the atmosphere. To prevent smoke and toxic gases from being spread throughout the structure, the system should be turned off. Large area and multistory structures will have systems that are *zoned*. Each zone may have thermostats and controls to the temperature within each area. Building codes also require that HVAC ducts be equipped with smoke detectors and carbon monoxide monitors that will activate an alarm, close fire-stops at fire-rated walls, and turn off the HVAC system.

It is sometimes counterproductive to arbitrarily turn off the HVAC system in a large building because it can, under controlled conditions, be used as part of the ventilation effort by expelling smoke and toxic gases from the building. This procedure helps reduce smoke damage and may limit the spread of fire. Controlling the HVAC system is usually achieved by emergency responders working closely with the building engineer.

The company officer advises the building engineer on what needs to be accomplished, and the building engineer operates the system controls accordingly. In most cases, emergency responders should not attempt to operate the system controls themselves.

Using a Heating, Ventilating, and Air-Conditioning (HVAC) System for Ventilation

To effectively use an HVAC system to control smoke movement, firefighters should use the following guidelines:

- Have a qualified building engineer (not emergency responders) operate the system.
- Use the system to assist in locating the seat of the fire.
- Use the system to limit the extension of fire and smoke to the smallest possible area.
- Do not allow the system to spread fire or smoke beyond the area of origin.
- Provide fresh, uncontaminated air to any occupants who are trapped or located in a designated safe refuge area within the building.

The fire officer should also have a basic understanding of HVAC systems in the event a building engineer is not able to respond to assist in the shutdown process. An instruction sheet should be with the system to assist in this situation.

Salvage

The *salvage* process includes all actions taken to protect structures and contents from preventable damage and can be applied at any time during the implementation of the *RECEO* model **(Figure 20.8, p. 470)**. It may occur during the confinement or extinguishment phases or following the extinguishment phase. During the extinguishment phase, salvage can best be achieved by minimizing the amount of water applied to extinguish the fire.

Salvage may consist of removing property from a hazardous environment or protecting it in place. Assigning personnel to perform salvage is a judgment decision based on the resources available, completion of the other *RECEO* model tasks, and the value or importance of the property involved.

Figure 20.8 Water should be removed as soon as possible following extinguishment of a fire. The weight of water used to control a fire can stress structural members to the point of collapse.

Size-up Application

As mentioned earlier, the size-up process actually begins before an incident is reported and continues throughout the incident. This section discusses the application of size-up theory to three specific time periods: preincident, on arrival, and during the incident.

Preincident

The size-up process begins well before an incident is reported. The information gathered in the preincident planning process discussed in Chapter 17, Preincident Planning, is an extremely important part of size-up. This information is gathered at a time when there is no reason to hurry, and data can be carefully reviewed, analyzed, recorded, and distributed.

When decisions are made regarding resources that will be needed to resolve certain hypothetical incidents at specific locations, these decisions can be translated into operational plans for those anticipated incidents. These plans provide facts that will help personnel make decisions during an incident at any of the surveyed locations. Regardless of whether preincident plans have been developed for a particular site, the size-up process still begins before an alarm is sounded and continues during the response.

Before an Alarm

Each day, as company officers and their personnel travel to work, they should begin a general size-up of the situation that day. They should observe road maintenance or construction areas as well as designated detours **(Figure 20.9)**. They should review the weather forecast and ask themselves how and to what extent the weather might affect any emergency to which they are called. They should consider answers to the following questions:

- Will response time be slowed because rain, snow, or ice has made the roads slick and dangerous?

- Will detours be necessary because of construction or other factors — parades, demonstrations, etc.?

- Will ventilation crews be at additional risk because of wet or icy roofs or high winds?

- Will wind combined with high temperature and low humidity increase the likelihood of wildland fires?

- Will these conditions make wildland fires burn more intensely and difficult to extinguish?

- Will extreme weather adversely affect trapped or injured victims?

- Are there any extremes of temperature that could make it more difficult and perhaps dangerous for personnel working outside?

Emergency responders performing strenuous work while wearing protective clothing in hot weather can be especially vulnerable to heat-related illnesses such as heat exhaustion or even heatstroke **(Figure 20.10)**. Company officers should be aware of the possible effects of weather and other factors on the abilities of their units to perform effectively and safely.

Figure 20.9 Company officers should be aware of changes in road conditions in their response areas. Temporary or permanent road closures require the use of alternate travel routes during emergency responses.

Figure 20.10 Company officers must monitor the conditions of their subordinates during emergency operations. Personnel who show signs of heat exhaustion or stress must go to the rehabilitation section or medical unit to receive water and proper medical attention.

While Responding

When an alarm is sounded, the size-up process then continues during the response. Company officers should consider the time of day when the alarm is received and how the incident will be affected by considering the answers to the following questions:

- Is it morning when burning conditions will become more extreme as the day goes on?

- Is it already late afternoon or evening when burning conditions can be expected to moderate?

- Is it during a time of day when the address at which the incident was reported is likely to be occupied?

- Are the occupants likely to need help getting out of the building?

- Is it the middle of the night when occupants may be sleeping?

- Is it during school hours on a weekday?

- How are the month, day of the week, and time of day likely to affect traffic congestion along the response route?

Company officers should continue to evaluate such variables as they respond to the scene of a reported incident. Additionally, company officers should factor in any other data that they can gather before arriving at the scene of an emergency. For example, the following information could be considered at a fire incident:

- Review the preplan of the building (if available) to more thoroughly prepare for what responders may encounter.

- Observe cloud formations to anticipate the possible effects of weather on fire behavior.

- Observe the amount, color, and movement of any smoke produced by the fire (**Figure 20.11, p. 472**).

This information, combined with knowledge of fire behavior and the building or area where the fire is burning, can help company officers better assess resource needs. Company officers should also evaluate any additional information provided by the telecommunications center over the radio during the response. Based on knowledge of the

Figure 20.11 The internal condition of a structure on fire, type of fuel load, and stage of the fire may be determined by the color and amount of smoke visible from outside. *Courtesy of District Chief Chris Mickal.*

Figure 20.12 After conducting an initial sizeup of the scene, the first-arriving company officer transmits a radio report describing the unit's status and any visible conditions. Instructions to other units assigned to the incident may also be given in this transmission.

response area, the units assigned, and the radio communications, the company officer should be able to determine which unit will arrive first and establish the NIMS-ICS. This knowledge base grows along with historical perspective, trial and error, and experience.

On Arrival

The most intense part of the size-up process may occur when the unit arrives at the emergency incident scene. The first-arriving officer may find a scene of utter chaos. In addition to the emergency situation and those directly involved in it, numerous spectators may be gathered at the scene, making it difficult to distinguish them from occupants or victims. These bystanders may be hysterical or irrational and screaming for responders to do something. Some may be attempting to extinguish the fire, assist victims, or perform a rescue — actions that may place them in direct danger.

Upon arrival, the company officer in charge of the first unit must transmit a *condition* or *arrival report* over the radio **(Figure 20.12)**. Many fire and emergency services organizations mandate this action in their operations standard operating procedure (SOP). This report does not replace the complete size-up or full appraisal of the incident. It is simply the first impression of the existing hazardous conditions and report of initial actions taken by the officer and unit.

The report provides other responding units with an idea of what they will encounter. Besides the hazardous conditions, the report can also include the type and location of any barriers such as parked cars or construction that could impede access.

The next step is to communicate the plan to all on-scene personnel. Communicating the plan usually starts with the first-arriving officer transmitting a report on incident scene conditions over the radio and formally assuming command of the incident. The officer names the incident and specifies the location of the incident command post (ICP) or describes the optional command activity that is in use.

For example, an initial alarm assignment (perhaps two engines, a truck, a rescue squad, and a chief officer) is dispatched to a reported structure fire. After performing an initial size-up, the first-arriving company officer might transmit the following information:

Company officer: *Dispatch, Engine 39.*

Dispatch: *Go ahead, Engine 39.*

Company officer: *Dispatch, we have a working fire involving one apartment on the ground floor of a* *four-story, wood-frame apartment building in the 9000 block of Alcosta Boulevard. Engine 39 is Incident Command and the incident command post is at the corner of Brockton and Alcosta. Engine 39 will make an offensive attack on the fire as soon as the RIT is in place and begin a primary search for victims. We will need to establish a water supply and start a vertical ventilation operation. Sound a second alarm.*

Dispatch: *Copy. Engine 39 is Alcosta incident command and you want a second alarm. Channel 24 is your tactical channel.*

This brief exchange accomplishes several things. It confirms that the call on which units have been dispatched is, in fact, an emergency: a working structure fire in an occupied (as opposed to abandoned) building where there is a potential life-safety hazard if residents are at home. Depending upon the time of day, day of the week, month of the year, and other variables, there may be many residents to evacuate or there may be none. In any case, other incoming units will know that a search of the building will be necessary.

Responding units will also know to switch their radios to the assigned tactical channel for incident traffic (in this case, Channel 24). This frequency gives the units assigned to the incident a clear radio channel on which to communicate and keeps the primary channel available for other traffic. Some types of communication systems permit the telecommunications center to perform this function automatically without verbally stating that it has been done.

Depending upon the organization's policies and procedures, if responders from the first-arriving engine do not lay a supply hoseline from the nearest hydrant (or otherwise ensure a water supply), responders from the next arriving engine will have to perform this operation **(Figure 20.13)**. Again depending upon policy, this procedure may be automatic or it may have to be assigned by the IC. In the latter case, providing the water supply would be part of the IAP and one more decision that the first-arriving officer must make.

The officer must make every effort to look at the scene from all sides **(Figure 20.14)**. The officer must focus on the situation and answer the question, *Can the resources at the scene and en route handle this situation?* If the answer is *no*, or even *maybe*, then additional resources must be requested *immediately*. Addressing this critical question is why the initial size-up sets the tone for the balance of the incident.

When the size-up is accurate and the needed resources are either at the scene, en route, or requested early in the incident, the incident can be handled successfully and in a timely manner. However, when there are not enough resources initially and the request for additional ones is delayed,

Figure 20.13 Local policies and procedures determine whether the second-arriving unit will automatically provide a supply hoseline to the first unit or wait at the hydrant for orders.

Figure 20.14 The first-arriving company officer should collect information on the incident by making a tour of the site if possible. If there are no visible indicators such as smoke and no eyewitnesses, the officer should make a firsthand evaluation of the situation before committing resources.

personnel are likely to start the incident *behind the curve*. This type of situation will take immense work and organization to overcome. Therefore, it is critically important for the initial size-up to be done with an attention to detail and focus on the desired outcome and the activities needed to attain that outcome.

Upon arrival at the incident, the company officer must make many decisions, usually in rapid succession. Considerations must be given to the level of acceptable personnel risk and which operational mode to initiate. Properly interpreting condition indicators can help an officer make the correct decisions.

Initial Risk Assessment

Based on the initial assessment of the incident scene, company officers must make decisions based on acceptable risk. This concept is clearly stated in a decision-making model developed by the Phoenix (AZ) Fire Department (PFD). The model is a departmental SOP that is used to help PFD officers make reliable emergency response decisions. The essence of the model is as follows:

- Each emergency response is begun with the assumption that *responders can protect lives and property.*

- Responders will *risk their lives a lot, if necessary, to save savable lives.*

- Responders will *risk their lives a little, and in a calculated manner, to save savable property.*

- Responders will *NOT risk their lives at all to save lives and property that have already been lost.*

Phoenix Model Simplified
- Risk a lot to save a lot.
- Risk a little to save a little.
- Risk nothing to save nothing.

Condition Indicators

Initial decisions must be made on accurate and complete information. Visual clues provide the company officer with condition indicators upon which to make the initial report and base the initial decisions. Condition indicators vary widely depending on the type of emergency incident the officer encounters. For instance, the presence of multiple unconscious victims may indicate the presence of a toxic or contaminated atmosphere. However, the lack of a visible cloud may raise the question of whether the indicators point to a chemical leak or biological contamination. Company officers should never rely on only one indicator to make a decision.

During the Incident

Once past the initial phase of an incident, emergency responders will be busy performing their assignments and making progress toward resolving the problem. This phase (between arrival and problem resolution) can be relatively short or last for a considerable length of time. When the problem is relatively small and/or officers make good decisions, the problem may be resolved in a few minutes. If not, additional assistance from other officers may be needed to resolve the situation.

During this phase, the situation changes as it either improves or worsens. In either case, the initial decisions that were based on the initial size-up may or may not remain valid; therefore, constant reassessment of incident conditions and the effect that operations have on the problem is critical. The IC must continue to size up the situation and make changes to the IAP as needed.

For example, if an emergency situation continues to deteriorate, the IC may need to request additional resources or transition from an aggressive attack to an operational mode that simply contains the status quo until additional resources arrive. When the situation is gradually improving but will take a long time to resolve, the IC may need to plan for responder rehabilitation and relief, logistical needs, etc. **(Figure 20.16, p. 476)**. As the situation improves, the IC should continually reassess (size up) the resource needs and release those that are no longer needed as soon as possible.

Structural Fire Condition Indicators

In the book *3D Fire Fighting: Training, Techniques, and Tactics*, by Paul Grimwood and others, the authors provide the following numerous indicators of structural fire conditions based on the appearance of smoke, air track, heat, and flame visible to the first-arriving officer:

- **Smoke**— Visible products of combustion. *Indicators:*

  - *Color and density:* Varies depending on the type of fuel and amount of air feeding the fire. *Examples:*

    ○ Light-colored smoke: Indicates that pyrolysis (chemical change) is occurring in areas adjacent to the main body of fire and that fire is developing.

    ○ Dark-colored smoke: Generally indicates burning synthetic or petrochemical materials or a reduction in the air available to the fire.

    ○ Smoke density: Thick dense smoke indicates burning petroleum-based material such as plastic or rubber; a thin smoke can indicate burning natural fiber materials.

    Smoke will also become lighter in density and color as water is applied to the fire and steam is released **(Figures 20.15 a–c)**.

  - *Volume and location:* Volume of smoke depends on the size of the fire and amount of air available to it. The more air available to the fire, the greater the quantity of smoke produced. Location of smoke may be an indicator of the location of the fire or a false indicator caused by movement of smoke through a structure.

  - *Height of the neutral plane (separation between the underpressure [lighter air] and overpressure [heavier air] regions of a compartment):* Also known as *thermal balance;* the neutral plane lowers as a fire develops and density of fire gases (smoke) increases. Interior attack teams must observe the level of the neutral plane very carefully and prepare to withdraw when there is a rapid change in conditions causing the neutral plane to lower. *Levels:*

    ○ High neutral plane: May indicate that the fire is in the early stages of development.

    ○ Midlevel neutral plane: Could indicate that the compartment has not ventilated yet and that flashover is approaching.

    ○ Very low-level neutral plane: May indicate that the fire is reaching backdraft conditions.

(Continued on next page)

Figures 20.15 a–c The ability to correctly *read* smoke comes with experience based on knowledge of the color and density of smoke that is generated by particular types of fuels and the change that occurs when water is introduced. (a) Dark smoke can indicate that available air is rapidly being consumed. (b) Light smoke may indicate that the fire is still growing. (c) Very light smoke or steam can indicate that water has been applied to the fire. *Photo c courtesy of District Chief Chris Mickal.*

- **Air track** — Movement of fresh air toward the base of a fire and movement of smoke and heated air out of a compartment; understanding this phenomenon can help in the ventilation of a fire. *Indicators:*
  - *Velocity and direction:* Slow, smooth movement of air toward a fire indicates that it is in the early stages and still fuel-controlled. Air movement is rapid and turbulent when a fire becomes ventilation-controlled. A sudden and total rush of fresh air into a compartment can indicate that a backdraft condition is imminent. The direction of air flow can indicate the location of the seat or base of the fire.
  - *Pulsations:* Fuel-rich and oxygen-deficient conditions result in smoke pulsing out of openings in a closed structure. Opening the structure improperly or at the wrong location can rapidly add fresh oxygen to the compartment, resulting in a backdraft.
  - *Noise:* Whistling noise created by the movement of the air into the structure indicates that a backdraft condition may be imminent.
- **Heat** — Form of energy transferred from one body to another as a result of a temperature difference; assists in an accurate assessment of the conditions within a burning structure. *Indicators:*
  - *Blackened or crazed (patterns of short cracks) glass:* Blackening indicates rich fuel conditions, while crazing indicates high interior temperatures. Caution should be taken when opening a structure with these indicators.
  - *Blistered paint:* Indicates both temperature extreme and location of the neutral plane.
  - *Sudden heat buildup:* Gives a very late indicator of flashover at the ceiling level. When operating inside a structure, personnel must be aware of a rapid increase in temperature.
- **Flame color** — Indicates the type of material that is burning, although the color may change, depending on the burning process.
  - *Yellow flame:* Generally indicates a reasonable air supply is reaching the fire.
  - *Reddish-orange flame:* Indicates that less air is reaching the fire and the fire is fuel-driven.
  - *Light yellow* to *clear flame:* Indicates that materials exposed to the main body of fire are beginning to ignite through pyrolysis.
  - *Blue flame:* Indicates incomplete combustion near the neutral plane and the high presence of unburned materials at that level; can also indicate a fire that is fueled by natural gas.

Figure 20.16 Providing water, shade (in hot weather), and a place to rest are important functions of the rehabilitation section.

Operational Implementation

With the initial size-up complete, the company officer must implement the operational decisions that have been made. Goals and objectives must be established, appropriate resources must be assigned, and the need for additional resources must be considered. The officer must determine the best form of command to assume and the most effective operational mode to implement. These actions are based on the company officer applying the knowledge gained from experience, study, and training along with strong leadership skills. An essential leadership trait is the application of a command presence that was discussed in Chapter 2, Leadership.

Goals and Objectives

As described previously, the goal of an incident is the overall desired outcome and the objectives are the activities used to reach that outcome. Both are included in the IAP and must be communicated to all personnel involved in the operation.

Strategic goals are the overall plans for controlling an incident. They are broad, general statements of the final outcomes to be achieved. These goals are dictated by the three overall priorities of life safety, incident stabilization, and property conservation. These priorities apply to all emergency situations. Strategic goals are based on the Layman decision-making model *RECEO-VS*.

Tactical objectives are statements of measurable outcomes. Achieving tactical objectives leads to the completion of strategic goals. Tactical objective statements are less general and more specific than strategic goal statements. Examples of some common tactical objectives are as follows:

- Initiate search and rescue.
- Provide a water curtain to protect exposures.
- Contain a hazardous materials spill.
- Use salvage covers to route water from the building's second floor.

Units and personnel are assigned specific tasks to accomplish each tactical objective. For instance, ladder personnel might be assigned the search and rescue task, while the second-arriving engine company would deploy hoselines and a master stream appliance to protect exposures.

Strategic goals and tactical objectives must be constantly evaluated to ensure that they are being accomplished. This evaluation is done by the continual process of size-up described previously. As goals and objectives are met, and situations change, so do the priorities. Company officers must be flexible enough to cope successfully with rapidly changing situations.

Command Activities

With the priorities established and a decision-making model ready for use, the company officer must be ready to take command of the situation. The first-arriving officer has the following three optional command activities available:

- *Nothing-showing* — When the problem generating the response is not obvious to the first-arriving unit, the company officer should assume command of the incident and announce that *nothing is showing.* The officer should direct the other responding units to stage at the last intersection in their route of travel before the reported incident location (**Figure 20.17**). The officer then accompanies unit personnel on an investigation of the situation and maintains command using a portable radio. Staging in this way allows for a maximum of deployment flexibility. This approach applies to all types of emergencies.

- *Fast-attack* — When the company officer's direct involvement is necessary for the unit to take immediate action to save a life or stabilize the situation, the officer should take command and announce that the unit is initiating a *fast attack.* Personnel will continue the fast attack, which usually lasts only a short time, until one of the following situations occurs:

— Incident is stabilized.

— Incident is not stabilized, but the officer must withdraw to outside the hazardous area to establish a formal incident command post (ICP). Depending upon the incident, the balance of the unit may be left inside the hazardous area when they can function safely and effectively *and* have radio communications capability.

— Command is transferred.

Figure 20.17 The first-arriving company officer may order other units to remain at the nearest intersection when there are no visible indicators at the response address.

NOTE: Under no circumstances may fewer than two responders be left in a hazardous area. When only two responders (including the company officer) are in the hazardous area and the company officer must leave, both must leave.

- *Command* — Because of the nature and/or scope of some incidents, immediate and strong overall command is needed. In these incidents, the first-arriving officer should assume command by naming the incident and designating an ICP, giving an initial report on conditions, and requesting the additional resources needed. *Types:*

  — *Combat command:* Involves the company officer performing multiple tasks such as serving as incident commander (IC), developing the incident action plan (IAP), and performing active tasks such as advancing a hoseline **(Figure 20.18a)**.

  — *Formal command:* Involves the company officer remaining at the mobile radio in the apparatus, assigning tasks to unit personnel, communicating with other responding units, and expanding the NIMS-ICS as needed by the complexity of the incident **(Figure 20.18b)**. In addition, the company officer must decide how to deploy the remainder of the unit. Three options are normally available:

    ○ Appoint one unit member as the acting officer to supervise the rest of the unit, provide a portable radio, and make an assignment such as performing a search of the incident site.

    ○ Assign unit members to work under the supervision of another company officer, performing the tasks assigned to that officer by the IC.

    ○ Use unit members to perform staff functions in support of command such as the incident safety officer (ISO) or accountability officer.

When a company officer IC needs to transfer command of an incident to another officer, the transfer must be done correctly. Otherwise, there could be confusion about who is really in command of an incident. The officer assuming com-

Figures 20.18 a and b The first-arriving company officer may elect to assume command while performing other activities such as (a) performing combat command or (b) remaining at the apparatus and establishing a formal command.

mand must communicate with the officer being relieved by radio or face to face (face-to-face communication is preferred) **(Figure 20.19)**. *Command should never be transferred to anyone who is not on the scene.* When transferring command, the officer being relieved should brief the relieving officer on the following items:

Figure 20.19 Transfer of command should be done in person if possible. Command is never passed to an officer who is not at the incident.

- Name of incident
- Incident status (such as fire conditions, number of victims, etc.)
- Safety considerations
- Goals and objectives listed in the incident action plan (IAP)
- Progress toward completion of tactical objectives
- Deployment of assigned resources
- Assessment of the need for additional resources

A simple analogy that can be used in transferring command is to provide a *CAN* report as follows:

- *Conditions* — State the current situation based on observations, preincident knowledge, and reports.
- *Actions* — State the actions that have been taken and allocation of resources.
- *Needs* — State the needs that still must be met, including additional resources and actions required to meet the goals of the IAP.

Operational Modes

The first and most important part of the IAP deals with life safety, and this part must be implemented as soon as possible. Addressing life safety involves a series of decisions that the IC must make. One of the first decisions relates to choosing one of the first two possible modes of operation: *offensive* or *defensive*. The third operational mode, *transitional*, is used when it is necessary to shift from an offensive to defensive mode.

Offensive Operational Mode

The offensive operational mode involves taking direct action to resolve the problem such as suppressing a structure fire, performing a rescue (when properly trained), containing a hazardous materials release, extricating the occupants of a wrecked vehicle, or providing life-support for a victim of a medical emergency. The IC must decide how to deploy the available resources in a way that will be the most effective. Apparatus, equipment, and personnel must be close to the operational area. Offensive operational mode situations are those that can be controlled by the resources available (**Figure 20.20, p. 480**).

Structure fire incident. The offensive operational mode at a structure fire usually means conducting an aggressive interior attack from the unburned side of the structure by one or more engine companies. In the meantime, ladder/truck personnel are assigned to perform forcible entry, initial search, utility control, salvage, and ventilation (**Figure 20.21, p. 480**). Countless possible variations exist for this scenario, depending upon the following conditions:

- Size of the structure
- Amount of fire involvement
- Whether the fire is on the ground floor or an upper floor
- Whether the building is occupied
- Whether the building contains toxic or explosive materials
- Whether the building has built-in fire-suppression systems
- Proximity of the burning building to uninvolved exposures

Figure 20.20 The concept of offensive operations can apply to nonfire incidents. In the case of a motor vehicle accident, apparatus are placed close to the incident to provide hoselines, tools, auxiliary power for extrication equipment, and lighting. *Courtesy of San Ramon Valley Fire District.*

Figure 20.21 Offensive operations at structure fires are symbolized by aggressive actions on the part of the emergency responders.

- Number of resources at the scene and number that will be available with some delay

- Other variables

By talking to building occupants who have escaped the fire, neighbors, or other witnesses, the IC may be able to determine whether there are any occupants still inside and, if so, whether there is a reasonable chance that any of them are still alive. When occupants who may be trapped inside and possibly alive are unaccounted for, an offensive operational mode is then indicated. When personnel resources permit, an aggressive fire attack would be started simultaneously with a search and rescue operation. If not, the search might have to be delayed until the fire is at least confined.

Nonfire rescue incident. The offensive operational mode in a nonfire rescue incident usually means deploying rescuers into the environment where the victim is trapped such as the following:

- Assigning personnel to assemble a mechanical-advantage system (assembly of ropes, pulleys, and anchors) with which to raise or lower a victim from a higher or lower elevation to grade level

- Rappelling down the face of a building or a cliff to reach a stranded victim

- Installing emergency shoring in a collapsed trench to facilitate entry by rescuers

- Sending a rescue team into any type of confined space

- Sending rescuers into water or onto ice to rescue victims in danger of drowning **(Figure 20.22)**

Defensive Operational Mode

Operating in a defensive operational mode is essentially intended to isolate or stabilize an incident and keep it from getting any worse or larger. In the

Figure 20.22 Performing ice rescues is a very specialized task requiring personal protective clothing that is designed for extremely cold temperatures. Placing personnel at risk is not justified if the victim is known to have perished. *Courtesy of Iowa Fire Service Training Bureau.*

case of a structure fire, a defensive mode may mean sacrificing a building that is on fire to save others that are not burning. A defensive operational mode is usually (but not always) an exterior operation that is chosen because not enough resources are available to conduct a safe and effective offensive attack (**Figure 20.23**).

Personnel and apparatus must be kept at a distance until further resources arrive because the incident is large or hazardous (such as large structure and wildland fires, transportation accidents, hazardous materials releases, and structural collapses). For example, protecting exposures from

Figure 20.23 Master stream appliances deployed on aerial devices, pumping apparatus, or ground mounts are traditionally used for defensive operations involving large or multiple structures that are involved in fire. *Courtesy of District Chief Chris Mickal.*

the spread of a large fire then becomes the primary mission of responders. Defensive operations are justified in the following conditions involving a structure fire:

- *Volume of fire* — Amount of fire exceeds the ability of a single unit to deliver minimum gpm or l/min. The water flow capability of the on-scene crew is insufficient to absorb the heat being produced by the fire and thus the crew is incapable of controlling the fire.

- *Structural deterioration* — Structure is unsound due to age, condition, or exposure to fire and an imminent safety hazard to operating crews.

- *Collapse probability* — Structure has been weakened by fire or natural causes (earthquake, tornado, high winds, or hurricane), creating a likelihood of collapse. Apparatus must be positioned away from the collapse area.

A defensive operational mode may also reflect a decision by the IC that a burning building is not worth the risk to responders to perform an aggressive interior attack. One reason may be because the burning building is an abandoned derelict. Another may be because the building is so heavily involved in fire that it is not reasonable to expect that anyone inside could still be alive, so it would not be prudent to put firefighters in jeopardy by ordering them to attack the fire inside the building. It may also reflect an assessment by the IC that there are too few resources at the scene to mount an effective fire attack.

In this case, the IC might assign the first-available engine companies to apply water to the exterior of exposures. If resources are extremely limited, the IC may decide to allow the building of origin to burn until additional resources arrive. When additional resources arrive, master streams can be assembled to attack the fire in the burning building from the outside.

Likewise, if a swimmer or boater has not been seen for several hours, the search should be conducted in a defensive operational mode, slowly and carefully, and without placing personnel in undue risk **(Figure 20.24)**. When the victim of a trench wall cave-in has been under tons of debris for so long that the likelihood of survival is extremely re-

Figure 20.24 Fire and emergency services organizations that are located near rivers, lakes, or coastal areas may have dive or water rescue teams. Generally, these units will be assigned to defensive-type operations such as body recovery when it is apparent that there is no hope of locating a victim alive.

mote or the trench filled with water after the cave-in, the operation should probably be conducted as a recovery and not a rescue.

In general, defensive and offensive operational modes should *not* be attempted concurrently. The offensive operational mode may involve rescue or extinguishment or both. In some fire incidents, rescue and extinguishment will occur simultaneously with engine crews attacking the seat of the fire, while other personnel search for victims. In extreme cases, where a victim is known to be trapped, rescue will become the *primary* activity and fire attack will be performed only to protect the rescuers and the victim.

In a still-developing incident such as a working fire, the IC may be forced to use a defensive operational mode in the early stages because of resource limitations. But as additional resources arrive at the scene, it will be possible at some point to switch from a defensive to an offensive operational mode.

NOTE: In some organizations the shift from defensive to offensive is referred to as *transitional attack mode*. This term should not be confused with the transitional operational mode discussed in the Transitional Operational Mode section that involves the shift from offensive to defensive operations and involves the withdrawal of forces from hazardous situations.

Transitional Operational Mode

When emergency responder fatalities and injuries occur at emergency incidents, they are often the result of rapid changes in the situation such as the following:

- Change in wind direction and velocity can turn a wildland fire in the direction of hoseline crews.

- Change in wind direction can cause an ignitable vapor to envelop personnel.

- Structural member weakening can cause a ceiling or wall to collapse.

- Introduction of fresh air into a superheated compartment can cause a backdraft to occur.

When a rapid change in the hazard is indicated, it is necessary for the operation to shift from an offensive to a defensive operational mode. The IC must be prepared to order that change and communicate the order to all personnel and units operating at the incident. The process of shifting from offensive to defensive is called the *transitional operational mode* (**Figure 20.25**).

How the transition occurs depends on the speed at which the situation is changing. In any case, the transition must be orderly. All personnel must be told to make the transition. Units that must remain in place to protect the withdrawal of other units

Figure 20.25 Rapid changes in the conditions of an emergency incident may require the company officer to implement a transitional mode of operation. *Courtesy of San Ramon Valley Fire District.*

must be aware of their duty to provide protection for units that are disengaging. Supervisors must be aware of the location of personnel assigned to them and account for them when withdrawal is complete. Hoselines should *not* be abandoned unless absolutely necessary. Abandoned hoselines do not provide any protection during a withdrawal. Rapid intervention crew (RIC) personnel must be ready to assist any units that require protection during the transition.

Obviously, for a transition to be efficient and effective, it must occur as soon as the need becomes apparent. To meet this requirement, the IC must have current and accurate knowledge of the situation. The use of observers on all sides of the incident as well as inside structures is needed. Situation or status reports must be made to the IC regularly.

Additional Resource Allocation

Regardless of the nature of an incident, the IAP should anticipate the need for calling additional resources if it appears that the incident will be protracted or has the potential to be a long-term operation. These additional resources may be held in reserve, used to relieve first-arriving units that have become fatigued, or assigned tactical objectives on the incident.

If additional resources are called, one or more staging areas may have to be established. On relatively small incidents or when the actual location, nature, and scope of the incident are not yet confirmed, the IC can often manage the staging function.

Apparatus Placement and Positioning

Proper placement and positioning of apparatus at an emergency scene is an important part of scene management and safety. Some emergency vehicles need to be closer to the scene than others. The goal of apparatus placement and positioning is to get vehicles that need to be closest to the operation into position.

For example, at some incidents, aerial apparatus and vehicles used to supply electrical power, operate hydraulic tools, or furnish emergency scene lighting need to be close in order to operate effectively. Apparatus that do not need to be close to the incident scene should be positioned to allow room for later-arriving vehicles that are needed to resolve the problem.

Apparatus placement based on operational mode can be applied to most types of emergency incidents. The sections that follow give guidelines for apparatus placement and positioning based on the type of incident that may be encountered. However, guidelines are never enough to prevent accidents, injuries, or fatalities. Policies and procedures must be developed based on the requirements found in NFPA 1500, *Standard on Fire Department Occupational Safety and Health Program*. It is the responsibility of the organization and company officer to ensure that all personnel adhere to established safety policies.

NOTE: While the physical operation of the apparatus is under the control of the driver/operator, the operation and placement of the apparatus, which may be dictated by organizational policy such as ladder truck placement at a building fire, is always the responsibility of the company officer.

Structural Fire Scenes

When operating at a structural fire scene, vehicles directly involved in fire suppression (engines, aerial apparatus, etc.) should be positioned in locations that support fire-suppression operations. Hoselines should be placed so that apparatus can be repositioned without shutting down hoselines or driving over them. These vehicles provide the tools and equipment needed to gain access, affect search and rescue, apply extinguishing agents, and protect property through ventilation and loss control activities. Additional apparatus that provide power for electric or hydraulic tools or incident scene lighting may also be found in this area.

Aerial devices should be strategically positioned so that they can be quickly placed into operation to provide access to upper stories or place elevated fire streams in operation **(Figure 20.26)**. The length and type of aerial device as well as the existence of overhead obstructions such as power lines, streetlights, or trafficker control devices must be taken into consideration when placing these devices. Of considerable importance is the need for the aerial device to be properly stabilized before the

aerial device is operated. Narrow, crowded streets or uneven terrain can affect the stability of these vehicles. See the IFSTA **Aerial Apparatus Driver/ Operator Handbook** for additional information.

Support vehicles such as rescue apparatus and ambulances should be positioned in a staging area where they will not interfere with fire-suppression operations but their equipment will still be readily available. Tools and equipment that might be needed from support vehicles can be carried to the scene.

A staging area also provides a good location for establishing a medical treatment area for victims or firefighters and makes it easier to coordinate with ambulances. It would be unsafe to treat people in a rescue vehicle parked in an area that may be exposed to smoke or other airborne particulates.

Figure 20.26 Aerial apparatus are usually positioned on flat, hard surfaces. The actual location depends on overhead obstructions, barriers that may hamper deploying the stabilizer jacks properly, and wind direction. *Courtesy of District Chief Chris Mickal.*

Command vehicles should be placed in a safe location so that they do not interfere with operating apparatus yet still give the IC a good view of one or two sides of the scene.

Wildland Fire Scenes

Placement of apparatus at wildland fires will be determined by the operational mode of attack established by the IC and off-road capability of the apparatus. The offensive operational mode will require that Type II, III, or IV apparatus be placed along the fireline (area where fire-suppression activities occur). These apparatus will operate from the burned and upwind side of the fire. See Chaper 19, Incident Scene Management, for apparatus type details.

This location can result in a direct attack on the flanks (sides) or head (forward-advancing point) of the fire. Type I (structural) apparatus should not be taken off-road, but it can be used for offensive operations from a hard-surface road on the burned side of the fire.

When the IC implements a defensive operational mode such as protecting structures, any type of apparatus may be used. The apparatus should be backed into driveways facing the street for quick withdrawal if necessary. The IC should also locate and announce a safety zone where apparatus can be parked so that they do not block or inhibit operations.

Apparatus should not be parked in and around tall trees or heavy brush (potential fuel for the fire), on soft ground, near small creeks and streams, in open trenches, on residential lawns or yards (with possible septic tanks and lateral lines), and on roads that are halfway up slopes and susceptible to a fire moving uphill rapidly. Basically, apparatus should be positioned so that it is safe and convenient for responders.

Proper apparatus placement and positioning can be accomplished by using the following guidelines:

- Park apparatus off roadways or back into driveways to avoid blocking other fire apparatus or evacuating vehicles; notice soft shoulders or deep edges along roads.

- Use amber flashers when parking apparatus on a roadway or shoulder. Mark both the front and rear of the apparatus with traffic cones to warn motorists of the presence of apparatus and personnel.

- Park apparatus in a designated safety zone and do not leave it unattended at fires.

- Park apparatus on the side of the fire from which the wind is blowing to minimize its exposure to heat and blowing embers (**Figure 20.27**).

- Avoid blocking access ways with hoselines.

- Do not park apparatus next to or under hazards such as the following:
  — Power lines
  — Flammable trees or snags (standing dead trees)
  — Liquefied petroleum gas (LPG) tanks or other pressure vessels

- Use wheel chocks when apparatus is parked.

In addition to proper positioning, other guidelines that can protect the apparatus include the following:

- Keep apparatus compartment and cab doors closed and windows rolled up to keep out burning materials.

- Ensure that fire hose bed covers are capable of protecting fire hose from blowing embers.

Figure 20.27 Apparatus must always be located on the windward side of the fireline at wildland incidents. Company officers must also keep in mind that wind direction and velocity can change rapidly, which could require relocating personnel and apparatus. *Courtesy of San Ramon Valley Fire District.*

- Ensure that a fire protection hoseline is connected and available for rapid deployment from the apparatus.

- Maintain communication/coordination with the rest of the fireground organization to ensure apparatus operations are safe and effective.

- Lay supply hoselines only on road shoulders.

- Do not lock apparatus doors or leave the apparatus unattended.

- Place the air-conditioning system of the apparatus in recirculation mode to avoid drawing in smoke from the outside.

- Leave the engine running and maintain a high engine idle to reduce apparatus stalling potential.

- Keep apparatus headlights turned on to maintain its visibility.

- Do not remove or deploy nonessential equipment from the apparatus.

- Remain on the burned side of the fireline.

Company officers should remember that Type I structural fire-suppression apparatus are not designed for off-road use. The distance from ground level to the bottom of the apparatus is too short to clear some obstacles, and the height of the apparatus can cause it to roll over on slight inclines due to a higher center of gravity. Even though all-wheel- or four-wheel-drive vehicles have superior climbing ability, they also have a high center of gravity that makes them susceptible to rollover. The weight of an apparatus can also result in it becoming stuck in soft, loose, or wet soil.

Hazardous Materials Incidents

Hazardous materials incidents can pose very complex problems that can change rapidly. The company officer must determine apparatus placement and positioning based on information that may be incomplete, incorrect, or altered. Apparatus placement and positioning considerations for incidents that involve the release of hazardous materials include the following:

- *Danger to personnel* — Safety is the primary consideration when determining apparatus placement and positioning during hazardous materials incidents. Once the level of risk has been determined based on the type of chemical, all other considerations can then be addressed.

- *Type of hazard* — Quantity and flammability of the material and whether it is unignited or ignited determine the placement and positioning of apparatus. While not all hazardous materials are flammable, some (such as caustic or corrosive chemicals) can injure personnel or damage apparatus if they approach too closely to the spill or release. When the type of chemical or hazardous material is unknown, the IC must adopt a defensive operational mode and keep apparatus and personnel at a safe distance.

- *Topography* — Configuration of the surface of the land that a spill or release covers is considered because heavier-than-air gases can accumulate in depressions, increasing the potential for accidental ignition from apparatus engines or electrical systems. Liquid spills or releases will also seek the lowest points and flow downhill.

- *Weather conditions* — Wind direction and velocity, rain, high-pressure areas, and other conditions could spread contamination or reduce the effectiveness of the suppressing agent chosen.

- *Incident location* — Hazardous material spills or releases may occur anywhere hazardous materials are manufactured, stored, used, transported, or disposed of. Potential locations include petroleum or chemical processing plants, storage tanks, populated or rural areas, along highways, in tunnels, on bridges, or in railroad yards. Apparatus placement and positioning are determined by the following:

  — Access to the area (ability to move apparatus close to the hot zone)

  — Proximity to exposures (close or at a distance)

  — Condition of the site (remote rugged area or developed area with streets, sewers, and water supply systems)

- *Operational mode* — Choice of an offensive or a defensive operational mode affects or helps determine the placement of apparatus (see earlier discussion on operational modes).

- **Available resources** — Minimum resources that any company officer initially has are personnel and apparatus. The apparatus can be placed close enough to the spill or release to apply a foam blanket with hoselines or master streams. The apparatus should also be placed far enough away to protect the apparatus and personnel if there is an explosion or rapid ignition. Before attacking any hazardous materials spill or fire, the correct type and quantity of extinguishing agent must be available to control the situation. See the IFSTA **Principles of Foam Fire Fighting** manual for additional information.

- **Level of training** — When the company officer and members of the unit are not trained and certified to handle hazardous materials spills or fires, they must position the apparatus at a safe distance and apply extinguishing agents to protect exposures or control the spill. They must wait for personnel who are trained and certified as hazardous materials technicians to arrive before advancing further.

General apparatus placement and positioning guidelines for hazardous materials incidents include the following:

- Park apparatus upwind of the incident scene and uphill whenever possible.

- Position apparatus well away from downed power lines, damaged transformers, or escaping flammable gas **(Figure 20.28)**.

- Place apparatus so that it can be repositioned easily and quickly.

- Place or position apparatus so that its hoselines can protect the route of egress through the spill when rescue is required.

- Consider the slope of the ground and wind direction.

High-Rise Incidents

Incidents in multistory or high-rise structures create special apparatus placement and positioning requirements. The structures may be located in a series or row of similar structures with only the front and rear of the structure accessible. They may also be independent of other structures and located on individual parcels of land surrounded by parking lots or connected to parking structures. They may range in height from two stories (approximately 20 feet [6 m]) to over 110 stories (over 1,400 feet [442 m], including communications towers).

High-rise structures are generally considered to be 7 stories (70 feet [21 m]) or more in height from grade level **(Figure 20.29, p. 488)**. Some of the characteristics that influence apparatus placement and positioning at high-rise structures are as follows:

Figure 20.28 Electrical power lines may be damaged by storms or structure fires. Apparatus must be located away from downed power lines, and personnel must be aware that lines may become detached during an incident. *Courtesy of District Chief Chris Mickal.*

Figure 20.29 High-rise structures may have features that prevent the placement of apparatus close to the base of the building. One such feature could be trees as shown in this photograph.

- Limited ground-level access with personnel-access doors located only in the front and rear walls (when the building is in a series of structures)

- Intermediate parking garage areas between grade level and upper occupied floors, which increase the distances that personnel must climb and equipment must be transported (parking levels will also be filled with vehicles that can be a source of ignition or fire)

- Below grade mechanical spaces that may include a fire control room or sprinkler control valves

- Windows that cannot be opened for use in rescue or ventilation operations

- Fences, planting beds, decorative walls, or other barriers near the base of independently located structures

- Limited street frontage

- Building setbacks from the street, parking areas, or driveways, which may be obstructed by barriers in the setback area

The first-arriving company officer must determine the location and type of emergency within or near the structure, select the appropriate operational mode, establish lobby command post, and ensure that the initial apparatus placement provides the best access to the structure without creating a barrier to other units. All responding units should follow organizational policies regarding apparatus placement and positioning at the base of the structure. These policies may be generic for all structures over a specified height or specific to each high-rise structure based on the preincident survey and plan.

In a high-rise incident, equipment, fire hose, and tools should be dropped off at the base location and unneeded apparatus parked in the designated staging area. Apparatus supplying sprinkler or standpipe systems through fire department connections (FDCs) located on the structure's exterior wall should be positioned so that they do not block access to the structure.

Technical Rescue Incidents

Proper placement and positioning of emergency apparatus at technical rescue incidents depends upon a number of variables. Placement and positioning of apparatus and/or resources is generally different from that normally found at a fire scene, hazardous materials incident, or high-rise incident.

At a technical rescue scene (water, ice, confined-space, structural collapse, trench, or high-angle), rescue vehicles (or apparatus carrying rescue tools and equipment) should be positioned nearest the incident. Rescue and extrication equipment may be the most important items in an emergency situation and need to be readily available. Apparatus used for fire-suppression operations (engines, ladders/trucks) should be located in the staging area.

While it is important to place apparatus close enough to unload or support power tools and equipment, it is also important that the weight of the apparatus not add to the problem. The weight of the apparatus and engine vibration can cause

Figure 20.30 At incidents that involve the use of volunteers or recalled career personnel, personal vehicles should be parked in a staging area that is remote from the incident.

soil in a trench-collapse area to cave in. Vehicles that do not need to be close to the scene, including Command vehicles and privately owned vehicles (POVs), should be parked in a staging area farther from the incident **(Figure 20.30)**.

Some general guidelines for the placement and positioning of apparatus at technical rescue incidents are as follows:

- Park apparatus between an incident and oncoming traffic to protect both personnel and victims when the incident is on or adjacent to a roadway or bridge.

- Park apparatus close enough to the incident to ensure its equipment is readily available with a minimum carrying distance.

- Do not position apparatus so close to the incident that it exposes victims or emergency responders to vehicle exhaust, vibration, or noise.

- Do not block an emergency scene. Allow access for ambulances and other emergency vehicles and normal flow of traffic when the incident is not in the roadway.

- Coordinate closely with on-scene law enforcement officials to address safety issues and concerns for emergency personnel, victims, bystanders, and other traffic.

Aircraft Incidents

Emergency personnel who may respond to aircraft incidents should be familiar with their organization's standard emergency response procedures or airport emergency plans. Most fire and emergency services organizations have SOPs for *standard*

emergency response involving normal aircraft activities: approaching, landing, taxiing, taking off, or while parked. *Unannounced* emergency responses involve onsite or offsite aircraft accidents that occur without prior warning.

NFPA 402, *Guide for Aircraft Rescue and Fire Fighting Operations,* states that there are no standardized categories for describing aircraft emergencies. The U.S. Federal Aviation Administration (FAA) and the International Civil Aviation Organization (ICAO) use similar terms as those given in the previous paragraph, while many local airports may use locally developed terms.

When the crew of an aircraft becomes aware of potential danger to the aircraft, crew members alert the nearest air traffic control tower (ATCT) about the nature of the emergency. The ATCT in turn alerts the airport fire department or the nearest municipal department. The FAA recommends that local airports classify known aircraft emergencies by the seriousness of the emergency.

Three common types of FAA notifications for an impending aircraft incident or emergency are *Alerts I, II,* and *III.* See the information box for descriptions. The U.S. military uses the classification terms of *standbys, ground emergencies, in-flight emergencies,* and *crashes* to designate the various types of emergencies.

U.S. Federal Aviation Administration Alert Classifications

1. *Alert I* — Indicates that an aircraft approaching the airport is in minor difficulty, for example, feathered propeller, oil leak, etc. Emergency equipment and crews would stand by at the equipment house for further instructions.

2. *Alert II* — Indicates that an aircraft approaching the airport is in major difficulty, for example, engine on fire, faulty landing gear, no hydraulic pressure, etc. Emergency equipment and crews would proceed to a predetermined location (end of runway, taxiway, access road, etc.) to await development of the potential emergency.

3. *Alert III* — Indicates that an aircraft is involved in an accident on or near the airport and emergency equipment and crews should proceed immediately to the scene.

Standard Emergency Response

The aircraft crew is aware of a problem and notifies the airport authorities of the emergency before it prepares to land. Runway standby positions for fire and emergency services vehicles in anticipation of an emergency are predetermined in SOPs and include predetermined response routes unless unforeseen conditions dictate otherwise (**Figure 20.31**).

While promptness and safety are equally important response considerations, responders must also consider weather, visibility, terrain, and vehicular traffic. Structural fire-fighting units that respond to airport incidents must be in communication with the ATCT or ground control and not enter the site until given permission to do so.

Airport fire-fighting apparatus and/or responding structural fire-fighting units must be positioned correctly if rescue and fire-fighting operations are to be successful. Because aircraft rescue and fire-fighting (ARFF) apparatus often respond single file, the first-arriving apparatus may establish a responding route onto the airport property for other vehicles and dictate their fire-fighting positions.

The following guidelines can be used to position apparatus for a standard aircraft emergency:

- Consider the slope of the ground and wind direction (generally park apparatus upwind of the scene and uphill). Do not place or position apparatus in a hazardous position downhill or downwind of a fuel spill.

- Do not place or position apparatus so that it blocks the entry to or exit from the emergency site, which is especially important when there is only one access route into the site.

- Place and stagger several apparatus on the shoulder of a taxiway so that they may operate effectively in the event of fire.

Figure 20.31 Apparatus placement at aircraft standby emergencies is regulated by local standard operating procedures (SOPs) and airport regulations.

- Place or position apparatus so that it does not hinder the egress or rescue of persons from the aircraft.

- Place apparatus so that it can be repositioned easily and quickly to respond to any change in the landing location of the aircraft such as a reassignment of runway or landing direction.

- Place or position apparatus so that its hoselines can protect the route of egress from the aircraft.

Once an aircraft is on the ground and has come to a complete halt, use the following guidelines:

- Communicate with the aircraft commander or air traffic control tower (ATCT) about intentions to taxi aircraft to a designated area, evacuate passengers, or shut down the aircraft.

- Position personnel with hoselines to protect the primary escape route for passengers and crews.

- Surround the aircraft with apparatus and personnel because passenger emergency exits are located on both sides and sometimes under the rear of the aircraft. Assist with securing evacuation slides to the ground while passengers slide down to safety.

- Apply a foam blanket to prevent vapor ignition if fuel is leaking.

- Suppress the fire if fuel has ignited, and push it away from the routes of escape.

- Proceed with fire extinguishment from the fuselage of the aircraft outward (away from the fuselage) once rescue operations are complete.

Unannounced Emergency Response

Unannounced aircraft emergencies may occur on or off the airport site. These emergencies may be the result of an overheated landing gear causing a tire to blowout upon landing or an aircraft skidding off the runway. Far more devastating are the emergencies that result in a high-speed impact by the aircraft into the earth.

Fire and emergency services units are dispatched immediately to the scene of an unannounced emergency incident by the most direct route, and the ATCT continues to keep responding units informed while they are en route. Apparatus should approach the scene with caution to avoid hitting persons who may have escaped from the aircraft or been thrown clear as well as witnesses who are attempting to rescue or locate victims.

In darkness or when vision is obscured, responders can use the Driver's Enhanced Vision System (DEVS), Forward-Looking InfraRed (FLIR) camera system, or other thermal imaging devices or have a person on foot precede the apparatus cautiously to ensure that the way is clear. Respond in a way that avoids damaging the responding apparatus and equipment. In case of an aircraft crash, avoid running over aircraft debris scattered around the accident scene. Position apparatus to indicate the perimeter of the debris field caused by the impact (**Figure 20.32**).

Figure 20.32 Apparatus responding to an aircraft crash site must be careful during the approach to prevent striking victims or debris.

Medical Incidents

The placement and positioning of apparatus and ambulances at medical incidents are critical factors to efficient and immediate patient care. Many medical emergencies are time-critical, requiring that a specific level of care be provided as quickly as possible. Cardiac arrest, asphyxiation, and massive blood loss are just three medical emergencies that demand immediate care. To reduce the amount of time required to reach patients, carry life-support equipment, and transport the patient to the ambulance, the company officer must carefully consider the placement of the apparatus.

Some considerations about apparatus and ambulance placement and positioning during medical incidents include the following:

- Place apparatus and ambulances as close to the incident as possible (**Figure 20.33**).

- Units that are designed for patient transport should be parked in such a way as to provide clear access to the loading door.

- Do not place or position apparatus so that it blocks the entry to or exit from the emergency site, making movement of the patient gurney difficult or time-consuming.

Figure 20.33 Ambulances should be located as close as possible to the incident in order to speed loading of victims and decrease the size of the operational area. *Courtesy of San Ramon Valley Fire District.*

- Do not position apparatus so close to victims or emergency responders that it exposes them to vehicle exhaust, vibration, or noise.

- Use amber flashers when parking apparatus on a roadway or shoulder. Mark both the front and rear of the apparatus with traffic cones to warn motorists of the presence of apparatus and personnel.

- Apparatus should be placed on the side of the road and positioned to protect the victim and emergency responders while the patient is being stabilized and loaded for transport (**Figure 20.34**).

Incident Termination

The termination phase of an emergency operation involves activities such as retrieving equipment used in the operation, determining the cause of the incident, releasing the scene to those responsible for it, performing medical evaluations of personnel involved in the incident, and returning the unit to service. Postincident activities including fire cause determination and postincident analysis are included in Chapter 21, Postincident Activities.

Equipment Retrieval

Company officers are responsible for preparing their unit and personnel to return to service and be available for other assignments. To prepare for

Figure 20.34 The safety of victims and responders can be improved by using apparatus as barriers to traffic at roadway incidents. Portable signs and traffic cones can also be used to alert drivers of emergency activities and apparatus.

active duty, the company officer and unit members must locate, identify, and retrieve all tools and equipment belonging to the unit **(Figure 20.35)**. Equipment that cannot be located or retrieved may be abandoned.

Depending on the size, complexity, and length of time involved in the operation, the job of retrieving all of the various pieces of equipment used may

be very easy or it may be very difficult and time-consuming. For instance, it may not be worth the effort to dig for equipment that is buried under the debris of a collapsed building. Equipment that is contaminated will have to be decontaminated before returning it to service.

Identification

The process of identifying and collecting pieces of equipment assigned to the various pieces of apparatus on scene is much easier when each piece of equipment is clearly marked. However, it may be necessary for the driver/operators of emergency apparatus on the scene to conduct an inventory of their equipment before leaving the scene. If the operation was large enough to require the establishment of a demobilization unit (part of the Logistics function of the NIMS-ICS), that unit will coordinate the recovery of loaned items such as portable radios and then document lost or damaged pieces of apparatus and equipment.

Abandonment

In some cases, the environment within the emergency scene may be too hazardous to justify sending personnel back to retrieve pieces of equipment, even expensive ones. Rather than putting personnel at risk to retrieve tools and equipment in a hazard zone, the equipment is simply abandoned in place **(Figure 20.36)**.

Figure 20.35 Before units are returned to service, all hose, tools, and equipment must be located and retrieved. At incidents that involve multiple units, it may take some time to sort out the ownership of items and load them on the appropriate units.

Figure 20.36 Retrieving tools and equipment from structures that have been totally destroyed may not be possible. The value of the equipment and its possible condition must be weighed against the risk personnel must take to retrieve it. *Courtesy of District Chief Chris Mickal.*

Equipment may be retrievable after the scene has been restored or it may be possible to recover the cost of replacing the abandoned equipment from the owner of the property, insurance, or government assistance. The process of recovering the costs of abandoned equipment and the need to replace lost or damaged equipment quickly underscores the need to fully document every emergency incident.

During hazardous materials incidents for example, equipment and personal protective equipment (PPE) may become contaminated. If equipment and PPE cannot be decontaminated, it will have to be disposed of according to the organization's policy **(Figure 20.37)**. Disposal procedures usually require sealing contaminated materials in salvage drums and sending them to a certified hazardous materials collection company.

Figure 20.37 Any equipment that cannot be decontaminated must be disposed of in accordance with local policy and federal regulations.

The definition and requirements for salvage drums is found in Title 49 (Transportation) *Code of Federal Regulations (CFR)*, Part 171.8 and 173.3. See the information box for the definition.

Salvage Drum

In Title 49 *CFR* 173.3, salvage packaging, including salvage drums, is defined as *special packaging conforming to 173.3 of this subchapter into which damaged, defective, or leaking hazardous materials packages, or hazardous materials that have spilled or leaked, are placed for the purposes of transport for recovery and disposal.*

The term *overpack drum* is sometimes used in the fire and emergency services to identify a salvage drum. This is an incorrect use of the term as defined by the *CFR*. While a salvage drum can be an overpack drum, an overpack drum cannot be a salvage drum. Overpack drums do not meet the requirements of 49 *CFR* 173.3 such as passing a pressure test to ensure they are leakproof.

The definition of overpack packaging is *an enclosure that is used by a single consignor to provide protection or convenience in handling of a package or to consolidate two or more packages.*

Scene Release

Once a fire and emergency services organization responds to an emergency incident scene, its personnel assume control of the scene and immediate surrounding area. Within certain limits, the organization can deny access to anyone, including the owner of the property.

Legitimate members of the news media have certain constitutionally protected rights of access, but the interpretation of these rights varies from state/province to state/province and from country to country. Company officers should be guided by local protocols; but at the very least, they should communicate with incident command to maintain safety and ensure that coordinated and accurate information is released.

The process of releasing control of the scene back to the owner or responsible party is sometimes not as straightforward as it might seem. The owner or responsible party should be escorted on a tour of the scene, or as close to it as safely possible, and given an explanation of any remaining hazards. If the scene is too hazardous to leave unattended, the owner may be required to post a security guard, erect a security fence around the hazard area, or do both. Before the scene is released, the organization may require the owner to sign a written release that describes the hazards and stipulates the conditions the owner must meet to secure the scene.

Medical Evaluation

Before returning personnel or units to service or releasing individual personnel called to the scene, a medical evaluation may be required. Any personnel who have shown signs or symptoms of heat stress or injury but remained at the scene must be evaluated. Some organizations are now requiring medical checks for anyone who participates in a working incident before they are allowed to return to service. Evaluations would be the responsibility of medical personnel assigned to a rehabilitation unit, and results would be reported to the incident safety officer.

Return to Service

The IC should return units to service as soon as they have retrieved equipment, personnel are fully rehabilitated, and units are no longer needed. Units that have been on the scene the longest may be returned to service, while units that have only been engaged for a short period of time may remain to complete the operation. Mutual aid units should also be returned to service as soon as possible. The IC may decide to return units to service but have them remain in staging until all operations are complete.

Off-duty personnel who were called should be released before personnel in active units are released. Off-duty personnel may have already worked a prior shift and could be fatigued. Personnel who are showing signs of fatigue must be evaluated before they are allowed to leave the scene.

Summary

The ability to quickly and accurately take command of an emergency situation is a critical skill for company officers. Because company officers are in charge of the units who are most often the first to arrive on an emergency scene, they must be able to remain calm in the midst of chaos. They must be able to quickly identify the nature and scope of the problem, assess the current and future resource needs, and gather the information needed to develop an IAP. The plan must be communicated to all emergency personnel.

The company officer must be able to apply the Layman decision-making model based on information gained during size-up, deploy resources, and direct the placement and positioning of apparatus and personnel to resolve the situation. The company officer must also select the appropriate command activity and determine the operational mode based on immediate resources.

When the decisions have been implemented, the officer manages the incident until it is terminated or command is transferred. The officer's final activities involve terminating the incident by preparing the unit to return to service and returning the property to the control of the owner/occupant.

Postincident Activities

Chapter Contents

Learning Objectives

1. Select facts about scene security.

2. Define *chain of custody*.

3. Distinguish between an interview and an interrogation.

4. Place in order the steps of an interview.

5. Identify characteristics of an incident report.

6. Identify the common causes of fires.

7. Select correct responses about fire growth and development.

8. Select facts about determining the point of origin for various types of fires.

9. Apply the evaluation process to the fire cause and determination task.

10. Identify the most common sources of contamination at fire scenes.

11. Select facts about the elements of a postincident analysis and critique.

12. Conduct a postincident analysis.

Job Performance Requirements

This chapter provides information that addresses the following job performance requirements of NFPA 1021, *Standard for Fire Officer Professional Qualifications* (2003):

Chapter 4 Fire Officer I

4.5

4.5.1

4.5.1(A)

4.5.1(B)

4.5.2(A)

4.6.4

4.6.4(A)

Chapter 21
Postincident Activities

When an emergency incident has been controlled and terminated, the company officer must still perform two very important activities: Determining the cause of the incident and preparing a postincident analysis (PIA) (also known as an *after-action report*). Both activities are essential because they provide information that can be used to reduce loss due to fires and other emergencies and improve responder safety. The information gathered is used to reinforce proper response activities or correct improper activities. A PIA focuses on the actual activities of responders and does not place blame or find fault.

The analysis is presented to all participants during a postincident critique, which is a gathering of the incident's participants to review the incident and discuss the outcome. The critique can be considered a training activity since it takes responders through the incident and allows them to see how various activities depend on each other for a successful conclusion to the incident.

NOTE: Many organizations have stopped using the word *critique* in relation to a postincident critique, preferring to call it a *postincident analysis (PIA)*. The reason is that there is a tendency for the meeting to become negative when it changes from a format of critiquing to criticizing.

The company officer will be primarily concerned with determining the cause of fires. Determining the cause of a fire provides data that are used to develop the local as well as the national fire risk status. It helps to focus on behavioral, technological, natural, and intentional problems that cause fires and determine trends that may indicate a wider problem.

When the information gathered is analyzed, programs can be created to provide a solution to the problem. In the case of behavioral causes, public fire and life-safety programs can be developed that make the population aware of the need to change dangerous habits such as smoking in bed. Changes in technology such as automatic gas shutoffs on commercial stoves linked to a fire-suppression system can decrease the loss due to cooking fires.

While natural causes cannot be altered, public education and changes in zoning laws can reduce the likelihood that people will live in areas that may be prone to wildland or urban interface fires. If the fire cause is determined to be intentional or malicious, similarities between the evidence and behavior may indicate the existence of a pattern that can be used to assist in locating and prosecuting arsonists or altering the behavior of juvenile firesetters.

While fire cause determination is the focus of most company officers, other types of emergencies should not be ignored. Information that is gathered on the National Fire Incident Reporting System (NFIRS) and other reporting systems should also be analyzed to determine causes of other emergency incidents. These results should be distributed to the appropriate organizations and community leaders.

For instance, some incident reports may indicate an increase in motor vehicle accidents at a particular intersection. Determining the cause of each accident may point to the need for a better traffic control system at that location or removal of a barrier that limits a driver's view of oncoming traffic. Even the cause of natural disasters, which may be obvious, should be

Figure 21.1 Torrential rain can cause washouts and mudslides as well as flooding in low-lying areas. *Courtesy of U.S. Federal Emergency Management Agency, Robert J. Alvey, photographer.*

analyzed. Mudslides or landslides in a particular area may indicate the need to prohibit rebuilding in that area or change the surface water runoff system **(Figure 21.1)**.

Emergency Cause Determination

Company officers must be able to make a preliminary determination of the cause of any fire, explosion, hazardous material spill, or other emergency to which they respond. Determining the cause of an emergency consists of basic detective work. Basic incident scene procedures include scene security, on-scene interviews, and report development. The company officer gathers data based on interviews, personal observations, and physical evidence and then compares the information to personal experiences and knowledge. In the case of non-fire emergencies, a detailed investigation into the cause may not be necessary. However, all pertinent information should be gathered and recorded on the appropriate forms.

Basic Incident Scene Procedures

The company officer can apply some basic procedures to determining the cause of all emergency incidents. The first activity is to ensure scene security, which is simply an extension of the security that was established during the emergency operations that separated the public from the hazardous condition and divided the area into control zones (see Chapter 19, Incident Scene Management).

The second procedure that the company officer should be aware of is how to conduct on-scene interviews of participants, responders, and witnesses. Besides the general recommendations included in this chapter, the company officer must be familiar with the local policies regarding interviews.

Finally, the company officer must know how to prepare and complete reports regarding the cause of an emergency. These reports may be prepared in essay format or on a prepared form such as the NFIRS forms where information is inserted into numbered spaces.

Scene Security

A secure perimeter must be established within which only those responsible for determining the cause of the emergency are allowed. In the case of a fire, this perimeter can be the same one used to define the hot zone established during the suppression or control phase of the operation. Rope or some form of barrier tape may be used to establish this perimeter **(Figure 21.2)**. In the case of nonfire emergencies such as hazardous materials spills or natural disasters, the perimeter may be far larger and may require the use of apparatus, road barriers, or law enforcement or military personnel to secure it.

When it is necessary to call law enforcement officials or a fire investigator, fire and emergency services personnel should secure the scene and preserve any evidence until the appropriate individuals arrive. Emergency responders should not move or handle evidence unless it is absolutely necessary in order to preserve it. However, there may be times when it is necessary because of the immediate unavailability of law enforcement officials or fire investigators. To reduce uncertainty, emergency responders should write a description of the evidence and draw/sketch or photograph the site where it was found.

Evidence of the cause of an emergency incident may need to be protected by additional means until it can be properly investigated. Depending upon the size of the evidence and the nature of its surroundings, it may be possible to protect it by covering it with a salvage cover or cardboard box **(Figure 21.3)**.

Figure 21.2 Barrier tape can be used to define an unsafe area, restrict access, and safeguard evidence such as tire or footprints that might be disturbed by personnel or onlookers. *Courtesy of District Chief Chris Mickal.*

Figure 21.3 Evidence should be protected and not moved until it is photographed and its condition, location, and significance recorded.

The most thorough investigation to determine the cause of an emergency incident can be wasted completely if the evidence chain of custody is broken because the scene was not properly secured. When law enforcement officials or fire investigators are not immediately available, the property must remain under the control of the fire and emergency services organization until all evidence has been collected.

Chain of Custody

The term *chain of custody* is a legal term that refers to the handling and integrity of real evidence, that is, physical materials. The term also denotes the documentation of the custody, including the acquisition or seizure, control, transfer, analysis, and final disposition of the evidence. To be acceptable in a court of law, the chain of custody must authenticate the location of evidence at all times and who had access to it. The term *chain of evidence* is sometime used interchangeably with *chain of custody.*

All evidence must be marked, tagged, and photographed before the scene is released by the organization. This action is mandatory because the U.S. Supreme Court has decreed that an administrative warrant or a signed consent form will be needed for any entries after the initial entry for the emergency. See **Appendix L** for sample consent forms.

Case Law

Two legal cases have established the requirement for warrants or consent before the investigation of a fire scene. The first is the 1978 case titled *Michigan v. Tyler and Robert Tompkins.* The Michigan Supreme Court held that investigators entering the premises after emergency response units had left the scene violated the Fourth Amendment of the U.S. Constitution because a warrant had not been obtained. The U.S. Supreme Court upheld the Michigan ruling.

In the 1984 case, *Michigan v. Clifford,* the U.S. Supreme Court ruled that Fourth-Amendment protection extends to burned properties. Therefore, all entries into a residence following the extinguishment of a fire to search for and remove evidence required either an administrative or criminal warrant. See **Appendix M** for a complete review of these two cases.

In most fire incidents, the fire and emergency services organization has the authority to deny access to any building during fire-fighting operations and for as long afterward as deemed reasonably necessary. However, company officers should be aware of any local laws pertaining to the right of access by owners, occupants, or members of the news media. The U.S. Supreme Court has ruled that a fire department has the authority to remain at a scene for a reasonable amount of time to investigate a fire. However, this investigation must be part of the continuation of the initial response to the emergency.

After a fire incident, no one, including the property owner or occupant, should be allowed to enter the premises before it is released unless they are accompanied by a fire officer or emergency responder. A written log of any such entry should be kept, showing the person's name, times of entry and exit, and a description of any items moved or taken from the scene. The company officer must restrict access from multiple-entry points to a single-entry control point to protect and not disturb any material that may be considered evidence.

On-Scene Interviews

The objective of PIA interviews is to gather information related to the incident. The company officer should start interviews as soon as possible during the termination phase of the incident. Witnesses at a fire or any other emergency incident scene with valuable information may leave the area without being identified or they may be unavailable at a later time. The following people are among those that need to be interviewed at the scene:

- Fire and emergency services responders
- Law enforcement personnel
- Building, facility, or vehicle owner
- Building or vehicle occupants
- Neighbors
- Witnesses

While a company officer can use the interview process to help determine the cause of an emergency incident and gather essential background information on the structure, facility, vehicle, or other emergency site, the officer must never interrogate a witness. It is important to understand the following differences between an interview and interrogation:

- **Interview** — Questioning of an individual for the purpose of obtaining information related to an investigation; nonaccusatory in nature.

- **Interrogation** — Formal line of questioning of an individual who is suspected of committing a crime or who may be reluctant to provide answers to an investigator's questions; accusatory in nature (the individual being questioned is a suspect in the commission of a crime such as arson). Interrogations are the responsibility of fire investigators and law enforcement personnel who have the authority and training to use them.

A company officer conducting an interview should always keep in mind that the purpose of an interview is to collect useful and accurate information about a fire or other emergency incident and its cause (**Figure 21.4**). The company officer can apply the following steps during an interview:

Step 1: Introduce yourself to the witness and provide proper identification.

Step 2: Set the tone of the interview during the early stage. The approach can be casual, friendly, businesslike, or authoritative, depending on the type of interview and the person being interviewed.

Step 3: Positively identify the person being interviewed before asking any questions. Use an official witness interview form such as that suggested in NFPA 921, *Guide for Fire and Explosion Investigations* (2004), or a similar form developed by the jurisdiction to record the following information for each person interviewed (**Figure 21.5, p. 504**):

— Full name

— Social Security number (optional; cannot be required)

— Date of birth

— Home address

— Home telephone number

— Work address

— Work telephone number

— Physical description (optional)

— Date, time, and location of the interview

— Name of the officer conducting the interview

Step 4: Begin the interview by outlining the objectives of the interview, which is to get the person being interviewed to give the investigator information regarding the incident.

Step 5: Be positive, professional, and objective; focus on getting as much information as possible.

Step 6: Actively listen while making eye contact while the witness is responding to questions. *Active listening skills:*

— Maintain eye contact with the witness.

— Stay focused and involved.

— Avoid emotional involvement.

— Remain objective and open-minded.

— Concentrate on what is being said.

Step 7: Avoid talking too much during the interview and not allowing the witness to answer questions or tell a story (two common mistakes). Do not provide the witness with more information about the incident than was known before the interview.

Step 8: Always be alert to nonverbal indicators that the witness is under stress or acting in a deceptive mode. *Stress indicators:*

— Depression

— Denial

— Bargaining

— Acceptance (absence of fight-or-flight response)

Nonverbal indicators (body language that may indicate that the witness is stressed by the interview and may or may not suggest that the person is being untruthful):

— Head position (chin down as though avoiding the interviewer's gaze)

— Facial color (pale and lacking color or flushed as though embarrassed)

— Facial expressions (frowns, pursed lips, or tight facial muscles)

— Covering or blocking mouth

— Scratching nose

— Touching head

— Yawning

— Biting, cleaning, or filing fingernails

— Playing with hands or rings

— Exhibitions of anger

— Defensive postures

— Breaking eye contact

— Sitting postures (slouching or tense)

— Placing chairs as barriers

Step 9: Inform the interviewee at the close of the interview that the information provided will only be used as part of the investigation and is considered confidential.

Figure 21.4 Once an incident is resolved, the company officer should interview witnesses, participants, and property owners/occupants.

Tompkins Fire Department
City of Tompkins, East Virginia

Witness Interview Form

INCIDENT RESPONSE NUMBER	INCIDENT DATE	FILE NUMBER
INCIDENT ADDRESS		INCIDENT TIME

WITNESS IDENTIFICATION

NAME			
STREET ADDRESS		CITY, STATE	COUNTY
HOME PHONE		MOBILE PHONE	
DATE OF BIRTH	SOCIAL SECURITY NO. (Optional)	DRIVER'S LICENSE NO.	OTHER I.D. NO.
RACE	AGE	SEX	WORK PHONE
PLACE OF EMPLOYMENT		WORK ADDRESS	
RELATIONSHIP TO INCIDENT			
MAY BE CONTACTED AT:			
STATEMENT TAKEN BY:		LOCATION, DATE, TIME OF STATEMENT	

PHYSICAL DESCRIPTION OF WITNESS

HEIGHT	WEIGHT	COLOR OF EYES
COMPLEXION	TATTOOS	HAIR COLOR AND LENGTH
DISTINGUISHING MARKS		

Witness Statement

Continue witness statement on back if necessary.

Figure 21.5 Sample witness interview form based on examples in NFPA 921.

Report Development

For all types of emergency responses, the company officer will be required to submit a company-level incident report (sometimes called a *run report*). The report will become part of the statistical data reflecting the jurisdiction's fire and emergency response history for any given period. It can also be used to help the organization determine where and how to focus fire prevention, life-safety programs, hazard preparedness, and public education efforts.

The report about a fire ultimately may be used as evidence in a legal case if the fire is determined to be intentional or conflict occurs between an owner/occupant and the insuring company. In the case of a nonfire report, for example, a description of a motor vehicle accident and the behavior of participants may conflict with official statements made initially. Therefore, it is essential that incident reports have the following characteristics:

- *Completeness* — The report must describe all pertinent details of the company's involvement in an incident beginning from the time of alarm dispatch and continuing until the company was released from the incident. Remembering and recording this information can sometimes be a challenge, but it is a very important part of the report's credibility. If any important point is omitted, the obvious question that follows is *what else has been left out?* If necessary, the company officer should use a checklist to ensure that all important points have been addressed.

- *Clarity* — Even when a report is very comprehensive, if it is written in a way that intentionally or unintentionally obscures important information, its value will be greatly diminished and authenticity may be challenged. The company officer must use words and phrases that are least likely to be misinterpreted or misunderstood. A good habit for company officers when writing reports is to have a dictionary and thesaurus available.

- *Objectivity* — Objective reports are based on facts and not on opinions or emotions. The company officer must record the events as they were experienced or reported by witnesses or other participants. Company officers must avoid making assumptions. The report should describe what company officers and other personnel saw, not what they may have assumed because of what they personally saw.

- *Factuality* — While the first three writing characteristics are important, they pale in comparison to the factuality of the report. In this context, factuality has nothing to do with the writer's honesty; it has to do with assumptions and interpretations. Ensuring factuality can be a difficult task, especially when attempting to record the cause of a fire or estimating the loss value to a structure or its contents. Equally important to the report's factuality is that when documenting their involvement in an incident, company officers must report only the facts and not attempt to interpret them.

Report forms may be found in NFPA 921. This document contains numerous report forms that may be used for structural, wildland, and vehicle incidents as well as those involving injuries or fatalities. The NFIRS forms are also sources for recording incident information for all types of incidents.

Fire Emergencies

Company officers may have the greatest experience determining the cause of fires. Fire cause determination and investigation have been parts of the company officer's responsibilities for decades if not longer. When a fire has been extinguished, the company officer must determine the events or conditions that caused it. Armed with the basic knowledge of how fire causes are categorized, the conditions required for a fire to start, and how fires grow and develop, the company officer uses a systematic approach to fire cause determination. The most successful method is to use a process of elimination.

Given that fires may be accidental, natural, or incendiary, the company officer can eliminate categories that do not apply. For instance, if the structure did not have electrical service or service was turned off at the time of the fire, an electrical short circuit in wiring or equipment could then be eliminated as a possible cause. If the fire occurred on a clear day with calm winds, lightning or high winds would not be considered contributing factors.

As the various possible causes are eliminated, an officer is able to focus on obvious indicators to first determine the point of origin of the fire and second determine the cause. For instance, a cone-shaped pattern and heavy damage to the walls and ceiling may indicate the point of origin (**Figure 21.6**). If this pattern is over a stove or cooking appliance, the officer then starts looking for evidence of equipment malfunction or operator negligence.

When accidental causes such as leaving food cooking on a stove unattended are eliminated, the officer must then consider indicators of an incendiary fire. These indicators may be items that are out of place under normal circumstances. For instance, a gasoline can in a bedroom or remotely located multiple points of origin are very strong indicators of a fire deliberately set. Primary visual indicators are upright hourglass-shaped burn patterns or inverted *V* patterns, lines of demarcation, trailers, timing devices, floor discoloration left by accelerants, and odors of accelerants in areas where none should be present.

NOTE: The company officer must remember that postflashover burning can result in burn patterns that are similar to those caused by accelerants. When in doubt, a fire investigator should complete the investigation.

Figure 21.6 Generally, an interior fire will create a distinctive cone-shaped pattern on vertical surfaces adjacent to the fire's ignition point.

The company officer must be able to secure the incident scene to preserve any evidence or potential evidence of the fire cause and point of origin (where the fire began) and request a fire investigator if needed. To accomplish these tasks, company officers must also be familiar with the common causes of fires and how they grow and develop.

Common Causes of Fires

NFPA defines *fire cause* as *the circumstances, conditions, or agencies that bring together fuel, ignition source, and oxidizer (such as air or oxygen) resulting in a fire or a combustion explosion.* NFPA 921 lists the following potential classifications of fire cause (**Figure 21.7**):

- *Accidental* — Fires that do not involve a deliberate human act to ignite or spread into an area where fire is not normally found

- *Natural* — Fires such as those caused by lightning, storms, or floods where human intervention has not been involved in the ignition process

- *Incendiary* — Fires set deliberately under circumstances in which the responsible party knows a fire should not be ignited

- *Undetermined* — Classification used when the specific cause of a fire cannot be determined. *Factors:*

  — May be used as an interim classification as the fire investigation is proceeding, or it may be the final outcome when additional information cannot be obtained that identifies the specific cause

  — Does not mean, however, that if each of the specific components of the fire tetrahedron is not specifically identified, the fire should be called *undetermined*

A cause should be given if sufficient information is available. For example, when there is a known natural gas leak that resulted in an explosion and the specific source of ignition is not known, the fire may be assigned to the *accidental* classification and the source of ignition listed as *undetermined.* When evidence points to the intentional use of ignitable liquids as an accelerant and the specific ignition source is not determined or found, the fire should be assigned to the *incendiary* classification and the source of ignition listed as *undetermined.*

NOTE: Many times *arson* is listed as a cause for a fire, but arson is not given as a fire cause. Listing it as a fire cause is inaccurate. The term *arson* applies to a statute or law that prohibits the intentional setting of a fire or malicious use of an incendiary device. When a fire is intentionally set (incendiary), the act of arson is committed.

The company officer must understand that the accurate collection of information on fire cause actually affects the statistics used to report the fire problem locally and nationally. According to statistics collected by the U.S. Fire Administration (USFA), the leading cause of fires is undetermined or unknown.

Many reasons exist for the undetermined category dominating the statistics. Primary among them is a lack of evidence remaining after a fire has completely engulfed a structure or vehicle. Another factor is the lack of investigative training on the part of the reporting officer. While determining the cause of an all-consuming fire may be impossible, the second factor can be

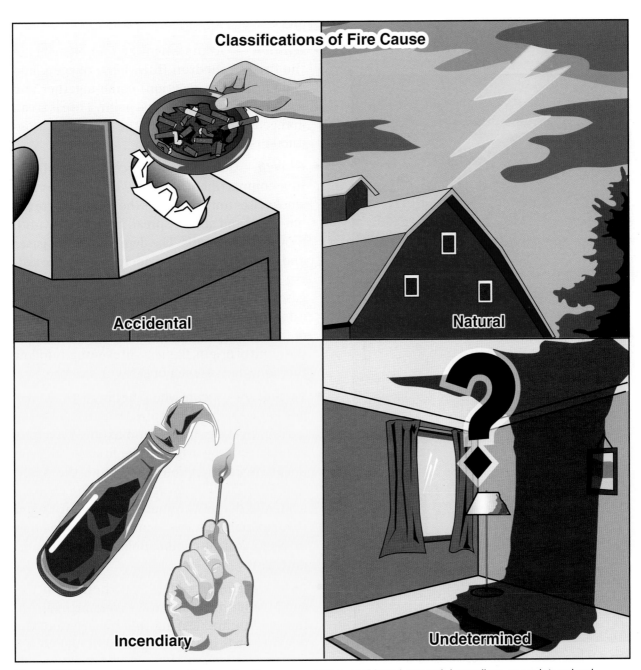

Figure 21.7 Four categories used to describe the cause of fires: accidental, natural, incendiary, or undetermined.

reduced by requesting an investigator as soon as possible and securing the area to preserve evidence.

An analysis of the causes of fires in the U.S. indicates that the most common cause in commercial properties is intentional (incendiary). In residential properties, the leading cause is cooking-related fires. Cooking fires, which may be considered accidental, also result in the highest rate of injuries and occur because of human error (**Figure 21.8**).

The leading cause of fire-related deaths in residential properties is the careless use of smoking materials, while heating equipment ties with incendiary as the second highest cause of fatalities in residences. These statistics can assist the company officer in narrowing the possible causes and determining (as near as possible) the actual cause of a fire.

Fire Growth and Development

To locate the point of origin and determine the cause of a fire, company officers must understand the basic concept of fire growth and development. When a fire begins inside an enclosed room or compartment, it generally develops in a predictable way. The following five stages of fire development have been identified through research (**Figure 21.9**):

- *Ignition* — Occurs when the four elements of the fire tetrahedron (fuel, heat, oxygen, and chemical chain reaction) come together and combustion begins. At this point, a fire is small and generally confined to the fuel that was ignited first.

- *Growth* — Occurs as the fire continues to burn. In a compartment, a plume of hot gases and smoke rises until it reaches the ceiling where the hot gases and smoke spread horizontally until they reach the walls. The depth of the hot gases and smoke then begins to increase from the ceiling downward toward the floor. When the hot gases and smoke encounter an opening such as a doorway or window, they will travel up and out of the opening. As the fire continues to grow at the point of origin, flames will eventually follow the same path as the hot gases and smoke.

- *Flashover* — Occurs when the hot gases, smoke, and flames at the ceiling of a compartment cause radiant heating of the combustible materials remote from the origin of the fire. When these materials reach ignition temperature, they spontaneously ignite or *flash over*. The fire changes from one that is dominated by the burning of the materials that were ignited first to one that involves *all* of the combustibles within the compartment.

- *Fully developed* — Occurs when all of the combustible materials in the compartment are involved in fire. During this time period, the burning fuels in the compartment release the maximum amount of heat possible for the available fuel.

Figure 21.8 Human error is a contributing factor in cooking-related fires in the U.S.

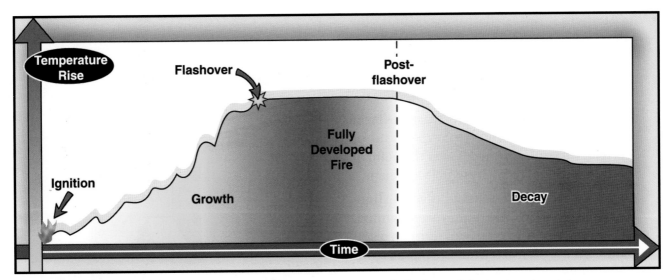

Figure 21.9 Stages of fire development in a compartment: ignition, growth, flashover, fully developed, and decay.

• *Decay* — Occurs when the available fuel in the compartment is consumed by the fire and the rate of heat release begins to decline. The fire becomes fuel-controlled, the amount of fire diminishes, and the temperatures within the compartment begin to decline.

Many of the following factors may affect fire growth and development in a compartment:

• Size, number, and arrangement of ventilation openings in the compartment

• Volume of the compartment

• Thermal properties of the compartment enclosures (walls, ceiling, and floor)

• Ceiling height of the compartment

• Size, composition, and location of the fuel that was ignited first

• Availability and locations of additional fuel

Note that under normal conditions in a closed structure, the highest levels of heat will be found at ceiling level and the lowest levels of heat will be found at floor level. ASTM International (originally known as the American Society for Testing and Materials [ASTM]) developed a time-temperature curve to illustrate the increase in temperature of a fire in a compartment over a period of time. The model is used to test the fire-retardant properties of building materials.

Although the testing model has remained relatively unchanged, changes in the fire environment have brought the accuracy of the test into question.

The test itself does not take into consideration the effects of sprinkler systems in relation to the tested product, the curve represents only a fully developed fire, and the size of tested components is limited by the size of the test furnace.

Point of Origin

The point of origin of any type of fire in a structure, wildland, or vehicle incident will be evident by a number of factors. A common approach to determining the point of origin is to begin with the area that exhibits the least amount of damage and then proceed to the area of greatest damage.

Structure fires. Because the point of origin is where a fire starts and has burned the longest, this area will be the most damaged area inside a structure. Several indicators of the point of origin inside a structure include the following:

• *Charring* — *Char* is the carbon-based remains of burned organic material. The location of char can indicate the direction the fire burned (usually up, but not always), while the depth of char can indicate which area burned the longest **(Figure 21.10, p. 510)**. Charring is usually deepest near the point of origin. Vertical surfaces of items, doors, or walls that face the direction the fire approached from will have the deepest char, while the reverse sides will exhibit less charring. Low charring may indicate lower-level burning and could indicate ignitable liquids were used as accelerants.

- **Burn pattern** — Burn pattern is a good indicator of the point of origin of a fire *inside* a structure. Structural fires behave in a predictable way because they are not subject to the elements of weather such as wind or rain. *Examples:*

  — Normal burn patterns inside structures form a cone-shaped pattern from the point of origin. On vertical surfaces near the point of origin, the pattern will resemble a *V* shape.

  — Fires started with accelerants leave a distinctive burn pattern where they were ignited. For example, an hourglass pattern can result from the use of an accelerant such as an ignitable liquid or any other material that releases heat at a high rate (**Figure 21.11**).

- **Swollen lightbulbs** — When incandescent lightbulbs are exposed to heat, they soften and swell. The swelling usually points toward the source of heat.

- **Floor damage** — Floors are typically less damaged than ceilings because fire usually burns in an upward direction. Heavily charred flooring may be an indicator of the point of origin. Sharp-edged flooring burns may indicate high heat at a low level, which could point to a mattress, couch, or sofa as added fuel.

Wildland fires. Unlike structural fires, outdoor fires are influenced by environmental factors such as topography, wind, and other weather conditions. Although these factors make determining the point of origin more difficult, the following predictable elements can be considered when attempting to locate the point of origin of a wildland fire (**Figure 21.12**):

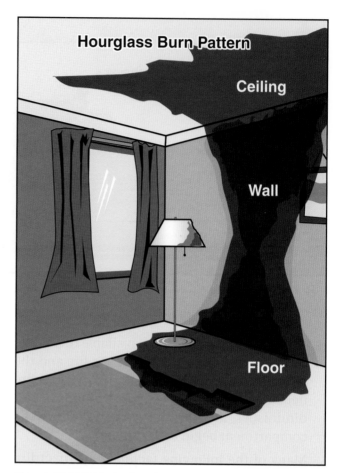

Figure 21.11 An hourglass burn pattern may be an indicator of the use of accelerants in starting a fire.

Figure 21.12 In densely wooded areas, fires are fueled by fine fuels such as dead leaves, dry grass, and rotten wood that may cover the ground under the trees. These conditions increase the fire's intensity, resulting in destruction of ignition evidence. Locating the exact point of origin becomes much more difficult. *Courtesy of U.S. Federal Emergency Management Agency, Liz Roll, photographer.*

Figure 21.10 Charring may provide clues about which direction the fire burned and may indicate the area that burned the longest. *Courtesy of Donny Howard, Yates & Associates.*

- Fire generally spreads away from the point of origin due to slope (incline), aspect (direction slope faces), and fuel moisture.

- Fire spreads faster uphill than downhill; consider ladder fuels (vertical continuity from the ground).

- Fire spreads faster with the wind than against it.

- Fire spreads faster in fine fuels (for example, grass spreads fire faster than timber).

- Point of origin is almost always nearer the heel (rear) than the head (forward advancing part) of a wildland fire. When viewed from above, the burn pattern will generally form a *V* shape with the point of origin located at the narrowest point.

Vehicle fires. Determining the point of origin of a vehicle fire is similar to determining the point of origin of a structural fire. The company officer should thoroughly examine the exterior of the vehicle and the surrounding area and then follow up with an examination of the interior. The following areas are included in the examination of a vehicle after a fire:

- Driver and passenger areas
- Engine compartment
- Fuel system
- Electrical systems

The company officer should interview the owner of the vehicle and any witnesses, if available, to determine whether the fire occurred when the vehicle was moving or parked. Fires that occur while a vehicle is being driven are usually caused by electrical or mechanical malfunctions or careless use of smoking materials by occupants. If the vehicle was moving, the following points should be considered:

- Mechanical fires typically start in the engine compartment, exhaust system, or wheel-and-brake assembly. These fires can result from fuel leaks, friction, and combustibles.

- Fires caused by electrical malfunctions usually begin under the dashboard or in the engine compartment **(Figure 21.13)**. Generally, the fire will not extend through the firewall.

Figure 21.13 Fires that start in the passenger compartment of automobiles generally result from electrical problems or improper use of smoking materials.

- Fires started by smoking materials may start in the upholstery.

A fire in a parked vehicle may have started while the vehicle was moving but was detected only after the vehicle was parked. When this situation is the case, the fire is likely to have started in the same areas listed for moving vehicles. When a fire starts in a vehicle that has been parked for several hours or days, it is wise to consider that the fire may have been set intentionally.

Vehicle fires may be set to hide the theft of parts or collect insurance claims. Indicators will include missing parts such as batteries, alternators, or engines in the engine compartments or radios, audio tape or compact disc (CD) players, steering wheels, seats, or other trims in interiors.

Fire Investigators

When conditions indicate that a fire may have been set intentionally, a more thorough investigation is warranted. The company officer must follow organizational protocols for calling a fire investigator. Pending the arrival of an investigator, the company officer's responsibilities are to secure and control the scene, protect the evidence, and prepare to inform the investigator of what has been found. For more information about fire and arson investigation, see the IFSTA **Introduction to Fire Origin and Cause** and **Fire Investigator** manuals or NFPA 921.

Even after a fire investigator arrives on scene and assumes control of the investigation, the company officer's job is not finished. The company officer and subordinates may be asked to assist with the investigation. If so, they have a tremendous opportunity to learn about the art and science of fire investigation. But even if company personnel are not included in the investigation, they still have tasks to perform — they must write the required reports regarding the incident in a chronological sequence.

Evidence Preservation

If the initial fire cause determination by the company officer indicates that a fire or explosion was the result of malicious, intentional, and possibly criminal intent, a fire investigator must be called to the scene. To assist the fire investigator, the company officer must identify and preserve any physical evidence.

The physical evidence found at a fire scene can be in many forms, including the following:

- Liquids thought to be accelerants
- Broken glass
- Portions of incendiary or explosive devices
- Liquid containers
- Appliances involved in the ignition of the fire
- Clothing/fabrics
- Tire or foot impressions
- Tool marks on doors or windows
- Bodily fluids
- Cigarette butts
- Papers or documents
- Samples of charred wood, carpet, or other fuel involved in the fire
- Paints
- Hairs
- Metal objects, such as broken locks

Physical evidence such as a device used to set a fire or materials that show specific fire patterns may be directly related to the fire. Some physical evidence collected may also be *exclusionary evidence* that shows that a particular device or scenario can be excluded in relation to the fire-ignition or fire-spread scenario. Most evidence collected at a fire scene will be in the form of *artifacts* that are the remains of materials involved in the fire that

Figure 21.14 Remains (artifacts) of a time-delay ignition device were recovered in this fire and may indicate the fire cause and may also be essential to the prosecution of the person responsible for starting the fire. *Courtesy of Bill Lellis.*

in some way are related or contributed to ignition, development, or spread of the fire or explosion **(Figure 21.14)**.

A major concern of fire investigators when collecting physical evidence is to prevent cross-contamination of the evidence. Contamination of the scene or samples being collected at a scene can occur from many sources. Some of the most common sources include the following:

- *Hand tools used by firefighters and investigators at the scene* — Pike poles, axes, or shovels used in the overhaul process can alter the appearance of or completely destroy evidence of forcible entry or incendiary ignition.

- *Protective equipment worn by firefighters and investigators working at the scene* — Once evidence has been located and identified, company officers and personnel should make every effort to isolate the evidence and stay away from it until the fire investigator arrives. Boots and gloves used in fire-fighting operations are potential sources of contamination, especially when they have been in contact previously with flammable or combustible liquids **(Figure 21.15)**.

- *Fuel-powered equipment used at the scene during fire-suppression and investigation operations* — After fire-suppression operations are completed, the company officer should document where this type of equipment was used and whether it was refueled while it was in place. *Procedures:*

— Take precautions to prevent contamination beyond the area in which the equipment is located when the use of this type of equipment is necessary during an investigation.

— Relate information regarding the operation of power tools and equipment to the investigator.

Company officers should work closely with their personnel and the fire investigator to ensure that evidence is undisturbed before collection and processing. The keys to minimizing potential evidence contamination or destruction are as follows:

• Good scene security

• Maintenance of the chain of custody (tracking) of items collected

• Careful monitoring of those who enter the scene for possible contamination on their clothing, tools, or equipment

Figure 21.15 Personnel who are investigating a fire scene should wear appropriate personal protective equipment. However, they must be careful to not allow residue that might be on boots and gloves to contaminate the area.

A *chain of custody* tracks an item of evidence from the time it is found until it is ultimately disposed of or returned to its owner. Maintaining this chain of custody is essential if the evidence is going to be of any value in a court of law. Each person who has possession of an item of evidence must be able to attest to the fact that the item was not subject to tampering or contamination while it was in the person's custody.

Company officers and their personnel are the first persons in the chain of custody **(Figure 21.16)**. When the fire investigator arrives at the incident scene and takes charge of the investigation, the following information regarding the evidence is obtained:

• Name and address of both the current and prior custodian

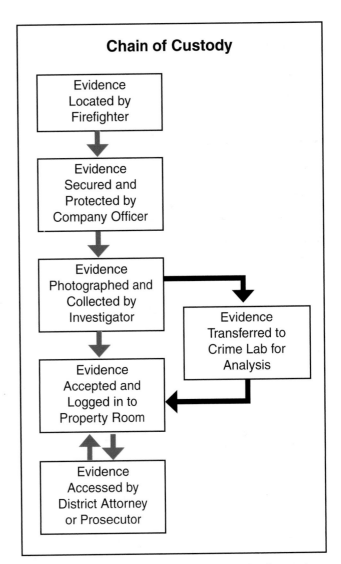

Figure 21.16 Illustration of the evidence chain of custody.

- Description of any modification, handling, testing, or other alteration that occurred while in the custody of the current custodian
- Condition of the item or its packaging when it was transferred to a new custodian

The greatest threats to the recovery of evidence or any physical indication of the cause of the fire or explosion are the overhaul activities of fire-suppression personnel. While it is essential that the fire be completely extinguished, including any hidden fires within concealed spaces or under debris, every effort must be made to protect evidence when it is located and identified. The use of water and movement of debris at a scene should be minimized to protect such evidence. The lack of evidence or indicators to the cause of a fire is a contributing factor in the high percentage of fires classified as *undetermined*.

Nonfire Emergencies

Along with the information given earlier in this section, the company officer can also use the basic accident investigation process described in the Investigation Policies section of Chapter 10, Safety and Health Issues, to determine causes of nonfire emergencies. Information is gathered from interviews, observations, and reports and then analyzed to determine the root cause of the incident. When provided to the appropriate authority, this information can determine how an emergency incident can be prevented or reduce its effects in the future. For instance, an analysis of the aftermath of a tornado might indicate the need for an improved notification system or a provision for strategically placed community storm shelters.

Because the fire and emergency services profession is now considered an all-hazards response profession, it is important that accurate and detailed information be collected on all types of emergencies. Although the company officer may only be involved in the collection of the information, that information may be the basis for changes that can affect the entire country. What may appear as an isolated incident in one municipality may actually be part of a much wider overall trend.

Postincident Analysis and Critique

The PIA and postincident critique are tools that are intended to determine whether an emergency incident was conducted in the safest and most efficient manner. The information that was gathered by the company officer is combined with the information gathered by the overall incident commander (IC) and incident safety officer (ISO) and then analyzed. The resulting PIA is used during a formal postincident critique involving all participants. In the case of a multiunit emergency, those participating in the critique include the responding units as well as staff officers, branch and division supervisors, and off-duty personnel who were called to the scene.

Analysis

The company officer may be assigned the responsibility of gathering information required to prepare a PIA. The officer must be objective in the gathering and recording of the data used. The analysis or report is not intended to place blame or punish personnel for perceived infractions of policies or procedures. Its purpose is to improve the effectiveness and efficiency of responders and increase scene safety. Two primary areas of analysis are the application and effectiveness of the operational strategy and tactics and personnel safety. Generally, when an incident is large and complex, two different members of the National Incident Management System-Incident Command System (NIMS-ICS) Command Staff are assigned to these topic areas.

Strategy and Tactics

The IC is responsible for assigning an officer to write the postincident analysis dealing with strategy and tactics. This individual may be a member of the Command Staff, a section chief, or other fire officer who was present at the incident.

Information is gathered from interviews of witnesses, participants, news media (photographs and video), operational procedures contained in the incident action plan (IAP), communication logs and tapes, preincident site plans and inspections, structural reports, and owner/occupant statements. A clear description of the site before the incident is required as a matrix over which to lay the development of the emergency and the actions of the responding units and agencies.

Safety Issues

The responsibility for collecting safety-related information for a postincident analysis is assigned to the ISO according to NFPA 1500, *Standard on Fire Department Occupational Safety and Health Program,* and NFPA 1521, *Standard for Fire Department Safety Officer*. This officer collects data from interviews of witnesses and participants, response and casualty reports, incident action and safety plans, and communication logs and tapes. The ISO then analyzes the data, reconstructs the incident, and provides recommendations to the organization's health and safety officer and the chief executive officer or manager of the organization. The primary concerns for this portion of the analysis are to identify the following elements:

- Violations of the organization's standard operating procedures/standard operating guidelines (SOPs/SOGs)
- Future topics for company training
- Poorly defined operational procedures
- Unforeseen situations
- Training deficiencies

The health and safety officer also evaluates the use of personal protective equipment (PPE), the personnel accountability system, rehabilitation operations, hazardous conditions, and any other issues that pertain to the personal safety of personnel at the incident **(Figure 21.17)**. A written report containing recommendations is created and forwarded to the chief executive officer or manager of each organization when multiple organizations were involved. Safety of all personnel must be seen as a major responsibility within each element of the NIMS-ICS structure and should get considerable attention before, during, and after any emergency incident regardless of size.

Critique

A postincident critique is a meeting that generally involves all participating units and agencies. The critique is based on the PIA. In this critique, honesty is the key to making it work, and all egos

Figure 21.17 The health and safety officer evaluates the use of personal protective equipment (PPE). Contaminated and damaged PPE such as that shown here must be cleaned, repaired, or discarded.

need to be left outside the room. The goal of the critique is to acknowledge any weaknesses and applaud strengths that were evident in the analysis. Safety issues are highlighted as well as strategic and tactical concerns. A critique can involve only the company officer and members of the unit if the incident was small.

The results of the critique should be recorded and recommendations added to the PIA. The final document should be distributed to interested parties in the organization or other participating agencies.

The company officer may want to hold an informal critique before returning the unit to service. Tailboard critiques are helpful in identifying and addressing aspects of an operation that could have been performed better. Before leaving the scene, on-scene personnel should gather together to briefly discuss what went right and what could or should have been done better.

A formal critique should be held as soon as all necessary information is gathered and reviewed by the organization. Generally, the critique should occur within a week of the incident. This timing ensures that the events are fresh in the minds of the participants and that needed corrections are not delayed.

When a large-scale incident occurred that involved multiple units, jurisdictions, or agencies, representatives of each group should attend rather than all of the participants. See **Appendix N** for a list of points to be addressed in a postincident critique.

Recommended Changes

When the analysis and critique are complete for a multiorganization incident, each organization's chief executive officer, manager, or administrative staff makes any necessary changes to the operational strategy, tactics, policies, and procedures. Changes to written policy and procedures are announced to each organization's membership, and the news media publicizes changes that affect the general public. Any weaknesses in skills must be corrected through additional training. Training may be applied to just the units that participated in the operation or to each individual organization. Recommendations are included in a report for the organization's management staff.

Summary

The company officer must be able to determine the cause of fires, explosions, hazardous materials spills, and other emergencies. In the case of fire cause determination, the company officer must be familiar with the cause of fires, fire behavior, indicators of the point of origin, and the procedures for requesting a fire investigator. While statistical evidence indicates that the cause of the majority of fires is reported as undetermined, it is the company officer's responsibility to do everything possible to determine the exact cause. The officer must also be able to secure the fire scene and preserve evidence.

The same process of gathering information also applies to all emergency incidents. The information from all emergencies is collected into a PIA that includes information regarding the activities of fire and emergency services personnel as well as observations of the incident and statements of witnesses and participants. The PIA is used as the basis for the postincident critique.

Both the analysis and critique are used to improve the way responders operate at similar emergencies. The analysis also provides information that can be used to eliminate hazards or reduce the effect of hazards through the development of codes, changes in personal habits, or the construction of facilities or devices that will protect the population from hazards.

Types of Forensic Analysis

Evidence that a company officer or fire investigator gathers is usually sent to a laboratory for analysis. Many types of analyses are used to determine the cause of a fire or explosion, the identity of victims or suspects, motive, or other information that will provide a clear picture of the incident. From a legal point of view, the results of each analysis are woven together to provide a sound body of evidence in a criminal case. Even if the incident is not an incendiary fire, analysis may point to a malfunction in a piece of equipment that can result in a design change in the equipment.

Some of the types of analyses that are available in forensic investigations are as follows:

- **Fire debris analysis** — Determines the presence of materials such as ignition devices or ignitable liquids that may have been used as accelerants

- **Forensic analysis of explosives evidence** — Determines the composition of an explosive and type of detonation device employed

- **Microanalysis** — Examines items such as damaged electrical wiring, fibers, tool marks, and impressions from tires and shoes found at the incident scene

- **Biological analysis** — Examines human hair and skin samples; includes deoxyribonucleic acid (DNA) analysis that compares samples with victim or suspect DNA data

- **Latent fingerprint analysis** — Compares fingerprints found at the scene to those of potential suspects or fingerprints on file in national databases

- **Serology** — Analyzes body fluids such as blood, urine, semen, or saliva.

- **Forensic anthropology** — Identifies deceased victims

- **Forensic pathology** — Determines the cause of death of victims

- **Forensic toxicology** — Determines the presence of poisons in victims or at the incident scene

- **Firearms analysis** — Classifies or identifies firearms and their projectiles; includes ballistics (marks on the projectile), chemistry (powder residue), and wound (physical injury from gunshot) analyses

- **Forensic drug analysis** — Determines the presence and type of drugs found at the incident scene; has become increasingly important with the production of methamphetamines and their relation to fires in structures

- **Forensic image analysis** — Analyzes photographic (both film and digital) images and video images such as those provided by surveillance cameras

Although not incident-scene related, forensic linguistic analysis can be used to compare voice patterns and sounds on audiotapes of people reporting an incident in the event of a potential criminal action. This science is also used when analyzing the cockpit voice recorder from aircraft crash incidents. A final type of non-incident-scene analysis is the analysis of digital information found on computers such as electronic files, e-mail, and Internet activity. This analysis can be used to determine motive or participation in a crime.

Management Activities

Chapter Contents

Learning Objectives

1. Define the term *managing*.

2. Identify the resources a company officer may have available for use.

3. Recall the functions of management.

4. Select skills of an effective manager.

5. Identify motivational methods a manager may use.

6. Define *span of control*.

7. Recall facts about the four stages of the change process.

8. Match change types to their definitions.

9. Identify the causes of resistance to change.

10. Select facts about the basic steps for overcoming resistance to change.

11. Recall information about change agents.

12. Identify characteristics of a policy to implement change.

13. Select from a list the reasons that change can fail to occur.

Job Performance Requirements

This chapter provides information that addresses the following job performance requirements of NFPA 1021, *Standard for Fire Officer Professional Qualifications* (2003):

Applies to all management requirements rather than specific JPRs.

Chapter 22
Management Activities

This part of the manual focuses on the duties performed by Fire Officer II as defined in NFPA 1021, *Standard for Fire Officer Professional Qualifications*. The Fire Officer II still performs supervisory functions and commands single and multiple unit emergency response activities. However, the position is also considered a management position and, therefore, has additional authority and responsibilities. When assigned to a multiunit emergency incident scene, the Fire Officer II or managing fire officer will take command from a Fire Officer I and allocate the resources available until or unless relieved of command by a chief officer. The Fire Officer II may also fulfill the duties assigned to nonemergency line or staff functions, such as training, public fire and life safety education, fire investigation, or administration.

To fulfill these additional responsibilities, the company officer must apply proven leadership skills, as presented in Chapter 2, and management principles. These principles are based on management theories that have been developed, applied, and validated over the past century. A detailed presentation of the development of management principles may be found in **Appendix O**.

Managing is the act of influencing, controlling, monitoring, or directing a project, program, situation, or organization through the use of authority, discipline, or persuasion. To be an effective manager, a company officer should be able to:

- Understand the development of management theories.

- Know the various management functions that managers perform.

- Recognize the skills necessary to manage.

- Understand the management of change within the organization.

With a workforce that has become more diverse over the years and now includes two and three generations, the company officer has to understand the validated aspects of all management theories. As a manager, the company officer is responsible for achieving the organization's goals and objectives through the effective and efficient use of its resources. Every level of management (from chief of the department to company officer) is affected by or uses these resources. The company officer should always remember that the citizens of the service area provide the resources through their political and economic support. Those resources are generally considered to be as follows (**Figure 22.1, p. 522**):

- *Human resources* — Personnel assigned to the company officer

- *Financial resources* — Funds that are allocated to the organization and, subsequently, to each division or branch for the completion of its assigned tasks

- *Physical resources* — Facilities, apparatus, tools, equipment, extinguishing agents, EMS supplies, and daily operating materials of the organization that are required to perform the assigned tasks

- *Informational resources* — Data that are compiled by the organization concerning its operation such as incident reports, attendance reports, exposure reports, and injury reports

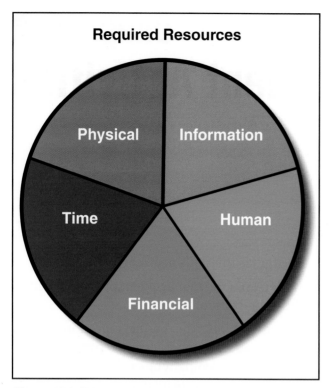

Required Resources

Figure 22.1 Citizens of the service area provide resources through their political and economic support.

to name a few; also includes the demographics of the community, political environment, economic climate, and trends in the fire and emergency services industry as well as the systems and processes used to manage the organization's information

- *Time resources* — Time required for completion of any project, which competes with the time required for other projects; must be invested wisely and prioritized with priority given to the most important projects

In the NFPA 1021 standard, the term *management* is used in conjunction with Level I and II Fire Officer responsibilities such as information management, incident management, and human resources management. Even though the standard defines the Level I officer as a supervisor and the Level II officer as a manager, it is essential for both Level I and Level II officers to fully understand the theories and methods used in the act of managing. Many will appear similar to the information provided in the chapters on leadership and supervision because they are, as mentioned in Chapter 2, linked together.

This chapter provides the company officer with a basic knowledge of the management functions, the skills required to be an effective manager, and the process for managing change. The company officer must realize that management, like leadership and supervision, is a broad topic and cannot be completely presented in one chapter of a manual like this. It is recommended that company officers either pursue a course of self-study based on the references listed in the Suggested Readings at the end of this manual or enroll in college-level management courses at their local colleges or universities. Company officers can also take courses online from an accredited educational organization. Courses are also available from the National Fire Academy (NFA) as well as regional and state/provincial fire academies.

Management Functions

Contemporary management principles include four functions that are similar to those defined in the classical management theories of Henri Fayol almost 100 years ago. It is a generally accepted business principle that the management process includes four functions: planning, organizing, leading, and controlling.

- *Planning* — Setting goals and objectives and determining the direction the organization or unit will take to achieve those results; it is both the broadest view of the organization (creation of the mission statement) and the narrowest (development of tactical plans for accomplishing a specific objective).

- *Organizing* — Coordinating tasks and resources to accomplish the unit's goals and objectives; accomplished by establishing the internal structure of the unit or organization that creates divisions of labor, coordinating the allocation of resources, and taking responsibility for tasks and flow of information within the department. Organizing includes staffing, which is the filling of positions with qualified people.

- *Leading* — Influencing, inspiring, and motivating employees to achieve the goals and objectives; also referred to as *directing* in some business definitions. Leading is a proactive approach to managing and was presented in Chapter 2, Leadership.

- *Controlling* — Establishing and implementing the mechanisms to ensure that objectives are attained; includes setting performance standards, measuring and reporting the actual performance, comparing the performance standard with the actual performance, and taking preventive or corrective action to close the gap between the two levels of performance.

These four functions are essential to the management of fire and emergency services organizations. Company officers must develop the skills necessary to apply each function to the duties assigned to them. It should be evident that these four functions can be applied to both emergency or nonemergency operations and duties.

Management Skills

Proper application of the management functions requires the company officer to possess certain management skills. While most company officers or officer candidates may have the knowledge to perform the technical tasks of the fire and emergency services, they may lack the interpersonal and management skills to be an effective company officer.

Skills

An effective manager must possess the following management skills:

- *Technical skills* — Methods and techniques required to perform certain tasks as a manager such as computer skills; knowledge of laws, codes, ordinances, and labor/management agreements; report writing skills; data analysis skills for problem and risk identification, and other skills that will be used to prepare budgets, create reports, or develop specifications **(Figure 22.2)**. These are in addition to the skills required of the officer as an emergency responder, such as the ability to manage an incident, apply strategic and tactical concepts to situations, and the knowledge of specialized emergency response skills.

- *Human and communication skills* — Interpersonal skills that include the ability to work with other people and supervise subordinates; success or failure often hinges on the ability to communicate.

Figure 22.2 An effective company officer should have computer skills to review codes and ordinances.

- *Conceptual and decision-making skills* — Skills that include the ability to understand abstract ideas and solve problems through a variety of ways; also the ability to understand the organization as a whole and recognize how the various parts are interrelated. *Details:*
  - Includes the analytical and evaluative skills discussed in Chapter 25
  - Includes the use of logic discussed in Chapter 4

Motivation

The company officer, like the captain of an athletic team, is responsible for inspiring and motivating the members of the unit. The leadership skills discussed in Chapter 2 are important for accomplishing this task. As a supervisor or manager, the company officer must find and apply methods to motivate unit personnel to achieve both the unit goals and their own personal goals.

Motivational Methods

In the private sector, there are many motivational methods or tools available for managers to use. The following are some proven methods:

- *Training* — Training motivates employees by:
  - Giving them the feeling the organization considers them valuable and trustworthy by investing in them

Seven Habits of Highly Effective People for Company Officers

The company officer will benefit from the concepts developed by Stephen Covey in his books *Seven Habits of Highly Effective People* and *The 8ᵗʰ Habit*. Covey details how a value-based personality can effectively improve leadership styles, which in turn motivates others to become proactive rather than reactive, allowing for others to affect one's lifestyle and behaviors. These actions include the following:

- **Be proactive.** Company officers must be able to work within and expand their circle of influence as opposed to focusing on their circle of concern, which causes reactive behavior. This is critical in emergency operations as well as nonemergency activities. When stressful occurrences develop, the company officer must realize that engaging the situation in a manner that allows for competent decision making rather than reacting with emotion will benefit the outcome of the incident for all parties involved.

- **Focus on the results.** The company officer must be able to conceptualize the variables related to an activity or operation to make the decisions necessary to accomplish it.

- **Prioritize.** The company officer must focus on accomplishing the primary objectives first.

- **Focus on a win-win outcome.** This process is the most important part of effective leadership or management because it is based on shared achievements and emphasizes team effort.

- **Mutual understanding.** The company officer must apply good interpersonal communication techniques to understand the needs and abilities of subordinates and for the unit members to understand the company officer.

- **Synergize.** This is the application of the concept that more can be accomplished by a team than by an individual.

- **Learn from the past.** The company officer must be able to apply the results of past experiences to current challenges.

- **Inspire others to their maximum abilities.** Once the company officer has achieved personal and leadership abilities then the officer should help others achieve it too.

— Providing them with new knowledge, skills, and abilities and giving them the feeling that they are progressing in their careers

- *Career planning* — Assisting the employee in selecting a career path that will benefit the organization and the employee **(Figure 22.3)**.

- *Pride in accomplishment* — Instill a feeling of accomplishment in the quality of service or product the employee generates.

- *Respect the humanity of the employee* — Remember that the employee has commitments and responsibilities outside of normal working hours. Support the employee and listen to personal concerns with an empathetic ear. Suggest solutions to personal problems within the constraints of organizational policy.

- *Mutual trust* — Do not micromanage employees. Delegate responsibility and allow workers to be creative in their ideas, without compromising organizational policies. Trust in their decision-making abilities by supporting and allowing them to present ideas to management. Create an atmosphere of trust through leadership.

Figure 22.3 Company officers can provide career counseling to their subordinates.

- *Assign authority with responsibility*— Delegate tasks to qualified members of the unit along with the commensurate amount of authority to allow the members to complete the tasks assigned.

- *Remain committed to high quality in service and products*— This will motivate the employee to attempt to reach the same level of results. High expectations yield high results.

- *Focus on the safety and well-being of the employee* — Ensure that the employees feel that managers and supervisors have the employees' best interest in mind.

Actions that Can Destroy Employee Motivation

The actions of a manager or supervisor can also destroy employee motivation and damage relationships and unit cohesion. The company officer should be aware of the negative results the following actions can have on employees and the unit:

- *Micromanage*— Indicates a lack of trust by the supervisor/manager and results in an inefficient use of resources

- *Be vague about the employee's role in the unit and organization*— Causes the employee to be uncertain of his or her duties and contribution to the unit's goals and objectives

- *Permit employees to compete in an unfriendly manner* — Can destroy the unit integrity and result in a loss of unit effectiveness

- *Permit employees to criticize each other*— Will destroy the unit and kill mutual respect

Span of Control

Historically, *span of control* has been known as the number of employees supervised by one supervisor. Although there has never been a definitive study to determine what exactly the perfect span of control is, the fire and emergency services have considered it to be three to seven subordinates, with five being optimum. This number comes from the classical management writers of the 1930s who taught that supervisors should maintain tight control over their subordinates and dictated that superiors should oversee a limited number rather then a large number of subordinates. In order to maintain this control, they taught that supervisors should have no more than six subordinates report-

ing to any one supervisor. This has been referred to as the Classical School of Management Theory developed by Fayol in 1916. See **Appendix O**.

Current management literature based on the Contemporary Management Theory advocates higher spans of control and flatter structures. Most advocates of the Contemporary Management Theory suggest that a higher span of control, ratios ranging from 15 to 25 subordinates per supervisor, is advantageous. Several of the Contemporary Management Theory authors also suggest that there should be no more than five organizational levels in any organization. See Chapter 11 for a discussion of organizational structure.

While the wider span of control can have advantages in nonemergency operations, it is not recommended for the majority of emergency operations. The ICS model is based on a span of control ratio of one supervisor to five subordinates or functions.

Managing Change Issues

One management challenge many fire officers may be faced with is managing change in the unit or organization. As an unknown author wrote, *Change is a part of every life*. The threat of change can have either a devastating effect or motivating effect on the organization. To successfully manage change, the company officer must know the forces that create and cause change and the change process itself. It is likely that the company officer will be the individual who implements change at the operational level. As the fire chief's change agent, the company officer must always maintain a positive posture toward the change, even when the officer does not necessarily agree with it. Knowing the types of change and how to overcome resistance to change, implement the change process, and use a follow-up plan can lead to successful change management.

The forces of change that affect the unit or organization can originate in two areas: inside and outside. The first force is within the organization and includes changes that are created by the delegation of responsibility, periodic performance reviews, organizational restructuring, and realignment of duties and tasks to meet the second or outside force of change. The second force from outside the organization takes the form of political decisions, economic trends, community service demands, changes in technology, and changes in the demographics of the community, among others.

All people experience the change process regardless of whether the change is work-related or personal. Changes that are perceived as a threat or loss are particularly challenging. Life changes such as the birth of a child, the death of a loved one, a divorce, or having one's children grow up and leave home all cause people to pass through the change process. Some change is immediate and affects people greatly, while most change is slow and gradual based upon numerous factors. The prospect of change causes people to go through the following four change process stages:

1. *Denial* — People refuse to believe that they will be affected by the change.

2. *Resistance* — When the threat of change becomes real, people start to resist it, which can be manifested in anger and dissatisfaction with management or the organization.

3. *Exploration* — People start to gain a better understanding of the potential change through training.

4. *Commitment* — Increased understanding in the third stage leads to an increased commitment to the new process, procedure, or structure that results from the change.

Change Types

Each type of change can be managed to create a new and effective organization as long as the fire officers involved are open to change. Support for change must come from the top down in order for it to be successful, but those affected by the change must take ownership through involvement and commitment or it will be a difficult and painful process. The types of change that an organization will have to undergo because of the forces of change are as follows:

- *Strategic* — Change in the short- or long-range plan of the organization; might include the location of future facilities or the types of service deliveries provided by the organization

- *Structure* — Change in the organizational design of the organization; may consist of unifying the command structure, division of labor, or size of the workforce

- *Technology* — Change may include the addition of new equipment, apparatus, communications systems, extinguishing agents, or computerization

- *People* — Change in the skills, performances, attitudes, behaviors, or cultures of the workforce to meet the force of change (for example, the new recruits hired this year have a very different cultural and educational background than those hired 20 years ago)

Resistance Issues

Research indicates that organizational change can fail because of employee resistance. To be a successful agent of change, the company officer must understand the reasons for employee resistance and the methods used to overcome those reasons. Resistance to change is caused by the following reasons (**Figure 22.4**):

- *Uncertainty* — Employees' routines or environments are disrupted, which causes them to feel insecure and not know how the changes will affect them or other members of the workforce. This fear is one of the most common reasons for resistance to change.

- *Loss of control or power* — Employees resent the feeling that they have lost control over their lives.

- *Fear of loss* — Employees experience layoffs, work-schedule changes, or transfers between workgroups.

- *Self-interest* — Employees are more concerned about their own situations than with the organization.

- *Learning anxiety* — Employees experience anxiety when they need to learn a new skill, technique, process, procedure, or equipment operation.

- *Lack of trust* — Employee distrust can be directed toward the organization's leaders and based on prior history or future concerns.

- *Lack of shared vision* — Employees are not aware of or do not hold the same vision for the goals of the organization.

By recognizing the resistance to change and taking steps to reduce it, the company officer can increase the opportunity for success in the process. Business analysts have determined that resistance to change can be overcome by the following seven basic steps:

1. ***Create a climate for change*** — Encourage employees to suggest changes and implement those changes. This step is founded on good interpersonal relations between the supervisor and members of the work group; they must have mutual trust and respect. Positive change can be a part of the organization's culture as the supervisor and employees look for better ways to accomplish tasks. With this type of climate in place, the organization will be better prepared to face external changes.

2. ***Plan for change*** — Have a plan and prepare to follow it in order to effectively implement change.

   Planning Steps:
   a. Analyze the current conditions.
   b. Identify the resistance factors.
   c. Define change objectives and clearly communicate them to the work group.
   d. Identify, acquire, and provide the necessary resources for change to the work-group.
   e. Change is not linear; it should have a feedback loop for corrective action.

3. ***Communicate the advantages and effects of change*** — State factually the advantages and effects of change to prevent unfounded rumors from eroding the trust between the supervisor

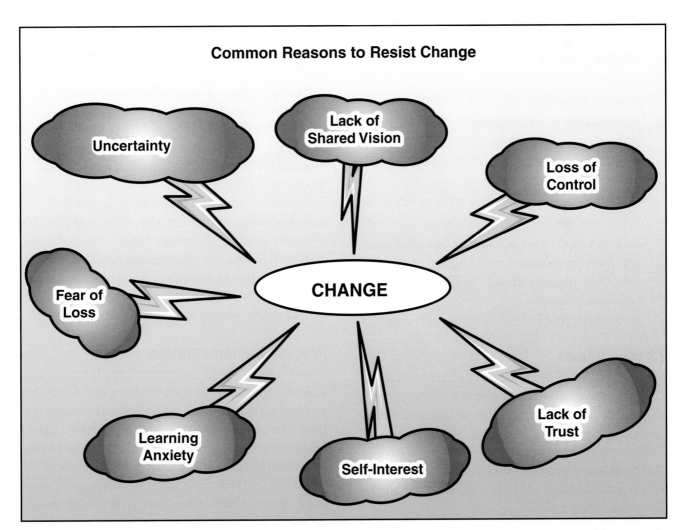

Figure 22.4 The company officer must recognize and understand the common reasons for employee resistance to change to avoid organizational failure.

and employees. Communication is the basis for all good management practice and is essential in the change process.

4. ***Meet the needs of both the organization and employees*** — See the change from the employees' viewpoints. Then, focus on their concerns and try to balance the good of the employees with the good of the organization. Share benefits equally in order to create a *win-win* situation.

5. ***Involve employees in the change process*** — Employees like to know that their perspectives on issues are taken into consideration when changes are considered. Involve employees in the change process, keep them informed, focus on their needs, and implement their suggestions. This involvement gives organizations a greater chance of success, and employees who participate in the change process are more likely to be committed to the change.

6. ***Provide support for employees during the change*** — Make a firm commitment to the change.

   Support Steps:
   — Listen to employees' concerns, resistances, and suggestions.
   — Provide the necessary resources, including training.
   — Help employees cope with unexpected change.

7. ***Seek the input and support of "opinion leaders" in the organization*** — Use informal leaders of the organization to help influence the opinions of others.

   Example: leaders of the labor organization

Change Agents

Company officers can effect or cause change by assuming the role of a change agent. A *change agent* is a person who leads a change project or initiative by defining, researching, planning, building support, and carefully selecting members of a change team. A change agent must possess three qualities — attitude, knowledge, and skills — that can ensure the success of the project.

Because bringing about change can be time consuming and involve complex issues and barriers, the change agent must have commitment and persistence. The officer must be committed to the vision that will result from the change. To attain this vision, the officer must be able to exert all the effort required throughout the time frame of the project. Diplomacy, tactfulness, and political awareness are also positive traits that the officer must have and use. Finally, the officer must rely on an ethical foundation that will ensure that the change is morally sound.

The officer who is leading a change team also needs to be a subject matter expert in the area that the change will occur. Therefore, if the change involves new apparatus specifications, it is important that the officer have a background in apparatus design, specifications development, and the purchasing process. Further knowledge in small group relations and interaction is also important for success of the change process. Additionally, the officer should have an established network within the organization and the community. Relationships in the political arena can also be important to success.

Change creates stress in both the change agent and the organization. To combat this stress, the officer must have skills that will reduce or eliminate stress. First and foremost, interpersonal skills are essential. Those are the skills that people need to interact effectively with others. Chapter 4 contains information essential to developing this skill. Besides the ability to interact, the officer must be able to communicate effectively with individuals and groups. In short, the officer must be able to *sell* the change to the organization and the community. Finally, the officer must have time management skills and the ability to prioritize the project.

Process Implementation

Even though change can come from both internal and external sources, establishing and following a specific change process benefits the organization. Having a policy for implementing change leads to success, and it makes change a part of the organization's culture. That policy needs to include methods for analyzing the current processes used by the organization, methods for suggesting change from the bottom up and from the top down, methods for implementing change, and a follow-up plan to ensure that the change met the needs it was intended to meet. All company officers should be aware of and familiar with the implementation policy and process.

Force Field Analysis

The concept of force field analysis was developed in the early 1950s by Kurt Lewin as part of his research into change management. Lewin determined that change is affected by two forces: driving and restraining. Driving forces may be internal or external, positive or negative. Restraining forces are opposing forces that create barriers that restrict change. The force field analysis model is used to help recognize the need for change, determine which driving forces can be used to support the change, and recognize the barriers to change and develop means of overcoming them.

One approach to using the model is to assemble a task group of internal and external stakeholders and customers. The group leader creates a chart with the current situation and the desired situation or goal described on it. The members of the group freely brainstorm the driving forces, which are listed in the appropriate column, and the restraining forces. Then the group generates ideas on how to maximize the positive driving forces and minimize the restraining forces. This session can help to overcome resistance within the task group as well as determine how to implement the necessary change.

For example, the current situation may be a community served by a volunteer fire department that provides only fire suppression protection. The goal may be to provide additional emergency services that demand 24-hour staffing that can be achieved by a combination-type department.

Driving forces may include the following:

- Available financial resources
- Greater public support for the additional services
- State mandate for EMS trained personnel in all fire departments.

Restraining forces may include:

- Lack of new volunteers to expand the existing department
- Lack of time for training new volunteers

- Lack of advancement within volunteer ranks

By listing these (and other) opposing forces on a chart, the group can determine how to use public support, for instance, to offset the lack of new volunteers. The financial resources and state mandate can be used to move the department toward a combination-type department, creating advancement opportunities and formal training situations. The advantages can be used to overcome the barriers.

There are three options that may exist once the force field analysis is complete.

Depending on restraining and driving forces, they are as follows:

1. Move ahead with the process if there are significant driving forces to overcome the restraining forces.

2. Move ahead at a slower pace if there is equilibrium between the two forces. Focus on weakening the restraining forces.

3. If the restraining forces exceed the driving forces, it may be necessary to abandon the efforts to make the change.

Implementation

Once the need for change has been recognized, resistance has been overcome, and an innovative solution has been agreed upon, it is time to implement the change. Many change implementation models have been developed. One model that has been available in the private sector since the 1950s is the Lewin Change Model, which consists of the three following phases (**Figure 22.5, p. 530**):

1. *Unfreezing* — Managers demonstrate to work groups the difference between the current level of performance and the desired or new level.

2. *Moving* — Work groups learn new behaviors, values, processes, or procedures. Sometimes referred to as *Changing*.

3. *Refreezing* — Changes become permanent.

Because change is a continuing process, it must be monitored to determine the effectiveness of the new process or procedure. It is important to remember that initial implementation of a change and institutionalizing that change are usually two different things. Since the development of the Lewin Change Model, the business environment has changed and become more technical and fast-

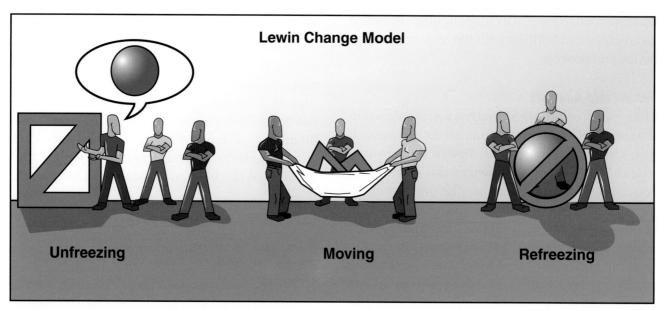

Figure 22.5 The Lewin Change Model.

paced. Likewise, the environment in which the fire and emergency services operate has changed in a similar fashion. Therefore, a new model for change has been created to facilitate most forms of change facing an organization; it is based on the following five steps:

1. ***Recognize the need for change.*** Clearly state the need for change and establish objectives. Consider the effects the change will have on other parts of the organization.

2. ***Identify resistance and overcome it.*** Identify potential resistance to the change and determine the best method for overcoming it.

3. ***Plan the change interventions.*** Recognize that a variety of change agents or interventions exist that can help in implementing the change.

Some Change Interventions:

— *Training and development*: Use to develop skills, behaviors, and attitudes that will be used in the workplace; may include technical skills, interpersonal skills, or communication skills to name a few.

— *Team building:* Focus on how to get the job done. The team approach (one of the most widely used intervention forms) allows for member involvement in defining the needed change and how to implement it.

— *Job design*: Change or alter the types of tasks members of the organization perform. It in-cludes enhancement, enrichment, simpli-fication, rotation, or expansion of the tasks to improve efficiency or effectiveness.

— *Direct feedback*: Use an outside agent such as a manufacturer's representative to train members in the use of new equipment or techniques.

— *Survey feedback*: Use a written question-naire that is designed to gather data from members of the organization. Analyze the data and determine recommended changes.

4. ***Implement the change.*** Use the appropriate change agent and put the change into opera-tion.

5. ***Control the change.*** Enforce, review, monitor, and analyze the change model. Take corrective action if change objectives are not met.

Work System and Task Analyses

Periodic systems analysis of the organization and the service area (including demographics, po-litical, environmental, and economic conditions) are necessary to determine two things: need for change and potential for change. First, the need for change based on shifts in the various elements analyzed must be determined. By having a baseline or benchmark to compare with periodic analysis, the manager can determine trends that require a corresponding change. For example, the presence of an aging population may warrant a change in service delivery that shifts its primary focus from structural fire fighting to providing emergency medical services. This shift may also require the purchase and use of personal protective equipment specific to hazards associated with medical responses. Second, the potential for change due to anticipated future changes must be evaluated. An example of this change would be federal mandates that require a local organization to assume added responsibilities in the area of national security. The implementation of the National Incident Management System (NIMS) is an example of change generated from outside the local fire and emergency services organizations.

With systems analysis a part of the organization's daily operation, it becomes commonplace and accepted as a preparation for change. It creates the climate of a proactive, change-oriented organization and not a reactive one. It is very important to maintain records that can be used to illustrate trends, which is especially important when justifying additional funding or requesting grants from other agencies.

Innovative Opportunities

Change, whether voluntary or forced on the organization, is an opportunity for innovation (use of creative thinking to develop new ideas and solutions). Innovation may include new types of extinguishing agents, new fire suppression tactics, new types of suppression equipment, or new staffing methods. Leaders anticipate industry, community, and organizational changes and position their organizations to their best advantage as opportunities occur.

When an analysis indicates that a change is necessary, the best approach is a proactive one. A useful method is to gather representatives of the affected groups together for a brainstorming session. These representatives may include community leaders, member organization leadership, work groups, senior staff, or political leaders. A facilitator leads the session and keeps the group focused and on schedule. The session needs to have a clearly defined goal such as meeting the impending budget shortfall or improving life and safety conditions in residences. All ideas are accepted and then ranked by consensus. The top three innovations are then critically reviewed to determine cost, effectiveness, and legality. The final result may then be applied to the situation.

Because fire and emergency services organizations do not exist in a vacuum, brainstorming committees must include all external groups that have an interest in the organization or the specific change that is being considered. For example, a change in work schedules may only appear to affect the members of the work group. However, union representatives, family members, finance personnel, and human resources personnel also have an interest in the decision that is made and need to have some representation on the committee.

Follow-Up Program Plan

The follow-up program is a formal part of the process that continues to monitor the effect of the change. The follow-up is applied to behavioral changes by individuals as well as structural changes to the organization. The follow-up program becomes part of the annual performance evaluation for personnel and the periodic review of programs, operations, or policies. The change process should be viewed as cyclical rather than linear; that is, the process is continuous and never-ending. The follow-up is the feedback that takes the results and loops them back to the first portion of the process, becoming the current level of performance. As first-line supervisors, company officers monitor the change process as it affects the company personnel and operations. When feedback indicates that the process requires alteration, the company officer should inform the organization's administration.

Reasons That Change Fails

Managers may not always succeed in implementing a change. John Kotter, an organizational researcher, determined in the 1990s that there are eight reasons that change processes fail. They are as follows:

1. The change process is too complex.

2. The change process lacks universal support.

3. Lack of a clear vision and not understanding the importance of having one.

4. The failure to communicate the vision to the organization.

5. Allowing barriers to be placed in the way of the vision and change process.

6. Not planning for and recognizing the short-term results.

7. Declaring completion of the change process prematurely.

8. Failure to make the change a permanent part of the organization's culture.

To minimize the effect of these reasons for failure, the company officer may apply the following strategies:

- Simplify the change process by dividing it into attainable segments and involving a diverse group of people to participate in the process.

- Gain support for the change from the *key actors* in the organization and community. The key actors are influential members such as the chief of the department, president of the labor organization, branch/division heads, members of the governing board, or heads of other departments, depending on the type of change that is required.

- Define the desired results and state them clearly. This is the vision statement that allows everyone to understand what the change is, why it is important, and how it will affect the organization and community.

- Communicate the vision to all members of the organization and all customers and stakeholders in the community.

- During the planning process try to determine the arguments against the change and develop strategies to answer these arguments logically and factually. Take a proactive approach and never allow the arguments to become barriers to change.

- Include limited objectives or milestones in the planning process. When these are attained, celebrate the accomplishment and use the enthusiasm to move onward to the next objective and ultimate goal.

- Ensure that all objectives have been met and that the final goal is complete before declaring victory. Prematurely declaring that the goal has been met will reduce credibility and lessen the team's enthusiasm and motivation.

- Implement the change and monitor the results of the change to ensure that it becomes permanent. If the change is insufficient, determine what is lacking and start the process over.

Summary

Company officers must prepare themselves to be effective supervisors and managers. They must study the principles of supervision of individuals and management of programs, projects, situations, and organizations. This chapter presented principles and the skills that are required to apply them to emergency and nonemergency duties. The company officer or officer candidate can use this material as a springboard to further studies through college-level classes, workshops, seminars, and reading on the various subjects covered here. Company officers must know and be able to apply supervisory and management skills to gain the greatest advantage from subordinates and the organization. This may at times seem overwhelming. However, the company officer has the most influential position in the fire service. The company officer must be able to effectively manage projects and lead subordinates at the same time with skills gained through experience, education, and trial and error. Finally, the company officer must be able to manage change and overcome the barriers that may occur in the unit and the organization when change is needed.

Time Management

One of the resources the company officer manages is time. So important is the efficient use of time that some organizations offer internal courses on time management. One thing should be obvious about time, though: it is a limited and finite quantity. Time cannot be created, only used. Therefore, the company officer must be able to use time wisely and efficiently.

Company officers should be aware of the pressure that time places on emergency responders. It is a known fact that a person will die if CPR is not administered within a certain period of time after the heart stops beating or that a fire will double in size every four minutes. This pressure, like the deadlines associated with nonemergency projects, can be managed if the company officer uses some accepted methods for time management.

The first approach for effective time management is to prioritize the tasks that must be accomplished. Lloyd Layman's theories introduced in Chapter 20, Incident Scene Operations, are a broad approach to emergency incident time management. The tasks of Rescue, Exposure, Confinement, Extinguishment, Overhaul, Ventilation, and Salvage (RECEO/VS) are prioritized over the duration of the incident. Likewise, the ABCs of cardiopulmonary resuscitation are prioritized to accomplish the correct task in the correct order and amount of time.

Nonemergency time management requires the company officer to prioritize tasks too. The steps for prioritizing are:

Step 1: Develop an idea of the tasks that need to be accomplished. Write all the tasks on a list in no particular order. Include every activity that will require time to complete. Assign estimates of the time that will be required to complete each task.

Step 2: Organize the tasks based on both urgency and importance. Tasks that are urgent and important, such as completing the annual budget by a certain date, are placed at the top of the list. Tasks that are neither important nor urgent should be placed at the bottom of the list. All others are spread between the two extremes.

Step 3: Using the priority list, establish a timetable for completion of the tasks. It may be possible that smaller, less important tasks can be performed at the end of the day or while waiting for others to complete tasks that are necessary to the higher priority tasks.

Step 4: Divide large tasks into smaller units that can be accomplished quickly. These short-term objectives provide a sense of accomplishment as they are completed. Note also any tasks from the priority list that must be accomplished prior to starting other tasks.

Step 5: Determine any tasks that can be delegated to subordinates or other unit members. Ensure that they have the knowledge, skills, and abilities, as well as the authority, to accomplish the tasks.

Prioritizing tasks will help the company officer to efficiently manage the time required to complete the task. By managing time, the officer can reduce the pressure that comes from working with deadlines and can permit the officer to focus on the task.

Types and Forms of Government

Chapter Contents

Learning Objectives

1. Identify the three types of local government commonly found in North America.

2. Compare and contrast the three primary types of municipal government.

3. Define other types of municipal government.

4. Compare and contrast the three forms of county and parish government.

5. Recall information about the lawmaking process of local governments.

6. Identify other agencies at the local level that interact with the fire and emergency services organization.

7. Select facts about the organization of state governments, provincial and territorial governments, and tribal governments.

8. Identify other agencies at the state/provincial level that interact with the fire and emergency services organization.

9. Recall information about the lawmaking process of the U.S. Federal Government.

10. Identify the U.S. federal agencies that are involved in fire protection.

11. Select facts about the structure of the Canadian Federal Government.

12. Recall information about the lawmaking process of the Canadian Federal Government.

13. Identify the Canadian agencies that are involved in fire protection.

Job Performance Requirements

This chapter provides information that addresses the following job performance requirements of NFPA 1021, *Standard for Fire Officer Professional Qualifications* (2003):

Chapter 5 Fire Officer II

5.1.1

Fire and emergency services organizations provide important and basic services in their response areas, and in all levels of government **(Figure 23.1)**. The organization must be an effective part of the local community and must work with other governmental and nongovernmental agencies. The company officer has an essential role in this relationship. Key to this role is an understanding of how governments operate and a familiarity with other agencies that are involved directly or indirectly in the fire protection process. This chapter discusses the types of local, state/provincial, and federal governments and their effect on fire and emergency services organizations. Private and nongovernmental organizations that have an effect on the emergency services are included in **Appendix P.**

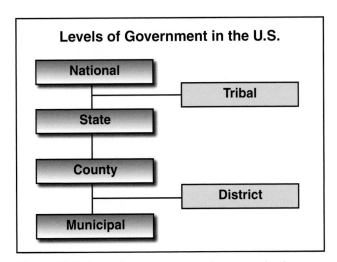

Figure 23.1 Fire and emergency services organizations provide important and basic services at all levels of government.

Local Government

Most citizens have more direct contact with the departments and divisions of the local level of government than with any other level. Citizens attend board meetings, pay utility bills, take tours of facilities, use public transportation, actively participate in various local elections, and, in some cases, have direct contact with their political representatives in local government. The following paragraphs address local government at several levels:

* Municipal
* County
* District

These terms used to describe these levels of government are not standard across North America, and their precise meaning varies greatly from one region to another.

This section gives an overview of typical governmental structures at the local level. Company officers should become acquainted with the organizational structure of the government bodies that oversee their jurisdiction and other jurisdictions with which they may interact.

Municipal (City) Government

In most of the United States and Canada, communities either have no formal government system or use designated officials to conduct those affairs that are of common interest to the residents of the community. The officials are generally elected by the eligible voters in the community, though some officials may be hired. In communities with formal governments, the three most common structures are as follows:

- Council-mayor government
- Council-manager government
- Commission government

These three forms of government differ primarily in how the actual administration of municipal operations occurs. However, they also share certain similar characteristics. The main common characteristic is the use of an elected body, whether a council or a commission, to represent the citizens in conducting the business of the community. The councilors or commissioners may be elected at large or as representatives of specific geographic areas of the municipality. In an at-large election, candidates can reside in any part of the city, with all eligible voters being able to vote for one or more candidates. The at-large system is intended to free the legislators from undue influence by any particular constituency or neighborhood group. This system is most common in smaller towns, while larger communities tend to be divided into districts, wards, or precincts (**Figure 23.2**). These subdivisions are generally intended to consist of approximately equal numbers of citizens, or a relatively equal division of racial demographics, who elect one or more councilors or commissioners to represent them. The use of political subdivisions is an attempt to ensure that each area of the city and each segment of the population will receive equal representation. Most municipalities use either an at-large or ward form of representation, though a few have both at-large and ward councilors or commissioners.

In addition to the three primary types of municipal government, other variations of municipal government exist in North America. They include townships, town meetings, boroughs, and villages. A brief description of each is included in this chapter (**Figure 23.3**).

On occasion, the type of government changes by a vote of the community. When this change occurs, everyone (citizens, elected and appointed officials, and the municipality's workforce) is affected by the *learning curve* that accompanies such a change. As the new political organization takes power, officials must learn the new duties and responsibilities. At the same time, government employees must learn how to function within the new framework.

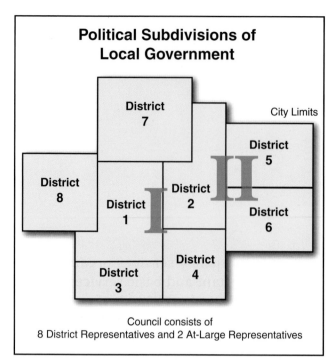

Figure 23.2 This political subdivision of local government is most common in smaller towns.

Council-Mayor Government

The council-mayor form of city government generally consists of a mayor elected at large and a group of representatives who normally serve districts, wards, or precincts, though some city councils are elected at large. This type of government may further be classified as a weak- or strong-mayor form. Under the weak-mayor concept, the council actually administers the business of the city while the mayor serves primarily as a figurehead and often has another full-time job or business. In some weak-mayor systems, the mayor does not even have a vote in matters placed before the council and frequently serves only as an ambassador of the city to welcome distinguished visitors and to serve in ceremonies. Other weak-mayor systems allow the mayor to vote in the event of a tie in a council vote or in all proceedings with the mayor's vote carrying no more weight than that of any other council member.

A mayor in strong-mayor systems is generally the official head of the city's government and often serves in a full-time capacity. Such mayors tend to set policy for the conduct of the community's business and often have substantial influence over council proceedings and actions, frequently serving as the head of the council and voting on all

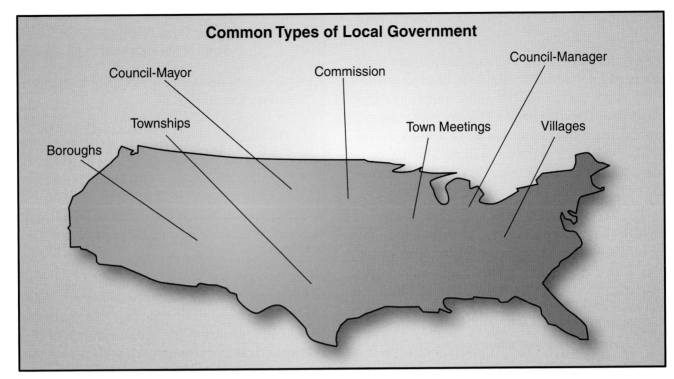

Figure 23.3 Common types of local government.

matters before the council. Strong mayoral systems commonly assign the mayor a great deal of authority in the hiring or appointing of other city officials, and the mayor often serves as the supervisor of department heads, including the fire chief or fire commissioner. It is also common for mayors in this system of government to appoint a Chief Administrative Officer (CAO) to serve as his or her designee in day-to-day operations **(Figure 23.4)**.

The council-mayor form of government tends to be found in older, larger cities or in very small cities with populations under 25,000 people. It is most popular in the Mid-Atlantic and Midwestern states. The following cities have variations in the mayor-council form of government:

- Los Angeles, California
- Richmond, Virginia
- Houston, Texas
- Topeka, Kansas
- Minneapolis, Minnesota
- Tulsa, Oklahoma

The council-mayor form with a strong mayor is perhaps the most common form of city government in Canada, where the elected head may be referred to as a *mayor, reeve, warden,* or *overseer*. Sometimes

---

Characteristics of the Council-Mayor Form of Government

- Separation of powers between directly elected mayor and city council

- Mayor has executive powers while council has legislative powers

- Mayor is directly elected to office, often full-time and paid

Figure 23.4 Characteristics of council/mayor form of government.

councilors are given specific functional roles similar to the commissioner concept and may be referred to as *controllers, aldermen (alderpersons),* or *councilors*.

Council-Manager Government

As cities continued to grow in area and population, their governing bodies began to recognize two key concepts:

1. It is often desirable to maintain a separation between the political planning of the city and its day-to-day administration.

2. Proper municipal administration requires formal training.

Consequently, many metropolitan areas have adopted a council-manager form of government. Under this concept, the voters elect representatives to serve on the city council. The city may also have an elected mayor comparable to a weak mayor within the council-mayor system. The mayor is basically a figurehead who may or may not vote on council issues.

The key characteristic of this form of government is that the council hires a professional public administrator to manage the daily affairs of the city. The manager reports to the council and advises them on various matters but usually does not get to vote on council agenda items. The manager's principal duty is to see that the council's policies are carried out in an efficient manner and within budget. The manager depends on the goodwill of the council to remain employed by the municipality. City managers tend to move from location to location, averaging tenure of 6.4 years per city **(Figure 23.5)**.

A total of 3,625 cities use this form of government. It is common in cities of population over 10,000, located mainly in the Southeast and Pacific coast areas. In cities with populations in excess of 100,000, 112 (out of 119) have council-manager governments. Cities that have this form of government include:

- Phoenix, Arizona
- San Diego, California
- Salt Lake City, Utah
- Rockville, Maryland
- Dallas, Texas
- Cincinnati, Ohio
- Kansas City, Missouri
- San Antonio, Texas

Commission Government

The commission form of government is similar to a council system and may or may not have a mayor. The current trend is away from commission forms, but some older cities and some other political divisions still use this approach. The largest city that still has a commission form of government

---

Characteristics of the Council-Manager Form of Government

- City council oversees the general administration, makes policy, sets budget

- Council hires a city manager to carry out day-to-day administrative operations

- Often the mayor is chosen from among the council on a rotating basis

Figure 23.5 Characteristics of council/manager form of government.

---

is Portland, Oregon. Commissions tend to be three- to five-member boards elected at-large within the municipality. The unique aspect of this system is that responsibility for the various functional operations of the city are generally divided among the commissioners. For example, a city may have a three-person commission such as the following:

- *A finance commissioner*—oversees the budget, tax collections, and related matters

- *A maintenance commissioner* — responsible for maintenance of the infrastructure; includes maintaining and expanding the streets, sewer system, city buildings, water system, and other physical structures as necessary

- *A services commissioner* — responsible for the police and fire departments, refuse collection, health department, and social services

Consequently, under this concept, each commissioner is like a city manager for a portion of the community's operations, but they are also elected officials like council members. Because the commissioners are generally less trained than a city manager and often have other full-time jobs, they usually rely more directly on the department heads for the day-to-day operation and planning for their departments.

Although over 500 cities once had this form of government, less than 150 municipalities still have commission governments. One of the weaknesses of the commission form of government is the combining of administrative responsibilities and legislative authority. This situation tends to lead to turf wars between the members of the commission who may become protective of the departments they administer **(Figure 23.6)**.

The commission form of government exists in only a few cities, such as:

- Sunrise, Florida
- Fairview, Tennessee

Variations of Municipal Government

While the previous forms of municipal government are the most popular in North America, other types exist as well. Variations that may be found include townships, town meetings, boroughs, and villages.

Township. Township governments are generally commission-type bodies, consisting of an elected mayor/supervisor and three to five commissioners/trustees; however, a common term for the commission is *board of trustees* **(Figure 23.7)**. Responsibilities for operation of the township are divided among the trustees. One distinction between boards of trustees and commissions that is often valid is that terms of office are sometimes less rigid among trustees. The commissioners in most city commissions serve for a prescribed period of time, usually two, four, or six years. Position elections are generally offset so that only one or two posts are filled during any given election. This helps to maintain continuity within the governing body. There is a tendency for more variation in the election intervals of trustees. Some boards use offset election periods while others open all positions during periodic elections. Frequently, each position on the board is designated as a *seat* or *place*, and candidates file for a specific seat and run against only the persons who file for the same seat. Senior trustees may not face opposition when seeking re-election and often serve until they resign.

Town meeting. Some municipalities are governed by a board of officers (called *selectmen*) who are elected during an annual meeting of all qualified voters in the community. At the meeting, voters also establish policies for the community that the board must then administer. A city manager may be appointed by the board to manage the daily operations of the community. Generally, town meetings are found in smaller communities in the Northeastern part of the U.S. This form of govern-

---

Characteristics of the Commission Form of Government

- Voters elect individual commissioners to a small governing board.

- Each commissioner is responsible for one specific area of service, which may include police and fire departments, refuse collection, health department, and social services.

- One commissioner is designated as chairman or mayor, who presides over meetings. (The mayor may be elected at-large as a strong mayor presiding over the commission.)

- The commission has both legislative and executive functions.

Figure 23.6 Characteristics of commission form of government.

Figure 23.7 A township sign at the city limits.

ment may also be applied to special governmental entities such as school boards and water boards **(Figure 23.8)**.

Representative town meeting. In communities that are too large for the direct representation found in town meetings, the representative town meeting is used to elect the board and make policy. The general voting public elects representatives that attend the annual meeting. Although the meeting is open to all members of the community, only the elected representatives may vote on issues.

Borough. The borough form of government is unique to New Jersey, although it may also exist in other locations within that area of the U.S. Generally, it is a council-mayor form of government in which the mayor and councilors are elected at-large (some boroughs may be divided into wards with councilors elected by ward). The mayor presides over council meetings and votes in the event of a tie. Department heads are appointed by the mayor or council. Some New Jersey cities that have the borough form of government are Allendale, Middlesex, and Saddle River.

Village. Similar to the township form of government, and unique to New Jersey, the village form of government consists of a board of trustees which is elected at large. One of these board members serves as the board president with the powers of a mayor. The board of trustees is the legislative body of the municipality. Lock Arbour, New Jersey, is currently the only community with a purely village form of government.

County/Parish Government

County and parish governments were originally formed in order to decentralize state and provincial governments. Before modern transportation, and even today in some remote areas, traveling to the state capital to conduct business was difficult. Consequently, county and parish offices tended to reflect the state-level organization. However, increasing urban populations and a decline in agriculture have meant that the nature of counties as a political unit has changed. Some cities have grown to occupy entire counties, and land that once was farmland has given way to houses, multifamily dwellings, shopping centers, and manufacturing plants. As a result, many counties have adopted a municipal form of government rather than reflect the state or provincial organization **(Figure 23.9)**. Thus, the three most prevalent forms of county and parish government today parallel the common forms of municipal government:

- County commission
- County commission-manager
- County commission-executive

County Commission

The commission form of government continues to be the most common form of county and parish government. This form takes one of two prevalent structures:

Figure 23.8 The town meeting form of government may also be applied to special governmental entities, such as school boards and water boards, that meet regularly.

Figure 23.9 In a county government, the municipal form of government is conducted in the county courthouse.

1. Commissioners or board of supervisors are elected at large and assume responsibility for a specific set of operational functions.

2. The county is divided into districts, and commissioners are responsible for the operation of their represented district and jointly are responsible for overall operations.

In actual practice, most routine matters within a district or in an assigned area are handled by the responsible commissioner, while county-wide matters and larger issues are decided by the whole commission.

County Commission-Manager

Equivalent to the council-manager form of municipal government, the commission-manager or commission-administrator concept in county and parish government is motivated by the perceived need to provide separation between county politics and administration of county business. It consists of an elected commission that hires an administrator to manage the affairs of the county and implement the policies of the commission. In a few instances, the manager is also an elected official.

County Commission-Executive

The strong-mayor form of the council-mayor government is largely duplicated in the county commission-executive structure. The commission is equivalent to the council and the executive or chief executive takes the place of the strong mayor. Under this concept, there are essentially two branches of government: the commission as the legislative branch and the executive as the executive branch. The commissioners generally represent a district within the county or parish and enact policies and ordinances; the executive is elected at large and prepares the budget, oversees the department heads (and often appoints them), and sees to the day-to-day operation of the county. The county executive often has a staff, which may include a professional administrator. The executive generally conducts commission meetings.

Special Districts

Some fire and emergency services organizations are established to provide service to areas known as *fire districts*. In many instances, such districts are governmental bodies empowered by their state or province to implement and enforce regulations and to raise and administer revenues. Fire districts are legal entities that can enter into contracts and agreements with other government bodies and corporations, impose taxes and fees, borrow money, and own property. Most fire districts operate under an elected board of directors. Occasionally, when a fire district overlaps the jurisdictions of several local governments, the board will be an appointed body with one or more representatives from each of the encompassed government entities.

In most cases, the state or province will designate one of its existing agencies, such as the forestry department, to oversee and coordinate the actions of fire districts. This level of support may simply consist of informal training and networking for the districts, or it may go to the extent of setting standards for the districts and verifying their compliance with those standards.

Several factors, including a scarcity of funds, successful examples in other types of districts, and the benefit of consolidation, have increased the popularity of fire districts, especially in rural areas (**Figure 23.10**). Virtually all levels of government face a scarcity of funds that can be partially offset through cooperative efforts, such as the pooled resources of fire districts. The effective operations of other types of districts, including school, hospital, and water districts, have set precedents for expansion of the concept. U.S. federal regula-

Figure 23.10 Several factors have increased the popularity of fire districts, especially in rural areas.

tions such as the Superfund Amendments and Reauthorization Act (SARA) of 1986 and the Department of Homeland Security have placed more responsibility for emergency preparedness and response at the local level and have emphasized the need for interagency cooperation. Such cooperation frequently leads to closer planning and the elimination of duplicated services among fire and emergency services organizations. Consolidating numerous small emergency services organizations into larger, more efficient fire districts is often the next logical step because it reduces or eliminates costly duplication.

Effect of Local Government on Fire and Emergency Services

The operation of local municipal and county/parish government affects emergency services organizations in two primary ways. First, governing bodies make decisions that directly relate to the operations of these organizations, such as allocating funds, approving or disapproving purchase and staffing requests, implementing ordinances related to fire protection and other emergency services, and reviewing and approving agreements with other fire protection agencies and governments. Second, local governments oversee other agencies with whom the emergency services organizations must work, which can affect policies, procedures, responsibilities, resource requirements, and other factors **(Figure 23.11)**.

How Local Government Affects the Emergency Services Organization	
Directly	**Indirectly**
• Allocates funds	• Oversees the operation of other internal agencies and departments
• Approves purchases	
• Approves staffing levels	
• Implements ordinances	
• Approves interagency agreements	

Figure 23.11 How local government affects the emergency services organization.

Lawmaking Process of Local Governments

Although the actual process of enacting laws varies from one form of local government to another, it is essential that company officers understand the process. Such understanding is a requirement of NFPA 1021, *Standard for Fire Officer Professional Qualifications*. An emergency service organization's effectiveness in accomplishing its mission can be directly affected by how well its officers and members understand the legislative process at all levels of government and how involved they are in trying to influence that process.

At the local level, legislation is enacted by the council, commission, or board that has authority over the jurisdiction and matters being regulated. In terms of emergency services issues, the local government will generally consider any information presented by the organization. Therefore, it is imperative that the organization be aware of the potential effects of such legislation and take an active role in advising the governing body. Company officers should also be aware of impending legislation that may not initially appear to have a direct effect on the organization's operations. For example, the local government may be considering zoning changes that would interrupt emergency response and evacuation routes or that would allow construction of a high-risk facility beyond the reasonable response of existing resources. Expansion of the city water system may not include consideration of hydrant requirements, or the pending contract with the city's fuel supplier may not contain provisions for diesel fuel being available at all hours of the day or night. Thus, company officers should not only be familiar with the lawmaking process but should also actively monitor it and be involved in the process as both professionals and citizens.

Agencies of Local Government

In addition to the fire and emergency services organization, a local government is likely to include a variety of departments, each structured to provide specific services. Examples of these departments include the following **(Figure 23.12)**:

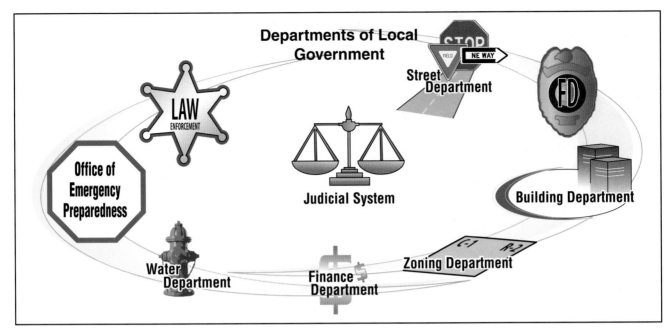

Figure 23.12 Departments of local government.

Law Enforcement

Local police and sheriff's departments work with emergency services organizations in the shared responsibility of protecting the public. These agencies may even share the same department head or supervisor, such as the commissioner of public safety. Law enforcement agencies support emergency service efforts through crowd and traffic control, with large-scale evacuations, by providing protection to emergency responders during civil unrest **(Figure 23.13)**, and through fire investigation activities. In some communities and jurisdictions, law enforcement agencies operate the emergency communications and dispatch centers for the entire governmental entity.

Building Department

In most localities, the building department is responsible for ensuring that building codes, including fire codes, are enforced during construction and renovation. This is the first step in the fire prevention process and precedes the fire and life-safety inspection program. The building department can also be a useful resource to fire protection personnel by assisting with the emergency planning process. The building department frequently maintains files of building floor plans that indicate structural layout, locations of entrances and exits,

Figure 23.13 Law enforcement agencies support emergency service efforts through crowd and traffic control.

fire suppression systems, and other features that can assist with the emergency response **(Figure 23.14, p. 546)**.

Most building departments have an appeal process for citizens who have been denied a building permit. Fire and emergency services personnel may be responsible for providing accurate documentation to support the decision to deny the permit if it is based on fire protection requirements.

Figure 23.14 In most localities, the building department is responsible for ensuring that building codes, including fire codes, are enforced during construction and renovation.

Water Department

The need for a good working relationship between the fire and emergency services organization and the water department is fairly obvious. During the water service planning phase, the two agencies must ensure that hydrant locations, pressure, pumping and storage capacities, and other factors support fire protection requirements (**Figure 23.15**). This coordination must continue during the day-to-day operations of the two agencies. Then, the emergency services organization can be informed of any planned or unexpected interrup-

tions in water service, and the water department can be informed of any unusual usage requirements of the emergency services organization (because of a major fire or a water-intensive exercise, for example). Local water departments often have responsibility for the sewer and storm drain systems within a community as well as the waste water treatment facilities. These systems are particularly important to emergency services organizations tasked with the control and cleanup of hazardous material spills.

Zoning Commission

The zoning commission (or board) coordinates use of land within the jurisdiction and determines the types of structures that can be located within a given area, such as single-family housing, multiple-family housing, business, agricultural, light industrial, and heavy industrial. The use of land affects its fire prevention and protection requirements and, thus, emergency services planning (**Figure 23.16**). The zoning commission is often involved in the selection and allocation of sites for

Figure 23.16 The zoning commission (or board) coordinates use of land within the jurisdiction and determines the types of structures that can be located within a given area.

Figure 23.15 During the water service planning phase, it is essential that hydrant locations, pressure, pumping and storage capacities, and other factors support fire protection requirements.

fire stations and support buildings such as training centers and maintenance facilities. The zoning commission also hears appeals from citizens who have been denied applications for locating a certain type of business in a certain location based on local restrictions. For instance, the zoning code may prohibit the location of a high hazard processing plant within a specific distance of a residential neighborhood. Emergency services personnel may be responsible for providing recommendations for or against such appeals.

Street or Road Department

Municipal street departments and county road departments maintain streets, alleys, and roads in their jurisdictions. At the same time, they keep the emergency services organization informed of planned repairs that will result in road closures or detours and other traffic problems that might affect emergency responses. They often involve the emergency services organization in the planning of fire lanes, bridges (including load capacities based on apparatus weights), intersections, entrances and exits for facilities, and other factors that may affect the operation and maneuverability of response apparatus. The street department can further assist the emergency services organization through the installation of automatic traffic signal control

devices that assist with a prompt response. Finally, the street department usually has a role in hazardous material incidents on public thoroughfares by assisting with the clean up and removal of the material, providing inert absorption materials, and blocking and detouring traffic **(Figure 23.17)**.

Judicial System

Local courts have the authority to render decisions in cases of arson, insurance fraud, failure to comply with building and fire codes, and other issues that may require testimony by emergency services personnel. Emergency incidents are sometimes the scenes of crimes and other events that require adjudication and that also may result in the presence in court of emergency responders. One division of the emergency services organization that often works closely with the courts is the fire marshal's office. Fire marshals may obtain inspection warrants to compel businesses to allow inspectors to inspect their premises or obtain court orders to force compliance with building or fire code requirements or to cease operation.

Office of Emergency Preparedness

Since September 11, 2001, the number of agencies within local government that are responsible for emergency preparedness has increased drasti-

Figure 23.17 The street department provides sand at a spill. *Courtesy of Chris E. Mickal.*

cally. Most comm unities have an agency that is responsible for preparing for and responding to disasters caused by terrorism, natural occurrences, or hazardous materials incidents. This office may be part of the fire and emergency services organization or may be a separate agency, such as the office of emergency preparedness or civil defense. Because these emergencies will require response by fire, rescue, and emergency medical personnel, the emergency services organization must work with this agency to define roles and responsibilities during large-scale disasters. In some jurisdictions, the head of the emergency preparedness agency may be empowered to command law enforcement, fire, rescue, and EMS operations when a major emergency is declared.

State and Provincial Government

Although fire and emergency services are largely a local issue, emergency services organizations are affected by state and provincial legislation and must sometimes work with agencies of the state and provincial governments. For these reasons, company officers should be familiar with the structure and operation of this next level of government.

State Government

In the United States, state and similarly territorial governments are generally modeled after the structure of the federal government with three functional branches (**Figure 23.18**):

- *Legislative* — The legislative branch is responsible for enacting laws. Members of the legislative branch are elected to represent their counties, parishes, or districts. All states except Nebraska have bicameral legislatures (consisting of two houses); Nebraska's legislature is unicameral (one house).

- *Executive* — The head of the state's executive branch is called the *governor.* A governor serves as the head of state and is granted certain powers and responsibilities that vary from state to state. Generally, these powers include the right to veto or approve legislation, call the legislature into session, serve as commander of the state's militia and law enforcement agencies, and perform similar duties.

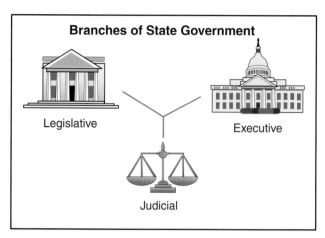

Figure 23.18 Branches of state government.

- *Judicial* — The judicial branch is responsible for interpreting state constitutions and overseeing the state's court system. Each county has a state courthouse and judges assigned to it. The state maintains a Supreme Court that is the last court of appeals for state issues. Court cases may be criminal or civil, as defined in Chapter 5.

The term *commonwealth* is also used to describe four states and one of the territories, Puerto Rico. (**NOTE:** Territories currently administered by the United States are Guam, Midway, American Samoa, Puerto Rico, and the U.S. Virgin Islands.) By definition, a commonwealth is a state in which the government functions with the common consent of the people. Those states that consider themselves to be commonwealths are Kentucky, Massachusetts, Pennsylvania, and Virginia.

Provincial and Territorial Governments

Canada is divided into ten provinces and two territories. Though both provinces and territories have governments, the powers of the territorial governments are more limited than those of the provinces. Provincial governments consist of three branches that include a unicameral legislative assembly (or National Assembly in Quebec), an executive branch headed by a premier, and a court system. Each province also has a lieutenant governor appointed by Canada's governor general; however, the position is largely honorary and carries no real legal authority. The duties of each branch are similar to those of the corresponding sections of U.S. state governments.

The political head of the Yukon Territory is the leader of the majority party and carries the title of government leader. In the Northwest Territories, a commissioner appointed by the federal government provides political leadership. Each territory has a legislative assembly and a court structure similar to the provincial systems.

Tribal Governments

The Native American or Aboriginal Peoples of North America maintain tribal governments to oversee the large areas of land formerly known as reservations **(Figure 23.19)**. These governments have structures similar to the federal government although the leader is called the *chief*. In the U.S., the Bureau of Indian Affairs (Department of the Interior) is the primary agency responsible for management of Indian lands and resources. Other federal departments that have programs that support the Native American culture include the departments of defense, labor, commerce, and agriculture, to name a few. FEMA, through the Department of Homeland Security, even manages programs that are specifically intended to aid Native Americans following a disaster.

Figure 23.19 The Native Americans of North America maintain tribal governments, structures similar to the federal government, to oversee the large areas of land formerly known as reservations.

Agencies of State and Provincial Governments

Because the structure and function of agencies vary greatly among the states and provinces, company officers must make an effort to become familiar with the exact agencies that are active in their political subdivision and their responsibilities. The following section contains brief summaries of some of the more common agencies that influence fire and emergency services in the United States and Canada.

NOTE: Remember that not all the agencies listed are to be found in all states and provinces and that in some areas, agencies not listed may be of even more importance than those included here. Also, agencies with the same or similar names may have different responsibilities and objectives in different jurisdictions. Not all the organizations described are government-sponsored, but each supports or affects the implementation of fire and emergency services within the states and provinces.

Fire Marshal

Most states and provinces maintain a fire marshal's office **(Figure 23.20)**. In as many as 47 of the states, the fire marshal serves as the principal authority on fire protection. Under some government structures, the fire marshal's office is an independent agency, while in others the position is part of another department, such as the state police. The responsibilities of the fire marshal vary greatly from state to state and province to

Figure 23.20 A state fire marshal takes notes while investigating a fire.

province. However, a key responsibility under most state and provincial governments is to advise the legislature or assembly on fire and life safety-related legislation and to oversee the fire prevention program. In cases of fire involving state or provincial property, or private property located outside a municipal boundary, the fire marshal generally conducts cause and origin investigations. The fire marshal commonly serves on panels and committees tasked with state and provincial planning for hazardous materials control and disaster preparedness.

Fire Training Programs

Many states and provinces deliver fire training programs through their fire marshal's office, colleges and universities, or vocational training systems. Training is provided at the institution's facilities or, in some cases, at local fire and emergency service facilities. These programs often provide technical advice and planning assistance to local fire protection agencies.

Fire Commission

A few states and provinces have established commissions to conduct fire and emergency services training and certification programs. Most receive funding from the legislature or assembly to support operation of the commission. The agency is headed by a commissioner or director who oversees the commission's operations and influences its objectives.

State or Provincial Police

Fire and emergency services organizations often have to respond to emergency incidents outside the jurisdiction of their local law enforcement agency. In such cases, state or provincial police often serve in the law enforcement role to provide traffic and crowd control, conduct large-scale evacuations, and protect firefighters during civil unrest **(Figure 23.21)**. State and provincial police, or *highway patrol*, may also assist with arson investigations and other legal matters that cross jurisdictional boundaries. As stated earlier, in some states, the state fire marshal's office is under the jurisdiction of the state police.

Figure 23.21 Highway patrol vehicles respond to emergencies.

Highway Department or Turnpike Authority

Roadway planning, maintenance, and control at the state or provincial level generally fall to the highway department or turnpike authority. Consequently, these agencies have a role in providing fire and emergency services organizations with usable thoroughfares to support emergency responses and to accommodate the required apparatus. Similarly, these agencies need to keep local emergency service officials informed of highway closures, detours, and repair work that might impede a response. The highway department and turnpike authority usually participate in state- or provincial-level disaster and hazardous materials incident planning, with local offices participating at the city and county level.

Environmental Protection Agency

Many states and provinces have established agencies to oversee environmental protection. In addition to serving in inspection, enforcement, and training roles, personnel from these agencies often assist in the development of response plans and frequently deploy to incident sites to support local response efforts. Company officers who are responsible for developing live-burn training must be familiar with the requirements of this agency. In most areas, the release into the atmosphere of carbon particles and contaminates, such as foam extinguishing agents, is closely monitored and controlled.

Health Department

When a fire involves a medical facility, food vendor, place of lodging, or public building, the health department frequently inspects the facility after the incident to evaluate its suitability for continued service. The agency may request information or assistance from the local fire and emergency services organization that responded to the emergency. At the same time, the health department can supply information on biological hazards, immunization, and quarantine procedures.

The city, county, or state/provincial health department may also have authority over and responsibility of the EMS in the jurisdiction. This authority may include the certification testing for all personnel and the setting of prehospital care and treatment protocols (**Figure 23.22**).

Forestry Department

Local fire and emergency services organizations often establish mutual aid agreements with the state or provincial forestry department and the logging industry (**Figure 23.23**). Under these agreements, the local fire and emergency services organization may assist in fighting fires that involve forest or other public lands. In reciprocation, the forestry department may make resources such as personnel and heavy equipment available to the local fire and emergency services organization, especially to assist in suppressing rural and urban interface fires.

Office of Emergency Preparedness or Homeland Security

Patterned after the national Department of Homeland Security, most states have established an Office of Homeland Security, Office of Domestic Preparedness, Office of Emergency Services, or a similar office. Regardless of the title, these agencies are responsible for preventing, preparing for, responding to, mitigating, and recovering from all types of disasters. Because local fire and emergency services organizations respond to large-scale disasters or other emergency situations, they must be able to work with these state-level agencies. Further, such agencies may provide personnel, management, equipment, and other support to local resources for smaller emergencies. Additionally, these agencies can be an excellent funding source for departmental training activities.

Other State and Provincial Agencies

Company officers should become familiar with the responsibilities, organization, and operations of other state and provincial agencies that may have some effect on local responses. For example, if a jurisdiction includes or is near a state or provincial park, interaction with the park and recreation department is important. If the jurisdiction includes navigable waterways, coordination with state-level agencies responsible for controlling and maintaining these systems is vital. Local emergency services organizations should identify these and other

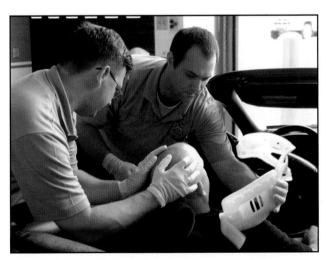

Figure 23.22 Students preparing for EMS certification.

Figure 23.23 The local fire and emergency services organization may assist in fighting fires that involve forestry on public lands.

special needs within or near their jurisdiction and ensure that coordination with these other agencies is addressed in planning and operating procedures as necessary.

U.S. Federal Government

The U.S. federal government has acknowledged its roles in providing for public safety through the establishment of departments and agencies and the passage of legislation to protect citizens in emergencies and to reduce the risk of life-threatening incidents. These agencies operate within the structure of the government through the support of public funds and under the direction of elected or appointed officials. The legislation that governs these agencies has been introduced and approved under the federal government's lawmaking process.

Legislation enacted by Congress often requires some means of implementation, such as obtaining funding for a specific program. To carry out the requirements of various legislative acts, numerous agencies have been created, such as the Federal Emergency Management Agency (FEMA) or the National Aeronautics and Space Administration (NASA). These agencies exist as part of the executive branch, and the president appoints the administrators or directors who manage them. However, the Senate must approve all presidential appointees and, if they are removed from office, the president must inform the Senate of the reason for their removal.

Lawmaking Process of the U.S. Federal Government

Congressional sessions in the United States last for two years. During that time, thousands of potential laws are introduced in the form of bills **(Figure 23.24)**. A *bill* is the written description of the legislation that is presented to Congress. All bills must be sponsored by a member of Congress, although most are actually written by Congressional staff specialists called *legislative counsels* or by lawyers representing special-interest groups. The idea for a bill may come from the public, press, a special-interest group, Congress, the president, or another part of the government. However, any bills dealing with taxes and spending must originate in the House of Representatives. The sponsor of the bill gives it to the house clerk, who reads the title of the bill publicly so that it will appear in the Congressional record. The bill then goes to the Government Printing Office for duplication and distribution.

Congress maintains committees that have responsibility for various segments of government operations. The bill is assigned for review to a House committee by the Speaker of the House and to a Senate committee by the Senate majority leader. The committee studies the bill and often calls experts, as well as other interested persons or groups, to testify about the bill. The committee may send the bill on to the rest of the originating house, revise it and release it to the house, or *table it;* that is, take no action.

Released bills are placed on the Congressional calendar for debate and vote by the members of the originating house. On the specified date, the bill is read aloud. Members are then allowed to express their opinions about the bill and to debate its perceived merits and flaws. Members can propose amendments to the bill. These proceedings continue until there is no more discussion or for as long as the House Rules Committee permits or, in the Senate, until the members vote to limit debate. The members then vote on the bill, with a simple majority of voting members being required for approval of most bills.

The approved bill is passed on to the other house of Congress, where a sponsor introduces the bill by being recognized by the presiding officer and announcing it to the other members. The presiding officer assigns it to a committee. As in the originating house, the bill is then subject to study and, if approved by the committee, debate by the members in the legislative chamber. If the bill is approved by the second house, it goes to a conference committee, which includes representatives of both houses of Congress. Their task is to work out the differences between the Senate and House versions of the bill and to prepare a final draft approved by the committee. The revised version of the bill is submitted to both houses for another vote.

Once both houses approve the bill, the Government Printing Office prints the final version, and the bill is enrolled as an act. The clerk of the house

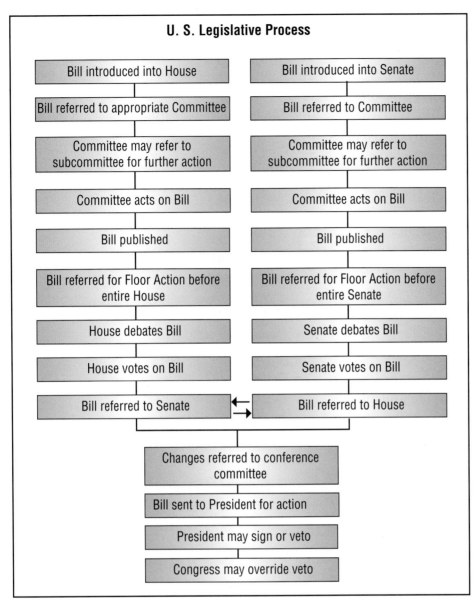

U. S. Legislative Process

Bill introduced into House	Bill introduced into Senate
Bill referred to appropriate Committee	Bill referred to Committee
Committee may refer to subcommittee for further action	Committee may refer to subcommittee for further action
Committee acts on Bill	Committee acts on Bill
Bill published	Bill published
Bill referred for Floor Action before entire House	Bill referred for Floor Action before entire Senate
House debates Bill	Senate debates Bill
House votes on Bill	Senate votes on Bill
Bill referred to Senate	Bill referred to House

Changes referred to conference committee

Bill sent to President for action

President may sign or veto

Congress may override veto

Figure 23.24 The U.S. legislative process.

that originated the bill certifies it and obtains the signatures of the presiding officers of both houses.

Congress sends the act to the President, who has ten days (excluding Sundays) to review the document. During this time, one of four following actions may take place:

1. The President can approve the act by signing and dating it and marking it as approved. The act then becomes law.

2. The President can veto the act by returning it to Congress with an explanation as to why it was rejected. If an act is vetoed by the President, Congress can override the veto with a yes vote of two-thirds of the members present. The act then becomes law without the approval of the President.

3. If Congress fails to override the veto, the act is dead and must begin again as a bill if it is to be reconsidered.

4. Finally, the President can choose to take no action on the act. Chief executives sometimes choose this method to show their disagreement with parts of the legislation. If the President fails to approve or veto the act within the allotted time, it will become law without the chief executive's signature if Congress is still in session at the end of the 10 days. However, if Congress submits legislation to the President with fewer than 10 days remaining in the ses-

sion and the president refuses to sign it, the proposed law is effectively disapproved in an action called a *pocket veto*.

Once a law is approved, responsible departments and agencies are then required to implement the law within their interpretation of the legislation and guidelines set forth in the act. Any citizen or group can use the judicial system to challenge legislation that has been passed by Congress and enacted as law. A case that requires the court to rule on the constitutionality of the law must be brought. The case can proceed through appeals all the way to the Supreme Court, which can take one of three actions:

- Choose not to hear the case, which in effect declares the challenge invalid without actually ruling on constitutionality.

- Hear the case and find in favor of the law.

- Hear the case and determine that all or some of the law is not consistent with the Constitution.

In the event that a law (including state and local laws) is overturned by the Supreme Court, the law is no longer enforceable, and legislative bodies which have approved the law or similar laws must address the issue through other laws.

U.S. Federal Agencies Involved in Fire Protection

In 1974, Congress passed the Federal Fire Prevention and Control Act (15 U.S.C. 2201) to provide improved training, assistance, coordination, and standards for fire protection. The act also established the United States Fire Administration. This legislation marked the federal government's first extensive regulatory efforts in the field of fire protection.

Over the years, this involvement has intensified as a result of a growing awareness of modern threats to public safety, including terrorism, the increased use and transport of flammable and hazardous materials, continuing developments in fire suppression technology, improved communications, and a growing trend toward interorganizational cooperation among both government and private agencies.

Fire and emergency services personnel play a substantial role on both sides of these efforts. They must comply with and often enforce the laws and regulations, and they frequently benefit from the improved training, safety, and operating procedures that develop through such cooperation. They also contribute to defining these agencies and their operations by testifying before Congress and serving on committees as individuals and as representatives of professional organizations.

United States Government Departments

The following departments are represented in the Cabinet:

- Department of State
- Department of Treasury
- Department of Interior
- Department of Justice
- Department of Agriculture
- Department of Commerce
- Department of Labor
- Department of Defense
- Department of Health and Human Services
- Department of Housing and Urban Development
- Department of Transportation
- Department of Energy
- Department of Education
- Department of Veterans Affairs
- Department of Homeland Security

Department of Homeland Security

The most drastic change in the organization of the federal government occurred in 2002 with the creation of the Department of Homeland Security (DHS) **(Figure 23.25)**. Agencies that were previously part of other departments were moved into the DHS in an attempt to consolidate intelligence gathering efforts to prevent further acts of terrorism. Among the fire and emergency services agencies that were absorbed into the DHS were the Federal Emergency Management Agency (FEMA) and with it the United States Fire Administration

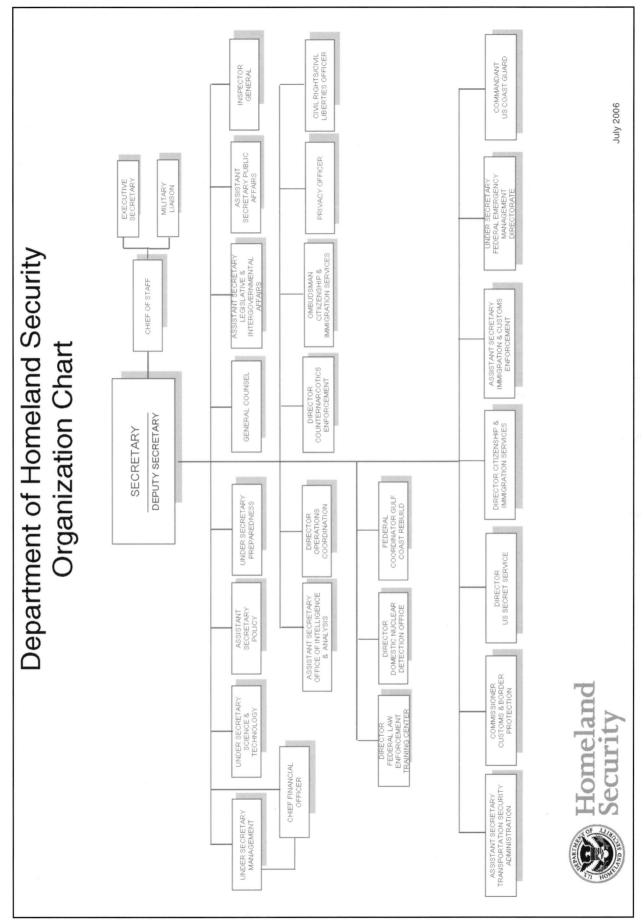

Figure 23.25 Department of Homeland Security Organizational Chart.

(USFA) and National Fire Academy (NFA). The U.S. Coast Guard, formerly part of the Treasury Department, Citizen and Immigration Services and U.S. Secret Service, formerly part of the Department of Justice, and the newly created Transportation Security Administration (TSA) were also added to DHS.

Federal Emergency Management Agency (FEMA). FEMA is an agency that serves as a single point of contact within the federal government for emergency management activities. Its role is that of a supporting partner to organizations within and outside the fire and emergency services that are involved in emergency management. FEMA's organizational structure reflects the functions of emergency management: preparedness, response, mitigation, and recovery **(Figure 23.26)**. In addition to these emergency management functions, the agency also supports risk-reduction and loss-prevention programs.

United States Fire Administration (USFA). Headquartered in Emmitsburg, Maryland, the USFA administers an extensive fire data and analysis program and provides overall fire policy and coordination. USFA acts as the lead agency in federal fire prevention and arson control programs, along with state and local fire service and law enforcement agencies. In conjunction with the National Institute of Occupational Safety and Health (NIOSH), the USFA administers a program concerned with firefighter health and safety.

National Fire Academy (NFA). The NFA is the training arm of the United States Fire Administration and is located in Emmitsburg, Maryland. The NFA provides training programs ranging from fire service management to the hazard mitigation of various materials and from arson investigation techniques to fire code application by architects and local building officials. The NFA delivers resident programs in Emmitsburg, as well as provides field programs through a partnership with state fire training systems and metro size fire departments (TRADE).

Emergency Management Institute (EMI). Some fire-related training is also provided by EMI **(Figure 23.27)**. The main focus of EMI, however, is on the training of emergency management professionals which include members of the fire service.

Figure 23.26 FEMA at an emergency incident. *Courtesy of Bri Rodriguez/FEMA News Photo.*

Figure 23.27 The EMI facility trains emergency management professionals. *Courtesy of Bill Koplitz, FEMA.*

U.S. Department of Agriculture (USDA)

The fire protection programs of the U.S. Department of Agriculture (USDA) are aimed at fire prevention and education in rural areas and are carried out by the USDA Forest Service, more commonly known as the U.S. Forest Service (USFS), and the Farmers' Home Administration (FHA).

Known to millions through its familiar symbol Smokey Bear, the USFS provides fire protection to more than 200 million acres of forests, grasslands, and nearby private lands (National Forest System) **(Figure 23.28)**. It also conducts research and develops improved methods in forest fire management (forest fire and atmospheric research) and provides

Figure 23.28 Smokey Bear poster.

technical and financial assistance to state forestry organizations to improve fire protection efficiency on nonfederal wildlands (cooperative fire protection). Research is also conducted on wood and wood-based products.

The Farmers' Home Administration makes loans to public bodies and nonprofit corporations in rural areas for the construction of fire stations, the provision of water supplies, and the purchase of fire suppression apparatus and equipment.

Department of Housing and Urban Development (HUD)

The Manufactured Housing and Construction Standards Division of the Department of Housing and Urban Development (HUD) promulgates and enforces rules regarding the safety and durability of manufactured housing, including fire safety standards. These rules are for consumer protection and to determine eligibility for HUD loans and mortgage insurance policies.

Department of the Interior (DOI)

The Bureau of Land Management (BLM) within the DOI provides protection against wildfires on 545 million acres of public land and services and supports the Interagency Fire Center in Boise, Idaho. The center provides logistic support for the U.S. Forest Service; the U.S. Department of Commerce's National Oceanic and Atmospheric Administration (NOAA); Bureau of Land Management; Bureau of Indian Affairs; National Park Service (NPS); and the Fish and Wildlife Service. The NPS also provides presuppression and suppression services and administers a fire safety program to protect national park visitors, employees, resources, and facilities.

Department of Labor (DOL)

In 1970, Congress established the Occupational Safety and Health Administration (OSHA) within the DOL to develop and promulgate mandatory occupational safety and health standards—rules and regulations applicable at the workplace. As part of the enforcement of its rules, OSHA conducts investigations and inspections, and it cites and penalizes companies for violations of the standards.

Department of Transportation (DOT)

Ten major operational units within the DOT investigate, research, analyze, and provide for the safety of vehicles, avenues, the environment, passengers, and cargoes in all modes of transportation. All these functions heavily involve fire safety. The organizational units are as follows:

- Three divisions within the Federal Aviation Administration (airports, special programs, and aircraft safety and airport technology) **(Figure 23.29, p. 558)**

- Federal Highway Administration (interstate highways)

- Federal Railroad Administration

- National Highway Traffic Safety Administration (on-road vehicle safety hazards and accidents)

- Maritime Administration (merchant marine)

- Urban Mass Transportation Administration (buses and subways)

- Materials Transportation Bureau (hazardous materials)

Figure 23.29 Airports are a division within the Federal Aviation Administration.

- Transportation Safety Institute (safety and security management, training)
- Transportation Systems Center (applied research)

Related to but independent from the DOT, the National Transportation Safety Board investigates and makes recommendations with respect to traffic accidents, including vehicular fire incidents.

Department of Justice

Through its network of agents across the United States, the Bureau of Alcohol, Tobacco, Firearms, and Explosives (ATF) conducts a vigorous arson investigation program, including training and technical assistance to state and local law enforce-

ment and fire authorities. The ATF's firearms and explosives programs protect interstate and foreign commerce from interference and disruption by reducing hazards to persons and property stemming from the insecure storage of explosives.

Consumer Product Safety Commission (CPSC)

The CPSC's Fire and Thermal Burn Program encompasses the investigation of injury patterns, data collection, research, and the promulgation and enforcement of mandatory standards with respect to consumer products.

Other U.S. Federal Agencies

Federal agencies, such as the Nuclear Regulatory Commission, U.S. Coast Guard, and Federal Aviation Administration, can play important roles in fire protection and emergency response procedures and planning. For example, while most jurisdictions will have little or no contact with the Nuclear Regulatory Commission (NRC), interaction with the NRC may be a normal part of a department's operations if its jurisdiction includes a nuclear power plant. Company officers must acquaint themselves with those federal agencies that may become involved in incidents that are likely to occur within the jurisdiction and in neighboring jurisdictions.

Canadian Federal Government

The Canadian federal government is modeled after the national structures of both the United States and Great Britain. Canada is a federation of self-governing provinces and territories, much as the United States is a federation of self-governing states, with a federal government consisting of three branches (**Figure 23.30**). Canada's legislature is called Parliament and consists of two houses: the House of Commons and the Senate. The most apparent differences in the structures of the U.S. and Canadian federal governments exist in the Executive Branch. Although Canada is an independent nation, it recognizes the sovereign of Great Britain as its official head of state. Thus, the king or queen of Great Britain presides in the same role over Canada, although no real powers are granted to the monarch. The British sovereign is officially represented in Canada by an appointed

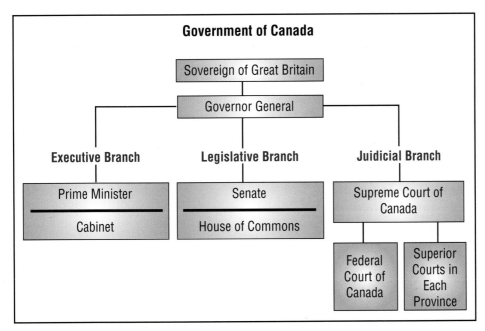

Government of Canada

Sovereign of Great Britain

Governor General

Executive Branch

Prime Minister

Cabinet

Legislative Branch

Senate

House of Commons

Juidicial Branch

Supreme Court of Canada

Federal Court of Canada

Superior Courts in Each Province

Figure 23.30 Structure of Canadian government.

official termed the Governor General. However, the true chief executive of the Canadian government is the Prime Minister. The Prime Minister is assisted by a cabinet of 27 ministers for various functional areas of the government in 2006.

Like the U.S. federal government, the Canadian government is responsible for the enacting of laws and the establishment and management of agencies that provide for the safety of the citizens. How the laws are enacted, however, differs between the two nations.

Lawmaking Process of the Canadian Federal Government

The Canadian Parliament recognizes two types of bills: public bills that affect the general population and private bills that affect individuals or small groups. Although any bill that does not involve spending may originate in either house, in actual practice virtually all bills are first introduced in the House of Commons and follow the steps described in this section.

All public bills begin the lawmaking process when a Cabinet minister requests that a bill be published in the *Notice Paper*. If the bill involves taxes or spending, a minister must still sponsor the legislation but only at the request of the Governor General in Council. After this notice, the minister requests permission in Parliament to introduce the bill through a first reading. Upon approval of the

request, the bill is read for the first time without discussion. This is followed by a second reading during which members may debate the bill's principal objectives but not the details of the legislation. At the end of the debate, the House votes on the bill. If the bill passes, the presiding officer forwards it to an appropriate committee.

The committee discusses the bill and returns it to the House with a written evaluation of the bill, its effect, suggested changes, and other information. The House may accept the committee report or return it to the committee for revision. Once the House accepts the committee report, the bill is debated on the floor. Amendments may be proposed and voted upon until such time as the presiding officer determines that the bill should be put to a vote. At this time, there is a third reading with some limited debate allowed and the proposal of additional amendments permitted.

If the bill receives the approval of the House, it goes to the Senate. There it undergoes a process similar to its introduction and review in the House. The Senate can take only limited actions on bills dealing with taxes and spending, but Senate committees can offer amendments to *reduce* spending or make amendments on other types of bills. When the bill goes to the floor of the Senate for its third reading, one of three actions can be taken. If the House version is approved without amendment, the bill goes to the Governor General. If the Senate votes the bill down, it must be resubmitted for a first reading and the process repeated. While the Senate cannot defeat a spending bill, it can delay passage of the bill for up to 180 days in this manner. Finally, the Senate may pass the bill with amendments. In this case, the bill is returned to the House for review of the Senate amendments.

If the bill is returned to the House, members review and vote on the Senate amendments. If they do not accept the amended bill, the House convenes a joint committee meeting with representatives of the Senate to work out compromises. The final version of the compromise legislation goes through three readings and a vote in each house. However, if the committee is unable to agree to compromises, the legislation is dead.

Legislation approved by Parliament goes to the Governor General for signature, who signs the bill into law. The legislation becomes effective immediately or at a time determined by the Cabinet.

Canadian Agencies Involved in Fire Protection

Numerous Canadian federal agencies have some form of interaction with the fire and emergency services. The following sections highlight these agencies and the relationship they have with the fire and emergency services.

Public Safety and Emergency Preparedness Canada (PSEPC)

As a result of the increasing terrorist threat to North America, the Canadian government created Public Safety and Emergency Preparedness Canada as the nation's primary department for public safety. The department is responsible for reducing the threat and effect of all types of emergencies including natural disasters, industrial accidents, terrorism, and computer viruses. As part of this responsibility, PSEPC develops national policy, response systems and standards, issues timely alerts and similar products to help protect Canada's critical infrastructure, and works closely with emergency management organizations by providing first responders with funds, tools, and training. The Royal Canadian Mounted Police (RCMP) is part of PSEPC.

Other responsibilities include the following:

- Operation of the Government Operations Centre, which is an advanced communications center for monitoring and coordinating the federal response to an emergency

- Management of the Canadian Emergency Preparedness College, providing training courses and educational resources to Canada's emergency management community

- Producing and distributing guides for citizens, businesses, and emergency services personnel on means for dealing with emergencies such as power outages, flooding, bomb threats, and other situations that may disrupt normal life

- Management of the Joint Emergency Preparedness Program, which funds projects that enhance the capacity of communities or provinces/territories to respond to emergencies through planning, training, and logistical support

- Management of the National Exercise Program, which develops and coordinates exercises that simulate emergency scenarios such as natural disasters, health threats, and terrorist attacks

- Management of the National Emergency Response System, which provides effective coordination of the numerous national agencies that must respond during national emergencies

- Management of the Urban Search and Rescue (USAR) program providing trained and equipped emergency responders to rescue victims from major structural collapse or other entrapments

Industry Canada

Industry Canada manages the Canadian Centre for Occupational Health and Safety. The centre oversees regulations intended to protect workers, including firefighters and emergency responders, in the workplace. Because these regulations also affect the use and storage of dangerous goods (hazardous materials) in the workplace, centre actions can influence how fire and emergency services organizations respond to emergencies within such facilities.

Public Works and Government Services Canada

Responsible for the construction and maintenance of public thoroughfares, bridges, and public buildings, Public Works and Government Services Canada and its field offices work closely with fire and emergency services organizations to ensure that their structures promote effective emergency response and fire safety. The department must keep fire and emergency services organizations informed of road closures, detours, and other situations that may prevent an effective and timely response. Canada's waterways and harbors also fall under the purview of the public works department so that specific coordination may be required for the fire protection of watercraft and marine facilities within a jurisdiction **(Figure 23.31)**.

Treasury Board

The comptroller general oversees all federal spending in Canada as part of the Treasury Board. The office is also responsible for government-sponsored economic development and regulatory affairs. Thus, fire and emergency services organizations are affected by both the level of financial support provided to relevant programs and by specific regulatory actions taken by the office.

Transport Canada

Transport Canada (TC) oversees virtually all transportation and communications within the country. Because many transportation systems within Canada are government-owned, TC's responsibilities include maintenance and operation of the national railway company, St. Lawrence Seaway Authority, Canadian Aviation Safety Board, and the Northern Pipeline Agency. The department is involved in the regulation of hazardous materials transport on land, in the air, and on water.

Environment Canada

Environment Canada plays a role in hazardous materials incident response planning and the use of chemicals and methods of fire suppression. The department also has responsibility for maintaining certain public and historical sites within Canada and, thus, must coordinate fire protection planning with local agencies.

Agriculture and Agri-Food Canada

The primary fire protection concerns that are within the purview of Agriculture and Agri-Food Canada are the offices for forestry and mines. These offices are responsible for the maintenance of government-owned forests and mining opera-

Figure 23.31 Canadian Port Facility.

tions and for the regulation of commercial timber and mining operations. Thus, the department is able to work with local fire and emergency services organizations to establish mutual aid agreements and to assist in response planning.

Human Resources and Social Development Canada

The Department of Human Resources and Social Development Canada is responsible for improving the standard of living and the quality of life of all Canadians by promoting a highly skilled and mobile workforce as well as an efficient and inclusive labor market. It is responsible for labor programs, homeless issues, vocational training, and educational grants and loans, to name a few areas.

National Research Council Institute for Research in Construction (NRC-IRC)

The NRC-IRC develops codes and standards for the construction industry. In particular, the institute researches and tests construction materials and processes to create cost-effective buildings, provides fire modeling and tests products for fire resistance, and develops technologies to improve the infrastructure of urban areas.

Other Canadian Federal Agencies

Many of the other departments have lesser roles in influencing fire and emergency operations in Canada. However, within a particular province or district, the importance of any given agency may be more pronounced, and fire officers need to become familiar with the need for coordination with particular agencies within their department jurisdiction.

Summary

Fire and emergency services organizations do not exist in a vacuum. They are an integral part of the local community and of the state or province in which they are located. They must interact with other local, regional, state, and national agencies and departments. In order to provide the best level of service to the community, company officers need to be aware of the governmental structure of which their organization is a part, and of the myriad other organizations that may be able to assist in the delivery of services at the local level. Resources are available from all levels of government depending on the type of emergency or the amount of assistance required. Company officers should establish working relationships with their counterparts in the agencies with which they will interact.

Political Neutrality

Government in North America is composed of citizens, elected or selected officials, and the bureaucracy. Fire and emergency services personnel are both citizens and members of the bureaucracy. As such, fire officers and emergency responders must weigh the responsibilities of citizens to be politically active with the responsibilities and constraints of being members of the bureaucracy.

All fire officers and emergency responders should remain politically neutral. The benefits of remaining politically neutral include the ability to work for elected officials who may represent the opposing party or view, maintain mutual respect between the elected officials and members of the organization, and maintain an unbiased image. Political neutrality is so important that the International City Management Association (ICMA) has included it in its code of ethics: Members will . . .

Refrain from all political activities, which undermine public confidence in professional administrators. Refrain from participation in the election of the members of the employing legislative body.

Fire officers should consider these statements as guidelines for their own activities and those of the members of their organizations. To remain politically neutral, fire and emergency services personnel should use the following guidelines:

- Treat all candidates and elected officials impartially and equally.

- Refrain from publicly criticizing any elected official or decision.

- Refrain from publicly supporting any candidate for elected office.

- Refrain from donating to any political party or candidate.

- Refrain from signing or circulating petitions.

- Refrain from participation in political fund-raising activities.

- Do not run for elected office while employed by the organization.

- Exercise the constitutionally established right to vote in all elections.

The company officer should not attempt to influence the political activities of subordinates or peers, however. The right to political action and opinions is firmly grounded in the Constitution. It is important, though, to remember that the political arena is fluid and that elected officials change. Remaining politically neutral is the best way to advance the interests of the local organization and the fire service as a whole.

Interagency and Intergovernmental Cooperation

Chapter Contents

Learning Objectives

1. Select facts about internal aid agreements.

2. Identify the types of external aid agreements.

3. Select from a list the items that should be included in a formal intergovernmental agreement.

4. Recall facts about jurisdictional authority.

5. Identify the components of area contingency plans.

6. Select from a list the criteria for declaring a federal disaster.

7. Recall the benefits of the National Response Plan.

8. Identify representative federal agencies that may interact with the fire and emergency services organization in the U.S. or Canada.

9. Select facts about areas that the company officer may be involved in during emergency management activities.

Job Performance Requirements

This chapter provides information that addresses the following job performance requirements of NFPA 1021, *Standard for Fire Officer Professional Qualifications* (2003):

<u>Chapter 5 Fire Officer II</u>

5.1.1

5.1.2

5.6.1

5.6.1(A)

5.6.1(B)

Chapter 24
Interagency and Intergovernmental Cooperation

The fire and emergency services administration is responsible for the development and management of interagency and intergovernmental agreements. To form agreements for management of large or complex incidents, the chief/manager of the organization and senior or administrative staff members meet with departmental representatives from within the jurisdiction and from other jurisdictions and levels of government. This interaction involves planning, training, implementing, monitoring, and evaluating these written agreements.

The interagency and intergovernmental agreements usually take the form of automatic aid, mutual aid, outside aid, and multiagency and multijurisdiction incident response and cooperation. The company officer must be aware of the existence of these agreements and the local protocols required to activate them. The concepts of mutual and automatic aid as well as outside aid have been presented in the Fire Officer I part of this manual. They are briefly recapped here.

The Fire Officer II may be assigned the following tasks or duties:

- Acting as the organization's representative in planning the agreement

- Creating training scenarios

- Implementing the process within the organization

- Monitoring the results or evaluating the effectiveness of the agreement

At the same time, the company officer may be involved in incidents that will escalate to the point that agreements must be activated. In all cases, the company officer must have a working knowledge of the existing agreements with the fire and emergency services organization.

The National Incident Management System (NIMS) outlines the requirements for multiagency and multijurisdictional cooperation and standardizes interagency and intergovernmental operations at emergency incidents. The company officer should review local protocol and how it relates to NIMS.

Local Aid Agreements

Local aid agreements provide additional resources to the fire and emergency services organization. These resources may supplement, replace, or augment the existing resources of the organization. The decision to activate the aid agreement will depend on the type of agreement, its terms, and who has the authority to request the aid. The source of the aid may also vary depending on whether the aid comes from within the jurisdiction or outside of it. All company and chief officers must be familiar with the local aid agreements, the protocols for activating them, how to respond when assigned to fulfill an aid agreement, and the responsibilities assigned in the Incident Command System (ICS).

Internal Aid Agreements

An internal aid agreement may be a simple function of the local government and not require a written document to verify it. Various departments within the jurisdiction will be required to respond when requested (**Figure 24.1, p. 568**). The following are examples of internal resources:

- *Street department* — provide inert materials for controlling liquid spills

Figure 24.1 This law enforcement vehicle provides traffic control by blocking traffic at the incident.

- *Public works* — provide heavy equipment for collapse or trench rescue operations
- *Law enforcement* — provide traffic or crowd control or investigative resources
- *Fire and emergency services department* — provide ventilation for nonemergency services workers entering a confined space
- *Emergency medical services* — provide medical support for firefighters and civilians

Representatives from these and other internal departments are usually involved in local emergency management planning and development meetings. The local emergency management plan should include contact information, types of resources, and response protocol.

Authority to request these resources may be distributed between the Incident Commander (IC), operations chief, or communication center. Obviously, the on-scene commander has the authority to request any resources when the need becomes apparent. This authority means that a Fire Officer I responding to a single-unit incident can request traffic control from the police department or sand from the street department to contain a spill. If the incident is complex, the battalion/district chief or assistant/deputy chief who has operational authority may request additional resources that may be retained at staging until needed. Finally,

the communication center can request the aid immediately if it is apparent that it will be needed by the first-arriving units.

If a fire and emergency services unit is assigned to provide internal aid to another department, the company officer should determine the following considerations prior to or while responding:

- Is the situation hazardous or life threatening?
- Should the response include the use of warning devices?
- Is the response a service call that does not require warning devices?
- What tools and equipment will be required to perform the aid?
- Who is responsible for or in charge of the situation?
- Will the unit be taken out-of-service during the assignment?

Providing internal aid or assistance builds goodwill and a sense of cooperation between departments within the jurisdiction. It is also a good form of public relations when the citizens become aware of the variety of services they can rely on from the jurisdiction.

Finally, the internal aid agreement helps build a network of internal relations between company officers and their counterparts in other departments. Whether the assistance is a service call or an emergency situation, the company officer must always approach it as a positive situation that will benefit the public. New internal relationships can be developed and existing ones strengthened by the application of basic interpersonal skills. The company officer should take the following steps to build strong relationships:

- Treat personnel, supervisors, and managers in other departments with courtesy, respect, and dignity.
- Offer positive comments and give compliments sincerely.
- Handle complaints about service in private and with tact.
- Never make derogatory remarks about individuals or groups in other departments.

- Comply with the guidelines of the organization for requests for assistance.
- Follow the Golden Rule, and it will provide positive benefits.

External Aid Agreements

Agreements with other neighboring jurisdictions are generally created to provide additional resources, provide coverage in adjacent areas, or reduce the cost of providing specialized services within a region. These external agreements are normally formal, written plans that define the roles of the participants and can be categorized as *automatic aid*, *mutual aid*, or *outside aid* agreements.

Automatic Aid

Automatic aid is a formal, written agreement between jurisdictions that share a common boundary. The authority to request automatic aid is understood and the communication center alerts the correct unit or jurisdiction. Automatic aid occurs whenever certain predetermined conditions occur. Examples of predetermined conditions include the following:

- Whenever an emergency is reported along a mutual jurisdictional boundary; closest unit is dispatched regardless of jurisdiction
- Any fire or emergency involving or exceeding a given number of alarms
- At specific facilities such as airports, oil refineries, or chemical manufacturing plants

- When an incident is likely to require the commitment of the majority of the jurisdiction's resources, and units are required to protect uncovered areas
- When jurisdictions share a unique resource like a heavy rescue unit or hazardous materials team **(Figure 24.2)**

Company officers who respond to automatic aid incidents operate in the same manner as when they respond to any emergency incident. If the incident involves activities that place them under the operational control of another jurisdiction, the company officer should perform the following:

- Determine the proper operational radio frequency.
- Determine the location of the command post.
- Report to the IC at the command post or by radio.
- Adhere to the personnel accountability system that is used by the other agency.

If the company officer is in charge of an incident that will involve automatic aid units from other jurisdictions, the officer is responsible for the following:

- Requesting that all responding units acknowledge that they are on the assigned radio frequency
- Assigning units based on arrival time and capabilities

Figure 24.2 Automatic aid response may involve the response of a heavy rescue unit. *Courtesy of Bob Esposito.*

- Establishing and communicating the location of staging areas

All company officers should have a list of the resources that will automatically respond to various target hazards or facilities and the circumstances under which automatic aid will be activated. It is a good idea to list these resources in the preplan for a particular building or hazard.

Mutual Aid

Mutual aid is a reciprocal agreement between two or more fire and emergency services organizations (**Figure 24.3**). The agreements may be local, regional, statewide, or interstate so the organizations may or may not have contiguous boundaries. The agreement defines how the organizations will provide resources in various situations and how the actions of the shared resources will be monitored and controlled. Responses under a mutual aid agreement are usually on an on-request basis. Response is not, however, guaranteed. If the jurisdiction that receives the request has also been affected by the disaster, such as a tornado or hurricane, then the request can be denied.

Company officers should have a list of all external mutual aid resources available to them. Availability information can be accessed by radio communication with the communication center, a hard copy list, or a computer terminal in the apparatus. During the size-up process, the company officer makes the decision about the type of aid required and where it should be sent. Company officers requesting or responding to mutual aid requests should follow the procedures listed under automatic aid.

Outside Aid

Outside aid is similar to mutual aid except that payment rather than reciprocal aid is made by one agency to the other. Outside aid is normally addressed through a signed contract under which one agency agrees to provide aid to another in return for an established payment, which is normally an annual fee but which may be on a per-response basis. Otherwise, the outside agreement differs little from the mutual aid agreement.

An outside aid agreement may be with a jurisdiction or with a commercial vendor. Emergency management officials may determine that large quantities of materials may be required in the event of an emergency incident (**Figure 24.4**). A contract would be executed with a vendor to provide a specified amount of materials within a specified length of time. For instance, the fire and emergency services organization responsible for protecting a flammable liquids storage facility may arrange for a specific quantity of Class B foam extinguishing agent to be provided within one hour of request. During hurricane season, the local emergency management agency may request that drinking water, tents, and blankets be prepositioned in the event they are needed to supply displaced persons. Another example of outside aid might be translators or sign language specialists .

Figure 24.3 This incident involves a mutual aid response.

Figure 24.4 Outside agreements arrange for necessities such as fresh water during hurricane season. A fresh water tanker responds after Hurricane Katrina. *Courtesy of Chris E. Mickal.*

Company and chief officers should have access to the outside aid contracts that their jurisdiction maintains. Contracts with vendors should be listed with the name of the vendor, contact information (including after-hours phone numbers), and services or materials to be provided. The list should be in multiple forms including alphabetical vendor names and by service or material.

Interagency and Intergovernmental Relations

While chief officers are in direct contact with the management of other departments and agencies, company officers will work closely with the members of those agencies. Company officers should base their relationships with these agencies on mutual respect, common goals, open communication, and a team approach.

To meet the increasing demands, challenges, and threats of the twenty-first century, agencies and organizations at all levels of government and in both the public and private sectors must work together. The following are some of the challenges and threats of this century that all levels of government must deal with:

- Natural disasters such as wildfires, hurricanes, and tornados.

- Human-caused emergencies such as terrorist attacks. These attacks may take the form of bombings, biological or chemical releases, or the use of weapons of mass destruction (WMD).

- Attacks on government agencies and businesses through the use of the Internet have continued to increase with the introduction of computer viruses and worms that destroy information and data collection systems.

The creation of emergency management agencies, such as the Federal Emergency Management Agency (FEMA) and the Office of Grants and Training (formerly ODP), has occurred at all levels of government. One result is the establishment of the National Incident Management System (NIMS), which standardizes interagency and intergovernmental operations at emergency incidents. States/provinces and local governments have established similar emergency management offices

and adopted incident command and management systems that allow them to meet national requirements. See **Appendix Q** for a copy of HSPD-5, the document that created NIMS.

Interagency and Intergovernmental Agreements

Formal agreements between the fire and emergency services organization and various levels of government and agencies are important to ensure a coordinated response in time of crisis. The agreements are the result of intergovernmental/agency planning sessions and training simulations designed to recognize conflicts and support needs **(Figure 24.5)**. Formal intergovernmental agreements should include the following items:

- Agency authority and responsibility

- Funding and reimbursement procedures

- Response procedures

- Communication systems, protocol, and procedures

- Preincident planning and training

- Postincident evaluations

- Notification procedures

Types of agreements range from local mutual aid agreements between departments/organizations to agreements between local departments/organizations and the state and federal government in the event of a declared state of emergency. Because these agreements are legal documents, the juris-

Figure 24.5 Fire and emergency services organizations and various agencies plan interagency and intergovernmental agreements.

diction's legal department should be involved in their development. In addition, these agreements should be reviewed and revised by representatives of each signatory agency as needed on a periodic basis just like other types of plans.

Jurisdictional Authority

Agreements, regardless of type, must establish jurisdiction over the emergency incidents in which the participants will be involved **(Figure 24.6)**. Jurisdiction or *who is in charge here* can be illustrated in two ways: vertical or horizontal. *Vertical jurisdiction* occurs when multiple levels of government are involved. For instance, the municipal fire and emergency services organization responds to a hazardous materials spill that leaks into a river. While the fire and emergency services organization is in initial command of the incident, the arrival of state water resources agency personnel may mean that its jurisdiction takes priority. State authority may be overridden when representatives of the U.S. Environmental Protection Agency (EPA) arrive on the scene.

An example of *horizontal jurisdiction* is an incident that covers multiple jurisdictions such as a wildland fire that crosses county or state borders. Agencies from different states must agree who will be in charge of the operation or form a multiagency emergency scene management team to provide a Unified Command (UC) system. FEMA recommends the creation of area contingency plans (ACPs) to prepare for responding to multijurisdictional incidents.

The National Incident Management System (NIMS)-based ICS/UC can be used as the model for response management in the ACP to ensure an effective response. Jurisdictions should consider the following items when developing ACPs:

- Jurisdictional responsibilities
- Roles of all levels of government in the Unified Command (federal, state/provincial, and local)
- Relationship between the federal on-site coordinators (FOSC) and other officials who also have decision-making authority but are not part of the UC

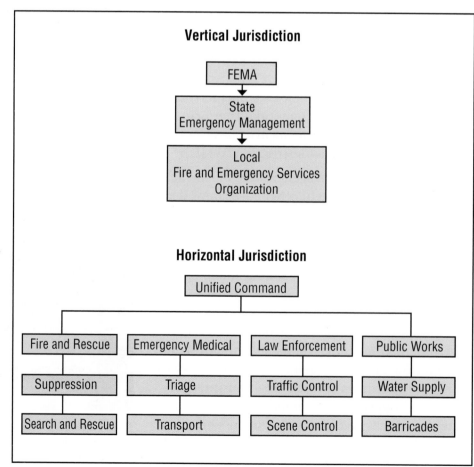

Figure 24.6 Vertical and horizontal jurisdictions.

- Financial agreements
- Information dissemination
- Communications
- Training and exercising
- Logistics
- Lessons learned

An important application of the ICS/UC concept to a response action can be seen in federal or provincial response to major disasters for the purposes of assisting local governmental agencies. Legislation has been created in both the U.S. and Canada that allows the highest levels of government to provide federal or state/provincial resources response to mitigate a disaster.

The Robert T. Stafford Disaster Relief and Emergency Assistance Act, 42 U.S.C. 5121-5206, established the programs and processes for the U.S. federal government to provide disaster and emergency assistance to states, local governments, tribal nations, individuals, and qualified private nonprofit organizations. The provisions of the Stafford Act cover all hazards including natural disasters and terrorist events. Relevant provisions of the Stafford Act include the following:

In the United States, the federal government has established a process for state governors to request federal disaster and emergency assistance from the President. The President may declare a major disaster or emergency:

(1) If an event is beyond the combined response capabilities of the state and affected local governments; and

(2) If based on the findings of a joint federal-state-local Preliminary Damage Assessment (PDA), the damages are of sufficient severity and magnitude to warrant assistance under the Act. (**NOTE:** In a particularly fast-moving or clearly devastating disaster, DHS may defer the PDA process until after the declaration.)

   a. If an emergency involves an area or facility for which the federal government exercises exclusive or preeminent responsibility and authority, the President may unilaterally direct the provision of emergency assistance under the Stafford Act. The governor of the affected state will be consulted if practicable.

   b. DHS can pre-deploy personnel and equipment in advance of an imminent Stafford Act declaration to lessen or avert the effects of a disaster and to improve the timeliness of disaster response.

   c. When an incident poses a threat to life and property that cannot be effectively dealt with by the state or local governments, the governor may request the Department of Defense (DoD) to use its resources after the incident occurs but prior to a Stafford Act declaration to perform any emergency work *essential for the preservation of life and property* under Section 403 of the Stafford Act.

National Response Plan

In the U.S., Homeland Security Presidential Directive (HSPD)-5, *Management of Domestic Incidents*, required the creation of the National Response Plan (NRP) to integrate federal government prevention, preparedness, response, recovery and mitigation plans into one all-discipline, all-hazard approach to domestic incident management. This plan was developed through an inclusive interagency, interjurisdictional process incorporating the expertise and recommendations of federal, state, local, tribal, and private-sector stakeholders. Similar efforts have occurred in Canada and its provinces.

The NRP and National Incident Management System (NIMS) provide the framework and processes that weave all of the capabilities and resources of the jurisdictions, disciplines, and levels of government and the private sector into a cohesive, unified, coordinated, and seamless national approach to domestic incident management. To accomplish a successful interagency team, the U.S. Department of Homeland Security (DHS) adopted NIMS in 2004. The benefits of these team approaches are as follows:

- Establish a common, agreed-upon set of goals.
- Reduce jurisdictional conflicts or *turf wars*.
- Create a forum to critique the team's performance in incident management.
- Create a controlled environment for the discussion of operational issues.

- Encourage sharing of resources.
- Build personal and professional relationships between participants.
- Increase understanding and respect between agencies.

The NRP (using NIMS) provides the core organizational structure and operational mechanisms for the following:

- Federal support to state and local authorities
- Implementation of direct federal incident management authorities and responsibilities under the law
- Full coordination of resources among federal departments and agencies

Key local government personnel, such as chief officers, elected officials, police chiefs, and others, should become familiar with the implementation of the NRP through their local emergency management agency.

The plan also calls for ongoing coordination among federal, state, local, tribal, private sector, and nongovernmental organization partners in an effort to keep the NRP current, incorporate best practices, and leverage emerging technologies and systems over the long term. The NRP calls for maximum integration and coordination at all levels of government and between government and private entities to optimize resources and better inform crisis decision-makers.

In the U.S., fire and emergency services personnel will have relationships with the following federal agencies:

- Department of Homeland Security (DHS)
- Bureau of Indian Affairs (BIA)
- Environmental Protection Agency (EPA)
- Department of Agriculture, Forest Service
- Department of the Interior (DOI)
- Department of Defense (DoD)
- Department of Justice (DOJ)
- Occupational Safety and Health Administration (OSHA)
- National Institute for Occupational Safety and Health (NIOSH)

- Department of the Treasury
- Centers for Disease Control and Prevention (CDC)

Canadian fire and emergency services organizations likewise are involved with the following organizations:

- Canadian Transport Emergency Centre (CANUTEC)
- Office of Critical Infrastructure Protection and Emergency Preparedness (OCIPEP)
- Joint Emergency Preparedness Program (JEPP)
- Department of National Defense and the Canadian Forces

Relationships with federal agencies can provide increased benefits and opportunities if the fire and emergency services organization recognizes and pursues them. Information, grants, funding, equipment, and support are available both during emergency preparedness planning and during a declared emergency. Company officers who are assigned the task of researching the availability of grants or locating information of response plans should have a list of federal resources available to them.

Company Officer Participation

All company officers will have some participation in interagency and intergovernmental relations. Knowledge of the existing agreements and the process that creates the agreements is important for all officers. However, the Fire Officer II must have the requisite knowledge of interagency and intergovernmental relations to develop operational plans involving multijurisdictional responses.

The company officer may be assigned to the planning, training, implementing, monitoring, evaluating, and/or revising of interagency and intergovernmental agreements **(Figure 24.7)**. As the representative of the fire and emergency services organization, the company officer must keep the interests of the organization in mind while also considering the best interests of the community. Representing the organization often requires knowledge of politics and the key players, as well as skills in diplomacy and collaboration. At the same time, the officer must have full knowledge of the resources and commitment that the organization can offer and the resources that other agencies or jurisdictions will be required to provide.

Planning

The company officer who is assigned to the planning process must be familiar with the assets and resources of the organization and the needs of the community. Working with representatives of other local, state/provincial, and federal agencies and organizations, the representatives create an inventory list of their total assets. The representatives prepare a list of the types of threats to their area and the specific targets that are at risk. They may also list the consequences that could occur in the event that one or more of these threats occurs.

For instance, the committee would list as a community asset the local water supply including the original source (river, lake, underground spring, or desalination plant), the purification system, storage facilities, and distribution system. It would then list any possible threats to the system. One threat might be the disruption of the local water supply caused by an earthquake. This consequence would require a response plan that would mitigate the threat. The resources that might be used to address this consequence would be the assignment of water tenders and commercial tank trucks for the transportation of water or the establishment of a contract with a vendor to provide bottles of drinking water (**Figure 24.8**).

When the emergency response plan and contingency plans are developed, the interagency and intergovernmental agreements are written to provide the method and circumstances for implementing the plans. All participating organizations must then ratify and sign the agreements.

Training

Once the agreements have been adopted by the participating agencies, personnel from each agency must be trained in their responsibilities. First, each separate agency or organization communicates the agreement to its membership. Each agency or organization assigns responsibility for implementation and then trains its personnel in the various aspects of the agreement. All agencies and their members must be informed of their responsibilities and authority once the agreement is signed and adopted.

Joint training exercises must be held after each agency or organization has trained in its assigned tasks and is familiar with the NIMS/ICS that will be used at each type of emergency. Company officers may be responsible for planning these scenarios and will participate in them in some fashion. Post-training critiques must be part of the exercises to permit participants the opportunity to learn from their experience.

Figure 24.7 While working on an aid agreement, the company officer must keep in mind the interests of the organization as well as the community.

Figure 24.8 Outside vendors provided bottles and cans of drinking water during the aftermath of Katrina. *Courtesy of Mark Wolfe, FEMA.*

During Hurricane Katrina, fire department chief officers thought they were naturally in charge of rescue and fire suppression functions. However, they learned that Louisiana State Wildlife and Fisheries was in charge of rescue and Agriculture was in charge of fire fighting. Fire agencies didn't know this prior to the event and neither did Agriculture or Wildlife and Fisheries. This lack of communication cost precious time in coordination efforts and resulted in increased suffering for the victims. The time for the first training event shouldn't be the first emergency event where the plan is implemented.

Figure 24.9 All fire officers must be prepared to work the triage area at an incident.

Implementing

The agreements will be implemented when conditions warrant, which may include situations such as the following:

- Terrorism threat level reaches a specified level.

- Intelligence indicates a threat may be imminent.

- Weather conditions indicate a threat is imminent.

- An emergency incident has already occurred.

- The Incident Commander or other authority requests implementation.

All fire officers within the organization must know their assigned duties in the event the agreement is implemented. In some cases, their assignment may not be their normal duty assignment **(Figure 24.9)**.

Monitoring

The agreements are monitored throughout their existence. Records are maintained on the planning process, the results of training scenarios and postincident critiques, and on the strengths and weaknesses exhibited during the actual implementation of the agreement.

Company officers must write accurate training and emergency incident reports. These reports provide a basis to assist in the evaluation of the effectiveness of the agreement and of the training provided to the participants. Postincident critiques

Figure 24.10 Interagency postincident critique.

held after training scenarios and actual incidents provide data that can be used in the evaluation of the agreements **(Figure 24.10)**.

Evaluating

To be effective, the agreement must be evaluated periodically and after each use. Periodic evaluation, usually annually, allows the participating agencies or organizations to report any changes in their needs or their resources. New hazards or facilities in the affected area, the reduction in personnel or equipment due to budget cuts, or the discovery of a new and potent threat will all require that the agreement be altered, augmented, or perhaps abandoned and replaced by a different agreement.

The company officer may be assigned the duty of evaluating the needs and resources of the organization and comparing them to the provisions of the agreement. Information gathered from a postincident critique may also point to the need to make changes in the agreement. The company officer may be responsible for writing an objective report and making a recommendation based on the results of the evaluation.

Revising

The evaluation may result in retaining the agreement as is, replacing it completely, or revising it. Retaining the agreement will require no action while replacing it completely will require the process to begin over in the planning stage. Revising the agreement will be similar to the planning phase.

Revising the agreement will require that the planning committee made up of representatives of each agency or organization review the evaluation report and determine the appropriate action. By considering the strengths and weaknesses found in the evaluation, the committee can determine what changes must be made. Once the changes have been made to the agreement, it must be approved by the participating organizations. The changes are then communicated to the personnel who use the agreement and training is provided to them.

Summary

Company officers will be in contact with representatives from other agencies, organizations, and governmental bodies often during their careers. The interaction may be with local law enforcement personnel at traffic accidents, state/provincial authorities at a hazardous materials spill, or federal officials at a major natural disaster. In every case, the interaction company officers and their organizations have with other agencies and jurisdictions must include planning, training, and practice. They must be prepared to establish ICS, recognize and adhere to jurisdictional authority, and to request the correct assistance from the appropriate agency or governmental entity.

Analyses, Evaluations, and Statistics

Chapter Contents

Learning Objectives

1. Define *analysis*.

2. Select facts about the analysis process.

3. Identify the types of analysis.

4. Identify the steps in the analysis process.

5. Analyze scenarios and make recommendations about reports involving accidents, injuries, illnesses, or fatalities.

6. Define *evaluation*.

7. Compare the terms effective and efficient.

8. Select facts about evaluating personnel.

9. Recall information about evaluating personnel.

10. Select facts about evaluating information.

11. Define *statistics*.

12. Identify the importance of statistics.

13. Match statistical terms to their definitions.

14. Select facts about the process of gathering data.

15. Identify visual aids and how they are used.

Job Performance Requirements

This chapter provides information that addresses the following job performance requirements of NFPA 1021, *Standard for Fire Officer Professional Qualifications* :

Chapter 25
Analyses, Evaluations, and Statistics

In life as well as in the fire and emergency services, people use analysis and evaluation daily. Comparing the price of food in the market, evaluating the effectiveness of a tool or process, or deciding what to order at a restaurant all require the application of analytical or evaluative thinking.

At emergency incidents, company officers analyze each piece of information during the size-up to determine the most appropriate action to take. When the incident is terminated, they perform a postincident analysis to determine what actions were effective and those that were ineffective.

Likewise, company officers evaluate personnel, processes, and equipment. Personnel evaluation takes place informally on a daily basis and formally on an annual basis. Processes, such as unit training, are evaluated for their ability to provide personnel with the correct skills and knowledge in the most efficient manner. Evaluating equipment, tools, apparatus, and materials is required when the company officer is tasked with recommending the purchase of these items.

To be able to apply the concepts of analysis and evaluation, the company officer must know what they are, how they differ, and when and how to apply them. Additionally, the use of statistics is also important. Because statistics is a very involved topic, it is recommended that company officers who are going to use it frequently go beyond the brief introduction provided in this chapter. Courses in statistical analysis are available at community colleges and universities in most areas or online through distance learning programs. The National Fire Academy also has courses and resource material available to the company officer.

Analysis Process

Analyzing is the process of methodically examining the various parts of an item, project, or incident. This analysis is then used to determine how the item or project works or how an incident occurred or was controlled. Analysis implies an objective study of the widest array of facts, statistics, or data. It involves looking at each piece or component to determine how it interacts with other parts and how they work together to create the whole. Analysis may require looking at the facts repeatedly to try to make all the pieces fit, much like assembling a massive jigsaw puzzle (**Figure 25.1**). In some in-

Analysis is Making the Pieces Fit

Figure 25.1 Analyzing a problem is similar to putting a jigsaw puzzle together. To make sense of the big picture, all the parts must fit.

stances, it also means analyzing the data compiled by opposition forces to determine if it is valid.

A very graphic example of analyzing an incident is the meticulous review of the *Challenger* and *Columbia* space shuttle tragedies by the U.S. National Aeronautics and Space Administration (NASA). Each available piece of debris and evidence was reviewed to determine how the incidents occurred **(Figure 25.2)**. When all the various parts were analyzed, the information was gathered into final reports that were evaluated to determine the root cause of the incidents and to recommend corrective actions to be taken.

According to the USFA *Fire Data Analysis Handbook*, analysis is the process of transforming raw data into information, information into understanding, and understanding into decisions. For the process to produce effective decisions, the raw data must be accurate and as complete as possible. Tools like the NFIRS report forms help the company officer to record the data in a consistent format that will permit it to be retrieved as needed.

Obviously, analysis precedes evaluation, and both precede drawing any conclusions or making a decision. Conclusions based on solid analysis and evaluation have a strong foundation and are defendable against speculation and criticism. Therefore, it is important to understand the types of analyses that a company officer may be required

to perform, the general steps in the analytical process, and the application of these steps to the various tasks assigned to that officer.

Types

There are numerous types of analysis, many more than the company officer will be required to perform. Those analysis types that benefit the company officer are those that concern cost/benefit, process, policy, program, needs, and risk.

Cost/Benefit

Cost/benefit analysis is based on the relationship between the effort (cost) and the result (benefit). To be successful or effective, the benefit must match or exceed the cost to justify the program, process, or purchase; however, justification is difficult when the expenditures are based on an existing risk rather than a likely event (possibility vs. probability). Public officials sometimes refer to this benefit as *return on investment* (ROI). It can be applied to the purchase of a new piece of equipment; staffing; facility construction, design, or location; and many other situations. One example of a cost/benefit analysis would be comparing the cost of purchase, installation, maintenance, testing, and user training for a new breathing air compressor to the cost of an annual contract with an outside vendor to supply the same service **(Figure 25.3)**. Another example is weighing the cost of hiring, training, and equipping new personnel against the cost of maintaining the current staffing level and paying overtime or associated sick leave benefits that may result from an increase in injuries or illnesses.

Two other elements of the cost/benefit analysis are cost avoidance and financial consequences. Cost avoidance occurs when a person or organization takes action that will prevent a future expense. The action can be as simple as scheduled periodic oil changes on an apparatus that prevent the need to replace a burned-out engine or retire an apparatus earlier than projected. Financial consequences, on the other hand, are costs that will occur by not taking a specific action or by purchasing a high-maintenance piece of equipment. For example, the financial consequences of installing carpet into a fire station, which would require frequent cleaning or short-life expectancy, would have to be consid-

Figure 25.2 Following the space shuttle *Columbia* disaster, NASA was faced with the task of determining the cause by analyzing all the factors that contributed to the incident. Each fragment of the shuttle that could be recovered was inspected and placed on a grid that represented the original location of the part in the shuttle. *Courtesy of the National Aeronautics and Space Administration.*

and the program is available from the USFA. It can help communities develop objective, quantifiable risk-reduction policies. Risk analysis is another analysis tool that relies on determining probability.

Steps

The steps in the analysis process progress from specific items to general items; that is, from the smallest part or element to the complete subject item, program, or process. Once the results of the analysis are known and collected, they can be evaluated for worth and a decision can be made. The steps may vary slightly depending on the application. In general, however, the steps needed to accomplish the analysis process are as follows:

- Determine each of the components that compose the larger item, program, or process.

- Follow a systematic process each time an analysis is made, using the same steps so that they become familiar.

- Try to remain objective and not come to a conclusion before all the facts are known.

- Go over all the various components and look for a pattern or relationship between the components.

- Seek the advice of others by discussing the analysis with them or involving them in the process.

- Attempt to look at the item, program, or process from the viewpoint of others who will be affected by it, which would include both service providers and customers.

- Set the analysis aside for a short time and take a break unless there is a definite deadline for completion. This action allows for a fresh view and may generate a new approach.

- Try to develop at least two approaches to the problem so that multiple approaches can be evaluated for effectiveness and value. This approach generates a minimum of three options: the best, a compromise, and status quo (no action at all).

Evaluation Process

While analyzing is determining how the various parts of the whole work and fit together, *evaluating* is establishing the worth or value of each of those parts (or the whole) based on the desired outcome. Evaluation determines how effective and efficient a person, a program, a process, or an item is compared to a benchmark or established set of criteria (**Figure 25.6**). While analysis is objective, evaluat-

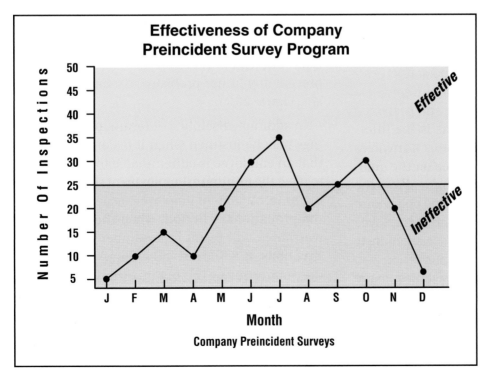

Figure 25.6 Benchmarks can be used to determine the effectiveness of a program. In this example, it is apparent that the company preincident survey program has not been as effective as the organization might like.

ing is subjective, depending on the knowledge and experience of the evaluator. Although evaluation is defined as the appraisal of persons, projects, or organizations in relation to stated criteria or standards, the interpretation of the criteria or standards is subject to personal bias.

Evaluating Personnel

As supervisors and managers, company officers must periodically evaluate the personnel who work for them. Formal personnel evaluations are conducted when employees are hired, continually during the probationary employment period, annually as part of a performance review, for promotional purposes, or for disciplinary or termination purposes. Each of these evaluations will be discussed in length in Chapter 26 of this manual.

While the organization's formal personnel evaluation program is necessary to maintain complete and documented personnel files, the preferred approach to personnel evaluations is the informal approach. The informal approach involves providing feedback to the employee on the quality of work that person is performing. It allows the supervisor to correct performance and behavioral problems quickly, and it provides the employee with the knowledge that the supervisor is genuinely concerned. This type of personal interaction also allows the employee to ask for assistance, make suggestions, and learn more about the job.

The informal personnel evaluations then become the basis for the formal periodic performance review. Performance objectives that were agreed upon in the informal evaluation are included in the formal review to indicate that they have been accomplished. The personnel evaluation program has the following advantages:

- Creates a permanent record of the employee's achievements for the purpose of awards, promotions, transfers, discipline, and termination

- Makes the need for additional training apparent; if warranted, new programs can be developed to address the deficiency if it appears to be widespread

- Helps the supervisor become more familiar with the personnel being evaluated

- Motivates personnel to improve

- Increases the awareness of higher levels of management of the abilities of lower-level supervisors and managers

- Illuminates the specific talents of individuals who may be used in other areas of the organization

- Improves the efficiency of both employees and the organization as a whole

All personnel evaluations should be timely. That is, they should occur when the need becomes apparent. The informal approach allows for this to happen. If the employee is performing at or above the anticipated level, personal recognition will help to instill pride in the employee. If there is a need to correct a work habit that is not meeting the required standard, immediate attention to the issue will lessen the effect of the work habit and prevent any future problems associated with the act **(Figure 25.7)**.

In addition, discipline or termination proceedings may be justified when it becomes apparent that an employee is either unable to or unwilling to meet the minimum employment standard. Failing to terminate an employee, especially during the probationary period, when the reasons are warranted will result in a number of unwanted situations. It will cause other employees to view the supervisor or the organization as being inconsistent with established policies. It will create resentment within the work force and create the impression that the organization is unwilling to deal with this type of situation. It will send the

Figure 25.7 Informal personnel evaluations are continuous and should provide the subordinate with immediate feedback on skills and behaviors.

message to other employees that nothing will happen to them if they too break rules, regulations, policies, and/or procedures. Discipline should be constructive and remedial and not punitive. See Chapter 26 for additional information on the discipline process.

Some organizations have a *Sunset Policy* that retires or eliminates minor disciplinary action from personnel records after a specified length of time or after the completion of required counseling or other activities. The company officer must be aware of any policies that eliminate such records and adhere to them.

Evaluating Equipment/Materials

All equipment used by fire and emergency services organizations should be evaluated for its ability to perform specific functions. These evaluations usually occur when specifications are developed or when the equipment is purchased. Evaluations of in-service equipment or materials, such as apparatus or extinguishing agents, may occur periodically to determine whether the item still meets the original requirements. Periodic evaluations are also required by the NFPA standards for apparatus or equipment.

New equipment. To evaluate new equipment, tools, or materials, it is necessary to determine what their use will be **(Figure 25.8)**. These criteria are developed from a job/task analysis or a risk

Figure 25.8 Prior to purchasing new equipment, such as a vehicle extrication system, the organization should perform an evaluation. The evaluation should be based on the actual use the equipment is intended to have.

analysis. The job or task analysis is a review of the various functions for which the item will be used. Examples of criteria are as follows:

- How many people will be required to operate the item?

- How much should the item weigh?

- Is the item to be used for prying, cutting, battering, or pulling?

- How much storage space is required for the item if carried on a vehicle?

A risk analysis is used to establish criteria for items such as extinguishing agents, respiratory protection equipment, or protective clothing. In this case, the minimum acceptable level of performance (or maximum acceptable level of risk) is determined and the equipment evaluated against that level. Equipment or materials must meet or exceed that level to be acceptable to the organization. These criteria are normally available from national organizations or from the federal government.

Additionally, new equipment, tools, or materials may be evaluated on a cost/benefit basis. In this case, the cost of a specific quantity or item is compared to the effectiveness of the item. For instance, one gallon of foam concentrate costs **X** dollars and will produce **Y** gallons of solution. The solution will extinguish **Z** square feet or meters of a Class B fire when applied through a compressed air foam system. Similar types of foam can then be compared to each other based on this data.

In-service equipment. Some in-service evaluations are common practice in the fire and emergency services. Annual hose, ground ladder, aerial ladders, PPE, and pump tests are used to determine if the equipment is still effective and meeting predetermined criteria. Other evaluations may include the sampling of extinguishment agents for laboratory testing, field tests of foam agents on live fires, and visual examinations of life safety ropes and harnesses **(Figure 25.9)**. In each instance a minimum level of acceptable service is established and the equipment/material is tested to that standard. The records of each year's testing are used to compare and determine the wear of materials and the remaining useful life of the material.

Evaluating Information

It is very important for the company officer to be able to critically evaluate information. This information may come from any of a variety of sources: peers, subordinates, personal observations, surveys, the Internet, vendors, etc. The types of information gathered from these sources may include product information, personnel behaviors, program effectiveness, or emergency incident situations. The challenge for the company officer is to objectively determine what information is accurate, factual, and reliable and what is inaccurate, false, or unreliable.

One approach is to always be cautious. Never take any information at face value. Is the source reliable? Is the source biased? The company officer should always remember that there are two sides to every story and that some *facts* may be perceived differently by the participants or observers. Performing additional research on the subject matter provides the company officer with better information on which to base an opinion or decision **(Figure 25.10)**.

A second approach is to use variety. To use variety is to compare and contrast various sources for the same information. In addition to asking the previous questions listed, gather the same information from other participants, observers, competitors, or peers. Similar responses will help to validate the information that was initially gathered.

The types of data or information that is collected, along with the sources, will depend on the program, project, item, or situation that is being evaluated. However, all evaluations should follow a similar plan to ensure consistency.

Figure 25.9 Field tests on the use of various types of extinguishing agents can be performed during training activities.

Evaluating Information in a Book, Journal Article, or Internet Web Site

Ask the following questions:

- Is the author credible?
- What is the reputation of the publisher?
- Is there a bibliography and is it annotated?
- Are the facts and statistics verifiable?
- Are the facts and statistics complete or only the portion that supports the author's thesis?
- Is the information biased?
- Is the information current?
- Is there peer review or consensus validation?

Figure 25.10 When evaluating resource materials used for research, the company officer must be careful to ensure the validity and factualness of the information.

Evaluation Plan

The basic framework for all types of evaluations should be maintained in a written evaluation plan adopted by the organization. This plan will contain the step-by-step process for the various types of evaluations. It ensures that the process is carried out in the same manner each time it is implemented. The plan should contain enough information for anyone to understand and follow it.

When the appropriate evaluation plan is applied to a program, project, individual, or item, it can be used as the basis for the evaluation report. That is, it can act as the outline upon which the information is developed. Records must be kept on all formal evaluations. Not only is this mandated in some jurisdictions, it is also good business practice. The company officer should remember that, with a few exceptions, the records maintained by the organization are open to the public. However, it is important to note that personnel and medical records are *not* open to the public.

Statistics

The term *statistics* has three meanings. First, it is a science within the field of mathematics. Second, it is a mathematical process consisting of concepts, rules, and processes for collecting, organizing, and interpreting numerical data that is used to determine trends, make decisions, and compare information. Finally, the term is used to describe the resulting numerical information that is developed from the analysis of the raw data **(Figure 25.11)**.

As mentioned previously, the statistics that result from the analysis process are only as accurate as the raw data that is entered into the process. If the input data is flawed, inaccurate, or incomplete,

the statistics will be inaccurate and unusable. The result could also be costly and even result in loss of life.

The company officer should have a working knowledge of statistics. At the very least, the officer should be able to recognize the terms and concepts associated with the statistical process. The ability to recognize statistics that are biased or inaccurate will also help the company officer make informed decisions when purchasing materials and equipment. Company officers who must use and rely on statistics in the completion of their duties are encouraged to take college-level courses in statistics.

Importance of Statistics

While many decisions do not require the use of statistical analysis, such as personnel decisions, grievance proceedings, promotions, and emergency incident decisions, the efficient use of resources demands the decisions be supported by statistics. Statistics can provide the justification required for staffing, station location, apparatus purchases, and service levels.

According to the *Fire Data Analysis Handbook*, there are three good reasons for relying on statistics:

1. To gain insights into fire and emergency service needs

2. To improve resource allocation for providing emergency services

3. To identify training needs

Probably the most compelling reason is that analysis gives insight into fire and life safety problems, which in turn can affect the organization's operations.

Collecting data on response times and analyzing it can provide an accurate view of how often the organization meets the national average for responses. It will also indicate the geographic areas of the community where the actual response time is higher than the target time. For example, the average response time to emergency incidents in an area is 6 minutes, compared to less than 4 minutes overall. This comparison may be helpful in justifying the relocation of apparatus and personnel or in the construction of an additional fire station.

Statistics

Statistics can be defined as:

- A branch of mathematics concerned with the collection of numerical facts.
- A set of concepts, rules, and procedures used to analyze numerical information and organize and illustrate it in the form of tables, graphs, and charts.
- Data that can be represented numerically.

Figure 25.11 The word *statistics* can have three meanings.

NFPA 1710 Response Criteria

As an example of how the fire and emergency services use statistics, the following is provided. NFPA 1710, *Standard for the Organization and Deployment of Fire Suppression Operations, Emergency Medical Operations, and Special Operations to the Public by Career Fire Departments*, establishes the following response criteria in Chapters 4 and 5:

4.1.2.1 The fire department shall establish the following time objectives:

(1) One minute (60 seconds) for turnout time

(2)*Four minutes (240 seconds) or less for the arrival of the first arriving engine company at a fire suppression incident and/or 8 minutes (480 seconds) or less for the deployment of a full first alarm assignment at a fire suppression incident

(3) Four minutes (240 seconds) or less for the arrival of a unit with first responder or higher level capability at an emergency medical incident

(4) Eight minutes (480 seconds) or less for the arrival of an advanced life support unit at an emergency medical incident, where this service is provided by the fire department

5.2.4.1 Initial Arriving Company.

5.2.4.1.1 The fire department's fire suppression resources shall be deployed to provide for the arrival of an engine company within a 4-minute response time and/or the initial full alarm assignment within an 8-minute response time to 90 percent of the incidents as established in Chapter 4 (4.1.2.1).

5.2.4.2 Initial Full Alarm Assignment Capability.

5.2.4.2.1* The fire department shall have the capability to deploy an initial full alarm assignment within an 8-minute response time to 90 percent of the incidents as established in Chapter 4 (4.1.2.1).

A fire and emergency services organization would collect response data based on turn out time, arrival time of first unit, and arrival time of each of the remaining units. This information would be collected for all fire suppression and medical responses made by all emergency units in the organization. The data would be averaged and the results compared to the criteria listed above. Any results that did not meet the criteria would be investigated to determine the cause for the delay (unit out of service requiring longer response distance, traffic congestion, etc.) and corrective action would be taken.

Reviewing data on the number of emergency responses can provide an overview of the effect that the time of day has on the frequency of calls. For instance, the center of an urban area may be congested with people during the workday and relatively empty at night and on weekends. This data could be used to justify relocating personnel and apparatus during the less active times and increasing the number of units available in the residential areas.

Finally, job-related injury reports may indicate a trend in back and shoulder strains and injuries (**Figure 25.12**. By quantifying the activities that personnel were performing when they were injured, an effective response could be developed to reduce or eliminate the injuries. Depending on the data, solutions might range from providing training in proper lifting techniques, purchasing back support braces, or relocating heavy tools to lower compartments on the apparatus.

Without accurate and timely reports, trends and problem areas may not be recognized, and potentially dangerous situations may be allowed to exist.

It is essential for the company officer to collect, compile, record, and submit accurate data on all unit activities including emergency and nonemergency responses and daily station training and activities. The company officer has the opportunity to ensure that data gathered at the company level is complete and, therefore, valuable.

Process

Statistics are generated through a process that involves the gathering of data. There are three generally accepted methods of research: survey, observation, and experimentation. Each method has its advantages and disadvantages.

Survey

The survey is the most commonly used method for gathering information (**Figure 25.13**). It can take the form of a face-to-face interview or a telephone, mail, or internet survey. The personal interview is the best method for obtaining personal, detailed, or in-depth information. It allows the interviewer to ask detailed open-ended questions while the

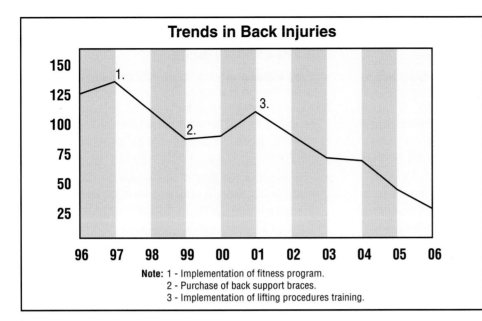

Figure 25.12 Tracking trends is particularly important to the decision-making process and for determining the effectiveness of a procedure, policy, or program.

Trends in Back Injuries

Note: 1 - Implementation of fitness program.
2 - Purchase of back support braces.
3 - Implementation of lifting procedures training.

OMB #3067-0260 EXPIRES NOVEMBER 30, 2005

NATIONAL FIRE ACADEMY
Long-Term Evaluation Form for Supervisors

This two-sided form concerns the course recently completed by the fire service professional (the "attendee") identified in the cover letter to this questionnaire. Please respond to the items as best you can. All responses will be *completely* confidential. Although each questionnaire has an identification number, it is used only to track the return of the form and to link it to the form returned by the attendee. After your questionnaire has been processed, it will be destroyed. Your answers will be reported along with those of other supervisors, and no one will know what you specifically have said. Do not write your name on this form.

*Public reporting burden for this form is estimated to average 10 minutes per response. The burden estimate includes the time for reviewing instructions, searching existing data sources, gathering and maintaining the needed data, and completing, reviewing and submitting the form. You are not required to respond to this collection of information unless a valid OMB control number appears in the upper right corner of this form. Send comments regarding the accuracy of the burden estimate and any suggestions for reducing the burden to: Information Collections Management, Federal Emergency Management Agency, 500 C Street, SW, Washington, DC 20472. **Note: Do not send the completed form to the above address.***

USE NO. 2 PENCIL ▦ or BLUE or BLACK INK PEN
CORRECT MARK ○ ● ○

Part I: Evaluation of Training Impacts

Please indicate your level of agreement or disagreement with each statement by filling in the appropriate bubble.

	Strongly Agree			Strongly Disagree	Don't Know or Not Applicable
1. The NFA training course has improved the job performance of this attendee.	○	○	○	○	○
2. This course contributed to the attendee's professional development.	○	○	○	○	○
3. This course has prepared the student for the next level of responsibility in our organization.	○	○	○	○	○
4. Material from this training has been incorporated into the prevention work of this department.	○	○	○	○	○
5. This training has helped the department address fire-related problems in our community's *high risk* areas.	○	○	○	○	○
6. The information gained in this class is likely to improve the performance of this department.	○	○	○	○	○
7. This NFA training course has met the expectations we had in sending our department member to the NFA.	○	○	○	○	○
8. The attendee's participation in this course has led to reductions in the overall fire-related risks in our community.	○	○	○	○	○
9. The benefit to the department of having the attendee go to the training outweighed the costs involved.	○	○	○	○	○
10. The attendee has trained (formally or informally) other colleagues in the procedures learned at NFA training.	○	○	○	○	○
11. I am likely to recommend NFA training to other department personnel.	○	○	○	○	○

FF, 95-58, NOV 02 *Please continue on the reverse side of this form.*

Figure 25.13 Example of a survey used to evaluate course effectiveness. *Courtesy of the U. S. National Fire Academy.*

Terminology

To understand statistics, the company officer should know a few of the terms that are used to describe the subject. Some of the terms, such as *validity* and *reliability*, may be familiar from Instructor I certification courses. These terms are used in the creation of test items used in training evaluation examinations. Other terms, such as *norm* and *median*, may be familiar from general usage.

- *Validity* refers to the accuracy or truthfulness of a measurement. Is the experiment measuring what it is intended to measure? This may seem like a simple concept, but it is extremely difficult to determine if a measurement is valid. Generally, validity is based solely on the judgment of the researcher.

- *Reliability* is synonymous with repeatability. A measurement that yields consistent results over time is said to be reliable. When a measurement is prone to random error, it lacks reliability. The reliability of an instrument places an upper limit on its validity because if it lacks reliability it will also lack validity.

- The *average* or *norm* is a statistic describing the location of a distribution. For instance, the average response time in the community is 4.5 minutes. The average is derived at by adding all identical quantities and dividing by the number of quantities.

- The *statistical method or procedure* is the method used to analyze or represent statistical data. For instance, determining the number of fires in a community per capita requires that the population be divided by 1,000. The total number of fires is then divided by the resulting number. For example, the city of Harterville has a population of 50,000. Last year the city had 500 fires. To determine the per capita number of fires, divide 50,000 by 1,000, which results in the number 50. Then divide 500 by 50, which indicates that the per capita number of fires is 10.

- *Statistical distribution* refers to the arrangement of values of a variable showing their observed or theoretical frequency of occurrence. The distribution may be illustrated with a line or dot chart. See Visual Aids section at the end of this chapter.

- *Deviation* is the difference between an observed value and the expected value of a variable or function. For instance, if the expected response time is 4 minutes and the actual time is 5 minutes there is a deviation of 1 minute.

- *Statistical analysis* is sometimes used to determine the *central tendency*, which is a typical or representative value for a set of data. It can be reported as the *mean*, the *median*, or the *mode*, depending on the data or the purpose of the experiment.

- The *mean* is the sum of the values divided by the number of values. It may also be referred to as the average or the norm. To determine the mean:
  — Add all of the values together.
  — Divide by the number of values to obtain the mean.
  — Example: The mean of 7, 12, 24, 20, 19 is (7 + 12 + 24 + 20 + 19) / 5 = 16.4.

- The *median* is the value which divides the values into two equal halves, with half of the values being lower than the median and half higher than the median. To determine the median:
  — Sort the values into ascending order.
  — If you have an odd number of values, the median is the middle value.
  — If you have an even number of values, the median is the arithmetic mean (halfway between) the two middle values.

  Example: The median of the same five numbers (7, 12, 19, 20, 24) is 19.

- The *mode* is the most frequently occurring value or values in the dataset. It is determined by:
  — Calculating the frequencies for all of the values in the data
  — The value (or values) with the highest frequency

  Example: For an ambulance having the following number of responses per day, 18, 18, 19, 20, 20, 20, 21, and 23, the mode is 20.

- *Ratio* is an expression of the relative size of two numbers by showing one divided by the other. The relation between two quantities expressed as the quotient of one divided by the other: *The ratio of water to foam concentrate in a 6% solution is 94 parts water to 6 parts concentrate or 6/100.*

respondent has the ability to provide detailed answers. Telephone interviews are similar to face-to-face interviews and are a more efficient use of time and funds. A disadvantage is that they are limited in the amount of in-depth questioning that can be accomplished. Additionally, in the telephone interview the interviewer cannot see the nonverbal responses of the subject, reducing the quality of the answers. Mail and internet surveys are generally the most cost-effective interview methods. This is offset by the low return rate of survey forms.

Observation

Observation research is used to monitor the subject's actions without directly interacting with them (**Figure 25.14**). Direct observation can provide insight into how people use tools or products, communicate with each other, or behave in public. Indirect observation is used to determine the buying habits of consumers. Research companies track the sale of items by the bar code printed on the package that is scanned into the cash register at time of purchase. This type of observation can also indicate the popularity of items based on geographic areas and seasons of the year.

Experiment

In an experiment, the researcher changes one or more independent variables over the course of the research. When all other dependent variables remain constant (except the one being manipulated), changes in the dependent variable can be explained by the change in the independent variable. It is usually very difficult to control all the variables in the environment. Therefore, experiments are generally restricted to laboratory models where the investigator has more control over all the variables.

Visual Aids

When the statistics have been generated, they must be used in some meaningful and easily read form to be of value. Commonly accepted visual aids permit the statistics to be presented to decision makers or the public in such a way that the importance of the information is obvious. Visual aids that can be used to describe statistics and their relationships include histograms, bar charts, line charts, pie charts, dot charts, pictograms, and hot charts.

Histogram

A *histogram* is a column graph where the height of the columns indicates the relative numbers or frequencies or values of a variable (**Figure 25.15**). The values may be numeric, such as response times, or nonnumeric, such as days of the week. Histograms provide a much better method for getting the feel of a list of numbers and answering

Figure 25.14 Company officers can use observation techniques and checklists to evaluate the skill level of subordinates.

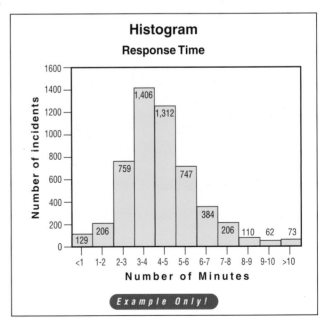

Figure 25.15 Sample histogram.

several questions about relationships. The patterns in a histogram are especially important, such as high and low frequencies and trends indicated by spikes, outliers, and gaps. Histograms give quick graphic representations of the data that otherwise would be hidden and hard to dig out of a table of numbers.

When viewing a histogram, the following patterns may be observed:

- Spikes are high or low points that stand out in a histogram.
- Gaps are spaces in a histogram reflecting low frequency of data.
- Outliers are extreme values isolated from the body of data.

Each of these patterns can be of value in the overall interpretation of the graph.

Bar Chart

A *bar chart* is one of the simplest and most effective ways to display data. In a bar chart, a bar is drawn for each category of data allowing for a visual comparison of the results (**Figure 25.16**). Interest in a list of this type usually centers on how the items compare to each other. Use a bar chart with categorical data when the objective is to show how the items in a category rank. Most fire and emergency

response data can be grouped in categories, such as cause of ignition, property use, area of origin, type of injury, etc. These categories are reflected on the NFIRS form as types of data that must be collected and submitted.

Column Charts

Column charts show frequency distributions that allow for easy identification of trends and other characteristics, particularly with time series data (**Figure 25.17**). The horizontal scale defines the natural groupings for the chart and the columns give the frequencies.

Another good application of column charts is to show comparisons across sets of data. Column charts of this type are particularly useful in demonstrating change over time. Where is the series increasing, decreasing, or staying about the same? If the analysis shows change over time, then column charts are particularly beneficial in presenting the changes.

Line Charts

Line charts are used to demonstrate increases, decreases, and fluctuations over time (**Figure 25.18**). An example of a line chart might be one that depicts the line-of-duty deaths (LODD) in the U.S. over a period of 25 years. Another version

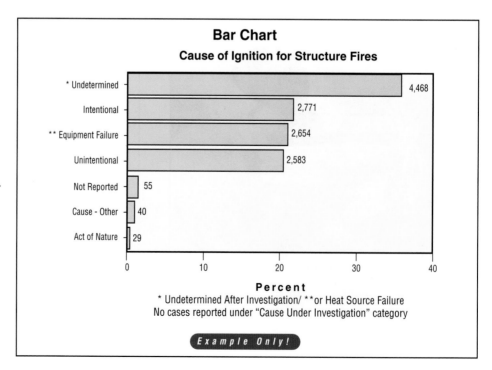

Figure 25.16 Sample Bar Chart.

could be used to show the same data by month for a particular year.

The column or line chart is used for data with a natural order, such as hours, months, or age groups. The chart depicts the general pattern and indicates points of special interest, such as spikes, gaps, and outliers.

Pie Charts

A pie chart is an effective way of showing how each component contributes to the whole (**Figure 25.19**). In a pie chart, each wedge represents the amount for a given category. The entire pie chart accounts for all of the categories. The percentages are included with each wedge label. Although the percentage numbers are not necessary, they aid in comparisons of the wedges.

For example, a pie chart could be used to illustrate the total budget for the organization. The pie chart might emphasize the fact that the largest percentage of the budget is dedicated to personnel costs including wages and benefits. In addition,

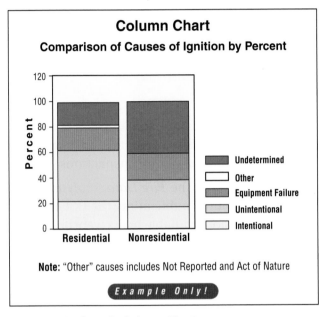

Figure 25.17 Sample Column Chart.

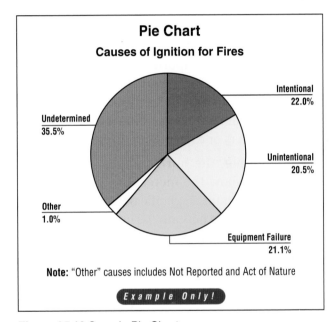

Figure 25.19 Sample Pie Chart.

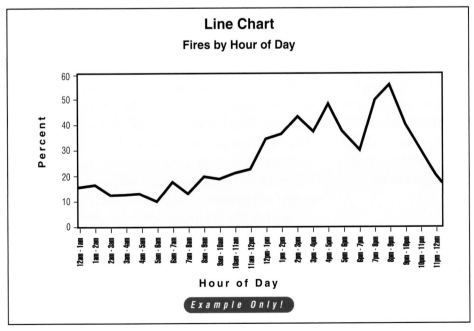

Figure 25.18 Sample Line Chart.

operating costs such as fuel, tools and equipment, PPE, and other noncapital purchases could be shown in relation to the cost of personnel.

A pie chart is beneficial when the objective is to show how the components relate to the whole. It is recommended that the number of components be kept to six or less and that the forming of several pie charts for comparison purposes be avoided.

Dot Charts

Dot charts or *scatter diagrams* emphasize the relationship between two variables (**Figure 25.20**). Generally, these variables are continuous rather than categorical. The pattern between the two variables is the important aspect for a dot chart. The pattern is more important than the individual dots on the chart. The horizontal axis of the chart reflects the cause while the vertical axis reflects the resulting variable. Dot charts are a very good way to show outliers or extremes in the data.

For example, the horizontal axis of the dot chart might show the increase in population of the service area for a specific period of time. The vertical axis might contain the number of medical responses in increments of 1,000. The location of the dots would indicate the relationship between the number of medical responses and the population at any given time.

Pictograms

Pictograms use pictures or maps to display data (**Figure 25.21**). Data by geographical areas, such as counties, census tracts, states/provinces, or fire districts can be presented on maps showing the boundaries of the areas. A pictogram is a pictorial representation of the data. The breakdown by geographic areas displays the relationship between the area and the type of information collected. For example, the number of tornados that various states experience in a specified period of time could be used in emergency management planning.

Hot Charts

Hot charts are another type of visual aid display, similar to a histogram (**Figure 25.22**). A hot chart is a diagram or map that highlights the occurrence of certain types of events. For example, by illustrating where fires occurred in the jurisdiction over a

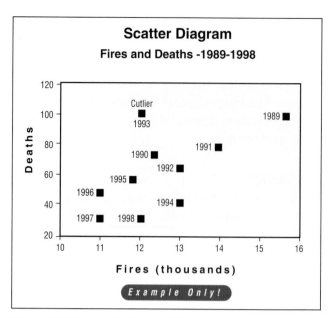

Figure 25.20 Sample Scatter Diagram.

six-month period, the organization can target that area with fire and life safety education, free smoke detectors, or voluntary home inspections.

NOTE: Although the *Fire Data Analysis Handbook* (1995) is out of publication, the USFA/FEMA has a 2003 version available on its website. Access is free, and the document is worth downloading

Determining Which Type to Use

When deciding which type of visual aid to use, the company officer should attempt to answer two questions:

- What are the main conclusions from the analysis?

- What is the best way to display the conclusions?

Answering these questions can assist in the selection and development of the appropriate graph or chart. In addition, it is best to consider the audience when selecting the visual aid to use. The audience may be an internal group including chief officers or other officials, an outside association or group of citizens, or even the own city or county governing body. The audience itself influences the type of chart that is selected.

Therefore, the first step is to determine the key results from the data. Once they have been identified, a selection of the best type of chart to convey to them must be made. Often it is helpful to try

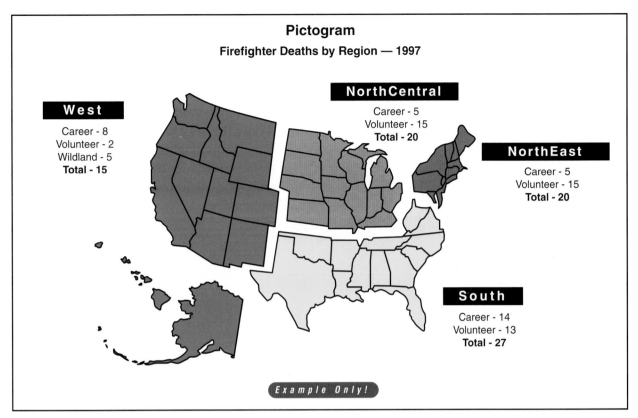

Figure 25.21 Sample Pictogram.

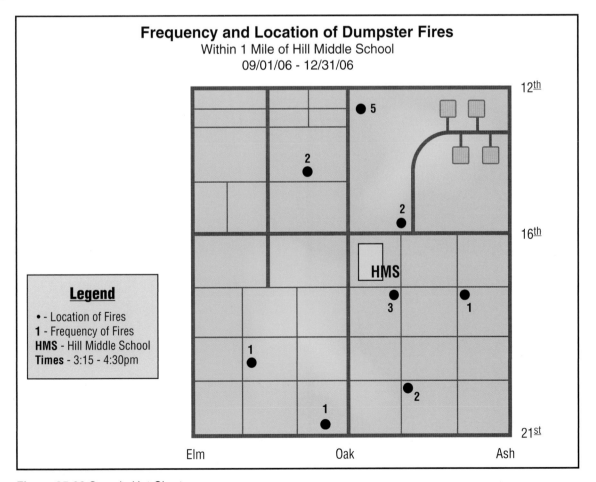

Figure 25.22 Sample Hot Chart

different charts to determine the best presentation format for a particular set of data and for a particular audience. The relationship of the data and its importance to the audience must be immediately evident to anyone who sees the visual aid.

Summary

The managing company officer will be required to analyze situations, evaluate personnel and equipment, and use statistics regularly while performing administrative functions. The ability to accurately and objectively report the results of these processes will be essential to the decision-making activities of the fire chief and senior management staff. They must also be able to understand statistics and identify the most appropriate type of visual aid to represent topics statistically. This chapter has provided only the very basic overview of these three subjects. The managing company officer must seek additional knowledge through independent study, research, and advanced courses at local colleges and universities.

Factors that Affect Personnel Evaluations

Personnel evaluations are performed by human beings, a fact that is not likely to change. The human factor is always difficult to control, and the potential for error by the company officer is always present. However, the company officer can avoid making errors by being aware of them. The following are the most common errors in personnel evaluations:

- *Halo effect* — This effect is a phenomenon of assessment in which the company officer's judgment of a subordinate's ability is biased by an evaluation of some previously observed action or behavior. The company officer tends to allow the subordinate's performance in one area influence ratings in another area. The company officer must pay careful attention to all behaviors and objectively justify the rating to avoid the halo effect. The opposite, called the horns effect, can also occur: The company officer observes one poor performance of a task and assumes other tasks will be performed just as poorly.

- *Leniency effect* — This effect is the tendency to give a subordinate the benefit of the doubt. A tendency to assign more than the usual number of higher ratings is the normal result of this type of error. The opposite (severity effect) can also occur.

- *Central-tendency effect* — This effect is the general tendency for judgments, ratings, or estimates to gravitate toward the center of a scale. The company officer tends to play it safe or avoid giving extreme ratings. However, it is important to make distinctions among subordinates, and the full use of the rating scale is the way to achieve this.

- *Similar-to-me effect* — Some subordinates remind the company officer of themselves. When the subordinate is similar to the company officer or approaches situations in the same way, it is tempting to award high ratings, even when the subordinate really didn't earn them. Company officers should remember that subordinates who are different can do a good job and that there are several effective ways to approach and accomplish any task.

- *Contrast effect* — The company officer must often rate several subordinates who are very dissimilar. A subordinate whose behavior is average can look extremely good or extremely poor in contrast to a very low-scoring or very high-scoring subordinate. Company officers must keep in mind that they are rating subordinates' actual behavior compared to the performance standard or criteria and not to the behavior of other personnel.

- *First-impression effect* — This effect is closely related to the halo effect. Sometimes a subordinate performs very well in the beginning and then falters, but the company officer has already formed an opinion based on the first impression. Company officers must consider the subordinate's performance during the entire evaluation period.

- *Recency effect* — Many times the company officer remembers events or performance that occurred recently. If the recent performances or events were good, the company officer may rate the subordinate better than the actual performance justifies. Conversely, if the recent performance was poor, the company officer may rate the subordinate worse.

- *Stereotype effect* — This particular type of effect can be a very difficult error to avoid since it can involve closely held and sometimes subconscious personal values. Sometimes company officer assigns ratings, not because of observed behavior but because they fit with the behavior associated with the stereotype. The company officer may have preconceived ideas or prejudices about the stereotyped individual, which the officer may use unconsciously in rating the subordinate.

These factors that occur in personnel evaluations may also occur in other types of evaluations. For example, when the company officer is evaluating requests for proposal (RFP), products, or bids, these factors may influence the officer's recommendation. The officer may consider the most recently reviewed product to be better than earlier items that were reviewed. Or, the officer might have a good first impression of one product and then evaluate all others against it rather than against the standard or criteria set forth in the RFP or specifications.

Human Resources Management II

Chapter Contents

Learning Objectives

1. Define *groups*.

2. Compare formal and informal groups.

3. Select facts about the essential characteristics of a group.

4. Identify the importance of the group as individuals.

5. Match leadership styles in group dynamics to their definitions.

6. Match behavior management terms to their definitions.

7. Select facts about counseling.

8. Select facts about coaching.

9. Recall information about mentoring.

10. Select from a list the characteristics of personnel-evaluation programs.

11. Select facts about the personnel-evaluation process.

12. Respond to scenarios involving human resources policies and procedures.

13. Respond to scenarios regarding the evaluation of the job performance of employees.

14. Select facts about discipline.

Job Performance Requirements

This chapter provides information that addresses the following job performance requirements of NFPA 1021, *Standard for Fire Officer Professional Qualifications* (2003):

<u>Chapter 5 Fire Officer II</u>

5.2

5.2.1

5.2.1(A)

5.2.1(B)

5.2.2

5.2.2(A)

5.2.2(B)

Chapter 26
Human Resources Management II

The Fire Officer II not only manages programs and multiunit emergency incident scenes but also supervises personnel. An understanding of the elements of group dynamics is vital for company officers because there is a direct connection between informal group support and formal group success or failure of the unit. A company officer's role in the group becomes one of meshing the goals of the formal and informal groups. In pursuing this role, company officers influence group behavior to meet the goals of both the company and the informal group.

The managing company officer is also responsible for evaluating personnel behavior and helping personnel to achieve their highest level of success. Knowledge of the organization's performance evaluation program and the common errors that can occur when evaluating subordinates is also essential. The officer should also be familiar with the formal coaching, mentoring, and counseling programs that the organization uses for improving work habits and increasing employee success.

Groups Defined

A *group* is usually defined as a collection consisting of a number of people who share certain traits, interact with one another, accept rights and obligations as members of the group, and share a common identity. In this definition, society itself can appear as a large group (**Figure 26.1**).

Society is composed of many formal and informal groups, and fire and emergency services organizations are a reflection of the society of which they are a part. An emergency response unit can be described as a subdivision of a fire and emergency

Society is Composed of a Multitude of Groups

Figure 26.1 An example of some of the many groups that make up society.

services organization or simply as an organized group of emergency responders. For purposes of this discussion, a group is defined as two or more persons who interact with regard to common goals; the goals may or may not be explicitly stated.

How formal the group is depends on how definite and specific the stated goals are. Formal groups usually define common goals in writing. An emergency response unit is a formal group of responders who interact to meet common goals as outlined by the organization's policies and its mission statement. Informal groups, on the other hand, define common goals in a less formal manner. A friendship can be described as an informal group: two persons who interact with the common goal of mutual respect and interests.

Within each formal group, it is common for informal subgroups to form and exist. For instance, two coworkers in an emergency response unit may form an informal group with the unstated goal of mutual friendship. Many potential informal subgroups exist within each formal group. These subgroups are limited only by the common interests of the individual members of the group. Informal groups most often form around common interests such as hobbies, political interests, social interests, religious beliefs, or sports activities **(Figure 26.2)**. Research on formal and informal groups has revealed two important facts:

- Informal subgroups form within all formal groups.

- The informal subgroup may have greater influence on the productivity and success of the formal group than does any other factor.

The point is that each informal subgroup has an effect upon the formal group, the unit. The effect may be positive if the members encourage each other to support the unit's activities. The effect may be negative if the individuals regard their informal group's goals as more important than or contrary to the goals of the unit.

A company officer is the leader of a formal group by the authority vested in the position by the organization; however, the company officer's position in any informal group and the ability to deal with the informal group are determined by group dynamics. For this reason, company officers must learn to work with the relationships within the unit.

The dynamics of a group include complex social forces that act within and upon every group and that together determine group behavior. Groups have relatively static aspects such as their names (for example, Ladder 7 or Rescue 3), their overall functions, and perhaps a fixed number of members **(Figure 26.3)**. Every group also has dynamic aspects that change, interact, and react. Changes in a group's composition, modifications of organizational structure, and specific events all bring about group change. Changes may be caused by promotions, transfers, retirements, or deaths. The directions in which groups move are determined by both internal and external forces. It is beyond the scope of this manual to attempt a complete explanation of group dynamics, but addressing the subject and creating an awareness of group dynamics can help company officers manage their units and the informal groups within them more effectively.

Figure 26.3 An engine crew composed of individuals which form the team.

Group Dynamics

The group structure of an emergency response unit is not significantly different from the structure of any other formal or informal group. Every group tends to have the five essential characteristics of a group. The members of the group must have the following:

- Common binding interest

- Vital group image

- Sense of continuity

Factors that Motivate People to Join Groups	
Interpersonal Factors	**Professional Factors**
Increased self-esteem	Goal achievement
Inclusion	Leadership opportunities
Personal status	Increased power created by the group
Emotional support	Increased productivity
Personal identity	Provides encouragement and support
Social development	
Enjoyment	Higher quality work
Affection	Results in better decisions
Relationships	

Figure 26.2 Examples of why people join groups.

- Shared set of values
- Different roles within the group

The effects of these five basic elements on the group members are what make up group dynamics. A study of group dynamics involves recognizing the internal and external pressures that affect these basic elements and learning to deal with them.

Common Binding Interests

For a group to exist, the members must be drawn together by some common interest that is important to them on some level. Hobby clubs grow out of their members' shared interest in the hobby. Union members are drawn together by a need for collective strength in matters relating to their employment. Religious groups form out of common beliefs. Local governments are formed because of the common needs of the citizens for security, safety, and other services.

The interests of individuals change, causing their participation in various groups to change. Some groups have interests, such as religious affiliations, that are binding to the individual for a lifetime **(Figure 26.4)**. Other groups hold an interest for the members only for a given period of time, such as membership in a school fraternity or sorority. Emergency responders' interests may change with their personal and professional growth and with their changing goals and aspirations within the organization and the fire and emergency services. Therefore, company officers should view the unit's members' interests as transitory. That is, company officers must strive to not only maintain their subordinates' interest in the unit and its mission but also recognize that those interests may change over time.

In the fire and emergency services, binding interests of the group may include:

- Desire to serve the community
- Sense of professionalism
- Sense of adventure
- Affiliation with a high-risk profession
- Desire for a secure career

Volunteer and combination organizations must determine, communicate, and support the common binding interests of their members if they are to retain them. The loss of motivation to be part of the group can be a factor in the loss of personnel and support of the unit and the organization.

Vital Group Image

The members of the group must share a vital group image. That is, the members of the group must recognize the existence of their group and take pride in it. This pride contributes to group spirit and high morale. This feeling of pride must extend beyond the unit to the entire organization.

In addition to being essential to the cohesion of the group, the group image is one of the greatest influences on the success of the group. A group tends to produce according to its image of itself. Groups that have a positive self-image tend to be higher achievers. Groups that have low group images tend to be poor producers. A positive self-image is sometimes called *esprit de corps*. This French term refers to the common spirit existing in the members of a group that inspires enthusiasm **(Figure 26.5, p. 606)**. However, company officers must not allow this group spirit to evolve into an unhealthy rivalry with other units. They must remind their subordinates that their first loyalty is to the organization and not the unit.

Figure 26.4 Types of groups people may join.

Figure 26.5 Esprit de corps may be expressed through pride in one's appearance and one's commitment to the organization.

Sense of Continuity

A sense of continuity is very important to group integrity. If the members of a group have doubts about the group's continued existence, then their commitment to the group may diminish. By disturbing the members' sense of continuity, the group can be fragmented, and the members may begin to think and act more independently. The members may become very individualistic and even somewhat territorial. This is one way that management sometimes deals with what they perceive as *problem* groups. However, company officers are concerned with how to maintain their subordinates' sense of continuity even though they are subject to being transferred to another unit or even to another shift. Company officers must continually remind their subordinates and themselves that they are part of a larger group: the emergency services organization.

Common Values

Common values are a part of the cohesive structure of most groups. They are sometimes a composite of individual perception of reality, responsibility, and integrity. The values of individual members surface as various subjects are confronted on a day-to-day basis in the normal interaction within the group structure. The values shared by a group can change as the membership of the group changes. This change usually occurs gradually and is related to group acceptance of new members' differing values. While individuals within the group have some values in common with the rest of the group, they are likely to have other values that differ. Company officers must recognize and respect these differences as long as they are not in conflict with the values of the organization.

Group values are also affected by the values of the organization (**Figure 26.6**). The values of the organization usually are reflected in the attitudes and actions of individuals and groups within the organization. For example, organizational values of the fire and emergency services require that emergency responders must be trustworthy and honest. This is an organizational imperative because responders must sometimes enter homes and businesses when the owners or occupants are not present. Company officers must exemplify and reinforce this and other organizational values within their units.

Roles Within the Group

Within each group, different individuals act in different roles. In formal groups, the leader is usually either assigned or elected. In informal groups, a natural or indigenous leader emerges regardless of whether any formal selection process is used. In an emergency response unit, the company officer is the assigned leader but may not be the indigenous leader. It is obviously desirable that the company officer be the leader of both the formal and informal groups, but if this is not the case, the company officer must recognize and deal with that fact.

Roles of the Company Officer

Company officers function in various roles both on and off the job. At work, emergency responders expect their company officer to fulfill the role of supervisor and manager (**Figure 26.7**). At home,

Examples of Ethical Core Values	
• Honesty	• Perseverance
• Integrity	• Frugality
• Impartiality	• Faithfulness
• Fairness	• Heroism
• Loyalty	• Patriotism
• Dedication	• Courage
• Responsibility	• Professionalism
• Accountability	• Trust

Figures 26.6 Core values that might be listed in an organization's mission statement.

Figures 26.7 A company officer working with a department employee.

their roles may include that of spouse, parent, sports team member, or neighbor. Most people play several roles simultaneously. For example, the fire officer is superior and subordinate at the same time: superior in rank and authority to the unit members but subordinate to the next higher level of supervision or management.

Role Expectations

As mentioned earlier, a company officer's subordinates expect the officer to be a supervisor. Officers and responders alike are guided in performing their duties by what others expect of them. This is called *role expectation*. A company officer's perception of that role is influenced by the role expectations of the formal organization, by group members, and by the officer's own concept of what it means to be a company officer.

It is important for company officers to realize that the ability to positively influence a group is not dependent upon being its informal leader. Generally, any member of the group can, to some extent, influence the group. Therefore, the officer must know how to fit into the informal group and learn to use the influence of that role. Ultimately, the company officer must strive to become the informal leader as well as the appointed leader by earning the respect of subordinates.

The most detrimental thing a company officer can do is to remain at a distance from the informal group. When this happens, the officer has little potential influence except from the formal authority of the position. Gaining the respect of the unit members and acceptance into the informal group can take time and effort on the part of the officer.

Member's Roles

The members of the group must agree to follow the rules and guidelines of the organization as well as the informal rules of the group. The members agree on who is the leader and the mutual status of the rest of the group (**Figure 26.8, p. 609**). Other areas of responsibility for the group members include:

• Mutual respect

• Openness

• Dependability

• Integrity

• Ethical conduct

• Ability to work without constant supervision

• Ability to communicate

• Goal oriented

The group members must be ready to acknowledge the authority of the company officer. By recognizing the officer's authority, the officer will be less prone to have to exert the authority. Control over the group will result from a more democratic approach to leadership than a more authoritarian approach. At emergency incidents, the group members will be able to carry out orders, tasks, and assignments with minimum supervision. This will permit the company officer to focus on the overall operation and the coordination of major resources.

Rules and Guidelines

Each group has its own rules and guidelines. For the emergency response unit, the rules and guidelines are the organization's rules, regulations, policies, and procedures. In some cases, the informal group develops its own rules and guidelines. The informal rules can be much stronger or persuasive than the formal rules. The traditions of the group are one form of informal rules or guidelines, but these rules may be very complex. Regardless of their complexity, company officers must learn to recognize when their unit members are behaving according to these rules and guidelines. Company officers should respect these informal rules and guidelines as long as they are not in conflict with the formal rules of the organization.

For example, if, in the company officer's judgment, the good-natured hazing that the informal rules prescribe for new members gets out of hand, the company officer must maintain order and discipline as mandated in the organization's rules, regulations, and policies by ordering the hazing stopped. If it does not stop, the company officer must use the coercive power of the position to discipline those who are doing it.

The Group as Individuals

To understand how the five basic elements of group dynamics influence the emergency response unit, company officers must understand that the total production of the group is determined by the interaction of the group members on an individual basis **(Figure 26.9)**. In other words, there is a synergistic effect within the group that produces a total that is greater than the sum of its parts. This total can be either positive or negative, depending upon the makeup of the group at the time. When company officers attempt to analyze how or why their unit is behaving in a certain way, they should consider the individuals within the unit and their relationships to each other.

One basic element to understanding the unit's members is the factors that motivated them to become fire and emergency services responders. There are many reasons why people join the fire and emergency services. Understanding these reasons will help company officers understand the motivations for personal behaviors of their subordinates. Some of these reasons are as follows:

- Desire for achievement
- Need for a sense of belonging
- Personal recognition
- Financial reward
- Security
- Guaranteed retirement benefit
- Personal challenge
- Advancement

Some Characteristics of Effective Work Groups

- Focus on the development and accomplishment of common goals and purposes.
- Be consciously inclusive by expecting and requiring participation of all members.
- Focus on behavioral rather than personality changes.
- Focus on the effect of behaviors rather than reason for the changes.
- Allow and expect members to discuss differences that impede full participation.
- Support the efforts of people to establish reasonable boundaries with other members.
- Avoid power or authority as a means of resolving group problems.
- Realize that square pegs can fit into round holes… but only for so long. That is, people will try to fit into a mold if they think it is expected or to their benefit. However, over time, they will revert to their normal pattern of behavior.
- Do not shoot messengers.
- Understand that all people, regardless of how high their position, feel vulnerable.
- Understand and accept that while group members have a right to ask for what they need, they won't always get it.
- Understand that conflict that has been suppressed, concealed, or avoided is likely to be destructive.
- Recognize that in conflict there is opportunity to improve relationships.

Figures 26.8 Group members acknowledge the leadership role of the company officer.

- Responsibility
- Helping the community
- Family tradition
- Increased sense of self-worth
- Fun
- Excitement
- Enjoyment of the benefits of departmental/organizational membership

Not all of these reasons or motivations are present in all personnel, and some motivations may not be a guarantee for a successful fire fighting or emergency-response career. Service as a family tradition or heritage does not ensure that every member of the family will perform well in an emergency service organization. Volunteer and combination organizations must understand the personal motivations of their members as a means to ensure continued retention and advancement.

Applying Leadership Styles in Group Dynamics

The company officer should apply the situational leadership styles to the group process. Depending on the readiness of the group or each individual, the company officer can use the appropriate style of leadership to gain the best results. The reader is reminded of the four-stage model developed by B.W. Tuckman for creating a cohesive team (see Chapter 3, Supervision). The basic four-stage model

Figures 26.9 Teams are composed of individuals who support their team through their efforts.

includes formation, control, work, and ending. The process was further expanded to include a fifth stage, adjourning. Tuckman refers to them using slightly different terms as the following five stages of development:

- *Forming* — Employees are uncertain of their roles in the group in this initial stage. They are not certain that they can trust or work with the other members. As relationships within the group grow, trust and respect develop, and the members begin to see themselves as a part of the group. At the same time, group members are enthusiastic about the challenges of a new project or task. This phase is critical within the team-development process and one in which the company officer can have a significant effect. The leadership style is directive, outlining the process and establishing the group structure. The company officer must also provide training and information on diversity issues to team members.

- *Storming* — Conflict may result at this stage as members jockey for informal leadership or attempt to exert their own individual influence over the group. This may occur when a new officer joins an existing company that contains older, more experienced firefighters. The most critical aspect of successful team development is to reduce the amount of time the group spends in the storming phase. The leader is supportive in this stage, actively listening to members and providing explanations for decisions.

- *Norming* — The group establishes its own sets of norms and values that each member accepts and adheres to during this stage. The members become closer and more cohesive. The company officer again must be aware of team norms and values as much as possible to make sure that those norms don't violate the sense of decency. The leader transitions into the role of team member, allowing leadership to be shared by the members.

- *Performing* — The supervisor works to maintain the team spirit as the group moves toward accomplishing the objectives in this fourth stage. At this point, the group is a true team with leadership shared by all members. The company officer must monitor progress in this area as well because team members can develop certain behaviors and attitudes that can work to destroy the team concept. It is critical for leaders to insist that team members act as equals and treat each other as equals. Involving all of the team members in team activities to the level that can be expected is critical to team growth. The end result is when everyone plays in the game; everyone is happy and involved in most cases.

- *Adjourning* — The final stage is the planned (and sometimes unplanned) termination of the group task. It includes the acknowledgement of the group's accomplishments and the participation of the individual members. Additionally, it is an opportunity to debrief the group members and determine if any changes in the process should be made. By bringing the process to a formal conclusion, the participants can feel satisfied by the results that have been achieved.

The company officer should also refer to Chapter 2, Leadership, for a detailed description of situational leadership.

Behavior Management

Behavior management can be a difficult skill for a new company officer to master. It is, however, one of the most important skills for an officer to acquire and maintain. Some company officers may believe that they do *not* need to perform behavior management because peer pressure will control the actions of the unit's members. They may even believe that membership in the fire and emergency services will automatically result in the highest level of behavior by their subordinates.

While it is a fact of human nature that the members of a group may respond to peer pressure, the company officer cannot shirk responsibility and depend on peer pressure to take care of disruptive behavior. In some situations, peer pressure does work. Along with effective peer pressure, the company officer may still need to privately counsel a disruptive subordinate.

Company officers who fail to control disruptive behavior will lose the respect of the other unit members when a disruptive individual is allowed to continue exhibiting inappropriate behavior. Behavior management begins with *prevention* of disruptive behavior. Prevention requires the officer to communicate behavioral expectations based on the organization's policies, provide a positive example through personal behavior, and create a positive atmosphere in the unit.

The company officer must review the organization's policies to determine how to best address the disruptive or inappropriate behavior. The review should include the specific policy or procedure that was violated and the policy that describes how violations should be handled. The company officer should also review the labor/management agreement to determine the appropriate steps mandated within.

Company officers have a number of tools available to help manage the behavior of individual unit members. They may choose to use any of the following ways to assist their subordinates in reaching their full potential:

- *Counseling* — Guidance starts with a counseling session between the company officer and a new member of the unit. The officer's expectations are stated positively and behavioral limitations are set (**Figure 26.10**). New members contribute their expectations and how they feel that they can fit into the unit. Counseling may be used to establish boundaries and set expectations, or it may be used in the context of discipline and used to determine the cause of inappropriate behavior and establish a means of correcting it.

- *Coaching*— In a coaching session, the company officer guides the individual member through any new activities, reinforces correct behaviors, and redirects incorrect behaviors (**Figure 26.11**).

- *Providing peer assistance*— Providing peer assistance may begin with assigning a more experienced member to work with the new member who is having difficulty becoming part of the group or learning the required duties.

- *Mentoring*— A supervisor or other superior acts as a trusted and friendly advisor or guide (mentor) to the member who is new to a particular role.

Reviewing Policies

One of the first priorities for a company officer managing behavior is to review with subordinates the policies, rules, and regulations of the organization, as well as the officer's personal expectations. The company officer must consistently promote, support, and enforce policies, rules, and regulations so that all personnel understand, respect, and adhere to them. These policies that are generally addressed include the following:

- Safety
- Facility or station layout
  - Use and cleanup requirements
  - Safety plan
  - Emergency reporting procedures
  - Evacuation plan
  - Disinfection area
  - PPE cleaning area
- Attendance, absenteeism, and tardiness
- Expectations and regulations for responding to emergencies
- Storage and care of PPE
- Station/facility care, cleaning, and maintenance
- Apparatus care, cleaning, and maintenance
- Equipment and tool care, cleaning, and maintenance
- Company-level training participation
- Physical fitness program participation

Figures 26.10 A counseling session between a company officer and a new crew member.

Figures 26.11 Company officers can help their subordinates learn through coaching sessions.

- Radio or communication watch
- Daily work assignment
- Dress/grooming regulations
- Smoking areas (if permitted)
- Procedures for accommodating with visitors or citizen inquiries
- Response procedures for volunteers in personally owned vehicles (POVs)

Counseling

Counseling is a broad term used for a variety of procedures designed to help individuals adjust to certain situations and a means of either reinforcing correct behavior or eliminating improper behavior. Counseling involves resolving behavior issues through such actions as:

- Giving advice
- Having discussions
- Recommending career path choices
- Providing professional development opportunities

Company officers must *not* assume the role of therapist when a subordinate appears to have a psychological/emotional problem. In this situation, the company officer's responsibility is to refer the subordinate to a professional therapist. Most employers have some sort of professional counseling available through their employee assistance program (EAP).

Attempts to force individuals into acceptable behavior will generally fail. Force causes resistance, and people do not like to be disciplined. Company officers must learn and practice appropriate counseling and positive reinforcement methods that stimulate and motivate subordinates to perform properly.

Fire and emergency services organizations have a formalized process to follow when documenting behavior issues. One of the steps in the process may include completing a type of counseling form. It is important for all company officers to be familiar with the organization's policies and procedures relating to counseling. Compliance with the proper counseling procedures will also require knowledge of the labor/management agreement and the correct documentation procedures **(Figure 26.12)**.

Company officers must consult with their superiors and follow the specific policies on counseling individuals and completing the counseling form. The company officer should use the following general guidelines:

- Meet and talk with the subordinate in private.
- List the exact facts of what behavior the individual is displaying on the form.
- State behavioral objectives that clearly and concisely communicate what is expected of the individual.
- Discuss and agree with the individual on solutions.
- Explain what actions will be taken if the individual does *not* comply with the objectives and solutions.
- Give a copy of the counseling form to the individual and retain the original.
- Forward a copy of the form to the next level of supervision.

Legal and ethical issues may require or dictate that company officers have supervisory authority before conducting a counseling session to correct behavior. At the same time, the labor/management agreement may stipulate that the subordinate have a union representative present during the counseling session. Company officers must understand and not act beyond their levels of responsibility and authority as directed by local policy.

Once all attempts to correct inappropriate behavior have been exhausted, the company officer may have to treat the problem as a disciplinary situation. When disciplinary action becomes necessary, the company officer will have to rely on documentation to support the corrective action. Organizations have policies to follow, and the company officer must be familiar with them.

When discipline becomes necessary, company officers must perform it privately, in a calm manner, and with an atmosphere that shows a willingness to help. The officer must begin these sessions with encouragement and praise for good work, suggest a constructive course of action, and focus on the mistake instead of the individual. In most situations, company officers who show a sincere interest in the subordinate do more toward solving problems than any action that intensifies the

PERFORMANCE IMPROVEMENT PLAN

Employee's Name   **Date** _____

1. **Description of Performance/Incident:**

2. **Measurable Improvement Goals:**

3. **Training/Direction Recommended/Required (Specify):**

4. **Improvement Time Frame:**

5. **Consequences:**

6. **Employee Input / Rebuttal:** (Optional)

X _____   X _____   _____
   I acknowledge the PIP   I disagree with the PIP   Date

X _____   X _____   _____
   Supervisor   Witness (*if necessary*)   Date

A print out or photo-copy of this completed form should be made for (1) the employee, (2) the immediate supervisor, and (3) Human Resources.

Figures 26.12 An example of a form used to document a counseling session.

individual's feelings of inferiority or inadequacy. It is always wise in these type situations to remember the saying: *Discipline should be remedial and not punitive*. In other words, the main goal is not to punish the individual but to change the unwanted behavior.

Coaching

Coaching can be described as an intensive process of directing the skills performance of an individual. For the company officer, coaching is the process of giving motivational correction, positive reinforcement, and constructive feedback to subordinates in order to maintain and improve their performance. To be effective, the feedback needs to be positive, immediate, direct, and frequent (**Figure 26.13**). It can either be as simple as telling the subordinate how well a task has been completed or involve a formal counseling session when a change in negative or inappropriate behavior is desired. Disruptive behavior often results from frustration or confusion, and company officers can help subordinates overcome these behaviors through coaching techniques.

Private industry generally subscribes to a formal coaching model that contains the following four steps:

- *Describe the current level of performance* — Describe levels in a positive manner. Specify behaviors that could be improved using specific examples. Do *not* state that the subordinate is doing something wrong; simply say that it can be done better, safer, or more efficiently.

- *Describe the desired level of performance* — State exactly what is required in detail to provide clear direction for the subordinate.

- *Gain a commitment for change* — Ensure that the subordinate agrees to the new level of performance. In some cases this commitment could be considered a contract and become part of the subordinate's formal personnel record.

- *Follow up the commitment* — Observe the subordinate to determine whether performance has improved or schedule a follow-up meeting to discuss progress. When change does not occur, subsequent coaching sessions may be required. The next step would be formal counseling by a counseling professional.

Figures 26.13 The four components of effective feedback.

Process

Even though the term *coaching* usually refers to an activity associated with sports and athletics, it is also an intensive kind of tutoring given to subordinates to improve skills in an activity or increase unit teamwork and effectiveness. Coaching can take place in a group setting or individually. The company officer should identify the problem source through observation and questioning and then guide the subordinate(s) to an appropriate solution.

The company officer must be able to clearly recognize, constructively criticize, and carefully correct flaws in actions of subordinates. They must also effectively praise and positively reinforce those actions that are being performed properly. To generate subordinates' enthusiasm about their performances, company officers must strike a balance between correcting what is performed wrong and praising what is performed right. Too much weight on either side of the scale unbalances the learning process and limits or inhibits it.

Techniques

Feedback from company officers also must be objective and precise in its description of the elements that are good or bad. The officer must not fall into the trap of just providing critical phrases such as *that's wrong — do it again — but the right way this time*. This type of feedback does not inform the subordinate of the error or how to correct it. A better example would be as follows: *Before you go further, do you remember what the rope needs to have on the running end before you tighten it?*

A questioning process allows subordinates to stop, think, and recall or build into their memory the information that they are attempting to apply. Some people perform this thought-construction process quickly while some take more time, but they remember better because they recalled it themselves. When a subordinate does not recall the information, the company officer can then carefully review the steps and coach the subordinate through the steps again.

Providing Peer Assistance

In society as well as the fire and emergency services, a *peer* is someone who is equal in status either socially or psychologically to another. *Peer assistance* refers to a process that involves having members of the unit assist each other in learning teamwork or perfecting new skills **(Figure 26.14)**. Some subordinates, in particular new unit members, are intimidated or afraid to perform in front of the company officer until they feel confident in their abilities. These subordinates may feel more comfortable practicing with a peer.

More experienced or mature members of the unit can often provide peer assistance to new members. Unit members who have specialized knowledge and skills can provide training in those areas. The peer assistance approach can be used as a basis for a buddy system that pairs an experienced member with a new employee during the probationary period.

Mentoring

Mentoring is a process that places a new subordinate under the guidance of a more experienced professional who acts as tutor, guide, and motivator. Mentoring situations are popular in both the public and private work environment. Many chief and company officers have acted as mentors, either formally or informally.

Typically, a mentor is usually someone other than the instructor who guides subordinates' actions in real experiences on the job. Mentors must be chosen carefully and selected for their experience, interest, patience, and communication abilities.

The primary purpose of mentoring is to prepare employees for advancement within the organization through the direction of a positive role model **(Figure 26.15)**. Mentoring programs enhance management skills, improve productivity, and encourage diversity. Instructors can mentor in the following ways:

- Provide role models for personnel.
- Provide guidance in career planning.

Figures 26.14 Members of a person's peer group can provide valuable assistance.

Figures 26.15 A mentoring session between a chief officer and a company officer.

- Assist in gaining specialized training.
- Provide outside resources.
- Make challenging work assignments.
- Monitor the achievements of personnel.

Personnel-Evaluation Programs

As managers and supervisors, company officers must periodically evaluate the personnel who work for them. Personnel might be formally evaluated in the following situations:

- When they are hired
- During their probationary period
- Annually as part of a performance review
- For promotional purposes
- For disciplinary or termination purposes

The formal evaluation schedule should not deter company officers from providing feedback on performance on an ongoing basis. Some organizations require performance feedback be provided on a quarterly or semi-annual basis. This allows the individual to alter or improve performance before an annual evaluation. It also provides the supervisor with documentation of the individual's performance during the evaluation period in terms of strengths, weaknesses, and improvements. General procedures for the process plus advantages and characteristics of personnel-evaluation programs are given in the sections that follow along with legal considerations.

Company officers should remember that the personnel evaluation process can be one of the most subjective activities that they perform. It must be approached as objectively as possible and with as much information as they can gather and document. They must also remember that the evaluations they perform can have a career-long effect on their subordinates. Improperly handled evaluations can result in the loss of motivation, personal resentment, or the tarnishing of an individual's professional, and sometimes personal, reputation.

Advantages

Personnel-evaluation programs are formal systematic procedures for appraising the abilities and accomplishments of employees at all levels within the organization. A variety of benefits can be derived from a well-organized personnel-evaluation program. The benefits include the following:

- The strength and weaknesses of each employee become part of a permanent record. This record is typically used for awards, promotions, transfers, discipline, and termination.

- The need for additional training becomes apparent. Weaknesses can be addressed with specific existing training programs. If it is warranted, new programs can be developed to address the deficiency if it appears to be widespread.

- The company officer who is performing the evaluation becomes more familiar with the personnel being evaluated. This familiarity allows for more effective use of personnel and a better succession system.

- The evaluation program is motivation for improvement by the person being evaluated.

- Higher levels of management become more aware of the abilities of lower-level managers and supervisors. However, the company officer must never use the evaluation process for personal advantage or gain.

- Personnel evaluations help to illuminate the specific talents of individuals who may be used in other areas of the organization.

- The program helps to improve the efficiency of both employees and the organization as a whole.

Characteristics

Personnel evaluations, like the other types of evaluations, have specific guidelines to which the company officer should adhere. If these standards are applied properly to the process, then personnel evaluations can be effective tools in the management of the organization. These guidelines are as follows (**Figure 26.16**):

- *Timely* — Perform performance evaluations that are linked to a specific incidence of unsatisfactory performance or inappropriate behavior in a timely manner. The evaluation should occur as soon as possible following the inappropriate behavior._

- *Clearly stated criteria* — State goals and objectives clearly and concisely. Maintain written job-performance criteria for review at each successive evaluation.

- *Not discriminatory* — Apply job-performance standards regardless of gender, race, ethnicity, age, or other classifications.

- *Consistency* — Apply job-performance standards equally throughout the organization based on the type of job or duty performed.

- *Thorough records* — Maintain thorough and complete records of each evaluation in the employee's personnel file. Give a copy of the evaluation to the employee; however, these records are not public so maintain confidentiality.

- *Trained supervisors* — Properly train company officers who are required to perform personnel evaluations

- *Objectivity* — Overcome personal bias and make the evaluation based on the established criteria. Objectivity is essential in personnel evaluations.

Guidelines for Personnel Evaluations	
• Timely • Clearly stated criteria • Nondiscriminatory • Consistent • Objective	• Performed by trained supervisors • Resulting in thorough and accurate records

Figures 26.16 Supervisors must follow specific guidelines when performing personnel evaluations.

Evaluation Processes

The personnel-evaluation process begins with an initial meeting between the company officer and the subordinate. At this point, the organization's expectations for the job performance of the employee are established. Performance standards are outlined and agreed upon by both parties. The job-performance evaluation is an opportunity to generate positive change in the organization. The company officer can accomplish this change by focusing on the positive accomplishments of the employee, involving the employee in setting goals and objectives, and creating an atmosphere in which the employee can feel comfortable and

accepted. Fire and emergency services personnel should also be familiar with the concept of a 360-degree feedback evaluation.

Fire and emergency services organizations generally have a six-, twelve-, or eighteen-month probationary period for newly hired employees. The job-performance expectations that were established initially provide the basis for performance evaluations during this period. The company officer must continually monitor the job performance of newly hired personnel and provide appropriate feedback. Feedback may be either additional information about what is expected or praise for meeting or exceeding expectations. This probationary period can be difficult if the supervisor does not provide enough information or if the new employee fails to ask questions or clarify misunderstandings. Company officers must ensure that every step of the probationary employee's performance is well documented and that the employee has been made aware of any deficiencies.

Periodic job-performance evaluations. Following the probationary period, formal, periodic job-performance evaluations are established on an annual basis. These evaluations are opportunities for both the company officer and employee to review the quality of work and established performance goals and objectives. The current trend in personnel evaluation is to provide continuous feedback to the employee through informal evaluations. The formal evaluation is then used to reinforce the continuous feedback. To ensure that evaluations are successful, take the following actions:

- Ensure that the employee is aware of the relationship of the position within the organization, authority the position has, and responsibilities assigned to the position.

- Allow the employee to contribute to the establishment or altering of performance goals and objectives.

- Conduct the evaluation like a formal interview: Select a predetermined time in the privacy of the evaluator's office and prohibit interruptions. There should be no surprises regarding performance or expectations of the employee during this interview.

- Include the signatures of both the company officer and employee on the final evaluation to indicate that the employee has received the evaluation. The employee's signature does not necessarily indicate agreement with the content of the evaluation. It simply indicates that the comments of the evaluator were reviewed with the employee.

360-degree feedback evaluations. Fire and emergency services personnel should also be familiar with the concept of a 360-degree feedback evaluation. It is similar to the type of size-up that occurs at an emergency incident when the Incident Commander (IC) requests situation reports from all sides of the incident. The need for tactical changes becomes apparent quickly, and the IC then responds accordingly.

When the concept is applied to the human resources program, the process and the results are similar. The information used in the performance evaluation is gathered from people who have direct professional contact with the person who is being evaluated. This evaluation would include peers, subordinates, employees, members of other agencies, and members of the public who are in reasonably constant contact with the individual. The information that is gathered is based on the performance they observe. Responses must remain confidential to protect the people who are providing the information. It also ensures that they will speak freely and not hesitate to provide constructive criticism.

The feedback should also be supported by a plan for the improvement of any behaviors that are perceived to be below standard. Coaching, mentoring, continuing education, and specialized skills training are just some of the ways to help an individual improve to meet the performance expectations. These evaluations and the interpretation of results should be administered and performed by a professional trained in this technique.

Legal Considerations

Personnel evaluations must adhere to the guidelines provided by the local authority having jurisdiction, the state/province, and the federal government. When a fire or emergency services organization first establishes a personnel-evaluation program, it must research the various legal requirements for such a program. Company officers must be familiar with all statutory requirements relevant to personnel evaluations. This information should be provided when initial personnel-evaluation training is provided by the organization. Some of the factors that have been emphasized in recent court decisions that influence the evaluation process are similar to the guidelines listed earlier. These factors are as follows:

- Evaluations must be significantly related to the work behavior or skills that the employee is assigned to perform. The individual cannot be judged on tasks that are not assigned or the person is not trained to perform.

- Evaluations must include definite identifiable criteria based on the quality or quantity of work or on specific performances that are supported by a documented record.

- Evaluations must be objective and not based on subjective observations.

- Evaluations must be supported by documentation.

Besides the legal requirements of federal, state/provincial, and local statutes, the company officer must also be aware of the requirements mandated by the labor/management agreement. Union representation, grievance procedures and reporting procedures may control the evaluation process and require certain actions on the part of the company officer and establish a specific time frame for the process.

Grievance Procedures

Grievance (complaint) procedures are usually included in the labor/management agreement or they are part of the organization's policy and procedures manual. As part of management, managing company officers are part of the grievance process. The topic of grievances was covered in Chapter 14, Labor/Management Relations. As a brief recap, a grievance is a complaint by an employee on one of the following issues:

- Demotion

- Suspension without pay

- Termination with cause

- Work assignments that violate the labor/management agreement, law, or departmental/organizational policy

- Conditions of work or employment that violate the labor/management agreement, law, or departmental/organizational policy

Because state labor laws or the labor/management agreement define grievance procedures, examples may vary widely. However, all model procedures contain the same general elements such as filing period, testimony, witnesses, representation, and review steps. The grievance procedure needs to be effective, consistent, and provide an equitable resolution.

Discipline

Discipline is often thought of as punishment; however, the vast majority of the discipline imposed is done to correct inappropriate behavior, not to punish the person. The word *discipline* comes from the root word *disciple* — a *learner*. One dictionary definition of discipline is *training that corrects;* therefore, the main purpose of discipline is to educate. Discipline in the fire and emergency services is designed to do the following:

- Educate and train

- Correct inappropriate behavior

- Provide positive motivation

- Ensure compliance with established policies, rules, regulations, standards, and procedures

- Provide direction

Therefore, discipline consists of corrective action that is used to get employees to meet standards and adhere to standing (policy) plans. Disciplinary actions should be taken in a manner that is corrective, progressive, and lawful. Several types of discipline are available, all stemming from positive or negative approaches.

Types

Generally speaking, there are two types of discipline: positive and negative. Positive discipline (sometimes called *constructive discipline*) results when management establishes reasonable rules of conduct that are fairly and consistently applied. Most fire and emergency services personnel realize that rules are necessary if the assigned work is to be completed safely, according to standard, and on time. As long as they know what is required, most personnel willingly conform to the rules through self-discipline **(Figure 26.17)**.

On the other hand, negative discipline involves corrective action when an employee disobeys or reluctantly obeys the established rules or performance requirements. There are many possible reasons why personnel may break the rules or not comply with procedures. Some (but not all) of these reasons include the following:

- *Resentment* — Created when wages and working conditions are (or perceived to be) substandard, bitter labor/management disputes have occurred, difficult contract negotiations have occurred, or rules are being unfairly or inconsistently applied.

Figures 26.17 A company officer disciplining a subordinate.

- *Boredom* — Caused when there is too little work or too little interest in the work.

- *Ignorance* — Occurs when there is a lack of knowledge of the job requirements and/or the rules of conduct.

- *Stress* — Caused by personal problems (on or off the job) that affect job performance.

When an established policy, rule, regulation, procedure, or standard has been violated, the company officer is obligated to correct the inappropriate behavior. If the violation is relatively minor, the company officer needs to promptly do whatever the organization requires in order to correct the behavior (usually by counseling in an informal private discussion between the officer and the employee). But in many organizations when violations are serious, such as safety violations that caused injuries or property losses, the company officer may be required to recommend more severe action. Company officers may or may not be empowered to administer formal discipline, such as a written reprimand or suspension of an employee with pay pending the outcome of investigations. Because state/provincial and federal laws are designed to protect employees from arbitrary and capricious disciplinary actions, company officers must recognize that employees are entitled to the following information and considerations:

- Written *notice of proposed action*

- The *reasons therefore*

- Copy of the charges and the material upon which the action is based

- The *right to respond* (either orally or in writing) to the authority initially imposing discipline

Once these requirements have been met, the discipline may be imposed without a hearing where evidence is provided or given, unless the employee requests one. If a hearing is held, it is not intended to be an adversarial proceeding. Instead, it is intended to be informational — to minimize the risk of error in a supervisor/manager's initial decision because of a lack of information. The employee, or designated legal or union representative, may provide additional information and respond to the specific charges before the discipline is imposed.

Progressive

Most public entities have laws requiring some form of progressive discipline, although it may not be called by that name. In general, progressive discipline usually starts with training/education to correct the first instance an employee fails to meet performance standards or violates the rules of conduct. It then progresses to punitive measures if there are additional offenses. However, even in organizations using progressive discipline, a sufficiently serious first offense (theft, assault, gross negligence, etc.) may result in termination. Because the action should always fit the offense, the initial response may be corrective or punitive. Progressive leadership and participatory management can help to ensure that punitive discipline is seldom used within the department/organization. Progressive discipline usually involves the following three levels:

- *Preventive action* — Attempt to correct the inappropriate behavior as soon as it is discovered. The idea is to prevent it from becoming a pattern or progressing to a more serious offense. Start preventive action with an individual counseling interview. During the interview, the company officer ensures that the employee understands both the rule that was violated and the organizational necessity for the rule. The company officer explains exactly what is expected of the employee in the future and what may happen if the rule is violated again.

- *Corrective action* — Use the second step when an employee repeats a violation for which preventive action was taken or commits a different violation. It may also be used if an employee commits a serious violation as a first offense. Corrective action differs from preventive action primarily in that it is always done in writing. Give the employee a letter in person or send one by certified mail with a return receipt requested to guarantee that it is received. The letter includes the following information:

  — Description of what transpired in the preventive interview if one occurred

  — Description of what the employee is or is not doing that violates organizational policies

  — Review of organizational policy regarding

the possible consequences if the behavior is continued or change in behavior fails to meet organizational standards

— Statement informing the employee that a copy of the letter will be placed in the employee's file

- ***Punitive action*** — Use this step when an employee either continues to exhibit inappropriate behavior despite earlier corrective efforts or commits a very serious violation of organizational rules as a first offense. The employee is given notice that this behavior cannot and will not be tolerated. After meeting all mandated procedural rules and safeguards, consider the range of possible sanctions as follows:

— Formal written reprimand

— Fine (specific monetary payment)

— Suspension (time off without pay)

— Demotion (reduction in rank)

— Termination (dismissal from department/organization)

— Prosecution (legal action that may result in a large fine or jail time)

Although most company officers will only be responsible for the first step, preventive action, they must be familiar with the remaining steps should they become necessary. In most organizations, corrective and punitive actions are the responsibility of the organization's administration and are strictly controlled by the labor/management agreement.

Summary

The human resources program is a major segment of any public or private fire and emergency services organization. Group dynamics, which are central to all human interaction in groups, should be understood by company officers as a background to human resources management. Company officers must also be familiar with the various components of a human resources program including the steps for evaluating and disciplining employees. Effective personnel evaluations will reduce the need for corrective discipline within the unit.

Administrative Responsibilities

Chapter Contents

Learning Objectives

1. Select facts about developing policies and procedures.

2. Develop a fire service policy or procedure.

3. Define the term *budget*.

4. Identify the three functions that a budget fulfills.

5. Define the terms *budget system* and *budget type*.

6. Select facts about various budget systems.

7. Compare and contract operating and capital budgets.

8. Identify the stages of a budget cycle.

9. Identify various revenue sources.

10. Select facts about the budget-development process.

11. Develop and justify a project budget.

12. Select facts about the steps in the purchasing process.

Job Performance Requirements

This chapter provides information that addresses the following job performance requirements of NFPA 1021, *Standard for Fire Officer Professional Qualifications* (2003):

Chapter 27
Administrative Responsibilities

Management of any fire and emergency services organization is a major undertaking. It requires the efforts of many people, both uniformed and nonuniformed. Some of the activities require highly specialized skills, such as the care of the organization's computers and electronic equipment. Other tasks can be handled by emergency responders as either a full-time assignment or as a part-time duty. These tasks may include logistics, personnel, or finance management.

Managing company officers will find themselves involved in the day-to-day administration of the organization, sometimes to the exclusion of emergency response duties. Part of the administrative tasks assigned to the Fire Officer II includes policy and procedures development, budget development, and purchasing activities.

This chapter provides an overview of each of these topics. All fire and emergency services organizations will have some or all of these administrative programs available to them. Larger career organizations may have separate sections within the administration that are responsible for providing them. Small volunteer, combination, or career organizations may depend on outside agencies, such as municipal purchasing departments, to provide support. In any case, company officers must be aware of the functions in order to manage them internally or monitor the required support from external sources.

Policy and Procedure Development

Written policies and procedures are essential for the effective and efficient operation of any fire and emergency services organization. Policies and pro-cedures place into writing the expectations of the organization based on the organizational model and the strategic and operational plans. They are known by a variety of names, including Standard Operating Procedures (SOP), Standard Operating Guidelines (SOG), Operating Instructions (OI), Administrative Policies and Procedures, and simply Policies and Procedures. Regardless of the title, they must contain information that is current and appropriate. Therefore, the organization should have a process to evaluate the need for new policies and procedures and a process for revising existing policies and procedures.

The majority of company officers will be required to enforce policies, rules, regulations, and procedures. However, NFPA 1021 states that the Fire Officer II must have the ability to identify a problem, determine the appropriate solution, and develop a policy or procedure that will rectify the problem. The company officer will have to apply the knowledge provided in Chapter 24, Analyses, Evaluations, and Statistics. Steps for determining the need for a new policy or procedure include the following:

- *Identify the problem or requirement for a policy or procedure* — Determine if a policy or procedure is actually necessary to address the problem. Some problems may be best addressed on an individual basis that does not require a formal policy.

- *Collect data to evaluate the need* — Use data that may be quantitative or qualitative and may come from personnel interviews, product literature, or activity reports.

- *Select the evaluation model* — Use one of the evaluation models: goals-based, process-based, or outcome-based.

- ***Establish a timetable for making the needs evaluation*** — Consider the length of time required to evaluate the problem, which depends on the complexity of the problem and the amount of information that must be evaluated (**Figure 27.1**).

- ***Conduct the evaluation*** — Follow the recommended steps for the model that is most appropriate for the problem.

- ***Select the best response to the need*** — Determine the best policy or procedure to solve the problem. Remember that this selection may include no policy or procedure at all.

- ***Select alternative responses*** — Select a second best choice if a contingency is indicated. External influences may make it necessary to select a policy or procedure other than the first choice. Personal safety, however, should not be compromised.

- ***Establish a revision process or schedule*** — Create a revision process as part of the policy or procedure. This process may be general for all policies and procedures or one that is specific to the policy that has been selected.

- ***Recommend the policy or procedure that best meets the need*** — Consider that because policies and procedures may have legal ramifications, they may need to be formally adopted by the jurisdiction. Formal approval requires that the policy or procedure be supported by documentation.

The policies and procedures of the organization, like most elements of the administrative function, must be continually monitored for effectiveness.

Personal Protective Clothing Project Timetable				
Process Step	**Date**	**Estimated Time**	**Actual Time**	**Responsibility**
Form Clothing Committee	01/15/07	1 day	1 day	Committee Chair
Establish Need	01/15/07	1 day	1 day	Committee
Determine Quantity Requirements	01/22/07	1 day	1 day	Bill & Tom
Research Legal Mandates and Technical Requirements	02/01/07	5 days	7 days	Joe, Bill, and City Legal
Develop Specifications	02/10/07	3 days	5 days	Committee
Write Request for Proposal	02/15/07	3 days	6 days	Committee
Review Responses	03/30/07	5 days	5 days	Committee
Evaluate Submitted Samples	04/10/07	15 days	15 days	Committee
Issue Bid Request	05/01/07	1 day	1 day	Committee
Review Bids	06/01/07	3 days	4 days	Committee
Select Best Bid	06/05/07	1 day	1 day	Committee
Issue Contract	06/07/07	1 day	3 days	Committee
Receive PPC	09/01/07	2 days	3 days	Bill, Tom, & Joe
Evaluate Products Against Bid Specifications	09/02/07	3 days	3 days	Committee
Place Clothing into Stock	09/05/07	3 days	4 days	Bill with Supply Section
Issue Clothing as Needed	09/10/07			Supply Section

Figure 27.1 A timetable such as this one can be a valuable resource during a needs evaluation.

Policies and procedures are most effective if they are considered dynamic documents, that is, documents that are subject to constant scrutiny, review, and revision. Responsibility for the monitoring of all policies and procedures rests with the chief officers of the organization. They should be familiar with the content, application, and effects of the policies they use to manage the organization. They should also be aware of the proper procedures for performing the tasks assigned to them and to the members of their command. Company officers who are assigned the task of assisting chief officers in the development and revision of policies and procedures should also be familiar with how the policies are applied and enforced.

Budget Preparation and Development

The term *budget* can be defined as a planned quantitative allocation of resources for specific activities. Therefore, in the broadest of definitions, it is the allocation of all resources to the completion of a task. Those resources include, among others, time, space, equipment, facilities, apparatus, personnel, funding, and research. In this manual, budgets refer to the narrow financial budget that lists both proposed expenditures of funds and expected revenue sources **(Figure 27.2)**. Developing and managing budgets are highly specialized skills usually performed by financial officers who work for the jurisdiction. Some large fire and emergency services organizations may have internal budget departments staffed by nonemergency employ-

ees and managed by a chief officer. Volunteer fire and emergency services organizations may have an accountant or financial advisor as part of the governing board. No matter the arrangement, all managing company officers should have substantial knowledge of the budget process that applies to their organizations.

According to the job performance requirements of NFPA 1021, *Standard for Fire Officer Professional Qualifications*, Level II fire officers must be able to develop a project or divisional budget. To accomplish these tasks, the company officer must understand the types of budgets normally used in public administration, types of revenue sources available, and the budget process itself. Local laws and ordinances vary, but the basic budgetary theory remains the same among jurisdictions.

Systems and Budget Types

The budget of government jurisdictions is more than a list of proposed expenditures and expected revenue. Budgets perform the following three vital functions for government:

- ***Describe and identify the relationship between different tasks*** — The budget is used to allocate limited resources to the various services that are provided by each division of the government and between those divisions. Therefore, the budget illustrates which of the tasks are considered essential, receiving the greater share of the resources, and which are considered less essential, receiving the smaller portion of the resources.

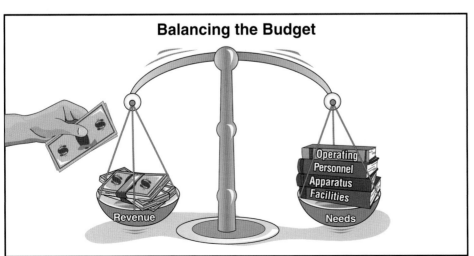

Balancing the Budget

Revenue

Operating
Personnel
Apparatus
Facilities
Needs

Figure 27.2 Budgets are necessary to balance organizational funds with organizational needs.

- **Provide assistance in the decision-making process** — Because the budget includes the projected available resources for the fiscal year, it provides the administration with an idea of how much money has been allotted to the organization. This allows the administration to decide on which services and programs are the most important.

- **Clarify political power** —Budget allocations are generally based on the perception of which services are most important. The political body that is ultimately in charge, whether a state/provincial legislature, Congress/Parliament, or municipal elected officials, will base the budget on what is politically important to them. If the officials currently place the greatest importance on security, then the budget will reflect this view.

Most budgets do the following:

- Anticipate future expenditures based on the goals and objectives of the jurisdiction or organization.

- Review the effectiveness of past budget performance.

- Establish and reinforce governmental policy.

- Assign responsibility for the accomplishment of goals and objectives.

In both the governmental and business sectors in North America, many terms are used to describe budgets. The terms vary depending on the source or the organization using them. In general the following two phrases define budgets:

- **Budget system** — Model or format to which the budget process conforms

- **Budget type**— How costs or revenues are divided between capital and operational purchases

Budget Systems

Budget systems are the general formats to which the jurisdiction's budget process conforms. Each system provides the same result through a variety of approaches. Some may contain elements of other systems. Company officers will generally not be involved in establishing a budget system, although they may participate in evaluating a current system and recommending changes to the system. Members of volunteer or combination organizations may have greater involvement in establishing a system, especially if the organization is new. Typically, those systems are known by the following names:

- **Line-item budgeting** — Consists of a list of revenue sources and a list of proposed expenditures for the budget cycle. It is also known as an object class budget because each line contains a specific object (such as apparatus) or class (such as salaries). The total of the revenue and expenditures must be equal for the budget to balance. This budgeting system is the most common system used in North America. This system may be applied to the entire jurisdiction or to the operating budget of an individual department/organization.

- **Zero-based budgeting (ZBB)** — Requires all expenditures to be justified at the beginning of each new budget cycle, as opposed to simply explaining the amounts requested that are in excess of the previous cycle's funding. During the ZBB budget planning, it is assumed that there is zero money available to operate the organization or program. The organization must justify the contribution that it makes to the jurisdiction.

ZBB is generally recognized as beneficial to public organizations because expenditures can get out of control when it is automatically assumed that the amount required during the last budget cycle is the amount that will be required during the subsequent cycle. One variation of ZBB has many organizations using 80 percent of the previous year's budget as a starting point rather than zero.

- **Matrix budgeting** — Members of independent divisions, branches, or sections are assigned to a project headed by a project manager in this system associated with the theory of matrix departmentalization. Matrix budgeting is used to fund programs or projects that involve a variety of departments, divisions, branches, or sections. The project is usually for a limited duration (such as the construction of a new fire station). Project team members may come from the fire, public-works, finance, legal, or street departments. Matrix budgeting has two identifying features:

— It permits double budgeting and imposes responsibility to gain consensus agreement, thus some view it as a key to collaboration between various departments.

— Project funds are vested in the partner departments, and allocation of other resources such as time and personnel must be shared.

• *Program budgeting* — Categorized by a program or activity; often a form of line-item budgets that use categories different from the classic line-item budget. In a fire and emergency services organization, each program — fire suppression, emergency medical services (EMS), fire prevention, public fire education, fire administration — is a separate category in the budget **(Figure 27.3)**. The line item for each program shows how much of the overall budget is allocated to that program — salaries, equipment, possible overtime, etc. Program budgeting often goes hand-in-hand with program evaluation. The relationship between the two helps administrators identify how much of the budget can be saved by abandoning costly, ineffective programs.

Figure 27.3 Program budgets provide funding for functions such as this plans review office.

• *Performance budgeting* — Categorized by function or activity (also called *outcome-based budgets*) similar to program budgets; however, these budgets fund each activity based on projected performance. For example, the budget for fire prevention is based upon conducting a specified number of inspections in various types of occupancies. Also included in a performance budget is a breakdown of the cost of each unit of performance — per inspection, plans review, EMS call, fire call, etc. Obviously, this budget can be very complicated and labor-intensive to develop and use.

• *Planning programming budgeting system (PPBS)* — Provides a framework consistent with the organization's goals, objectives, policies, and strategies for making decisions about current and future programs through three interrelated phases: planning, programming, and budgeting. The purpose of PPBS is to subject the budgetary process to intense, systematic, and continuous analysis. PPBS provides an overall management philosophy and a specific management process for policy development and implementation. It translates the erratic and unpredictable aspects of routine decision-making into a rational and quantified management scheme. Additional information regarding PPBS includes the following:

— PPBS is an effort to link planning and budgeting through the development of programs designed to achieve stated goals and objectives. Program effectiveness is determined through analysis based on cost-effective criteria.

— The PPBS system was developed in the 1970s in an attempt to coordinate planning, program development, and budget processes.

— Presently, PPBS is used in industry and by the U.S. Department of Defense and the U.S. Armed Forces. The original PPBS, although still in use by the military, has evolved into a service-based budgeting system in some jurisdictions.

Budget Requests

Managing company officers are responsible for preparing budget requests to obtain the items needed to operate their division or to manage a project. Preparation of a division budget request usually involves the relatively simple process of updating the requests from the previous year's budget to reflect current needs. Project requests may be more difficult if the project is new or a one-time event.

Budget requests from the various projects, battalions/districts, divisions, branches, and sections are combined to form a single budget request for the organization. A percentage that represents the rate of inflation based on the federal government's cost of living estimate is usually added to the request. It is important that all fire officers participate in this process. The chief officer and the company officer can share the workload and reduce the chances that something is omitted. Once a budget is approved, it is difficult to purchase anything that was not requested.

Budget Types

In general, two types of budgets are used by public organizations: capital budgets (projected major purchases) and operating budgets (recurring expenses of day-to-day operation).

Capital. A capital budget includes projected major purchases — items that cost more than a certain specified amount of money and are expected to last more than one year (usually three or more years). Fire apparatus and vehicles, equipment, and facilities are typical capital items for fire and emergency services organizations **(Figure 27.4)**. Many jurisdictions have multiyear capital improvement plans or projects (CIPs) for these and other major investments. A typical CIP may include a multiyear plan for replacing apparatus or

equipment or building a new training center. With a CIP, each year's capital budget represents that year's portion of the expenditures included in the CIP. Because capital budgets typically span several years, competing priorities between departments and changes in elected and/or appointed officials cause capital budgets to be dynamic and somewhat competitive.

The revenues for capital purchases may come from a variety of sources. The amount may be a set percentage of the annual revenues used to operate the jurisdiction. These funds are shared between the various departments of the jurisdiction. The final decision on what is purchased will be made by the governing body based on the justification provided by the representatives of each department. Another source may be a special tax dedicated to capital purchases such as a multi-year CIP or a dedicated sales tax. Special grants, assessments, or bond issues may also provide the necessary funds.

Operating. Unlike the capital budget that is used to pay for one-time, long-term purchases, the organization's operating budget is used to pay for the recurring expenses of day-to-day operations. The largest, single item in the operating budget of most career organizations is personnel costs — salaries and benefits. In many organizations, personnel costs (sometimes called *personnel services*) represent as much as 90 percent of the operating budget. Considering that noncash (fringe) benefits cost some jurisdictions an amount equal to 50 percent of a person's

Figure 27.4 A new fire station would be a capital budget item.

base salary, it is easy to understand why the personnel-services category represents such a high percentage of the budget.

Operating budgets also pay for utilities, office supplies, apparatus and vehicle fuel, janitorial supplies, and countless other items needed to function on a daily basis **(Figure 27.5)**. Contract services for the maintenance of apparatus and facilities are also a part of the operating budget.

Capital and operating budgets are normally separated for the following reasons:

- *Funding* — Capital purchases are funded by one-time, earmarked funds. One source of funds is the sale of bonds for the purchase of capital items. Separation ensures that the funds will not be used for other expenditures. Operating budgets are funded from general revenue sources such as property or sales taxes that are then as-

signed to the various departments, programs, or categories (personnel, training, etc).

- *Decision-making process* — Capital budgets involve a listing of all potential projects and a ranking in order of priority. As a project is funded and completed, it leaves the list and a new one is added. Operating budgets generally do not require ranking because the programs they fund usually continue from year to year.

- *Planning and implementation time frames* — Capital budgets involve a longer development time and may require many years for completion. Detailed planning is critical to prevent costly errors that result in change orders to the project documents. Operating budgets are generally developed over a period of six months before adoption of the new budget. Operating budgets do not require the high level of monitoring that the capital-budget projects require.

Budget Cycle

The term *budget cycle* is used to identify major events or activities in the development and implementation of the budget **(Figure 27.6, p. 632)**. The exact definition will vary from jurisdiction to jurisdiction but, generally, the following four stages will apply to most budgets.

Stage 1: **Budget formulation** — The administration develops the jurisdiction's budget. The budget development process may begin four to six months before the official beginning of the budget year.

Stage 2: **Budget enactment** — The council, commission, or legislative branch of the jurisdiction officially adopts the budget.

Stage 3: **Budget execution** — This is the implementation stage. Each division or department of the jurisdiction expends funds according to the adopted budget plan.

Stage 4: **Budget auditing and assessment** — In this stage the use of the funds is accounted for and the effectiveness of their use is evaluated.

The entire process is monitored, usually by the jurisdiction's finance and revenue department, to ensure that all legal mandates are met. Documentation is essential to the effectiveness of monitoring, auditing, and assessing the budget process.

Figure 27.5 Examples of items that would be funded through an operating budget.

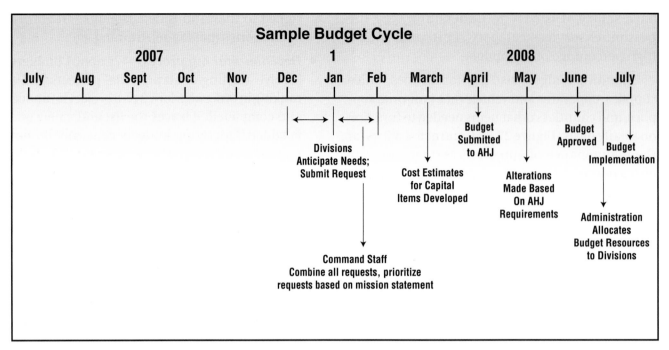

Figures 27.6 Many fire and emergency services organizations operate on a budget cycle similar to this one.

Budgets are usually annual, beginning on a specific date. Generally, there are three budget cycles used in North America. The budget cycle may begin and end on the following dates:

- January 1 – December 31 (calendar year)
- July 1 – June 30 (budget year)
- October 1 – September 30 (U. S. federal government year)

Revenue Sources

All government jurisdictions depend on some type of revenue to provide the services that citizens require. The majority of jurisdictions depend on property, sales, or income taxes (or a combination of these) as the primary source of revenue. Trust funds, enterprise funds, bond sales, grants/gifts, or fund-raising may supplement or replace this revenue (**Figure 27.7**).

Tax Revenues

Traditional sources of revenue that government organizations depend on include property taxes, use fees, sales taxes, and income taxes. These taxes tend to provide a rather stable and predictable source of revenue that is available to all levels of government. These traditional sources of revenue are not, however, completely immune to changes in

the economy or taxpayer revolts. Company officers must be aware of the trends in revenue collection in order to develop realistic budget projections and program goals. It may be necessary to actively support an increase in taxation by justifying it based

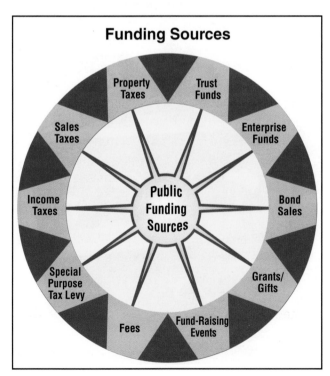

Figures 27.7 Many funding sources exist for public services.

on the required level of services. Gaining support for tax increases requires accurate data collection and public presentations that are objective and factual. Descriptions of the various revenue sources are as follows:

- **Property taxes** — Ad valorem (Latin for *according to value*) tax levied against the owner of real or personal property. Property ad valorem taxes are the major source of revenues for state and municipal governments. They generally have been very dependable, increasing with the value of property as determined by the most recent sale price or periodic evaluations by tax assessors. However, because of voter disapproval, the past 25 years have seen changes that have resulted in stagnation or regression in property-tax revenues. Some states have placed a ceiling or limit on the annual increases in property taxes and even require a vote of the people to approve any increases over a specified amount.

- **Sales taxes** — Levied by a state or city on the retail price of an item, collected by the retailer. Sales taxes are generally levied at municipal and state levels of government and may be the primary revenue source for operating budgets. They are also a target for citizen groups who demand tax reform.

- **Personal income taxes** — Collected by the federal government, most state/provincial governments, and some municipal governments. Income taxes, like other forms of revenue, have been the subject of some voter concern and are directly affected by the economy and political trends. Layoffs, reductions in work hours, loss of overtime benefits, and tax cuts have all resulted in decreased revenues for all jurisdictions.

- **Special purpose tax levy** — Based on the assessed value of property specified as *millage* ($1/$1,000 property valuation) and collected by the local government for a specified government purpose, such as the operation of the fire department or ambulance service. The tax levy, which runs for a specified time period, is submitted to voters for approval. Another approach is the special taxing authority used to support rural fire-protection districts.

- **Fees** — Collected for building permits, plans review, reports, vehicle registrations, building inspections/reinspections, hazardous-materials response, EMS response, and even fire protection (subscription services for emergency response) to support services. The individual department/organization or the finance and revenue department may collect fees and then credit them to the appropriate organization.

Trust Funds

A *trust fund* is an account whose assets are managed by a trustee or a board of trustees for the benefit of another party or parties. Funds are governed by applicable federal and state/provincial laws and the legal document that established the trust. Funds that are derived from donations and gifts are placed into the account. Donations and gifts may be further divided into categories such as undesignated gifts, broadly designated gifts, and specifically designated gifts, depending on the wishes of the donor. Thus a donation may be designated for the purchase of a new piece of equipment, construction of a new facility, or simply for operation of the organization.

There are two types of trust funds: general and specific. *General* trust funds can be either perpetual or long-term: Perpetual trusts are funds from which only income (interest) from capital may be expended. Long-term trusts are funds from which both income and capital may be expended. Any capital spent from long-term trusts must be defined as expendable. *Specific* trust funds are short-term funds that are spent in the current year for some expressed purpose. Trust funds are usually intended for one-time purchases and not for recurring operating expenses.

Another form of trust fund is the employee pension fund that provides retirees with an income based on years of service, age, and contributions. Both the jurisdiction and the employee usually make contributions to the fund over the length of the employee's service.

Enterprise Funds

An *enterprise fund* is established to finance and account for the acquisition, operation, and maintenance of government facilities and services, such as water and sewer services, that are entirely or pre-

Figures 27.8 An ambulance service such as this one might be funded by an enterprise fund.

dominantly self-supporting by user fees. Enterprise funds may also be established when the jurisdiction has decided that periodic determination of revenues earned, expenses incurred, and/or net income is appropriate. Government-owned utilities and hospitals are ordinarily accounted for by enterprise funds. The ambulance transportation component of EMS is often sustained or supplemented by an enterprise fund, if the service is provided by a government agency **(Figure 27.8)**.

An *auxiliary enterprise* is an entity that exists to furnish services to the population of a service area and that charges a fee related to the cost of the service. Auxiliary enterprise accounts are operated on an annual budget based on the estimate of operating income and expense, including bond-interest expense and provisions for bond retirement if applicable. Fire-protection subscriptions (annual dues or fees paid by residents for fire protection similar to homeowner's insurance) may be used to create auxiliary enterprise funds.

Restricted Funds

Restricted funds receive money from a single source, such as building or smoke detector inspections. The fire department collects the money and deposits it into a restricted account. Only the fire department can withdraw funds from that account. These funds can only be used for very specific expenses, such as fire and life safety program costs.

Sinking Fund

Although not a source of revenue, sinking funds are part of the budget of most state/provincial and municipal governments. A *sinking fund* is an account that receives a specified amount of revenue that will be used in the future to pay off the jurisdiction's indebtedness. That is, when a municipality sells bonds to build a new fire station, funds must be accumulated from sales or property tax to buy the bonds back with interest at a specific date in the future.

Bond Sales

A *bond* is a certificate issued by a governmental entity or jurisdiction that promises to repay the principal along with interest on a specified date, that is, when the bond reaches maturity. Some bonds do not pay interest, but all bonds require a repayment of principal. When an investor buys a bond, that person becomes a creditor of the jurisdiction that sold the bond. The federal government, states/provinces, counties/parishes, municipalities, public corporations, and many other types of institutions sell bonds to fund programs and projects.

Bonds are divided into different categories based on tax status, credit quality, issuer type, maturity, and whether they are secured or unsecured, as well as other classification methods. U.S. government treasury bonds (T-Bonds) are generally considered the safest unsecured bonds because the possibility of the U.S. Treasury defaulting on payments is almost zero. Some bonds are tax-exempt such as those typically issued by municipal, county/parish, or state/provincial governments. These interest payments are not subject to federal income tax and sometimes are not subject to state or local income tax.

In some jurisdictions, members of the electorate must approve the sale of bonds. Bond sales are linked to specific purchases such as apparatus or land. This type of single-use funding may be an alternative to tax revenues when there is strong voter sentiment against property, sales, or income tax increases.

Grants

Many fire and emergency services organizations supplement their general budgets with grants that are either private or corporate donations or subventions (subsidies) from the national or state/provincial governments to these organizations to meet specific needs. For example, in some states a portion of all fire-insurance premiums paid into the insurance industry is returned to local fire and emergency services organizations to pay for training and training-related materials. In many jurisdictions, service clubs and other civic organizations have donated funds to purchase specialized equipment such as hydraulic rescue tools or semiautomatic defibrillators. It is important that funds donated for capital purchases are used for that purpose only, and not for operating expenses.

Government and nongovernment grants. Grants are available from both governmental and nongovernmental organizations (NGO) for specific purposes. Government grants, such as those provided by the U.S. Fire Administration (USFA), the U.S. Department of Homeland Security (DHS), or U.S. Department of Transportation (DOT), provide local emergency responders with the training and equipment necessary to deal with a variety of incidents. Nongovernment organizations or nonprofit organizations provide grant money to fund programs, such as civilian cardiopulmonary resuscitation (CPR) training, through fire and emergency services organizations **(Figure 27.9)**. The application process for obtaining grants can be challenging, especially for small organizations.

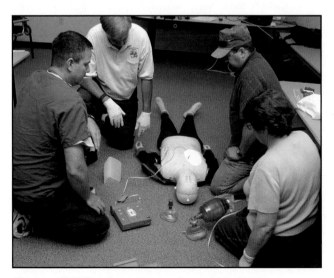

Figures 27.9 Grant money may be used to fund a defibrillator training program.

Block grants. While many grants are based on specific needs, such as hazardous-materials response training, other federally and state/provincial supported programs operate largely through consolidated funding streams, normally referred to as *block grants*. Under this methodology, funding is made available for defined purposes but with minimum conditions. The use and support for block grants have increased in recent years. They meet the need for flexibility at the program level. Block-grant funding minimizes the bureaucratic aspects of the budgeting process because those outside the performance chain are presumed accountable for fund expenditures. The increasing use of block grants recognizes that those who do the work and spend the funds are accountable, responsible, and best qualified to make such decisions. At the same time, block grants ensure community involvement in the application process. An example of a program funded by a block grant is a senior-citizen safety awareness program that provides education as well as smoke detectors or fire extinguishers to participants.

Foundations

The fire service is not as familiar with foundations as a source of revenue. However, in certain situations they can provide considerable funding to the fire service. When researching available foundations, company officers should realize that foundations want to make a difference. As such, the foundation's scope is limited and the application requirements quite extensive.

Foundations usually focus on specific projects or innovative ideas. They usually have a specific target area of interest and geographic area in which to support projects. It is a waste of time to solicit funds from a foundation if the department is not within its scope or geographic area. There are several different types of foundations and are organized as private, corporate, community, and operating. They usually have a board of directors and will give potential recipients information on their scope and geographic distribution area. Many state governments publish an annual listing of foundations operating within their jurisdictions. These reports contain valuable information including the scope of the grants, the target area and audience, the value of the grants, application deadlines, and the contact person for the foundation.

Fund-Raisers

Fund-raising is most often an activity used by volunteer or combination organizations to supplement or provide their own operating revenue. Fund-raising usually takes the form of local events such as social events, bingo, raffles, and requests for donations. Some organizations have annual bean or pancake suppers that serve as public-relations events as well as fund-raisers **(Figure 27.10)**. In some areas, fire and emergency services organizations sponsor circuses and other events and share the proceeds with organizers of the events. The greatest danger in these cosponsored events is that the telephone solicitations required to sell tickets may result in negative responses from the public, which will focus on the organization and not the telephone marketers. Fund-raisers can also be very time consuming, which often requires additional staff-hours from already taxed volunteer members.

Budget-Development Process

Company officers work together along with chief officers, other staff members, and citizen representatives to create annual budgets. To help ensure successful adoption, both internal and external

Figures 27.10 An example of a flyer for a fund-raising event.

customers should be involved in the process. Because the process is involved and ongoing, it should be divided into understandable steps. In general, six steps are involved in the budget process: planning, preparation, implementation, monitoring, evaluating, and revising.

Budget Planning

Throughout the year, the chief officers and managing company officers who are responsible for budget preparation should keep records and make notes on the implementation of the current budget. Depending on local conditions or legal requirements, the budget process begins in earnest three to five months before the end of the current fiscal year. At this point, a jurisdiction should have a fairly clear idea of estimated revenues, based upon tax projections; expected grants and subsidies from the state/provincial or federal government; expected fees for services; bond sales; and other sources.

Budget planning is part of the strategic-planning process. The financial resources necessary to implement elements of the strategic plan must be determined in order to include them in the budget process. A budget project-management team assists in evaluating the effectiveness of the current budget, determining funding requirements to meet the annual objectives of the strategic plan, and analyzing any trends that may affect the budget such as taxpayer unrest. A budget project-management team may consist of representatives from the following areas:

- *External customers (community)* — Involvement of community members is very important. The organization serves external customers who, in turn, provide a source of funding which the organization depends on to operate.

- *Internal customers (employees)* — Internal customers are the human resources expected to implement the budget. If they do not have an opportunity to participate in the process, they will not understand how the final budget was developed and why certain programs/projects were funded ahead of others. It is also essential that representatives of the labor organization be involved so that they are aware of the available revenue and personnel costs.

Figures 27.11 A fire department officer describing a budget request to a group of citizens.

- *External stakeholders* — Leaders of civic or nonprofit organizations, who may partner with the organization or business leaders, may require additional services. Therefore, they may have a stake in the operation of the organization during the year (**Figure 27.11**).

Budget Preparation

The jurisdiction's finance and revenue department estimates revenues from all sources into preliminary budget priorities. The chief/manager of the organization may be informed of the general fiscal conditions and what parameters to work within during departmental budget planning and preparation sessions. The jurisdiction may require that the department/organization submit the same budget as the current year with an adjustment for inflation. The chief/manager may be told to submit a budget that reflects an across-the-board increase or decrease of a specified percentage based on projected revenues as determined by the financial department of the jurisdiction. In any case, those chief officers, company officers, and other participants responsible for preparing the organization's budget request must begin preparing a budget-request proposal.

Budget requests. Budget requests should not be inflated or overestimated. To help the taxpayers and their elected representatives make informed decisions about how tax revenues are spent, fire and emergency services organization officers have a responsibility to make every budget request as accurate and realistic as possible. These officers should present the budget request in the format expected by administrators and elected officials.

At this point, the chief and the administrative staff must decide the level and type of services the organization can and should provide during the upcoming year. In most cases, the organization's budget request reflects the same services and service levels as the previous year. However, there may be a need to add new services or delete existing services because of changes in the needs of the service area.

Funding requests. The decisions regarding services and service levels must be translated into firm program proposals, and a funding request must be developed for each program. Each program must be described in terms of personnel, equipment, and material needs as well as other costs. Chief officers and managing company officers are responsible for describing these programs and developing the funding request for each one. Some jurisdictions require the use of specific types of program-justification forms in the budget-development process. Company officers must be familiar with these forms and the information required to complete them.

All requests should be kept as simple as possible. The simplest, most direct language should be used. In the narrative description of the services and their funding requirements, the language should be written so that anyone can understand it — no acronyms or fire and emergency services jargon. Those who ultimately decide to approve or disapprove these requests may have little or no knowledge of fire and emergency services terms. If a request is disapproved or reduced, it should be done on the merits of the program — not because the request could not be understood.

In most jurisdictions, funding requests for capital items are separated from operating expenses as mentioned earlier. Even though these two categories must be separated, they are submitted as part of the same organizational budget request. Once all this data are compiled and translated into specific requests for specific programs and activities, the first draft of the budget request is finished. Because this request will be thoroughly scrutinized along with the requests from every other organization in the jurisdiction, its chances for approval are increased if the document is as complete and correct as

possible. Therefore, before it is submitted for external review (by the jurisdiction), prudent administrators insist that each departmental/organizational budget request go through a diligent internal review first.

A complete budget contains information that supports the requests based on valid and accurate justification. Additionally, the systems approach may be used to illustrate the budget. Prudent administrators also insist that each organizational budget request go through a diligent internal review before it is submitted for external review (by the jurisdiction).

Justification. Justifying a budget request requires documentation and supporting evidence that proves to even the most casual listener that the request is valid. Thorough research is the basis for this documentation. This information is not only used to justify the budget request, it is also the information that was used to prepare the budget in the first place. Accurate research and internal records maintenance provide strong bases for both activities. Sources to be researched include the following (**Figure 27.12**):

- *Organizational financial history* — Primary source of data to support the budget request based on the actual cost of providing the services required by the jurisdiction. This history includes (but is not limited to) the costs of fuel, maintenance, utilities, parts, training, operating supplies, and a multitude of other expenditures. It can be used to justify the operating budget or a capital request such as the replacement of an apparatus or vehicle.

- *Market studies* — Surveys of similar service areas and organizations, which provide foundations for personnel salary increases, changes in benefits, or the hiring of additional personnel. Lists of fire and emergency services organizations that may be used for comparison are available from the IAFF.

- *Actual equipment, material, or service costs* — Information available from vendors, which reflects the average cost of an item or product. Information may also be based on existing contracts the jurisdiction has for materials or services.

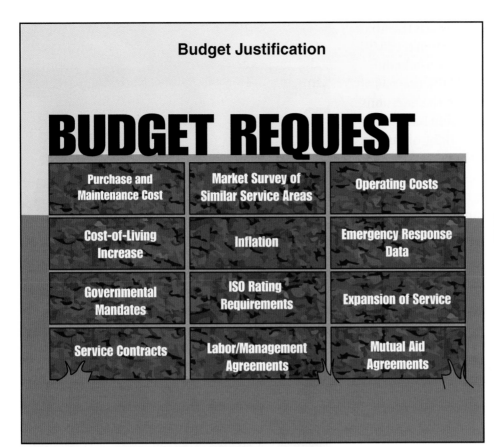

Budget Justification

BUDGET REQUEST

Purchase and Maintenance Cost	Market Survey of Similar Service Areas	Operating Costs
Cost-of-Living Increase	Inflation	Emergency Response Data
Governmental Mandates	ISO Rating Requirements	Expansion of Service
Service Contracts	Labor/Management Agreements	Mutual Aid Agreements

Figures 27.12 A variety of justifications for budget requests.

- *Performance data* — Information provides a clear understanding of inadequate resources based on actual response data.

- *Government economic reports* — Information provides an idea of the cost-of-living increase based on inflation or the estimated revenue potential for the service area.

- *Insurance information* — Information from the state/provincial insurance commission, which includes fire-related claims, insurance premiums, Insurance Services Office, Inc. (ISO) rating figures, and projections based on service levels.

- *Governmental mandates* — Essential documentation when higher levels of government place requirements on local services and then fail to provide adequate funding.

- *Contractual requirements* — Contracts with the labor organization and contracts for services that the department/organization is obligated to provide such as mutual or automatic aid response.

Internal review. In this context, *internal* refers to the fire and emergency services organization as well as the parent organization, such as the Department of Public Safety, to which it may be assigned. The administrator of the parent organization, the chief/manager of the organization, or staff of both organizations thoroughly review the fire and emergency services organization's budget request. At this stage of the process, the budget is critically reviewed to determine if the data available justify the request. It is also an opportunity to consider alternative approaches to providing the same services or alternative sources of revenue. The fire and emergency services administrator should consider potential questions that the governing body may ask and develop answers based on sound arguments. After a thorough internal review, the fire and emergency services organization's budget is incorporated into the combined budget request for the entire Department of Public Safety. This document is then submitted to the jurisdiction's governing body for an external review.

External review. The *external* review is the final review that the budget-request document receives. The governing body of the jurisdiction schedules one or more public hearings so that the citizens of the jurisdiction can have input into the decisions on the budget. The budget may be sent back to the administrator to be reworked in light of citizen concerns. The governing body then considers both revenues and expenditures and may adjust either or both to balance the budget and meet the needs of the citizens. When the concerns of citizens have been addressed and the budget is balanced, the governing body approves the budget and it becomes law. However, many municipalities schedule the public hearing at the same meeting as the vote for budget adoption, which limits the amount of public input on the document. In some communities, certain factions of the electorate may view this negatively and as a result influence how they view the various departments within the organization.

Budget Implementation

Once the budget has been approved, the administrator, department heads, managing company officers, and supervising company officers now have the funds with which to turn the vision reflected in the budget into reality. They must use their administrative and managerial skills to implement the budget. In addition to important fiscal details, the approved and adopted budget represents a plan for the organization's operation for the fiscal year. Company officers should take this opportunity to meet with subordinates to review the budget and explain what it means to the project and the organization's operation **(Figure 27.13)**.

The budget informs those who must function within its limitations if new personnel can be hired, staff cuts will be necessary, vacant positions can be filled, and new equipment can be purchased. In addition, the budget requests that were approved or disapproved may provide an indication about how the jurisdiction perceives the services provided by the organization — or they may simply reflect fiscal reality. The budget message should include any specific praise or criticism by the jurisdiction of the organization's operation. While the praise may be gratifying, the criticism may be more valuable. If

Figures 27.13 A company officer reviewing a budget with crew members.

criticism is viewed objectively, it can serve as a way to focus future priorities and performance within the fire and emergency services organization.

Budget Monitoring

The budget process does not end with the implementation of the budget. It must be monitored to determine its effectiveness and prevent a budgetary crisis in the event of a change in the economic environment. Typically, the individual organizations within the jurisdiction are only informed of the expenditures of their allotted budgets. Most jurisdictions print and distribute monthly account statements that indicate the account balance in each program, line item, or category of the budget. This accounting allows the officer who is responsible for budget administration to track the purchasing trends and ensure that accounts are not overspent. With the addition of computer-based accounting programs, this monitoring control can become a more frequent check performed on a weekly or daily basis with feedback provided to budget managers. In addition, many organizations now keep such budget-accounting information in electronic form on computer servers accessible to department managers. This electronic version provides more current information and eliminates the need for much of the printing and distribution that was done in the past (**Figure 27.14**).

When a trend appears that indicates that an account lacks sufficient funds to last the remainder of the fiscal year, the officer will have to determine the best option to address the problem. The legal options in order of preference include the following:

- Transfer funds from an underutilized account while maintaining a balanced total in the budget.

- Restrict further purchases from the account to an amount that can be evenly spread over the remainder of the year.

- Request a budget adjustment from the jurisdiction.

- Do nothing while continuing to monitor the account until it is empty or the trend ceases.

Through these options, the fire and emergency services organization has the ability to manage its budget efficiently. Unfortunately, the organization will not be aware of or have any control over changes in revenue collections. It may also take a month or more for the jurisdiction's finance and revenue department to determine that a trend is developing that will result in a revenue shortfall. At that point it may be necessary to require the individual organizations to take action. The decision to implement any actions must be made based on the primary mission of the organization. Because they are all drastic moves and have long-range consequences, they must be made only after a risk analysis. Aside from the previously listed options, the organizations may be required to implement the following actions:

- Limit all capital purchases.
- Reduce operating services.
- Reduce or eliminate overtime pay options.
- Eliminate positions, cease hiring replacement personnel, lay off employees, or make other personnel changes within the limits of the labor/management agreement.
- Close facilities.
- Eliminate preventive maintenance for apparatus, vehicles, and facilities.
- Seek alternative funding.

Typical Monthly Operating Budget Report

Report for July 2005

Account Number	Title	July Expenditures	July Encumbered	July Balance Remaining	Approved Monthly Allowance	Current Year to Date	Current Year Total
1002003001230	Janitorial	$ 5,000	$ 2,000	$ 1,000	$ 8,000	$ 35,000	$ 96,000
1002003001231	Tools	1,000	1,500	500	3,000	15,000	36,000
1002003001232	Supplies	5,000	2,000	3,000	10,000	40,000	4,000
1002003001233	Professional Services	4,000	2,500	1,000	7,500	21,000	90,000
1002003001234	Training	3,000	4,000	2,000	9,000	40,000	108,000
1002003001235	Personal Protective Equipment	10,000	5,000	5,000	20,000	120,000	240,000
Total		$28,000	$17,000	$12,500	$57,500	$271,500	$654,000

Figures 27.14 Budget spreadsheets such as this one are useful in tracking expenditure trends.

Budget Evaluations

Evaluating the effectiveness of a budget is part of the monitoring process. Applied to the purchase of materials, an evaluation can be as simple as determining that the proper amount and quality of materials are available in a reasonable amount of time. When it is applied to programs and performance, it requires a cost/benefit analysis that compares the total effort necessary to produce desired results. The individual project manager assigned by the jurisdiction may perform evaluations. The results of the evaluation can be used to justify program changes, additional funding for programs, or elimination of programs that are deemed cost-prohibitive.

Budget Revisions

There is always the possibility that a budget will have to be revised during the budget cycle. Causes may include the following:

- Decrease in revenue
- Increase in operating costs
- Budget underestimated actual costs
- Increase in service requirements
- Change in labor/management agreement
- Unforeseen or catastrophic occurrence

Because the budget expenditures must be in line with actual revenue, the most likely result of a change will be to revise the costs of operations or capital purchases. The process for revising the budget is defined by local ordinance or policy. However, the options and actions listed in the Budget Monitoring section can be applied to each of these reasons for revisions. Records should be maintained on all changes and revisions in the budget during the cycle. These records are necessary for improving the accuracy of future budget preparations and provide a history of the current budget.

Purchasing Process

A budget provides the organization with the funds necessary to perform its assigned mission. Part of this mission is to purchase materials, equipment, and apparatus necessary to perform that mission. The following personnel may be responsible for purchasing:

- Supply chief
- Apparatus chief
- Logistics chief
- Managing company officer
- Nonuniformed employee
- Member of the Central Purchasing Department of the jurisdiction **(Figure 27.15)**

This section of the chapter provides an overview of the purchasing process.

While large fire and emergency services organizations may have internal purchasing capabilities, small organizations may rely on a centralized purchasing department within the jurisdiction. In either case, the purchasing process possesses certain characteristics. The process for selecting and procuring apparatus, equipment, and materials must be objective, logical, methodical, and repeatable. An objective process must be based on fact and not emotion or gut-feelings. It must have a logical, stepping-stone pattern that allows each decision to be based firmly on the preceding decision.

Methodical means that it adheres to an existing, well-established pattern that has been used successfully by other organizations. Finally, it must be repeatable by future company officers who are given the task of providing logistical support through this process.

Figures 27.15 Many modern purchase orders can be completed on a computer.

The selection and procurement process provided in this chapter is applicable for all types of apparatus, equipment, personal protective equipment, and some types of expendable materials. The managing company officer who is responsible for purchasing apparatus, equipment, or materials directly from vendors or who generates purchase requests for a central supply source to fill should use the following steps as necessary to ensure that the proper supplies are provided. These steps apply to both capital items and operating equipment and materials, although the purchasing procedures may vary as indicated later in this section. The process steps include the following:

- Determine the needs of the organization.
- Conduct research on the equipment, manufacturers, and any applicable standards/regulations.
- Evaluate and field-test proposed equipment.
- Review product data.
- Conduct the purchasing process.
- Conduct acceptance procedures.

Determine Needs

A needs assessment takes place once during the budget-preparation process and again before purchasing the approved equipment and materials. Once a list of equipment and materials is developed, it is necessary to research the quality and quantity that is available for purchase and the vendors who can provide them. The organization's needs may be determined in a variety of ways such as the following:

- *Perform a needs assessment* — Evaluation based on the programs and services provided by the organization to the jurisdiction. Each program manager (suppression, prevention, training, etc.) can provide a list of the equipment and materials required to complete the programs during the fiscal year based on past experience and future projections. The compatibility of equipment should also be taken into account.
- *Review standards and regulations that mandate the purchase of specific types of equipment* — Legal mandates created by the local, state/provincial, or federal governments for the operation of a fire and emergency services organization.

- *Review the current purchases* — Indicates the effectiveness of the current equipment and materials in meeting the service requirements of the response area. It also helps to determine if the correct quantities of materials are available in a timely fashion.
- *Perform a hazards analysis of the response area* — Helps to focus on any changes in the service area and the need for changes in programs, services, or equipment.
- *Determine the amount of funds available in each budget account* — If an account does not contain sufficient funds to purchase the required quantity of materials, follow the options outlined in the earlier section on budget monitorship.

Conduct Research

The time required to conduct research depends on the type of equipment or materials being purchased. The managing company officer must ensure that there is sufficient time allowed to gather and evaluate the information. Expendable items such as janitorial supplies may require only a review of product literature, while apparatus or personal protective equipment may require from a few months to a year for research. The research process for capital purchases may include the following:

- Survey other jurisdictions.
- Review manufacturers' business histories.
- Request references.
- Review standards and regulations.
- Review industry trends.
- Compare various products.
- Determine equipment compatibility.
- Review purchasing ordinances and laws.
- Develop request for proposal.

Survey Other Jurisdictions

Research can begin by surveying fire and emergency services organizations in other jurisdictions about the type of apparatus or equipment that they use. Survey topics should include:

- Types of equipment used
- Problems encountered with the equipment

- Ability of the equipment manufacturer to meet specifications
- Equipment service or maintenance difficulties
- After-sales support by manufacturers or vendors

Send the survey to various members of the organization, including the maintenance, training, and emergency-response personnel; labor organization representatives; and the person in charge of the purchasing function. Allow each responder sufficient time to complete the survey. This approach provides a wider and more comprehensive view of the equipment by a multitude of personnel in other organizations rather than the opinion of one individual **(Figure 27.16)**. A sample survey form used for self-contained breathing apparatus (SCBA) is included in **Appendix R**, SCBA Survey Form. This form can be used or adapted for other equipment.

Review Manufacturers' Business Histories

Perform a review of the business histories of the various manufacturers and the vendors representing them. Annual reports, articles in trade journals, financial statements, and business reports published by companies such as Dunn and Bradstreet can provide an image of the company and some insight into its ability to supply the desired system or equipment. Consider the share of the market that the manufacturers hold and why they have that share.

Figures 27.16 Survey information may be gathered by telephone.

Request References

Another important source of information is references from other organizations, including both public and private purchasers that have purchased the equipment. Request a list of the most recent purchasers of equipment that is similar to the type under consideration from the manufacturers.

Review Standards and Regulations

Review all applicable standards and regulations. These standards/regulations include not only the equipment's operational requirements but also design and testing requirements. This review allows the company officer to develop specifications that meet or exceed the standards/regulations. A thorough understanding of the relevant standards/regulations also allows the officer to better judge the products that are submitted for evaluation.

Review Industry Trends

Manufacturers are continually making changes in the design of fire and emergency services equipment to meet changes in the standards/regulations. In addition, changes are made to improve the equipment based on internal research projects and improvements in technology. Therefore, a company officer must review the latest industry trends in equipment design. Trade journals, trade shows, and press releases by the manufacturers' marketing divisions all provide opportunities to keep up with current developments **(Figure 27.17)**. In some cases, online Internet sites have product reviews that may assist in the decision-making process.

Compare Various Products

Competition is very strong among fire protection equipment manufacturers. Unlike the automobile industry, there are few fire protection equipment manufacturers and limited customers. Therefore, a company officer must compare the various products based on the following:

- Similar characteristics
- Sales and technical support
- Parts availability
- Length of time before equipment may become obsolete or have a major design change

Figures 27.17 Exhibits at tradeshows are useful for identifying the latest trends in fire apparatus and equipment.

- Available warranties and warranty support
- Local manufacturer representation
- Manufacturer's ability to fill orders within a specified time frame

This information can be entered into a matrix or computer database for ease of comparison. Competition in the marketplace can be used to an organization's advantage when negotiating terms of contracts.

Determine Equipment Compatibility

Information gained during the needs assessment relating to compatibility is now applied to the equipment under consideration. Compatibility includes both physical compatibility and equipment usability. The equipment must meet the operational procedures of the organization without drastic changes in training and operational procedures. For example, if an organization is issuing individual respiratory protection facepieces that can be used with both self-contained breathing apparatus (SCBA) and supplied-air respirator (SAR) units, compatibility concerns must be included in the evaluation. As well, when the operational standard calls for 24-foot (7.3 m) extension ladders, the purchase of A-frame folding ladders will have a negative effect on ladder operations and training.

Review Purchasing Ordinances and Laws

Once all the essential data has been collected, review the purchasing ordinances and laws of the jurisdiction. Most jurisdictions are bound by state/provincial purchasing requirements. Involving members of the jurisdiction's legal, finance, or purchasing departments in the process prevents any errors in the development of specifications or bid development.

Develop Request for Proposal

If the jurisdiction permits, it is a good idea to develop a request for proposal (RFP) before sending bid notices. An RFP defines the needs of the organization and allows manufacturers or their authorized distributors to decide if they can meet bid specifications. An RFP must have a specific schedule outlined, including bid dates, delivery dates, provisions for supplying equipment for scheduled evaluations, and training dates for maintenance technicians and training officers. An RFP also allows the jurisdiction to have control over the companies that can bid, based on responses to the RFP and participation in prebid meetings. Companies are eliminated from consideration for the following reasons: failure to meet delivery deadlines or provide required performance bonds, lack of established financial support to complete the contract, or a documented history of contract violations. The RFP process reduces the number of bidders to those companies that are capable of meeting the bid specifications.

Before writing an RFP, the company officer should consult both legal counsel and the authority's purchasing laws to determine what kinds of controls can legally be placed on bids or bidders. The selection of bidders may not be subjective or arbitrary. A sample RFP is found in **Appendix E**.

NOTE: Fire and emergency services organizations cannot be subjective or arbitrary in the selection of bidders for fire protection equipment, apparatus, or materials: Open and fair purchasing laws regulate all government organizations. Company officers must respect these laws and operate within them.

Once a specific product is determined to be the most appropriate for the organization, it can be established as the standard for the organization.

Thus the organization does not have to rewrite specifications the next time identical equipment needs to be purchased. Another approach is to establish a renewable contract in the bid specifications. The contract may be negotiated for one year with three subsequent annual renewals based on a set increase for inflation if both parties agree. However, due to rapid changes in the standards/regulations for respiratory protection, protective clothing, and apparatus, the purchasing organization must be prepared to rewrite the specifications based on recent changes. Ensure that contract language also reflects this possibility.

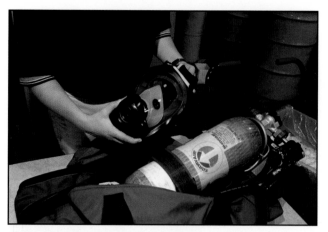

Figures 27.18 Equipment evaluations help determine if new equipment will meet the department's needs.

Evaluate Equipment

The RFP should contain language requiring a physical evaluation of fire protection equipment and accessories that each manufacturer is planning to submit for bid. This physical evaluation is an opportunity for the organization to test the proposed equipment in controlled training exercises and in actual daily operations. The physical evaluation, like the prebid meeting, should be a requirement for participation in the official bid process. Companies that do not participate should not be certified to continue the bidding process. Each manufacturer should provide a specified number of units, usually enough to outfit at least one emergency-response unit. Before the actual evaluations, the manufacturer must provide training for personnel participating in the testing of the equipment. In the case of respiratory protection equipment, individual facepieces must be supplied for the testing personnel and properly fit tested. The facepieces must be provided in a variety of sizes in order to fit all possible facial configurations. A manufacturer's sales or technical representative should be present during the equipment evaluations to answer questions or provide additional training **(Figure 27.18)**.

The physical evaluation should include both training evolutions and actual field tests. Therefore, the RFP must specify the total amount of time that the equipment is needed for evaluation, specific dates and times for training evolutions, and language releasing the organization from responsibility for any damage or wear to the equipment.

Regardless of the types of training evolutions, a company officer must have an objective grading system for the equipment. Establish criteria and assign points based on the equipment's ability to meet the standard/regulation. Grades may be numerical from *best* to *worst*, or terms such as *excellent, good, fair,* or *poor* may be used. Include a comments section on the grade form for any additional information or opinions by users. A sample form for the evaluation of respiratory protection equipment is included in **Appendix S**, Equipment Evaluation Form. Evaluation criteria may include (but are not limited to) the following factors:

- Maneuverability
- Flexibility
- Effect on vision
- Ease of donning
- Ease of doffing
- Impact on workload
- Comfort
- Durability
- Ease of operation
- Compatibility with operational procedures

Once the controlled training evaluations are complete, the evaluation units are assigned to active emergency-response units. Depending on the activity level of the units, this portion of the evaluation may take a month or more. Personnel are given equipment evaluation forms to complete after each use. Field evaluations under actual use conditions provide additional data for the company officer and also allow personnel who will be using the final product to have a part in the selection process. Therefore, personnel (other than those who participated in the controlled training evaluations) should be chosen to conduct field tests. The managing company officer compiles and analyzes the information gained from the physical evaluations. All grading forms and comments are retained in the specifications files in case the final purchase decision is questioned. The importance of maintaining thorough and complete records cannot be overemphasized.

Review Product Data

Once field evaluations are complete, the company officer can consider other facts about the various equipment systems, materials, or apparatus. Some areas of concern and factors to consider are as follows:

- *Features* — List the various features and accessories available with the particular equipment.

- *Durability* — Answer the following questions: How sturdy is the equipment? Are plastic parts easily broken? Will the equipment withstand rough treatment?

- *Life-cycle cost* — Include the initial purchase price (which may have to be estimated based on the list price) and costs of annual maintenance, parts, and support amortized over the life expectancy of the equipment to determine life-cycle cost.

- *Maintenance requirements* — Determine maintenance requirements by considering the manufacturer's suggested maintenance schedule, the level of technician certification and training, and whether maintenance can be done in-house or by a contract vendor approved by the manufacturer.

- *Infrastructure* — Answer the following questions: What is the existing infrastructure that supports the current brand of equipment? What changes or investments are required to redesign the equipment maintenance facility, modify existing systems, and retrofit apparatus mounting hardware?

When all the data is collected and reviewed, the company officer should recommend the system, equipment, or apparatus that best meets the established needs of the organization. Equipment that does not meet the criteria should be eliminated from consideration. The company officer must be fully aware of purchasing ordinances or laws in the event that specifications are too restrictive and legally prohibited. If specific equipment is determined to meet the organization's needs, thereby precluding an open-bid process, the jurisdiction's purchasing and legal departments may require a variance or exemption from the approved purchasing process. See Create Bid Specifications section for more information.

Conduct Purchasing Process

The purchasing procedure for fire protection equipment depends on the process adopted and regulated by the authority having jurisdiction. Most equipment such as SCBA, SAR systems, ventilation fans, vehicles and apparatus, and power extrication tools are considered capital purchases and must have funds specifically allocated for those purposes. Other items such as high efficiency particulate air (HEPA) filter masks, equipment parts, air-purifying respirator (APR) cartridges, hand tools, equipment accessories, and janitorial supplies may be purchased from operating funds **(Figure 27.19, p. 648)**. Some purchases may require a formal bid process while others may be purchased on a purchase order form that does not require an official bid. The company officer must be aware of the process and conform to it. Generally, the purchasing process consists of the following steps:

1. Determine the funds available and the source of the funds.

2. Create bid specifications based on the evaluation process.

3. Evaluate the certified bid proposals.

4. Score the bid proposals.

5. Award purchase contract.

Two possible alternatives for purchasing equipment are the group or cooperative purchasing arrangements and piggyback bids. The group-purchasing arrangement permits small organizations

Figures 27.19 Some products and materials may be purchased at local stores.

to benefit from lower purchase prices that result from large-quantity purchases of similar types of equipment. This arrangement is especially helpful if an organization has limited staff or does not have the expertise to draft requests for proposals. In the piggyback bids, contract language is included that allows other organizations to use existing bids for a specified period of time. An advantage is that it reduces the time required for preparing and accepting a bid.

Determine Funding Sources

The first step in the purchase process is to determine the funding source. Some of the more common sources were mentioned in the budget sections. Another option that is based on local purchasing laws may be available — lease or lease/purchase arrangement. Funding sources include the following:

- *Operating funds* — Designated in an annual budget for purchasing perishable items such as disposable filter masks, cartridges, repair parts,

and janitorial supplies. The value of a purchased item is usually restricted to a specific value such as *less than $1,000.*

- *Capital funds* — Designated in an annual budget for purchasing capital items for items that are over a fixed value. An example might be an item that costs *more than $1,000* with a life expectancy of more than one year. These items are requested specifically during budget preparation and purchased through the bid process if approved.

- *Bonds* — Provide specific funds for particular projects or purchases. Voters must approve bonds that are issued by a jurisdiction and purchased by investors. Bonds are set for a fixed amount, a specified time period, and specific items. Bond proposals are used for high-cost projects such as replacement of the entire respiratory protection system in use by an organization. Because they depend on the approval of voters, bond proposals must be supported by good documentation and justified to the population.

- *Grants* — Funds provided by government agencies and nongovernment organizations. Grants provide equipment that an organization may not have the funds to purchase. For instance, in the U.S., an organization that must respond to transportation incidents that involve hazardous materials on an interstate highway can apply for a grant from the U.S. Department of Transportation. This grant would fund hazardous materials response protective clothing and the appropriate level of respiratory protection equipment. Grant funds do not have to be paid back, but the jurisdiction receiving the grant must be accountable for how the funds are spent.

- *Lease or lease/purchase* — Another method of obtaining or purchasing capital items, although not a funding source as such. A *lease* is used when equipment is needed only for a short duration or for extended evaluations. A *lease/purchase* arrangement allows the cost to be spread over several years. Purchasing ordinances and laws of the jurisdiction govern this method. In some cases it may be illegal to encumber funds in the subsequent budget cycle, thereby preventing a lease. The company officer must research this form of acquisition or purchase before including it in bid specifications. A cost/benefit analysis must be made to compare the direct purchase of equipment with the lease/purchase process cost.

Create Bid Specifications

Once the funding source is established and committed, the company officer must develop the actual bid specifications. Bid specifications include specific fire protection equipment requirements of the organization plus the legal requirements of the finance or purchasing officer of the jurisdiction. Most manufacturers provide sample specifications forms as a guide. The purchasing department prepares the wording of the basic legal requirements, sometimes referred to as *boilerplate*, which is required in all bid specifications. Boilerplates define the legal obligations that are necessary to meet the specifications. These requirements may include vendor attendance at a prebid meeting, warranties, liability or performance bonds, specified delivery times, payment schedules, and financial statements.

When developing product-specific specifications, the company officer in charge of purchasing or procurement should be aware of the legal-requirements sections of the specifications and their influence on potential bidders. The specifications language must be clear and concise. Each detail of the design requirement must be included, and nothing should be assumed **(Figure 27.20)**. Some of the items that should be included in bid specifications are as follows:

- Requirements for National Institute for Occupational Safety and Health/Mine Safety and Health Administration (NIOSH/MSHA) (current standard) or American National Standards Institute (ANSI) certification for the intended use, if applicable
- Requirements for NFPA compliance, if applicable
- Number of purchases
- Design requirements
- Delivery date
- Warranty
- Accessories
- Training for maintenance technicians

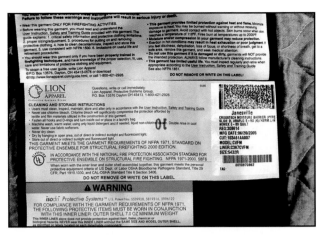

Figures 27.20 This label identifies the specifications for this particular product.

- Training for operational personnel
- Startup parts inventory
- Acceptance testing
- Technical support
- Penalties for nondelivery
- Length of time for which the quoted price is good

If a specific feature that meets valid operational requirements is available only from a single manufacturer, an option for bidding an equal alternative or a method to take exception to the specifications must be included. Purchasing ordinances or laws of the jurisdiction may prohibit a restrictive bid that includes too many specifications that only one manufacturer can meet. If a specific brand of equipment is the only type that meets the needs of the organization, then the finance or purchasing officer of the jurisdiction may grant a variance or exemption for a sole-source bid and declare that specific brand as the jurisdiction's standard.

The jurisdiction's finance or purchasing officer usually has to approve specifications. Once approved, the purchasing department issues the bid requests to qualified bidders and sets a date for the opening of the bids. The bids may only be returned to and handled by the purchasing department.

Evaluate and Score Proposals

Qualified bids are given to the company officer who is responsible for evaluating them. The evaluation process of the qualified bids is based on the original bid specifications. A matrix or spreadsheet can be created with the specific requirements listed down the side and individual bidders listed across the top. Values can be assigned to each requirement and written into the corresponding box, depending on whether or not the bidder exceeded, met, or failed to meet the specification. (See **Appendix S**, Equipment Evaluation Form.) Personnel involved in evaluating and scoring proposals must be aware of what behaviors are and are not appropriate during the bidding and procurement processes.

Award Purchase Contract

After the company officer has reviewed the bids, evaluated the bids, and made a recommendation to the chief/manager of the organization, the jurisdiction awards a purchase contract to the supplier with the winning bid. The legal department usually writes the contract, which binds both the supplier to meet the specifications and the jurisdiction to pay for the goods or services. The purchasing department administers the contract for the fire and emergency services organization that receives the goods or services. The fire and emergency services organization is responsible for accepting, testing, inventorying, storing, maintaining, and placing the equipment, materials, or apparatus into service.

The purchasing procedures of the organization, like most elements of the administrative function, must be continually monitored for effectiveness. Policies and procedures are most effective if they are considered *dynamic documents*; that is, documents that are subject to constant scrutiny, review, and revision. The chief officers and managing company officers of the organization are responsible for the monitoring of all policies and procedures. They should be familiar with the content, application, and effects of the purchasing procedures they use.

Summary

The administration of any fire and emergency services organization can be challenging. The company officer must be familiar with the process used to write and revise policies, procedures, rules, and regulations. The officer must also be able to evaluate the policies and procedures to ensure that they are fair, equitable, and up to date. Providing the equipment, apparatus, and operating supplies required to accomplish the organization's mission requires that the managing company officer be familiar with the concepts of the budgeting and purchasing functions as well as the specific policies and procedures adopted by the AHJ. While each of these functions may not seem as challenging as those encountered at emergency incidents, they are equally important and necessary for providing the services demanded by the public.

Material Safety Data Sheet (MSDS) Policies

Some policies that the company officer may be responsible for are mandated by federal or state/provincial law. One of those policies is based on the Hazardous Communications Standard (HCS) provided in parts 1910.1200 of the Code of Federal Regulations (CFR) of Chapter XVII of Title 29 under the Department of Labor (a.k.a. 29CFR1910.1200). HCS applies to nearly all employers and is applicable to most work operations where hazardous materials are present.

The HCS and the policies based on it require that a Material Safety Data Sheet (MSDS) be maintained on-site for each chemical or hazardous material located at the work site. In many instances, the material safety data sheets are based on OSHA Form-20, or a form that is essentially similar to Form-20.The forms are generally maintained in a binder in the office or watch booth of the facility. The standard requires that the binder be current and that any new materials used at the facility have their material safety data sheets added to the binder.

In the age of computers and electronic networks, OSHA permits the information to be maintained online or on computers rather than in paper format. If a paperless system is used, the employer must comply with the following requirements:

a. MSDSs must be readily accessible with no barriers to employee access. This means reliable devices accessible at all times without the employee needing to ask anyone for permission.

b. Workers must be trained in the use of these devices, including specific software.

c. There must be an adequate back-up system and written plan for rapid access to hazard information in the event of an emergency including power outages, equipment failure, online access delays, etc.

d. Employees and emergency response personnel must be able to immediately obtain hard copies of the MSDSs, if needed or desired.

Company officers must be familiar with the requirements of the Hazardous Communications standard and the local policies. They must also be responsible for seeing that the MSDS binders are current, that all materials on site that require MSDS forms have the forms, and that all personnel understand the policy and how to access the MSDS forms.

Fire and Life Safety Inspections

Chapter Contents

Learning Objectives

1. Select from a list the steps in assessing the potential risks to a community or service area.

2. Define *risk*.

3. Define *hazard*.

4. Identify the steps in assessing risk.

5. Match hazard categories to their definitions.

6. Select facts about private fire protection systems, water supply sources, automatic/mutual aid sources, and building construction types as they apply to risk assessment.

7. Choose correct responses about a company officer's authority to perform inspections.

8. Select facts about various ordinances, codes, and standards that are used to ensure fire and life safety.

9. Identify the company officer's responsibilities in the inspection process.

10. Select facts about preparing for inspections.

11. Select facts about conducting inspections.

12. Identify general inspection categories.

13. Match contents-hazard classifications to their definitions.

14. Select facts about hazardous materials labeling.

15. Select facts about inspecting/testing fire protection systems.

16. Match fire detection/signaling systems to their definitions.

17. Identify the three types of standpipe and hose systems.

18. Identify types of fire extinguishing systems.

Job Performance Requirements

This chapter provides information that addresses the following job performance requirements of NFPA 1021, *Standard for Fire Officer Professional Qualifications* (2003):

<u>Chapter 5   Fire Officer II</u>

5.5

5.5.1(A)

5.5.1(B)

Chapter 28
Fire and Life Safety Inspections

Reducing losses caused by hazardous conditions requires both a proactive and a reactive approach. For many years, the reactive approach took precedence. Resources were committed to the training of personnel and the purchasing of equipment and materials required to extinguish fires, extricate trapped victims, and provide medical treatment. The proactive approach was confined to fire prevention programs that included fire inspections, education, and investigations.

The Station Club Fire in West Warwick Rhode Island, 2003

The tragic deaths of 100 people in the February 20, 2003, fire at the Station Club in West Warwick, Rhode Island, resulted in changes not only at the state level but nationally. The state of Rhode Island passed and enacted a fire code safety law that:

- Adopted the NFPA 101® *Life Safety Code®*
- Removed the grandfather clause from RI fire codes
- Required sprinklers in high-risk assembly occupancies by 2006
- Authorized an increase in the number of state fire and life safety inspectors
- Required the application of the active alarm code
- Mandated that occupancy rates (number of people per square foot of space) be reduced until occupancies become compliant
- Required the presence of an on-duty firefighter in assembly occupancies during events
- Approved nighttime inspections of assembly occupancies and strengthened enforcement requirements

The Rhode Island fire service altered its operating procedures based on a review of the incident by:

- Increasing aggressive preincident planning
- Increasing the review of all public occupancies for fire and life safety violations
- Increasing company-level inspections and providing a visible presence

- Increasing mass-casualty training and planning
- Improving EMS site communications with area hospitals
- Purchasing additional mass-casualty equipment
- Improving communications equipment and procedures

Nationally, the NFPA Standards Council met and recommended the following changes in NFPA 101® and NFPA 5000®:

- Install fire sprinklers in new nightclubs and similar assembly occupancies and in existing facilities that accommodate more than 100 people.
- Inspect exits to ensure they are free of obstructions and to maintain records of each inspection.
- Employ at least one trained crowd manager for all gatherings, except religious services. For larger gatherings, additional crowd managers are required at a ratio of 1:250.
- Prohibit festival seating for crowds of more than 250 unless a life-safety evaluation approved by the authority having jurisdiction has been performed. Festival seating, according to NFPA 101®, is a form of audience/spectator accommodation in which no seating, other than a floor or ground surface, is provided for the audience to gather and observe a performance.

In addition, numerous states and municipalities have reviewed and revised their sprinkler requirements and occupancy codes in the wake of the Station Club fire. The Commonwealth of Pennsylvania required all of its fire inspectors and plans examiners to go through a refresher training and requalification process.

In recent years the proactive approach has gained more attention and, consequently, more resources. Fire prevention has expanded to include life-safety topics, public education has added information targeted at specific at-risk groups of people, and investigations have increased the use of advanced technology and subject profiling. It has been recognized that funds spent on a proactive preventive approach can significantly reduce the funds required for emergency responses and restoration of facilities and services following an emergency.

At the same time, communities have attempted to shift the responsibility for fire and life safety to the owners and occupants of structures. Stronger building codes have required improvements in the passive and active fire protection elements of building construction and process control. Suppression systems have been required in new construction buildings of a given size or occupancy type, hazardous processes have been eliminated from certain types of construction, and building ventilation systems have been designed with controls to permit their use in moving contaminated atmospheres out of the structure.

As a basis for the proactive approach, the fire and emergency services organization must know what hazards the community might be exposed to and the risks that those hazards create. Managing company officers may be responsible for the administration of the organization's risk management plan, fire and life safety inspection program, public education program, or investigations program (**Figure 28.1**). This chapter focuses on the community risk analysis and the fire and life safety inspection program. Information on public education may be found in the Fire Officer I portion of this manual while the investigation program is included in Chapter 29.

Community Risk Analysis

In everyday conversation, the terms *hazard* and *risk* are often used interchangeably; however, technically, they describe two different things. The term *hazard* usually refers to the source of a risk. A *risk*, on the other hand, is the likelihood of suffering harm from a hazard. Risk can also be thought of as the potential for failure or loss. In other words,

Figure 28.1 Inspecting new construction sites is one of the duties of personnel assigned to the code enforcement function.

risk is the exposure to a hazard. A *hazard* is a condition, substance, or device that can directly cause an injury or loss.

Assessing the potential risks to a community or service area involves the following steps:

- Applying a risk management model
- Determining the existing and potential hazards
- Cataloging and inspecting private fire protection systems in local facilities
- Determining the available water supply sources in the area
- Recognizing the types of building construction that are prevalent in the area
- Evaluating the existing and potential mutual aid agreements from regional fire and emergency services organizations

This information is critical in the development of a fire prevention and life safety program that the organization manages. Thorough research, data collection, and data analysis provide a framework upon which to build the program.

All-Hazards Risk Reduction Model

Traditionally, risk management has been associated with the NFPA model. However, this model is best suited for industrial environments and does not suit the needs of the modern community where an all-hazards approach to risk management and reduction is needed. For this reason, the National Fire Academy (NFA) developed, teaches, and advocates the all-hazards approach to risk reduction.

This approach gathers community risk into two broad categories: natural and man-made risks. Natural risks are those hazards that are caused by natural acts, such as hurricanes, tornados, blizzards, floods, earthquakes, and droughts (**Figure 28.2**). Man-made (better termed *human-caused*) risks are those that result from the acts of humans, such as fires, hazardous materials spills, explosions, vehicle accidents, and household accidents (**Figure 28.3**). Man-made risks may be intentional or unintentional, but they still pose a threat to people and can result in injuries, fatalities, and property loss. Community risk is the total sum of all natural and human-caused risks that a community may suffer.

Community risk reduction is the process of eliminating or reducing these risks. This process begins at the neighborhood level with the activities of the company officer and the emergency response personnel assigned to the unit. The company officer must be familiar with the steps in assessing the community or neighborhood risk:

Step 1: Identify the risks.

Step 2: Describe the people affected by the risk.

Step 3: Describe the cause of the risk.

Step 4: Prioritize the risks.

Identify the Risks

The first step in the process is to identify the risks in the neighborhood. The company officer can develop this list of risks from both traditional and nontraditional sources.

Traditional Sources of Information	Nontraditional Sources of Information
Fire and emergency incident reports	Discussions, both official and unofficial, with neighborhood leaders
Emergency medical service incident reports	Discussions with members of neighborhood groups and organi-

(Continued on p. 658)

Figure 28.3 Motor vehicle accidents can be classified as human-caused risks because they result from human error or behavior. Many result from drivers drinking alcohol prior to or while driving the vehicle. *Courtesy of Bob Esposito.*

Figure 28.2 Tornados annually strike many areas in North America. They are a particularly frequent and devastating natural risk to communities in the Central United States. *Courtesy of George Armstrong, photographer, FEMA.*

Traditional Sources of Information	Nontraditional Sources of Information
	tions, such as the Lions Clubs, Senior Citizens' Associations, and Neighborhood Associations
Fire and life safety inspection reports	Reports for government agencies and nongovernment organizations (NGO) serving the target groups and neighborhoods, such as Meals on Wheels, Neighbor for Neighbor, and Habitat for Humanity
Public fire and life safety education reports	Discussions with emergency response personnel who serve the neighborhood
Reports by fire investigators	Insurance reports, both property and automotive
Hospital emergency room data	Station logs listing the activities of the company during each shift
State fire marshal reports	Reports on sociocultural trends in the areas served
Reports and data from the U.S. Fire Administration such as the National Fire Incident Reporting System (NFIRS)	
Reports on fires and fire trends from the National Fire Protection Association (NFPA)	
Reports on public health trends from the Centers for Disease Control and Prevention (CDC)	
Reports from the local and state public health department	

The primary type of information is associated with emergency responses and has traditionally been the data and information used to plan community-wide prevention programs. This type of information includes the following data:

- Number of emergency responses by emergency units

- Frequency of each specific type of emergency

- Specific types of emergencies, for example, car fires, careless cooking fires, and heart attacks

- Types of structures where fires occur

- Amount of loss as a result of fire

- Types of injuries

- Addresses or fire demand zones where the emergencies occur

- Types of hazardous materials located in the neighborhood, including transportation, processing, and storage activities

- Types of requests for service by the public, such as assistance with opening car doors, removing water from flooded basements following a rain storm, and taking food or medicine to the elderly during a natural disaster

- Fire department personnel relaying customer comments to the company officer through the chain of command.

- Nonemergency activities such as going to schools, nursing homes, or day care centers

- Information on customer needs from other agencies and organizations working in the neighborhood

- Feedback from residents in the neighborhood

- Identified trends in the fire service, locally, statewide, and nationally

The information on the neighborhood risks is then divided into four categories: neighborhood information, local (community) information, state/provincial information, and national information. Some of the information will be specific to the neighborhood while other information will reflect a national trend. For instance, a simple example of risk by category might be as follows:

- *Neighborhood* — The majority of single-family residential structures were built prior to 1940.

- *Local* — The majority of families live at or below the poverty level.
- *State/provincial* — The state/province is in a region that is prone to drought conditions.
- *National* — Increased threat of possible terrorist attacks.

The end result of categorizing and analyzing the information is an all-hazard picture of the neighborhood within the community, state, and nation. The next step is for the company officer to determine each of the groups that are at risk.

Describe the People Affected by the Risk

In the all-hazard approach to risk reduction, the company officer must know who is at risk. Some hazards, such as flooding from a nearby river, will affect all members of the neighborhood (**Figure 28.4**). Other hazards, such as broken bones resulting from falls by elderly residents, may affect only a portion of the neighborhood.

The company officer must be aware of the demographics of the neighborhood and how those demographics change over time. For instance, as the residents of a neighborhood age, they may move to nursing or retirement homes. Younger families with children may move to the neighborhood. The needs of each group are different, and the company officer must be prepared to provide the correct service to each group.

Figure 28.4 Flooding may be a continuous community risk or a seasonal one depending on the geographic location of the community. *Courtesy of Arron Skolnik, FEMA photographer.*

Sources for demographic information include social services, census records, and public health records. Some of the demographic categories include the following information:

- Age
- Ethnicity
- Socioeconomic status
- Family type and configuration
- Cultural heritage
- Group values
- Religion
- Language

Describe the Cause of the Risk

Risks may have many apparent causes. There may be a primary cause or various secondary causes, but there will always be a root cause. The root cause may not be obvious at first, but the company officer must locate it in order to recommend the appropriate response to the risk.

For instance, a risk may have been identified as cooking fires that occur in the early evening. The majority of the victims may be people between 18 and 24 years of age. These fires may be the result of the person's starting to cook food on the stove and then leaving the kitchen area. On the surface, this may appear simply to be a problem caused by unattended cooking. However, national studies of this type of fire clearly indicate that the underlying factor causing these persons to fail to attend to the cooking is often their impairment due to alcohol or drug use. By misunderstanding this underlying factor, the prevention message may fail to address the dangers of cooking when impaired in such a way.

The company officer must identify the root cause for each of the types of risks that have been identified for each of the groups that are at risk. This may be a very time-consuming process, but the result will be an accurate picture of the all-hazard problem in the neighborhood and, ultimately, in the community.

Prioritize the Risks

The final step in the risk reduction process is to prioritize the risks in the neighborhood. The company officer should prioritize the risks based on severity and frequency. That is, how severe the result will be based on human suffering, economic cost, and environmental devastation. At the same time, the company officer must consider how often the hazard might occur: daily, weekly, monthly, annually, etc.

A very real and recent example of severity and frequency is the 2005 hurricane season in the Gulf of Mexico. Hurricane Katrina was very severe, causing extreme and long-lasting damage to the region, human lives, the environment, and the economy **(Figure 28.5)**. However, the potential frequency of a Category 5 hurricane (Katrina made landfall as a Category 3 storm) has been rare. Generally, the number of hurricanes within one season is also much lower than the 28 that occurred in 2005, exceeded only by 31 storms in 1931.

Prioritizing risks permits the company officer and the organization to allocate resources to meet the risks. Because the all-hazard model is broader in scope than the traditional fire and life safety prevention programs, it will be necessary for the company officer and the organization to address the risks through partnerships.

Partnerships include efforts between other municipal departments, nongovernmental organizations (NGO), and members of the community groups defined as at risk in Step 2 of the process. Each of these groups can provide resources, including personnel, funds, media support, and

materials in an effort to create an awareness of the risks and the steps to be taken to mitigate the risks.

Hazard Categories

The two broad community risk categories may be further divided into four specific subcategories: behavioral, intentional, natural, and occupancy-related. Obviously, not all of these hazards will result in fires or emergency incidents, but all are potentially life threatening to the population of the service area. A fire prevention and life safety program can be designed to reduce the threat posed by many of these hazards.

Behavioral

Behavioral hazards are caused by the perceived careless actions of individuals or groups **(Figure 28.6)**. Examples include storing ignitable liquids improperly, smoking in bed, and drinking and driving (personal habits that may result in injury, illness, or death). While the first example may be addressed with a strong inspection and code enforcement program, all three behaviors may be altered through a public fire and life safety education program. Collecting data on these hazards involves reviewing the organization's response history and categorizing the types of responses and the causes. Additional data sources include the local Red Cross and safety council, national safety organizations

Figure 28.5 Hurricane Katrina caused massive amounts of physical damage to the coastal regions around New Orleans in 2005. In addition, hundreds of thousands of people were displaced, unable to return to their homes. *Courtesy of Chief Chris E. Mickal.*

Figure 28.6 Careless behavior, such as using fuel near an open flame, can result in fatalities, injuries, and property loss.

such as the Home Safety Council (HSC), Centers for Disease Control and Prevention (CDC), and the medical profession.

Intentional

Intentional hazards result from actions that are meant to cause property destruction or life loss **(Figure 28.7)**. These hazards may include — but not are limited to — vandalism, arson, or terrorism, and the reasoning may include revenge, anger, or personal gain. In any case, an effective fire cause determination or investigation program helps to pinpoint the causal factor and provide evidence for a judicial case. Inspection and public education can also reduce the potential for such incidents. If the public is aware of a trend, they can provide information that may prevent future incidents. Data is gained through the review of previous investigations, an understanding of the local society that may indicate the existence of gang or criminal activity, or information from national sources that may provide trends that are similar to local events.

Figure 28.7 Terrorists, especially in the Middle East, have become extremely creative in the design of explosive and incendiary devices. The one shown here is inside an orange juice container.

Natural

Natural hazards consist of incidents that are generally out of the control of humans **(Figure 28.8)**. Tornados, hurricanes, earthquakes, floods, landslides, and forest fires are just a few that come to mind. Many of these incidents may be regional in nature, although some have occurred in unexpected areas. Most natural disasters would not be considered disasters if humans had not chosen to build, live, work or travel there. In fact, human activities can even exacerbate the severity of some natural events, such as landslides, floods, and forest fires.

Fire and emergency services personnel may not be able to prevent the effects of natural hazards, but they can reduce the consequences. Building and fire codes, along with zoning restrictions (such as those that prevent structures from being built in areas that are prone to natural hazards), can help reduce the potential effects of these hazards. Public fire and life safety education can also help reduce the number of deaths and injuries by training people in the proper response to various disasters. An example of educating the public is to remind drivers not to enter rapidly moving water that is crossing roadways. Information on these types of hazards may be obtained from the National Weather Service, historical documentation sources, and local geographical and population-spread data, which may be available through the library system or agencies of the local government.

Figure 28.8 Natural disasters including earthquakes, hurricanes, and tornados are out the control of humans. Potential damage can be reduced, however, by the enforcement of strict zoning and building codes. *Courtesy of FEMA News.*

The effect natural disasters have on the infrastructure of emergency services organizations is often overlooked in the planning stage.

Occupancy Related

The local or state/provincial building codes determine the occupancy-use categories such as assembly, residential, commercial, etc. Each of these categories is not only a criterion for building construction but also an indication of the potential hazard the structure presents. While the occupancy designations are usually determined by the building inspector or plans review personnel of the building department, the fire and emergency services organization is responsible for ensuring that the owner/occupant continues to adhere to the requirements of the building code. This adherence is accomplished through the enforcement of a particular fire code that has been adopted by the jurisdiction. In some jurisdictions, the fire prevention division may also be responsible for the duties normally assigned to a building department, including plans review.

The first step in determining occupancy-related hazards is to understand the building and fire codes and any local amendments in effect in the service area. The next step is to survey all structures (except single-family dwellings) and list the types of occupancies and hazards they create. This data can then be included in a community or service area hazards assessment and used to develop a complete fire prevention and life safety program.

Although single-family dwellings may be exempt from mandatory fire and life safety inspection requirements, they may be included in two programs that can reduce loss. (On military installations, single-family dwellings can be inspected.) First, a voluntary home inspection program can be established that doubles as a public education opportunity. Fire and emergency services personnel visit every home in their response area and offer voluntary home safety surveys. The surveys include the distribution of safety-related information, suggestions for safe storage of ignitable liquids, home escape plans, and tests of smoke detection equipment. Some jurisdictions even provide free smoke detectors or replacement batteries to residents of

target areas **(Figure 28.9)**. These target areas are determined by the frequency of fires, the economic status of the residents, and the age or infirmity of the residents.

The second program is a physical survey of all residential neighborhoods in the response area to determine the potential risks from natural hazards. Streets and highways are designated and marked as escape routes, recommendations for sheltering in place are made, and an inventory of the number of potential evacuees is developed. Facilities within the neighborhood, such as schools and recreation centers, are designated as evacuation sites and stocked with the appropriate supplies. Company officers may be assigned to assist emergency planners by gathering information on the neighborhoods. Emergency planners and managers use this information to establish a state/provincial, regional, or national plan for the evacuation of large numbers of people in the event of a major natural disaster, terrorist attack, or act of war.

Figure 28.9 Voluntary home inspections can help to eliminate hazards, such as improperly installed or maintained water heaters, and provide an opportunity to educate the public on safety issues.

Private Fire Protection Systems

The occupancy-use survey also provides information on the existence of private fire protection systems in structures in the service area. These systems may include fire detection and alarm systems, fire-suppression systems, private water distribution systems (private or yard hydrants), and auxiliary pumping systems **(Figure 28.10)**. Private fire protection systems usually exist when the local building code or insurance carrier requires them. In some cases, systems are installed when the owner/occupant determines that the savings in insurance premiums greatly offsets the cost of the installation.

Plans examiners review plans for the installation of private fire systems. Fire inspection personnel conduct field verifications to ensure installation of the system is being accomplished according to the approved plans. Fire investigators may also be involved by collecting information when a system fails to activate during an incident. The organization can also take a proactive approach through education by demonstrating the value of private fire protection systems in certain types of structures including single-family dwellings.

An issue that requires significant future fire service support and education is the installation of home fire sprinkler systems. From a life-safety standpoint, home fire sprinkler systems installed in all new residential construction would improve the fire safety profile of a community.

Figure 28.10 Private fire protection systems include fire-suppression systems as well as fire detection and alarm systems. Inspectors should be familiar with the suppression system components and code requirements for testing the systems.

Information to assist managing company officers with programs and publicity decisions relating to sprinkler systems in all types of occupancies is available through organizations such as the:

- Home Fire Sprinkler Coalition (HFSC)
- National Fire Protection Association (NFPA)
- National Fire Sprinkler Association, Inc. (NFSA)
- American Fire Sprinkler Association (FSA)
- International Fire Sprinkler Association (IFSA)
- Canadian Automatic Sprinkler Association (CASA)

Water Supply Sources

A survey of the available sources of water required for fire-suppression operations in the service area may be available from the water department or Insurance Services Office (ISO) grading service. If not, a physical survey of the service area may be necessary. Potential sources include the municipal water system, ponds and lakes, streams, rivers, bays, and oceans. Capturing and using water from each source requires a variety of approaches, including pumping apparatus connections to hydrants, drafting or hard suction intake hoses, or auxiliary pumping stations. The company officer should make a record of the capacities of sources and accesses to them. It is also important to determine the flow capacity for each hydrant in the municipal system. This information is also included in the emergency response map book provided to all units in the organization.

Automatic/Mutual Aid Sources

Depending on population density and the geographic arrangement of communities and jurisdictions, most fire and emergency services organizations have other similar public organizations in the surrounding area. Industrial fire brigades or military fire departments may also be within or adjacent to the boundaries of a municipality. Each of these organizations is a potential source of automatic/mutual aid in the event of a major emergency. Aircraft fire fighting or hazardous materials response teams are also potential resources for services not provided by the local fire and emergency services organization. The authority having jurisdiction is responsible for the creation and maintenance of the contracts and agreements that result in automatic or mutual aid. The managing company officer may be delegated the responsibility for overseeing these contracts and agreements for the fire and emergency services organization. The AHJ should survey adjacent fire and emergency service organizations to determine their potential need for assistance and ability to provide assistance. The AHJ should provide similar information on needs to neighboring organizations as an indication of reciprocal capabilities.

Fire and emergency services organizations that have automatic/mutual aid agreements with neighboring jurisdictions should schedule and hold training scenarios regularly. Joint preincident surveys and planning sessions can also be beneficial to participating organizations.

Building Construction Types

As discussed in Chapter 17, the type of building construction used in an area is determined by the building code that has been adopted by the jurisdiction. In many instances (old areas in particular), existing structures may not be required to meet the current building code unless a significant amount of renovation is being performed. Therefore, it is important to conduct individual building inspections to determine the type of construction, the current occupancy use, what alterations have been made, and potential hazards that the structure may present to occupants and emergency responders **(Figure 28.11)**. This survey can also assist in the development of preincident plans discussed in Chapter 17, Preincident Planning.

Inspections

Fire and life safety inspections have a two-fold purpose. The first is to ensure that fire and life safety code requirements are adhered to within publicly accessible facilities. This is a proactive approach intended to reduce the potential for and severity of fires and other incidents. Historically, the majority of fire and life safety codes were created as a result of tragic events in the past and are, therefore, reactive. The Triangle Shirtwaist Company fire in 1911 and the Coconut Grove Nightclub fire in 1942 are specific examples of fires that cost many lives and

Figure 28.11 Inspections of buildings under construction not only determine if the work meets code requirements but also helps to familiarize personnel with the types of construction and materials in use in the buildings.

could have been prevented by strong fire and life safety codes and enforcement. More recently, fatality fires at the Beverly Hills Supper Club (Southgate, KY, 1977), the Happy Land Social Club (New York City, NY, 1990), and The Station Club (West Warwick, RI, 2003) have contributed to changes in state and local fire and life safety codes and inspections **(Table 28.1)**. While one of these fires was determined to have been intentional (arson), the others were the result of improper code enforcement and inspection procedures.

The second purpose of fire and life safety inspections is to provide the owner/occupant with safety education materials and information. The information can simply explain why an act or condition is unsafe, like the storage of ignitable liquids near an open-flame water heater, or information regarding the type and size of first aid kit that is appropriate for the occupancy. Either way, the inspection is an opportunity to provide a service to the public.

| \multicolumn{3}{c}{**Table 28.1**} |
| \multicolumn{3}{c}{**High Life Loss Fires in the U.S. During the**} |
| \multicolumn{3}{c}{**20th Century**} |

Year	Name of Occupancy	Fatalities
1908	Lakeview Grammar School, Collingwood, OH	175
1911	Triangle Shirtwaist Company, NY	196
1937	New London School, New London, TX	294
1942	Coconut Grove Nightclub, Boston MA	492
1958	Our Lady of Angels elementary school, Chicago, IL	95
1977	Beverly Hills Supper Club, Southgate, KY	165
1990	The Happy Land Social Club, New York City, NY	87
2003	The Station Club, West Warwick, RI	100

and permission for its emergency responders to enter has been granted by that organization.

Exigent Circumstances

Exigent circumstances are conditions that allow emergency responders and law enforcement officers to enter a structure without a warrant. In this condition, people must be in imminent danger, evidence may face imminent destruction, or a suspect may escape.

According to the California Supreme Court case *People v. Ramsey*, 545 P.2d 1333,1341 (Cal. 1976), an *exigent circumstance* is: An emergency situation requiring swift action to prevent imminent danger to life or serious damage to property or to forestall the imminent escape of a suspect or destruction of evidence. There is no ready litmus test for determining whether such circumstances exist, and in each case the extraordinary situation must be measured by the facts known by officials.

According to NFPA 1021, Level II Fire Officers are responsible for conducting fire and life safety inspections. To effectively perform this function, managing company officers must recognize the authority and the limits of that authority permitting them to make inspections. They must also be familiar with the ordinances, codes, and standards that the building owner/occupant is required to meet. The officer must know the steps to take in preparing for and conducting the inspection, how to conduct exit drills, and how to inspect and test private fire protection and signaling systems.

Authority

In general, unless an emergency is in progress on the property, fire and emergency responders cannot enter private property without obtaining permission from the owner or occupant. Under common law and most statutory law (see Information box), the existence of an emergency constitutes implied permission to enter. Exceptions to this fundamental rule of law are in the cases of military emergency responders on base and of members of industrial fire brigades on company property. In these cases, all property is under the ownership or control of the parent organization,

When no life-threatening emergency condition exists, the owner/occupant or local ordinance must grant the right to enter private property. This situation applies specifically to fire and life safety inspections performed by fire and life safety inspectors. The local governing body (city or borough council, county board of supervisors, etc.) must adopt an ordinance that authorizes the fire chief and designated representatives to enter private property within the jurisdiction, at any reasonable hour, to conduct fire and life safety inspections. This ordinance should contain a section that specifically authorizes inspection personnel to enter and provides for the issuance of an inspection warrant if the occupant refuses to allow inspectors to enter.

Ordinances, Codes, and Standards

In most cases, local jurisdictions adopt one or more ordinances delegating authority to the fire chief for protecting the public from fires and other life-safety hazards. Through these ordinances, it usually adopts national model building and fire codes and standards by reference. For example, rather than write its own fire code, the governing body may choose to adopt the current edition of the

International Code Council's *International Fire Code* (IFC) or the NFPA 1 *Uniform Fire Code*™. In adopting a particular edition of a model code, the governing body also may choose to amend it to make it more applicable to local conditions. The ordinance would adopt that specific edition of the code, as amended, as the law within the jurisdiction. This edition of the code would continue to be applicable within the jurisdiction, even after a more recent edition was published, unless the governing body chose to formally adopt the newer edition in the same way it adopted the first one.

Likewise, the local governing body may choose also to adopt other codes and standards on the recommendation of the fire chief or local building officials. The following are some of the more common of these standards:

- International Building Code
- International Residential Code
- International Plumbing Code
- ICC Electrical Code
- International Zoning Code
- Existing Building Code
- International Wildland-Urban Code
- NFPA 10 *Standard for Portable Fire Extinguishers*
- NFPA 12 *Standard on Carbon Dioxide Extinguishing Systems*
- NFPA 13 *Standard for the Installation of Sprinkler Systems*
- NFPA 14 *Standard for the Installation of Standpipe and Hose Systems*
- NFPA 17 *Standard for Dry Chemical Extinguishing Systems*
- NFPA 25 *Standard for the Inspection, Testing, and Maintenance of Water-Based Fire Protection Systems*
- NFPA 70 *National Electrical Code® (NEC)*
- NFPA 72® *National Fire Alarm Code®*
- NFPA 101®, *Life Safety Code®*
- NFPA 5000® *Building Construction and Safety Code®*

When inspecting buildings and facilities, the company officer may need to refer to the previously adopted editions of the codes and standards as well as similar codes and standards as amended by the local governing body. Enforcement, however, is based solely on the currently adopted fire prevention code. The company officer must be thoroughly familiar with the locally adopted codes and standards.

The company officer must also be aware that certain national requirements will influence the design and construction of buildings that are open to the public. Among these are the Americans with Disability Act Accessibility Guidelines (ADAAG) and the ICC/ANSI A117.1, *American National Standard for Accessible and Usable Buildings and Facilities* (1998). These documents are intended to improve the ability of persons with physical impairments to access and use all structures and buildings. Portions of ICC/ANSI A117.1 define the requirements for audible and visible fire and emergency alarm systems. Both documents describe corridor and door widths that are greater than standard widths.

Inspection Responsibilities

The company officer may be responsible for performing fire and life safety inspections as either a primary or a secondary responsibility. If the responsibility is primary, the officer will hold the position of fire prevention inspector conducting inspections individually. The officer's primary duty is to conduct the inspection and enforce the codes. If the officer's primary duty is as the manager/supervisor of an emergency response unit, then the inspection function is secondary to emergency response duties. The inspection is performed by the members of the unit with the knowledge that the inspection may be interrupted at any time by an emergency.

When managing company officers inspect buildings or facilities within their jurisdiction either alone or with a unit, they carry with them certain responsibilities. Primary among these is a responsibility to act on known violations and to ensure that fire and life safety hazards are mitigated. To do this, the company officer must be thoroughly prepared for the inspection and conscientious while conducting it.

While private citizens have the right to ignore hazardous conditions they may see, on-duty company officers have no such right. In fact, all emergency responders have a duty, both legal and moral, to act when confronted by a hazardous condition. When the local jurisdiction adopts one of the national model codes, the fire and emergency services organization's responsibility to inspect all buildings and facilities (other than private residences) within the jurisdiction is identified clearly in the code. While the exact terminology may differ among codes, each of these model codes specifies that the fire chief is responsible for ensuring that these buildings and facilities are inspected. The fire chief delegates this responsibility to the fire marshal who usually delegates the actual inspections to fire prevention officers or personnel at the unit level.

Most fire codes require each building or facility to be inspected at least once each year. Certain high hazard occupancies, such as places of public assembly, may require more frequent inspection. Inspections may also be required when a Certificate of Occupancy (*C of O*) is requested by a new occupant, there is substantial renovation to the structure, or after repairs are made following a fire in the structure. Numerous agencies may be involved in the inspections for issuing a C of O. These agencies could include, but are not limited to, the fire, building, water, and planning and zoning departments.

When conducting fire and life safety inspections, company officers must identify hazardous conditions that might cause a fire or contribute to its spread (**Figure 28.12**). They must also identify conditions that might impede the occupants' egress from the structure if there is an emergency. Any of these conditions is a violation of one or more sections of the applicable code. It is the inspector's responsibility to identify the specific code section that applies and to see that the building owner or occupant takes appropriate and timely action to bring the occupancy into compliance with the code by eliminating the hazardous condition.

In some cases, violations must be corrected immediately. For example, if access to an exit door is obstructed or the door is found to be locked, this clear life-safety hazard must be corrected before the inspector leaves the premises. These are types of hazards that the occupant can eliminate immediately (**Figure 28.13**). However, some violations

Figure 28.12 Penetrations in fire walls may occur during the initial construction of a building, during remodels, or with the installation of new services such as communication systems.

Figure 28.13 Life safety hazards must be corrected immediately. Among these are locked or blocked designated exit doors. *Courtesy of Jeff Kilfoyle.*

may require more time to correct. For example, if the inspection tag on a fire extinguisher is found to be outdated, the occupant must be given a reasonable amount of time in which to comply **(Figure 28.14)**. Other violations may be of less immediate concern and the occupant may be incapable of complying with the code immediately. For example, if one or more of the fire extinguishers in the building appear to be operative but are due for annual service, the inspector should allow the occupant a reasonable amount of time to arrange for a fire extinguisher service company to service the extinguishers. The amount of time allowed for correcting any particular violation varies depending upon the nature of the violation and the locally adopted code and amendments.

When the occupant has been notified of the existence of a violation and the required corrective action explained, a written notice is issued including the date and time of the follow-up or reinspection. The company officer is responsible for ensuring that the follow-up inspection is made on the specified date. If the follow-up inspection reveals that the hazard has been eliminated, the code enforcement inspection process has served its purpose and is virtually over. All that remains is to thank the occupant and to complete the necessary

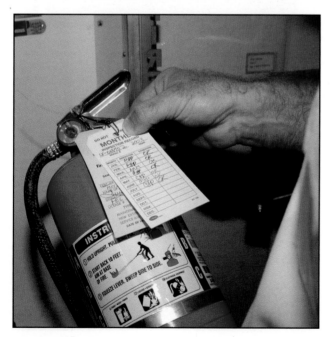

Figure 28.14 Owners and occupants may be given time to correct some violations such as having fire extinguishers inspected by a third party inspection company.

paperwork. However, if nothing has been done to correct the violation or if a halfhearted attempt was made and the hazard still exists, then the inspector must follow the organization's guideline regarding how to gain compliance of the code. A number of possible avenues are available. These range from making another attempt to convince the occupant of the necessity for compliance and scheduling a second follow-up inspection or issuing the responsible party a citation. In some cases, the inspector may be empowered to force the business to cease operation or vacate the occupancy until compliance with the code is obtained. Whether to take this action depends on the situation and organization's policy. The company officer is responsible for knowing local code enforcement policy and applying it appropriately.

NOTE: The inspector must not attempt to apply code requirements that have not been adopted by the jurisdiction. Also, the company officer should not attempt to apply current code requirements to existing structures unless the code states that it covers *all* or *all new and existing structures.*

Preparing for Inspections

A major factor in the success of any fire and life safety inspection is preparation. All fire and life safety inspections have certain characteristics in common. However, each class of occupancy has characteristics that make it different from all other classes, and within each class there are differences among individual occupancies. The extent to which the company officer prepares to inspect a particular occupancy often determines the quality of the results of the inspection.

The purpose of any fire and life safety inspection is to leave the occupancy safer than before the inspection and the occupants more knowledgeable about protecting themselves and their property from fires. With this in mind, when a company officer is assigned a particular occupancy to inspect, preparation for the inspection begins by gathering information. The information needed may come from a variety of sources and varies with the type of occupancy and the officer's level of expertise.

Except for information about completely new occupancies, one of the best sources of useful information about a particular occupancy is the record of previous inspections made there. This record provides background information about the building or facility's ownership and occupancy and includes other critical information such as phone numbers and emergency contacts. The record also shows the types of activities that are conducted within the facility, as well as any previous code violations and their nature. Information about previous inspections may reveal patterns of compliance or noncompliance that can indicate the owner's level of commitment to fire and life safety. For example, if there are fewer and less serious violations found each time the building is inspected, it probably means that management is making a conscientious attempt to comply with the code. On the other hand, a record showing the same number and types of violations every time the occupancy is inspected may indicate that the ownership and management do not take safety issues very seriously. At the very least, the record indicates a need for more public education with the owner or occupant of the building.

The most specific and authoritative sources of information about any particular class or type of occupancy are the model building and fire codes adopted by the jurisdiction. In addition to general fire and life safety requirements that apply to all occupancies, model codes specify in detail exactly what is required for various processes in many different types of occupancies.

Company officers should consult the locally adopted building and fire codes and any other sources needed to become familiar with the requirements for the type of occupancy they have been assigned to inspect (**Figure 28.15**). For further information, see the IFSTA **Inspection and Code Enforcement** manual.

Once the preparation is complete, the inspection is ready to be scheduled. It is a good practice to contact each business in advance to make an appointment for the inspection. This allows the owner/occupant to prepare for the inspection and reduces the possibility of inconveniencing employees by disrupting work schedules. Some organizations require a systematic scheduling of inspections by geographical area to ensure the public that the inspection process is consistent and not selective. Other organizations inspect similar

Figure 28.15 Building and fire codes may be found online or stored on office computers for easy access to the company officer.

types of occupancies at the same time. Company officers must know the inspection policy and follow it.

During an inspection, the company officer must dress and act in a completely professional manner. The officer's appearance will reflect on the jurisdiction, the organization, and the officer. Career organizations usually require that a dress uniform be worn for inspections. Coveralls and protective clothing are used to protect the uniform as mentioned previously. Badges and official identification are mandatory for all inspection personnel.

If the inspection is performed by an emergency response unit, all members must be briefed thoroughly on what is expected of them during the inspection. They should present a businesslike appearance by being well-groomed and wearing clean uniforms (**Figure 28.16, p. 670**). A large part of the success of the inspection depends on how the business owner and the employees perceive the emergency responders conducting the inspection.

Conducting Inspections

The inspection begins as the inspector approaches the building or facility. The inspector should drive around the facility, or the block on which it is located, to observe the surrounding area. The officer should make note of or photograph the hydrants, potential exposures, overhead obstructions, business name and address as displayed on the front of the building, and anything else that might impede or improve the ability to locate and gain access to the building or facility.

If an emergency response unit makes the inspection, the apparatus should be parked in a way that does not interfere with employees or customers and allows the unit to respond quickly if called during the inspection. Most organizations require that one member of the unit remain with the apparatus during the inspection. This allows the apparatus to be moved if necessary and provides some security for the apparatus and the tools and equipment carried on it.

The inspector should enter the business through the main entrance and go directly to the main office or reception desk. The officer should contact the person responsible for the safety and security of the building or facility **(Figure 28.17)**. In small businesses, this may mean dealing directly with the business owner; in larger firms, the designated representative may be a manager or maintenance supervisor. The company officer should introduce himself and the members of the unit, if present. The inspector states the reason for the visit — to conduct a fire and life safety inspection as required by the code. Finally, the company officer explains to the representative the purposes of the inspection, how it is conducted, and the possible outcomes.

Before starting the inspection tour, ask the representative to review the background data listed in the inspection record (address, ownership of the building, ownership of the business, both business and emergency phone numbers, etc.) to

Figure 28.16 Company officers should always dress in an appropriate and professional manner when making building inspections and surveys.

Figure 28.17 Before making any building inspection or survey, the company officer should meet with the building owner, occupant, or representative.

ensure the information is still current. In the case of a new business, this data should be compiled at this time.

At the beginning of the inspection, the representative should be asked to either accompany the inspector throughout the tour or designate someone else to do so. Having a representative of the business with the inspector is very important to the success of the inspection. The representative can answer any questions that the inspector might have, open locked doors, and explain processes or activities in the facility.

The inspector's primary concern is life safety. Therefore, it should be made clear to the representative that the inspector is interested in more than just the fire extinguishers. It also should be explained to the representative that the inspector must be able to inspect every room, space, or compartment by direct, visual observation. If the inspector would have to don special clothing to avoid contaminating *clean rooms* or other environmentally controlled areas, then they should do so. If the business is concerned about the security of trade secrets being compromised during the inspection, some reasonable accommodation must be made that allows the inspector to inspect the sensitive room or area. To facilitate this, the inspector should sign an agreement of confidentiality. It is not uncommon for private firms doing business under contract with the federal government to require inspection personnel to complete a personal data form before being allowed to enter the premises.

There is no set pattern for conducting fire inspections. However, whatever pattern is chosen must be systematic and thorough. Some businesses are so small that inspecting their premises is relatively simple and takes only a few minutes. Others are quite large and complex, often occupying more than one building and covering large areas of land, and they take several hours to inspect. Even though the inspector has surveyed the exterior of the building and its surroundings in general, the officer may choose to start the formal inspection from the outside. This allows the inspector to measure the building, make notes or take pictures of important features such as the existence of fire department connections (FDC), or security gates

or window coverings that may prevent access or egress from the structure. If the company officer knows that the occupancy has a sprinkler system, he or she may want to check the post indicator valve (PIV) to ensure it is in the open position before going inside the building. If the PIV is closed, the company officer can address this with the building supervisor **(Figure 28.18)**.

Once inside the building, inspectors may choose to start at the lowest level and systematically work their way to the roof, or vice versa. Some inspectors feel that starting from the roof gives them another opportunity to see the entire building or facility from a different vantage point and can expose features that were missed from grade level. Regardless of where the inspection starts, the most important consideration is to ensure that it is done in a way that results in each and every compartment within the building or facility is inspected. The floor plan should be checked against the previous one to see whether any major remodeling has been done or additions have been made to the building. If no

Figure 28.18 Post indicator valves must be in the open and locked position indicating that water is available to the fire suppression system in the building or site.

floor plan exists, one should be drawn during the inspection tour. The representative accompanying the inspector should be asked to open any doors that are found to be locked.

General Inspection Categories

In all occupancies, regardless of size or classification, there are certain general fire and life safety items that must be inspected. Many fire and emergency services organizations have these common violations listed on their inspection form so that the inspector only needs to check the appropriate box to indicate a violation of that section of the code. These items fall into the following categories:

- Means of egress
- Housekeeping
- Processes
- Storage
- Waste management
- Fire protection

Means of Egress

The means of egress from the building is the single most important life-safety item to be inspected. The means of egress consists of three parts: the access to the exit, the exit itself, and the exit discharge. The exit may discharge into a public way or lead to a point of safety or area of refuge. According to NFPA 101®, NFPA 1, and ICC/ANSI A117.1, all means of egress must be *usable by a person with a severe mobility impairment*. See the Information Box for the exact NFPA definitions for each of the components of the means of egress plus other related terms.

The inspector should look for obstructions, markings, lighting, door swing, hardware, and stairwells.

- *Obstructions* — Any permanent or moveable object that will reduce the width of the original exit passageway. Obstructions may include furniture, plants, or storage of materials, which block or partially block the pathway. These obstructions must be removed immediately. Walls or other construction features that have been added that reduce or alter the passageway would also be considered obstructions. These violations, if severe, may result in the tempo-

rary closing of the facility until corrections are made.

- *Markings* — Exit doors and the passageways to them must be marked with signs that are visible in the dark. Signs are usually electrified and have auxiliary power in the event of a power failure **(Figure 28.19)**. Some reflective, self-luminous signs are permitted by some fire codes. Signs are traditionally over the door, although additional alternate signs may be at floor level to permit people who are crawling under smoke to see them. In occupancies that require them, exit path maps must be displayed at various locations.

- *Lighting* — Auxiliary emergency lighting systems that operate during power failures should also be checked for operation. In some cases, rechargeable hand lights may also be required for use by staffs of medical facilities.

- *Door swing* — Depending on the occupancy type, exit doors usually swing in the direction of travel. On the exit discharge side of the door, the door opening should not result in the width of the exit passage being reduced. That is, when the door is open, it should not extend into the passageway.

- *Door hardware* — Exit doors must remain unlocked from the inside whenever the building is occupied, and they must be capable of being opened from the inside with a single motion that

Figure 28.19 Exit signs and emergency lighting should be tested to ensure proper operation and visibility.

Definitions

Means of Egress — A continuous and unobstructed way of travel from any point in a building or structure to a public way consisting of three separate and distinct parts: (1) the exit access, (2) the exit, and (3) the exit discharge.

Accessible Means of Egress — A path of travel, usable by a person with a severe mobility impairment, that leads to a public way or an area of refuge.

Means of Escape — A way out of a building or structure that does not conform to the strict definition of *means of egress* but does provide an alternate way out.

Exit Access — That portion of a means of egress that leads to an exit.

Exit — That portion of a means of egress that is separated from all other spaces of the building or structure by construction or equipment as required to provide a protected way of travel to the exit discharge.

Horizontal Exit — A way of passage from one building to an area of refuge in another building on approximately the same level, or a way of passage through or around a fire barrier to an area of refuge on approximately the same level in the same building that affords safety from fire and smoke originating from the area of incidence and areas communicating therewith.

Level of Exit Discharge — (1) The lowest story from which not less than 50 percent of the required number of exits and not less than 50 percent of the required egress capacity from such a story discharge directly outside at grade; (2) the story with the smallest elevation change needed to reach grade where no story has 50 percent or more of the required number of exits and 50 percent or more of the required egress capacity from such a story discharge directly outside at grade.

Public Way — A street, alley, or other similar parcel of land essentially open to the outside air deeded, dedicated, or otherwise permanently appropriated to the public for public use and having a clear width and height of not less than 3 m (10 ft).

Point of Safety — A location that (a) is exterior to and away from a building; or (b) is within a building of any type construction protected throughout by an approved automatic sprinkler system and that is either (1) within an exit enclosure meeting the requirements of this *Code*, or (2) within another portion of the building that is separated by smoke barriers, with not less than a ½-hour fire resistance rating, and that portion of the building has access to a means of escape or exit that conforms to the requirements of this *Code* and does not necessitate return to the area of fire involvement; or (c) is within a building of Type I, Type II(222), Type II(111), Type III(211), Type IV, or Type V(111) construction and is either (1) within an exit enclosure meeting the requirements of this *Code*, or (2) within another portion of the building that is separated by smoke barriers, with not less than a ½-hour fire resistance rating, and that portion of the building has access to a means of escape or exit that conforms to the requirements of this *Code* and does not necessitate return to the area of fire involvement.

Area of Refuge — An area that is either (1) a story in a building where the building is protected throughout by an approved, supervised automatic sprinkler system and has not less than two accessible rooms or spaces separated from each other by smoke-resisting partitions; or (2) a space located in a path of travel leading to a public way that is protected from the effects of fire, either by means of separation from other spaces in the same building or by virtue of location, thereby permitting a delay in egress travel from any level.

Reprinted with permission from the NFPA *Glossary of Terms*, © 2005, National Fire Protection Association, Quincy, MA 02169.

does not require a key or any special knowledge. Depending upon the occupancy type and occupant load served (maximum number of people), exit doors may be required to swing open in the direction of exit travel and be equipped with panic hardware (**Figure 28.20, p. 674**).

- *Stairwells* — The condition of exit stairs should be inspected. Stair treads and handrails must be secure to prevent tripping and falling. If required, reentry onto all floors should not be prevented by interior locks. (Reentry permits sheltering in place on selected floors). Lights and signs must be in place and operational.

Housekeeping

Accumulations of trash and litter in the workplace can be hazardous in several ways. Trash and litter can obscure or block access to the means of egress (**Figure 28.21, p. 674**). Even though trash

Figure 28.20 Designated exit doors are equipped with opening hardware that require only a single movement to open.

Figure 28.21 Cluttered work areas may contain and conceal potential hazards such as open ignitable liquid containers, oily rags, and open electrical receptacles.

and litter rarely start a fire (except in the case of spontaneous combustion), they can provide additional fuel to any fire that does start. They can also create trip and fall hazards and conceal the existence of other hazards such as leaking pipes or exposed wiring. Housekeeping is also an indication of how owners and employees feel about a safe work environment.

Processes

There are countless ways in which industrial processes can create hazards to human life. They can start fires or contribute to their spread or contaminate the environment. Because there are so many ways, requirements for each of the various classes of occupancies have been developed and included in the various codes. The hazards specific to each of the major occupancy classifications are discussed later in this chapter. It is critically important that the company officer thoroughly research the code requirements applicable to the occupancies before inspecting them.

Storage

Storage areas come in all sizes and may contain a variety of items, some hazardous. Small storage rooms may contain janitorial supplies, office supplies, or miscellaneous materials. Larger store rooms may contain retail merchandise such as toys, clothing, maintenance parts, or ignitable liquids. Storage buildings may contain the raw materials used to produce finished

Figure 28.22 Warehouses and storage buildings may contain high concentrations of combustible materials. Building codes may require the installation of in-rack fire suppression systems in certain types of storage shelving.

products, boxes containing the finished products, or both. In any case, flammable materials, such as cardboard boxes, packing materials, or ignitable liquids, must be kept separate from sources of ignition (**Figure 28.22**). This may include prohibiting smoking and/or welding and cutting operations in storage areas. Storage also must not interfere with automatic sprinklers or other built-in fire protection devices or systems. High-stack storage may require in-rack automatic sprinkler systems. Exit passageways must be marked and not obstructed by stored materials.

Waste Management

Besides being potential environmental hazards, accumulations of flammable or combustible waste

Figure 28.23 Proper waste management is important to preventing fires and accidents. Rags that are contaminated with ignitable liquids should be discarded in self-sealing cans.

such as wastepaper or oily rags can be a significant fire and life safety hazard. Just as with ignitable liquids storage, these materials must be kept separate from sources of ignition. With flammable wastes, this most often means proper containment such as putting oily rags into approved, self-closing containers to putting flammable trash in metal containers in sprinklered enclosures (**Figure 28.23**).

Fire Protection

This item is based on the assumption that the other parts of the system may not always be successful in preventing fires. Fire protection includes many components such as:

- Employees' knowledge of how to recognize and report a fire
- Employees' knowledge of the capabilities and limitations of various types of portable fire extinguishers and how to use them safely
- Built-in fire detection and alarm systems
- Automatic sprinklers and other built-in fire suppression systems

Company-level personnel must be sufficiently knowledgeable to answer employee questions related to fire prevention and protection. They also must be able to assist plant safety and security personnel in these areas when asked. Company-level personnel also must be capable of inspecting and, if required, testing built-in fire detection and suppression systems.

There is no substitute for the preinspection research that company-level personnel must do to prepare for the inspection of any occupancy that they are assigned. However, such preparation is even more important if the company is assigned to inspect some highly complex and very specialized occupancies. The inspection criteria peculiar to the most common of these occupancies are discussed in the following section.

Model Code Families

The majority of model codes relating to buildings and fire safety currently used in North America are based on the type of occupancy or use of the building or structure. All model codes classify buildings in this manner. The primary fire and life safety codes in use are those developed by the National Fire Protection Association (NFPA), International Code Council (ICC), and National Building and Fire Codes of Canada (NBFCC). The occupancy classifications for each of these are provided in **Table 28.2, p. 676.**

Hazard of Contents

In addition to the preceding categories of occupancy classification, NFPA 5000® and NFPA 1 further classify each individual occupancy according to the relative fire hazard of its contents. These classifications are based on a subjective evaluation of the relative danger of the start and spread of fire, the danger of smoke or gases generated, and the danger of explosion or other occurrence potentially endangering the lives and safety of occupants of the building or structure. There are three contents-hazard classifications:

- *Low hazard* is the classification for contents of such low combustibility that a self-propagating fire cannot occur in them. Examples of such materials might include fiberglass insulation or minerals that do not contain hydrocarbons.

Table 28.2
Occupancy Classifications

This table is a general comparative overview of the occupancy categories for three major model code systems. Readers must consult the locally adopted code and amendments for complete information regarding each of these occupancies.

Occupancy	ICC	NFPA	NBCC
Assembly	**A-1** - occupancies with fixed seating that are intended for the production and viewing of performing arts or motion picture films. **A-2** - those that include the serving of food and beverages; occupancies have nonfixed seating. Nonfixed seating is not attached to the structure and can be rearranged as needed. **A-3** - occupancies used for worship, recreation, or amusement, such as churches, art galleries, bowling alleys, amusement arcades, as well as those that are not classified elsewhere in this section. **A-4** - occupancies used for viewing of indoor sporting events and other activities that have spectator seating. **A-5** - outdoor viewing areas; these are typically open air venues but may also contain covered canopy areas as well as interior concourses that provide locations for vendors and other commercial kiosks.	**Assembly Occupancy** - An occupancy (1) used for a gathering of 50 or more persons for deliberation, worship, entertainment, eating, drinking, amusement, awaiting transportation, or similar uses; or (2) used as a special amusement building, regardless of occupant load.	**Group A Division 1** - Occupancies intended for the production and viewing of the performing arts. **Group A Division 2** - Occupancies not classified elsewhere in Group A. **Group A Division 3** - Occupancies of the arena type. **Group A Division 4** - Occupancies in which occupants are gathered in open air.
Business	***Business Group B*** - Buildings used as offices to deliver service-type or professional transactions, including the storage of records and accounts. Characterized by office configurations to include: desks, conference rooms, cubicles, laboratory benches, computer/data terminals, filing cabinets, and educational occupancies above the 12th grade.	***Business*** - Occupancy used for the transaction of business other than mercantile.	**Group D** - Business and personal services occupancies

Table 28.2
Continued

Occupancy	ICC	NFPA	NBCC
Educational	***Educational Group E -*** Buildings providing facilities for six or more persons at one time for educational purposes in grades kindergarten through twelfth grade. Religious educational rooms and auditoriums that are part of a place of worship, which have occupant loads of less than 100 persons, retain a classification of Group A-3.	**Educational Occupancy -** Occupancy used for educational purposes through the twelfth grade by six or more persons for 4 or more hours per day or more than 12 hours per week.	Covered under Group A
Factory Industrial	***Factory Industrial Group F -*** Occupancies used for assembling, disassembling, fabrication, finishing, manufacturing, packaging, repair, or processing operations. - ***Factory Industrial F-1 Moderate Hazard*** (examples include but not limited to: aircraft, furniture, metals, and millwork) - ***Factory Industrial F-2 Low Hazard*** (examples include but not limited to: brick and masonry, foundries, glass products, and gypsum) ***High Hazard Group H -*** Buildings used in manufacturing or storage of materials that constitute a physical or health hazard. - ***High-hazard Group H-1 -*** detonation hazard - ***High-hazard Group H-2 -*** deflagration or accelerated burning hazard - ***High-hazard Group H-3*** - materials that readily support combustion or pose a physical hazard - ***High-hazard Group H-4 -*** health hazards - ***High-hazard Group H-5 -*** hazardous production	**Industrial Occupancy -** Occupancy in which products are manufactured or in which processing, assembling, mixing, packaging, finishing, decorating, or repair operations are conducted.	**Group F Division 1 -** High-hazard industrial occupancies **Group F Division 2 -** Medium-hazard occupancies **Group F Division 3 -** Low-hazard industrial occupancies

Table 28.2
Continued

Occupancy	ICC	NFPA	NBCC
Occupancy Institutional (Care and Detention)	***Institutional Group I*** **Group I-1 -** Assisted living facilities holding more than 16 persons on a 24 hour basis. These persons are capable of self rescue. **Group I-2 -** Medical, surgical, psychiatric, or nursing care facilities for more than 5 people who are not capable of self-preservation or need assistance to evacuate. **Group I-3 -** Prisons and detention facilities for more than 5 people under restraint. **Group I-4 -** Child and adult day care facilities.	**Ambulatory Health Care -** Building (or portion thereof) used to provide outpatient services or treatment simultaneously to four or more patients that renders the patients incapable of taking action for self-preservation under emergency conditions without the assistance of others. **Health Care -** An occupancy used for purposes of medical or other treatment or care of four or more persons where such occupants are mostly incapable of self-preservation due to age, physical or mental disability, or because of security measures not under the occupants' control. **Residential Board and Care** - Building or portion thereof that is used for lodging and boarding of four or more residents, not related by blood or marriage to the owners or operators, for the purpose of providing personal care services. **Detention and Correctional -** An occupancy used to house one or more persons under varied degrees of restraint or security where such occupants are mostly incapable of self-preservation because of security measures not under the occupants' control.	**Group B Division 1 -** Care or detention occupancies in which persons are under restraint or are incapable of self-preservation because of security measures not under their control. **Group B Division 2 -** Care or detention occupancies in which persons having cognitive or physical limitations require special care or treatment.
Mercantile	***Mercantile Group M.-*** Occupancies open to the public that are used to store, display, and sell merchandise with incidental inventory storage.	**Mercantile -** An occupancy used for the display and sale of merchandise.	**Group E -** Mercantile occupancies
Residential	***Residential Group R*** **R-1 -** Residential occupancies containing sleeping units where the occupants are primarily transient in nature (boarding houses, hotels, and motels) **R-2 -** Residential occupancies containing sleeping units or more than 2 dwelling units where the occupants are primarily permanent in nature (apartments, convents, non-transient hotels, etc.)	**Residential Occupancy –** Provides sleeping accommodations for purposes other than health care or detention and correctional. **One- and Two-Family Dwelling Unit -** Building that contains not more than two dwelling units with independent cooking and bathroom facilities.	**Group C -** Residential occupancies

Table 28.2
Continued

Occupancy	ICC	NFPA	NBCC
Residential (continued)	**R-3 -** Residential occupancies where the occupants are primarily permanent in nature and not classified as Group R-1, R-2, R-4, or I **R-4 -** Residential occupancies shall include buildings arranged for occupancy as residential care/ assisted living facilities for more than 5 but less than 16 occupants (excluding staff)	**Lodging or Rooming House -** Building (or portion thereof) that does not qualify as a one- or two-family dwelling, that provides sleeping accommodations for a total of 16 or fewer people on a transient or permanent basis, without personal care services, with or without meals, but without separate cooking facilities for individual occupants. **Hotel -** Building or groups of buildings under the same management in which there are sleeping accommodations for more than 16 persons and primarily used by transients for lodging with or without meals. **Dormitory -** A building or a space in a building in which group sleeping accommodations are provided for more than 16 persons who are not members of the same family in one room, or a series of closely associated rooms, under joint occupancy and single management, with or without meals, but without individual cooking facilities. **Apartment Building -** Building (or portion thereof) containing three or more dwelling units with independent cooking and bathroom facilities.	**Group C -** Residential occupancies
Storage	**Storage Group S –** Structures or portions of structures that are used for storage and are not classified as hazardous occupancies. - *Moderate-hazard storage, Group S-1* (examples include but not limited to: bags, books, linoleum, and lumber) - *Low-hazard storage, Group S-2* (examples include but not limited to: asbestos, bagged cement, electric motors, glass, and metal parts)	**Storage Occupancy -** An occupancy used primarily for the storage or sheltering of goods, merchandise, products, vehicles, or animals.	Covered under Group F
Utility/ Miscellaneous	*Utility/Miscellaneous Group U* - These are accessory buildings and other miscellaneous structures that are not classified in any specific occupancy (agricultural facilities such as barns, sheds, and fences over 6 ft [2m])	—	—

- *Ordinary hazard* is the classification for contents that are likely to burn with moderate rapidity or give off a considerable volume of smoke. Examples of these materials might include paper, cardboard, textiles, and some plastics.

- *High hazard* is the classification for contents that are likely to burn with extreme rapidity or from which explosions are likely. Examples of these materials might include flammable liquids or highly reactive substances.

NOTE: The preceding hazard levels are incorporated within the ICC and Canadian codes under each occupancy classification.

Hazardous Materials Labeling

Fire and life safety inspectors and company-level personnel must be familiar with the marking systems that are used to identify hazardous materials and processes. In addition to Department of Transportation (DOT) placards, labels, and markings, a number of other markings, marking systems, labels, labeling systems, colors, color codes, and signs may indicate the presence of hazardous materials at fixed facilities, on piping systems, and on containers. These other markings may be as simple as the word *chlorine* stenciled on the outside of a fixed-facility tank or as complicated as a site-specific hazard communication system using a unique combination of labels, placards, emergency contact information, and color codes. Some fixed-facility containers may have identification numbers that correspond to site or emergency plans that provide details on the product, quantity, and other pertinent information.

Inspectors need to be familiar with some of the more widely used specialized marking systems for hazardous materials. This section highlights the most common specialized systems in North America, including NFPA 704, common hazardous communication labels, piping systems, and color codes. For additional detailed information, see IFSTA **Hazardous Materials for First Responders** manual.

Hazardous materials labels may be found on the exterior of the building, on fences surrounding a storage area, on doors into storage rooms, and on packages or containers. The inspector should note the types of materials indicated and determine if the label is still appropriate to the material in storage. Old labels should be removed and current ones applied as needed.

NFPA 704. The information in NFPA 704 gives a widely recognized method for indicating the presence of hazardous materials at commercial, manufacturing, institutional, and other fixed-storage facilities. Use of this system is commonly required by local building and fire codes for all occupancies that contain hazardous materials. It is designed to alert fire and emergency services responders to health, flammability, instability, and related hazards (specifically, oxidizers and water-reactive materials) that may be present as short-term, acute exposures resulting from a fire, spill, or similar emergency.

The NFPA 704 system contains the following information:

- Provides the appropriate indication to first responders and the inspector that hazardous materials are present. The fire and emergency services personnel who see the NFPA 704 marker on a structure can determine the hazards of a single material in a marked container or the relative combined hazard severity of the collection of numerous materials in the occupancy.

- Identifies the general hazards and the degree of severity for health, flammability, and instability.

- Provides immediate information necessary to protect the lives of both the public and emergency response personnel.

Be Aware!

NFPA 704 markings provide very useful information, but the system does have its limitations. For example, an NFPA diamond doesn't state exactly what chemical or chemicals may be present in specific quantities. Nor does it tell exactly where they may be located when the sign is used for a building, structure, or area (such as a storage yard) rather than an individual container. Positive identification of the materials needs to be made through other means such as container markings, employee information, company records, and preincident surveys.

Specifically, the NFPA 704 system uses a rating system of numbers from 0 to 4 **(Figure 28.24)**. The number 0 indicates a minimal hazard, whereas the number 4 indicates a severe hazard. The rating is assigned to three categories: health, flammability, and instability. The rating numbers are arranged on a diamond-shaped marker or sign. The health rating is located on the blue background, the flammability hazard rating is positioned on the red background, and the instability hazard rating appears on a yellow background. As an alternative, the backgrounds for each of these rating positions may be any contrasting color, and the numbers (0 to 4) may be represented by the appropriate color (blue, red, and yellow). Special hazards are located in the six o'clock position and have no specified background color; however, white is most commonly used. Only two special hazard symbols are presently authorized for use in this position by the NFPA: W̶ and OX (respectively, indicating unusual reactivity with water or that the material is an oxidizer). However, the inspector may see other symbols on old placards, including the trefoil radiation symbol.

Hazard communications labels and markings.
The OSHA *Hazard Communication Standard* (HCS) (Subpart Z, Toxic and Hazardous Substances, 29 *CFR* 1910.1200) requires employers to identify hazards in the workplace and train employees how to recognize those hazards. It also requires the employer to ensure that all hazardous material containers are labeled, tagged, or marked with the identity of the substances contained in them, along with appropriate hazard warnings. The standard does not specify what system (or systems) of identification must be used, leaving that to be determined by individual employers. Inspectors and company-level personnel, then, may encounter a variety of different (and sometimes unique) labeling and marking systems in their jurisdictions. Conducting preincident surveys will also assist emergency responders in identifying and understanding these systems.

A variety of labeling systems is used to comply with the requirements of HCS **(Figure 28.25, p. 682)**. Some of these systems are available commercially to the general public; individual companies or organizations develop others for their private

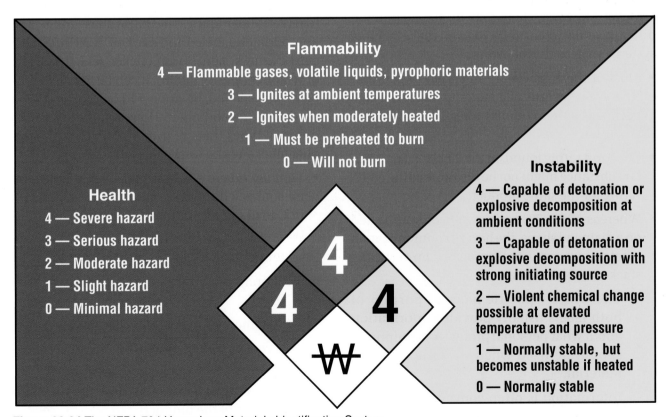

Figure 28.24 The NFPA 704 Hazardous Materials Identification System.

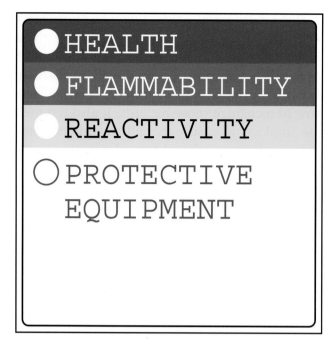

○ HEALTH

○ FLAMMABILITY

○ REACTIVITY

○ PROTECTIVE
  EQUIPMENT

Figure 28.25 Example of the OSHA Hazard Communication System. *Courtesy of Lab Safety Supply, Inc.*

use. Many of these systems resemble NFPA 704 in that they are color-coded/numerical rating systems based on a rating scale of 0 to 4, with 0 indicating the lowest level of hazard and 4 indicating the highest level. However, there may be some common differences between NFPA 704 and these labeling systems such as the following:

- Most of these labels are intended to communicate the hazards of a material under normal, occupational conditions rather than emergency conditions.

- The 0 to 4 rating found on the label for a particular substance might not be the same as the NFPA rating for the same product.

- Whereas NFPA 704 ratings are communicated on a diamond shape, the hazard communication label ratings are usually provided on vertically stacked bars. Details:

  — The white (specific hazard) portion of both labels usually provides information about what personal protective equipment should be used when working with the material.

  — Information is often conveyed by a letter code, sometimes supplemented by pictograms. For example, the letter A in the white

box/bar might indicate that safety glasses should be worn.

- Different systems may use colors to indicate different things. For example, whereas blue generally indicates Health and red indicates Flammability, NFPA uses yellow to indicate Instability, while the *Hazardous Materials Information Guide* (HMIG) system (a commercial labeling system marketed by Lab Safety Supply), uses yellow to indicate Reactivity.

- An asterisk (*) or other symbol is sometimes used to indicate that the material has chronic health effects.

Again, the inspector should be aware that many employers have devised their own hybrid labeling systems that are often very similar looking but may have significant differences in how they should be interpreted. Besides information gathered during inspections, it is important that emergency responders use preincident surveys to become familiar with the systems used at facilities in their jurisdictions.

Canadian Workplace Hazardous Materials Information System. Like the U.S. HCS, the Canadian Workplace Hazardous Materials Information System (WHMIS) requires that hazardous products be appropriately labeled and marked. A WHMIS label can be a mark, sign, stamp, sticker, seal, ticket, tag, or wrapper **(Figure 28.26)**. It can be attached, imprinted, stenciled, or embossed on the controlled product or its container. However, there are two different types that are used most often: the supplier label and the workplace label.

- ***Supplier labels.*** A supplier label must appear on all controlled products received at workplaces in Canada and contain the following information:

  — Product identifier (name of product)

  — Supplier identifier (name of company that sold it)

  — Statement that an MSDS is available

  — Hazard symbols (pictures of the classifications)

  — Risk phrases (words that describe the main hazards of the product)

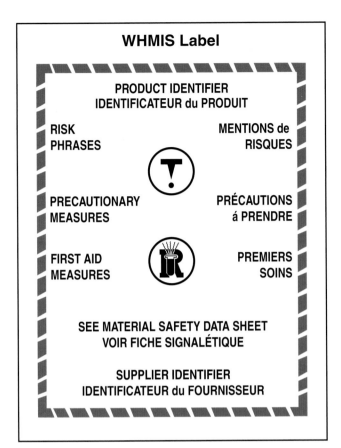

WHMIS Label

PRODUCT IDENTIFIER
IDENTIFICATEUR du PRODUIT

RISK PHRASES

MENTIONS de RISQUES

PRECAUTIONARY MEASURES

PRÉCAUTIONS á PRENDRE

FIRST AID MEASURES

PREMIERS SOINS

SEE MATERIAL SAFETY DATA SHEET
VOIR FICHE SIGNALÉTIQUE

SUPPLIER IDENTIFIER
IDENTIFICATEUR du FOURNISSEUR

Figure 28.26 Example of the Canadian Workplace Hazardous Materials Information System (WHMIS).

— Precautionary measures (how to work with the product safely)

— First aid measures (what to do in an emergency)

— All text in English and French

— WHMIS hatched border

If the product is always used in the container with the supplier label, no other label is required (unless the supplier label is lost or becomes unreadable). However, if the material is moved into another container for use in the workplace, this new container must have a workplace WHMIS label.

- *Workplace labels.* A workplace label must appear on all controlled products produced in a workplace or transferred to other containers by the employer and must provide the following information:

  — Product identifier (product name)

  — Information for the safe handling of the product

  — Statement that the MSDS is available

The employer may wish to put more information on the labels such as the WHMIS hazard symbols or other pictograms, but it is not required under the law. Workplace labels may appear in placard form on controlled products received in bulk from a supplier.

U.S. and Canadian safety color codes. Colors can provide clues to the nature of hazardous materials in buildings and facilities. For example, the inspector can determine that the material inside a container is some type of oxidizer if the placard background color is yellow. If the placard color is red, it can be determined that the material is flammable.

Most flammable liquid storage cabinets are painted yellow as well as many portable containers of corrosive or unstable materials. Flammable liquid safety cans and portable containers are often red.

ANSI Z535.1 sets forth the following safety color code that is recommended for use in the U.S. and Canada:

- ***Red***—Means Danger or Stop; is used on containers of flammable liquids, emergency stop bars, stop buttons, and fire-protection equipment

- ***Orange*** — Means Warning; is used on hazardous machinery with parts that can crush or cut energized equipment

- ***Yellow*** — Means Caution; solid yellow, yellow and black stripes, or yellow and black checkers may be used to indicate physical hazards such as tripping hazards; also used on containers of corrosive or unstable materials

- ***Green*** — Marks safety equipment such as first-aid stations, safety showers, and exit routes

- ***Blue*** — Marks safety information signage such as labels or markings indicating the type of required personal protective equipment (PPE)

Closing Interview

When the inspection has been completed, the inspector's findings should be discussed with the business owner or designated representative during a closing interview. If no violations were found, the inspector should congratulate the owner/occupant and thank the individual for assisting with the inspection. If any violations were found, the inspector should review and discuss them. As mentioned earlier, immediate threats to life safety, such as locked or obstructed exits, must be corrected immediately before the inspector leaves the premises. For other, less critical violations the inspector should point them out to the representative and explain the necessary corrective measures. A reasonable amount of time should be allowed for the corrections to be made. As discussed earlier in this chapter, the amount of time allowed varies depending upon the nature of the violations and the difficulty involved in their correction. During the closing interview, the inspector should establish a date and time for a follow-up inspection. The inspector should develop a plan of correction with the representative if correcting the violations will take some time (for example, installing a fire detection and alarm system). The plan should include reinspections at specified intervals to ensure that reasonable progress is made and that full compliance is eventually obtained.

Documentation

As with other fire and emergency services organization activities, documenting fire and life-safety inspections is extremely important. This documentation creates the inspection history of each individual occupancy that the organization inspects. The documentation may be needed to force reluctant property owners to comply with the code requirements, or it may be needed as evidence should there be a fire in a particular occupancy. This data may also be needed for statistical purposes at the state/provincial level. Therefore, it is also extremely important that the documentation be as complete, accurate, and readable as possible **(Figure 28.27)**.

Besides providing documentation for inspection files and state/provincial reports, reports can also be provided to the operational units that respond to the building or facility. Changes in the floor plan, use or processes, access, and occupancy status are all important to the emergency responders. This information can be used to update the preincident plans or generate a preincident survey by the responding units.

Conducting Exit Drills

Inspectors or company-level personnel may be required to conduct exit drills in some occupancies. Exit drills are particularly important in schools and similar occupancies where large numbers of people are gathered **(Figure 28.28)**. These drills are used to familiarize the occupants with the procedures to follow and the route to take when exiting the building in an emergency. Emergency response units can also be involved in the drill to familiarize them with the locations of exit discharges, exterior safe havens, and interior areas of refuge. The occupants benefit from this coordinated activity by being aware of the possible access routes the emergency response units will take to enter the facility. The company officer must be aware of situations that will prevent conducting exit drills in educational occupancies. Coordination and communication with school officials are essential to ensure that all life safety and educational requirements are met.

In hospitals and nursing homes, only the staff should participate in these drills. Plans must be in place for evacuating the patients or moving them to an area of refuge. Because these facilities typically operate 24 hours a day, drills should be conducted with all shifts.

Figure 28.27 An effective code enforcement and inspection program depends on accurate data collection and storage. Company officers must complete all required inspection forms and enter the data into the organization's data base.

Figure 28.28 School exit drills provide company personnel with the opportunity to observe the exit procedures in use by the school, distribute fire and life safety to the students, and familiarize the students and teachers with the locations apparatus will be at during an emergency.

Inspection personnel also may be involved in helping certain occupancies develop their emergency exit plans. Regardless of how well-written these plans may be, they should be tested periodically through a series of realistic exercises. From time to time, it may be appropriate to conduct these drills without prior notification.

Inspecting/Testing Fire Protection Systems

Inspecting and testing fire protection systems is a very technical process. For system certification inspections and tests, the building owner will contract with a fire protection service firm to perform the tests. Fire and emergency services inspectors and sometimes company-level personnel may be responsible for witnessing these tests or assisting in the test under the supervision of the contracted firm.

Generally, inspectors and/or company-level personnel will only be required to check the system service tag to ensure that it has been inspected and tested within the time interval specified in the code (**Figure 28.29**). When inspecting these systems, the inspector should look for evidence of damage to any part of the system and for anything that might obstruct the system's operation. They also should look for any remodeling of the building or additions to it to ensure that newly created spaces are covered by the protective system. At the same

Figure 28.29 Company officers should look for the inspection tag to ensure that the fire suppression system has been tested in the proper time frame.

time, the addition of walls or storage racks can alter the original sprinkler coverage and require the addition or relocation of sprinkler heads.

Several different types of systems may be installed in occupancies to comply with building code requirements. The types most often inspected and tested by fire and emergency services personnel are fire detection/signaling systems, water supplies, stationary fire pumps, public fire alarm systems, standpipe systems, fire extinguishing systems, and portable fire extinguishers.

Fire Detection/Signaling Systems

Different types of fire detection and signaling systems are installed in various types of occupancies. Regardless of the type of system or the means of activation, each must meet the requirements of NFPA 72®, *National Fire Alarm Code®*. Inspectors and company-level personnel must be familiar with how these systems operate and how to test them. The most common types of systems are local, auxiliary, remote station, proprietary, central station, and emergency voice/alarm communica-

tions. Additional information can be found in the IFSTA **Fire Detection and Suppression Systems** manual.

Local alarm systems. Local alarm systems may be activated by a number of different means, but they all have one feature in common: they initiate an alarm signal only on the premises where they are installed. They do not transmit a signal to the fire and emergency services organization or to any other location (**Figure 28.30**). These systems primarily are intended to alert the occupants of the building to a fire so that they will leave the building. They are also intended to alert passersby to a fire in the building so that they will report the fire. These systems may be activated manually or by sensors that detect heat, smoke, or flame.

Auxiliary alarm systems. These systems are used only in communities that have municipal alarm box systems. Auxiliary alarm systems are installed within a building and connected directly to a municipal alarm box located on the street adjacent to the building. When the system is activated by a fire in the protected premises, the system transmits a signal to the fire and emergency services organization by the same means as an alarm from any other street box.

Remote station systems. These systems are similar to auxiliary systems in that they also are connected directly to the fire and emergency services organization communications/dispatch center (**Figure 28.31**). However, remote station systems transmit an alarm by some means other than the municipal fire alarm box circuits, usually over a leased telephone line. Where permitted, a radio signal on a dedicated fire and emergency services organization frequency may be used instead. Commonly used in communities that are not served by a central station system, remote station systems may be of the coded or noncoded type. A *noncoded system* may be used where only one building is covered by the system; a *coded system* is necessary in occupancies consisting of buildings at different locations. Up to five buildings may be covered by one remote station system, and it may or may not have local alarm capability.

Proprietary systems. A proprietary system is used to protect large commercial and industrial buildings, high-rise buildings, and groups of com-

Figure 28.30 Local area alarms are intended to alert the occupants of an emergency. One component of the system is manual pull stations located at all exits from the structure.

Figure 28.31 Central telecommunication centers receive alarms from monitored buildings or sites and dispatch emergency responders to the site. *Courtesy of Jason Pack, photographer, FEMA.*

monly owned buildings in a single location such as a college campus or an industrial complex. Each building in the complex is protected by a separate system connected to a common receiving point somewhere on the premises. The receiving point must be in a separate structure or in a part of a structure that is remote from any hazardous operations. The receiving point must be staffed constantly by an employee of the occupant who is trained in system operation and the protocol for handling system alarms. In addition to fire and life safety functions, some proprietary systems also are used to monitor plant security systems.

Central station systems. A central station system is basically the same as a proprietary system with two differences. First, the receiving point is not on the protected premises, and second, the person receiving the alarm is not an employee of the owner of the protected premises. The operator works in a receiving point called a *central station* and is an employee of the alarm service company that contracts with the owner/occupant of the protected premises. When an alarm is received in the central station, the operator notifies the fire and emergency services organization and a representative of the property owner/occupant.

Because the central station may be located in another state, it is critically important that the operator provide the fire and emergency services organization with the correct address of the property and accurately identify what area of the protected property is involved. Some fire and emergency services organizations require that the central station provider be listed by Underwriters Laboratories (UL).

Emergency voice/alarm communications systems. These are supplementary systems installed in properties in addition to one of the other types of systems previously listed. Their purpose is to increase the capability of transmitting detailed information to occupants and/or emergency responders who are on the premises. These systems may be separate from or integrated into the main fire detection/signaling system protecting the premises. They may be one-way communication systems in which information can be announced to but not received from the occupants; they may be two-way systems in which communications also can be received from the occupants.

Water Supplies

Inspectors or company-level personnel may be assigned to inspect occupancies that have their own private water supply that is intended to operate required sprinklers and/or standpipes. In the absence of a municipal water system, or if the water pressure in the municipal system is too low to adequately supply the fire protection system, the owner/occupant may have installed an elevated water tank on the roof of the building or a freestanding water tank on the property. In either case, the inspector or company-level personnel will not be involved in determining the adequacy of the system but only in how well it is maintained. Inspectors should look for signs of rust or corrosion around valves and fittings and should check the pressure readings of any gauges. Even though the owner/occupant should have flow data available, the inspector may have to conduct flow tests to verify these figures. For more information on inspecting water supplies, see the IFSTA **Fire Inspection and Code Enforcement** manual.

Stationary Fire Pumps

Stationary fire pumps may be installed in some occupancies where it is impractical or impossible to maintain water storage for fire protection. These installations must conform to NFPA 20, *Standard for the Installation of Stationary Fire Pumps for Fire*

Protection (2007). The pumps are used to increase the pressure in the fire protection system when needed. They are almost always electrically-driven centrifugal pumps with a discharge capacity from 500 to 4,500 gpm (2 000 L/min to 18 000 L/min). As with stored water supplies, inspection personnel usually are not required to test these pumps, but they may be present when the tests are performed or make a visual inspection of the pumps during regular visits **(Figure 28.32)**. Inspectors should be familiar with the types of pumps installed in the occupancies in the response area. When inspecting these installations, they should check the owner/occupant's pump maintenance and test records; NFPA 20 requires these pumps to be run for at least 30 minutes per week. The inspector should also look for signs of water or oil leaks and for rust, corrosion, or damage to the pumps or associated piping. For more information on inspecting stationary fire pumps, see the IFSTA **Fire Detection and Suppression Systems** manual.

Public Fire Alarm Systems

Unlike the other fire protection systems discussed in this chapter, public fire alarm systems are usually owned and maintained by the municipality or other entity of which the fire and emergency services organization is a part. They may consist of a number of dedicated fire alarm circuits connected to street fire alarm boxes or consist of street boxes that are individual radio transmitters on a

Figure 28.32 Facilities like petroleum refineries and chemical processing plants may have stationary fire pumps intended to produce a specified water flow and pressure. *Courtesy of ConocoPhillips.*

dedicated fire alarm frequency. These systems are classified as either Type A (manual retransmission) or Type B (automatic retransmission). In Type A systems, the alarm operator must manually retransmit alarms received from the street boxes to the designated fire stations. In Type B systems, alarms received from the street boxes are automatically retransmitted to all fire stations within the jurisdiction. Type A systems are necessary in jurisdictions with a large call volume to keep the stations from being inundated with fire calls for which they are not part of the assigned initial response.

The routine maintenance and testing of these systems are often done by technical personnel other than company-level personnel, but not always. In some cities, line personnel are assigned these duties. For more information on the installation, maintenance, and testing of these systems, see NFPA 1221, *Standard for the Installation, Maintenance, and Use of Emergency Services Communications Systems* (2007).

Standpipe and Hose Systems

Standpipe and hose systems are required in single-story buildings, in large area buildings, on each floor of structures that are greater than four stories, and in industrial facilities such as petroleum refineries. The purpose of these systems is to provide a quick and convenient source of water for the manual application of water for fire fighting. These systems must be installed according to NFPA 14, *Standard for the Installation of Standpipe and Hose Systems*, and to be effective, they must be supplied with water in sufficient volume and at adequate pressure. NFPA 14 classifies standpipe systems as Class I, II, or III according to their intended use **(Figures 28.33 a-c)**:

- Class I systems are intended to be used by fire fighting personnel who are trained in handling large handlines (2½-inch [65 mm] hose). They usually consist of strategically located valve-controlled 2½ -inch (65 mm) outlets attached to the standpipe riser. Class I systems do not have permanently attached hoses or nozzles.

- Class II systems are intended to be used by building occupants who have no specialized fire training. These systems are intended to allow occupants to control the spread of fire until the arrival of the fire department or fire brigade. They are usually equipped with a rack or reel of 1½-inch (38 mm) fire hose (with nozzle) connected to a valve-controlled outlet. Usually referred to as *house lines,* these systems are not intended for emergency responder use and are not a substitute for the organization's nozzles and hoses.

Figure 28.33 a-c The company officer should be familiar with the types of standpipes located in structures in the response area: (a) Class I, (b) Class II, and (c) Class III.

- Class III systems combine the features of both of the other classes and are intended to be used by firefighters, brigade members, and untrained occupants. The system must be designed to permit both the 2½-inch outlet and the 1½-inch house line to be used simultaneously. This combination allows the occupants to apply water to a fire until firefighters or brigade members arrive, and it allows the trained firefighters to attack the fire with heavy hose streams.

When inspecting any of these systems, the inspector should perform the following duties:

- Check the hose cabinets to see that they are free of trash and debris.

- Check the hose to see that it is not showing signs of deterioration including water stains, cuts, or abrasions on its surface.

- Feel the hose between the connection and the first fold to see whether water has accumulated in the hose, which is an indication that the valve is partially open or is leaking.

- Disconnect the hose on 1½ -inch (38 mm) hose connections, and test the valve by opening it to allow water to flow into a bucket held close to the outlet.

- Check the condition of the hose threads and gasket while the hose is disconnected.

- Remove the hose nozzle and check its operation and gasket.

- Remove the cap and check the threads on 2½- inch (65 mm) hose connections, and connect a pressure gauge to the outlet so that the valve can be opened to test it.

- Check the system's fire department connection (FDC) to ensure that the threads are undamaged and the inlets are free of debris.

For more information on inspecting standpipe systems, see the IFSTA **Fire Inspection and Code Enforcement** manual.

Fire Extinguishing Systems

Inspectors and company-level personnel may have to inspect and test a variety of fire extinguishing systems and equipment. The most common of these are automatic sprinkler systems, special-agent fixed fire extinguishing systems, and portable fire extinguishers.

Automatic sprinkler systems. An automatic sprinkler system consists of a water source, distribution piping, and one or more individual sprinklers (**Figure 28.34**). Depending on the particular situation, either a wet system or a dry system may be installed.

In wet-pipe systems, the piping is constantly full of water under pressure. Heat from a fire causes one or more sprinkler heads to activate (sometimes referred to as *fused* or opened) at a specified temperature allowing water to be discharged directly onto the fire. Wet-pipe systems can apply water onto a fire faster than dry systems, but the water in the piping is subject to freezing. Frozen distribution piping can burst and the linkage in individual sprinklers can be broken. When frozen piping thaws, water flows through the open sprinklers and piping, possibly causing considerable water damage. Therefore, in cold-storage units and occupancies in cold climates, dry sprinkler systems are required.

In dry-pipe systems, the distribution piping is filled with air. This allows the system to remain functional during freezing temperatures, but it delays the application of water onto a fire. There are three types of dry sprinkler systems — dry-pipe systems, preaction systems, and deluge systems.

In dry-pipe systems, conventional sprinklers are installed in the distribution piping, which is filled with air under pressure. The air pressure in the piping is greater than the pressure of the water supplying the system, and the air pressure keeps the main water control valve (dry-pipe valve) closed. When a sprinkler activates because of a fire, the air within the piping is released, allowing water from the source to flow into the system. After the air in the piping has been discharged, water begins to be applied to the fire through the activated head or heads.

In preaction systems, conventional sprinklers are used in combination with heat-sensing devices. When a fire starts, the heat-sensing devices allow water to enter the distribution piping and be discharged through those sprinklers that have fused due to the heat of the fire. These systems are used where preventing or limiting water damage is important.

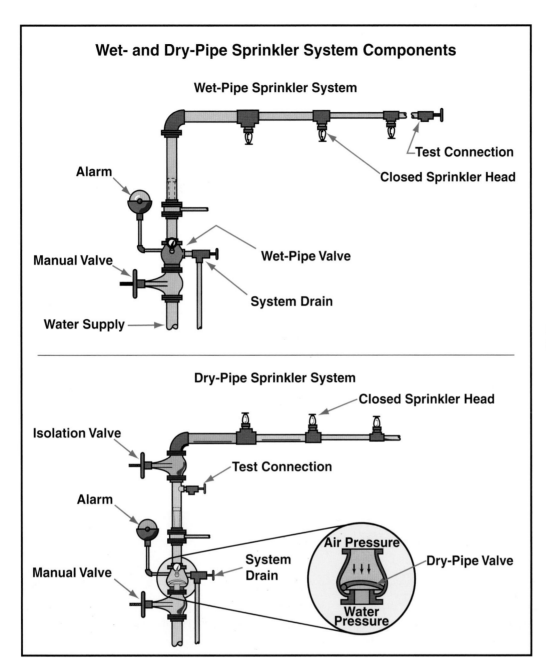

Wet- and Dry-Pipe Sprinkler System Components

Wet-Pipe Sprinkler System

Test Connection

Closed Sprinkler Head

Alarm

Wet-Pipe Valve

Manual Valve

System Drain

Water Supply

Figure 28.34 Sprinkler system components.

Dry-Pipe Sprinkler System

Closed Sprinkler Head

Isolation Valve

Test Connection

Alarm

Air Pressure

Dry-Pipe Valve

System Drain

Manual Valve

Water Pressure

In deluge systems, heat-sensing devices are used to control the flow of water to the distribution piping in which the individual sprinklers are installed. However, in this type of system, all the sprinklers are open-type heads. Therefore, when any heat-sensing device activates, water discharges from all the sprinkler heads at once. Obviously, this type of system is used where overwhelming a fire with massive amounts of water is more important than preventing water damage **(Figure 28.35, p. 692)**.

Dry chemical systems. Dry chemical systems must conform to NFPA 17, *Standard for Dry Chemical Extinguishing Systems*. They are used in areas where a rapid extinguishment of the fire is required but where reignition of the fire is unlikely. These systems may be either engineered or preengineered. Engineered systems are specifically calculated and constructed for a particular occupancy; preengineered systems are designed to protect a given amount of area in any type of occupancy.

Fixed dry chemical systems use the same fire extinguishing agents as portable dry chemical fire extinguishers. These agents are nontoxic and nonconducting, but they leave a very fine powdery residue that is extremely difficult to clean up. In some systems, the agent and expellant gas are stored in the same tank; in others, they are stored in separate tanks. There are two main types of dry chemical systems: local application and total flooding.

Local application is the most common type of dry chemical system. These systems are designed to discharge agent directly onto a relatively small area such as the cooking surfaces in a commercial kitchen **(Figure 28.36)**. If installed over a deep fryer or commercial range, these systems are designed also to shut off the flow of gas to the unit when the extinguishing system actuates. Inspectors or company personnel inspecting these systems should perform the following:

- Check the discharge nozzles to see that they are not so heavily coated with grease or other material that they would not function as designed.

- Check the manual controls to see that the safety seals have not been broken.

- Check the fusible link(s) to see that they are clean and intact.

- Check the pressure gauge on the agent tank(s) to see that it is within the operating range, and

check the service tag to see that the system has been serviced within the preceding year.

Total flooding dry chemical systems are installed in areas, such as paint spray booths, where a heavy cloud of agent is needed to fill the entire space when it is discharged. Like local application

Figure 28.36 Building codes require the installation of dry chemical extinguishment systems in range ventilation hoods over cooking surfaces in commercial kitchens.

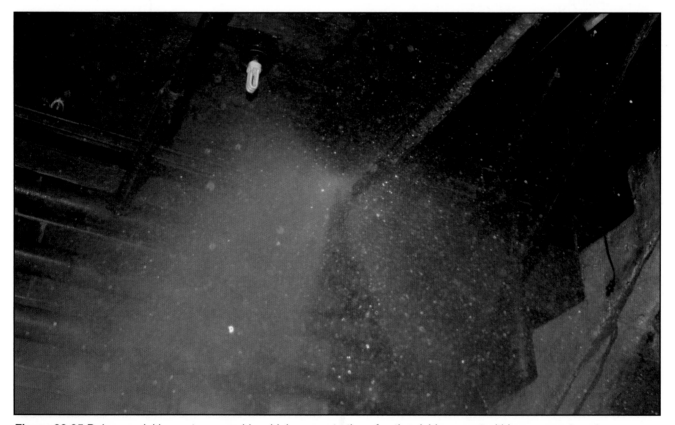

Figure 28.35 Deluge sprinkler systems provide a high concentration of extinguishing agent within a compartment.

systems, total flooding systems may be actuated manually or automatically. Automatic actuation is by means of a fusible link holding a spring-loaded cable to the system controls. The same items that were listed for the local application systems should be inspected on total flooding systems.

The inspector should also ensure that the manual activation (pull station) devices are unobstructed, that seals and tamper indicators are intact, and that the occupants are familiar with the operation of the system. In some installations, multiple manual activation devices may be required at various exits from the compartment or area.

Wet chemical systems. These systems are designed to be installed in commercial range hoods, plenums, and ducts. They must conform to the requirements of NFPA 17A, *Standard for Wet Chemical Extinguishing Systems*. Similar to dry chemical systems in operation, wet chemical systems use an agent that is typically a mixture of water and either potassium carbonate or potassium acetate that is delivered in the form of a spray. Wet chemical systems are especially well-suited for cooking oil-related applications because the agent reacts to animal and vegetable oils by forming a noncombustible soap. This extinguishes a fire by denying it fuel. The components of a wet chemical system are essentially the same as dry chemical systems, as are the items to be inspected. Portable fire extinguishers in the immediate area must be compatible with the wet chemical agent (K-rated).

Carbon dioxide systems. The installation of these systems must conform to NFPA 12, *Standard on Carbon Dioxide Extinguishing Systems*. Like dry chemical systems, carbon dioxide (CO_2) systems are designed as either local application or total flooding systems; the type of system used in a particular area depends upon the situation.

Because CO_2 extinguishes fire by excluding oxygen (smothering), the total flooding systems can be hazardous to anyone in the compartment that is flooded. Therefore, total flooding CO_2 systems must have a predischarge alarm to warn anyone in the room of an impending discharge so that they can immediately leave the compartment. Both the automatic and manual operation activate the predischarge alarm before discharging the agent. But, in addition, these total flooding systems also

have emergency manual activation devices that discharges (dumps) the agent into the room immediately and without warning. In the automatic mode, these systems are actuated by any type of detector: heat, rate-of-rise, smoke, or flame.

Local application CO_2 systems are usually supplied from one or more small cylinders, similar to portable extinguisher cylinders, located near the area to be protected. Total flooding systems are usually supplied by much larger tanks or a bank of cylinders. In either case, the agent is discharged through a system of piping from the supply to the point of discharge. The items to be inspected are essentially the same as for types of fixed extinguishing systems.

Halogenated agent systems. Halons and the halogenated extinguishing agents contain atoms from one of the halogen series of chemical elements: fluorine, chlorine, bromine, and iodine. The halogenated agents are principally effective on Class B and Class C fires **(Figure 28.37)**. Halon

Figure 28.37 Halon and halon replacement systems are designed to protect equipment and materials that could be damaged by water or dry chemical extinguishing systems.

was originally developed and used because it was considered a *clean agent*, namely one that leaves no residue. Because Halon has been proven to be harmful to humans and to the earth's ozone layer, however, international restrictions have been placed on its production. Although the Montreal Protocol of 1987 provided for a phaseout of Halons and forbade the manufacture of new Halon agents after January 1, 1994, limited production continues because there are some exceptions to the phaseout plan.

Caution

Avoid prolonged exposure to the Halons. These substances break down under fire conditions and liberate toxic substances such as chlorine, bromine, hydrogen chloride, and hydrogen bromide. These are irritating gases and their presence is readily apparent to the extinguisher user.

ⓘ Use of Halons

Locations where Halon agent use is deemed to be *essential* may be granted an exemption from the phaseout, and Halon systems installed prior to the Montreal Protocol may remain in use until such time as they are discharged on a fire or the gas "leaks off." The criteria for this exemption are as follows:

- Halon agent use is necessary for human health and safety or critical for the functioning of society. One such use is in aircraft engine fire suppression systems.

- There are no technically or economically feasible alternatives.

- All feasible actions must be taken to minimize emissions from use.

- The supply of substitute Halon agents from existing banks or recycled stocks is not sufficient to accommodate the need.

In portable fire extinguishers, two Halons are still in use:

- Halon 1211 (bromochlorodifluoromethane — CF$_2$BrCl) — Is the one most commonly found in portable fire extinguishers.

- Halon 1301 (bromotrifluoromethane — CF$_3$Br) — Is used in some portable fire extinguishers, but it is more commonly found in fixed system applications.

Like dry chemical systems, Halon systems may be engineered or preengineered. Except for some local application systems, most Halon systems are engineered for the particular occupancy in which they are installed. However, regardless of the design or installation, all Halon systems have the same component parts: agent tanks and associated piping, valve actuators, nozzles, detectors, manual releases, and control panels. One feature unique to Halon systems is an abort switch to cancel an inadvertent actuation of the system so that these very expensive agents are not wasted by being dumped accidentally.

When inspecting these systems, the inspector should check the agent storage tanks for loss of agent. Some systems have a dipstick-type gauge to indicate the amount of agent in the tank. The inspector should ensure that the detectors and discharge nozzles are not obstructed. The service tags should be checked to ensure the system has been serviced by a licensed service firm within the time interval specified in the code.

Halon replacement agents. There has been considerable research and development on new clean agents that extinguish fires in the same manner as Halon agents but that cause no significant damage to the atmosphere. NFPA 2001, *Standard on Clean Agent Fire Extinguishing Systems* (2004) defines a clean agent as *an electrically nonconducting, volatile, or gaseous fire extinguishant that does not leave a residue upon evaporation* **(Table 28.3)**. Consult NFPA 2001, *Clean Agent Fire Extinguishing Systems,* (2004), for more information.

NOTE: State and local codes may vary with respect to conversion to Halon replacement agents, which cannot usually be put directly into an existing Halon extinguishing system or portable extinguisher without certain precautions. For more information, see NFPA 2001.

Table 28.3
Clean Agents

FC-3-1-10	Perfluorobutane	C_4F_{10}
FK-5-1-12	Dodecaflouro-2	$CF_2CF_2C(O)CF(CF_3)_2$
	Methylpentan-3-one	
HCFC Blend A	Dichlorotrifluoroethane	$CHCl_2CF_3$
	HCFC-123 (4.75%)	
	Chlorodifluoromethane	$CHClF_2$
	HCFC-22 (82%)	
	Chlorotetrafluoroethane	$CHClFCF_3$
	HCFC-124 (9.5%)	
	Isopropenyl-1-	
	Methylcyclohexene (3.75%)	
HCFC-124	Chlorotetrafluorethane	$CHClFCF_3$
HFC-125	Pentafluoroethane	CHF_2CF_3
HFC-227ea	Heptafluoropropane	CF_3CHFCF_3
HFC-23	Trifluoromethane	CHF_3
HFC-236fa	Hexafluoropropane	$CF_3CH_2\,CF_3$
FIC-13I1	Trifluoroiodide	CF_3I
IG-01	Argon	Ar
IG-100	Nitrogen	N_2
IG-541	Nitrogen (40%)	N_2
	Argon (40%)	Ar
	Carbon Dioxide (8%)	CO_2
IG-55	Nitrogen (50%)	N_2
	Argon (50%)	Ar

Notes:

1. Other agents could become available at later dates. They could be added via the NFPA process in future additions or amendments of the standard.

2. Composition of inert gas agents are given in percent by volume. Composition of HCFC Blend A is given in percent by weight.

3. The full analogous ASHRAE nomenclature for FK-5-1-12 is FK-5-1-12mmy2.

- Halotron® is a "clean agent" hydrochlorofluorocarbon which, when discharged, is a rapidly evaporating liquid. Halotron® leaves no residue and meets Environmental Protection Agency (EPA) minimum standards for discharge into the atmosphere. The agent does not conduct electricity back to the operator, making it suitable for Class C fires. Halotron® has a limited Class A rating for extinguishers over 9 pounds (4 kg). A 28-pound (13 kg) Halotron® extinguisher is given a UL rating of 2A:10BC. It may be found in telecommunication facilities, clean rooms, computer rooms, and even vehicles.

- FM-200 is a hydrofluorocarbon that is considered to be an acceptable alternative to Halon 1301 because it leaves no residue and is not harmful to humans or the environment. This agent does require significantly more agent to achieve extinguishment than Halon 1309 did.

- Inergen is a blend of three naturally occurring gases: nitrogen, argon, and carbon dioxide. It is stored in cylinders near the facility under protection. Inergen is environmentally safe and does not contain a chemical composition like many other proposed Halon alternatives.

Systems inspections should conform to the manufacturer's recommendation. Generally, these systems have the same components and actuation devices found in the older Halon systems.

Foam systems. Foam systems are used in locations where the application of water alone, such as from a conventional automatic sprinkler system, may not be effective in extinguishing a fire. Such locations include facilities for the processing or storage of flammable or combustible liquids, aircraft hangars, and facilities in which rolled paper or textiles are stored **(Figures 28.38 a and b, p. 696)**. Foam systems may be designed to produce protein, fluoroprotein, film forming fluoroprotein (FFFP), or aqueous film forming foam (AFFF) in low-, medium-, or high-expansion ratios; the design in use depends on the hazards present in the particular occupancy. Systems designed to produce low-, medium-, and high-expansion foam must conform to NFPA 11, *Standard for Low-, Medium-, and High-Expansion Foam* (2005). Some systems are designed to produce ATC (alcohol-type concentrate) foams for polar solvents and other flammable

Figures 28.38 a and b High-expansion foam generating systems (a) are installed in aircraft hangars and (b) are designed to flood the compartment with high-expansion foam. (b) *Courtesy of United States Air Force.*

liquids that are miscible with water. These various types and ratios of foam may be delivered through deluge nozzles or through special foam sprinklers. For additional information on foam systems, see IFSTA **Principles of Foam Fire Fighting** and **Fire Detection and Suppression Systems**.

Portable fire extinguishers. Part of the process of inspecting any occupancy involves checking the portable fire extinguishers on the premises. Regardless of the type of occupancy, all portable fire extinguishers must be installed and maintained according to NFPA 10, *Standard for Portable Fire Extinguishers.* Depending upon the types of flammable or combustible materials that are in the particular occupancy, a variety of types and sizes of portable fire extinguishers may be present.

Portable fire extinguishers use different methods to expel the extinguishing agent and can be broadly classified according to the method used. These include the following **(Figures 28.39 a-c)**:

- *Stored-pressure*—Contains an expellant gas and an extinguishing agent in a single chamber. The pressure of the gas forces the agent out through a siphon tube, valve, and nozzle assembly.

- *Cartridge-operated* — Has the expellant gas stored in a separate cartridge, while the extinguishing agent is contained in an adjacent cylinder, called an *agent cylinder* or *tank.*

- *Pump-operated* — Discharges its agent by the manual operation of a pump.

Extinguishers must be properly distributed throughout an occupancy to ensure that they are readily available during an emergency. To be effective, extinguishers cannot be located at great travel distances from where they may be needed. In the same manner, they cannot be effective if there are not enough extinguishers provided for the hazard involved. The proper selection and distribution of extinguishers is determined by several factors, including the size of the extinguisher and the hazard protected. Requirements for extinguisher distribution are contained in NFPA 10; these requirements are separated into specifics for Class A, Class B, Class C, Class D, and Class K hazards. Because local codes and ordinances can be more restrictive, they should be reviewed along with the requirements contained in NFPA 10. The following elements are important in the selection and distribution of fire extinguishers:

- Chemical and physical characteristics of the combustibles that might be ignited

- Potential severity (size, intensity, and rate of advancement) of any resulting fire

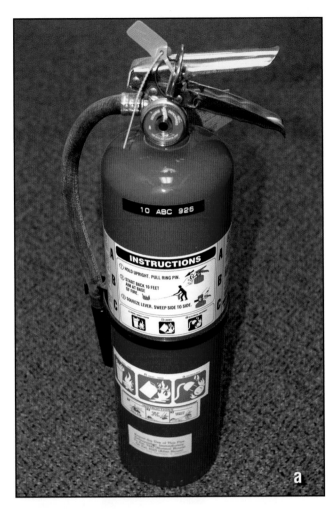

Figure 28.39 a-c Three common types of portable hand-held extinguishers are (a) stored pressure, (b) cartridge-operated, and (c) pump-operated units.

- Location of the extinguisher
- Effectiveness of the extinguisher for the hazard in question
- Personnel available to operate the extinguisher, including their physical abilities, emotional characteristics, and any training they may have in the use of extinguishers
- Environmental conditions that may affect the use of the extinguisher (temperature, winds, presence of toxic gases or fumes)
- Any anticipated adverse chemical reactions between the extinguishing agent and the burning material
- Any health and occupational safety concerns such as exposure of the extinguisher operator

to heat and products of combustion during fire fighting efforts

- Inspection and service required to maintain the extinguishers

In addition to proper selection and distribution, effective use of fire extinguishers requires that they be readily visible and accessible. Proper extinguisher placement is an essential but often overlooked aspect of fire protection. Extinguishers should be mounted properly to avoid injury to building occupants and to avoid damage to the extinguisher. Some examples of improper mounting would be an extinguisher mounted where it protrudes into a path of travel or one that is sitting on top of a workbench with no mount at all. To minimize these problems, extinguishers are frequently placed in cabinets or wall recesses for protection of both the extinguisher and people who might walk into them. If an extinguisher cabinet is placed in a rated wall, then the cabinet must have the same fire rating as the wall assembly. Proper placement of extinguishers should provide for the following:

- Extinguishers should be visible and well signed.
- Extinguishers should not be blocked by storage or equipment.
- Extinguishers should be near points of egress or ingress.
- Extinguishers should be near normal paths of travel.

Although an extinguisher must be properly mounted, it must be placed so that all personnel can access it. The extinguisher should not be placed too high above the floor for safe lifting. The standard mounting heights specified for extinguishers are as follows:

- Extinguishers with a gross weight not exceeding 40 pounds (18 kg) should be installed so that the top of the extinguisher is not more than 5 feet (1.5 m) above the floor.
- Extinguishers with a gross weight greater than 40 pounds (18 kg), except wheeled types, should be installed so that the top of the extinguisher is not more than 3½ feet (1 m) above the floor.
- The clearance between the bottom of the extinguisher and the floor should never be less than 4 inches (100 mm).

In most occupancies, extinguishers are used so infrequently that there is a natural tendency to ignore them until a fire occurs. Therefore, regular inspections of extinguishers are very important to ensure their readiness. Unless they are inspected

regularly, some of the following situations can impair extinguisher readiness:

- An extinguisher can be stolen or misplaced.
- An extinguisher can be damaged as a result of being struck by a vehicle such as a forklift truck.
- An extinguisher may have lost its pressure for a variety of mechanical reasons.
- An extinguisher may have been used on a fire and then replaced on its mount without anyone notifying the proper authorities or the unit being properly serviced or recharged.

During an inspection, the inspector or company-level personnel should perform the following:

- Check that the extinguisher is in its proper location (**Figure 28.40**).
- Ensure that access to the extinguisher is not obstructed by boxes, clothing, storage items, or is otherwise inaccessible.

Figure 28.40 Portable extinguishers should be located in cabinets or mounted on wall brackets.

- Check the inspection tag to determine if maintenance is due.

- Examine the nozzle or horn for obstructions.

- Check lock safety pins or tamper seals to make sure that they are intact.

- Check for signs of physical damage.

- Check that the extinguisher is full of agent.

- Check that the pressure gauge indicates proper operating pressure.

- Check collar tag for current information and/or damage.

- Check that required signage is in place.

- Check to see if the operating instructions on the extinguisher nameplate are legible.

- Check that the extinguisher is suitable for the hazard protected.

Summary

One of the most effective ways of preventing fires and other emergencies is through the adoption and enforcement of appropriate building fire codes and standards. Code enforcement helps to ensure that structures and facilities are maintained in a fire-safe condition and that owners and occupants follow prescribed behaviors that maintain a safe environment. The enforcement of these regulations may be done by a Fire Officer II inspector or by company-level personnel through a conscientiously applied and managed fire prevention and life safety inspection program. Company officers must be able to develop a fire risk analysis for the community or response area, perform fire and life safety inspections, enforce applicable codes and standards, and supervise company-level personnel in inspections. The result will be a proactive approach to fire and life safety that should result in a reduction in life and property loss due to fires and other emergencies.

Fire Investigations

Chapter Contents

Learning Objectives

1. Select facts about locating the point of origin of a fire.

2. Select facts about the four classifications of fire cause.

3. Identify evidence that would indicate that a fire was intentional and malicious.

4. Identify the four core elements of the crime of arson.

5. Select facts about the analysis or investigative findings.

6. Choose correct responses about various motives that cause a person to set a fire.

7. Identify evidence that indicates who had opportunity to set a fire.

8. Recall various means of setting fires.

9. Select facts about juvenile firesetters and pyromania.

10. Analyze scenarios to determine the point of origin and preliminary cause of a fire.

Job Performance Requirements

This chapter provides information that addresses the following job performance requirements of NFPA 1021, *Standard for Fire Officer Professional Qualifications* (2003):

Chapter 5   Fire Officer II

5.5.2

5.5.2(A)

5.5.2(B)

Chapter 29
Fire Investigations

All fires and explosions are evaluated to determine the cause and the sequence of events that resulted in the fire or explosion. The Fire Officer I makes the first evaluation following the mitigation of the incident. If the officer is able to determine that the incident was caused by accident or nature or if there was no loss of life or high-content loss, then the investigation will end at that point.

If, however, loss of life or high-content loss has occurred or if there is an indication that the fire or explosion was intentional or malicious, then the officer must request a fire investigator to evaluate the scene. The position of fire investigator is defined simply as an individual who has demonstrated the skills and knowledge necessary to conduct, coordinate, and complete an investigation. The individual may be a Fire Officer II or an NFPA 1033, *Standard for Professional Qualifications for Fire Investigator*, certified fire investigator.

According to the NFPA 1021 requirements for Fire Officer II, the investigation at this level is focused on determining if the crime of arson has occurred. Because of the complexity of arson crimes, the officer must know the methods used by adult and juvenile firesetters, recognize the common causes of fire, isolate the basic origin and cause determination, understand fire growth and development, and be skilled in preliminary fire investigative documentation procedures. (As a Fire Officer I, some of this knowledge has already been acquired regarding fire cause, locating point of origin, and understanding the development and growth of fires.) This chapter provides a more detailed look at each of these areas and then proceeds into information concerning the motives and methods used by arsonists.

CAUTION

One of the most important aspects of fire investigation is awareness by company officers and unit members of the importance of preserving evidence. Emergency responders must be careful during suppression operations not to needlessly disturb or destroy potential evidence of the fire cause. In addition, company officers must not allow the overhaul process to begin before the cause of the fire has been determined and any evidence protected. Because overhaul is the final step of the extinguishment process, deciding when to stop to preserve evidence and when to proceed to complete extinguishment requires good judgment on the part of the company officer.

Basic Fire Cause Knowledge

With training and experience, the company officer will become skilled in locating the point of origin of structural, vehicular, and exterior fires. Determining the cause of explosions will require additional training because of the specialized nature of explosives recognition. This area is outside the realm of this manual and is not specifically included in the NFPA 1021 requirements. Therefore, this section will look at the steps required to locate the point of origin of the fire, discuss the main causes of fires, and create the basic foundation for investigations of fires that are presumed to be intentional or malicious.

Locating the Point of Origin

The first step in the fire investigation process is to locate the point of origin. Some of the most important sources of information about the point of origin are those who reported the fire and those who fought it **(Figure 29.1)**. To determine where the fire was burning when it was first seen, the company officer should interview the reporting party and any other witnesses. The initial-attack firefighters also should be asked the same questions.

In the absence of meaningful eyewitness information, company officers can estimate where, in general, the fire started by applying the principles of basic fire behavior. However, this part of the process can be very different depending upon whether the fire being investigated is a structure fire, a vehicle fire, or a fire in the wildland. Even though the chemistry and physics involved are exactly the same, there are different environmental influences on fires burning within a confined space and those burning outdoors. Outdoor fires are affected by topography where interior structure fires are not and outdoor fires are influenced by weather to a much greater degree than interior fires. Regardless of whether a fire was inside a structure or out in the wildland, the burn pattern left by the fire is an indicator of the point of origin.

Structure Fires

A fire inside a structure also behaves in predictable ways, and the burn pattern it leaves is one of the most important indicators of the point of origin. Because there is usually no wind to influence how the fire spreads, burn patterns tend to be vertical from the point of origin and are often V-shaped **(Figure 29.2)**. Also, because of the natural convection of fire, many times the area of origin will be located at or near the lowest level of burning. However, burning debris falling or dropping down from the ceiling or upper stories can result in a condition that is referred to as a *false indicator*. That is, there is greater damage at a lower point than at the actual point of origin. If accelerants were used, their characteristic burn pattern is often obvious. Just as in the wildland, the deepest char on structural members appears on the side from which the fire spread. Also, because the fire burns longer at the point of origin, it is usually the area of greatest fire damage.

Vehicle Fires

Fires in vehicles behave according to the same physical laws as any other fire, and they may present the same challenges to those investigating them. In general, vehicle fires fall into one of two broad categories: those that occur while the vehicle is being driven, and those that occur while the vehicle is parked. However, due to the large concentrations of plastic materials in the construction of

Figure 29.1 A good source of information about the fire is the emergency responders who arrived first at the scene.

Figure 29.2 Burn patterns in structural fires can assist the investigator in tracking the development of the fire and locating the most likely point of origin.

vehicle interiors and the high intensity of burning, company officers should expect to see a complete destruction of the interiors and any potential evidence (**Figure 29.3**).

Fires that occur while a vehicle is being driven are most often due to mechanical or electrical malfunctions, or to carelessness with smoking materials. Fires that result from a mechanical malfunction are usually rather easily traced to their source. They occur most often in the engine compartment, in the exhaust system, or in the wheel-and-brake assembly. These fires often result from fuel leaks, combustibles too close to catalytic converters, or friction from overheated brakes or worn-out bearings and drive belts. Fires caused by electrical malfunction are most likely to be in the engine compartment or under the dashboard. Electrical fires may also start in the trunk area that may contain audio sound system components, combustible materials such as blankets or clothing, or the filler pipe that leads to the fuel tank. Fires that result from carelessness with smoking materials often occur when someone inside the vehicle attempts to throw out lighted material but the wind blows the material back into the vehicle. This may go unnoticed by the vehicle occupants until a fire starts in the upholstery or seat cushions.

Vehicle fires that occur when the vehicle is parked may simply be the delayed result of something that happened while the vehicle was being driven. The driver may park the vehicle and leave it unattended with smoking material smoldering in the back seat. Malfunctioning mechanical or electrical components that had been kept below their ignition temperature by the cooling effect of the wind while the vehicle was in motion may overheat and cause a fire when the vehicle is parked. However, if a fire starts in a vehicle that has been parked for several hours or days, the likelihood of the fire being of incendiary origin increases significantly.

Wildland Fires

In general, a wildland fire spreads away from the point of origin in predictable ways: it spreads faster uphill than down; it spreads faster with the wind than against it; and it spreads faster in fine fuels, such as grass, than in heavier fuels, such as timber. Therefore, the point of origin is almost always nearer the heel of the fire than the head (**Figure 29.4, p. 706**). The remains of fence posts, trees, and stumps show the deepest char on the side that was exposed to the advancing flame front. So, the depth of char indicates the direction *from which* the fire spread. For more information on wildland fire investigation, see the IFSTA **Wildland Fire Fighting for Structural Firefighters** manual.

Regardless of whether a fire occurred inside a structure, in a vehicle, or in the wildland, once the point of origin is located, the company officer must protect that part of the fire scene until the specific cause of the fire is determined or longer if further investigation is warranted.

Determining the Cause of the Fire

Once the point of origin has been located and any obvious evidence protected, company officers also must apply their understanding of basic fire behavior to determine the specific cause of the fire. Company officers and unit members must work together in this process. For example, as the company officer searches for any physical evidence, one responder may assist by taking notes while another makes a sketch of the scene and another photographs the evidence found (**Figure 29.5, p. 706**). If the company officer cannot determine the specific cause, an investigator should be called. If the fire appears to be the result of a malicious or negligent act, an investigator must be called.

Figure 29.3 Determining the point of origin or cause of a vehicle fire can be hampered by the complete destruction that often occurs.

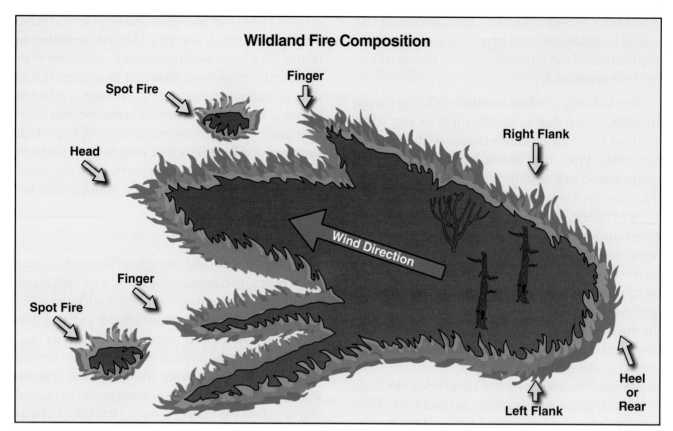

Figure 29.4 Terms used to describe the development and spread of a wildland fire.

Figure 29.5 Photographing the fire scene and evidence while it is in place can provide additional information for determining the cause of the fire.

NFPA 921, *Guide for Fire and Explosion Investigations*, defines *fire cause* as "the circumstances, conditions, or agencies that bring together a fuel, ignition source, and oxidizer (such as air or oxygen) resulting in a fire or a combustion explosion." Generally, fires may be classified as accidental, natural, incendiary, or undetermined.

- *Accidental fires* are those that did not result from intentional or malicious human activity.

- *Natural fires* are those that result from phenomena such as lightning strikes and earthquakes and not from human activity.

- *Incendiary fires* are those that involve human activity and are deliberately set. The intent may or may not be malicious. A fire started in a wood-burning stove is intentional and thus incendiary without any malicious intent. Malicious intent is involved only if the fire is a criminal act.

- *Undetermined* is the classification used when the specific cause of a fire cannot be determined. This classification may be used as an interim classification as the fire investigation is proceeding, or it may be the final outcome if additional information cannot be developed that identifies the specific cause. This does not, however, mean that if each of the specific components of the fire tetrahedron is not specifically identified, the fire should be called undetermined. A cause should be given if sufficient information is available.

Fire cause determination requires the identification of the circumstances and factors that were necessary for the fire to have occurred. These circumstances and factors include, but are not limited to, a reliable ignition source, the material first ignited, and the actions that brought them together. The mere presence of a readily ignitable fuel and a competent ignition source does not establish a fire cause. The fire cause is the sequence of events that allowed the fuel and the source of ignition to come together.

If doubt about the cause of a fire exists, the company officer or investigator first must eliminate all possible accidental or natural causes before concluding that the fire was incendiary in nature. The term *suspicious* should not be used as a fire cause classification. Mere suspicion concerning a fire's cause is an unacceptable level of proof, and it should not be used in fire reports. As mentioned earlier, if the cause cannot be determined with a reasonable degree of certainty, it should be listed as *undetermined*.

Accidental Fires

Many accidental fires are started by human activity, but they differ from incendiary fires in that there was no malicious intent on the part of the person who started the fire. Some accidental fires start as what the fire insurance industry calls *friendly fires*. These fires are started intentionally for a legitimate purpose, such as burning leaves, yard debris, or other refuse, but they get out of control and spread to adjacent combustibles. If someone started such a fire on a windy day or during an official ban on outside burning, that person may be subject to prosecution for negligence. In many communities, open burning is either banned or requires a permit. Company officers should be familiar with the local ordinances that control open burning.

Other common accidental fire causes are such things as people falling asleep while smoking; refueling gasoline-powered equipment near a source of ignition, such as a pilot light; placing combustibles too close to a furnace register or other heat source; or putting fireplace ashes into a paper bag, cardboard box, or combustible trash container **(Figure 29.6)**. Sparks from welding and cutting operations also can start fires accidentally, as can those from unscreened fireplaces. There are countless ways in which fires start accidentally; however, a significant number of accidental fires involve electricity and electrical appliances.

Smoking-related fires. Numerous conditions involve smoking materials that result in accidental fires. Many fatality fires occur when the occupant goes to sleep, inadvertently allowing lighted smoking materials to come into contact with lightweight combustibles, such as cotton bedding. In other situations, the smoking material becomes lodged between a cushion or pillow and the body of a chair or sofa. The smoking material is insulated between the fabric and smolders until full ignition occurs. Another cause of smoking-related fires occurs when someone dumps an ashtray into a wastebasket or allows an unattended cigarette to fall from an ashtray onto bedding, carpet, or upholstered furniture. Fatalities often occur in these fires if the occupant is incapacitated by alcohol or other drugs and either falls asleep or passes out. An ashtray, the metal parts of a cigarette lighter, or other evidence of smoking may be found in the ashes at the point of origin.

Figure 29.6 Unsafe behaviors, such as placing fireplace ashes in a paper bag or cardboard box, often results in accidental fires.

Pyrophoric ignition. These fires occur under conditions that appear to be without an identifiable heat source. However, when wood or other cellulose material is more or less continuously subjected to a low level of heat over a long period, the material can be converted to pyrophoric carbon through pyrolysis **(Figure 29.7)**. As this conversion takes place, the ignition temperature of the material is gradually lowered until autoignition occurs. A common example is the autoignition of wood framing in walls adjacent to metal fireplace boxes and flues. The following items are common heat sources for ignition pyrophoric carbonized materials and may be found near the point of origin:

- Steam pipes
- Flue pipes (wood-burning stoves and fireplaces)
- Fluorescent light ballasts

NOTE: In an appellate court ruling in the case of *Truck Insurance Exchange v. MagneTek, Inc.,* 2004 WL 348936 (10th Cir., February 25, 2004), the court upheld a lower court ruling that pyrolysis, as an element of fire causation theory, had not been subjected to sufficient testing, and that without such testing there were few reliable principles about it to determine when pyrolysis might occur. This court case does not mean that pyrolysis is not a cause, only that the scientific basis for the theory must be proven if it is to be used in a court of law.

Electrical fires. Electrical conductors (wiring) and appliances rarely cause fires if they are used as intended and are protected by functioning fuses or circuit breakers of the appropriate size. The mere presence of electrical wiring or appliances near the point of origin does not necessarily mean that the fire was electrical in nature. However, heat generated by electrical wiring and equipment can ignite adjacent combustibles, so it should be considered along with other possible sources of ignition.

Perhaps the most common cause of electrical fires involves misuse of the electrical system by the building occupants. This often involves the use of lightweight extension cords, sometimes called *zip cords*. Electrical fires also commonly result from the use of a multiple-outlet device commonly called an *octopus* **(Figure 29.8)**. When all the appliances that are plugged into the device

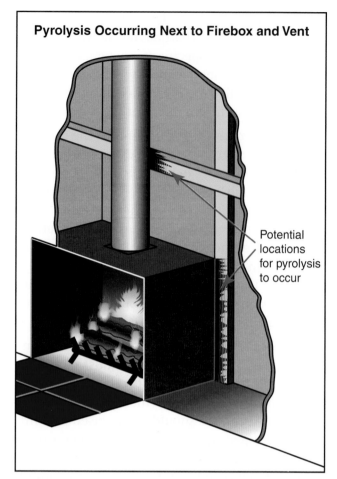

Figure 29.7 Example of pyrolysis occurring in the structural members adjacent to a fireplace.

Figure 29.8 An overloaded receptacle can cause overheating in the wiring or receptacle resulting in a fire.

are operated simultaneously, the wiring and/or the fixture can overheat and eventually ignite. A further example of the misuse of a simple electrical appliance is leaving a clothes iron on and in contact with fabric.

Another very common scenario involves an automatic coffeemaker or similar appliance inadvertently being left on when the occupants leave the premises. As long as liquid remains in the unit, evaporation keeps it from overheating. However, after a few hours all the liquid evaporates, and the unit begins to overheat. If the automatic temperature control within the unit fails, the plastic parts of the unit will eventually reach their ignition temperature and catch fire. If the unit is sitting on or near combustible materials, they may become involved and spread the fire. Therefore, one of the most important things to check during the fire investigation is the position of the power switch on any electrical appliance found at the point of origin.

Clothes dryers, both electric and gas, sometimes start fires because of a failure of the high-temperature control or the timing mechanism. If a malfunction of either of these devices occurs, abnormal heat buildup can result, possibly igniting clothing or accumulated lint. However, fires in clothes dryers may simply be the result of accumulated lint ignited during normal operation of the machine.

Another common scenario in which electricity is the fire cause involves improperly installed wiring or equipment. Homeowners and business owners who lack the training to properly install electrical wiring and fixtures sometimes try to save money by doing the work themselves instead of calling a licensed contractor or electrician. The results can be far more expensive than the cost of paying a trained professional. Interviewing the property owner or occupant often confirms improper installation as the real cause of the fire.

The company officer must first determine if the electrical service to the structure was turned on. Then it must be determined if the wiring or equipment that was involved in fire was energized. Circuit breakers, fuse panels, and electric meters can help to determine the availability of electricity to the structure or item. The company officer should photograph the position of the breaker and the condition of the fuses as a record for determining the possible involvement in the fire.

Natural Fires

Nature can cause fires in a variety of ways. Fires may result from lightning strikes, earthquakes, and other natural phenomena. One of the most common of these is a lightning strike.

Lightning-related fires. When lightning strikes a building, it can instantly overload the building's entire electrical system by introducing several thousand volts into it and thus cause multiple fires. It can destroy heating and air conditioning units, television sets, stereo sound systems, computers, and other appliances that normally remain plugged in all the time. In these fires, the main fuses or circuit breakers may be melted (**Figure 29.9**). If a lightning strike cannot be confirmed by

Figure 29.9 An inspection of the electrical service to the structure, including the weatherhead, meter, circuit box, and wiring, can provide evidence of a possible electrical cause for the fire.

a witness or by finding an obvious point of contact, the fire scene must be examined carefully for evidence of a strike. However, there are incidents where lightning strikes have produced no visible damage. Some of the most likely contact points are as follows:

- Roof peaks with metal flashing
- Any metal object of significant size, such as tanks, blowers, and air-handling units, on or near the top of the structure
- Antennas affixed to and serving the structure
- Electrical service weather head
- Trees near the structure

Earthquake-related fires. Earthquakes occur daily in some parts of North America, but they may occur anywhere at any time. When major earthquakes occur, structures may suffer serious damage or may even collapse (**Figure 29.10**). The movement can break gas pipes and cause electrical equipment and systems to short out. This resulting combination of abundant fuel and a competent ignition source often results in fires starting, sometimes in numerous locations simultaneously.

Earthquakes can sometimes do damage that is not obvious in a cursory inspection but that can cause a fire later. For example, if the terra-cotta flue liner in a fireplace chimney is cracked by earthquake movement, a subsequent fire started in the fireplace may ignite combustibles adjacent to the chimney. A diligent amount of investigation may be required to determine the cause of these fires as the fire may occur several months after the quake event.

Other natural fires. While fires caused by lightning strikes and earthquakes may be the most common and most spectacular of those caused by natural forces, they are not the only ones. Other examples include fires caused by wind damage to electrical conductors and transmission lines. The wind also can cause fires by blowing electrical lines into contact with tree limbs. Hurricanes and the resulting flooding can cause fires as electrical systems short out and ignite combustibles (**Figure 29.11**).

An obscure but not uncommon natural cause of fires is the heat generated by the friction between dehydrating logs piled on a sawmill log deck. If rain water dampens powdered swimming pool chemicals, the reaction can generate enough heat to ignite adjacent combustibles. Company officers may have to do a diligent amount of investigation to determine the fire cause in these situations.

> **WARNING!**
> Company-level personnel and other fire investigators should consider any exposed electrical wiring or equipment as energized unless the power has been shut off by utility company personnel.

Figure 29.10 Earthquakes can cause all types of structures, including elevated highways, to fail and collapse. Natural gas supply lines attached to or supplying the structure can rupture providing fuel that can result in a fire or explosion. *Courtesy of FEMA News.*

Figure 29.11 High winds associated with hurricanes, tornadoes, and other storms can cause trees to fall on power lines igniting nearby combustibles. *Courtesy of Chief Chris E. Mickal.*

Incendiary Fires

Incendiary fires are caused by the same combination of a reliable ignition source and an ignitable material that causes accidental and natural fires. The most obvious difference between these types of fires, though, is that incendiary fires are started intentionally and may involve malicious intent. Some fires that are intentional result in the accidental spread of the fire. Although intentional, these fires lack the malicious intent that would be classified as arson incidents. It should be noted that even though intent is nice to know, it is not something a company officer, or fire investigator, must prove in order to state a fire was of an incendiary nature.

When the company officer has eliminated accidental and natural causes for a particular fire having started, the possibility that the fire is of incendiary origin involving malicious intent must be considered. In many cases, this conclusion may be obvious. Other differences between incendiary fires and those of accidental or natural origin are that the firesetters often do one or more of the following:

- Use accelerants to increase the rate at which the fire develops and spreads
- Disable fire detection systems and equipment to delay the fire being reported (**Figure 29.12**)

Figure 29.12 Disabled smoke detectors are an indication that a fire may have been intentionally set.

- Disable fire suppression systems and equipment to allow the fire to develop
- Employ some means of delaying ignition
- Employ some means of delaying the emergency service's response

Some other indicators that a fire was of incendiary origin and involved malicious intent are the following:

- ***Multiple points of origin*** — Evidence of separate fires in different rooms or areas. The company officer or investigator must be able to prove that the seemingly multiple points of origin were separate and distinct and were not the result of the normal propagation of the fire or a secondary ignition source such as curtains igniting and dropping to a lower level (**Figure 29.13, p. 712**).

- ***Timing devices*** — Devices designed and used to start a fire. Most incendiary timing devices leave evidence of their existence, especially the metal parts of electrical or mechanical devices. More than one device may be used, and sometimes a faulty device can be found. The following are examples of devices used to start a fire:

  — Cigarette-match combinations and candles are frequently used timing devices.

  — Wax from a candle often soaks into the floor and can be detected on the scene or by a laboratory test. The spot beneath the candle often is not burned as badly as the surrounding floor.

  — Alarm clocks are not often used but should not be discounted. The metal parts of alarm clocks and similar devices are seldom destroyed by fire.

- ***Trailers*** — Term used to describe the patterns that result when materials are used to intentionally spread the fire from one area of a structure to another or from one floor level to another (**Figure 29.14, p. 712**). They are usually ordinary combustibles often soaked with ignitable liquids. The resulting pattern may appear elongated, like a trail, and contain residue of the ignitable liquid or solid material that was used to spread the fire. Items used to make trailers may include the following:

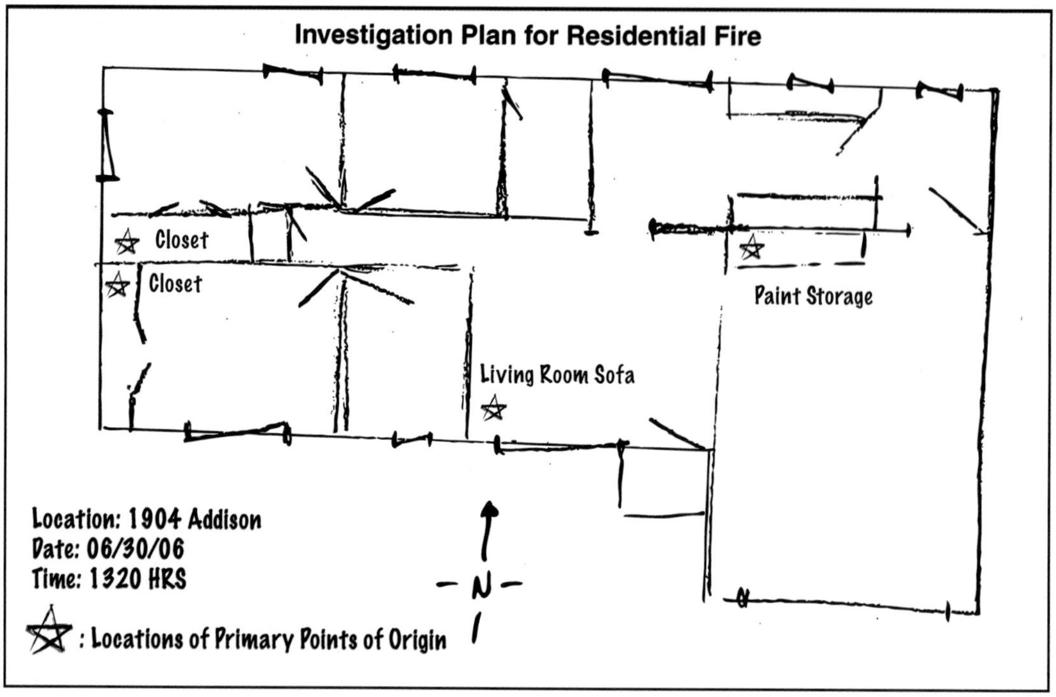

Investigation Plan for Residential Fire

Figure 29.13 Multiple unrelated points of origin are another indication that the fire cause may be intentional and incendiary.

Closet

Closet

Paint Storage

Living Room Sofa

Location: 1904 Addison
Date: 06/30/06
Time: 1320 HRS

— N —

☆ : Locations of Primary Points of Origin

Figure 29.14 Trailers are a means used to spread fire from one area of a structure to another. They may consist of paper or cloth that has been soaked in ignitable liquids.

— Toilet paper

— Newspapers

— Gunpowder

— Wax paper

— Excelsior

— Blasting fuse

— Oil-soaked string, cord, or rope

— Cotton, wool, and similar materials

• *Chemicals* — Phosphorous, metallic sodium, potassium permanganate, or glycerin.

• *Matches* — They are not always consumed by the fire, and even if they are, the staple from a matchbook will remain if the matchbook was left at the scene. Unburned matchbook covers may yield fingerprints, so they must be handled carefully.

• *Ignitable liquids*— Gasoline, kerosene, solvent, alcohol, carbon disulfide, paint thinner, acetone, ether, and other flammable or combustible accelerants. Pronounced and irregular damage to a floor may indicate the use of an ignitable liquid. (**NOTE:** Oftentimes these are false indicators as it can be created by carpet and concentrated fuel loads such as furniture and ventilation). Ignitable liquid flows to the lowest level possible; therefore, corners and the base of walls should be checked for an unconsumed accumulation.

- **Bottles** — These often are used to make Molotov cocktails. Unburned cloth may be found in the bottle's neck. Some remains of the bottle almost always can be found.

- **Rubber items** — Balloons, condoms, latex gloves, hot-water bottles, and similar rubber items used to hold flammable liquids or phosphorous and water sometimes can be recovered at the scene (**Figure 29.15**).

- **Other containers** — Those that may have held ignitable liquids often can be found in or around the scene.

- **Glass** — Sometimes used to focus the sun's rays on combustible materials, glass may be found at the scene, especially in wildland fires.

- **Butane lighters** — Even if the plastic fuel reservoir is consumed, the metal parts of the lighter are usually identifiable.

- **Altered heating equipment** — Improperly adjusted draft controls, deliberate breaks in flue and stove pipes, or oil or gas lines deliberately damaged.

- **Electrical appliances** — Lamps or heating equipment intentionally placed in contact with combustibles; deliberate overloads on circuits.

- **Tools** — Those used for forcible entry, such as crowbars, screwdrivers, hammers, etc.

- **Oily rags** — The ash from an oily rag retains its shape and may be identifiable.

- **Newspapers** — These often are used as the initial fuel. Undisturbed ash may still be readable, and headlines, dates, etc., can be photographed.

- **Burn patterns** — They may be consistent with the use of ignitable liquids.

- **Highway flares (fusees)** — Striker can be used to trace the source of the flare and may yield fingerprints. The nail contained in some highway flares also may be located.

- **Financial papers** — Demands for payments, etc., may have been left intentionally where they would burn.

- **Valuable items replaced with cheaper ones** — Sometimes valuable furnishings are listed on the inventory, but only inexpensive furnishings are found in the debris.

- **Items present/missing** — Things that should not be there, but are; things that should be there, but are not. A gasoline can in a bedroom closet requires explanation. Outbuildings and storage areas may contain valuable items or those with sentimental value that were removed from the building before the fire.

- **Signs of forced entry** — Jimmy marks on doors or windows, doors broken in (**Figure 29.16, p. 714**)

- **Anything unusual or out of place** — Combustibles arranged in a way that makes them more susceptible to ignition; items in rooms where they are not normally found — for example, a gasoline can in a bedroom closet.

- **Bridges or access roads blocked, damaged, or destroyed; address numbers removed or obliterated; gates or doors locked or barricaded** — Anything that might impede the response of the emergency services organization.

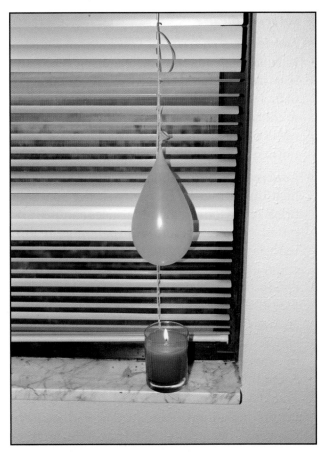

Figure 29.15 Ballons, latex gloves, or other rubber items filled with ignitable liquids and suspended above candles are used as delayed ignition devices.

Figure 29.16 Broken glass that does not exhibit fire damage is an indication of forcible entry. Glass that broke as a result of the fire will be smoke stained and crazed.

- *Smoke/heat detectors removed or disabled, or automatic sprinklers shut off.*

- *Windows covered or blacked out to delay discovery of the fire.*

- *Low levels of charring* — Low levels of charring indicate high amounts of heat at low levels and may indicate the introduction of ignitable liquids. However, the investigator must not jump to conclusions. Low-level burning may also be a result of the fire fighting tactics, flashover igniting existing fuels, or ventilation factors.

- *Concrete spalling* — Spalling is caused by high heat liberating the moisture in the concrete, brick, or masonry leaving surfaces chipped and pitted. Newer concrete will spall more readily than does older concrete. Concrete spalling may occur as a result of burning ignitable liquid. If conditions are right, Class A or D combustibles may also cause concrete spalling. Many factors such as the type of aggregate and the age of the concrete affect spalling. Spalling may be caused by other situations such as the rapid cooling of heated concrete when fire streams are applied. The fact that spalling can be caused by other factors, including the application of extinguishing agents (water) on heated concrete, brick, or masonry materials, means that spalling is not proof of the presence of a liquid fuel accelerant. Spalling must be taken in context with

other indicators in the analysis of a possible heat source. See NFPA 921, *Guide for Fire and Explosion Investigations* (2004), for additional information.

- *Inverted V-patterns* —These may indicate the introduction of ignitable liquids. The inverted V-pattern is narrower at the apex (top) than it is at the base. These patterns are generally found on walls and originate at the floor. They often result from pooled ignitable liquids; however, other factors such as fall-down, ventilation, or fuel arrangement may also explain these findings. The company officer or investigator must rule out these other possibilities before concluding that the inverted V-patterns were caused by ignitable liquids.

- *Hourglass patterns* — Hourglass-shaped patterns are formed as a result of air movement from the side of the fire, cooling the wall surface where air enters the flame zone. These patterns may be the result of an ignitable liquid or any other material that releases heat at a high rate.

If any of these conditions are found at the scene, a more thorough investigation is warranted. The company officer must follow departmental protocols for calling an investigator. Pending the arrival of the investigator, the company officer's responsibilities are to control the scene, protect the evidence, and gather the information about what has been found to give to the investigator. For more information about fire and arson investigation, see the IFSTA **Introduction to Fire Origin and Cause** manual or NFPA 921, *Guide for Fire and Explosion Investigations*.

Even after a fire investigator arrives on scene and assumes control of the investigation, the company officer's job is not finished. The company officer and unit members may be asked to assist with the investigation. If so, this is a tremendous opportunity for them to learn about the art and science of fire investigation **(Figure 29.17)**.

Incendiary Fire Investigation

Malicious incendiary fires are a major problem in North America and the cause of numerous fatalities and injuries as well as high property loss. As a crime, intentionally set malicious fires are termed *arson*, which is generally defined as the act of intentionally and maliciously destroying or damaging property through the use of fire. The legal definition may differ between states/provinces and local jurisdictions. In some jurisdictions, arson only involves the destruction of a house. In others, the crime can involve the destruction of personal property such as the burning of one's clothing or books (**Figure 29.18**). And, in other jurisdictions, it must be the property of another person or group.

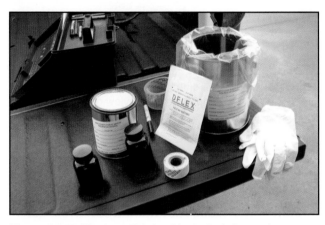

Figure 29.17 Fire investigation kits include latex gloves, containers for storing evidence, tape, labels, and markers.

Figure 29.18 Arson is considered to be the intentional destruction of another person's property through the use of fire.

In any case, the crime of arson must include four core elements:

- *Lighting of fire* — Fire is the fundamental element of arson. If there is no fire lit, then arson has not occurred.

- *Willful intent* — The firesetter must have intentionally lit the fire.

- *Malice* — The firesetter must have intentionally lit the fire with a desire to do damage or to collect insurance as a result of the fire. This allows the investigator to exclude fires started intentionally with positive or legitimate intent, such as the burning of trash or debris.

- *Property* — An object, item, or structure must be burned. The description of this element varies between jurisdictions.

Similar to the NFIRS, the Uniform Crime Reporting (UCR) program provides the law enforcement community with a data-reporting and trend-analysis process. The UCR is the source of information on the numbers of arson-related fires and the resulting loss value from the fires. The UCR Program reported the following data for 2002:

- Approximately 75,000 suspected arson cases were reported.

- Arson fires in residential, commercial, industrial, or other types of structures were the most frequently reported and accounted for 41.3 percent of the reported arsons.

- Mobile properties, such as motor vehicles and trailers, made up 33.1 percent of arsons.

- Other properties (crops, timber, etc.) accounted for 25.7 percent of arson offenses.

The period between 2001 and 2004 saw a drop in arson offenses from each previous year.

Within the structural arson category, the fires in residential properties accounted for 60.7 percent of those offenses. Single occupancy residences comprised 71.0 percent of the residential arsons. At the time of the arson, 18.2 percent of structural properties were uninhabited, vacant, or not in use. In terms of mobile property arsons, motor vehicles comprised 94.6 percent of that type of arson.

According to the USFA, in 2004 an estimated 36,500 intentionally set structure fires resulted in 320 civilian deaths. Intentionally set structure fires resulted in an estimated $714 million in total property damage. During the UCR reporting period, the average dollar loss associated with arson offenses was $11,253. The average dollar loss for structural property arsons was $20,818, and the average dollar loss for mobile property arson offenses was $6,073. Other property type arson offenses had an average dollar loss of $2,536. The seemingly low dollar-loss per structure and the difficulty in proving arson based on the four core elements contribute to the low prosecution rate in some jurisdictions.

Because of these obviously high total losses and the need for the prosecution and conviction of adult and juvenile firesetters, company officers and investigators must collect and accurately analyze fire scene data. This data includes information collected from participants and witnesses, reports, and evidence. The company officer must also know the motives for firesetters and the characteristics of the firesetter.

The Analysis of Investigative Findings

Up to this point in the fire scene investigation, the company officer or investigator has been primarily focused on the fire scene with activities involving scene documentation, collecting physical evidence, and taking statements from witnesses. Once the thorough examination of a fire scene has been completed, the company officer moves into a phase of the investigation that involves the organization and analysis of the available information with the ultimate objective of determining the origin and cause of the fire. When it is determined that a fire was intentionally set, the company officer may also be involved in determining who was responsible for the fire.

The analysis phase of the fire investigation can be very simple and may be completed during the scene examination if the origin and cause are easily determined **(Figure 29.19)**. When the determination of the origin and cause is not readily made during the examination of the scene, the post-scene investigation can be complex and time-consuming. The post-scene investigation may include compilation of records such as:

- Police reports regarding the incident
- Fire and emergency services incident reports

Figure 29.19 Analysis of the evidence about suspicious fires includes the compilation and review of records from multiple agencies and sources.

- Reports developed by private investigators or insurance company representatives
- Photos and videos obtained from investigative and other sources, such as television stations or bystanders at the fire scene

Depending on the incident complexity, other elements of the post-scene investigation may include:

- Conducting additional interviews of involved parties or individuals who might possess information essential to the investigation
- Submitting evidence for laboratory analysis [later it will be necessary to compare the results of the analysis with the reported fire scene observations]
- Developing data necessary to assist in the determination of the fire cause
- Seeking experts to assist in the development and/or analysis of investigative information
- Reviewing and analyzing records and documents related to the incident and/or the involved parties

The objective of the post-scene investigation is to develop additional information regarding the origin and cause of a fire. The need for this information is determined after a careful evaluation of the information obtained from the scene investigation. To make a final determination of the origin and cause of a fire, the company officer or investigator needs to answer each of the following questions:

- What factors or circumstances brought the components of the fire tetrahedron (heat, fuel, oxygen, and chemical chain reaction) together?

- What were the spread characteristics of the fire once it was ignited? How did the fire spread? Were the fire protection systems adequate? Did the building construction and interior finish or contents contribute to the spread of the fire?

- What factors were responsible for injuries or fatalities resulting from the fire? These factors may include the adequacy of the means of egress, fire alarm systems or defend in-place building components, and the role of specific products that may have emitted toxic by-products during the fire. If there were firefighter injuries or fatalities, the factors that contributed to those injuries should also be determined.

- What human factors were involved in the ignition of this fire? These factors may include fires that result from unsafe acts or negligence as well as those that are maliciously set.

- If the fire appears to be intentionally set, are the four core elements required to establish the potential for an arson case present?

After the elimination of all accidental and natural causes, the investigator can use the following *red flags* to assist in the investigation (**Figure 29.20**).

- Have contents been removed or moved out of place?

- Is there an absence of personal items?

- Is there evidence of other crimes in the structure? If so, was the crime related to the fire or was it *staged* to distract the company officer or investigator into thinking it was fire related?

- Was the second fire in the same structure?

- Was there structural damage before the fire?

- Was the fire department access blocked?

- Did the fire occur at an unusual time of day?

- Were there signs of forced entry?

- Does the owner's/occupant's story match the circumstances?

- Did the fires occur during inclement weather causing a delayed response or providing a possible excuse for the fire?

Figure 29.20 Red Flags that may indicate a fire was intentionally set. *Photo courtesy of Chief Chris E. Mickal*

In any case that may result in a legal action, criminal or civil, the importance of proper documentation cannot be overstressed. Chain of evidence, complete interview reports, photographs, and certified original copies of documents must be gathered and recorded into an incident investigation report. Each item, its location, and time and date of acquisition are recorded. The previous list of questions can act as an outline for gathering and organizing the information in the report.

The Evaluation of Interview Information

One step in the investigative process is an evaluation of the interviews that were taken from participants, witnesses, property owners, or other involved parties. The company officer or investigator should review the interview information and identify the data that supports the findings. Also, it is important to identify areas for further investigation where interview information conflicts with information from the scene or other interviews.

During this step of the process, the company officer or investigator evaluates the information provided by the various individuals interviewed and judges the reliability of that information. An example of this type of judgment would be descriptions of the fire from occupants, witnesses, and firefighters. Based on their experience and knowledge, the description provided by the firefighter would probably be the most accurate. Information provided by parties who are suspect in criminal investigations should be evaluated with caution. To assist in this evaluation, the investigator might use an index to rank the validity and reliability of the information available.

NOTE: The company officer must be knowledgeable regarding the law when interviewing subjects regarding a fire. The company officer must know how to properly advise a subject of the rights outlined in the Miranda Rights. If this is not done correctly, anything told to the company officer will not be admissible in a court of law during a criminal arson trial.

As the interview information is organized and evaluated, the company officer can begin to develop hypotheses or conclusions based on the

Miranda Rights Questions

The following questions must be read to any person that is suspected of involvement in a crime. If the suspect does not speak English, the questions must be read by a translator in the suspect's common language.

WARNING OF RIGHTS

1. You have the right to remain silent and refuse to answer questions. Do you understand?

2. Anything you do say may be used against you in a court of law. Do you understand?

3. You have the right to consult an attorney before speaking to the police and to have an attorney present during questioning now or in the future. Do you understand?

4. If you cannot afford an attorney, one will be appointed for you before any questioning if you wish. Do you understand?

5. If you decide to answer questions now without an attorney present you will still have the right to stop answering at any time until you talk to an attorney. Do you understand?

6. Knowing and understanding your rights as I have explained them to you, are you willing to answer my questions without an attorney present?

facts that emerged during the investigation. The conclusion may include indicators as to the intent or motive that would cause a person to set the fire. The company officer will need to know the characteristic motives, opportunities, and means that are associated with firesetters.

Motives

The National Center for the Analysis of Violent Crimes (NCAVC) has determined that there are six general categories of motives that may individually or in combination cause a person to set a fire. Adult firesetters are usually motivated by revenge, vandalism, profit (fraud), crime concealment, excitement (vanity), or extremism (terrorism). Fires are generally set in a location and manner unique to a specific motive. Identification of the motive provides valuable assistance in the identification of the person responsible for setting the fire.

Revenge

Fires set because of personal or professional vendettas fall into the largest category of arson fires and account for half of the total arson problem. Targets of revenge include individuals, institutions, society in general, or specific groups. The attacks may be combined with other types of vandalism and include graffiti or other types of symbols that are intended to convey a message to the victim or to society at large.

Generally, the victim is able to provide information regarding the suspect's identity. Personal property is often the target, and ignitable liquids are seldom used because most often the fire is not planned. Rather, the fire occurs without planning and in reaction to an incident or perceived insult. Normal targets are vehicles, storage rooms or outbuildings, and fences. Fires set to homes or businesses are often set to the exterior or through a broken window. Molotov cocktails or *firebombs* may also be employed **(Figure 29.21)**. Revenge fires set in homes as a result of a spouse believed to be unfaithful are often set to that person's clothing or to the bed. Often a history of domestic disputes precedes the fire.

Vandalism

Vandalism fires are most often set by two or more individuals (usually juveniles) for no apparent reason other than for excitement. Schools are prime targets while other common locations include vacant buildings, trash containers, and vegetation **(Figure 29.22)**. Forced entry to buildings is present, and property damage and graffiti are often done before the fire. Historical data indicates that vandalism is usually the result of boredom or frustration and is committed by those who are undereducated or people with below-average intelligence.

Figure 29.21 Molotov cocktails, bottles filled with ignitable liquids and stuffed at the neck with a rag, are often used to set intentional fires.

Figure 29.22 Vacant buildings are often the target of vandals. *Courtesy of Chief Chris E. Mickal.*

Profit (Fraud)

Monetary gain is the primary motivator for this type of fire, and total destruction of property is the ultimate goal. The key to this fire is the desire to cause the most possible damage in the least possible time. For that reason, multiple fires and ignitable liquids are commonly used. Holes broken in the walls or ceilings and trailers are often used to assist in the fire spread. The use of time-delay ignition devices is common. Fires set by the property owners are often elaborate in nature and require a significant setup time. No other motive allows a firesetter unlimited access and time to the interior of a structure without fear of discovery. Premeditation is a definite factor in fires that are set for profit. Profit from fires in commercial properties may result from:

- Insurance payments based on actual or inflated value of the property

- Destruction of a structure that is worth less than the land it sits on

- Destruction of business or inventory records that indicate fraud, theft, or embezzlement

- Destruction of old equipment or goods in storage that would be unprofitable to repair or sell

Fires in residential properties may be motivated by insurance payments or as a result of increased repair or ownership costs that cannot be met by the owner/occupant.

In premeditated fires in residences, the arsonist may remove pets or irreplaceable personal property before starting the fire. The property owner is frequently absent from the building, and doors are found locked. Fires that are motivated by fraud or personal gain are classically set because of poor financial status; however, the motivation for arson for profit may be quite abstract and as varied as the imagination of the firesetter. An example would include a profitable and well-established business set on fire for fraudulent reasons; that is, a successful nightclub needs to be remodeled because of worn carpet and tobacco-smoked ceilings. If the owner were to close for the week required to complete the remodeling, revenue would be lost. If a fire were set to a business with adequate insurance, the overhead expenses, lost revenues, and remodeling fees would be paid through the business interruption insurance.

Other reasons for fraud-related fires do not involve the property owners. The fires are generally not elaborate and if set to the interior, require the firesetter to force entry. The following are examples of fires set for economic gain by persons other than the owners or insured:

- Competitors attempting to drive the victim out of business

- Contractors attempting to secure a contract for rebuilding the loss

- Insurance agents wanting to sell insurance to uninsured/underinsured persons in the area

- Persons wishing to devalue the property so they can purchase it at a lower price

- Firefighters wanting to obtain overtime or call-out pay

Crime Concealment

Arson used as a tool to destroy evidence of another crime is most generally associated with burglary, homicide, and embezzlement. The attempt to cover a burglary is most common with the fire set at the location where evidence, such as fingerprints or blood, was believed to have been left. Most often the location is at the point of entry or where an item has been removed. The fire is generally set with combustibles on hand and rarely involves ignitable liquids **(Figure 29.23)**; a burglar usually

Figure 29.23 Bottles of paint stripper or charcoal lighter fluid may be used to start fires because they are ordinarily present in many structures or may be purchased without raising suspicion.

enters a structure with the intent to steal and not to set a fire. The fire is set after entry and after it is decided that incriminating evidence may have been left behind.

Homicide concealment fires, however, often involve the use of ignitable liquids in an attempt to destroy the body and, therefore, evidence of the manner and cause of death. These fires are generally set on and around the body. Besides an attempt to conceal the homicide, some studies indicate that the fire may be set as part of the killer's desire for complete destruction of the victim.

Embezzlement fires are set to erase or destroy documents, files, records, or computer systems that may contain evidence of criminal activities. Therefore, the paperwork, computer, and surrounding area are the origin for the fire. Often the paperwork itself is used as the fuel with ignitable liquids sometimes used to assist in the destruction of the documents.

Excitement (Vanity)

The ability to create a situation requiring the response of the fire service and law enforcement to a fire gives some people a feeling of empowerment over society. The spur-of-the-moment fires, however, develop as a recognizable pattern over a period of time. Examples of pattern development include the following:

- *Dates and day of the week* — Paydays, normal work days, or days spent consuming alcohol are believed to help stimulate these individuals in firesetting.

- *Time of day* — The time of day or night may correspond with travel to and from work or other activity. Most excitement fires are set during the hours of darkness.

- *Type of structure* — The arsonist is often consciously or subconsciously attracted to a certain type of structure — for example, schools, churches, vacant structures, etc.

- *How the fire is set* — The arsonist rarely plans to set a fire; therefore, combustibles on hand are most often used. They often become comfortable with a certain method and tend to stay with the method that has worked in the past. Elaborate

or sophisticated ignition devices are rarely used, while easily obtainable items like matches and lighters are preferred.

- *Where the fire is set* — The arsonist tends to set these fires in similar locations (for example, under a crawl space) as prior fires at that location resulted in the required emergency response and lack of detection.

Firesetters who seek recognition or wish to be viewed as heroes may set and then *discover* and report the fires. These individuals are always present at the fire scene and often attempt to assist in fire fighting activities. They may be from any background; however, it has been noted that some have been employed as security guards, career and volunteer firefighters, and reserve law enforcement officers. These same individuals may often be seen at multiple fire scenes, and if their presence is observed, the investigator should check their background for past examples of firesetting behavior **(Figure 29.24)**.

Extremism (Terrorism)

Social protest by an individual or group may target a government facility, ethnic or religious group, or a facility that operates in opposition to the protester's cause. Fires or explosions are carried out with the intent to advertise or advance the firesetter's purpose. Although the firesetter wishes to remain personally anonymous, it is

Figure 29.24 Company officers and fire investigators should take a moment to observe people who are present at fires. Individuals who are present at numerous fires without good reason may be linked to the fire.

important that the group or cause be identified as the responsible party. Graffiti or signs may be left at the scene, and phone calls or letters to the press are common. Fires and explosives are most often set to the exterior of buildings or are propelled (as is a Molotov cocktail, for example) into the interior through broken windows or doorways.

Attacks within the United States have included fire bombings of abortion clinics, churches, government buildings, and commercial institutions. Explosive devices have also been used as was the case with the 1993 World Trade Center attack and the 1995 Oklahoma City Murrah Federal Building attack (**Figure 29.25**). The use of roadside bombs, either contained in parked vehicles or buried under or next to the roadway, have become a popular means of inflicting injury and damage in the Middle East. The potential for such attacks in North America should always be considered possible.

Figure 29.25 Both domestic and international terrorism have occurred in the United States in the past two decades including the 1995 bombing of the Murrah Federal Building in Oklahoma City.

Opportunity

The evaluation and correlation of various pieces of evidence may indicate the people who had an opportunity to set the fire. Opportunity involves the firesetter actually being on the property at the time the fire started. Unless a witness or video image can place the suspected firesetter at the point of origin, conviction can be very difficult. Evidence to be considered may include the following:

- *Personal items found at the scene* — personal property that can be directly linked to the suspect such as tools used to force entry or a gasoline can

- *Building security* —the lack of security or the ability by the suspect to gain entrance without being noticed

- *Latent prints* — finger, hand, or footprints that can be directly linked to the suspect

- *Impressions* — marks made by tools used to force entry, vehicle tire tracks, footprints leading to or from the structure

- *Phone records* — calls from home, office, or cellular phones that might have triggered a remote ignition device or that might pinpoint the location of the suspect at the time the fire started

- *Witness statements* — eyewitness statements that can place the suspect at the fire scene or at some other location

- *Alarm system printout* — can provide the exact times that entry was made into the building, if the alarm was shut off, or when the fire detection system activated; some structures or compartments that require pass card access record the identity of the person gaining access

- *Security or surveillance cameras* — may provide an image of the suspect at time of entry or ignition (**Figure 29.26**)

- *Traffic citations* — can place the suspect near the site of the incident or provide an alibi if the citation and the incident times coincide

While this information can connect a person to the scene, it can also be used to eliminate potential suspects by providing evidence that they did not have the opportunity to commit the crime. A third piece to any case is for the suspect to have the means to commit the crime.

Figure 29.26 Surveillance cameras can provide the investigator with visual evidence of activities surrounding the emergency incident scene prior to the fire or explosion.

Figure 29.27 Matches are available in a variety of types and may be acquired in many locations, including bars, restaurants, hotels, and retail outlets. Matchbooks have been used for free advertising for many years.

Means

The term *means* is generally used to describe the methods used by firesetters to bring the fuel and the ignition source together to start the fire. The company officer or investigator uses the knowledge of these means to determine if they are present at the point of ignition, establish patterns linking similar types of fires, and attribute the means to a particular suspect or suspect group. As mentioned previously, firesetters become comfortable with a specific means (also referred to as the *method of operation, modus operandi*, or *MO*) for starting a fire and routinely use it.

Once the means has been determined, the company officer must protect, secure, and document the evidence as the beginning of the chain of evidence. All evidence must be controlled from the time of discovery until it is used in a court of law. Any interruption in the chain of evidence can jeopardize the arson case.

Matches

The most common source of ignition, and one that is readily available, is matches. Matches are manufactured in a number of forms including *safety matches,* which only ignite when struck against an abrasive surface, and *strike anywhere* matches, which ignite through friction against any rough surface **(Figure 29.27)**. The matches may be packaged in small booklets with card stock stems or individually in boxes with wood stems. Match-

books have been used as timed ignition devices that permit the firesetter to leave the area before full ignition. Otherwise, the firesetter must be present for ignition to occur when using matches. Residue from the match or matchbook may be present at the point of origin.

Lighters

Cigarette lighters provide an ignition source and, in one form, a sustained fuel source for the firesetter. Lighters may contain the following: an electric element (the type found in vehicles) or a fuel source such as propane, butane, or liquid lighter fluid. The fuel-type lighters may be small, approximately 2 inches long (5 cm) or larger hand torches used for lighting fireplaces and grills that are approximately 12 inches long (30 cm). The larger units can produce flames that are longer and more sustained than the cigarette-type lighters **(Figure 29.28, p. 724)**. The remains of lighters may or may not be present at the point of origin.

Candles

Candles are the cause of many accidental fires and have been used as ignition sources for malicious incendiary fires. Firesetters will use one or more candles located on or adjacent to solid ignitable fuels. When the candle burns down, it ignites the fuel, which then spreads the fire. Another approach is to light a candle in one area and open a gas valve

Figure 29.28 Propane, butane, and liquid lighters are available in many sizes.

Figure 29.29 Electric space heaters may be found in many types of occupancies and have been used as ignition sources for incendiary fires. Combustibles can be stuffed into the heaters in contact with the heating coils.

in another area. As the fuel fills the space it comes in contact with the candle flame and ignites in a gas explosion. Candles are often used because the remains appear to indicate an accidental fire cause. They also permit the firesetter to establish an alibi by being at another location at the time the fire actually starts. Company officers should consider the evidence closely when trying to determine if a candle caused an accidental ignition or was used intentionally as an ignition source.

Appliances

Small and large appliances can be used as intentional ignition sources in an attempt to create the appearance of an accidental fire. The appliances may be electric or gas powered and may or may not produce flames. For instance, a hair curling iron can be left in contact with ignitable materials, heating it to its ignition temperature. Evidence of an incendiary source of ignition may include intentional damage to electric power cords or a small appliance that appears to be out of place at the point of origin.

A gas valve can be left open with the supply hose disconnected or severed. The gas regulator on a range or oven can be removed or damaged to prevent the gas from being shut off. The company officer should look for open gas valves, disconnected gas supply lines, or other sources that could feed or contribute to the ignition and development of the fire.

Heaters

Space heaters may be permanently attached to the structure, such as wall heaters, or freestanding units, such as electric or kerosene units. Freestanding units can be used as ignition sources in a similar way to candles. The firesetter may turn up the fire to a maximum setting and then leave. The heater can ignite combustibles piled near the face of the heater or ignitable liquids in open containers **(Figure 29.29)**. If the structure is closed, the heater can consume all the air and self-extinguish before complete combustion occurs. The company officer should check the heater to determine if it was on and what the temperature setting was when the fire occurred.

Ignition Devices

Professional firesetters use very imaginative devices that create ignition. Generally, though, the company officer will encounter devices that are composed of readily available materials, such as mirrors used to focus sunlight on ignitable solids. Timers may consist of an alarm clock or kitchen timer that is wired to an ignition source. Chemical combinations that can cause a fire through a chemical reaction may also be used. Company officers should be suspicious of any device, item, or material that is at or near the point of origin. When in doubt, the officer should contact the department/county/state/provincial fire marshal's office or the national agency responsible for determining the cause of intentionally set fires for assistance.

Juvenile Firesetters and Pyromania

Pyromania is a term that has be associated with fires and firesetters for many years. Traditionally, pyromania is considered a mental or behavioral disorder that results in the setting of fires for no apparent reason. The NCAVC contends that all firesetters have motives, such as those previously listed. At the same time, the psychology profession states that pyromania is an impulse-control disorder. Most small children under the age of 7 years experiment with fire out of curiosity usually resulting in accidental fires **(Figure 29.30)**. Between the ages of 8 and 12 years, the majority of fires set by children are the result of psychosocial conflicts, such as revenge, anger, or need for attention. Parents and teachers are usually responsible for recognizing the symptoms and altering the inappropriate behavior.

The last phase of juvenile firesetter is the crisis phase. This phase is considered between 13 and 18 years and usually involves the arrest and detention of the firesetter. These firesetters have a long history of playing with fire or intentionally using fire for revenge or to gain attention. In 2003, it was estimated that 51 percent of all arson-related fires were set by juveniles under 18 years of age. For individuals under age 21, that estimate rises to 60 percent. Canadian figures for 2001 indicate that 47 percent of arson-related fires were set by individuals under age 18.

Pyromania is then applied to any person who has an impulse to deliberately and purposely set fires. The act of setting the fire is usually accompanied by sexual arousal and gratification. Indications that a person may be a pyromaniac include:

- The person deliberately sets a series of fires.
- The person is aroused or excited prior to setting the fire.
- The person is interested in or attracted to fire, fire equipment, or fire fighting.
- The person experiences pleasure or relief following the setting of the fire.
- The fires are not set for profit, to conceal a crime, or to express a political statement.

Setting fires is simply an end in itself that brings pleasure to the firesetter. The majority of juvenile firesetters are male, and many have poor social skills. The company officer should be aware of the presence of the same juveniles at fires and visiting the fire station.

Summary

Determining the true cause of a fire can be extremely difficult. The point of origin may not be obvious, the structure or vehicle may be completely destroyed, or the fire suppression activities may have eliminated much of the evidence as to the cause. The company officer must gather together as much information as possible from witness and participant interviews, inspection histories of the facility (if available), and physical evidence to determine the point of origin. Then, by eliminating the less likely causes, focus on the potential cause. If the information indicates that the fire was intentional and malicious, the officer should request the assistance of fire investigators from the jurisdiction, county/parish, state/province, or national government. Every effort should be made to determine the true cause of the fire and, if it is determined to be intentional, locate the firesetter and bring him or her to justice.

Figure 29.30 Small children will usually experiment with fire, hiding in closets or unused rooms.

Multiunit Emergency Scene Operations

Chapter Contents

Learning Objectives

1. Identify the characteristics of an Incident Command System (ICS).

2. Match operational positions within the ICS structure to their definitions.

3. Select facts about implementing the ICS. [NFPA 1021, 5.6.1(A)]

4. Identify how resources are tracked in the ICS.

5. Recall the three levels of command in the ICS.

6. Define *division* and *groups* according to the ICS model.

7. Select facts about establishing divisions/groups.

8. Define *operational plans*.

9. Identify the components of an operational plan.

10. Compare and contrast an initial attack and a sustained attack.

Job Performance Requirements

This chapter provides information that addresses the following job performance requirements of NFPA 1021, *Standard for Fire Officer Professional Qualifications* (2003):

Chapter 5 Fire Officer II

5.6

5.6.1

5.6.1(A)

5.6.1(B)

Chapter 30
Multiunit Emergency Scene Operations

The Fire Officer I is usually responsible for an emergency incident involving only one unit from arrival to termination of the incident. If the incident involves more units, the officer is responsible for the operation until the arrival of a senior officer and transfer of command takes place. The officer initially establishes command and the basic framework of the Incident Command System (ICS) adopted by the local jurisdiction.

The Fire Officer II has even greater authority and responsibility for multiunit emergency scene operations. Besides the responsibilities assigned to a Fire Officer I, NFPA 1021 states that the Level II officer must be able to produce operational plans that effectively utilize all resources that are available in a safe manner and result in the mitigation of the incident **(Figure 30.1)**. Producing operational plans involves the application of information gath-

ered from preincident surveys of the structure or facility, knowledge of the jurisdiction's ICS procedures, knowledge of incident scene safety policies, and the strategy required to control incidents using the various available resources. This chapter looks at both operational plan development and the advanced organization of an ICS including the command positions and functions and the organization of the incident scene.

Incident Command System

The Incident Command System (ICS) model adopted by many jurisdictions in North America is based on NFPA 1561, *Standard on Emergency Services Incident Management System*. The ICS provides guidance and direction for the management and control of all types of emergency incidents ranging from single company responses to mul-

Figure 30.1 During a rapidly developing incident, company officers must be able to manage and assign multiple resources to control the incident.

tiple agency and jurisdiction incidents. In March 2004, the U.S. government officially adopted ICS as part of the National Incident Management System (NIMS), and all federal agencies or state and local agencies that receive federal funding must use it.

Additional information on the NIMS ICS model and its application may be found in the Department of Homeland Security National Incident Management System document and the *Model Procedures Guide* series developed by the National Fire Service Incident Management Consortium and published by Fire Protection Publications.

NIMS Compliance

Many firefighters and emergency services organizations have confused NIMS compliance with just having to take ICS courses. This is not true. ICS is part of the requirements within NIMS. An individual's responsibility in the organization determines the level of ICS training that individual must receive. Chief Officers should be at the ICS 400 level while company officers can be at the ICS 300 level. However, to be fully compliant with NIMS, organizations need to ensure that they have met the six components of NIMS. They are as follows:

- Command and Management
- Preparedness
- Resource Management
- Communications and Information Management
- Supporting Technologies
- Ongoing management and maintenance

If company officers and their crews have not taken the IS-700 program they are not compliant according to NIMS.

NIMS-ICS Training

All personnel should receive NIMS-ICS training as part of their entry-level training, recurring proficiency training, and professional development. NIMS-ICS courses are offered through the National Fire Academy, the Federal Emergency Management Agency, many state/tribal and local agencies, as well as online. **Table 30.1** identifies the appropriate courses for each level of responsibility.

Company officers who have completed the Fire Officer I certification training should be familiar with the basics of the ICS in use by their jurisdiction. As a Fire Officer II, knowledge of the ICS evolves as the responsibility for larger and more complex incidents increases. This section includes a review of some of the basic information and then applies it to the Fire Officer II responsibilities. The ICS has a number of interactive components that

Table 30.1	
Responder	**Courses**
Entry Level Responders and Disaster Workers	FEMA IS-700: NIMS, An Introduction
	ICS-100: Introduction to ICS (or equivalent)
First Line Supervisors	FEMA IS-700: NIMS, An Introduction
	ICS-100: Introduction to ICS (or equivalent)
	ICS-200: Basic ICS (or equivalent)
Middle Management	FEMA IS-700: NIMS, An Introduction
	FEMA IS-800: National Response Plan (NRP), An Introduction
	ICS-100: Introduction to ICS (or equivalent)
	ICS-200: Basic ICS (or equivalent)
	ICS-300: Intermediate ICS (or equivalent)
Command and General Staff	FEMA IS-700: NIMS, An Introduction
	FEMA IS-800: National Response Plan (NRP), An Introduction
	ICS-100: Introduction to ICS (or equivalent)
	ICS-200: Basic ICS (or equivalent)
	ICS-300: Intermediate ICS (or equivalent)
	ICS-400: Advanced ICS (or equivalent)

provide the basis for clear communication and effective operations:

- Common terminology
- Modular organization
- Integrated communications
- Unified command structure
- Consolidated action plans
- Manageable span of control
- Predesignated incident facilities
- Comprehensive resource management

Operational Positions

To understand the application of ICS, company officers should know the major operational position descriptions within the ICS structure (**Figure 30.2, p. 732**). These include Command, Command Staff, and the General Staff Sections which consists of Planning, Operations, Logistics, and Finance/Administration. Following transfer of command, the company officer may be assigned to any of these positions based on that officer's knowledge, skills, and ability.

Command

The fire officer in overall command of an incident is the Incident Commander (IC). The IC is ultimately responsible for all incident activities, including the development and implementation of a strategic plan. This process may include making a number of critical decisions and being responsible for the results of those decisions. The IC has the authority to request resources to the incident and to release them from it. If the size and complexity of the incident require it, the IC may delegate authority to others, who together with the IC form the Command Staff.

Command Staff

The Command Staff reports directly to the IC by providing management support in functions that are not directly involved with the operational tasks. Command staff positions include the Safety Officer, Liaison Officer (LO), and Public Information Officer (PIO) (**Figure 30.3, p. 733**).

- *Safety Officer* — Assesses hazardous conditions and unsafe situations and develops an incident safety plan that ensures the safety of personnel

at the incident. The Incident Safety Officer (ISO) has the authority to alter, suspend, or terminate activities that are imminently dangerous to the life of an occupant or responder.

- *Liaison Officer* — Acts as a point of contact for other agencies and jurisdictions and coordinates the activities with them.

- *Public Information Officer* —The PIO provides accurate and complete information on the incident to the media. During larger incidents, the PIO provides information to other governmental agencies that need information concerning the incident.

Planning

Planning is responsible for the collection, evaluation, dissemination, and use of information concerning the development of the incident. Planning is also responsible for tracking the status of all resources assigned to the incident. Command uses the information compiled by Planning to develop strategic goals and contingency plans (**Figure 30.4, p. 733**). Specific units under Planning include the Resource Unit, Situation Status Unit, Demobilization Unit, and any technical specialists whose services are required.

Operations

The Operations Officer reports directly to the IC and is responsible for managing all operations that directly affect the primary mission of mitigating the incident. The Operations Officer directs the tactical operations to meet the strategic goals developed by the IC. Operations may be subdivided into as many as five branches if necessary (**Figure 30.5, p. 733**).

Logistics

Logistics is responsible for providing the facilities, services, and materials necessary to support the incident. There are two branches within Logistics: the Support Branch and the Service Branch (**Figure 30.6, p. 733**). The Support Branch includes medical, communications, and food services. The Service Branch includes supplies, facilities, and ground support (vehicle services).

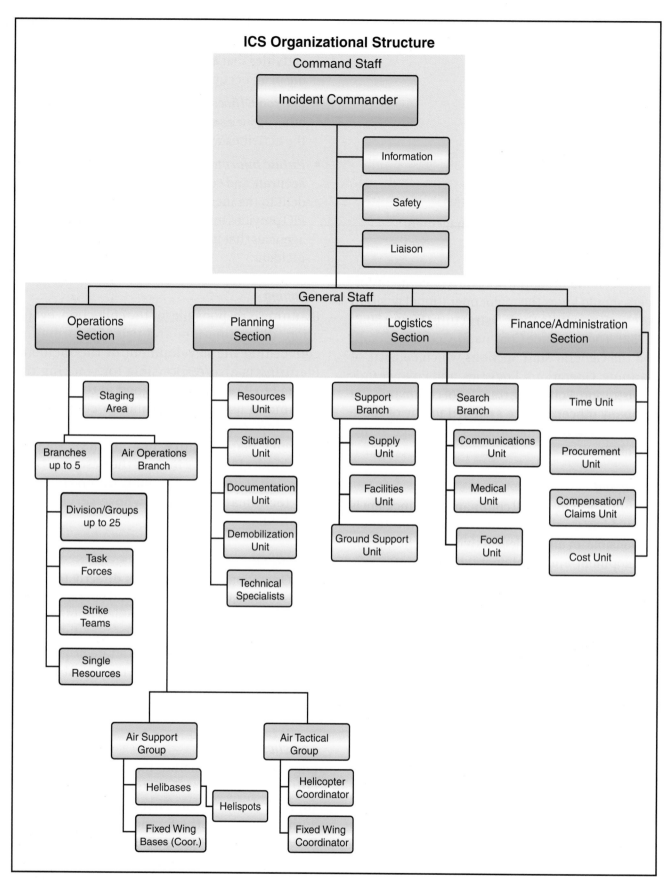

ICS Organizational Structure

Figure 30.2 The Incident Command System designates functions that are necessary to control all types of incidents. As the incident evolves, additional functions are filled by personnel assigned to the incident.

Figure 30.3 ICS vests are worn by the Command staff to designate functions and make them readily identifiable.

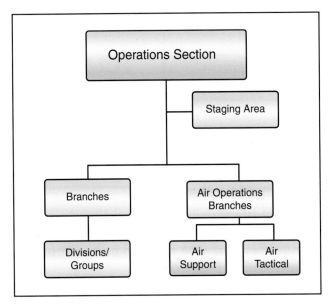

Figure 30.5 Operations Section units.

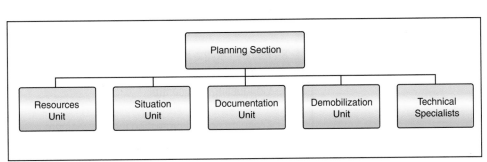

Figure 30.4 Planning Section units.

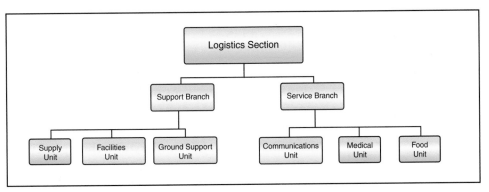

Figure 30.6 Logistics Section branches and units.

Finance/Administration

Finance/Administration has the responsibility for tracking and documenting all costs and financial aspects of the incident. Generally, Finance/Administration will be activated only on large-scale, long-term incidents. Day-to-day mutual aid and automatic aid responses are usually considered to be reciprocal and do not require interagency reimbursement. Administration is also responsible for the legal aspects of the incident, such as monitoring contracts with vendors, agreements with other agencies, and compliance with state/provincial, and national laws **(Figure 30.7, p. 734)**.

NIMS also provides for an Intelligence Officer, Section, or Unit which may be part of the Command staff, the Planning section, or a completely separate section.

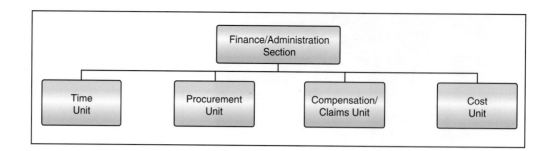

Figure 30.7 Finance Section units.

Implementing the System

The first fire officer arriving at the emergency incident scene establishes the ICS. This officer begins to evaluate the situation by answering the following questions:

- What has occurred?
- What is the current status of the emergency?
- Is anyone injured or trapped?
- Can the emergency be handled with the resources on scene or en route?
- Does the emergency fall within the scope of the individual's training?

Incident Action Plan

If no life-threatening situation demands immediate action, the IC should begin to formulate an Incident Action Plan (**Figure 30.8**). The plan should reflect the following priorities:

1. Ensuring personnel safety and survival
2. Rescuing or evacuating endangered occupants
3. Eliminating the hazard
4. Conducting loss control
5. Cleaning up and protecting the environment

With advice from the Operations Officer, the IC gathers enough resources to handle the incident and organizes information to ensure that orders can be carried out promptly, safely, and efficiently. Having sufficient resources on scene will help to ensure the safety of all involved personnel. The incident must be structured so that all available resources can be utilized to achieve the goals of the IAP.

All incident personnel must function according to the IAP. Company officers or Crew/Division/Group/Branch Leaders should follow standard

The Incident Action Plan

The IAP establishes the following priorities:

1. Ensuring personnel safety and survival

2. Rescuing or evacuating endangered occupants

3. Eliminating the hazard

4. Conducting loss control

5. Cleaning up and protecting the environment

Figure 30.8 The incident action plan establishes the priorities for the emergency incident.

operating procedures, and incident personnel should direct every action toward achieving the goals and objectives specified in the plan. When all members (from the IC to the lowest ranking member of the team) understand their positions, roles, and functions in the ICS, the system can serve to safely, effectively, and efficiently use resources to accomplish the plan.

Chain of Command

Whenever the ICS is implemented, there should be only **ONE** Incident Commander except in a multijurisdictional incident when a unified command is appropriate. A multi-jurisdictional incident involves agencies beyond the jurisdiction of one organization or agency. Even when a unified command is used, the chain of command must be clearly defined. One person should issue all orders through the chain of command to avoid confusion caused by conflicting orders.

If the Fire Officer II arrives subsequent to the establishment of the ICS, that officer may determine that the current IC is capable of retaining command or request that command be transferred. At the same time, the Fire Officer II may transfer command to another more experienced officer or an officer of higher rank. In either case, the transfer of command must be done in person at the initial command post.

The first IC provides the relieving officer with all the information that has been gathered on the situation and the actions that have been taken to this point in time. This can be accomplished by giving a situation status report (size-up), which is an updated version of the incident evaluation performed on arrival. The officer assuming command should acknowledge receipt of the information by repeating it back to the current IC. If the reiteration is accurate, the recipient is ready to accept control of and responsibility for the management of the incident. The former IC can then be reassigned to an operating unit or retained at the Command Post (CP) as an aide or as a member of the Command or General Staff.

Situation Status Report

The situation status report should include the following information:

- Description of what happened
- Whether anyone was/is injured or trapped
- What has been done so far
- Whether the problem has stabilized or is getting worse
- What resources are on scene or en route
- Whether it appears that current resources are adequate for the situation or that more resources need to be called
- What functions of the ICS have been implemented and what additional functions should be considered

The new IC should assess the situation and determine if the operation is reaching the objectives that have been established in the Incident Action

Plan (IAP). If the initial Command Post is located within the hot zone, the new IC should consider relocating the Command Post to a location that provides a better view of the overall incident. That location should be in the warm zone and in an area that does not interfere with suppression or mitigation activities. It should also have space for the support functions of the command and general staffs. Finally, it should be safe from contaminated atmosphere and runoff.

Tracking Resources

One of the most important functions of an ICS is to provide a means of tracking all personnel and equipment assigned to the incident. Most units responding to an incident arrive fully staffed and ready to be assigned an operational objective; other personnel may have to be formed into units as they arrive at the scene. In order to manage these resources, the IAP must contain a tracking and accountability system with the following elements (**Figure 30.9**):

- Procedure for checking in at the scene
- Way of identifying the location of each unit and all personnel on scene
- Procedure for releasing units no longer needed

Unit Tracking

The IC must be able to locate, contact, deploy, and reassign the units that are assigned to the emergency incident. These tasks are accomplished

Figure 30.9 The Incident Commander can use a site plan or plotting chart to identify the location and assignments of units at the incident.

through the ICS procedures that assign units to Crews, Divisions, and Groups based on location within the operating area. As units arrive at the scene, the IC or Operations Chief assigns them to the part of the incident where they are most needed. The units may be held in a staging area until needed or until they are released from the incident. If staging has not been implemented, company officers must check in with the IC and wait for an assignment for the system to work.

Communications between units will be through the jurisdiction's emergency radio communication system or through direct face-to-face communication **(Figure 30.10)**. As units are assigned to the incident, the central communications center announces the command frequency in use or automatically places all radios on that frequency. Units that have been assigned to the incident must contact the IC to ensure that they have complete communication with the command post. Face-to-face communication occurs as personnel without radios arrive at the incident and are formed into units.

Figure 30.10 When the situation permits, the most effective method for giving orders is face-to-face. *Courtesy of San Ramon Valley Fire District.*

The IC can use a number of visual aids to help manage the arriving units. The visual aid can be as simple as a preprinted form to sketch the incident scene and the location of units as they arrive, or it can be an elaborate tracking board with magnetic symbols identifying each of the units. Regardless of the tracking device, it should be simple to read and contain as much information as necessary about the activities of all the units on scene. The visual aid may contain the following information:

- Assigned radio frequencies
- Assigned units
- Activated ICS functions
- Site plan
- Staging areas
- Logistics location
- Control zones

Personnel Accountability System

Each organization must develop its own system of accountability that identifies and tracks all personnel working at an incident. The organization should standardize the system so that it is used at every incident. All personnel must be familiar with the system and participate in the system when operating at an emergency incident. The system must also account for those individuals who respond to the scene in vehicles other than emergency response apparatus, including staff vehicles and personally owned vehicles (POVs).

Accountability is vital in the event of a change in the emergency incident. At a structure fire, that change might be the extension of the fire through a concealed space, the rapid increase in the volume of fire due to the ignition of a flammable or combustible liquid, or a flashover or backdraft situation. The IC must know who is at the incident and where each person is located. For example, SCBAs can malfunction or run out of air; firefighters can get lost in mazes of rooms and corridors. Without having an accountability system, it is impossible to determine who and how many may be trapped inside or injured. Too many firefighters have died because they were not discovered missing until it was too late.

Wildland and urban interface fires have also claimed many lives when emergency responders were trapped by a change of direction of the fire. At the same time, emergency responders have suffered heart attacks that were fatal because they could not be located in time to provide medical treatment.

Company officers are responsible for keeping track of the members of their units. When operating in the hot zone, the unit should be within visible range of each other (**Figure 30.11**). When the atmosphere is obscured, they should be in physical contact of each other.

Company officers must be aware that the ISO and Accountability Officer (AO) do not perform the same function. While both the AO and the ISO report to the IC, they serve two different purposes. The AO remains in a single location that funnels personnel in and out of the operational area. The ISO must be able to move freely around the incident scene and monitor operations to ensure the safety of all personnel.

The IC is responsible for managing the personnel accountability system employed by the organization. The system may be assigned to the AO, if one is available, as part of the planning section. The system should indicate the individuals assigned to each apparatus, the names of people responding individually, such as staff personnel and volunteers, the time of arrival, the assigned duty or unit, and the time of release from the scene. Various systems, such as the tag system, SCBA tag system, and bar code readers, are available for tracking individuals at the emergency incident.

Tag system. A simple tag system can aid in accounting for personnel within the incident scene perimeter. Personnel can be equipped with a personal identification tag (**Figure 30.12**). Upon entering the outer perimeter, emergency responders leave their tags at a given location or with a designated person (command post, apparatus compartment, company officer, or incident safety officer). Tags can be attached to a control board or personnel identification (ID) chart for quick

///////////////////////////

CAUTION

Personnel who arrive individually at an incident must always check in at the command post or staging if it has been implemented. Personnel must not *freelance* or assign themselves to a task. Freelancing is unsafe and can result in fatalities or injuries.

Figure 30.11 Company officers should remain in close contact with their crews when operating in the hot zone.

Figure 30.12 The tag accountability system permits the Incident Commander to keep track of all personnel operating at the emergency incident.

reference. Upon leaving the incident perimeter, the emergency responders collect their tags. This system enables officers to know exactly who is operating at the incident scene.

SCBA tag system. An SCBA tag system provides closer accountability for personnel inside a structure. All personnel entering a hazardous atmosphere are required to wear full personal protective clothing with SCBA. Each SCBA is provided with a tag containing the name of the user and the air pressure in the SCBA air tank. Upon entering a building, personnel give their tags to a designated supervisor. The company officer records time of entry and expected time of exit. This officer also does a brief check to ensure that all protective equipment is properly worn, used and activated, including the personal alert safety system (PASS) device **(Figure 30.13)**. This provides complete accountability for those inside the structure and ensures that they are wearing the proper gear. Responders leaving the danger area retrieve their tags so that the control officer knows who is safely outside and who is still inside the structure or danger area.

Bar code readers. Some organizations have adopted bar code readers for tracking personnel at emergency incident scenes. Similar to the inventory control devices used by retail outlets, the systems involves the assignment of a unique bar code number to each member of the organization.

Figure 30.13 Prior to entering the hot zone, the company officer should check the PASS devices of all unit members to ensure that it is turned on and operating properly.

When that person arrives at the incident, the bar code is scanned into a computer which registers the presence of the individual at the scene. When the person leaves the scene, the bar code is scanned a second time and the person's name is removed from the site. Depending on local policies, the bar code may be attached to the helmet, protective clothing, or other equipment that is permanently assigned to each member of the organization. It may also be on a personal identification card.

Releasing Resources

As control is gained over the emergency situation, personnel and units can be released from the incident. It the personnel or units have been committed to mitigating the incident, they should be sent to the rehabilitation unit prior to being released. This helps to ensure that all personnel have an opportunity to rest, receive nourishment, and be examined by a medical professional. This can help to prevent heart attacks by allowing a monitored cooldown time for each person who has been actively involved in the incident.

Before leaving the scene, units that have been engaged in the incident must be inspected by the company officer to ensure that they are ready to return to service. Missing equipment must be located, and damaged equipment must be replaced or repaired. If critical equipment is not available, the unit may have to remain out of service until the equipment can be replaced.

Decontamination may be required before placing the personnel or units back into service. This can take place at the incident site or when the unit returns to the station. Small tools, medical equipment, and personal protective equipment must be decontaminated in accordance with local policy and NFPA 1581, *Standard on Fire Department Infection Control Program*. Contaminated clothing and equipment may not be cleaned in kitchen or bathroom sinks or showers **(Figure 30.14)**.

Assigning Multiunit Resources

The Incident Command System is designed to permit the control and allocation of any number of units or agency at an emergency incident. The Fire Officer II may be responsible for an entire initial response that may consist of multiple engines,

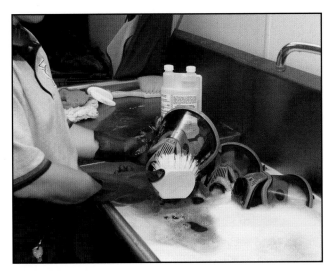

Figure 30.14 Decontaminate equipment in designated sinks following manufacturer's recommendations or local SOPs.

Level	Responsibilities
Strategic	The overall direction and goals of the incident.
Tactical	Objectives that must be achieved to meet the strategic goals. The Tactical Level supervisor/officer is responsible for completing assigned objectives.
Task	Specific tasks assigned to units that lead toward meeting Tactical Level requirements.

Table 30.2
The Three Levels of Command

ladders/trucks, rescue, and ambulance units. If the initial assignment is insufficient to control the incident, then the officer may be responsible for transferring command to a superior officer and assuming one of the ICS command or general staff positions or commanding a single unit. The company officer must be familiar with the general configuration of a multiunit incident and the terms used by the ICS to describe duties and functions.

Command Organization

The Command organization must develop at a pace that stays ahead of the tactical deployment of personnel and resources. The IC must be able to direct, control, and track the locations and functions of all operating units in order to efficiently manage the incident. Building a Command organization is the best support mechanism the IC can use to achieve the harmonious balance between managing personnel and incident needs (**Table 30.2**).

Strategic Level

The strategic level involves the overall command of the incident. The IC is responsible for the strategic level of the Command structure. The Incident Action Plan (IAP) should cover all strategic responsibilities, tactical objectives, and support activities needed during the entire operational period **(Figure 30.15)**. The IAP defines where and when resources will be assigned to the incident to

Figure 30.15 The Incident Commander communicates the IAP to units and personnel operating at the emergency incident.

control the situation. The IAP is the basis for developing a Command organization, assigning all resources, and establishing tactical objectives.

Strategic level responsibilities include the following:

- Determination of the appropriate strategy
- Establishment of overall incident objectives
- Setting of priorities
- Development of an Incident Action Plan

- Obtainment and assignment of resources
- Planning
- Prediction of outcomes
- Assignment of specific objectives to tactical level management units

Tactical Level

Tactical level supervisors direct operational activities toward specific objectives. Tactical level supervisors supervise grouped resources and are responsible for specific geographic areas or functions **(Figure 30.16)**. A tactical level assignment comes with the authority to make decisions and assignments within the boundaries of the overall plan and safety conditions. The accumulated achievements of tactical objectives should accomplish the strategy as outlined in the Incident Action Plan.

Task Level

The task level refers to those activities normally accomplished by individual units or specific personnel **(Figure 30.17)**. The task level is where the work is actually done. Task level activities are routinely supervised by company officers. The accumulated achievements of task level activities should accomplish tactical objectives.

Basic Organization

The most basic organization combines all three levels of the Command structure. For example, the company officer on a single-engine response to a dumpster fire determines the strategy and tactics and supervises the crew doing the task. The basic structure for an initial response incident involving a small number of units requires only two levels of the Command structure. In this situation, the IC directly handles strategic and tactical levels. Emergency response units report directly to Command and operate at the task level.

The NIMS/ICS terms Divisions and Groups are tactical level management components that assemble units and/or resources for a common purpose. *Divisions* represent geographic operations and *Groups* represent functional operations. The following examples illustrate the use of these terms.

Figure 30.16 Tactical level operations, such as the ventilation of a roof, combine together to accomplish the overall strategic goals of the operation.

Figure 30.17 Specific tasks may be assigned to individuals or to units, such as laddering the building.

NOTE: For ease of reading in this document, the abbreviation *DG* will be used when referencing a Division/Group hereafter. The term *DG Supervisor* will refer to the person in charge of a Division/Group.

Divisions are the organizational level having responsibility for operations within a defined geographic area **(Figure 30.18)**. The Division level is organizationally between Single Resources, Task Forces, or Strike Teams and the Branch. For situa-

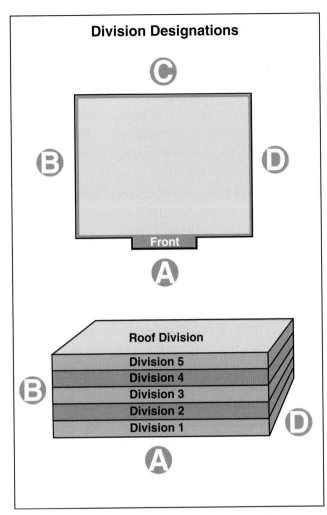

Division Designations

Roof Division

Division 5
Division 4
Division 3
Division 2
Division 1

Figure 30.18 Division is used to designate operations based on the side of the structure or the floor within the structure.

tions where the incident has an odd geographical layout (no obvious North, South, East, or West), the front of the building is designated *Division A*, and the remaining sides are given a designation of B, C, or D in a clockwise manner. For clarity of purpose during radio communications, the phonetic designations of *Alpha, Bravo, Charlie,* and *Delta* are suggested. For example, *Command from Division Delta.*

In multistory occupancies, Divisions will usually be indicated by floor number (Division 6 indicates 6th floor). When operating in levels below grade, Divisions will usually be indicated by a descriptive term such as Basement Division 2 or Parking Garage Division 4.

Groups are an organizational level responsible for a specific functional assignment **(Figure 30.19)**. The Group level is also organizationally between Single Resources, Task Forces, or Strike Teams and the Branch. Examples are Salvage Group, Search Group, Rescue Group, Haz-Mat Group, and Medical Group.

Establishing Divisions/Groups (DG)

A major incident will initially have more tasks that need to be completed than the available resources can accomplish. There is a tendency to start performing these tasks immediately upon arrival,

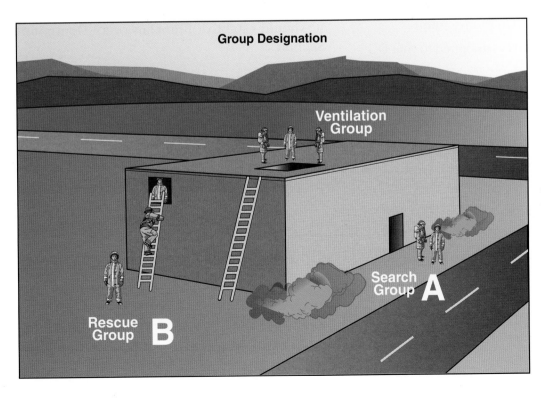

Group Designation

Ventilation Group

Rescue Group **B**

Search Group **A**

Figure 30.19 The term *Group* is used to define functional assignments.

thereby postponing the establishment of ICS. *This is a major error.* The lack of direction will result in confusion and lack of coordination. This increases the risks to emergency personnel and decreases the likelihood of a successful operation.

The IC should begin to assign DGs based on the following factors:

- Situations that will involve a number of units or functions beyond the IC's span of control. As additional chief officers become available, they may relieve the company officer of responsibility for the area or function.

- When units are involved in complex operations (large interior or geographic areas, hazardous materials operations, high-rise fires, technical rescues, etc.).

- When units are operating from tactical positions that Command has little or no direct control over (e.g., they are out of IC's sight).

- When the situation presents special hazards and close control is required over operating units (e.g., unstable structural conditions, heavy fire load, marginal offensive situations, etc.).

When establishing DGs, the IC will assign/advise each unit:

- Tactical objectives
- A radio designation (Division/Group)
- The identity of resources assigned to that DG

Span of Control

Complex emergency situations often exceed the capability of one officer to effectively manage the entire operation. The span of control must be reduced by creating organizational tactical-level components to direct operations in specific geographic areas or to manage incident-related functions. This is accomplished by establishing Divisions/Groups (DGs).

DGs reduce the span of control to more manageable, smaller-sized units. DGs allow the IC to communicate principally with these organizational levels rather than multiple individual company officers. DGs provide an effective Command structure and incident scene organization (**Figure 30.20**).

The officer of the first company assigned to a geographic area or function typically assigns DG responsibilities early in the incident. This early establishment of DGs provides an effective organizational framework on which the operation can be built and expanded.

The number of resources that the IC can effectively manage varies. Normal span of control is three to seven. In fast-moving, complex operations, a span of control of no more than five DGs is recommended. In slower moving, less-complex operations, the IC may effectively manage more DGs. When the span of control is exceeded, the IC should establish Branches or an Operations Section.

Figure 30.20 The use of Divisions and Groups reduces the span of control for the Incident Commander to a manageable size.

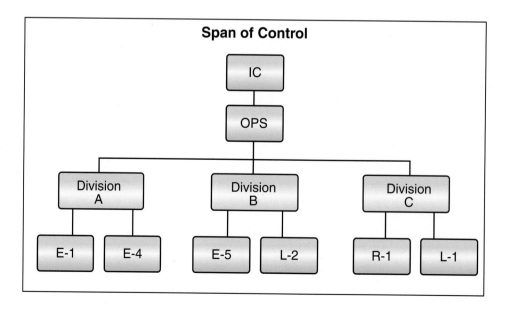

The DG procedures provide an array of major functions that may be selectively implemented according to the needs of a particular situation. This places responsibility for the details and execution of each particular function on the DG.

Division/Group Supervisors

When effective DGs have been established, the IC can concentrate on overall strategy and resource assignments, allowing the DG Supervisor to supervise the assigned resources. The IC determines strategy and assigns tactical objectives and resources to each DG. Each DG Supervisor is responsible for the tactical deployment of the resources at his or her disposal in order to complete the tactical objectives assigned by the IC. DG Supervisors are also responsible for communicating their needs and progress to Command.

In some cases, a DG Supervisor may be assigned to an area/function initially to evaluate and report conditions and advise Command of needed tasks and resources. This DG Supervisor will then assume responsibility for directing resources and operations within an assigned area of responsibility.

The DG Supervisor must be in a position to directly supervise and monitor operations (**Table 30.3**). This will require the DG Supervisor to be equipped with the appropriate personal protective clothing and equipment as well as a means of communication. DG Supervisors assigned to operate within the hazard zone must be accompanied by a partner at all times.

The primary function of company officers working within a DG is to direct the operations of their individual units in performing assigned tasks. Company officers will advise their DG Supervisor of work progress, preferably face-to-face. All requests for additional resources or assistance within a DG must be directed to the DG Supervisor. These Supervisors will communicate with the next higher level of supervision. Command is responsible for obtaining resources and prioritizing their commitment.

Each DG Supervisor will keep the Incident Commander informed of conditions and progress in their DG through regular progress reports. The Supervisors must limit progress reports to essential information only. Command must be advised immediately of significant changes, particularly those involving the ability or inability to complete an objective, the existence of hazardous conditions, accidents, imminent structural collapse, etc.

The DG Supervisor should avoid becoming involved in physical task activities because doing so compromises his or her ability to manage effectively. While participation in these physical activities may be required and allowable in the early stages of an incident when few resources are on scene, as additional units arrive, the Supervisor must resume the command role.

When a unit is assigned from Staging to an operating DG, the unit will be told what DG they will be reporting to and the name of the DG Supervisor (**Figure 30.21, p. 744**). The DG Supervisor will be informed of which resources have been assigned to him by the IC. It is then the responsibility of the Supervisor to contact the assigned unit to transmit any instructions relative to the specific action requested.

DG Supervisors will monitor the conditions of the crews operating in their areas of responsibility. Relief crews will be requested in a manner that ensures the safety of personnel and maintains progress toward the DG's objectives. Supervisors will ensure an orderly and thorough reassignment of crews to incident rehab. Crews must report to the incident rehab intact to facilitate accountability.

Table 30.3	
DG Supervisor Responsibilities	
Complete objectives assigned by Command.	Coordinate actions with related activities and adjacent DGs.
Account for all assigned personnel.	Monitor welfare of assigned personnel.
Ensure that operations are conducted safely.	Request additional resources as needed.
Monitor work progress.	Provide the IC with essential and frequent progress reports.
Redirect activities as necessary.	Reallocate or release resources within the DG.

NOTE: The DG Supervisor should be readily identifiable and maintain a visible position *in the area of responsibility* as much as possible.

Figure 30.21 Staging officers keep the Incident Commander aware of the status of available resources and direct those resources to assigned locations at the request of the IC.

Communications

The use of DGs reduces the overall amount of radio communications. Most routine communications within a DG unit should be conducted in a face-to-face manner between company officers and the DG Supervisor (**Figures 30.22 a and b**). This process reduces unnecessary radio traffic and increases the ability to transmit critical radio communications.

The safety of fire fighting personnel represents a major reason for establishing DGs. Each DG Supervisor must maintain communication with assigned units to control both their location and function. The DG Supervisor must constantly monitor all hazardous situations and risks to personnel and take appropriate action to ensure that units are operating in a safe and effective manner.

As previously stated, DGs will be commanded by chief officers, company officers, or any other emergency responders designated by the IC. Regular transfer of command procedures should be followed in transferring DG responsibility when necessary.

Implementing an Incident Action Plan

NFPA 1021 requires the company officer to produce operational plans to ensure *that required resources and their assignments are obtained and plans are carried out in compliance with approved*

Figures 30.22 a and b During large or complex operations, face-to-face communications may not be possible. When radio communications are necessary, proper radio protocol must be used to reduce the amount of radio traffic and to ensure that orders are received and understood.

safety procedures resulting in the mitigation of the incident. In most fire and emergency services organizations, operational plans (also called *prefire plans, preincident plans,* or *incident action plans*) identify the specific resources needed to successfully deal with a variety of hypothetical incidents at a particular location or type of occupancy. The incident scenarios analyzed are those that are considered to be the most likely to occur at the location or occupancy in question. For example, if an occupancy uses or stores large quantities of toxic or highly flammable materials, scenarios involving these materials are created and analyzed. Likewise, if an occupancy houses a large number of elderly or infirm residents, scenarios that require the evacuation of these residents or moving them to areas of safe refuge are created and analyzed **(Figure 30.23)**. This process is applied to as many target hazards as time and staffing allow.

Operational Plans

Operational plans often include possible resource deployments. In the most likely scenarios at a given location, possible options for deploying the initial alarm resources are studied, as well as options for the deployment of those resources that would respond only if called. Scenarios based on increasingly larger and more complex hypothetical incidents help planners to identify the resources that may be needed and to identify how they can by deployed to the best advantage.

Operational plans often include provisions for a number of possible contingencies. Some possible variations include:

• Operational plans might include a variety of responses based on unusually severe weather conditions that could greatly increase the potential for wildland fires starting and increase the likelihood of these fires spreading at a greater-than-normal rate. An operational plan might specify an increase in the initial alarm resources at certain points on the daily burning index.

• Operational plans might specify different initial alarm resource levels for a given occupancy if the number of people normally in the building is significantly different at different times of the day or night. For example, the operational plan for an elementary school might specify

Figure 30.23 Some emergency incidents, such as floods and chemical spills, may require the evacuation of people who are not able to move themselves. Additional personnel will be required for an efficient evacuation of nonambulatory patients. *Courtesy of Jocelyn Augustino, photographer, FEMA.*

that the initial alarm assignment be doubled if an alarm is received from the school during the hours when it is normally in operation. However, it might also specify that a lesser response be dispatched at other hours.

• The operational plans for occupancies that store large quantities of ignitable liquids might specify that crash/rescue vehicles from the local airport be a part of the initial alarm assignment so that their foam-making capabilities are immediately available if needed **(Figure 30.24, p. 746)**.

• The operational plans for large industrial complexes might specify that the first-arriving unit is to respond directly to the fire alarm panel or the plant security station but that other responding units are to stage at the facility gates and await directions from the first-in unit.

Figure 30.24 Operational plans should list additional resources that are available to the Incident Commander, such as foam units from the local airport. *Courtesy of United States Air Force.*

In essence, the data gathered at any particular target hazard is used to project the strategic and tactical possibilities and probabilities at that location. Based on these scenarios, the resources needed are compared to the resources available in the organization. If resources indicated are more than or different from what the organization has, planners can then recommend the purchase of the needed resources or the development of mutual aid or automatic aid agreements with nearby organizations that do have the needed resources.

Operational Plan Components

The operational plan consists of information gathered from a number of sources. The initial component is the preincident survey combined with any fire and life safety inspection data. Combined, these two sources provide a picture of the actual conditions that exist at the location or occupancy. This information must be current and accurate to be of value in the planning process.

The next component is the analysis of the fire and emergency services organization's assets and abilities. This is an inventory of such items as:

- Staffing levels

- Apparatus types and quantity

- Station locations

- Response times

- Training and certification of personnel

- Water supply

- Types and quantity of specialized extinguishing agents

- Specialized response units

- Automatic and mutual aid agreements

- Dispatch and communications system

The final component is the jurisdiction's Incident Command System. This is the organizational framework for all single and multiunit emergency incidents. It establishes functions and assigns duties based on the complexity of the incident. The Fire Officer II must be familiar with the system used locally and how it fits into the state/provincial and national system, NIMS/ICS.

Resource Allocation

Even though the company officer is able to accurately calculate the fire flow required, it is still necessary to provide that amount of water in either an initial attack or a sustained attack. These two attacks are defined as (**Figures 30.25a and b**):

- *Initial attack* — an aggressive offensive attack against the fire.

- *Sustained attack* — a heavy defensive attack intended to prevent the fire from spreading by containing the fire to the structure or area of origin.

Figures 30.25 a and b The company officer must be able to calculate the quantity of water that will be required for both (a) an initial attack and (b) a sustained attack.

The company officer, as Incident Commander (IC), must be able to determine if the available resources can support the initial or sustained attack. If the available fire flow is equal to or greater than the estimated need, an initial, aggressive offensive attack can be made. If the fire flow requirement exceeds the available amount, a defensive or sustained attack must be implemented. If the initial offensive attack is unsuccessful in controlling the fire or if the fire increases in intensity, the IC must shift to a defensive attack until the additional resources become available or the incident is terminated. The shift from offensive mode to defensive mode is called the transitional mode. All personnel and units as well as the communication center must be notified of the change, and attacking units must be given time to disengage in an orderly manner. Personnel accountability is essential for a safe and efficient transition to the defensive mode.

Initial Attack

Operational plans should include the ability of the initial assignment of apparatus and personnel to properly control a fire within 10 minutes of the receipt of the alarm **(Figure 30.26)**. The quantity of water required to accomplish this is stated in gpms. The ability to make an initial attack includes not only suppression but also search and rescue activities, forcible entry, ventilation, and salvage operations.

Sustained Attack

The fire and emergency services organization should be able to provide the required fire flow for a sustained attack for at least 30 minutes. The time frame includes the time allowed for the initial assignment to arrive, begin operations, request ad-

Figure 30.26 Small handlines can be used for an initial attack as long as they supply the quantity of water required to quickly control the incident. The use of foam extinguishing agents can increase the effectiveness of small handlines in the initial attack.

Figure 30.27 A sustained attack may involve the use of large diameter attack handlines, master stream appliances, and elevated fire streams. *Courtesy of Major Danny Atchley, Oklahoma City (OK) Fire Department.*

ditional resources, and for those resources to arrive and begin operations **(Figure 30.27)**.

NFPA 1410, *Standard on Training for Initial Emergency Scene Operations*, contains evaluation criteria for determining the effectiveness of units in the initial attack mode. All types of apparatus and emergency scene activities are included from donning self-contained breathing apparatus to providing ventilation. NFPA 1710, *Standard for the Organization and Deployment of Fire Suppression Operations, Emergency Medical Operations, and Special Operations to the Public by Career Fire Departments*, also provides response criteria for career organizations. See the following Information box for initial response requirements found in this standard.

NFPA 1710, *Standard for the Organization and Deployment of Fire Suppression Operations, Emergency Medical Operations, and Special Operations to the Public by Career Fire Departments*

4.1.2.1 The fire department shall establish the following time objectives:

(1) One minute (60 seconds) for turnout time

(2)* Four minutes (240 seconds) or less for the arrival of the first arriving engine company at a fire suppression incident and/or 8 minutes (480 seconds) or less for the deployment of a full first alarm assignment at a fire suppression incident

5.2.4.2 Initial Full Alarm Assignment Capability.

5.2.4.2.1* The fire department shall have the capability to deploy an initial full alarm assignment within an 8-minute response time to 90 percent of the incidents as established in Chapter 4.

5.2.4.2.2 The initial full alarm assignment shall provide for the following:

(1) Establishment of incident command outside of the hazard area for the overall coordination and direction of the initial full alarm assignment. A minimum of one individual shall be dedicated to this task.

(2) Establishment of an uninterrupted water supply of a minimum 1520 L/min (400 gpm) for 30 minutes. Supply line(s) shall be maintained by an operator who shall ensure uninterrupted water flow application.

(3) Establishment of an effective water flow application rate of 1140 L/min (300 gpm) from two handlines, each of which shall have a minimum of 380 L/min (100 gpm). Each attack and backup line shall be operated by a minimum of two individuals to effectively and safely maintain the line.

(4) Provision of one support person for each attack and backup line deployed to provide hydrant hookup and to assist in line lays, utility control, and forcible entry.

(5) A minimum of one victim search and rescue team shall be part of the initial full alarm assignment.

Each search and rescue team shall consist of a minimum of two individuals.

(6) A minimum of one ventilation team shall be part of the initial full alarm assignment. Each ventilation team shall consist of a minimum of two individuals.

(7) If an aerial device is used in operations, one person shall function as an aerial operator who shall maintain primary control of the aerial device at all times.

(8) Establishment of an IRIC that shall consist of a minimum of two properly equipped and trained individuals.

5.2.4.3 Additional Alarm Assignments.

5.2.4.3.1 The fire department shall have the capability for additional alarm assignments that can provide for additional personnel and additional services, including the application of water to the fire; engagement in search and rescue, forcible entry, ventilation, and preservation of property; accountability for personnel; and provision of support activities for those situations that are beyond the capability of the initial full alarm assignment.

5.2.4.3.2 When an incident escalates beyond an initial full alarm assignment or when significant risk is present to fire fighters due to the magnitude of the incident, the incident commander shall upgrade the IRIC to a full rapid intervention crew(s) (RIC) that consists of four fully equipped and trained fire fighters.

5.2.4.3.3 An incident safety officer shall be deployed to all incidents that escalate beyond an initial full alarm assignment or when significant risk is present to fire fighters.

5.2.4.3.4 The incident safety officer shall ensure that the safety and health system is established as required in Section 6.1.

Reprinted with permission from NFPA 1710, *Standard for the Organization and Deployment of Fire Suppression Operations, Emergency Medical Operations, and Special Operations to the Public by Career Fire Departments*, Copyright© 2004, National Fire Protection Association, Quincy, MA 02269. This reprinted material is not the complete and official position of the National Fire Protection Association on the referenced subject, which is represented only by the standard in its entirety.

ICS Forms

NIMS – ICS provides approximately 26 forms to assist in the establishment of an incident command. Examples of completed forms are included in **Appendix K**. The primary forms that are contained in most IAPs are the following ones:

- *Incident Objectives (ICS 202)* — Clearly stated and measurable objectives to be achieved in the specific time interval

- *Organization Assignment List (ICS 203)* — Description of the ICS table of organization, including the units and agencies that are involved

- *Assignments List (ICS 204)* — Specific unit tactical assignments divided by Branch, Division, and Group

- *Incident Radio Communications Plan (ICS 205)* — Lists the basic radio channel assignments for use during the incident

- *Medical Plan (ICS 206)* — Provides information on the location and staffing of the incident medical aid station, the types of ambulance resources available, the location of on-site ambulances, and the contact information for hospitals that are available to the IC

Summary

By applying the basic concepts of the Incident Command System, the company officer will be able to manage multiunit operations. Deployment of the initial assignment and requests for additional assistance can ensure that the appropriate amount of resources are available to control the incident. As a member of the Command or general staff, the company officer will be able to provide assistance to the Incident Commander or manage Divisions, Groups, or as assigned. The company officer must know the components of the local ICS and practice its use in single and multiunit operations.

Postincident Analysis and Critique

Chapter Contents

Learning Objectives

1. Define *postincident analysis* (PIA).

2. Select from a list objectives of a PIA.

3. Identify sources for PIA information.

4. Recall areas of concern when analyzing response information.

5. Select facts about a postincident critique.

6. Develop a postincident analysis.

7. Conduct a postincident critique.

Job Performance Requirements

This chapter provides information that addresses the following job performance requirements of NFPA 1021, *Standard for Fire Officer Professional Qualifications* (2003):

<u>Chapter 5 Fire Officer II</u>

5.6.2

5.6.2(A)

5.6.2(B)

Chapter 31
Postincident Analysis and Critique

The postincident analysis (PIA), evaluation (PIE), or review (PIR) is essential to the successful and safe operations of the fire and emergency services. Properly developed and written, the PIA determines the strengths and weaknesses of the organization's response to an emergency. It provides a training tool as well as the basis for future planning for emergency responses. The postincident analysis also motivates change in policies and procedures that may be outdated or ineffectual in meeting the current needs of the response area **(Figure 31.1)**.

NFPA 1021 states that the Fire Officer II will *develop and conduct a postincident analysis* for a multiunit incident. At the same time the standard assigns the Fire Officer I the same responsibility for single-unit incidents. This chapter looks at the PIA, defines it, provides a process for developing it, and describes how to use it in a postincident critique. The Fire Officer II should realize that the PIA is the foundation for strengthening the emergency response activities of the organization.

Importance of the Postincident Analysis

- Recognizes organizational strengths

- Identifies organizational weaknesses

- Provides an example for training

- Motivates changes in operational policies and procedures

Figure 31.1 This list identifies some of the benefits of conducting postincident analysis.

Postincident Analysis Defined

The postincident analysis is a written document that is compiled by the Incident Commander (IC) or a designated member of the Incident Command or general staff, such as the Incident Safety Officer (ISO). The PIA should be written for all incidents, whether small or large. If the results of the PIA indicate that a postincident critique be held, all participants should be included in the critique.

The PIA objectives are the following:

- Provide an opportunity for participants to objectively review operations in a constructive manner.

- Identify effective procedures (strengths) for future emergency operations.

- Identify areas needing improvement (weaknesses) and recommend changes to improve effectiveness.

The analysis is intended to focus on the activities of the participants, the elements of the emergency, and the decisions made that were intended to control the incident. The PIA is *not* intended to place blame or find fault with the participants. It must not be used to punish any of the participants and must not be perceived as a fault-finding process.

The term *postincident analysis* is sometimes confused with the term *postincident critique*. Even the NFPA 1021 standard infers that the analysis is both the written record and the activity that makes up the critique. For better understanding, this manual will use the term PIA to mean only the written report. The postincident critique will be the meeting of participants that may be required based on the results of the analysis **(Figures 31.2 a and b, p. 754)**.

Figure 31.2a A company officer conducting postincident analysis.

Figure 31.2b A company officer performing a postincident critique with his crew members.

Data Collection

The PIA is a critical and objective assessment of the emergency incident based on all available information about the incident (**Figure 31.3**). Information sources include the following:

- *Preincident survey or fire and life safety inspection report* — Provides background information on the structure, facility, or occupancy (if available).

- *Size-up* — Provides information on the structure, facility, occupancy, or location based on the impressions of the first-arriving company officer and crew.

- *Incident Action Plan* — Provides information on the actions that were taken to mitigate the incident. These actions may or may not have actually occurred.

- *Command and general staff records* — Provide a detailed view of the activities of each of the ICS functions during the incident.

- *Outside agency reports* — Provide information on the assistance provided by other agencies.

- *Interviews* — Provide a narrative of the actions of each of the participants as well as the impressions of witnesses; some information may be provided by the fire investigator.

- *Site plan* — Provides a visual aid in placing the responding units and personnel as well as casualties and occupants (**Figure 31.4**).

- *Incident safety plan* — Provides information gathered by the Incident Safety Officer on all safety- and health-related issues.

- *Personnel accountability system* — Provides an accurate record of the participants and their time of arrival and release from the incident.

- *Weather reports* — Provide information on weather conditions that may have contributed to fire spread or hampered unit access. This is particularly important when analyzing wildland and urban interface incidents.

- *Communications records* — Provide accurate dispatch times and transcripts of radio communications at the incident.

- *Miscellaneous reports* — Provide additional information that may be of value, such as apparatus or equipment maintenance records of vehicles or equipment that may have broken down during the incident.

The use of the NIMS-ICS forms, provided in **Appendix K**, can assist in the collection of much of this data (see Chapter 19 for more information). These forms are designed for use in all types of emergency incidents and can be acquired from the FEMA website or other similar sources.

The information from each of these sources is then compiled into a chronological report of the incident. Photographs and sketches can help to illustrate the situation both before and after the incident. Appendices are used to provide copies of the essential reports.

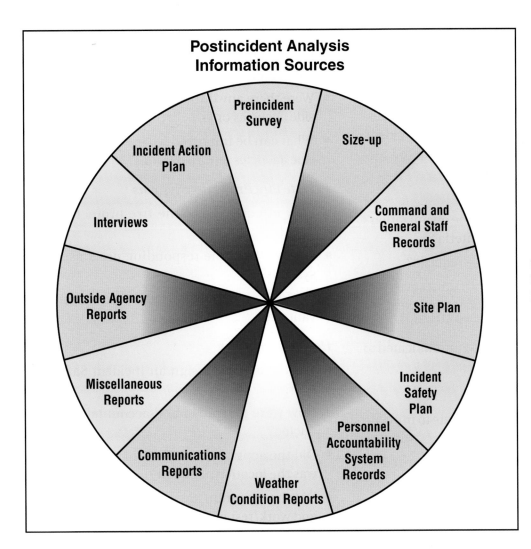

**Postincident Analysis
Information Sources**

Preincident Survey

Size-up

Command and General Staff Records

Site Plan

Incident Safety Plan

Personnel Accountability System Records

Weather Condition Reports

Communications Reports

Miscellaneous Reports

Outside Agency Reports

Interviews

Incident Action Plan

Figure 31.3 Sources of information to be used in postincident analysis.

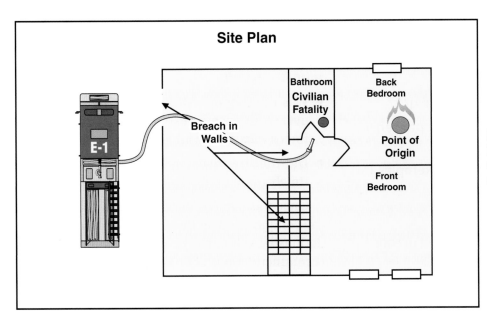

Site Plan

E-1

Breach in Walls

Bathroom
Civilian Fatality

Back Bedroom

Point of Origin

Front Bedroom

Figure 31.4 This site plan identifies the locations of various equipment, personnel, and events at an incident.

Analysis

With all the information compiled into one report, the company officer must then look for the strengths and weaknesses in the response. The company officer can develop a checklist of questions to help focus on each aspect of the incident. The following areas should be considered and addressed:

Dispatch

- Was the response time within the organization's minimum/maximum time criteria?

- How can the response time be reduced?

- Were there any extenuating circumstances that resulted in an increased response time (weather, traffic, road construction, etc.)?

- Was all available information communicated to the responding units?

Initial Attack

- Was the initial assignment adequate to mitigate the incident?

- What additional resources were required to mitigate the incident?

- Was the ICS properly implemented?

- Was the ICS adequate for the incident?

- Was all available information communicated from the incident scene to other responding units?

- What improvements could be made to the initial attack?

- What weaknesses should be corrected?

- What procedures need to be updated or changed?

- What strengths can be used as examples for similar situations?

Subsequent Resource Assignments

- Were additional resources requested in time to be effective?

- Was a Staging Area established and a Staging Area Manager (SAM) assigned?

- Were IC duties delegated according to the ICS?

- Were communications with automatic and mutual aid units and other support resources adequate?

- Were there any difficulties in dealing with outside agencies or jurisdictions?

- What can be improved when dealing with outside agencies or jurisdictions?

Private Fire Protection Systems

- How effective were the fire protection systems?

- How well did the responding units use these systems?

- Could the systems have been used to better advantage?

Health and Safety

- Did the activity assign an Incident Safety Officer?

- How were personnel and accountability conducted?

- Did the activity necessitate for a REHAB; if so, was the location adequate?

- Did the operation identify operational periods and work/rest cycles?

- Was the 2-In/2-Out program placed in operation?

- Were there rapid intervention teams and/or a backup assigned if needed?

Post Fire Activity

- Was the property properly secured or turned over to the fire investigator after suppression forces vacated the area?

- Did the fire investigations unit respond in a timely manner?

Once these and other questions are answered, the company officer develops a set of recommendations based on the results of the analysis. The recommendations should be included in the PIA and in an executive summary that is provided to the organization's administration. The executive summary is a brief overview of the incident along with the recommendations. If a critique is warranted, the company officer should recommend that one be held.

Postincident Critique

Postincident critiques can be informal or formal. As mentioned in Chapter 21, the informal critique can be held by the company officer and members of the unit following any single-unit incident. Weather permitting, this critique occurs immediately after termination of the incident and prior to leaving the incident scene. By discussing the incident while at the scene, the unit members can provide their impressions of the initial attack, suggest alternative approaches to the attack, and learn methods to improve their actions at similar incidents. In inclement weather, the critique can take place at the station immediately after returning from the incident. In essence, an informal critique can be used as a training exercise for the unit (**Figure 31.5**).

CAUTION

Postincident critiques must always be positive in nature. Personnel, units, agencies, or organizations must not be criticized for their actions, procedures, or policies. Simply state the facts and focus recommendations on improving emergency responses and interagency relationships.

The formal critique is held if the PIA indicates that it is necessary or if the incident involves an interagency or interjurisdictional response. If the incident involved only units from one jurisdiction, then all participants should participate in the critique. If the incident was interjurisdictional, representatives of each agency or jurisdiction should be in attendance.

Provide copies of the analysis before the critique to allow the participants time to read the report. Hold the critique in a classroom setting that provides comfortable seating, work space, audiovisual aids, and privacy (**Figure 31.6**). A set agenda and sufficient time are also important to a productive critique.

Following an overview of the incident, each unit commander or agency representative should present a brief report of their participation in the incident in order of arrival. The PIA recommendations can be reviewed and procedures for implementing them can be developed. Any additional recommendations can also be discussed and addressed.

The greatest failure of both the postincident analysis and postincident critique is the failure to learn from and apply the results and recommendations. Whether the critiques are informal or formal, the participants must be assured that any necessary changes will be made and that successes will be celebrated. Celebrations are in order when the incident was mitigated according to ICS and local protocol and without injuries or fatalities to responders.

Figure 31.5 An informal postincident critique can be an effective training tool for crew members involved in an incident.

Figures 31.6 A formal postincident critique being conducted using a projection system in a large classroom.

Summary

It is very important for company officers to realize the importance of the postincident analysis and critique. Both provide an opportunity for the organization, unit, officer, and unit members to improve the way they respond to emergency incidents. The company officer should emphasize the importance to subordinates and stress the positive nature of the PIA and critique. If unit members and other participants view the PIA and the critique as a learning experience and not as punishment, the results will be evident in the quality of service provided by the organization.

Training and the Postincident Analysis and Critique

In the text, the postincident analysis (PIA) and critique (PIC) are mentioned as possible training aids. That is, the analysis is used to identify behaviors, skills, or processes that need to be improved. Training programs or exercises can then be developed and implemented with the objective of improving personal and unit skill levels. The critique can be used as a training exercise for the unit as its actions are reviewed and possible alternative actions discussed.

The company officer, however, should also consider using practical training exercises as a means to improving the skills needed to generate an effective analysis and critique. Therefore, a PIA should be developed following multiunit training exercises and presented to participants in the PIC.

The following are skills that can be developed when training includes a PIA/PIC:

- *Observation* — the company officer should practice observing the activities of crew members along with the development of the emergency. Safety-related concerns should be noted.

- *Interviewing* — the company officer should practice interviewing participants and asking questions that will result in a complete picture of the training exercise. Developing this skill will also help when it is necessary to interview witnesses during a fire cause investigation.

- *Analysis* — the company officer can develop analytical skills while reviewing the results of the interviews, personal observations, and other data.

- *Report writing* — the company officer can improve writing skills. Translating actions and observations into words that accurately convey the events takes planning and practice.

- *Presentation* — the company officer can practice making the presentation of the incident to other participants during the critique. This includes planning and preparing for the presentation as well as presenting it.

- *Discussion* — the company officer can practice leading a small group discussion during the PIC. Brainstorming and consensus-making are skills that can be refined during the discussion process.

Even a simple practical training evolution involving only one unit can be used to practice these skills. Rather than preparing a detailed analysis, the company officer can hold a tailboard critique (See Chapter 21) to discuss the evolution and methods for improving skills and behaviors. A tailboard critique has the advantage of providing instance feedback for personnel and an opportunity for them to provide suggestions.

The company officer must keep in mind that both the PIA and the PIC are intended to improve skills and abilities, correct unsafe practices, and increase unit proficiency. They are not intended to place blame or criticize the performance of unit members or other participants.

Safety Investigations and Analyses

Chapter Contents

Learning Objectives

1. Identify initiatives of the *Everyone Goes Home* project.

2. Select facts about the risk-management model and the development steps of the risk-management plan.

3. Identify sources of information when identifying a personnel risk.

4. Recall information regarding frequency and severity when evaluating risks.

5. Identify various risk-control techniques.

6. Select facts about implementing and evaluating the risk-management plan.

7. Define the term *accident*.

8. Select from a list the reasons to investigate workplace accidents.

9. Select facts about the human factors that often contribute to accidents.

10. Identify the initial responsibility of the company officer when dealing with any injury, illness, or exposure.

11. Identify the questions that must be answered when analyzing an accident report.

12. Recall how HIPAA affects the analysis process.

13. Analyze scenarios and make recommendations about reports involving accidents, injuries, illnesses, fatalities, or health exposures.

This chapter provides information that addresses the following job performance requirements of NFPA 1021, *Standard for Fire Officer Professional Qualifications* (2003):

Chapter 32
Safety Investigations and Analyses

It is generally acknowledged that the fire and emergency services are high risk professions. Emergency responders enter hazardous conditions and situations to protect other citizens, eliminate the hazards, and restore the incident scene to a safe environment. In accomplishing these tasks, fire and emergency service responders sustain casualties that are high by many standards. Line-of-duty deaths have consistently numbered around 100 per year, and injuries have been over 80,000 per year over the past decade. These numbers have resulted in an increased focus on ways that fire and emergency services organizations can provide a safe work environment and reduce responder casualties.

One of those ways is the *Everyone Goes Home* project sponsored by the Fallen Firefighters Foundation. Of the sixteen initiatives listed (See Infor-

EVERYONE GOES HOME

Firefighter Life Safety Initiatives Program

1. Define and advocate the need for a cultural change within the fire service relating to safety; incorporating leadership, management, supervision, accountability and personal responsibility.

2. Enhance the personal and organizational accountability for health and safety throughout the fire service.

3. Focus greater attention on the integration of risk management with incident management at all levels, including strategic, tactical, and planning responsibilities.

4. All firefighters must be empowered to stop unsafe practices.

5. Develop and implement national standards for training, qualifications, and certification (including regular recertification) that are equally applicable to all firefighters based on the duties they are expected to perform.

6. Develop and implement national medical and physical fitness standards that are equally applicable to all firefighters, based on the duties they are expected to perform.

7. Create a national research agenda and data collection system that relates to the initiatives.

8. Utilize available technology wherever it can produce higher levels of health and safety.

9. Thoroughly investigate all firefighter fatalities, injuries, and near misses.

10. Grant programs should support the implementation of safe practices and/or mandate safe practices as an eligibility requirement.

11. National standards for emergency response policies and procedures should be developed and championed.

12. National protocols for response to violent incidents should be developed and championed.

13. Firefighters and their families must have access to counseling and psychological support.

14. Public education must receive more resources and be championed as a critical fire and life safety program.

15. Advocacy must be strengthened for the enforcement of codes and the installation of home fire sprinklers.

16. Safety must be a primary consideration in the design of apparatus and equipment.

mation box), the following six can be addressed directly by the company officer. The company officer can:

- Create, implement, and support a change in the organization's culture that emphasizes the importance of safety, health, and wellness.

- Adhere to and support personal accountability for choices that result in a healthy lifestyle and safe work environment.

- Apply the risk management model to safety, health, and wellness in the organization.

- Empower subordinates to stop unsafe behaviors and practices and provide a positive role model for subordinates.

- Thoroughly investigate all employee fatalities, injuries, and accidents.

- Insist on safe design, maintenance, and operation of all apparatus and equipment.

As a supervisor, the Fire Officer I provides a positive role model for safe behavior and applies the organization's safety policies and regulations to the operation of the unit. As a manager, the Fire Officer II is responsible for investigating and analyzing the accidents, injuries, health exposures, and fatalities that members of the organization may sustain. The Fire Officer II can use this analysis to accomplish some of the *Everyone Goes Home* program initiatives.

Though the primary safety and health duty assigned to the Fire Officer II in NFPA 1021 is that of *reviewing injury, accident, and health exposure reports, identifying unsafe work environments or behaviors, and taking approved action to prevent reoccurrence*, the officer may also be assigned other tasks that are associated with this duty **(Figure 32.1)**. Those tasks may be to act as the organization's Health and Safety Officer (HSO) and manage the health and safety program. To perform any health and safety duties effectively, the officer must have an understanding of risk management as it is applied to health and safety. An overview of that topic is included in this chapter. Additionally, the steps for performing an accident investigation and analysis are also included to help meet the primary safety responsibility of the Fire Officer II.

Figure 32.1 A review of accident reports may lead to actions that can be taken to prevent reoccurrences of similar accidents.

Risk Management

The terms *hazard* and *risk* have been used previously in this manual. In those instances, they have been used to describe the hazards that exist in the community or service area and the risk that they pose to the population. In this chapter, these terms are applied to the members of the fire and emergency services organization. The hazards are those that an individual faces while carrying out the duties of firefighter or emergency responder. These hazards include those found en route, while operating at, and when returning from an emergency scene as well as those that exist in the organization's facilities, apparatus, and nonemergency operations. The risks that must be minimized include the ones that are caused by the high physiological and psychological nature of the profession.

The chief executive officer of the organization is responsible for the development of a risk-management plan for the organization. Responsibility for this task may be delegated to the organization's HSO, however. Regardless of whether it is a chief officer or a company officer who is responsible for the plan, it is important that all members of the organization be familiar with the plan. Personnel who fill the HSO position must be capable of performing multiple skills such as training, investigating, evaluating, analyzing, implementing, and communicating. Each of these skills can be applied to the tasks required of the HSO. In each task, however, the HSO is a risk manager, applying the elements of risk management to each of the various tasks.

Risk-Management Model

To understand how the risk management model works, it is necessary to understand the risk-management model incorporated in NFPA 1500. The risk-management model adopted by NFPA has been successfully used by general industry for decades. In the 2002 edition of the standard, the safety and health components of risk management are outlined in Chapter 4 and applied to emergency operations in Chapter 8. The role of the HSO in the risk-management process is defined in Chapter 5 of NFPA 1521.

The risk-management plan described in NFPA 1500 is a process that incorporates several components that can be applied to the operations of a fire and emergency services organization. This plan is not a stagnant document that is developed, described in a printed document, and placed in a manual on a shelf and used only occasionally. Essentially, a risk-management plan serves as documentation that risks have been identified and evaluated and that a reasonable control plan has been implemented and followed. An effective risk-management plan has a positive effect on the organization from the operational, safety, financial, and liability standpoints.

Risk-Management-Plan Development Steps

1. Risk identification — For every aspect of the operation of the fire department at the station, list potential problems. The following are examples of sources of information that may be useful in the process:

- List of the risks to which members are or may be exposed

- Records of previous accidents, illnesses, and injuries (both locally and nationally)

- Facility and apparatus survey/inspection results

2. Risk evaluation — Evaluate each item listed in the risk-identification process using the following two questions:

- What is the potential frequency of occurrence?

- What is the potential severity and expense of its occurrence?

Use this information to set priorities in the control plan (needs assessment). Some sources of information include the following:

- Safety audits and inspection reports

- Prior accident, illness, and injury statistics

- Application of national data to local circumstances

- Professional judgment in evaluating risks unique to the jurisdiction

3. Risk control — Once the risks are identified and evaluated, determine which control should be implemented and documented. The two primary methods of controlling risk, in order of preference, are the following:

- Wherever possible, totally eliminate/avoid the risk or the activity that presents the risk. For example, if the risk is falling on ice, then do not allow members to go outside when icy conditions are present.

- Where it is not possible or practical to avoid or eliminate the risk, take steps to control it. In the previous example, methods of control would be applying sand/salt or wearing proper footwear.

Also consider the specific development of safety programs, standard operating procedures, training, and inspections as control methods.

4. Risk-management monitoring and follow-up — Periodically evaluate the selected controls to determine whether they are working satisfactorily. If not, identify and implement new control measures.

Reprinted with permission from NFPA 1500, *Standard on Fire Department Occupational Safety and Health Program*, Copyright © 2002, National Fire Protection Association, Quincy, MA 02269. This reprinted material is not the complete and official position of the National Fire Protection Association on the referenced subject, which is represented only by the standard in its entirety.

In Chapter 4 of NFPA 1500, the requirements of the risk-management plan are simply stated. The fire and emergency services organization adopts an official written risk-management plan that covers administration, facilities, training, vehicle operations, protective clothing and equipment, operations at emergency incidents, operations at nonemergency incidents, and other related activities. At a minimum, the plan shall include risk identification, risk prioritization, risk evaluation, risk-control techniques, and risk monitoring.

An understanding of the concepts of risk management and system safety is essential to fire officers and especially the personnel who fill the position of HSO for the organization. These concepts are the basis for the majority of the roles and responsibilities for those officers who plan, develop, and manage the safety and health program. Company officers who investigate and analyze accidents within the organization will benefit from an understanding of the risk management model.

Personnel-Risk Analysis

The company officer is responsible for the safety of all personnel assigned to the unit or under the command of the officer at an emergency incident. This responsibility exists throughout the work shift and includes emergency and nonemergency situations (**Figure 32.2**). The officer uses the risk management model to determine the appropriate responses to the health, safety, and wellness risks faced by the unit.

Figure 32.2 The company officer should review safety information with his assigned personnel on a frequent basis.

Risk Identification

To identify the risks, the fire officer compiles a list of all emergency and nonemergency operations and duties in which the organization participates. Ideally, the officer should take into consideration the worst possible conditions or potential events, including major disasters, multiple events, pandemics, and acts of terrorism. There are many sources to assist with this identification process.

The first (and possibly the most effective) is the organization's internal records on accidents, injuries, illnesses, fatalities, physical fitness tests, and daily attendance reports. In addition, incident response reports provide the basis for an understanding of the most frequent types of emergency responses. Although most organizations are too small to rely on their own database for a statistically valid trend, national averages and trends are available from a number of sources.

National sources for information and statistics on safety-related risks include:

- *The Centers for Disease Control and Prevention (CDC)* — Provides statistics on illnesses and injuries that have been reported nationally and issues warnings on potential trends that may affect the health of the nation.

- *National Institute for Occupational Safety and Health (NIOSH)* — Investigates fire and emergency responder fatalities; issues an evaluation of each incident and a list of recommendations for preventing a recurrence of the incident.

- *Fire Department Safety Officers Association (FDSOA)* — Professional organization that promotes safety in the fire and emergency services. Information is available on all aspects of safety activities.

- *National Fire Protection Association (NFPA)* — Collects injury and fatality statistics from fire and emergency services, compiles the information, and issues an annual report based on the results.

- *National Fire Academy (NFA)* — Maintains data on safety, health, and wellness initiatives based on the annual statistics.

- ***National Fallen Firefighters Foundation*** — Tracks and maintains information on line-of-duty deaths and provides support to survivors and family members (**Figure 32.3**).

- ***National Fire Fighter Near-Miss Reporting System*** — Sponsored jointly by the IAFF, IAFC, and the VCOS, this initiative collects, compiles, and provides reports on incidents that are defined *as an unintentional, unsafe occurrence that could have resulted in an injury, fatality, or property damage.* This is a voluntary reporting system that provides information on the types of incidents that are not reported to other organizations.

- ***Close Calls.Com*** — FirefighterCloseCalls.Com and EMSCloseCalls.Com are both web-based sources of information on near tragic incidents reported to these sights. Many include photos or videos of the incident and can be used as training aids (**Figure 32.4**).

The company officer should monitor all of these sources to be aware of trends, obtain suggestions for safety training, and be aware of new threats to the safety of themselves and their personnel. It must be remembered that national data is not always complete or accurate due to collection inconsistencies, and a time lag of one to two years is required to collect, analyze, and publish it. At the same time, it is better than no data at all.

Risk Evaluation

Once the risks are identified, they can be evaluated from both frequency and severity standpoints. *Frequency,* referred to by OSHA as *incidence rate,* addresses the likelihood of occurrence. Typically, if a particular type of incident such as injuries related to lifting has occurred repeatedly, it will continue to occur until a job hazard or task analysis has been performed to identify the root causes and effective control measures have been implemented. In this example, the HSO or company officer would develop and implement guidelines that outline proper lifting techniques and physical-fitness requirements, provide mechanical aids for lifting, or establish a requirement for a minimum number of personnel needed to lift a specific weight (**Figure 32.5, p. 768**).

Severity addresses the degree of seriousness of the incident and can be measured in a variety of ways such as lost time away from work, cost of damage, cost of and time for repair or replacement of equipment, disruption of service, or legal costs. Refer to **Appendix S** for the formula for calculating frequency and severity. Incidents of high frequency

Figure 32.4 Organizations like FireFighter Close Calls.com post information on accidents and incidents on line.

Figure 32.3 The National Fallen Firefighters Memorial located on the campus of the National Fire Academy in Emmitsburg, Maryland.

Figure 32.5 Additional safety training, such as proper lifting and carrying techniques, may be necessary to prevent future accidents.

> ## Tompkins Valley Fire and Rescue Service
> ### Accident Frequency and Severity Analysis
>
> **Highest Priority** *(High Frequency/High Severity)*
> - Heart Attack/Stroke
> - Asphyxiation
> - Strains, back
>
> **Medium Priority**
> **— *(High Frequency/Low Severity)***
> - Burns
> - Strains, ankle
>
> **— *(Low Frequency/High Severity)***
> - Trauma
> - Strains, neck
>
> **Lowest Priority** *(Low Frequency/Low Severity)*
> - Cuts or abrasions

Figures 32.6 As a result of frequency and severity analysis, company officers should develop a prioritized list of actions required to correct the problems identified.

---

and high severity are given the highest priority in the risk analysis while those of low frequency and low severity receive the lowest priority. The method for calculating the risk may vary from one organization to another.

Risk Prioritization

Taken in combination, the results of the frequency and severity assessments help to establish priorities for determining action. Any risk that has both a high probability of occurrence and serious consequences deserves immediate action and is considered a high-priority item. Nonserious incidents with a low likelihood of occurrence are lower priorities and can be placed near the bottom of the *action-required* list **(Figure 32.6)**.

Risk-Control Techniques

When the risks have been prioritized, it is time to apply risk-control measures. Several approaches can be taken in risk control, including the following:

- **Risk avoidance** — The best risk-control choice is risk avoidance. Simply put, avoid the activity that creates the risk. In a fire and emergency services organization, this approach frequently is impractical.

  Examples:

  — Lifting a stretcher presents a serious back injury risk, but personnel cannot avoid this risk and still provide effective service. Training in the use of safe-lifting techniques and/or safer equipment would be more acceptable solutions.

  — Risk avoidance could include a policy prohibiting smoking by organization candidates when they are hired, thereby reducing the potential for lung cancer and other smoking-related illnesses among members.

- **Risk transfer** — This approach can be accomplished in one of two primary ways: physically transferring the risk to someone else and through the purchase of insurance. Transfer of risk may be difficult if not impossible for a fire or emergency medical services (EMS) organization.

Examples:

— Contracting the cleanup and disposal of hazardous waste would transfer risks to a private contractor who is trained and equipped to remove the waste and accepts the liability of the risks associated with those activities **(Figure 32.7)**.

— The purchase of insurance transfers financial risk only and does nothing to affect the likelihood of occurrence. Buying fire insurance for the station – while highly recommended to protect the assets of the organization – does nothing to prevent the station from burning. Insurance is no substitute for effective control measures such as installing an automatic sprinkler system.

- *Control measures* — Effective control measures (risk reduction) is the most common method used for the management of risk. While control measures will not eliminate the risk, they can reduce the likelihood of occurrence or mitigate the severity. Effective control measures include safety, health, and wellness programs; ongoing training and education programs; and well-defined standard operating procedures or guidelines (SOPs/SOGs).

Examples:

— Changes in station apparatus bay design and apparatus-backing procedures have been very practical. The risks associated with backing apparatus into station bays are well-documented. The simplest solutions are improved driver/operator training, painted guidelines on the apparatus bay floors, and a policy that requires a second person to guide the backing operation from the rear of the vehicle. A more expensive solution would be the replacement of old single-door stations with new drive-through stations.

— Typical control measures instituted to control incident-scene injuries include use of accountability systems, use of full-protective clothing, mandatory respiratory-protection plans, training and education sessions, and health and wellness SOP/SOGs.

Implementation

Implementation of the risk-management plan requires communication, training, and application. The plan, produced in written form as part of the organization's SOPs/SOGs, is distributed to the membership of the organization. The distribution includes the public acknowledgement by the administration and the leadership of the jurisdiction of the importance of the plan. Administration support of the risk-management plan is essential

Figure 32.7 This picture illustrates how risk can be transferred to another agency. In this case, a private contractor has been hired to clean up and dispose of hazardous waste. *Courtesy of Chad Love.*

to membership acceptance and support. Communication of this support helps to ensure a positive response from not only the internal customers but also the external customers and stakeholders.

After communicating the plan and its importance, use, and intended results, training sessions on the plan should be conducted. Training is organization wide and begins in the entry-level training for new employees **(Figure 32.8)**. Training sessions for changes in the plan as well as refresher training sessions are provided periodically to current members of the organization. The effectiveness of the program depends on proper training.

The application of the plan takes place daily as fire officers and members follow the prescribed policies and procedures. The risk-control techniques must become second nature to all personnel. Whether these techniques involve applying proper lifting techniques when picking up heavy objects or donning respiratory protection when entering a contaminated atmosphere, they must be performed naturally without questions.

Monitoring

The effectiveness of the plan becomes evident through monitoring. This step ensures that the system is dynamic and facilitates periodic reviews of the entire program. Any problems that occur in the process have to be revised or modified. The

Figure 32.8 Risk management training must be conducted throughout the organization and include entry-level training for new personnel.

intent of the risk-management plan is to develop a strategy for reducing the inherent risks associated with fire and emergency services operations. Regardless of the size or type of the organization, every emergency services organization should operate within the parameters of a risk-management plan. Operation of this plan is a dynamic and aggressive process that the HSO and all fire officers must monitor. Monitoring leads to the evaluation of the effectiveness of the program and possible revisions. Revisions should be made at least annually or as needed.

Evaluation

Applying the evaluation techniques discussed earlier in Chapter 26, the company officer or HSO compares the desired results with the actual results of the plan. Data for making the comparisons include injury and fatality reports, amount of participation in safety training, fitness testing results, preemployment physical fitness reports, and alterations that have been made to address preplan risks. The sources for the data are the same ones used to identify the hazards and reduce the risks initially. These sources include the target hazards or risks, policies, and procedures intended to eliminate the risks; emergency incident reports; daily attendance reports; medical leave requests; training records; and physical fitness reports.

The results of the comparisons, which may indicate an increase, decrease, or no change in the risks, determine the effectiveness of the risk-management plan. If there is a decrease in the risk, indicated by a reduction in medical leave taken or lost-time injuries, for example, then the plan may be considered effective. If, however, the evaluation indicates that there is no change or an increase in the number of injuries, then the implemented risk-control techniques must be reviewed and alternate solutions applied.

When the risk management plan is initially implemented, there may be an increase in some types of injuries. For instance, at the very beginning of a mandatory physical-training (PT) program, there may be a temporary increase in on-the-job injuries. This increase may be due to improper warm-up techniques, improper exercise techniques, inadequate training, or even attempts

Figure 32.9 A firefighter participating in a fire department physical-training program.

to make the program fail **(Figure 32.9)**. An analysis of the types and frequency of these injuries will need to be made to determine the root cause and the appropriate response.

It will also be important to determine if the cost/benefit is appropriate; that is, is the cost of the risk-control techniques less than the cost of the results of the risk. For example, if the cost of altering apparatus storage compartments is greater than the cost of lost-time injuries due to back strains resulting from removing equipment from the compartments, then it may not be worth the control cost.

Revision

Revision procedures are included in the risk-management plan when it is developed. The revision process involves following the same steps that the initial risk-management plan followed, although it only focuses on those risks that require revision and not the entire plan. Company officers should be aware of the reasons why revisions may be necessary and be able to recognize these reasons when they appear in the plan evaluation.

Some reasons may include the following:

- Increase in injuries, fatalities, or loss due to the target risks
- Increase in medical leave requests
- Increase in risk-related costs
- No apparent change in the risk results
- Ineffective cost/benefit
- Changes in the target risks
- Ineffective training

When a trend becomes apparent, the plan must be revised. To be effective, the plan must continually provide the organization with a means to create a safe working environment. If it does not, the status quo that existed before the plan was developed will establish itself again and an unsafe environment will develop.

Health and Safety Investigations

Managing company officers are responsible for reviewing and analyzing injury, accident, and health exposure reports. The Fire Officer II is also responsible for identifying unsafe work environments or behaviors and taking approved action to prevent reoccurrence. In some organizations, this duty is assigned to the HSO. In others, it may be the responsibility of all company officers to monitor the health and safety of the personnel assigned to them.

Besides understanding the risk-management process, the organization's health and safety program, and the basic causes of accidents and injuries, the company officer must also be skilled in investigation and analysis techniques. Much like the skills required to investigate and determine the cause of a fire, determining the cause of accidents, injuries, illnesses, and exposures requires good research skills and basic detective work. The analysis process has been covered in Chapter 26 and should be referred to when needed.

Accident Investigations

As defined, *accidents* are unplanned, uncontrolled events resulting from unsafe acts and/or unsafe occupational conditions, either of which may result in injury, death, or property damage. Accidents may result from adverse conditions in the environment (weather, terrain, or situation), equipment/material malfunction (design, age, lack of maintenance), or the result of human error (ignorance, carelessness, or mental/emotional/physical difficulties) **(Figures 32.10 a-c)**. To reduce the potential for accidents to occur or to reduce the severity of accidents, the organization must develop and implement an accident investigation policy and procedure.

The policy should define accidents, establish the authority for investigating each type of accident, and establish a procedure for accident investigation. The HSO and the safety and health committee will have the ultimate authority for accident analysis. The company officer, however, will have the responsibility for doing the initial accident investigation based on the procedure.

Accident investigations are not limited to accidents according to NFPA 1500. Also included in events that must be investigated by the company

officer and referred to the HSO are job-related injuries and illnesses, fatalities, and health exposures. These will be addressed in later sections.

Conducting Accident Investigations

When an accident occurs, an investigation is conducted to determine the *root cause* of the accident. The root cause is the most basic reason and the source or origin for the accident. Accident investigations should be objective, impartial, and

Figure 32.10b This ruptured handline will prevent the handline crew from performing their assignment until the ruptured section of hose is replaced.

Figure 32.10a Adverse environmental conditions (in this case, the weather) contributed to this accident. *Courtesy of Mike Mallory.*

Figure 32.10c Human error caused this accident. *Courtesy of Mike Mallory.*

directed toward fact-finding, not fault-finding. Workplace accidents are investigated to identify:

- The behavior or condition that caused the accident (root cause)
- Previously unrecognized hazards
- Apparatus/equipment defects or design flaws
- Additional training needs
- Improvements needed in safety policies and procedures
- Facts that could have a legal effect on an accident case
- Trends

When a workplace accident investigation is conducted, the company officer should interview all participants and witnesses and document all relevant factors **(Figure 32.11)**. Prominent among these is the human factor. To conduct a thorough and comprehensive investigation, the company officer must understand human behavior and how it contributes to the occurrence of accidents.

Understanding Human Factors

Safety research in private industry has shown that accidents happen frequently to some people and infrequently to others. This indicates that accidents are not uniformly distributed throughout the workforce. Workers who fail to control the factors leading to an accident because of mental, psychological, or physical reasons will be involved in accidents more often than other workers. These workers are sometimes described as *accident prone*, a condition that can more accurately be explained by *human factors*.

Human factors are an individual's attributes or personal characteristics that cause the individual to be involved in more or fewer accidents than other individuals. In most cases, an organization can mitigate negative human factors through motivation, training, or technical revision. Human factors that often contribute to accidents have been classified into three broad categories:

- ***Improper attitude.*** This includes willful disregard, recklessness, irresponsibility, laziness, disloyalty, uncooperativeness, fearfulness, oversensitivity, egotism, jealousy, impatience, obsession, phobia, absentmindedness, excitability, inconsideration, intolerance, or mental unsuitability in general. Readjusting any of these attitudes or personality traits through counseling, coaching, mentoring, training, or discipline can lead to accident reduction **(Figure 32.12)**.

- ***Lack of knowledge or skill.*** This includes insufficient knowledge, misunderstandings, indecision, inexperience, poor training, or failure to recognize potential hazards. These problems can be reduced or eliminated through training, coaching, and mentoring **(Figure 32.13, p. 774)**.

Figure 32.11 This company officer is gathering information from an individual who witnessed an accident.

Figure 32.12 A company officer counseling a subordinate who displayed an improper attitude that contributed to an accident.

- *Physically unsuited.* This includes problems of hearing, sight, weight, height, illness, allergies, slow reactions, disabilities, intoxication, or physical limitations in general. Correcting these physical limitations can often reduce accident rates. If they cannot be corrected, personnel should not be assigned to tasks where their limitations might create a hazard or be potentially dangerous to themselves or others (**Figure 32.14**).

An organization's effectiveness in mitigating the human factors that lead to accidents often depends upon a number of other factors. Some of

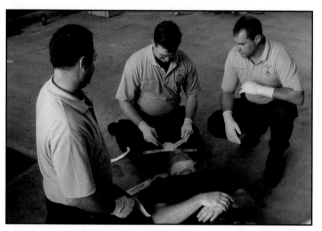

Figure 32.13 Lack of knowledge or skill can be corrected through training.

Figure 32.14 The prescription lens inserts being placed in this SCBA facepiece help the wearer overcome a physical limitation.

these factors include time and resources committed to developing and implementing safety, policies and procedures, safety training, and certification on the safe use of equipment. The training must be documented and the policies and procedures enforced.

In conducting an investigation, supervising company officers collect basic information about the participants, event, or incident. The investigation should provide the managing company officer with the following information:

- *General information* — Items:
    - Date and time of incident
    - Type of incident, illness, injury, exposure, fatality
    - Location and emergency response type
    - Names of witnesses and their accounts of the situation
- *Employee characteristics (participant)* — Items:
    - Name and unit assignment (company/shift)
    - Age and gender
    - Rank/function
    - Personal protective clothing or equipment in use
- *Environmental information* — Items:
    - Weather and temperature
    - Day or night conditions
    - Noise and visibility
    - Terrain
- *Apparatus/equipment information* — Items:
    - Type of equipment involved
    - Age and condition
    - Location
    - Maintenance history
    - Distinguishing characteristics

A narrative description of the incident is the final portion of the investigation report. This narrative includes observations on the part of the officer, eyewitness reports, participant interviews, and information from other sources such as law-enforcement reports and dispatch information.

Injury, Illness, and Exposures

The initial responsibility of the company officer when dealing with any injury, job-related illness, or health exposure is to provide medical assistance to the affected responder. No matter where the incident occurs, the health and safety of the responder takes precedence over investigating the cause. Once the victim is stabilized, transported, or treated locally, the company officer can gather the necessary information needed for the investigation **(Figure 32.15)**.

The investigation process is identical to the one used for accidents. The same general questions should be asked of the victim, witnesses, and participants. At the same time, gathering incident specific information is very important for all incidents, even though no injuries, illnesses, or exposures are immediately apparent.

While an injury is obvious at the time that it occurs, job-related illnesses or the symptoms of health-related exposures may not become evident for hours, days, weeks, or longer. For instance, the exposure to asbestos may not produce symptoms related to cancer for many years. Therefore, maintaining accurate information on the emergency response is essential. If there is a suspicion that asbestos or any other contaminant is present, it should be noted and the employee informed. In situations where it is likely that exposure to a contaminate will not produce symptoms of an occupational illness, it may be more appropriate to enroll the employee in a medical surveillance program (including a base-line medical evaluation) to document any health changes that may be directly related to the earlier exposure.

Job-related illnesses and health exposures can result from a number of situations throughout the work shift and a various work sites. Some situations and illnesses may include:

- *Headaches* — result from stress, noise, or physical back strains
- *Nausea* — results from exposure to flu or viruses, contaminated food, or stress
- *Virus* — results from exposure to others carrying the virus
- *Hepatitis* — results from contact with the body fluids of an infected person
- *HIV* — results from contact with the body fluids of an infected person
- *Allergies* — results from exposure to pollen, dust, mold, or mildew
- *Hearing Loss* — results from exposure to loud or continuous high noise levels
- *Stress* — results from exposure to noise, heat, high levels of activity, or situations involving fatalities or casualties

Gathering information on these types of illnesses and exposures will take a great deal of effort because the root cause may not be obvious at first. This is especially true of delayed symptoms. The company officer will have to research incidents, situations, and personal attendance histories over an extended period of time. Off-duty situations that may have resulted in the illness or exposure will also have to be considered. It may be difficult to determine if the employee was exposed to a virus during a response, at the station, or at home. The more information that can be compiled, the greater the chance of pinpointing the root cause of the illness.

Analyzing Safety and Health Reports

The analysis of safety and health reports provides the organization with an opportunity to prevent future accidents, injuries, illnesses, or exposures. When a specific root cause has been determined

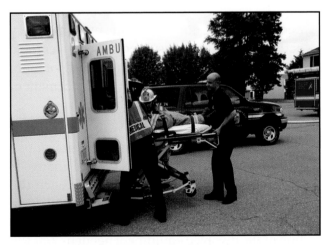

Figure 32.15 A company officer ensuring an injured firefighter is being transported for medical care.

and documented, specific policies or procedures can be developed to mitigate it. The Fire Officer II or HSO is responsible for determining the cause through analysis and recommending a solution. Determining the cause is accomplished through analyzing accident, injury, illness, and health exposure reports.

NOTE: While NFPA 1021 is specific about the investigation and analysis of accident, injury, illness, and health exposure incidents, it does not mention fatalities other than as part of the accident investigation. Generally, fatalities involving fire and emergency responders are investigated by the organization's chief officers and the jurisdiction's medical examiner, as well as OSHA and NIOSH investigators.

Accident Reports

After all data have been compiled following an accident, the information must be analyzed. A careful analysis of an accident report can have some very positive effects on workplace safety in the future. However, just as with the initial investigation, the analysis must be conducted in an objective and impartial way. The point is to glean useful information from the report to determine the root cause and not to find fault or fix blame. The report should be carefully scrutinized to see whether any patterns emerge or whether there were common elements in the sequence of events leading to the accident.

All workplace accidents are the result of unsafe acts, unsafe conditions, or both. The point of the accident analysis is to determine how these factors combined to create one root cause and what can be learned from the particular incident. Unsafe acts may result from inadequate training and supervision or from improper attitudes of the individual(s) involved. Unsafe acts may be the result of a well-intentioned attempt to save time by *cutting corners*. Or, they may result from a careless attitude that reflects the low morale of those involved.

Unsafe conditions are common at most emergency incident scenes and during emergency responses. Most organizations have SOPs designed to reduce the risks to fire and emergency responders in these situations. However, if the circumstances were beyond those anticipated in the SOPs, the

procedures may be inadequate. Unsafe conditions also exist during training exercises and daily non-emergency activities.

In conducting an analysis of an accident report, company officers should attempt to find answers to a number of basic questions. Some of these questions are as follows:

- **Who was involved?** Is this the first time this individual has been involved in an accident, or is this just the latest in a series? Is this individual accident-prone? Were individuals assigned a task that was beyond their capabilities/limitations? Is there a need for more/different training? Were others involved in the accident?

- **What was involved?** Was the individual operating machinery or equipment? If so, was it being operated according to the manufacturer's recommendations and the organization's established policies and procedures? If not, why not? Did the situation justify not following established procedures? Does the procedure need to be changed, or is a new procedure needed? Was the equipment adequate for the job, or is more/better/different equipment needed? Was the required level of personal protection in use? If not, why not?

- **What were the circumstances?** Was inclement weather or darkness a contributing factor? Is more/better lighting or other equipment needed? Did a drug/alcohol screening determine the presence/absence of these substances? Did the accident occur during an emergency or during routine activities? If during an emergency, was the accident reasonably preventable? Accidents occurring during routine, nonemergency activities should be assumed to be preventable until proven otherwise. Is there a need for more training or for more aggressive enforcement of established procedures?

- **What was the root cause?** Was the accident the result of equipment failure? Do preventive maintenance procedures need to be changed? Was operator carelessness or negligence the cause? Was excessive speed involved and, if so, was it justified? Is more training on the operation of the involved equipment needed? Was the accident caused by a breakdown in communications? Is more/better/different communications equipment needed? Are the established communications procedures adequate? Are different communications procedures needed? Was the accident the result of a lack of training? If so, what kind of training is required or what should be changed in the current training? Is the root cause a result of the organization's culture? How can the culture be changed to eliminate its influence?

Conclusions

What conclusions can be drawn from this report? Is this an isolated incident or is this part of a trend? Are there any recognizable patterns? Were the same personnel involved in a number of accidents or near misses? Was the same equipment involved? Were the same operations/evolutions involved? What can be done to prevent similar accidents in the future?

The analysis will provide the company officer with a number of potential responses to the root cause. First, the analysis may indicate a need for more personnel, more and better equipment, or more training. Additional funding, a realignment of resources, mutual aid agreements, or the purchase or creation of new training programs will require an effort on the part of the administration and the political authority to which the organization reports. Some responses may result in shifting of the risk to the private sector and requiring changes in building codes, traffic laws, or building design. These approaches will take time to develop and implement **(Figure 32.16)**.

However, not every safety problem can be solved by allocating more money. A certain amount of risk is inherent in fire fighting and other emergency response activities. Making changes in an emergency responder's personal behavior or changing the organization's culture will require conscious effort on the part of the administration and membership of the organization.

Changing the attitude and behavior of fire and emergency responders is the duty of the company officer. Especially in the area of safety, company officers have a responsibility to take action. First and foremost, the company officer must be a role model by providing personnel with an example

Figure 32.16 This intersection control device was installed in response to a need identified through accident analysis.

of correct safe behavior. Second, the company officer must insist that subordinates adhere to the organization's safety policies and procedures. Finally, the company officer must support and enforce all safety-related decisions made by the administration.

Injury, Illness, and Exposure Reports

Analyzing injury, job-related illnesses, and health exposures is much the same as analyzing accident reports. Pertinent information is gathered, the root cause is determined, and, if indicated, a recommendation for change is made. The primary difference in the process is the length of time that may exist between the incident and the investigation.

Starting an investigation months or even years after the incident can be difficult. Participants and witnesses may have been transferred, retired, or died. Reports or records may be incomplete or have been lost or destroyed **(Figure 32.17, p. 778)**. The site of the original incident to which the illness or exposure is linked may have been torn down or redeveloped. The reason for the investigation may not have the urgency that it would have had at the time of the incident.

At the same time, some information may not be available to the company officer. Medical records of those suffering from the illness or exposure will be private and only available to the individual or a designated family member. The Health Insurance Portability and Accountability Act of 1996 (HIPAA,

Figure 32.17 This file has a specific date identifying when the records contained within are to be destroyed.

Title II) required the Department of Health and Human Services (HHS) to establish national standards for the security of health care information. Accessing information that may help in determining the illness or symptoms from which the individual is suffering may be impossible, removing an essential element from the investigation. To get around this potential barrier, the investigating company officer should work with the individual or the individual's family, the fire and emergency services organization's physician, and the legal department of the jurisdiction to access those portions of the individual's medical records that relate to the health problem.

It may also be difficult to obtain information on materials that may have produced the health exposure problem. Chemical compounds, mixtures of various compounds that create further compounds, and the lack of documentation can present a barrier to analysis. In particular, personnel responding to illegal drug labs may be exposed to highly toxic materials that can cause immediate or delayed reactions.

In the end, the investigating company officer works with the data that is available. When necessary, the officer should consult with experts in various fields that may be able to explain how and why certain symptoms occur. Other experts may include the organization's physician, the HSO, law enforcement laboratory technicians, chemists, and hazardous materials technicians. Once

the information is in an understandable form, the officer can work from the illness or health-related problem back to the cause by linking logical components together.

Recommendations

When the company officer has completed the analysis and determined the root cause of the accident, injury, job-related illness, or health exposure, the officer should identify a solution to resolve the problem. As part of the investigation, the officer writes a report outlining the problem, the investigation process, and one or more recommended solutions.

Although most investigations may result in one very obvious solution, others may require multiple solutions. For instance, a firefighter may be exposed to airborne contaminants while performing overhaul after a fire has been extinguished. The investigation determines that the individual had disconnected the SCBA facepiece hose during overhaul and inhaled the contaminants while working. This is determined to be an infraction of the organization's respiratory protection policy. Therefore, the recommendation would be to have the individual participate in a respiratory protection refresher course.

A situation that may require multiple solutions might involve the rollover of a water tender while en route to an incident. The investigation indicated that the driver/operator lost control of the vehicle and failed to recover before the vehicle rolled over **(Figure 32.18)**. Contributing factors uncovered in the investigation might include lack of baffles in the water tank causing the weight of the water to throw off the center of balance, inexperience on the driver's part, location of the overflow pipe that allowed water to spill in front of the rear tires, excessive speed, and the lack of a response policy for water tenders. Recommended solutions might be the following:

- Purchase of new water tender with properly constructed tank and overflow pipe

- Installation of baffles in existing tank

- Relocation of water overflow pipe away from rear wheels

Figure 32.18 Incidents such as this water tanker accident may require more than one solution to prevent reoccurrences.

- Improved driver/operator training
- Development of policy and procedures for operating water tenders including maximum speed limits to be adhered to during response.

In some cases, contingency recommendations should be developed. In the case of the water tender, the primary recommendation might be the purchase of a new apparatus. This may not be politically or economically feasible. Therefore, the installation of baffles and relocation of the water overflow pipe may help to resolve the design flaw while the remainder of the recommendations addresses the unsafe behavior.

One area that can have a long-lasting effect on the safety and health of emergency responders is the wellness component of the safety and health program. Statistics verify that cardiac arrest (heart attacks) and strokes are the leading cause of fire and emergency responder fatalities. While the wellness program may be of little help to the victim of a heart attack or stroke, it is a strong preventive for others.

An effective wellness program, including proper nutrition, physical fitness, periodic medical evaluations, ceasing tobacco use, and stress relief and control, will help to reduce this needless loss of life. The company officer should not hesitate to recommend this as a solution when it is evident that physical and/or psychological stress was the root cause of the injury or fatality.

Summary

The Fire Officer II holds a unique position in the organization based on the health and safety requirements of NFPA 1021. Because the officer is responsible for reviewing and analyzing injury, accident, and health exposure reports, the officer can effect changes that will result in a safer work environment. Knowledge of the risk management model, the organization's health and safety program, and the steps required to investigate and analyze the information and determine trends are basic to the officer's success in providing a safe environment.

Appendices

Contents

NFPA 1021 (Levels I & II) JPR Numbers	Chapter References*	Page References
4.1.1	3, 4, 9, 11, 14, 19	55–68, 77–92, 193–215, 235–258, 313–327, 435–459
4.1.2	8	167–189
4.2	13	285–308
4.2.1	6, 18	123–138, 413–430
4.2.2	6	123–138
4.2.3	12	263–281
4.2.4	13	285–308
4.2.5	7, 13	143–163, 285–308
4.2.6	3, 13	55–68, 285–308
4.3	15	331–353
4.3.1	15	331–353
4.3.2	15	331–353
4.3.3	7, 9, 15	143–163, 193–215, 331–353
4.3.4	15	331–353
4.4.1	7, 9	143–163, 193–215
4.4.2	16, 17	357–374, 379–409
4.4.3	9	193–215
4.5	21	495–517
4.5.1	21	495–517
4.5.2	21	495–517
4.6	20	463–495
4.6.1	7, 17	143–163, 379–409
4.6.2	7, 19, 20	143–163, 435–459, 463–495
4.6.3	7, 19	143–163, 435–459
4.6.4	7, 21	143–163, 495–517
4.7.1	7, 10	143–163, 219–231
4.7.2	7, 10	143–163, 219–231
5.1.1	23, 24	537–563, 567–577

NFPA 1021 (Levels I & II) JPR Numbers	Chapter References*	Page References
5.1.2	24	567–577
5.2	26	603–621
5.2.1	2, 26	31–50, 603–621
5.2.2	25, 26	581–598, 603–621
5.4.1	27	625–650
5.4.2	27	625–650
5.4.3	27	625–650
5.4.4	7, 8	143–163, 167–189
5.4.5	8	167–189
5.5	28	655–699
5.5.1	28	655–699
5.5.2	29	703–725
5.6	30	729–749
5.6.1	24, 30	567–577, 729–749
5.6.2	25, 31	581–598, 753–779
5.7	32	763–779
5.7.1	25, 32	581–598, 763–779

*Company Officer Chapter Titles:

Part A Fire Officer Level I
Chapter 1:   Transition to the Role of Company Officer
Chapter 2:   Leadership
Chapter 3:   Supervision
Chapter 4:   Logic, Ethics, and Decision-Making
Chapter 5:   Legal Responsibilities and Liabilities
Chapter 6:   Interpersonal Communications
Chapter 7:   Oral Communications
Chapter 8:   Written Communications
Chapter 9:   Administrative Functions
Chapter 10: Safety and Health Issues
Chapter 11: Organizational Structure
Chapter 12: Company-Level Training
Chapter 13: Human Resources Management
Chapter 14: Labor/Management Relations
Chapter 15: Community Relations and Public Fire and Life-Safety Education
Chapter 16: Records Management
Chapter 17: Preincident Planning

Chapter 18: Incident Scene Communications
Chapter 19: Incident Scene Management
Chapter 20: Incident Scene Operations
Chapter 21: Postincident Activities

Part B Fire Officer Level II
Chapter 22: Management Activities
Chapter 23: Types and Forms of Government
Chapter 24: Interagency and Intergovernmental Cooperation
Chapter 25: Analyses, Evaluations, and Statistics
Chapter 26: Human Resources Management II
Chapter 27: Administrative Responsibilities
Chapter 28: Fire and Life-Safety Inspections
Chapter 29: Fire Investigations
Chapter 30: Multiunit Emergency Scene Operations
Chapter 31: Postincident Analysis and Critique
Chapter 32: Safety Investigations and Analyses

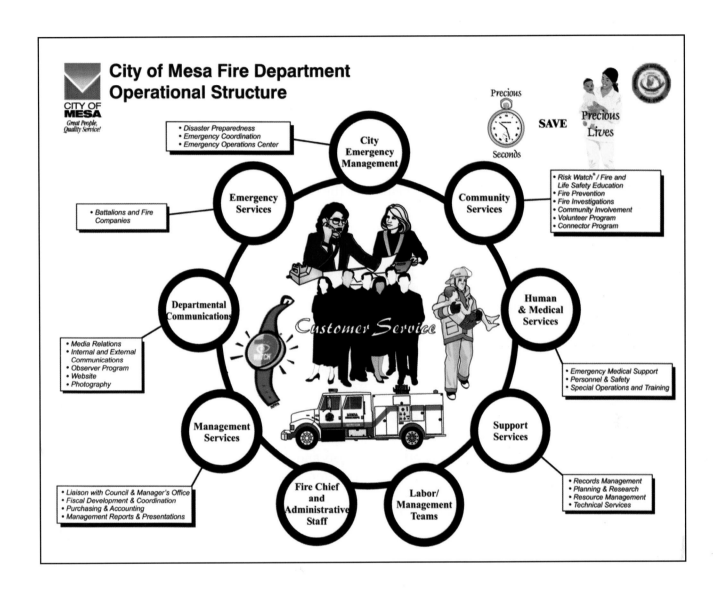

Appendix C
Code of Ethics as Department Directive

Policy Directive 1007
CHFD Ethics

EFFECTIVE DATE: JULY 1, 2002
REVISION DATE:

GENERAL INFORMATION

Objective

It is the purpose of this Policy Directive to help guide the Cherry Hill Fire Department and its employees in emphasizing ethics as an approach to everyday business. As in any similar type policy, the laws that govern our community, state and federal government belie the principles within this document.

All personnel will be governed by these publications and shall be aware of the contents of same and their responsibilities for compliance when appropriate. Officers will review this information with all assigned members at the start of their shift. A copy of this Order will be posted for 30 days from the date issued.

POLICY

We believe working at the Cherry Hill Fire Department is a public trust. The vitality and stability of an organization like ours rely on the public's confidence in the integrity of our members. Whenever the public perceives a conflict between the private interests and the public duties of an appointed government employee or staff personnel in a public organization, that confidence is imperiled.

Ethics and integrity are the cornerstones of the Department's ability to serve the public interest. They are also the cornerstones of developing, earning and maintaining the trust and respect of the citizens of Cherry Hill.

The Cherry Hill Fire Department has the duty both to provide the citizens they serve with standards by which they may determine whether public duties are being performed and to apprise their employees and members of the behavior which is expected of them while conducting their duties.

Our goal is to provide a method of assuring a standard of ethical conduct for the Cherry Hill Fire Department members and employees that is clear, consistent and uniform in its application, and to provide its members and employees with advice and information concerning possible conflicts of interest which might arise in the conduct of their public duties. Further, it requires its members and employees to be independent, impartial, and responsible to the public.

This document will be liberally construed in favor of protecting the public's interest in full disclosure of conflicts of interest and promoting ethical standards of conduct for Department members and employees.

RESPONSIBILITY

Personal responsibility is important for every member of the Department. If mediocrity in ethics is allowed to become the normal operating procedure for a department, then the integrity of the department is compromised.

Accordingly, this policy establishes standards of conduct for all members and employees of the Cherry Hill Fire Department under the jurisdiction of the Board of Fire Commissioners, District 13, Cherry Hill, whether elected or appointed, paid or unpaid, and they shall comply with the following provisions.

1. **Disqualification From Acting on Department Business**

   a) Engage in any transaction or activity, which is, or would to a reasonable person appear to be, in conflict with or incompatible with the proper discharge of official duties, or which impairs, or would to a reasonable person appear to impair, the member's or employee's independence of judgment or action in the performance of official duties and fail to disqualify him or herself from official action in those instances where the conflict occurs;

   b) Have a financial or other private interest, direct or indirect, personally or through a member of his or her immediate family, in any matter upon which the member or employee is required to act in the discharge of his or her official duties, and fail to disqualify himself or herself from acting or participating;

   c) Fail to disqualify himself or herself from acting on any transaction which involves the Department and any person who is, or at any time within the preceding twelve (12) month period has been a private client of his or hers, or of his or her firm or partnership;

   d) Have a financial or other private interest, direct or indirect, personally or through a member of his or her immediate family, in any contract or transaction to which the Department or any Department agency may be a party, and fails to disclose such interest to the appropriate Department authority prior to the formation of the contract or the time the Department or Department agency enters into the transaction; provided, that this paragraph shall not apply to any contract awarded through the public bid process in accordance with applicable law.

2. **Improper Use of Official Position**

   a) Use his or her official position for a purpose that is, or would to a reasonable person appear to be primarily for the private benefit of the member or employee, rather than primarily for the benefit of the Department; or to achieve a private gain or an exemption from duty or responsibility for the member or employee or any other person;

   b) Use or permit the use of any person, funds, or property under his or her official control, direction, or custody, or of any Department funds or Department property, for a purpose which is, or to a reasonable person would appear to be, for other than a Department purpose; provided, that nothing will prevent the private use of Department property which is available on equal terms to the public generally, the use of Department property in accordance with municipal policy for the conduct of official Department business (such as the use of a Department automobile), if in fact the property is used appropriately; or the use of Department property for participation of the Department or its officials in activities of associations of governments or governmental officials;

c) Except in the course of official duties, assist any person in any Department transaction where such Department member or employee's assistance is, or to a reasonable person would appear to be, enhanced by that member or employee's position with the Department; provided that this subsection; but shall not apply to: any member or employee appearing on his or her own behalf or representing himself or herself as to any matter in which he or she has a proprietary interest, if not otherwise prohibited by ordinance;

d) Regardless of prior disclosure thereof, have a financial interest, direct or indirect, personally or through a member of his or her immediate family, in a business entity doing, or seeking to do, business with the Department, and influence or attempt to influence the selection of, or the conduct of business with, such business entity by the Department.

3. Accept Gifts or Loans

a) Solicit or receive any retainer, gift, loan, entertainment, favor, or other thing of monetary value from any person or entity where the retainer, gift, loan, entertainment, favor, or other thing of monetary value has been solicited, or received or given or, to a reasonable person, would appear to have been solicited, received or given with intent to give or obtain special consideration or influence as to any action by such member or employee in his or her official capacity; provided, that nothing shall prohibit contributions which are solicited or received and reported in accordance with applicable law.

4. Disclose Privileged Information

a) Disclose or use any privileged or proprietary information gained by reason of his or her official position for a purpose which is for other than a Department purpose; provided, that nothing shall prohibit the disclosure or use of information which is a matter of public knowledge, or which is available to the public on request.

5. Hold Financial or Beneficial Interest in Department Transaction

a) Regardless of prior disclosure thereof, hold or acquire a beneficial interest, direct or indirect, personally or through a member of his or her immediate family, in any contract which, in whole or in part, is, or which may be, made by, through, or under the supervision of such member or employee or which may be made for the benefit of his or her office; or accept, directly or indirectly, any compensation, gratuity, or reward in connection with such contract from any other person or entity beneficially interested therein, in violation law;

b) Regardless of prior disclosure thereof, be beneficially interested, directly or indirectly, in any contract or transaction which may be made by, through or under the supervision of such member, in whole or in part, or which may be made for the benefit of his office, or accept, directly or indirectly, any compensation, gratuity or reward in connection with such contracts or transaction from any other person beneficially interested therein.

6. Prohibited conduct after leaving the Department

a) No former member or employee shall disclose or use any privileged or proprietary information gained by reason of his/her Department employment unless the information is a matter of public knowledge or is available to the public on request;

b) No former member or employee shall, during the period of one (1) year after leaving Department Office or employment:

- Assist any person in proceedings involving the agency of the Department with which he or she was previously employed, or on a matter in which he or she was officially involved, participated or acted in the course of duty
- Represent any person as an advocate in any matter in which the former member or employee was officially involved while a Department member or employee;
- Participate as a competitor in any competitive selection process for a Department contract in which he or she assisted the Department in determining the project or work to be done or the process to be used.

c) A Department member, who contracts with a former Department member or employee for expert or consultant services within one (1) year of the latter's leaving Department office or employment, shall promptly inform the Administrator about the agreement.

BY ORDER OF THE CHIEF OF DEPARTMENT

Courtesy of Cherry Hill (NJ) Fire Department

Appendix D
Information Officer Checklist

November 1, 1981   ICS 220-2

CHAPTER 1 CHECKLIST

1.1 *CHECKLIST USE* The checklist presented below should be considered as a minimum requirement for this position. Users of this manual should feel free to edit this list as necessary.

1.2 *INFORMATION OFFICER'S CHECKLIST*

a. Contact the jurisdictional agency to coordinate public information activities.

b. Establish single incident information center whenever possible.

c. Arrange for necessary work space, materials, telephones, and staffing.

d. Obtain copies of current INC-209s (Situation Status Summary Reports).

e. Prepare initial information summary as soon as possible after arrival.

f. Observe constraints on the release of information imposed by incident commander.

g. Obtain approval for information release from incident commander.

h. Release news to news media and post information in command post and other appropriate locations.

i. Attend meetings to update information released.

j. Arrange for meetings between media and incident personnel.

k. Provide escort service to the media and VIPs.

l. Provide fire retardant clothing for media and VIPs (as appropriate).

m. Respond to special requests for information.

n. Maintain unit log (ICS Form 214).

November 1, 1981   ICS 220-2

2.1 *ORGANIZATION* The information officer, a member of the command staff, is responsible for the information and release of information about the incident to the news media and other appropriate agencies and organizations. The information officer reports to the incident commander (see Figure 2-1).

2.2 *MAJOR RESPONSIBILITIES AND PROCEDURES* The major responsibilities of the information officer are stated below. Following each responsibility is procedure for accomplishing the activity.

a. Identify Information Officer Activities

    1. Contact the jurisdictionally responsible agency to determine what other external public information activities are being performed for this incident.

    2. Take actions required to establish coordination of information acquisition and dissemination activities.

    3. Compile the information obtained and maintain records.

b. Establish Incident Information Center as Required

    1. Establish information center adjacent to command post area where it will not interfere with command post activities .

    2. Contact facilities unit for any support required to set up information center.

c. Prepare Press Briefing

    1. Identify from the incident commander any constraints on the release of information.

    2. Select information to be released (e.g., size of incident, agencies involved, etc.).

    3. Prepare material for release (obtained from incident briefing (ICS Form 201), situation unit status reports, etc.).

    4. Obtain incident commander's approval for release. (The commander may give blanket release authority.)

    5. Release information for distribution to the news media.

6. Release information to press representatives at incident information center.

7. Post a copy of all information summaries in the command post area and other appropriate incident locations, e.g., base, camps.

d. Collect and Assemble Incident Information

1. Obtain the latest situation status and fire behavior prediction information from appropriate situation unit leader.

2. Observe incident operations.

3. Hold discussions with incident personnel.

4. Identify special event information (e.g., evacuations, injuries, etc.).

5. Contact external agencies for additional information.

6. Review the current incident action plan (ICS Form 202).

7. Repeat procedures as necessary to satisfy media needs.

e. Provide Liaison Between Media and Incident Personnel

1. Receive requests from the media to meet with incident personnel and vice versa.

2. Identify parties involved in the request (e.g., incident commander for TV interviews, air operations director for availability of helicopters for photos, etc.).

3. Determine if policies have been established to handle requests and, if so, proceed accordingly.

4. Obtain any required permission to satisfy request (e.g., incident commander).

5. Fulfill request or advise the requesting party of inability to do so, as the case may be.

6. Upon arrival of the incident commander, coordinate with air operations director for news media flights into the incident area.

f. Respond to Special Requests for Information

　　1. Receive request for information.

　　2. Determine if the requested information is currently available and, if so, provide it to the requesting party.

　　3. If information is not currently available, determine if it can be reasonably obtained by contacting incident personnel.

　　4. Assemble desired and available information and provide it to the requesting party.

g. Maintain Unit Log

　　1. Record information officer actions on unit log (ICS Form 214).

　　2. Collect and transmit information summaries and unit logs to documentation unit at the end of each operational period.

Appendix E
Sample Request for Proposal

Introduction

The _____ Department is pursuing the evaluation and subsequent purchase of SCBA. To accomplish this, the department is requesting SCBA meeting the specifications shown in this request for proposal.

Through each of the major steps of the evaluation process, the SCBA evaluated will be assigned points based on a point system in the categories as follows:

SCBA Provider Support	30 points
Actual and/or Simulated Use Conditions	35 points
Classroom/Maintenance	35 points

Throughout the evaluation process each evaluation team member will review the features of the SCBA submitted and complete an evaluation form. The forms will be tabulated and totaled in each category.

The evaluation process will begin with distributor presentations and training of firefighters who are assigned to evaluate the SCBA. At the time of the presentation, the supplier must submit _____ SCBA meeting the specifications shown in this request for proposal and at least one spare cylinder for each SCBA to be used by the department for the evaluation period.

Each supplier is requested to complete the attached questionnaire and return it to:

_____

(Department Contact Person and Address)

The completed questionnaire should be returned no later than_____.

Pre-Qualification Questionnaire

All questions will be answered in detail on a separate sheet.

1. Location of Corporate/Business Headquarters:

   Company Name:
   Street:
   City, State, Zip:
   Phone:
   FAX:
   SCBA Supplied:

2. Location of the nearest office or distribution center with repair capabilities. Prompt facilitation of repairs will be a critical factor in pre-qualification. Describe in this section your ability to effectively perform maintenance service and repair functions.

    Company Name:

    Name of Person in Charge:

    Street:

    City, State, Zip:

    Phone:

    FAX:

3. Provide contact individuals, titles, and phone numbers of persons within your organization who will be responsible for supporting the department through the evaluation process as well as subsequent use and maintenance of SCBA.

4. How long has your firm been in the business of supplying SCBA and service?

5. What major fire department or industrial SCBA owner does your firm currently support? How many SCBA does this department/company own? How long has your firm supported this customer?

6. Indicate the approximate number of self-contained breathing apparatus sold during each of the past two years.

7. Indicate the approximate number of self-contained breathing apparatus overhauled/serviced during each of the past two years.

8. Will you furnish a finance program for this purchase? If so, include details of program.

9. Indicate if you will provide facepiece fit testing, equipment identification, and record format. Please provide details of how each process is conducted.

10. Will you furnish a written guarantee that sufficient replacement apparatus and/or replacement parts and components will be available at your facility if requested within a minimum 24-hour period?

11. Will your firm provide support including training and technical information for the evaluation units and subsequent purchased SCBA?

12. Will you provide a written copy of the manufacturer's warranty on the entire SCBA unit? State length of standard warranty and portions of unit covered as well as all requirements for the department to remain within warranty compliance.

13. Provider must state estimated ability to meet current and future NFPA standards.

14. Include any information that may be of interest to the _____ Department in this process.

15. Prospective provider must submit "Current Customer Profile" to allow the _____ Department full range of communication with current distributor customers.

Appendix F
Sample Customer-Satisfaction Survey Form

 CITY OF
MESA
Great People, Quality Service!

||||

BUSINESS REPLY MAIL
FIRST-CLASS MAIL   PERMIT NO. 299   MESA, AZ

POSTAGE WILL BE PAID BY ADDRESSEE

NO POSTAGE
NECESSARY
IF MAILED
IN THE
UNITED STATES

FIRE DEPARTMENT ADMINISTRATION
CITY OF MESA
PO BOX 1466
MESA AZ 85211-9957

You have just been assisted, or have had recent contact with the City of Mesa Fire Department. You can support us in our efforts to provide exceptional customer service by returning this survey.

Please indicate which of our services you have used:

❏   Emergency Medical   ❏   Inspections/Partners in Prevention

❏   Fire   ❏   Education/Car Seats/Junior Fire Setter

❏   Observer Program   ❏   Other: _____

Were our personnel friendly and caring?   ❏ Yes ❏ No

Were our personnel knowledgeable in their field of expertise? ❏ Yes ❏ No

Were you kept informed and your questions answered?   ❏ Yes ❏ No

Please rate our service on the following scale: (Low) 1 2 3 4 5 (High)

How can we improve/comments: _____

_____

_____

Richmond (VA) Fire and Emergency Services Safety Stand Down

On June 21, 2005, Richmond Fire and Emergency Services (VA) implemented its version of the "Safety Stand Down" to refocus members of the organization on working safely. The program lasted just over six weeks and included a multi-dimensional approach to maximize the fire chief's message.

The program used the department's daily training schedule to provide members with a different safety subject each shift day. This component of the "Safety Stand Down" gave the company officers the latitude of scheduling the training when it best fit into the schedule of the day.

The second training component was video training over the city's cable television channel. The department's training staff used various safety videos played on a repeating schedule to ensure that members could view the training at different times of the day. This approach prevented members in the busier companies from missing the training because of emergency responses.

The final component was face-to-face training with the department's shift safety officers. Stations were placed out of service (one at a time, and on a rotating basis) for approximately three hours while the safety officer assigned to that shift presented members with information on everything from fireground safety to fire station safety. The face-to-face presentations concluded with information sharing by one of the department's peer fitness trainers.

An evaluation of the program by ESU (the department's EMS/safety unit) showed that almost the entire department membership felt that the program was helpful and that it should become an annual training program.

Analysis of the department's occupational injuries, illnesses, and motor vehicle collisions showed a sharp decline in all three categories immediately following the "Safety Stand Down" and a consistent reduction (though less dramatic) in reported incidents throughout the remainder of the calendar year.

Below are graphs that illustrate the impact of the program:

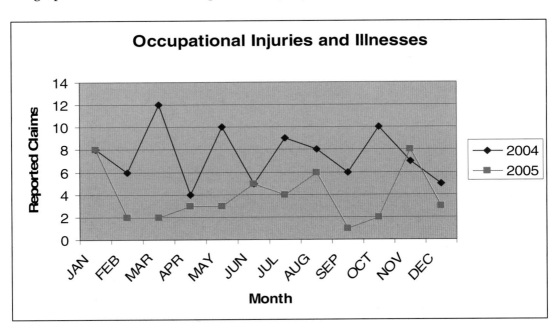

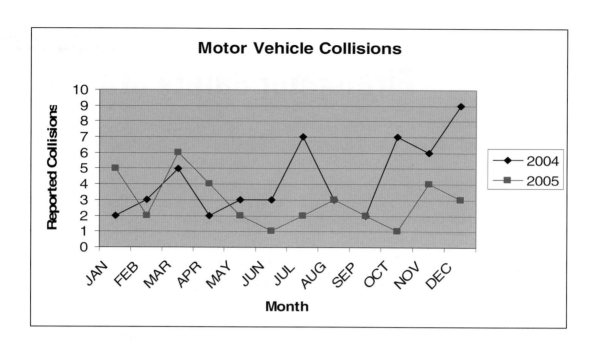

Guidelines for Media
at Emergency Incidents

EPHRATA FIRE DEPARTMENT

REVISED JULY 2006

Introduction

One of the first and most fundamental considerations of this nation's founders in drafting the Bill of Rights was to provide for a free press as an essential element of the First Amendment to the Constitution. They recognized that a well-informed citizenry is vital to the effective functioning of a democracy.

Ephrata Fire Department operations profoundly affect the public and therefore arouse substantial public interest. Likewise, public interest and public cooperation bear significantly on the successful accomplishment of our mission.

The Ephrata Fire Department will make every reasonable effort to serve the needs of the media in informing the public about fire and life safety issues, and other fire hazards. This will be done with an attitude of openness and frankness whenever possible.

The media will be told all that can be told *except*:

1. identities of juveniles involved in an incident,
2. identities of medical emergency patients or their protected healthcare information, or
3. information related to a criminal investigation.

Information will be given which will not impinge on these three areas. If asked to divulge this information, we will simply state that nothing more can be said.

In all other matters in our relationship with the media in dealing with current news, we will make every reasonable effort in providing the media representatives with full and accurate material.

We appreciate your assistance in broadcasting the activities of the Ephrata Fire Department and assisting us in preventing fires and injuries.

Guidelines for Media at Emergency Incidents

As a member of the working media, you may travel to various emergency incidents to report the event.

The Ephrata Fire Department is an all hazard department, responding not only to fires, but also auto accidents, medical emergencies, hazardous materials releases and brush fires, for example.

To assist you in quickly gathering the information you need in a manner that will guard your safety, we request you follow the guidelines below.

1. You have access to the Ephrata Fire Department Public Information Officer. Should you have a question related to an emergency event in Ephrata, contact Public Information Officer, Battalion Chief Kyle Foreman, at 509-771-0875, or the Fire Station at 509-754-4666 Monday – Friday, 8am-5pm.

2. When driving to the scene of an emergency, please follow all traffic laws. Do not try to keep up with an emergency vehicle should one pass you.

3. When you arrive on the emergency scene, park your vehicle on the same side of the road as the emergency responders, at least a block away as to not interfere with incoming apparatus..

4. Dress for the conditions. Emergency scenes are usually wet, muddy or full of debris.

5. Report to the Command Post to locate the Public Information Officer (PIO). The Command Post is usually marked by a green strobe light or flag indicating "Command Post." From here you will be directed to the media area and information officer. If you are unsure, ask any firefighter to assist you, or look for a firefighter with a white helmet, which indicates a command officer.

6. Understand that during an emergency incident, the primary objective is to save lives and protect property. Information will be relayed to the press as quickly as possible. Persons assigned to assist you understand the deadlines you work under and will provide information as it becomes available.

7. When you report to the media area and PIO, he/she will brief you as to dangers on the scene. In addition to emergency scenes being wet and muddy, they are also very dangerous. Walls can fall, power lines can come down and explosions may occur. You will not be restricted in your movements other than to keep you alive and uninjured.

8. Following the incident, should additional information become available, it will be forwarded to your newsroom.

9. After each significant incident, the EFD will post a news release on the City of Ephrata website at www.ephtrata.org .

Media Relations Program

The information we can and will release differs depending upon the nature of the emergency.

A. FIRE INCIDENTS

- Property owner or occupant names
- Address
- Cause of the fire
- Origin of the fire
- Dollar estimate of damage and contents saved
- Injuries
- Numbers of firefighters, fire equipment involved
- Special accomplishments, hazards
- Other information as requested

B. NON-FIRE INCIDENTS

- Release of property owner, occupant or victims names, as allowed by law
- Address of incident
- Cause of accident, as allowed by law
- Injury report
- Hospital location where victims were transported
- Numbers of firefighters, fire equipment involved
- Special accomplishments, hazards
- Other information as requested

By Washington State law, we cannot release the following information:

- Names of juveniles involved in an incident.
- Identities of medical emergency patients.
- Information related to a criminal incident or investigation.
- Generally, victim names are released by law enforcement agencies after the immediate family is notified.

The **Public Information Officer (PIO)** is charged with dissemination of information to the news media on the scene of an incident, as well as follow-up information that is not readily available on the scene (i.e. damage estimate, cause, etc.). This person is also available to augment existing communications and assist in contacting other Fire Protection Department personnel for media interviews.

The Fire Department enforces two policies pertaining to media relations that must be adhered to at all times:

1. With the exception of the chief officers, the only Fire Department personnel authorized to relay information to the news media, without prior approval, are the PIO or the Incident Commander (IC) of the emergency.
2. At any time during the course of an incident involving private property, if the property owner asks that media representatives leave the premises, Fire Department personnel will see that news media adhere to the property owner's request. In the event this occurs, Fire Department personnel will relay information to media outlets at a separate time and location.

Ephrata Fire Department Fact Sheet

Population Served: 6,875
Area Served: 10.1 Square Miles
Number of Alarms Annually: 400 (average)
Personnel: 1 career Fire Chief, 40 volunteers, 1 Admin. Assistant
Number of Apparatus: 16

Fire Station Location

Station 21
800 A Street SE
Ephrata, WA 98823-2200

Helmet Color Code

The Ephrata Fire Department uses a helmet color code system for identification of personnel on the scene of an emergency. The system is as follows:

White Helmet – Chief, Assistant Chief, Battalion Chief
Red Helmet – Captain
Yellow Helmet – Firefighter

Vehicle Number System

Each vehicle in the Department has an assigned number. The first number in the sequence represents the station where the apparatus is stationed. The next two numbers indicate the vehicle's use. Example: 2111 - Station 21 Engine; 2172 - Station 21 Command Unit.

    2111, 2112, 2113 - Engine
    2121, 2122, 2123, 2124, 2125 – Wildland Engine
    2131 – Water Tender
    2141 - Rescue Unit
    2161, 2162, 2163 – Support/Utility Units
    2171, 2172 – Command Units
    2195 – Ladder Truck

Radio Identifiers:

20-01	Fire Chief
20-02 20-03	Batt'n Chiefs
20-04 20-05 20-06	Captains
20-08	Safety Officer
20-09	Medical Officer
20-48	Chaplain

Emergency Incidents

Emergency incidents are usually categorized by the amount of equipment used. Equipment is dispatched according to the severity of the emergency.

A. STILL ALARM

An alarm called into the fire station rather than the 911 dispatch center.

B. FIRST ALARM

A supply of engine companies and tankers supplemented by a ladder, a rescue squad and a chief. Usually two or three engines, one or two tankers, one ladder and one chief respond to a first or box alarm. This is the standard response, whether the structure is residential or commercial.

C. SECOND OR ADDITIONAL ALARMS

An additional supply of engines, tenders and/or ladders to supplement equipment already involved in fire fighting operations. A general rule is that often the same numbers of units are sent on additional alarms as responded to the first alarm.

Alarm Types

RESIDENTIAL STRUCTURE FIRE: A fire in any single-family dwelling. Usual response includes: one engine, one ladder truck, one rescue unit, and mutual aid assistance from Fire District 13.

COMMERCIAL STRUCTURE FIRE: Any structure fire involving a multiple family dwelling or commercial business. Usual response to this incident includes: one engine, one ladder truck, one rescue unit and mutual aid assistance from Grant County FD 13.

TECHNICAL RESCUE: Any situation in which a life may be in danger (i.e. drowning, building collapse, climbing accident, etc.). Usual response includes: one engine, one rescue unit and one ambulance unit.

ACCIDENT WITH EXTRICATION: An automobile accident in which the occupants are trapped. Usual response includes: one ENGINE, one RESCUE UNIT.

ACCIDENT WITH INJURIES: A vehicle accident with injured persons. Usual response includes: one RESCUE and one ENGINE.

MEDICAL EMERGENCY: Any incident involving illness or trauma not related to a motor vehicle accident or rescue. Usual response includes: One RESCUE.

INVESTIGATION: Any incident in which actual emergency situation may be unknown, such as smoke in the area.

ASSIST A CITIZEN: Any incident in which a citizen needs assistance (i.e. water in the basement, person locked in car, etc.). Usual response includes: one ENGINE or one RESCUE, depending on the situation.

OUTSIDE FIRE: An incident involving burning grass, weeds or other natural ground cover. Response generally includes: 2 WILDLAND ENGINES, one WATER TENDER.

VEHICLE FIRE: An incident involving fire in a motor vehicle. Usual response includes one engine.

HAZARDOUS MATERIALS INCIDENT: An incident involving the uncontrolled release or spill of a designated hazardous material. This event may present risk to persons or the environment. Usual response includes: one engine, one support unit with hazmat equipment.

MISCELLANEOUS INCIDENTS: Include carbon monoxide detector soundings, gas odors outside, etc. Response generally includes one engine and the Duty Officer.

Helicopter Operations

The Ephrata Fire Department occasionally uses helicopters in its emergency operations. The most frequently used aircraft is Northwest MedStar, the air medical helicopter based in the Tri-Cities and Spokane.

If a medical emergency warrants helicopter transport, the helicopter is requested by the Fire Department and responds. Firefighters on the scene locate and establish a landing zone and provide assistance to the helicopter and medical flight crew as needed.

Basic criteria for requesting the helicopter can include, but is not limited to:

- life threatening traumatic injury from an auto accident;
- life threatening illness such as cardiac arrest;
- distance from hospital.

If you are on the scene of an emergency when the helicopter is arriving or departing please follow these safety guidelines.

- Do not take flash photographs or shoot video using a floodlight. This can blind the pilot and flight crew at night.
- Hold onto personal belongings such as hats. The rotor wash can blow these off.
- Do not approach the helicopter unless told to do so by the pilot or flight crew.
- NEVER approach from the rear due to the danger of the tail rotor.
- Follow other directions of firefighters or flight crew.

Ambulance Locations Serving Ephrata
Services Provided by Grant County Fire Department 5 of Moses Lake

Medic 54	Alder St. NW, Ephrata (Sta 5-14)
Medic 58	Patton Blvd., Moses Lake (Sta 5-8)
Medic 51	Nelson Rd., Moses Lake (Sta 5-1)

Glossary

AIR PACK, SCBA (Self-Contained Breathing Apparatus): Respiratory protective mask and tank worn by firefighters that contain their own breathing air supply.

AIRWAY: A medical term referring to the passageway from the mouth/nose to the lungs of a patient. Also refers to the plastic devices used by medical personnel to keep this passage open.

ALARM: A notification to respond to an emergency.

APPARATUS: Any fire department vehicle.

APPARATUS OPERATOR: Engineer, driver, aerial ladder operator or anyone acting in any one of these positions.

APPARATUS BAY: The portion of a fire station on which fire trucks are parked.

ARSON: The willful and malicious burning of the property of another. Can also refer to the intentional burning on one's own property.

ATTACK: Any action to control a fire.

AUDIBLE ALARM: An alarm actuated by heat/smoke, flame-sensing devices or the water flow in a sprinkler system.

BACKDRAFT: An explosion of a hot, smoldering fire caused by a sudden inrush of oxygen into the previously smoldering fire.

BATTALION: A division within the fire department, usually containing a number of companies.

BLEVE (Boiling Liquid Expanding Vapor Explosion): Catastrophic explosion of pressurized vapors from pressurized tank such as propane or anhydrous ammonia tanks.

BOOSTER LINE: Small diameter hose wound onto a reel on a fire apparatus. Generally used for small fires such as brush and trash.

BOOSTER TANK: Water tank built into a fire apparatus. Usually holds between 500 and 1,000 gallons of water. This water can be used until hose lines are laid to a hydrant.

CATCH A HYDRANT/PLUG: To dismount from fire apparatus at a hydrant, connect fire hose to the hydrant and supply the engine company with water.

CHARGED LINE: A line of hose loaded with water under pressure and ready to use.

CHECKING THE BUILDING: Fire size-up term used when equipment arrives on the scene of an incident and no fire or smoke are visible. The act of determining if there is an actual fire. Same as Investigation.

CHIEF: The chief administrative officer of the fire department and chief command officer at any fire.

COMMAND POST: A location, established by the Incident Commander of an incident, at which management directs fire operations. Normal location for Public Information Officer or Press Liaison.

COMPANY: A designated number of emergency equipment. Typically, a fire engine is considered an engine company. A tanker is considered a tanker company.

DELUGE GUN/DECK GUN/MONITOR: A master stream appliance (hose) on top of an engine.

DRAFT: The process of taking water from a static source (i.e. pond, lake, portable tank, etc.) with an engine.

EMS: Emergency Medical Services

ENGINE: Firefighting vehicle that carries water and hose. Also referred to as a Pumper.

ENGINE COMPANY: Firefighting unit that provides extinguishment and basic emergency medical service.

EXPOSURE: An object, such as a building or other structure, in the proximity of a fire and in danger of being ignited by the fire's heat.

FALSE ALARM: An alarm given with malicious intent or without reason.

FIRE DEPARTMENT CONNECTION/SPRINKLER CONNECTION: Connections provided at ground level on a building through which the fire department supplies water to a building for fire suppressions.

FIRST ALARM: The initial alarm assignment.

FLASHOVER: The stage of a fire in which a room or other confined area becomes heated to the point that flames flash over the entire surface of the area igniting all contents.

IMMEDIATE FAMILY: Father, mother, brother, sister, spouse or child.

INCIDENT COMMANDER: The person in charge of the emergency scene.

INCIDENT COMMAND SYSTEM (ICS): Method of managing resources at the scene of an emergency.

IN-SERVICE: When an apparatus is available to respond to an alarm.

INVESTIGATION: See Checking the Building.

KNOCK DOWN: Phase of fire extinguishment where the fire is reduced to a semi-extinguished state, inhibiting its spread.

LADDER: A piece of fire fighting apparatus that carries an aerial ladder used for rescue and positioning of personnel on upper floors of a building. Also called Truck or Aerial.

MOVE-UP: Signal for a station to move apparatus to another fire station in the Department when the first station has exhausted its personnel and apparatus on an incident. This occurs primarily when more than one emergency is occurring in adjoining geographical areas.

MUTUAL AID: An agreement with neighboring fire departments that provides for mutual assistance in the event additional equipment is needed.

NURSE TANKER: A water tanker used to supply a Pumper and other tankers in turn supply that.

OPEN-UP: The process of effecting entry into a burning structure. The opening of windows and doors and cutting holes for ventilation.

OUT-OF-SERVICE: A piece of apparatus is not in a position to respond to an alarm. Generally, the apparatus needs fuel or water or is out for routine maintenance.

OVERHAUL (aka MOP UP): The final operation at a fire. Investigating the entire premise to determine that no more fire exists. There is also removal of some building contents for this purpose.

PLUG: Fire hydrant.

PUBLIC INFORMATION OFFICER (PIO): Officer responsible for relaying information to the media on the scene of an incident.

PUMPER: See Engine.

PRECONNECT/PRECONNECTED LINE/CROSS LAY: An attack line of any size that is pre-attached to a discharge outlet of an engine. Cross lays are normally 1-½ inches or 1 3/4 inches in size.

RELAY: The use of two or more pumpers to move water distances that would require excessive pressure if only one Pumper was used.

REVERSY LAY: A hose layout from the fire to the water supply that places a Pumper at the water supply.

RUN: The action of a fire company responding to an alarm. Usually includes its return. Same as Call.

SAR: Search and rescue

SALVAGE: Operation of reducing the damage to non-damaged goods within a structure that has burned. Example: covering furniture with salvage covers to prevent water damage.

SIZE-UP: The verbal appraisal via radio of conditions at the scene of an incident by the first-in company or officer. May be updated as command officers arrive on the scene.

STEAMER CONNECTION: A fire hydrant connection usually from 4 ½ inches to 6 inches in diameter.

STRAIGHT LAY/FORWARD LAY: A hose layout from the water supply to the fire that places an engine at the fire.

TANKER SHUTTLE: The act of transferring water from a direct water supply via tankers to the fire.

VENTILATE: The operation of opening windows, doors and cutting holes in a building for the purpose of removing smoke, heat and fire gases. This action facilitates an improved working environment for firefighters, as well as reducing smoke and fire damage to the contents of the building.

WATERGUN: A pressurized water fire extinguisher.

WORKER: A fire that requires a major fire fighting effort to extinguish. Also called a Working Fire.

Appendix I
Fire Flow Calculations

Calculating Fire Flow Requirements

Experienced company officers recognize the fact that the amount of extinguishing agent available for controlling a fire will determine the success of the operation. Water must be available and applied to a fire in sufficient quantity to completely extinguish it. Early application, through private fire-suppression systems, will help control a fire and reduce the amount of water damage that can occur if application is delayed. Therefore, the company officer must be able to determine the quantity of water required to control a fire in a specific structure through the application of mathematical formulas.

The National Fire Academy uses the term *fire flow* to describe the amount of water needed to extinguish a fire in an occupancy. Fire flow is not just the amount of water but also the available pressure (either from the water supply system or from a fire pump), available personnel needed to deploy, handle, and advance hose lines, and the number and type of apparatus needed to pump, transport, or support the application of the water. Fire flow is always stated in gallons per minute (gpm) **(L/min)** and should be available for a specified time period.

Fire flow calculations apply to the use of handlines in structures that do not have private fire suppression systems. Structures that have private fire suppression systems will require a specific fire flow for the system. If the system is operating properly, the number and size of handlines and fire flow required for them may be less.

A number of formulas are available to the company officer when trying to calculate the fire flow required for a location or occupancy. In each case, a safety factor should be added to the estimate to allow for any changes in the fire development at the location. The company officer should also understand that each formula has its weaknesses and is only an estimate of the quantity of water required.

The formulas were originally developed in the 1940s when fuel loads were smaller and the use of synthetic materials was less common. Therefore, the formulas are based on area of the structure and not the contents. Results are on the conservative side since they do not take into consideration the high flammability of new products.

Cubic Foot Formula (C)

The cubic foot or Iowa State formula is used to estimate the required fire flow for the initial attack on the fire. This formula is based on the ability of water to absorb heat and turn to steam. This estimate is made during the preincident survey. The largest single area in the building is measured and its cubic foot capacity is determined. The number of cubic feet is then divided by 100 to obtain the total number of gallons of water needed for extinguishment.

For example, a space 50 feet (15.24 m) by 20 feet (6.10 m) by 10 (3.05 m) feet high would contain 10,000 cubic feet (283.54 cubic meters). Dividing this figure by 100 would result in an estimated 100 gpm (379 l/min) fire flow. Experiments indicate that the greatest efficiency results from the water being applied to the hottest part of the fire for only 30 seconds. This would mean that the calculation should be divided by half, resulting in a 50 gpm (0.70 l/min) requirement.

National Fire Academy Quick Calculation Formula (C)

The next formula is known as the *National Fire Academy Quick Calculation Formula*. While the cubic foot (cubic meters) formula can be used in preincident planning, the NFA formula is intended for use by the first arriving company officer at a fire incident. It is intended to provide the fire flow for initial attack situations.

This basic formula is based on the square footage (square meters) of the structure. The result is divided by 3 and the resulting figure is the gpm (l/min) required to control a one story structure that is fully involved in fire. For multistory structures, the square footage (square meters) is multiplied by the number of floors of the structure. The resulting figure is divided by 3 and that number is multiplied by the percent expressed as a decimal of the total building that is involved in fire. One additional adjustment must be made to provide the required fire flow. An additional 25 percent must be added for each exposure to the building.

Fire Fighter Fatality Investigation and Prevention Program

Death in the line of duty...

A summary of a NIOSH fire fighter fatality investigation   July 6, 1998

Single-Family Dwelling Fire Claims the Lives of Two Volunteer Fire Fighters--Ohio

SUMMARY

On February 5, 1998, two male volunteer fire fighters (Victim #1 and Victim #2) died of smoke inhalation while trying to exit the basement of a single-family dwelling after a backdraft occurred. A volunteer Engine company composed of four fire fighters and one driver/operator were the first responders to a structure fire at a single-family dwelling 3 miles from the fire department. When the Engine company arrived, one fire fighter on board reported light smoke showing from the roof. The four fire fighters (including Victim #1) entered the dwelling through the kitchen door and proceeded down the basement stairs to determine the fire's origin. The four fire fighters searched the basement which was filled with a light to moderate smoke. A few minutes later, a fifth fire fighter from Rescue 211 (Victim #2) joined the group. After extinguishing a small fire in the ceiling area, Victim #2 raised a ceiling panel and a backdraft occurred in the concealed ceiling space. The pressure and fire from the backdraft knocked ceiling tiles onto the fire fighters, who became disoriented and lost contact with each other and their hoseline. Two fire fighters located on the basement staircase exited the dwelling with assistance from two fire fighters who were attempting rescue. One fire fighter was rescued through an exterior basement door and the two victims' SCBAs ran out of air while they were trying to escape. Both fire fighters died of smoke inhalation and other injuries. Additional rescue attempts were made by other fire fighters but failed due to excessive heat and smoke and lack of an established water supply. NIOSH investigators concluded that, in order to prevent similar incidents, fire departments should:

● **utilize the first arriving engine company as the command company and conduct an initial scene survey**

Figure: Basement where fatalities occurred.

The **Fire Fighter Fatality Investigation and Prevention Program** is conducted by the National Institute for Occupational Safety and Health (NIOSH). The purpose of the program is to determine factors that cause or contribute to fire fighter deaths suffered in the line of duty. Identification of causal and contributing factors enable researchers and safety specialists to develop strategies for preventing future similar incidents. To request additional copies of this report (specify the case number shown in the shield above), other fatality investigation reports, or further information, visit the Program Website at:

http://www.cdc.gov/niosh/firehome.html

or call toll free **1-800-35-NIOSH**

Single-Family Dwelling Fire Claims the Lives of Two Volunteer Fire Fighters--Ohio

- *implement an incident command system with written standard operating procedures for all fire fighters*

- *provide a backup hose crew*

- *provide adequate on-scene communications including fireground tactical channels*

- *train fire fighters in the various essentials of, but not limited to, how to operate in smoke-filled environments, basement fire operations, dangers of ceiling collapse, ventilation practices, utilizing a second hoseline during fire attack, and identifying pre-backdraft, rollover, and flashover conditions*

- *appoint an Incident Safety Officer.*

INTRODUCTION

On February 5, 1998, five male volunteer fire fighters, including the two victims, ages 43 and 29 years old, entered a single-family dwelling that had light smoke showing from the roof. The fire fighters entered the dwelling through the kitchen door and proceeded down the basement stairs to determine the fire's origin. After extinguishing a small ceiling fire, a ceiling tile was lifted and a backdraft occurred in the concealed ceiling space which disoriented the fire fighters. Two fire fighters died of smoke inhalation and other injuries, one fire fighter had to be rescued, and the other two fire fighters escaped with some assistance.

On February 10, 1998, Richard Braddee and Tommy Baldwin, Safety and Occupational Health Specialists from the Division of Safety Research, traveled to Ohio to conduct an investigation of this incident. Meetings were conducted with fire department officers, the surviving three volunteer fire fighters of the initial fire attack crew, and a representative from the local Fire Investigation Task Force. Copies of photographs of the incident site and the transcription of dispatch tapes were obtained, and a site visit was conducted. The 33-member volunteer fire department involved in the incident serves a population of 7,800 in a geographic area of 84 square miles. The fire department requires all new fire fighters to complete Fire Fighter Level I training which consists of 36 hours of training and is required by the State of Ohio. The required training is designed to cover personal safety, forcible entry, ventilation, fire apparatus, ladders, self-contained breathing apparatus, search and rescue, and hose practices. Recertification in-service training is conducted on an annual basis. The victims had approximately 5 and 10 years of fire fighting experience, respectively. The fire department had an active equipment inspection and maintenance program. Any equipment found to be defective was repaired or replaced immediately.

The site of the incident was a 20-year-old, one-story, single-family residence measuring 28' x 50'. The ranch-style residence was constructed of wood framing, had a shingled roof and hardboard siding. The residence had a 26-foot-long deck attached to the west side and a full basement about 8 ½-feet high with a 16-inch dropped ceiling. Access to the basement was gained through either an interior stairway from the kitchen or an exterior stairway which was located on the north side of the residence. The residence

Page 2

Single-Family Dwelling Fire Claims the Lives of Two Volunteer Fire Fighters--Ohio

contained a full kitchen both upstairs and in the basement, had full carpeting, and was heated by a natural gas furnace. Three smoke detectors were present in the residence, but the occupant stated they did not operate. The residence was about 3 miles from the fire department involved in the incident.

Although eight volunteer fire departments were involved in this incident, only those directly involved up to the time of the fatal incident are mentioned in this report.

INVESTIGATION

On February 5, 1998, at 0210 hours, a fire call was received by the Sheriff's Office from the occupant of a private residence near the incident site. The Sheriff's Office dispatched the automatic response group for structure fires which consisted of three local volunteer fire departments. At 0220, Engine 211 with four fire fighters and a driver/operator, including Victim #1, responded to the alarm. Rescue 211 with the Chief and two fire fighters, including Victim #2 also responded. Additionally Squad 211 (ambulance), and Tanker 211 responded with six personnel. Altogether 4 pieces of equipment and 13 personnel arrived at the fire scene between 0226 and 0231 hours. By 0238 hours, all three automatic response fire department units were on the scene.

Engine 211 crew were first to arrive at 0226 hours and reported that smoke was showing from the roof. A 1¾-inch crosslay handline was pulled and laid to the kitchen door. Information was relayed by a relative of the owner of the dwelling to the Engine 211 crew that heavier smoke had been observed in the southwest corner of the basement, possibly at the circuit breaker box under the stairway. The Engine 211 crew

prepared to enter the house by arming their PASS devices, turning on their SCBAs, and checking each others' gear. The 1¾-inch handline was charged, and upon entry into the kitchen, they noticed light smoke. Rescue 211 arrived at 0227 hours with the Chief and two fire fighters, including Victim #2, and the Chief assumed command. The Engine 211 driver/operator requested a supply line be laid to the tanker and the Chief assisted in laying the line. The Chief returned to the residence and saw light gray smoke emanating from the kitchen door. While inside the residence, four of the fire fighters from Engine 211 encountered a closed, interior door leading to the basement. The fire fighters opened the basement door and proceeded down the basement steps. Victim #1 and another fire fighter, who carried a two-way VHF radio, stayed at the top of the steps and helped advance hose. Three fire fighters, two of whom were carrying the charged hoseline, began a right-hand search pattern to locate the circuit breaker box. After finding no fire at the breaker box, the crew moved to another part of the basement. As the crew progressed back around the steps, their hoseline became caught between the legs of a metal folding chair. As they advanced the hoseline further into the basement, the chair was pulled under the staircase and collapsed onto the hose which pinched off the water supply. In the interim, Victim #2, who also carried a two-way VHF radio, broke the window from the exterior basement door then opened the door and yelled to the interior crew that this was a second way out. Victim #2 went back up the exterior stairwell then entered the kitchen on the first floor and met another fire fighter who yelled down the stairs that he and Victim #2 would search the first floor. A second 1¾-inch hoseline was pulled off Engine 211, taken into the first floor kitchen through the interior door and laid partially down the steps into

Page 3

Single-Family Dwelling Fire Claims the Lives of Two Volunteer Fire Fighters--Ohio

the basement. The line was charged in anticipation of being used in the basement fire attack. The fire fighters in the basement saw light to moderate gray, puffing smoke at the basement ceiling and then lazy orange flames from the ceiling area. The two fire fighters including Victim #2, went down the interior stairs and followed the hoseline and joined the three fire fighters in the basement. They were advised to get down because the fire was in the ceiling area. They saw a small fire at a fluorescent light fixture midway in the basement between the interior staircase and the northeast corner (see Figure). This fire was extinguished with the last available water due to the hose being pinched off. The crew, unaware of the water situation, waited a moment to watch conditions. Fire then traveled across the ceiling and re-entered the walls and several fire fighters saw the smoke puffing out from between the ceiling and wall. Victim #2 then passed by the crew and used an axe to lift a ceiling tile in the center of the basement to check flame spread. The concealed ceiling space had reached the smoldering stage (i.e., high temperatures and considerable quantities of soot and combustible fire gases had accumulated) and when the ceiling tile was lifted, oxygen was introduced into the ceiling space and a backdraft occurred. Seconds after the backdraft, visibility went black and ceiling tiles collapsed onto the fire fighters from the pressure created by the backdraft. Disoriented from the heat and smoke and fallen ceiling tiles, the fire fighters began crawling out of the basement following the hoseline, but soon lost the hose. Victim #2 told a fire fighter to hit the fire with water from the hoseline, which he attempted, but there was no water in the hose. At 0243 hours a radio transmission was given "In the basement...send water" (charge the hoseline with water). Fire had vented up the stairway and burned through both

hoselines, causing them to burst and freely flow water. The crew began to crawl back toward the staircase with Victim #1 in front, and the other fire fighters following. The PASS devices of Victims #1 and #2 began to sound due to heat activation and the SCBA low-air alarms also began to sound. At 0243 hours, Victim #2 radioed for help and the Chief ordered the apparatus air horns sounded for all to evacuate the house. The crew in the basement heard the horns. At 0244 hours, another radio transmission "Need water!" was received from the basement. One fire fighter, suffering from the intense heat, became unconscious and collapsed to the floor. Another fire fighter remembered the direction of the second exit and continued to feel for the hose as he tried to orient himself. He then found another fire fighter and they went up the steps and were assisted out of the house by the rescue team. At 0245 hours, the radio transmission "Guys inside to IC" (Incident Command) was received. The Chief began to advance a 2½-inch hoseline down the exterior basement stairwell to assist with fire extinguishment and heard PASS devices sounding from inside the basement. He was driven back by heat and smoke. He advised his Assistant Chief of the situation, relinquished command to the Assistant Chief, and went to Squad 211 to recover.

One of the fire fighters who had just exited the residence informed the rescuers that other fire fighters were still inside. A two-person rescue crew entered the basement from the exterior door and rescued the unconscious fire fighter who was about 3 feet from the door. At 0303 hours, a radio transmission was received from Squad 211: "We have two fire fighters that are in critical condition." Four additional attempts were made to rescue the victims but the rescuers were driven back due to intense heat and fire. The bodies

Single-Family Dwelling Fire Claims the Lives of Two Volunteer Fire Fighters--Ohio

were later recovered after the fire was extinguished. A post-incident investigation revealed the point of origin of the fire was in the area of the furnace.

CAUSE OF DEATH

The cause of death listed by the medical examiner was asphyxiation due to smoke inhalation, burns and crushing trauma injuries to the chest.

RECOMMENDATIONS/DISCUSSION

Recommendation #1: Fire departments should utilize the first arriving engine company as the command company and conduct an initial scene survey. [2, 3, 4]

Discussion: Since incident command and size-up are the responsibility of the first officer on-scene, the first arriving engine company should concentrate its efforts on establishing a command post, performing initial size-up, coordinating communications, and relaying information and additional requirements to dispatch. Scene safety is greatly enhanced by waiting to perform operations until adequate resources are on-scene. An initial scene survey, or size-up, should occur at each incident. Size-up is an evaluation made by the officer in charge which enables him to determine his course of action and to accomplish his mission. A fire situation can change drastically and rapidly. The commanding officer must quickly survey and analyze the situation and quickly weigh the various factors. Factors to consider include: the type of occupancy, nature of the fire situation, structure involved, and the fire itself. Based on evaluation of these factors, the commanding officer should decide what action should be taken to control the emergency. The next step is to formulate a plan of operation given the resources available, and implement that plan.

Recommendation #2: Fire departments should implement an incident command system with written standard operating procedures for all fire fighters. [1, 2, 4]

Discussion: The system should establish roles and responsibilities for all personnel involved. It should ensure personnel accountability and safety and should provide a well-coordinated approach to all emergency activities. All fire department personnel should be thoroughly trained on this system and receive periodic refresher training. All training should be documented.

Recommendation #3: Fire departments should provide a back-up hose crew. [1, 2, 3, 5, 6]

Discussion: A second manned attack hoseline should be established to provide back-up for the initial attack line to assist with fire extinguishment and fire fighter rescue. The National Fire Protection Association (NFPA) and the Occupational Safety and Health Administration recommend that four persons (two-in and two-out), each with protective clothing and respiratory protection be provided when interior operations are taking place. Also, a rapid intervention team should be established to effect fire fighter rescue. NFPA 1500, 6-5.2 states that "A rapid intervention crew shall consist of at least two members and shall be available for rescue of a member or a team if the need arises. Rapid intervention crews shall be fully equipped with the appropriate protective clothing, protective equipment, SCBA, and any specialized rescue equipment that might be needed given the specifics of the operation under way."

Recommendation #4: Fire departments should provide adequate on-scene communications

Page 5

Single-Family Dwelling Fire Claims the Lives of Two Volunteer Fire Fighters--Ohio

including fireground tactical channels.[1, 2, 4, 6]

Discussion: Communication should be an on-going component of on-scene operations. NFPA 1561 states that the communications system shall meet the requirements of the fire department for routine and large-scale emergencies. Emergency scenes become very hectic within a short period of time. Radio communications occurring between incident command, attack crews, pumper operators, mutual aid companies, and dispatch can easily be missed. It is imperative that on-scene operations be given fireground tactical radio channels which are separate from the normal dispatch frequencies. Fire fighters operating on-scene must be capable of communicating between themselves and incident command without being "talked over" by dispatch or other companies. In a small fire department, one radio channel for dispatch and one fire ground communications channel might be sufficient for most situations. A larger fire department requires several additional radio channels to provide for the volume of communications relating to routine incidents and for the complexity of multiple alarm situations. Interior attack crews should have adequate radio communication with incident command and with other attack crews to provide for personnel accountability, coordination of efforts, report on flame spread, fire extinguishment, and other pertinent information. As incident command becomes aware of changing conditions, vital information can be given directly to the attack crews. The radio capabilities should also provide for communications with mutual aid resources or other agencies that could be expected to respond to a major incident. The system should be developed to provide reserve capacity for unusually complex situations where effective communications could become critical.

***Recommendation #5:** Fire departments should train fire fighters in the various essentials of how to operate in smoke-filled environments, basement fire operations, dangers of ceiling collapse, ventilation practices, utilizing a second hoseline during fire attack, and identifying pre-backdraft, rollover, and flashover conditions.*[2, 3, 6, 7]

Discussion: The essentials of fire fighting are numerous and varied, and require initial and refresher training on a monthly, annually, or an as needed basis. NFPA 1500 recommends that all personnel who may engage in structural fire fighting participate in training at least monthly. Ideally, this monthly training will serve to reinforce safe practices until they become automatic. Other types of training are required on an "as needed" basis. For example, training is required when new procedures or equipment are introduced.

***Recommendation #6:** Fire departments should appoint an Incident Safety Officer.*[3, 4, 8]

Discussion: The Incident Safety Officer (ISO) is appointed by the Incident Commander at each emergency scene. The duties of the ISO are to monitor the scene and report the status of conditions, hazards, and risks to the incident commander, ensure fire fighter rehabilitation occurs, the personnel accountability system is being utilized, and monitor radio communications to ensure all areas of the scene are capable of communicating to incident command.

References:

1.   29 Code of Federal Regulations 1910.120(q)(3), Hazardous Waste Operations and Emergency Response. (Incident Command, Two-In/Two-Out

Page 6

Rule, Communications).

2.   Essentials of Fire Fighting, 3rd edition, Fire Protection Publications, 1998. (Incident Command, Back-Up Hose Crew, Rapid Intervention Team, Communications).

3.   National Fire Protection Association. NFPA 1500,* Standard on FireDepartment Occupational Safety and Health Program. National Fire Protection Association, Quincy, MA. (Back-Up Hose Crew, Rapid Intervention Team) 1997 Edition.

4.   National Fire Protection Association. NFPA 1561, Standard on Fire Department Incident Management System. National Fire Protection Association, Quincy, MA. (Incident Command, Communications), 1995 Edition.

5.   Dunn Vincent. Hoseline Placement at Structural Fires, Firehouse, August 1997

.
6.   Dunn Vincent. Safety and Survival on the Fireground, PennWell, Tulsa, Oklahoma, 1992.

7.   Dunn Vincent. Collapse of Burning Buildings, PennWell, Tulsa, Oklahoma, 1988.

8.   National Fire Protection Association. NFPA 1521, Standard for Fire Department Safety Officer. National Fire Protection Association, Quincy, MA,

1997 Edition.

Page 7

Figure: Basement where fatalities occurred.

Single-Family Dwelling Fire Claims the Lives of Two Volunteer Fire Fighters--Ohio

Figure. Fire Dwelling
Basement Floor Plan
FACE 98F06

One-story, 20-year old single-family dwelling with full basement measuring 28' x 50'. Wood-frame construction with shingle roof and hardboard siding. Three smoke detectors present-none operable.

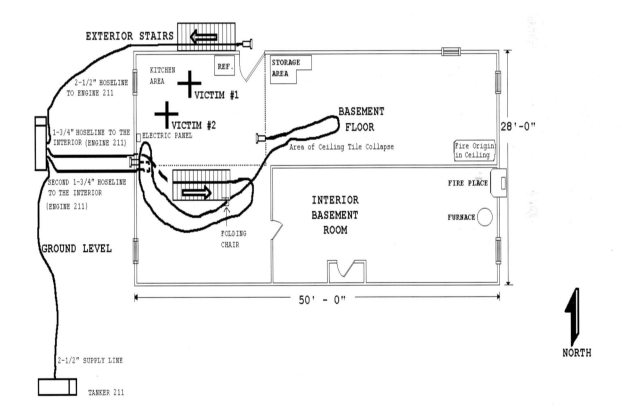

Appendix K
NIMS-ICS Forms

INCIDENT OBJECTIVES	1. INCIDENT NAME	2. DATE PREPARED	3. TIME PREPARED

4. OPERATIONAL PERIOD (DATE/TIME)

5. GENERAL CONTROL OBJECTIVES FOR THE INCIDENT (INCLUDE ALTERNATIVES)

6. WEATHER FORECAST FOR OPERATIONAL PERIOD

7. GENERAL SAFETY MESSAGE

8. ATTACHMENTS (✔ IF ATTACHED)

☐ ORGANIZATION LIST (ICS 203)   ☐ MEDICAL PLAN (ICS 206)   ☐ _____
☐ ASSIGNMENT LIST (ICS 204)   ☐ INCIDENT MAP   ☐ _____
☐ COMMUNICATIONS PLAN (ICS 205)   ☐ TRAFFIC PLAN   ☐ _____

9. PREPARED BY (PLANNING SECTION CHIEF)	10. APPROVED BY (INCIDENT COMMANDER)

202 ICS (1/99)   NFES 1326

ORGANIZATION ASSIGNMENT LIST

1. INCIDENT NAME	2. DATE PREPARED	3. TIME PREPARED

POSITION	NAME	4. OPERATIONAL PERIOD (DATE/TIME)

5. INCIDENT COMMANDER AND STAFF

INCIDENT COMMANDER

DEPUTY

SAFTEY OFFICER

INFORMATION OFFICER

LIAISON OFFICER

6. AGENCY REPRESENTATIVES

AGENCY	NAME

7. PLANNING SECTION

CHIEF

DEPUTY

RESOURCES UNIT

SITUATION UNIT

DOCUMENTATION UNIT

DEMOBILIZATION UNIT

TECHNICAL SPECIALISTS

8. LOGISTICS SECTION

CHIEF

DEPUTY

a. SUPPORT BRANCH

DIRECTOR

SUPPLY UNIT

FACILITIES UNIT

GROUND SUPPORT UNIT

b. SERVICE BRANCH

DIRECTOR

COMMUNICATIONS UNIT

MEDICAL UNIT

FOOD UNIT

9. OPERATIONS SECTION

CHIEF

DEPUTY

a. BRANCH I- DIVISION/GROUPS

BRANCH DIRECTOR

DEPUTY

DIVISION/GROUP

DIVISION/GROUP

DIVISION/GROUP

DIVISION/GROUP

DIVISION/GROUP

b. BRANCH II- DIVISION/GROUPS

BRANCH DIRECTOR

DEPUTY

DIVISION/GROUP

DIVISION/GROUP

DIVISION/GROUP

DIVISION/GROUP

DIVISION/GROUP

c. BRANCH III- DIVISION/GROUPS

BRANCH DIRECTOR

DEPUTY

DIVISION/GROUP

DIVISION/GROUP

DIVISION/GROUP

DIVISION/GROUP

DIVISION/GROUP

d. AIR OPERATIONS BRANCH

AIR OPERATIONS BR. DIR.

AIR TACTICAL GROUP SUP.

AIR SUPPORT GROUP SUP.

HELICOPTER COORDINATOR

AIR TANKER/FIXED WING CRD.

10. FINANCE/ADMINISTRATION SECTION

CHIEF

DEPUTY

TIME UNIT

PROCUREMENT UNIT

COMPENSATION/CLAIMS UNIT

COST UNIT

PREPARED BY(RESOURCES UNIT)

203 ICS (1/99)

NFES 1327

1. BRANCH	2. DIVISION/GROUP	**ASSIGNMENT LIST**

3. INCIDENT NAME	4. OPERATIONAL PERIOD
	DATE _____ TIME _____

5. OPERATIONAL PERSONNEL

OPERATIONS CHIEF _____ DIVISION/GROUP SUPERVISOR _____

BRANCH DIRECTOR _____ AIR TACTICAL GROUP SUPERVISOR _____

6. RESOURCES ASSIGNED THIS PERIOD

STRIKE TEAM/TASK FORCE/ RESOURCE DESIGNATOR	EMT	LEADER	NUMBER PERSONS	TRANS. NEEDED	PICKUP PT./TIME	DROP OFF PT./TIME

7. CONTROL OPERATIONS

8. SPECIAL INSTRUCTIONS

9. DIVISION/GROUP COMMUNICATIONS SUMMARY

FUNCTION		FREQ.	SYSTEM	CHAN.	FUNCTION		FREQ.	SYSTEM	CHAN.
COMMAND	LOCAL				SUPPORT	LOCAL			
	REPEAT					REPEAT			
DIV./GROUP TACTICAL					GROUND TO AIR				

PREPARED BY (RESOURCE UNIT LEADER)	APPROVED BY (PLANNING SECT. CH.)	DATE	TIME

204 ICS (1/99)

NFES 1328

INCIDENT RADIO COMMUNICATIONS PLAN

1. INCIDENT NAME	2. DATE/TIME PREPARED	3. OPERATIONAL PERIOD DATE/TIME

4. BASE RADIO CHANNEL UTILIZATION

SYSTEM/CACHE	CHANNEL	FUNCTION	FREQUENCY/TONE	ASSIGNMENT	REMARKS

5. PREPARED BY (COMMUNICATIONS UNIT)

205 ICS (9/66)

NFES 1330

MEDICAL PLAN

	1. INCIDENT NAME	2. DATE PREPARED	3. TIME PREPARED	4. OPERATIONAL PERIOD

5. INCIDENT MEDICAL AID STATIONS

MEDICAL AID STATIONS	LOCATION	PARAMEDICS	
		YES	NO

6. TRANSPORTATION

A. AMBULANCE SERVICES

NAME	ADDRESS	PHONE	PARAMEDICS	
			YES	NO

B. INCIDENT AMBULANCES

NAME	LOCATION	PARAMEDICS	
		YES	NO

7. HOSPITALS

NAME	ADDRESS	TRAVEL TIME		PHONE	HELIPAD		BURN CENTER	
		AIR	GRND		YES	NO	YES	NO

8. MEDICAL EMERGENCY PROCEDURES

206 ICS 8/78	9. PREPARED BY (MEDICAL UNIT LEADER)	10. REVIEWED BY (SAFETY OFFICER)

NFES 1331

OPERATIONAL PLANNING WORKSHEET

1. INCIDENT NAME	2. DATE PREPARED	3. OPERATIONAL PERIOD (DATE/TIME)
	TIME PREPARED	

4. DIVISION OR OTHER LOCATION	5. WORK ASSIGNMENTS	6. RESOURCE	RESOURCES BY TYPE (SHOW STRIKE TEAM AS ST)	7. REPORTING LOCATION	8. REQUESTED ARRIVAL TIME
		TYPE			
		REQ			
		HAVE			
		NEED			
		REQ			
		HAVE			
		NEED			
		REQ			
		HAVE			
		NEED			
		REQ			
		HAVE			
		NEED			
		REQ			
		HAVE			
		NEED			
		REQ			
		HAVE			
		NEED			
		REQ			
		HAVE			
		NEED			
		REQ			
		HAVE			
		NEED			

9. TOTAL RESOURCES REQUIRED	SINGLE RESOURCES		
	STRIKE TEAMS		
TOTAL RESOURCES ON HAND			
TOTAL RESOURCES NEEDED			

10. PREPARED BY (NAME AND POSITION)

215 ICS 9-86

NFES 1338

Appendix L
Scene Entry Consent Forms

(NOTE): The following Consent to Search Fire-Damaged Premises and Consent to Search Fire-Damaged Vehicle forms were developed by Kevin Smith, Agency Legal Specialist, North Carolina Justice Academy and my be reproduced for training and investigative purposes.

CONSENT TO SEARCH FIRE-DAMAGED PREMISES

1. Name of Owner/Occupant:

_____

_____

2. Description of Premises:

_____

_____

I, the undersigned, hereby state that I am the above occupant, or that I am authorized to give this consent on behalf of the owner, tenant, or other party occupying or possessing the above described premises.

I hereby give my consent and permission to any fire department member, any law enforcement officer, or any other person assisting an official engaged in the determination of the cause of a fire, to enter, re-enter, and remain on the above described premises, from time to time, for the purpose of conducting an investigation into the cause and origin of a fire occurring on or within the above described premises, and to seize evidence related to the cause and origin of that fire, regardless of the nature of that evidence.

This consent and permission extends to and includes the entire premises above described, whether or not the same are fire damaged or are immediately involved in fire damaged caused by the fire. All areas of the above described premises, near to or remote from the point of the fire's origin are included within the scope of this permission.

This consent and permission shall be valid for such period of time as the above designated officers and officials deem necessary or appropriate for any investigative purpose or administrative purpose, and includes entry and re-entry over time and from time to time, without limitation.

This consent and permission is given freely and voluntarily. I acknowledge that no threats or promises have been made to induce me to give this consent and permission. I understand that any object or evidence seized during this search may be used in court of law in either a civil or criminal proceeding against any person.

Date: _____

Signature of Consenting Party_____

Witness:_____

_____ Title or Authority

CONSENT TO SEARCH FIRE-DAMAGED VEHICLE

1. Name of Registered Owner or Person in Control of Vehicle: _____

_____

2. Description of Vehicle:_____

_____

I, the undersigned, hereby state that I am the above registered owner of the above described vehicle to be searched, or that I am in control of its operation and contents and I am authorized to give this consent on behalf of the owner, or other party possessing the above described vehicle.

I hereby give my consent and permission to any fire department member, any law enforcement officer, or any other person assisting an official engaged in the determination of the cause of a fire, to enter, re-enter, and remain within the above described vehicle, from time to time, for the purpose of conducting an investigation into the cause and origin of a fire occurring on or within that vehicle, and to seize evidence related to the cause and origin of that fire, regardless of the nature of that vehicle.

This consent and permission extends t and includes the entire vehicle above described, whether or not the same is fire damaged or is immediately involved in fire damage caused by the fire. All areas of the above described vehicle, near to or remote from the point the fire's origin are included within the scope of this permission.

The consent and permission shall be valid for such period of time as the above designated officers and officials deem necessary or appropriate for any investigative purpose or administrative purpose, and includes entry and re-entry from time to time, without limitation.

This consent and permission is given freely and voluntarily. I acknowledge that no threats or promises have been made to induce me to give this consent and permission. I understand that any object or evidence seized during this search may be used in a court of law in either a civil or criminal proceeding against any person.

Date: _____

Signature of Consenting Party_____

Witness: _____

Title or Authority_____

Source: http://www.jus.state.nc.us/NCJA/w-mw-1099.htm

Appendix M
Court Cases on Warrants

Fire Scene Searches

Search and Seizure/General Principles

The Fourth Amendment to the United States Constitution protects persons from unreasonable searches and seizures. A search made without a warrant is presumed to be unreasonable and therefore unconstitutional *unless* the search is conducted pursuant to a recognized exception to the warrant requirement. Search by authorities is deemed unreasonable and therefore unconstitutional only if it unduly infringes upon an individual's reasonable expectation of privacy. No reasonable expectation of privacy is recognized in the following:

- Abandoned property
- Open fields
- Buildings completely destroyed by fire

Fire scenes are subject to Fourth Amendment protections against unreasonable search and seizure and Fourth Amendment warrant requirement. To make lawful entry onto premises, firefighters and investigators must have a search warrant, valid consent, or exigent circumstances.

Fourth Amendment rights may be waived by voluntary consent.

Components of valid consent:

- Must be obtained from proper person
- Must be freely and voluntarily given and should be in writing
- Exigent circumstance — Where emergency exists, warrantless entry onto premises is permissible

A burning building constitutes exigent circumstances sufficient to permit warrantless entry; fire itself is the emergency and no further justification is necessary.

Firefighters may enter to:

- Save lives
- Protect property
- Suppress fire

While present at a fire, firefighters may properly search without a search warrant for accelerant on the premises, if they are engaged in any continuing activity to control or extinguish the fire or prevent rekindling. (See State v. Langley). Absent valid consent or exigent circumstances, an administrative search warrant (North Carolina General Statutes [N.C.G.S.] 15-27 [a]) or criminal search warrant (N.C.G.S. 15a-221-223) is required for lawful entry and search of fire damaged premises.

Case Law

Michigan v. Tyler and Robert Tompkins, 436 U.S. 499 S.CT. 1942 (1978). Fire scenes are subject to the warrant requirement of the Fourth Amendment. A burning building presents an emergency of sufficient proportions to render a warrantless entry reasonable under the Fourth Amendment. Subsequent detached entries are unlawful unless made pursuant to a warrant, consent, or exigent circumstances.

In Michigan v. Tyler, the major legal points are: A burning building is a sufficient exigency to allow a non-consensual warrantless entry into a building. After the suppression of a fire, crews may remain in the building for a reasonable remaining-on period of time to look for cause and origin. This remaining-on period of time can sometimes be extended by conditions at the scene. A commercial building can house an expectation of privacy for purposes of Fourth Amendment search and seizure law.

436 U.S. 499, 56 L.Ed.2d 486. State of MICHIGAN, Petitioner, v. Loren TYLER and Robert Tompkins. No. 76-1608. Argued January 10, 1978. Decided May 31, 1978.

A judgment of the Michigan Supreme Court, 399 Mich. 564, 250 N. W. 2d 467, granted a new trial to defendants convicted of conspiring to burn real property, one defendant having been also convicted of burning real property and of burning insured property with intent to defraud. The State of Michigan sought review by way of certiorari. The Supreme Court, Mr. Justice Stewart, held that:

(1) An entry to fight a fire requires no warrant, and, once in the building, officials may remain there for a reasonable time to investigate the cause of the blaze;

(2) Thereafter, additional inquiries to investigate cause of the fire must be made pursuant to the warrant procedures governing administrative searches, and

(3) Evidence of arson discovered in the course of such investigations is admissible, but if investigating officials find probable cause to believe that arson has occurred and require further access to gather evidence for possible prosecution, they may obtain a warrant only upon traditional showing of probable cause applicable to searches for evidence of crime.

Application of Law to Facts

Michigan v. Clifford, 464 U.S. 287, 104 S.CT. 641 (1984). The court analyzed the searches made at the Clifford residence (subsequent to the initial entry for suppression) as two separate searches: the search of the basement and the search of the rest of the house. The Cliffords retained a reasonable expectation of privacy in their home; their personal belongings remained in the house and they had made an effort to secure the premises, as evidenced by the work crew on the scene.

The postfixed searches were therefore subject to the warrant requirement and were valid only if officers had a warrant, consent, or exigent circumstances to justify their entry and search. There were no exigent circumstances. The fire had been completely extinguished, police and their units had left the scene, and water was being pumped from the house.

The investigator's search was not a continuation of an earlier investigation, as in *Tyler*. Investigators did not have an administrative warrant to autho-

rize the reentry into the Clifford house. The Cliffords had not consented to the search. There was no emergency such as a rekindling of the fire. For these reasons, the reentry and search of the basement was unlawful and the evidence found there should not have been admitted at trial. Reasonable expectation of privacy may remain in fire damaged premises, necessitating a warrant for re-entry to determine cause and origin of fire.

The major legal points are: In *Michigan v. Clifford* entry into a private home by firefighters requires either an exigency, consent, or administrative inspection warrant or criminal search warrant based on a probable cause. The reasonable remaining-on period of time is limited to the earliest of the following: discovery of the cause and origin of the fire or a reasonable length of time.

Fourth Amendment protections encompass burned premises; no lawful warrantless entry or search of such premises may be made absent a showing of valid consent or exigent circumstances. A burning building presents an emergency of sufficient proportions to render an initial warrantless entry reasonable. Once in a building for the purpose of suppression, firefighters may seize evidence of arson which is in plain view.

It is the duty of firefighters not only to extinguish fires but to determine the cause of such fires. A prompt determination of the cause and origin of a fire may be necessary to prevent its re-ignition; also, immediate investigation may be necessary to preserve evidence from destruction (intentional or accidental). Firefighters do not need a warrant to remain on burned premises for a reasonable time to investigate the cause of a fire after it has been extinguished.

Any warrantless seizure of evidence is constitutional if made during the course of inspection of premises for purposes of suppression and determination of cause and origin. If an investigation into cause and origin is begun pursuant to initial entry for suppression, but the investigation is hindered by and briefly terminated due to conditions such as smoke, steam, and darkness which prevent further investigation, then a return to the premises and continuation of the investigation as soon as possible is considered to be a continuous course of action and no warrant is required.

Additional entries made after and detached from the initial emergency and warrantless entry may be made only if done pursuant to consent or a search warrant. Any evidence seized as a result of such warrantless or non-consensual reentry must be suppressed as obtained in violation of the Fourth Amendment. Additional entries to investigate must be made pursuant to an administrative search warrant.

If evidence of arson is discovered during the course of such investigation, then the evidence is admissible; however, if fire investigators find probable cause to believe that arson has occurred and require further access to gather evidence for a possible prosecution, then they must obtain a criminal search warrant and may continue their search pursuant to such warrant. If it is determined by the warrantless search that the fire is of incendiary origin (i.e., at the point that probable cause has been established), then investigators may not expand the scope of their search to other areas for the purpose of gathering criminal evidence without first obtaining a criminal search warrant to justify an expanded search.

If an investigator discovers evidence which establishes probable cause to suspect arson (or other unlawful burning) during the course of an administrative search for cause and origin, then he or she should:

- Stop the search. Do not continue the search for the purpose of gathering more evidence of the crime.

- Secure the scene. Leave personnel on the scene to guard against destruction of evidence.

- Control access to the scene. Request assistance of the local law enforcement agency, if necessary.

- Obtain a criminal search warrant. If you are not a sworn law enforcement officer, request assistance from the appropriate law enforcement agency.

- Continue the search for criminal evidence pursuant to the authority of the criminal search warrant. This procedure should be followed whether criminal evidence is found during the initial warrantless search or a later search after reentry conducted pursuant to an administrative search warrant.

In many cases, there will be no bright line rule separating the firefighters' investigation into the cause of a fire from a search for evidence of arson. Thedistinction will vary with the circumstances of the particular fire and generally will involve more than the lapse of time or the number of entries and re-entries. For example, once the cause of a fire in a single-family dwelling is determined, the administrative search should end, and any broader investigation should be made pursuant to a criminal warrant. A fire in an apartment, on the other hand, may present complexities that make it necessary for officials to conduct more expansive searches, to remain on the premises for longer periods of time, and to make repeated entries and re-entries to the building.

464 U.S. 287, 78 L.Ed.2d 477 MICHIGAN, Petitioner. v. Raymond CLIFFORD and Emma Jean Clifford. No. 82-357. Argued October 5, 1983. Decided January 11, 1984. Rehearing denied March 5, 1994. (See 465 U.S. 1084, 104 S.CT. 1457). Homeowners were charged with arson. The state trial court denied their motion to suppress evidence and interlocutory appeal was taken. The Michigan Court of Appeals affirmed. The Supreme Court, Justice Powell, held that: (1) if reasonable expectations of privacy remain in fire-damaged premises, search directed to cause and origin of a fire is subject to warrant requirement; (2) administrative warrant will suffice if primary object is to determine cause and origin of fire; (3) criminal warrant is required when primary object of search is to gather evidence of criminal activity; (4) defendants had reasonable expectation of privacy in fire-damaged home which they had arranged to have secured in their absence, and (5) once fire investigators had determined cause of fire, additional search of home could only have been for the purpose of finding evidence of arson and thus criminal warrant was required.

Administrative Search Warrant

Individuals have especially strong expectations of privacy in their homes. A private residence may retain significant expectations of privacy, despite fire damage. Where a reasonable expectation of privacy remains in the premises, administrative search (a non-continuation search made after the initial entry for suppression has been completed and firefighters have relinquished the scene) to determine cause and origin of the fire is subject to the warrant requirement, absent a showing of exigent circumstances or valid consent. If a warrant is necessary, then the purpose of the search determines what type of warrant is required.

An administrative search warrant is proper for circumstances wherein the primary objective of a proposed search is to determine cause and origin of a fire. To obtain an administrative search warrant, an officer must show that a fire of undetermined origin has occurred on the premises, that the scope of the proposed search is reasonable and will not be unnecessarily intrusive, and that the search will be executed at a reasonable time.

In making the determination to obtain an administrative search warrant the issuing official must consider:

- Number of prior entries
- Scope of the proposed search
- Time of the proposed search
- Lapse of time since the fire
- Continued use of the building
- Owner's offers to secure the premises

The warrant serves to provide the property owner with sufficient information to assure him or her of the legality of the entry. To secure an administrative search warrant, investigators must show more than the bare fact that a fire occurred (see *Michigan v. Tyler*).

Criminal Search Warrant

A criminal search warrant is proper for circumstances wherein the primary objective of a search is to gather evidence of a crime. To obtain a criminal search warrant, an officer must establish probable cause to believe that the evidence will be found in the place to be searched. If during an administrative inspection warrant search the fire is determined to be of incendiary origin (i.e., at the point that probable cause has been established), then investigators may not expand the scope of their search to other areas for the purpose of gathering criminal evidence without first obtaining a criminal search warrant to justify an expanded search.

Evidnce may be used to establish probable cause for issuance of a criminal search warrant, which must be obtained before continuation of the search for criminal evidence. If an investigator discovers evidence which establishes probable cause to suspect arson (or other unlawful burning) during the course of an administrative search for cause and origin, then he or she should:

- Stop the search. Do not continue the search for the purpose of gathering more evidence of the crime.
- Secure the scene. Leave personnel on the scene to guard against destruction of evidence. Control access to the scene and obtain a criminal search warrant.

Dog Trained in Detection of Fire Accelerants

State v. Buller, 517 N.W.2d 711 (Iowa 1994) Dog trained in detection of fire accelerants qualifies as expert witness in State of Iowa, Appellee, v. Roy Laverne Buller, Appellant. No. 93-701, Supreme Court of Iowa, May 25, 1994. Defendant was convicted in the district court, Muscatine County, Jack L. Burns, J., of arson and he appealed. The Supreme Court. Harris, J., held that dog handler's expert testimony concerning reaction at fire scene of dog trained in fire accelerant detection was admissible because foundation for expert testimony had been shown by evidence establishing handler's expertise, dog's training and general accuracy of dog's reaction during investigations. Affirmed.

Firefighters may search for accelerants at a fire scene

State v. Langley, 64 N.C. App. 674, 308 S.E.2d 445, rev. den. 310 N.C. 310, 321 S.E.2d 653 (1984). Firefighters may search for accelerants at a fire scene while present and engaged in any continuing activity to control or extinguish a fire or to prevent re-ignition. State of North Carolina v. Charles Sidney Langley. No. 837SC104. Court of Appeals of North Carolina. November 1, 1983. Defendant was convicted before the Superior Court, Nash County, Charles Winberry, J., of conspiring to burn and burning personal property of others and burning of a building used for trade or business, and he appealed. The court of appeals, Wells, J., held that: (1) evidence was sufficient for jury, and (2) while firemen are present at a fire and engaged in any continuing activity to bring under control or extinguish a fire, or prevent re-ignition, a search for the possible presence of accelerants on the premises may reasonably be conducted without a search warrant and without regard to how or why any accelerants may have been placed or stored on the premises, and the fruits of such a search are admissible in evidence against any person charged with an unlawful burning of or upon the premises.

Summary

This information gives basic knowledge of the fire/arson problem and a general overview of the legal aspects of fire/arson investigations. It is suggested to obtain copies of *Michigan v. Tyler and Robert Tompkins* and *Michigan v. Clifford*. Also obtain landmark fire/arson cases (case law) within the applicable jurisdictions and study them. Check with the local district attorney, legal advisor, Federal Bureau of Investigation, insurance agencies, etc., and ascertain legal advice in reference to duties and responsibilities.

Appendix N
Post Incident Analysis

Clark County Fire District 6
Post Incident Review Procedure

Objectives
The objectives of a post incident review (PIR) are to:

1. Evaluate:

   - Efficiency and effectiveness of operations

   - Proper use of the incident command system

   - Safety

   - Size-up

   - Strategy and tactics

2. Determine training needs based on PIR evaluations.

Criteria
All working structure fires in District 6

All incidents requiring more than one company to mitigate (Engine 61 and Rescue 61 will be considered one company)

Any incident deemed appropriate by personnel

Procedure
A formal PIR should take place as soon as possible after the incident. The shift battalion chief/shift officer will instruct incident participants to write brief narratives of the incident. These should include, but not be limited to, the following:

- Situation observed upon arrival

- Size-up, if appropriate

- Initial orders/actions

- Progress of events

- Safety issues

- Strategy and tactics

- General questions or concerns

The training battalion vhief or his/her designee will lead the PIR whether or not he/she was present at the incident. Prior to the PIR the battalion chief or his/her designee should gather together such documentation as in necessary to properly review the incident. That documentation should include, but not be limited to, the following:

- CRCA radio communication of the incident (must be ordered by a chief officer)
- Copies of all reports obtainable for the incident
- Photos of occupancy/incident area indicating location and extent of fire (if applicable)

At the conclusion of reviewing the photos and radio communication the following shall be discussed:

- Strategic and tactical issues
- Safety issues
- Important points of the discussion
- What went well
- What needs to be improved upon
- Conclusions

Discussion should begin with the officer on the first arriving unit and his/her crew. Discussion should include the establishment of command, the incident action plan (IAP), and the subjects included in each individual's narratives. Each officer and his/her crew will be afforded time to lead the discussion according to their arrival sequence.

After a complete discussion of the incident has occurred, the battalion chief will call for individuals to comment on safety issues, ask questions concerning tactics used, or make comments concerning the incident.

Appendix O
Management Theories

As the United States and Western Europe entered the Industrial Age, organizational researchers and theorists began to develop theories intended to help businesses produce more products, more efficiently. While scientists and engineers designed and created machines and streamlined manufacturing, organizational theorists (university professors who studied how organizations work) developed management concepts that would allow the industrial businesses to get the most out of the labor force.

Simultaneously, in the Industrial Age, working conditions and new innovations created by the business effect of machines and the application of some of the management concepts led to the rise and popularity of labor organizations. Only the late twentieth century would see management theory start to focus on the benefits derived from a satisfied and happy workforce.

Many management theories are similar to the leadership theories discussed in Chapter 2. In some cases, these theories were derived from the same research and written by the same authors. Each of these many management theories reflects a particular view of workers – primarily, what motivates them and what does not. The following are the major theories in the twentieth century:

- Scientific management
- Human relations
- Motivation-hygiene theory
- Management by objectives
- Total quality management

This section discusses the development and evolution of management theories in the twentieth century. Many have been applied to functions of public administration and the fire and emergency services in particular.

Scientific Management Theory

At the beginning of the twentieth century, Europe and North America had entered the Industrial Age. Companies were building machines and streamlining manufacturing processes. The worker now was part of the manufacturing process and less skill was needed to produce a product. Skilled labor was becoming less desirable and work was composed of ongoing, routine tasks. In the United States, people placed a high regard on scientific and technical advances, including careful measurement and specification of activities, processes, and results. An early theorist, Frederick Winslow Taylor, applied this careful specification and measurement of all types of organizational tasks in an attempt to increase productivity and improve efficiency. As a result, tasks were standardized to increase output and workers were rewarded and punished according to their productivity. The resulting theory, termed Scientific Management, was popular from 1890 to 1940 and has continued to influence the development of organizational theory through the rest of the century.

- Clear delineation of authority
- Responsibility
- Separation of planning from operation
- Incentive schemes for workers
- Management by exception
- Task specialization

Although Taylor's theory has been largely replaced by others that emphasize employee satisfaction and involvement, there are some aspects of the theory that are evident in today's fire service – especially at the company level. Taylor's idea about breaking each task down into its most fundamental steps is the same thing that a "job breakdown" does in curriculum development. The job breakdown is not only the basis for all psychomotor (manipulative) lesson plans, it serves as the basis for many of the standard operating procedures or guidelines (SOP/SOGs) that are used daily at the company level. For instance, a list of the steps involved in inspecting or donning an SCBA is an example of a job breakdown – which is an application of Taylor's theory.

Classical School of Management Theory

While Taylor emphasized gaining the maximum from the physical efforts of the worker, French engineer Henri Fayol advocated a consistent set of principles that successful organizations should use

Fourteen Principles of Management

Another result of Fayol's work was the creation of the following Fourteen Principles of Management that are also basic to current organizational concepts:

1. *Specialization or the division of labor* — Specialization encourages continuous improvement in skills and the development of improvements in methods. The division of labor leads to efficient use of human resources. In the fire service, specialization exists within the individual unit, divided between the firefighters, driver/operator, and company officer, and between units such as engine, ladder, and rescue companies.

2. *Authority with responsibility* — Includes the right to give orders and require compliance. This is the concept that gives all fire officers their authority of command.

3. *Discipline* — The establishment of rules and regulations and the adherence to them. Discipline is the basis for most policies and procedures developed by fire and emergency services organizations.

4. *Unity of command* — A subordinate reports to only one supervisor; basic concept used by the fire service.

5. *Unity of direction* — All efforts are directed toward one common goal.

6. *Subordination of individual interests* — The employee concentrates on work during shift. Given the realities of station life, this may be the least applicable to the fire service.

7. *Remuneration* — Equal pay for equal work resulting in a fair wage. Basic to career, combination, and paid-on-call organizations.

8. *Centralization* — Consolidation of all management functions with decisions made at the top of the organization. The scalar organization that the fire service has traditionally been based upon is modeled on centralization.

9. *Scalar chain or line of authority* — Formal chain of command from the bottom to the top of the organization. This concept is also basic to the majority of fire service organizations.

10. *Order* — All resources, human and physical, have a defined place in the organization and must remain in that location. Modern organizational theory has altered this concept somewhat although it is still applicable in some situations.

11. *Equity* — All employees are treated equally but not necessarily identically. This is a concept that most supervisors and managers strive for, although it is not always perceived by members as having been attained.

12. *Lifetime jobs* — Productive workers are ensured lifetime employment, resulting in limited turnover of employees, employee security, and lowered company training costs. This is another concept that has changed over the past century. In the career fire service, lifetime may mean the length of time required to become vested in a pension program. In other situations, personnel may complete a full career with one organization and move on to a higher rank in another, thereby giving a lifetime of work to the profession rather than to a single job.

13. *Initiative* — Employees are encouraged to develop a plan to confront a problem and then make it happen. Within the limits imposed by operational requirements, this concept may be applied to nonemergency projects and assignments.

14. *Esprit de corps* — Loyalty to the organization and peers resulting in greater organizational cohesion and harmony. This is a concept that the organization's leadership would like to make a permanent part of the culture. Younger generations of employees may be less supportive of the concept.

The most important elements of these are specialization, unity of command, scalar chain, and coordination by managers (the combining of authority and unity of direction). Their presence in the fire and emergency services has been, and continues to be, the foundation for most tables of organization.

to operate. His theories, published in 1916, are part the *Classical School of Management* theory and include views on the implementation of authority in the business process.

Fayol divided modern management into five functions that are still applicable in the twenty-first century. Experienced fire and emergency services personnel will recognize these functions as they are applied to their profession. The functions include the following:

- Planning
- Organizing
- Commanding
- Coordinating
- Controlling

Human Relations Theory

In response to the scientific approach to management as well as the growth of the labor movement, organizational theorists began paying more attention to workers and their unique capabilities in the organization. The new approach was based on the belief that the organization would benefit if its workers were satisfied. As a result, human resource departments were added to organizations to provide services and benefits to employees.

The human relations theory of management was based on the research of Elton Mayo of Harvard University. His best-known contribution to the research into worker productivity came from a study, known as the Hawthorne Study, conducted at Western Electric's Hawthorne plant in Cicero, Illinois, between 1927 and 1932. This study provided the first documented evidence to support the theory that workers are more productive when they are treated decently and given good working conditions.

For company officers, one lesson that can be learned from the Hawthorne study is evident. By showing a genuine concern for their subordinates' welfare, they will respond by being as creative, cooperative, and productive as possible. A more current example of the application of Mayo's theory – and one that company officers should apply daily – is what the Hewlett Packard Corporation calls *management by walking around* (MBWA). MBWA simply means that managers and supervisors should not be bound to their desks. They should take every opportunity to leave their offices and walk around the workplace, observing what is and is not going on, and talking with the workers.

Motivation-Hygiene Theory

After the hiatus in research into management and supervision caused by the Great Depression and World War II, Frederick Herzberg, a professor at Case Western Reserve University in Cleveland, Ohio, and two research assistants developed what they called the Motivation-Hygiene Theory or Two-Factor Theory in 1959. They interviewed hundreds of working professionals about what gave them satisfaction on the job and what made them feel dissatisfied. At the time, many managers still believed that money was the best motivator – give workers a raise, and their morale would improve, and they would be more productive. Likewise, if they were given more time off, they would be more satisfied and more motivated to work hard. However, the research did not support these assumptions.

What Herzberg found was that if pay, time off, and similar benefits were substandard for the industry or the area, they had a much greater potential for creating *dissatisfaction* than for producing satisfaction among workers – except in the short term. Giving workers a raise, more time off, or other similar benefits temporarily improves morale, satisfaction, and productivity. But after a relatively short time, these new pay scales, vacation schedules, etc., are perceived as the norm, and their motivational value disappears. Herzberg came to refer to pay and similar benefits as *hygiene factors* because they are necessary to prevent worker dissatisfaction. He found that compensation and other benefits are of little long-term motivational value.

According to Herzberg, the things that create and sustain long-term worker satisfaction (true motivators) are inherent in the work itself. If workers feel that what they are doing is important and that there is an opportunity for achievement, they derive considerable personal satisfaction from the job. In addition, if they receive appropriate recognition for doing the job well and are rewarded with increased responsibility and opportunities for advancement, they tend to be very satisfied and highly motivated

Company officers can apply Herzberg's theory on a daily basis. They should take every opportunity and, if necessary, *create* opportunities to remind their subordinates how important their work is to the citizens of the community. The company officer should remind subordinates of the importance of performing their duties well.

Management by Objectives

Peter Drucker, a contemporary of both Herzberg and Dr. Douglas McGregor, first described his theory of Management by Objectives (MBO) in 1954. This theory was based on the proposition that if workers could see the *big picture* — or the goal that was to be achieved — they could more readily understand how their individual roles fit into the overall plan. This vision would motivate workers by showing them how important their individual contributions were to achieving organizational goals. In addition, if everyone has a specific objective to achieve, they can plan for and work toward achieving their part of the overall goal. If individual objectives are achieved, collectively the goals and objectives of the organization will be achieved. One caution should be understood: Not all objectives are measurable. While the objective of *securing funding* is measurable, *satisfying customer needs* is not.

Another concept that was introduced by Drucker and can be applied to check the validity of any objective is the SMART concept – which states that objectives must be:

- Specific
- Measurable
- Achievable
- Realistic
- Time-related

SMART Example

The Rinkerville Fire Department's Fire and Life Safety Bureau will provide and install battery operated smoke detectors in all single family dwellings located within the city limits of Rinkerville. Two smoke detectors per residence will be provided and installed near the sleeping area and kitchen. The Rinkerville Chamber of Commerce will donate 1,500 smoke detectors. The completion of the project will be within one year of the beginning date, January 1, 2007.

Modern Management Theory

Although known by a variety of names, modern management is based on a very participative and democratic style of leadership. Like McGregor's Theory Y, it relies on a belief in the value of every worker's ideas and experience, that workers want to do a good job, and that they will derive great satisfaction from doing a good job. It is also based on a belief that decisions will be better if everyone has an opportunity to contribute to them.

Modern management is also based on a relentless pursuit of quality in both performance and products. The person who is most associated with this emphasis is the late Dr. W. Edwards Deming. Often cited as the architect of the post-World War II economic revival of Japanese industry, Deming is considered by many to be the father of Total Quality Management (TQM).

Total Quality Management

Between the end of World War II and his death in 1993, Dr. W. Edwards Deming was the creator and spokesperson for the concept of TQM. In the post-war period, Deming applied his theories of management to industry in war-torn Japan and is credited with helping Japan rebuild and achieve the world economic status it has in the twenty-first century. In the 1970s and 1980s, industry in the United States started to apply his theories in response to the rise in Japan's economic power.

Also known as *Continuous Quality Improvement (CQI)*, TQM has been adopted by many private businesses and public organizations. It is based on the following four elements:

- **Customer identification and feedback.** Organizations must continually monitor the needs of their customers and modify, innovate, or abandon programs or services as necessary to meet customer needs.

- **Tracking performance.** This requires a *process* orientation, rather than a *results* orientation. TQM focuses on the process of how something gets done and not on the individual who does it. Therefore, the purpose is to monitor the performance of the process to identify changes needed to improve quality.

- **Constant and continuous improvement.** TQM is based on a continuous effort to improve the organization's process for producing and delivering programs, services, and products. Quality service is consistently helpful, accurate, timely, and complete.

- **Employee participation in all processes.** The most important element of a successful TQM program is changing traditional ideas about managing people. To make TQM work, it is essential for the management to value and respect all employees and their opinions, encourage employee contributions, and provide employee training and education. Organizations that attempt to use TQM without true good intentions or sincerity will do more damage than had they had never embraced the process of employee participation.

Although Deming's theories are primarily focused on the management aspect of businesses, his central ideas, found in the book *Out of the Crisis*, have been adopted as key points of leadership. Over the 25 years since the book was published, the theories have become proven models in industry. The theory, and the model, is based on the 14 points shown in the following Information Box.

In the current decade, a new management model called *Six Sigma* has become popular, particularly in the computer industry. Six Sigma is an outgrowth of the TQM theory. It can be defined as a management philosophy, a statistic, or a process, depending on how the term Six Sigma is used. With many benefits, it can be a useful tool for the fire service. Currently, the Nashville (TN) Fire Department is applying Six Sigma to its daily nonemergency operations.

Six Sigma

As a management philosophy, Six Sigma is a customer-based approach that emphasizes that defects in manufacturing or services are expensive. Less defects results in lower operating costs and higher customer satisfaction. In the economic marketplace, the producer with the lowest cost and highest value is the most competitive provider of goods and services.

In the public sector, the ability to provide services on a cost-effective basis increases the support of the external customers and stakeholders. When the term *defects* is used in this situation, it can mean unacceptable response times, high out-of-service times, high maintenance costs, high job-related injuries, or inefficient use of staffing. The application of the Six Sigma management philosophy can help to minimize these types of defects.

The Six Sigma process consists of defining, measuring, analyzing, improving, and controlling the elements of the production process. This

Deming's 14 Points

1. Create constancy of purpose towards improvement through long-term planning.
2. Adopt the TQM philosophy by management as well as the workforce.
3. End dependence on inspection of products and processes. Inspections will be unnecessary since quality will be assured through the TQM philosophy.
4. To reduce variations (and cost) in supplies, use a single supplier for any one item.
5. Improve constantly and forever by working to reduce variation.
6. Institute training on the job in order to make processes consistent.
7. Institute leadership, which is employee-focused (supervision is output-focused according to Deming).
8. Cease the use of management by fear.
9. Break down barriers between departments by implementing the concept of the internal customer; each department serves the other departments that use its products or services.
10. Eliminate slogans; they are counter-productive and only serve to intimidate employees..
11. Eliminate management by objectives (MBO).
12. Remove barriers to pride of workmanship.
13. Institute education and self-improvement that can increase employee satisfaction.
14. The transformation to a TQM philosophy is everyone's job – workers and management.

is not a new process. These process components are found in the TQM system. Six Sigma is simply the application of these components to a product or service provider. In the public sector, Six Sigma can be used to address issues and problems that may include station location, budget allocations, or communication problems.

The many benefits of Six Sigma include the following:

- Decrease in defects that reach the external customer
- Decreased waste of resources
- Improved supply-chain management efficiency
- Reduced costs to provide goods and services
- Development and application of standard operating procedures
- Improved safety performance
- Reductions of accidents and lost-time injuries
- Focus on external customer and stakeholders
- Improved customer relations
- Reduction in customer complaints
- Improved external customer loyalty
- Success measurements based on customer requirements

- Better understanding of processes
- Improved time management
- Employee motivation
- Improved team building
- Development of leadership skills
- Improved management training
- Improved supervisor training
- Improved project management skills
- Decisions based on accurate data
- Sustained improvements
- Systematic problem solving
- Better decision making
- Data analysis performed before decision making
- Better strategic planning
- Breaks down barriers between divisions and functions
- Alignments with strategic vision, values, and mission statement

The company officer should examine the application of Six Sigma management philosophy and consider its use in fire and emergency service organizations and decreases injuries on the fire ground, hence the reason for more information.

Appendix P
Private and Nongovernmental Organizations

There are a large number of private and professional organizations with which company officers should be familiar. Each of these organizations has a specific role in the fire service, and the company officer should understand what those roles are and when they can be of assistance.

Congressional Fire Services Caucus

With more than 300 dedicated members, the Congressional Fire Services Caucus is the largest congressional caucus on Capitol Hill. Providing a bipartisan representation, the members of the caucus are drawn together by a mutual concern for the safety of our citizens and a respect for those who respond to fires and other emergencies.

Congressional Fire Services Institute

The Congressional Fire Services Institute is a nonpartisan, nonprofit organization dedicated to the task of educating the members of both houses of Congress on issues of importance to the emergency services. Because of its nonpartisan nature and the expertise of its members, the institute is often consulted by members of Congress who need objective information about the emergency services and related issues.

International Fire Service Accreditation Congress (IFSAC)

IFSAC is an accreditation system operated by member organizations. Its purpose is to accredit entities that provide certification of fire service personnel, utilizing professional qualification standards at the state, province, or territory level. IFSAC accredits training organizations in numerous states, provinces, and foreign nations. Within IFSAC there are two separate and distinct assemblies, each with its own board of governors. The Degree Assembly accredits qualifying programs at degree-granting institutions such as community colleges and four-year institutions. The Certificate Assembly accredits training entities that certify those successfully completing specified training courses according to recognized standards.

International Fire Service Training Association (IFSTA)

IFSTA is an educational alliance formed in 1934 to develop training materials for the fire service. Committees meet each July (and at other times as needed) to review existing or proposed manuals. All validated manuals are published by the Fire Protection Publications division of Oklahoma State University. IFSTA's objectives are to:

- Develop training materials and visual aids for publication.
- Add new techniques and developments.
- Delete obsolete and outmoded methods.
- Validate training material for publication.
- Provide materials for students and instructors to assist in certification.
- Upgrade the fire service through training.

IFSTA publications are used in all the U.S. states and Canadian provinces. A number of federal government agencies and several foreign countries have adopted the IFSTA publications as their official training manuals.

International Municipal Signal Association (IMSA)

IMSA was organized in 1896 as an educational, nonprofit organization dedicated to conveying knowledge, technical information, and guidance to its membership. Its current membership of more than 3,000 consists of municipal signal and communication department heads and their first assistants. The range of communications covered includes traffic control, fire alarms, and police alarms. There are sixteen sections of IMSA based on geographical areas in the United States and Canada and a sustaining section to serve the regional needs of its members. The *IMSA Signal Magazine* is the association's bimonthly publication.

International Society of Fire Service Instructors (ISFSI)

Organized in 1960, the International Society of Fire Service Instructors is composed of people responsible for training firefighters, fire officers, and rescue and emergency medical personnel. Its goal is to develop uniform professional standards for fire service instructors, to assist in the development of fire service instructors through better training and educational opportunities, to provide the means for continual upgrading of such instructors through in-service training, and to actively promote the role of the fire service instructor in the total fire service organization. It has members in all fifty states and ten foreign countries.

National Board on Fire Service Professional Qualifications (NBFSPQ)

The National Board on Fire Service Professional Qualifications (NBFSPQ) was created to improve life safety and fire protection through a national system of fire service professional qualifications certification and accreditation. The NBFSPQ supports the development of NFPA standards (NFPA 1000 series) on certification and accreditation, the utilization of such standards, a National Registry of Fire Service Professional Qualifications certification, and the NFPA Fire Service Professional Qualification Standards. Accreditation of certifying organizations is carried out by the National Professional Qualifications Board (NPQB) under the direction of the board of the directors of the NBFSPQ. The board of directors receives advice from an advisory council made up of representatives of those organizations utilizing the system.

The board of directors represents the organizations appointed August 2, 1989, by the former Joint Council of National Fire Service Organizations to a select committee for determining the future for a national fire service certification accreditation program. The work of the select committee in establishing the NBFSPQ constituted the last activity of the former Joint Council.

National Volunteer Fire Council (NVFC)

The NVFC was organized in 1976 as an organization of various state volunteer firefighters associations and of individual volunteer firefighters. Its purpose is to represent and pursue the interests of volunteer firefighters and volunteer fire departments throughout the United States. Among its objectives are to provide a forum for the formulation of unified positions concerning developments nationally affecting volunteers and to support fire prevention education in the lower grades of school systems.

International Association of Arson Investigators (IAAI)

The International Association of Arson Investigators was formed at Purdue University, West Lafayette, Indiana, in 1949, when insurance industry, fire service, and law enforcement personnel from the United States and Canada met to discuss the growing arson problem and the need for training and education in fire investigation. The association has the following objectives:

- To unite for mutual benefit those public officials and private persons engaged in the control of arson and kindred crime

- To provide for exchange of technical information and developments

- To cooperate with other law enforcement agencies and associations to further fire prevention and the suppression of crime

- To encourage high professional standards of conduct among arson investigators

- To continually strive to eliminate all factors that interfere with administration of crime suppression

Active membership in the IAAI is open to any representative (21 years of age or older) of government or of a governmental agency and to any representative of a business or industrial concern who is actively engaged in some phase of the suppression of arson and whose qualifications meet the requirements of the membership committee of the association. Associate membership is open to persons not qualified for active membership after determination of their qualification by the membership committee. The IAAI publishes a quarterly bulletin, *The Fire and Arson Investigator*, and conducts an annual meeting in conjunction with a conference on arson, normally as part of a state arson seminar. Various committees are organized to assist the association in its attack on the arson problem, such as the Fire Marshal Advisory Committee, the Fraud Fires and Organized Crime Committee, the Insurance Advisory Committee, the Legislative Committee, the Photography Committee, the Police Advisory Committee, the Riots and Civil Disorders Committee, and the Technical Advisory and Training Committee.

International Association of Black Professional Fire Fighters (IABPFF)

The IABPFF was organized in 1970 with the following goals:

- To create a liaison among black firefighters across the nation

- To compile information concerning injustices that exist in the working conditions in the fire service and to implement action to correct them

- To collect and evaluate data on all deleterious conditions where minorities exist

- To see that competent blacks are recruited and employed as firefighters where they reside

- To promote interracial progress throughout the fire service

- To aid in motivating African-Americans to seek advancement to elevated ranks (Figure 8.22)

The organization is a life member of the National Association for the Advancement of Colored People.

International Association of Fire Chiefs (IAFC)

The IAFC was organized in 1873 to further the professional advancement of the fire service and to ensure and maintain greater protection of life and property from fire. Its purposes are fulfilled by:

- Conducting research and studies of major problems affecting the fire service at community, state, provincial, regional, national, and international levels

- Developing and implementing an active program vital to the continued well-being of the fire service

- Serving as the recognized organization for the exchange of ideas, information, knowledge, and experience in areas affecting the safety of life and property from fire

- Encouraging and developing public education in fire prevention to preserve human life and material resources

- Promoting educational programs in the best interests of the fire service.

Active membership includes the following classifications: chief of department and all chief officers of regularly organized public, governmental, or industrial fire departments; state and provincial fire marshals; fire commissioners and/or fire directors who devote full time to administration and fire fighting operations. Associate membership includes fire commissioners and/or fire directors not responsible for administration or for fire-fighting operations; directors of public safety; public officials; officers and members of fire departments; individuals interested in the protection of life and property from fire; and officers of recognized fire prevention organizations. Sustaining membership includes individuals and/or concerns engaged in the manufacture or sale of emergency apparatus or equipment and/or individuals or concerns otherwise interested in the field of fire protection. Other membership categories are active life members, associate life members, and honorary life members.

The IAFC also has more than twenty committees, or interest groups, that function for the organization including the Metropolitan Committee (chiefs of the major cities) who serve the association in the special areas of their concern. These committees include arson, communications, emergency medical services, fire prevention, hazardous materials, health and safety, industrial and federal fire departments, professional development, urban search and rescue, and volunteers. The IAFC holds an annual conference with a major technical and educational exhibition each year and offers a series of publications on fire service matters to all interested persons. It has a membership of more than 10,000 and a headquarters staff of approximately 15.

Metropolitan Committee of the IAFC

The Metropolitan Committee of the International Association of *Fire Chiefs*, also commonly known as the Metro Chiefs, was organized in 1965. The membership of the Metropolitan Committee is limited to active fire chiefs of cities or jurisdictions having a population of more than 200,000 or a minimum of 400 career members and who are current members of the International Association of Fire Chiefs. The mission of the Metropolitan Committee is to assist the International Association of Fire Chiefs in developing and propagating policy relating to major fire departments.

Emergency Medical Services (EMS)

Almost 90 percent of all fire protection agencies in the United States provide some level of emergency medical service. This service may be first responder, emergency medical technician-basic (EMT-B), or paramedic. A growing number of these agencies provide cardiac defibrillation as well. The IAFC established an EMS section to assist local fire chiefs with the challenges presented by this very worthwhile community service.

International Association of Fire Fighters (IAFF)

Organized in 1918, the IAFF has approximately 175,000 members in the United States and Canada. The IAFF is affiliated with the American Federation of Labor and Congress of Industrial Organizations in the United States and the Canadian Labor Congress (AFL-CIO/CLC). Any person who is engaged as a permanent and paid employee of a fire depart-

ment is eligible for active membership through the chartered local, state, or provincial associations and joint councils. Conventions of the association are biannual. The IAFF headquarters provides a variety of services to the membership including technical assistance.

National Registry of Emergency Medical Technicians (NREMT)

NREMT registers emergency medical services providers across the United States. It is a private not-for-profit agency. The NREMT board of directors is comprised of members from national EMS organizations or who have expertise in the field. Established in 1970, the NREMT has tested more than 750,000 emergency medical technicians.

Underwriters Laboratories Inc.

Underwriters Laboratories Inc. (UL) in the U.S. and Underwriters' Laboratories of Canada (ULC) are not-for-profit corporations having as their sole objective the promotion of public safety through the conduct of "scientific investigation, study, experiments, and tests, to determine the relation of various materials, devices, products, equipment, constructions, methods, and systems to hazards appurtenant thereto or to the use thereof affecting life and property and to ascertain, define, and publish standards, classifications, and specifications for materials, devices, products, equipment, constructions, methods, and systems affecting such hazards, and other information tending to reduce or prevent bodily injury, loss of life, and property damage from such hazards." Formed separately by the same founder, these two organizations have now joined. An independent public service corporation, UL/ULC has no capital stock or shareholders and exists solely for the service it renders in the field of fire, crime, and casualty prevention.

Factory Mutual Research Corporation (FMRC)

The research function of Factory Mutual Research Corporation (FMRC) is to conduct research and development in the field of property loss control. This activity serves the needs of the Factory Mutual System and is available to other entities, such as government agencies, trade associations, and individual businesses, through contracts.

The scope of the research ranges from basic investigation into the nature of fire to the development of standards for direct use by industry in establishing practices designed to minimize loss. Although such standards are intended primarily for Factory Mutual System members, they are recognized and widely used by others. Between the extremes of basic research and standards, major effort is made in the area of applied research. This activity includes studies, surveys, operations research, experimentation, laboratory-scale testing, and full-scale testing to evaluate hazards and protection of storage, manufacturing operations, and construction arrangements.

Building and Fire Research Laboratory (BFRL)

Formerly the National Bureau of Standards' Center for Fire Research, the Building and Fire Research Laboratory (BFRL) of the National Institute of Standards and Technology (NIST) is located in the NIST complex at Gaithersburg, Maryland. The laboratory conducts research designed to improve codes and standards. This work is done by developing improved or new test methods and by using large-scale tests to validate the test method developments. Work is also conducted on acquiring knowledge of the properties of materials and their performance in fire conditions. The laboratories also create mathematical models to predict performance of materials under fire conditions.

Society of Fire Protection Engineers (SFPE)

Organized in 1950, the Society of Fire Protection Engineers is the professional society for engineers involved in the multifaceted field of fire protection engineering. The purposes of the society are to advance the art and science of fire protection engineering and its allied fields, to maintain a high ethical standing among its members, and to foster fire protection engineering education. Its worldwide members include engineers in private practice, industry, and local, regional, and national government, as well as technical members of the insurance industry. Forty chapters of the society are located in the United States, Canada, Europe, and Australia.

Membership in the society is open to those possessing engineering or physical science qualifications coupled with experience in the field and to those in associated professional fields.

The society serves as an international clearinghouse for fire protection engineering state-of-the-art advances and information. It publishes the *SFPE Bulletin*, a newsletter with regular features; the *Journal of Fire Protection Engineering*; and a series of "Technology Reports" covering technical developments of interest to the engineering community. It also publishes occasional special reports.

Appendix Q
HSPD-5

the
White House
President George W. Bush

For Immediate Release
Office of the Press Secretary
February 28, 2003

Homeland Security Presidential Directive/HSPD-5

Subject: Management of Domestic Incidents

Purpose

(1) To enhance the ability of the United States to manage domestic incidents by establishing a single, comprehensive national incident management system.

Definitions

(2) In this directive:

(a) the term "Secretary" means the Secretary of Homeland Security.

(b) the term "Federal departments and agencies" means those executive departments enumerated in 5 U.S.C. 101, together with the Department of Homeland Security; independent establishments as defined by 5 U.S.C. 104(1); government corporations as defined by 5 U.S.C. 103(1); and the United States Postal Service.

(c) the terms "State," "local," and the "United States" when it is used in a geographical sense, have the same meanings as used in the Homeland Security Act of 2002, Public Law 107-296.

Policy

(3) To prevent, prepare for, respond to, and recover from terrorist attacks, major disasters, and other emergencies, the United States Government shall establish a single, compre-hensive approach to domestic incident management. The objective of the United States Government is to ensure that all levels of government across the Nation have the capability to work efficiently and effectively together, using a national approach to domestic incident management. In these efforts, with regard to domestic incidents, the United States Government treats crisis management and consequence management as a single, integrated function, rather than as two separate functions.

(4) The Secretary of Homeland Security is the principal Federal official for domestic incident management. Pursuant to the Homeland Security Act of 2002, the Secretary is responsible for coordinating Federal operations within the United States to prepare for, respond to, and recover from terrorist attacks, major disasters, and other emergencies. The Secretary shall coordinate the Federal Government's resources utilized in response to or recovery from terrorist attacks, major disasters,

or other emergencies if and when any one of the following four conditions applies: (1) a Federal department or agency acting under its own authority has requested the assistance of the Secretary; (2) the resources of State and local authorities are overwhelmed and Federal assistance has been requested by the appropriate State and local authorities; (3) more than one Federal department or agency has become substantially involved in responding to the incident; or

(4) the Secretary has been directed to assume responsibility for managing the domestic incident by the President.

(5) Nothing in this directive alters, or impedes the ability to carry out, the authorities of Federal departments and agencies to perform their responsibilities under law. All Federal departments and agencies shall cooperate with the Secretary in the Secretary's domestic incident management role.

(6) The Federal Government recognizes the roles and responsibilities of State and local authorities in domestic incident management. Initial responsibility for managing domestic incidents generally falls on State and local authorities. The Federal Government will assist State and local authorities when their resources are overwhelmed, or when Federal interests are involved. The Secretary will coordinate with State and local governments to ensure adequate planning, equipment, training, and exercise activities. The Secretary will also provide assistance to State and local governments to develop all-hazards plans and capabilities, including those of greatest importance to the security of the United States, and will ensure that State, local, and Federal plans are compatible.

(7) The Federal Government recognizes the role that the private and nongovernmental sectors play in preventing, preparing for, responding to, and recovering from terrorist attacks, major disasters, and other emergencies. The Secretary will coordinate with the private and nongovernmental sectors to ensure adequate planning, equipment, training, and exercise activities and to promote partnerships to address incident management capabilities.

(8) The Attorney General has lead responsibility for criminal investigations of terrorist acts or terrorist threats by individuals or groups inside the United States, or directed at United States citizens or institutions abroad, where such acts are within the Federal criminal jurisdiction of the United States, as well as for related intelligence collection activities within the United States, subject to the National Security Act of 1947 and other applicable law, Executive Order 12333, and Attorney General-approved procedures pursuant to that Executive Order. Generally acting through the Federal Bureau of Investigation, the Attorney General, in cooperation with other Federal departments and agencies engaged in activities to protect our national security, shall also coordinate the activities of the other members of the law enforcement community to detect, prevent, preempt, and disrupt terrorist attacks against the United States. Following a terrorist threat or an actual incident that falls within the criminal jurisdiction of the United States, the full capabilities of the United States shall be dedicated, consistent with United States law and with activities of other Federal departments and agencies to protect our national security, to assisting the Attorney General to identify the perpetrators and bring them to justice. The Attorney General and the Secretary shall establish appropriate relationships and mechanisms for cooperation and coordination between their two departments.

(9) Nothing in this directive impairs or otherwise affects the authority of the Secretary of Defense over the Department of Defense, including the chain of command for military forces from the President as Commander in Chief, to the Secretary of Defense, to the commander of military forces, or military command and control procedures. The Secretary of Defense shall provide military support to civil authorities for domestic incidents as directed by the President or when consistent with military readiness and appropriate under the circumstances and the law. The Secretary of Defense shall retain command of military forces providing civil support. The Secretary of Defense and the Secretary shall establish appropriate relationships and mechanisms for cooperation and coordination between their two departments.

(10) The Secretary of State has the responsibility, consistent with other United States Government activities to protect our national security, to coordinate international activities related to the prevention, preparation, response, and recovery from a domestic incident, and for the protection of United States citizens and United States interests overseas. The Secretary of State

and the Secretary shall establish appropriate relationships and mechanisms for cooperation and coordination between their two departments.

(11) The Assistant to the President for Homeland Security and the Assistant to the President for National Security Affairs shall be responsible for interagency policy coordination on domestic and international incident management, respectively, as directed by the President. The Assistant to the President for Homeland Security and the Assistant to the President for National Security Affairs shall work together to ensure that the United States domestic and international incident management efforts are seamlessly united.

(12) The Secretary shall ensure that, as appropriate, information related to domestic incidents is gathered and provided to the public, the private sector, State and local authorities, Federal departments and agencies, and, generally through the Assistant to the President for Homeland Security, to the President. The Secretary shall provide standardized, quantitative reports to the Assistant to the President for Homeland Security on the readiness and preparedness of the Nation -- at all levels of government -- to prevent, prepare for, respond to, and recover from domestic incidents.

(13) Nothing in this directive shall be construed to grant to any Assistant to the President any authority to issue orders to Federal departments and agencies, their officers, or their employees.

Tasking

(14) The heads of all Federal departments and agencies are directed to provide their full and prompt cooperation, resources, and support, as appropriate and consistent with their own responsibilities for protecting our national security, to the Secretary, the Attorney General, the Secretary of Defense, and the Secretary of State in the exercise of the individual leadership responsibilities and missions assigned in paragraphs (4), (8), (9), and (10), respectively, above.

(15) The Secretary shall develop, submit for review to the Homeland Security Council, and administer a National Incident Management System (NIMS). This system will provide a consistent nationwide approach for Federal, State, and local governments to work effectively and efficiently together to prepare for, respond to, and recover from domestic incidents, regardless of cause, size, or complexity. To provide for interoperability and compatibility among Federal, State, and local capabilities, the NIMS will include a core set of concepts, principles, terminology, and technologies covering the incident command system; multi-agency coordination systems; unified command; training; identification and management of resources (including systems for classifying types of resources); qualifications and certification; and the collection, tracking, and reporting of incident information and incident resources.

(16) The Secretary shall develop, submit for review to the Homeland Security Council, and administer a National Response Plan (NRP). The Secretary shall consult with appropriate Assistants to the President (including the Assistant to the President for Economic Policy) and the Director of the Office of Science and Technology Policy, and other such Federal officials as may be appropriate, in developing and implementing the NRP. This plan shall integrate Federal Government domestic prevention, preparedness, response, and recovery plans into one all-discipline, all-hazards plan. The NRP shall be unclassified. If certain operational aspects require classification, they shall be included in classified annexes to the NRP.

(a) The NRP, using the NIMS, shall, with regard to response to domestic incidents, provide the structure and mechanisms for national level policy and operational direction for Federal support to State and local incident managers and for exercising direct Federal authorities and responsibilities, as appropriate.

(b) The NRP will include protocols for operating under different threats or threat levels; incorporation of existing Federal emergency and incident management plans (with appropriate modifications and revisions) as either integrated components of the NRP or as supporting operational plans; and additional opera-tional plans or annexes, as appropriate, including public affairs and intergovernmental communications.

(c) The NRP will include a consistent approach to reporting incidents, providing assessments, and making recommendations to the President, the Secretary, and the Homeland Security Council.

(d) The NRP will include rigorous requirements for continuous improvements from testing, exercising, experience with incidents, and new information and technologies.

(17) The Secretary shall:

(a) By April 1, 2003, (1) develop and publish an initial version of the NRP, in consultation with other Federal departments and agencies; and (2) provide the Assistant to the President for Homeland Security with a plan for full development and implementation of the NRP.

(b) By June 1, 2003, (1) in consultation with Federal departments and agencies and with State and local governments, develop a national system of standards, guidelines, and protocols to implement the NIMS; and (2) establish a mechanism for ensuring ongoing management and maintenance of the NIMS, including regular consultation with other Federal departments and agencies and with State and local governments.

(c) By September 1, 2003, in consultation with Federal departments and agencies and the Assistant to the President for Homeland Security, review existing authorities and regulations and prepare recommendations for the President on revisions necessary to implement fully the NRP.

(18) The heads of Federal departments and agencies shall adopt the NIMS within their departments and agencies and shall provide support and assistance to the Secretary in the development and maintenance of the NIMS. All Federal departments and agencies will use the NIMS in their domestic incident management and emergency prevention, preparedness, response, recovery, and mitigation activities, as well as those actions taken in support of State or local entities. The heads of Federal departments and agencies shall participate in the NRP, shall assist and support the Secretary in the development and maintenance of the NRP, and shall participate in and use domestic incident reporting systems and protocols established by the Secretary.

(19) The head of each Federal department and agency shall:

(a) By June 1, 2003, make initial revisions to existing plans in accordance with the initial version of the NRP.

(b) By August 1, 2003, submit a plan to adopt and implement the NIMS to the Secretary and the Assistant to the President for Homeland Security. The Assistant to the President for Homeland Security shall advise the President on whether such plans effectively implement the NIMS.

(20) Beginning in Fiscal Year 2005, Federal departments and agencies shall make adoption of the NIMS a requirement, to the extent permitted by law, for providing Federal preparedness assistance through grants, contracts, or other activities. The Secretary shall develop standards and guidelines for determining whether a State or local entity has adopted the NIMS.

Technical and Conforming Amendments to National Security Presidential Directive-1 (NSPD-1)

(21) NSPD-1 ("Organization of the National Security Council System") is amended by replacing the fifth sentence of the third paragraph on the first page with the following: "The Attorney General, the Secretary of Homeland Security, and the Director of the Office of Management and Budget shall be invited to attend meetings pertaining to their responsibilities.".

Technical and Conforming Amendments to National Security Presidential Directive-8 (NSPD-8)

(22) NSPD-8 ("National Director and Deputy National Security Advisor for Combating Terrorism") is amended by striking "and the Office of Homeland Security," on page 4, and inserting "the Department of Homeland Security, and the Homeland Security Council" in lieu thereof.

Technical and Conforming Amendments to Homeland Security Presidential Directive-2 (HSPD-2)

(23) HSPD-2 ("Combating Terrorism Through Immigration Policies") is amended as follows:

(a) striking "the Commissioner of the Immigration and Naturalization Service (INS)" in the second sentence of the second paragraph in section 1, and inserting "the Secretary of Homeland Security" in lieu thereof ;

(b) striking "the INS," in the third paragraph in section 1, and inserting "the Department of Homeland Security" in lieu thereof;

(c) inserting ", the Secretary of Homeland Security," after "The Attorney General" in the fourth paragraph in section 1;

(d) inserting ", the Secretary of Homeland Security," after "the Attorney General" in the fifth paragraph in section 1;

(e) striking "the INS and the Customs Service" in the first sentence of the first paragraph of section 2, and inserting "the Department of Homeland Security" in lieu thereof;

(f) striking "Customs and INS" in the first sentence of the second paragraph of section 2, and inserting "the Department of Homeland Security" in lieu thereof;

(g) striking "the two agencies" in the second sentence of the second paragraph of section 2, and inserting "the Department of Homeland Security" in lieu thereof;

(h) striking "the Secretary of the Treasury" wherever it appears in section 2, and inserting "the Secretary of Homeland Security" in lieu thereof;

(i) inserting ", the Secretary of Homeland Security," after "The Secretary of State" wherever the latter appears in section 3;

(j) inserting ", the Department of Homeland Security," after "the Department of State," in the second sentence in the third paragraph in section 3;

(k) inserting "the Secretary of Homeland Security," after "the Secretary of State," in the first sentence of the fifth paragraph of section 3;

(l) striking "INS" in the first sentence of the sixth paragraph of section 3, and inserting "Department of Homeland Security" in lieu thereof;

(m) striking "the Treasury" wherever it appears in section 4 and inserting "Homeland Security" in lieu thereof;

(n) inserting ", the Secretary of Homeland Security," after "the Attorney General" in the first sentence in section 5; and

(o) inserting ", Homeland Security" after "State" in the first sentence of section 6.

Technical and Conforming Amendments to Homeland Security Presidential Directive-3 (HSPD-3)

(24) The Homeland Security Act of 2002 assigned the responsibility for administering the Homeland Security Advisory System to the Secretary of Homeland Security. Accordingly, HSPD-3 of March 11, 2002 ("Homeland Security Advisory System") is amended as follows:

(a) replacing the third sentence of the second paragraph entitled "Homeland Security Advisory System" with "Except in exigent circumstances, the Secretary of Homeland Security shall seek the views of the Attorney General, and any other federal agency heads the Secretary deems appropriate, including other members of the Homeland Security Council, on the Threat Condition to be assigned."

(b) inserting "At the request of the Secretary of Homeland Security, the Department of Justice shall permit and facilitate the use of delivery systems administered or managed by the Department of Justice for the purposes of delivering threat information pursuant to the Homeland Security Advisory System." as a new paragraph after the fifth paragraph of the section entitled "Homeland Security Advisory System."

(c) inserting ", the Secretary of Homeland Security" after "The Director of Central Intelligence" in the first sentence of the seventh paragraph of the section entitled "Homeland Security Advisory System".

(d) striking "Attorney General" wherever it appears (except in the sentences referred to in subsections (a) and (c) above), and inserting "the Secretary of Homeland Security" in lieu thereof; and

(e) striking the section entitled "Comment and Review Periods."

GEORGE W. BUSH

Appendix R
SCBA Survey Form

1. Primary Use Applications:

Fire fighting operations	Yes	No
Rescue operations	Yes	No
HAZ MAT operations	Yes	No
Other:	Yes	No

2. What features are most important for new SCBA?

NFPA compliance	Yes	No
Capable of future NFPA upgrade	Yes	No
Comfort	Yes	No
Communications	Yes	No
Individual facepiece and sizes	Yes	No
Electronic features	Yes	No
Low lifecycle cost	Yes	No
Ease of use while wearing protective clothing	Yes	No
Ease of cleaning/disinfecting	Yes	No
Proven performance	Yes	No
Distributor service and support	Yes	No
SCBA warranty	Yes	No
SCBA maintenance requirements	Yes	No

3. SCBA working pressure:

4 500 psig cylinders: • Lighter weight • Low profile • Choice of duration (30-45-60 minutes) 2 216 psig cylinders: • Lightweight (composite cylinders) • Refill capability – cascade *vs.* compressor	4 500 psig	2 216 psig
Fill station capability	4 500 psig	2 216 psig

4. What accessory options are important?

Integrated PASS alarms	Yes	No
Buddy-breathing capabilities	Yes	No
Airline capabilities for extended duration – HAZ MAT/Confined space	Yes	No
Rapid cylinder refill option	Yes	No
Communications	Yes	No
● Amplification	Yes	No
● Radio interface	Yes	No

5. How many SCBA are required?

Total number of SCBA required	
Total number of spare cylinders required	
Rated duration: 30 Minute	
45 Minute (4 500 psig)	
60 Minute (4 500 psig)	

6. How will the department pay for this purchase?

Cash purchase	Yes	No
Lease-purchase options	Yes	No
● City/county/township finance	Yes	No
● Vendor finance programs	Yes	No
Other:	Yes	No

7. How many different SCBA will be considered?

Scott Air-Pak 2.2	Yes	No
Scott Air-Pak 3.0	Yes	No
Scott Air-Pak 4.5	Yes	No
MSA MMR	Yes	No
Survivair Panther	Yes	No
Draeger	Yes	No
ISI Viking	Yes	No
Interspiro	Yes	No

8. Which SCBA distributors will be considered?

Distributor	Contact Person and Phone	SCBA Supplied

9. Who will provide SCBA training after purchase?

SCBA distributor	Yes	No
Department training officer	Yes	No

10. Who will provide service and testing of SCBA after purchase?

SCBA distributor	Yes	No
Department personnel	Yes	No

11. Who will initiate SCBA?

Record format	Department	Distributor
SCBA identification	Department	Distributor
Facepiece fit testing and records	Department	Distributor

12. Will current SCBA be:

Kept for backup/training?	Yes	No
Traded in to offset purchase price?	Yes	No
Disposed of by SCBA distributor?	Yes	No
Sold by department?	Yes	No
Donated by department?	Yes	No

Appendix S
Equipment Evaluation Form

Rank _____   Name _____

Date _____   Location _____

(1) Strongly Disagree
(2) Disagree
(3) No Opinion or Not Applicable
(4) Agree
(5) Strongly Agree

1. The SCBA was easy to don.   1   2   3   4   5

_____

2. After donning, the SCBA fit comfortably.   1   2   3   4   5

_____

3. The facepiece is easy to don.   1   2   3   4   5

_____

4. The facepiece and head harness do not interfere
    with head protection.   1   2   3   4   5

_____

5. It is easy to breathe with the regulator undocked
    from the facepiece.   1   2   3   4   5

_____

6. The regulator is easy to dock/undock and
    remains secure.   1   2   3   4   5

_____

7. It is easy to breathe with air flowing.   1   2   3   4   5

_____

8. The purge/bypass is easy to operate.   1   2   3   4   5

_____

9. It is easy to determine when *my* PASS device activates.   1   2   3   4   5

10. The PASS device is easy to reset.   1   2   3   4   5

11. I felt balanced wearing the SCBA while:
    A. Walking   1   2   3   4   5
    B. Climbing ladder   1   2   3   4   5
    C. Crawling   1   2   3   4   5
    D. Raising arms and pulling   1   2   3   4   5

12. The air-pressure gauge is easy to read.   1   2   3   4   5

13. The low-air alarm is easy to hear and identify.   1   2   3   4   5

14. The cylinder valve is easy to turn off.   1   2   3   4   5

15. The cylinder is easy to change.   1   2   3   4   5

16. Communication is clear with the facepiece on.   1   2   3   4   5

17. The communication system is clear.   1   2   3   4   5

Total Points _____ /100 possible

Formula for Calculating Frequency and Severity of Risk

The following formulas may be used to calculate the frequency or incident rate and the severity of incidents.

The Occupational Safety and Health Administration (OSHA) calculates the frequency (incident rate) as follows:

$$N/EH \times 200{,}000 = IR$$

Where:

N = number of injuries and/or illnesses

EH = total hours worked by all employees during the calendar year

$200{,}000$ = base for 100 full-time equivalent employees (provides *standardization between agencies and companies*)

IR = incident rate

OSHA calculates the severity as follows:

$$LWD/EH \times 200{,}000 = S$$

Where:

LWD = loss work days

EH = total hours worked by all employees during the calendar year

$200{,}000$ = base for 100 full-time equivalent employees

S = severity rate

Another method is to assign values to the frequency and severity in the following formula:

$$R = S \times IR$$

Where:

R = risk

S = severity

IR = incident rate

Assessment of Severity

8.	Extreme	Multiple deaths or widespread destruction may result from hazard.
7.	Very High	Potential death or injury or severe financial loss may result.
6.	High	Permanent disabling injury may result.
5.	Serious	Loss time injury greater than 28 days or considerable financial loss.
4.	Moderate	Loss time injury of 4 to 28 days or moderate financial loss.
3.	Minor	Loss time injury up to 3 days.
2.	Slight	Minor injury resulting in no loss of time or slight financial loss.
1.	Minimal	No loss of time injury or financial loss to organization.

Assessment of Incident Rate

7.	Frequent	Occurs weekly.
6.	Very Likely	Occurs once every few months.
5.	Likely	Occurs about once a year.
4.	Occasional	Occurs annually in the United States.
3.	Rare	Occurs every 10 to 30 years.
2.	Exceptional	Occurs every 10 to 30 years in the United States.
1.	Unlikely	May occur once in 10,000 years within the global fire service.

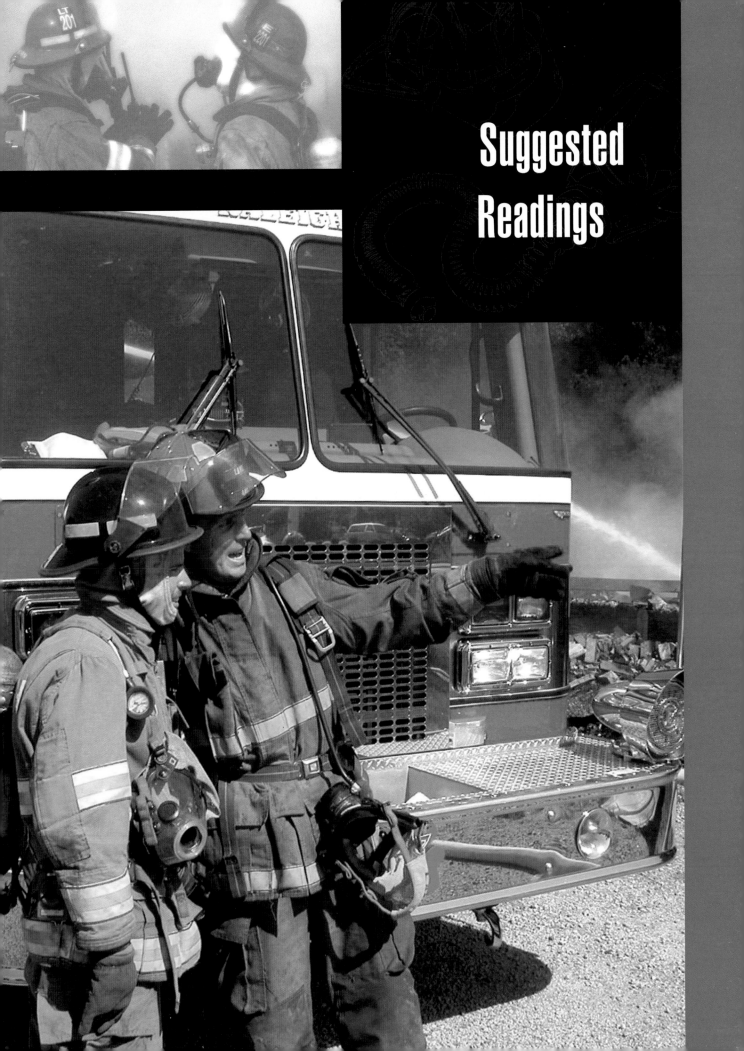

Suggested
Readings

Suggested Readings

Anderson, Gregory M., and Robert L. Lorber, Ph.D. *Safety 24/7: Building an Incident-Free Culture.* Plano: Back Porch Creative, 2006.

Badaracco, Joseph L. *Defining Moments: When Managers Must Choose Between Right and Right.* Boston: Harvard Business School Press, 1997.

Beebe, Steven A., and Susan J. Beebe. *Public Speaking: An Audience-Centered Approach.* Needham Heights: Pearson, Allyn & Bacon, 2002.

Bennett, Lawrence T. *Fire and EMS Law for Officers: Employment Best Practices.* Oklahoma State University: Fire Protection Publications, 2005.

Bennett, Lawrence T. *Fire and EMS Law for Officers: Safety (Including Lights and Sirens).* Oklahoma State University: Fire Protection Publications, 2005.

Brill, Laura. *Business Writing Quick & Easy,* 2nd Edition. New York: AMACOM, 1989.

Bruce, Andy. *Project Management.* New York: Dorling Kindersley, 2000.

Brunacini, Alan. *Essentials of Fire Department Customer Service.* Oklahoma State University: Fire Protection Publications, 1996.

Brunacini, Alan. *Fire Command.* Oklahoma State University: Fire Protection Publications, 2002.

Bryson, John M. *Strategic Planning for Public and Nonprofit Organizations: A Guide to Strengthening and Sustaining Organizational Achievement.* San Francisco: Jossey-Bass, John A. Wiley & Sons, 1995.

Cantonwine, Sheila. *Safety Training That Delivers — How to Design and Present Better Technical Training.* Des Plaines: American Society of Safety Engineers, 1999.

Carter, Harry, Ph.D. *Fire Fighting Strategy and Tactics.* Oklahoma State University: Fire Protection Publications, 1998.

Chetkovich, Carol. *Real Heat: Gender and Race in the Urban Fire Service.* New Brunswick: Rutgers University Press, 1997.

Cole, Robert, Robert Crandall, and Jerold Bills. *Firefighter's Complete Juvenile Firesetter Handbook.* Pittsford: Fireproof Children Company, May 1999.

Collins, Jim. *Good to Great.* New York: HarperCollins, 2001.

Compton, Dennis, and John Granito, editors. *Managing Fire and Rescue Services.* Washington: International City/County Managers Association, 2002.

Compton, Dennis. *Mental Aspects of Performance for Firefighters,* 2nd Edition. Oklahoma State University: Fire Protection Publications, 2004.

Compton, Dennis. *When in Doubt, Lead!* Oklahoma State University: Fire Protection Publications, 1999.

Compton, Dennis. *When in Doubt, Lead . . . Part 2.* Oklahoma State University: Fire Protection Publications, 2000.

Compton, Dennis. *When in Doubt, Lead! Part 3.* Oklahoma State University: Fire Protection Publications, 2002.

Covey, Stephen R. *The Seven Habits of Highly Effective People.* New York: Simon and Schuster, 1990.

Covey, Stephen R. *Principle-Centered Leadership.* New York: Simon and Schuster, 1992.

Covey, Stephen R. *The 8th Habit: From Effectiveness to Greatness.* New York: Simon and Schuster, 2004.

Dehaan, John D. *Kirk's Fire Investigation,* 5th Edition. Upper Saddle River: Prentice-Hall, 2002.

DePree, Max. *Leadership is an Art.* New York: Dell Publishing, 1989.

Devito, Joseph A. *The Interpersonal Communication Book,* 10th Edition. Needham Heights: Pearson, Allyn & Bacon, 2003.

Edwards, Steven T. *Fire Service Personnel Management,* 2nd Edition. Upper Saddle River: Prentice-Hall, 2004.

Fanning, Fred. *Basic Safety Administration: A Handbook for the New Safety Specialist.* Des Plaines: American Society of Safety Engineers, 2003.

— *Fire Data Analysis Handbook.* Federal Emergency Management Agency, U.S. Fire Administration, U.S. Government Printing Office 1995 (620-956/82068 Out of print. See FEMA web site for public access version in PDF file).

— *Fire Department Safety Officer.* Oklahoma State University: International Fire Service Training Association, 2001.

— *Fire and Emergency Services Instructor,* 7th Edition. Oklahoma State University: International Fire Service Training Association, 2006.

— *Fire Inspection and Code Enforcement,* 7th Edition. Oklahoma State University: International Fire Service Training Association, 2007.

— *Fire Investigator.* Oklahoma State University: International Fire Service Training Association, 2000.

— *Fire and Life Safety Educator,* 2nd Edition. Oklahoma State University: International Fire Service Training Association, 1997.

— *Fire Risk Analysis: A Systems Approach.* Emmitsburg: National Fire Academy, 1984.

Gaston, James M., Ph.D., CAE, and Dr. Riley Harvill. *Fire Officer Coaching.* Oklahoma State University: Fire Protection Publications, 2005.

Gaynor, Gerard H. *What Every New Manager Needs to Know.* New York: AMACOM, 2003.

Grimwood, Paul, Ed Hartin, John McDonough, and Shan Raffel. *3D Fire Fighting: Training, Techniques, and Tactics.* Oklahoma State University: Fire Protection Publications, 2005.

— *Harvard Business Review on Decision Making.* Boston: Harvard Business School Press, 2001.

Hersey, Paul, Kenneth H. Blanchard, and Dewey E. Johnson. *Management of Organizational Behavior: Leading Human Resources,* 8th Edition. Upper Saddle River: Prentice Hall, 2001.

— *Incident Management System Model Procedures Guide for Emergency Medical Incidents.* National Fire Service Incident Management System Consortium and Oklahoma State University: Fire Protection Publications, 2002.

— *Incident Management System Model Procedures Guide for Hazardous Materials Incidents.* National Fire Service Incident Management System Consortium and Oklahoma State University: Fire Protection Publications, 2000.

— *Incident Management System Model Procedures Guide for High-Rise Firefighting.* National Fire Service Incident Management System Consortium and Oklahoma State University: Fire Protection Publications, 2003.

— *Incident Management System Model Procedures Guide for Structural Collapse and US&R Operations.* National Fire Service Incident Management System Consortium and Oklahoma State University: Fire Protection Publications, 1998.

— *Incident Management System Model Procedures Guide for Structural Firefighting.* National Fire Service Incident Management System Consortium and Oklahoma State University: Fire Protection Publications, 2000.

— *Incident Management System Model Procedures Guide for Wildland Firefighting.* National Fire Service Incident Management System Consortium and Oklahoma State University: Fire Protection Publications, 2000.

Janing, Judy, and Gordon M. Sachs. *Achieving Excellence in the Fire Service.* Upper Saddle River: Prentice-Hall, 2002.

Kipp, Jonathan D., and Murrey E. Loflin. *Emergency Incident Risk Management: A Safety and Health Perspective.* New York: John Wiley and Sons, 1996.

Klaene, Ben, and Russell Sanders. *Structural Fire Fighting.* Batterymarch Park: National Fire Protection Association, 2002.

Klein, Gary. *Sources of Power: How People Make Decisions.* Cambridge: MIT Press, 1998.

Krieger, Gary R., and John F. Montgomery, editors. *Accident Prevention Manual for Business and Industry,* 12th Edition. Itasca, IL: National Safety Council, 2001.

Lacey, Brett, and Paul Valentine. *Fire Prevention Applications.* Oklahoma State University: Fire Protection Publications, 2005.

Linsky, Martin, and Ronald A. Heifetz. *Leadership on the Line: Staying Alive Through the Dangers of Leading.* Boston: Harvard Business School Press, 2002.

Lussier, Robert N., Ph.D. *Management Fundamentals: Concepts, Applications, Skill Development,* 2nd Edition. Mason: Thomson South-Western Publishers, 2003.

Macoby, Michael. *The Gamesman.* New York: Bantam Doubleday Dell Publishing Group, 1977.

Maira, Arun, and Peter Scott-Morgan. *The Accelerating Organization: Embracing the Human Face of Change.* New York: McGraw-Hill, 1997.

— *Many Faces, One Purpose: A Manager's Handbook on Women in Firefighting.* Federal Emergency Management Association/U.S. Fire Administration, date unknown.

Markel, Mike. *Technical Communication,* 6th Edition. New York: St. Martin's Press, 2001.

Marks, Michael E. *Emergency Responder's Guide to Terrorism: A Comprehensive Real-World Guide to Recognizing and Understanding Terrorist Weapons of Mass Destruction.* Chester: Red Hat Publishing, 2003.

Northouse, Peter Guy. *Leadership: Theory and Practice.* Thousand Oaks: Sage Publications, 1997.

Osborne, David, and Ted Gaebler. *Reinventing Government.* Reading: Addison-Wesley Publishing Company, Inc., 1992.

Pearsall, Thomas E. *The Elements of Technical Writing.* Boston: Allyn and Bacon, 2001.

Phelps, Burton, and Robert Murgallis. *Command and Control 2: ICS, Strategy Development and Tactical Selections.* Oklahoma State University: Fire Protection Publications, 2004.

Phelps, Burton, and Robert Murgallis. *Command and Control: ICS, Strategy Development and Tactical Selections.* Oklahoma State University: Fire Protection Publications, 2001.

— *Retention & Recruitment in the Volunteer Fire Service — Problems and Solutions.* NVFC & USFA, Final Report 1998.

Robey, Cora L. *New Handbook of Basic Writing Skills.* Ft. Worth, TX: Harcourt College Publishers, 2001.

Smith, James P. *Strategic and Tactical Considerations on the Fireground.* Upper Saddle River: Prentice-Hall, 2002.

Snook, Jack W., Jeffery D. Johnson, and Mary Jo Wagner. *Cooperative Service Through Consolidations, Mergers and Contracts — Making the Pieces Fit.* West Linn: Emergency Services Consulting Group, 1997.

Snook, Jack W., Jeffery D. Johnson, Daniel C. Olsen, and John Buckman. *Recruiting, Training, and Maintaining Volunteer Firefighters,* 3rd. Edition. West Linn: Emergency Services Consulting Group, 1998.

Wallace, Mark. *Fire Department Strategic Planning: Creating Future Excellence.* Saddlebrook: Fire Engineering Books & Videos, PennWell Publishing Co., 1998.

Weiss, Joseph W., and Robert K. Wysocki. *5-Phase Project Management: A Practical Planning and Implementation Guide.* Boulder: Perseus Books Group, 1992.

Wieder, Mike. *The Sourcebook for Fire Company Training Evolutions,* 2nd Edition. Oklahoma State University: Fire Protection Publications, 2000.

Wood, Julia T. *Everyday Encounters: An Introduction to Interpersonal Communication.* Florence: Wadsworth Publishing, 2001.

Wysocki, Robert K., Robert Beck, Jr., and David B. Crane. *Effective Project Management,* 2nd Edition. New York: John A. Wiley and Sons, Inc., 2000.

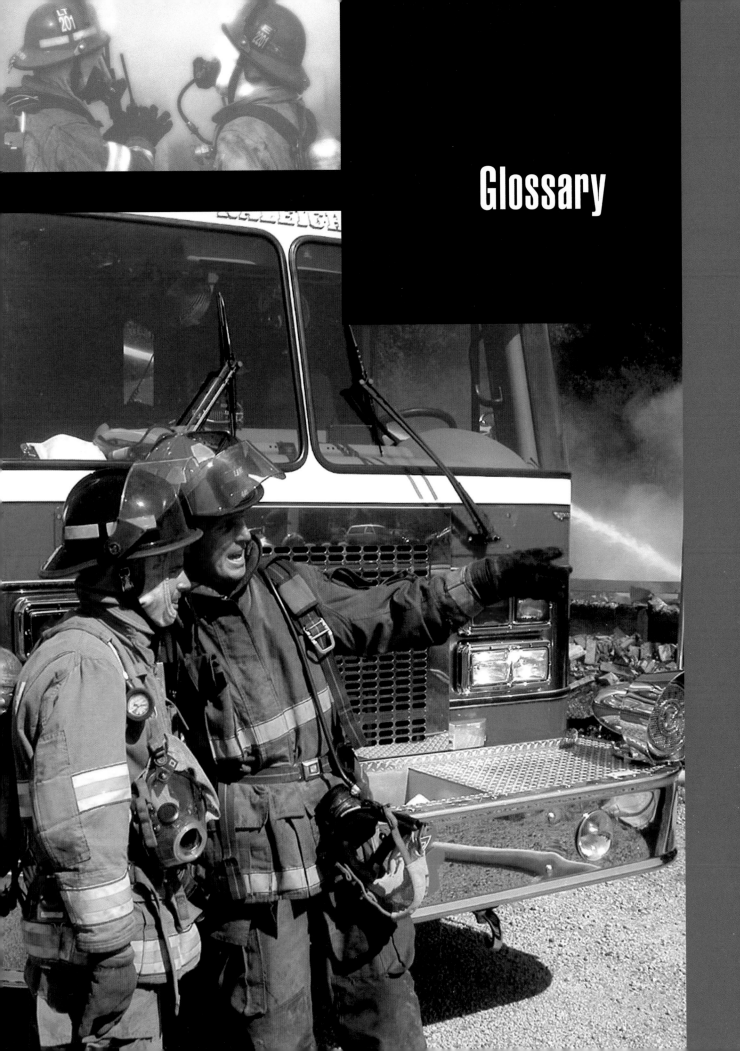

Glossary

Glossary

A

Abstract — *See* Executive Summary.

Accident Investigation — Fact-finding rather than fault-finding procedure that looks for causes of accidents, which leads to analyzing causes in order to prevent similar accidents. *Also see* Accident.

Accident — Sequence of unplanned or uncontrolled events that produces unintended injury, death, or property damage; the results of unsafe acts by persons who are unaware or uninformed of potential hazards, are ignorant of safety policies, or fail to follow safety procedures. *Also see* Hazard.

ADA — Abbreviation for Americans with Disabilities Act.

Administrative Law — Body of law created by an administrative agency in the form of rules, regulations, orders, and decisions to administer regulatory powers and duties of the agency. *Also see* Law, Legislative or Statutory Law, and Judiciary Law.

Affirmative Action Policy — Employment program required by federal statutes and regulations designed to correct past and current discriminatory practices in hiring and promoting members of underutilized and minority groups. *Also see* Affirmative Action Program.

Affirmative Action Program — Employment program designed to remedy discriminatory practices in hiring and promoting of members of underutilized and minority groups. *Also see* Affirmative Action Policy.

AHJ — Abbreviation for Authority Having Jurisdiction.

American National Standards Institute (ANSI) — Voluntary, private, nonprofit membership standards-setting organization that examines and certifies existing standards and new standards with the mission of making the U.S. economy more competitive in the world market.

American Society for Testing and Materials (ASTM) — Voluntary standards-setting organization that establishes characteristics and performance criteria for materials, products, systems, and services.

American Society of Safety Engineers (ASSE) — Professional safety organization composed of members who manage, supervise, and consult on safety, health, and environmental issues in industry, insurance, government, and education.

Americans with Disabilities Act (ADA) — U.S. federal law that prohibits discrimination against a qualified individual with a disability in application, hiring, advancement, discharge, compensation, job training, and other terms, conditions, and privileges of employment; prohibits asking certain questions of job applicants, including those about medical history, workers' compensation or health insurance claims, absenteeism due to illness, mental illness, and past treatment for alcoholism.

Analogical Reasoning — Mental process that is used to reach a conclusion by comparing two similar cases. *Also see* Causal Reasoning, Deductive Reasoning, and Inductive Reasoning.

Analysis — Ability to divide information into its most basic components. *Also see* Analyzing, Hazard/Risk Analysis, Job Analysis, Risk Analysis, and Task Analysis.

Analyzing — Process of methodically examining the various parts of an item, project, program, or incident. *Also see* Analysis.

ANSI — Acronym for American National Standards Institute.

ASSE — Abbreviation for American Society of Safety Engineers.

ASTM — Abbreviation for American Society for Testing and Materials.

Attending — Element of the listening process that involves paying attention to a message; focusing on the speaker (sender) and ignoring other distractions. *Also see* Listening, Message, and Sender.

Authority Having Jurisdiction (AHJ) — Organization, office, or individual responsible for approving equipment, an installation, or a procedure.

B

B.C.E. — Abbreviation for Before the Common Era.

Before the Common Era (B.C.E.) — Term used to designate the time period before the Common Era (C.E.); replaces the previously used B.C. *(before Christ)*, and covers the period of history before the birth of Christ.

Behavioral Hazard — Condition caused by unintentional actions of individuals or groups. *Also see* Accident, Hazard, Intentional Hazard, and Natural Hazard.

Boilerplate — Standardized language for the wording of legal requirements in contracts; defines the legal obligations necessary to meet specifications and is required in all bid specifications; prepared by purchasing departments.

Bond — Promise to repay the principal sum along with interest on a specified date; that is, when the bond reaches *maturity*; form of investment in which an individual purchases the bond with the intention of selling it upon maturity.

Brainstorming — Decision-making method in which a group of people is given a problem or situation and then given time to determine a solution to it.

Buckley Amendment — *See* Privacy Act.

Budget — Planned quantitative allocation of resources for specific activities. In this manual, budget refers to the narrower financial statement that lists both the proposed expenditures and expected revenue sources. *Also see* Budget Cycle, Capital Budget, Operating Budget, Performance Budget, and Zero-Based Budget (ZBB).

Budget Cycle — Time period in which an organization's annual budget is developed, presented, enacted, and executed. *Also see* Budget.

C

Canadian Centre for Occupational Health and Safety Administration (CCOHC) — Canadian federal agency responsible for workplace health and safety issues; similar to U.S. Occupational Safety and Health Administration (OSHA).

Capital Budget — Statement that includes funds for projected major purchases — items that cost more than a certain specified amount of money and are expected to last more than 1 year, usually 3 or more years. *Also see* Budget, Line-Item Budget, Operating Budget, Performance Budget, and Zero-Based Budget (ZBB).

Cardiopulmonary Resuscitation (CPR) — Application of rescue breathing and external cardiac compression used on patients in cardiac arrest to provide an adequate circulation and oxygen to support life.

Case Law — *See* Judiciary Law.

Causal Reasoning — Mental process based on the relationship between two or more events in such a way that it is obvious one caused the other to occur. Also called *cause-and-effect reasoning. Also see* Analogical Reasoning, Deductive Reasoning, and Inductive Reasoning.

Cause-and-Effect Reasoning — *See* Causal Reasoning.

CBRNE — Abbreviation for Chemical, Biological, Radiological, Nuclear, or Explosive.

CDC — Abbreviation for U.S. Centers for Disease Control and Prevention.

CD-ROM — Abbreviation/acronym for compact disc-read-only memory.

Centers for Disease Control and Prevention (CDC) — U.S. government agency responsible for the collection and analysis of data regarding disease and health trends.

Certified — Condition in which a person has successfully completed specific criteria and has been designated as capable of performing specific functions, duties, or tasks.

CFR — Abbreviation for U.S. *Code of Federal Regulations*.

Chemical, Biological, Radiological, Nuclear, or Explosive (CBRNE) Device — *See* Weapons of Mass Destruction (WMD).

Chronemics — Use of time. Eurocentric cultures view time *monochronically;* that is, time is compartmentalized with events scheduled in succession and allotted specific amounts of time. Cultures that are *polychronic* (such as some Middle Eastern and Latin American societies) do not place these same restrictions on time.

Clarity — Ability to precisely and clearly explain concepts and processes through a systematic presentation of material.

Clear-Text — Use of plain English (or language) in radio communications transmissions; replaces ten-signal or agency-specific coded systems. *Also see* Communication.

Coaching — Process in which supervisors direct the skills performance of subordinates by observing, evaluating, and making suggestions for improvement of their work or personal habits and skills.

Code — Body of law established either by legislative or administrative agencies with rule-making authority; designed to regulate (within its scope) the topic to which it relates. *Also see* Law.

Code of Ethics — Organized group of ethical behavior guidelines that govern day-to-day activities of a profession, an organization, or an individual. *Also see* Ethics.

Code of Federal Regulations (CFR) — Formal name given to the books or documents containing the specific U.S. regulations provided by law; the complete body of federal law. *Also see* Law.

Communication — Two-way process of transmitting and receiving some type of message. *Also see* Interpersonal Communication, Message, Receiver, Sender, and Speech Communication.

Compact Disc-Read-Only Memory (CD-ROM) — Electronic media data storage device.

Comprehension — Ability to understand the meaning of information.

Consistency — Concept that information is *not* contradictory and conforms to the principles that a course is attempting to teach.

Contingency Plan — Alternative procedure or set of procedures implemented in the event of uncontrollable circumstances.

Controlling — Management process for establishing and implementing mechanisms to ensure that objectives are attained. *Also see* Management and Managing.

Coordinating — Exchanging information within an organization in order to relate and adjust interdependent activities and programs.

Copyright Law — Legal document that protects the works of artists, photographers, and authors and gives them exclusive rights to publish their works or determine who may publish or reproduce them. *Also see* Law.

Counseling — Advising subordinates on their educational progress, career opportunities, personal anxieties, or sudden crises in their lives; broad term used for a variety of procedures designed to help individuals adjust to certain situations.

CPR — Abbreviation for Cardiopulmonary Resuscitation.

Customer-Relationship Management (CRM) — Methodologies and tools that help product and service providers manage customer relationships in an organized way; sometimes called *customer-service management*. *Also see* Customer Service.

Customer Service — Concept providing a product or service that meets the needs of a group of people, called *customers*, who use and consume the product or service. *Also see* Customer-Relationship Management (CRM), External Customers, and Internal Customers.

Customer-Service Management — *See* Customer-Relationship Management (CRM).

D

Deductive Reasoning — Mental process of reaching a specific conclusion based on a general statement or principle. *Also see* Analogical Reasoning, Causal Reasoning, and Inductive Reasoning.

Demographics — Data related to population: size, components of change, and characteristics such as age, education, sex, income, etc.

Demonstration — Act of showing how to perform a procedure or activity or how an item operates, works, or acts.

Department of Homeland Security (DHS) — Administrative body of the executive branch of the U.S. federal government responsible for the security of the nation against terrorist attacks. Similar state agencies also exist to assist in coordinating efforts on a local level.

Department of Transportation (DOT) — Administrative body of the executive branch of a state/province or federal government responsible for transportation policy, regulation, and enforcement.

DHS — Abbreviation for U.S. Department of Homeland Security.

Digital Versatile (or Video) Disc (DVD) — Electronic media storage disc used for storing and replaying videos or movable images.

Disability — Term used in connection with workers' compensation acts; composite of actual incapacity to perform the usual tasks of one's employment and the resulting wage loss as well as the physical impairment of the body that may or may not be incapacitating.

Disaster — Occurrence that inflicts widespread destruction or distress.

Discussion — Organized, possibly unstructured, two-way dialog between members of a group.

Diversity — Condition of being different or having differences; recognizing, valuing, and using those differences in employees and subordinates to make the organization more efficient and effective.

DOT — Abbreviation for Department of Transportation.

Duty — Obligation that one has by law or contract.

DVD — Abbreviation for Digital Versatile (or Video) Disc.

E

EAP — Abbreviation for Employee Assistance Program.

EEO — Abbreviation for Equal Employment Opportunity.

EEOC — Abbreviation for U.S. Equal Employment Opportunity Commission.

Effective — Efforts or conditions that produce the desired result or meets its intended purpose, which could be considered *doing the right thing.*

Efficient — Condition that exists when results are produced with a minimum of effort, waste, or expense; that is, minimum cost for maximum effect.

Electronic Mail (E-Mail) — Form of electronic communication based on Internet and intranet connections between computer systems. *Also see* Communication.

E-Mail — Abbreviation for Electronic Mail.

Emergency Medical Services (EMS) — Publicly or privately funded immediate medical care that extends hospital emergency room treatment into the community in order to provide care to the victims of illness and injury as quickly as possible.

Emergency Medical Technician (EMT) — Qualified provider of basic life support medical care.

Empathy — Ability to understand the feelings and attitudes of another person.

Employee Assistance Program (EAP) — Program designed to provide employees with counseling services ranging from financial counseling to substance-abuse programs and domestic-violence prevention.

EMS — Abbreviation for Emergency Medical Services.

EMT — Abbreviation for Emergency Medical Technician.

Environmental Protection Agency (EPA) — U. S. government agency that creates regulations and enforces laws designed to protect air, water, and soil from contamination.

Enterprise Fund — Fund established to finance and account for acquisition, operation, and maintenance of government facilities and services that are entirely or predominantly self-supporting by user fees.

EPA — Abbreviation for U.S. Environmental Protection Agency.

Equal Employment Opportunity (EEO) — Process required by law in the U.S. that requires fair and equitable access to jobs through the hiring and promotional process.

Equal Employment Opportunity Commission (EEOC) — U.S. government agency that reviews and enforces fair hiring and promotional standards.

Equal Employment Opportunity Laws — Laws that apply to protected groups of individuals who have experienced past workplace discrimination. *Also see* Law.

Ethics (Ethos) — Philosophical principles that are used to determine correct and proper behavior by members of a society. Sometimes called *moral philosophies*. *Also see* Code of Ethics.

Evaluating — Act of establishing the worth or value of each part or the sum total of the whole based on the desired outcome, which therefore determines how effective or efficient an item, program, or process is compared to a benchmark or established set of criteria. In the communication process, it is the act of critically analyzing a message to determine how factual it really is; the receiver (or listener) must be able to separate facts from opinions. *Also see* Communication, Effective, Efficient, Receiver, and Message.

Executive Summary — Brief review of the key points in a report, a technical paper, a list of specifications, or an analysis; also called *abstract*.

External Customers — General population of the service area. *Also see* Customer Service and Internal Customers.

F

FAA — Abbreviation for U.S. Federal Aviation Administration.

Fact — Verifiable piece of data that can be used to support the decision-making process.

Fallacy — False reasoning that occurs when someone attempts to persuade others without sufficient supporting evidence or uses irrelevant or inappropriate arguments.

Fax — Term that refers to the act of sending (verb) a copy of a document via the telephone system; also used as a noun to mean the item that is transmitted; originally an acronym for *facsimile*.

Federal Aviation Administration (FAA) — Subdivision of the U.S. Department of Transportation that is responsible for the regulation of civil aviation.

Federal Emergency Management Agency (FEMA) — U.S. federal agency responsible for emergency preparedness, mitigation, and response activities including natural, technological, and attack-related emergencies; part of the U.S. Department of Homeland Security (DHS).

Feedback — In the communication process, responses that clarify and ensure that a message was received and understood by the receiver (or listener); also used to mean comments by a supervisor to a subordinate regarding the subordinate's abilities or achievements. *Also see* Communication, Receiver, and Message.

FEMA — Acronym for U.S. Federal Emergency Management Agency.

Fire and Life-Safety Education Program — Plan that informs members of the community or service area about fire and life-safety hazards and what they can do to mitigate those hazards — that is, help them change their behavior in ways that result in fewer fires, injuries, and property losses within the community. *Also see* Hazard and Mitigation.

Fire Prevention and Life Safety — Proactive approach to reducing the loss of life and property and meeting the fire and emergency services organization's mission statement.

Foreseeability — Legal concept that reasonable people should be able to foresee the consequences of their actions and take reasonable precautions.

G

Government Infrastructure — Entity that has the responsibility of providing the citizens or customers within the jurisdiction an agreed-upon level of service.

Grant — Source of funds provided by governmental agencies and nongovernmental organizations; provides equipment that an organization may not have the funds to purchase.

Grievance — Complaint against management by one or more employees concerning an actual, alleged, or perceived injustice; may concern a breach of the labor/management agreement if employees are members of a bargaining unit.

H

Hazard — Condition, substance, or device that can directly cause an injury or loss; usually refers to the source of a risk. *Also see* Accident, Behavioral Hazard, Intentional Hazard, Natural Hazard, and Risk.

Hazards Assessment — Review of the types of occupancies and facilities within a service area and the types of hazards each creates for the community and the fire and emergency services organization. *Also see* Hazard.

Hazard/Risk Analysis — Determines the potential safety threats that may be encountered during training and emergency operations; the analysis process identifies potential problem areas and is the foundation for a risk-management plan. *Also see* Analysis, Hazard, Risk, and Risk-Management Plan.

Hearing — Physiological process that involves sound waves striking the eardrums.

Health and Safety Officer (HSO) — Member of the fire and emergency services organization who is assigned and authorized by the administration as the manager of the health and safety program and performs the duties, functions, and responsibilities found in NFPA 1521, *Standard for Fire Department Safety Officer.*

Heating, Ventilating, and Air-Conditioning (HVAC) — Air-handling system within a building consisting of fans, ducts, dampers, and other equipment necessary to make the system function.

Home Safety Council (HSC) — National nonprofit organization dedicated to preventing home-related injuries through national programs, partnerships, and the support of volunteers by educating people of all ages how to be safer in and around their homes.

HSC — Abbreviation for Home Safety Council.

HSO — Abbreviation for Health and Safety Officer.

HVAC — Abbreviation for Heating, Ventilating, and Air-Conditioning.

I

IAFC — Abbreviation for International Association of Fire Chiefs.

IAFF — Abbreviation for International Association of Fire Fighters.

IAP — Abbreviation for Incident Action Plan.

IC — Abbreviation for Incident Commander.

ICMA — Abbreviation for International City/County Managers Association.

ICS — Abbreviation for Incident Command System.

IFSAC — Acronym for International Fire Service Accreditation Congress.

IFSTA — Acronym for International Fire Service Training Association.

IMS — Abbreviation for Incident Management System.

Incident Action Plan (IAP) — Written or unwritten set of procedures for the disposition of an incident; establishes the strategic goals and tactical objectives of the operation or scenario for a specific time period. *Also see* Strategy.

Incident Commander (IC) — Person in charge of the incident command/management system and responsible for the management of all incident operations during an emergency. *Also see* Incident Command System (ICS).

Incident Command System (ICS) — Process that provides for a systematic development of a complete, functional command organization and increases the effectiveness of fire and emergency services organizations; also provides the base for multiagency and multijurisdictional incident management systems. It is a part of the National Incident Management System (NIMS). Also called *Incident Management System (IMS). Also see* National Incident Management system (NIMS).

Incident Management System (IMS) — *See* Incident command System (ICS).

Incident Safety Officer (ISO) — Member of the Incident Command System (ICS) Command Staff responsible for monitoring and assessing safety hazards and unsafe conditions during an incident, and developing measures for ensuring personnel safety. *Also see* Hazard, Hazards Assessment, and Incident Command System (ICS).

Incident Safety Plan (ISP) — Program based on the Incident Commander's (IC's) strategy and tactics as described in the incident action plan (IAP) and the type of hazard involved at the incident. *Also see* Incident Commander (IC), Incident Action Plan (IAP), Strategy, and Hazard.

Inductive Reasoning — Process that arrives at a general conclusion based on a foundation of specific examples or data. *Also see* Analogical

Reasoning, Causal Reasoning, and Deductive Reasoning.

Information Management — *See* Records Management and Record Keeping.

Insurance Services Office (ISO) — Private national organization that evaluates and establishes insurance rates for communities based on fire protection services available to them.

Integrity — Personal quality that is based on the values and morals of an individual.

Intentional Hazard — Condition that results from actions that are meant to cause property destruction or loss of life. *Also see* Hazard, Behavioral Hazard, and Natural Hazard.

Interference — In the communication process, those factors that prevent the receiver from fully receiving a message; may be created by either internal or external sources. *Also see* Communication, Receiver, and Message.

Internal Customers — Employees and membership of the fire and emergency services organization. *Also see* External Customers and Customer Service.

International Association of Fire Chiefs (IAFC) — Professional organization that represents the interests of fire and emergency services chief officers.

International Association of Fire Fighters (IAFF) — Professional organization that represents the interests of fire and emergency services personnel through professional development and labor/management relations.

International City/County Managers Association (ICMA) — Professional and educational organization that provides technical and management assistance, training, and information resources to members and the local government community.

International Fire Service Accreditation Congress (IFSAC) — Nonprofit organization that accredits both fire service certification programs and higher education fire-related degree programs.

International Fire Service Training Association (IFSTA) — Nonprofit educational association that develops and provides training materials to the fire and emergency services internationally.

Interpersonal Communication — Communication that takes place between two people who have established a relationship; occurs on a daily basis in the lives of all people who live in groups. *Also see* Communication and Speech Communication.

Inventory Control — Process of tracking physical assets that an organization purchases from the date it is received until it is consumed or retired from service.

ISO — Abbreviation for Incident Safety Officer or Insurance Services Office.

ISP — Abbreviation for Incident Safety Plan.

J

Job — Grouping of similar functions within a block in a task analysis. *Also see* Analysis, Job Analysis, and Task Analysis.

Job Analysis — Process of determining types of duties required for a specific position and qualifications needed to fill that position. *Also see* Analysis, Job, and Task Analysis.

Job Performance Requirement (JPR) — Statement that describe the performance required for a specific job.

JPR — Abbreviation for Job Performance Requirement.

Judicial Legislation — *See* Judiciary Law.

Judiciary Law — Usually the result of a legal precedent or a judicial decision; decisions that serve as rules for future determinations in similar cases; also known as *judicial legislation* or *case law*. *Also see* Administrative Law, Law, and Legislative or Statutory Law.

K

Kinesics — Use of body motion and position in the nonverbal component of the communication process. *Also see* Communication, Nonverbal Cue, and Speech Communication.

Knowledge — Ability to remember previously learned information.

L

Law — Legal document that sets forth rules that govern a particular type of activity; also used to mean a rule or body of rules of conduct inherent in human nature and essential to the operation of society; used broadly and commonly to address many legal concepts. *Also see* Administrative Law, Legislative or Statutory Law, and Judiciary Law.

Leadership — Art of influencing and directing people to accomplish a mission or task. *Also see* Leading and Motivation.

Leading — Act of controlling, directing, conducting, guiding, and administering through the use of personal behavioral traits or personality characteristics that motivate employees to the successful completion of an organization's goals. *Also see* Leadership and Motivation.

Legislative or Statutory Law — Legal document made by federal, state/provincial, or local legislative bodies that pertains to civil and criminal matters. *Also see* Administrative Law, Law, and Judiciary Law.

Lesson — Planned and organized learning experience that is developed to guide students through a course of study. *Also see* Lesson Plan.

Lesson Plan — Instructional document that outlines the information and skills to be taught (prelude to instruction); makes effective use of available resources (personnel, time, space, and materials). *Also see* Lesson.

Liability — Broad, comprehensive term that describes legal responsibility. *Also see* Negligence and Vicarious Liability.

Line Function — Personnel or units that deliver services such as fire suppression and fire-prevention and life-safety programs directly to external customers. *Also see* External Customers and Staff Function.

Line-Item Budget — Lists of revenue sources and proposed expenditures for a budget cycle; most common budget system used in North America. *Also see* Budget, Budget Cycle, Capital Budget, Operating Budget, Performance Budget, and Zero-Based Budget (ZBB).

Listener — *See* Receiver.

Listening — Active process that includes receiving, attending, understanding, remembering, evaluating, and responding to a message from a speaker (sender). *Also see* Attending, Remembering, Sender, Receiver, and Message.

Literacy — Individual's ability to read, write, speak in English, and compute and solve problems at levels of proficiency necessary to function on the job, in the family of the individual, and in society.

Live-Fire Training — Training activity that involves a simulated fire-suppression activity. May take place in a purpose-built structure, acquired structure, or in the open.

Logic (Logos) — Ability to reason and present strong arguments in favor of or against a position.

Logistics — Procurement, distribution, maintenance, and replacement of material and equipment.

M

Management — Administration and control of projects, programs, systems, resources, or organizations. *Also see* Managing and Controlling.

Managing — Act of controlling, monitoring, or directing a project, program, system, or organization through the use of authority, discipline, or persuasion. *Also see* Management, Managing, and Controlling.

Mastery — High-level or nearly complete degree of proficiency in the performance of a skill based on criteria stated in objectives.

Mean — Average of a set of scores; found by adding the set of scores (values) and dividing by the total number of scores. *Also see* Median and Mode.

Median — Middle score in a set of scores (values) that are arranged or ranked in size (order) from high to low. *Also see* Mean and Mode.

Medium — In the communication process, path that the message takes between the sender and receiver. *Also see* Communication, Sender, Receiver, and Message.

Mentor — Trusted and friendly adviser or guide for someone who is new to a particular role. *Also see* Mentoring and Role Model.

Mentoring — Activity that matches a mentor with a new employee to provide guidance, motivation, and a positive role model for the new person. *Also see* Mentor and Role Model.

Message — In the communication process, information or idea transmitted and received through all or most of the senses. *Also see* Communication, Nonverbal Cue, and Speech Communication.

Mitigation — Act of making less severe or intense; process of finding solutions to reduce the severity of hazards or emergencies. *Also see* Hazard.

Mode — Most frequent score (value) in a set of scores. *Also see* Mean and Median.

Moral Philosophies — *See* Ethics.

Motivation — Internal state or condition that activates and directs behavior toward a goal. *Also see* Leadership and Leading.

N

National Board on Fire Service Professional Qualifications (Pro Board) — Certification and accreditation organization with the purpose of establishing an internationally recognized means of acknowledging professional achievement in the fire and emergency services; primary goal is the accreditation of organizations that certify uniform members of career and volunteer public fire departments.

National Fire Academy (NFA) — Educational component of the U.S. Fire Administration (USFA) providing training to members of the fire and emergency services nationally.

National Fire Incident Reporting System (NFIRS) — U.S. government agency that collects and analyses information about fires in the U.S.

National Fire Protection Association (NFPA) — Nonprofit educational and technical association devoted to protecting life and property from fire by developing fire protection standards and educating the public.

National Incident Management System (NIMS) — Process that provides for the systematic establishment of a complete, functional command organization for multiagency incidents that involve the U.S. government as well as state and local agencies.

National Institute for Occupational Safety and Health (NIOSH) — U.S. government agency of the Centers for Disease Control and Prevention (CDC) that helps ensure that workplaces and associated equipment are safe; also investigates workplace injuries, reports results, and makes recommendations.

National Volunteer Fire Council (NVFC) — Nonprofit membership association representing the interests of the volunteer fire, emergency medical services (EMS), and rescue services; serves as the information source regarding legislation, standards, and regulatory issues that affect the volunteer emergency services.

Natural Hazard — Condition that is generally out of the control of humans. *Also see* Hazard, Behavioral Hazard, and Intentional Hazard.

Needs Assessment — Survey of the types of services required or desired by the community or service area.

Negligence — Breach of duty where there is a responsibility to perform. *Also see* Duty, Liability, and Vicarious Liability.

NFA — Abbreviation for U.S. National Fire Academy.

NFIRS — Abbreviation for National Fire Incident Reporting System.

NFPA — Abbreviation for National Fire Protection Association.

NIMS — Acronym for the National Incident Management System.

NIOSH — Acronym for U.S. National Institute for Occupational Safety and Health.

Nonverbal Cue — Message without words often transmitted in gestures, posture or body language, eye contact, facial expression, tone of voice, and appearance. *Also see* Message, Communication, Kinesics, and Speech Communication.

NVFC — Abbreviation for National Volunteer Fire Council.

O

Occupational Safety and Health Administration (OSHA) — U S. federal agency that develops and enforces standards and regulations for occupational safety in the workplace.

Operating Budget — List of funds that are used to pay for the recurring expenses of the day-to-day operation of the fire and emergency services organization. *Also see* Budget, Capital Budget, Line-Item Budget, Performance Budget, and Zero-Based Budget (ZBB).

Operational/Administrative Plan — Program that focuses on *how* objectives will be accomplished as opposed to a strategic plan that focuses on *what* the organization will do. *Also see* Strategic Plan.

Opinion — Generalization that may *not* be verifiable without additional data.

Ordinance — Local law that applies to persons, things, and activities in a jurisdiction and has the same force and effect as legislative or statutory law. *Also see* Law and Legislative or Statutory Law.

Organizational Flowchart — *See* Organizational Structure.

Organizational Structure — Framework that permits an organization to accomplish its mission, strategy, goals, and objectives; defines the functions of each portion of the organization and establishes the communication and control lines associated with the operation of the organization; visualized in an *organizational flowchart* or *table of organization (TO)*.

Organizing — Activity that involves coordinating tasks and resources to accomplish established goals and objectives.

OSHA — Acronym for U.S. Occupational Safety and Health Administration.

P

Paraphrasing — Restating a message in different words while keeping the meaning.

Partnership — Formal or informal agreement between the fire and emergency services organization and other public or nonprofit agencies and private companies to provide mutual services for a common good.

Pathos — Ability to have empathy or sympathy for another person and make arguments based on emotional appeals.

Peer — Someone who is equal in status either socially or psychologically to another.

Performance Budget — Type of budget categorized by function or activity; each activity is funded based on projected performance; similar to *program budgets, performance budgets,* or *outcome-based budgets*. *Also see* Budget, Capital Budget, Line-Item Budget, Operating Budget, and Zero-Based Budget (ZBB).

Performance Evaluation — Assessment of the behavior, knowledge, skills, and abilities of an employee; may be informal or formal.

PERT — Acronym for Program Evaluation and Review Technique.

PIO — Abbreviation for Public Information Officer.

Planning — Act of setting goals and objectives and determining the direction an organization or unit will take to achieve those results.

Privacy Act — Prohibits invasion of a person's right to privacy or unwanted publicity; restricts access to personal information such as personnel files and student grades; guarantees access to records only by the covered student or eligible parent or guardian; prohibits disclosure of personal information without consent. Also called *Buckley Amendment*.

Pro Board — Unofficial name for the National Board on Fire Service Professional Qualifications.

Profession — Vocation that requires specialized knowledge and long, intense preparation that includes (1) learning scientific, historical, or scholarly principles that apply to specific skills, processes, and methods; (2) maintaining high standards of personal achievement and conduct; and (3) committing to continued study and educational advancement.

Program Evaluation and Review Technique (PERT) Chart — Chart that plots a project and evaluates the success of each step; depicts the individual tasks, time required for each task, and interrelationship or dependency of the various steps with each other.

Promulgate — To officially develop, file, publish, announce, and put into effect a law, ordinance, rule, or regulation. *Also see* Law, Ordinance, and Regulation.

Public Information Officer (PIO) — Member of the fire and emergency services organization who provides the public, via the media, with information about the organization and its operations.

Q

Qualified — Person who meets the proper standards, requirements, training, and certifications to perform a task or fill a position.

R

Rapid Intervention Crew (RIC) — Two or more fully equipped and immediately available firefighters designated to stand outside the hazard zone ready to enter and affect rescue of firefighters inside if necessary. Also called *rapid intervention team (RIT)*.

Rapid Intervention Team (RIT) — *See* Rapid Intervention Crew (RIC).

Reasonable Accommodation — Making facilities readily accessible to and usable by individuals with disabilities.

Receiver — In the communication process, the individual who receives the message and decodes or interprets it. Also called *listener*. *Also see* Communication, Message, and Speech Communication.

Record — Permanent account of known or recorded fact that is used to recall or relate a past event or action taken by an individual, unit, or organization. *Also see* Record Keeping and Records Management.

Record Keeping — Storage of records and reports accumulated by an organization. Also known as *information management. Also see* Record and Records Management.

Records Management — Process of planning, controlling, directing, organizing, training, and conducting other managerial activities required for maintaining an organization's records. Also known as *information management. Also see* Record and Record Keeping.

Regulation — Rule or similar directive issued by an administrative agency.

Remembering — Element of the listening process that involves retaining the message in the receiver's memory. *Also see* Listening, Receiver, and Message.

Report — Written or verbal accounting of an event based on facts surrounding the incident, response, or activity.

Request for Proposal (RFP) — Document that defines the specific requirements for an item that an organization intends to purchase through the bid process.

Research — Collection of facts, data, and evidence that are analyzed or evaluated to determine an answer to a problem or situation.

Responding — In the communication process, the action of the receiver who completes the process, which means an exchange of roles has occurred (the receiver becomes the sender and vice versa). *Also see* Communication, Receiver, and Sender.

Revenue — Yield of income sources that a political unit collects and receives for public use; includes property taxes, sales taxes, and income taxes.

RFP — Abbreviation for Request for Proposal.

RIC — Abbreviation for Rapid Intervention Crew.

Risk — Exposure to a hazard that may result in injury, loss of life, or loss of property. *Also see* Hazard, Hazard/Risk Analysis, Risk Analysis, and Risk-Management Plan.

Risk Analysis — Level of risk a fire and emergency services organization is willing to accept in order to protect the lives and property of the community or service area. *Also see* Analysis, Risk, and Hazard/Risk Analysis.

Risk-Management Plan — Written program that identifies and analyzes the exposure to hazards, selects appropriate risk-management techniques to address exposures, explains how to implement chosen techniques, and explains how to monitor the results of those techniques. *Also see* Analysis, Hazard, Risk, Hazard/Risk Analysis, and Risk Analysis.

RIT — Abbreviation for Rapid Intervention Team.

Role Model — Individual who others look to as an example while learning or adopting a new role or job; the part a company officer plays, image a company officer portrays, and actions a company officer demonstrates to subordinates and peers. *Also see* Mentor.

Safety Guidelines — Rules, regulations, or policies created and/or adopted by an organization that list steps or procedures to follow that will aid in reducing or eliminating accidents or injuries. Also called *safety plan*.

Safety Plan — *See* Safety Guidelines.

Scalar — Organization having an uninterrupted series of steps or chain of authority with authority centralized at the top such as paramilitary, hierarchal, or pyramid-type organizations.

Semantics — Study of meaning in words and symbols; refers to language, word meanings, and meaning changes due to context, all of which may be affected by individual background, knowledge, and experience.

Sender — In the communication process, the person who originates a message by encoding or turning thoughts and mental images into words. Also referred to in some speech communication texts as *speaker*. *Also see* Communication, Message, and Speech Communication.

Single-Use Plan — Procedure or set of procedures written to accomplish a specific objective within a short period of time such as development of a program, project, or budget. *Also see* Budget.

SOG — Abbreviation for Standard Operating Guideline.

SOP — Abbreviation for Standard Operating Procedure.

Speaker — *See* Sender.

Speech Anxiety — Fear of public speaking that manifests itself with increased breathing rates, rapid heartbeats, excess perspiration, upset stomachs, and quivering voices.

Speech Communication — Process of presenting formal oral presentations to groups. *Also see* Communication and Interpersonal Communication.

Staff Function — Nonemergency personnel or organizational units (such as human resources, finance, maintenance, and logistics) that provide advice and support efforts to line-function units and personnel. *Also see* Line Function and Internal Customers.

Stakeholder — Member of the political body that governs fire and emergency services organizations or influences them through legislation, nongovernment agencies, community groups, standards-making organizations, and businesses that provide services.

Standard — Rule, principle, criterion, or measure established by authority.

Standard of Care — Degree of care that a reasonably prudent person should exercise in similar or the same circumstances.

Standard Operating Guideline (SOG) — Standard method, procedure, or rule in which a fire and emergency services organization operates to perform a routine function; usually contained in a written policy and procedures handbook. Also called *standard operating procedure*.

Standard Operating Procedure (SOP) — *See* Standard Operating Guideline.

Standing Plan — Program that leads to the development of policies, procedures, and rules that are used frequently.

Statutory Law — *See* Legislative or Statutory Law.

Strategic Plan — Long-range program that charts the course of an organization over an indefinite future that is divided into definite time components. *Also see* Operational/Administrative Plan.

Strategy (or Strategic Goal) — Overall plan for controlling an incident or situation. *Also see* Incident Action Plan, Incident Safety Plan, and Tactic.

Substantive Right — Freedom that everyone has such as the right to equal enjoyment of fundamental rights, privileges, and immunities.

Supervising — Act of directing, overseeing, or controlling the activities and behavior of employees who are assigned to a particular supervisor. *Also see* Supervision.

Supervision — Act that includes the processes of directing, overseeing, and controlling the activities of other individuals who are assigned to a particular supervisor. *Also see* Supervising.

T

Table of organization (TO) — *See* Organizational Structure.

Tactic (or Tactical Objective) — Action taken to achieve a chosen strategy. *Also see* Strategy.

TO — Abbreviation for Table of Organization.

Task Analysis — Detailed review of each physical task or job that is performed by emergency personnel; each task is divided into steps that are required to complete it. *Also see* Analysis, Hazard/Risk Analysis, Job, and Job Analysis.

Training Aid — *See* Training Prop.

Training Prop — Permanent structure or portable device used to simulate specific types of emergency situations and teach fire and emergency related-subjects. Sometimes called *training aid*.

Trust Fund — Account whose assets are managed by a trustee or board of trustees for the benefit of another party or parties.

U

Understanding — Element of the listening process that consists of the receiver decoding the message and assigning meaning to it. *Also see* Message, Receiver, and Listening.

Underwriters Laboratories Inc. (UL) — Independent fire research and testing laboratory that certifies equipment and materials. *Also see* Underwriters' Laboratories of Canada.

Underwriters' Laboratories of Canada (ULC) — Canadian branch of Underwriters Laboratories Inc. (UL). *Also see* Underwriters Laboratories Inc.

UL — Abbreviation for Underwriters Laboratories Inc.

ULC — Abbreviation for Underwriters' Laboratories of Canada.

U.S. Fire Administration (USFA) — Agency of the U.S. Department of Homeland Security (DHS) whose mission is to reduce life and economic losses due to fire and related emergencies through leadership, advocacy, coordination, and support.

USFA — Abbreviation for U.S. Fire Administration.

V

Vicarious Liability — Liability imposed on one person for the conduct of another based solely on the relationship between the two persons. Indirect legal responsibility for acts of another (liability of an employer for acts of an employee). *Also see* Liability and Negligence.

W

Weapons of Mass Destruction (WMD) — Weapons that cause large-scale destruction; generally use chemical, biological, radiological, nuclear, or explosive (CBRNE) devices. Also known as *chemical, biological, radiological, nuclear, or explosive (CBRNE) devices*.

World Wide Web (WWW) — Information system using the Internet to access information stored on computers worldwide.

WMD — Abbreviation for Weapons of mass destruction.

WWW — Abbreviation for World Wide Web.

Z

Zero-Based Budget (ZBB) — Budget type where all expenditures must be justified at the beginning of each new budget cycle as opposed to simply explaining the amounts requested that are in excess of the previous cycle's funding. During ZBB planning, it is assumed that there is zero money available to operate the organization or program, thus the contribution that the organization or program makes to the jurisdiction must be justified. *Also see* Budget, Budget Cycle, Capital Budget, Line-Item Budget, Operating Budget, and Performance Budget.

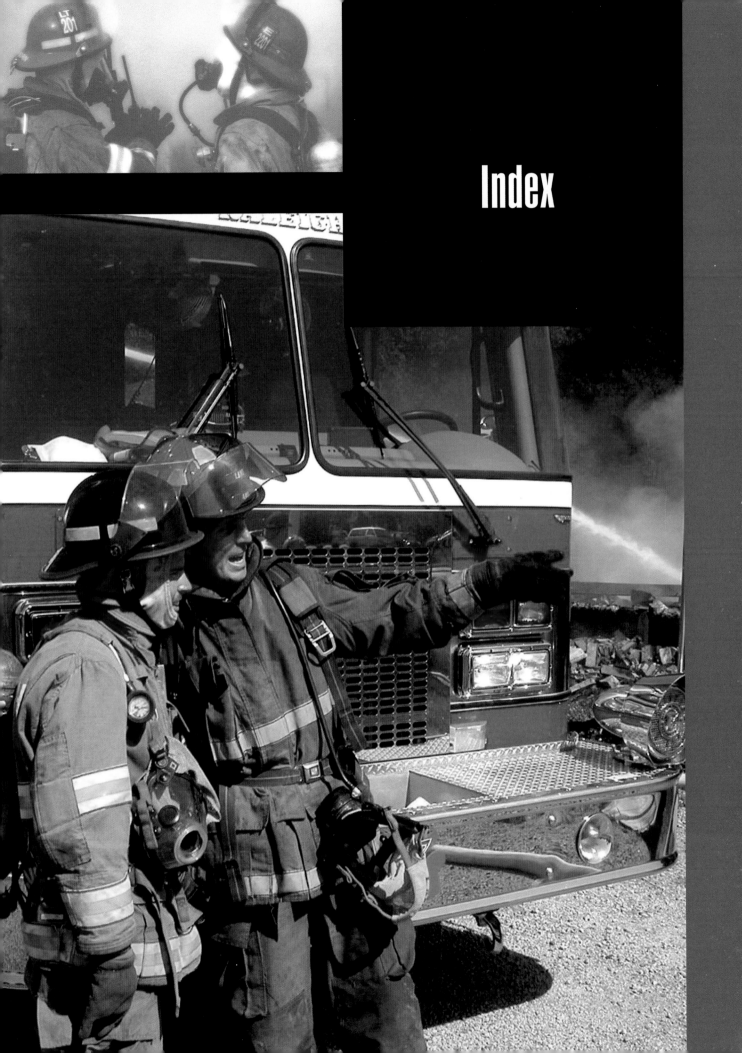

Index

Executive summary, 183–184, 185
Exigent circumstances, 665
Exit
    exit drills, 684–685
    inspections, 672–673
    markings, 672
Expectations of company officers, 20–21
Experiments, statistical, 593
Expert, power type, 48–49
Exploitive mentality, 80
Explosions, 703
Exposures
    Layman decision-making model, 464, 466, 467
    during practical training evolutions, 279
    safety investigations, 775, 777–778
    safety recommendations, 778
Exterior survey, 394–395
External aid agreements
    automatic aid, 569–570
    described, 570–571
    mutual aid, 570
Extinguishment, Layman decision-making model, 464, 467
Eye contact
    kinesics, 131–132
    during speech delivery, 155, 161

F

FAA. *See* Federal Aviation Administration (FAA)
Facial expression
    kinesics, 132, 133
    during speech delivery, 155, 161
Facility exterior survey, 394–395
Facility survey equipment, 390–391
Fair Labor Standards Act (FLSA), 114, 202, 316
Fallacies, 76–78
False indicator, 704, 712
Family Education and Privacy Act, 373
Family Medical Leave Act (FMLA), 112
Farmers' Home Administration (FHA), 556, 557
Fax machines, 423
FCC (Federal Communications Commission), 414
FDSOA (Fire Department Safety Officers Association), 766
Fear, as barrier to decision-making, 89
Federal Aviation Administration (FAA)
    airport supervision, 557, 558
    alert classifications, 489
    functions, 558
Federal Communications Commission (FCC), 414
Federal Emergency Management Agency (FEMA)
    creation of agency, 552
    FEMA Incident and Response Support Team (FIRST), 431
    functions, 556
    Mobile Emergency Response Support (MERS), 431
    as part of DHS, 554, 556
Federal government
    bill, defined, 552
    in Canada. *See* Federal government, Canadian
    Consumer Product Safety Commission (CPSC), 558
    Department of Housing and Urban Development (HUD), 557
    Department of Labor (DOL), 557
    Department of the Interior (DOI), 557
    Department of Justice (DOJ), 558
    Department of Transportation (DOT), 557–558
    DHS. *See* Department of Homeland Security (DHS)
    FAA. *See* Federal Aviation Administration (FAA)
    fire protection agencies, 554–558
    functions, 552
    lawmaking process, 552–554
    legislative counsels, 552
    National Fire Academy (NFA), 5, 203, 556, 766
    Nuclear Regulatory Commission (NRC), 558
    services, 246, 249
    U.S. Coast Guard, 556, 558
    U.S. Department of Agriculture (USDA), 556–557
    U.S. Fire Administration (USFA), 5, 556

Federal government, Canadian
    Agriculture and Agri-Food Canada, 561–562
    Environment Canada, 561
    fire protection agencies, 560–562
    Human Resources and Social Development Canada, 562
    Industry Canada, 560
    lawmaking process, 559–560
    National Research Council Institute for Research in Construction (NRC-IRC), 562
    Public Safety and Emergency Preparedness Canada (PSEPC), 560
    Public Works and Government Services Canada, 561
    Royal Canadian Mounted Police, 560
    structure, 558–559
    Transport Canada, 561
    Treasury Board, 561
Federal law
    ADA. *See* Americans with Disabilities Act (ADA)
    adverse impact, 109–110
    affirmative action, 109–112
    CFR. See Code of Federal Regulations
    Civil Rights Act, 108, 110–112
    constitutions, 98, 100
    differential treatment, 109
    disparate treatment, 109
    Environmental Protection Agency (EPA), 108, 550
    Equal Employment Opportunity Commission (EEOC), 108–109
    Fair Labor Standards Act (FLSA), 114, 202, 316
    Family Education and Privacy Act, 373
    Family Medical Leave Act (FMLA), 112
    hostile work environment, 110–111
    OSHA. *See* Occupational Safety and Health Administration (OSHA)
    Pregnancy Discrimination Act of 1978, 112
    quid pro quo, 110
    reasonable accommodation, 112
    sexual harassment, 110–112
    supervisory roles and responsibilities, 111–112
Federal services, 246, 249
Fee revenue, 208–209, 633
Feedback
    coaching, 614–615
    communications, 125, 127, 144
    from customers, 197–200
    360-degree feedback evaluation, 45, 618
FEMA. *See* Federal Emergency Management Agency (FEMA)
FESHE (Fire and Emergency Services Higher Education) model curriculum, 5
FHA (Farmers' Home Administration), 556, 557
Field sketch, 393, 394
Finance/Administration Section, 438, 733–734
Financial consequences, 582–583
Financial resources, 521, 522
Fire and Emergency Services Higher Education (FESHE) model curriculum, 5
Fire and life-safety inspections
    all-hazards risk reduction model, 657–660
    authority for entrance, 665
    automatic aid, 663–664
    behavioral hazards, 660–661
    building construction types, 664
    closing interview, 683–684
    community risk analysis, 656–664
    conducting inspections, 669–672
    definitions, 673
    documentation of inspections, 684
    exit drills, 684–685
    fire detection/signaling systems, 686–687
    fire extinguishers, 668
    fire extinguishing systems, 690–699
    fire protection inspection, 675
    fire protection system inspections/testing, 685–699
    hazard of contents, 675, 680
    hazardous materials labeling, 680–683
    home inspections, 662
    housekeeping, 673–674
    inspection responsibilities, 666–668
    intentional hazards, 661

I

J

Jargon, 6
Jealousy, as barrier to decision-making, 89
Job interest, 63–66
Job-centered leadership style, 34
Judicial branch of government, 98
Judicial system, 545, 547
Jurisdictions
    horizontal, 572
    interagency and intergovernmental authority, 572–573
    for services, 245
    surveys, for purchases, 643–644
    vertical, 572
Justification
    for budget requests, 213, 214, 638–639
    practical training evolutions, 278
    as unethical conduct, 80–81
Juvenile firesetters, 725

K

Katrina, Hurricane. *See* Hurricane Katrina
Kinesics, 131–133
Knowledge
    company officer requirements, 4–5, 7
    power, 48–49

L

Labor unions
    arbitration, 322
    bargaining session schedule, 320
    collective bargaining, 317, 318–319
    contract content, 320–321
    contract negotiations, 320–324
    employee involvement, 323–324
    fact-finding, 322
    firefighter unions, 320
    history of, 313
    impasse, 321–322
    mediation, 322
    negotiation process, 320–321
    open communications, 321–323
    preparation of contract, 321
    private labor unions, 317, 318–320
    proposal presentation, 321
    public labor unions, 317–320
    representation, 321
    scope of bargaining, 321
    strike. *See* Strike
    union, defined, 317
    union shop, defined, 317
Labor/management relations
    arbitration, 322
    bargaining session schedule, 320
    bargaining unit, 313
    contract content, 320–321
    contract negotiations, 320–324
    definitions, 317
    employee involvement, 323–324
    fact-finding, 322
    Fair Labor Standards Act (FLSA), 114, 202, 316
    grievances, 324–326, 618–619
    history of labor movement, 314–317
    history of labor organizations, 313
    impasse, 321–322
    job performance requirements, 312
    Labor-Management Reporting and Disclosure Act, 317
    Landrum-Griffin Act, 317
    learning objectives, 311
    mediation, 322
    National Industrial Recovery Act (NIRA), 315
    negotiation process, 320–321
    Norris-La Guardia Act, 315
    open communications, 321–323
    overview, 313–314, 326–327
    preparation of contract, 321
    private labor unions, 317, 318–320

proactive meetings, 324
    proposal presentation, 321
    public labor unions, 317–320
    representation, 321
    scope of bargaining, 321
    strike. *See* Strike
    Taft-Hartley Act of 1947, 316, 317
    Wagner-Connery Act, 315–316
Laissez-faire leadership style, 34
Landrum-Griffin Act, 317
Landslides, 500
Languages, 335–336, 341
Law. *See also* Legal responsibilities; Liability
    ADA. *See* Americans with Disabilities Act (ADA)
    administrative laws, 99, 100
    civil laws, 101
    Civil Rights Act, 108, 110–112
    classifications, 99–101
    common law (case law), 99, 100
    criminal (penal) laws, 100, 101
    defined, 98
    English Common Law, 106
    Fair Labor Standards Act (FLSA), 114, 202, 316
    Family Education and Privacy Act, 373
    Family Medical Leave Act (FMLA), 112
    federal. *See* Federal law
    federal lawmaking process, 552–554
    government agencies, 99
    investigation warrants, 501
    judicial decisions, 99
    judicial system, 545, 547
    Labor-Management Reporting and Disclosure Act, 317
    Landrum-Griffin Act, 317
    law enforcement department, 545
    legal definitions, 98, 102
    legislative actions, 98
    liability. *See* Liability
    local government lawmaking process, 544
    Municipal Freedom of Information and Protection of Privacy Act (MFIPPA), 373
    national consensus standards. *See* National consensus standards
    National Industrial Recovery Act (NIRA), 315
    Norris-La Guardia Act, 315
    overview, 97, 119
    Pregnancy Discrimination Act of 1978, 112
    procedural laws, 100
    for purchases, 645
    right-to-work law, 317
    Robert T. Stafford Disaster Relief and Emergency Assistance Act, 573
    sources of, 98–99
    state constitutions, 98, 100
    statutory law, 100
    substantive laws, 99–100
    Superfund Amendments and Reauthorization Act (SARA), 543–544
    Taft-Hartley Act of 1947, 316, 317
    Wagner-Connery Act, 315–316
Layman, *Fire Fighting Tactics*, 446–451
Layman decision-making model
    background, 463
    confinement, 464, 466–467
    exposures, 464, 466, 467
    extinguishment, 464, 467
    overhaul, 464, 467
    overview, 464
    rescue, 464–466
    salvage, 464, 469–470
    ventilation, 464, 468–469
Leadership
    actions and attitudes, 51
    alpha leadership model, 44
    basic leadership model, 41–42
    behavioral leadership, 33–37
    challenges of, 16
    coercive power type, 48
    command presence, 49–50

concepts, 46–47
expert, power type, 48–49
of groups, 609–610
identification, power type, 48
job performance requirements, 30
leadership-continuum theory, 37–38
leading, defined, 32, 55
leading by example, 20
learning objectives, 29
legitimate, power type, 49
levels, 40–41
manager vs. leader, 47
managing, defined, 32
models, 41–44
overview, 31–32, 50
power types, 47–49
principle-centered leadership, 40
reward power type, 47–48
situational leadership, 37–40, 42–43
skills development, 44–46
social-change model, 43–44
styles, 38, 39
supervising, defined, 32
theories. *See* Theories of leadership
total quality management (TQM), 37
traits, 32–33, 51
Lease or lease/purchase, 648–649
Legal responsibilities. *See also* Law; Liability
boilerplate, 188, 649
discipline, 307
learning objectives, 95
overview, 97, 119
personnel evaluations, 618
during practical training evolutions, 278–279
purpose of the law, 97–98
Legal system, defined, 98. *See also* Legal responsibilities
Legislative branch of government, 98
Legitimate, power type, 49
Leniency effect, 599
Letters, written communication, 176–179
Level 1 leader, 40
Level 2 leader, 40
Level 3 leader, 40
Level 4 leader, 40
Level 5 leader, 40
Level I fire officer. *See* Fire Officer I
Level II fire officer. *See* Fire Officer II
Level III fire officer. *See* Fire Officer III
Level IV fire officer. *See* Fire Officer IV
Lewin Change Model, 529–530
Liability. *See also* Law; Legal responsibilities
civil liability, 102–103
criminal liability, 102
defined, 101
Fireman's Rule, 101, 105–106
governmental immunity, 105, 106–107
malfeasance, 102
misfeasance, 104
for negligence, 103–105
nonfeasance, 104
overview, 97, 119
personal liability, 105
protection with e-mails, 172
punitive damages, 103, 106–107
sovereign immunity, 106–107
tort liability, 103, 114
Liaison officer, 731
Life safety inspections. *See* Fire and life-safety inspections
Lighters as fire ignition source, 723, 724
Lightning-related fires, 709–710
Line and staff personnel, 235, 237–238
Line charts, 594–595
Line functions, 3
Listening skills
attending, 134–135
barriers to listening, 136–137, 138
evaluating, 135–136
guidelines, 139
hearing vs. listening, 134
improving skills, 136–138
remembering, 135, 136
responding, 136
understanding, 135
Literature readings for skills development, 46
Local aid agreements
automatic aid, 569–571. *See also* Automatic aid
external aid agreements, 569–571
internal aid agreements, 567–569
mutual aid, 570. *See also* Mutual aid agreement
outside aid, 258, 570–571
purpose, 567
Local alarm systems, 686
Local government
borough, 542
building department, 545–546
commission government, 540–541
council-manager government, 539–540
council-mayor government, 538–539
county commission, 542–543
county commission-executive, 543
county commission-manager, 543
county government, 542–543
effect on fire and emergency services, 544–548
fire district, 246–247, 248, 543–544
judicial system, 545, 547
law enforcement department, 545
lawmaking process, 544
municipal (city), 537–542. *See also* Municipal (city) government
office of emergency preparedness, 545, 547–548, 551
overview, 537
parish government, 542–543
representative town meeting, 542
street or road department, 545, 547
town meeting, 541–542
township, 541
village, 542
water department, 545, 546
zoning commission, 545, 546–547
Lockout, defined, 317
Logic
analogical reasoning, 74, 76
causal reasoning, 74, 75–76
deductive reasoning, 74, 75
defined, 73
fallacies, 76–78
inductive reasoning, 73–75
learning objectives, 71
overview, 73, 92
reasoning, 73–76
Logistics Section, 438, 731, 733
Logs (dehydrating), as cause of fires, 710
London (England) Fire Brigade, 2
Long-term trusts, 209, 633
Loyalty, leadership trait, 19, 51

M

MABAS (Mutual Aid Box Alarm System), 257
Maintenance
corrective maintenance, 365
preventive maintenance, 363, 365, 366
records management, 363, 365–366
Malfeasance, 102
Management
Board of Trustees, 541
change issues, 525–532. *See* Change issues.
Classical School of Management Theory, 525
of conflict, 300–304
defined, 55, 521
force field analysis, 529
functions, 521–523
incident scenes. *See* Incident scene management

Management *(continued)*
    information systems. *See* Management information system (MIS)
    job performance requirements, 520
    leader vs. manager, 47
    learning objectives, 519
    Level II officer as manager, 6
    Lewin Change Model, 529–530
    managing, defined, 32, 55
    motivation, 523–525
    participatory, 86
    of records. *See* Records management
    resistance to change, 526–528
    skills, 523–525
    span of control, 525
    time management, 533
    work system and task analyses, 530–531
Management information system (MIS), 358–362
    acquiring data, 358–359
    active files, 360
    activity records, 367
    analyzing data, 359–360
    archives, 360, 362
    budget records, 363
    computer backups, 362
    filing system, 362
    information distribution, 360
    inventory records, 363, 365
    maintenance records, 363, 365–366
    organizing information, 360, 361
    personnel records, 367–368
    storage. *See* Information storage
    topics in record types, 364
Manual organization, 5–6
Manufacturers of purchases, 644
Mapping Applications for Response, Planning, and Local Operational Tasks (MARPLOT®), 404
MARPLOT® (Mapping Applications for Response, Planning, and Local Operational Tasks), 404
Master stream appliances, 481
Matches as fire ignition source, 723, 724
Material Safety Data Sheet (MSDS) policies, 651
Materials, evaluation of, 587–588
Maturity of employees, 42–43
MDC (Mobile data computer), 424
MDT (Mobile data terminal), 424
Mean, defined, 592
Means of egress, 672–673
Media. *See* News media
Median, defined, 592
Medical emergency. *See also* Health issues
    apparatus placement and positioning, 491–492
    assessment, 448
    personnel evaluations, 495
Medical records, 368
Medium or channel, in communications, 124, 125, 126, 144
Meeting minutes, 184, 186
Memos, written communication, 172–176
Mental preparation for emergency response, 57
Mentors
    for behavior management, 611, 615–616
    for creating job interest, 63
    defined, 63, 291
    of employees, 65–66
    for skills development, 46
MERS (Mobile Emergency Response Support), 431
Message, in communications, 124, 125, 144
Methamphetamine labs, 450
MFIPPA (Municipal Freedom of Information and Protection of Privacy Act), 373
Michigan v. Clifford, 501
Michigan v. Tyler and Robert Tompkins, 501
Minutes of meetings, 184, 186
Miranda rights, 718
MIS. *See* Management information system (MIS)
Misfeasance, 104
Mobile data computer (MDC), 424

Mobile data terminal (MDT), 424
Mobile Emergency Response Support (MERS), 431
Mobile radios, 418
Mobilization/staging areas, 443, 484–485
Mode, defined, 592
Models
    all-hazards risk reduction model, 657–660
    customer service, 347
    decision-making, 85–87
    Layman. *See* Layman decision-making model
    leadership. *See* Models of leadership
    Lewin Change Model, 529–530
    model code families, 675–685
    NIMS-ICS. *See* Incident scene management
    Phoenix risk assessment model, 474
    RECEO-VS, 464–470
    risk analysis, 584
    risk management, 765–766
Models of leadership
    alpha leadership model, 44
    basic leadership model, 41–42
    situational leadership model, 42–43
    social-change model, 43–44
Modems, 423–424
Modular organization, 439
Molotov cocktails, 719, 722
Monitoring
    agreements, 576
    budgets, 215, 640–641
    policies and procedures, 203
    risk-management plan, 770
    safety investigations, 770
    service delivery, 200
Monitors for ventilation, 400
Monochronic view of time, 134
Monroe's Motivated Sequence Pattern, 147
Motivation
    destructive actions, 525
    by management, 523–525
    methods, 523–524
    Seven Habits of Highly Effective People, 40, 524
Motives for incendiary fires
    crime concealment, 720–721
    excitement (vanity), 721
    extremism (terrorism), 721–722
    profit (fraud), 720
    revenge, 719
    vandalism, 719
Motor vehicles. *See* Vehicles
Moving, change phase, 529
MSDS (Material Safety Data Sheet) policies, 651
Mudslides, 500
Multiunit emergency scenes
    assigning resources, 738–744
    ICS. *See* Incident Command System (ICS)
    ICS forms, 440, 442, 749
    incident action plan (IAP), 744–749
    initial attack, 746, 747
    job performance requirements, 728
    learning objectives, 727
    operational plans, 286, 745–746
    overview, 729, 749
    resource allocation, 746–749
    sustained attack, 746, 747–748
Municipal (city) government
    borough, 542
    commission government, 540–541
    council-manager government, 539–540
    council-mayor government, 538–539
    Municipal Freedom of Information and Protection of Privacy Act (MFIPPA), 373
    overview, 537–538
    representative town meeting, 542
    services, 245–247
    town meeting, 541–542

NFPA 1521, *Standard for Fire Department Safety Officer*, 515

NFPA 1561, *Standard for Fire Department Incident Management System*, 440, 729

NFPA 1581, *Standard on Fire Department Infection Control Program*, 227, 738

NFPA 1620, *Recommended Practice for Pre-Incident Planning*, 380, 404

NFPA 1710, *Standard for the Organization and Deployment of Fire Suppression Operations, Emergency Medical Operations, and Special Operations to the Public by Career Fire Departments*, 590, 748–749

NFPA 2001, *Standard on Clean Agent Fire Extinguishing Systems*, 694

NFPA 5000, *Building Construction and Safety Code ®*, 675

NIMS-ICS. *See* National Incident Management System-Incident Command System (NIMS-ICS)

NIOSH. *See* National Institute for Occupational Safety and Health (NIOSH)

NIRA (National Industrial Recovery Act), 315

Non sequitur fallacy, 77

Nonaggressive behavior, 300

Nonemergency activity planning, 289

Nonfeasance, 104

Nongovernment grants, 211, 635

Nonprofit fire and emergency services organizations, 252

Nonverbal communications. *See also* Communication
    cultural customs, 337
    interpersonal communications, 131–134
    during speech delivery, 155, 161–162

Norm, defined, 592

Norming stage of team development, 61, 610

Norris-La Guardia Act, 315

Notes, defined, 7

NPS (National Park Service), 557

NRC (Nuclear Regulatory Commission), 558

NRC-IRC (National Research Council Institute for Research in Construction), 562

NRP (National Response Plan), 573–574

NTSB (National Transportation Safety Board), 558

O

Objectives. *See* Goals and objectives

Observation research, 593

Occupancy
    Certificate of Occupancy, 667
    classifications, 676–679
    occupancy related hazards, 662
    occupant services, 458–459

Occupational Safety and Health Administration (OSHA)
    creation of agency, 557
    Hazard Communication Standard, 681–682
    hazardous materials labeling, 681–682
    laws, 100, 101
    Title 29 (Labor) regulations, 107–108
    two-in/two-out rule, 107, 465

Offensive operational mode, 479–480, 486

Office of emergency preparedness, 545, 547–548, 551

Oklahoma City federal building bombing, 413, 422, 450

On-scene occupant services, 458–459

Open shop, defined, 317

Operating funds for purchases, 648

Operational modes
    defensive, 480–482, 486
    offensive, 479–480, 486
    transitional, 482–483

Operational plans, 286, 745–746

Operations officer, 731, 733

Operations Section, 438

Orders, 204

Organization
    application of skills, 57
    authority power, 49
    career organizations, 252–254, 285
    centralized authority, 239
    chain of command, 241
    classifications, 245–252
    county services, 246, 247–248
    decentralized authority, 239
    decision-making authority, 235, 238–240

    delegation of authority, 239–240
    division of labor, 236, 243–244, 259
    external barriers to decision-making, 90–91
    federal services, 246, 249
    fire district, 246–247, 248
    flow chart, 236
    for-profit services, 251–252
    functional supervision, 241
    Incident Command System (ICS), 732, 739–741
    incident scene management levels, 436–437
    industrial fire brigades, 250–251
    job performance requirements, 234
    labor organizations. *See* Labor/management relations
    learning objectives, 233
    line and staff personnel, 235, 237–238
    municipal services, 245–247
    nonprofit services, 252
    overview, 258
    private services, 250–252
    public services, 245–250
    purposes, 244
    resource allocation, 255–258
    scalar structure, 235, 236–237
    span of control, 236, 241–242
    staffing, 252–255
    state/provincial services, 246, 248
    structure based on rank, 1–2
    structure overview, 235
    tribal, 246, 250
    unity of command, 235, 240–241

OSHA. *See* Occupational Safety and Health Administration (OSHA)

Outside aid agreement, 258, 570–571

Overhaul, Layman decision-making model, 464, 467

Overpack drum, 494

Own situation, 451

P

Pagers, 419–420

Paralanguage, 131

Paraphrasing, 135

Pareto's Principle (80/20 Rule), 44

Parish government
    county commission, 542–543
    county commission-executive, 543
    county commission-manager, 543
    overview, 542–543
    services, 246, 247–248

Parking lots and garages
    apparatus placement and positioning, 488
    traffic control, 455, 456

Participating leadership style, 43

Participative leadership style, 38, 39

Participatory management style, 86

PASS device, 738

Passive behavior, 300

Passwords, computer, 369

PATCO (Professional Air Traffic Controllers Organization), 318

Path-goal theory, 38, 39

Payoffs, 80

Peer assistance, 611, 615

Peer Fitness Training (PFT) Certification Program, 324

Pension trust funds, 209, 633

People v. Ramsey, 665

Perceptions, challenges of, 18–19

Performance evaluations, 295, 367–368

Performing stage of team development, 61, 610

Perimeter control
    cold zone, 452–453
    control zones, 452–454
    hot zone, 452, 453
    warm zone, 452, 453

Permit and license issuance, 26

Perpetual trusts, 209, 633

Personal alert safety system (PASS) device, 738

Personal factors, challenges of, 19–20

Personal income taxes, 208, 633

Risk *(continued)*
    equipment and materials analysis, 587
    evaluation of, 767–768
    frequency, 767–768
    identification of, 657–659, 766–767
    management of, 764–771
    manmade, 657
    natural, 657
    personnel-risk analysis, 766–769
    Phoenix risk assessment model, 474
    prioritization, 768
    reduction of, 769
    risk-management model, 765–766
    risk-management plan, 769–771
    severity, 767–768
    sources of information, 657–658
    transfer of, 768–769
RIT (rapid intervention team), 453
Road department, 545, 547
Roadway constrictions during emergencies, 455–456
Robert T. Stafford Disaster Relief and Emergency Assistance Act, 573
Roles
    company officer, 606–607
    expectations, 607
    federal laws, 111–112
    within groups, 606–608
    of members, 607, 609
    rules and guidelines, 608
    supervisory, 111–112
    transitions. *See* Transition to role of company officer
Roof types
    arched roof, 387
    automatic roof vents, 400, 401
    concrete roof, 387–388
    flat roof, 385–386
    metal roof, 388
    panelized roof, 388
    pitched roof, 386–387
    purlins, 388
    Type II construction, 383
Royal Canadian Mounted Police, 560

S

Safe haven, 465–466
SAFER (Staffing for Adequate Fire and Emergency Response) Grant, 211
Safety. *See also* Health issues
    building conditions, 397
    Canadian Centre for Occupational Health and Safety, 560
    cardiac arrest, 219, 737, 779
    casualties, 219–223
    close call, 222
    at emergency scenes, 220–221, 224–225
    en route to and from scene, 225
    Everyone Goes Home initiative, 222, 763–764
    exposures, 775, 777–778
    facilities, 225–226
    federal agencies, 554–558
    Firefighter Safety Stand Down, 222–223
    fuel load, 397–398
    hazard communications symbols, 396
    initiative, 222
    inspections. *See* Fire and life-safety inspections
    investigation policies, 227–231
    investigations. *See* Safety investigations
    job performance requirements, 218
    learning objectives, 217
    Level I and Level II officer duties, 26
    life safety, incident priority, 445
    MSDS (Material Safety Data Sheet) policies, 651
    NFIRS (National Fire Incident Reporting System), 229
    NFPA standards, 223
    NIOSH (National Institute for Occupational Safety and Health), 229
    nonemergency safety, 219, 221
    overview, 231

    policies and procedures, 223
    postincident analysis, 756
    practical training evolutions, 278
    preincident planning hazard survey, 396–398
    Project Safe Place, 197
    public safety departments, 246, 353
    safety and health program, 226, 227
    safety officer, 731
    safety stand down, 26, 222–223
    ventilation systems, 398–402
    in the workplace, 223–226
Safety Connection program, 341
Safety investigations
    accident investigations, 228–230, 772–774, 776–777
    evaluation of plan, 770–771
    Everyone Goes Home initiative, 222, 763–764
    information collected, 774
    injury, illness, and exposures, 775, 777–778
    job performance requirements, 762
    learning objectives, 761
    overview, 763–764
    personnel-risk analysis, 766–769
    plan monitoring, 770
    policies and procedures, 227–231
    recommendations, 778–779
    report analysis, 775–779
    revisions of risk-management plan, 771
    risk. *See* Risk
Sales taxes, 208, 633
Salvage, Layman decision-making model, 464, 469–470
Salvage drum, 494
SARA (Superfund Amendments and Reauthorization Act), 543–544
Satellite
    Internet, 424
    telephones, 423
Scalar structure, 235, 236–237
Scatter diagrams, 596
SCBA (self-contained breathing apparatus) tag system, 738
SCC (Standards Council of Canada), 114, 118
Scene control, 451–459
    crowd control, 456–457
    defined, 452
    on-scene occupant services, 458–459
    perimeter control, 452–454
    traffic control, 454–456
Scope of manual, 6
Section, defined, 436–437
Selectmen, 541
Self-contained breathing apparatus (SCBA) tag system, 738
Self-esteem
    as barrier to decision-making, 89
    as reason for unethical conduct, 80
Self-gratification, as reason for unethical conduct, 80
Self-presentation, 131
Selling leadership style, 38, 43
Seminars for skills development, 46
Sender, in communications, 124, 125, 127, 144, 145
September 11, 2001. *See* World Trade Center attack
Seven Habits of Highly Effective People, 40, 524
Sex, defined, 332
Sexual harassment, 110–112, 297–298
Shelter in place, 465–466
Short-term trusts, 209, 633
Shutout, defined, 317
Sick leave, 296
Signaling systems. *See* Fire detection and alarm systems; Fire protection systems
Similar-to-me effect, 599
Simple training evolutions, 275–276
Single-use plans, 286
Sinking funds, 210, 634
Site plan, 754, 755
Situation status report, 735
Situational leadership
    leadership-continuum theory, 37–38
    model, 42–43

Index by Nancy Kopper